Essentials of Conservation Biology
Fifth Edition

ESSENTIALS OF
CONSERVATION
BIOLOGY

FIFTH EDITION

Richard B. Primack

Boston University

 Sinauer Associates, Inc., Publishers
Sunderland, Massachusetts U.S.A.

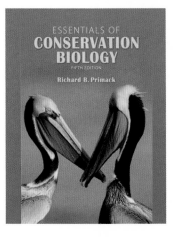

About the Cover

Brown pelicans (*Pelecanus occidentalis*) represent a conservation success story. Pelican numbers had declined in the United States, with the pesticide DDT identified as the cause of thinning eggshells and a lack of reproduction. Since its listing under the U.S. Endangered Species Act in 1970 and the banning of DDT, brown pelican numbers have increased substantially. Because of this recovery, the brown pelican was removed from listing under the Act in 2009. (Photograph © Tom Vezo/Minden Pictures.)

Essentials of Conservation Biology, *Fifth Edition*

Copyright © 2010 by Sinauer Associates, Inc.

For information, address:
Sinauer Associates, Inc., 23 Plumtree Road, Sunderland, MA 01375 USA
Fax: 413-549-1118
E-mail: orders@sinauer.com; publish@sinauer.com
Internet: www.sinauer.com

Library of Congress Cataloging-in-Publication Data

Primack, Richard B., 1950-
  Essentials of conservation biology / Richard B. Primack. — 5th ed.
      p. cm.
   ISBN 978-0-87893-640-3 (alk. paper)
  1. Conservation biology. I. Title.
  QH75.P752 2010
  333.95'16—dc22

                                                2010011325

Printed in China

5 4 3 2 1

To my family, Margaret, Dan, Will, and Jasper,
and the teachers who inspired me,
Carroll E. Wood Jr. (1921–2009) and Janis Antonovics

Brief Contents

Contents

PART IV   Conservation at the Population and Species Levels   245

PART VI   Conservation and Human Societies   459

Preface

After decades of public interest in nature and the environment, the United Nations focused worldwide attention on conservation by declaring 2010 to be the International Year of Biodiversity. The general public has absorbed this message and is asking its political leaders to provide the policy changes needed to address this issue. Conservation biology is the field that seeks to study and protect the living world and its biological diversity (or biodiversity in its shortened form). The field emerged during the last 35 years as a major new discipline to address the alarming loss of biological diversity. The threats to biodiversity are all too real, as demonstrated by the recent recognition that fully one-third of amphibian species are in danger of extinction. At the same time, our need to remain hopeful is highlighted, for example, by increasing sea turtle populations at many locations throughout the world following comprehensive conservation efforts. Many examples described in this book show that governments, individuals, and conservation organizations can work together to make the world a better place for nature.

Evidence of the explosive increase of interest in conservation biology is shown by the rapidly increasing membership in the Society for Conservation Biology, the great intellectual excitement displayed in many journals and newsletters, and the large numbers of new edited books and advanced texts that appear almost weekly. International conservation organizations have emerged to tackle conservation issues with a multi-disciplinary approach, and an *Encyclopedia of Life* is being developed as an online resource to provide the needed information for conservation issues.

University students continue to enroll enthusiastically and in large numbers in conservation biology courses. Previous editions of *Essentials of Conservation Biology* have provided a comprehensive textbook for this subject. (The *Primer of Conservation Biology*, in its Fourth Edition, continues to fill the need for a "quick" guide for those who want a basic familiarity with conservation biology.) The Fifth Edition of *Essentials* provides a thorough introduction to the major concepts and problems of the field. Like its predecessors, it is designed for use in conservation biology courses, and also as a supplemental text for general biology, ecology, wildlife biology, and environmental policy courses. The book is also intended to serve as a detailed guide for professionals who require a comprehensive background in the subject. Readers should enjoy and benefit from the updated full-color illustration and photo program. Highlighted synopses of major points in the text have been added as sidebars and serve as useful study aids.

This Fifth Edition reflects the excitement and new developments in the field. It provides coverage of the latest information available on a number of topics, including the expanding system of marine protected areas and linkages between conservation and global change. It also highlights new approaches culled from the literature on topics such as species reintroductions, population viability analysis, protected areas management, and payments for ecosystem services. Also new to this edition is an Instructor's Resource CD, available to qualified adopting instructors of the text. This IRCD includes electronic versions of all the figures, photos, and tables from the textbook.

In keeping with the international approach of conservation biology, I feel it is important to make the field accessible to as wide an audience as possible. With the assistance of Marie Scavotto and the staff of Sinauer Associates, I have arranged an active translation program, beginning in 1995 with translations into German and Chinese in 1997. It became clear to me that the best way to make the material accessible was to create regional or country-specific translations, identifying local scientists to become coauthors and to add case studies, examples, and illustrations from their own countries and regions that would be more relevant to the intended audience. To that end, in the past 12 years, editions of *Essentials* have appeared in Arabic, Hungarian, Romanian, and Spanish with a Latin American focus; and the *Primer* has appeared in Brazilian Portuguese, Chinese (two editions), Czech, Estonian, French with a Madagascar focus, Greek, Indonesian (two editions), Italian, Japanese (two editions), Korean (two editions), Mongolian, Romanian, Russian, Spanish, and Vietnamese. New editions of the *Primer* for France, South Asia, Pakistan, Turkey, and the Czech Republic are currently in production. It is my hope that these translations will help conservation biology develop as a discipline with a global scope. At the same time, examples from these translations find their way back into the English language editions, thereby enriching the presentation.

I hope that readers of this book will want to find out more about the extinction crisis facing species and ecosystems and how they can take action to halt it. I encourage readers to take the field's activist spirit to heart—use the Appendix to find organizations and sources of information on how to help. If readers gain a greater appreciation for the goals, methods, and importance of conservation biology, and if they are moved to make a difference in their everyday lives, this textbook will have served its purpose.

Acknowledgments

I sincerely appreciate the contribution of everyone who helped make this book accurate and clear. Individual chapters in this edition were reviewed by Dana Bauer, Patrick Bohlen, Katrina Brandon, Sue Bratton, Phil Cafaro, Linus Chen, Richard Corlett, Chris Elphick, Richard Frankham, Elizabeth Freeman, Richard Griffiths, Susan Jacobson, Christopher Johnson, Jeff McNeely, Michael Reed, Tom Ricciardi, Marcos Robles, Eric Seabloom, Jodi Sedlock, Howard Snell, and Navjot Sodhi. Les Kaufman of Boston University provided expertise on marine systems in all chapters.

Numerous people offered specialized input that helped make the boxes and case studies current and accurate. I would particularly like to recognize the contributions of Kamal Bawa, Steve Bousquin, Marlin Bowles, David Bray, Jim Estes, Ed Guerrant, Shen Guozhen, Kayri Havens, Rob Horwich, Daniel Janzen, Lukas Keller, Cheryl Knot, Tom Kunz, Kerry Lagueux, Laurie Bingaman Lackie, Rodrigo Gamez Lobo, Kathy MacKinnon, Elizabeth Marquard, Carlos Peres, Tom Power, Robert Simmons, Lisa Sorenson, Michael Thompson, Sebastian Troenig, David Western, Tony Whitten, Peter Wrege, Miriam Wyman, and Truman Young.

Rachel Morrison was the principal research assistant and organizer for the project, with additional help from Jin Chung, Libby Ellwood, Elysia Heilig, Heather Lieb, Farah Mohammedzadeh, Rebecca Norklun, Caroline Polgar, and Lily Smith. Sydney Carroll and Kathaleen Emerson provided invaluable help in the production of the book, with numerous suggestions on how to make the book friendlier to student readers. Andy Sinauer, Chris Small, David McIntyre, Joan Gemme and the rest of the Sinauer staff helped to transform the manuscript into a finished book.

Special thanks are due to my wife Margaret and my children Dan, Will, and Jasper for encouraging me to fulfill an important personal goal by completing this book. I would like to recognize Boston University for providing me with the facilities and environment that made this project possible and the many Boston University students who have taken my conservation biology courses over the years. Their enthusiasm and suggestions have helped me to find new ways to present this material. And lastly, I would like to express my great appreciation to my coauthors in other countries who have worked with me to produce conservation biology textbooks in their own languages, which are critical for spreading the message of conservation biology to a wider audience.

Richard Primack
Boston, Massachusetts
April, 2010

Media and Supplements to accompany Essentials of Conservation Biology, Fifth Edition

Instructor's Resource Library (ISBN 978-0-87893-638-0)
(Available to qualified adopting instructors.)

The *Essentials of Conservation Biology* Instructor's Resource Library includes all of the textbook's figures (including photos) and tables, in several formats. Each figure has been formatted and optimized for excellent legibility when projected in the classroom. Images are provided as both low-resolution and high-resolution JPEGs, and a PowerPoint® presentation of all figures and tables is provided for each chapter, making it easy to quickly incorporate figures into lecture presentations.

MAJOR ISSUES THAT DEFINE THE DISCIPLINE

Chapter 1

What Is Conservation Biology?

Popular interest in protecting the world's biological diversity—including its amazing range of species, its complex ecosystems, and the genetic variation within species—has intensified during the last few decades. It has become increasingly evident to both scientists and the general public that we are living in a period of unprecedented biodiversity* loss. Around the globe, biological communities that took millions of years to develop, including tropical rain forests, coral reefs, temperate old-growth forests, and prairies, are being devastated by human actions. Thousands, if not tens of thousands, of species and millions of unique populations are predicted to go extinct in the coming decades (MEA 2005). Unlike mass extinctions in the geological past, in which tens of thousands of species died out following massive catastrophes such as asteroid collisions with the Earth and dramatic temperature changes, today's extinctions have a human face. Never before in the history of life have so many species and ecosystems been threatened with extinction in so short a period of time. Never before has such devastation been caused by beings who claim reason, a moral sense, and free will as their unique and defining characteristics. The overwhelming cause of all this loss is the rapidly expanding human population.

*Biological diversity is often shortened to biodiversity.

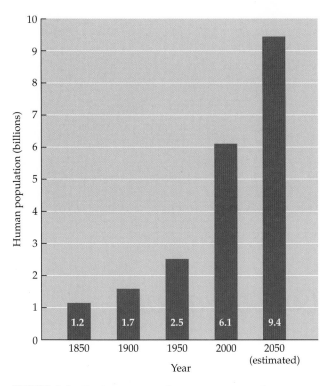

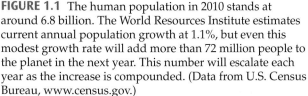

FIGURE 1.1 The human population in 2010 stands at around 6.8 billion. The World Resources Institute estimates current annual population growth at 1.1%, but even this modest growth rate will add more than 72 million people to the planet in the next year. This number will escalate each year as the increase is compounded. (Data from U.S. Census Bureau, www.census.gov.)

During the last 160 years, the human population has exploded. It took more than 10,000 years for the number of *Homo sapiens* to reach 1 billion, an event that occurred sometime around the year 1850. Estimates for 2011 put the number of humans at 7 billion, with an estimated 9.4 billion by 2050 (Rosenberg 2009); at this size, even a modest rate of population increase adds tens of millions of individuals each year (**Figure 1.1**). The threats to biodiversity are accelerating because of the demands of the rapidly increasing human population and its rising material consumption. People use natural resources such as firewood, coal, oil, timber, fish, and game, and they convert natural habitats to land dominated by agriculture, cities, housing developments, logging, mining, industrial plants, and other human activities.

Worsening the situation is the fact that as countries develop and industrialize, the consumption of resources by their citizens increases. For example, the average citizen of the United States uses five times more energy than the average global citizen, ten times more than the average Chinese citizen, and 28 times more than the average Indian citizen (Worldwatch Institute 2008; Encyclopedia of the Nations 2009). The ever-increasing number of human beings and their intensifying use of natural resources have direct and harmful consequences for the diversity of the living world.

Unless something is done to reverse the trend of human-caused extinctions, wonderful species that exemplify the natural world for us—such as giant pandas, butterflies, songbirds, and whales—soon will be lost forever from their wild habitats. Additionally, many thousands, possibly millions, of less conspicuous plant, fungi, and invertebrate species and uncountable numbers of microorganisms will join them in extinction unless their habitats and populations are protected. The loss of these inconspicuous species may prove to be devastating to the planet and its human inhabitants because of the roles these species play in maintaining ecosystems.

In addition to species extinctions, the natural hydrologic and chemical cycles that people depend on for clean water and clean air have been disrupted by deforestation and land clearing. Soil erosion and pollution from agriculture and sewage discharges cause massive damage to rivers, lakes, and oceans. The very climate of our planet Earth has been disrupted by a combination of atmospheric pollution and deforestation. Genetic diversity within species has decreased as populations are reduced in size, even among species with seemingly healthy populations.

The main threat humans pose to the diversity of life is our destruction of natural habitat, which stems from the growth of the human population and our ever-increasing use of resources (Papworth et al. 2009). Such habitat destruction includes the clear-cutting of old-growth forests in the temperate zone and in rain forests in the tropics, overuse of grasslands for pasture, draining of wetlands, and pollution of freshwater and marine ecosystems. Even when parcels of natural habitat are preserved as national parks, nature reserves, and marine protected areas, extreme vigilance is required to prevent the extinction of their remaining species, whose numbers have been so dramatically reduced in the past that they are now particularly vulnerable to extinction. Also, the environment in the preserved habitat fragments is so altered from its original condition that a site may no longer be suitable for the continued existence of certain species.

There are many other threats facing modern ecosystems, including climate change and invasive species. Efforts to protect a species in one area may be severely crippled as a result of a rapid climate change to which the species cannot adapt (see Chapter 9). Also, biological communities have been particularly devastated by the introduction of exotic species, some of which have been deliberately brought in from other areas and established by people, such as domesticated animals and ornamental plants, and some of which have been brought in accidentally, such as weed species, insect pests, and new diseases. In many cases, particularly on islands, these species have become invasive (see Chapter 10) and have displaced and eliminated native species.

Another major threat to biological diversity is the use of modern technology to overharvest animals and plants for local and international markets. Hunters in tropical forests now use guns and motorized vehicles, where before they used bows and arrows and walked on foot. Fishing has changed from small wind- and hand-powered boats to large motorized fleets with freezers that can stay at sea for weeks or months at a time. Entire forest, grassland, and ocean communities have been emptied of their animal life and, in many cases, cleared of their plant life as well.

Powerful technologies allow alteration of the environment on a regional and even a global scale. Some of these transformations are intentional, such as the creation of dams and the development of new agricultural land, but other changes, such as air pollution, strip-mining of entire hills, and damage to seabed habitats during fishing, are by-products of our activities. Unregulated dumping of chemicals and sewage into streams, rivers, and lakes has polluted major freshwater and coastal marine systems throughout the world and has driven significant numbers of species toward extinction. Pollution has reached such high levels that even large marine environments, such as the Mediterranean Sea, the Gulf of Mexico, and the Persian Gulf, which were once assumed to be able to absorb pollution with no negative effects, are threatened with the loss of whole suites of formerly common species. Some inland water bodies, such as the Aral Sea, have been completely destroyed, along with the many unique fish species that lived in them. Air pollution from factories and cars has turned rainwater into an acid solution that weakens and kills mountain trees downwind of industrial centers and, in turn, removes habitat for the animals that depend on those plants. Scientists have warned that levels of air pollution have become severe enough to alter global climate patterns and strain the capacity of the atmosphere to filter out harmful ultraviolet radiation. The impacts of these events on ecosystems are enormous and ominous; they have also stimulated the growth of conservation biology.

Scientists now realize that many of the threats to biological diversity are synergistic—that is, the negative effects of several independent factors such as logging, fire, poverty, and overhunting combine additively or even multiplicatively. Scientists also know that the threats to biological diversity directly threaten human populations because people are dependent on the natural environment for raw materials, food, medicines, and even the water they drink. And the poorest people are the ones who will experience the greatest hardship from damaged environments.

The New Science of Conservation Biology

Many of us feel discouraged by the avalanche of species extinctions and the wholesale habitat destruction occurring in the world today. But it is possible—and indeed necessary—to feel challenged in order to find ways to stop the destruction (Orr 2007). Actions taken—or bypassed—during the next few decades will determine how many of the world's species and natural areas will survive. People may someday look back on the first decades of the twenty-first century as an extraordinarily exciting time, when a collaboration of determined people acting locally and internationally saved large numbers of species from extinction and even entire ecosystems from destruction. Examples of such conservation efforts are described later in this chapter and throughout this book.

Conservation biology is an integrated, multidisciplinary scientific field that has developed in response to the challenge of preserving species and ecosystems. It has three goals:

- to document the full range of biological diversity on Earth

- to investigate human impact on species, genetic variation, and ecosystems

- to develop practical approaches to prevent the extinction of species, maintain genetic diversity within species, and protect and restore biological communities and their associated ecosystem functions

The first two of these goals involve the dispassionate search for factual knowledge typical of scientific research. The third goal, however, defines conservation biology as a **normative** discipline—that is, it embraces certain values and attempts to apply scientific methods to achieving those values. Like medical science, which applies knowledge gleaned from physiology, anatomy, biochemistry, and genetics to the goal of achieving human health and eliminating illness, conservation biologists intervene to prevent the human-enhanced loss of biodiversity, because they believe the preservation of species and ecosystems to be an ultimate good (Nelson and Vucetich 2009).

Conservation Biology Complements the Traditional Disciplines

Conservation biology arose in the 1980s because the traditional applied disciplines of resource management alone were not comprehensive enough to address the critical threats to biological diversity. Agriculture, forestry, wildlife management, and fisheries biology have been concerned primarily with developing methods to manage a small range of species for the marketplace and for recreation. These disciplines generally were not concerned with the protection of the full range of species and ecosystems, or at best, they regarded this as a secondary issue. Conservation biology complements the applied disciplines and provides a more general theoretical approach to the protection of biological diversity. It differs from these disciplines in its primary goal of long-term preservation of entire ecosystems, with economic factors secondary.

> Conservation biology merges applied and theoretical biology and incorporates ideas and expertise from a broad range of fields outside the natural sciences, toward the goal of preserving biodiversity.

The academic disciplines of population biology, taxonomy, ecology, and genetics constitute the core of conservation biology, and many conservation biologists have been drawn from these ranks. Others come from backgrounds in the applied disciplines, such as forestry and wildlife management. In addition, many leaders in conservation biology have come from zoos and botanical gardens, bringing with them experience in locating rare and endangered species in the wild and then maintaining and propagating them in captivity.

Conservation biology is also closely associated with **environmentalism**, a widespread movement characterized by political and educational activism with the goal of protecting the natural environment from destruction and pollution. Conservation biology is a scientific discipline whose findings often contribute to the environmentalist movement but differs from it by being based in biological research.

Because much of the biodiversity crisis arises from human pressures, conservation biology also incorporates ideas and expertise from a broad range of other fields (**Figure 1.2**) (Groom et al. 2006). For example, environmental law and policy provide the basis for government protection of rare and endangered species and critical habitats. Environmental ethics provides a rationale for preserving species. Ecological economists provide analyses of the economic value of biological diversity to support arguments for preservation. Ecosystem ecologists and climatologists monitor the biological and physical characteristics of the environment and develop models to predict environmental responses to disturbance. Social sciences, such as anthropology, sociology, and geography, provide methods to involve local people in actions to protect their immediate environment. Conservation education links academic study and fieldwork to solve environmental problems, teaching people about science and helping them realize the value of the natural environment. Because it draws on the ideas and skills of so many separate fields, conservation biology can be considered a truly multidisciplinary approach.

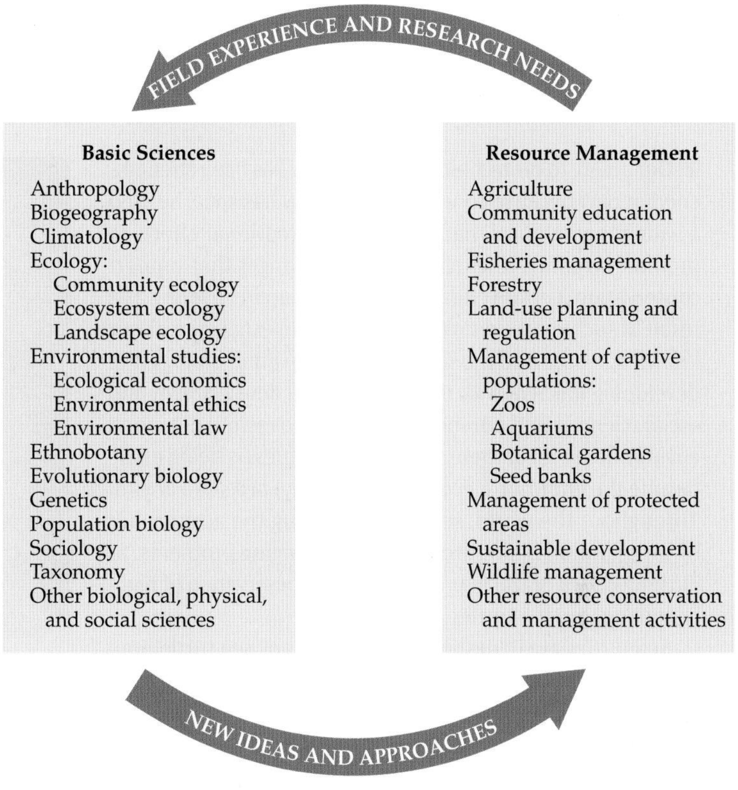

Another crucial difference between conservation biology and other purely academic disciplines is that conservation biology attempts to address specific issues with solutions that can be applied to actual threats to biodiversity (**Box 1.1**). These issues involve determining the best strategies for protecting rare species, designing nature reserves, developing programs to maintain genetic variability in small populations, and reconciling conservation concerns with the needs of

FIGURE 1.2 Conservation biology represents a synthesis of many basic sciences (left) that provide principles and new approaches for the applied fields of resource management (right). The experiences gained in the field, in turn, influence the direction of the basic sciences. (After Temple 1991.)

local people. The critical test for conservation biology is whether it can preserve and restore species and ecosystems (Hall and Fleishman 2010). While much of conservation research remains overly academic, the goal is still to provide practical solutions that managers can use in real situations.

Conservation Biology Is a Crisis Discipline

In many ways, conservation biology is a crisis discipline. Decisions about park design, species management, and other aspects of conservation are made every day under severe time pressure (Marris 2007). Conservation biologists and scientists in related fields are well suited to provide the advice that governments, businesses, and the general public need in order to make crucial decisions, but because of time constraints, scientists are often compelled to make recommendations without thorough investigation. Decisions must be made, with or without scientific input, and conservation biologists must be willing to express opinions and take action based on the best available evidence and informed judgment (Chan 2008). They must also articulate a long-term conservation vision that extends beyond the immediate crisis (Redford and Sanjayan 2003; Nelson and Vucetich 2009).

Conservation Biology's Ethical Principles

Earlier in the chapter, we mentioned that conservation biology is a normative discipline in which certain value judgments are inherent. Conservation biology rests on an underlying set of principles that are generally accepted by members of the discipline (Soulé 1985):

BOX 1.1 *Conservation Biology's Interdisciplinary Approach: A Case Study with Sea Turtles*

■ Our ability to protect biological diversity has been strengthened in part because conservation biology has spearheaded a wide range of local, national, and international efforts to promote scientific research and policy changes that support conservation. Certain endangered species are recovering as a result of such measures. We can point to an expansion of our knowledge base and the science of conservation biology, the developing linkages with the fields of rural development and social sciences, and our increased ability to restore degraded environments. All of these suggest that progress is being made despite the enormous, even overwhelming, tasks still ahead. Throughout the world, scientists are using the approaches of conservation biology to address challenging problems, as illustrated by a Brazilian program for the conservation of highly endangered sea turtles.

Sea turtles are in desperate trouble. Many sea turtle populations have shrunk to less than 1% of their original sizes, devastated by a combination of factors that includes destruction of their nesting habitat, hunting of adult turtles and collecting of turtle eggs for food, and high mortality due to entanglement in fishing gear. The nation of Brazil's comprehensive approach to saving these fascinating, mysterious creatures provides an illustration of the interdisciplinary nature of conservation biology.

> Interdisciplinary approaches, the involvement of local people, and the restoration of important environments and species all attest to progress in the science of conservation biology.

Sea turtles spend their lives at sea, with only the females returning to land to lay eggs on sandy beaches. When the Brazilian government set out to design a conservation program, planners discovered that no one knew exactly which species of sea turtles were found in Brazil, how many turtles there were, where they laid their eggs, and how local people were affecting them. To overcome this lack of basic information, in 1980 the Brazilian government established the National Marine Turtle Conservation Program, called Projeto TAMAR* (Marcovaldi and Marcovaldi 1999; Marcovaldi and Chaloupka 2007). The project began with a 2-year survey of Brazil's 6000 kilometers of coastline, using boats, horses, and foot patrols, combined with hundreds of interviews with villagers. TAMAR divers aided in these efforts by tagging and monitoring sea turtle populations in the water. This data-gathering phase is an important initial step in many conservation projects.

In a protected feeding and nesting area around Rocas Atoll, about 220 km from the coast of Brazil, Brazilian scientists measure the length of an endangered green turtle (*Chelonia mydas*). They will permanently tag the turtle as part of a comprehensive conservation effort by Projeto TAMAR. (Photograph courtesy of Projeto TAMAR Image Bank.)

The TAMAR survey found that turtle nesting beaches fell into three main zones along 1100 km of the coastline between Rio de Janeiro and Recife, with loggerhead turtles (*Caretta caretta*) the most abundant species and four other species also present. The green turtle (*Chelonia mydas*) was the only species nesting on Brazil's offshore islands.

Interviews with villagers and observations of beaches revealed that adult turtles and turtle eggs were being harvested intensively, with people often collecting virtually every turtle egg laid. In many areas, the construction of resorts, houses, commercial developments, and beach roads had damaged and reduced the available nesting area on beaches. Shadows cast by the buildings changed the temperature of the sand in which the eggs incubated, which biologists now know to be a critical factor in determining the sex of a developing turtle embryo. On some beaches, almost all of the emerging turtles were females, affecting the ability of the species as a whole to reproduce successfully. Additionally, the light from the buildings at night disoriented emerging hatchlings: instead of heading straight to the ocean, they often wandered in wrong directions and became exhausted. Of the young turtles that did make it to sea, many were caught in the nets of fishermen, where they suffocated and died.

*TAMAR is an acronym for "TArtarugas MARinas," which is Portuguese for "marine turtles."

BOX 1.1 *(continued)*

Information from the TAMAR survey was critical to legislation passed in 1986 in Brazil that led to the complete protection of sea turtles and the establishment of two new biological reserves and a marine national park to protect important nesting beaches. While creating protected areas is important in conservation efforts, ongoing management activities are also needed. Projeto TAMAR chose an innovative and comprehensive approach to protecting the turtles on the ground. They established conservation stations at each of 21 main nesting beaches. The Brazilian government grants TAMAR complete responsibility for and control of the beaches within these stations. Each station has a manager, several university interns, and local employees. More than 85% of TAMAR's 1000 employees live on the coast; many are former fishermen who bring their knowledge of sea turtles to bear on conservation. These local employees have become strong advocates for the turtles because their wages from Projeto TAMAR and the related tourist industry are linked to the continuing presence of these animals.

The stations' personnel regularly patrol the conservation areas on foot and by vehicle, measuring turtles for size and permanently flipper-tagging all adults observed on the beach. In places where predators are abundant, some nests are covered with wire mesh fitted with small gaps to protect the eggs and then allow movement of the baby turtles after they hatch. Alternatively, the eggs are collected and brought to nearby hatchery areas, where they are reburied (Almeida and Mendes 2007). These measures allow baby turtles emerging from protected nests or hatcheries to enter the ocean just as if they had emerged from natural nests. TAMAR protects over 4000 turtle nests each year and has protected around 100,000 nests and approximately 7 million hatchlings in the years since its inception. On average, the number of turtle nests on the beaches has also been increasing by an impressive 20% a year (Marcovaldi and Chaloupka 2007).

TAMAR is also working with the Brazilian government to protect and manage the nesting beaches on the offshore islands. The project has extended its mission to include preventing turtles from getting caught in fishing nets while feeding in coastal waters. TAMAR provides fishermen with information about the importance of turtles and about fishing gear designed to prevent turtle capture. Fishermen are also taught techniques for reviving turtles caught in their nets so the turtles will not suffocate. Their increasing appreciation of turtles and their awareness of the new laws lead most fishermen to cooperate with these policies. However, accidental capture remains a leading cause of turtle mortality.

Projeto TAMAR plays a positive role in the villages where it operates. In many areas, TAMAR is the primary source of income for the local people, often providing child care facilities and small medical and dental clinics. Villagers are employed in making turtle-themed crafts to sell to tourists. To increase awareness of the program at the local level, TAMAR personnel give talks about marine conservation in village schools and organize hatchling release ceremonies.

The project reaches a wide audience in Brazil through coverage in popular articles and on television programs. In addition, TAMAR operates sea turtle educational centers where hundreds of thousands of tourists, most of whom are from Brazil, visit each year. The tourists get to see con-

Projeto TAMAR generates publicity for sea turtle conservation by staging festive events involving tourists, school groups, and local people, such as this release of hatchlings that were incubated in the safety of a protected hatchery. (Courtesy of Projeto TAMAR Image Bank.)

servation in action and receive a large dose of conservation education; in turn, they support the project through their purchase of souvenirs.

Projeto TAMAR has tried to involve the next generation of concerned conservationists in current projects, helping student interns experience success with a real-life conservation project. Hopefully, the awareness raised by Projeto TAMAR will extend gradually to other conservation programs.

As a result of Projeto TAMAR's efforts in protecting thousands of adult turtles, tens of thousands of nests, and millions of hatchlings, sea turtle numbers in Brazil have stabilized and even show signs of increasing. The project has changed people's attitudes, both in coastal villages and in the wider Brazilian society. By integrating conservation goals with community education and development, Projeto TAMAR has improved the future for sea turtles and for local people involved with their conservation.

- *The diversity of species and ecosystems should be preserved.* The rich diversity of life should be protected. In general, most people agree with this principle because they enjoy biological diversity. The hundreds of millions of visitors each year to zoos, national parks, botanical gardens, and aquariums testify to the general public's interest in observing different species and ecosystems (**Figure 1.3**). Genetic variation within species also sparks popular interest, as shown by the wide appeal of pet shows, agricultural expositions, flower exhibitions, and large numbers of specialty clubs (African violet societies, rose societies, etc.). Home gardeners pride themselves on how many types of plants they have in their gardens, while bird-watchers compete to see how many species they can identify in one day or in their lifetimes. It has even been suggested that humans may have a genetic predisposition to like biological diversity, called **biophilia**, from the Greek root words *bio* or "life" and *philia* or "loving"; that is, to love living things (Kellert 1997; Corral-Verdugo et al. 2009).

- *The untimely extinction of populations and species should be prevented.* The ordinary extinction of species and populations as a result of natural processes is an ethically neutral event. Through the millennia of geological time, the natural extinction of each species has tended to be balanced by the evolution of new species. The local loss of a population of a species likewise is usually offset by the establishment of a new population through dispersal. However, as a result of human activity, the rate of extinction has increased by more than a hundredfold (see Chapter 7). Virtually all of the hundreds of vertebrate species—and the presumed tens of thousands of invertebrate species—that have gone extinct in the last few centuries have been wiped out by humans. Many people now recognize their role and responsibility in causing and, more important, in preventing extinctions.

FIGURE 1.3 People enjoy seeing the diversity of life, as shown by the growing popularity of butterfly gardens. (Photograph by Richard B. Primack.)

- *Ecological complexity should be maintained.* Many of the most interesting properties of biological diversity are only expressed in natural environments. For example, complex coevolutionary and ecological relationships exist among some tropical flowers, the hummingbirds that visit the flowers to drink nectar, and the mites that live in the flowers and use the hummingbirds' beaks as "buses" to travel from flower to flower. These relationships would no longer exist if the hummingbirds, mites, and plants were housed separately and in isolation at zoos and botanical gardens. While the biological diversity of species may be partially preserved in zoos and gardens, the ecological complexity that exists in natural communities will be largely lost without the preservation of wild lands and aquatic environments.

> There are ethical reasons why people want to conserve biological diversity, such as a belief that species have intrinsic value. Also, people may be naturally disposed to appreciate and value biodiversity.

- *Evolution should continue.* Evolutionary adaptation is the process that eventually leads to new species and increased biological diversity. Therefore, it is important to allow populations to continue to evolve in nature. Human processes that limit or even prevent populations from evolving, such as elimination of unique mountain populations or populations at the northern edge of a species range, should be avoided. Preserving species in captivity when they are no longer able to survive in the wild is a possible stopgap means of rescue, but such species are then cut off from the ecological processes that allowed them to evolve. In those cases, the species may no longer be able to survive in the wild if released. Such evolution is particularly important in the modern world, with a rapidly changing climate and other human impacts.

- *Biological diversity has intrinsic value.* Species and the ecosystems in which they live possess value of their own ("intrinsic value") regardless of their economic, scientific, or aesthetic value to human society. This value is conferred not only by their evolutionary history and unique ecological role, but also by their very existence (see Chapter 6 for a more complete discussion of this topic). This position is in sharp contrast to an economic viewpoint, which would assign a monetary value to each species or ecosystem on the basis of the goods and services that it provides or potentially could provide to humans. A purely economic viewpoint often leads to a decision to move forward with a highly destructive development project and to ignore the intrinsic value of biological diversity.

These principles cannot be proved or disproved, and accepting all of them is not a requirement for conservation biologists. Religious people who are active in the conservation movement but do not believe in the theory of evolution, for instance, may not accept some of these principles. Nonetheless, this set of ethical and ideological statements forms the philosophical foundation of the discipline and suggests research approaches and practical applications. As long as one or two of these principles are accepted, there is enough rationale for conservation efforts.

The Origins of Conservation Biology

The origins of conservation biology can be traced to religious and philosophical beliefs concerning the relationship between human societies and the natural world (Dudley at al. 2009; Higuchi and Primack 2009; also see Chapter 6). In many of the world's religions, people are seen as both physically and spiritually connected to the plants and animals in the surrounding environment (**Figure 1.4**). In Chinese Taoism, Japanese Shintoism, Indian Hinduism, and Buddhist philosophies, some sacred wilderness areas and natural settings are valued and protected for their capacity to provide intense spiritual experiences. Many Christian monastaries and

FIGURE 1.4 Tanah Lot Temple is a Hindu temple on the island of Bali in Indonesia. Its coastal setting allows worshippers to experience the connection of the human spirit with the natural world. (Photograph © Hemis/Alamy.)

religious centers similarly protect the surrounding nature as an important part of their mission. These philosophies see a direct connection between the natural world and the spiritual world, a connection that breaks when the natural world is altered or destroyed by human activity. Strict adherents to the Jain and Hindu religions in India believe that *all* killing of animal life is wrong. In Islamic, Judaic, and Christian teachings alike, people are given the sacred responsibility to be guardians of nature. Many of the leaders of the early Western environmental movement that helped to establish parks and wilderness areas did so because of strong personal convictions that developed from their Christian religious beliefs.

Biological diversity often has immediate significance to traditional societies whose people live close to the land and water. In Native American tribes of the Pacific Northwest, hunters undergo purification rituals in order to be considered worthy of hunting animals. The Iroquois, a Native American group, considered how their actions would affect the lives of their descendants after seven generations. Hunting and gathering societies, such as the Penan of Borneo, give thousands of names to individual trees, animals, and places in their surroundings to create a cultural landscape that is vital to the well-being of the tribe. This type of relationship to the natural world was described eloquently at the Fourth World Wilderness Congress in 1987 by the delegate from the Kuna people of Panama (Gregg 1991):

> For the Kuna culture, the land is our mother and all living things that we live on are her brothers in such a manner that we must take care of her and live in a harmonious manner with her, because the extinction of one thing is also the end of another.

In an ecological and cultural history of the Indian subcontinent, Gadgil and Guha (1992) argue that the belief systems, religions, and myths of hunter-gatherer societies and stable agricultural societies tend to emphasize conservation themes and the wise use of natural resources because these groups have learned over time to live within the constraints of a fixed resource base. In contrast, the belief systems of communities that raise livestock, and rapidly expanding agricultural and industrial societies, emphasize the rapid consumption and destruction of natural resources as a way to maximize growth and assert control over other groups. These groups move to new localities when the resources of any one place are exhausted. Modern industrial states represent the extreme of such societies. Their excessive and wasteful consumption requires the transportation of resources to urban centers in ever-widening circles of resource depletion. However, what will we do when the resources are all gone?

European Origins

To the European mind, the prevalent view has been that God created nature for humans' use and benefit. In Genesis, the first book of the Bible, God instructs Adam and Eve to "be fruitful and multiply and fill the Earth and subdue it; have dominion over every living thing that moves upon the Earth." The biblical instruction supports a dominant tenet of Western philosophy: Nature should be converted into wealth as rapidly as possible and used for the benefit of humans. This point of view justifies nearly all land uses and implies that to leave land unused is to misuse God's gift—a foolish, if not downright sinful, mistake. In medieval Europe, wilderness generally was perceived to be useless land and was often believed to be inhabited by evil spirits or monsters, in contrast to the orderly qualities and appearance of agricultural landscapes. This perspective of nature was not true in all places and in every period, but it describes a general perception that is different from our view today.

This anthropocentric (human-centered) view of nature led to the exploitation and degradation of vast resources in the regions colonized by European countries from the sixteenth century onward (Diamond 1999). In practice, the wealth and benefits that came from this policy accrued primarily to the citizens of the colonial powers, while the needs of non-European native peoples were largely disregarded. The long-term ramifications for the forests, fisheries, and other natural resources themselves were not considered at all; the unexplored territories of the Americas, Asia, Africa, and Australia seemed so vast and rich that it was inconceivable to the colonial powers that their natural resources could ever be depleted.

An important element of the conservation movement did develop in Europe, however, based on the experiences of scientific officers—often imbued with Romantic idealism—who were sent to assist in the development of colonies in the eighteenth and nineteenth centuries (Subashchandran and Ramachandra 2008). These scientists were trained to make detailed observations on the biology, natural history, geography, and anthropology of the colonial regions. Many of them expected to find the indigenous people living in wonderful harmony with nature. Instead, they found devastated forests, damaged watersheds, and newly created poverty.

In European colonies throughout the world, perceptive scientific officers came to see that protection of forests was necessary to prevent soil erosion, provide water for irrigation and drinking, maintain wood supplies, and prevent famine. Some colonial administrators also argued that certain intact forests should remain uncut because of their necessary role in ensuring a steady supply of rainfall in adjacent agricultural areas—foreshadowing modern concern with global climate change. Such arguments led directly to conservation ordinances. On the Indian Ocean island of Mauritius, for example, the French colonial administration in 1769 stipulated that 25% of landholdings should remain forested to prevent erosion, degraded areas should be planted with trees, and forests growing within 200 meters of water should be protected. In order to prevent water pollution and the destruction of fish populations, various colonial governments passed laws in the late eighteenth century regulating the pollutants being discharged by sugar mills and other factories. On a larger scale, British scientists working in India issued a report in 1852 urging the establishment of forest reserves throughout the vast subcontinent, managed by professional foresters, in order to avert environmental calamities and economic losses. In particular, the report linked deforestation to decreased rainfall and water supplies, which resulted in famine among the local people. The report was embraced by the leadership of the British East India Company, who could see that conservation made good economic sense. This system of forest reserves was widely adopted in other parts of the colonial world, such as Southeast Asia, Australia, and Africa, and it influenced forestry in North America as well. It is also true that many of these new systems of resource management, implemented with a command-and-control mentality, resulted in dramatic failures when reality did not conform to management plans. A further irony is that, prior to colonization, indigenous peoples in these regions often had well-developed systems of natural resource management that were swept aside by the colonial governments (Subashchandran and Ramachandra 2008).

Many of the themes of contemporary conservation biology were established in European scientific writings of a century or more ago. The possibility of species extinction was demonstrated by the loss of wild cattle (*Bos primigenius*, also known as the aurochs) from Europe in 1627 and the extinction of the dodo bird (*Raphus cucullatus*) in Mauritius in the 1680s (**Figure 1.5**). To address the problem of the decline and possible extinction of the wisent, also known as the European bison (*Bison bonasus*), the Polish king in 1561 established a nature reserve that prohibited hunting. The Białowieża Forest represented one of the earliest deliberate European efforts to conserve a species. While this action failed to preserve the original population of wild wisent, the wisent was reintroduced into the forest in 1951. The Białowieża Forest, which extends from modern Poland into Belarus, remains today one of Europe's most important nature reserves, preserving one of the last remaining stands of the great forests that formerly covered Europe.

In Europe, expression of concern for the protection of wildlife began to spread widely in the late nineteenth century (Galbraith et al. 1998). The combination of both an increasing area of land under cultivation and more widespread use of firearms for hunting led to a marked reduction in wild animals. In Britain, many

(A)

(B)

FIGURE 1.5 (A) Roland Savery's figure of the dodo in his picture of the Fall of Adam, in the Royal Gallery at Berlin. This illustration was painted using a live dodo which was brought to Europe in the early seventeenth century before the species went extinct. (B) One of Europe's first nature reserves was established to protect the wisent in Poland. (B, photograph © Liz Leyden/istockphoto.com.)

culturally and ecologically significant species—great bustards (*Otis tarda*), ospreys (*Pandion haliaetus*), sea eagles (*Haliaeetus albicilla*), and great auks (*Pinguinus impennis*)—became extinct in the wild around this time. Other species showed similar rapid declines. These dramatic changes stimulated the formation of the British conservation movement, leading to the founding of the Commons, Open Spaces and Footpaths Preservation Society in 1865, the National Trust for Places of Historic Interest or Natural Beauty in 1895, and the Royal Society for the Protection of Birds in 1899. Altogether, these groups have preserved about 900,000 hectares* (ha) of open land. In the twentieth century, government action produced laws such as the National Parks and Access to the Countryside Act, passed in 1949 for the "protection and public enjoyment of the wider countryside," and the Wildlife and Countryside Act, passed in 1981 for the protection of endangered species, their habitat, and the marine environment. Because of the intensive human use of the British landscape, conservation efforts in Britain have traditionally emphasized the preservation and management of relatively small fragments of land. Rare and declining habitats, such as the chalk grasslands and old growth forests, continue to be a major concern in conservation efforts.

Many other European countries also have strong traditions of nature conservation and land protection, most notably Denmark, Austria, the Netherlands, Germany, and Switzerland. In these countries as well, conservation is enacted by both the government and private conservation organizations. Over the last two decades, regional initiatives to protect species, habitats, and ecosystem processes have been expanded and coordinated by the European Union. Similar efforts have been made in other countries settled by European peoples, such as Australia, New Zealand, and Canada.

> As demonstrated by the conservation tradition in Europe, habitat degradation and species loss can catalyze long-lasting conservation efforts.

*For an explanation of the term *hectare* and other measurements, see **Table 1.1**.

TABLE 1.1 Some Useful Units of Measurement

Length

1 meter (m)	1 m = 39.4 inches = ~3.3 feet
1 kilometer (km)	1 km = 1000 m = 0.62 mile
1 centimeter (cm)	1 cm = 1/100 m = 0.39 inch
1 millimeter (mm)	1 mm = 1/1000 m = 0.039 inch

Area

square meter (m^2)	Area encompassed by a square, each side of which is 1 meter
1 hectare (ha)	1 ha = 10,000 m^2 = 2.47 acres
	100 ha = 1 square kilometer (km^2)

Mass

1 kilogram (kg)	1 kg = 2.2 pounds
1 gram (g)	1 g = 1/1000 kg = 0.035 ounce
1 milligram (mg)	1 mg = 1/1000 g = 0.000035 ounce

Temperature
°C = 5/9(°F − 32)

degree Celsius (°C)	0°C = 32° Fahrenheit (the freezing point of water)
	100°C = 212° Fahrenheit (the boiling point of water)
	20°C = 68° Fahrenheit ("room temperature")

American Origins

Among the first major intellectual figures in the United States arguing for the protection of natural areas were the nineteenth-century philosophers Ralph Waldo Emerson and Henry David Thoreau (Callicott 1990). Emerson, in his transcendentalist writings, saw nature as a temple in which people could commune with the spiritual world and achieve spiritual enlightenment (Emerson 1836). Thoreau was both an advocate for nature and an opponent of materialistic society, believing that people needed far fewer possessions than they sought. To prove his point, he lived simply in a cabin near Walden Pond, writing about his ideas and experiences in a book—*Walden*, published in 1854—that has had a significant impact on many generations of students and environmentalists. Thoreau believed that the experience of nature was a necessary counterweight to the weakening tendencies of civilization. In his collection of essays (1863) he argued emphatically that

> [in] wilderness is the preservation of the world. . . . The story of Romulus and Remus [the founders of the Roman Empire] being suckled by a wolf is not a meaningless fable. The founders of every state which has risen to eminence have drawn their nourishment and vigor from a similar wild source.

This concern for preserving wilderness, large areas that remain essentially unoccupied, unmanaged, and unmodified by human beings, is a continuing and dominant theme in the American conservation movement up to the present time (Congressional Research Service and Saundry 2009). It contrasts sharply with the traditional European view that because landscapes developed over thousands of years of human interaction, further management is appropriate in attempts to reach conservation objectives (Cooper 2000).

Eminent American wilderness advocate John Muir used the transcendental themes of Emerson and Thoreau in his campaigns to preserve natural areas. According to Muir's **preservationist ethic**, natural areas such as forest groves, mountaintops, and waterfalls have spiritual values that are generally superior to the tangible material gain obtained by their exploitation (Muir 1901). This philosophy emphasized the needs of philosophers, poets, artists, and spiritual seekers—who require the beauty and stimulus of nature for their development—over the needs of ordinary people, who require jobs and material goods from the natural environment. Some see this view as undemocratic and elitist, arguing that it disregards the very real material needs of food, clothing, shelter, and employment, which may require economic exploitation of the wilderness. Yet one does not have to be a member of the elite in order to appreciate natural beauty: All human beings share these impulses, and Muir's arguments for the spiritual and artistic value of nature did not limit its accessibility or its benefits to a single stratum of society. That wilderness can benefit all of society can be seen today in special programs, such as Outward Bound, that use experiences with nature and wilderness to challenge and enrich the character development and self-confidence of teenagers and young adults, some of whom might otherwise succumb to drugs, crime, despair, or apathy.

In addition to advocating the preservation of nature on the grounds of human spiritual needs, Muir was among the first American conservationists to explicitly state that nature has **intrinsic value**—value in and of itself, apart from its value to humanity. Muir argued on biblical grounds that because God had created nature and individual species, to destroy them was undoing God's work. In Muir's view, species have an equal place with people in God's scheme of nature (Muir 1916, p. 139):

> Why should man value himself as more than a small part of the one great unit of creation? And what creature of all that the Lord has taken the pains to make is not essential to the completeness of that unit—the cosmos? The universe would be incomplete without the smallest transmicroscopic creature that dwells beyond our conceitful eyes and knowledge.

JOHN MUIR
(1838–1914)

Muir also viewed biological communities as assemblages of species evolving together and dependent on one another, foreshadowing the views of modern ecologists.

An alternative view of nature, known as the **resource conservation ethic**, was developed by Gifford Pinchot, the dynamic first head of the U.S. Forest Service (Meine et al. 2006; Ebbin 2009). According to Pinchot, the world consists essentially of two components, human beings and natural resources. He defined natural resources as the commodities and qualities found in nature, including timber, fodder, clean water, wildlife, and even beautiful landscapes (Pinchot 1947). The proper use of natural resources, according to the resource conservation ethic, is whatever will further "the greatest good of the greatest number [of people] for the longest time." Its first principle is that resources should be fairly distributed among present individuals, and between present and future generations. In this definition, we see the origins of sustainable use doctrines and modern attempts by ecological economists to put a monetary value on natural resources. As defined by the World Commission on Environment and Development (1987), "sustainable development is development that meets the needs of the present without compromising the ability of future generations to meet their own needs." From the perspective of conservation biology, **sustainable development** is development that best meets present and future human needs without damaging the environment and biological diversity (Davies 2008; Czech 2008).

GIFFORD PINCHOT
(1865–1946)

The second principle of the resource conservation ethic is that resources should be used with efficiency—that is, they should be put to the best possible use and not wasted. Efficiency implies that there can be an ordering of uses, with some favored over others, or possibly a "multiple use" of resources. In this view, appreciation of natural beauty and other aesthetic and intellectual experiences can be considered competing uses of nature, which in some situations will take precedence over material uses, although in practice, "multiple use" land managers have usually given precedence to material uses.

Although the resource conservation ethic can be linked to resource economics to determine the "best" or most profitable use of the land, such methods use market forces to determine value and thus have a tendency to minimize or even disregard the costs of environmental degradation and to discount the future value of resources. Consequently, Pinchot argued that government bodies are needed to regulate and control natural resources such as forests and rivers with a long-term perspective to prevent their destruction. The resource conservation ethic came to dominate American thinking in the twentieth century because of its democratic social philosophy and because it supported American efforts to increase control over nature. Government bodies that manage natural resources for multiple use, such as the Bureau of Land Management and the U.S. Forest Service, are the legacy of this conservationist approach, in contrast to the generally preservationist philosophy of the National Park Service.

The resource conservation ethic was the philosophy initially embraced by the influential biologist Aldo Leopold in his early years as a government forester. Eventually, however, he came to believe that the resource conservation ethic was inadequate because it viewed the land merely as a collection of individual goods that can be used in different ways. Leopold began to consider nature as a landscape organized as a system of interrelated processes (Leopold 1939a) and remarked:

> The emergence of ecology has placed the economic biologist in a peculiar dilemma: with one hand he points out the accumulated findings of his search for utility, or lack of utility, in this or that species; with the other he lifts the veil from a biota so complex, so conditioned by interwoven cooperations and competitions, that no man can say where utility begins or ends.

Leopold eventually came to the conclusion that the most important goal of conservation is to maintain the health of natural ecosystems and ecological processes (Leopold

ALDO LEOPOLD
(1887–1948)

2004). As a result, he and many others lobbied successfully for certain parts of national forests to be set aside as wilderness areas (Shafer 2001). He also considered humans part of the ecological community rather than standing apart from and exploiting nature, as the proponents of the resource conservation ethic argued. Despite Leopold's philosophical shift, he remained committed to the idea that humans should be involved in land management, seeking a middle ground between overexploitation and total control over nature, on the one hand, and complete preservation of land with no human presence or activity, on the other.

> Discussions of natural resources, ecosystem management, and sustainable development are major themes throughout the field of conservation biology.

Leopold's synthesis has been termed the **land ethic**. In his writings and in practice at his family farm, Leopold advocated a land use policy in which human use of natural resources was compatible with, or even enhanced, biological diversity (Leopold 1939b, 1949). Integrating human activity into preservationist philosophy also makes practical sense because complete exclusion of human impact from natural reserves has always been very difficult and is now becoming impossible because of human population growth, air pollution, and global climate change. An approach that combines ideas of both Leopold and Pinchot has been developed, known as **ecosystem management**, which places the highest management priority on cooperation among businesses, conservation organizations, government agencies, private citizens, and other interested parties to provide for human needs and to maintain the health of wild species and ecosystems.

Development of these philosophies has taken place alongside the growth of many U.S. conservation organizations, such as the Wilderness Society, the Audubon Society, Ducks Unlimited, and the Sierra Club; the development of the national and state park systems; and the passing of numerous environmental laws. Elements of each of these differing philosophies are present in contemporary writings, the stated goals of conservation organizations, and government policy in both the United States and other countries. Disagreements over policy and practice among and within conservation organizations, individual conservationists, and government departments continue to reflect these long-term philosophical differences. This continuing debate over elements of conservation philosophy and ethics is necessary in deciding how to balance the long-term needs of protecting biological diversity with the more immediate needs of modern society for natural resources.

Environmental activists, writers, and educators have applied these diverse philosophies in ways that have benefited and transformed society. Ellen Swallow Richards (1842–1911) was one such influential individual, though she had great difficulty obtaining a professional position as a chemist, a field not open to women at that time. After being appointed as chemistry instructor at the Massachusetts Institute of Technology, she developed the first course in the new subject of ecology. In her many public activities she emphasized the need to protect the natural environment as a key element in maintaining public health. Richards was particularly concerned with how water quality was affected by sewage and industrial wastes, and she began to test the quality of water in rivers and lakes. Her procedures led to the first water quality standards in the country and eventually to the development of modern sewage treatment plants that help protect public drinking supplies as well as the natural environment.

ELLEN SWALLOW
RICHARDS
(1842–1911)

Another key figure was Rachel Carson (1907–1964). In her widely read book *Silent Spring* (1962), she documented the role of pesticides and the chemical industry in the loss of bird populations. At first she was heavily criticized by representatives of the chemical industry. However, her tireless campaigning led to bans on DDT in many countries and to better regulation of other toxic chemicals, and it was crucial to the development of the modern environmental movement. The recovery of numerous bird species, such as falcons, eagles, and ospreys, in the years following the ban on DDT proved that her observations were correct (see Box 9.1). Carson was especially effective in changing public opinion through writing popular books, some specifically written for children.

Within the American conservation movement, other writers have prophetically warned about the increasing destruction of biological diversity and the natural environment (Meine 2001). Key authors extend from G. P. Marsh, with his *Man and Nature: Or, Physical Geography as Modified by Human Action* (1864), and Fairfield Osborn, author of *Our Plundered Planet* (1948), up to former U.S. Vice President Albert Gore, author of *An Inconvenient Truth: The Planetary Emergency of Global Warming and What We Can Do About It* (2006), and Jared Diamond, with his decisive historical analysis *Collapse* (2005). These authors have found a receptive general audience and have galvanized citizens by the millions to join efforts to protect birds and other wildlife; to conserve mountains, seashores, wetlands, and other habitats; and to limit environmental pollution (Leisher 2008). Over the past decade, a new crop of writers has emerged to address growing concern with global climate change and damage to the world's oceans.

RACHEL CARSON
(1907–1964)

A New Science Is Born

By the early 1970s, scientists throughout the world were aware of an accelerating biological diversity crisis, but there was no central forum or organization to address the issue. The growing number of people thinking about conservation issues and conducting research needed to be able to communicate with each other to develop new ideas and approaches. Ecologist Michael Soulé organized the First International Conference on Conservation Biology in 1978, which met at the San Diego Wild Animal Park, so that wildlife conservationists, zoo managers, and academics could discuss their common interests. At that meeting, Soulé proposed a new interdisciplinary approach that could help save plants and animals from the threat of human-caused extinctions. Subsequently, Soulé, along with colleagues including Paul Ehrlich of Stanford University and Jared Diamond of the University of California at Los Angeles, began to develop conservation biology as a discipline that would combine the practical experience of wildlife, forestry, and fisheries management with the theories of population biology and biogeography. In 1985, this core of scientists founded the Society for Conservation Biology.

Conservation Biology: A Dynamic and Growing Field

The field of conservation biology has set itself some imposing—and absolutely critical—tasks: to describe the Earth's biological diversity, to restore what is degraded, and to protect what is remaining. Fortunately, the field is up to such tasks. The indicators listed below show just how dynamic the field is today.

- *Conservation biology has resulted in government action, both nationally and internationally.* The protection of biological diversity has emerged as a major goal of many national governments, as shown by the widespread government action being taken on behalf of conservation biology: laws such as the U.S. Endangered Species Act; Red Lists of endangered species in the European Union; new national parks and protected areas; international treaties, such as the Convention on Biological Diversity; and increased regulations on trade and harvesting of endangered species, most notably the Convention on Trade in Endangered Species (CITES).

- *Conservation biology programs and activities are being funded as never before.* Major funding agencies have made conservation biology a primary recipient for funding. For example, the Global Environment Facility, a special program

2010 International Year of Biodiversity

FIGURE 1.6 The United Nations has declared 2010 to be the International Year of Biodiversity. (Courtesy of the Secretariat of the Convention on Biological Diversity.)

established by the United Nations and the World Bank, has allocated $8.6 billion in funding and $36 billion in cofinancing for more than 2400 projects in over 165 countries involving conservation and environmental protection (www.thegef.org/gef). Major foundations, such as the MacArthur Foundation, the Ford Foundation, and the Pew Charitable Trusts, also make conservation activities a major priority.

- *Conservation biology's goals have been adopted by traditional conservation organizations.* Large, established conservation organizations such as The Nature Conservancy, the World Wildlife Fund, and Birdlife International, which formerly had a restricted set of priorities, have embraced the broader goals of conservation biology, making science central to decision making.

- *Conservation biology's goals are being incorporated into international scientific activities and policy.* For example, in 2005, over 1300 scientists from 95 countries completed the Millennium Ecosystem Assessment, promoting the value of biodiversity to the public, government officials, and funding agencies as well as describing actions needed to protect it. The United Nations has declared 2010 to be the Year of Biodiversity (**Figure 1.6**). In addition, innovative, open-access projects such as Encyclopedia of Life, Tree of Life, and the Global Biodiversity Information Facility are producing a comprehensive list of all known species and related databases of species distribution, evolutionary relationships, conservation status, habitat, and documented museum specimens.

- *Conservation biology's aims and goals are reaching a broader audience through increased media coverage* (Morrell 1999). The latest findings of the field reach an even wider audience through popular magazines such as National Geographic, National Wildlife, Scientific American, and Environment; newspapers such as the New York Times; and nature television programs such as those found on Nova and on the National Geographic Channel. The prominence of environmental concerns was highlighted by the award of the 2007 Nobel Peace Prize to former U.S. Vice President Al Gore and the Intergovernmental Panel on Climate Change (IPCC) for bringing the issue of global climate change to public attention.

> Since its formal inception in 1985, the field of conservation biology has continued to grow in scope and influence. The United Nations has even designated 2010 as the Year of Biodiversity.

- *Conservation biology courses and curricula are expanding.* More than 150 American, Canadian, European, and Australian colleges and universities, and numerous universities in other countries, have established graduate programs in conservation biology and biological diversity; large numbers of courses are being taught at all levels (see also www.gradschools.com). This development in higher education is driven by the interests of students (Van Heezik and Seddon 2005), the changing research activities of professors, and the willingness of foundations to support new programs.

- *Conservation biology has a rapidly expanding professional society.* The Society for Conservation Biology (SCB) has become one of the fastest-growing and most exciting societies in biology (**Figure 1.7**). The SCB now has more than 10,000 professional members in 120 countries (www.conbio.org), equaling the size of the Ecological Society of America, which was founded more than 90 years ago. The growing membership in the SCB reflects the perceived relevance of this new discipline.

Despite the threats to biological diversity, we can detect many positive signs that allow conservation biologists to remain cautiously hopeful. The number of people living in extreme poverty has been in decline since the Industrial Revolution, and the rate of human population growth has slowed (Sachs 2008). The number of protected areas around the globe continues to increase, with a dramatic expansion in the number of marine protected areas. In just 2006, the South Pacific country of Kiribati established the world's largest marine sanctuary. Moreover, our ability to protect biological diversity has been strengthened due to a wide range of local, national, and international efforts. Certain endangered species are now recovering as a result of conservation measures. We can point to an expansion of our knowledge base and the science of conservation biology, the developing linkages with rural development and social sciences, and our increased ability to restore degraded environments. All of these suggest that progress is being made despite the enormous tasks still ahead.

FIGURE 1.7 The Society for Conservation Biology has a simple, yet powerful, logo showing the circle of life, within which we live. The ocean waves in the center symbolize the changes that lie ahead. The logo can also be viewed as a bird, which provides us with beauty; on closer look, we see that its wings are really rustling leaves. (Courtesy of the Society for Conservation Biology.)

Summary

1. Thousands of species are going extinct, genetic variation is being lost, millions of populations are disappearing, and entire ecosystems are being destroyed as a result of human activities. Conservation biology is a synthetic discipline combining basic and applied research to describe biological diversity, document the threats it faces from human activities, and develop methods to protect and restore biological diversity.

2. Conservation biology rests on a number of underlying assumptions that are accepted by most conservation biologists: biological diversity, including the range of species, genetic variation, biological communities, and ecosystem interactions, should be preserved; the extinction of species by human activities should be prevented; the complex interaction of species in natural communities should be maintained; evolutionary change should continue; and biological diversity has value in and of itself.

3. Conservation biology draws on both scientific and religious/philosophical traditions. European scientists in the eighteenth and nineteenth centuries reacted to the destruction of forests and water pollution in their colonies by proposing some of the first environmental legislation. The decline and extinction of species in Europe led to the establishment of the first nature reserves and an active popular interest in conservation. In the United States, Henry David Thoreau and John Muir argued for the preservation of wilderness and the intrinsic value of species. Gifford Pinchot proposed developing a balance among competing natural resource needs for present and future societies. Aldo Leopold advocated striking a balance between managing land for ecological processes and satisfying human needs. These philosophies still guide land management, and elements of them can be found in the current doctrines of conservation organizations and government departments.

For Discussion

1. How is conservation biology fundamentally different from other branches of biology, such as physiology, genetics, or cell biology? How is it different from environmentalism?

2. What do you think are the major conservation and environmental problems facing the world today? What are the major problems facing your local community? What ideas for solving these problems can you suggest? (Try answering this question now, and once again when you have completed this book.)

3. Consider the public land management and private conservation organizations with which you are familiar. Would you consider their guiding philosophies to be closest to the resource conservation ethic, the preservation ethic, or the evolutionary–ecological land ethic? What factors allow them to be successful or limit their effectiveness? Learn more about these organizations through their publications and Web sites.

4. How would you characterize your own viewpoint about the conservation of biodiversity and the environment? Which of the religious or philosophical viewpoints of conservation biology stated here do you agree or disagree with? How do you, or could you, put your viewpoint into practice?

Suggested Readings

Chan, K. M. A. 2008. Value and advocacy in conservation biology: Crisis discipline or discipline in crisis? *Conservation Biology* 22: 1–3. Conservation biologists need to be more effective advocates on behalf of biodiversity.

Czech, B. 2008. Prospects for reconciling the conflict between economic growth and biodiversity conservation with technological progress. *Conservation Biology* 22: 1389–1398. Is it possible to balance ever greater human use of natural resources with the need to protect biodiversity?

Diamond, J. 2005. *Collapse: How Societies Choose to Fail or Succeed.* Viking Press, New York. An eminent biologist describes patterns of environmental catastrophe that have destroyed human societies in the past and that threaten us today.

Dudley, N., L. Higgins-Zogib, and S. Mansourian. 2009. The links between protected areas, faiths, and sacred natural sites. *Conservation Biology* 23: 568–577. In many places, local people are already protecting biodiversity.

Hall, J. A. and E. Fleishman. 2010. Demonstration as a means to translate conservation science into practice. *Conservation Biology* 24: 120–127. Conservation biologists need to demonstrate to the public and government how their ideas work in practice.

Leisher, C. 2008. What Rachel Carson knew about marine protected areas. *BioScience* 58: 478–479. The key to effective MPAs is often getting local people involved.

Leopold, A. 1949. *A Sand County Almanac.* Oxford University Press, New York. Leopold's evocative essays articulate his "land ethic," defining human duty to conserve the land and the living things that thrive upon it.

Marris, E. 2007. What to let go. *Nature* 450: 152–155. In this time of crisis, scientists are identifying species and ecosystems that are the highest priorities for funding and conservation action.

Millennium Ecosystem Assessment (MEA). 2005. *Ecosystems and Human Well-Being.* 4 vols. Island Press, Washington, D.C. Detailed report and summary by the world's leading scientists documenting the importance of ecosystem services.

Morell, V. 1999. The variety of life. *National Geographic* 195 (February): 6–32. Special issue includes beautifully illustrated articles about biodiversity, threats to its existence, and key conservation projects.

Nelson, M. P. and J. A. Vucetich. 2009. On advocacy by environmental scientists: What, whether, why, and how. *Conservation Biology* 23: 1090–1101. Scientists have a responsibility to be advocates as well as researchers.

Orr, D. W. 2007. Optimism and hope in a hotter time. *Conservation Biology* 21: 1392–1395. Hope means to learn the truth and then have the courage to act accordingly.

Papworth, S. K., J. Rist, L. Coad, and E. J. Milner-Gulland. 2009. Evidence for shifting baseline syndrome in conservation. *Conservation Letters* 2: 93–100. People often forget what biodiversity was like in the past.

Van Heezik, Y. and P. J. Seddon. 2005. Conservation education structure and content of graduate wildlife management and conservation biology programs: An international perspective. *Conservation Biology* 19: 7–14. Conservation education programs are increasing and are highly diverse.

World Resources Institute (WRI). 2005. *World Resources 2005: The Wealth of the Poor—Managing Ecosystems to Fight Poverty.* World Resources Institute, Washington, D.C. Massive body of data on biodiversity and the human condition.

KEY JOURNALS IN THE FIELD *Biodiversity and Conservation, Biological Conservation, BioScience, Conservation Biology, Conservation Letters, Ecological Applications, Journal of Applied Ecology, National Geographic*

What Is Biological Diversity?

The protection of biological diversity is central to conservation biology. Conservation biologists use the term **biological diversity**, or simply **biodiversity**, to mean the complete range of species and biological communities, as well as the genetic variation within species and all ecosystem processes. By this definition, biodiversity must be considered on three levels:

1. *Species diversity.* All the species on Earth, including single-celled bacteria and protists as well as the species of the multicellular kingdoms (plants, fungi, and animals)

2. *Genetic diversity.* The genetic variation within species, both among geographically separate populations and among individuals within single populations

3. *Ecosystem diversity.* The different biological communities and their associations with the chemical and physical environment (the ecosystem) (**Figure 2.1**)

All three levels of biological diversity are necessary for the continued survival of life as we know it, and all are important to people (Levin 2001; MEA 2005). **Species diversity** reflects the entire range of evolutionary and ecological adaptations of species to particular environments. It provides people with

FIGURE 2.1 Biological diversity includes genetic diversity (the genetic variation found within each species), species diversity (the range of species in a given ecosystem), and community/ecosystem diversity (the variety of habitat types and ecosystem processes extending over a given region). (After Palumbi 2009.)

resources and resource alternatives—for example, a tropical rain forest or a temperate swamp with many species produces a wide variety of plant and animal products that can be used as food, shelter, and medicine. **Genetic diversity** is necessary for any species to maintain reproductive vitality, resistance to disease, and the ability to adapt to changing conditions (Laikre et al. 2010). In domestic plants and animals, genetic diversity is of particular value in the breeding programs necessary to sustain and improve modern agricultural species and their disease resistance. **Ecosystem diversity** results from the collective response of species to different environmental conditions. Biological communities found in deserts, grasslands, wetlands, and forests support the continuity of proper ecosystem functioning, which provides crucial services to people, such as water for drinking and agriculture, flood control, protection from soil erosion, and filtering of air and water. We will now examine each level of biodiversity in turn.

Species Diversity

Species diversity includes the entire range of species found on Earth. Recognizing and classifying species is one of the major goals of conservation biology (Morell 1999). How do biologists identify individual species among the mass of living organisms on Earth, many of them small in size and with few distinguishing features? And what is the origin of new species? Identifying the process whereby one species evolves into one or more new species is one of the ongoing accomplishments of modern biology. The origin of new species is normally a slow process, taking place over hundreds, if not thousands, of generations. The evolution of higher taxa, such as new genera and families, is an even slower process, typically lasting hundreds of thousands or even millions of years. In contrast, human activities are destroying in only a few decades the unique species built up by these slow natural processes.

What Is a Species?

A species is generally defined in one of two ways:

1. A group of individuals that is morphologically,* physiologically, or biochemically distinct from other groups in some important characteristic is the **morphological definition of species**.

2. A group of individuals that can potentially breed among themselves in the wild and that do not breed with individuals of other groups is the **biological definition of species**.

Because the methods and assumptions used are different, these two approaches to distinguishing species sometimes do not give the same results. Increasingly, differences in DNA sequences and other molecular markers distinguish species that look almost identical, such as types of bacteria (Janzen et al. 2009).

The morphological definition of species is the one most commonly used by **taxonomists**, biologists who specialize in the identification of unknown specimens and the classification of species (**Figure 2.2**). In practice, the biological definition of species

---

*An individual's morphology is its form and structure—or, to put it more simply (if not totally accurately), its appearance.

(A)
(B)

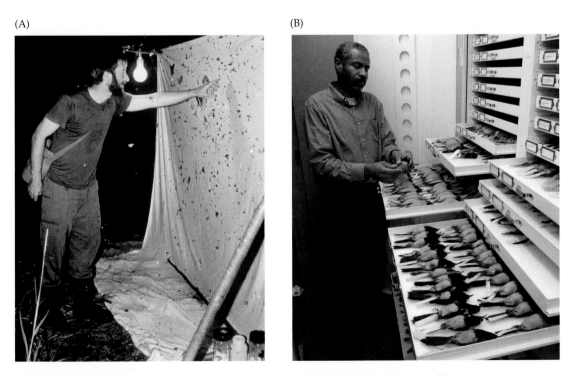

FIGURE 2.2 (A) An entomologist collects moth specimens that land on a lighted white sheet. (B) An ornithologist at the Museum of Comparative Zoology, Harvard University classifying collections of orioles: Black-cowled Oriole (*Icterus prosthemelas*) from Mexico and Baltimore Orioles (*Icterus galbula*) which occur throughout eastern North America. (A, photograph © The Natural History Museum/Alamy; B, photograph courtesy of Jeremiah Trimble, Museum of Comparative Zoology, Harvard University © President and Fellows of Harvard College.)

is difficult to use, because it requires a knowledge of which individuals actually have the potential to breed with one another and their relationships to each other—information that is rarely available. As a result, practicing field biologists learn to recognize one or more individuals that look different from other individuals and might represent a different species, sometimes referring to them as **morpho-species** or another such term until taxonomists can give them official scientific names (**Box 2.1**; Norden et al. 2009).

Problems in distinguishing and identifying species are more common than many people realize (Bickford et al. 2007; Haig et al. 2006). For example, a single species

> Using morphological and genetic information to identify species is a major activity for taxonomists; taxonomists have only described about one-third of the earth's species.

may have several varieties that have observable morphological differences, yet the varieties are similar enough to be considered a single biological species. Different varieties of dogs, such as German shepherds, collies, and beagles, all belong to one species and readily interbreed despite the conspicuous morphological differences among them (**Figure 2.3**). Alternatively, closely related "sibling" species appear very similar in morphology and physiology, yet they are biologically separate and do not interbreed. In practice, biologists often find it difficult to distinguish variation *within* a single species from variation *between* closely related species. For example, genetic analysis of New Zealand's unique reptile, the tuatara (*Sphenodon punctatus*), revealed that there are actually two distinct species of tuatara, both deserving scientific recognition and conservation protection (Hay et al. 2003). And scientists are still debating whether the African elephant is one widespread, variable species or is actually three separate species: a savanna species, a forest species, and a desert species.

Taxonomists are now aware that in many cases what were thought to be separate populations of the same species are in fact genetically distinct, different species. Increasingly, differences in DNA sequences and other molecular markers are being used to distinguish species that look virtually identical, including many species of bacteria, plants, and even animals. Conservation biologists and taxonomists are now developing a system that will identify the species of a living organism based on the DNA from any tissue sample, a method termed **DNA barcoding** (Valentini et al. 2009). Using such an approach, researchers found that a common small black wasp in Costa Rica that was thought to parasitize many different species of catepillar, was actually composed of many distinct wasp species, each of which parasitized different caterpillar species (Janzen et al. 2009).

Such a situation has been dubbed **cryptic biodiversity**—the widespread existence of undescribed species that have been wrongly classified and grouped with a similar-appearing species (Seidel et al. 2009).

To further complicate matters, individuals of related but distinct species may occasionally mate and produce **hybrids**, intermediate forms that blur the distinction between species. Sometimes hybrids are better suited to their environment than either parent species, and they can go on to form new species. Hybridization is particularly common among plant species in disturbed habitats. Hybridization in both plants and animals frequently occurs when a few individuals of a rare species are surrounded by large numbers of a closely related species. For example, the endangered Ethiopian wolf (*Canis simensis*) frequently mates with domestic dogs, and declining British populations of the European wildcat (*Felis silvestris*) are being swamped with genetic material due to matings with domestic cats. In the United States, protection of the endangered red wolf (*Canis rufus*) was almost withdrawn because morphological and genetic evidence demonstrated that many of the remaining individuals are hybrids formed

FIGURE 2.3 Breeds of dogs have been bred for different characteristics, including size, shape, color, and behavior, yet they still interbreed and are considered one species. (Photograph © Moodboard/Photolibrary.com.)

BOX 2.1 *Naming and Classifying Species*

■ **Taxonomy** is the science of classifying living things. The goal of modern taxonomy is to create a system of classification that reflects the evolution of groups of species from their ancestors. By identifying the relationships between species, taxonomists help conservation biologists identify species or groups that may be evolutionarily unique and/or particularly worthy of conservation efforts. Information about the taxonomy, ecology, morphology, distribution, and status of species is being organized into central databases accessible via the Internet, such as the Tree of Life (www.tol web.org). In modern classification, the following groupings apply:

Similar species are grouped into a **genus** (plural, **genera**): the Blackburnian warbler (*Dendroica fusca*) and many similar warbler species belong to the genus *Dendroica*.

Similar genera are grouped into a **family**: all wood warbler genera belong to the family Parulidae.

Similar families are grouped into an **order**: all songbird families belong to the order Passeriformes.

Similar orders are grouped into a **class**: all bird orders belong to the class Aves.

Similar classes are grouped into a **phylum** (plural, **phyla**): all vertebrate classes belong to the phylum Chordata.

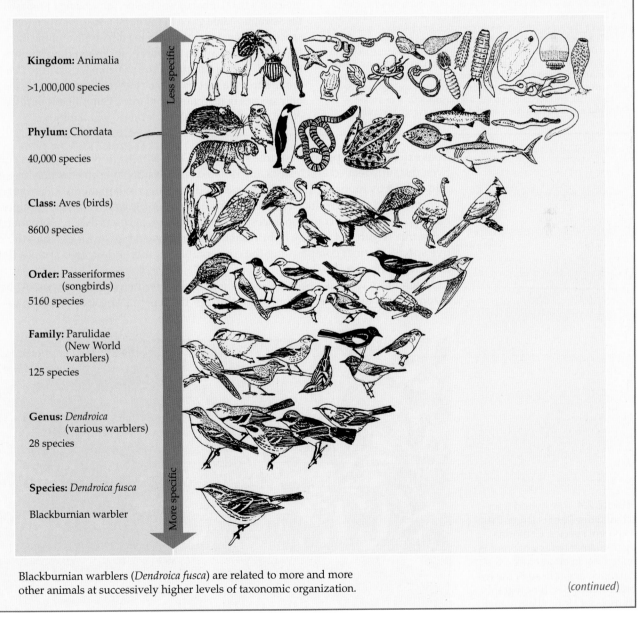

Kingdom: Animalia

>1,000,000 species

Phylum: Chordata

40,000 species

Class: Aves (birds)

8600 species

Order: Passeriformes (songbirds)

5160 species

Family: Parulidae (New World warblers)

125 species

Genus: *Dendroica* (various warblers)

28 species

Species: *Dendroica fusca*

Blackburnian warbler

Less specific / More specific

Blackburnian warblers (*Dendroica fusca*) are related to more and more other animals at successively higher levels of taxonomic organization.

(continued)

BOX 2.1 (*continued*)

Similar phyla are grouped into a **kingdom**: all animal classes belong to the kingdom Animalia.*

Biologists throughout the world have agreed to use a standard set of scientific, or Latin, names when discussing species. The use of scientific names avoids the confusion that can occur when using common names; the Latin names are standard across countries and languages. Scientific species names consist of two words. This naming system, known as **binomial nomenclature**, was developed in the eighteenth century by the Swedish biologist Carolus Lin-

naeus. In the scientific name for the Blackburnian warbler, *Dendroica fusca*, *Dendroica* is the genus name and *fusca* is the species name. The genus name is somewhat similar to a person's family name in that many people can have the same family name (Sullivan), while the species name is similar to a person's given name (Margaret).

Scientific names are written in a standard way to avoid confusion. The first letter of the genus name is always capitalized, whereas the species name is almost always lowercased. Scientific names are italicized in print or underlined when handwritten. Sometimes scientific names are followed by a person's name, as in *Homo sapiens* Linnaeus, indicating that Linnaeus was the person who first proposed the scientific name given to the human species. When many species in a single genus are being discussed, or if the identity of a species within a genus is uncertain, the abbreviations spp. or sp., respectively, are sometimes used (e.g., *Dendroica* spp.). If a species has no close relatives, it may be the only species in its genus. Similarly, a genus that is unrelated to any other genera may form its own family.

*Until recently, most modern biologists recognized five kingdoms in the living world: plants, animals, fungi, monerans (single-celled species without a nucleus and without mitochondria, such as bacteria), and protists (more complex single-celled species with a nucleus and mitochondria). With the increasing sophistication of molecular techniques, many biologists now use a system of classification with six kingdoms within three domains: Bacteria (common bacteria), Archaea (ancient bacteria that live in extreme environments, such as hypersaline pools, hot springs, and deep sea vents), and the Eucarya (all organisms with a membrane-bound nucleus, including animals, plants, fungi, and protists).

---

from extensive mating with common coyotes (*Canis latrans*) (www.redwolves.com). Even distantly related and historically isolated species may interbreed when brought into contact by humans. The endangered California tiger salamader (*Ambystoma californiense*) and the introduced barred tiger salamander (*A. mavortium*) are thought to have evolved from a common ancestor 5 million years ago, yet they readily mate in California (**Figure 2.4**). These hybrid salamanders have a higher fitness than the native species, further complicating the conservation of this endangered species (Fitzpatrick and Shaffer 2007).

Much more work is needed to catalog and classify the world's species. At best, taxonomists have described only one-third of the world's species, and perhaps as

FIGURE 2.4 The hybrid tiger salamander (left) is larger than its parent species, California tiger salamander (right), and is increasing in abundance. Note the much larger head of the hybrid salamander. (Photograph courtesy of H. Bradley Shaffer.)

little as a few percent. The inability to clearly distinguish one species from another, whether due to similarities of characteristics or to confusion over the correct scientific name, often slows down efforts at species protection. It is difficult to write precise, effective laws to protect a species if scientists and lawmakers are not certain what name should be used. At the same time, species are going extinct before they are even described. Tens of thousands of new species are being described each year, but even this rate is not fast enough. The key to solving this problem is to train more taxonomists, especially for work in the species-rich tropics (Wilson 2003). We'll return to this topic in Chapter 3.

The Origin of New Species

The biochemical similarity of all living species and the uniform use of DNA as the genetic code indicate that life on Earth originated only once, about 3.5 billion years ago. From one original species came the millions of species found on Earth today. The process of new species formation, known as **speciation**, continues today and will most likely continue into the future.

This process, whereby one original species evolves into one or more new and distinct species, was first described by Charles Darwin and Alfred Russel Wallace more than 100 years ago (Darwin 1859; Futuyma 2009). Their theory of the origin of new species is widely accepted today in the scientific community* and continues to be further refined and developed, along with the science of genetics. The wealth of new information that is continuously provided by the fossil record, along with the extensive modern research in molecular biology, has provided additional support for the ideas of Darwin and Wallace.

The theory of evolution is both simple and elegant. Imagine a population of a species—mountain rabbits living in Canada, for example. Individuals in the population tend to produce more offspring than can survive in that place. Most offspring will die before reaching maturity. In the population, each pair of rabbits will produce numerous litters of six or more offspring, yet on average, in a stable population, only two of those offspring will survive to adulthood. Individuals in the population show variations in certain characteristics (such as fur thickness), and some of these characteristics are inherited; that is, they are passed from parents to offspring via genes. These genetic variations are caused both by mutations—spontaneous changes in the chromosomes—and by the rearrangement of chromosomes that occurs during sexual reproduction. Within the rabbit population, some individuals have thicker fur than others because of such genetic differences. These differences will enable some individuals to grow, survive, and reproduce better than others, a phenomenon sometimes referred to as survival of the fittest. Our hypothetical thick-furred rabbits will be more likely to survive cold winters than rabbits with thinner fur. As a result of the improved survival ability associated with a certain genetic characteristic, the individuals possessing that characteristic will be more likely to produce offspring than the others; over time, the genetic composition of the population will change. After a series of cold winters, more thick-furred rabbits will have survived and produced thick-furred offspring, while more thin-furred rabbits will have died. Consequently, more rabbits in the population will have thicker fur than in previous generations. At the same time, another population of the same species living in a lowland area or further south could be undergoing selection for individuals with thinner fur in response to warming conditions.

In the process of evolution, populations often genetically adapt to changes in their environment. These changes may be biological (new food sources, new com-

---

*That evolution occurs is regarded by virtually all biologists as fact. Several popular and scholarly books (e.g., Futuyma 2009; Shanks 2004) discuss religion-based arguments (and intelligent-design arguments) against evolution and why most scientists do not accept such arguments.

petitors, new predators) as well as environmental (climate, water availability, soil characteristics). When a population has undergone so much genetic change that it is no longer able to interbreed with the original species from which it derives, the population can be considered a new species. This gradual transformation of one species into another is termed **phyletic evolution**.

In order for two or more new species to evolve from one original ancestor, there is usually a geographical barrier that prevents the movement of individuals between the various populations of a species (Futuyma 2009). For terrestrial species, these barriers may be rivers, mountain ranges, or oceans that the species cannot readily cross. Aquatic species adapt to particular lakes, rivers, or estuaries, which are separated from one another by land. Speciation is particularly rapid on islands. Island groups, such as the Galápagos and the Hawaiian Islands, are homes to many examples of insects and plants that were originally local populations of a single colonizing species. These local populations adapted genetically to the distinctive environments of particular unoccupied islands, mountains, and isolated valleys. Often in the absence of the competitors, predators, and parasites that affected them on the mainland, they diverged sufficiently from the original species to be considered separate species. This process of local adaptation and subsequent speciation is known as **adaptive radiation**. One of the best-known examples of adaptive radiation is that of the Hawaiian honeycreepers, a group of specialized bird species that apparently derives from a single pair of birds that arrived by chance in the Hawaiian Islands tens of thousands of years ago (**Figure 2.5**). Over this time period, honeycreeper species have evolved bill shapes and behaviors that are specialized to particular food resources.

The origination of new species is normally a slow process, taking place over hundreds, if not thousands, of generations. The evolution of new genera and families is an even slower process, lasting hundreds of thousands, or even millions, of years. However, there are mechanisms whereby new species can arise in just one generation without geographical separation. Unusual, unequal divisions of chromosome sets during reproduction may result in offspring with extra sets of chromosomes; these offspring are known as **polyploids**. Polyploid individuals may be morphologically and physiologically different from their parents and, if they are well suited to the environment, may form a new species within the range of the parent species. Hybrids that result from mating between individuals of two different species can also form new species, especially when they have different characteristics from their parents and mate among themselves. New polyploid species are particularly common in plants.

Even though new species are arising all the time, the present rate of species extinction is probably more than 100 times faster than the rate of speciation and may even be 1000 times faster. The situation is actually worse than this grim statistic suggests. First, the rate of speciation may actually be slowing down because so much of the Earth's surface has been taken over for human use and no longer supports evolving biological communities. As habitats decline, fewer populations of each species exist, and thus there are fewer opportunities for evolution. Many of the existing protected areas and national parks may be too small to allow the process of speciation to occur (**Figure 2.6**). Second, many of the species threatened with extinction in the wild are the sole remaining representatives of their genus or family; examples include the gorilla (*Gorilla gorilla*), rapidly declining throughout its range in Africa, and the giant panda (*Ailuropoda melanoleuca*) in China. The extinction of taxonomically unique species representing ancient lineages is not balanced by the appearance of new species that are closely related to existing species.

Measuring Species Diversity

Conservation biologists often want to identify locations of high species diversity. In the broadest sense, species diversity is simply the number of different species in a place. However, there are many other specialized, quantitative definitions of species diver-

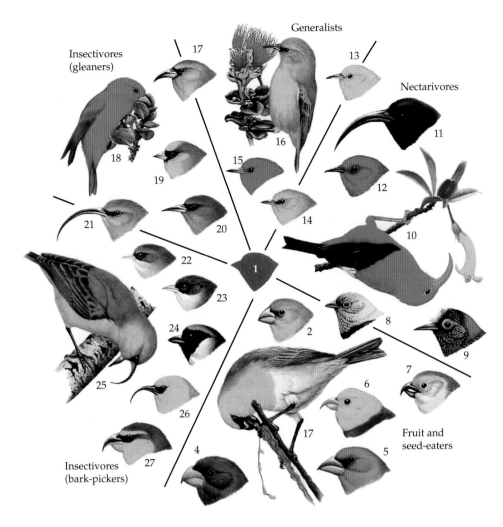

Insectivores (gleaners)

17

Generalists

13

Nectarivores

18

19

15

16

11

12

14

10

21

20

22

23

24

2

8

9

25

26

7

6

17

5

Fruit and seed-eaters

27

4

Insectivores (bark-pickers)

1

FIGURE 2.5 The Hawaiian honeycreeper family, a spectacular example of adaptive radiation, is thought to have arisen from one pair of birds that arrived on the Hawaiian Islands (indicated by #1). The shape and size of the bill are related to foods eaten: sharp for eating insects or long and thin for bark-pickers, thick for cracking seeds and eating fruit, long and curved for feeding on nectar and generalists with short, sharp bills. Black lines separate different feeding habits. Different color patterns represent adaptations for mating behavior. Numbered birds indicate different species, both living and recently extinct. (Courtesy of Doug Pratt.)

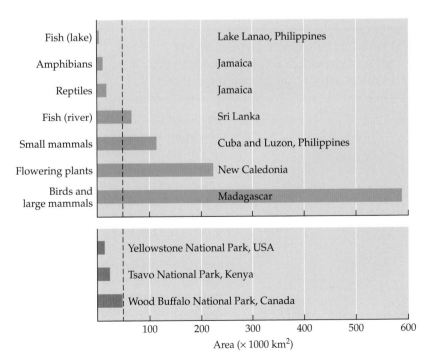

FIGURE 2.6 Certain groups of organisms apparently need a minimum area in order to undergo the process of speciation (upper graph). For example, for small mammals, the smallest islands (Cuba and Luzon) on which a single species is known to have given rise to two species are 100,000 km². The bottom graph shows the areas of some national parks. Even the largest national park shown (dotted line) is probably too small to allow for the evolution of new species of river fish, flowering plants, birds, or mammals, although it might be large enough for the continued evolution of lake fishes, amphibians, and reptiles. (After Soulé 1980.)

Fish (lake) — Lake Lanao, Philippines
Amphibians — Jamaica
Reptiles — Jamaica
Fish (river) — Sri Lanka
Small mammals — Cuba and Luzon, Philippines
Flowering plants — New Caledonia
Birds and large mammals — Madagascar

Yellowstone National Park, USA
Tsavo National Park, Kenya
Wood Buffalo National Park, Canada

100   200   300   400   500   600

Area (× 1000 km²)

sity that ecologists have developed as a means of comparing the overall diversity of different communities at varying geographical scales (Legendre et al. 2005; Thiere et al. 2009). Ecologists have used these quantitative measures to test the assumption that increasing levels of diversity lead to increasing community stability and biomass production. In controlled experiments in greenhouses or gardens, or in grassland plant communities, increasing the number of species growing together generally leads to greater biomass production and resistance to drought. However, the significance of this result to the broader range of natural communities, such as forests and coral reefs, still needs to be convincingly demonstrated. Measures of biological diversity used by field ecologists are often most useful for comparing particular groups of species within or among communities and determining patterns of distribution. These researchers typically consider the diversity of plants, birds, or frogs separately.

At its simplest level, diversity has been defined as the number of species found in a community, a measure often called **species richness**. Quantitative indexes of biodiversity have been developed primarily to denote species diversity at three different geographical scales. The number of species in a certain community or designated area is described as **alpha diversity**. Alpha diversity comes closest to the popular concept of species richness and can be used to compare the number of species in particular places or ecosystem types, such as lakes or forests. For example, a 100 ha deciduous forest in New York or England has fewer tree species than a 100 ha patch of the Amazon rain forest; that is, the alpha diversity of the rain forest is greater. More highly quantitative indexes such as the Shannon diversity index take the relative abundance of different species into account and assign the highest diversity to communities with large numbers of species that are equally abundant and the lowest scores to communities in which there are either few species, or a large number of species, one or a few of which are much more abundant than the others.

Gamma diversity applies to larger geographical scales. It refers to the number of species in a large region or on a continent. Gamma diversity allows us to compare large areas that encompass diverse landscapes or a wide geographical area. For example, Kenya, with 1000 species of forest birds, has a higher gamma diversity than Britain, which has only 200 species.

Beta diversity links alpha and gamma diversity. It represents the rate of change of species composition along an environmental or geographical gradient. For example, if each lake in a region contained different fish species, or if the bird species on one mountain were entirely different from the birds on neighboring mounts, then beta diversity would be high. However, if the species composition along the gradient did not change much ("the birds on this mountain are the same as the birds on the mountain we visited yesterday"), then beta diversity would be low. Beta diversity is sometimes calculated as the gamma diversity of a region divided by the average alpha diversity, though other measures also exist.

> Identifying patterns of species diversity helps conservation biologists establish which locations are most in need of protection.

We can illustrate the three types of diversity with a theoretical example of three mountain ranges (**Figure 2.7**). Region 1 has the highest alpha diversity, with more species per mountain on average (six species) than the other two regions. Region 2 has the highest gamma diversity, with a total of ten species. Dividing gamma by alpha shows that region 3 has a higher beta diversity (2.7) than region 2 (2.5) or region 1 (1.2) because all of its species are found on only one mountain each.

These quantitative definitions of diversity are useful for talking about patterns of species distribution and for comparing regions of the world. They are also valuable for highlighting areas that require conservation protection. As an example, artificial wetlands in agricultural landscapes in Sweden were evaluated for their aquatic invertebrate diversity, including snails, insects, and worms. It was found that over 80% of species richness was attributed to beta diversity (Thiere et al. 2009). This result indicates that protecting many wetlands is needed, rather than focusing on just a few sites.

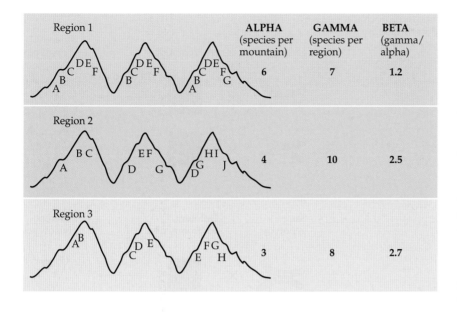

	ALPHA (species per mountain)	GAMMA (species per region)	BETA (gamma/ alpha)
Region 1	6	7	1.2
Region 2	4	10	2.5
Region 3	3	8	2.7

FIGURE 2.7 Biodiversity indexes for three regions, each consisting of three separate mountains. Each letter represents a population of a species; some species are found on only one mountain, while other species are found on two or three mountains. Alpha, gamma, and beta diversity values are shown for each region. If funds were available to protect only one *mountain range*, Region 2 should be selected because it has the greatest gamma (total) diversity. However, if only one *mountain* could be protected, a mountain in Region 1 should be selected because these mountains have the highest alpha (local) diversity, that is, the greatest average number of species per mountain. Each mountain in Region 3 has a more distinct assemblage of species than the mountains in the other two regions, as shown by the higher beta diversity. If Region 3 were selected for protection, the relative priority of the individual mountains should then be judged based on the relative rarity of the assemblages.

Genetic Diversity

At each level of biological diversity—genetic, species, and ecosystem—conservation biologists study the mechanisms that alter or maintain diversity. Genetic diversity within a species is often affected by the reproductive behavior of individuals within populations. A **population** is a group of individuals that mate with one another and produce offspring; a species may include one or more separate populations. A population may consist of only a few individuals or millions of individuals, provided that the individuals actually produce offspring. A single individual of a sexual species would not constitute a population. Neither does a group of individuals that cannot reproduce; for example, the last ten dusky seaside sparrows (*Ammodramus maritimus nigrescens*), native to the southeastern United States, did not constitute a true population, because all of them were male.

Individuals within a population usually are genetically different from one another. Genetic variation arises because individuals have slightly different forms of their **genes** (or **loci**), the units of the chromosomes that code for specific proteins. These different forms of a gene are known as **alleles**, and the differences originally arise through **mutations**—changes that occur in the deoxyribonucleic acid (DNA) that constitutes an individual's chromosomes. The various alleles of a gene may affect the development and physiology of an individual organism.

Genetic variation increases when offspring receive unique combinations of genes and chromosomes from their parents via the **recombination** of genes that occurs during sexual reproduction. Genes are exchanged between chromosomes, and new combinations are created when chromosomes from two parents combine to form a genetically unique offspring. Although mutations provide the basic material for genetic variation, the random rearrangement of alleles in different combinations that characterizes sexually reproducing species dramatically increases the potential for genetic variation.

The total array of genes and alleles in a population is the **gene pool** of the population, while the particular combination of alleles that any individual possesses is its **genotype** (Winker 2009). The **phenotype** of an individual represents the morphological, physiological, anatomical, and biochemical characteristics of the individual that result from the expression of its genotype in a particular environment

FIGURE 2.8 The physical, physiological, and biochemical characteristics of an individual—its phenotype—are determined by its genotype and by the environment (e.g., hot vs. cold climate; abundant vs. scarce food) in which the individual lives. (After Alcock 1993.)

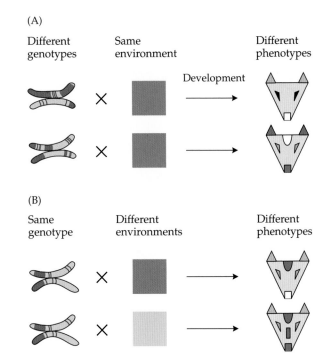

(**Figure 2.8**). Some characteristics of humans, such as the amount of body fat and tooth decay, are strikingly influenced by the environment, while other characteristics, such as eye color, blood type, and forms of certain enzymes, are determined predominantly by an individual's genotype.

Sometimes individuals that differ genetically also differ in ways related to their survival or ability to reproduce—such as their ability to tolerate cold, as in our hypothetical thick-furred rabbits; their resistance to disease; or the speed at which they can run away from danger. If individuals with certain alleles are better able to survive and produce offspring than individuals without these alleles, then **gene frequencies** in the population will change in subsequent generations. This phenomenon is called **natural selection**. Our hypothetical rabbits in the cold climate are experiencing natural selection against thin, short fur.

> Genetic variation within a species can allow the species to adapt to environmental change; genetic variation can also increase the value of domestic species to people.

The amount of genetic variability in a population is determined by both the number of genes that have more than one allele (**polymorphic genes**) and the number of alleles for each of these genes (**Figure 2.9**). The existence of a polymorphic gene also means that some individuals in the population will be **heterozygous** for the gene; that is, they will receive a different allele of the gene from each parent. On the other hand, some individuals will be **homozygous**: they will receive the same allele from each parent. All these levels of genetic variation contribute to a population's ability to adapt to a changing environment. Rare species often have less genetic variation than widespread species and, consequently, are more vulnerable to extinction when environmental conditions change (Frankham et al. 2009). The importance of genetic variability to conservation biology is discussed at length in Chapter 11.

In a wide variety of plant and animal populations, it has been demonstrated that individuals that are heterozygous have greater **fitness** than comparable homozygous individuals. This means that heterozygous individuals have greater growth, survival, and reproduction rates than homozygotes. The reasons for this appear to be that (1) having two different alleles gives the individual greater flexibility in deal-

FIGURE 2.9 Genetic variation occurs within individuals due to variation in the alleles found at particular loci, or genes, and variation between chromosomes. Genetic variation also occurs between individuals within populations and among separate populations. (After Groom et al. 2006.)

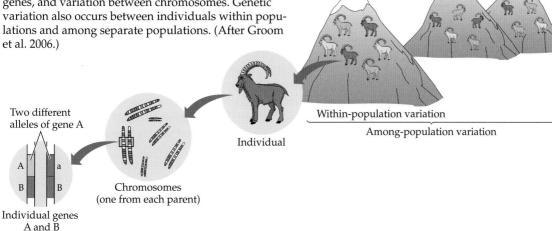

ing with life's challenges, and (2) nonfunctional or harmful alleles received from one parent are masked by the functioning alleles received from the other parent. This phenomenon of increased fitness in highly heterozygous individuals, also referred to as **hybrid vigor**, or **heterosis**, is widely known in domestic animals. As populations of wild species get smaller because of habitat destruction and other human activities, genetic variation will be lost and individuals will have a lower average fitness. Genetic variation within a species can also affect the abundance and distribution of other species. For example, genetic variation in bark characteristics among individuals in a widespread tree species can enhance the regional diversity of bark-inhabiting insects (Barbour et al. 2009).

Populations of a species may differ genetically from one another in relative frequencies of alleles and even in types of allele forms for particular genes. These genetic differences may result from adaptation of each population to its local environment or simply from random chance. Unique populations of a species, particularly those found at the edges of a species range, are considered an important component of biological diversity, and conservation biologists often recommend their protection (Thompson et al. 2010). Such populations are sometimes designated as distinct varieties or subspecies, especially when they are morphologically distinct. Furthermore, distinctive alleles from these populations can sometimes be used as markers to determine the geographical origin of individuals collected in the wild (Wasser et al. 2008).

Although most mating occurs within populations, individuals occasionally move from one population to another, resulting in the transfer of new alleles and genetic combinations between populations. This genetic transfer is referred to as **gene flow**. Natural gene flow between populations is sometimes interrupted by human activities, causing a reduction in the genetic variation in each population (Wofford et al. 2005).

Genetic variation also occurs within domesticated plants and animals. In traditional agricultural societies, people preserved new plant forms that were well suited to their needs. Through generations of this process of **artificial selection**, varieties of species were developed that were high yielding, reliable, and adapted to local conditions of soil, climate, and crop pests. This process has greatly accelerated in modern agriculture, which makes use of scientific breeding programs that manipulate genetic variation to meet present human needs. Without genetic variation, improvements in agriculture would be more difficult. Advanced techniques of biotechnology enable even more precise use of genetic variation by allowing the transfer of genetic material between unrelated species. Thousands of varieties of crops, such as rice, potatoes, and wheat, have been incorporated into the breeding programs of modern agriculture. Among animals, the huge numbers of breeds of domestic dogs, cats, chickens, cattle, sheep, and pigs are evidence of the ability of artificial selection to alter gene pools for the benefit of people (see Figure 2.3).

Genetic variation is also maintained in specialized collections of species used in scientific research, such as the *Drosophila* fruit fly stocks used in genetic studies; the tiny, fast-growing *Arabidopsis* mustard plants that are used in plant research; and the mice used in physiological and medical research.

Human activities are already causing artificial selection in wild species, as seen by pesticide resistance in many agricultural pests and drug resistance in disease-causing bacteria (Myers and Knoll 2001). Evidence also suggests that the intensive harvesting of fish in the ocean is imposing artificial selection on fish populations; targeting the largest fish in the population, among other negative effects, causes selection to favor individuals that reproduce at an earlier age and smaller size (Fenberg and Roy 2008).

Ecosystem Diversity

Ecosystems are diverse, and this diversity is apparent even across a particular landscape. As we climb a mountain, for example, the structure of the vegetation and kinds of plants and animals present gradually change from those found in a tall forest to those found in a low, moss-filled forest to alpine meadow to cold, barren rock. As we move across the landscape, physical conditions (soil, temperature, precipitation, and so forth) change, and one by one the species present at the original location drop out, and we encounter new species that were not found at the starting point. The landscape as a whole is dynamic and changes in response to the overall environment and the types of human activities that are associated with it.

What Are Communities and Ecosystems?

A **biological community** is defined as the species that occupy a particular locality and the interactions among those species. A biological community, together with its associated physical and chemical environment, is termed an **ecosystem**. Many characteristics of an ecosystem result from ongoing processes, including water cycles, nutrient cycles, and energy capture. Water evaporates from leaves, the ground, and other surfaces, to fall again elsewhere as rain or snow and replenish terrestrial and aquatic environments. Soil is built up from parent rock material and decaying organic matter. Photosynthetic plants absorb light energy, which fuels the plants' growth. This energy may be captured by animals that eat the plants, and it may be released as heat when the plants (or the animals that eat them) die and decompose. Plants absorb carbon dioxide and release oxygen during photosynthesis, while animals and fungi absorb oxygen and release carbon dioxide during respiration. Mineral nutrients, such as nitrogen and phosphorus, cycle between the living and the nonliving compartments of the ecosystem. These processes occur at geographical scales that range from square meters to hectares to square kilometers and all the way to regional scales involving tens of thousands of square kilometers (see Table 1.1 for definitions of these metric terms).

The physical environment, especially annual cycles of temperature and precipitation and the characteristics of the land surface, affects the structure and characteristics of a biological community and profoundly influences whether a site will support a forest, grassland, desert, or wetland. In aquatic ecosystems, physical characteristics such as water turbulence and clarity, as well as water chemistry, temperature, and depth, affect the characteristics of the associated **biota** (a region's flora and fauna). In turn, the biological community can also alter the physical characteristics of an environment. For example, wind speeds are lower and humidity is higher inside a forest than in a nearby grassland. Marine communities such as kelp forests and coral reefs (**Box 2.2**) can affect the physical environment as well, by buffering wave action.

Within a biological community, species play different roles and differ in what they require to survive (Marquard et al. 2009). For example, a given plant species might grow best in one type of soil under certain conditions of sunlight and moisture, be pollinated only by certain types of insects, and have its seeds dispersed by certain bird species. Similarly, animal species differ in their requirements, such as the types of food they eat and the types of resting places they prefer (**Figure 2.10**). Even though a forest may be full of vigorously growing green plants, an insect species that feeds only on one rare and declining plant species may be unable to develop and reproduce because it cannot get the specific food that it requires. Any of these requirements may become a **limiting resource** when it restricts population size of the species. For example, a bat species with specialized roosting requirements—forming colonies only in small grottoes on the ceilings of limestone caves—will be restricted by the number of caves with the proper conditions for roosting sites. If people damage the caves to collect limestone,

> Within a community, each species has its own requirements for food, temperature, water, and other resources, any of which may limit its population size and distribution.

BOX 2.2　*Kelp Forests and Sea Otters: Shaping an Ocean Ecosystem*

■ Although the effects of human activities on the world's tropical and temperate forests have been given a lot of media attention in recent years, a third kind of forest has received very little notice—marine kelp forests. Although unsung in magazines and newspapers, these forests provide essential habitat for a diversity of species. Kelp forests are communities that develop mostly in the high-latitude coastal waters of the world's oceans around any of a number of species of marine brown algae, such as giant kelp (*Macrocystis pyrifera*). Enormous numbers of ocean fish, shellfish, and invertebrates depend on these forests for food and shelter (McClanachan and Branch 2008; Schaal et al. 2009). Like terrestrial forests, kelp and seaweed communities inhibit erosion: the presence of kelp reduces the impact of waves and currents upon the shoreline, preventing destruction of coastal land. Despite their recognized value, kelp forests have disappeared over the last century at many localities in Alaska, British Columbia, and the Pacific Northwest of the United States.

The source of reduction is not as apparent as clear-cutting of terrestrial forests. Kelp is harvested in many countries by local people for subsistence, but this type of exploitation is fairly small-scale and does little harm to the kelp beds. Even large-scale harvesting of kelp for the food-processing industry appears to have little long-term effect.

The principal cause for kelp forest declines began over a century ago, with the harvesting of sea otters.

Sea otters (*Enhydra lutris*), once widespread throughout the Pacific, were all but exterminated by fur traders. Sea otters eat large quantities of shellfish—as much as 25% of their body weight each day. In the absence of otters, populations of mussels, abalone, other shellfish, and sea urchins exploded, providing a greater harvest for the shellfish industry. However, sea urchins feed voraciously on kelp; unchecked by predators, they created large "urchin barrens" where kelp forests were previously common.

Confined mostly to the far northern Pacific islands for decades, the sea otter is now protected in the United States and has begun to recolonize parts of its former range. The return of the sea otters has initiated a cascade of effects throughout the ecosystem with implications for the economy of the region's fisheries. Reductions in shellfish populations from sea otter predation have angered fishermen (Fanshawe et al. 2003), but at the same time, the reduced herbivory by sea urchins has allowed kelp and other algae to grow back. Wherever otters have returned or have been reintroduced, significant changes have taken place in kelp communities: Within one, two, or more years of the otters' return, formerly deforested areas are again dominated by kelp. Enhanced production of kelp has increased fish

(continued)

BOX 2.2 (continued)

production and growth rates of suspension feeders, benefiting commercial and recreational fishing, though in many areas fish populations have been significantly reduced by overharvesting (Paddack and Estes 2000). The disappearance of kelp beds in the last century and their subsequent recovery following the restoration of the sea otter demon-

> A change in one species in an ecosystem sometimes changes the connections among species at different trophic levels, a phenomenon known as a trophic cascade.

strates an important feature of ocean ecosystems: The loss of a single keystone species, no matter what its position on the food chain, can have a profound effect on every aspect of the system's ecological interactions. The sea otter recovery is still fragile, however. Over the last decade, off the coast of western Alaska, killer whales have switched to feeding on sea otters because their preferred prey of seals and sea lions has declined, perhaps in part because of overfishing or as an indirect effect of whaling (Estes et al. 2009). As a consequence, certain former kelp forests are again reverting to sea urchin–dominated barrens.

Forests of giant kelp provide the starting point and structure for a diverse biological community off the Pacific coast of North America. Sea otters are vital to the kelp community because they feed on invertebrates, such as sea urchins, that graze on the kelp. When the sea otters decline in number, sea urchin populations soar, resulting in grave damage to the kelp forests. (Illustration © Abigail Rorer. Reproduced with permission from *The Work of Nature* by Yvonne Baskin, Island Press, Washington, D.C.)

then the bat population will likely decline; however, if the bats are able to adapt to human presence and roost under bridges, their population might increase.

In many ecosystems, there may be occasional episodes of extreme environmental conditions when one or several resources become limited and vulnerable species are eliminated from the site. For example, although water is not normally a limiting resource to organisms living in a rain forest, episodes of drought lasting for weeks and even months occasionally do occur, even in the wettest forests. At these times, animal and plant species that need a constant supply of water may vanish. Or, bird species that are specialized to feed on flying insects may be unable to eat or to feed their young during days or weeks when unusually cold, wet, or windy weather prevents insects from flying; in this situation, the flying insects suddenly become the limiting resource for the bird population. Unfortunately, such episodes of extreme conditions are predicted to become more common in coming decades because of global climate change (see Chapter 9).

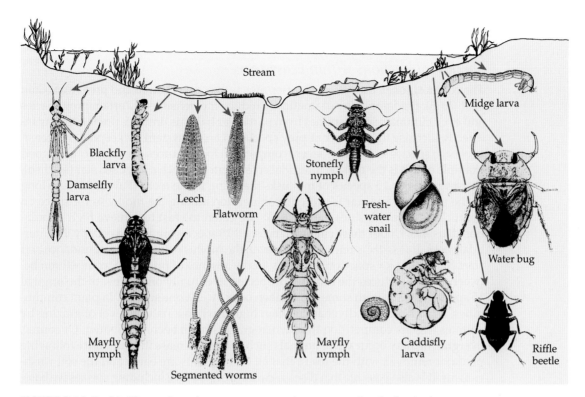

FIGURE 2.10 In this illustration of a stream community cross-section in the Andean mountains, each animal species lives at different water depths and in association with certain structural features of rocks, plants, and sediment. (From Roldán 1988.)

Ecological Succession

As a result of its particular requirements, behaviors, or preferences, a given species often ends up appearing in a given site at a particular time during the process of ecological succession. **Succession** is the gradual process of change in species composition, community structure, soil chemistry, and microclimatic characteristics that occurs following natural and human-caused disturbance in an ecosystem. For example, sun-loving butterflies and annual plants most commonly are found early in succession, in the months or few years immediately following a hurricane or after a logging operation has destroyed an old-growth forest. At this time, with the tree canopy disrupted, the ground is receiving high levels of sunlight, with high temperatures and low humidity during the day. Over the course of decades, the forest canopy is gradually reestablished. Different species, including shade-tolerant, moisture-requiring wildflowers, butterflies whose caterpillars feed on these plants, and birds that nest in holes in dead trees, thrive in these mid- and late-successional stages. Similar cases of species firmly associated with early, mid, or late succession are found in other ecosystems, such as grasslands, wetlands, and the intertidal zones of oceans. Human management patterns often upset the natural pattern of succession; for instance, grasslands that have been overgrazed by cattle and forests from which all the large trees have been cut for timber no longer contain certain late-successional species.

Successional processes in modern landscapes might represent a combination of natural and human-caused disturbances. A grassland and forest ecosystem in the Rocky Mountains of Colorado, for instance, might be affected by natural fires, cycles of drought, and grazing by elk. Now succession in such an ecosystem is increasingly dominated by human-caused fires, cattle grazing, and road construction.

Often, the largest number of species occurs in landscapes with intermediate levels of disturbance and a mixture of early, mid, and late stages of succession.

Species Interactions within Ecosystems

The composition of ecosystems is often affected by **competition** and **predation** (Cain et al. 2008). Predators may dramatically reduce the densities of certain prey species and even eliminate some species from particular habitats. Indeed, predators may indirectly increase the number of prey species in an ecosystem by keeping the density of each species so low that severe competition for resources does not occur. A good example of this is the marine intertidal ecosystem in which a large sea star (starfish), *Pisaster*, feeds on 15 species of mollusks that cling to the rocks (Paine 1966). As long as the predatory sea star is present, competition among the mollusks for space on the rocks is reduced, since the mollusks are eaten too fast to achieve high population densities. Under these circumstances, all 15 species are able to occupy the intertidal rocks. If *Pisaster* is removed, however, the mollusks increase in abundance and start competing for space on the rocks. In the absence of predation, competition between species reduces the number of species; eventually only a few of the original 15 species remain, with some rocks taken over by just one species. In plant communities, as well, species diversity is often higher when a natural level of grazing by animals lessens competition than when grazers have been eliminated. Of course, overgrazing may occur when animals such as deer increase in abundance following predator removal, with the result that all of the plants are eaten and the soil washes away. It is also possible that disease-causing organisms, including species we barely notice unless they attack us directly, profoundly influence community structure, reducing certain ecologically important species to low densities.

In many ecosystems, predators keep the number of individuals of a particular prey species below the number that the resources of an ecosystem can support, a number termed the habitat's **carrying capacity**. If the predators (e.g., wolves) are removed by hunting, poisoning, or some other human activity, the prey population (e.g., deer) may increase to carrying capacity, or it may increase beyond carrying capacity to a point at which crucial resources are overtaxed and the population crashes.

In addition, the population size of a species may often be controlled by other species that compete with it for the same resources; for example, the population size of terns that nest on a small island may decline or grow if a gull species that uses the same nesting sites becomes abundant or is eliminated from the site. When the population of a species is sufficiently large to have an impact on the other species in an ecosystem, it is termed **ecologically functional**.

Community composition is also affected when two species benefit each other in a **mutualistic relationship**. Mutualistic species reach higher densities when they occur together than when only one of the species is present. Common examples of mutualism are fruit-eating birds and plants with fleshy fruit, flower-pollinating insects and flowering plants, the fungi and algae that together form lichens, and plants that provide both food and homes for the ants that protect them from pests (**Figure 2.11**). Two species that are always found in close long-term association are said to form a **symbiotic relationship**. (In some cases these relationships are mutualistic and the species apparently cannot survive without each other.) For example, the death of certain types of coral-inhabiting algae following unusually high water temperatures in tropical areas, due to natural causes or human activities, may be followed by the weakening and subsequent death of their associated coral species.

Principles of Community Organization

Examining the feeding relationships among species provides an important way to understand how an ecosystem is organized. Further investigations demonstrate how these relationships can be disrupted by human activities.

(A)

(B)

FIGURE 2.11 Two examples of mutualistic relationships. (A) Certain species of ants in a tropical savanna live on *Acacia* shrubs, feeding on the nectar and food bodies produced by the plant; the ants in turn attack any animal that tries to feed on the plant. (B) In Peru, a white-necked Jacobin hummingbird (*Florisuga mellivora*) feeds on a brightly colored legume flower. (A, courtesy of D. Morris; B, courtesy of L. Mazariegos.)

TROPHIC LEVELS   Ecosystems can be organized into trophic levels that represent ways in which energy is obtained from the environment (**Figure 2.12**).

- **Photosynthetic species** (also known as **primary producers**) obtain their energy directly from the sun. In terrestrial environments, higher plants, such as flowering plants, gymnosperms, and ferns, are responsible for most photosynthesis, while in aquatic environments, seaweeds, single-celled algae, and cyanobacteria (blue-green algae) are the most important. All of these species use solar energy to build the organic molecules they need to live and grow. Without the primary producers, species at the higher levels could not exist.

- **Herbivores** (also known as **primary consumers**) eat photosynthetic species. For example, in terrestrial environments, gazelles and grasshoppers eat grass, while in aquatic environments, crustaceans and fish eat algae. Because much plant material, such as cellulose and lignin, is indigestible to many animal species or is simply not eaten, only a small percentage of the energy captured by photosynthetic species is actually transferred to the herbivore level. The intensity of grazing by herbivores often determines the relative abundance of plant species and even the mass of plant material present.

- **Carnivores** (also known as **secondary consumers** or **predators**) kill and eat other animals. Primary carnivores (e.g., foxes) eat herbivores (e.g., rabbits), while secondary carnivores (e.g., bass) eat other carnivores (e.g., frogs). Because carnivores do not catch all of their potential prey, and because many body parts of the prey are indigestible, again only a small percentage of the energy of the herbivore trophic level is transferred to the carnivore level. Carnivores usually are predators, though some combine direct predation with scavenging behavior, and others, known as **omnivores**, include a substantial proportion of plant foods in their diets. In general, predators are larger and stronger than the species they prey on, but they usually occur in lower den-

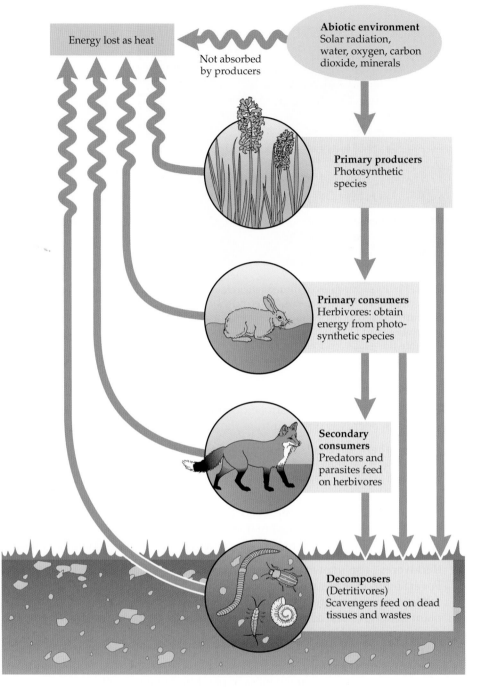

FIGURE 2.12 A model of a field ecosystem showing its trophic levels and simplified energy pathways.

sities than their prey. In many biological communities, carnivores play a crucial role in keeping herbivore numbers in check and preventing overgrazing of plants.

- **Parasites** form an important subclass of predators. Parasites of animals, including mosquitoes, ticks, intestinal worms, protozoans, bacteria, and viruses, are small in size and do not kill their hosts immediately, if ever. Plants can also be attacked by parasites, including fungi, other plants (such as mistletoe), nematode worms, insects, bacteria, and viruses. The effects of parasites range from imperceptibly weakening their hosts to totally debilitating or even killing their hosts over time. The term *parasite* applies to many of the organisms that cause disease, and that we call pests. Parasites can strongly affect the density of host species. When host densities are low, parasites are less able to move from one host to another, and their effects on the host population are correspondingly weak. When host populations are at a high density, parasites spread readily from one host individual to the next, causing an intense local infestation of the parasite and a subsequent decline in host density. High densities of host populations are sometimes maintained in zoos and small nature reserves, making these places hazardous for many endangered species because of the easy spread of parasites.

- **Decomposers** and **detritivores** are species that feed on dead plant and animal tissues and wastes (detritus), breaking down complex tissues and organic molecules. In the process, decomposers release minerals such as nitrates and phosphates back into the soil and water, where they can be taken up again by plants and algae. The most important decomposers are fungi and bacteria, but many different kinds of other species play roles in breaking down organic materials. For example, vultures and other scavengers tear apart and feed on dead animals, dung beetles feed on and bury animal dung, and worms break down fallen leaves and other organic matter. Crabs, worms, mollusks, fish, and numerous other organisms eat detritus in aquatic environments. If decomposers were not present, organic material would accumulate, and plant growth would decline greatly.

FOOD CHAINS AND FOOD WEBS Because less and less energy is transferred to each successive trophic level in biological communities, the greatest **biomass** (living weight) in a terrestrial ecosystem is usually that of the primary producers. In any community there tends to be more individual herbivores than primary carnivores, and more primary carnivores than secondary carnivores. For example, a forest community generally contains more insects and insect biomass than insectivorous birds, and more insectivorous birds than raptorial birds (birds such as hawks that feed on other birds). Most energy accumulated by each level is eventually broken down by decomposers.

Although species can be organized into these general trophic levels, their actual requirements or feeding habits within the trophic levels may be quite restricted. For example, a certain aphid species may feed on only one type of plant, and a certain lady beetle species may feed on only one type of aphid. These specific feeding relationships are termed **food chains**. The more common situation in many biological communities, however, is for one species to feed on several other species at the lower trophic level, to compete for food with several species at its own trophic level, and, in turn, to be preyed upon by several species at the next higher trophic level. Consequently, a more accurate description of the organization of biological communities is a **food web**, in which species are linked together through complex feeding relationships (Yodzis 2001) (**Figure 2.13**). Species at the same trophic level that use approximately the same environmental resources are considered to be a **guild** of competing species. For example, the many bird species that eat fruit in the temperate woodland make up a guild.

Humans can substantially alter the relationships in food webs (Levy 2007). For example, in urban settings, bird populations may increase due to reduced numbers of predators, reducing insect abundance in the process (Faeth et al. 2005).

FIGURE 2.13 A simple food web in a traditional agricultural ecosystem. Photosynthetic plants are eaten by people, ducks, and insects. Insects and aquatic invertebrates are eaten by ducks and fish, which are then eaten by people.

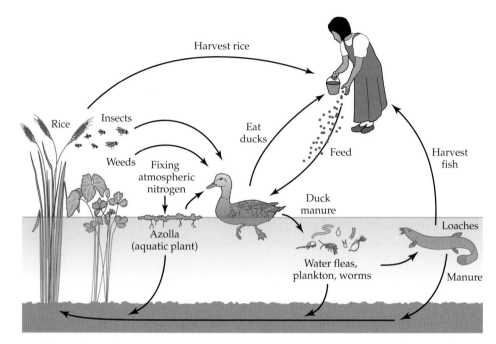

Keystone Species and Guilds

Within biological communities, a particular species or groups of species with similar ecological features (guilds) may determine the ability of large numbers of other species to persist in the community. These **keystone species** affect the organization of the community to a far greater degree than one would predict, if considering only the number of individuals or the biomass of the keystone species (**Figure 2.14**) (Letnic et al. 2009). Protecting keystone species and guilds is a priority for conser-

FIGURE 2.14 Keystone species determine the ability of large numbers of other species to persist within a biological community. Although keystone species make up only a small percentage of the total biomass, a community's composition would change radically if one of them were to disappear. Rare species have minimal biomass and seldom have significant impact on the community. Dominant species constitute a large percentage of the biomass and affect many other species in proportion to this large biomass. Some species, however, have a relatively low impact on the community organization despite being both common and heavy in biomass. (After Power et al. 1996.)

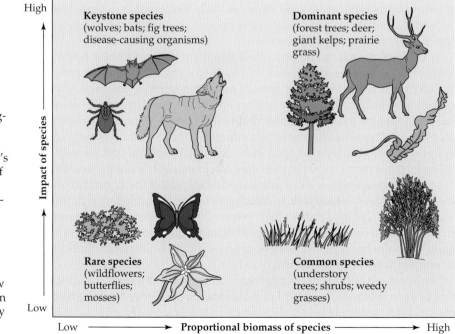

vation efforts, because loss of a keystone species or guild will lead to loss of numerous other species as well (see Box 2.2).

While we can sometimes identify such keystone species, it is also true that less obvious species may be significant for ecosystem functioning in ways that are not immediately obvious. Top predators are often considered keystone species because predators can markedly influence herbivore populations (Wallach et al. 2009). The elimination of even a small number of individual predators, even though they constitute only a minute amount of the community biomass, may result in dramatic changes in the vegetation and a great loss in biological diversity sometimes called a **trophic cascade** (Bruno and Cardinale 2008; Beschta and Ripple 2009). For example, the common plant-eating marsh crab (*Sesarma reticulatum*) found on Cape Cod, Massachusetts, salt marshes has increased dramatically since populations of predators such as blue crab have been reduced by overharvesting and water pollution. The subsequent increase in grazing pressure of the *Sesarma* has denuded 70% of the salt marsh cordgrass on Cape Cod (Bertness et al. 2009), leading to soil erosion and a loss of protection for other species inhabiting the salt marsh. In some other localities, where gray wolves and other predators have been hunted to extinction by humans, deer populations have exploded. The deer severely overgraze the habitat, eliminating many herb and shrub species. The loss of these plants, in turn, is detrimental to the deer and to other herbivores, including insects. The reduced plant cover may lead to soil erosion, also contributing to the loss of species that inhabit the soil.

> If scientists can identify the keystone species in a community affected by human activity, those species can be carefully protected and even encouraged.

Bats called flying foxes, of the family Pteropodidae, are another example of a keystone species (**Figure 2.15**). These bats are the primary pollinators and seed dispersers of many economically important tree species in the Old World tropics and Pacific Islands (Nyhagen et al. 2005). When bat colonies are overharvested by hunters, and when the trees in which the bats roost are cut down, the bat populations decline. As a result, many of the tree species in the remaining forest fail to reproduce.

Species that extensively modify the physical environment through their activities, often termed ecosystem engineers, are considered keystone species also (Beyer et al. 2007). For example, beavers build dams that flood temperate forests, creat-

FIGURE 2.15 Flying foxes—bats in the family Pteropodidae, such as this *Pteropus samoensis*, a fruit bat—are vital pollinators and seed dispersers in Old World tropical forest communities. (Photograph © Barry Bland/Alamy.)

ing new wetland habitat for many species. Earthworms may turn over many tons of soil per hectare each year, dramatically affecting soil fertility and thereby the plant and animal community. Leaf-cutter ants in tropical and subtropical American forests dig extensive tunnels through the soil to build fungal gardens and, in the process, create new habitats for many subterranean species; their leaf-cutting activities also have a profound effect on the vegetation.

The importance of grazing animals in physically shaping communities is illustrated by the case of Caribbean coral reefs (Alvarez-Filip et al. 2009). On these reefs, many species of fish and sea urchins of the genus *Diadema* included algae in their diets, particularly those species of large, fleshy algae that were fairly uncommon prior to 1980. However, in the 1980s, overharvesting greatly depleted fish populations, and there was a massive die-off of *Diadema*, apparently caused by a viral epidemic. Without the fish and *Diadema* to control their numbers, the fleshy algae increased dramatically in abundance, covering and damaging the coral reefs. Pollution of coastal waters by human activities may have helped tip the ecological balance in favor of the algae by providing abundant nutrients for growth.

The importance of a keystone species or guild may hinge upon highly specialized relationships between the keystone species and other organisms. In many tropical forests, fig trees and fig vines (*Ficus* spp.) appear to be keystone species in the functioning of vertebrate communities. Fig flowers are pollinated by small, highly specialized fig wasps, which mature inside the developing fig fruit. Mature fig trees produce continuous fig crops, and generations of wasps are continually coming to maturity. As a consequence of this continuous fruit production, figs provide a reliable source of fruit to primates, birds, and other fruit-eating vertebrates throughout the year, even during dry seasons. While fig fruits do not have the high energy content of many preferred lipid-rich fruits or the high protein content of an insect diet, during periods of drought the fig fruits serve as "famine food," which allows vertebrates to survive until their preferred foods are once more available. Even though fig trees and vines may be uncommon in the forest and the fruit may constitute only a small percentage of the total vertebrate diet, their persistence is necessary to the continued functioning of many species in the vertebrate community. In this case, the fig trees are a keystone guild because so many other species rely on them for food, and the health of the fig tree populations rests on the health of their wasp pollinators. The mutualistic relationship between the trees and the wasps forms the foundation of the entire community's health.

Many keystone species play less obvious roles that are nevertheless essential to maintaining biological diversity. In addition to worms, other inconspicuous detritivores also play a significant role in the functioning of communities. For example, dung beetles exist at low density levels in tropical forests and constitute only a fraction of the biomass (Lewis 2009), yet these beetles are crucial to the community because they create balls of dung and carrion and bury them as a food source for their larvae (**Figure 2.16**). These buried materials break down rapidly, making nutrients available for plant growth. Seeds contained in the dung of fruit-eating animals are also buried, which facilitates seed germination and the establishment of new plants. In addition, by burying and feeding on dung, the beetles kill the vertebrate parasites contained in the dung, thus helping to keep the vertebrate populations healthy. Disease-causing organisms and parasites can also be examples of inconspicuous but nevertheless crucial species, because their presence reduces the density of their host species and keeps the biological community in balance.

As should be evident from our discussion thus far, the identification of keystone species has several important implications for conservation biology. First, the elimination of a keystone species or group from a community may precipitate the loss of other species (Letnic et al. 2009). Losing keystones can create a series of linked extinction events, known as an **extinction cascade**, that results in a degraded ecosys-

FIGURE 2.16 Dung beetles, also known as scarabs, are important keystone species in many communities. The beetles disperse and bury balls of dung and carrion, allowing the waste material to decompose quickly and making nutrients available for plant growth. Seeds are dispersed along with the dung, allowing new plants to flourish. (Photograph by David McIntyre.)

tem with much lower biological diversity at all trophic levels. This may already be happening in tropical forests where overharvesting has drastically reduced the populations of birds and mammals that act as predators, seed dispersers, and herbivores (Nunez-Iturri et al. 2008). While such a forest appears to be green and healthy at first glance, it is really an "empty forest" in which ecological processes have been irreversibly altered such that the species composition of the forest will change over succeeding decades or centuries (Redford 1992).

In the marine environment, the loss of key structural species such as sea grasses and seaweeds can lead to the loss of specialized species that inhabit such communities, such as delicate sea dragons and sea horses (Hughes et al. 2009). If the few keystone species in a community being affected by human activity can be identified, sometimes they can be carefully protected or even encouraged. For example, during selective logging operations, figs and other important fruit trees should be protected, while common trees that are not keystone species could be reduced in abundance with little permanent loss of biological diversity. Likewise, hunting of keystone animal species in the logging area should be limited or stopped altogether.

Keystone Resources

Often nature reserves are compared and valued in terms of their size because, on average, larger reserves contain more species and habitats than smaller reserves. However, area alone does not ensure that a nature reserve contains the full range of crucial habitats and resources. Particular habitats may contain critical **keystone resources**, often physical or structural, that occupy only a small area yet are crucial to many species in the ecosystem (Kelm et al. 2008). Consider these examples:

- *Salt licks and mineral pools* provide essential minerals for wildlife, particularly in inland areas with heavy rainfall. The distribution of salt licks can determine the abundance and distribution of vertebrates in an area.

- *Deep pools* in streams and springs may be the only refuge for fish, certain plant species, and other aquatic species during the dry season, when water levels drop. For terrestrial animals, these water sources may provide the only available drinking water for a considerable distance.

- *Hollow tree trunks* are needed as breeding sites for many bird and mammal species. Suitable tree cavities are the limiting resource on the population size of many vertebrate species. The significance of nesting sites is demonstrated by the increase in breeding pairs that occurs when nesting boxes are provided and by the decline in population size of many species when dead and hollow trees are removed in managed forests. In one study of a forest–pasture mosaic in Costa Rica, 10 species of bats colonized nest boxes within a few weeks, and they dispersed the seeds of over 60 plant species (Kelm et al. 2008).

- *Rotting wood* provides habitat for a wide range of animals, plants, and fungi in both terrestrial and aquatic environments (Gurnell et al. 2005). Fallen trees in streams are important refuges for fish; they provide shelter from predators and also create well-oxygenated ripples that nourish both fish and their invertebrate prey. When such wood is cleared away, the species richness of the system declines.

> There are many different types of keystone resources specific to their own ecosystems. These are essential for the maintenance of ecosystem structure and function and the persistence of many species.

Keystone resources may occupy only a small proportion of a conservation area, yet they are of crucial importance in maintaining many animal populations. The loss of a keystone resource could mean the rapid loss of animal species, particularly certain birds and mammals. When vertebrate species are lost, there could be an extinction cascade of plant species that depend on those animals for pollination and seed dispersal.

Ecosystem Dynamics

In the interaction of the biological community with the physical and chemical environment, key ecosystem processes include transfer of energy; production of biomass; cycling of carbon, nitrogen, and other nutrients; and the movement of water. The concept of **ecosystem integrity** is important to conservation (but is challenging to evaluate objectively and quantitatively). Ecosystem integrity is the condition in which an ecosystem is complete in terms of species composition, structure, and function (Tierney et al. 2009). An ecosystem that has been damaged by human activity and has lost some of its species and certain processes, such as the ability to retain water after storms and then release it slowly, has lost some of its integrity (Vaughn 2010).

An ecosystem in which the processes are functioning normally, whether or not there are human influences, is referred to as a **healthy ecosystem**. In many cases, ecosystems that have lost some of their species will remain healthy because there is often some redundancy in the roles performed by ecologically similar species. Ecosystems that are able to remain in the same state are referred to as **stable ecosystems**. These systems remain stable either because of lack of disturbance or because they have special features that allow them to remain stable in the face of disturbance. Such stability despite disturbance could result from one or both of two features: resistance and resilience. **Resistance** is the ability to maintain the same state even with ongoing disturbance; that would be the case if after an oil spill, a river ecosystem retained its major ecosystem processes. **Resilience** is the property of being able to return to the original state quickly after disturbance has occurred; that would be true if following contamination by an oil spill and the deaths of many animals and plants, a river ecosystem eventually returned to its original condition. For example, when non-native fish are introduced in previously fish-free ponds, the number of native animal species declines, indicating low resistance; but when the fish die out, the number of native species soon recovers, indicating high resilience (Knapp et al. 2005).

Conclusion

The concepts of biological diversity described in this chapter can help identify species and places in need of protection. In addition, ecological principles are being used to formulate management strategies for the conservation and restoration of ecosystems. These topics will be further developed in later chapters. The next chapter will explore the global distribution of biological diversity.

Summary

1. The Earth's biological diversity includes the entire range of living species, the genetic variation that occurs among individuals within a species, and, at a higher level, the biological communities in which species live and their ecosystem-level interactions with the physical and chemical environment.

2. Species richness, one component of species diversity, refers to the number of species found in a particular location. Species diversity is also measured across landscapes and at regional scales with the goal of examining and comparing large-scale patterns of species distribution. These measures are used chiefly for examining particular groups of species.

3. Genetic variation within species arises through the mutation of genes and the recombination of genes during sexual reproduction. Species with high levels of genetic variation may adapt most readily to a changing environment through the process of natural selection. In some cases, this process leads to the evolution of new species. In artificial selection, people alter gene pools to make domestic plants and animals more suitable for human use.

4. Within ecosystems, species interact through processes such as competition, predation, and mutualism, and they occupy distinct trophic, or feeding, levels that represent the ways in which they obtain energy. Individual species often have specific feeding relationships with other species that can be represented as food chains and food webs.

5. Certain keystone species or groups may determine the ability of other species to persist in an ecosystem. These keystone species are sometimes top carnivores but also may be inconspicuous species. The loss of a keystone species from an ecosystem might result in a cascade of extinctions of other species.

6. Certain keystone resources, such as, nesting sites, and salt licks, may occupy only a small fraction of a habitat, but they can be crucial to the persistence of many species in an area.

For Discussion

1. How many species of birds, plants, insects, mammals, and mushrooms can you identify in your neighborhood? How could you learn to identify more? Do you believe that the present generation of people is more or less able to identify species than past generations?

2. Conservation efforts usually target genetic variation, species diversity, biological communities, and ecosystems for protection. Can you think of other components of natural systems that need to be protected? What do you think is the most important component of biological diversity?

3. Some examples of keystone species are top predators. Can examples of keystone species be found at all trophic levels and in each kingdom of the living world?

4. How could you manage a property, such as a degraded rangeland, a forest plantation, or a polluted lake, to restore all levels of biological diversity?

Suggested Readings

Alvarez-Filip, L., N. K. Dulvy, J. A. Gill, I. M. Côté, and A. R. Watkinson. 2009. Flattening of Caribbean coral reefs: Region-wide declines in architectural complexity. *Proceedings of the Royal Society*, Series B 276: 3019–3025. Human impacts have simplified and degraded coral reefs.

Beschta, R. L. and W. J. Ripple. 2009. Large predators and trophic cascades in terrestrial ecosystems of the western United States. *Biological Conservation* 142: 2401–2414. Keystone species can have a dramatic impact on the structure of biological communities.

Estes, J. A., D. F. Doak, A. M. Springer, and T. M. Williams. 2009. Causes and consequences of marine mammal population declines in Southwest Alaska. *Philosophical Transactions of the Royal Society* Series B 365: 1647–1658. Complex species interactions can change over decades, affecting multiple trophic levels.

Janzen, D. H. and 45 others. 2009. Integration of DNA barcoding into an ongoing inventory of complex tropical biodiversity. *Molecular Ecology Resources* 9(s1): 1–26. DNA techniques can reveal large numbers of cryptic species.

Kelm, D. H., K. R. Wiesner, and O. von Helversen. 2008. Effects of artificial roosts for frugivorous bats on seed dispersal in a Neotropical forest pasture mosaic. *Conservation Biology* 22: 733–741. Putting up artificial roosts can dramatically increase the number of seeds being dispersed by bats.

Laikre, L. and 19 others. 2010. Neglect of genetic diversity in implementation of the Convention on Biological Diversity. *Conservation Biology* 24: 86–88. A greater emphasis on genetic diversity needs to be part of conservation efforts.

Legendre, P., D. Borcard, and P. R. Peres-Neto. 2005. Analyzing beta diversity: Partitioning the spatial variation of community composition data. *Ecological Monographs* 75: 435–450. Biological diversity can be measured at varying scales using different methods.

Letnic, M., F. Koch, C. Gordon, M. S. Crowther, and C. R. Dickman. 2009. Keystone effects of an alien top-predator stem extinctions of native mammals. *Proceedings of the Royal Society*, Series B 276: 3249–3256. Removal of the dingo increases herbivore activity and then results in the loss of grass cover and native small mammals.

Levin, S. A. (ed.). 2001. *Encyclopedia of Biodiversity*. Academic Press, San Diego, CA. A comprehensive guide to the whole field.

Marquard, E. and 8 others. 2009. Plant species richness and functional composition drive overyielding in a six-year grassland experiment. *Ecology* 90: 3290–3302. Plant species richness and functional diversity increases biomass in a grassland ecosystem.

Myers, N. and A. Knoll. 2001. The biotic crisis and the future of evolution. *Proceedings of the National Academy of Sciences USA* 98: 5389–5392. Human alteration of the world is changing the process of evolution and may lead to unpredictable results.

Thompson, J. D., M. Gaudeul, and M. Debussche. 2010. Conservation value of site of hybridization in peripheral populations of rare plant species. *Conservation Biology* 24: 236–245. Sites with two closely related species may contain high levels of genetic variation and may be appropriate for special conservation efforts.

Valentini, A., F. Pompanon, and P. Taberlet. 2009. DNA barcoding for ecologists. *Trends in Ecology and Evolution* 24: 110–117. DNA technology can be used in species identification.

Vaughn, C. C. 2010. Biodiversity losses and ecosystem function in freshwaters: Emerging conclusions and research directions. *BioScience* 60: 25–35. The loss of species will have complex and unpredictable impacts on ecosystem function.

Wilson, E. O. 2003. The encyclopedia of life. *Trends in Ecology and Evolution* 18: 77–80. One of the founders of conservation biology argues that there is an urgent need for more taxonomists to describe new species.

Where Is the World's Biological Diversity Found?

Although the planet Earth has an abundance of biological diversity, certain ecosystems have far more species than others. Certain groups of organisms are also especially rich in species, and scientists are discovering entire new biological communities in previously unexplored places. In this chapter we will examine the factors that determine the abundance and distribution of species throughout the world, which is one of the major components of biological diversity.

The most species-rich environments appear to be tropical rain forests and deciduous forests, coral reefs, large tropical lakes, and perhaps the deep sea (MEA 2005). Much of the diversity of tropical forests is due to their great abundance of insects, but they also have many species of birds, mammals, amphibians, and plants. In coral reefs and the deep sea, diversity is spread over a much broader range of phyla and classes. These marine systems contain representatives of 28 of the 35 animal phyla that exist today; one-third of these phyla exist only in the marine environment (Grassle 2001). In contrast, only one phylum is found exclusively in the terrestrial environment. Diversity in the ocean may be due to great age, enormous water volume, the degree of isolation of certain seas by intervening landmasses, the stability of the environment, and specialization

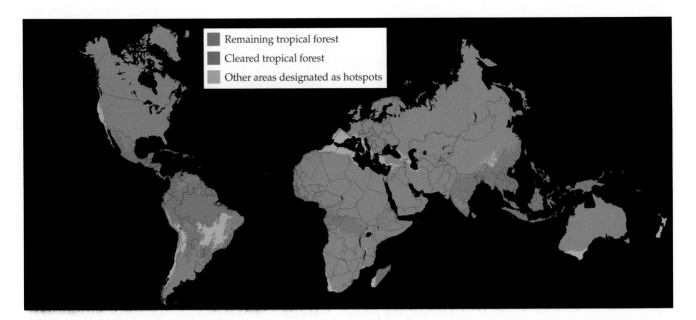

FIGURE 3.1 The current extent of tropical forests, and the areas that have been cleared of tropical forests. Note the extensive amount of land that has been deforested in northern and southeastern South America, India, Southeast Asia, Madagascar, and western Africa. The map also shows hotspots of biodiversity, a subject that will be treated in further detail in Chapter 15. Many of the biodiversity hotspots in the temperate zone have a Mediterranean climate, such as southwestern Australia, South Africa, California, Chile, and the Mediterranean basin. This map is a Fuller Projection, a type of map that has less distortion of the size and shapes of continents than typical maps. (Map created by Clinton Jenkins; originally appeared in Pimm and Jenkins 2005.)

on particular sediment types and water depths (adding a third dimension to the space occupied). However, the traditional view of the "unchanging" sea is being reevaluated as a result of evidence that shows decreased deep sea biodiversity during postglacial episodes and recent shifts in species distribution associated with global climate change. Diversity in large tropical lakes is accounted for by the rapid evolutionary radiation of fishes and other species in a series of isolated, productive habitats. High freshwater diversity is also found in complex river systems, with individual species having restricted distribution.

In temperate communities, great diversity is found among plant species in southwestern Australia, the Cape Region of South Africa, California, central Chile, and the Mediterranean basin, all of which are characterized by a Mediterranean climate of moist winters and hot, dry summers (**Figure 3.1**). The Mediterranean basin is the largest in area (2.1 million km²) and has the most plant species (22,500) (Conservation International and Caley 2008); the Cape Floristic Region of South Africa has an extraordinary concentration of unique plant species (9000) in a relatively small area (78,555 km²). The shrub and herb communities in these areas are apparently rich in species due to their combination of considerable geological age, complex site characteristics (such as topography and soils), and severe environmental conditions. The frequency of fire in these areas also may favor rapid speciation and prevent the domination of just a few species.

Two of the Most Diverse Ecosystems on Earth

Species richness is greatest in tropical ecosystems. Tropical rain forests on land and coral reefs in marine systems are among the most biologically diverse ecosystems on Earth and have become the focus of popular attention.

Tropical Rain Forests

Even though the world's tropical forests occupy only 7% of the land area, they contain over half the world's species (Corlett and Primack 2010). This estimate is based on limited sampling of insects and other arthropods, groups that are thought to contain the majority of the world's species. Reasonable estimates of the number of insect species in tropical forests range from 5 million to 10 million, though some estimates have been as high as 30 million species (Gaston and Spicer 2004). Such numbers suggest that insects found in tropical forests may constitute the majority of the world's species. Information on other groups, such as plants and birds, is much more accurate. For flowering plants, gymnosperms, and ferns, about 40% of the world's 275,000 species occur in the world's tropical forest areas in the Americas, Africa, Madagascar, Southeast Asia, New Guinea, Australia, and various tropical islands.

About 30% of the world's bird species—1300 species in the American tropics, 400 species in tropical Africa, and 900 in tropical Asia—depend on tropical forests. This figure is probably an underestimate, since it does not include species that are only partially dependent on tropical forests (such as migratory birds), nor does it reflect the high concentrations of tropical forest birds living in restricted habitats, such as islands, that may be more vulnerable to habitat loss. In forested islands such as New Guinea, 78% of the nonmarine birds depend on the tropical forest for their survival.

> Species diversity is greatest in the tropics, particularly in tropical forests and coral reefs. The Amazon basin in South America has the largest area of tropical forests. The southwestern Pacific has the greatest diversity of coral reef species.

Coral Reefs

Colonies of tiny coral animals build the large coral reef ecosystems—the marine equivalent of tropical rain forests in both species richness and complexity (Knowlton and Jackson 2008) (**Figure 3.2**). One explanation for this richness is the high primary productivity of coral reefs, which produce 2500 grams of biomass per square meter per year, in comparison with 125 g/m²/yr in the open ocean. The clarity of the water in the reef ecosystem allows sunlight to penetrate deeply so that high levels of photosynthesis occur in the algae that live mutualistically inside the coral.

FIGURE 3.2 Coral reefs are built up from the skeletons of billions of tiny individual animals. The intricate coral landscapes create a habitat for a diversity of other marine species, including many different kinds of fish. This reef is in the Maldives, an island nation in the equatorial Indian Ocean. (Photograph © Wolfgang Amri/istock.)

Extensive niche specialization among coral species and adaptations to varying levels of disturbance may also account for the high species richness found in coral reefs.

The world's largest coral reef is Australia's Great Barrier Reef, with an area of 349,000 km². The Great Barrier Reef contains over 400 species of coral, 1500 species of fish, 4000 species of mollusks, and 6 species of turtles, and it provides breeding sites for some 252 species of birds. Although the Great Barrier Reef occupies only 0.1% of the ocean surface area, it contains about 8% of the world's fish species. The Great Barrier Reef is part of the rich Indo–West Pacific region. The great diversity of species in this region is illustrated by the fact that more than 2000 fish species are found in the Philippine Islands, compared with 448 species found in the mid-Pacific Hawaiian Islands, and 500 species around the Bahama Islands. In comparison to tropical coral reefs, the number of marine fishes in temperate areas is low: the mid-Atlantic seaboard of North America has only 250 fish species, and the Mediterranean has fewer than 400 species.

Most of the animals inhabiting coral reefs are small in size and not yet studied; tens of thousands of species still await discovery and description. Scientists are also now beginning to learn about deep sea corals that live in deep, cold environments without light (Roark et al. 2006). These deep sea coral communities are still poorly known, but they appear to be rapidly declining due to destructive trawling practices.

One notable difference between the species of tropical forests and coral reefs is that, unlike many species of tropical forests that occur only in a specific part of the world, species of coral reefs are often widely dispersed, yet they occupy a tiny percentage of the ocean's surface area. Only isolated islands, such as Hawaii, Fiji, and the Galápagos, have numerous restricted-range **endemic** species—species that are found in a particular location and nowhere else; fully 25% of Hawaiian coral species are endemic to the area (Pacific Whale Foundation 2003). Because most coral reef species are more widely distributed than rain forest species, they may be less prone to extinction by the destruction of a single locality. However, this assertion may be a taxonomic bias, because coral reef species are not as well known as terrestrial species. Recent research suggests that some widely distributed tropical marine species have genetically unique populations in certain geographical areas (Knutsen et al. 2009); eventually certain of these populations might be considered to be distinct species and warrant protection for that reason.

Patterns of Diversity

Patterns of diversity are known primarily through the efforts of taxonomists, who have methodically collected organisms from all areas of the world. These patterns, however, are known only in broad outline for many groups of organisms, because the great majority of species-rich groups, such as beetles, bacteria, and fungi, remain undescribed. It is clear that local variation in climate, environment, topography, and geological age are factors that affect patterns of species richness (Harrison et al. 2006).

Variation in Climate and Environment

In terrestrial communities, species richness tends to increase with decreasing elevation, increasing solar radiation, and increasing precipitation; that is, hot, rainy lowland areas have the most species. These factors act in combination; for example, deserts are species poor because of their low precipitation, even though they have high solar radiation. In some localities, species abundance is greatest at mid elevations. The lower richness of plants and animals in Africa, in comparison with South America and Asia, may be due to a combination of lower past and present rainfall, the smaller total area of rain forest, and a longer period of human impact in Africa (Corlett and Primack 2010). Even within tropical Africa itself, areas of low rainfall in the Sahel have fewer species than forested areas with higher rainfall to the south. However, the extensive savanna areas of east and central Africa have a richness and abundance of antelopes and other ungulate grazers not found on other continents. The greatest abundance of mammal species may occur at intermediate levels of precipitation rather than in the wettest or driest habitats. In the open ocean, species diversity reaches a peak at 2000 to 3000 m, with lower diversity closer to the surface and at greater depths.

Variation in Topography, Geological Age, and Habitat Size

Species richness can be greater where complex topography and great geological age provide more environmental variation, which allows genetic isolation, local adaptation, and speciation to occur. For example, a species able to colonize a series of isolated mountain peaks in the Andes during a period of favorable climate may eventually evolve into several different species, each adapted to its local mountain environment. A similar process could occur for fish and invertebrates occupying large drainage systems and lakes that become divided into several smaller systems. Examples include the Tennessee River system in the United States, the Mekong River in Southeast Asia, and Lake Baikal in Siberia. Geologically complex areas can produce a variety of soil conditions with very sharp boundaries between them, leading to multiple communities and species adapted to one specific soil type or another.

At various spatial scales, there are concentrations of species in particular places, and there is a rough correspondence in the distribution of species richness between different groups of organisms (Lamoreux et al. 2006; Xu et al. 2008). For example, in South America, concentrations of amphibians, birds, mammals, and plants are greatest in the western Amazon, with secondary concentrations in the highlands of northeastern South America and the Atlantic forests of southeastern Brazil (**Figure**

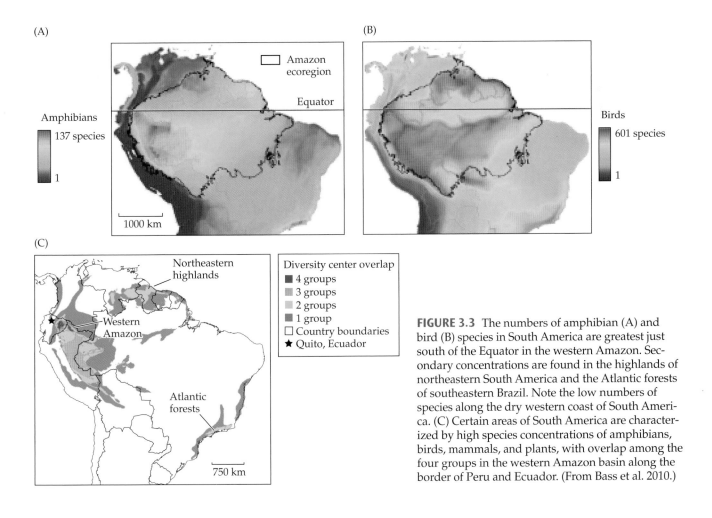

FIGURE 3.3 The numbers of amphibian (A) and bird (B) species in South America are greatest just south of the Equator in the western Amazon. Secondary concentrations are found in the highlands of northeastern South America and the Atlantic forests of southeastern Brazil. Note the low numbers of species along the dry western coast of South America. (C) Certain areas of South America are characterized by high species concentrations of amphibians, birds, mammals, and plants, with overlap among the four groups in the western Amazon basin along the border of Peru and Ecuador. (From Bass et al. 2010.)

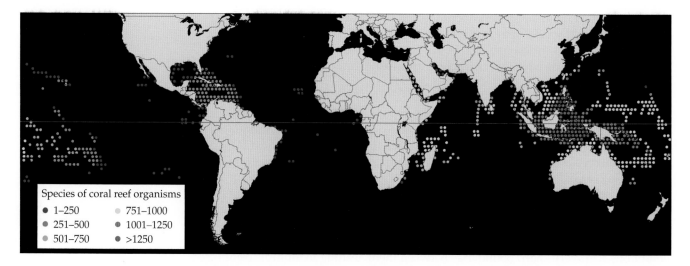

FIGURE 3.4 Number of species of coral reef organisms, including fish, corals, snails, and crustaceans, found in different regions of the world. Note the greater richness of species in the southwestern Pacific Ocean in comparison with the Caribbean, and the decline in the number of species farther away from the equator. (Map created by Clinton Jenkins with permission, using data from Callum Roberts and colleagues.)

3.3). In North America, large-scale patterns of species richness are highly correlated for amphibians, birds, butterflies, mammals, reptiles, land snails, trees, all vascular plants, and tiger beetles; that is, a region with numerous species of one group will tend to have numerous species of the other groups (Ricketts et al. 1999). On a local scale, this relationship may break down; for example, amphibians may be most diverse in wet, shady habitats, whereas reptiles may be most diverse in drier, open habitats. At a global scale, each group of living organisms may reach its greatest species richness in a different part of the world because of historical circumstances or the suitability of the site to its needs.

Larger areas also can provide a greater range of habitats in which species can evolve and live. For example, coral species richness is several times greater in the Indian and West Pacific oceans than in the western Atlantic Ocean, which is much smaller in area (**Figure 3.4**). More than 50 genera of coral exist in many of the Indo–Pacific areas, but only about 20 genera occur in the reefs of the Caribbean Sea and the adjacent Atlantic Ocean.

Why Are There So Many Species in the Tropics?

Almost all groups of organisms show an increase in species diversity toward the tropics. For example, Thailand has 241 species of mammals, while France has only 104, despite the fact that both countries have roughly the same land area (**Table 3.1**). The contrast is particularly striking for trees and other flowering plants: 10 ha of forest in Amazonian Peru or Brazil might have 300 or more tree species, whereas an equivalent forest area in temperate Europe or the United States would probably contain 30 species or less. Within a given continent, the number of species increases toward the equator.

Patterns of diversity in terrestrial species are paralleled by patterns in marine species, again with an increase in species diversity toward the tropics. For example, the Great Barrier Reef off the eastern coast of Australia has 50 genera of reef-building coral at its northern end where it approaches the tropics, but it has only 10 genera at its southern end, farthest away from the tropics. These increases in rich-

TABLE 3.1	Number of Native Mammal Species in Selected Tropical and Temperate Countries Paired for Comparable Size				
Tropical country	Area (1000 km^2)	Number of mammal species	Temperate country	Area (1000 km^2)	Number of mammal species
Brazil	8456	604	Canada	9220	207
DRC^a	2268	425	Argentina	2737	378
Mexico	1909	529	Algeria	2382	84
Indonesia	1812	471	Iran	1636	150
Colombia	1039	443	South Africa	1221	278
Venezuela	882	363	Chile	748	147
Thailand	511	241	France	550	104
Philippines	298	180	United Kingdom	242	75
Rwanda	25	111	Belgium	30	71

Source: Data from IUCN Red List 2009.
^{a}DRC = Democratic Republic of the Congo.

ness of coastal species toward the tropics and in warmer waters are paralleled by increases in open ocean species, such as plankton and predatory fish (Rombouts et al. 2009), though there are some groups of species that are most diverse in temperate waters.

Many theories have been advanced to explain the greater diversity of species in the tropics (Pimm and Brown 2004). Following are some of the most reasonable theories:

> High species diversity in the tropics may be due to greater productivity and stability, warmer temperatures, and more niche specialization, allowing many species to flourish and co-exist.

1. Tropical regions receive more solar energy over the course of a year than temperate regions, and many of them also have abundant rainfall. As a result, many tropical communities have a higher rate of productivity than temperate communities, in terms of the number of kilograms of living material (biomass) produced each year per hectare of habitat. This high productivity results in a greater resource base that can support a wider range of species.

2. Species of tropical communities have had longer periods of stability than species of temperate communities, which have had to disperse in response to periods of glaciation. This greater stability has allowed the processes of evolution and speciation to occur uninterrupted in tropical communities in response to local conditions. In temperate areas, the scouring actions of glaciers and the frigid climate destroyed many local species that might have evolved, and it favored those species able to disperse long distances. Thus, a relatively more stable climate has allowed a greater degree of evolutionary specialization and local adaptation to occur in tropical areas.

3. The warm temperatures and high humidity in many tropical areas provide favorable conditions for the growth and survival of many species. Entire communities of species can also develop in the tree canopies. In contrast, species living in temperate zones must have physiological mechanisms that allow them to tolerate cold and freezing conditions. These species may also have specialized behaviors, such as dormancy, hibernation, burrowing into the ground, or migration, to help them survive the winter. The inability of many groups of plants and animals to live outside the tropics suggests that adaptations to cold do not evolve easily or quickly.

4. Due to a predictable environment, species interactions in the tropics are more intense, leading initially to greater competition among species and later to niche specialization. Also, tropical species may face greater pressure from parasites and disease because there is no freezing weather in winter to reduce pest populations. Ever-present populations of these parasites prevent any single species or group of species from dominating communities, creating an opportunity for numerous species to coexist at low individual densities. For example, tree seedlings are often killed by fungi and insects when they grow near other trees of the same species, often leading to wide spaces between adult trees of the same species. In many ways, the biology of the tropics is the biology of rare species. In contrast, temperate zone species may face reduced parasite pressure because the winter cold suppresses parasite populations, allowing one or a few competitively superior species of plants and animals to dominate the community and exclude many other, less competitive species.

5. The large geographical area of the tropics, in comparison with the temperate zone, may account for the greater rates of speciation and lower rates of extinction in the tropics (Chown and Gaston 2000). This follows from the fact that the tropical areas north and south of the equator are next to each other, while the temperate areas outside the tropics are divided in two by the tropics themselves.

How Many Species Exist Worldwide?

At present, about 1.5 million species have been described. At least two to three times this number of species (primarily insects and other arthropods in the tropics) remain undescribed (**Figure 3.5A**). Our knowledge of species numbers is imprecise because inconspicuous species have not received their proper share of taxonomic attention. For example, spiders, nematodes, and fungi living in the soil and insects living in the tropical forest canopy are small and difficult to study. These poorly known groups could number in the hundreds of thousands, or even millions, of species. Our best estimate is that there are between 5 and 10 million species (Gaston and Spicer 2004).

New Species Are Being Discovered All the Time

Amazingly, about 20,000 new species are described each year. While certain groups of organisms such as birds, mammals, and temperate flowering plants are relatively well known, a small but steady number of new species in these groups are being discovered each year (Peres 2005). Even among a group as well studied as primates, ten new monkey species have been found in Brazil over the past 20 years, and three new species of lemurs have been discovered in Madagascar. Every decade, 500 to 600 new species of amphibians are described.

In groups such as insects, spiders, mites, nematodes, and fungi, the number of described species is still increasing at the rate of 1%–2% per year (Donoghue and Alverson 2000). Huge numbers of species in these groups, mostly in tropical areas but also in the temperate zone, have yet to be discovered and described (**Figure 3.5B**). Compounding the problem is the fact that, though most of the world's remaining undescribed species are probably insects and other invertebrates, only one-third of the world's 5000 taxonomists are now studying these groups.

Species are typically discovered when taxonomists collect specimens while on field trips but are unable to identify them despite looking at all available published descriptions. Taxonomists will then make a description of each new species and give it a new scientific name. New species are also discovered when further research,

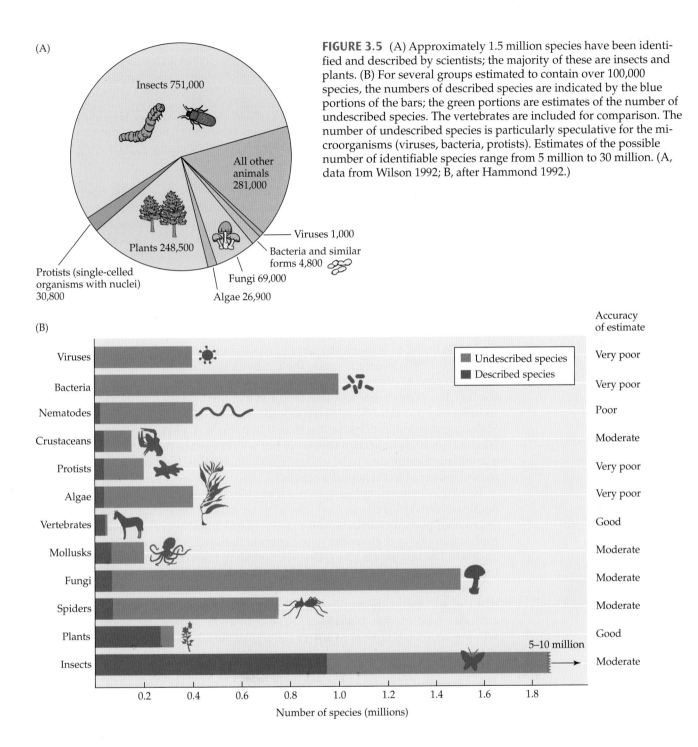

FIGURE 3.5 (A) Approximately 1.5 million species have been identified and described by scientists; the majority of these are insects and plants. (B) For several groups estimated to contain over 100,000 species, the numbers of described species are indicated by the blue portions of the bars; the green portions are estimates of the number of undescribed species. The vertebrates are included for comparison. The number of undescribed species is particularly speculative for the microorganisms (viruses, bacteria, protists). Estimates of the possible number of identifiable species range from 5 million to 30 million. (A, data from Wilson 1992; B, after Hammond 1992.)

often involving the techniques of molecular systematics and DNA analysis, reveals that what was originally thought to be a single species with a number of geographically distinct populations is really two or more species.

Sometimes new species are discovered as "living fossils"—species known only from the fossil record and believed to be extinct until living examples are found in modern times. In 1938, ichthyologists throughout the world were stunned by the report of a strange fish caught in the Indian Ocean. This fish, subsequently named *Latimeria chalumnae*, belonged to a group of marine fish known as coelacanths that were common in ancient seas but were thought to have gone extinct 65 million years

FIGURE 3.6 Researchers first encountered *Laonastes aenigmamus* being sold as a delicacy in Laotian food markets. This recently discovered species belongs to a group of rodents previously believed to have been extinct. In 2006, David Redfield of Florida State University led an expedition that was able to obtain the first photographs of a living *L. aenigmamus*. (Photograph by Uthai Treesucon, courtesy of *Research in Review*, FSU.)

ago (Thomas 1991). Coelacanths are of particular interest to evolutionary biologists because they show certain features of muscles and bones in their fins that are comparable to the limbs of the first vertebrates that crawled onto land. Biologists searched the Indian Ocean for 14 years before another coelacanth was found, off Grand Comore Island between Madagascar and the African coast. Subsequent investigation has shown that there is a single population of about 300 individuals living in underwater caves just offshore of Grand Comore (Fricke and Hissmann 1990). In recent years, the Union of the Comores implemented a conservation plan to protect the coelacanths, including a ban on catching and selling the fish. In a remarkable footnote to this story, in 1997 a marine biologist working in Indonesia was astonished to see a dead coelacanth for sale in a local fish market. Subsequent investigations demonstrated that this was a new species of coelacanth (Inoue et al. 2005) unknown to science but well known to the local fishermen, with a population estimated to be about 10,000, illustrating how much is still waiting to be discovered in the world's oceans.

In 2002, scientists exploring in the remote Brandberg Mountains of Namibia in southwestern Africa discovered insects in an entirely new order, distantly related to grasshoppers, stick insects, and praying mantids, subsequently named the Mantophasmatodea and given the new common name of "gladiator insects" (Klass et al. 2002). The last time a new order of insects had been described was in 1915. Further searches in other African countries have found additional species in this order.

New species may be discovered in unexpected places, as members of an international research team found when they noticed an unusual entrée on the grill in a Laotian food market. Natives called it "kha-nyou"; although clearly a rodent, it was not an animal known to any of the researchers. In 2006, after several years of studying skeletons and dead specimens, taxonomists deemed *kha-nyou* to be a heretofore unknown species belonging to a rodent family thought to have been extinct for 11 million years (Dawson et al. 2006). The newly discovered species was given the scientific name *Laonastes aenigmamus*, or "rock-dwelling, enigmatic mouse." More commonly called the Laotian rock rat or rock squirrel, this rodent is neither a mouse nor a rat nor a squirrel, but a unique species (**Figure 3.6**).

Recently Discovered Communities

In addition to new species, entire biological communities continue to be discovered, often in extremely remote and inaccessible localities. These communities often consist of inconspicuous species, such as bacteria, protists, and small invertebrates, that have escaped the attention of earlier taxonomists. Specialized exploration techniques have aided in these discoveries, particularly in the deep sea and in the forest canopy. Some recently discovered communities include the following:

(A)

(B)

FIGURE 3.7 (A) An entomologist (wearing a helmet and safety harness linked to climbing ropes) checks a suspended sheet containing fallen insects and leaves from a rainforest tree. He is holding a "pooter," which he sucks on to capture insects in a small bottle. (B) A dirigible lowers its inflatable platform base into the dense Guiana rainforest canopy. Scientists will later gain access to the canopy by climbing on the platform. (A, photograph by Philippe Psaila/Photo Researchers, Inc.; B, photograph © Raphael Gaillarde/Gamma/Eyedea/Zuma Press.)

- Diverse communities of animals, particularly insects, are adapted to living in the canopies of tropical trees and rarely, if ever, descend to the ground (Lowman et al. 2006). Technical climbing equipment, canopy towers and walkways, tall cranes, and even dirigibles are being used to open up this habitat to exploration (**Figure 3.7**).

- The floor of the deep sea has unique communities of bacteria and animals that grow around geothermal vents (**Box 3.1**). Undescribed, active bacteria unrelated to any known species have even been found in marine sediments at depths of up to 6.5 km (4 mi.), where they undoubtedly play a major chemical and energetic role in this vast ecosystem (Li et al. 1999; Scheckenback et al. 2010). Drilling projects have shown that diverse bacterial communities exist even 2.8 km deep in the Earth's crust, at densities ranging from 100 to 100 million bacteria per gram of solid rock. These bacterial communities in extreme environments are being actively investigated as a source of novel chemicals, for their potential usefulness in degrading toxic chemicals, and for insight into whether life could exist on other planets.

- Using DNA technology to investigate the interior of leaves of healthy tropical trees has revealed an extraordinarily rich group of fungi, consisting of thousands of undescribed species (Arnold and Lutzoni 2007). These fungi appear to aid the plant in excluding harmful bacteria and fungi, in exchange for receiving a place to live and perhaps some carbohydrates.

- The human body is populated by millions of viruses, bacteria, fungi, and mites. The density of bacteria growing in our armpits may reach 10 million cells per cm^2. One study of six people discovered that there were 182 distinct species of bacteria living on their arms. Some of these bacteria may play a beneficial role in secreting antimicrobial compounds that control harmful bacteria. We might also expect to find comparable levels of microbial abundance and diversity on other animals.

BOX 3.1 *Conserving a World Unknown: Hydrothermal Vents and Oil Plumes*

■ Biologists are aware that many species exist that have not been adequately studied and described, a fact that frequently hampers conservation. In recent years, it has become apparent that there are entire ecosystems that remain undiscovered in the more remote parts of the Earth. It is clear from the example of deep sea hydrothermal vents that species, genera, and even families of organisms exist about which scientists know nothing and in places where little life was predicted to occur. The biota of these vents were investigated in detail only in the last 30 years with the invention of technology that enables scientists to photograph and collect specimens from depths of over 2000 meters (German et al. 2008). Such organisms pose a significant problem for conservationists: How does one go about conserving undiscovered or barely known species and ecosystems?

Hydrothermal vents are temporary underwater openings in the Earth's crust. Extremely hot water (in excess of 150°C), sulfides, and other dissolved minerals escape from these vents and support a profusion of species in the deepest parts of the ocean. Specialized chemosynthetic bacteria are the primary producers of the vent community, using the minerals as an energy source. Communities of large animals such as clams, crabs, fishes, and 2 m long tube worms (also known as pogonophorans) in turn feed on the bacteria directly, or the bacteria live symbiotically inside their bodies. The vents themselves are short-lived, spanning a few decades at most; however, the ecosystems supported by these vents are thought to have evolved over the past 200 million years or more. Until deep sea submersibles were developed in the 1970s, scientists were completely unaware of the communities that live around the vents. Since 1979, however, when the submersible *Alvin* was first used to examine the vents around the Galápagos rift in the Pacific Ocean, 150 new species, 50 new genera, and 20 new families and subfamilies of animals—not including microorganisms—have been described. As investigation of deep sea vents continues, more families will certainly be discovered, encompassing many new genera and species.

Like many terrestrial ecosystems, hydrothermal ecosystems vary according to differences in their local environment. Distribution of hydrothermal ecosystems is dependent upon the character of the vents, including the temperature, chemical composition, and flow pattern of hydrothermal fluid issuing from the vents. Scientists studying hydrothermal species may work for decades yet acquire only minimal knowledge of the dynamics of these ecosystems, because of the unique nature of the study sites: the vents are ephemeral, sometimes existing for only a few years, and inaccessible—they can be reached only with the use of expensive, specialized equipment. Work is just starting on the genetics of these species to determine their ability to disperse and colonize new vents.

Scientists continue to make remarkable discoveries in nature. Conservation strategies, such as reducing pollution, sometime need to be implemented even when little is known about the species or ecosystem in question

Diversity Surveys: Collecting and Counting Species

Describing the diversity of major groups of organisms represents an enormous undertaking. Large institutions and teams of scientists often undertake biological surveys of entire countries or regions, which may involve decades—such work includes specimen collection in the field, identification of known species, descriptions of new species, and finally, publication of the results so that others can use the information. Two such examples are the massive Flora of North America project, based at the Missouri Botanical Garden, and the Flora Malesiana in the Indo–Pacific region, organized by the Rijksherbarium in the Netherlands.

In conducting such surveys, scientists determine the identity and numbers of species present in an area by means of a thorough collection of specimens that has been compiled over an extended period of time. The collection is then carefully sorted and classified by specialists, often at museums. For example, a team from the Natural History Museum in London collected over 1 million beetles from a 500 ha lowland rain forest in the Dumoga Bone National Park on Sulawesi, Indonesia, in 1985. This effort led to an initial list of 3488 species, large numbers of which were previously unknown to science. Subsequent museum work allowed the identifi-

BOX 3.1 *(continued)*

Part of a hydrothermal vent community on the ocean bottom. Large tube worms (*Riftia pachyptila*) dominate the ecosystem. Crabs and mussels also make their home here. The energy and nutrients that support this community are derived from the hydrogen sulfide and minerals emitted by volcanic vents. (Photograph courtesy of Cindy Lee Van Dover.)

Petroleum-seep communities, another little-known ecosystem like the assemblages at hydrothermal vents, can exist at ocean depths far below the reach of sunlight. In these areas, the initial source of energy comes from petrochemicals—oil—seeping from cracks in the ocean floor, and this energy supports a variety of organisms, some of which are similar to those that comprise hydrothermal communities. Some of the same species that congregate around hydrothermal and petroleum-seep vents may also colonize the carcasses of large fish and marine mammals, such as whales, that sink to the bottom of the ocean floor (Little 2010). These unpredictable bonanzas of organic matter may provide crucial stepping-stones for organisms to disperse among widely scattered hydrothermal vents and petroleum seeps.

Despite the inaccessibility of the sites and the cost of investigation, biologists nevertheless need to think ahead to conservation problems that might face these unique marine ecosystems in the future. Water pollution and trawling, for example, have damaged ocean species in shallower waters and in theory could harm these ecosystems as well. Is it possible to develop conservation programs for such deep sea ecosystems despite our lack of information? At this stage, there is only one definitive statement that can address these dilemmas: we know that restricting and regulating pollution, degradation from trawling, and other damaging human activities have broadly positive effects on natural ecosystems, so programs that protect the marine environment may offer the best conservation strategy in these situations, even when the ecosystems themselves are not thoroughly understood.

cation of 1000 more species, with as many as 2000 species remaining to be identified over the coming years and decades. The goal of many such surveys is to keep sampling until most of the species have been collected. Even careful surveys miss many species, particularly when they are rare or inconspicuous, or if they only occur in the soil.

Estimating the Number of Species

Worldwide, the most diverse group of organisms appears to be the insects, with about 750,000 species described already—about half the world's total species (see Figure 3.5A). If we assume the number of insect species can be accurately estimated in tropical forests where they are most abundant, then it may be possible to estimate the total number of species in the world. Various entomologists have attempted this by sampling entire insect communities in tropical forests, using insecticidal fogging of whole trees and intensive hand collection (**Figure 3.8**) (Ødegaard 2000; Novotny et al. 2002; Gering et al. 2007). These studies have revealed an extremely rich and largely undescribed insect fauna in the tree canopies. Using the results of such intensive collecting, these entomologists have attempted to calculate the number of insect species. In one approach, they began with the fact that there are 55,000

(A)

(B)

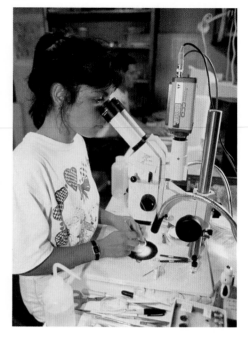

FIGURE 3.8 (A) A researcher uses insecticidal fog to sample the vast number of insect species in a tropical tree canopy. Dead insects will be collected on sheets when they fall out of the tree canopy. (B) In the lab, a Costa Rican researcher begins the process of sorting, describing, and identifying insects taken from the tree canopy. (Photographs courtesy of John Longino and Robert Colwell.)

species of tropical trees and woody vines (lianas). Based on detailed field sampling, entomologists estimated that there are on average 9 species of specialized beetle feeding on each distinct plant species, leading to an estimated 400,000–500,000 species of canopy beetles. Canopy beetles represent about 44% of all beetle species, yielding an estimate of about 1 million beetle species. Because beetles are about 20% of all insects, it can be estimated that there are about 5 million insects in tropical forests. Such calculations give values comparable to earlier estimates of 5 to 10 million species for the entire Earth (Gaston and Spicer 2004).

> Many scientists are working to determine the number of species in the world. The best estimate is that there are about 5–10 million species, with about half of them being insects.

Such "rules" can be used to determine how many species are involved in other biological relationships (Schmit et al. 2005). For example, in Britain and Europe, where species have been extensively studied, there are about six times more fungus species than plant species. If this general ratio is applicable throughout the world, there may be as many as 1.5 million fungus species, in addition to the estimated 250,000 plant species worldwide. Since only 69,000 fungus species have been described so far, it is possible that there are over 1.4 million fungus species waiting to be discovered, most of them in the tropics. If it turns out that fungal diversity increases more rapidly toward the equator, as some scientists have suggested (Frohlich and Hyde 1999), there may be as many as 9 million undescribed fungus species.

Yet another approach is to assume that each species of plant and insect, which together form the majority of currently known species, has at least one species of specialized bacteria, protist, and nematode (roundworm); hence the estimate of the number of total species worldwide should be multiplied by 4—bringing it to 20 million, using the figure of 5 million species as the starting point, or to 40 million if 10 million species is the starting point. Developing such preliminary approaches allows estimates to be made of the numbers of species in communities while more rigorous sampling and identification is being performed.

UNDERREPRESENTED SPECIES   The difficulty of making estimates of species numbers is exacerbated by the fact that inconspicuous species have not received their proper share of taxonomic attention. Since inconspicuous species constitute the majority of species on Earth, the difficulty of finding and cataloging them delays a thorough understanding of the full extent of the planet's biological diversity (Caron 2009).

Inconspicuous organisms, including small rodents, most insects, and microorganisms, are much less likely to be observed by chance outside their natural habitats, as the coelacanth was, or even *within* their native environments (Wilson 2010). For example, mites in the soil, soft-bodied insects such as bark lice, and nematodes in both soil and water are small and hard to study. If properly studied, these groups could be found to number in the hundreds of thousands of species, or even millions. Since demonstrating the role of nematode species as root parasites of agricultural plants, scientists have dramatically increased their efforts to collect and describe these minute roundworms. Consequently, the catalog of this one group of organisms has grown from the 80 species known in 1860 to about 20,000 species known today; some experts estimate that there may be millions more species waiting to be described (Boucher and Lambshead 1995). As is the case with so many other taxonomic groups, the number of trained specialists is the limiting factor in unlocking the diversity of this enormous group of species.

Bacteria are also very poorly known (Azam and Worden 2004) and thus underrepresented in estimates of the total species on Earth. Yet, at the densities at which they occur, they must have an important role to play in ecosystem functioning. For example, the density of bacteria in seawater is astonishing; upward of 100 million cells per liter can exist, with a large diversity of species. Only about 5000 species of bacteria are currently recognized by microbiologists, because they are difficult to grow and identify. However, work analyzing bacterial DNA indicates that there may be from 6400 to 38,000 species in a single gram of soil and 160 species in a liter of seawater (Nee 2003). Such high diversity in small samples suggests that there could be tens of thousands or even millions of undescribed bacteria species. Many of these unknown bacteria are probably very common and of major environmental importance. In the ancient kingdom of Archaea, which has been less studied in the past, even new bacteria *phyla* continue to be discovered.

> DNA analyses suggest that many thousands of species of bacteria have yet to be described. The marine environment also contains large numbers of species unknown to science.

Many inconspicuous species that live in remote habitats will not be found and cataloged unless biologists search for them. A lack of collecting, especially, has hampered our knowledge of the species richness of the marine environment—a great frontier of biological diversity, with huge numbers of species and even entire communities still unknown—at least in part because it poses challenges for study (Brandt et al. 2007). Marine invertebrate animals such as polychaete worms, for instance, are not well studied because they make the ocean bottom their home. Additionally, an entirely new animal phylum, the Loricifera, was described in 1983 based on specimens from the deep sea (Kristensen et al. 2007), and another new phylum, the Cycliophora, was first described in 1995 based on tiny, ciliate creatures found on the mouthparts of the Norway lobster (**Figure 3.9**) (Funch and Kristensen 1995). Undoubtedly, more species, genera, families, orders, classes, and phyla (and perhaps even kingdoms!) are waiting to be discovered.

Considering that about 20,000 new animal species are described each year and perhaps 5 million more are waiting to be identified, the task of describing the world's

FIGURE 3.9 A new phylum, the Cycliophora, was first described in 1995. The phylum contains one vase-shaped species, *Symbion pandora* (about 40 of which are shown in the inset). The individuals attach themselves to the mouthparts of the Norway lobster, *Nephrops norvegicus*. (Photographs courtesy of Reinhardt Kristensen, University of Copenhagen.)

species will not be completed for over 250 years if continued at the present rate! This underlines the absolutely critical need for more taxonomists.

The Need for More Taxonomists

A major problem the scientific community faces in describing and cataloging the biological diversity of the world is the lack of trained taxonomists able to take on the job. At the present time, there are only about 5000 taxonomists in the world, and only about 1500 of them are competent to work with tropical species, plus many of *them* are based in temperate countries. Unfortunately, this number is declining rather than increasing. When academic taxonomists retire, universities have a tendency to either close the position due to financial difficulties or replace the retiring biologist with a nontaxonomist. Many members of the younger generation of taxonomists are so preoccupied with the technology of molecular systematics and associated data analysis that they are neither interested in nor capable of continuing the great tradition of discovering and cataloging the world's biological treasures. A substantial increase in the number of field taxonomists focused primarily on describing and identifying tropical and marine species is needed to complete the task of describing the world's biological diversity. Much of this effort should be directed to lesser-known groups, such as fungi, bacteria, and invertebrates. And where possible, these taxonomists need to be based in tropical countries where this diversity is located. Natural history societies and clubs that combine professional and amateur naturalists also can play a valuable role in assisting these efforts and in exposing the general public and student groups to the issues and excitement of biological diversity and encouraging people to become taxonomists.

Summary

1. In general, species richness is greatest in tropical rain forests, coral reefs, tropical lakes, the deep sea, and shrublands with a Mediterranean climate. In terrestrial habitats, species richness tends to be greatest at lower elevations and in warmer areas with abundant rainfall. Areas that are geologically old and topographically complex also tend to have more species.

2. Tropical rain forests occupy only 7% of the Earth's land area, yet they are estimated to contain most of the Earth's species. The great majority of these species are insects not yet described by scientists. Coral reef communities are also rich in species, with many of the species widely distributed. The deep sea also appears to be rich in species but is still not adequately explored.

3. About 1.5 million species have been described, and more than twice that number remain to be described. Intensive collecting of insects in tropical forest has yielded estimates of species numbers ranging from 5 to 10 million, but it could be higher.

4. While conspicuous groups, such as flowering plants, mammals, and birds, are reasonably well known to science, other inconspicuous groups, particularly insects, bacteria, and fungi, have not been thoroughly studied. New biological communities are still being discovered, especially in the deep sea and the forest canopy. For example, spectacular communities that occupy deep sea hydrothermal vents are major, recent discoveries.

5. There is a vital need for more taxonomists and field biologists to study, collect, classify, and help protect the world's biological diversity before it is lost.

For Discussion

1. What are the factors promoting species richness? Why is biological diversity diminished in particular environments? Why aren't species able to overcome these limitations and undergo the process of speciation?

2. Develop arguments for both low and high estimates of the total number of species in particular groups, such as bacteria, fungi, or nematodes. Read more about groups that you don't know well. Why is it important to identify and name all the species in a particular group?

3. If taxonomists are so important to documenting and protecting biological diversity, why are their numbers declining instead of increasing? How could societal and scientific priorities be readjusted to reverse this trend? Is the ability to identify and classify species a skill that every conservation biologist should possess?

4. Some scientists have argued that life may have existed on Mars, and recent drilling demonstrates that bacteria actually flourish in rocks deep under the Earth's surface. Speculate, as wildly as you can, about where to search for previously unsuspected species, communities, or novel life forms.

Suggested Readings

Arnold, A. E. and F. Lutzoni. 2007. Diversity and host range of foliar fungal endophytes: are tropical leaves biodiversity hotspots? *Ecology* 88: 541–549. Fungi living inside leaves are incredibly diverse and appear to benefit the plants that they inhabit.

Brandt, A. A. and 20 others. 2007. First insights in the biodiversity and biogeography of the Southern Ocean deep sea. *Nature* 447: 307–311. Hundreds of new species were found on this recent expedition.

Caron, D. A. 2009. New accomplishments and approaches for assessing protistan diversity and ecology in natural ecosystems. *BioScience* 59: 287–299. New molecular approaches have greatly advanced the study of microbial diversity and ecological roles.

Corlett, R. and R. B. Primack. 2010. *Tropical Rainforests: An Ecological and Biogeographical Comparison*, Second Edition. Wiley-Blackwell Publishing, Malden, MA. Rain forests on each continent have distinctive assemblages of animal and plant species.

Donoghue, M. J. and W. S. Alverson. 2000. A new age of discovery. *Annals of the Missouri Botanical Garden* 87: 110–126. In this article and others in the same special issue, scientists describe new species still being discovered throughout the world.

Groombridge, B. and M. D. Jenkins. 2002. *World Atlas of Biodiversity: Earth's Living Resources in the 21st Century*. University of California Press, Berkeley. Description of the world's biodiversity, with lots of maps and tables.

Knowlton, N. and J. B. C. Jackson. 2008. Shifting baselines, local impacts, and global change on coral reefs. *PLoS Biology* 6: e54. There are no truly "pristine" coral reef ecosystems; they are all affected by major human impacts.

Lamoreux, J. F. and 6 others. 2006. Global tests of biodiversity concordance and the importance of endemism. *Nature* 440: 212–214. Concentrations of species are found in similar places for many major groups of organisms.

Lowman, M. D., E. Burgess, and J. Burgess. 2006. *It's a Jungle Up There: More Tales from the Treetops*. Yale University Press, New Haven, CT. Anecdotes and adventures while exploring the diversity of the tropical forest canopy.

Ødegaard, F. 2000. How many species of arthropods? Erwin's estimate revised. *Biological Journal of the Linnean Society* 71: 583–597. An analysis of tropical insect diversity allows an estimate of the number of insect species.

Pimm, S. L. and J. H. Brown. 2004. Domains of diversity. *Science* 304: 831–833. Various theories of global diversity are critically examined.

Scheckenbach, F., K. Hausmann, C. Wylezich, M. Weitere, and H. Arndt. 2010. Large-scale patterns in biodiversity of microbial eukaryotes from the abyssal sea floor. *Proceedings of the National Academy of Sciences USA* 107: 115–120. Large numbers of mostly unknown species are found at depths of 5000 m.

Wilson, E. O. 2010. Within one cubic foot: miniature surveys of biodiversity. *National Geographic* 217(2): 62–83. A study of the remarkable amount of life that can be found in a mere cubic foot on land or in the sea.

Chapter 4

Ecological Economics and Direct Use Values

Decisions on protecting species, communities and ecosystems, and genetic variation often come down to arguments over money: How much will it cost? And how much is it worth? The economic value of something is generally accepted as the amount of money people are willing to pay for it. But this is only one possible way of assigning value to things, including biological diversity. Ethical, aesthetic, scientific, and educational methods of valuation are available as well. However, government and corporate officials currently base major policy decisions on economic valuation. As a result, conservation biologists now use the methodology and vocabulary of economics in their arguments for the protection of diversity: It is easier to convince governments and corporations to protect biological diversity when there is an economic incentive to do so. When the loss of biological diversity is perceived to cost money, governments and corporations may act more aggressively to prevent it.

An awareness of, and involvement in, assigning economic value to biological diversity is increasingly important for conservation biologists. Some people would argue that any attempt to place a strictly monetary value on biological diversity is inappropriate and potentially corrupting, since many aspects of the natural world are unique and thus truly priceless (Redford and Adams 2009). Supporters of this position point out that there is no way to assign monetary value to the wonder people experience when they see an animal in the wild or a beautiful natural landscape; nor can economic value realistically be assigned to the human lives that have been and will be saved through the medicinal compounds derived from wild species. In fact, economic models contribute much to the debate over the protection of biological diversity. It is to the advantage of conservationists to develop economic models—both to improve such models' accuracy and to appreciate their limitations—since these models often provide surprisingly strong support for the crucial role of biological diversity in local economies and for the need to protect ecosystems. Economic models need to be presented to policy makers and incorporated into the regulations that will affect how development proceeds.

Why Economic Valuation Is Needed

A major problem for conservation biology is that natural resources have often been undervalued. Thus, the costs of environmental damage have been ignored, the depletion of natural resource stocks disregarded, and the future value of resources discounted (MEA 2005). Because the underlying causes of environmental damage are so often economic in nature, the solution must incorporate economic principles (Shogren et al. 1999). **Ecological economics** is an emerging discipline that studies the interaction between economic and ecological systems. It facilitates understanding between economists and ecologists and seeks to integrate their thinking into a transdiscipline aimed at developing a sustainable world (Sachs 2008).

> Arguments for the protection of biodiversity are often strengthened by evidence provided by ecological economics.

One of the core agenda items of this new discipline is to develop methods to value biological diversity by integrating economic valuation with ecology, environmental science, sociology, and ethics and then, based on those new valuations, design better public policies related to conservation and environmental issues (Nunes et al. 2003; Common and Stagl 2005). Governments need to allocate their resources in the most efficient manner possible, and a well-considered argument for the conservation of biological diversity that is grounded in economics will often effectively support arguments based on biological, ethical, and emotional grounds (Balmford et al. 2002).

Before the trend of biodiversity loss can be reversed, its fundamental causes must be understood. What factors induce humans to act in a nonsustainable—and therefore destructive—manner? Usually, environmental degradation and species loss occur as by-products of human economic activities. Forests are logged for revenue from timber sales. Species are hunted for personal consumption, sale, and sport. Marginal land is converted into cropland because people have nowhere else to farm. Species, either transported accidentally by commercial vessels or brought purposefully by people, invade islands and continents, often killing the local flora and fauna. Factories and towns release their pollutants into nearby water bodies.

An understanding of a few fundamental economic principles will clarify the reasons why people treat the environment in what appears to be a shortsighted, wasteful manner. One of the most universally accepted tenets of modern economic thought centers on the "voluntary transaction"—the idea that a monetary transaction takes place only when it is beneficial to both of the parties involved. For example, a baker who sells his loaves of bread for $40 will find few customers. Likewise, a customer who is willing to pay only 4 cents for a loaf will soon go hungry. A transaction between seller and buyer will only occur when a mutually agreeable price is set that benefits both parties: perhaps $4 for that loaf of bread, for instance. Adam Smith, the eighteenth-century philosopher whose ideas are the foundation of much modern economic thought, wrote, "It is not upon the benevolence of the butcher, the baker, or the brewer that we eat our daily bread, but upon his own self-interest" (Smith 1909). All parties involved in an exchange expect to improve their own situation. The sum of each individual acting in his or her self-interest results in a more prosperous society. Smith likened this effect to an "invisible hand" guiding the market—turning selfish, uncoordinated actions into increased prosperity and relative social harmony.

However, there are exceptions to Smith's principle that directly apply to environmental issues. For example, Smith assumed that all the costs and benefits of free exchange are accepted and borne by the participants in the transaction. In some cases, however, associated costs or benefits befall individuals not directly involved in the exchange. These hidden costs or benefits are known as negative and positive **externalities** (Buckley and Crone 2008). Where externalities exist, the market may fail to maximize the net benefits to society as a whole. **Market failure** occurs when resources are misallocated, which allows a few individuals or businesses to benefit at the expense of the larger society. As a result, the society as a whole becomes *less* prosperous from certain economic activities, not more prosperous.

Perhaps the most important and frequently overlooked negative externality is the environmental damage that occurs to **open-access resources**, such as water, air, and soil, as a consequence of human economic activity. Open-access resources are collectively owned by society at large or owned by no one, with availability to everyone who is part of that society. Open-access resources are available for everyone to use. Because of the lack of property rights, these resources are essentially free. When there are no regulations, then people, industries, and governments use and damage these resources without paying more than a minimal cost, or sometimes they pay nothing at all. This is a situation in which market failure occurs, also described as **the tragedy of the commons**—the value of the open-access resource is gradually lost to all of society (Hardin 1985; WRI 2005; Lant et al. 2008). For example, consider the dumping of industrial sewage into a river as a by-product of manufacturing. The externalities of this activity are degraded drinking water and in increase in disease, loss of opportunity to bathe and swim in the water, fewer fish that are safe to eat, and the loss of many species unable to survive in the polluted river.

> Aspects of biodiversity are often damaged or lost because society does not value them appropriately.

Market failure can also occur when there is a lack of enforcement of regulations relating to **common property**, that is, resources owned by society but regulated for common benefit; for example, harvesting of fish in an area may be managed according to a sustainable system. However, if this system is not adequately enforced, overharvesting may occur, leading to a collapse of the fishing stock and damage to the ecosystem.

The fundamental challenge facing conservation biologists is to ensure that all the costs of economic behavior, as well as all the benefits, are understood and taken into account when decisions are made that will affect biological diversity (Hoeinghaus et al. 2009). Companies, individuals, or other stakeholders involved in production that results in ecological damage generally do not bear the full cost of their activities but gain substantial private economic benefits. For example, the company that owns an electric power plant that burns coal and emits toxic fumes benefits from the sale of low-cost electricity, as does the consumer who buys this electricity. Yet the hidden costs of this transaction—decreased air quality and visibility, increased respiratory disease for people and animals, damage to plant life, and a polluted environment—are distributed throughout society and do not affect decisions made by the company.

Another example is the almost unstoppable movement to convert undeveloped land into agricultural land, residential neighborhoods, and industrial sites. Such activities create great individual and corporate wealth, often increasing the value of the land by 200 to 2500 times (Hulse and Ribe 2000). Yet the loss in species, ecosystem services, and quality of life for the surrounding human community is rarely considered in the rush to make a profit, and it is borne by the society as a whole. Understanding this imbalance is central to understanding market failure: the wide distribution of economic cost, often combined with the concentrated benefit to a small group of owners (or a large group of consumers), creates conflict between private and social benefits and costs, and it results in the overuse of natural resources, loss of biodiversity and ecosystem services, and even harm to the welfare of the society.

When individuals and organizations must pay for the consequences of their actions—that is, be forced to take into account the negative externalities that result from their activities—they will be much more likely to stop damaging, or at least minimize their damage to, the environment (Loucks and Gorman 2004). Some suggestions designed to discourage behavior that damages the environment include charging taxes on air pollution caused by using fossil fuels; charging higher rates for water use and sewage discharge; preserving open land as compensation when another nearby site is developed; and paying for the damage caused when insecticides, herbicides, and fertilizers are released into the environment. Many countries have already put such ideas into action. In addition, policy makers could create penalties for damaging biological diversity and subsidies for preserving it, to make individuals and industries more mindful of how their actions affect the environment.

Evaluating Development Projects

In order to ensure that the full costs of development are taken into account and carefully weighed, it is essential to review new projects and evaluate their potential effects *before* they proceed. Such reviews are the standard practice in most developed countries and are increasingly carried out in developing countries as well. International donor agencies, such as the World Bank, often require such evaluations before projects are funded.

Cost-Benefit Analysis

Economists evaluate large development projects using **environmental** and **economic impact assessments**, which consider the present and future effects of the projects on the environment and the economy. The environment is often broadly defined to include not only harvestable natural resources but also air and water quality, the quality of life for local people, and the preservation of endangered species. In its most comprehensive form, **cost-benefit analysis** compares the values gained against the costs of the project or resource use (Atkinson and Mourato 2008; Newbold and Siikamäki 2009). For example, during feasibility studies for a large logging operation that would remove a forest, an economist might compare the income obtained from logging with the income and resources lost due to damage to game animals, medicinal plants, clean water, fish habitat, a scenic walk through a grove of large trees, rare bird species, and wildflower populations. Alternatively, an economist might estimate what it would cost to restore the ecosystem or resource to its original condition after logging ceased. These different strategies are likely to have very different costs and benefits and produce very different results.

> Many conservation biologists are turning to "green" accounting methods to ensure that the elements of biodiversity are properly valued by society.

In one cost-benefit analysis, the competing uses of the terrestrial and marine environments in Bacuit Bay, Palawan, Philippines, were modeled for three development alternatives (**Table 4.1**). In the first option, intensive logging, tourism, and fishing would occur together. While logging provides more revenue than tourism and fishing do when all three activities occur simultaneously, logging has strong negative impacts on the fishing industry and on tourism, because it results in increased sedimentation that kills coral communities and the fish that depend on

TABLE 4.1 Cost-Benefit Analysis of Three Development Options in Bacuit Bay, Palawan, Phillippines

Development option	Amount of revenue[a] generated by			
	Tourism	Fisheries	Logging	Total revenue
Option 1: Intensive logging until timber depleted[b]	$6	$9	$10	$25
Option 2: Logging banned; protected area established[c]	$25	$17	$0	$42
Option 3: Sustainable logging[d]	$24	$16	$4	$44

Source: After Hodgson and Dixon 1988.

[a]Revenues are in millions of dollars over a 10-year period.

[b]In this option, intensive logging substantially decreases the revenues from tourism and fisheries. Timber is completely depleted after 5 years.

[c]In this option, tourism and fisheries are major sustainable industries; no logging.

[d]In this option, logging is allowed to proceed in an environmentally responsible manner. A buffer of trees is maintained near wetlands and streams, logging does not occur on steep slopes, construction of logging roads is minimized, and hunting is banned. There is minimal impact on fisheries and tourism, and the overall economic benefits are enhanced. (Real-life logging practices are rarely as benign as portrayed here.)

them. The second option would protect forests through a ban on logging; the fishing and tourist industries provide more revenue in that situation than when all three industries operate together. The third possible option involved the techniques of sustainable logging. Logging would be undertaken in a responsible and limited way (such as by logging in small patches and avoiding steep slopes, streams, rivers, and the coast) to minimize environmental damage. If this third option were chosen, fishing, tourism, and sustainable logging might coexist without one industry compromising the economic benefits of the others. Although, based on this analysis, sustainable forestry appeared to be the best long-term option, ultimately this was not considered realistic. In the end, Bacuit Bay was established as a marine sanctuary and has become a major tourist resort (Ong 2002).

In theory, the outcome of such analysis is simple: If cost-benefit analysis shows that a project will be profitable, it should go forward, while unprofitable projects should be stopped. In practice, though, cost-benefit analyses are notoriously difficult to calculate, because benefits and costs change over time and are hard to measure. For example, when a new paper mill is being constructed in a forested area, it is difficult to predict the future price of paper, the profitability of the industry, the future need for clean water, and the value of other plant and animal species in the forests being harvested. In the past, the natural resources used or damaged by large development projects were either ignored or were grossly undervalued. Now, there is an increasing tendency by governments, conservation groups, and economists to apply the **precautionary principle**; when there is uncertainty about the risks associated with a project, it is better to err on the side of doing no harm to the environment. In some cases this may mean not approving a project.

It would be highly beneficial to apply cost-benefit analysis to many of the basic industries and practices of modern society. Many economic activities appear to be profitable even when they are actually losing money, because governments subsidize industries involved in environment-damaging activities with tax breaks, direct payments or price supports, cheap fossil fuels, free water, and road networks—sometimes referred to as **perverse subsidies** (Myers and Kent 2001; Bagstad et al. 2007; Myers et al. 2007). These government subsidies promote specific industries, such as agriculture, fishing, automobile manufacturing, and energy production, and they may amount to trillions of dollars per year, or roughly 5% of the world economy. Subsidies in agriculture and fisheries can be as high as 20%–30% of the production value (MEA 2005). Without these subsidies, many environmentally damaging or expensive activities—such as farming in areas with high labor, energy, and water costs; overfishing in the ocean; and inefficient and highly polluting energy use—would be reduced.

In evaluating development projects, conservation biologists and ecological economists also need to address **discount rates**, which are commonly used by economists to calculate the present value of natural resources that will be harvested or used at some point in the future (Naidoo and Adamowicz 2006). Economists use discount rates to assign a *lower current value* to resources or materials that will be used in the future, on the grounds that it is better for the society to have money now and invest it for greater wealth rather than leave natural resources unused. Such investments might include building schools, hospitals, factories, roads, port facilities, and other infrastructure. Economists often assign high discount rates (higher discount rates = lower current values) to natural resources (trees, wood, water, fish, wild game, etc.) in developing countries because their meeting day-to-day needs are more critical than in developed countries and thus they have a higher preference for current consumption over future consumption; that is, resources harvested at some point in the future have a much lower value to the citizens of a developing country than equivalent resources harvested now. Such an approach often leads to shortsighted decisions to use resources right away, and it minimizes the value of resources used in the future. This use of discounting propels development projects forward, when a more cautious approach would be to use lower discount rates for natural resources in general, especially in developing countries, where local people rely on natural resources to survive.

Assigning monetary values to species, communities, and ecosystems has strengthened the conservation movement (Jenkins et al. 2004; MEA 2005). Researchers, governments, and corporations are now starting to assign economic values to ecosystem variables such as the actions and resources that contribute to the reduction of atmospheric carbon dioxide and other greenhouse gases (van Kooten and Sohngen 2007), the protection of water resources (Benítez et al. 2007), and the future use of presently unused or even unknown species. Increasingly, the hidden costs of environmental degradation that occur during income-producing activities, such as logging, agriculture, commercial fishing, and development of wetlands for commercial use, are now being incorporated into discussions of the costs of large-scale projects.

Natural Resource Loss and the Wealth of Societies

Attempts have been made to include the loss of natural resources in calculations of gross domestic product (GDP) and other indexes of national production. The problem with GDP is that it measures economic activity in a country without accounting for all the costs of nonsustainable activities (such as overfishing of coastal waters and poorly managed strip-mining), which causes the GDP to increase, even though these activities may be destructive to a country's long-term economic well-being. In actuality, the economic costs associated with environmental damage can be considerable, and they often offset the gains attained through agricultural and industrial development.

Unsustainable activities such as clear-cut logging, strip mining, and overfishing may cause a country's apparent productivity to increase for the present moment but are generally destructive to long-term economic well-being.

In Costa Rica, for example, the value of the forests destroyed during the 1980s greatly exceeded the income produced from forest products, so the forestry sector actually represented a drain on the wealth of the country. In the United Kingdom, hidden environmental costs in agriculture, including soil erosion and water pollution, are estimated to be worth about $2.6 billion per year, or 9% of the value of the country's agriculture (MEA 2005). Such hidden costs of environmental damage are enormous by any standard—and all such costs are underappreciated and excluded from GDP calculations. If farmers were paid a subsidy based on how well their land provided soil protection and flood con-

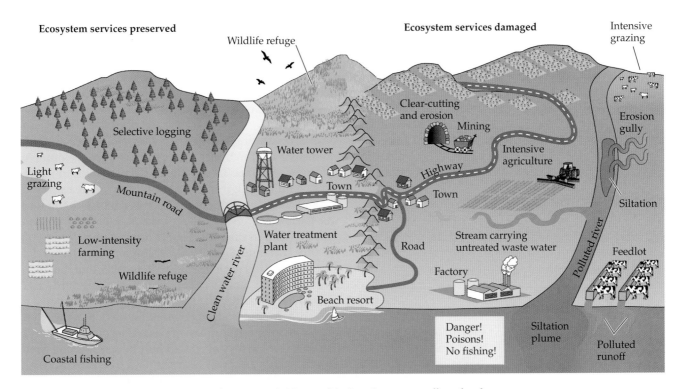

Ecosystem services preserved

Wildlife refuge

Ecosystem services damaged

Intensive grazing

Selective logging

Clear-cutting and erosion

Mining

Erosion gully

Light grazing

Water tower

Intensive agriculture

Highway

Mountain road

Town

Town

Siltation

Low-intensity farming

Water treatment plant

Road

Stream carrying untreated waste water

Feedlot

Wildlife refuge

Clean water river

Factory

Polluted river

Beach resort

Danger! Poisons! No fishing!

Siltation plume

Coastal fishing

Polluted runoff

FIGURE 4.1 Agricultural ecosystems, forestry activities, and industries are usually valued by the products that they produce. In many cases these activities have negative externalities in that they erode soil, degrade water quality, and contribute to flooding (right side of figure). But farms, forests, and other human activities could also be valued on the basis of their public benefits, such as flood control, soil retention, and water quality, and their owners might receive subsidies for these benefits (left side of figure).

trol and contributed to water quality, they might improve their farming practices (Robertson and Swinton 2005) (**Figure 4.1**).

By excluding environmental costs and the loss of natural resources from economic analyses, many countries that appear to be achieving impressive economic gains actually may be on the verge of economic collapse. Unregulated national fisheries are a classic example of the need to monitor assets. Increased investment in fishing fleets may result in higher short-term catches and impressive profits, but it gradually leads to the overharvesting and destruction of one commercial species after another and, eventually, to the collapse of the entire industry. It would be easier to justify this activity if the profits were used to improve society through increased infrastructure, industrial development, job training, and education. However, often a small number of people or companies take most of the profits, while society as a whole realizes only minor and temporary improvements.

The hidden costs associated with superficial economic gains are effectively demonstrated by the case of the *Exxon Valdez* oil spill in Alaska in 1989. The spill cost billions of dollars to clean up; damaged the environment; killed a large number of birds, fish, and marine mammals; and wasted 42 million liters (or 260,000 barrels) of oil. Even 20 years later, oil from the spill still contaminates many of Alaska's beaches. Yet the event was recorded as a *net economic gain* because expenditures associated with the cleanup increased the U.S. GDP and provided employment for cleanup crews hired throughout the United States. Without consideration of the hidden environmental costs and long-term damage to natural resources, a disaster like the *Exxon Valdez* spill can easily be misrepresented as economically beneficial!

In the more complete systems of "green" accounting (such as national resource accounting) that are being developed, the costs of depleting and damaging resources are included as part of the *internal cost* of doing business instead of being regarded as externalities. When such accounting methods are used, the value of maintaining natural resources is often greater than the short-term benefit realized through resource extraction (**Box 4.1**).

Another attempt to account for natural resource depletion, pollution, and unequal income distribution in measures of national production is the development of the Index of Sustainable Economic Welfare (ISEW), the updated version of which

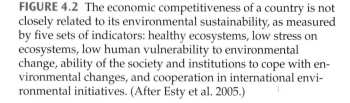

New measures of national productivity take environmental sustainability into account. These include both the benefits and costs that result from human activities.

is called the Genuine Progress Indicator (GPI) (van de Kerk and Manuel 2009). This index includes factors such as the loss of farmlands, the loss of wetlands, the impact of acid rain, the number of people living in poverty, and the effects of pollution on human health. Using the GPI, the U.S. economy apparently did not improve during the period from 1956 to 1986, and it actually declined from 1986 to 1997, even though the standard GDP index showed a dramatic gain. The GPI suggests what conservation biologists have long feared: Many modern economies are achieving their growth only through the nonsustainable consumption of natural resources. As these resources run out, the economies on which they are based may be seriously disrupted (Talberth et al. 2007; Brennan 2008).

A third measure is the Environmental Sustainability Index (ESI), which uses 21 environmental indicators to rank countries according to the health of, and threats to, their ecosystems, the vulnerability of their human population to an adverse environment, the ability of their society to protect the environment, and participation in global environmental protection efforts (Siche et al. 2008; van de Kerk et al. 2009; http://sedac.ciesin.columbia.edu/es/epi/).There is a concern among many economists and businesspeople that a country that rigorously protects its environment as shown by a high ESI may not be competitive in the world economy as measured by a competitiveness index that includes worker productivity and a country's ability to grow and prosper. However, **Figure 4.2** shows that environmental sustainability is not linked to a country's economic competitiveness. Countries such as Finland can have an economy that is both sustainable and competitive, whereas Belgium is competitive but ranks poorly in sustainability. The rapidly growing economies of China and India are intermediate in competitiveness but rank low in environmental sustainability.

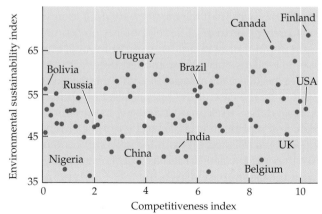

FIGURE 4.2 The economic competitiveness of a country is not closely related to its environmental sustainability, as measured by five sets of indicators: healthy ecosystems, low stress on ecosystems, low human vulnerability to environmental change, ability of the society and institutions to cope with environmental changes, and cooperation in international environmental initiatives. (After Esty et al. 2005.)

BOX 4.1 *Industry, Ecology, and Ecotourism in Yellowstone Park*

■ Yellowstone National Park is the oldest and most famous of the protected areas of the U.S. national parks system. While federal policies affecting the natural landscape of the park often attract intense public scrutiny, policies that support the extraction of timber, oil, natural gas, and other natural resources within the greater Yellowstone ecosystem surrounding the park, in Wyoming, Montana, and Idaho, often are difficult to stop.

The industries that benefit from these policies argue that such activities are necessary for the economic health of the local communities surrounding the park and even the entire country, but studies indicate that this argument is increasingly less valid. The economic health of the communities surrounding Yellowstone has gradually become primarily dependent on the tourism industry and on the new residents and businesses that have moved to the area because of a perceived higher quality of life (Power 1991; Power and Barrett 2001; Gude et al. 2006). Though extractive industry was a significant force in the regional economy half a century ago, it may now be detrimental to the economic well-being of local residents because it harms what has become their major economic resource: the wildlife and natural landscapes of Yellowstone Park and its surrounding wildlands.

> The economy of Yellowstone National Park, like many places in the world, has shifted from a focus on extractive activities to an emphasis on less destructive activities, including ecotourism.

One of the industries in Yellowstone that presently provides the largest boost to the economy of the region—ecotourism—is also the one that does the least damage to the ecosystem of the park. Ecotourism is not without drawbacks. The noise and pollution brought by the passage of millions of tourists annually, the disruption and alteration of animal behavior from constant exposure to the human presence, and the threat of human-caused soil erosion and fire are all side effects of the tourist trade. Accidental fires are perhaps the most visible and fearsome form of disturbance related to ecotourism; nevertheless, even the damage caused by these anthropogenic fires pales in comparison to the damage done by logging and mining activities. The reason that extractive industry is so much more damaging than ecotourism is simple: ecotourism, while it can pollute and alter habitats, does not actively destroy them.

In contrast, logging and mining have many detrimental effects. Clear-cutting, a common logging practice in

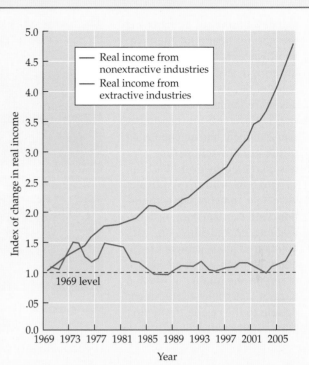

In the greater Yellowstone region, real income from extractive industries has fluctuated widely over the last 35 years but has not grown significantly, while real income from the rest of the economy—including recreation industries, tourism, service industries, and new residents, including retirees—has grown steadily, expanding by almost 400%. The region's economy has become increasingly independent of the extractive industries. The two income lines shown in the graph are standardized to equal a value of 1 in 1969, when extractive industries provided about 23% of the region's total income. By 2007 extractive industries provided only 8% of the region's total income. (After Power 1991, with updates from author.)

which forested slopes are simply cleared of trees, can induce massive sheet erosion, particularly if steps are not immediately taken to replace the vegetation removed during logging. The eroded silt builds up in streams, killing fish and other aquatic species, and the loss of nutrients retards regrowth of vegetation. Mining practices often introduce into the environment harmful chemical by-products, including cyanide. These practices are ultimately not cost-effective for several reasons: (1) they lower the potential for future extraction by damaging the soil and water resources needed to regenerate timber; (2) they lower the region's potential for tourism, retirement communities,

(continued)

BOX 4.1 *(continued)*

and new businesses by damaging the natural beauty of the area; and (3) they create hidden costs by lowering water quality for residents of the area, who must then pay more to have clean drinking water. However, the previously sparse resident human population of the greater Yellowstone area has increased by over 60% from 1970 to 2009, with an even greater increase in rural housing construction. With exurban housing development encroaching on park boundaries, management of residential growth is now needed to maintain the quality of life and natural landscapes that brought people to the region in the first place (Gude et al. 2006).

Many people and businesses have been moving to the Yellowstone National Park area because of its natural beauty. People like these visitors to the Midway and Lower Geyser Basin, value a lifestyle filled with outdoor experiences. (Photograph courtesy of U.S. National Park Service.)

Assigning Economic Value to Biological Diversity

A number of frameworks have been developed to assign economic values to genetic variability, species, communities, and ecosystems. Assignment of economic value can be done on three levels—the marketplace (or harvest) value of resources, the value provided by unharvested resources in their natural state, and the future value of resources (Kareiva and Levin 2003). For example, we can assign economic value to the Southeast Asian wild gaur (*Bos frontalis*), a wild relative of domestic cattle, based on: the meat currently harvested from its wild populations, the animal's value in the wild for nature tourism, and its future potential in domestic cattle breeding programs. As yet there is no universally accepted framework for assigning values to biological diversity, but a variety of approaches have been proposed. Among the most useful is the framework used by McNeely et al. (1990) and Barbier et al. (1994), in which economic values are first divided into **use values** and **non-use values**. Use values of biodiversity are divided between **direct use values** (also known in other frameworks as **commodity values**, and **private goods**) and **indirect use values**. Direct use values are products harvested by people, such as timber, seafood, and medicinal plants from the wild, while indirect use values are benefits provided by biological diversity that do not involve harvesting or destroying the resource. Indirect use values provide current benefits to people, such as recreation, education, scientific research, and scenic amenities, and include the benefits of ecosystem services such as water quality, pollution control, natural pollination and pest control, ecosystem productivity, soil protection, and regulation of climate. **Option value** is also part of indirect use value and is determined by the prospect for possible future benefits for human society, such as new medicines, possible future food sources, and future genetic resources. **Existence value** is the non-use value that can be as-

Total Economic Value of a Tropical Wetland Ecosystem

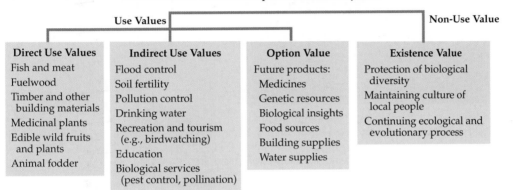

Use Values			Non-Use Value
Direct Use Values	**Indirect Use Values**	**Option Value**	**Existence Value**
Fish and meat	Flood control	Future products:	Protection of biological diversity
Fuelwood	Soil fertility	Medicines	Maintaining culture of local people
Timber and other building materials	Pollution control	Genetic resources	Continuing ecological and evolutionary process
Medicinal plants	Drinking water	Biological insights	
Edible wild fruits and plants	Recreation and tourism (e.g., birdwatching)	Food sources	
Animal fodder	Education	Building supplies	
	Biological services (pest control, pollination)	Water supplies	

FIGURE 4.3 Evaluating the success of a development project must incorporate the full range of its environmental effects. This figure shows the total economic value of a tropical wetland ecosystem, including direct and indirect use value, option value, and existence value. A development project such as an irrigation project lowers the value of the wetland ecosystem when water is removed for crop irrigation. When that lowered value is taken into account, the irrigation project may represent an economic loss. (From Groom et al. 2006; based on data in Emerton 1999.)

signed to biodiversity—for example, economists can attempt to measure how much people are willing to pay to protect a species from going extinct or an ecosystem from being destroyed. A category of existence value is **bequest value**, which is how much people are willing to pay to protect something for their children or future generations. The combination of all these individual values can be used to calculate the **total economic value** of biodiversity. **Figure 4.3** describes how these different values can be applied to a tropical wetland ecosystem. (Indirect use value, option value, and existence value are discussed further in Chapter 5.)

Direct Use Values

Direct use values can often be readily calculated by observing the activities of representative groups of people, by monitoring collection points for natural products, and by examining import and export statistics. Direct use values are further divided into **consumptive use value**, for goods that are consumed locally, and **productive use value**, for products that are sold in markets.

Consumptive Use Value

Goods such as fuelwood and game that are consumed locally and do not appear in the national and international marketplace are assigned consumptive use value

(A)

(B)

FIGURE 4.4 (A) A wide variety of animals, plants, and other natural products, such as these fried grasshoppers, are used throughout the world as sources of food or medicine. (B) Wild animals, such as this wild bearded pig in Borneo, provide people with a crucial source of protein in many areas of the world. (A, photograph © Alan Tobey/istockphoto.com; B, photograph by R. Primack.)

(Davidar et al. 2008). People living close to the land often derive a considerable proportion of the goods they require for their livelihood from the surrounding environment. These goods do not appear in the GDP of countries, because they are neither bought nor sold. However, if rural people are unable to obtain these products, as might occur following environmental degradation, overexploitation of natural resources, or even creation of a protected reserve, their standard of living will decline, possibly to the point where they are forced to relocate.

Studies of traditional societies in the developing world show how extensively these people use their natural environment to supply themselves with fuelwood, vegetables, fruit, meat, medicine, rope and string, and building materials (Balick and Cox 1996; Davidar et al. 2008). Studies of Amazonian Indians have found that most rain forest trees are used for some specific product other than fuel (Dobson 1995). About 80% of the world's population still relies principally on traditional medicines derived from plants and animals as their primary source of treatment (Shanley and Luz 2003). More than 5000 species are used for medicinal purposes in China, 6000 species are used in India, and 2000 species are used in the Amazon basin.

One of the most crucial requirements of rural people is protein, which they obtain by hunting and collecting wild animals for meat (**Figure 4.4**). In some places, this is called bushmeat. In many areas of Africa, bushmeat constitutes a significant portion of the protein in the average person's diet—about 40% in Botswana and about 75% in the Democratic Republic of the Congo (formerly Zaire) (Rao and McGowan 2002). In Nigeria, over 100,000 tons of giant rats (*Cricetomys* sp.) are consumed each year, while in Botswana over 3 million kg of springhare (*Pedetes capensis*) are eaten per year. Estimates of annual harvesting rates are about 100,000 tons (about 200 million pounds) for the Brazilian Amazon and an astonishing 1 to

4 million tons (2 to 8 billion pounds) for central Africa (Fa et al. 2002). Extraction rates for Africa are definitely unsustainable, perhaps by a factor of 6. This wild meat includes not only birds, mammals, and fish but adult insects, spiders, snails, caterpillars, and grubs. In certain areas of Africa, insects may constitute the majority of the dietary protein and supply critical vitamins.

In areas along coasts, rivers, and lakes, wild fish represent an important source of protein. Throughout the world, 130 million tons of fish, crustaceans, and mollusks, mainly wild species, are harvested each year, with 100 million tons constituting marine catch and 30 million tons constituting freshwater catch (Chivian and Bernstein 2008). Much of this catch is consumed locally. In coastal areas fishing is often the most important source of employment, and seafood is the most widely consumed protein. Even though fish farming is increasing rapidly, much of the feed used is fish meal derived from wild-caught fish (Gross 2008a).

Consumptive use value can be assigned to a product by considering how much people would have to pay if they had to buy an equivalent product when their local source was no longer available. This is sometimes referred to as a **substitute cost approach**.

> Consumptive use value can be calculated by considering how much people would have to pay to buy an equivalent product if their local source were no longer available.

In many cases local people do not have the money to buy products in the market. For example, the amount of bushmeat could be estimated for a family or village in Africa by recording what they eat and counting how many animals they catch per month (Peres 2007). The value of this meat could be estimated by determining how much it would cost the family to buy an equivalent amount of meat from domestic animals in a local market. In remote regions, markets may not exist at all. When the local resource is depleted, local people may be forced to change their livelihoods or migrate to other rural areas or cities, or they may simply be faced with rural poverty.

Consumptive use value can also be assigned to fuelwood used for heating and cooking, which is gathered from forests and shrublands (**Figure 4.5**). About 2.6 billion people rely on fuelwood as the primary energy source for heating and cooking (MEA 2005). This accounts for over half of all global wood use. The value of these fuels, in places such as Nepal, Tanzania, and Peru, can be determined by considering how much people would have to pay for kerosene or other fuels if they were unable to obtain fuel from their environment. In many areas of the world, rural people have consumed all local fuel sources but do not have the money to buy fuel from the market. This situation, the "poor man's energy crisis," forces the poor—in particular poor women—to walk ever greater distances to obtain fuel and leads to ever-widening circles of deforestation. People also end up burning crop remains and dung for fuel, leading to a loss of mineral nutrients needed to maintain agricultural productivity.

In the past, people developed ways of extracting common property resources from the natural environment that prevented overuse of renewable resources (Berkes 2001). Certain

FIGURE 4.5 A woman in India returns to her village with a load of wood. Fuelwood is one of the most important natural products consumed by local people, particularly in Africa and southern Asia. (Photograph © Borderlands/Alamy.)

species of wild fruit trees were never allowed to be cut down; the breeding season of the year was taboo for hunting certain animals; families owned hunting territories that other families were not allowed to enter. These systems were organized at the village and tribal levels and were enforced through strong social pressures. For example, traditional Sherpa villages in Nepal had the custom of *shingo nava*, in which men were elected to be forest guards. These men determined how much fuelwood people could collect and what trees could be cut and hence protected the common resources. People violating the village rules were made to pay fines, which were used to fund village activities.

Many of these traditional conservation systems have broken down as populations have grown and cash economies and national governments have developed. Local conservation strategies have also been eliminated by centralized or "top-down" government decisions that take control of natural resources, such as forests, coastal fisheries, and wildlife. Rather than consuming products locally, people now frequently sell natural resources in town markets for money. As social controls break down at the village level, the villagers, as well as outsiders, may begin to extract local resources in a destructive and nonsustainable manner. If the resources become depleted, many villagers may be forced to pay high prices in town markets for many of the products that they formerly obtained free from their natural environment. It is also true that access to town markets sometimes provides advantages to villagers that balance the loss of some local resources. For example, it sometimes allows local people to obtain higher prices for their products. With the cash, people may be able to establish their own businesses, educate their children, and have access to modern medical care.

Although dependency on local natural products is primarily associated with the developing world, there are rural areas of the United States, Canada, Europe, and other developed countries where hundreds of thousands of people are dependent on fuelwood for heating and on wild game and seafood for their protein needs. Many of these people would be unable to survive in these locations if they had to buy these necessities.

Productive Use Value

Resources that are harvested from the wild and sold in both national and international commercial markets are assigned productive use value. Standard economic methods value these products at the price paid at the first point of sale minus the costs incurred up to that point. Some studies value the resourse at the final retail price of the products. The two methods give a wide range of values for the same resource. For example, bark from the wild cascara (*Rhamnus purshiana*) gathered in the western United States is the major ingredient in certain brands of laxatives. The purchase price of the bark is about $1 million, but the final retail price of the medicine is $75 million (Prescott-Allen and Prescott-Allen 1986). In this case, the value of the wild cascara bark as an input to the production of laxatives is $1 million, while the $75 million includes the values of all inputs (labor, energy, other materials, R & D, and cascara bark).

The productive use value of natural resources is significant, even in industrial nations. Approximately 4.5% of the U.S. GDP ($14 trillion)—about $630 billion for the year 2008—depends in some way on wild species. The percentage would be far higher for developing countries that have less industry and a higher percentage of the population living in rural areas.

The range of products obtained from the natural environment and sold in the marketplace is enormous: fuelwood, construction timber, fish and shellfish, medicinal plants, wild fruits and vegetables, wild meat and skins, fibers, rattan (a vine used to make furniture and other household articles), honey, beeswax, natural dyes, seaweed, animal fodder, natural perfumes, and plant gums and resins (Baskin 1997; Chivian and Bernstein 2008). Ad-

A wide variety of natural resources are sold commercially and have enormous total market value. They can be considered as the productive value of biodiversity.

ditionally, there are large international industries associated with collecting tropical cacti, orchids, and other plants for the horticultural industry, and birds, mammals, amphibians, and reptiles for zoos and private collections. The value of ornamental fish in the aquarium trade is estimated at $1 billion per year, with wild-caught fish representing 15%–20% of the total. A surprisingly large area within 23 countries in sub-Saharan Africa is managed for trophy hunting by foreigners (Lindsey et al. 2007).

In many cases, species have to be collected just once or a few times, because then they can be propagated in captivity. Only a few individuals are needed to establish entirely new populations, to be used for display purposes, to be used in the development of new medicines and industrial products, and to be used as biological control agents (Chivian and Bernstein 2008). Wild relatives of domesticated crops can be collected and incorporated into modern breeding programs for genetic improvement. This occasional collection can be considered productive use value, or perhaps as option value, for its ability to maintain and improve economic activity. Species collected only in small numbers from the wild will be treated in Chapter 5, in the section on option value. Products gathered in large quantities from the wild are described below.

FOREST PRODUCTS Wood is one of the most significant products obtained from natural environments, with an export value of about $135 billion per year (WRI 2003). The total value of timber and other wood products is far greater, perhaps about $400 billion per year, because most wood is used locally and is not exported. Wood products from the forests of tropical countries, including timber, plywood, and wood pulp, are being exported at a rapid rate to earn foreign currency, to provide capital for industrialization, to pay foreign debt, and to provide employment. In tropical countries such as Indonesia, Brazil, and Malaysia, timber products earn billions of dollars per year (Corlett and Primack 2010) (**Figure 4.6A**).

Nonwood products from forests, including bushmeat, fruits, gums and resins, rattan, and medicinal plants, also have a large productive use value (**Figure 4.6B**).

(A)

(B)

FIGURE 4.6 The timber industry is a major source of revenue in many tropical countries. (A) Timber is being shipped on a barge on the Amazon River near Iquitos, Peru. (B) Nonwood products are often important in local and national economies. Many rural people supplement their incomes by gathering natural forest products to sell in local markets. Here a Land Dayak family in Sarawak (Malaysia) sells wild honey and edible wild fruits. (A, photograph © Morley Read/Alamy; B, photograph by R. Primack.)

These nonwood products are sometimes erroneously called "minor forest products"; in reality they are often very important economically and may even rival the value of wood. In India, nonwood forest products account for 40% of forestry revenues and 55% of the forestry employment. One study from rural Zimbabwe demonstrated that 35% of village income was derived from natural products. What was especially noteworthy was that dependence on the sale of natural products was even greater in the poorest households, showing the value of ecosystems in providing resources to people with nothing else (WRI 2005).

Many other studies similarly show that natural ecosystems provide resources to rural people in goods and services that do not appear in official government figures. When the ecosystem value of the forest as a source of drinking water, flood control, and soil protection is combined with the value of nonwood products, maintaining and utilizing natural communities may still prove to be more productive than intensive logging, converting the forest into commercial plantations, or establishing cattle ranches (WRI 2005). In particular, the role of forests in absorbing atmospheric carbon dioxide is now being assigned monetary value (van Kooten and Sohngen 2007). Careful tree harvesting that minimizes damage to the surrounding biological community and the ecosystem services it provides, combined with gathering nontimber products, may be a profitable approach that justifies maintaining the land in forest.

THE NATURAL PHARMACY Effective drugs are needed to keep people healthy, and they represent an enormous industry, with worldwide sales of about $300 billion per year (Chivian and Bernstein 2008). The natural world is an important source of medicines currently in use and possible future medicines. One species with great medicinal use is the rose periwinkle (*Catharanthus roseus*) from Madagascar (**Table 4.2**). Two potent drugs derived from this plant are effective in treating Hodgkin's disease, leukemia, and other blood cancers. Treatment using these drugs has increased the survival rate of childhood leukemia from 10% to 90%. How many more such valuable plants will be discovered in the years ahead—and how many will go extinct before they are discovered?

Even in the case of medicines that are now produced synthetically by chemists, many were first discovered in a wild species used in traditional medicine (Cox 2001; Chivian and Bernstein 2008) (**Figure 4.7**). Extracts of willow tree bark (*Salix* sp.) were used by the ancient Greeks and by tribes of Native Americans to treat pain, leading to the discovery of acetylsalicylic acid—the painkilling ingredient in modern aspirin, one of our most important and widely used medicines. Similarly, the use of coca (*Erythroxylum coca*) by natives of the Andean highlands eventually led to the development of synthetic derivatives such as Novocain, procaine, and lidocaine, commonly used as local anesthetics in dentistry and surgery. Many other important medicines were first identified in animals. Venomous animals such as rattlesnakes, bees, and cone snails have been especially rich sources of chemicals with valuable medical and biological applications.

All of the 20 most frequently used pharmaceuticals in the United States are based on chemicals first identified in natural products. These drugs have a combined sales revenue

FIGURE 4.7 In much of the world, medical treatment relies on natural products found in the immediate environment. Here Hortense Robinson, a village healer and midwife in Belize, gives a demonstration re-creating the application of a medicinal poultice made of leaves from the palm *Chamaedorea tepejilote*. (Photograph courtesy of Michael J. Balick.)

TABLE 4.2 Twenty Drugs from the Plant World First Discovered in Traditional Medical Practice

Drug	Medical use	Plant source	Common name
Ajmaline	Treats heart arrhythmia	*Rauwolfia* spp.	Rauwolfia
Aspirin	Analgesic, anti-inflammatory	*Spiraea ulmaria*	Meadowsweet
Atropine	Dilates eyes during examination	*Atropa belladonna*	Belladonna
Caffeine	Stimulant	*Camellia sinensis*	Tea plant
Calanolide	Anti-HIV agent	*Calophyllum* spp.	Bintangor
Cocaine	Ophthalmic analgesic	*Erythroxylum coca*	Coca plant
Codeine	Analgesic, antitussive	*Papaver somniferum*	Opium poppy
Digitoxin	Cardiac stimulant	*Digitalis purpurea*	Foxglove
Ephedrine	Bronchodilator	*Ephedra sinica*	Ephedra plant
Ipecac	Emetic	*Cephaelis ipecachuanha*	Ipecac plant
Morphine	Analgesic	*Papaver somniferum*	Opium poppy
Pseudoephedrine	Decongestant	*Ephedra sinica*	Ephedra plant
Quinine	Antimalarial prophylactic	*Cinchona pubescens*	Chinchona
Reserpine	Treats hypertension	*Rauwolfia serpentina*	Rauwolfia
Sennoside A, B	Laxative	*Cassia angustifolia*	Senna
Scopolamine	Treats motion sickness	*Datura stramonium*	Thorn Apple
Strophanthin	Treats congestive heart failure	*Strophanthus gratus*	Rose Allamanda
THC	Antiemetic	*Cannabis sativa*	Marijuana
Toxiferine	Relaxes muscles during surgery	*Strychnos guianensis*	Strychnos plant
Tubocurarine	Muscle relaxant	*Chondrodendron tomentosum*	Curare
Vincristine	Treats pediatric leukemia	*Catharanthus roseus*	Rose periwinkle
Warfarin	Anticoagulant	*Melilotus* spp.	Sweet clover

Sources: After Balick and Cox 1996; Chivian and Bernstein 2008.

of $6 billion per year. About 25% of the prescriptions filled in the United States contain active ingredients derived from plants, and many of the most important antibiotics, including penicillin and tetracycline, are derived from fungi and other microorganisms (Chivian and Bernstein 2008). More recently, the fungus-derived drug cyclosporine has proved to be a crucial element in the success of heart and kidney transplants. As will be discussed in the next chapter, the natural world is being actively searched for the next generation of medicines and industrial products.

Multiple Uses of a Single Resource: A Case Study

Horseshoe crabs provide an example of the diverse values that can be provided by just one species. They are usually noticed only as clumsy creatures that seem to move with difficulty in shallow seawater (**Figure 4.8**). In the United States, commercial fishermen harvest these animals in large quantities for use as cheap fishing bait. In recent years, however, we have realized that horseshoe crab eggs and juveniles are extremely important as a food source for shorebirds and coastal fish, which have a major role in local tourism related to bird-watching and sportfishing. Without horseshoe crabs, bird populations and sport fish decline in abundance (Niles 2009). Additionally, the blood of horseshoe crabs is collected to make limulus amebocyte lysate (LAL), a highly valuable chemical used to detect bacterial contamination in injection-administered medications and vaccines (Odell et al. 2005). This chemical cannot be manufactured synthetically, and horseshoe crabs are its only source. With-

> Sometimes a specific species or ecosystem can provide a diversity of goods and services to human society. Compromises are occasionally needed to balance competing uses.

FIGURE 4.8 Horseshoe crabs (*Limulus polyphemus*) gather in great numbers to reproduce in shallow coastal waters. These aggregations have significant value for contending groups of people. (Photograph © FLPA/Mark Newman/AGE Fotostock.)

out this natural source of LAL, our ability to determine the purity of injected medicines would be compromised.

Currently, commercial fishing and sportfishing interests, environmental groups, bird-watching groups, and the biomedical industry are competing for control of horseshoe crabs along U.S. coastlines. Each group can make a good argument for its own right to use or protect horseshoe crabs. Hopefully, the final result will be a working compromise that allows the crabs a place in a functioning ecosystem and still provides for the needs of people living in the area.

Summary

1. Conservation biologists and ecological economists are developing new methods to assign monetary value to biological diversity and, in the process, are providing arguments for its protection. While some conservation biologists would argue that biological diversity is priceless and cannot and should not be assigned economic value, economic justification for biological diversity will play an increasingly important role in debates on the use of natural resources.

2. Many countries that appear to have annual increases in gross domestic product may have stagnant or even declining economies when the costs of development—depletion of natural resources and damage to the environment—are included in the calculations. Increasingly, large development projects are being analyzed through environmental and economic impact assessments and cost-benefit analyses before being approved. In addition, assigning economic value gives both the public and policy makers a frame of reference for understanding the magnitude of environmental degradation.

3. A number of frameworks have been developed to assign economic value to biological diversity. In one framework, resources are divided between use values and non-use values. Use values include direct use values, which are assigned to products harvested by people; indirect use values, which are assigned to benefits provided by biological diversity that do not involve harvesting or destroying the resource; and option value, which is assigned to the potential future value of biological diversity. Non-use values include existence value and bequest value, based on the willingness of society to pay for the protection of biological diversity.

4. Direct use values can be further divided into consumptive use value and productive use value. Consumptive use value is assigned to products that are consumed locally, such as fuelwood, wild meat, fruits and vegetables, medicinal plants, and building materials. These goods can be valued by determining how much money people would have to pay for them if they were unavailable in the wild. When these wild products become unavailable, the living standard of the people who depend on them declines. Productive use value is assigned to products harvested in the wild and sold in markets, such as commercial timber, fish and shellfish, and wild meat.

For Discussion

1. Find a recent large development project from your area, such as a dam, sewage treatment plant, shopping mall, highway, or housing development, and learn all you can about it. Estimate the costs and benefits of this project in terms of biological diversity, economic prosperity, and human health. Who pays the costs and who receives the benefits? Consider other projects carried out in the past, and determine their impact on the surrounding ecosystem and human community. (These are challenging questions that may be appropriate to tackle as a group activity.)

2. How do traditional (or rural) societies use and value biological diversity? What is the relative importance of biological diversity in both traditional and modern societies? How do these societies value biodiversity knowledge?

3. Suppose a medicinal plant used by traditional people in a remote area in Indonesia is investigated by a European pharmaceutical company and found to have huge potential as a new cancer medicine. Who will profit from the sale of this medicine under current practices? Can you suggest alternative methods to distribute the profits in a way that would be more equitable and that would increase the possibility of preserving Indonesia's biological diversity?

Suggested Readings

Balick, M. J. and P. A. Cox. 1996. *Plants, People and Culture: The Science of Ethnobotany.* Scientific American Library, New York. Fascinating story of traditional use of plants, filled with anecdotes and beautifully illustrated.

Balmford, A. and 18 others. 2002. Economic reasons for conserving wild nature. *Science* 297: 950–953. Ecosystem services provide strong economic arguments for conserving biodiversity.

Chivian, E. and A. Bernstein (eds.). 2008. *Sustaining Life: How Human Health Depends on Biodiversity.* Oxford University Press, New York. Great examples, and beautifully illustrated.

Common, M. and S. Stagl. 2005. *Ecological Economics: An Introduction.* Cambridge University Press, New York. Assumes no prior knowledge of economics.

Davidar, P., M. Arjunan, and J. P. Puyravaud. 2008. Why do local households harvest forest products? A case study from the southern Western Ghats, India. *Biological Conservation* 141: 1876–1884. The unsustainable harvest of forest products for domestic consumption and sale is partially responsible for tropical deforestation.

Hoeinghaus, D. J. and 7 others. 2009. Effects of river impoundment on ecosystem services of large tropical rivers: Embodied energy and market value of artisanal fisheries. *Conservation Biology* 23: 1222–1231. Dams often negatively affect native fish species, with significant economic consequences.

Lant, C. L., J. B. Ruhl, and S. E. Kraft. 2008. The tragedy of ecosystem services. *BioScience* 58: 969–974. Laws need to be changed to value common property.

Lindsey, P. A., P. A. Roulet, and S. S. Romañach. 2007. Economic and conservation significance of the trophy hunting industry in sub-Saharan Africa. *Biological Conservation* 134: 455–469. Land managed for trophy hunting in Africa is larger in area than the national parks.

Myers, N. and J. Kent. 2001. *Perverse Subsidies: How Tax Dollars Can Undercut the Environment and the Economy.* Island Press, Washington, D.C. Governments are paying for destructive industries to continue.

Naidoo, R. and W. L. Adamowicz. 2006. Modeling opportunity costs of conservation in transitional landscapes. *Conservation Biology* 20: 490–500. Information about land prices and discount rates is needed to protect biological diversity.

Niles, L. J. 2009. Effects of horseshoe crab harvest in Delaware Bay on red knots: Are harvest restrictions working? *BioScience* 59: 153–164. Restrictions have not been effective at preventing overharvesting of horseshoe crabs, leading to a drop in shorebird populations.

Redford, K. H. and W. M. Adams. 2009. Payment for ecosystem services and the challenge of saving nature. *Conservation Biology* 23: 785–787. The ecosystem services concept is widely used in conservation strategies but is not without problems.

Sachs, J. D. 2008. *Common Wealth: Economics for a Crowded Planet*. Penguin Press, New York. Poverty, climate change, and environmental destruction can be addressed for a moderate cost right now, with huge future benefits.

Shanley, P. and L. Luz. 2003. The impacts of forest degradation on medicinal plant use and implications for health care in Eastern Amazonia. *BioScience* 53: 573–584. The loss of traditional medicinal plants threatens the health of people.

Indirect Use Value

I ndirect use values can be assigned to aspects of biodiversity —such as environmental processes and ecosystem services— that provide both present and future economic benefits without being harvested or destroyed during use (**Figure 5.1**). Because these benefits are not goods or services in the usual economic sense, they do not typically appear in the statistics of national economies, such as the GDP. They are often called public goods because they belong to the society in general, without private ownership. However, these benefits may be crucial to the continued availability of the natural products on which the economies depend. If natural ecosystems are not available to provide these benefits, substitute sources must be found—often at great expense—or local and even regional economies may face collapse (Srinivasan et al. 2008; Granek et al. 2010).

Nonconsumptive Use Value

The great variety of environmental services that biological communities provide can be classified as having a particular type of indirect use value, known as **nonconsumptive use value** (because the services are not consumed). Economists are just beginning to

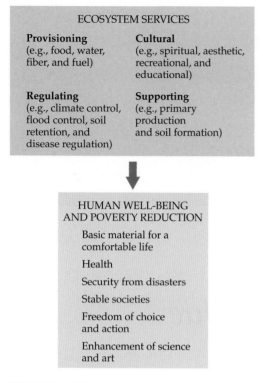

ECOSYSTEM SERVICES

Provisioning
(e.g., food, water, fiber, and fuel)

Cultural
(e.g., spiritual, aesthetic, recreational, and educational)

Regulating
(e.g., climate control, flood control, soil retention, and disease regulation)

Supporting
(e.g., primary production and soil formation)

HUMAN WELL-BEING AND POVERTY REDUCTION

Basic material for a comfortable life

Health

Security from disasters

Stable societies

Freedom of choice and action

Enhancement of science and art

FIGURE 5.1 Natural ecosystems provide many important products and services that are essential for human well-being. (After MEA 2005.)

calculate the nonconsumptive use value of ecosystem services at regional and global levels (Naeem et al. 2009; Peterson et al. 2010). One such calculation suggests that the nonconsumptive use value of ecosystem services is enormous, about $33 trillion per year in 1997, greatly exceeding the direct use value of biodiversity (Costanza et al. 1997). Because this amount was almost double the value of the world economy at the time, the point could be made that human societies are totally dependent on natural ecosystems, and societies would not persist if these ecosystem services were permanently degraded or destroyed. Especially important in this regard are wetland ecosystems, including coastal marshes, bayous, swamps, and riverbank and lakeshore communities (**Table 5.1**). It is only in recent decades that scientists have realized the crucial importance of these land–water interfaces in the complex and essential processes of water purification and nutrient recycling, as well as their tremendous role in flood control (see the section Protection of Water and Soil Resources below). Some of these crucial ecosystems, especially coastal marshes, are vulnerable to global climate change and associated rising sea levels.

Many ecological economists sharply disagree about how value calculations should be done, or if they even should be done at all (Peterson et al. 2010). Using different approaches, Pimentel et al. (1997) and Balmford et al. (2002) came up with much lower estimates than those of Costanza et al. (1997) described above, but they still amounted to trillions of dollars a year. The disparity in these various estimates indicates that much more work needs to be done on this topic.

The great variety of environmental services that ecosystems provide can be separated into particular types of indirect use value. The following sections discuss some of the specific use values derived from conserving biodiversity that do not usually appear on the balance sheets of environmental impact assessments or in national GDPs. Later in the chapter, we will consider two other ways of valuing biodiversity: option value, the value that biodiversity may have in the future, and existence value, the amount that people are willing to pay to protect biodiversity.

TABLE 5.1	**Estimated Value of the World's Ecosystems Using Ecological Economics**		
Ecosystem[a]	Total area (millions of ha)	Annual local value (dollars/ha/year)	Annual global value (trillions of dollars/year)
Coastal	3102	4052	12.6
Open ocean	33,200	252	8.4
Wetlands	330	14,785	4.9
Tropical forests	1900	2007	3.8
Lakes, rivers	200	8498	1.7
Other forests	2955	302	0.9
Grasslands	3898	232	0.9
Cropland	1400	92	0.1

Source: After Costanza et al. 1997

[a]Desert, tundra, urban, and ice/rock ecosystems not included.

Ecosystem Productivity and Carbon Sequestration

The photosynthetic capacity of plants and algae allows the energy of the sun to be captured in living tissue. The energy stored in plants is sometimes harvested by humans for use as food, fuelwood, and hay and other fodder for animals. This plant material is also the starting point for innumerable food chains, from which many animal products are harvested by people. Human needs for natural resources dominate approximately half of the productivity of the terrestrial environment (MEA 2005). The destruction of the vegetation in an area through overgrazing by domestic animals, overharvesting of timber, or frequent fires will destroy the system's ability to make use of solar energy. Eventually it will lead to the loss of production of plant biomass, loss of the animals that live at that site, and loss of a place where people can make a living.

Likewise, coastal estuaries are areas of rapid plant and algal growth that provide the starting point for food chains leading to commercial stocks of fish and shellfish. The U.S. National Marine Fisheries Service has estimated that damage to estuaries has cost the United States more than $200 million per year in lost productive value of commercial fish and shellfish and in lost value of fish caught for sport (McNeely et al. 1990). Even when degraded or damaged ecosystems are rebuilt or restored at great expense, they often do not function as well as before and almost certainly do not contain their original species composition or species richness.

Scientists are actively investigating how the loss of species from biological communities affects ecosystem processes such as the total growth of plants, the ability of plants to absorb atmospheric carbon dioxide (CO_2), and the ability to adapt to global climate change (Flombaum and Sala 2008; Egoh et al. 2009; Luck et al. 2009). This question was addressed experimentally at grasslands in Minnesota and Germany in which from 1 to 24 species were grown on 3 m × 3 m plots (Tilman 1999; Marquard et al. 2009). The growth of plant material and the uptake of soil nutrients such as nitrogen were greater in plots with more species, clearly demonstrating the importance of species diversity to productivity (**Figure 5.2**). These results were

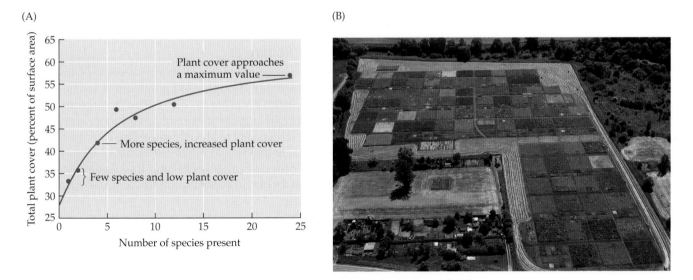

FIGURE 5.2 (A) Varying numbers of grassland species were grown in experimental plots. The plots containing the most species had the greatest overall amount of growth, as measured by the total plant cover (the percentage of the total surface area occupied by plants). (B) View of grassland research plots in Germany. Plots vary by color and shading depending on the species present and the density of planting. The experimental field is 300 m across the top, with individual squares being 20 m on a side. (A, after Tilman 1999; B, photograph by Dr. Alexandra Weigelt.)

further supported by similar observations of nearby native grasslands. Plots with greater diversity of species showed an increased ability to withstand drought and resist invasion by outside species. This research has been extensively replicated in grasslands, pasture communities, and wetlands at other locations with similar results and is also being extended to marine systems (Palumbi et al. 2009).

We know that species diversity is being reduced in major ecosystems as a result of human activities (Foley et al. 2005). At what point will the productivity of these ecosystems decline as well? We need to know the answer to this question before the world's forestry, ranching, agriculture, and fishing industries become critically damaged by the consequences of species decline. In many places, these industries are already operating with relatively few species and are often sustained with external inputs of mineral fertilizer. It is safe to assume that ecosystems with a lower diversity of species will be less able to adapt to the altered weather conditions associated with rising CO_2 levels and global climate change. For example, temperate forest ecosystems with few tree species to start with will likely show the effects of species loss quickly as their resident species are eliminated by drought and exotic diseases and insects.

> Ecosystems with reduced species diversity may be less able to adapt to the altered conditions associated with rising carbon dioxide levels, higher temperatures, and other aspects of global climate change.

The value of intact and restored forests in retaining carbon and absorbing atmospheric carbon dioxide is now being recognized by environmental economists (van Kooten and Sohngen 2007; Butler et al. 2009). As countries and corporations reduce their carbon dioxide emissions as part of the worldwide effort to address global climate change, they are paying to protect and restore forests and other ecosystems (Berkessy and Wintle 2008; Venter et al. 2010). The payments for carbon reduction offset their own carbon production. In some cases, the value of ecosystems for carbon sequestration and watershed management can be greater than their ability to produce harvestable products. Regenerating forests in the temperate zone, especially in North America, appear to play a particularly important role in slowing the increase of atmospheric carbon dioxide. The current market in carbon sequestration payments is about $350 million per year but is projected to increase by 30 to 100 times over the next 5 years. However, this carbon market is quite volatile because of problems in regulating and defining the market.

Protection of Water and Soil Resources

Biological communities are of vital importance in protecting watersheds, buffering ecosystems against extremes of flood and drought, and maintaining water quality (Pimentel et al. 1995; Foley et al. 2007; Thorp et al. 2010). Plant foliage and dead leaves intercept the rain and reduce its impact on the soil; plant roots and soil organisms aerate the soil, increasing its capacity to absorb water. This increased water-holding capacity reduces the flooding that would otherwise occur after heavy rains and allows a slow release of water for days and weeks after the rains have ceased. The value of just the U.S. national forests in contributing to the water supply has been estimated at $4 billion per year.

When vegetation is disturbed by logging, farming, and other human activities, the rates of soil erosion, and even occurrences of landslides, increase rapidly, decreasing the value of the land for human activities (Quist et al. 2003). Damage to the soil limits the ability of plant life to recover from disturbance and can render the land useless for agriculture. In addition, silt (soil particles suspended in water from runoff) can degrade aquatic habitats and kill freshwater fish and other animals, coral reef organisms, and the marine life in coastal estuaries. Erosion and flooding also contaminate drinking water supplies for humans in the communities along the rivers, leading to an increase in human health problems. Soil erosion increases sediment loads into the reservoirs behind dams, causing a loss of electrical

FIGURE 5.3 A flooded area with only rooftops showing along the Mississippi River, Missouri. The river channel can be seen in the upper left. (Photograph by Andrea Booher/FEMA Photo.)

output, and creates sandbars and islands, which reduces the navigability of rivers and ports.

Floods are currently the most common natural disaster in the world, killing thousands of people per year (**Figure 5.3**). The incidence of major floods has increased manyfold during the last few decades, which can be attributed to the concentration of people living in coastal areas and to the destruction of wetlands and upland ecosystems (Barbier et al. 2008; Ewel 2010). Unprecedented catastrophic floods and landslides in Bangladesh, India, the Philippines, Thailand, and Central America have been associated with recent extensive logging in watershed areas. Flood damage to India's agricultural areas has led to massive government and private tree-planting programs in the Himalayas. Removal and filling in of coastal mangrove swamps is part of the explanation for the severe devastation associated with the 2004 Indian Ocean tsunami, in which about 300,000 people lost their lives. In the industrial nations of the world, wetlands protection has become a priority in order to prevent flooding of developed areas. In certain locations, wetlands are estimated to have a value of $6,000 per ha per year in reducing flood damage and other ecosystem services, which is three times the value of farmland created on the same site (MEA 2005). The conversion of floodplain habitat to farmland along the Mississippi, Missouri, and Red rivers, and along the Rhine River in Europe, is considered a major factor in the massive, damaging floods in past years. The most dramatic example is the devastating flooding of New Orleans in 2005 after Hurricane Katrina struck the Mississippi Delta, which has undergone heavy conversion for urban, industrial, and agricultural development (**Box 5.1**). The risk of flooding would be substantially reduced if even a small proportion of the wetlands along these rivers were restored to their original condition.

> Wetland ecosystem services whose value is typically not accounted for in the current market system include waste treatment, water purification, and flood control—all of which are essential to healthy human societies.

In many areas of the developing world, people settle near natural water sources to obtain water for drinking, washing, and irrigation. As hydrologic cycles are disrupted by deforestation, soil erosion, and dam projects, and as water quality de-

BOX 5.1   *Prophecy Fulfilled: How Ecosystem Services Became Front Page News*

"As the whirling maelstrom approached the coast, more than a million people evacuated to higher ground. Some 200,000 remained, however—the carless, the homeless, the aged and infirm. . . . The storm hit Breton Sound with the fury of a nuclear warhead, pushing a deadly storm surge into Lake Pontchartrain. . . . As it reached 25 feet (eight meters) over parts of the city, people climbed onto roofs to escape it. Thousands drowned in the murky brew that was soon contaminated by sewage and industrial waste. . . . It took two months to pump the city dry, and by then the Big Easy was buried under a blanket of putrid sediment, a million people were homeless. . . . It was the worst natural disaster in the history of the United States."

■ This *National Geographic* excerpt might be any of the now-familiar narratives of the devastation wreaked on New Orleans by Hurricane Katrina but for one fact: it was published in October 2004, almost a year before its description became reality on August 29, 2005 (Bourne 2004). Other major scientific publications and newspapers, including *Scientific American*, *Popular Mechanics*, and the *Houston Chronicle*, had written similar articles warning of the pending catastrophe, echoing an earlier 1998 Louisiana task force report by government officials, engineers, and scientists.

How did New Orleans reach the point at which impending disaster could be so clearly predicted? The answer lies partly in the geological and ecological processes by which the Mississippi Delta and its marshes were formed, and part-

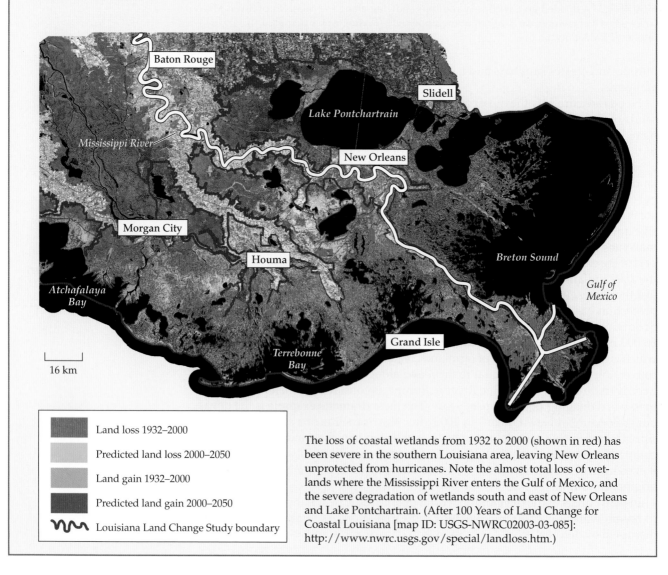

Land loss 1932–2000

Predicted land loss 2000–2050

Land gain 1932–2000

Predicted land gain 2000–2050

Louisiana Land Change Study boundary

The loss of coastal wetlands from 1932 to 2000 (shown in red) has been severe in the southern Louisiana area, leaving New Orleans unprotected from hurricanes. Note the almost total loss of wetlands where the Mississippi River enters the Gulf of Mexico, and the severe degradation of wetlands south and east of New Orleans and Lake Pontchartrain. (After 100 Years of Land Change for Coastal Louisiana [map ID: USGS-NWRC02003-03-085]: http://www.nwrc.usgs.gov/special/landloss.htm.)

BOX 5.1 *(continued)*

ly in the man-made systems that carved dry land from the marsh.

The delta surrounding New Orleans would have long ago sunk below sea level but for the contributions of the river. For millennia, the sediment load carried by the muddy Mississippi River was deposited in the delta marshes and swamps, nourishing the plants that grow there; these plants acted as anchors to protect the landscape against erosion, and the added new sediment and new plant matter compensated for the tendency of the old sediment to subside. Until recently, these wetlands absorbed the fury of storms before they reached New Orleans. The construction of levees, or raised walls, along the river margin in the twentieth century to prevent flooding, however, changed the equation. As the levees prevented sediment from reaching the coastal wetlands, the balance between land lost and land gained was tipped, and the the landscape subsided below the water level. Because New Orleans was continually pumping out water to stay dry, the city itself was subsiding below the level of the river even faster than the marshes.

To make matters worse, the remaining wetlands along the coast south of New Orleans were being filled in for coastal development and carved up by engineers creating canals for ship traffic and oil drilling. Over 12,800 km (8000 miles) of canals were cut into the marshes, increasing soil erosion and introducing saltwater into the freshwater wetlands—saltwater that further degraded the health of the wetland ecosystems.

By the 1990s, New Orleans had become a shallow depression almost 5 m (14 feet) below sea level, ringed by levees to protect it from the Mississippi River to its south and Lake Pontchartrain to the north. Proposals to repair the wetlands were delayed and underfunded; these early efforts were small in scale and experimental in nature—nothing to match the 64 square kilometers of wetlands that were lost each year. When the hurricane struck in 2005, New Orleans was virtually an island, its marshes gone, exposed to the full impact of the ocean's wrath.

> The importance of ecosystem services to modern society has often been underestimated, at great cost to humans. Rebuilding lost ecosystems is sometimes a high priority.

Katrina has left behind great damage, and its horrific destruction has shown indelibly the great value of the ecosystem services provided by coastal wetlands. If coastal wetlands had been in place to absorb the storm surge, much of the damage to property and the loss of life and livelihoods could have been avoided. As the rebuilding of New Orleans gets slowly underway, government authorities are asking questions about how to protect the city from another disaster—and are recognizing that spending $10 billion or more to restore the ecosystem services provided by wetlands is an urgent priority.

teriorates because of pollution, people are increasingly unable to meet their water needs from natural systems. Water scarcity affects over 1 billion people throughout the world (MEA 2005). The cost of boiling water, buying bottled water, or building new wells, rain catchment systems, water treatment plants, pipes, and water pumps gives some measure of the consumptive use value of water from surface sources. The government of New York City, for instance, paid $1.5 billion in the late 1980s to county and town governments in rural New York State to maintain forests on the watersheds surrounding its reservoirs and to improve agricultural practices in order to protect the city's water supply. Water filtration plants doing the same job would have cost $8 to $9 billion (www.nyc.gov/watershed). Wetlands can also be valued by the amount that developers have to pay to create new wetlands in compensation for ones destroyed in large projects; in the Chicago area, the value of one hectare of wetlands averages about $51,000 (Robertson 2006).

Increases in waterborne disease and intestinal ailments such as cholera and dysentery, which currently affect half of the world's population, and the subsequent deaths and lost days of work that result from such illnesses add to estimates of the economic value of water and the natural systems that provide it.

There is growing recognition of the fact that development of dams, reservoirs, and new croplands needs to include protection measures for natural communities located on the highlands above these projects, in order to ensure a steady supply of high-quality water. For example, in Sulawesi, the Indonesian government established the Dumoga Bone National Park to protect the watershed above a major agricultural project in the adjacent lowland. Similarly, in many places, governments are paying farmers and other landowners to maintain such ecosystem services (Sánchez–Azofeifa 2007).

Waste Treatment and Nutrient Retention

Aquatic communities such as swamps, lakes, rivers, floodplains, tidal marshes, mangroves, estuaries, the coastal shelf, and the open ocean are capable of breaking down and immobilizing toxic pollutants, such as heavy metals and pesticides that have been released into the environment by human activities. Fungi and bacteria are particularly important in this role. The waste treatment services performed by these biological communities are estimated to be valued at about $2.4 trillion per year (Costanza et al. 1997; Balmford et al. 2002). When these ecosystems are damaged and degraded, expensive pollution treatment facilities must be installed and operated to assume these functions.

Aquatic biological communities also play an important role in processing, storing, and recycling the large amount of nutrients that enter the ecosystem as sewage or agricultural runoff, allowing these nutrients to be absorbed by photosynthetic organisms. These communities also provide a matrix for the bacteria that fix atmospheric nitrogen. These roles in nutrient processing and retention have an estimated value of $15.9 trillion per year, with coastal marine areas accounting for most of the total (Costanza et al. 1997).

An excellent example of the value of such an ecosystem is provided by the New York Bight, a 5200 km^2 (2000 square mile) bay at the mouth of the Hudson River. For hundreds of years, the New York Bight provided a free sewage disposal system into which was dumped the waste produced by the millions of people in the New York metropolitan area (Pearce 2000). However, as the volume of sewage increased in the 1960s and 1970s, the water quality and species diversity of the bight began deteriorating, and the region was becoming less suitable for swimming and sportfishing. To deal with this situation, the ocean disposal of sewage sludge was stopped by the government in 1987, and the water quality began to improve, beaches became more acceptable for swimming, and marine species increased in abundance. However, the government had to spend billions of dollars on alternative waste treatment facilities.

Climate Regulation

Plant communities are important in moderating local, regional, and probably even global climate conditions (Foley et al. 2007). At the local level, trees provide shade and transpire water, and these things reduce the local temperature in hot weather. This cooling effect reduces the need for fans and air conditioners and increases people's comfort and work efficiency. Trees are also locally important because they act as windbreaks for agricultural fields, reducing soil erosion by wind and reducing heat loss from buildings in cold weather.

At the regional level, plants capture water that falls as rain and then transpire it back into the atmosphere, from which it can fall as rain again. At the global level, loss of vegetation from large forested regions such as the Amazon basin and western Africa may result in a reduction of average annual rainfall or greatly altered weather patterns. In both terrestrial and aquatic environments, plant growth is tied to the carbon cycle. A reduction in plant life results in reduced uptake of carbon dioxide, contributing to the rising carbon dioxide levels that lead to global warming (IPCC 2007). Further, plants are the "green lungs" of the planet, producing the oxygen on which all animals, including people, depend for respiration.

All of the ecosystem services mentioned so far will be directly impacted by global climate change in coming decades. For example, rising sea levels will reduce the area of coastal tidal marshes, and rising temperatures will cause many forests to die back. A decline in ecosystem services is a likely consequence of such changes (Marshall et al. 2008; Craft et al. 2009).

Species Relationships

Many of the species harvested by people for their productive use value depend on other wild species for their continued existence. For example, the wild game and fish harvested by people are dependent on wild insects and plants for their food. A decline in insect and plant populations will result in a decline in animal harvests. Thus, a decline in a wild species of little immediate value to humans may result in a corresponding decline in a harvested species that is economically important.

Crop plants also benefit from wild insects, and other animals (Cleveland et al. 2006; Gardiner et al. 2009; Philpott et al. 2009). For example, many species of birds, bats, and predatory insects such as lady beetles (**Figure 5.4**), feed on pest insect species that attack the crops (**Box 5.2**). Insects act as pollinators for numerous crop species (Priess et al. 2007). About 150 species of crop plants in the United States require insect pollination of their flowers, often involving a mixture of wild insects and domestic honeybees (Kremen and Ostfeld 2005). The value of these pollinators to overall crop yield has been estimated to be about $20 billion to $40 billion per year. The value of wild insect pollinators will increase in the near future if they take over the pollination role of domestic honeybees, whose populations are declining in many places because of disease and pests. Many useful wild plant species depend on fruit-eating animals, such as bats, birds, and primates, to act as seed dispersers. Where these animals have been overharvested, fruits remain uneaten, seeds are not dispersed, and species head toward local extinction (Sethi and Howe 2009). However, it should be noted that there is redundancy in guilds of similar species, and the service of one pollinator or seed disperser may be carried out equally well by another species.

(A)

(B)

FIGURE 5.4 Wild species benefit crop plants. (A) A house wren feeds on white cabbage butterflies whose caterpillars are a major pest of vegetable crops, such as cabbage and broccoli. (B) A bumblebee visiting apple blossoms; without such pollination, the apple fruits would not develop. (A © Steve Byland/istockphoto.com; B © Sergey Ladanov/Shutterstock.)

BOX 5.2 How Much Are Bats Worth? A Case Study of Texas Bats

■ Imagine a pest control service on such a large scale that it eradicates about 250 tons of flying insect pests above farms in less than 24 hours. Now imagine that this service is not only free but also currently in operation throughout the southwestern United States. If this idea sounds unusual or downright unbelievable to you, you're not alone. The lightweight (12 gram) Brazilian free-tailed bat (*Tadarida brasiliensis*) is just beginning to receive its due as one of nature's best pest controllers. These bats form enormous summer breeding colonies in the U.S. Southwest, with the millions of bats at Bracken Cave in San Antonio, Texas, comprising one of the largest known bat colonies in the world. The bats' main economic value to humans stems from their voracious appetite for a variety of agricultural pests, with each bat capable of eating more than half its weight in insects every night. Bats are especially fond of eating flying

Mexican long-tailed bats eat enormous numbers of moths and in the process provide a free pest-control service. (Photograph © Merlin D. Tuttle, Bat Conservation International, www.batcon.org.)

> Bats provide surprisingly important ecosystem services in the form of agricultural pest control.

moths whose offspring are destructive caterpillars that feed on key crops. These pests include the fall armyworm (*Spodoptera frugiperda*), cabbage looper (*Trichoplusia ni*), tobacco budworm (*Heliothis virescens*), and cotton bollworm (*Helicoverpa zea*). The cotton bollworm in particular is one of the most destructive agricultural pests in all of the Americas, and farmers in the United States spend over $1 billion per year applying pesticides to kill them.

Without these bats, more moths would be laying more eggs on the crops and the farmers would have to pay more money for pesticides or lose more of their crops to the growing populations of caterpillars. Researchers working on this system have estimated the bats' value as pest control for just cotton production in this one area of Texas at $741,000 per year, which is about 15% of the value of the crop (Cleveland et al. 2006). The importance of bats and birds as pest control agents is currently being estimated in other agricultural areas of the world, and the value is similarly high in many places. Besides their newly recognized importance to agriculture, the bat colony at Bracken Bat Cave is also being developed as a tourist attraction by Bat Conservation International with the combined goal of protecting the world's largest bat colony and educating the public about the immense value of bats to human society.

One of the most economically significant relationships in ecosystems is the one between many forest trees and crop plants and the soil organisms that provide them with essential nutrients (Hart and Trevors 2005). Fungi and bacteria break down dead plant and animal matter, which they use as their energy source. In the process, the fungi and bacteria release mineral nutrients such as nitrogen into the soil. These nutrients are used by plants for further growth. The filaments of mycorrhizal fungi that extend from the soil into tree roots greatly increase the ability of plant roots to absorb water and minerals, and certain mutualistic bacteria convert nitrogen into a form that can be taken up by plants (**Figure 5.5**). In return, the plants provide the mutualists with photosynthetic products that help them grow. The poor growth and dieback of many trees in certain areas of North America and Europe is attributable in part to the deleterious effects of acid rain and air pollution on soil fungi. With-

> Interspecies relationships are often essential for preserving biodiversity and providing value to people. For example, many insects pollinate the crops on which people depend for food.

out fungi in their root systems, these plants are more susceptible to drought, disease, and insect attack.

Environmental Monitors

Species that are particularly sensitive to chemical toxins serve as "early warning indicators" for monitoring the health of the environment. Some species can even substitute for expensive detection equipment. Among the best-known indicator species are lichens, which live on rocks and trees and absorb chemicals in rainwater and airborne pollution (Jovan and McCune 2005). High levels of toxic materials kill certain lichens, so the distribution and abundance of lichens can identify areas of contamination around sources of air pollution, such as smelters and urban areas. Conversely, certain conspicuous lichens grow only in old-growth forests and can be used to identify areas likely to contain rare and endangered species that are less conspicuous. Aquatic filter feeders, such as mollusks, are also effective in monitoring pollution, because they process large volumes of water and concentrate toxic chemicals such as poisonous metals, PCBs, and pesticides in their tissues. The U.S. National Oceanic and Atmospheric Administration (NOAA) has a Mussel Watch program, started in 1986, that now includes 300 coastal and freshwater sites in which mussel (*Mytilus* sp.) and clam (*Corbicula fluminea*) tissues are sampled and analyzed for toxic compounds, highlighting areas of serious water pollution. Monitoring algal blooms in shallow marine waters can provide a warning of the contamination of shellfish by toxic species and potential health impacts on swimmers from encounters with harmful and dangerous species (Anderson 2009).

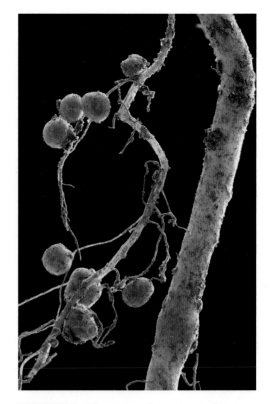

FIGURE 5.5 A bean root–bacteria symbiosis. These round nodules are formed by the roots of the common bean (*Phaseolus vulgaris*) and are inhabited by nitrogen-fixing bacteria (*Rhizobium* sp.). (Photograph courtesy of David McIntyre.)

Recreation and Ecotourism

Ecosystems provide many recreational services for humans, such as the nonconsumptive enjoyment of nature through hiking, photography, and bird-watching (Buckley 2009). The monetary value of these activities, sometimes called their **amenity value**, can be considerable (**Figure 5.6**). In the United States, there are 350 million visitors each year to U.S. national parks, wildlife refuges, and other protected public lands. These visitors engage in nonconsumptive activities such as enjoying nature and camping, and in the process they spend $4 billion on fees, travel, lodging, food, and equipment. Recreation represents over 75% of the value of the U.S. national forests, far greater than the value of the wood being extracted (Groom et al. 2006).

In national and international sites known for their conservation value or exceptional scenic beauty, nonconsumptive recreational value often dwarfs the value generated or captured by all other economic enterprises, including extractive industries. This value is even larger when the money spent off-site on food, lodging, equipment, and other goods and services purchased in the local area is included. Even sportfishing and hunting, which in theory are consumptive uses, are in practice nonconsumptive because the food value of the animals caught by fishermen and hunters is insignificant compared with the time and money spent on these activities. The increasingly common practice among sport fishermen of releasing fish rather than keeping them emphasizes the recreational and nonconsumptive aspect of the activity. In many rural economies, such as those of East Africa, Alaska, and even many areas of developed countries, sportfishing and hunting are sources of tens of thousands of jobs. In the United States, the recreational hunting and fishing industries have been estimated to be worth about $100 billion per year (MEA 2005). The potential value of these recreational activities may be even greater than

Consumptive Uses
Commercial hunting • Sport hunting • Subsistence hunting • Commercial fishing • Sportfishing • Subsistence fishing • Fur trapping • Hunting for animal parts and pet trade • Indirect kills through other activities (pollution, bycatch, road kills) • Eradication programs for animals posing real or perceived threats

Low-Consumptive Uses
Zoos and animal parks • Aquariums • Scientific research

Nonconsumptive Uses
Bird-watching • Whale-watching • Photography trips • Nature walks • Commercial photography and cinematography • Wildlife viewing in parks, reserves, and recreational areas

FIGURE 5.6 Wildlife is used in a variety of consumptive and nonconsumptive ways by both traditional and modern societies. The range of this use and the value of wildlife to people are increasing all the time. (After Duffus and Dearden 1990.)

this number suggests, because many park visitors, fishermen, and hunters indicate that they would be willing to pay even higher usage fees to continue their activities.

Ecotourism is a special category of recreation that involves people visiting places and spending money wholly or in part to experience unusual biological communities (such as rain forests, African savannas, coral reefs, deserts, the Galápagos Islands, and the Everglades) and to view particular "flagship" species (such as elephants on safari trips) (www.ecotourism.org; Balmford et al. 2009). Tourism is among the world's largest industries (on the scale of the petroleum and motor vehicle industries). Ecotourism currently represents about 20% of the $600 billion dollar per year tourist industry.

Ecotourism is growing rapidly in many developing countries because people want to experience tropical biodiversity for themselves. One example of ecotourism's potential is Rwanda, which developed a gorilla tourism industry that at one point was the country's third largest foreign-currency earner. Ecotourism has traditionally been a key industry in East African countries such as Kenya and Tanzania and is now a large and growing part of tourism in many countries in Asia and the Americas.

The revenue provided by ecotourism has the potential to provide one of the most immediate justifications for protecting biological diversity, particularly when ecotourism activities are integrated into overall management plans (Fennell 2007). In integrated conservation development projects (ICDPs), local communities develop accommodations, expertise in nature guiding, local handicraft outlets, and other sources of income; the revenue income from ecotourism allows the local people to give up unsustainable or destructive hunting, fishing, or grazing practices (**Figure 5.7**). The local community benefits from the learning of new skills, employment opportunities, greater protection for their environment, and the development of additional community infrastructure such as schools, roads, medical clinics, and stores.

To help protect biological diversity, ecotourism must provide a significant and secure income for its destination location (Reynisdottir et al. 2008). However, in a typical ecotourist package, only 20%–40% of the retail price of the trip remains in the destination country, and only 0.01%–1% is paid in entrance fees to native parks (Gössling 1999; Balmford et al. 2009). For example, for a 2-week trip costing $4000, somewhere between 40 cents and $40 would typically be paid in entrance fees. Even in well-known destinations, such as Komodo National Park in Indonesia, tourist revenues account for less than 10% of the park management budget. Obviously, raising entrance fees and increasing tourist spending in parks and adjacent countryside is a priority for this industry if local communities are to benefit from these activities.

> The rapidly developing ecotourism industry can provide income to protect biodiversity, but possible costs must be weighed along with benefits.

A danger of ecotourism is that tourists themselves will unwittingly damage these sites—by trampling wildflowers, breaking coral, or disrupting nesting bird colonies, for instance—thereby contributing to the degradation and disturbance of sensitive areas (Walker et al. 2005; Nash 2009). To take one example, hatching success was reduced by 47% when Adelie penguins (*Pygoscelis adeliae*) in the Antarctic were exposed to the typical activities of tourists (Giese 1996). Tourists might also indirectly damage sites by creating a demand for fuelwood for heating and cooking, thus contributing to deforestation. In addition, the presence, affluence, and demands of tourists

(A)

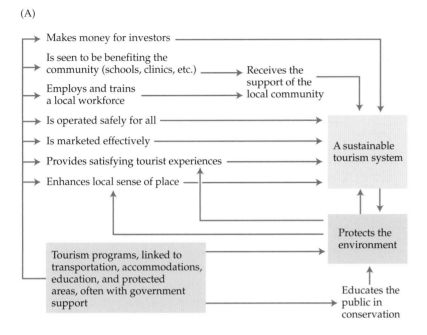

(B)

FIGURE 5.7 Ecotourism can provide an economic justification for protecting biodiversity and also can provide benefits to people living nearby. (A) The diagram illustrates some of the main elements in a successful ecotourism program. (B) Ecotourists who visit the African nation of Botswana experience its unique biota and contribute hugely to the country's economy. Here travelers are shown an ancient baobob tree (*Andansonia digitata*) that measures 25 meters around. (A, after Braithwaite 2001; B, photograph by A. Sinauer.)

can transform traditional human societies in tourist areas by changing employment opportunities and often serving as a magnet for outside people looking for work (Dahles 2005). As local people increasingly enter a cash-based economy, their values, customs, and relationship to nature may be lost along the way. A final potential danger of this industry is that ecotourist facilities may provide a sanitized fantasy experience rather than help visitors understand the serious social and environmental problems that endanger biological diversity (**Figure 5.8**). To respond to these problems, travel companies are promoting measures to minimize their impacts and provide increased benefits to local people. The key to a successful project is making sure that enough tourist money is paid to the local people to maintain and improve their way of life and to park authorities for park protection. Ecotourism activities can even become certified as sustainable through programs such as Green Globe 21.

Courtesy: EG Magazin

FIGURE 5.8 In developing countries, facilities for ecotourists sometimes create a fantasyland that disguises and ignores the real problems those countries face. (From E. G. Magazin, Germany.)

Educational and Scientific Value

Many books, television programs, and movies produced for educational and entertainment purposes are based on nature themes (Osterlind 2005). These natural history materials are being incorporated continually into school curricula. Such educational materials are probably worth billions of dollars per year. These represent a nonconsumptive use value of biodiversity because nature is used as intellectual content in these materials. A considerable number of professional scientists, as well as highly motivated amateurs, are engaged in making ecological observations and preparing educational materials. In rural areas, these activities often take place in scientific field stations, which are sources of training and employment for local people. While these scientific activities provide economic benefits to the areas surrounding field stations, their real value lies in their ability to increase human knowledge, enhance education, and enrich the human experience.

The Long-Term View: Option Value

In addition to the indirect values discussed already, option value is another ways of valuing biological diversity. Later in the chapter we will discuss existence value.

Recall from Chapter 4 that a species' potential to provide an economic benefit to human society at some point in the future is its **option value**. As the needs of society change, so must the methods of satisfying those needs, and such methods often lie in previously untapped animal or plant species. For example, the continued genetic improvement of cultivated plants is necessary, not only for increased yield, but also to guard against pesticide-resistant insects and more virulent strains of fungi, viruses, and bacteria (Sairam et al. 2005). Catastrophic crop failures often can be directly linked to low genetic variability: the 1846 potato blight in Ireland, the 1922 wheat failure in the Soviet Union, and the 1984 outbreak of citrus canker in Florida were all related to low genetic variability among crop plants. To overcome this problem, scientists are constantly substituting new, resistant varieties of agricultural species for susceptible varieties. The source of resistance often comes from genes obtained from wild relatives of crop plants and from local varieties of the domestic species grown by traditional farmers.

The genetic improvement of crops is an ongoing process, and past improvements can give an indication of the potential for future improvements. Development of new crop varieties has a huge economic impact, and the option value of future improvements is similarly great (Nabhan 2008). Genetic improvements in U.S. crops are responsible for increasing harvest values by an average of $8 to $15 billion per year (Frisvold et al. 2003). In developing countries, genetic improvements of rice, wheat, and other crops have increased harvests by an estimated $6 to $11 billion per year. As one example, the discovery of a wild perennial relative of corn in the Mexican state of Jalisco has a huge option value: It is potentially worth billions of dollars to modern agriculture because it could lead to the development of a high-yielding perennial corn crop, thus eliminating the need for annual plowing and planting. This example demonstrates the considerable option value of biodiversity for agricultural improvement alone.

Wild species also have option value as biological control agents. Biologists often can control exotic, invasive species by searching the pest species' original habitat for a control species that limits its population. This control species is then brought to the new locality, where it can be released to act as a biological control agent. A classic example is the case of the prickly pear cactus (*Opuntia inermis*), a South American species introduced into Australia for use as a hedgerow plant. The cactus spread out of control and took over millions of hectares of rangeland. In the prickly pear's native habitat, the larvae of a particular moth species (*Cactoblastis cactorum*) feed on the cactus. The moth was successfully introduced into Australia, where it has reduced the cactus to comparative rarity and allowed native species to recover. Thus pristine habitats can be of great value as reservoirs of natural pest control agents.

> The potential economic or human health value of natural resources motivates people and countries to protect biodiversity.

As was discussed in Chapter 4, we are continually searching the biological communities of the world for new plants, animals, fungi, and microorganisms that can be used to fight human diseases or to provide some other economic value,* an activity referred to as **bioprospecting** (**Box 5.3**) (Lawrence et al. 2010). These searches are generally carried out by government research institutes and pharmaceutical companies. The U.S. National Cancer Institute has been carrying out a program to test extracts of thousands of wild species for their effectiveness in controlling cancer cells and the AIDS virus. To facilitate the search for new medicines and to profit financially from new products, the National Biodiversity Institute (INBio) was established in Costa Rica to collect biological products and supply samples to drug companies and medical reseach agencies (**Figure 5.9**). The Merck Company signed

---

*We discussed the productive use value of natural materials in Chapter 4; however, their future value as new products also gives them value in the present time, so in this chapter we will discuss their option value.

FIGURE 5.9 Taxonomists and technicians at INBio sort and classify Costa Rica's rich array of species. In the offices shown here, many species of plants and insects are cataloged. Many of these species are also being tested for their effectiveness in treating diseases. (Photograph by Steve Winter.)

BOX 5.3   *Mighty Multitudes of Microbes: Not to Be Ignored!*

■ They're out there, and there are billions of them. They occupy cities, suburbs, countrysides, and forests; they're equally at home in spiffy high-rise hotels, filthy shanty towns, and barren deserts. They live in hospitals, restaurants, parks, theaters, and your digestive tract, as well as on mountaintops, in rain forests, and on seashores. They can be found swimming in the ocean's depths and warming themselves near volcanoes—they may even exist on Mars. These are the living world's quintessential jet-setters; we find them everywhere we look—or we would, if we could see at the microscopic level. Fortunately for the peace of mind of most people, we can't, so the billions of microbes that inhabit our world go unnoticed, out of sight and out of mind, except when we're bothered by a cold or have gone too long without cleaning out the vegetable drawer in the refrigerator.

The word *microbe* is a catchall for thousands of species of bacteria, yeasts, protozoans, fungi, and the bacterialike species in the primitive kingdom Archaea.* A handful of soil can contain thousands, millions, even billions of each of these different types of microbes, except for the Archaea, which at present are known only from extreme environments such as deep sea thermal vents, coal deposits, highly salty environments, and hot springs (see Box 3.1). Few people realize how utterly essential these invisible critters are to our day-to-day existence. We tend to look on microbes as nuisances that pose a potential threat to our health—hence the proliferation of antibacterial soaps and antibiotic sprays on supermarket shelves.

In truth, most microbes either actively help us or at the very least do us little harm. Those microbes that do harm us—pathogens that range from the annoying fungus that causes athlete's foot to the deadly viruses and protozoans that cause killer diseases such as AIDS and malaria—are fairly few in number when compared with the total collection of microbes present in the world. On the other hand, we literally could not live without some of them. Microbes play a vital role in the production of foods such as bread, cheese, vinegar, yogurt, soy sauce, and tofu and in alcoholic beverages such as beer and wine. Bacteria in our gastrointestinal tract help break down the food we eat. A few species of bacteria perform the vital biochemical function of transforming nitrogen gas from the atmosphere into a form that

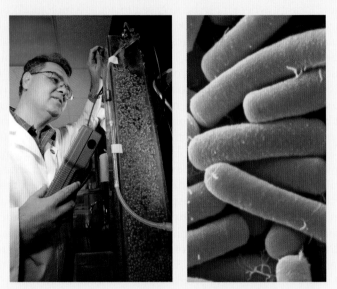

A soil scientist monitors conditions in an experimental bioreactor, testing the potential use of bacteria to remove nitrates from agricultural effluents; a scanning electron micrograph of *Bacillus thuringiensis*, a species increasingly being used to control agricultural insect pests. (Photograph courtesy of Peggy Greb/USDA ARS; micrograph © Medical-on-Line/Alamy.)

plants can take up from the soil as a nutrient. Such "fixed" nitrogen is essential for plant growth. Bacteria and fungi in the soil also aid in the decomposition of organic wastes, freeing up more nutrients such as phosphates, nitrates, carbon dioxide, and sulfates for plants to use as they grow (Coleman 2008). In short, without bacteria, there would be no plants—and thus no food or oxygen available for the animal kingdom, including humans.

> Bacteria are not only critical to ecosystem function and human existence, but also can be incorporated into conservation strategies.

In recent years, scientists have begun to appreciate that these organisms are important, not only to sustain life as we know it, but also to assist in the conservation of threatened species. Some microbes have uses that may ultimately help reduce environmental pollution and habitat degradation. For instance, a major cause of the decline of many insect and bird species is the presence of harmful compounds in sprays used to control agricultural pests and pathogens. These chemicals harm important nonpest

*The term *microbe* also encompasses viruses, fragments of genetic material surrounded by a protective protein coat, which can invade the cells of other species and make copies of themselves. Viruses are not generally considered to be living, independent organisms.

BOX 5.3 *(continued)*

species either by killing them outright or by interfering with their ability to forage and reproduce; at the same time, many pests and pathogens have grown resistant to the compounds. As pesticides have become less effective, agronomists have begun turning to microbial solutions to solve pest problems. For example, the bacterial species *Bacillus thuringiensis* produces a toxin that kills some insect pests, and *Agrobacterium radiobacter* inhibits the growth of a bacterial pathogen that attacks several important fruit and flower species. These bacteria can be sprayed on crops. Or by using the techniques of molecular biology, we can incorporate specific genes from bacteria into the cells of crop plants such as corn, potato, and tomato. The use of transgenic crops has improved crop yield, but some people believe that such dramatic alteration of species is morally wrong and potentially dangerous because of its unknown

effects on other species and the potential spread of pesticide resistence to weedy species.

In addition, scientists are currently developing technologies involving bacteria to extract metals from ore in mines, and even to generate electricity from wastewater (Burton 2005). Bioengineering has also allowed us to "train" microbes to perform tasks that are not feasible by technological means. For example, bacteria engineered to attack pollutants such as cyanide, crude oil, and creosote are used more and more often in cleaning up toxic waste sites. This use of microbes may become an important factor in reclaiming damaged habitat, possibly an essential component of future conservation efforts. It is ironic that the simplest, "lowest" life forms on Earth should be in a position to address problems created by the most complex and "highest" life form, humankind.

an early agreement to pay INBio $1 million for the right to screen samples, with an obligation to pay royalties to INBio on any commercial products that result from the research (Ragavan 2008; Bhatti et al. 2009). INBio has since signed more than 40 external agreements, resulting in substantial transfer of funds, training, and equipment to INBio and its staff. The GlaxoSmithKline corporation, a Brazilian biotechnology company, and the Brazilian government signed a contract in 1999 worth $3 million to sample, screen, and investigate approximately 40,000 plants, fungi, and bacteria from Brazil, with part of the royalties going to support scientific research and local community-based conservation and development projects. Another approach has been to target traditional medicinal plants and other natural products for screening, often in collaboration with local healers. Programs such as these provide financial incentives for countries to protect their natural resources and the biodiversity knowledge of their indigenous inhabitants.

One discovery in this search is a potent anticancer chemical in the Pacific yew (*Taxus brevifolia*), a tree native to North American old-growth forests. This chemical, called taxol, has greatly reduced the mortality rate from ovarian cancer. Another discovery is the ginkgo tree (*Ginkgo biloba*), a species that occurs in the wild in a few isolated localities in China. This species is widely grown for its edible seeds and as a street tree, with its leaves used in traditional Chinese medicine. During the last 30 years, an industry valued at $500 million a year has developed around the cultivation of the ginkgo tree (**Figure 5.10**) and the manufacture of medicines made from its leaves, which are widely used in Europe, Asia, and North America to treat circulatory problems, including strokes, and to restore and maintain memory function.

The search for valuable natural products is wide-ranging: entomologists search for insects that can be used as biological control agents, microbiologists search for bacteria that can assist in biochemical manufacturing processes, and wildlife biologists search for species that can potentially produce animal protein more efficiently and with less environmental damage than existing domestic species (Chivian and Bernstein 2008). The growing biotechnology industry is finding new ways to reduce pollution, to develop alternative industrial processes, and to fight diseases

(A)

(B)

FIGURE 5.10 (A) Ginkgo trees are widely grown as ornamental trees because of their beautiful leaves and long life. This species is the basis of a pharmaceutical business worth hundreds of millions of dollars each year. (B) Because of the valuable medicines made from their leaves, ginkgo trees are now cultivated as a crop. Each year the woody stems sprout new shoots and branches, which are harvested. (Photographs by Richard Primack and Peter Del Tredici, Arnold Arboretum of Harvard University.)

threatening human health. Gene-splicing techniques of molecular biology are allowing unique, valuable genes found in one species to be transferred to another species. Both newly discovered and well-known species are often found to have exactly those properties needed to address some significant human problem. If biological diversity is reduced, the ability of scientists to locate and utilize a broad range of species will also be reduced.

A question currently being debated among conservation biologists, governments, environmental economists, and corporations is, Who owns the commercial development rights to the world's biological diversity? In the past, species were freely collected from wherever they occurred (often in the developing world) by corporations (almost always headquartered in the developed world). Whatever these corporations found useful in the species found during bioprospecting was then processed and sold at a profit, which was entirely kept by the corporation. An excellent example is provided by the immunosuppressant drug cyclosporine. From the fungus *Tolypocladium inflatum*, the drug cyclosporine was developed into a family of drugs with sales of $1.2 billion per year by the Swiss company Sandoz, which later merged to become Novartis (Bull 2004). The fungus was in a sample of soil that was collected in Norway, without permission, by a Sandoz biologist on vacation. As of yet, Norway has not received any payment for the use of this fungus in drug production. Such past and present unauthorized collecting of biological materials for commercial purposes is now often termed **biopiracy**. Many developing countries have reacted to this situation by passing laws that require permits for collecting of biological material for research and commerical purposes, and they impose criminal penalties and fines for the violation of such laws (Bhatti et al. 2009). People collecting samples without the needed permits have been arrested for violating the law.

Countries in both the developing and developed world now frequently demand a share in the commercial activities derived from the biological diversity contained within their borders, and rightly so. Local people in developing countries who possess knowledge of the species, protect them, and show them to scientists should also share in the profits from any use of them. Writing treaties and developing procedures to guarantee participation in this process will be a major diplomatic challenge in the coming years.

How can the option value of species be determined? One way involves examining the impact on the world economy of wild species only recently utilized by humans. Consider a hypothetical example: Imagine that during the last 20 years, newly discovered uses of 100 previously unused plant species accounted for $100 billion of new economic activity in the form of increased agriculture, new industrial products, and improved medicines. Since there are presently 250,000 unused plant species, a rough calculation might demonstrate that each presently unused plant species has the potential to provide an average of $400,000 worth of benefits to the world economy in the next 20 years. These types of calculations are now at a very preliminary stage, and they assume, for the sake of convenience, that the average value of a species can be determined.

> A question currently being debated among conservation biologists, governments, ecological economists, corporations, and local individuals is, "Who owns the commercial rights to the world's biodiversity?"

While most species may have little or no direct economic value and little option value, a small proportion may have enormous potential value to supply medical treatments, to support a new industry, or to prevent the collapse of a major agricultural crop. If just one of these species goes extinct before it is discovered, it could be a tremendous loss to the global economy, even if the majority of the world's species were preserved. As Aldo Leopold commented:

> If the biota, in the course of aeons, has built something we like but do not understand, then who but a fool would discard seemingly useless parts? To keep every cog and wheel is the first precaution of intelligent tinkering.

The diversity of the world's species can be compared to a manual on how to keep the Earth running effectively. The loss of a species is like tearing a page out of the manual. If we ever need the information from that page in the manual to save ourselves and the Earth's other species, the information will have been irretrievably lost.

Existence Value

Many people throughout the world care about wildlife, plants, and entire ecosystems and are concerned for their protection. This concern may be associated with a desire to someday visit the habitat of a unique species and see it in the wild; alternatively, concerned individuals may not expect, need, or even desire to see these species personally or experience the wilderness in which they live. For this reason, option value is considered a non-use value: people value the resource without any intention to use it now or in the future. These individuals recognize an **existence value** in wild nature—the amount that people are willing to pay to prevent species from going extinct, habitats from being destroyed, and genetic variation from being lost (Martín-López et al. 2007). A component of existence value is **beneficiary value**,

FIGURE 5.11 For many people, the existence value of charismatic species, such as whales, is clear. Here people greet a minke whale that is being rescued after it became entangled in a trawler's gill net; the float behind the whale was attached to the net to keep the whale at the surface so it could breathe. Later, rescuers were able to release the whale from the netting. Most people find interacting with other species to be an educational and uplifting experience. Such meetings (which usually take place at greater distances, as in a more traditional "whale-watch" setting or on "photo safaris" in Africa) can enrich human lives. (Photograph by Scott Kraus, New England Aquarium.)

or **bequest value**, how much people are willing to pay to protect something of value for their own children and descendants, or for future generations.

Particular species, the so-called charismatic megafauna—such as pandas, whales, lions, elephants, bison, manatees, and many birds—elicit strong responses in people (**Figure 5.11**). Special groups have been formed to appreciate and protect butterflies and other insects, wildflowers, and fungi. People place value on wildlife and wild lands in a direct way by joining and contributing billions of dollars each year to conservation organizations that protect species. In the United States, billions of dollars are contributed each year to conservation and environmental organizations, with The Nature Conservancy ($1.1 billion in 2008), the World Wildlife Fund ($110 million), Ducks Unlimited ($180 million), and the Sierra Club ($51 million) high on the list. Citizens also show their concern by directing their governments to spend money on conservation programs and to purchase land for habitat and landscape protection. For example, the government of the United States has spent millions of dollars to protect a single rare species, the brown pelican (*Pelecanus occidentalis*), protected initially under the U.S. Endangered Species Act and now considered recovered. The citizens of the United States have indicated in surveys that they are willing to spend about $31 per person per year (more than $9 billion per year in total, if multiplied by the number of people in the United States) to protect a national symbol, the bald eagle (*Haliaeetus leucocephalus*), a bird whose populations have suffered significant declines in the past but are now rebounding (**Figure 5.12**) (Groom et al. 2006).

> People, governments, and organizations contribute large sums of money annually to ensure the continuing existence of certain species, such as birds and whales, and of ecosystems such as rain forests and lakes.

Existence value can be attached to biological communities, such as temperate old-growth forests, tropical rain forests, coral reefs, and prairie remnants, and to areas of scenic beauty. Growing numbers of people and organizations contribute large sums of money annually to ensure the continuing existence of these habitats. Over the last 20 years and continuing into the present, surveys taken in the United States and the United Kingdom show that the public regards environmental protection as a high priority for their government. Further, people want environmental education included in public school curricula (www.neetf.org; www.epa.gov/enviroed).

At present, many people do not extend existence value to include the full range of the world's species. Although a few insect species, such as the monarch butterfly (*Danaus plexippus*), receive protection and attention, the need to protect other invertebrates, much less single-celled bacteria and protists, is not even part of the public discussion. Conservation biologists need to continue to educate the public on the subject of biological diversity to raise awareness of the need to protect *all* species, not just mammals and birds. Similarly, people need to learn the value of protecting all biological communities, including ones that are not as well-known or popular, and populations that are genetically unique or have special value due to their proximity to urban centers.

FIGURE 5.12 The bald eagle is a symbol of the United States. Many people have indicated a willingness to pay to protect its continued existence. (Photograph © Stockbyte/PictureQuest.)

Is Economic Valuation Enough?

In summary, ecological economics has helped to draw attention to the wide range of goods and services provided by biodiversity. That has enabled scientists to account for environmental impacts that were previously left out of the equation. When analyses of large-scale development projects have finally been completed, some projects that initially appeared to be successful have been seen to be actually running at an economic loss. For example, to evaluate the success of a development project, such as an irrigation project using water diverted from a tropical wetland ecosystem, the short-term benefits (improved crop yields) must be weighed against the environmental costs. Figure 4.3 (page 81) shows the total economic value of a tropical wetland ecosystem, including its use value, option value, and existence value. When the wetland ecosystem is damaged by the removal of water, the ecosystem's ability to provide the services shown in the figure are curtailed, their value greatly diminishes, and the economic success of the project is called into question. It is only by incorporating the wetland's value into this equation that an accurate view of the total project can be gained.

Although the more complete systems of accounting being developed by ecological economics value common property resources and include them in the cost of doing business (instead of leaving them out, as in traditional accounting methods), many environmentalists feel that ecological economics does not go far enough. For some, the use of green accounting methods still means acceptance of the present world economic system. These environmental thinkers advocate much stronger changes in our current economic system, which is responsible for pollution, environmental degradation, and species extinctions at unprecedented rates.

They argue that the most damning aspect of this system is the unnecessary overconsumption of resources by a minority of the world's citizens while the majority of the world's people face poverty. Given a world economic system in which millions of children die each year from disease, malnutrition, warfare, crime, and other factors strongly correlated with poverty, and in which thousands of unique species go extinct each year because of habitat destruction, these thinkers suggest that major structural changes—not just minor adjustments—are needed.

As we will discuss in Chapter 6, proponents of this view favor an alternative approach, one that will dramatically lower the consumption of resources in the developed world, reduce the need to over exploit natural resources, and greatly increase the value placed on the natural environment and biological diversity. Some suggestions for bringing this about include stabilization or reduction of the number of people in the world, much higher taxes on fossil fuels, penalties for inefficient energy use and pollution, support for public transportation and fuel-efficient vehicles, and mandatory recycling programs. Lands on which endangered species are present would have to be managed for biodiversity; private landowners would receive a government subsidy for maintaining the habitat. One of the greatest inefficiencies in the agricultural economies of Western countries is the overproduction of meat and dairy products, so a switch to (or at least toward) vegetarianism would be more healthy for people and would reduce the impact on the environment. Restrictions could be placed on trade so that only those products derived from sustainable activities could be bought or sold on national and international markets. Debts of developing countries could be reduced or dismissed and investment redirected to activities that provide the most benefits to the greatest number of impoverished people. Finally, financial penalties for damaging biological diversity, and incentives for protecting biological diversity, could be established and made so compelling that industries would be forced to protect the natural world. Many of these policies exist in some form in many countries in the world today. While the political will to carry out these policies may not be present today in most countries, perhaps at some point in the future, such policies can be implemented and strengthened across the world and biological diversity can be truly protected.

Summary

1. Indirect use values can be assigned to aspects of biological diversity that provide economic benefit to people but are not harvested or damaged during use. One major group of indirect use values is the nonconsumptive use values of ecosystems. These include ecosystem productivity (important as the starting point for all food chains and carbon sequestration); protection of water resources and soils; regulation of local, regional, and global climates; waste treatment and nutrient retention; the enhancement of commercial crops by wild species; and recreation.

2. Biological diversity features prominently in the growing recreation and ecotourism industry. The number of people involved in nature recreation and the amount of money spent on such activities are considerable. In many countries, particularly in the developing world, ecotourism represents one of the major sources of foreign income. Even in industrialized countries, the economy in areas around national parks is increasingly dominated by the recreation industry. Educational materials and the mass media draw heavily on themes of biological diversity and create materials of considerable value.

3. Biological diversity also has an option value in terms of its potential to provide future benefits to human society, such as new and improved medicines, biological control agents, and crops. The biotechnology industry is developing innovative techniques to take advantage of new chemicals and genetic variation found in the living world.

4. People are often willing to pay money in the form of taxes and voluntary contributions to ensure the continued existence of unique species, biological communities, and landscapes; this amount represents the existence value of biological diversity.

For Discussion

1. Consider the natural resources people use where you live. Can you place an economic value on those resources? If you can't think of any products harvested directly, consider basic ecosystem services such as flood control, freshwater, and soil retention.

2. Ask people how much money they spend on nature-related activities. Also ask them how much they would be willing to spend each year to protect specific well-known species of birds and mammals, such as the polar bear; to save a rare, endangered freshwater mussel; and to protect water quality and forest health. Multiply the average values by the number of people in your city, your country, or the world to obtain estimates of how much these components of biological diversity are worth. Is this an accurate method for gauging the economic value of biodiversity? How might you improve this simple methodology?

3. Imagine that the only known population of a dragonfly species will be destroyed unless money can be raised to purchase the pond where it lives and the surrounding land. How much is this species worth? Consider different methods for assigning a monetary value to this species, and compare the different outcomes. Which method is best?

Suggested Readings

Balmford, A., J. Beresford, J. Green, R. Naidoo, M. Walpole, and A. Manica. 2009. A global perspective on trends in nature-based tourism. *PLoS Biology* 7: e1000144. Ecotourism is increasing throughout the world and may help to protect biodiversity.

Bhatti, S., S. Carrizosa, P. McGuire, and T. Young (eds.). 2009. *Contracting for ABS: The Legal and Scientific Implications of Bioprospecting Contracts*. IUCN, Gland. Comprehensive treatment of bioprospecting, with numerous case studies.

Butler, R., L. P. Koh, and J. Ghazoul. 2009. REDD in the red: Palm oil could undermine carbon payment schemes. *Conservation Letters* 2: 67–73. Certain tropical tree crops are more profitable for landowners than forest protection programs.

Craft, C. and 7 others. 2009. Forecasting the effects of accelerated sea-level rise on tidal marsh ecosystem services. *Frontiers in Ecology and the Environment* 7: 73–78. The loss of tidal marshes due to rising seas will have large economic costs.

Ewel, K. C. 2010. Appreciating tropical coastal wetlands from a landscape perspective. *Frontiers in Ecology and the Environment* 8: 20–26. Coastal wetlands provide important goods and services to local people living nearby.

Gardiner, M. M. and 9 others. 2009. Landscape diversity enhances biological control of an introduced crop pest in the north-central USA. *Ecological Applications* 19: 143–154. Natural enemies control populations of a soybean pest, reducing the need for insecticide.

Granek, E. F. and 16 others. 2010. Ecosystem services as a common language for coastal ecosystem-based management. *Conservation Biology* 24: 207–216. Ecosystem services provide a way to begin a public dialogue on the need to protect biodiversity.

Luck, G. W. and 21 others. 2009. Quantifying the contribution of organisms to the provision of ecosystem services. *BioScience* 59: 223–235. The authors provide a framework that values the ecosystem services provided by individual species.

Nabhan, G. P. 2008. *Where Our Food Comes From: Retracing Nicolay Vavilov's Quest to End Famine*. Shearwater Press. The security of our food supply depends on protecting the genetic diversity of our crop species.

Naeem S., D. E. Bunker, A. Hector, M. Loreau, and C. Perrings (eds.). 2009. *Biodiversity, Ecosystem Functioning, and Human Wellbeing: An Ecological and Economic Perspective*. Oxford University Press, Oxford, UK. Essays that describe the importance of biodiversity to human health.

Nash, S. 2009. Ecotourism and other invasions. *BioScience* 59: 106–110. The Galápagos Islands are relatively well managed but remain threatened by the pressures of increasing tourism.

Sánchez-Azofeifa, G. A., A. Pfaff, J. A. Robalino, and J. P. Boomhower. 2007. Costa Rica's payment for environmental services program: Intention, implementation, and impact. *Conservation Biology* 21: 1165–1173. Costa Rica is a leader in developing markets for environmental services, but their impacts on deforestation are still unclear.

Srinivasan, U. T. and 9 others. 2008. The debt of nations and the distribution of ecological impacts from human activities. *Proceedings of the National Academy of Sciences USA* 105: 1768–1773. Ecosystem services in poor countries are negatively affected by the activities of developed nations.

Venter, O., J. E. M. Watson, E. Meijaard, W. F. Laurance, and H. P. Possingham. 2010. Avoiding unintended outcomes from REDD. *Conservation Biology* 24: 5–6. Climate change programs have the potential to greatly increase the areas of protected tropical forests.

Thorp, J. H. and 8 others. 2010. Linking ecosystem services, rehabilitation, and river hydrogeomorphology. *BioScience* 60: 67–74. The authors describe the challenges of assigning economic values to wetland ecosystem services.

Chapter 6

Ethical Values

As was discussed in Chapters 4 and 5, the new discipline of ecological economics provides positive arguments in support of conservation that can be put to use in the policy arena. Although such economic arguments can be advanced to justify the protection of biological diversity, there are also strong ethical arguments for doing so (Novacek 2008; Justus et al. 2009). While economic arguments often are assumed to be more objective or more convincing, ethical arguments have unique power: They have foundations in the value systems of most religions and philosophies and are readily understood by the general public (Moseley 2009; Woodhams 2009). They may appeal to a general respect for life; a reverence for nature or specific parts of it; a sense of the beauty, fragility, uniqueness, or antiquity of the living world; or a belief in divine creation. Indeed, to many people, ethical arguments provide the most convincing reasons for conservation.

Environmental ethics, a vigorous new discipline within philosophy, articulates the ethical value of the natural world (Brennan and Lo 2008; Minteer and Collins 2008). As a corollary, it challenges the materialistic values that tend to dominate modern societies (Alexander 2009). If contemporary societies de-emphasized the pursuit of wealth and instead focused on furthering genuine human well-being, the preservation of the natural environment and the maintenance of biological diversity would likely become fundamental priorities, rather than occasional afterthoughts (Mills 2003).

Ethical Values of Biological Diversity

Environmental ethics provides virtues and values that make sense to people today. In an unprecedented moment in human history, ethical arguments can and do convince people to conserve biodiversity. Ethical arguments are also important because although economic arguments by themselves provide a basis for valuing some species and biological communities, economic valuation can also provide grounds for extinguishing species, or for saving one species and not another (Rolston 1994; Redford and Adams 2009). According to conventional economic thinking, a species with low population numbers, unattractive appearance, no immediate use to people, and no relationship to any species of economic importance will be given a low value. Such qualities may characterize a substantial proportion of the world's species, particularly insects and other invertebrates, fungi, and nonflowering plants. Halting profitable developments or making costly attempts to preserve these species may not have any obvious economic justification. In fact, in many circumstances, economic cost-benefit analyses will argue for destroying endangered species that stand in the way of "progress."

Despite any economic justification, though, many people would make a case against species extinction on ethical grounds, arguing that the conscious destruction of a natural species is morally wrong, even if it is economically profitable. Similar arguments would be advanced for protecting unique biological communities and genetic variation. Ethical arguments for preserving biological diversity resonate with people because they appeal to our nobler instincts or a belief in a divine creation, which do play a role in societal decision making (Fischer and van der Wal 2007). Human societies have often made decisions based more on ethical values than on economic ones. Outlawing slavery, limiting child labor, and preventing cruelty to animals are three examples. The linkages among environmental ethics, conservation, peace, and social and economic justice have been incorporated into a unique and uncompromising document, the Earth Charter, put forward by Mikhail Gorbachev, the former president of the Soviet Union, and other world leaders (www.earthcharterinaction.org).

> Ethical arguments can complement economic and biological arguments for protecting biodiversity. Such ethical arguments are readily understood by many people.

Ethical, noneconomic justifications for the protection of biodiversity are already incorporated into the legal system. For example, in the United States a de facto right of all species to continue to exist is strongly protected under the Endangered Species Act (ESA), and a judge ruling in a major court decision stated "that Congress intended endangered species to be afforded the highest of priorities" (Rolston 1988). The ESA states that the justification for this protection is the "aesthetic, ecological, educational, historical, recreational and scientific value" of species. As described below, the full range of ethical arguments includes many of these aspects of value. Significantly, economic value is not included in this legal rationale, and economic interests are explicitly stated to be of secondary importance when protecting species from extinction. According to the law, profits and economic values must be set aside when their pursuit threatens to extinguish a species. (The law does allow economic values to prevail in rare cases, but only if a so-called God squad of senior government officials rules that economic concerns are of overriding national interest.)

In addition to these legal measures, if modern society adopted ethical values that strongly support preserving the natural environment and maintaining biological diversity, we could expect to see lower consumption of scarce resources and greater care in the use of those resources (Naess 1989; Cafaro 2010). We would also see efforts to limit human population growth (Cafaro and Staples 2009). Unfortunately, however, modern consumer societies generally take a different view. While demanding that human beings treat one another ethically, their primary attitude toward nature is "anything goes"—people can use or destroy it as they see fit, as long as they do not harm human beings or take their property. In recent years, this attitude has been questioned by proponents of environmental ethics.

Ethical Arguments for Preserving Biological Diversity

Ethical arguments can form the basis for political action and changes in laws and corporate management (Rolston 1994; Minteer and Collins 2008; Teel and Manfredo 2010). The following arguments, based on the intrinsic value of species and on our duties to other people, are important to conservation biology because they provide the rationale for protecting all species, including rare species and species of no obvious economic value.

EACH SPECIES HAS A RIGHT TO EXIST   All species represent unique biological solutions to the problem of survival. All are the living representatives of grand historical lineages, and all have their own beauty and fitness. For these reasons, the survival of each species must be guaranteed, regardless of its importance to humans. This statement is true whether the species is large or small, simple or complex, ancient or recently evolved; whether it is economically important or of little immediate economic value to humans; and whether it is loved or hated by humans (**Box 6.1**). Each species has value for its own sake—an **intrinsic value** unrelated to human needs or desires (Agar 2001; Sagoff 2008). This argument suggests not only that we have no right to destroy any species, but also that we have a moral responsibility to actively protect species from going extinct as the result of our activities. It recognizes humans are part of the larger biotic community and reminds us that we are not the center of the universe.

> An argument can be made that people have a responsibility to protect species and other aspects of biodiversity because of their intrinsic value, not because of human needs.

Robert Elliot (1992) suggests that wild nature has the following properties that show its intrinsic value: "diversity, stability, complexity, beauty, harmony, creativity, organization, intricacy, elegance, and richness." These qualities of natural organisms are ones that we can appreciate—and that call forth responses of personal restraint and active protection. In addition, "naturalness" itself might be seen as a valuable property, particularly in a world where wild nature is becoming more rare.

Some people argue that recognizing an intrinsic value in nature leads to absurdity. Because we must use nature, they say, we cannot recognize its intrinsic value, since by definition that would limit the ways in which we use it. Even people who are sympathetic to environmentalism and appreciate wild nature often resist granting it intrinsic value, since this demands so much. If nature is wonderful and complex, as science and our own experiences tell us it is, how can we go on using it? But we must do so to survive. In addition, the world is already filled with rules limiting our actions; adding another layer is tiresome. Finally, since so many modern lifestyles (especially in the developed world) depend to such a large extent on an ecologically destructive economic system, many despair of protecting the world and give up trying to live in an environmentally responsible manner.

These are legitimate concerns. Still, effective action to protect biological diversity is both possible and desirable (Schmidtz 2005). First, it is possible to use natural resources in a respectful and limited way: *It is necessary to use nature, but not all use of nature is necessary.* Second, while no one likes more rules, growing up and living moral lives involves recognizing our duty to others. Finally, it is possible to live in an environmentally responsible manner even in industrialized countries: it requires making a personal commitment to use less resources, have less of an impact on the environ-

BOX 6.1 *Sharks: A Feared Animal in Decline*

■ Of the many plants and animals threatened by human exploitation, one of the least loved is the shark. Public perception of these animals is based almost entirely upon gruesome media images that portray sharks as merciless, indiscriminate killers (e.g., the movies *Jaws*, *Finding Nemo*, and *Open Water*) and on news reports of attacks on humans (which are actually quite rare; in the year 2007, only 71 shark attacks and one death were confirmed worldwide). For most people, a shark is little more than a terrifying triangular fin and a mouthful of very sharp teeth. For conservationists concerned with rapidly dwindling shark populations worldwide, the shark's bad reputation is a public relations nightmare. However, a recent international agreement to regulate trade in great white sharks is a major step in the right direction.

When we contrast the small number of people killed by sharks per year worldwide with the estimated 100 million sharks killed by people per year, it is clear that people, by far, are the more dangerous species (Perry 2009). Sharks actually help people far more than they harm them. For example, shark's liver oil was an important source of vitamin A until it was synthesized in 1947, it is used in cosmetics, and it is highly effective at shrinking human hemorrhoids and is widely used in medicines for that purpose. The chem-

> Sharks are being overharvested, but the ecological consequences of the decline of these top predators has yet to be appreciated by the public.

ical squalamine found in the internal organs of dogfish has the ability to inhibit the growth of certain brain tumors in humans, and shark cartilage is being used as an alternative treatment for kidney cancer. The immune system of sharks is being intensively studied to learn the secret of why sharks have an unusually low incidence of cancer even when experimentally exposed to known carcinogens; this information may prove invaluable to humans in our battle against cancer (Raloff 2005). Sharks' grace and power in the water, along with the medical benefits they provide or may provide in the future to people, would seem to warrant that they should be more appreciated by the public.

One quality that redeems these animals in the public eye is not one that encourages conservation: Shark fins are a popular item on menus in Chinese restaurants. In Asia, and Chinese restaurants around the world, shark fin soup is a delicacy that has created high demand for several species of shark (Clarke 2008). Consequently, shark fishing has become a booming business in the past decade. A single

Scalloped hammerhead shark (*Sphyrna lewini*) caught in a gill net in the Sea of Cortez. This species is listed as endangered by the IUCN. (Photograph © Stephen Frink Collection/Alamy.)

fin of the giant basking shark (also known as the whale shark) could bring up to $57,000 (Magnussen et al. 2007). The cruel and wasteful practice called finning, in which a captured shark is flung back into the water to die after its fins are amputated, has spurred some public sympathy for sharks and has led to a call for banning the practice. A more serious problem, however, is the tendency for sharks to become bycatch of commercial fishing using drift gill nets. More than half of the annual shark kills are related to accidental gill net catches; sharks caught in this manner are usually simply discarded.

High shark mortality has conservationists concerned for several reasons (Dicken et al. 2008; Dulvy et al. 2008). Sharks mature very slowly, have long reproductive cycles, and produce only a few young at a time. Fish such as salmon (which have also been overharvested) can recover rapidly because of the large numbers of offspring they produce annually; sharks do not have this ability. A second problem is that

BOX 6.1 *(continued)*

harvesting of sharks by commercial and private fishing concerns is largely unregulated in many countries. Sharks are increasingly harvested for their meat, often used in fish-and-chips. Sharks are also targeted by sport fishermen because of their size and fierce reputation. A few countries, notably the United States, Australia, New Zealand, and Canada, have enacted legislation to stem shark losses, including a ban on finning, but other countries involved in commercial shark fishing either see no need for action or are delaying proposed regulations. The recent ban on catching large coastal sharks in U.S. waters is a step in the right direction, but allowing continued harvesting of smaller individuals and open-ocean sharks may prevent vulnerable species from recovering to their original numbers.

Finally, the decimation of shark populations is occurring at a time when very little is known about more than a handful of individual species. Though more than 350 species of sharks exist, management proposals often treat all sharks as a single entity because, lacking specific information, management by species is impossible. Species in the heavily fished Atlantic Ocean that have been studied have demon-strated a precipitous decrease of 40% to 99% in the last 20 years (Dulvy et al. 2008).

The decline of shark populations is a matter for concern in and of itself, but it is also an important factor in a larger problem. Sharks are among the most important predators in marine ecosystems; they feed upon a variety of organisms and are distributed throughout oceans and seas worldwide. Terrestrial ecologists have already observed the benefits of predation for prey populations and the problems that occur when predators are removed from an ecosystem. The decline of sharks could have a significant, and possibly catastrophic, cascade effect upon marine ecosystems, allowing unwanted species to rapidly increase in numbers. Ironically, sharks have fulfilled their role for some 400 million years, making them one of the longest-lived groups of organisms on the planet; yet their future depends upon a change in human attitudes and perceptions. Conservationists have their work cut out for them. They must persuade world governments to look beyond the shark's terrifying aspect and act to preserve this diverse group of species that is vital to the health of the world's oceans.

ment, and help to change society in a positive manner. If nature does in fact have intrinsic value, we should respect that value—whether doing so is convenient or not.

Opponents to this view counter that, even though some people do value these qualities in nature, they are not morally required to do so (Ferry 1995). They argue that humans have a value beyond all other species' value because only we are fully conscious, rational, and moral beings, and unless our actions affect other people, directly or indirectly, any treatment of the natural world is morally acceptable. It might seem strange to assign rights of existence and legal protection to nonhuman species, especially simple organisms, when they lack the self-awareness that we usually associate with the morality of rights and duties. How can a lowly moss or fungus have rights when it doesn't even have a nervous system? However, whether or not we allow them rights, species carry great value as the repositories of the accumulated experience and history of millions of previous life forms through their continuous evolutionary adaptation to a changing environment (Rolston 2000). The premature extinction of a species due to human activities destroys this history and could be regarded as a "superkilling" (Rolston 1989) because it kills future generations of the species and eliminates the processes of evolution and speciation.

Other people, especially many animal rights activists, have difficulty assigning rights to species, even if they value the rights of individual animals (Regan 2004). Singer (1979), for one, argues that "species as such are not conscious entities and so do not have interests above and beyond the interest of individual animals that are members of a species." However, Rolston (1994) counters that on both biological and ethical grounds, species, rather than individual organisms, are the appropriate targets of conservation efforts. All individuals eventually die; it is the species that continues, evolves, and sometimes forms new species. In a sense, individuals are temporary representatives of species, thus species are more important than individuals.

This focus on species challenges the modern Western ethical tradition of individualism. But the preservation of biodiversity seems to demand that the needs of endangered species take precedence over the needs of individuals. For example, the U.S. National Park Service killed hundreds of rabbits on Santa Barbara Island to protect a few plants of the endangered species Santa Barbara Island live-forever (*Dudleya traskiae*); in this case, one endangered plant species was judged to be more valuable than hundreds of individual animals of a common species (**Figure 6.1**).

ALL SPECIES ARE INTERDEPENDENT   Species interact in complex ways in natural communities. The loss of one species may have far-reaching consequences for other members of the community (as described in Chapter 2). Other species may become extinct in response, or the entire ecosystem may become destabilized as the result of cascades of species extinctions. For these reasons, if we value some parts of nature, we should protect all of nature (Leopold 1949). We are obligated to conserve the system as a whole because that is the appropriate survival unit (Diamond 2005). Even if we only value human beings, our instincts toward self-preservation should impel us to preserve biodiversity. When the natural world prospers, we prosper. When the natural world is harmed, people suffer from widespread health problems—such as asthma, food poisoning, waterborne diseases, and cancer—that are caused or aggravated by environmental pollution.

>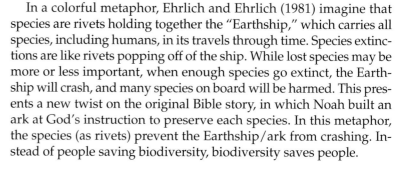
> All species and ecosystems are interdependent, and so all parts of nature should be protected. It is in the long-term survival interest of people to protect all of biodiversity.

In a colorful metaphor, Ehrlich and Ehrlich (1981) imagine that species are rivets holding together the "Earthship," which carries all species, including humans, in its travels through time. Species extinctions are like rivets popping off of the ship. While lost species may be more or less important, when enough species go extinct, the Earthship will crash, and many species on board will be harmed. This presents a new twist on the original Bible story, in which Noah built an ark at God's instruction to preserve each species. In this metaphor, the species (as rivets) prevent the Earthship/ark from crashing. Instead of people saving biodiversity, biodiversity saves people.

PEOPLE HAVE A RESPONSIBILITY TO ACT AS STEWARDS OF THE EARTH
Many religious adherents find it wrong to destroy species, because they are God's creations (Moseley 2009). If God created the world, then presumably the species God created have value. Within the Jewish and Christian traditions, human responsibility for protecting animal species is explicitly described in the Bible as part of the covenant with God. The Book of Genesis describes the creation of the Earth's biological diversity as a divine act, after which "God saw that it was good" and "blessed them." In the story of Noah's ark, God commanded Noah to save two of all species, not just the ones human beings found useful. God provided detailed instructions for building the ark, an early species rescue project, saying, "Keep them alive with you." The prophet Muhammad, founder of Islam, continued this theme of human responsibility: "The world is green and beautiful and God has appointed you as His stewards over it. He sees how you acquit yourselves." Belief in the value of God's creation supports a stewardship argument for preserving biodiversity: human beings have been given responsibility for God's creation and must preserve, not destroy, what they have been given.

Other religious traditions also support the preservation of nature (Bassett 2000; Science and Spirit 2001). For example, Hinduism locates divinity in certain animals and recognizes a basic kinship between humans and other beings (including the transmigration of souls from one species to another). A primary ethical concept in Hin-

FIGURE 6.1 Government agencies judged the continued existence of the endangered plant Santa Barbara Island live-forever (*Dudleya traskiae*, the tall plant) to be more valuable than the common rabbits on its island home. The rabbits, which fed on the plant's fleshy leaves (shown at the bottom), were killed to stop their destruction of this fragile plant species. (Photograph © 1985 California Native Plant Society.)

duism and other Indian religions, such as Jainism and Buddhism, is ahimsa—non-violence or kindness to all life. To live by this ideal, many religious people become vegetarians and live materially simple lives. Of course, some religions articulate views that put human beings at the center of creation, supporting a domineering attitude toward nature. Since many people base their ethical values on a religious faith, the development of religious arguments in support of conservation might be effective in motivating people to conserve biodiversity (Foltz et al. 2003; Wirzba 2003). Speakers for many major religions, in fact, have stated that their faiths mandate the conservation of nature (**Box 6.2**).

PEOPLE HAVE A DUTY TO THEIR NEIGHBORS   Humans must be careful to minimize damage to their natural environment, because such damage not only harms other species, it harms people as well. Much of the pollution and environmental degradation occurring today is unnecessary and could be minimized with better planning. Our duty to other humans requires us to live within sustainable limits (Norton 2003). This goal can be achieved by people in the industrialized countries taking strong actions to reduce their excessive and disproportionate consumption of natural resources. Why does an average person living in the United States or Canada need to use 9 times more energy per year than a person living in China, or 17 times more than a person living in India? If such energy use is not curbed, global warming could result in crop failures throughout the world, and the rise in sea level could flood low-lying areas from Bangladesh to the Mississippi Delta, with poor people bearing most of the harm. The government of the United States, where less than 5% of the world population uses 25% of the world's energy, has not yet joined recent international efforts to forestall global warming. But it is immoral for the government leaders of the United States and other countries to avoid serious action on global warming when their inactions risk the lives and livelihoods of their own citizens and poor neighbors at home and abroad (Gardiner 2004; Gardiner et al. 2010).

PEOPLE HAVE A RESPONSIBILITY TO FUTURE GENERATIONS   If in our daily living we degrade the natural resources of the Earth and cause species to become extinct, future generations will pay the price in terms of a lower standard of living and quality of life (Gardiner et al. 2010). As species are lost and wild lands developed, children are deprived of one of the most exciting experiences in growing up—the wonder of seeing "new" animals and plants in the wild. Rolston (1995) predicts, "[I]t is safe to say that in the decades ahead, the quality of life will decline in proportion to the loss of biotic diversity, though it is often thought that one must sacrifice biotic diversity to improve human life." To remind us to act more responsibly, we might imagine that we are borrowing the Earth from future generations who expect to get it back in good condition.

Over 150 years ago, reflecting on the depauperate ecological landscape around him in Concord, Massachusetts, the philospher and naturalist Henry Thoreau wrote in his journal (1856):

> When I consider that the nobler animals have been exterminated here, I cannot but feel as if I lived in a tamed, and, as it were, emasculated country. . . . I take infinite pains to know the phenomena of the spring, thinking that I have here the entire poem, and then, to my chagrin, I hear that it is but an imperfect copy that I possess and have read, that my ancestors have torn out many of the first leaves and grandest passages, and mutilated it in many places.

Like Thoreau, many of us believe that our descendants will "wish to know an entire heaven and an entire Earth." They have a right to know and explore wild nature. We shouldn't take that away from them.

BOX 6.2 *Religion and Conservation*

■ In September 1986, an interfaith ceremony was held in the Basilica of St. Francis, in Assisi, Italy. It included "Declarations on Nature" by representatives of the five participating religions—Buddhism, Christianity, Hinduism, Islam, and Judaism. For the first time in history, leaders of these faiths declared that their religions mandate the conservation of nature. Excerpts from the five declarations follow.*

> Leaders of the world's religions increasingly prioritize the conservation of natural resources and respect for all life.

THE BUDDHIST DECLARATION ON NATURE
Venerable Lungrig Namgyal Rinpoche, Abbot, Gyuto Tantric University

The simple underlying reason why beings other than humans need to be taken into account is that, like human beings, they too are sensitive to happiness and suffering. . . . Many have held up usefulness to human beings as the sole criterion for the evaluation of an animal's life. Upon closer examination, one discovers that this mode of evaluation of another's life and right to existence has also been largely responsible for human indifference as well as cruelty to animals.

We regard our survival as an undeniable right. As co-inhabitants of this planet, other species too have this right for survival. And since human beings as well as other non-human sentient beings depend upon the environment as the ultimate source of life and wellbeing, let us share the conviction that the conservation of the environment, the restoration of the imbalance caused by our negligence in the past, be implemented with courage and determination.

"All sentient beings, all breathing things, creatures without exception, may no evil befall them."
—Gradual Sayings of the Buddha

Source: Text excerpts from World Wildlife Fund 1999, used with permission. Art from Bassett 2000, used with permission.

THE CHRISTIAN DECLARATION ON NATURE
Father Lanfranco Serrini, Minister General, Order of Friars Minor (Franciscans)

To praise the Lord for his creation is to confess that God the Father made all things visible and invisible; it is to thank him for the many gifts he bestows on all his children. . . . By reason of its created origin, each creature according to its species and all together in the harmonious unity of the universe manifest God's infinite truth and beauty, love and goodness, wisdom and majesty, glory and power.

Man's dominion cannot be understood as license to abuse, spoil, squander or destroy what God has made to manifest his glory. That dominion cannot be anything other than a stewardship in symbiosis with all creatures. . . . Every human act of irresponsibility towards creatures is an abomination. According to its gravity, it is an offence against that divine wisdom which sustains and gives purpose to the interdependent harmony of the universe.

THE HINDU DECLARATION ON NATURE
Dr. Karan Singh, President, Hindu Virat Samaj

The Hindu viewpoint on nature is permeated by a reverence for life, and an awareness that the great forces of nature—the earth, the sky, the air, the water and fire—as well as various orders of life including plants and trees, forests and animals, are all bound to each other within the great rhythms of nature. The divine is not exterior to creation, but expresses itself through natural phenomena. The *Mahabharata* says that "even if there is only one tree full of flowers and fruits in a village, that place becomes worthy of worship and respect."

Let us declare our determination to halt the present slide towards destruction, to rediscover the ancient tradition of reverence for all life and, even at this late hour, to reverse the suicidal course upon which we have embarked. Let us recall the ancient Hindu dictum

"The Earth is our mother, and we are all her children."

RESPECT FOR HUMAN LIFE AND HUMAN DIVERSITY IS COMPATIBLE WITH A RESPECT FOR BIOLOGICAL DIVERSITY Some people worry that recognizing an intrinsic value in nature requires taking resources and opportunities away from human beings. But a respect for and protection of biological diversity can be linked to greater opportunities and better health for people (Jacob et al. 2009). Some of the most exciting developments in conservation biology involve supporting the economic development of disadvantaged rural people in ways that are linked to the protection of biological diversity.

BOX 6.2 (continued)

☪ THE MUSLIM DECLARATION ON NATURE
Dr. Abdullah Omar Nasseef, Secretary General, Muslim World League

The essence of Islamic teaching is that the entire universe is God's creation. Allah makes the waters flow upon the earth, upholds the heavens, makes the rain fall and keeps the boundaries between day and night. . . . It is God who created the plants and the animals in their pairs and gave them the means to multiply.

For the Muslim mankind's role on earth is that of a *khalifa*, viceregent or trustee of God. We are God's stewards and agents on Earth. We are not masters of this Earth; it does not belong to us to do what we wish. It belongs to God and He has entrusted us with its safekeeping. . . . The *khalifa* is answerable for his/her actions, for the way in which he/she uses or abuses the trust of God.

THE JEWISH DECLARATION ON NATURE
Rabbi Arthur Hertzberg, Vice President, World Jewish Congress

The encounter of God and man in nature is conceived in Judaism as a seamless web with man as the leader and custodian of the natural world. . . . Now, when the whole world is in peril, when the environment is in danger of being poisoned and various species, both plant and animal, are becoming extinct, it is our Jewish responsibility to put the defense of the whole of nature at the very centre of our concern.

We have a responsibility to life, to defend it everywhere, not only against our own sins but also against those of others. We are all passengers together in this same fragile and glorious world. Let us safeguard our rowboat—and let us row together.

"... and the rainbow shall be in the cloud; and I will look upon it, that I may remember the everlasting covenant between God and every living creature . . . that is upon the Earth."—Genesis 9:16

Helping poor people establish sustainable plots of cash crops and achieve a degree of economic independence sometimes reduces the need to overharvest wild species. Working with indigenous people to establish legal title to their land gives them the means to protect the biological communities in which they live (although they may not choose to do so in practice). In developed countries, the **environmental justice** movement seeks to empower poor and politically weak people, who are often members of minority groups, to protect their own environments; in the process their well-being and the protection of biological diversity are enhanced. Working for the social and political benefit of poor and powerless people is not only compatible with efforts to preserve the natural environment but also often a necessary component of an effective conservation program (Pellow 2005).

> Environmental justice and social justice are related, since both encourage broad respect for all kinds of life, both human and non-human.

Human maturity often leads to self-restraint and a respect for others. Environmentalists have argued that the further maturation of the human species will involve an "identification with all life forms" and "the acknowledgment of [their] intrinsic value" (Naess 1986). They envision an expanding circle of moral obligations, moving outward from oneself to include duties to relatives, local communities, one's nation, all humanity, animals, all species, ecosystems, and ultimately the whole Earth (**Figure 6.2**).

Conservation biologists need to be sensitive to the public perception that they care *more* about birds, turtles, or nature in general than they do about people. They need to look for win-win scenarios where the interests of people and nature can both be furthered. However, in some situations, protecting biological diversity may be incompatible with meeting human needs or promoting human interests. For example, if a tribe needs to hunt the last remaining individuals of an endangered animal to maintain its way of life, environmental protection would demand real sacrifices from that tribe. In such a situation, the need to preserve a species from extinction arguably should trump all other considerations (Rolston 1995).

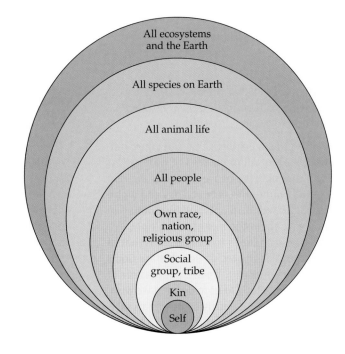

FIGURE 6.2 Environmental ethics holds that an individual has an expanding set of moral obligations, extending outward beyond the self to progressively more inclusive levels. (From Noss 1992.)

Enlightened Self-Interest: Biodiversity and Human Development

Economic arguments stress that preserving biological diversity *is in our material self-interest*. Ethical arguments based on the intrinsic value of wild nature and our duties to others stress that we should act altruistically toward nature *regardless of our material self-interest*. A second ethical framework appeals to our *enlightened self-interest*, arguing that preserving biodiversity and developing our knowledge of it will make us better and happier people (Sandler 2007). The following points describe how protecting biological diversity is in our enlightened self-interest.

AESTHETIC AND RECREATIONAL ENJOYMENT Nearly everyone enjoys wildlife and landscapes aesthetically, and this joy increases the quality of our lives. Nature-related activities are important in childhood development (Carson 1965; Kahn and Kellert 2002). The beauty of a field of wildflowers in Glacier National Park or a migrating warbler on a spring morning in a city park enriches people's lives. And for many people, experiencing nature means experiencing it in a natural setting—simply reading about species or seeing them in museums, gardens, or zoos does not suffice. Recreational activities such as hiking, canoeing, and mountain climbing are physically, intellectually, and emotionally satisfying. People spend tens of billions of dollars annually in these pursuits, proof enough that they value them highly. What if there were no more migratory birds or no more meadows filled with wildflowers and butterflies? Would we still enjoy nature as much?

ARTISTIC EXPRESSION AND PHILOSOPHICAL INSIGHT Throughout history, poets, writers, painters, and musicians of all cultures have drawn inspiration from wild nature (Thoreau 1854; Swanson et al. 2008). Nature provides countless forms and symbols for painters and sculptors to render and interpret (**Figure 6.3**). Poets have often found their greatest inspiration in either wild nature or the pastoral countryside. Preserving biological diversity preserves possibilities for all artists and for everyone who appreciates their works. Philosophers too go to nature to find insights into human existence and our place in the wider universe. A loss of biodiversity limits such experiences and diminishes our intellectual resources.

FIGURE 6.3 Rare wildflowers and butterflies are the inspiration for botanical sculptor Patrick O'Hara. In his studio in western Ireland, O'Hara molds, sculpts, and paints delicate porcelain scenes from nature that inspire an appreciation of conservation in a worldwide audience. (Photograph courtesy of Anna O'Hara; www.ohara-art.com.)

SCIENTIFIC KNOWLEDGE   Science and our growing knowledge of nature are among humanity's greatest achievements. This knowledge is facilitated by the preservation of wild nature. Wild areas allow the study of natural ecological interactions. Wild species preserve the record of evolution. Young people are inspired to become scientists by personal contacts with wild nature, and those who do not become professional scientists can apply their basic knowledge of science to understanding their own local fields, forests, and streams.

Three of the central mysteries in the world of science are how life originated, how the diversity of life interacts to form complex ecosystems, and how humans evolved. Thousands of biologists are working on these problems and are coming ever closer to the answers. New techniques of molecular biology allow greater insight into the relationships of living species as well as some extinct species, which are known to us only from fossils. However, when species become extinct and ecosystems are damaged, important clues are lost, and the mysteries become harder to solve. For example, if *Homo sapiens'* closest living relatives—chimpanzees, bonobos, gorillas, and orangutans—disappear from the wild, we will lose important clues regarding human physical and social evolution.

HISTORICAL UNDERSTANDING   Knowing nature, both scientifically and through personal experience, is key to an understanding of human history: In walking the landscapes our ancestors walked, we gain insight into how they experienced the world at a slower pace and without mechanized aids. We often forget just how recently humankind has moved to ultrafast transportation, fully illuminated cities that shut out the night, cell phones, computers, and other aspects of modern life. We need to preserve natural areas in order to develop our historical imaginations.

RELIGIOUS INSPIRATION   Many religions have traditions of "wandering in the wilderness" in order to commune with God or with spirits, or to purify themselves of the temptations and evils associated with life within human communities. From

FIGURE 6.4 Kinkaku-ji, the Golden Pavilion, in Kyoto, Japan. The spiritual link with nature is often apparent in the placement and landscaping of religious shrines such as this Buddhist temple. (Photograph by R. Primack.)

the Judeo-Christian tradition, Moses, Isaiah, St. John the Baptist, St. Francis of Assisi, and even Jesus all sought out the solitude of wilderness to obtain spiritual strength and receive the guidance of God. Generations of Sioux, Ute, Cheyenne, and other Native American vision seekers have done the same, albeit in accordance with different traditions. Being in nature allows us to clear and focus our minds and, sometimes, experience the transcendent (**Figure 6.4**). When we are surrounded by the artifacts of civilization, our minds usually stay fully focused on human purposes and our everyday lives. Religion probably would not disappear from an environment totally tamed by humans, but it might become diluted for many. Some of the most exciting conservation activities are those in which different communities come together, such as projects that link scientists, religious leaders, and recreational fishing groups (**Figure 6.5**).

> Maintaining the full diversity of life improves opportunities for scientific investigation and religious inspiration.

PROTECTING OUR LIFE-SUPPORT SYSTEMS AND OUR ECONOMY It cannot be repeated too often that biological diversity preserves our basic life-support systems of food production, water supply, oxygen replenishment, waste disposal, soil conservation, and more. People will be healthier and happier in a clean, intact environment. We depend on this and should value it. In addition to providing life-support, biodiversity allows us to create tremendous economic wealth, directly and indirectly, as detailed in Chapters 4 and 5.

For these reasons and more, degrading ecosystems and destroying species is almost always contrary to people's real interests. When it appears otherwise, that is usually because we are taking a short-term, selfish, or overly materialistic view of what those interests are (Norton 2003).

Deep Ecology

Recognition of both the economic value and the intrinsic value of biological diversity leads to new limits on human action. This can make it seem like conservation is simply a never-ending list of "thou shalt nots," but many environmentalists believe that an understanding of our true self-interest would lead to a different conclusion (Naess 1989):

> The crisis of life conditions on Earth could help us choose a new path with new criteria for progress, efficiency, and rational action. . . . The ideological change is mainly that of appreciating life quality rather than adhering to a high standard of living.

In the past 200 years, the Industrial Revolution, with its accompanying technological advances and social changes, has generated tremendous material wealth and improved the lives of millions of people. But the law of diminishing returns seems to apply: For many in the developed world, heaping up further wealth at the expense of life quality makes little sense (McKibben 2007; Ng 2008). This unsatisfying and unending pursuit of increasing material wealth has been termed **affluenza**. Similarly, the continued loss of biodiversity and taming of the natural landscape will not improve people's lives. What is being lost is unique and increasingly more precious as monetary wealth increases and opportunities to experience nature diminish. Human happiness and human development require preserving our remaining biodiversity, not sacrificing it for increased individual or corporate wealth.

During the last five decades, ecologists, nature writers, religious leaders, and philosophers have increasingly articulated an appreciation of nature and have spoken of the need for changes in human lifestyles in order to protect it. In the 1960s and 1970s, Paul Ehrlich and Barry Commoner demonstrated that professional biologists and academics could use their knowledge of environmental issues to create and lead political movements to protect nature. Former Vice President Al Gore has devoted himself to increasing public awareness of, and finding solutions to, global environmental problems. Today religious leaders are revitalizing their followers with calls to combine social activism with environmental protection. Political movements such as these, Green political parties, and activist conservation organizations such as Greenpeace and Earth First! exist throughout the world, with members numbering in the millions.

FIGURE 6.5 Different people and organizations appreciate nature for different reasons, such as this scientist, priest, and fisherman, but they can still work together to protect nature. (Photograph courtesy of Sudeep Chandra.)

One well-developed environmental philosophy that supports this activism is known as **deep ecology** (Barnhill et al. 2006; Naess 2008). Deep ecology builds on the basic premise of biocentric equality, which expresses "the intuition . . . that all things in the biosphere have an equal right to live and blossom and to reach their own individual forms of unfolding" (Devall and Sessions 1985). Humans have a right to live and thrive, as do the other organisms with whom we share the planet. Deep ecologists oppose what they see as the dominant worldview, which places human concerns above all and views human happiness in materialistic terms (**Table 6.1**).

> Deep ecology is an environmental philosophy that advocates placing greater value on protecting biodiversity through changes in personal attitude, life style, and even societies.

Deep ecologists see acceptance of the intrinsic value of nature less as a limitation than as an opportunity to live better lives. Because present human activities are destroying the Earth's biological diversity, existing political, economic, technological, and ideological structures must change. These changes entail enhancing the life quality of all people—emphasizing improvements in environmental quality, aesthetics, culture, and spirituality rather than higher levels of material consump-

TABLE 6.1 A Comparison of Beliefs of the Dominant Worldview and Those of Deep Ecology

Dominant worldview	Deep ecology
Humans dominating nature	Humans living in harmony with nature
Natural environment and species as resources for humans	All nature having intrinsic worth, regardless of human needs
A growing human population with a rising standard of living	A stable human population living simply
Earth providing unlimited resources	Earth providing limited resources that must be used carefully
Ever-higher technology bringing progress and solutions	Appropriate technology being used with respect for the Earth
Material progress as a goal	Spiritual and ethical progress as goals
Strong central government	Local control, organized according to ecosystems or bioregions

tion. Improving adult literacy; organizing active hiking, bird-watching, and natural history clubs; encouraging people to live healthier lifestyles; and lobbying to reduce air pollution and sprawling development are some practical examples. The philosophy of deep ecology includes an obligation to work to implement needed programs through political activism and a commitment to personal lifestyle changes, in the process transforming the institutions in which we work, study, pray, and shop (Bearzi 2009). Professional biologists, ecologists, and all concerned people (such as you?) are urged to escape from their narrow, everyday concerns and act and live "as if nature mattered" (Naess 1989).

Summary

1. Protecting biological diversity can be justified on ethical grounds as well as on economic grounds. The value systems of most religions, philosophies, and cultures provide justifications for preserving species. These justifications even support the protection of species that have no obvious economic or aesthetic value to people.

2. The most central ethical arguments assert that humans have a duty to protect species, biological communities, and other aspects of biodiversity based on their intrinsic value, unrelated to human needs. People do not have the right to destroy species and should take action to prevent their extinction.

3. Species, rather than individual organisms, are the appropriate target for conservation efforts; it is the species that evolves and undergoes speciation, whereas individuals are temporary representatives of the species.

4. Species interact in complex ways in biological communities. The loss of one species may have far-reaching negative consequences to that biological community and to human society.

5. People must learn to live within the ecological constraints of the planet, minimize environmental damage, and take responsibility for their actions, since they may harm humans as well as other species. People also have a responsibility to future generations to keep the Earth in good condition.

6. Protecting nature is in our enlightened self-interest. Biological diversity has provided generations of writers, artists, musicians, and religious thinkers with inspiration. A loss of species and natural areas cuts people off from this wellspring of creative experience and impoverishes human culture. It also curtails recreational enjoyment, scientific knowledge, and self-understanding.

7. Deep ecology is a philosophy that advocates major changes in the way society functions in order to protect biological diversity and promote genuine human growth. Advocates of this philosophy are committed to personal lifestyle changes and political activism.

For Discussion

1. Do living creatures, species, biological communities, and physical entities, such as rivers, lakes, and mountains, have rights? Can we treat them any way we please? Where should we draw the line of moral responsibility?

2. Do human beings have a duty toward individual animals, most of which lack self-awareness, and toward plants, which lack a nervous system? Toward species of plants and animals? Biological communities? Mountains and streams? If so, what is the source of this duty? What is the sort of protection or respectful use appropriate for each of these groups?

3. What roles do the consumption of resources, physical pleasure, the search for knowledge, artistic expression, recreation, and amusement play in your life? What roles should they play in human life in general? Does the preservation of biodiversity set limits on these human activities, or is it a prerequisite for our continued enjoyment of them?

4. What is your own environmental philosophy? What is the source of your ideas? Reason? Emotion? Faith? Does it affect your life in any important way? Is it easy or hard to live up to?

5. If your house were on fire, you would most likely try to rescue every family member inside. If even one person died, you would be devastated. Should we try to save every species threatened with extinction? Is the comparison valid?

6. Suppose the proposed management plan for one endangered species threatens the existence of a second endangered species. How can we decide on which course of action to take?

Suggested Readings

Bearzi, G. 2009. When swordfish conservation biologists eat swordfish. *Conservation Biology* 23: 1–2. Conservation biologists need to lead by personal example.

Cafaro, P. 2010. Economic growth or the flourishing of life: The ethical choice global climate change puts to humanity in the 21st century. *Essays in Philosophy* (online) 11(1), article 6. http://commons.pacificu.edu/eip/vol11/iss1/6. Global warming demands a rethinking of our fundamental economic goals.

Carson, R. L. 1965. *The Sense of Wonder*. Harper & Row, New York. Rachel Carson's final book urges adults to teach children about the natural world.

Gardiner, S., S. Caney, D. Jamieson, and H. Shue. 2010. *Climate Ethics: Essential Readings*. Oxford University Press, New York. Explores all aspects of climate ethics, including duties to future generations and to nonhuman species.

Justus, J., M. Coyvan, H. Regan, and L. Maguire. 2009. Buying into conservation: Intrinsic versus instrumental value. *Trends in Ecology and Evolution* 24: 187–191. Which is a better justification for preserving biodiversity?

Kahn, P. H., Jr. and S. R. Kellert (eds.). 2002. *Children and Nature: Psychological, Sociocultural, and Evolutionary Investigations*. The MIT Press, Cambridge, MA. Exposure to nature benefits children in many ways.

Leopold, A. 1949. *A Sand County Almanac and Sketches Here and There*. Oxford University Press, New York. Strong statement for the beauty and value of nature and the many benefits that accrue from protecting it.

McKibben, B. 2007. *Deep Economy: The Wealth of Communities and the Durable Future*. Henry Holt, New York. Eloquent argument that economic growth is neither sustainable nor improving our lives, with an exploration of alternatives.

Minteer, B. A. and J. P. Collins. 2005. Ecological ethics: Building a new tool kit for ecologists and biodiversity managers. *Conservation Biology* 19: 1803–1812. Ethical issues arise when managers need to control nonnative animal populations.

Moseley, L. (ed.). 2009. *Holy Ground: A Gathering of Voices on Caring for Creation*. Sierra Club Books, San Francisco. Religious leaders from many faiths find common cause in nature preservation.

Naess, A. (au.), A. Drengson, and B. Devall (eds.). 2008. *The Ecology of Wisdom: Writings by Arne Naess*. Counterpoint, Berkeley, CA. Essays by an influential thinker and a founder of the deep ecology movement.

Rolston, H., III. 1994. *Conserving Natural Value*. Columbia University Press, New York. A leading environmental philosopher lays out the ethical arguments for preserving biodiversity.

Sandler, R. 2007. *Character and Environment: A Virtue-Oriented Approach to Environmental Ethics*. Columbia University Press, New York. Discusses how we can change to create sustainable societies and preserve nature.

Swanson, F. J., C. Goodrich, and K. D. Moore. 2008. Bridging boundaries: Scientists, creative writers, and the long view of the forest. *Frontiers in Ecology and the Environment* 6: 499–504. Synergies result from communication between conservation biologists and creative people in other fields.

Teel, T. T. and M. J. Manfredo. 2010. Understanding the diversity of public interests in wildlife conservation. *Conservation Biology* 24: 128–139. The public has diverse attitudes toward wildlife that can impact government conservation efforts.

Thoreau, H. D. 1854. *Walden; or, Life in the Woods*. Ticknor and Fields, Boston. More than 150 years after its publication, still an eloquent personal statement for protecting nature.

Woodhams, D. C. 2009. Converting the religious: Putting amphibian conservation in context. *BioScience* 59: 463–464. Conservationists need to form a common cause with the religious community.

THREATS TO BIOLOGICAL DIVERSITY

Extinction

We live at a historic moment, a time in which the world's biological diversity is being rapidly destroyed. The present geological period has more species than any other, yet the current rate of extinction of species is greater now than at any time in the past million years (Mace 2005; Wake and Vredenburg 2008). Ecosystems and communities are being degraded and destroyed, and species are being driven to extinction. The species that persist are losing genetic variation as the numbers of individuals in populations shrink, unique populations and subspecies are destroyed, and remaining populations become increasingly isolated from one another.

The cause of this loss of biological diversity at all levels is the range of human activity that alters and destroys natural habitats to suit human needs. At present, approximately half of the net primary productivity of the terrestrial environment—roughly one-fourth of the total primary productivity of the world—is used or wasted in some way by people (Haberl et al. 2007). Genetic variation is being lost even in domesticated species, such as wheat, corn, rice, chickens, cattle, and pigs, as farmers abandon traditional agriculture. In the United States, about 97% of the vegetable varieties that were once cultivated

FIGURE 7.1 The Monteverde golden toad (*Bufo periglenes*) from Costa Rica was officially declared extinct in 2004 after repeated searches had failed to find any living individuals. (Courtesy of Charles H. Smith, U.S. Fish and Wildlife Service.)

are now extinct (Veteto 2008). In tropical countries, farmers are abandoning their local varieties in favor of high-yielding varieties for commercial sale. This loss of variability among food plants and animals and its implications for world agriculture are discussed further in Chapters 14 and 20.

E. O. Wilson, one of the leading advocates of conservation biology, has argued that the most serious aspect of environmental damage is the extinction of species. Biological communities can be degraded and reduced in area, and their value to people lessened, but as long as all of the original species survive, communities retain the potential to recover. Similarly, genetic variation within a species is reduced when population size drops, but species can regain genetic variation through mutation, natural selection, and recombination. Unfortunately, once a species is eliminated, the unique genetic information contained in its DNA and the special combination of characters that it possesses are forever lost—its populations cannot be restored, the communities that it inhabited become impoverished, and its potential value to humans will never be realized.

The word *extinct* has many nuances, and its meaning can vary somewhat depending on the context. A species is **extinct** when no member of the species remains alive anywhere in the world: "The Monteverde golden toad is extinct" (**Figure 7.1**). If individuals of a species remain alive only in captivity or in other human-controlled situations, the species is said to be **extinct in the wild**: "The Franklin tree is extinct in the wild but grows well under cultivation." In both of these situations the species are also considered to be **globally extinct**. A species is **locally extinct**, or **extirpated**, when it is no longer found in an area it once inhabited but is still found elsewhere in the wild: "The gray wolf once occurred throughout North America; it is now locally extinct in Massachusetts." A species may also be considered **regionally extinct** if it is extinct in a country or region but still persists in another part of its range. Some conservation biologists speak of a species as being **ecologically extinct** if it persists at such reduced numbers that its effects on the other species in its community are negligible (McConkey and Drake 2006): "Tigers are ecologically extinct because so few remain in the wild that their impact on prey populations is insignificant." In order to successfully maintain species, conservation biologists must identify the human activities that affect the stability of populations and drive species to extinction.

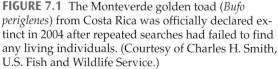

The current rate of species loss is unprecedented and irreversible. The loss of local populations, genetic variation, and ecosystems is also cause for the utmost concern.

Past Mass Extinctions

The diversity of species found on the Earth has been increasing since life first originated. This increase has not been steady; rather, it has been characterized by periods of high rates of speciation followed by periods of minimal change and episodes of mass extinction (Ward 2004). This pattern is visible in the fossil record, which has been examined by scientists interested in determining the number of species and families in particular geological periods.

The evolutionary history of marine animals is better studied than that of terrestrial organisms because marine animals often have hard body parts that are preserved in rocks formed from marine sediments. Marine animals first arose about 600 million years ago during the Paleozoic era. According to the fossil record, new families of marine animals appeared in rapid and steady succession during the next 150 million years. For the 200 million years that followed, the number of families was more or less constant at about 400, and then declined sharply to around 200

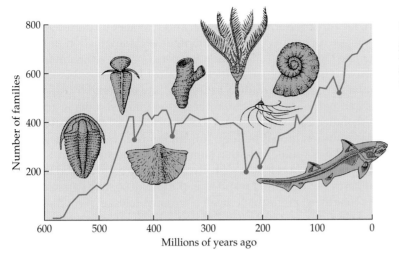

FIGURE 7.2 The number of families of marine organisms has been gradually increasing over geological time; this graph of their history clearly shows evidence of five episodes of mass extinction. (After Wilson 1989.)

families. For the last 250 million years of the Mesozoic and Cenozoic eras, the diversity of families steadily increased to its present number of over 700 families (**Figure 7.2**). The fossil record of marine animals demonstrates the slow pace of evolution, with the number of families increasing at a rate of roughly 2 per million years.

In addition to this overall increase in the number of animal families, there have been five episodes of mass extinction in the fossil record, occurring at intervals ranging from 60 to 155 million years (**Figure 7.3**). These episodes, which occurred dur-

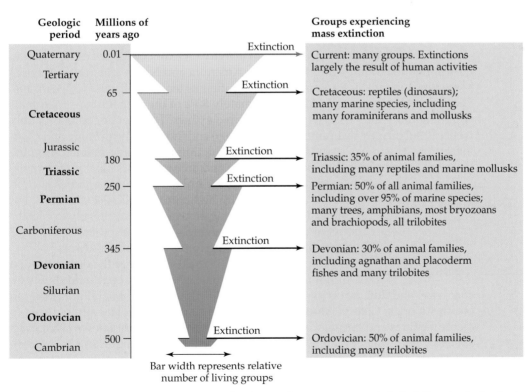

FIGURE 7.3 Although the total number of families and species of organisms has increased over the eons, during each of five episodes of natural mass extinction, a large percentage of these groups disappeared. The most dramatic period of loss occurred about 250 million years ago, at the end of the Permi-an period. A sixth episode, beginning about 30,000 years ago and continuing up to the present time, incorporates the effects of hunting and habitat loss as human populations have spread across the continents.

ing the Ordovician, Devonian, Permian, Triassic, and Cretaceous periods, could be called "natural mass extinctions." The most famous is the extinction of the dinosaurs during the late Cretaceous, 65 million years ago, after which mammals achieved dominance in terrestrial communities. The most massive extinction took place at the end of the Permian, 250 million years ago, when about 95% of all marine animal species and half of the animal families are estimated to have gone extinct (Wake and Vredenburg 2008). David Raup (1979) observed: "If these estimates are even reasonably accurate, global biology (for higher organisms at least) had an extremely close call." It is quite likely that some massive perturbation, such as widespread volcanic eruptions, a collision with an asteroid, or both, caused the dramatic change in the Earth's climate that resulted in the end of so many species. Another speculation is that there might have been a massive release of methane gas from beneath the ocean floor—a "big burp," if you will. Such an event not only would have released toxic plumes but almost certainly would have affected the climate, since methane is an even more potent greenhouse gas than carbon dioxide. It took about 80–100 million years of evolution for Earth's biota to regain the number of families lost during the Permian extinction.

The Current, Human-Caused Mass Extinction

The global diversity of species reached an all-time high in the present geological period. The most advanced groups of organisms—insects, vertebrates, and flowering plants—reached their greatest diversity about 30,000 years ago. Since that time, however, species richness has slowly decreased as one species has asserted its dominance. Humans have increasingly altered terrestrial and aquatic environments, at the expense of other species, in their need to consume natural resources. We are presently in the midst of a *sixth extinction episode*, this one caused by human activities rather than a natural disaster (Mace et al. 2005; Wake and Vredenburg 2008).

The first noticeable effects of human activity on extinction rates can be seen in the elimination of large mammals from Australia and North and South America at the time humans first colonized these continents tens of thousands of years ago. Shortly after humans arrived, approximately 80% of the megafauna—mammals weighing more than 44 kg (100 lb)—became extinct. These extinctions probably were caused directly by hunting (Johnson 2009) and indirectly by burning and clearing of forests and grasslands and the introduction of invasive species and new diseases. On all continents, paleontologists and archaeologists have found an extensive record of prehistoric human alteration and destruction of habitat coinciding with high rates of species extinctions. For example, deliberate burning of savannas, presumably to encourage plant growth for browsing wildlife and thereby improve hunting, has been occurring for 50,000 years in Africa.

> Many large mammal species became extinct when people arrived to each of the continents. These extinctions were almost certainly caused by human activity.

In the roughly 10,000 to 12,000 years since the domestication of herd animals such as goats, sheep, and cattle and of wheat, corn, rice, and other crop plants, the total area of natural grassland and forest in North America, Central America, Europe, and Asia has been steadily reduced to create pastures and farmlands to supply human needs. It is not known what exact species went extinct because of these landscape alterations, but these changes almost certainly had a significant impact upon wild species, just as they do today.

Extinction rates during the last 2000 years are best known for land vertebrates, especially birds and mammals, because these species are conspicuous, that is, relatively large and well studied. Scientists have noted when these species have no longer been found in the wild (**Table 7.1**). Extinction rates for the other 99% of the world's species are just rough guesses at present. However, extinction rates are un-

TABLE 7.1 Some Species That Have Gone Extinct from 1984 to 2006

Species	Common name	Date of extinction	Place of extinction
Amphibians			
Atelopus ignescens	Jambato toad	1988 (last record)	Ecuador
Bufo baxteri	Wyoming toad	Mid 1990s[a]	United States
Bufo periglenes	Golden toad	1989 (last record)	Costa Rica
Incilius holdridgei	Holdridge's toad	1986 (last record)	Costa Rica
Rheobatrachus vitellinus	Northern gastric brooding frog	1985 (last record)	Australia
Cynops wolterstorffi	Yunnan Lake newt	1986 (last record)	China
Birds			
Corvus hawaiiensis	Hawaiian crow	2002[a]	Hawaiian Islands
Crax mitu	Alagoas curassow	Late 1980s	Brazil
Cyanopsitta spixii	Spix's macaw	2000 (last record)	Brazil
Gallirallus owstoni	Guam rail	1987[a]	Guam
Melamprosops phaeosoma	Black-faced honeycreeper	2004 (last record)	Hawaiian Islands
Moho braccatus	Kaua'i	1987 (last report of vocalizations)	Hawaiian Islands
Myadestes myadestinus	Kama'o	2004	Hawaiian Islands
Podilymbus gigas	Atitlán grebe	1986	Guatemala
Mammals			
Diceros bicornis longipes	West African black rhinoceros	2006	Cameroon
Oryx dammah	Scimitar-horned oryx	1996[a]	Chad
Plants			
Argyroxiphium virescens	Silversword	1996	Hawaiian Islands
Commidendrum rotundifolium	Bastard gumwood	1986[a]	St. Helena Island
Nesiota elliptica	St. Helena olive	2003	St. Helena Island

Source: IUCN 2009 (www.iucnredlist.org).
[a]Species still exists in captivity.

certain even for birds and mammals because some species that were considered extinct have been rediscovered. For example, the Australian night parrot (*Pezoporus occidentalis*) was last seen in 1912 and presumed extinct before being rediscovered in 1979. Sometimes it is difficult to determine whether a species truly is extinct. In 2004, for example, ornithologists in North America dramatically announced the sighting of an ivory-billed woodpecker (*Campephilus principalis*) in an Arkansas swamp forest—decades after this bird was believed to have gone extinct. Since then, however, intensive efforts to find and conclusively identify existing individuals of the species have been unsuccessful (Stokstad 2007). It is also true that species presumed to be **extant** (still living) may actually be extinct; the Yangtze river dolphin (*Lipotes vexillifer*), for example, has not been officially declared extinct, but no individuals were found during an extensive survey in 2006. For many species, scientists have not revisited the remote sites where they occur, to determine if they still exist. In addition, in the last four centuries, many species may have existed and gone extinct before we even discovered them.

How has human activity affected extinction rates in more recent times? One set of estimates based on the best available evidence indicates, for example, that about 77 species of mammals and 129 species of birds have become extinct since the year

FIGURE 7.4 Rates of extinctions of birds during 25-year intervals since 1500. Extinction rates have been increasing from 1650 to the present. Initial extinctions were on islands, but extinctions of mainland species have been increasing since 1800. (After Baillie et al. 2004.)

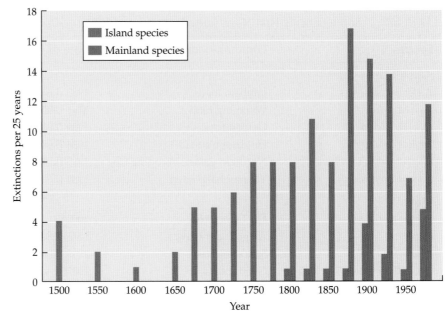

1600, representing 1.6% of known mammal species and 1.3% of known birds* (Baillie et al. 2004). While these numbers may not seem alarming initially, the trend of these extinction rates is on the rise, with the majority of extinctions occurring in the last 150 years (**Figure 7.4**). The extinction rate for birds was about 0 to 5 species every 25 years during the period from 1500 to 1725, but it rose to 8 to 12 species every 25 years from 1750 to 1850. After 1850, the extinction rate rose again to more than 16 species every 25 years. This increase in the rate of extinction indicates the seriousness of the threat to biological diversity. One trend to note is that all of the early extinctions were on islands. However, extinctions of birds in mainland areas were first observed about 1800, and they have been increasing since then. Some of these species are extinct in the wild but still remain alive in captivity. In the future, mainland species will be an increasing proportion of future extinctions.

The apparent decline in extinction rates since 1950 (see Figure 7.4) is due to the current practice of not declaring a species extinct until decades after any individuals of the species can no longer be found. In the coming years, numerous species will be declared extinct during the 1950–2000 period. In the last few years, a number of species not found despite intensive searches were finally declared extinct, including the Spix's macaw (2004) and the Hawaiian crow (2004). People have been looking for the golden toad of Costa Rica since 1989 without success. Also, Miss Waldron's red colobus monkey (*Procolobus badius waldroni*) was reported extinct from Ghana and Côte d'Ivoire, the first extinction of a primate in the last 100 years (Oates et al. 2000). Many species not yet listed as extinct—and some that have not yet been documented at all—have been decimated by human activities and persist only in very low numbers. Our inability to locate any extant populations of many rare species provides further evidence that extinction rates are accelerating.

Although for many species it is true that a few individuals in scattered small populations might persist for years, decades, or centuries (for woody plants in particular, isolated individuals can persist for hundreds of years), their ultimate fate is

---

*Only about 60 species of insects are known to have gone extinct, roughly 0.001% of the number of species in this taxon. However, this extremely low reported extinction rate is principally due to the poor state of our knowledge of this large group; many species may have gone extinct without scientists ever having been aware that they existed.

FIGURE 7.5 St. Helena ebony (*Trochetiopsis ebenus*) is endemic to the island of St. Helena in the southern Atlantic Ocean. The wild population has been reduced to just two individuals on the side of a cliff. Because of such low numbers, this species will almost certainly go extinct in the wild. The species will still remain alive in cultivation. (Photograph © fotoFlora/Alamy.)

extinction. Remaining individuals of species that are doomed to extinction following habitat destruction have been called "the living dead" or "committed to extinction" (**Figure 7.5**) (Gentry 1986; Janzen 2001). There are certainly many species in this category in the remaining fragments of forest in species-rich locations such as Madagascar and the Atlantic Forest of Brazil (Ferraz et al. 2003). Though technically such species are not extinct while these individuals live, the populations are no longer reproductively viable, hence the future of these species is limited to the life spans of the remaining individuals. Evidence from forest fragments and parks indicates that, following the destruction of the surrounding habitat, species diversity of vertebrates may actually show a temporary increase as animals flee into the few remaining patches of forest (Laurance 2007b). However, the number of species falls over the next few weeks, months, and years as species begin to go extinct on a local scale and are not replaced by other species. The predicted eventual loss of species following habitat destruction and fragmentation is called the **extinction debt** (Kuussaari et al. 2009). For example, it is estimated that 9% of Madagascar's species will eventually go extinct in coming decades and centuries because of the forest destruction that has already occurred (Allnutt et al. 2008).

Extinction rates will remain high in the coming century because of the large number of threatened species. About 12% of the world's remaining bird species are threatened with extinction. Mammal species are in even greater danger, with 27% of species under threat; 36% of amphibians are threatened (www.iucnredlist.org). **Table 7.2** shows certain animal groups for which the danger is even more severe, such as three orders that include turtles, manatees, and rhinos. Plant species are also at risk, with gymnosperms (conifers, ginkgos, and cycads) and palms among the especially vulnerable groups. For most species in the less well-known groups, such as fungi, fishes, and insects, the overall extinction risk has still not been determined. Extinction levels in marine species are much less studied than in terrestrial species. The scale of the threat to marine species has been highlighted by a recent survey suggesting that about one-third of coral species are at risk of extinction (Carpenter et al. 2008).

The threat of extinction is greater for some groups of species than for others (see Chapter 8). Some groups are especially vulnerable for a combination of reasons, including high levels of human exploitation. For example, 12 of the world's 23 crocodile and alligator species face extinction, not only because their habitat is

TABLE 7.2 Numbers of Species Threatened with Extinction in Major Groups of Animals and Plants			
Group	Approximate number of species	Number of species threatened with extinction	Percentage of species threatened with extinction
Vertebrate Animals			
Fishes	28,000	1722	6[a]
Amphibians	6248	2279	36
Reptiles	8240	622	8[a]
Crocodiles	23	12	52
Turtles	205	175	85
Birds	9865	2065	21
Anseriformes (waterfowl)	161	37	23
Petrels and albatrosses	128	74	58
Mammals	5414	1464	27
Primates	413	224	54
Manatees, dugongs	4	4	100
Horses, tapirs, rhinos	16	14	88
Plants			
Gymnosperms	18,000	727	4[a]
Angiosperms (flowering plants)	260,000	9115	4[a]
Palms	356	293	82
Fungi	100,000	3	0[a]

Source: Data from IUCN 2009 (www.iucnredlist.org).
[a]Low percentages reflect inadequate data due to the small number of species evaluated.

disappearing, but also because they are overhunted for their meat and skins. About 54% of the world's primate species and 58% of the petrel and albatross species are threatened with extinction for similar and additional reasons. Throughout the world, large cat species (family Felidae) are hunted for sport, for their fur, and because they are perceived to be a threat to domestic animals and people. Slipper orchids, which have restrictive habitat requirements, are overharvested by plant collectors. In Europe, more mollusks have gone extinct than birds, mammals, reptiles, and amphibians together (Bouchet et al. 1999).

> Many species today are represented only by scattered populations, each consisting of a few individuals. Although these isolated populations could persist for years or decades, the ultimate fate of such species is extinction.

In most past geological periods, the extinction of existing species was balanced or exceeded by the evolution of new species. However, the present rate of human-caused extinction far surpasses the known rate of evolution. The known examples of recent rapid evolution—fruit flies adapting to localized environments, or plants rapidly acquiring new characteristics when their chromosomes double during a peculiarity in meiosis—usually do not produce new families or orders. These unique evolutionary events require thousands of generations on a timescale over hundreds of thousands, if not millions, of years. The famous naturalist William Beebe said, "[W]hen the last individual of any race of living things breathes no more, another heaven and another earth must pass before such a one can be again."

Background Extinction Rates

To better understand how calamitous present extinction rates are, it is useful to compare them to the natural extinction rates that would prevail regardless of human activity. What is the natural rate of extinction in the absence of human influence? Natural "background" extinction rates can be estimated by looking at the fossil record. In the fossil record, an individual species lasts about 1 to 10 million years before it goes extinct or evolves into a new species (Mace et al. 2005; Pimm and Jenkins 2005). Since there are perhaps 10 million species on the Earth today, we can predict that 1 to 10 of the world's species would be lost per year as a result of a natural extinction rate of 0.0001% to 0.00001% per year. These estimates are derived from studies of wide-ranging marine animals, so they may be lower than natural extinction rates for species of narrow distribution, which are more vulnerable to habitat disturbance; however, they do appear to be applicable

> Ninety-nine percent of current extinctions are caused in some way by human activities.

for terrestrial mammals. The current observed rate of extinction of birds and mammals of 1% per century (or 0.01% per year) is 100 to 1000 times greater than would be predicted based on background rates of extinction. Putting it another way, about 100 species of birds and mammals were observed to go extinct between 1850 and 1950, but the natural rate of extinction would have predicted that, at most, only 1 species would have gone extinct. Therefore, the other 99 extinctions can be attributed to the effects of human activity.

Some scientists have sharply questioned the accuracy of these estimates, saying that they are based on unfounded assumptions, such as the validity of comparing animals known from fossils with living animals and the validity of comparing marine mammals and terrestrial animals (Regan et al. 2001). However, even using a much more conservative approach with the available data, Regan and colleagues came up with a modern extinction rate that is still 36 to 78 times the background rate. Despite questions about the exact rates, no one disagrees that current extinction rates are far above background levels and that they are caused by human activity.

Extinction Rates on Islands

It should not come as a surprise that the highest species extinction rates during historic times have occurred on islands. Island species often have limited areas, small population sizes, and small numbers of populations (Régnier et al. 2009; Clavero et al. 2009). The high extinction rates on islands include the extinctions of birds, mammals, and reptiles during the last 350 years of European colonization. Furthermore, numerous endemic plants of oceanic islands are extinct or in danger of extinction. (Endemic species—species found in one place and nowhere else—are particularly vulnerable to extinction; they are discussed in more detail in Chapter 8.)

Island species usually have evolved and undergone speciation with a limited number of competitors, predators, and diseases, and often have a high percentage of endemic species (**Table 7.3**). When predatory species from the mainland are introduced onto islands, they frequently decimate the endemic island species, which have not evolved any defenses against them (**Box 7.1**; see also Chapter 8). Species extinction rates peak soon after humans occupy an island and then decline after the most vulnerable species are eliminated (**Figure 7.6**). In general, the longer an island has been occupied by people, the greater the percentage of extinct biota. Island plant species are also threatened, mainly through habitat destruction. In Madagascar, 72% of the 9000 plant species are endemic, and 189 species are threatened with extinction. The numerous lemur species) are also endemic to Madagascar, and most of these unique primates are threatened.

FIGURE 7.6 The proportion of recently extinct (that is, since the arrival of Europeans) or currently endangered bird species decreases the longer non-European peoples have occupied an island group. This probably means that most sensitive species have already disappeared from those islands with long histories of human occupation. Hawaii has been occupied for a shorter time and has a high percentage of extinct and endangered species, such as the critically endangered black-faced honeycreeper. The seeming anomaly of the high rate of recent extinctions in the Marianas group is due to the devastation caused by the recent introduction of the brown tree snake (see Chapter 10). (After Pimm et al. 1995.)

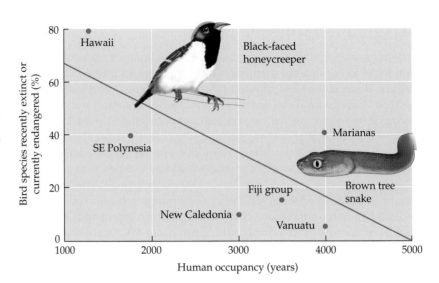

Island species have had higher rates of extinction than mainland species. Freshwater species are more vulnerable to extinction than marine species.

European colonization of islands has sometimes been more destructive than colonization by other peoples, because European colonization includes greater amounts of clearing and the wholesale introduction of nonnative species. For instance, between 1840 and 1880, more than 60 species of vertebrates, particularly grazing animals such as sheep, were deliberately introduced into Australia, where they displaced native species and altered many communities. In the 1500s, the first European visitors to the Mascarene Islands (Mauritius, Réunion, and Rodrigues) in the Indian Ocean east of Madagascar released monkeys and pigs. These animals, and subsequent hunting and colonization by Dutch settlers, led to the extinction of the dodo bird, 19 other species of birds, and 8 species of reptiles. The impact of introduced predators on island species is highlighted by the example of the flightless Stephen Island wren, a bird that was endemic to a tiny island off New Zealand. Every Stephen Island wren on the island was killed by a single cat that belonged to the lighthouse keeper. Even one introduced predator can eliminate an entire species.

The vulnerability of island species is further illustrated by the comparison of the number of species that have gone extinct in mainland areas, on islands, and in the oceans from 1600 to the present. Of the 726 species of animals and plants known to have gone extinct, 351 (about half of the total) were island species, even though islands represent only a small fraction of the Earth's surface (Baillie et al. 2004). Despite the documented danger to island species, however, in the coming decades a higher proportion of extinctions will occur in continental lowlands where many species occur and where human alteration of the landscape is rapid and extensive.

Extinction Rates in Aquatic Environments

In contrast with the large amount of information we have on extinct terrestrial species, there are no documented cases of marine fish or coral species that have gone extinct during the last few thousand years. Only about 14 species—four marine mammals, five marine birds, one fish, and four mollusks—are known to have gone extinct in the world's vast oceans during historic times (Régnier et al. 2009). This number of extinctions is almost certainly an underestimate, since marine species are not nearly as well known as terrestrial species (Edgar et al. 2005), but it may reflect a greater resiliency of marine species in response to disturbance. However,

TABLE 7.3 Number of Native Plant Species and Those Species That Are Endemic (Found There and Nowhere Else) for Various Islands and Island Groups

Island(s)	Native species	Endemic species	Percentage endemic
United Kingdom	1500	16	1
Solomon Islands	2780	30	1
Sri Lanka	3000	890	30
Jamaica	2746	923	33
Philippines	8000	3500	44
Cuba	6004	3229	54
Fiji	1307	760	58
Madagascar	9000	6500	72
New Zealand	2160	1942	90
Australia	15,000	14,074	94

Source: Data from WRI 1998.

BOX 7.1   *Invasive Species and Extinction in Island Ecosystems*

■ Evolutionary radiation from relatively few colonizing species can produce an array of new species in isolated island archipelagoes, such as has been seen in the Hawaiian Islands and the Galápagos (see Chapter 2). An extreme instance of this type of rapid evolution occurred in Hawaii, where one or two colonizing species of fruit fly evolved into more than 800 different species (Howarth 1990). In addition to their unusual diversity, island ecosystems have particular value for evolutionary biologists as natural laboratories for the study of evolution. Charles Darwin's observation of finches in the Galápagos—observation from which he developed and supported his theory of the origin of new species—is a classic study of the rapid speciation common to islands. While both archipelagoes have high percentages of endemic species, Hawaii has more species and a greater overall biodiversity due to its greater age, wetter climate, and more diverse topography.

Unfortunately, the same factors that make these island ecosystems so unique biologically also leave them particularly vulnerable to invasions by exotic species, in addition to habitat destruction and overexploitation. In Hawaii, an initial wave of introductions, including Polynesian pigs, dogs, Polynesian rats, and a variety of plants, accompanied the colonization of the islands by the Polynesians approximately 1300 years ago. At present, paleontologists have documented at least 62 species of birds that became extinct after the arrival of the Polynesians. Since the arrival of Europeans in 1778, the introduction of black rats, domestic non-Polynesian pigs, cats, sheep, horses, cattle, goats, mongooses, and an estimated 2000 species of arthropods have caused further declines and extinctions among birds,

insects, and plants in Hawaii. In addition, numerous plant species brought to the islands have become naturalized, often outcompeting endemic taxa. The impact of exotic species and habitat destruction has been so severe and the area occupied by many native species is so small that Hawaii has the dubious distinction of having more recorded species extinctions than the entire rest of the United States.

Invasive species are a major threat to island species. Controlling such invasive species is a conservation priority, and can result in the recovery of endemic species.

Until recently, the overall inhospitality of the arid, rocky Galápagos resulted in far less human colonization and impact than in Hawaii. Nonetheless, introduced goats, cattle, and pigs are now the primary culprits in the decline of many endemic plant species; populations of goats on some islands are as high as 80,000, a number far in excess of what native plant species can withstand. Pigs consume the eggs of iguanas and turtles, including those of the endangered Pacific green turtle, which nests on the islands. Introduced cultivated plants that have escaped into the wild, including guava (*Psidium guajava*) and raspberries (*Rubus niveus*), crowd out many native species. The number of introduced plant species continues to increase and is strongly correlated with the rise in the human population. Even Darwin's famous finches are in decline, with several species having already gone extinct (Grant et al. 2005). The government of Ecuador, which has jurisdiction over the

(continued)

BOX 7.1 (*continued*)

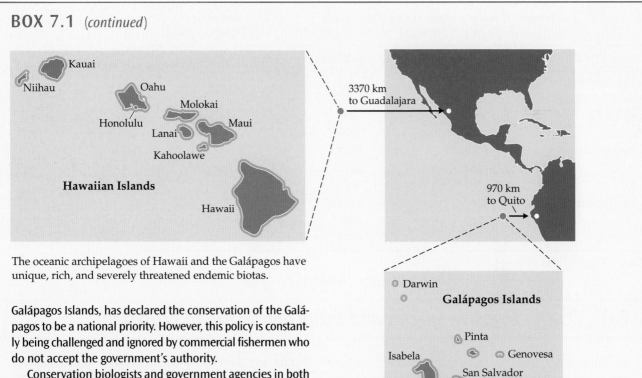

The oceanic archipelagoes of Hawaii and the Galápagos have unique, rich, and severely threatened endemic biotas.

Galápagos Islands, has declared the conservation of the Galápagos to be a national priority. However, this policy is constantly being challenged and ignored by commercial fishermen who do not accept the government's authority.

Conservation biologists and government agencies in both archipelagoes are trying to eradicate some of the more prominent and destructive invasive species, particularly introduced mammals (Cruz 2007). The hunting and removal of feral goats, pigs, and other ungulates is actively underway, while domestic stock is kept closely penned. The Galápagos rail has started to recover, following the removal and control of such invasive mammals (Donlan et al. 2007). Introduced herbs and trees are being eliminated in some places by herbicide sprays, felling, and burning. Over 75% of the management costs for Hawaii's protected areas are spent on the control of exotic species. Control of invasive insects and other invertebrates and many herbaceous weeds is often far more difficult be-

cause their small size makes detection difficult. Now that the problem of invasive species has been identified, the respective governments and conservation organizations are actively managing areas of the islands to protect, restore, and enlarge the original biological communities that remain.

(A)  (B)

(A) Native vegetation in the Galápagos can only persist inside of a fenced-off area where grazing by introduced goats and pigs has been excluded. (B) When goats and pigs are removed, the native vegetation can begin to recover outside of the fenced-off area. (Courtesy of Josh Donlan et al. 2007.)

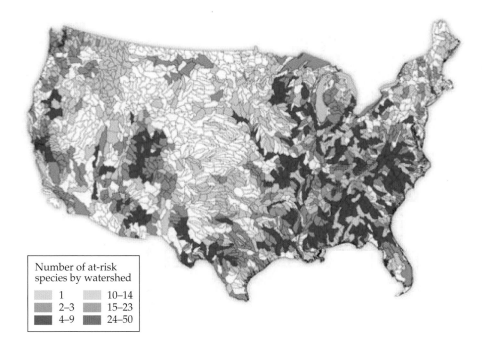

FIGURE 7.7 Number of fish and mussel species threatened with extinction in the United States, by individual watershed. The largest numbers of threatened species are in the southern Appalachian Mountains, with other concentrations in the Ozark Mountains of Arkansas and Missouri, Indiana, and southern Alabama. The major threats are from dams, irrigation systems, polluted runoff from industry and agriculture, introduced species, and habitat destruction. The most threatened species are in the places with the most species and the most human impact. (From Master et al. 1998.)

the significance of these losses may be greater than the numbers suggest. Many marine mammals are top predators, and their loss could have a major impact on marine communities. Some marine species are the sole species of their genus, family, or even order, so the extinction of even a few of them can possibly represent a serious loss to global biological diversity. The oceans were once considered so enormous that it seemed unlikely that marine species could go extinct; many people still share this viewpoint. However, as marine coastal waters become more polluted and species are harvested more intensely, even the vast oceans will not provide safety from extinction (Jackson 2008). Many species of whales and of large fish have declined by 90% or more because of overharvesting and other human activities and are in danger of extinction.

Also in contrast to terrestrial extinctions, the majority of freshwater fish extinctions have occurred in mainland areas rather than on islands, because of the vastly greater number of species in mainland waters. In North America, over one-third of freshwater fish species are in danger of extinction (Moyle and Cech 2004). The fish of California are particularly vulnerable because of the state's scarcity of water and its intense development—10% of California's 67 types of native fish are already extinct, and 58% are in danger of extinction. Large numbers of fish and aquatic invertebrates, such as mollusks, are in danger of extinction in the southeastern United States due to dams, pollution, irrigation projects, invasion of alien species, and general habitat damage (**Figure 7.7**).

Estimating Extinction Rates with the Island Biogeography Model

Studies of island communities have led to general rules on the distribution of biological diversity, synthesized as the **island biogeography model** by MacArthur and Wilson (1967). This model can be used to estimate future extinction rates, as we will see later in this section. The central observation that this model was built to explain is the **species–area relationship**: Islands with large areas have more species than islands with smaller areas (**Figure 7.8**). This rule makes intuitive sense because a large island will tend to have a greater variety of local environments and community

FIGURE 7.8 The number of species on an island can be predicted from the area of an island. In this figure, the number of species of reptiles and amphibians is shown for each of seven islands in the West Indies. The numbers of species on large islands such as Cuba and Hispaniola far exceeds those on the tiny islands of Saba and Redonda. (After Wilson 1989.)

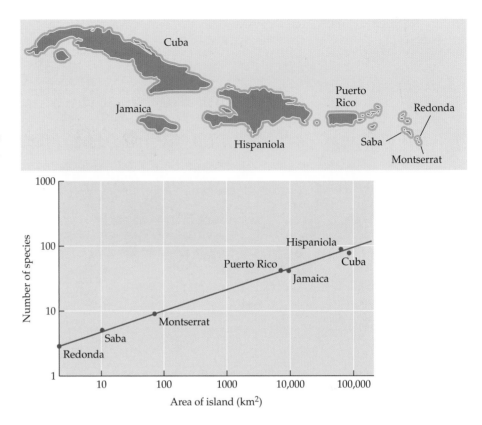

types than a small island. Also, large islands allow greater geographical isolation, a larger number of populations per species, and larger sizes of individual populations, increasing the likelihood of speciation and decreasing the probability of local extinction of newly evolved as well as recently arrived species. The species–area relationship can be accurately summarized by the empirical formula

$$S = CA^Z$$

where S is the number of species on an island, A is the area of the island, and C and Z are constants. The exponent Z determines the slope of the curve. The values for C and Z will depend on the types of islands being compared (tropical vs. temperate, dry vs. wet, etc.) and the types of species involved (birds vs. reptiles, etc.). Z values are typically about 0.25, with a range from 0.15 to 0.35 (Connor and McCoy 2001). Island species of restricted ranges, such as reptiles and amphibians, tend to have Z values near 0.35, while widespread mainland species tend to have Z values closer to 0.15. Values of C will be high in groups such as insects that are high in species numbers, and they will be low in groups such as birds that are low in species numbers.

The model has been empirically validated to the point of acceptance by most biologists (Quammen 1996; Triantis et al. 2008; Chen 2009): for numerous groups of plants and animals, it has been found to describe reasonably well the observed richness of species, explaining about half of the variation in numbers of species. Imagine the simplest situation, in which $C = 1$ and $Z = 0.25$, for raptorial birds on a hypothetical archipelago:

$$S = (1)A^{0.25}$$

The formula predicts that islands of 10, 100, 1000, and 10,000 km² in area would have 2, 3, 6, and 10 species, respectively. It is important to note that a tenfold in-

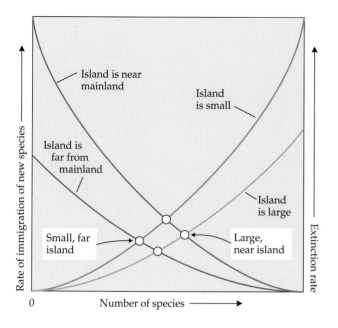

FIGURE 7.9 The island biogeography model describes the relationship between the rates of colonization and extinction on islands. The immigration rates (blue and red curves) on unoccupied islands are initially high, as species with good dispersal abilities rapidly take advantage of the available open habitats. The immigration rates slow as the number of species increases and sites become occupied. The extinction rates (green and gold curves) increase with the number of species on the island; the more species on an island, the greater the likelihood that a species will go extinct at any time interval. Colonization rates will be highest for islands near a mainland population source, since species can disperse over shorter distances more easily than longer ones. Extinction rates are highest on small islands, where both population sizes and habitat diversity are low. The number of species present on an island reaches equilibrium when the colonization rate equals the extinction rate (circles). The equilibrium number of species is greatest on large islands near the mainland and lowest on small islands far from the mainland. (After MacArthur and Wilson 1967.)

crease in island area does not result in a tenfold increase in the number of species; with this equation, each tenfold increase in island area increases the number of species by a factor of approximately 2. Actual data from three Caribbean islands can be used to illustrate the relationship: with increasing area, St. Nevis (93 km²), Puerto Rico (8959 km²), and Cuba (114,524 km²) have 2, 10, and 57 species of anolis lizard, respectively; with a C of 0.5 and a Z of 0.35, the islands would be predicted to have 2, 12, and 30 species, respectively.

In their classic text, MacArthur and Wilson (1967) hypothesized that the number of species occurring on an island represents a dynamic equilibrium between the arrival of new species (and also the evolution of new species) and the extinction rate of existing species. Starting with an unoccupied island, the number of species will increase over time, since more species will be arriving (or evolving) than are going extinct, until the rates of extinction and immigration are balanced (**Figure 7.9**). The arrival rates will be higher for large islands than small islands because large islands represent larger targets for dispersing animals to find and are more likely to have suitable open habitat available for colonization. The extinction rates will be lower on large islands than small islands because large islands have greater habitat diversity and greater numbers of populations. The rates of immigration of new species will be higher for islands near the mainland than for islands farther away, since mainland species are able to disperse to near islands more easily than to distant islands. The model predicts that for any group of organisms, such as birds or orchids, the number of species found on a large island near a continent will be greater than that on a small island far from a continent.

Extinction Rates and Habitat Loss

Species–area relationships have been used to predict the number and percentage of species that would become extinct if habitats were destroyed (Laurance 2007; Rompré et al. 2009). The calculation assumes that reducing the area of natural habitat on an island (or any habitat) would result in the island's being able to support only a number of species that could be supported on a smaller island (**Figure 7.10**). This model has great utility because it can be extended to national parks and na-

FIGURE 7.10 According to the island biogeography model, the number of species present in an area increases asymptotically—that is, it rises sharply and then levels off, as seen by the red curve in this example. The shape of the curve differs from region to region and for different species groups, but this model gives a general indication of the interrelationship of habitat loss and species loss. Here, if the area of habitat is reduced by 50%, then 10% of the species in the group will be expected to disappear; if the habitat is reduced by 90%, half the species will be lost. Stating this in another way, a system of protected areas covering 10% of a country could be expected to include 50% of the country's species.

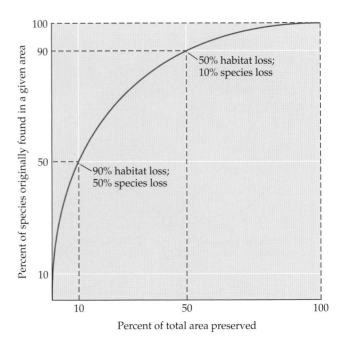

> The island biogeography model can be used to predict how many species will go extinct due to habitat loss. The model can also be used to predict how many species will remain in protected areas of different sizes.

ture reserves that are surrounded by damaged habitat (Chittaro et al. 2010). The reserves can be viewed as "habitat islands" in an inhospitable "sea" of unsuitable habitat. The model predicts that when 50% of an island (or habitat island) is destroyed, approximately 10% of the species occurring on the island will be eliminated. If these species are endemic to an area, they will become extinct. When 90% of the habitat is destroyed, 50% of the species will be lost; and when 99% of the habitat is gone, about 75% of the original species will be lost. The island of Singapore can be used as an example. Over the last 180 years, over 95% of its original forest cover has been removed; the model estimates that about 70% of its forest species would be lost. In fact, between 1923 and 1998, more than 90% of Singapore's native birds were lost, with higher rates of loss for large ground birds and for insectivorous birds of the forest canopy (Castelletta et al. 2005).

Predictions of extinction rates based on habitat loss vary considerably, because each species–area relationship is unique. Because insects and plants in tropical forests account for the great majority of the world's species, estimates of present and future rates of species extinction in rain forests give an approximation of global rates of extinction. Using the conservative estimate that 1% of the world's rain forests is being destroyed each year, Wilson (1989) estimated that 0.2% to 0.3% of all species—10,000 to 15,000 species, using a total of 5 million species worldwide—will be lost per year, or 34 species per day. This estimate predicts that over the next 10-year period, approximately 125,000 species will become extinct. The most recent estimates are that species extinctions by 2050 will be up to 35% in tropical Africa, 20% in tropical Asia, 15% in tropical America, and 8% to 10% elsewhere (MEA 2005). Extinction rates might in fact be higher because the highest rates of deforestation are occurring in countries with large concentrations of rare species, and large forest areas are increasingly being fragmented by roads and development projects (Laurance et al. 2007). We might lower extinction rates if these hotspot areas, particularly rich in endemic species, are targeted for conservation. Extinction rates may be higher than predicted if habitat destruction is nonrandom and is concentrated in such hotspots. Regardless of which estimate is the most accurate, all indicate that tens of thousands—if not hundreds of thousands—of species are headed for extinction within the next 50 years (Bradshaw et al. 2009). Such a rate of extinction is without precedent since the great mass extinction of the Cretaceous period 65 million years ago.

Assumptions and Generalizations in the Island Biogeography Model

Estimates of extinction rates based on the island biogeography model include a number of assumptions and generalizations that may limit the validity of this approach:

1. These estimates are based on typical values for the species–area curves. Groups of species with broad geographical ranges, such as marine animals and temperate tree species, will tend to have lower rates of extinction than species with narrow geographical distribution, such as island birds and freshwater fish.

2. The model assumes that all endemic species are eliminated from areas that have been largely cleared of forest. It is possible that many species can survive in isolated patches of forest and recolonize secondary forest that develops on abandoned land. A few primary forest species may also be capable of surviving in plantations and managed forests. Adaptation to managed forests is likely to be particularly significant in tropical forests that are being selectively logged on a large scale.

3. The species–area model assumes that areas of habitat are eliminated at random. In fact, areas of species richness are sometimes targeted for species conservation efforts and national park status. As a result, a greater percentage of species may be protected than is assumed in the species–area model. It is also true that lowland tropical rain forests are sometimes targeted for clearing because of their agricultural potential, even though they are rich in species.

4. The degree of habitat fragmentation may affect extinction rates. If remaining areas of land are divided into very small parcels or crossed by roads, then wide-ranging species or species requiring large population sizes may be unable to maintain themselves. Also, hunting, clearing land for agriculture, and the introduction of exotic species may increase in fragmented forests, leading to further loss of species.

Another approach to estimating extinction rates uses information on projected declines in habitat, numbers of populations, and the geographical range of well-known individual species (Mace 1995). This approach uses empirical information to give a more accurate estimate of extinction rates for a smaller number of species. Applied to 725 threatened vertebrate species, this method predicts that some 15 to 20 species (3%–5%) will go extinct in the world over the next 100 years. Extinction rates are expected to be much higher in certain groups; within 100 years it is likely that half of the 29 threatened species in the deer family (Cervidae) will be extinct, as will 3 of the world's 10 threatened hornbill species (family Bucerotidae). Applied to specific geographical areas, the numbers of species predicted to go extinct using the estimated loss of habitat and the island biogeography models closely correspond with the current number of species extinct or threatened with extinction (Brooks et al. 2002).

Time to Extinction

The time required for a given species to go extinct following a reduction in area or fragmentation of its range is a vital question in conservation biology, and the island biogeography model makes no prediction about how long it will take. Small populations of some species may persist for decades or even centuries in habitat frag-

FIGURE 7.11 Ringtail possums (*Pseudocheirus peregrinus*) are sensitive to fragment size. Populations in forest fragments less than 10 ha go extinct in under 10 years, and populations in fragments 40–80 ha persist for about 50 years on average. (Photograph © ANT Photo Library/Photo Researchers, Inc.)

ments, even though their eventual fate is extinction. One method used to estimate when extinctions will occur compares predictions of species loss with historical examples. Applying this method to forests in Kenya has allowed biologists to estimate the rates at which remaining forest fragments will lose their bird species. Of the species that will eventually be lost, the best estimates predict that half will be lost in 50 years from a 1000 ha fragment, while half will be lost in 100 years from a 10,000 ha fragment (Brooks et al. 1999). Certain forest mammals in Australia have an expected persistence time of 50 years in an 80 ha habitat fragment but of 100 years in a 300 ha fragment (**Figure 7.11**) (Laurance et al. 2008). In situations in which there is widespread habitat destruction followed by recovery, such as in New England and Puerto Rico over the last several centuries, species may be able to survive in small numbers in isolated fragments and then reoccupy adjacent recovering habitat. Even though 98% of the forests of eastern North America were cut down, the clearing took place in a patchwork fashion over hundreds of years, so forest always covered half of the area, providing refuges for mobile animal species such as birds.

Local Extinctions

In addition to the global extinctions that are a primary focus of conservation biology, many species are experiencing a series of local extinctions, or extirpations, across their range (Balmford et al. 2003; Rooney et al. 2004; Bilney et al. 2010). When habitats are degraded and destroyed, populations of plants and animals go extinct. Formerly widespread species are sometimes restricted to a few small pockets of their former habitat. For example, the American burying beetle (*Nicrophorus americanus*), once found all across central and eastern North America, is now found in only three isolated populations (**Figure 7.12**) (Muths and Scott 2000). Biological communities are impoverished by such local extinctions. Concord, Massachusetts, an intensively surveyed town, was first assessed for wildflower species in the 1850s by the famous naturalist and philosopher Henry David Thoreau. Twenty-seven percent of the native species could not be found when the area was surveyed 150 years later (Willis et al. 2008; Primack and Miller-Rushing 2008). A further 36% of the species now persist only in one or two populations and are vulnerable to extinction. In some cases, only a few individual plants remain of species that were formerly common. Certain groups, such as orchids and lilies, have shown particularly severe losses. A combination of forest succession, invasions by exotic species, air and water pollution, grazing by deer, habitat destruction and fragmentation, and now climate change have contributed to species losses in Concord. In the large Adelaide metropolitan area of Australia, 20 of 40 native mammal species and 89 of 1136 native plant species were lost between 1836 and 2002 (Tait et al. 2005).

According to surveys by the Natural Heritage programs in the United States, 4% to 8% of the plant species formerly found in Hawaii, New York, and Pennsylvania can no longer be found in these states. In Britain, where species distributions are

> Many species are experiencing the loss of populations across their range. Such local extinctions result in the loss of species richness at the local level, with potential implications for ecosystem function and the enjoyment of nature.

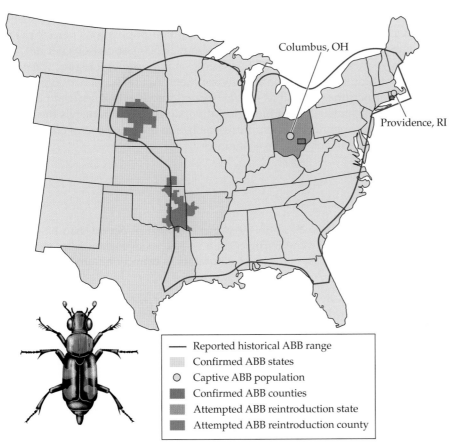

FIGURE 7.12 The American burying beetle (ABB) was once widespread in the eastern and central United States (outlined in green), but its range is now greatly reduced and it is found only in two separate areas of central United States and on Block Island in Rhode Island. Intensive efforts have been initiated to determine the cause of this decline and develop a recovery plan. The species is also being bred in captivity. (After O'Meilla 2004).

Columbus, OH

Providence, RI

— Reported historical ABB range
  Confirmed ABB states
○ Captive ABB population
  Confirmed ABB counties
  Attempted ABB reintroduction state
  Attempted ABB reintroduction county

often known with great accuracy due to decades of collecting and research, an analysis of butterflies showed that local extinctions over the last several decades had eliminated 13% of the previously known localities of species, a high rate of local loss (Thomas et al. 2004). And in a survey of one part of the Indonesian island of Sumatra, of 12 populations of Asian elephants known from the 1980s, only 3 populations were still present 20 years later (Hedges et al. 2005).

Such local extinctions break the ecological connections between species and could in turn lead to further extinctions. Also, the local loss of species diminishes the enjoyment of nature for people who visit these areas. Many people become excited when they see an abundance and diversity of birds, wildflowers, and other species groups. If they do not see much of interest during a visit to a natural area, perhaps they will be less likely to be inspired by the place and to become advocates for its protection.

LOST POPULATIONS The world's 5 million species are estimated to consist of 1 billion distinct populations, or about 200 populations per species (Hughes and Roughgarden 2000). While some species have just a few populations, other species might have thousands of populations. The loss of populations is roughly equal to the proportion of a habitat that is lost, so the world's populations are being lost at a far higher rate than the rate for the loss of species (see Figure 7.10). When 90% of an extensive grassland ecosystem is destroyed, 90% of the populations of plants, animals, and fungi there will also be lost. Tropical rain

Species-rich tropical rain forests are being lost at a rate of 1% a year, a rate believed to result in the destruction of more than 13,500 biological populations each day. Population losses eventually result in species extinctions.

forests contain at least half of the world's species, and they are being lost at the rate of about 1% per year. This represents a loss of 5 million populations per year (1% of 500 million tropical forest populations), or about 13,500 populations per day.

These large numbers of local extinctions serve as important biological warning signs that something is wrong with the environment. Action is needed to prevent further local extinctions, as well as global extinctions. The loss of local populations not only represents a loss of biological diversity, but it diminishes the value of an area for nature enjoyment, scientific research, and the provision of crucial materials to local people in subsistence economies.

Summary

1. There are more species on Earth in the present geological period than have ever existed in the past. However, the current rate of species extinction is rapid and is comparable to the five past episodes of natural mass extinction found at intervals in the geological record.

2. The effect of human activity has been to drive many species to extinction. Since 1600, about 1.6% of the world's mammalian species and 1.3% of its birds have gone extinct. The rate of extinction is accelerating, and many of the species still alive are teetering on the brink of extinction. The current observed rate of extinction for birds and mammals is estimated to be 100 to 1000 times greater than the rate that would be occurring naturally.

3. Individuals of long-lived species that remain alive in disturbed and fragmented habitats can be considered "the living dead." The species may persist for many years but will eventually die out because of a lack of reproduction.

4. Island species have a higher rate of extinction than mainland species. Among aquatic species, freshwater species apparently have a higher extinction rate than marine species.

5. An island biogeography model has been developed to predict the equilibrium number of species that might be found on islands of different areas and distances from the mainland. This model has been used to estimate how many species will go extinct if human activity continues to destroy habitats at the present rate. The best evidence indicates that about 2% to 3% of the Earth's species will be lost over the next 10 years, with a loss of about 10,000 to 15,000 species per year. Other empirical evidence on population declines and range reductions support the prediction that the rate of extinction will remain high over the coming decades.

6. Many species are experiencing a loss of populations across their ranges, leading to impoverished biological communities. These local extinctions, or extirpations, also represent a loss of biodiversity.

For Discussion

1. Calculate the number of species expected on islands of various sizes, using several values of *C* (0.5, 1, 2, 4, etc.) and several values of *Z* (0.15, 0.25, 0.35, etc.). How many species will be lost on the largest island if native habitat is completely destroyed on 30%, 70%, 97%, and 98% of the island? What are the assumptions on which these calculations are based?

2. Why should conservation biologists, or anyone else, care if species go locally extinct if they are still found somewhere else?

3. If 50% of the species present today went extinct within the next 200 years, what is your estimate of how long it would take for the process of speciation to replace the lost species?

Suggested Readings

Bilney, R. J., R. Cooke, and J. G. White. 2010. Underestimated and severe: Small mammal decline from the forests of southeastern Australia since European settlement, as revealed by a top-order predator. *Biological Conservation* 143: 52–59. Small mammals in Australia have undergone severe range contractions and local extinctions since European colonization.

Carpenter, K. E., M. Abrar, G. Aeby, R. B. Aronson, S. Banks, A. Bruckner, et al. 2008. One-third of reef-building coral faces elevated extinction risk from climate change and local impacts. *Science* 321: 560–563.

Chittaro, P. M., et al. 2010. Trade-offs between species conservation and the size of marine protected areas. *Conservation Biology* 24: 197–206. Species–area relationships can be used to establish marine protected areas.

Jackson, J. B. C. 2008. Ecological extinction and evolution in the brave new ocean. *Proceedings of the National Academy of Sciences USA* 105: 11458–11465. Anthropogenic impacts are degrading complex ocean ecosystems and may cause a mass marine extinction.

Johnson, C. 2009. Megafaunal decline and fall. *Science* 326: 1072–1073. The largest animals are often the most vulnerable to extinction.

Kuussaari, M., R. Bommarco, R. K. Heikkinen, A. Helm, J. Krauss, R. Lindborg, et al. 2009. Extinction debt: A challenge for biodiversity conservation. *Trends in Ecology and Evolution* 24: 564–571. The impact of current human activities will be seen in future extinctions.

Laurance, W. F. 2007. Have we overstated the tropical biodiversity crisis? *Trends in Ecology and Evolution* 22: 65–70. The increasing rate of rain forest destruction threatens enormous numbers of species.

Laurance, W. F., S. G. Laurance, and D. W. Hilbert. 2008. Long-term dynamics of a fragmented rainforest mammal assemblage. *Conservation Biology* 22: 1154–1164. Many species are lost over time in habitat fragments.

MacArthur, R. H. and E. O. Wilson. 1967. *The Theory of Island Biogeography.* Princeton University Press, Princeton, NJ. This classic text has been highly influential in shaping modern conservation biology.

Primack, R. B., A. J. Miller-Rushing, and K. Dharaneeswaran. 2009. Changes in the flora of Thoreau's Concord. *Biological Conservation* 142: 500–508. Human impacts can cause extensive local extinction even in a well-protected suburban landscape.

Quammen, D. 1996. *The Song of the Dodo: Island Biogeography in an Age of Extinctions.* Scribner, New York. Popular account of early and modern explorations and of island biogeography theory.

Régnier, C., B. Fontaine, and P. Bouchet. 2009. Not knowing, not recording, not listing: Numerous unnoticed mollusk extinctions. *Conservation Biology* 23: 1214–1221. Mollusks don't get much attention, but they are among the most threatened animals.

Stokstad, E. 2007. Gambling on a ghost bird. *Science* 317: 888–892. Leading ornithologists publically announced the discovery of an extinct woodpecker, but they were probably mistaken.

Wake, D. B. and V. T. Vredenburg. 2008. Are we in the midst of the sixth mass extinction? A view from the world of amphibians. *Proceedings of the National Academy of Sciences USA* 105: 11466–11473. As a result of intensive study, amphibians are now recognized as among the most threatened animal groups.

Chapter 8

Vulnerability to Extinction

Not all species have an equal chance of going extinct. Rare species are considered to be especially vulnerable to extinction, while common species are considered less so. But the term *rare* has a variety of meanings, each of which has a different implication for conservation biology (Feldhamer and Morzillo 2008).

Generally speaking, a species is considered rare if it (1) lives in a narrow geographical range, (2) occupies only one or a few specialized habitats, or (3) is found only in small populations (Harrison et al. 2008). The first criterion, based on geographical area, is the most obvious: The Venus flytrap (*Dionaea muscipula*) is rare because it occurs only on the coastal plain of the Carolinas in eastern North America. Many geographically rare species occupy islands, and some may also occupy isolated habitats, such as high mountain peaks in the middle of lowlands or lakes surrounded by a terrestrial landscape. Within their limited geographical range, however, a rare species may be locally abundant.

Related to the concept of rarity is the concept of **endemism**— the idea that some species are found naturally in a single geographical area and no other place. This concept may seem similar to the properties of those rare species that live in a narrow geographical range. But a species may be endemic to a large

FIGURE 8.1 The Iberian lynx (*Lynx pardinus*) is a critically endangered species. Though they were once found over the entire Iberian Peninsula, there are now believed to be fewer than 100 of these cats in a few scattered areas in Spain. The fragmentation of their habitat and decline of their prey populations have contributed to the lynx's decline. (Photograph © Carlos Sanz/VWPICS/Visual & Written SL/Alamy.)

> Species that occupy a narrow range, such as many island species, are particularly vulnerable to extinction.

area and abundant throughout it. In contrast, a rare species such as the Venus flytrap is typically found only in a limited area (and could be considered a narrowly distributed endemic). Or a rare species may be considered geographically rare in only part of its range. For example, the sweetbay magnolia (*Magnolia virginiana*) is reasonably common throughout the southeastern United States, but in the New England region this species is considered rare because it occurs in only one population of 100 individuals in one particular swamp in Magnolia, Massachusetts. Individual species may have always had a narrow geographical range, or they may have been more widespread at one time but became restricted because of human activities and habitat destruction, in which case they could be termed *artificially rare*.

A species may also be considered rare if it occupies only one or a few specialized habitats. Salt marsh cord grass (*Spartina patens*) is found only in salt marshes and not in other habitats, yet within this habitat, cord grass is quite common. This example contrasts with common species that are found in many different habitats, such as the dandelion (*Taraxacum officinale*), which occupies open meadows, roadsides, river edges, and mown lawns.

Finally, a species may be considered rare if it is found only in small populations. The Iberian lynx (*Lynx pardinus*) formerly occurred across Spain and Portugal, but their populations are now always small and isolated. A common species would have large populations at least in some locations. (**Figure 8.1**).

These three criteria of rarity—narrow geographical range, specific habitat requirements, and small population size—can be applied to the entire range of species or to the distribution and abundance of species in a particular place. Such an approach can highlight priorities for conservation. A species with a narrow geographical range and specific habitat requirements that is always found in small populations requires immediate habitat protection and, possibly, habitat management to maintain its few, fragile populations. This also applies, to a somewhat lesser degree, to species with larger populations. However, where species have a narrow geographical distribution but a broad habitat specificity, experiments in which individuals are transported to unoccupied but apparently suitable localities to create new populations may be a strategy worth considering (see Chapter 13); these species may have been unable to disperse outside of their narrow geographical areas because of factors such as geographic barriers or inherent inability to disperse. This suggestion is supported by observations showing that plant species with poor dispersal abilities (no adaptation for long-distance dispersal) tend to have more aggregated populations than do species with good dispersal ability (light, wind-dispersed seeds, or seeds dispersed by mammals and birds), which tend to have more widely dispersed populations (Quinn et al. 1994). Species with broad geographical ranges are less susceptible to extinction and less likely to need rescue efforts, since they tend to have more extant populations and more opportunities to colonize potentially suitable sites.

Endemic Species and Extinction

A species found naturally in a single geographical area and no other place is **endemic** to that location. Endemism is an extremely important factor in a species' risk of extinction. If the populations of an endemic species on Madagascar, or any isolated island, go extinct, the species will be globally extinct. In contrast, mainland species often have many populations distributed over wide areas, so the loss of one population is not catastrophic for a species. Even though 98% of the forests of eastern North America were logged or cleared for farming, for instance, no bird species went extinct because of habitat loss: presumably the remaining forest fragments were sufficient to allow these widespread species to survive until the forest grew back following the abandonment of farming.

Expansion of an endemic species' geographical distribution that is caused deliberately or accidentally by humans is not considered part of the species' natural distribution. For example, the giant panda (*Ailuropoda melanoleuca*) is endemic to China, even though it now lives in zoos throughout the world. The black locust tree (*Robinia pseudoacacia*) is native to the eastern and southern United States but has been widely planted elsewhere in North America, Europe, and other temperate regions as a timber tree and an ornamental, and it has spread aggressively into native vegetation in these regions. A species may be endemic to a wide geographical area; for example, the black cherry tree (*Prunus serotina*) is endemic to the Western Hemisphere and is found across North, Central, and South America. Or a species may be endemic to a small geographical area, such as the giant Komodo dragon (*Varanus komodoensis*), which is endemic to several small islands in the Indonesian archipelago. Species that occupy a small area because they have only recently evolved from closely related species are designated **neoendemics**; examples include the hundreds of species of cichlid fish that occupy Lake Victoria in East Africa. In contrast, **paleoendemics** are ancient species whose close relatives have all gone extinct; examples include the giant panda and the Indian Ocean coelacanth. All such narrowly distributed endemic species are of concern for their potential to become extinct.

Isolated geographical units, such as remote islands, old lakes, and solitary mountain peaks in deserts, often have high percentages of endemic species. A high level of endemism is also evident in geologically old, continental areas with Mediterranean climates, such as southern Africa and California (**Table 8.1**). The biota of the entire continent of Australia has evolved in almost complete isolation, with 94% of its native plant species endemic. In the United States, it is not surprising that the geographically isolated Hawaiian Islands have a large number of endemic species (**Figure 8.2**).

TABLE 8.1 Total Plant Species and Endemic Plant Species in Selected Regions

Region	Area (km²)	Total number of species	Number of endemic species	Percent endemic species
Europe	10,000,000	10,500	±3500	33
Australia	7,628,300	15,000	14,074	94
Texas	751,000	4694	379	8
California	411,000	5647	1517	27
Germany	349,270	2600	6	<1
North and South Carolina	217,000	3586	23	1
Cape Region of South Africa	90,000	8578	5850	68
Panama	75,000	9000	1222	14
Belgium	30,230	1400	1	<1

Source: After Gentry 1986; WRI 2000.

FIGURE 8.2 The number of plant species endemic to the different states varies greatly. For example, 379 plant species are found in Texas and nowhere else; New York, in contrast, has only 1 endemic plant species. California, with its large area and vast array of habitats, including deserts, mountains, seacoasts, old-growth forests, and myriad others, is home to more endemic species than any other state. There is a trend toward more endemic species in states farther south. The island archipelago of Hawaii, far from the mainland, hosts many endemic species despite its small area. (After Gentry 1986.)

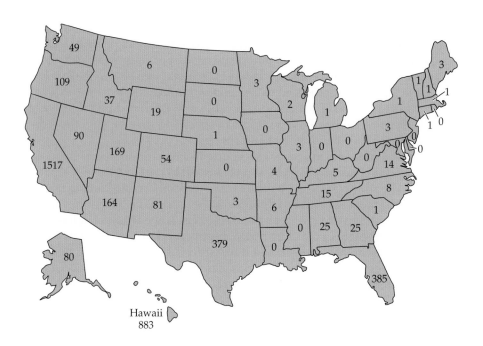

Areas that are not geographically isolated typically have much lower percentages of endemic species. For example, Germany and Belgium have few endemic species because virtually all of their species are found in neighboring countries. Similarly, the Carolinas in the southeastern United States share most of their species with adjoining areas. One of the most notable concentrations of endemic species is on the island of Madagascar, where the moist tropical forests are spectacularly rich in endemic species: 100% of its lemurs, 99% of the frogs, and over 92% of the 15,000 plant species on the island are found nowhere else but on Madagascar (Goodman and Benstead 2005). About 80% of Madagascar's land has been altered or destroyed by human activity, possibly putting almost half of the endemic species of birds and mammals in danger of extinction.

Species Most Vulnerable to Extinction

When ecosystems are damaged by human activity, the ranges and population sizes of many species will be reduced, and some species will go extinct. Rare species must be carefully monitored and managed in conservation efforts. Ecologists have observed that particular categories of species are most vulnerable to extinction, many of which have the defining characteristics of rare species (Hockey and Curtis 2009; Grouios and Mane 2009). The five categories most frequently used in conservation planning are as follows:

> Identifying characteristics of extinction-prone species allows conservation biologists to anticipate the needs of vulnerable species, even when detailed data is lacking.

- **Species with a narrow geographical range.** Some species occur at only one or a few sites in a restricted geographical range, and if that whole range is affected by human activity, the species may become extinct (Cardillo et al. 2008; Lawler et al. 2010). Bird species on oceanic islands are good examples of species with restricted ranges that have become extinct or are in danger of extinction; in many instances, a fish species confined to a single lake or a single watershed has also disappeared. Species with limited ranges are especially vulnerable to global climate change (see Chapter 9). Recent estimates suggest that numerous bird species, mainly those with narrow ranges, could become extinct as a result of climate change (Sekercioglu et al. 2008).

- **Species with only one or a few populations.** Any one population of a species may become extinct as a result of chance factors, such as earthquake, fire, an outbreak of disease, or human activity. Species with many populations are less vulnerable to extinction than are species with only one or a few populations. This category is linked to the previous category, because species with few populations will also tend to have narrow geographical ranges.

- **Species in which population size is small.** Small populations are more likely to go locally extinct than large populations because of their greater vulnerability to demographic and environmental variation and loss of genetic variability (see Chapter 11); species that characteristically have small population sizes, such as large predators or extreme specialists, are more likely to become extinct than species that typically have large populations (Bulman et al. 2007). At the extreme are species whose numbers have declined to just a few individuals.

Population size by itself seems to be one of the best predictors of the extinction rate of isolated populations (see Chapter 7). An excellent example is provided by studies of isolated forest fragments in Brazil: The persistence of individual bird species, after several decades of isolation, was related to the size of the forest fragment, the number of habitats found in the fragment, and the initial abundance of the species (Laurance 2008b). Larger fragments with more habitat diversity had more forest species than smaller, less diverse fragments, and species with high initial populations were far more likely to persist than species with low initial populations.

- **Species in which population size is declining.** Population trends tend to continue, so a population showing signs of decline is likely to go extinct unless the cause of decline is identified and corrected (Peery et al. 2004). As Charles Darwin pointed out almost 150 years ago in *On the Origin of Species* (1859):

  > To admit that species generally become rare before they become extinct, to feel no surprise at the rarity of the species, and yet to marvel greatly when the species ceases to exist, is much the same as to admit that sickness in the individual is the forerunner of death—to feel no surprise at sickness, but when the sick man dies, to wonder and to suspect that he died of some deed of violence.

- **Species that are hunted or harvested by people.** Overharvesting can rapidly reduce the population size of a species (see Chapter 10). If hunting and harvesting are not regulated, either by law or by local customs, the species can be driven to extinction. Utility has often been the prelude to extinction (**Figure 8.3**).

FIGURE 8.3 Yellow gentian (*Gentiana lutea*), a beautiful perennial herb of European mountain meadows, has roots that are collected for traditional medicine. Approximately 1500 tons of dried roots are used each year in a wide variety of preparations to stimulate digestion and to treat stomachache. Because of overharvesting and the resulting decline and destruction of many populations, the species is listed as endangered in Portugal, Albania, and certain regions of Germany and Switzerland and as vulnerable in other countries, according to the IUCN's classification categories. Despite official regulation that restricts collection to designated areas, illegal harvesting continues. (Photograph © Arco Images GmbH/Alamy.)

The following categories of species have also been linked to extinction, though they are not considered as all-encompassing as the previous five categories:

- *Species that need a large home range.* A species in which individual animals or social groups need to forage over wide areas is prone to die off when part of its range is damaged or fragmented by human activity.

- *Animal species with large bodies.* Large animals tend to have large individual ranges, have low reproductive rates, require more food, and be hunted by humans. Top carnivores, especially, are often killed by humans because they compete with humans for wild game, sometimes damage livestock, and are hunted for sport. Within groups of species, often the largest species will be the most prone to extinction—that is, the largest carnivore, the largest lemur, the largest whale (**Figure 8.4**). In Sri Lanka, for example, the largest species of carnivores—leopards and eagles—and the largest species of herbivores—elephants and deer—are at the greatest risk of extinction. For plants, species with large, short-lived seeds are more vulnerable than are species with smaller, long-lived seeds (Kolb and Diekmann 2005).

> Species most vulnerable to extinction have the following characteristics: narrow geographic range, only one or a few populations, small populations, declining population size, and being hunted or harvested by people.

- *Species that are not effective dispersers.* Environmental changes prompt species to adapt, either behaviorally or physiologically, to the new conditions of their

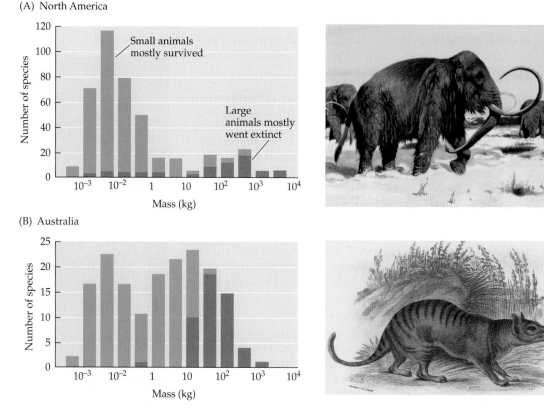

(A) North America

Number of species (y-axis: 0, 20, 40, 60, 80, 100, 120)
Mass (kg) (x-axis: 10^{-3}, 10^{-2}, 1, 10, 10^2, 10^3, 10^4)

Small animals mostly survived

Large animals mostly went extinct

(B) Australia

Number of species (y-axis: 0, 5, 10, 15, 20, 25)
Mass (kg) (x-axis: 10^{-3}, 10^{-2}, 1, 10, 10^2, 10^3, 10^4)

FIGURE 8.4 Body mass of herbivorous mammals from North America (A) and Australia (B) that survived (green area of bars) until historical times (the time of European arrival) and that died between the time of the first human arrival and historical times (red area of bars). Note that Australia has fewer mammals than North America, with a more even distribution of size classes. Most of the extinctions were of the largest animals such as (top image) a wooly mammoth and (bottom image) a Thylacine or Tasmanian tiger. (After Johnson 2009; A, © INTERFOTO/Alamy; B, a print from William Home Lizars.)

habitat. Species unable to adapt to changing environments must either migrate to more suitable habitat or face extinction. Species that are unable to cross roads, farmlands, and disturbed habitats are more likely to go extinct as their original habitat becomes affected by pollution, exotic species, and global climate change. Dispersal is important in the aquatic environment as well, where dams, point sources of pollution, channelization, and sedimentation can limit movement. Limited ability to disperse, as well as more specialized habitat requirements, may explain why in the United States 69% of the freshwater fauna of mussels and snails are extinct or threatened with extinction, in contrast to some 18% of dragonfly species (which can fly between the aquatic sites needed for their larval stages) (Stein et al. 2000). In another study that examined 16 nonflying mammal species in Queensland rain forests, the most important characteristic that determined the ability of species to survive in isolated forest fragments was their ability to use, feed on, and move through the intervening matrix of secondary vegetation (Laurance 1991). This study highlights the importance of maintaining secondary vegetation for the survival of certain primary forest species.

- *Seasonal migrants.* Species that migrate seasonally depend on two or more distinct habitat types. If either one of those habitat types is damaged, the species may be unable to persist. The billion songbirds of 120 species that migrate each year between the northern United States and the American tropics depend on suitable habitat in both locations to survive and breed. Also, if barriers to dispersal are created by roads, fences, or dams between the needed habitats, a species may be unable to complete its life cycle (Wilcove and Wikelski 2008). Salmon species that are blocked by dams from swimming up rivers and spawning are a striking example of this problem. Many animal species migrate among habitats in search of food, often along elevational and moisture gradients. Herds of wild pigs, grazing ungulates, frugivorous vertebrates, and insectivorous birds are all examples of these. If these species are unable to migrate and thus are confined to one habitat type, they may not survive, or if they do survive, they may be unable to accumulate the nutritional reserves needed to reproduce. Species that cross international barriers represent a special problem, in that conservation efforts must be coordinated by more than one country. Imagine the difficulties of conserving the tiny flock of Siberian cranes (*Grus leucogeranus*) that must migrate 4800 km each year from Russia to India and back, crossing six highly militarized, tense international borders.

- *Species with little genetic variability.* Genetic variability within a population can sometimes allow a species to adapt to a changing environment (see Chapters 2 and 11). Species with little or no genetic variability may have a greater tendency to become extinct when a new disease, a new predator, or some other change occurs in the environment.

- *Species with specialized niche requirements.* Once a habitat is altered, the environment may no longer be suitable for specialized species (Dunn et al. 2009; Van Turnhout et al. 2010). For example, wetland plants that require very specific and regular changes in water level may be rapidly eliminated when human activity affects the hydrology of an area. Species with highly specific dietary requirements are also at risk. For instance, there are species of mites that feed only on the feathers of a single bird species. If the bird species goes extinct, so do its associated feather mite species. Specialized insects that feed on only one type of plant species will go extinct if that plant species goes extinct. These types of linked extinctions are termed co-extinctions. Specialist tropical birds that follow army ants and feed on escaping insects are one such

FIGURE 8.5 The Barred antshrike (*Thamnophilus doliatus*) of Brazil is a specialist feeder on insects and other small animals fleeing from raiding swarms of army ant species. It may not be able to survive in a forest if army ants die out following logging and habitat fragmentation. (Photograph © Peter Arnold Images/Photolibrary.com.)

example; when army ants are eliminated from areas by habitat fragmentation, the ant birds also die out (**Figure 8.5**).

Some species are confined to a single unusual habitat type that is scattered and rare across the landscape. Unique species are found, for example, in vernal pools in California, granite outcrops in the southeastern United States, and isolated high mountains in the southwestern United States, illustrating the importance of habitat preservation to conserve species with specialized requirements.

- *Species that are characteristically found in stable, pristine environments.* Many species are found in environments where disturbance is minimal, such as in old stands of tropical rain forests and the interiors of rich temperate deciduous forests. When these forests are logged, grazed, burned, or otherwise altered, many native species are unable to tolerate the changed microclimatic conditions (more light, less moisture, greater temperature variation) and influx of exotic species. Also, species of stable environments tend to delay reproduction to an advanced age and produce only a few young. Following one or more episodes of habitat disturbance, such species are often unable to rebuild their populations fast enough to avoid extinction. When the environment is altered by air and water pollution, species unable to adapt to the destabilized physical and chemical environment will be eliminated from the community (**Box 8.1**). Coral reef species and freshwater invertebrates, such as crayfish, mussels, and snails, often cannot survive when their environments receive large inputs of sediment and sewage from human activities.

> Many species cannot tolerate the disturbances associated with human activity, and require undisturbed conditions to survive.

- *Species that form permanent or temporary aggregations.* Species that group together in specific places are highly vulnerable to local extinction (Reed 1999). For example, bats forage widely but typically roost together in particular caves. Hunters that enter these caves during the day can rapidly harvest every individual in the population. Herds of bison, flocks of passenger pigeons, and schools of spawning ocean fish all represent aggregations that have been exploited and completely harvested by people. Temporary aggre-

BOX 8.1 *Why Are Frogs and Toads Croaking?*

■ At the First World Congress on Herpetology in 1989 in Canterbury, England, what had previously seemed like casual findings began to take on a disturbing significance: Scientists from around the world were seeing a decline in amphibian populations. Frogs, toads, salamanders, and other amphibians that had been common less than two decades ago were becoming rare, with some species even going extinct. This led to a call for action, to determine what was happening and what could be done to stop it. In the years since the meeting, hundreds of studies have been published, in addition to dozens of review articles and books. To pull together this vast body of new information, a global amphibian assessment was carried out from 2000 to 2004 (Stuart et al. 2004). This report and a recent international survey (www.iucnredlist.org) show the astonishing conclusion: 43% of amphibian species are declining in numbers and 36% are threatened with extinction.

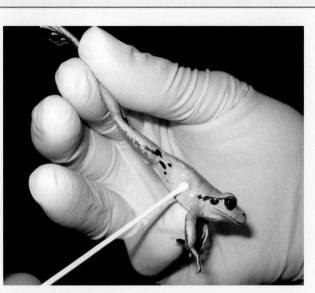

A researcher uses a cotton swab on an Australian frog. The swab will later be tested for the presence of the disease-causing chytrid fungus. (Photograph © KerryKriger/savethefrogs.com.)

> Worldwide studies have shown that amphibians face multiple threats. Infection by a waterborne fungus is a major contributor to amphibian decline.

These studies demonstrate that amphibians are particularly vulnerable to human disturbance, perhaps because many species require two separate habitats, aquatic and terrestrial, to complete their life cycles. If either habitat is damaged, the species will not be able to reproduce. Amphibians, like many other taxa, are also sensitive to pesticides, chemical pollution, and acid rain (see Chapter 9). The latter two factors may be particularly dangerous to these animals: Chemical pollution and pesticides can easily penetrate the thin epidermis characteristic of amphibians, while slight decreases in pH can destroy eggs and tadpoles.

The loss of wetland habitat is especially important. For instance, the number of farm ponds, a favorite habitat for amphibians in Britain, has declined by 70% over the last 100 years. Introduced predatory fish, drought, unusual climatic events, and increased ultraviolet radiation due to a decrease in the protective ozone layer have subsequently been blamed for the decline of individual species; in many cases, these stress factors have apparently made species

susceptible to fatal infections from a waterborne chytrid fungus (*Batrachochytrium dendrobatidis*) (Murray 2009). This deadly fungus may be spread around the world by global commerce, especially trade in live aquatic organisms (Picco and Collins 2008). Despite an abundance of recent studies, scientists are still not sure whether amphibian species are declining on a global scale because of global causes or if they are declining on a local scale because of numerous separate causes. In the past two decades, a huge effort on the part of the conservation and herpetology communities has provided evidence for the crises facing amphibians, and many of the causes. Now that this information is available, people need to develop and implement an effective course of action. Such a conservation program may include protecting wetlands from destruction and pollution, reducing the spread of the harmful fungus, establishing new populations of threatened species at unoccupied sites, and when all else fails, developing captive populations. For less well-known species, we cannot develop conservation strategies as long as the reasons for the declines remain unknown or beyond our control.

gations include schools of fish such as salmon and alewife moving up rivers to spawn; nets across rivers can catch virtually every fish and eliminate a species in a few days. Overly efficient harvesting of wild fruits from a cluster of neighboring trees for commercial markets can eliminate the seedlings that would have grown into the next generation. Even though sea turtles may swim across vast stretches of ocean, egg collectors and hunters on a few narrow nesting beaches can threaten a species with extinction, as shown in Box 1.1. Many species of social animals may be unable to persist when population size or density falls below a certain number, because they may be unable to forage, find mates, or defend themselves; this is termed the **Allee effect**. Such species may be more vulnerable to habitat destruction than asocial species in which individuals are widely dispersed.

- *Species that have not had prior contact with people.* As we discussed in relation to islands in Chapter 7, species that have experienced prior human disturbance and persisted have a lower current extinction risk than species encountering people—along with their associated animals and plants—for the first time (see Figure 7.6) (Balmford 1996). The rate of recent bird extinction is far lower on Pacific islands colonized in the past by Polynesians than on islands not colonized by Polynesians. Similarly, Western Australia, which has only recently experienced intense human impact, has a modern extinction rate for plant species that is ten times higher than the Mediterranean region, which has a long history of heavy human impact (Greuter 1995).

- *Species that have closely related species that are recently extinct or are threatened with extinction.* Often groups of species, such as primates, cranes, sea turtles, and orchids, are particularly vulnerable to extinction. The characteristics that make certain species vulnerable are often shared by related species.

Characteristics of extinction-prone species are not independent; rather, they group together into categories of characteristics. For example, many orchid species have specialized habitat requirements, have specialized relationships with pollinators, and are overharvested by collectors, and all of those characteristics lead to decline and extinction. A high percentage of seabirds are also in danger of extinction because they have low reproductive rates, they form dense breeding aggregations often in a small areas where their eggs and nestlings are prone to attack by introduced predators, they are killed by oil pollution and as bycatch during commercial fishing operations, and their eggs are overharvested by people (Munilla et al. 2007). The characteristics that make species vulnerable often vary among groups because of peculiarities of natural history. For instance, butterflies differ from jellyfish and cacti in the things that make them vulnerable to extinction. By identifying characteristics of extinction-prone species, conservation biologists can anticipate the need for managing populations of vulnerable species. Those species most vulnerable to extinction may have the full range of characteristics, as David Ehrenfeld (1970) imagined:

> Species may have multiple characteristics that make them vulnerable to extinction. Field studies are sometimes needed to identify these characteristics and formulate conservation measures.

> a large predator with a narrow habitat tolerance, long gestation period, and few young per litter [that is] hunted for a natural product and/or for sport, but is not subject to efficient game management. It has a restricted distribution but travels across international boundaries. It is intolerant of man, reproduces in aggregates, and has nonadaptive behavioral idiosyncrasies.

There is another great need for identifying characteristics of threatened species: Most threatened species that have been identified so far are also in the most well-studied groups, such as birds and mammals, highlighting the point that only when we are knowledgeable about a species can we recognize the dangers it faces (Duncan and Lockwood 2001). A lack of knowledge about a group of species, such as beetles, ocean fish, and fungi, should not be taken to mean that the species are not threatened with extinction; rather, a lack of knowledge should be an argument for urgent study of those species. The conservation status of amphibians, for example, was relatively unknown until 10 years ago, when intensive study revealed that a high proportion of species were in danger of extinction.

Conservation Categories

Identifying those species most vulnerable to extinction is essential to the work of protecting biodiversity. To mark the status of rare and endangered species for conservation purposes, the IUCN (formerly known as the International Union for Conservation of Nature) has established conservation categories (**Figure 8.6**); species in categories critically endangered (CR), endangered (EN), and vulnerable (VU) are considered to be threatened with extinction. For the three categories of threatened species, the IUCN has developed more quantitative measures of threat based on the probability of extinction (Mace et al. 2008; www.iucnredlist.org). These categories have proved to be useful in establishing protection at the national and international levels through published Red Data Books and Red Lists of threatened species and by directing attention toward species of special concern. Red Lists identify species threatened with extinction for protection through international agreements, such as the Convention on International Trade in Endangered Species (CITES). The conservation categories follow:

- *Extinct* (*EX*). The species (or other taxon, such as subspecies or variety) is no longer known to exist. The IUCN currently lists 717 animal species and 87 plants species as extinct.

- *Extinct in the wild* (*EW*). The species exists only in cultivation, in captivity, or as a naturalized population well outside its original range. The IUCN currently lists 37 animal species and 28 plant species as extinct in the wild.

- *Critically endangered* (*CR*). These species have an extremely high risk of going extinct in the wild, according to any of the criteria A to E (in Table 8.2).

- *Endangered* (*EN*). These species have a very high risk of extinction in the wild, according to any of the criteria A to E.

- *Vulnerable* (*VU*). These species have a high risk of extinction in the wild, according to any of the criteria A to E.

- *Near threatened* (*NT*). The species is close to qualifying for a threatened category but is not currently considered threatened.

- *Least concern* (*LC*). The species is not considered near threatened or threatened. (Widespread and abundant species are included in this category.)

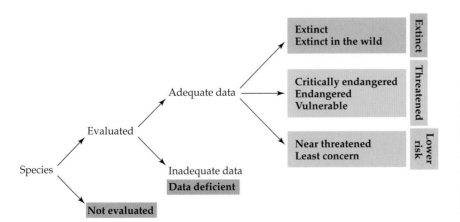

FIGURE 8.6 The IUCN categories of conservation status. This chart shows the distribution of the categories. Reading from left to right, they depend on (1) whether a species has been evaluated or not and (2) how much information is available for the species. If data are available, the species is then put into a category in the lower risk, threatened, or extinct area. (After IUCN 2001.)

- *Data deficient (DD)*. Inadequate information exists to determine the risk of extinction for the species.

- *Not evaluated (NE)*. The species has not yet been evaluated against the Red List criteria.

When used on a national or other regional level, there are two additional Red List categories:

- *Regionally extinct (RE)*. The species no longer exists within the country (region) but is extant in other parts of the world.

- *Not applicable (NA)*. The species is not eligible for the regional Red List because, for example, it is not within its natural range in the region (it has been introduced) or because it is only a rare migrant to the region.

> The IUCN uses quantitative information, including the area occupied by the species and the number of mature individuals presently alive, to assign species to conservation categories.

Species in the critically endangered, endangered, and vulnerable categories are considered to be **threatened** with extinction. For these three categories, the IUCN has developed quantitative measures of threat based on the probability of extinction. These **Red List criteria**, described in **Table 8.2**, are based on the developing methods of population viability analysis that will be described further in Chapter 12. These criteria focus on population trends and habitat condition. The advantage of this system is that it provides a standard method of classification by which decisions can be reviewed and evaluated according to accepted quantitative criteria, using whatever information is available.

Using habitat loss as a criterion in assigning categories is particularly useful for many species that are poorly known biologically, because species can be listed as threatened if their habitat is being destroyed even if scientists know little else about them. In practice, a species is most commonly assigned to an IUCN category based on the area it occupies, the number of mature individuals it has, or the rate of decline of the habitat or population; the probability of extinction is least commonly used (Kindvall and Gärdenfors 2003). In any case, the probability of a species' going

TABLE 8.2 IUCN Red List Criteria for the Assignment of Conservation Categories

Red List criteria A–E	Quantification of criteria for Red List "critically endangered" category[a]
A. Observable reduction in numbers of individuals	The population has declined by 80% or more over the last 10 years or 3 generations (whichever is longer), either based on direct observation or inferred from factors such as levels of exploitation, threats from introduced species and disease, or habitat destruction and/or degradation
B. Total geographical area occupied by the species	The species has a restricted range (<100 km² at a single location) *and* there is observed or predicted habitat loss, fragmentation, ecological imbalance, or heavy commercial exploitation
C. Predicted decline in number of individuals	The total population size is less than 250 mature, breeding individuals and is expected to decline by 25% or more within 3 years or 1 generation
D. Number of mature individuals currently alive	The population size is less than 50 mature individuals
E. Probability the species will go extinct within a certain number of years or generations	Extinction probability is greater than 50% within 10 years or 3 generations

[a]A species that meets the described quantities for *any one* of criteria A–E may be classified as critically endangered. Similar quantification for the Red List categories "endangered" and "vulnerable" can be found at www.iucnredlist.org.

extinct using population viability analysis is strongly correlated with its IUCN category and various other methods of risk assessment (O'Grady et al. 2004).

The present IUCN system can still devolve into arbitrary assignment if decisions have to be made with insufficient data. Gathering the data needed for proper assignment is expensive and time-consuming, particularly for developing countries and in rapidly changing situations. Regardless of this limitation, this system of species classification is a distinct improvement over past methods that were more subjective, and it will assist attempts to protect species.

Using criteria in Table 8.2 and the categories in Figure 8.6, the IUCN has evaluated and described the threats to plant and animal species in its series of Red Data Books and Red Lists of threatened species; these detailed lists of endangered species by group and by country can be seen at www.iucn.org. The IUCN Red Lists direct public attention toward threatened species that have been protected through national laws and international agreements (Donald et al. 2007; Fontaine et al. 2007). Species listed as threatened include 1464 of 5414 described mammal species, 2065 of 9865 bird species, and 2279 of 6248 amphibian species (see Table 7.2). In addition, Red Lists have been developed for individual countries (**Table 8.3**).

> The IUCN system has been used to identify Red Lists of threatened species, and to determine if species are responding to conservation efforts.

Although the IUCN evaluations have included numerous species of fish (1722), reptiles (1513), mollusks (2197), insects (1259), crustaceans (1735), and plants (12,041), they are still not extensive enough. Most bird, amphibian, and mammal species have been evaluated using the IUCN system, but the levels of evaluation are lower for reptiles, fish, and flowering plants. The evaluations of insects and other invertebrates, mosses, algae, fungi, and microorganisms are even less adequate (Régnier et al. 2009). A recent survey of dragonflies suggests that about 10%–15% can be considered threatened (Clausnitzer et al. 2009). Evaluating a greater number of species using the IUCN system is an urgent priority.

The IUCN system has been applied to specific geographical areas and groups of species as a way of highlighting conservation priorities. As a group, mammals face a greater degree of threat than birds. Comparing regions, in general, the species of Japan are more threatened than the species of South Africa, which are more threatened, in turn, than the species of the United Kingdom (see Table 8.3).

By tracking the conservation status of species over time, it is possible to determine whether species are responding to conservation efforts or are continuing to be threatened (Butchart and Bird 2010). One such measure is the Red List Index, which demonstrates that the conservation status of certain animal groups has continued to decline during the period from 1988 to 2004, with particularly sharp declines for albatrosses and petrels and for amphibians (Quayle et al. 2007; Baillie et al. 2008). However, the rates of extinction of critically endangered species have been less than predicted, most likely because of the positive effects of conservation interventions (Brooke et al. 2008). Another measure, the Living Planet Index, follows population sizes for 1686 vertebrate species; this index has shown a decline of 28% from 1970 to 2005 (Collen et al. 2009).

In Switzerland, a different approach is being used to identify those threatened (or Red List) species that are responding to conservation efforts (Gigon et al. 2000). The 317 species that have stable populations or are increasing in abundance as of 2007 are listed in a Blue List. The Blue List highlights successful conservation efforts and suggests further projects that might succeed (**Figure 8.7**) (www.bluelists.ethz.ch). While the Blue List approach has not been widely adopted, it remains an important concept in showing the way forward. A further development, suggested for other countries, is grouping together Red List species that occur in similar habitats so that they can be managed together (Pärtel et al. 2005).

TABLE 8.3 Percentage of Terrestrial, Freshwater, and Marine Species in Some Temperate Countries that Are Threatened[a] with Global Extinction

	Mammals		Birds	
	Number of species	Percent threatened	Number of species	Percent threatened
Argentina	374	9	974	5
Canada	206	4	536	3
China	555	13	1234	7
Japan	145	19	443	9
Russian Federation	299	11	601	1
South Africa	298	8	762	5
United Kingdom	75	7	268	1.5
United States	441	8	866	9

Source: Data from IUCN 2009 (www.iucnredlist.org); NatureServe 2009.

[a]Threatened species include those in IUCN's critically endangered, endangered, and vulnerable categories.

[b]Percentages are low for amphibians in Russia and for plants in all countries because most species have not yet been evaluated using the updated system of assigning categories. Once all species have been evaluated, these percentages will probably increase.

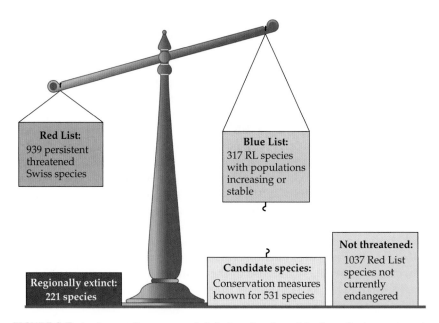

FIGURE 8.7 An innovative approach is being developed in three Swiss cantons to evaluate the current status of the species of plants and animals that are currently on the Red List of threatened and extinct species. Of these, 317 species have been identified as stable or increasing in abundance, thanks to conservation and protection measures; these species form a Blue List of recovering species that have been removed from the Red List. Protection and conservation techniques are locally successful or known for 531 species; these species are "candidate" species for the Blue List. There are 939 "persistent" Red List species that are still declining in size and for which recovery efforts are not yet known. There are 1037 species on the Red List not currently listed as threatened, but in some cases abundances are declining, data are inadequate, or species are not responding to current conservation measures. The goal is to shift the balance as the Blue List lengthens. (After Gigon et al. 2000.)

Reptiles		Amphibians[b]		Plants[b]	
Number of species	Percent threatened	Number of species	Percent threatened	Number of species	Percent threatened
220	2	158	18	9000	0.5
33	9	46	2	6889	0
340	9	326	27	30,000	1.5
66	18	56	34	4700	0.3
58	14	29	0[b]	11,400	0.1
299	6	116	18	23,000	0.3
5	0	8	0	1550	0.9
273	13	269	21	22,079	1

Natural Heritage Data Centers

A program similar to the efforts of the IUCN is the NatureServe network of Natural Heritage programs that covers all 50 of the United States, 3 provinces in Canada, and 14 Latin American countries (www.natureserve.org/explorer). This network, strongly supported by The Nature Conservancy, gathers, organizes, and manages information on the occurrence of "elements of conservation interest"—more than 64,000 species, subspecies, and biological communities (in addition to half a million precisely located populations) (De Grammont and Cuarón 2006). Elements are given status ranks based on a series of standard criteria: number of remaining populations or occurrences, number of individuals remaining (for species) or extent of area (for communities), number of protected sites, degree of threat, and innate vulnerability of the species or community. On the basis of these criteria, elements are assigned an imperilment rank from 1 to 5, ranging from critically imperiled (1) to demonstrably secure (5), on a global, national, and regional basis. Species are also classified as "X" (extinct), "H" (known historically with searches ongoing), and "unknown" (uninvestigated elements). Data on these conservation elements are available on the NatureServe Web site.

The results of NatureServe's conservation status assessment for the United States are detailed in *Precious Heritage: The Status of Biodiversity in the United States* (Stein et al. 2000; www.natureserve.org). The results demonstrate that aquatic species groups, including freshwater mussels, crayfish, amphibians, and fish, are in greater danger of extinction than well-known groups of insects and terrestrial vertebrates (**Figure 8.8**). Freshwater mussels are by far the most endangered species group, with 12% of these species presumed to be extinct already and almost 25% critically imperiled. Land plants are intermediate in degree of endangerment.

This system has also been applied to the 7101 distinct ecological communities recognized in the United States. Only 25% of these can be considered apparently secure, with 58% listed as vulnerable, less than 1% as potentially extinct, and 17% as not yet evaluated or not possible to evaluate (www.natureserve.org). Concentrations of endangered communities occur in Hawaii, the Willamette Valley of Oregon, and large areas of the Midwest and Southeast.

This system has proved extremely successful and useful in organizing hundreds of thousands of records of species and ecosystems occurrence (Pearman et al. 2006). Regional data centers are maintained by hundreds of workers and are consulted

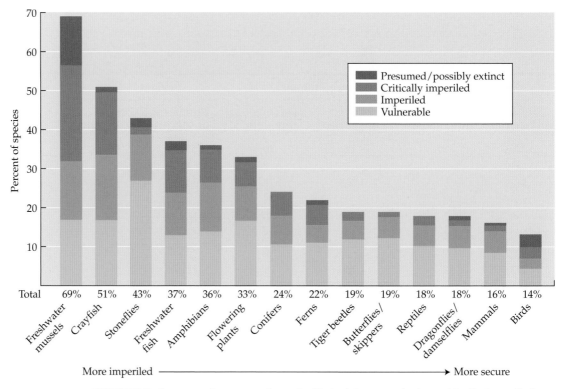

FIGURE 8.8 Some species groups from the United States ranked as critically imperiled, imperiled, or vulnerable according to criteria endorsed by The Nature Conservancy and coordinated by NatureServe. The graph also shows the percentage of species in each class that are presumed to be extinct. The groups are arranged with those at greatest risk on the left. (After Stein et al. 2000.)

approximately 200,000 times a year for information to assist with protection efforts on behalf of endangered species, environmental impact reports, scientific research, and land use decisions. Organizing vast amounts of conservation information is an expensive, labor-intensive activity, but it is a crucial component of conservation efforts. It is imperative to know what species and biological communities are in danger and where they occur, in order to protect them.

Summary

1. Rare species are more prone to extinction than common ones. A species can be considered rare if it has one of these three characteristics: it occupies a narrow geographical range, it occupies only one or a few specialized habitats, or it is always found in small populations. Isolated habitats such as islands, lakes, and mountaintops may have locally endemic species with narrow distributions.

2. Species most vulnerable to extinction have particular characteristics, including a very narrow range, one or only a few populations, small population size, declining population size, and an economic value to humans, which leads to overexploitation. Additional characteristics include low population density, a large home range, large body size, low rate of population increase, poor dispersal ability, migration among different habitats, little genetic variability, specialized niche requirements, a need for

a stable environment, or typically being found in large aggregations. An extinction-prone species may display several of these characteristics.

3. To highlight the status of species for conservation purposes, the IUCN has established nine conservation categories (plus two on the national level), including three categories of threatened species: critically endangered, endangered, and vulnerable. This system of classification is now widely used to evaluate the status of species and establish conservation priorities. Categorization depends on having quantitative information for species, such as number of individuals alive in the wild, number of extant populations, trends in population size, area occupied, and predicted future threats to the species.

4. Countries and regions of the world, as well as conservation organizations, are establishing additional lists of endangered species and biological communities.

For Discussion

1. Learn about a well-known endangered species, such as the Australian koala, the right whale, or the African cheetah. Why are these particular species vulnerable to extinction? Use the IUCN criteria (www.iucnredlist.org) to determine the appropriate conservation category for one or more species.

2. Develop an imaginary animal, recently discovered, that is extraordinarily vulnerable to extinction. Give your species a whole range of characteristics that make it vulnerable; then, consider what could be done to protect it. Give your species a hypothetical set of population characteristics, natural history, and geographical range. Then apply the IUCN system to the species to determine its conservation category.

Suggested Readings

Brooke, A. D., S. H. M. Butchart, S. T. Garnett, G. M. Crowley, N. B. Mantilla-Beniers, and A. Stattersfield. 2008. Rates of movement of threatened bird species between IUCN Red List categories and toward extinction. *Conservation Biology* 22: 417–427. Red Lists provide a standardized method to evaluate changing threats to species and conservation efforts.

Bulman, C. R., R. J. Wilson, A. R. Holt, A. L. Galvez-Bravo, R. I. Early, M. S. Warren, and C. D. Thomas. 2007. Minimum viable population size, extinction debt, and the conservation of declining species. *Ecological Applications* 17: 1460–1473. Many species with small populations are in danger of extinction.

Butchart, S. H. and J. P. Bird. 2010. Data deficient birds on the IUCN Red List: What don't we know and why does it matter? *Biological Conservation* 143: 239–247. The conservation status of birds is better known than other groups, but more information is still needed.

Cardillo, M., G. M. Mace, J. L. Gittleman, K. E. Jones, J. Bielby, and A. Purvis. 2008. The predictability of extinction: Biological and external correlates of decline in mammals. *Proceedings of the Royal Society*, Series B 275: 1441–1448. Species with certain characteristics are more vulnerable to extinction.

Donald, P. F., F. J. Sanderson, I. J. Butterfield, S. M. Bierman, R. D. Gregory, and Z. Walicky. 2007. International conservation policy delivers benefits for birds in Europe. *Science* 317: 810–813. Countries that implement protection show increases in bird populations.

Dunn, R. R., N. C. Harris, R. K. Colwell, L. P. Koh, and N. S. Sodhi. 2009. The sixth mass co-extinction: Are most endangered species parasites and mutualists? *Proceedings of the Royal Society*, Series B 276: 3037–3045. Every time a vertebrate species goes extinct, other species that live on or with it also face extinction.

Fontaine, B. and 70 others. 2007. The European Union's 2010 target: Putting rare species in focus. *Biological Conservation* 139: 167–185. The European Union's conservation efforts include classifying the level of threat for 130,000 species.

International Union for Conservation of Nature (IUCN). www.iucnredlist.org. This Web site has lists of threatened species and useful reports.

Lawler, J. J., S. L. Shafer, B. A. Bancroft, and A. R. Blaustein. 2010. Projected climate impacts for the amphibians of the Western Hemisphere. *Conservation Biology* 24: 38–50. Montane amphibians are especially vulnerable to the changing patterns of temperature and rainfall associated with climate change.

Mace, G. M., N. J. Collar, K. J. Gaston, C. Hilton-Taylor, H. R. Akcakaya, N. Leader-Williams, et al. 2008. Quantification of extinction risk: IUCN's system for classifying threatened species. *Conservation Biology* 22: 1424–1442. The IUCN has moved from a subjective system to a quantitative system for measuring threats to species.

NatureServe. 2009. http://natureserve.org. This Web site organizes and presents data on biodiversity surveys from North America.

Van Turnhout, C. A. M., R. P. B. Foppen, R. S. E. W. Leuven, A. Van Strien, and H. Siepel. 2010. Life-history and ecological correlates of population change in Dutch breeding birds. *Biological Conservation* 143: 173–181. Ground-nesting bird species in the Netherlands are declining in numbers because of agricultural intensification.

Wilcove, D. S. and M. Wikelski. 2008. Going, going, gone: Is animal migration disappearing? *PLoS Biology* 6: 1361–1364. Fences, roads, farms, and other human activities prevent the free movement of migratory species.

Habitat Destruction, Fragmentation, Degradation, and Global Climate Change

As we've seen in Chapters 7 and 8, the human population poses a serious and growing threat of extinction to species and entire biological communities. Massive disturbances caused by people have altered, degraded, and destroyed the natural landscape on a vast scale, driving species and even entire ecosystems to the point of extinction. The seven major threats to biological diversity that result from human activity are habitat destruction, habitat fragmentation, habitat degradation (including pollution), global climate change, the overexploitation of species for human use, the introduction of invasive species, and the increased spread of disease (**Figure 9.1**). In this chapter we will examine the first four threats we pose to the environment; in Chapter 10 we will discuss overexploitation, invasive species, and disease. Most threatened species face at least two of these threats, thus speeding their way to extinction and hindering efforts to protect them (Burgman et al. 2007). Typically, these threats develop so rapidly and on such a large scale that species are not able to adapt genetically to the changes or disperse to a more hospitable location. Moreover, multiple threats may interact additively or even synergistically such that their combined impact on a species or an ecosystem is greater than their individual effects.

FIGURE 9.1 The major threats to biodiversity (yellow boxes) are the result of human activities. These seven factors can interact synergistically to speed up the loss of biodiversity. (After Groom et al. 2006.)

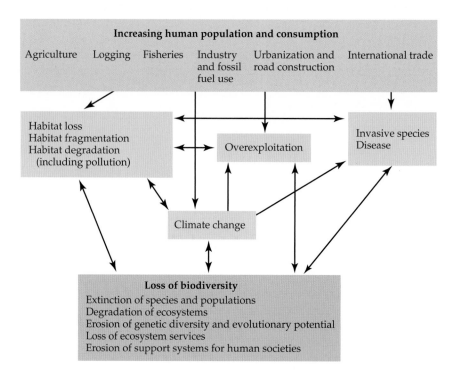

Human Population Growth and Its Impact

The seven major threats to biological diversity are all caused by an ever-increasing use of the world's natural resources by an expanding human population (**Table 9.1**). Up until the last 300 years, the rate of human population growth had been relatively slow, with the birthrate only slightly exceeding the mortality rate. The greatest destruction of biological communities has occurred over the last 150 years, during which time the human population exploded from 1 billion in 1850 to 7 billion in 2010. Humans have increased in such numbers because birthrates have remained high while mortality rates have declined—a result of both modern medical achievements (specifically the control of disease) and the presence of more reliable food supplies. Population growth has slowed in the industrialized countries of the world, as well as in some developing countries in Asia and Latin America,

---

TABLE 9.1 Three Ways Humans Dominate the Global Ecosystem

1. Land Surface

Human land use and need for resources, mainly agriculture and forestry, have transformed as much as half of the Earth's ice-free land surface.

2. Nitrogen cycle

Each year human activities, such as cultivating nitrogen-fixing crops, using nitrogen fertilizers, and burning fossil fuels, release more nitrogen into terrestrial systems than is added by natural biological and physical processes.

3. Atmospheric carbon cycle

By the middle of this century, human use of fossil fuels and cutting down forests will have resulted in a doubling of the level of carbon dioxide in the Earth's atmosphere.

Source: Data from MEA 2005; Kulkarni et al. 2008.

but it is still high in other areas, particularly in tropical Africa. If these countries implement immediate and effective programs of population control, human population numbers could possibly peak at "only" 8 billion in 2050 and then gradually decline. Because human population density is a good predictor of the intensity of threats to biodiversity, this increase in human population is predicted to cause an additional 14% of bird and mammal species to be threatened with extinction by the year 2050 (Gaston 2005).

People use natural resources, such as fuelwood, wild meat, and wild plants, and convert vast amounts of natural habitat for agricultural and residential purposes. Agricultural systems now occupy one-fourth of the Earth's land surface. All else being equal, more people equals greater human impact and less biodiversity (Laurance 2007; Clausen and York 2008). Nitrogen pollution is greatest in rivers flowing through landscapes with high human population densities, and rates of deforestation are greatest in countries with the highest rates of human population growth. Therefore, some scientists have argued strongly that controlling the size of the human population is the key to protecting biological diversity (Rockström et al. 2009).

Whether motivated by greed, desperation, or indifference, once a community or nation begins exploiting resources for short-term gain, it is difficult to stop the process. Biological communities can often persist close to areas with high densities of people as long as human activities are regulated by local custom or government. The sacred groves that are preserved next to villages in Africa, India, and China are excellent examples of locally managed biological communities (Wild and MacLeod 2008). Sometimes this regulation breaks down during war, political unrest, and social instability. When this happens, there may be a scramble to use up and sell resources that had been sustainably used for generations. The higher the density of people, the more closely their activities must be regulated, and the greater the destruction that can result from a breakdown in authority (Grimm et al. 2008). The devastation that occurred in China's forests during the Cultural Revolution is a revealing example: Strict regulations against cutting trees were no longer enforced, so farmers cut down trees at a tremendous rate, stockpiling wood for fuel, construction, and furniture making (Zhang et al. 2006).

In many developing countries, local farm owners are often forced off their land by large landowners, business interests, and even the government, which is often backed up by the police and army. These local farmers often have no choice but to move to remote, undeveloped areas and attempt to eke out a living through shifting cultivation, destroying natural habitats and hunting animals to local extinction. Political instability, lawlessness, and war also force farmers off their land and into remote, undeveloped areas where they feel safer. The 1 billion impoverished people of the world who live on less than $2 per day are too hungry and desperate to worry about protecting biodiversity. Until these people are given the opportunity to improve their lives in a sustainable manner, and until the present economic inequality between rich and poor people is addressed, the environments in which they live will continue to deteriorate (Holland et al. 2009).

Population growth is not the only cause of species extinction and habitat destruction: overconsumption of resources is also responsible. Species extinctions and the destruction of ecosystems are not necessarily caused by individual citizens obtaining their basic needs. The rise of industrial capitalism and materialistic modern societies has greatly accelerated demands for natural resources, particularly in the developed countries. Moreover, industrialized countries have served as role models for developing nations, which now increasingly aspire to attain the same levels of overconsumption as the industrial countries. China and India, in particular, have emerged as major importers of soybeans, palm oil, and timber, in the process contributing to tropical deforestation. Inefficient and wasteful use and overconsumption of natural resources are major causes of the decline in biological diversity.

FIGURE 9.2 Citizens of the wealthy, developed countries of the world often criticize the poorer, developing nations for a lack of sound environmental policies but seem unwilling to acknowledge that their own excessive consumption of resources is a major part of the problem. (Cartoon by Scott Willis © San Jose Mercury News.)

People in industrialized countries (and the wealthy minority in the developing countries) consume a disproportionate share of the world's energy, minerals, wood products, and food (Myers and Kent 2004), and therefore have a disproportionate impact on the environment (**Figure 9.2**). Each year, the United States, which has 5% of the world's human population, uses roughly 25% of the world's natural resources. Each year the average U.S. citizen uses 23 times more energy and 79 times more paper products than does the average citizen of India (Randolph and Masters 2008).

The impact (I) of any human population on the environment is captured by the formula $I = PAT$, where P is the number of people, A is the average income, and T is the level of technology (Ehrlich and Goulder 2007; Dietz et al. 2007). It is important to recognize that this impact is often felt over a great distance; for example, a citizen of Germany, Canada, or Japan affects the environment in other countries through his or her use of foods and other materials produced elsewhere. This increasing interconnectedness of resource and labor markets is termed **globalization**. The fish eaten quietly at home in Washington, D.C., perhaps came from Alaskan waters, where its capture contributed to the population decline of sea lions, seals, and sea otters; the chocolate cake and coffee consumed at the end of a meal in Italy or France were made with cacao and coffee beans grown in plantations carved out of rain forests in West Africa, Indonesia, or Brazil. This linkage has been captured in the idea of the **ecological footprint**, defined as the influence a group of people has on both the surrounding environment and locations across the globe (**Figure 9.3**) (Holden and Hoyer 2005). In the western United States, the human footprint is greatest in populated areas and in areas converted to agriculture (Leu et al. 2008).

A modern city in a developed country typically has an ecological footprint that is hundreds of times its area. For example, the city of Toronto in Canada occupies an area of only 630 km², but each of its citizens requires the environmental services of 7.7 ha (0.077 km²) to provide food, water, and waste disposal sites; with a population of 2.4 million people, Toronto has an ecological footprint of 185,000 km², an

> The major threats to biodiversity—habitat destruction, habitat fragmentation, pollution, global climate change, overexploitation of resources, invasive exotic species, and the spread of disease—are all rooted in the expanding human population.

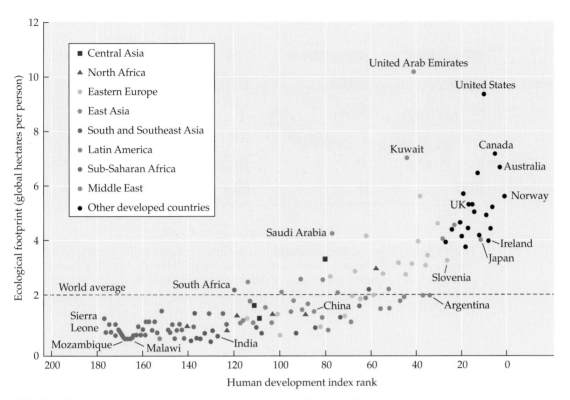

FIGURE 9.3 An ecological footprint for a nation is arrived at by calculations that estimate the number of global hectares needed to support an average citizen of that nation. Although the methods used to arrive at these calculations can be argued, the overall message is clear. When plotted against an economic development index of living standards, global footprints graphically illustrate the disproportionate use of natural resources by people in developed nations. (Data from Global Footprint Network and the United Nations Development Programme 2006.)

area equal to the state of New Jersey or the country of Syria. This excessive consumption of resources is not sustainable in the long term. Unfortunately, this pattern is now being adopted by the expanding middle class in the developing world, including the large, rapidly developing countries of China and India, and this increases the probability of massive environmental disruption (Grumbine 2007). The affluent citizens of developed countries must confront their excessive consumption of resources and reevaluate their lifestyles while at the same time offering aid to curb population growth, protect biological diversity, and assist industries in the developing world to grow in a responsible way.

> The enormous consumption of resources in an increasingly globalized world is not sustainable in the long term.

Habitat Destruction

The primary cause of the loss of biological diversity, including species, biological communities, and genetic variation, is not direct human exploitation or malevolence but the habitat destruction that inevitably results from the expansion of human populations and human activities (**Figure 9.4**). For the next few decades, land-use change will continue to be the main factor affecting biodiversity in terrestrial ecosystems, probably followed by overexploitation, climate change, and the introduction of invasive species (IUCN 2004). Consequently, the most important means of protecting biological diversity is habitat preservation. Habitat loss does not necessar-

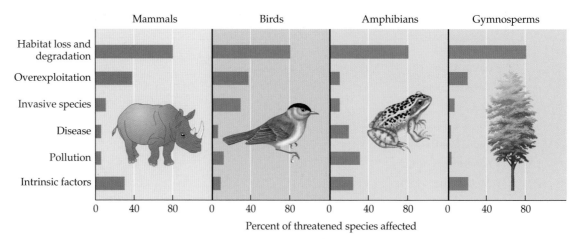

FIGURE 9.4 Habitat loss and degradation is the greatest threat to the world's species, followed by overexploitation. Groups of species face different threats; birds are more threatened by invasive species, whereas amphibians are more affected by disease and pollution. Percentages add up to more than 100% because species often face multiple threats. (After IUCN 2004.)

ily mean wholesale habitat destruction—habitat fragmentation and habitat damage associated with pollution can also mean that the habitat is effectively "lost" to species that cannot tolerate these changes, even though to the casual onlooker the habitat appears intact. A pond contaminated by acid rain may still look like a healthy wetland habitat, but for frogs sensitive to these chemicals, it can be considered a lost habitat. When a habitat is degraded and destroyed, the plants, animals, and other organisms living there will have nowhere to go and will just die off.

In many areas of the world, particularly on islands and in locations where human population density is high, most of the original habitat has been destroyed (MEA 2005) (**Figure 9.5**). Fully 98% of the land suitable for agriculture has already been transformed by human activity (Sanderson et al. 2002). Because the world's population will continue to increase, we will increase agricultural output by 30% to 50% over the next 30 years; thus, the need to protect biological diversity will be forced to compete directly against the need for new agricultural lands.

Habitat disturbance has been particularly severe throughout Europe; southern and eastern Asia, including the Philippines, China, and Japan; southeastern and southwestern Australia; New Zealand; Madagascar; West Africa; the southeastern and northern coasts of South America; Central America; the Caribbean; and central and eastern North America. In many of these regions, more than 50% of the natural habitats have been disturbed or removed. Only 15% of the land area in Europe remains unmodified by human activities, and in some regions of Europe, the figure is even lower. In Germany or the UK, for example, one can hardly find any habitat that has not been modified by humans at one time or another.

In the United States, only 42% of the natural vegetation remains, and in many regions of the East and Midwest, less than 25% remains (Stein et al. 2000). Certain biological communities in the United States have declined in area by 98% or more since European settlement (Noss et al. 1995): old-growth stands in eastern deciduous forests, old-growth longleaf pine (*Pinus palustris*) forests and savannas in the southeastern coastal plain, ungrazed dry prairie in Florida, native grasslands in California, ungrazed sagebrush steppe in the Intermountain West, and streams in the Mississippi River floodplain. The principal threats to habitat that affect endangered species, in order of decreasing importance, are agriculture (affecting 38% of endangered species), commercial developments (35%), water projects (30%), out-

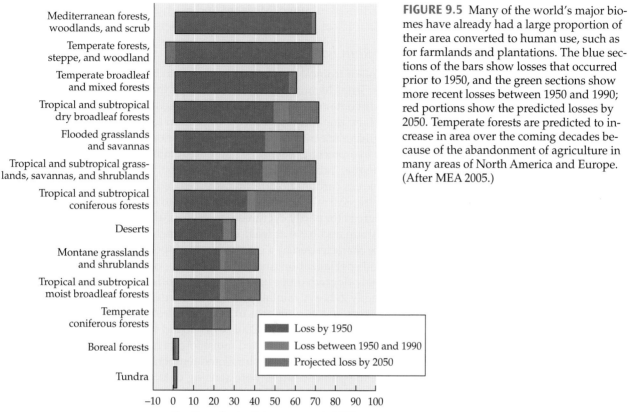

FIGURE 9.5 Many of the world's major biomes have already had a large proportion of their area converted to human use, such as for farmlands and plantations. The blue sections of the bars show losses that occurred prior to 1950, and the green sections show more recent losses between 1950 and 1990; red portions show the predicted losses by 2050. Temperate forests are predicted to increase in area over the coming decades because of the abandonment of agriculture in many areas of North America and Europe. (After MEA 2005.)

door recreation (27%), livestock grazing (22%), pollution (20%), infrastructure and roads (17%), disruption of fire ecology (13%), and logging (12%) (Stein et al. 2000; Wilcove and Master 2005).

More than 50% of the wildlife habitat has been destroyed in many tropical countries (Gallant et al. 2007). In tropical Asia, fully 65% of the primary forest habitat has been lost. The two biologically rich countries of Brazil and Indonesia still have about half of their primary forest habitats and have established extensive protected areas, but the forces of habitat destruction and degradation continue apace (Koh and Wilcove 2007; Laurance 2007). Sub-Saharan Africa has similarly lost a total of about 65% of its forests, with losses being most severe in Rwanda (80%), Gambia (89%), and Ghana (82%). The large and biologically rich Democratic Republic of the Congo (formerly Zaire) is relatively better off, retaining about half of its forests, although the recent civil war has halted efforts to protect and manage wildlife.

In the Mediterranean region, which has been densely populated by people for thousands of years, only 10% of the original forest cover remains. An important point to remember here is that wildlife populations are lost in proportion to the amount of habitat that has been lost; even though the Mediterranean forest still exists in places, approximately 90% of its populations of birds, butterflies, wildflowers, frogs, and mosses that once existed are no longer there.

For many important wildlife species, the majority of habitat in their original ranges has been destroyed, and very little of the remaining habitat is protected. For certain Asian primates, such as the Javan gibbon, more than 95% of the original habitat (and 95% of the populations!) has been destroyed, and some of these species are protected on less than 2% of their original ranges (WRI 2000). The orangutan, a great ape that lives in Sumatra and Borneo, has lost most of its range and is protected in only 35% of its range (Meijaard and Wich 2007). In North America, bison occupy less than 1% of their original range (Sanderson et al. 2008).

Threatened Rain Forests

The destruction of tropical rain forests has come to be synonymous with the rapid loss of species. Tropical moist forests occupy 7% of the Earth's land surface, but they are estimated to contain over 50% of its species (Bradshaw et al. 2009; Corlett and Primack 2010). Many rain forest species are important to local economies and have the potential for greater use by the entire world population. Rain forests also have regional importance in protecting watersheds and moderating climate, local significance as home to numerous indigenous cultures, and global importance as sinks to absorb some of the excess carbon dioxide that is produced by the burning of fossil fuels. About 40% of tropical rain forests are in the Brazilian Amazon (Rodrigues et al. 2009).

These evergreen (or partly evergreen) forests occur in frost-free areas below about 1800 m in altitude and have at least 100 mm (4 inches) of rain per month in most years. They are characterized by a great richness of species and a complexity of species interaction and specialization unparalleled in any other community. Tropical rain forests are easily degraded because the soils are often thin and nutrient poor, and they erode readily in heavy rainfall. At present, there is considerable discussion about the original extent and current area of tropical forests as well as rates of deforestation (see Figure 3.1) (Jenkins et al. 2003; Corlett and Primack 2010). The original extent of tropical rain forests and related moist forests has been estimated at 16 million km², based on current patterns of rainfall and temperature. A combination of ground surveys, airplane photos, and remote-sensing data from satellites showed that in 1990 only 11.5 million km² remained. A recent estimate from satellite imagery suggests that an additional 2.4% of the world's tropical rain forest was lost between 2000 and 2005 (Hansen et al. 2008b). More than 60% of that loss occurred in the Neotropics, with Brazil alone accounting for almost half. Another third occurred in Asia, with Indonesia second to Brazil in the absolute rate of forest loss. Africa contributed only 5.4% to the total area lost, reflecting the current absence of industrial-scale agricultural clearance. Strikingly, 55% of all forest losses occurred within only 6% of the total area, with these including an "arc of deforestation" in the south and southeast of the Brazilian Amazon, much of Malaysia, and Sumatra and parts of Kalimantan in Indonesia. The current rate of deforestation represents approximately 1% of the original forest area lost per year (Laurance 2007a).

Despite the difficulty in obtaining accurate numbers for rain forest deforestation rates, due to varying definitions of *forest cover* and *forest degradation* and differing methods, the consensus is that tropical deforestation rates are alarmingly high (Laurance and Luizão 2007). The loss of tropical forest habitat continues at a rate that guarantees that almost all tropical rain forests will be lost over the next few decades. The only forests that remain will be in protected areas and on rugged or remote terrain. The move to establish large new parks in many tropical countries is cause for some hope; however, these will need to be well funded and managed to be effective, as described in Chapters 15 and 17. In many cases, these are only "paper parks" with few employees or facilities.

On a global scale, the majority of rain forest destruction may still result from small-scale cultivation of crops by poor farmers, often forced to remote forest lands by poverty or sometimes moved there by government-sponsored resettlement programs) **(Figure 9.6A,B)**. Much of this farming is termed **shifting cultivation**, a kind of subsistence farming, sometimes referred to as slash-and-burn, or swidden, agriculture, in which trees are cut down and then burned away. The cleared patches are farmed for two or three seasons, after which soil fertility usually diminishes to the point where adequate crop production is no longer possible (Phua et al. 2008). The patches are then abandoned and new natural vegetation must be cleared. Shift-

(A)

(B)

(C)

FIGURE 9.6 The displacement of rain forest for agricultural purposes can take many forms. (A) In this case, members of the Pemon tribe indigenous to Brazilian Amazonia have cut down trees to build shelters and have burned forest cover in preparation for planting crops. Such settlements are usually abandoned after a few growing seasons as soil fertility decreases—a widespread practice known as "shifting cultivation" or "slash-and-burn agriculture." (B) Tropical forest has been cleared for small-scale crops on this hill in Sabah, Malaysian Borneo. Note the abrupt edge between the field and the intact forest. (C) Large areas of tropical forests have been cleared for oil palm plantations. From the air, these look somewhat like green seas. (A, photograph © David Woodfall/Alamy; B, photograph © Matthew Lambley/Alamy; C, photograph © jeremy sutton-hibbert/Alamy.)

ing cultivation is often practiced because the farmers are unwilling or unable to spend the time and money necessary to develop more permanent forms of agriculture on land that they do not own and may not occupy for very long. Included in this destruction is land degraded each year for fuelwood production, mostly to supply local villagers with wood for cooking fires. More than 2 billion people cook their food with firewood, so their impact is significant. Increasing human population in poor tropical countries will cause further loss of forests in coming decades (**Table 9.2**).

In an increasing proportion of the tropics, however, clearance by peasant farmers to meet subsistence needs is now dwarfed by clearance by large landowners and commercial interests, to create pasture for cattle ranching or to plant cash crops,

TABLE 9.2 Some Statistics Relevant for the Future of Rain Forests in Five Major Rain Forest Countries (Note the different dates to which they apply. What are the greatest threats to forests in each of these countries?)

	Brazil	DRC	Indonesia	PNG	Madagascar
Area of forest (thousand km²) (2005)[a]	4777	1336	885	294	128
Percentage forest cover (2005)[a]	57	59	49	65	22
Percentage of intact forest landscapes (c. 2000)[b]	32	29	20	35	8
Annual change in forest cover (%) (2000–2005)[a]	−0.6	−0.2	−2.0	−0.5	−0.3
Annual log production (million m³) (2008)[c]	25	0.3	34	3	0.1
Number of cattle (millions) (2007)[d]	200	1	11	0.1	10
Human population (millions) (2005)[e]	186	59	219	6	18
Population density (per km²) (2005)[e]	22	25	119	13	32
Human population growth rate (%) (2005)[e]	1.0	2.8	1.2	2.4	2.7
Projected human population in 2050[e]	219	148	288	13	43
Fertility (children per woman) (2005)[e]	1.9	6.1	2.2	4.1	4.8
Mortality before age 5 (per thousand) (2005)[e]	29	198	32	69	100
Life expectancy (2005)[e]	72	48	71	61	60
Per capita GDP (PPP) (US$) (2008)[f]	10,200	300	3900	2200	1000

Source: Corlett and Primack 2010.
[a] FAO Global Forest Resources Assessment 2005. Includes all forest types; in the case of Madagascar, most of this is not tropical rain forest.
[b] Potapov et al. 2008.
[c] International Tropical Timber Organization.
[d] FAOSTAT.
[e] United Nations Population Division.
[f] International Monetary Fund. GDP = gross domestic product; PPP = purchasing power parity.
DRC = Democratic Republic of the Congo; PNG = Papua New Guinea.

such as oil palm and soybeans (Butler and Laurance 2008) (**Figure 9.6C**). Cattle ranching and soybean cultivation are particularly important in tropical America, while plantations of tree crops are the major cause of deforestation in much of Southeast Asia and are increasing elsewhere. Commercial agriculture displaces poor farmers and justifies the expansion of roads. It is generally worse for biodiversity than clearance by peasant farmers, because large areas are maintained under a uniform crop cover. Large areas of rain forest are damaged during commercial logging operations, most of which are poorly managed selective logging. In many cases, logging operations precede conversion of land to agriculture and ranching.

The relative importance of these enterprises varies by geographical region: logging is a significant activity in tropical Asia and America, cattle ranching is most prominent in tropical America, and farming is more important for the rapidly expanding population in tropical Africa (Corlett 2009; Corlett and Primack 2010). In relative terms the deforestation rate is greatest in Asia, at about 1.2% per year, while in absolute terms tropical America has the greatest amount of deforestation because of its larger total area. Extending the projection forward in time reveals that, at the current rate of loss, there will be little tropical forest left after the year 2040, except in the relatively small national parks and remote areas of the Amazon basin, Congo River basin, and New Guinea. The situation is actually more grim than these projections indicate, because the world's population is still increasing and poverty is on the rise in many developing tropical countries, putting ever-greater demands on the dwindling supply of rain forest.

The destruction of tropical rain forests is caused frequently by demand in industrialized countries for cheap agricultural products, such as rubber, palm oil, cocoa,

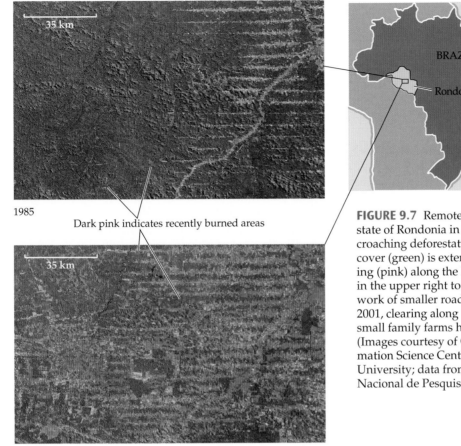

1985

Dark pink indicates recently burned areas

2001

FIGURE 9.7 Remote sensing images from the Brazilian state of Rondonia in the Amazon River basin show encroaching deforestation over a 15-year time frame. Forest cover (green) is extensive in 1985, with small areas of clearing (pink) along the highway from the town of Ariquemes in the upper right to the lower middle; an east–west network of smaller roads was built by the government. By 2001, clearing along the road for large cattle ranches and small family farms had removed most of the forest cover. (Images courtesy of Christopher Barber, Geographic Information Science Center of Excellence, South Dakota State University; data from U.S. Geological Survey and Instituto Nacional de Pesquisas Espaciais, Brazil.)

soybeans, orange juice, and beef, and for low-cost wood products (**Figure 9.7**) (Nepstad et al. 2006). During the 1980s, Costa Rica and other Latin American countries had some of the world's highest rates of deforestation as a result of the conversion of rain forests into cattle ranches. Much of the beef produced on these ranches was sold to the United States and other developed countries to produce inexpensive hamburgers. Adverse publicity resulting from this "hamburger connection," followed by consumer boycotts, led major restaurant chains in the United States to stop buying tropical beef from these ranches. The boycott was important in making people aware of the international connections that promote deforestation. Cattle ranching to produce beef for export is still a major contributor to rain forest destruction in Brazil and other Latin American countries. A priority for conservation biology is to help provide the information, programs, and public awareness that will allow the greatest amount of rain forest to persist once the present cycle of destruction ends. At present, most consumers in temperate countries are not aware of how their food choices affect land use. Many people would be surprised to learn how widely palm oil is used in food products, and the story of where it come from. It is also true that increasing proportions of these agricultural and wood products are consumed within the tropical countries themselves or exported to rapidly industrializing countries, such as China and India.

> The demand for coffee, chocolate, sugar, timber, and beef in the United States and other industrialized countries helps fuel the destruction of vast expanses of tropical rain forest.

The story of Indonesian Borneo and Sumatra in Southeast Asia illustrates how rapid and serious rain forest destruction can be. Between 1990 and 2005, an incredible 42% of the lowland forest of these two large islands was cleared. Most of the clearing was due to logging, both legal and illegal, and the development of cash crops, especially oil palm (Hansen et al. 2009).

Other Threatened Habitats

The plight of the tropical rain forests is perhaps the most widely publicized case of habitat destruction, but many other habitats are also in grave danger. We discuss a few of these threatened habitats below:

TROPICAL DECIDUOUS FORESTS   The land occupied by tropical deciduous forests is more suitable for agriculture and cattle ranching than is the land occupied by tropical rain forests. The forests are also easier than rain forests to clear and burn. Moderate rainfall in the range of 250 to 2000 mm per year allows mineral nutrients to be retained in the soil where they can be taken up by plants. Consequently, human population density is five times greater in dry forest areas of Central America than in adjacent rain forests. Today, the Pacific coast of Central America has less than 2% of its original forest remaining (WWF and McGinley 2009), and less than 3% remains in Madagascar which is home to the lemurs, an endemic group of primates (**Figure 9.8**) (Hogan et al. 2008).

> Between 1800 and 1950, as much as 97% of North America's tallgrass prairie was converted to farmland. The majority of European wetlands has been lost due to human activity.

GRASSLANDS   Temperate grassland is another habitat type that has been almost completely destroyed by human activity. It is relatively easy to convert large areas of grassland to farmland and cattle ranches. Between 1800 and 1950, as much as 97% of North America's tallgrass prairie was converted to farmland (White et al. 2000). The remaining area of prairie is fragmented and widely scattered across the landscape.

WETLANDS AND AQUATIC HABITATS   Wetlands are critical habitats for fish, aquatic invertebrates, and birds. They are also a resource for flood control, drinking water, and power production (MEA 2005). Although many wetland species are widespread, some aquatic systems are known for their high levels of endemism.

FIGURE 9.8 Verreaux's sifaka (*Propithecus verreauxi*) is a lemur, a lineage of primates found only on the large island of Madagascar. Virtually all of the numerous lemur species are endangered as a result of the destruction of Madagascar's forests. (Photograph © Kevin Schafer/Alamy.)

Wetlands are often filled in or drained for development, or they are altered by channelization of watercourses, dams, and chemical pollution (Coleman et al. 2008). All of these factors are affecting the Florida Everglades, one of the premier wildlife refuges in the United States, which is now on the verge of ecological collapse (and see Box 5.1 for the disastrous consequences of wetlands destruction in Louisiana). Over the last 200 years, over half of the wetlands in the United States have been destroyed, resulting in either extinction or endangerment of 40% to 50% of the freshwater snail species in the southeastern United States (Stein et al. 2000). More than 97% of the vernal pools in California's San Diego County have been destroyed; these unusual wetlands fill up with water in the winter and dry out in the summer, and they support a unique endemic biota. The majority of U.S. Pacific salmon stocks face moderate to high extinction risks as the rivers that they use to spawn are damaged and dammed (Laetz et al. 2009). In the United States, 98% of the country's 5.2 million km of streams have been degraded in some way to the point that they are no longer considered wild or scenic. Destruction of wetlands has been equally severe in other parts of the industrialized world, such as Europe and Japan. About 60% to 70% of wetlands in Europe have been lost. Only 2 of Japan's 30,000 rivers can be considered wild, without dams or some other major modification. In the last few decades, major threats to wetlands in developing countries have included massive development projects involving drainage, irrigation, and dams, organized by governments and often financed by international aid agencies.

The Three Gorges Dam on the Yangtze River of China is a recent example (see Box 21.2) (Stone 2008). The dam is the largest hydroelectric power plant in the world, generating much-needed clean and renewable energy. But by the time the reservoir is filled, the project will have displaced more than 1 million people and destroyed untold numbers of ecosystems and archeological sites. Additional millions of people may need to be moved in coming years. The economic benefits of such projects are important, but the rights of local people and the value of the ecosystem are often not adequately considered.

Marine Coastal Areas

Human populations are increasingly concentrated in coastal areas. Already 20% of marine coastal areas have been degraded or highly modified by human activity. Throughout the world, intensive harvesting of fish, shellfish, seaweeds, and other marine products is transforming marine environments (Halpern et al. 2007). They are also threatened by pollution, dredging, sedimentation, destructive fishing practices, invasive species, and now rising temperatures. Human impacts are less well studied than in the terrestrial environment, but they are probably equally severe, especially in shallow coastal areas. Two coastal habitats of special note are mangroves and coral reefs.

MANGROVES Mangrove forests are among the most important wetland communities in tropical areas. Composed of species that are among the few woody plants able to tolerate saltwater, mangrove forests occupy coastal areas with saline or brackish water, typically where there are muddy bottoms. Such habitats are similar to salt marshes in the temperate zone. Mangroves are extremely important breeding grounds and feeding areas for shrimp and fish (**Figure 9.9**). In Australia, for example, two-thirds of the species caught by commercial fishermen depend to some degree on the mangrove ecosystem.

Despite their great economic value and their utility for protecting coastal areas from storms and tsunamis, mangroves are often cleared for rice cultivation and commercial shrimp and prawn hatcheries, particularly in Southeast Asia, where as much as 15% of the mangrove area has been removed for aquaculture. Mangroves have also been severely degraded by overcollecting of wood for fuel, construction

FIGURE 9.9 Mangrove forests in Southeast Asia and elsewhere in tropical coasts are being removed for shrimp farms and other coastal development. Fragments of mangroves and the river channel are still visible. (Photograph © Tim Laman.)

poles, and timber throughout the region. Over 35% of the world's mangrove ecosystems have already been destroyed, and more are being destroyed every year (Martinuzzi et al. 2009). Of the vertebrates endemic to mangroves, 40% are threatened with extinction (Luther and Greenberg 2009).

CORAL REEFS Tropical coral reefs are particularly significant, as they contain an estimated one-third of the ocean's fish species in only 0.2% of its surface area (see Chapter 3). Already 20% of all coral reefs have been destroyed. A further 20% has been degraded by overfishing, overharvesting, pollution, and the introduction of invasive species (MEA 2005). The most severe destruction is taking place in the Philippines, where a staggering 90% of the reefs are dead or dying. The main culprits are pollution, which either kills the coral directly or allows excessive growth of algae; sedimentation following deforestation; overharvesting of fish, clams, and other animals; and finally, blasting with dynamite and releasing cyanide to collect the few remaining living creatures. Climate warming, discussed later in this chapter, also appears to be playing a role in the rapid degradation of coral reefs.

Extensive loss of coral reefs is expected within the next 40 years in tropical East Asia, the areas around Madagascar and East Africa, and throughout the Caribbean (**Figure 9.10**). In the Caribbean, overfishing, hurricane damage, coastal development, sedimentation, pollution, and disease combined are responsible for a dramatic decline of a large proportion of the coral reefs and their replacement by fleshy macroalgae (Carpenter et al. 2008; Mora 2009). Elkhorn and staghorn corals, which were formerly common in the Caribbean and gave structure to the community, have already become rare in many locations.

Over the last 10 years, scientists have discovered extensive reefs of coral living in cold water at depths of 300 m or more, many of which are in the temperate zone of the North Atlantic. These coral reefs are rich in species, with numerous species new to science. Yet at the same time these communities are first being explored, they are being destroyed by trawlers, which drag nets across the seafloor to catch fish; the trawlers destroy the very coral reefs that protect and provide food for young

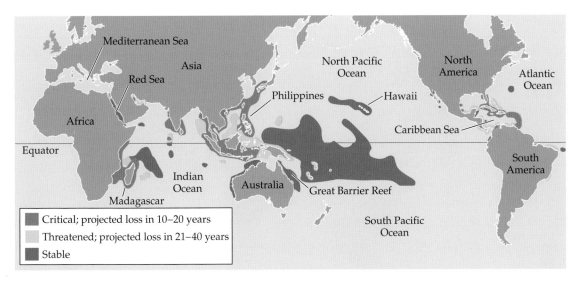

FIGURE 9.10 Extensive areas of coral will be damaged or destroyed by human activity over the next 40 years unless conservation measures can be implemented. (After Bryant et al. 1998.)

fish. The damage to these cold water reefs by careless harvesting is costing the industry its resource base in the long run.

Desertification

Many biological communities in seasonally dry climates are degraded by human activities into man-made deserts, a process known as **desertification** (Okin et al. 2009). These dryland communities include grasslands, scrub, and deciduous forest, as well as temperate shrublands, such as those found in the Mediterranean region, southwestern Australia, South Africa, central Chile, and California. Dry areas cover about 41% of the world's land area and are home to about 1 billion people. Approximately 10% to 20% of these drylands are at least moderately degraded, with more than 25% of the productive capacity of their plant growth having been lost (Neff et al. 2005). These areas may initially support agriculture, but their repeated cultivation, especially during dry and windy years, often leads to soil erosion and loss of water-holding capacity in the soil (**Figure 9.11**). Land may also be chronically overgrazed by domestic livestock, and woody plants may be cut down for fuel. Frequent fires during long dry periods often damage the remaining vegetation. The result is the progressive and largely irreversible degradation of the biological community and the loss of soil cover. Ultimately, formerly productive farmland and pastures take on the appearance of a desert. Desertification has been ongoing for thousands of years in the Mediterranean region, and was known even to ancient Greek observers.

Worldwide, 9 million km^2 of arid lands have been converted to man-made deserts. These areas are not functional desert ecosystems but wastelands, lacking the flora and fauna characteristic of natural deserts. The process of desertification is most severe in the Sahel region of Africa, just south of the Sahara, where most of the native large mammal species are threatened with extinction. The human dimension of the problem is illustrated by the fact that the Sahel region is estimated to have 2.5 times more people (100 million currently) than the land can sustainably support. The problem is magnified by the high population growth and poverty of people living in such areas, as well as by wars and civil unrest, which force thousands of people to eke out an existence using whatever resources and methods they can find, whether sustainable or not (MEA 2005). Further desertification appears to be almost inevitable,

(A)

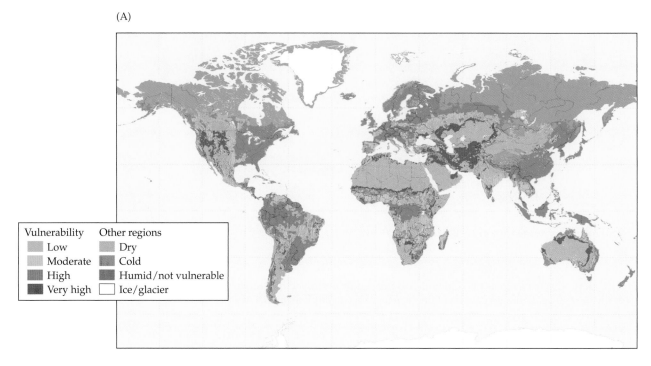

(B)

FIGURE 9.11 (A) Arid areas of the world are experiencing encroaching desertification, with increasing aridity and expanding deserts. The regions shaded in red, orange, and yellow are vulnerable to desertification and are potentially at risk of becoming desert over the next several decades. (B) Deserts are expanding as human activities stress semiarid ecosystems. (A, courtesy of the USDA Natural Resource Conservation Service; B, photograph © Images of Africa Photobank/Alamy.)

As the human population grows, people and domesticated animals move into drylands that can't support their numbers, turning semiarid areas into full-blown deserts.

especially when accompanied by the higher temperatures and lower rainfall associated with predictions of future climate change (Verstraete et al. 2009). In such areas, the solution will be programs involving improved and sustainable agricultural practices, the elimination of poverty, the stabilization of civil society, and population control.

Habitat Fragmentation

In addition to being destroyed outright, habitats that formerly occupied wide, un-broken areas are now often divided into pieces by roads, fields, towns, and a broad range of other human constructs. **Habitat fragmentation** is the process whereby a large, continuous area of habitat is both reduced in area and divided into two or more fragments (**Figure 9.12**). When habitat is destroyed, a patchwork of habitat fragments may be left behind. These fragments are often isolated from one anoth-er by a highly modified or degraded landscape, and their edges experience an al-

(A)

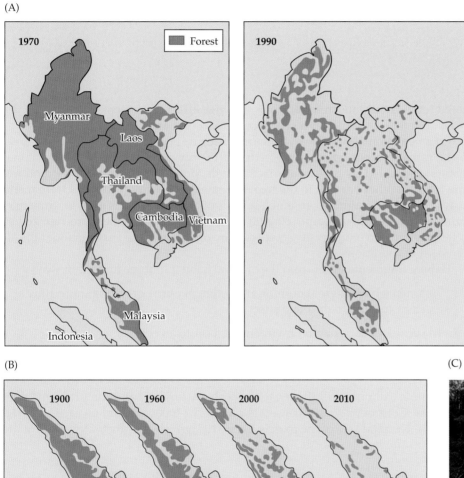

(B)

(C)

FIGURE 9.12 The forests of tropical Asia have experienced massive deforestation and fragmentation in recent decades. (A) Two forest maps of Southeast Asia from 1970 and 1990. (B) Sumatra, a large is-land of Indonesia, has experienced intense habitat destruction over the past 100 years, and this process was predicted to continue through 2010. (C) A wide path (note the car for scale) has been cut through rain forest to allow construction of a gas pipeline in Thai-land. Such disturbances often lead to the far-reaching effects of habi-tat fragmentation. (A,B, after Bradshaw et al. 2009; C, photograph © Mike Abrahams/Alamy.)

FIGURE 9.13 Rural development in Colorado has led to the expansion of the road network and the fragmentation of the habitat. Formerly widespread species are now restricted to small fragments. (From Knight et al. 2006.)

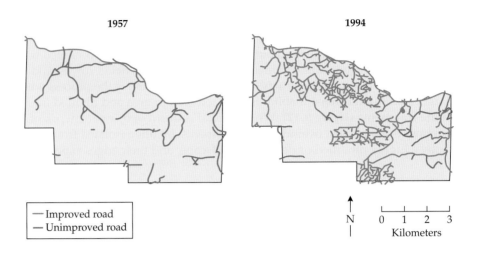

1957   1994

— Improved road
— Unimproved road

N   0   1   2   3
Kilometers

tered set of conditions, referred to as the **edge effect**. Fragments are often on the least desirable land, such as steep slopes, poor soils, and inaccessible areas.

Fragmentation almost always occurs during a severe reduction in habitat area, but it can also occur when area is reduced to only a minor degree if the original habitat is divided by roads, railroads, canals, power lines, fences, oil pipelines, fire lanes, or other barriers to the free movement of species (**Figure 9.13**). In many ways, the habitat fragments resemble islands of original habitats in an inhospitable, human-dominated landscape. Habitat fragmentation is now being recognized as a serious threat to biodiversity, as species are often unable to survive under the altered set of conditions.

Habitat fragments differ from the original habitat in three important ways:

1. Fragments have a greater amount of edge per area of habitat (and thus a greater exposure to the edge effect).

2. The center of each habitat fragment is closer to an edge.

3. A formerly continuous habitat hosting large populations is divided into pieces, with smaller populations.

A simple example will illustrate these characteristics and the problems they can cause. Consider a square conservation reserve 1000 m (1 km) on each side (**Figure 9.14**). The total area of the park is 1 km² (100 ha). The perimeter (or edge) of the

FIGURE 9.14 A hypothetical example shows how habitat area is severely reduced by fragmentation and edge effects. (A) A 1 km² protected area. Assuming edge effects (gray) penetrate 100 m into the reserve, approximately 64 ha are available as usable habitat for nesting birds. (B) The bisection of the reserve by a road and a railway, although taking up little in actual area, extends the edge effects so that almost half the breeding habitat is destroyed. Effects are proportionately greater when forest fragments are irregular in shape, as is usually the case.

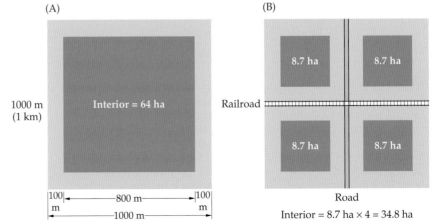

(A)

1000 m
(1 km)

Interior = 64 ha

100 m ——800 m—— 100 m
——1000 m——

(B)

8.7 ha   8.7 ha

Railroad

8.7 ha   8.7 ha

Road
Interior = 8.7 ha × 4 = 34.8 ha

park totals 4000 m. A point in the middle of the reserve is 500 m from the nearest perimeter. If the principle edge effect for birds in the reserve is predation from domestic cats and introduced rats, which forage 100 m into the forest from the perimeter of the reserve and prevent forest birds from successfully raising their young, then only the reserve's interior—64 ha—is available to the birds for breeding. Birds can move freely across this entire area. Edge habitat, unsuitable for breeding, occupies 36 ha.

Now imagine the park divided into four equal quarters by a north–south road 10 m wide and an east–west railroad track, also 10 m wide. The rights-of-way remove a total of 2 × 1000 m × 10 m of area (2 ha) from the park. Since only 2% of the park is being removed by the road and railroad, government planners argue that the effects on the park are negligible. However, the reserve has now been divided into four fragments, each of which is 495 m × 495 m in area. If birds are unable or unwilling to leave forest areas, what was formerly one population is now divided into four small populations. The distance from the center of each fragment to the nearest point on the perimeter has been reduced to 247 m, which is less than half of the former distance. Since cats and rats can now forage into the forest from along the road and railroad as well as the perimeter, birds can successfully raise young only in the most interior area of each of the four fragments. Each of these interior areas is now 8.7 ha, for a total of 34.8 ha. Even though the road and railroad removed only 2% of the reserve area, they reduced the habitat available to the birds by about half because of edge effects. The implications of this can be seen in the decreased ability of birds to live and breed in small forest fragments compared with larger blocks of forest (**Figure 9.15**). Comparable edge effects are known to impact many other groups of animals and plants in fragmented habitats.

LIMITS TO DISPERSAL AND COLONIZATION   Fragmentation may limit a species' potential for dispersal and colonization by creating barriers to normal movements (Laurance et al. 2008). In an undisturbed environment, seeds, spores, and animals move passively and actively across the landscape. When they arrive in a suitable but unoccupied area, new populations begin to develop at that site. Over time, populations of a species may build up and go extinct on a local scale as the species

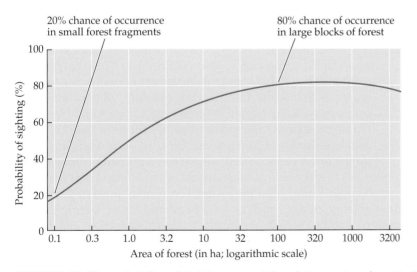

FIGURE 9.15 The probability of sighting a wood thrush in a mature forest in Maryland is only about 20% in a forest fragment of 0.1 ha; it increases to about 80% in a forest fragment over 100 ha in area. (After Decker et al. 1991; photograph © William Leaman/Alamy.)

disperses from one suitable site to another and the biological community undergoes succession. At a landscape level, a series of populations exhibiting this pattern of extinction and recolonization is sometimes referred to as a metapopulation (see Chapter 12).

When a habitat is fragmented, the potential for dispersal and colonization is often reduced. Many bird, mammal, and insect species of the forest interior will not cross even very short distances of open area (Laurance et al. 2009). If they do venture into the open, they may find predators such as hawks, owls, flycatchers, and cats waiting on the forest edge to catch and eat them. Agricultural fields 100 m wide may represent an impassable barrier to the dispersal of many invertebrate species. Roads in particular may be significant barriers to animal movement. Many species will avoid crossing roads, which represent a totally different environment for animals. For animals that attempt to cross roads, motor vehicles are a major source of mortality. To deal with such problems, highway officials are building animal underpasses, overpasses, and other improvements to minimize animal mortality (Grilo et al. 2009).

As species go extinct within individual fragments through natural successional and metapopulation processes, new species will be unable to arrive because of barriers to colonization, and the number of species present in the habitat fragment will decline over time (Beier et al. 2002). Extinction will be most rapid and severe in small habitat fragments. In Belgium, the area of heathland has declined by over 99% during the last 100 years, with the remaining habitat broken up into small fragments; the greatest loss of species is in the most isolated habitats, indicating the role of dispersal in maintaining species richness (Piessens et al. 2005). Dispersal can also be affected in aquatic environments when dams and artificial lakes prevent the migration of species such as salmon and river dolphins (Gross 2008).

Species that are able to live in and move across disturbed habitat will increase in abundance in small, isolated fragments of undisturbed habitat. This is particularly true when the spaces between forest fragments are occupied by secondary forests and tree plantations, rather than pastures and cultivated fields (Laurance 2008b). Most of the world's national parks and nature reserves represent fragments of the original ecosystems that are now too small and isolated to maintain populations of many of the original species.

RESTRICTED ACCESS TO FOOD AND MATES   Many animal species, as either individuals or social groups, need to move freely across the landscape to feed on widely scattered resources (Becker et al. 2010). A given resource may be needed only for a few weeks each year, or even only once in a few years, and when a habitat is fragmented, species confined to a single habitat fragment may be unable to migrate over their normal home range in search of that scarce resource. For example, gibbons and other primates typically remain in forests and forage widely for fruits. Finding scattered trees with abundant fruit crops may be crucial during episodes of fruit scarcity. Clearings and roads that break up the forest canopy may prevent these primates from reaching nearby fruiting trees, because the primates are unable or unwilling to descend to the ground and cross the intervening open landscape. Fences may prevent the natural migration of large grazing animals such as wildebeest and bison, forcing them to overgraze unsuitable habitat, which eventually leads to starvation and further degradation of the habitat (Dudley and Platania 2007).

Barriers to dispersal can also restrict the ability of widely scattered species to find mates, leading to a loss of reproductive potential for many animal species. Plants also may have reduced seed production if butterflies and bees are less able to migrate among habitat fragments to pollinate flowers.

> The barriers that fragment a habitat reduce the ability of animals to forage, find mates, migrate, and colonize new locations. Fragmentation often creates small subpopulations that are vulnerable to local extinction.

DIVISION OF POPULATIONS Habitat fragmentation may precipitate population decline and extinction by dividing an existing widespread population into two or more subpopulations in restricted areas. These smaller populations are then more vulnerable to inbreeding depression, genetic drift, and other problems associated with small population size (see Chapter 11). Deaths of animals killed while crossing roads will further depress population size. While a large area may support a single large population, it is possible that none of the smaller subpopulations will be sufficiently large to persist for a long period. Connecting the fragments with properly designed movement corridors may be the key to maintaining populations.

Edge Effects

Habitat fragmentation also changes the microenvironment at the fragment edge. Some of the more important edge effects include microclimatic changes in light, temperature, wind, humidity, and incidence of fire (Laurance 2008b). Each of these edge effects can have a significant impact on the vitality and composition of the species in the fragment and on ecosystem health.

MICROCLIMATE CHANGES Sunlight is absorbed and reflected by the layers of leaves in forest communities and other communities with dense plant cover. In rain forests, often less than 1% of the light energy may reach the forest floor. The forest canopy buffers the microclimate of the forest floor, keeping it relatively cool, moist, and shaded during the day, reducing air movement, and trapping heat during the night. When the forest is cleared, these effects are removed. As the forest floor is exposed to direct sunlight, the ground becomes much hotter during the day; without the canopy to reduce heat and moisture loss, the forest floor is also much colder at night and generally less humid. Increased wind movement at the forest edge further dries out the vegetation and soil, leading to the death of trees and ground plants. These effects will be strongest at the edge of the habitat fragment and decrease toward the interior of the fragment. In studies of Amazonian forest fragments, microclimate changes had strong effects up to 60 m into the forest interior, and increased tree mortality could be detected within 100 to 300 m of forest edges (**Figure 9.16**) (Laurance et al. 2002). Since species of plants and animals are often precisely adapted to temperature, humidity, and light levels, changes in these factors will eliminate many species from forest fragments. Shade-tolerant wildflower species of the temperate forest, late-successional tree species of the tropical forest, and humidity-sensitive animals such as certain insects and amphibians often are rapidly eliminated by habitat fragmentation because of altered environmental conditions, leading to a shift in the species composition of the community.

> Habitat fragmentation increases edge effects—changes in light, humidity, temperature, and wind that may be less favorable for the ecosystem there.

In response to these altered conditions, a dense tangle of vines and fast-growing pioneer species may grow up at the forest edge and may create a barrier that reduces the effects of environmental disturbance on the interior of the fragment. Over time, the forest edge may be occupied by species of plants and animals different from those found in the forest interior.

INCREASED INCIDENCE OF FIRE Increased wind, lower humidity, and higher temperatures make fires more likely. Fires may spread into habitat fragments from nearby agricultural fields that are being burned regularly, as in sugarcane harvesting, or from the irregular activities of farmers practicing slash-and-burn agriculture. Forest fragments may be particularly susceptible to fire damage when wood has accumulated on the edge of the forest where trees have died or have been blown down by the wind. In Borneo and the Brazilian Amazon, millions of hectares of tropical moist forest burned during unusually dry periods in 1997 and

FIGURE 9.16 Edge effects in the Amazon rain forest. The bars indicate how far into the forest fragment the specified effect occurs. For example, trees growing within 300 m of an edge have a higher mortality rate, and the average height of trees in the forest canopy (see drawing) is reduced within 100 m of the edge. (After Laurance et al. 2002.)

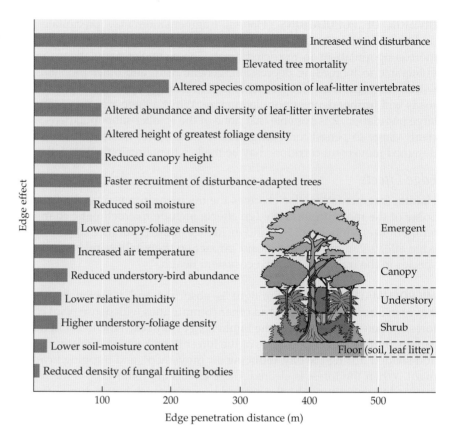

Increased wind disturbance

Elevated tree mortality

Altered species composition of leaf-litter invertebrates

Altered abundance and diversity of leaf-litter invertebrates

Altered height of greatest foliage density

Reduced canopy height

Faster recruitment of disturbance-adapted trees

Reduced soil moisture

Lower canopy-foliage density

Increased air temperature

Reduced understory-bird abundance

Lower relative humidity

Higher understory-foliage density

Lower soil-moisture content

Reduced density of fungal fruiting bodies

Emergent

Canopy

Understory

Shrub

Floor (soil, leaf litter)

Edge effect

100   200   300   400   500

Edge penetration distance (m)

1998 (Barlow and Peres 2004). A combination of factors contributed to these environmental disasters: forest fragmentation due to farming and selective logging, the accumulation of brush following selective logging, and human-caused fires (Le Page et al. 2007; Messina and Cochrane 2007). Once a forest burns, dead fuel accumulates and sunlight can more readily dry out the ground, leading to a greater likelihood of further fires. Eventually, a forest can be degraded into scrub.

INTERSPECIES INTERACTION   Habitat fragmentation increases the vulnerability of the fragment to invasion by exotic and native pest species (Flory and Clay 2009). The road edges themselves may represent dispersal routes for invasive species. The forest edge represents a high-energy, high-nutrient, disturbed environment in which many pest species of plants and animals can increase in number and then disperse into the interior of the fragment. For example, the seeds of invasive wind-dispersed plants may be blown great distances into the interior of the fragment and then colonize open, sunny areas where trees and shrubs have recently died, either from natural causes or because of the newly altered growing conditions. Butterflies that are adapted to disturbed habitats migrate up to 250 m into the forest interior.

In the temperate regions of North America, omnivorous native animals such as raccoons, skunks, and blue jays may increase in population size along forest edges, where they can eat foods, including eggs and nestlings of birds, from both undisturbed and disturbed habitats. (Similar increases in nest predation occur on the edges of fragmented tropical forests.) These aggressive feeders seek out the nests of interior forest birds, often preventing successful reproduction for many bird species hundreds of meters from the nearest forest edge (Lampila et al. 2005). Nest-parasitizing cowbirds, which live in fields and edge habitats, use habitat edges as invasion points, flying up to 15 km into forest interiors, where they lay their eggs in the nests of forest songbirds (Lloyd et al. 2005). The combination of habitat fragmentation, increased nest predation, and destruction of tropical wintering habitats is probably responsible for the dramatic decline of certain migratory songbird species of North America, such as the cerulean warbler (*Dendroica cerulea*), particularly in the eastern half of the United States (Valiela and Martinetto 2007). (In addition to these local effects, individual bird species in North America and Europe are both increasing and decreasing on regional scales in response to changing land use patterns, such as those caused by agricultural practices and forest management activities.) Populations of deer and other herbivores can also build up in edge areas, where plant growth is lush, eventually overgrazing the vegetation and selectively eliminating certain rare and endangered plant species for distances of several kilometers into the forest interior.

In settled areas with fragmented landscapes, domestic cats may be extremely important predators. In one area of Michigan, 26% of landowners had cats that went outside. Each cat killed an average of one bird per week, including species of conservation concern (Lepczyk et al. 2003). As an alternative, cat owners can buy specially designed, highly visible collars that can greatly reduce the ability of cats to catch birds, reptiles, and small mammals (Calver et al. 2007). In many areas of the world, human hunters are the most important predators. When habitat is fragmented by roads, hunters can use the road network to hunt more intensively in the habitat fragments and reach remote areas. Without controls on hunting, there is no refuge for the animals, and their populations decline.

POTENTIAL FOR DISEASE   Habitat fragmentation puts wild populations of animals in closer proximity to domestic animals. Diseases of domestic animals can then spread more readily to wild species, which often have no immunity to them. There is also the potential for diseases to spread from wild species to domestic plants, animals, and even people, once the level of contact increases. The effects of disease, and of exotic species in general, are more thoroughly examined in Chapter 10. One study of fragmented forest habitats shows high densities of white-footed mice and black-legged ticks and high rates of infection with Lyme disease, along with a corresponding increase in Lyme disease in people living in those areas (Killilea et al. 2008).

Two Studies of Habitat Fragmentation

An extensive literature on habitat fragmentation has developed over the last 10 years. These studies show that habitat fragmentation changes the local environment, often resulting in the decline and loss of original species. The following are two such studies:

- The impact of habitat fragmentation was examined for eight bird species occupying chaparral and coastal sage scrub in Southern California, an area undergoing rapid urban development (Crooks et al. 2001). In comparison with large fragments, small fragments (less than 10 ha in area) had higher rates of species extinction and lower rates of new species colonization. Bird species with high initial densities were less likely to go extinct in habitat fragments and were better able to persist in small fragments.

- Reindeer are one of the essential symbols of Scandinavian culture. The last remaining population of wild reindeer (*Rangifer tarandus tarandus*) lives in southern Norway (Vistnes et al. 2008). Prior to 1900, the reindeer lived as a continuous herd, freely migrating throughout the mountain ranges of this region. Infrastructure developments and the reindeer's tendency to keep 5 km away from human settlements and other structures, such as resort areas, roads, and power lines, have fragmented the population into 26 distinct herds

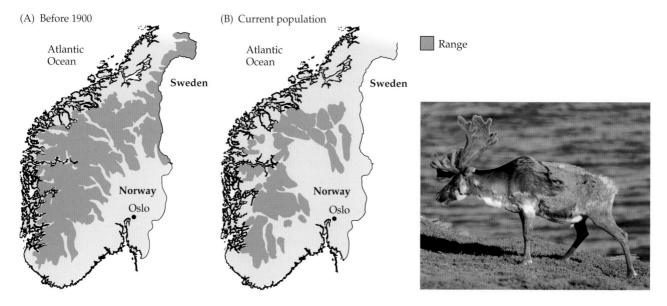

FIGURE 9.17 (A) Wild reindeer herds formerly roamed throughout the mountainous regions of southern Norway, with only one break in their range. (B) The range of reindeer has now been divided by roads, power lines, and other types of infrastructure, leading to 26 isolated subpopulations. (After Nelleman et al. 2001; photograph © Gerhard Zwerger-Schon Imagebroker/AGE Fotostock.)

(**Figure 9.17**). Only about 10% of the original range of reindeer is now found more than 5 km from such human structures. Because isolated herds are unable to migrate and consequently tend to overgraze the vegetation in their habitat fragments, herds must be actively managed by hunting to prevent local population increases. If additional roads, power lines, and resorts are built, the reindeer populations will undergo further fragmentation and the reindeer's long-term future will then be even more in doubt.

Habitat Degradation and Pollution

Even when a habitat is unaffected by overt destruction or fragmentation, the ecosystems and species in that habitat can be profoundly affected by human activities. Biological communities can be damaged and species driven to extinction by external factors that do not change the structure of dominant plants or other features in the community in a way that the damage is immediately apparent. For example, in temperate deciduous forests, physical degradation of a habitat might be caused by frequent, uncontrolled ground fires; these fires might not kill the mature trees, but the rich perennial wildflower community and insect fauna on the forest floor would gradually become impoverished. Keeping too many cattle in a grassland community gradually changes it, often eliminating many native species and favoring exotic species that can tolerate grazing and trampling. Frequent boating and diving among coral reefs degrade the community, as fragile species are crushed by divers' flippers, boat hulls, and anchors. Out of sight from the public, fishing trawlers drag across an estimated 15 million km² of ocean floor each year, an area 150 times greater than the area of forest cleared in the same time period. The trawling destroys delicate creatures such as anemones and sponges and reduces species diversity, biomass, and community structure (see Figure 9.19) (Hinz et al. 2009). Proposed deep sea mining operations have the potential to greatly increase the scale of this degradation (Halfer and Fujita 2007).

The most subtle and universal form of environmental degradation is pollution, commonly caused by pesticides, herbicides, sewage, fertilizers from agricultural fields, industrial chemicals and wastes, emissions from factories and automobiles, and sediment deposits from eroded hillsides (Relyea 2005). These types of pollution often are not visually apparent even when they occur all around us, every day, in nearly every part of the world. The general effects of pollution on water quality, air quality, and even the global climate are cause for great concern, not only because of the threats to biological diversity, but also because of their effects on human health (Kampa and Castanas 2008; Srinivasan and Reddy 2009; Dearborn and Kark 2010). Although environmental pollution is sometimes highly visible and dramatic, as in the case of the massive oil spill shown in **Figure 9.18**, it is the subtle, unseen forms of pollution that are probably the most threatening—primarily because they are so insidious.

> Pollution of the air, water, and soil by chemicals, wastes, and the by-products of energy production destroys species and habitats in insidious ways.

Pesticide Pollution

The dangers of pesticides were brought to the world's attention in 1962 by Rachel Carson's influential book *Silent Spring*. Carson described a process known as **biomagnification**, through which dichlorodiphenyltrichloroethane (DDT) and other organochlorine pesticides become concentrated as they ascend the food chain (Elliott et al. 2005; Kelly et al. 2007; Weis and Cleveland 2008). These pesticides, used on crop plants to kill insects and sprayed on water bodies to kill mosquito larvae, were harming wildlife populations, especially birds that ate large amounts of insects, fish, or other animals exposed to DDT and its by-products. Birds with high levels of concentrated pesticides in their tissues, particularly raptors such as hawks and eagles, became weak and tended to lay eggs with abnormally thin shells that cracked during incubation. As a result of the failure to raise young and the outright death of many adults, populations of these birds showed dramatic declines throughout the world (**Box 9.1**).

In lakes and estuaries, DDT, PCBs, and other pesticides became concentrated in predatory fish and in sea mammals such as dolphins. In agricultural areas, beneficial and endangered insect species were killed along with pest species. At the same time, mosquitoes and other targeted insects evolved resistance to the chemicals, so ever-larger doses of DDT were required to suppress the insect populations. Recognition of this situation in the 1970s led many industrialized countries to ban the use of DDT and other chemically related pesticides. The ban eventually allowed the partial recovery of many bird populations, most notably peregrine falcons (*Falco peregrinus*), ospreys (*Pandion haliaetus*), and bald eagles (*Haliaeetus leucocephalus*). Nevertheless, the continuing massive use of pesticides and even DDT itself in other countries is still cause for concern, not only for endangered animal species, but also for the potential long-term effects on people, particularly the workers who handle these chemicals in the field and the consumers of the agricultural products treat-

FIGURE 9.18 Birds, marine mammals, and many other ocean animals sicken and die when they are covered by oil following spills. These birds found in Kenai Fjords, Alaska perished following the Exxon Valdez oil spill. (Photograph © Accent Alaska.com/Alamy.)

BOX 9.1   *Pesticides and Raptors: Sentinel Species Warn of Danger*

■ Birds of prey such as the American bald eagle, the osprey, and the peregrine falcon are symbols evocative of power, grace, and nobility to people worldwide. When populations of these and other raptors began an abrupt decline in the 1950s, concern for the birds prompted urgent research into the cause. In retrospect, we see that these birds of prey were acting as sentinels, warning human society of a serious danger in the environment that was broadly affecting biological communities. The culprit was eventually identified as the chemical pesticide DDT (dichlorodiphenyltrichloroethane) and related organochlorine compounds such as DDE and dieldrin. DDT was first used as an insecticide during World War II to combat insect-borne diseases among the troops. After the war ended, domestic use of the chemical exploded in an effort to control agricultural pests and mosquitoes; consequently, raptor populations plummeted.

A male peregrine falcon feeding young on a city roof. (Photograph courtesy of the U.S. Fish and Wildlife Service.)

> A ban on the use of harmful pesticides resulted in the recovery of many raptor species.

Raptors are particularly vulnerable to these compounds because of their position at the top of the food chain. Toxic chemicals become concentrated at the top of the food chain through biomagnification: Pesticides are ingested and absorbed by insects and other invertebrates and remain in their tissues at fairly low concentrations. When fish, birds, or mammals eat a diet of these insects, the pesticides are further concentrated, eventually to highly toxic levels. For example, DDT concentrations might be only 0.000003 parts per million (ppm) in lake water and 0.04 ppm in zooplankton, but the concentrations rise to 0.5 ppm in minnows that eat zooplankton, 2.0 ppm in fish that eat the minnows, and 25 ppm in fish-eating birds. Birds such as the osprey (*Pandion haliaetus*) and the bald eagle (*Haliaeetus leucocephalus*) are particularly susceptible because they rely heavily on fish, which concentrate the toxins draining into rivers and lakes from agricultural watersheds. Peregrine falcons (*Falco peregrinus*), which frequently feed on insectivorous birds and bats, are also vulnerable to the effects of biomagnification. DDT and its breakdown products cause eggshell thinning, inhibit proper development of the embryo, change adult bird behavior, and may even cause direct adult mortality.

Dramatic evidence of the damage done to raptors by DDT is the rapidity with which many U.S. populations re-

ed with these chemicals. These chemicals are widely dispersed in the air and water and can harm plants, animals, and people living far from where the chemicals are actually applied (Daly et al. 2007). High concentrations of these toxins are found even in the tissues of polar bears in northern Norway and Russia, where they have a harmful impact on bear health. In addition, even in countries that outlawed these pesticides decades ago, chemicals persist in the environment, where they have a detrimental effect on the reproductive and endocrine systems of aquatic vertebrates (Oehlmann et al. 2009).

Water Pollution

Water pollution has negative consequences for people, animals, and all species that live in water: it destroys important food sources and contaminates drinking water with chemicals that can cause immediate and long-term harm to the health of people and other species that come into contact with the polluted water (Oehlmann et al. 2009). In the broader picture, water pollution often severely damages aquatic ecosystems (**Figure 9.19**). Rivers, lakes, and oceans are used as open sewers for in-

BOX 9.1 *(continued)*

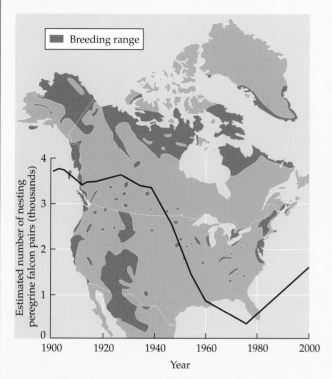

Peregrine falcons are now breeding in many areas across North America, and populations continue to increase. (After Canadian Wildlife Service and Connecticut Department of Environmental Protection.)

covered after DDT and other organochlorine pesticides were banned in 1972. The peregrine falcon has made an astonishingly strong recovery in many parts of the world (Hoffman and Smith 2003; Craig et al. 2004). Captive-bred peregrine falcons released within their former range have

successfully established new breeding populations, often nesting on skyscrapers in urban areas. Ospreys and bald eagles have made similar comebacks. There are now over 7000 breeding pairs of eagles in the lower 48 U.S. states, following a low of 417 pairs in 1963.

The unanticipated decline of raptor populations illustrates the dangers of indiscriminately introducing chemicals into the environment. The unique sensitivity of raptors to pesticides warned of potential danger to humans as well, though it should have been expected that a chemical toxic to insects might have a negative impact on other organisms. Chemicals known to be toxic to human and animal life are still being produced and finding their way into the environment. It has long been known that PCBs cause cancer, yet they continue to be used, for example, in the manufacture of electric transformers. As the use of new chemicals multiplies, so do the chances of unanticipated, harmful side effects. In addition, lead poisoning from spent ammunition and fishing weights, an old but little-recognized problem for humans and animals, is causing increased public concern because of the numbers of eagles, California condors, trumpeter swans, and other species dying from ingestion of lead shot and bullet fragments. Another emerging problem for wildlife is the widespread contamination of water with pharmaceuticals that affect hormonal balances, behavior, and reproduction.

Observation of sentinel species—in this case, top predators that accumulate contaminants—may alert us to rising levels of harmful chemicals in the environment. But it may take the threat of another "silent spring" to motivate humankind to stop contaminating the environment with chemicals.

dustrial wastes and residential sewage. And higher densities of people almost always mean greater levels of water pollution. Pesticides, herbicides, oil products, heavy metals (such as mercury, lead, and zinc), detergents, and industrial wastes directly kill organisms, such as insect larvae, fish, amphibians, and even marine mammals living in aquatic environments (Relyea 2005). Pollution is a threat to 90% of the endangered fishes and freshwater mussels in the United States. An increasing source of pollution in coastal areas is the discharge of nutrients and chemicals from shrimp and salmon farms.

Even if aquatic organisms are not killed outright, these chemicals can make the environment so inhospitable that species can no longer thrive. In contrast to a dump in the terrestrial environment, which has primarily local effects, toxic wastes in aquatic environments diffuse over a wide area. Toxic chemicals, even at very low levels in the water, can be lethal to aquatic organisms through the process of biomagnification. Many aquatic environments are naturally low in essential minerals, such as nitrates and phosphates, and aquatic species have

> Water pollution not only damages biodiversity, but also harms the health of people who use the water.

FIGURE 9.19 The aquatic environment faces multiple threats, as shown by this schematic view of damage to the ocean. Trawling is a fishing method in which a boat drags a net along the ocean bottom, harvesting commercial fish indiscriminately with noncommercial species and other sea life ("bycatch") and damaging the structure of the community. (After Snelgrove 2001.)

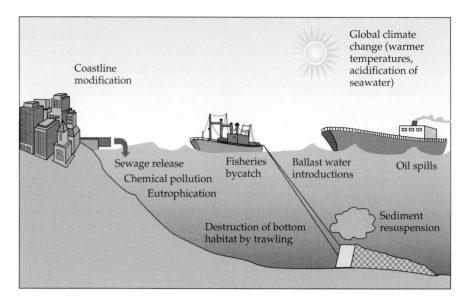

adapted to the natural absence of minerals by developing the ability to process large volumes of water and concentrate these minerals. When these species process polluted water, they concentrate toxic chemicals along with the essential minerals; the toxins eventually poison the plant or animal. Species that feed on these aquatic species ingest these concentrations of toxic chemicals. One of the most serious connections is the accumulation of mercury and other toxins by long-lived predatory fishes, such as swordfish and shark, and its impact on the nervous system of people who eat these types of fish frequently (**Figure 9.20**) (Campbell et al. 2008; Jaeger et al. 2009).

Essential minerals that are beneficial to plant and animal life can become harmful pollutants at high levels (Smith and Schindler 2009). Human sewage, agricultural fertilizers, detergents, and industrial processes often release large amounts of nitrates and phosphates into aquatic systems, initiating the process of **eutrophication**, the result of human activity. Humans release as much nitrate into the environment as is produced by all natural processes; and the human release of nitrogen is expected to keep increasing as the human population continues to increase. Even small amounts of these nutrients can stimulate plant and animal growth, and high concentrations of nutrients released through human activities often result in thick "blooms" of algae at the surface of ponds and lakes. These algal blooms may be so dense that they outcompete other plankton species and shade bottom-dwelling plant species. As the algal mat becomes thicker, its lower layers sink to the bottom and die. The bacteria and fungi that decompose the dying algae grow in response to this added sustenance and consequently absorb all of the oxygen in the water. Without oxygen, much of the remaining animal life dies off, sometimes visibly in the form of masses of dead fish floating on the water's surface. The result is a greatly impoverished and simplified community, a "dead zone" consisting of only those species tolerant of polluted water and low oxygen levels (**Figure 9.21**).

This process of eutrophication can also affect marine systems with large anthropogenic inputs of nutrients, particularly coastal areas and bodies of water in confined areas, such as the Gulf of Mexico, the Mediterranean, the North Sea and Baltic Sea in Europe, and the enclosed seas of Japan (Greene et al. 2009). In warm tropical waters, eutrophication favors algae, which grow over coral reefs and completely change the biological community.

Eroding sediments from logged or farmed hillsides can also harm aquatic ecosystems. The sediment covers submerged plant leaves and other green surfaces with a

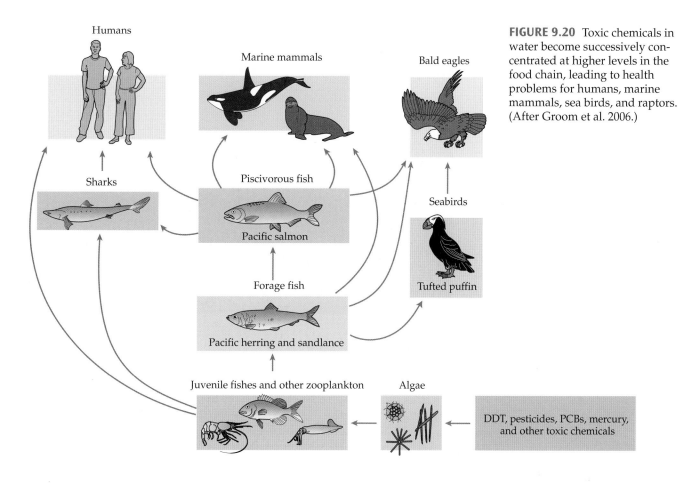

FIGURE 9.20 Toxic chemicals in water become successively concentrated at higher levels in the food chain, leading to health problems for humans, marine mammals, sea birds, and raptors. (After Groom et al. 2006.)

muddy film that reduces light availability and diminishes the rate of photosynthesis. Increasing water turbidity reduces the depth at which photosynthesis can occur and may prevent animal species from seeing, feeding, and living in the water. Sediment loads are particularly harmful to many coral species that require crystal-clear waters to survive. Corals have delicate filters that strain tiny food particles out of the clear water. When the water is filled with a high density of soil particles, the filters clog up and the animals cannot feed. Coral animals often have symbiotic algae that provide carbohydrates for the coral. When the water is filled with soil particles, there may be too little light for the algae to photosynthesize, and the corals will lose this source of energy.

Air Pollution

The effects of air pollution on forest communities have been intensively studied because of the great economic value of forests from wood production, protection of water supplies, and recreation (Bytnerowicz et al. 2007; Karnosky

FIGURE 9.21 Fish in the Salton Sea in California died off as a result of eutrophication. High nitrogen and phosphorus levels from human activity resulted in excessive algal growth, followed by algal death and decay leading to oxygen levels so low that fish could not survive. (Photograph © Mike Goldwater/Alamy.)

FIGURE 9.22 Forests in montane areas near and downwind of concentrations of power plants and heavy industry are experiencing diebacks, thought to be caused in part by the effects of acid rain combined with nitrogen deposition, ozone damage, insect attack, and disease. These dead trees were photographed in North Carolina. (Photograph © Bruce Coleman, Inc./ Alamy.)

et al. 2007). In certain areas of the world, particularly northern Europe and eastern North America, air pollution damages and weakens many tree species—apparently both directly and indirectly—and makes them more susceptible to attacks by insects, fungi, and disease (**Figure 9.22**). When the trees die, many of the other species in a forest also become locally extinct. Even when communities are not destroyed by air pollution, species composition may be altered as more susceptible species are eliminated. Lichens—symbiotic organisms composed of fungi and algae that can survive in some of the harshest natural environments—are particularly susceptible to air pollution. Because each lichen species has distinct levels of tolerance to air pollution, the composition of the lichen community can be used as a biological indicator of the level of air pollution.

In the past, people assumed that the atmosphere was so vast that materials they released into the air would be widely dispersed and their effects would be minimal. But today several types of air pollution are so widespread that they damage whole ecosystems. These same pollutants also have severe impacts on human health, demonstrating again the common interests shared by people and nature. We discuss specific air pollutants below.

ACID RAIN   Industries such as smelting operations and coal- and oil-fired power plants release huge quantities of nitrogen and sulfur oxides into the air, where they combine with moisture in the atmosphere to produce nitric and sulfuric acids. These acids become part of cloud systems and dramatically lower the pH (the standard measure of acidity) of rainwater, leading to the weakening and deaths of trees over wide areas. Acid rain, in turn, lowers the pH of soil moisture and water bodies, such as ponds and lakes, and also increases the concentration of toxic metals such as aluminum.

Acid rain is currently a severe problem in eastern North America, in central Europe and other parts of Europe, and in China and Korea and other parts of East Asia; within the next 50 years acid rain will also affect Southeast Asia, western coastal India, and south central Africa (Menz and Seip 2004). In the United States alone, about 40 million metric tons of these compounds are released into the atmosphere each year (Lynch et al. 2000). The heavy reliance of China on high-sulfur coal and the rapid increase in automobile ownership and industrialization in China,

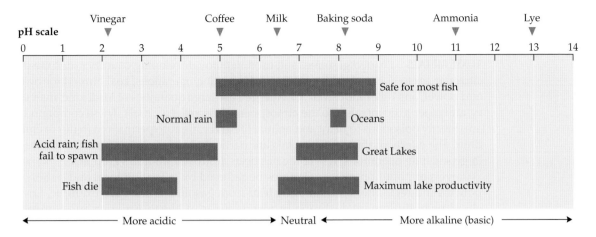

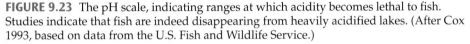

FIGURE 9.23 The pH scale, indicating ranges at which acidity becomes lethal to fish. Studies indicate that fish are indeed disappearing from heavily acidified lakes. (After Cox 1993, based on data from the U.S. Fish and Wildlife Service.)

India, and Southeast Asia represent serious threats to biological diversity in the region, with dramatic increases in acid rain and nitrogen deposition predicted over the next 50 years (Larssen et al. 2006).

Increased acidity alone damages many plant and animal species; as the acidity of water bodies increases, many fish either fail to spawn or die outright (**Figure 9.23**). Both increased acidity and water pollution are contributing factors to the dramatic decline of many amphibian populations throughout the world (Norris 2007). Most amphibian species depend on bodies of water for at least part of their life cycle, and a decline in water pH causes a corresponding increase in the mortality of eggs and young animals. Acidity also inhibits the microbial process of decomposition, lowering the rate of mineral recycling and ecosystem productivity. Many ponds and lakes in industrialized countries have lost large portions of their animal communities as a result of acid rain. These damaged water bodies are often in supposedly pristine areas hundreds of kilometers from major sources of urban and industrial pollution, such as the North American Rocky Mountains and Scandinavia. While acidity of rain is decreasing in many areas because of better pollution control, it still remains a serious problem. In developing countries, such as China, the acidity of rain is increasing as the country powers its rapid industrial development through the use of fuels high in sulfur.

Acid rain and other examples of air pollution are increasing rapidly in Asia as countries industrialize. Acid rain is particularly harmful to freshwater species.

OZONE PRODUCTION AND NITROGEN DEPOSITION Automobiles, power plants, and industrial activities release hydrocarbons and nitrogen oxides as waste products. In the presence of sunlight, these chemicals react with the atmosphere to produce ozone and other secondary chemicals, collectively called **photochemical smog**. Although ozone in the upper atmosphere is important in filtering out ultraviolet radiation, high concentrations of ozone at ground level damage plant tissues and make them brittle, harming biological communities and reducing agricultural productivity. Ozone and smog are detrimental to people and animals when inhaled, so both people and biological communities benefit from air-pollution controls. Smog can be so severe that people may avoid outside activities. When airborne nitrogen compounds are deposited by rain and dust, biological communities throughout the world are damaged and altered by potentially toxic levels of this nutrient (Brys et al. 2005). In particular, the combination of nitrogen deposition and acid rain is responsible for a decline in the density of soil fungi that form beneficial relationships with trees.

TOXIC METALS   Leaded gasoline (still used in many developing countries, despite its clear danger to human health), mining and smelting operations, coal burned for heat and power, and other industrial activities release large quantities of lead, zinc, mercury, and other toxic metals into the atmosphere (Driscoll et al. 2007). These compounds are directly poisonous to plant and animal life and can cause permanent injury to children. The effects of these toxic metals are particularly evident in areas surrounding large smelting operations, where life has been destroyed for miles around.

Levels of pollution may sometimes be reduced by enforcing local and national policies and regulations; eliminating lead from gasoline is one such example. Levels of air pollution are declining in certain areas of North America and Europe, but they continue to rise in many other areas of the world. Increases in air pollution will be particularly severe in many Asian countries with dense (and growing) human populations and expanding industrialization (Zhao et al. 2006). Hope for controlling air pollution in the future depends on building motor vehicles with dramatically lower emissions, increasing the development and use of mass transit systems, developing more efficient scrubbing processes for industrial smokestacks, and reducing overall energy use through conservation and efficiency measures. Many of these measures are already being actively implemented in European countries and in Japan. The United States lags far behind most other industrialized countries, especially in reducing automobile emissions and increasing fuel efficiency.

Global Climate Change

Carbon dioxide, methane, and other trace gases in the atmosphere are transparent to sunshine, allowing light energy to pass through the atmosphere and warm the surface of the Earth. These gases and water vapor (in the form of clouds) trap the energy radiating from the Earth as heat, slowing the rate at which heat leaves the Earth's surface and radiates back into space. These gases are called **greenhouse gases** because they function much like the glass in a greenhouse, which is transparent to sunlight but traps energy inside the greenhouse once it is transformed to heat. The similar warming effect of Earth by its atmospheric gases is called the **greenhouse effect** (**Figure 9.24**). We can imagine that these gases act as "blankets" on the Earth's surface: the denser the concentration of gases, the more heat trapped near the Earth, thus, the higher the planet's surface temperature.

The greenhouse effect allows life to flourish on Earth—without it the temperature on the Earth's surface would fall dramatically. Today, however, as a result of human activity, concentrations of greenhouse gases are increasing so much that scientists believe they are already affecting the Earth's climate (Karl and Trenberth 2003; Gore 2006; IPCC 2007). The term **global warming** is used to describe this increased temperature resulting from the greenhouse effect, and **global climate change** refers to the complete set of climate characteristics that are changing now and will continue to change in the future, including patterns of precipitation and wind.

During the past 100 years, global levels of carbon dioxide (CO_2), methane, and other trace gases have been steadily increasing, primarily as a result of burning fossil fuels—coal, oil, and natural gas (IPPC 2007; Kannan and James 2009). Clearing forests to create farmland and burning firewood for heating and cooking also contribute to rising concentrations of CO_2. Through these activities, humans currently release about 70 million tons of CO_2 into the atmosphere *every day*. Carbon dioxide concentration in the atmosphere has increased from 290 parts per million (ppm) to 387 ppm over the last 100 years (**Figure 9.25**), and it is projected to double at some point in the latter half of this century. Even if the plans to reduce CO_2 production that were agreed upon

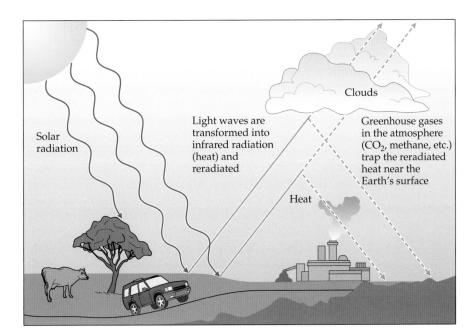

FIGURE 9.24 The greenhouse effect results when gases and water vapor form a blanket around the Earth that acts like the glass roof of a greenhouse, trapping heat near the Earth's surface. (After Gates 1993.)

by many countries at the 1997 Kyoto conference were implemented tomorrow, there would be little immediate reduction in present atmospheric CO_2 levels, because each CO_2 molecule resides in the atmosphere for an average of 100 years before being removed by plants and natural geochemical processes. Because of this time lag, levels of CO_2 in the atmosphere will continue to rise in the medium term.

Another significant greenhouse gas is methane, which has increased from 0.8 to 1.7 ppm in the last 100 years as a result of rice cultivation, cattle production, microbial activity in dumps, the burning of tropical forests and grasslands, and release during fossil fuel production. Methane is far more efficient at absorbing heat than carbon dioxide, so even at low concentrations, methane is an important con-

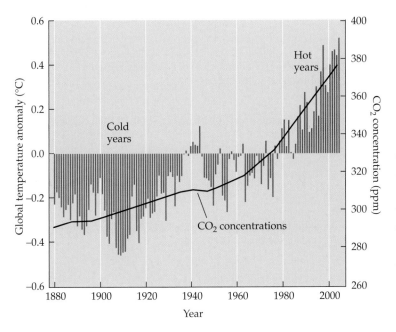

FIGURE 9.25 Over the last 130 years, atmospheric CO_2 concentrations in parts per million (ppm) have increased dramatically as a result of human activities. Global annual temperatures were colder than average prior to 1980 when annual temperatures began to be warmer than average. The average annual temperature is based on the period from 1961 to 1990. Results are reported as differences (anomaly) from this average temperature. Most scientists believe the observed increase in global temperature is caused by this increased atmospheric concentration of carbon dioxide and other greenhouse gases. (After Karl 2006.)

tributor to the greenhouse effect. Methane molecules persist in the atmosphere for even longer than carbon dioxide. Reductions in methane levels will require changes in agricultural practices and improved pollution controls.

There is a broad scientific agreement among the **Intergovernmental Panel on Climate Change** (**IPCC**), a study group of leading scientists organized by the United Nations, that the increased levels of greenhouse gases have affected the world's climate and ecosystems already and that these effects will increase in the future (**Table 9.3**) (Rosenzweig et al. 2008). An extensive review of the evidence supports the conclusion that global surface temperatures have increased by 0.6°C during the last century (IPCC 2007; Robinson et al. 2008). Temperatures at high latitudes, such as in Siberia, Alaska, and Canada, have increased by 2°C to 4°C. Some plant and animal species are changing their ranges and the timing of their reproductive behavior in response to these temperature changes (Kannan and James 2009). Evidence indicates that ocean water temperatures have also changed over the last 50 years: the Atlantic, Pacific, and Indian oceans have increased in temperature by an average of 0.06°C (Gillett et al. 2003). As a consequence, certain marine species are expanding their ranges to higher latitudes.

There is also a general consensus among climatologists that the world climate will increase in temperature by an additional 2°C to 4°C by 2100 as a result of increased levels of carbon dioxide and other gases (**Figure 9.26**). The increase could be even greater if carbon dioxide levels rise faster than predicted; conversely, it could be slightly less if all countries reduce their emissions of greenhouse gases in the very near future. The increase in temperature will be greatest at high latitudes and over

> There is a broad concensus among scientists that increased concentrations of carbon dioxide and other greenhouse gases in the atmosphere, produced as a consequence of human activities, have already resulted in warmer temperatures, and will continue to affect Earth's climate in coming decades.

TABLE 9.3 Some Evidence for Global Warming

1. Increased temperatures and incidence of heat waves

Examples: 2007 was the warmest year worldwide over the past 125 years; previously the warmest year was 2005. An August 2003 heat wave in France killed over 10,000 people as temperatures reached 40°C (104°F).

2. Melting of glaciers and polar ice

Examples: Arctic Sea summer ice has declined by 15% in area over the past 25 years. Since 1850, glaciers in the European Alps have disappeared from more than 30%–40% of their former range.

3. Rising sea levels

Example: Since 1938, one-third of the coastal marshes in a wildlife refuge in Chesapeake Bay have been submerged by rising seawater.

4. Earlier flowering of plants

Example: Two-thirds of plant species are now flowering earlier than they did several decades ago.

5. Earlier spring activity

Example: One-third of English birds are now laying eggs earlier in the year than they did 30 years ago, and oak trees are now leafing out earlier than they did 40 years ago.

6. Shifts in species ranges

Example: Two-thirds of European butterfly species studied are now found farther north by 35 to 250 km than recorded several decades ago.

7. Population declines

Example: Adélie penguin populations have declined over the past 25 years as their Antarctic sea ice habitat melts away.

Source: Union of Concerned Scientists (www.ucsusa.org) and NASA.

large continents (IPCC 2007; Kannan and James 2009). Rainfall has already started to increase on a global scale and will continue to increase but will vary by region, with some regions showing decreases in rainfall. There will also probably be an increase in extreme weather events, such as hurricanes, flooding, snow storms, and regional drought, associated with this warming (Jentsch et al. 2007). In dry forests and savannas, warmer conditions will result in an increased incidence of fire. In coastal areas, storms will cause increased destruction of cities and other human settlements and will severely damage coastal vegetation, including beaches and coral reefs. The series of hurricanes that devastated the southern United States in 2005, including Hurricane Katrina, could be an indication of what the future may bring.

The computer simulation models of future weather patterns are rapidly improving to include more variables: the role of the ocean in absorbing atmospheric carbon dioxide, how plant communities will respond to higher carbon dioxide levels and temperatures, the effects of increased levels of anthropogenic aerosols (airborne particles resulting from burning fossil fuels, wood, and other sources), and the role of cloud cover in reflecting sunlight. Even though details of global climate change

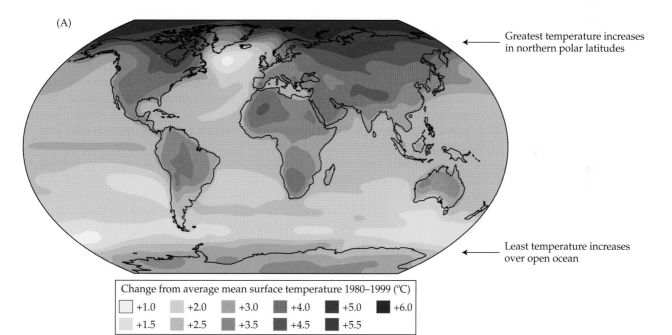

(A)

Greatest temperature increases in northern polar latitudes

Least temperature increases over open ocean

Change from average mean surface temperature 1980–1999 (°C)

+1.0	+2.0	+3.0	+4.0	+5.0	+6.0
+1.5	+2.5	+3.5	+4.5	+5.5	

(B)

FIGURE 9.26 (A) Computer models of global climate predict that temperatures will increase significantly when CO_2 levels double in the mid to late part of this century. Predicted temperature increases for the time frame 2080–2099 are shown, indicated as the amount of deviation (in °C) from mean surface temperatures recorded for 1980–1999. (B) All climate models predict that the greatest warming will take place in the northern polar regions. Polar ice caps are already melting at alarming rates, as these walrus in the Bering Sea off Alaska seem to attest. (A after IPCC 2007; B, photograph by Budd Christman, courtesy of NOAA.)

are being debated by scientists, there is a broad consensus that the world's climate has started to change already and will continue to change substantially in coming decades.

As governments and the public have become aware of the implications of climate change to human welfare and the natural environment, there has been a strong movement to reduce the output of carbon dioxide and other greenhouse gases. The principal world agreement governing this issue is the Kyoto Protocol of 1997, which commits its members to reductions in greenhouse gas emissions. Unfortunately, the United States, Russia, and most countries of Africa and the Middle East did not immediately agree to the provisions of the treaty. However, government representatives at the highest levels continue to develop a new agreement that more countries will accept. The award of the 2007 Nobel Peace Prize to former U.S. Vice President Al Gore and the IPCC has brought added public attention to this topic. It is widely accepted that efforts to reduce greenhouse gas emissions now will result in lesser climate change impacts later.

Changes in Temperate and Tropical Climates

Global climate change is not a new phenomenon. During the past 2 million years, there have been at least ten cycles of global warming and cooling. When the polar ice caps melted during warm periods, sea levels rose to well above their earlier levels, and species extended their ranges closer to the poles and migrated to higher elevations on mountains. During cold periods, the ice caps enlarged, sea levels dropped, and species shifted their ranges closer to the equator and to lower elevations. While many species undoubtedly went extinct during these repeated episodes of range changes, the species we have today are survivors of global climate change. If species could adjust to changes in global climate in the past, will species be able to adjust to the predicted changes in global climate caused by human alteration of the atmosphere?

It seems likely that many species will be unable to adjust quickly enough to survive this human-caused warming, which will occur far more rapidly than previous, natural climate shifts. Many species will be unable to disperse rapidly enough to track the changing climate and remain within their "climatic envelope" of temperature and precipitation (Jackson et al. 2009; Post et al. 2009). Habitat fragmentation caused by human activities will further slow or prevent many species from migrating to new sites where suitable habitat exists. Many species of limited distribution and/or poor dispersal ability, such as snakes, amphibians, and forest birds, will undoubtedly go extinct, with widely distributed, easily dispersed species being favored in the new communities (Sekercioglu et al. 2008). Extinction rates for species of restricted range could be 9% to 13%, with over 1 million species predicted to go extinct by 2050 (Thomas et al. 2004). Entire biological communities may become altered and degraded if the dominant species are not able to adapt to the changing conditions. Experimental warming experiments in mountain meadows to simulate the effects of global climate change show that there will be a loss of species from these communities. Certain biological communities of the United States, such as the spruce–fir and the aspen–birch communities, may decline in area by more than 90%. The loss could be even greater if warmer conditions and elevated carbon dioxide levels favor invasive species and outbreaks of pest species.

As a result of global climate change, climatic regions in the northern and southern temperate zones will be shifted toward the poles. This change has clearly begun already, with alpine plants found growing higher on mountains and migrating birds observed spending longer times at their summer breeding grounds. In the coming century, global climate change is predicted to have a great impact on arctic boreal and alpine ecosystems as a result of warmer conditions and a longer growing season.

The effects of global climate change on temperature and rainfall are also expected to have dramatic effects on tropical ecosystems (IPCC 2007). Many species and biological communities appear to have narrow tolerances for temperature and rainfall, so even small changes in the climate could have major effects on species composition, cycles of plant reproduction, patterns of migration, and susceptibility to fire (Robinson et al. 2008). Major contractions in the area of rain forest are quite likely (Colwell et al 2008). Such changes have already been linked to the decline and extinction of amphibians in the mountains of Costa Rica, and they will have comparable impacts on birds and other rain forest species. Especially, cool-adapted species that live atop tropical mountains could be highly vulnerable to increasing temperatures; as bands of vegetation move higher on mountains, the species at the top will have nowhere to go.

> As rainfall patterns change and most regions become warmer, many plant and animal populations may not be able to adapt quickly enough to survive, and habitat fragmentation may prevent them from migrating to more viable regions.

Plants and Climate Change

Plants are already responding to climate change, as seen by earlier flowering and leafing out times in the spring. In coming decades, some plant species will adapt to utilize the increased carbon dioxide levels and higher temperatures to increase their growth rates, whereas other, less adaptable species will not and will decrease in abundance. Vegetation patterns and the production of plant biomass will similarly change, but not in a consistent pattern (Goetz et al. 2007). Increased tree mortality is already occurring in some ecosystems and will continue in coming decades because of water stress (Breshears et al. 2009). Also, many areas of rain forest in the Amazon and elsewhere will change to savanna (Malhi et al. 2008). Shifts in the populations of herbivorous insect species and pollinators may be pronounced as their plant resources change.

Finally, the large areas where temperate agricultural crops, such as wheat, maize (corn), and soybeans, are now grown may show declining yields of 30% or more by the end of the century due to higher temperatures. Such farm areas may have to be moved farther from the equator and perhaps expanded just to maintain production levels (Schlenker and Roberts 2009). Many of the areas that will be potentially suitable for new agricultural land are currently protected conservation land such as national parks. A situation could develop in which the protection of biological diversity directly competes with supplying the food needs of people.

Rising Sea Levels and Warmer Waters

Warming temperatures are already causing mountain glaciers to melt and the polar ice caps to shrink, and this process will continue and accelerate. As a result of this release of water and the thermal expansion of ocean water, over the next 100 years sea levels are predicted by the IPCC to rise by 20 to 60 cm (8 to 24 inches) and flood low-lying, coastal communities (IPCC 2007). These predictions are considered by many scientists to be too conservative, with values of 80 to 130 cm (up to 4 ft) being posssible. Given such increases in sea level, much of the current land area of low-lying countries such as Bangladesh could be under water within 100 years. Somewhere between 25% and 80% of coastal wetlands could be altered by rising sea levels. Many coastal cities, such as Miami and New York will have to build expensive sea walls, or they will become flooded by the rising waters (**Figure 9.27**). There is evidence that this process has already begun; sea levels have already risen by about 20 cm over the last 100 years (IPCC 2007). Many low islands that were previously just above water are now just below the water level (McClanahan et al. 2009).

Sea level rise will occur so rapidly that many species will be unable to migrate quickly enough to adjust to changing water levels. The migration of species of coastal salt marshes, in particular, will be blocked where human settlements, roads, and

FIGURE 9.27 (A) A predicted 1-m sea level rise by the end of this century will flood many coastal areas of South Florida, including much of Miami and the Everglades. A 3-m sea level rise, which is possible within a few centuries, would put all of Miami, Tampa, Jacksonville, and many other communities and ecosystems under water. (From Robbins 2009; maps by J. Weiss and J. Overpeck.)

(A) 1-m sea level rise

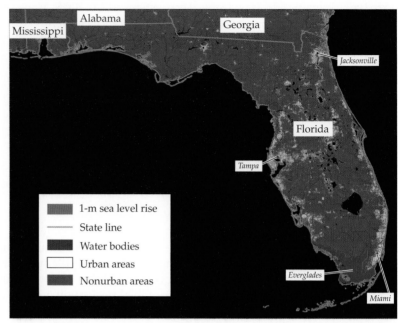

(B) 3-m sea level rise

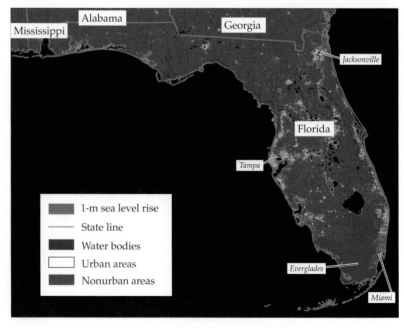

flood control barriers have been built. Squeezed between the rising sea and dense coastal developments, many species will no longer have a place to live (Feagin et al. 2005). This will have major economic impacts as well because salt marsh habitat is among the world's most productive habitat for plant and animal life, and it is a major breeding and nursery ground for commercial fish and shellfish.

Rising sea levels are potentially detrimental to many coral reef species, which grow at a precise depth in the water with the right combination of light and water movement. In coming decades, water levels may start to rise almost 1 cm per year—and

1 cm per year is about as fast as many coral species can grow. Slow-growing coral reefs will be unable to keep pace with the rise in sea level and will gradually be submerged and die; only fast-growing species will be able to survive. Compounding this, the pace of coral growth might be slower than normal; increasing absorption of CO_2 by the ocean will make the water more acidic and inhibit the ability of coral animals to deposit the calcium used to build the reef structure (De'ath et al. 2009).

Warming waters are already affecting the marine environment (Valdés et al. 2009). In the coastal waters off California, warm-water southern species are increasing in abundance while cold-water northern species are declining. Zooplankton are also declining in some areas because of warmer seas temperatures, with dire consequences for the marine animals that use them for food (Robinson et al. 2008). In addition, coral reefs are threatened by rising seawater temperatures (Carpenter et al. 2008; Thompson and van Woesik 2009). Abnormally high water temperatures in the Pacific Ocean and Indian Ocean in 1998 caused the coral animals to sicken and expel the symbi-

> Climate change is predicted to cause both rising sea levels and increasing seawater temperatures, with broad implications for marine ecology and coastal areas occupied by people.

otic algae that live inside the coral and provide them with essential carbohydrates; subsequently, these "bleached" coral then suffered a massive dieback, with an estimated 70% coral mortality in Indian Ocean reefs, though scattered patches did survive (**Figure 9.28**). Even-warmer conditions in the coming decades could be a disaster for many coral reefs, which are already stressed by pollution (Wooldridge and Done 2009).

The Overall Effect of Global Warming

Global climate change has the potential to radically restructure biological communities and change the ranges of many species. The pace of this change could overwhelm the natural dispersal abilities of species. There is mounting evidence that this process has already begun (see Table 9.3), with poleward movements in the distribution of bird and plant species and with reproduction occurring earlier in the spring (Parmesan and Yohe 2003; Cleland et al. 2007; Willis et al. 2008). Because the implications of global climate change are so far-reaching, biological communities, ecosystem functions, and climate need to be carefully monitored over the coming decades. Global climate change will also have an enormous impact on human populations in coastal areas affected by rising sea levels and increased hurricane impacts and in areas that are already experiencing drought stress and desertification. In much of sub-Saharan Africa, growing seasons will get shorter, and crop yields will decline (Lobell et al. 2008). The poor people of the world will be least able to adjust to these changes and will suffer the consequences disproportionately. However, all countries of the world will be affected, and it is time for people and their governments to recognize the urgent need to address global climate change.

It is likely that, as the climate changes, many existing protected areas will no longer preserve the rare and endangered species that currently live in them (McClanahan et al. 2008; Heller and Zavaleta 2009; Mawdsley et al. 2009). We need to establish new conservation areas now to protect sites that will be suitable for these species in the future, such as sites with large elevational gradients (**Figure 9.29**). Potential future migration routes, such as north–south river valleys, need to be identified and established now. If species are in danger of going extinct in the wild because of global climate change, the last remaining individuals may have to be maintained in captivity. Another strategy that we need to consider is to transplant isolated populations of rare and endangered species to new localities at higher elevations and farther from the poles, where they can survive and thrive. This has been termed "assisted migration." There is considerable debate within the conservation community about whether assisted migration represents a valid strategy or whether it is too problematic because of the potential for transplanted species to become invasive in their

FIGURE 9.28 Throughout the world, coral species are dying due to the combined effects of warming seawater, pollution, and the spread of diseases. This is sometimes seen in the "bleaching" or white patches in previously healthy, colorful coral, and their subsequent death. (Photograph © Georgette Douwma/Naturepl.com.)

new ranges. Even if global climate change is not as severe as predicted, establishing new protected areas can only help to protect biological diversity.

Although the prospect of global climate change is cause for great concern, it should not divert our attention from the massive habitat destruction that is the principal current cause of species extinction: Preserving intact communities and restoring degraded ones are the most important and immediate priorities for conservation, especially in the marine environment. Over the longer term, we need to reduce our use of fossil fuels and protect and replant forests in order to decrease levels of greenhouse gases.

(A) Now: Butterflies protected

(B) In 100 years: Butterflies not protected

(C) Better plan: Butterflies protected now and in the future

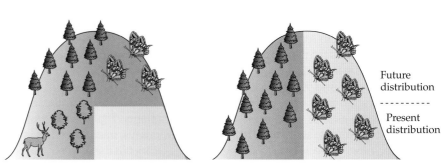

FIGURE 9.29 (A) A rare butterfly now lives inside a protected area. (B) However, because of a warming climate over the next 100 years, it migrates to a higher elevation where it is no longer protected. The alpine zone, with its associated plants and birds is completely lost. (C) The solution for butterflies is to establish, as soon as possible, more protected areas along elevational gradients and natural migration routes, in anticipation of future climate change. This plan does not provide a solution for the alpine plants and animals.

Summary

1. Massive disturbances to the environment caused by human activities are driving species, even ecosystems, to the point of extinction. These impacts will increase in the future, mostly in the species-rich tropical countries, as the human population increases to 8 to 10 billion by the year 2050. Slowing human population growth and reducing the overconsumption of resources are important elements of the solution to the biological diversity crisis.

2. The major threat to biological diversity is the loss of habitat, so to protect biological diversity, we must preserve habitat. Many unique and threatened species have lost most of their habitat and are protected on only tiny percentages of their original ranges. Species-rich tropical rain forests are currently being destroyed at a rapid rate. Extensive habitat destruction has occurred in tropical dry forests, wetlands in all regions of the world, coral reefs, and temperate grasslands.

3. Habitat fragmentation is the process whereby a large continuous area of habitat is both reduced and divided into two or more fragments. These fragments are isolated from one another by modified or degraded habitat. Habitat fragmentation leads to the rapid loss of remaining species because it creates barriers to the normal processes of dispersal, colonization, and foraging. Particular fragments may lack the range of food types and other resources necessary to support permanent populations of certain species, or they may contain altered environmental conditions and increased levels of pests, which make them less suitable for the original species.

4. Environmental pollution eliminates many species from biological communities, even where the structure of the community is not obviously disturbed. Pesticides, sprayed to control insects, become concentrated in the bodies of birds, particularly raptors, leading to a decline in populations. Water pollution by petroleum products, sewage, and industrial wastes can kill species outright or gradually eliminate them. Excessive nutrient inputs can cause harmful algal blooms that damage aquatic communities. Acid rain, high ozone levels near the surface of the Earth, and airborne toxic metals are all damaging components of air pollution.

5. Global climate patterns are predicted to change within the coming century because of the large amounts of carbon dioxide and other greenhouse gases produced by human activities, such as the burning of fossil fuels. Predicted temperature increases could be so rapid during this coming century that many species will be unable to adjust their ranges and will go extinct. Low-lying coastal communities will be submerged by seawater as the polar ice caps continue to melt. Conservation biologists need to monitor these changes and take action when species cannot adapt to climate change.

For Discussion

1. Human population growth is often blamed for the loss of biological diversity. Is this valid? What other factors are responsible, and how do we weigh their relative importance? Is it possible to find a balance between providing for increasing numbers of people and protecting biodiversity?

2. Excessive consumption of resources by people in developed countries is a major cause of the loss of biological diversity. An alternative is to "live simply, so that others may simply live" or to "live as if life mattered." Consider the absolute minimum of food, shelter, clothing, and energy that you and your family need to survive, and compare it with what you now use. Would you be willing to change your lifestyle to preserve the environment and help others? How could an entire society change enough to benefit the environment?

3. What can an individual citizen do to improve the environment and conserve biodiversity? Consider the options, which range from doing no harm to becoming actively involved in large conservation organizations.

4. Consider the most damaged and the most pristine habitats near where you live. Why have some been preserved and others been allowed to degrade?

5. Examine maps of parks and nature reserves. Have these areas been fragmented by roads, power lines, and other human constructs? How has fragmentation affected the average fragment size, the area of interior habitat, and the total length of edge? Analyze the effects of adding new roads or eliminating existing roads and developments from the parks, and consider their biological, legal, political, and economic implications.

Suggested Readings

Becker, C. G., C. R. Fonseca, C. F. B. Haddad, and P. I. Prado. 2010. Habitat split as a cause of local population declines of amphibians with aquatic larvae. *Conservation Biology* 24: 287–294. Isolated forest fragments show a marked decline in amphibian populations.

Carpenter, K. E. and 38 others. 2009. One-third of reef-building corals face elevated extinction risk from climate change and local impacts. *Science* 321: 560–563. Coral species may have a higher extinction risk than most terrestrial taxa, with Caribbean and the western Pacific species most at risk.

Gore, A. 2006. *An Inconvenient Truth.* Rodale Books, New York. This book (and movie) convinced people that climate change was really happening. As author and Nobel Laureate Al Gore phrased it, "inconvenient truths do not go away."

Heller, N. E. and E. S. Zavaleta. 2009. Biodiversity management in the face of climate change: A review of 22 years of recommendations. *Biological Conservation* 142: 14–32. Managers need to start dealing with climate change right now.

Intergovernmental Panel on Climate Change (IPCC). 2007. *Climate Change 2007: The Physical Science Basis.* Contribution of Working Group I to the Fourth Assessment Report. Cambridge University Press, Cambridge. Comprehensive presentation of the evidence for global climate change, along with predictions for the coming decades.

Jackson S. T., J. L. Betancourt, R. K. Booth, and S. T. Gray. 2009. Ecology and the ratchet of events: Climate variability, niche dimensions, and species distributions. *Proceedings of the National Academy of Sciences USA* 106(suppl. 2): 19685–19692. In coming decades, many species will not be able to survive in their present locations because of climate change.

Laurance, W. F., M. Goosem, and S. G. W. Laurance. 2009. Impacts of roads and linear clearings on tropical forests. *Trends in Ecology and Evolution* 24: 659–679. Tropical species are vulnerable to linear infrastructure such as roads, which fragment habitat and open up new areas to human colonization and exploitation.

Oehlmann, J. and 10 others. 2009. A critical analysis of the biological impacts of plasticizers on wildlife. *Philosophical Transactions of the Royal Society*, Series B 364: 2047–2062. Chemicals released by plastics affect hormone systems.

Sekercioglu, C. H., S. H. Schneider, J. P. Fay, and S. R. Loarie. 2008. Climate change, elevational range shifts, and bird extinctions. *Conservation Biology* 22: 140–150. Climate change is predicted to cause the extinction of hundreds of bird species by the end of the twenty-first century.

Smith, V. H. and D. W. Schindler. 2009. Eutrophication science: Where do we go from here? *Trends in Ecology and Evolution* 24: 201–207. While eutrophication is a significant water quality issue, many key questions remain unanswered.

Thompson, D. M. and R. van Woesik. 2009. Corals escape bleaching in regions that recently and historically expressed frequent thermal stress. *Proceedings of the Royal Society*, Series B 276: 2893–2901. Reduced recent bleaching is perhaps due to rapid die-off of sensitive corals in 1998.

Verstraete, M. M., R. J. Scholes, and M. S. Smith. 2009. Climate and desertification: Looking at an old problem through new lenses. *Frontiers in Ecology and the Environment* 7: 421–428. Arid lands will come under further threat in many areas due to rising temperatures and changing rainfall patterns.

Willis, C. G., B. Ruhfel, R. B. Primack, A. J. Miller-Rushing, and C. C. Davis. 2008. Phylogenetic patterns of species loss in Thoreau's woods are driven by climate change. *Proceedings of the National Academy of Sciences USA* 105: 17029–17033. Climate change is already affecting the distribution and abundance of plants in a temperate ecosystem.

Wooldridge, S. A. and T. J. Done. 2009. Improved water quality can ameliorate effects of climate change on corals. *Ecological Applications* 19: 1492–1499. Much of the present damage to coral species is still coming from pollution.

Chapter 10

Overexploitation, Invasive Species, and Disease

E ven when biological communities appear intact, they may be experiencing significant losses as a result of human activities. In this chapter, we will discuss three threats to biological communities that are less obvious, but not less damaging, than more apparent threats such as habitat destruction and loss. These three threats are overexploitation of particular species, introduction of invasive species, and increased levels of disease transmission. These threats often follow habitat fragmentation and degradation, or are made worse by such factors. Global climate change will also make biological communities more vulnerable to these threats in the future.

Overexploitation

Overexploitation by humans has been estimated to currently threaten about a fourth of the endangered vertebrates in the United States and fully three-fourths of the vertebrate species in China (Li and Wilcove 2005). The greater level of overexploitation in China results from its large, poor, rural population and the extensive use of wildlife for both food and traditional medicine. People have always hunted and harvested the food and other resources they need to survive, and as long as human populations were small and the methods of collection unsophisticated, people could sustainably harvest and hunt the plants

FIGURE 10.1 Intensive harvesting has reached crisis levels in many of the world's fisheries. These bluefin tuna are being transferred from a fishing trawler to a "factory ship," aboard which huge quantities of fish are efficiently processed for human consumption. Such efficiency can result in massive overfishing. (Photograph © Images&Stories/Alamy.)

and animals in their environment. However, as human populations have increased, our use of the environment has escalated, and our methods of harvesting have become dramatically more efficient (**Figure 10.1**) (Lewis 2004). In many areas, this has led to an almost complete depletion of large animals from many biological communities and the creation of strangely "empty" habitats.

Technological advances mean that, even in the developing world, guns are used instead of blowpipes, spears, or arrows for hunting in the tropical rain forests and savannas. Small-scale local fishermen now have outboard motors on their canoes and boats, allowing them to harvest wider areas more rapidly. Powerful motorized fishing boats and enormous "factory ships" harvest fish from the world's oceans and sell them on the global market. However, even in preindustrial societies, intense exploitation, particularly for meat, has led to the decline and extinction of local species of birds, mammals, and reptiles (Steadman et al. 2002). For example, ceremonial cloaks worn by the Hawaiian kings were made from feathers of the mamo bird (*Drepanis* sp.); a single cloak used the feathers of 70,000 birds of this now-extinct species.

Traditional societies sometimes have imposed restrictions on themselves to prevent overexploitation of jointly owned common property or natural resources (Cinner and Aswani 2007). For example, the rights to specific harvesting territories were rigidly controlled; hunting and harvesting in certain areas were banned. There were often prohibitions against harvesting female, juvenile, and undersized animals. Certain seasons of the year and times of the day were closed for harvesting. Certain efficient methods of harvesting were not allowed. (Interestingly enough, these restrictions, which allowed some traditional societies to exploit communal resources on a long-term, sustainable basis, are almost identical to the fishing restrictions regulators have imposed on or proposed for many fisheries in industrialized nations.) Among the most highly developed restrictions were those of the traditional or artisan societies of the Pacific islands (Cinner et al. 2005). In some of these societies, the resources of the reef, lagoon, and forest were clearly defined, and the possible consequences of overharvesting were readily apparent. This is still true today in

Tonga, where only the king is permitted to hunt flying foxes since their numbers have shrunk precipitously because of overharvesting.

Exploitation in the Modern World

Such self-imposed restrictions on using common property resources are often less effective today. In much of the world, resources are exploited opportunistically (de Merode and Cowlishaw 2006). In economic terms, a regulated common property resource sometimes becomes an open access resource and available to everyone without regulation. The lack of restraint applies to both ends of the economic scale—the poor and hungry as well as the rich and greedy. In previous chapters, we have seen how corporations and the developed world take advantage of natural resources for a profit. If a market exists for a product, local people will search their environment to find and sell it. Sometimes traditional groups will sell the rights to a resource, such as a forest or mining area, for cash to buy desired goods. In rural areas, the traditional controls that regulate the extraction of natural products have generally weakened. Whole villages are mobilized to remove systematically every usable animal and plant from an area of forest. Where there has been substantial human migration, civil unrest, or war, controls of any type may no longer exist. In countries beset with civil conflict, such as Somalia, Cambodia, the former Yugoslavia, the Democratic Republic of the Congo, and Rwanda, firearms have come into the hands of rural people. The breakdown of food distribution networks in countries such as these leaves the resources of the natural environment vulnerable to whoever can exploit them (Loucks et al. 2009). The most efficient hunter can kill the most animals, sell the most meat, and make the most money for himself and his family. Animals are sometimes even killed for target practice or simply to spite the government.

> Today's vast human population and improved technology have resulted in unsustainable harvest levels of many species and other biological resources.

On local and regional scales, hunters in most developing countries move into recently logged areas, national parks, and other areas near roads, where they legally and illegally shoot, trap, and collect wild mammals to sell as bushmeat. Populations of large primates, such as gorillas and chimpanzees, as well as ungulates and other mammals may be reduced by 80% or more by hunting, and certain species may be eliminated altogether, especially those that occur within a few kilometers of a road (Parry et al. 2009; Suárez et al. 2009). In many places, hunters are extracting animals at a rate six or more times greater than the resource base can sustain. The result is a forest with a mostly intact plant community that is lacking its animal community. The decline in animal populations caused by the intensive hunting of animals has been termed the **bushmeat crisis** and is a major concern for wildlife officials and conservation biologists, especially in Africa (**Figure 10.2**) (www.bushmeat.org). Eating primate bushmeat also increases the possibility that new diseases will be transmitted to human populations. In many coastal areas, people also intensely harvest sea turtles, whales, dolphins, and manatees for meat, leading to population declines (Clapham and van Waerebeek 2007). In areas of coastal Africa, the export of fish to supply European markets is creating even greater demand for bushmeat to supply local protein needs (Brashares et al. 2004).

Solutions involve restricting the sale and transport of bushmeat, restricting the sale of firearms and ammunition, closing roads following logging, extending legal protection to key endangered

FIGURE 10.2 Bushmeat hunters begin with the largest animals and successively remove medium-sized and small animals until there is an "empty forest." The monkey in this photograph is a red-tailed guenon (*Cercopithecus ascanius*). (Photograph © Martin Harvey/Alamy.)

species, establishing protected reserves where hunting is not allowed, and most important, providing alternative protein sources to reduce the demand for bushmeat (Bennett et al. 2007). Projects with these goals are being initiated, with the premise that "food secure, farm-based communities with alternative sources of income to illegal use of wildlife can contribute positively to wildlife protection" (Lewis 2004). However, it remains to be seen if regulating bushmeat markets and increasing domestic livestock production will reduce hunting pressure on (or halt declines in) wildlife populations.

International Wildlife Trade

The legal and illegal trade in wildlife is responsible for the decline of many species. Worldwide trade in wildlife is valued at over $10 billion per year, not including edible fish. One of the most pervasive examples of this is the international trade in furs, in which hunted species, such as the chinchilla (*Chinchilla* spp.), vicuña (*Vicugna vicugna*), giant otter (*Pteronura brasiliensis*), and numerous cat species, have been reduced to low numbers. Overharvesting of butterflies by insect collectors; of orchids, cacti, and other plants by horticulturists; of marine mollusks by shell collectors; and of tropical fish by aquarium hobbyists are further examples of targeting of whole biological communities to supply an enormous international demand (**Table 10.1**) (Uthicke et al. 2009). It has been estimated that 350 million tropical fish valued at $1 billion are sold worldwide for the aquarium market, and many times that number are killed during collection or shipping (Karesh et al. 2005). Many rare animals such as bears and tigers are killed to obtain specific organs or body parts that are considered useful for medicines and aphrodisiacs, particularly in East Asia. Major exporters are primarily in the developing world, often in the tropics; most major importers are in the developed countries and East Asia, including Canada, China, the European Union, Hong Kong, Japan, Singapore, Taiwan, and the United States. The international trade in other live animals

TABLE 10.1 Major Targeted Groups of the Worldwide Trade in Wildlife		
Group	Number traded each year[a]	Comments
Primates	40,000	Mostly used for biomedical research; also for pets, zoos, circuses, and private collections.
Birds	4 million	Zoos and pets. Mostly perching birds, but also legal and illegal trade of about 80,000 parrots.
Reptiles	640,000	Zoos and pets. Also 10–15 million raw skins. Reptiles are used in some 50 million manufactured products (mainly from the wild but increasingly from farms).
Ornamental fish	350 million	Most saltwater tropical fish come from the wild and may be caught by illegal methods that damage other wildlife and the surrounding coral reef.
Reef corals	1000–2000 tons	Reefs are being destructively mined to provide aquarium decor and coral jewelry.
Orchids	9–10 million	Approximately 10% of the international trade comes from the wild, sometimes deliberately mislabeled to avoid regulation.
Cacti	7–8 million	Approximately 15% of traded cacti come from the wild, with smuggling a major problem.

Source: Data from WRI 2005 and Karesh 2005.
[a]With the exception of reef corals, refers to number of individuals.

is similarly large: 640,000 reptiles, 4 million birds, and 40,000 primates are sold each year (Karesh et al. 2005).

In an attempt to regulate and restrict this trade, many declining species are listed as protected under the Convention on International Trade in Endangered Species (CITES; see Chapter 21). Listing species with CITES has often protected species or groups of species from further exploitation.

Besides a surprisingly large legal trade, billions of dollars are involved in the illegal trade of wildlife (Christy 2010). A black market links poor local people, corrupt customs officials, rogue dealers, and wealthy buyers who don't question the sources from whom they buy. This trade has many of the same characteristics, the same practices, and sometimes the same players as the illegal trade in drugs and weapons. Confronting those who perpetuate such illegal activities has become a major and dangerous job for international law enforcement agencies.

The pattern of overexploitation of plants and animals in many cases is distressingly similar: A wildlife resource is identified, a commercial market is developed for that resource, and the local human populace is mobilized to extract and sell the resource. Initial sales are used to buy guns, boats, trucks, tools, and whatever else will help extract the resource more quickly. A transportation network involving roads, cargo ships, and airplanes is built to connect harvesters, buyers, and stores. As the supply diminishes, the price rises, creating a strong incentive to overexploit the resource. The resource is extracted so thoroughly that it becomes rare or even extinct, and the market then turns to another species or another region to exploit. Commercial fishing and whaling demonstrates this pattern well, with the industry working one species after another to the point of diminishing returns, a process sometimes termed "fishing down the food web" (Link 2007) (**Box 10.1**). Often the average size of caught animals declines as there are fewer older animals to harvest (**Figure 10.3**) (McClenachan 2009). Top predators in particular are being removed at dramatic rates—a process that has poorly understood consequences for the rest of the food web; several formerly common species of

> Overharvesting of wildlife has increased to supply global markets, both legal and illegal.

(A) 1957

(B) 2007

FIGURE 10.3 Trophy fish caught in Key West, Florida. (A) In 1957 the fish were abundant, large, and diverse. (B) The fish were less abundant, smaller, and less diverse in 2007 after 30 years of overharvesting. (Photographs from McClenachan 2009.)

BOX 10.1   *Endangered Whales: Making a Comeback?*

■ Whales are among the largest and, possibly, most intelligent animals on Earth, with complicated social organization, large brains, and communication systems. The discovery of the humpback whale's intricate, unique songs captured the public imagination, resulting in strong public support for research on whales and for legal measures to protect them. But as public support has increased, has the situation for whales really improved?

Scientists have only recently begun to comprehend the complexity of whale behavior and ecology because studies of many whale species are difficult, for several reasons. First, radio tracking devices commonly used for land animals are difficult to attach to whales, making it difficult to observe individuals and populations. Second, whales are often very far-ranging, traveling throughout the year from tropical to polar seas. Finally, whales live in the open water, which greatly adds to the expense and logistical challenges of research studies.

Few ocean predators are capable of taking on the larger whales, so the greatest threat to all whale species for the last four centuries has been humans. Until as recently as three decades ago, commercial whaling had been the single most significant factor leading to the decline of the larger whale species—a threat from which many have not yet recovered (Morrel 2007).

Commercial whaling began in the eleventh century and reached its apex in the nineteenth and twentieth centuries. During the 1800s, baleen (whalebone), spermaceti (wax and oil from sperm whales), and oil made from whale blubber became important commercial products in the international marketplace. Several species that were hunted preferentially were pushed to the brink of extinction. Right whales—so named because they were slow and easy to capture and provided up to 150 barrels of blubber oil as well as abundant baleen, thus making them the "right" whales for whalers—were the first to bear the brunt. In the twentieth century, new technology allowed whalers to access the faster, more pelagic whales, and the slaughter was on. In the first half of the twentieth century, almost 2 million whales of many species were killed, primarily for soap, edible oils, and, finally, their meat.

> Certain whale species have recovered following protection on hunting. However, other species face different threats and require further conservation efforts.

Hunting of right and gray whales was made illegal by international agreement in 1935, by which point they had been reduced to less than 5% of their original abundance. By 1946, whaling nations created the International Whaling Commission (IWC) to try to sustain whale hunting. In the early 1960s, the IWC instituted partial bans on whaling for parts of the world (and for certain species). In 1982, the IWC passed a moratorium on all commercial killing of whales worldwide (instituted in 1986), against the protests of nations such as Japan, Norway, Russia, and Iceland. Some of these nations continued hunting by employing a technical loophole in the IWC agreement, allowing hunting for scientific studies, but hunters regularly kill more whales

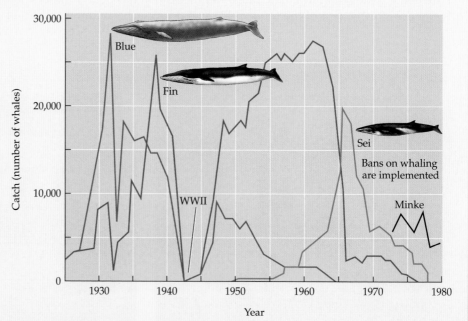

The annual catch of whales. Successively smaller whale species are exploited as populations of the larger species edge closer to commercial extinction. Commercial whaling was discontinued during World War II, and declined in the 1960s as bans on whaling were implemented.

BOX 10.1 (*continued*)

than the agreement permits (Gales et al. 2007). The Japanese fleet currently catches 1500 or more minke whales per year, as well as smaller numbers of sei, Bryde's, and sperm whales. Worse still, whalers frequently make kills of protected species, such as fins and humpbacks, often with the tacit approval of their governments (Alter et al. 2003). Nevertheless, annual killings of whales have dropped dramatically since the 1986 ban.

Since the ban was instituted, different species have had variable recovery rates. Right whales, protected since 1936, have not recovered in either the North Atlantic or North Pacific. Humpback numbers, on the other hand, have more than doubled in some areas since the late 1980s, an increase of 5%–10% annually. Eastern gray whales appear to have recovered to their previous levels of about 23,000 animals, after being hunted to less than 3000.

Though the whaling ban has greatly reduced the most direct threat, other factors now contribute to whale mortality. One species at great risk is the right whale. The North Atlantic right whale population is currently estimated at approximately 400 animals—far less than its original size (IUCN Red List). Right whales can be injured or killed by collisions with large ships or when they become tangled in fishing gear. Recent efforts to limit injury and deaths related to human activities have included bans on gill nets in Florida calving grounds and speed and area restrictions for ships. In addition, information about whale distribution, from bioacoustic monitoring, is being used to make fishing boats and commercial ships aware of critical feeding areas off the coast of New England.

Many whales too small for large-scale commercial use, such as dolphins and porpoises, have shown substantial population declines as a result of deliberate as well as accidental capture. As fish become scarce because of overharvesting, people are hunting dolphins for food in increasing numbers. Other rare marine animals, such as manatees, are also being targeted by fishermen. Nevertheless, acci-

Worldwide Populations of Whale Species Harvested by Humans

Species	Numbers prior to whaling[a]	Present numbers	Primary diet items	Status
Baleen whales				
Blue	200,000	10–25,000	Plankton	Endangered
Bowhead	56,000	25,500	Plankton	Least concern
Fin	475,000	60,000	Plankton, fish	Endangered
Gray (Pacific stock)	23,000	15–22,000	Crustaceans	Least concern
Humpback	150,000	60,000	Plankton, fish	Least concern
Minke	140,000	1,000,000	Plankton, fish	Least concern
Northern right	Unknown	1300	Plankton	Endangered
Sei	250,000	54,000	Plankton, fish	Endangered
Southern right	100,000	3–4000	Plankton	Least concern
Toothed whales				
Beluga	Unknown	200,000	Fish, crustaceans, squid	Near threatened
Narwhal	Unknown	50,000	Fish, squid, crustaceans	Near threatened
Sperm	1,100,000	360,000	Fish, squid	Vulnerable

Source: American Cetacean Society (www.acsonline.org); IUCN Red List.

[a]Preexploitation population numbers are highly speculative; recent evidence suggests the populations might have been even greater (Roman and Palumbi 2003; Alter et al. 2007).

dental catches by commercial fishing boats still account for a high proportion of dolphin deaths. Dolphins in tropical waters of the eastern Pacific Ocean are particularly vulnerable to fishing-related fatalities because they often travel with schools of tuna; thousands of dolphins die in tuna nets each year. One approach to limiting dolphin bycatch has been to establish international certification of tuna that have been caught by special fishing gear that reduces the accidental harvest of dolphins and then to label the tuna caught with such methods.

Small whales and dolphins living in estuarine and riverine habitats face additional threats—of indirect harm caused by dams and chemical and noise pollution and, because these areas are heavily used for shipping and boating, of direct harm from collisions or entanglements. One such species, the Baiji (Chinese river dolphin, *Lipotes vexillifer*), was declared extinct in 2007; this was the first human-caused extinction of a cetacean species, which occurred despite many international efforts to halt the species' decline. In general, whales and dolphins appear to be highly sensitive to pollutants and carcinogens (particularly heavy metals and pesticides), which are present in greater concentrations in

(*continued*)

BOX 10.1 *(continued)*

rivers and harbors than in the open sea. Tissue samples of St. Lawrence River belugas (*Delphinapterus leucas*), for example, contain concentrations of carcinogenic PCBs much higher than have been found in ocean-dwelling Arctic belugas (McKinney et al. 2006). Long-term exposure to high levels of pollutants exacts a heavy toll on the health of river-dwelling whales: autopsies of beluga whales from the St. Lawrence indicate a surprisingly high cancer rate and respiratory and gastrointestinal infections associated with parasites, bacteria, viruses, and protozoans, and their population has shown a corresponding decline during this period.

In the coming years, whales and people will come into increasing conflict over marine resources. Fin, humpback, minke, orca, and sperm whales eat some of the same fish and squid that commercial fishing fleets are harvesting intensively in the North Atlantic Ocean. Increasingly powerful sonar devices being tested by the U.S. Navy may be responsible for recent episodes of whale stranding on beaches (Parsons et al. 2008). As harvesting of marine resources becomes ever more efficient and as marine habitats are affected by human activities and destroyed, it will becoming even more challenging to find effective conservation strategies to protect whales and other marine species and to sustain ocean ecosystems.

A commercial whaling ship has harpooned and killed a whale, ostensibly for scientific study. The meat will be processed and sold. (Photograph © Jeremy Sutton-Hibbert/Alamy.)

sharks have declined by as much as 75% in recent decades, leading to cascading effects on lower trophic levels (Myers et al. 2007).

Any number of other examples could be given to illustrate this scenario of overexploitation: fisherfolk in the Philippines who supply ornamental fish to international buyers, and exploitation leading to the depletion of wild game at increasing distances around mining towns in Africa. A striking example is the enormous increase in demand for sea horses (*Hippocampus* spp.; **Figure 10.4**) in China. The Chinese use dried sea horses in their traditional medicine because they resemble dragons and are believed to have a variety of healing powers. About 45 tons of sea horses are consumed in China per year—roughly 16 million animals. Sea horse populations throughout the world are being decimated to supply this ever-increasing demand, with the result that international trade in sea horses is now carefully monitored and regulated by international treaty (Foster and Vincent 2005).

Another example is the worldwide trade in frog legs; each year Indonesia exports the legs of roughly 100 million frogs to western European countries for luxury meals. There is no information on how this intensive harvesting affects frog populations, forest ecology, and agriculture, and perhaps not surprisingly, the names of the frog species on the shipping labels are often wrong, which adds to

FIGURE 10.4 Seahorses have been overfished around the world for traditional medicines, aquarium displays, and curiosities. All exports are now regulated. (Photograph courtesy of ACJ Vincent/Project Seahorse.)

the difficulty in quantifying the extent of the problem (Warkentin et al. 2009; www.traffic.org). The United States similarly exports and imports millions of amphibians and reptiles every year for food, pets, and clothing products, and many shipments do not even identify the species involved (Schlaepfer et al. 2005). Such intense exploitation of plants and animals leads to decline, and it is unknown if species can recover when exploitation ceases (**Figure 10.5**).

FIGURE 10.5 *Neopicrorhiza* is a Himalayan medicinal plant that is declining rapidly because of overharvesting. In experimental plots, the density was reduced in Year 1 by various intensities of harvesting. Following no harvesting or light harvesting (25%), density increased over 3 subsequent years. Density remained low after intensive harvesting (75% and 100%); virtually all plants had been removed and other species had grown in their place. (After Ghimire et al. 2005; photograph courtesy of S. K. Ghimere.)

Commercial Harvesting

Governments and industries often claim that they can avoid the overharvesting of wild species by applying modern scientific management. As part of this approach, an extensive body of literature has developed in wildlife and fisheries management and in forestry to describe the **maximum sustainable yield**: the greatest amount of a resource, such as Atlantic bluefin tuna (*Thunnus thynnus*), that can be harvested each year and replaced through population growth without detriment to the population. Calculations using the maximum population growth rate (r) and the carrying capacity (B; the largest population or biomass that a given area can support) are used to estimate the maximum sustainable yield (Y_{max}), which typically occurs when the population size is at about half the carrying capacity, or when the biomass is half of its maximum value. The maximum sustainable yield can be estimated as

$$Y_{max} = rB/4$$

For a growing population with r having a value of 2 (meaning the population is capable of doubling each year until it reaches carrying capacity), half of the biomass could theoretically be harvested each year. In highly controlled situations where the resource can be quantified, such as with plantations of timber trees, it may be possible to approach maximum sustainable yield. However, in many real-world situations, industry representatives and government officials managing commercial operations (logging, fishing, etc.) may lack the key biological information that is needed to make accurate calculations. Not surprisingly, attempts to harvest at high levels can lead to abrupt species declines. Yield management of marine resources demonstrates some of the serious problems that can arise from unrealistic applications of maximum sustainable yield figures.

PROBLEMS WITH YIELD MANAGEMENT: THE FISHING INDUSTRY Eighty percent of the world's major fish stocks have been classified as overfished (Mora et al. 2009). As a consequence, consumption of fish, an important source of protein, has been declining in most developing countries. But fishing industry representatives use maximum sustainable yield calculations to support their position that harvesting levels of Atlantic bluefin tuna, for example, can be maintained at the present rate, even though the population of the species has declined by 97% in recent years (Safina and Klinger 2008; www.bigmarinefish.com). In order to satisfy local business interests, protect jobs, and generate revenue, governments often set harvesting levels too high, resulting in damage to the resource base (Dichmont et al. 2010). It is particularly difficult to coordinate international agreements and to monitor compliance with maximum sustainable yield limits when species migrate across national boundaries and through international waters. Illegal harvesting may result in additional resource removal not accounted for in official records (McClanahan et al. 2008), as has been occurring in the whaling industry and in fishing operations in Antarctic waters.

Furthermore, a considerable proportion of the remaining juvenile stock may be damaged during harvesting operations. Another difficulty presents itself if harvest levels are kept fairly constant—often based on overly optimistic estimates of resource biomass—even though the resource base fluctuates; a normal harvest of a fish species during a year when fish stocks are low because of variable or poor weather conditions may severely reduce or destroy the species. In order to protect species from total destruction, governments are more frequently closing fishing grounds in the hopes that populations will recover. For example, the Canadian fishing fleet continued to harvest large amounts of cod off Newfoundland during the 1980s, even as the population declined. As a result, cod stocks dropped to 1% of their original numbers, and the government was forced to close the fishery in 1992, eliminating 35,000 jobs (MEA 2005).

Many examples like these clearly demonstrate that management based on simplistic mathematical models of maximum sustainable yield is often inappropriate and invalid for the real world. Yield models should primarily be used to gain insight into fish stocks rather than to determine a single yield level that must be accepted. What *is* required is constant monitoring of stocks and the ability to adjust harvesting levels as appropriate. Once harvesting pressure is removed by government restrictions, fishing stocks may take years to recover, because fish density may be too low for successful reproduction, competing species may have established themselves, or most years may be unsuitable for reproduction. In some cases, fishing stocks have not recovered even many years after harvesting has been stopped completely. One hope is that pressure to keep exploiting wild stocks will decrease because of the rapid increase in commercial aquaculture production of fish and shellfish (Diana 2009). However, aquaculture has its own negative impacts, such as water pollution, and when domestic populations transmit parasites and novel genes to wild populations.

> Commercial fisheries have been overharvested due to pressures for high harvest levels, fluctuating fish populations, and illegal harvests. Many non-commercial species are caught and killed accidentally as bycatch during fishing activities.

For many marine species, direct exploitation is less important than the indirect effects of commercial fishing (Cox et al. 2007; Zydelis et al. 2009). Many marine vertebrates and invertebrates are caught incidentally as **bycatch** during fishing operations and are killed or injured in the process. Approximately 25% of the harvest in fishing operations is dumped back in the sea to die. The declines of skates, rays, and millions of seabirds have all been linked to their wholesale death as bycatch. The huge number of sea turtles and dolphins killed by commercial fishing boats as bycatch resulted in a massive public outcry and led to the development of improved nets to reduce these accidental catches. Even so, many marine animals die when they accidentally become entangled in discarded and lost fishing gear. The development of improved nets and hooks, as well as other methods to reduce bycatch, is an active area of current fisheries research (Carruthers et al. 2009).

What Can Be Done to Stop Overexploitation?

Perhaps, as many overexploited species become rare, it will no longer be commercially viable to harvest them, and their numbers will have a chance to recover. Unfortunately, populations of many species, such as the rhinoceroses and certain large wild cats, may already have been reduced so severely by the combination of hunting and habitat destruction that they will require vigilant conservation efforts to recover. In some cases, rarity even increases demand: As a rare species becomes more rare, the price often rises, making it an even more valuable commodity on the black market (Gault et al. 2008). In rural areas of the developing world, desperate people may search even more intensively for the last remaining marketable plants and animals to collect and sell, in order to buy food for their families.

Finding the methods to protect and manage the remaining individuals in such situations is a priority for conservation biologists. As described in Chapter 20, conservation projects linking the conservation of biodiversity and local economic development represent one possible approach. In some cases, this linkage may be made possible by acknowledging the sustainable harvesting of a natural resource with a special certification that allows producers to receive a higher price for their product. Certified timber products and seafoods are already entering the market, but it remains to be seen if they will have a significant positive impact on biodiversity, particularly among increasingly affluent

> Certifying timber, seafood, and other products as sustainable may be a way to prevent overharvesting.

consumers in China and other Asian countries (Butler and Laurance 2008). National parks, nature reserves, marine sanctuaries, and other protected areas can also be established to conserve overharvested species. When harvesting can be reduced or stopped by the enforcement of international regulations, such as CITES and comparable national regulations, species may be able to recover. Elephants, sea otters, sea turtles, seals, and certain whale species provide hopeful examples of species that have recovered, once overexploitation was stopped (Lotze and Worm 2009).

Invasive Species

Throughout the history of life, species have spread into new regions via natural processes of dispersal, but under human influence they are moving faster, farther, and in greater numbers than ever before (Ricciardi 2007). Every region of the world is affected; even the Antarctic continent and its surrounding islands have been invaded by nearly 200 plants, animals, invertebrates, and microbes, just within the past two centuries (Frenot et al. 2005). Human activities have distributed species throughout the world, obscuring past regional differences. This new, more homogeneous distribution of species is so significant that some scientists have proposed that we are entering a new era that could be called the Homogeocene.

Exotic species are species that occur outside their natural ranges because of human activity. The great majority of exotics do not become established in the places in which they are introduced, because the new environments are not suitable to their needs or because they have not arrived in sufficient numbers. However, a certain percentage of species do establish themselves in their new homes, and many of these can be considered **invasive species**—that is, they spread and increase in abundance rapidly, sometimes at the expense of native species (Davis 2009; Wilson et al. 2009). These invasive species may displace native species through competition for limiting resources. Introduced animal species may prey upon native species to the point of extinction, or they may alter the habitat so that many natives are no longer able to persist (**Figure 10.6**) (Gooden et al. 2009). Invasive exotic species represent threats to 42% of the endangered species in the United States, with particularly severe impacts on bird and plant species (Pimentel et al. 2005). The thousands of nonnative species in the United States are estimated to cause damages and losses amounting to $120 billion per year. Globally, over half of all recent animal extinctions are attributable in whole or in part to the effects of invasive species, according to the IUCN database (Clavero and García-Berthou 2005).

Many species introductions have occurred by the following means:

> Invasive species may displace native species through competition for limiting resources, they may prey upon native species to the point of extinction, or they may alter the habitat so that natives are no longer able to persist.

- *European colonization.* Settlers arriving at new colonies released hundreds of different species of European birds and mammals into places like New Zealand, Australia, North America, and South Africa to make the countryside seem familiar and to provide game for hunting. Numerous species of fish (trout, bass, carp, etc.) have been widely released to provide food and recreation.

- *Agriculture, horticulture, aquaculture.* Large numbers of plant species have been introduced and grown as ornamentals, agricultural species, pasture grasses, or soil stabilizers. Many of these species have escaped from cultivation or their original habitat and have become established in local communities. As aquaculture develops, there is a constant danger of more plant species escaping and becoming invasive in marine and freshwater environments (Chapman et al. 2003).

- *Accidental transport.* Species are often transported unintentionally (Lee and Chown 2009). For example, weed seeds are accidentally harvested with commercial seeds and sown in new localities; rats, snakes, and insects stow away aboard ships and airplanes; and disease-causing microbes, parasitic organ-

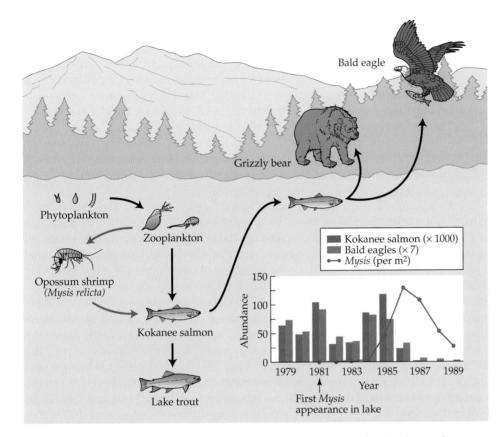

FIGURE 10.6 In Flathead Lake and its tributaries in Montana, the food web was disrupted by the deliberate introduction of opossum shrimp (*Mysis relicta*). The natural food chain consists of grizzly bears, bald eagles, and lake trout, which all eat kokanee salmon; kokanee eat zooplankton (cladocerans and copepods); and zooplankton eat phytoplankton (algae). Opossum shrimp, introduced as a food source for the kokanee salmon, ate so much zooplankton that there was far less food for the kokanee. Kokanee salmon numbers then declined radically, as did the eagle population that relied on the salmon. Eagle and salmon populations remained depressed as of 2005. (After Spencer et al. 1991 and Spencer, personal communication.)

isms, and insects travel along with their host species, particularly in the leaves and roots of plants and the soil of potted plants. Seeds, insects, and microorganisms on shoes, clothing, and luggage can be transported across the world in a few days by modern jet travelers. Ships frequently carry exotic species in their ballast tanks, releasing vast numbers of bacteria, viruses, algae, invertebrates, and small fish into new locations. Large ships may hold up to 150,000 tons of ballast water. Governments are now developing regulations to reduce the transport of species in ballast water, such as requiring ships to exchange their ballast water 320 km offshore in deep water before approaching a port (Costello et al. 2007).

- *Biological control.* When an exotic species becomes invasive, a common solution is to release an animal species from its original range that will consume the pest and hopefully control its numbers. While biological control can be dramatically successful, there are many cases when a biological control agent does not control its targeted pest or when the introduced species itself becomes invasive, attacking native species along with (or instead of) the intended target species (Elkington et al. 2006). For example, a parasitic fly species (*Compsilura cocinnata*) introduced into North America to control invasive gypsy moths has been found to parasitize more than 200 native moth species, in many cases dramatically reducing population numbers. In another example, an herbivorous weevil (*Rhinocyllus conicus*) introduced into North America to control invasive Eurasian thistles (*Carduus* spp.) has been found to attack native North American thistles (*Cirsium* spp.), and it is threatening populations of several uncommon and rare species (Louda et al. 2003). In order to minimize the probability of such effects, species being considered as biological control agents are tested before release, to determine whether they will restrict their feeding to the species intended as their targets.

Many areas of the world are strongly affected by exotic species. The United States currently has more than 20 species of exotic mammals, 97 species of exotic birds, 138 species of exotic fish, 88 species of exotic mollusks, 5000 species of exotic plants, 53 species of exotic reptiles and amphibians, and 4500 species of exotic insects and other arthropods (Pimental et al. 2005). Exotic perennial plants completely dominate many North American wetlands: purple loosestrife (*Lythrum salicaria*) from Europe dominates marshes in eastern North America, while Japanese honeysuckle (*Lonicera japonica*) forms dense tangles in bottomlands of the southeastern United States. Introduced annual grasses now cover extensive areas of western North American rangelands and increase the probability of ground fires in the summer. Europe has over 3700 naturalized alien species; half of these are completely alien to Europe, and the other half are growing outside their ranges in Europe. When invasive species dominate a community, the diversity and abundance of native plant species and the insects that feed on them show a corresponding decline (Heleno et al. 2009). Evidence also indicates that invasive plants can even reduce the diversity of soil microbe species (Callaway et al. 2004). Further, invasive species are many of the most serious agricultural weeds, costing farmers tens of billions of dollars a year in lost crop yield and extra weed control and herbicide expenses (**Box 10.2**).

Insects introduced both deliberately, such as European honeybees (*Apis mellifera*) and the biocontrol weevil (*Rhinocyllus conicus*), and accidentally, such as fire ants (*Solenopsis invicta*) and gypsy moths (*Lymantria dispar*), can build up huge populations (**Figure 10.7**). The effects of such invasive insects on the native insect fauna can be devastating. At some localities in the southern United States, the diversity of insect species declined by 40% following the invasion of exotic fire ants, and there was a similarly large decline in native birds (**Figure 10.8**). Introduced European earthworm species are currently outcompeting native species in soil communities across North America, with potentially enormous consequences to the rich underground biological communities and to the recycling of nutrients from the leaf litter to plants (Nuzzo et al. 2009). In areas of human settlement, domestic cats may be one of the most serious predators of birds and small mammals: A placid house cat may be a fearsome hunter when outdoors. Feral cats that must hunt for their own meals are especially damaging because of their ability to move far from human settlements.

Invasive Species on Islands

The isolation of island habitats encourages the evolution of a unique assemblage of endemic species (see Chapter 7), but it also leaves these species particularly vulnerable to depredations by invading species. Only a limited number of organisms are capable of crossing large expanses of water without human assistance. Thus, undisturbed island communities generally include few, if any, large mammalian grazers and predators, and organisms representing the highest trophic levels, such as mammalian carnivores, may be absent altogether. Because they evolved in the ab-

(A) Gypsy moth, *Lymantria dispar*

(B) Red imported fire ant, *Solenopsis invicta*

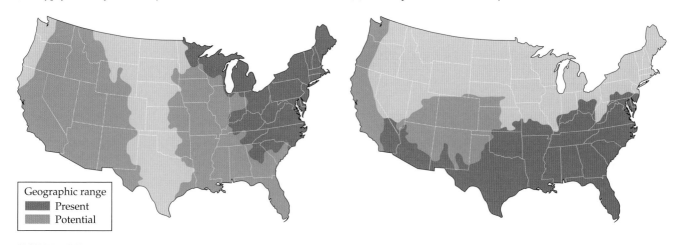

Geographic range
Present
Potential

FIGURE 10.7 Present and potential geographic ranges for two important invasive species in the United States. (A) Gypsy moths are predicted to spread widely across forest areas in the United States, damaging trees and reducing ecosystem services. (B) Fire ants will expand into the southwest and west coast, harming wildlife and creating a public health hazard for people. (After Crowl et al. 2008).

sence of selective pressures from mammalian grazers and predators, many endemic island plants and animals have evolutionarily lost or never developed defenses against these enemies and often lack a fear of them. Many island plants do not produce the bad-tasting, tough vegetative tissue that discourages herbivores, nor do they have the ability to resprout rapidly following damage. Some birds have lost the power of flight and simply build their nests on the ground.

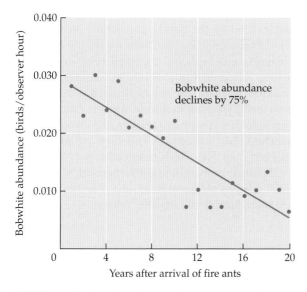

FIGURE 10.8 The abundance of northern bobwhites (*Colinas virginianus*) in Texas has been declining over a 20-year period following the arrival of the exotic red fire ant (*Solenopsis invicta*). The fire ants may directly attack and disturb bobwhites, particularly at the nestling stage, and may compete for food items, such as insects. (After Allen et al. 1995; bobwhite photograph courtesy of Steve Maslowski/U.S. Fish and Wildlife Service; fire ant photograph courtesy of Richard Nowitz/USDA ARS.)

BOX 10.2 *GMOs and Conservation Biology*

■ A special topic of concern for conservation biologists is the increasing use of genetically modified organisms (GMOs) in agriculture, forestry, aquaculture, the production of medicines, and toxic waste cleanups (Snow et al. 2005). In such organisms, genes from a source species have been added into the GMO using the techniques of recombinant DNA technology. In some cases, the transfer even occurs across kingdoms, as when a bacterial gene toxic to insects is transferred into a crop, such as corn. Already, enormous areas—especially in the United States, Argentina, China, and Canada—have been planted with GMOs, the main crops being soybeans, corn (maize), cotton, and oilseed rape (canola). GMO animals are still under development, with salmon and pigs showing commercial potential. There is a concern among some people, especially in Europe, that GMOs will hybridize with related species, leading to new, aggressive weeds and virulent diseases (Kuparinen et al. 2007). Also, the use of GMOs could potentially harm noncrop species, such as insects, birds, and soil organisms that live in or near agricultural fields. Further, some people want assurances that eating food from GMO crops will not harm their health and, especially, not cause unusual allergic reactions. The fact that many species being investigated for genetic engineering, including viruses, bacteria, insects, fungi, and shellfish, have not previously been used in breeding programs has many people worried, and it has resulted in governments' implementing special controls on this type of research and its commercial applications. It is also clear that GMO crop species have the potential to increase crop production and produce new and cheaper medicines;

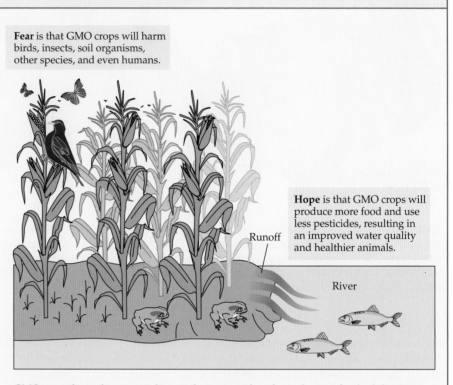

Fear is that GMO crops will harm birds, insects, soil organisms, other species, and even humans.

Hope is that GMO crops will produce more food and use less pesticides, resulting in an improved water quality and healthier animals.

Runoff

River

GMO crops have the potential to produce more abundant, cheaper food while using less pesticides. However, there is a concern that these crops will hybridize with wild species to create new weeds and diseases, that the crops will harm wild animals that eat them, and that eating food from GMO crops might harm people.

such benefits are clearly potentially important in providing abundant food for the human population, increasing efficiency of drug production, and reducing the use of pesticides on agricultural fields and the runoff associated with such use (but "Roundup Ready" herbicide-resistant genetically modified soybeans are actually treated with more, rather than less, glyphosate herbicide, which is sold as the weed killer Roundup®) (www.sourcewatch.org). In sum, the actual benefits of GMOs need to be examined and weighed against the potential risks. The best approach involves proceeding cautiously, investigating GMOs thoroughly before commercial releases are authorized, and monitoring environmental and health impacts after release.

Thriving endemic species on islands often succumb rapidly when the selective pressures that exotic invasive species represent are introduced. Animals introduced to islands often prey efficiently upon endemic animal species and have grazed some native plant species to extinction (Clavero et al. 2009). Introduced plant species with tough, unpalatable foliage are better able to coexist with the introduced grazers than are the more palatable native plants, so the exotics often begin to dominate the landscape as the native vegetation dwindles. Moreover, island species often have no natural immunities to mainland diseases. When exotic species (e.g., chickens, domestic ducks) arrive, they frequently carry pathogens or parasites that, though relatively harmless to the carriers, devastate the native populations (e.g., wild birds).

The introduction of just one exotic species to an island may cause the local extinction of numerous native species. Three examples illustrate the effects of introduced species on the biota of islands:

- *Plants of Santa Catalina Island.* Forty-eight native plant species have been eliminated from Santa Catalina Island off the coast of California, primarily because of grazing by introduced goats, pigs, and deer. One-third of the plant species currently found on the island are exotics. Almost complete removal of goats and pigs from part of the island has led to the reappearance of many rare wildflowers and the regrowth of woodlands.

- *Birds of the Pacific islands.* The brown tree snake (*Boiga irregularis*; **Figure 10.9**) has been introduced onto a number of Pacific islands where it is devastating endemic bird, bat, and reptile populations. The snake eats eggs, nestlings, and adult birds. On Guam alone, the brown tree snake has driven 10 of 13 forest bird species extinct (Perry and Vice 2009). Visitors have remarked on the absence of birdsong: "between the silence and the cobwebs, the rain forests of Guam have taken on the aura of a tomb" (Jaffe 1994). Perhaps in an attempt to locate new prey, brown tree snakes have even attacked sleeping people. The government spends $2 million per year on attempts to control the brown tree snake population, so far without success.

> Many island species have been driven to extinction by invasive species. Freshwater and marine ecosystems may also be altered by invasive species.

- *Society Island snails.* The deliberate introduction of a predatory snail onto the Society Islands as a biological control agent has resulted in the extinction of over 50 native snail species (www.zsl.org).

FIGURE 10.9 The brown tree snake (*Boiga irregularis*) has been introduced onto many Pacific islands, where it devastates populations of endemic birds. This adult snake has just swallowed a bird. (Photograph by Julie Savidge.)

Invasive Species in Aquatic Habitats

Freshwater communities are somewhat similar to oceanic islands in that they are isolated habitats surrounded by vast stretches of inhospitable and uninhabitable terrain. Exotic species can have severe effects on vulnerable lake communities and isolated stream systems. There has been a long history of introducing exotic commercial and sport fish species into lakes, such as the introduction of the Nile perch into Lake Victoria in East Africa, which was followed by the subsequent extinction of numerous endemic cichlid fish species. Often the introduced exotic fish are larger and more aggressive than the native fish fauna, and they may eventually drive the local fish to extinction. The invasion of sea lampreys into the Great Lakes of North America severely damaged the commercial and sport fisheries, particularly lake trout; the United States and Canada spend $13 million each year to control the lampreys. In Madagascar, surveys of freshwater habitats were able to locate only 5 of the 28 known native freshwater fish of the island, with introduced fish dominating all of the freshwater habitats. But once these invasive species are removed from aquatic habitats, the native species are sometimes able to recover (Vredenburg 2004).

Whereas invasions in freshwater environments are often more readily noticed, invasions also occur in marine and estuarine ecosystems. A recent survey found that there are 329 invasive marine species, with 84% of marine areas worldwide affected by at least one species (Molnar et al. 2008). The most impacted regions are northern Europe, especially the area around Britain; the Mediterranean; the U.S. west coast; and Hawaii. Shipping is the major cause of species introductions, especially the transport of ballast water, followed by aquaculture. The most common invasive species are crustaceans, followed by mollusks, algae, fish, worms, and plants. In the United States, every estuary that has been carefully surveyed has been found to contain between 70 and 235 exotic species; the actual numbers may be much higher because many of the species were probably not recognized as exotic or were absent from the specific locations surveyed (Carlton 2001).

The case of the comb jelly (*Mnemiopsis leidyi*) demonstrates the damage that can be caused by invasive species in the marine environment (Lehtiniemi et al. 2007). This species from North American coastal waters was first spotted in the Black Sea in eastern Europe in 1982, where it had presumably been discharged in ship ballast water. The Black Sea has no predators or effective competitors of this fish-eating comb jelly. Only 7 years later, in 1989, this species constituted 95% of the biomass of the Black Sea. The voracious appetite of this jellyfish for fish larvae and for the zooplankton on which fish feed, along with overfishing, contributed to the collapse of a $250 million fishing industry and disruption of the entire ecosystem (Boersma et al. 2007). However, in 1997, a second exotic comb jellyfish appeared and began feeding on *Mnemiopsis* populations, leading to signs of recovery for the fish populations.

One-third of the worst invasive species in aquatic environments are aquarium and ornamental species that are traded worldwide to the tune of $25 billion per year (Keller and Lodge 2007); the harmful impact of these species needs to be considered as part of the often-ignored cost of this trade. One such species is *Caulerpa taxifolia*, a highly invasive green alga used as a decorative plant in marine aquariums. This species is spreading in the northwestern Mediterranean, outcompeting native species of algae and reducing fish abundance. *Caulerpa* was discovered at many sites in California in 2000, and apparently an aggressive eradication program involving the release of bleach has successfully eliminated this invader there. A ban on the most harmful aquarium species and the creation of a "white list" of noninvasive alternative species could reduce the harm done by invasive aquatic species.

One of the most alarming recent invasions in North America was the arrival in the mid-1980s of the zebra mussel (*Dreissena polymorpha*) in the Great Lakes (Strayer 2009). This small, striped native of the Caspian Sea apparently was a stowaway

(A)

FIGURE 10.10 The zebra mussel (*Dreissena polymorpha*), a native of the Caspian Sea, was accidentally introduced into Lake Erie in 1988. (A) This current meter was retrieved from Lake Michigan after a crust of thousands of zebra mussels made it inoperable. Such encroachment is typical of the tiny mollusks, which also encrust and destroy native mussel species and other organisms. (B) The map shows distribution of zebra mussel and quagga mussel infestations throughout North America over the past 20 years and an estimation of the relative risk that these mussels will spread to additional streams and rivers. Each star indicates the location where a boat on a trailer was observed with live mussels on its hull. (A, photograph by M. McCormick, courtesy of NOAA/Great Lakes Environmental Research Laboratory; B based on data from Whittier et al. 2008 and the U.S. Geological Survey.)

(B)

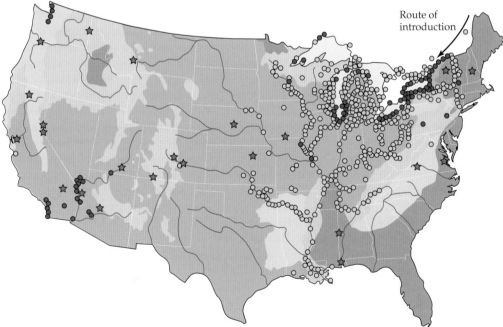

in the ballast tanks of a European cargo ship. Within 2 years, zebra mussels had reached almost unbelievable densities of 700,000 individuals per square meter in parts of Lake Erie, encrusting every hard surface and choking out native mussel species in the process (**Figure 10.10**). The zebra mussel has a prodigious capacity to reproduce: A single female can produce a million eggs per year, and the larval stage can disperse long distances in water currents. Zebra mussels and the related quagga mussel that arrived in 1989 are now spreading south via larval dispersal throughout the entire Mississippi River drainage, and they are spreading west across the Rocky Mountains, apparently by hitchhiking on the hulls of trailered recreational boats. As they continue to spread throughout the waters of the United States, these exotic species are causing enormous economic damage to fisheries, dams, power plants, water treatment facilities, and boats, estimated to be $1 billion per year, as well as devastating the aquatic communities they encounter (Pimentel et al. 2005). Merely keeping water intake pipes clear of zebra and quagga mussels represents a huge new maintenance cost.

The Ability of Species to Become Invasive

The great majority of introduced species do not survive outside of their native ranges, and of those that do survive in their new locations, only a small fraction (perhaps less than 1%) are capable of increasing and spreading there. Why are certain exotic species able to invade and dominate new habitats and displace native species so easily? One reason is the absence in the new habitat of their specialized natural predators and parasites that would control their population growth (Davis 2009). For example, in Australia, introduced rabbits spread uncontrollably, grazing native plants to the point of extinction, because there were no effective checks on their numbers. Australian control efforts have focused in part on introducing specific diseases that helped control rabbit populations elsewhere. In Hawaii, introduced Puerto Rican coqui frogs (*Eleutherodactylus coqui*) are reaching densities 100 times greater than in their native habitat, due in part to an absence of their predators, and in the process are decimating native insect populations and keeping people awake at night with their loud calls (Sin and Radford 2007).

Exotic species also may be better suited to taking advantage of disturbed conditions than native species (Leprieur et al. 2008). Human activity causes disturbances that may create unusual environmental conditions, such as higher mineral nutrient levels, increased incidence of fire, or enhanced light availability, to which exotic species sometimes are better adapted than are native species. In fact, the highest concentrations of invasive species are often found in the habitats that have been most altered by human activity. For example, in western North America, increased grazing (by cattle) and increased frequency of fire associated with humans provided the opportunity for the establishment of exotic annual grasses in areas formerly dominated by native perennial grasses. In North America, human-created ponds and lakes have a far greater probability of being occupied by certain invasive aquatic species than do natural water bodies, and these artifical water bodies enhance the spread of invasive species to nearby natural water bodies (Johnson et al. 2008). When habitats are altered by global climate change, they will become even more vulnerable to invasion (Hellman et al. 2008; Ibáñez et al. 2009; Walther et al. 2009). In one of the key generalizations of this field, we can say that of the enormous number of introduced species, the species most likely to become invasive and exert strong impacts in a new location are those species that have already been shown to do so someplace else (Ricciardi 2003).

Invasive species is generally defined as a species that has proliferated outside its native range, but some native species dramatically flourish within their home ranges because they are suited to the ways in which humans have altered the environment and are therefore almost as much a source of concern as exotic invasive species. Within North America, fragmentation of forests, suburban development, and easy access to garbage have allowed the numbers of coyotes, red foxes, and certain gull species to increase. Native jellyfish have become far more abundant in the Gulf of Mexico because they use oil rigs and artificial reefs for spawning and feed on plankton blooms stimulated by nitrogen pollution. As these aggressive species increase, they do so at the expense of other local native species, such as the juvenile stages of commercially harvested fish. These unnaturally abundant native species represent a further challenge to the management of vulnerable native species and protected areas.

A special class of invasive species is made up of those introduced exotic species that have close relatives in the native biota. When invasive species hybridize with the native species and varieties, unique genotypes may be eliminated from local populations and taxonomic boundaries may become obscured—a process called genetic swamping (Fox 2008). This appears to be the fate of native trout species when confronted by commercial species. In the American Southwest, the Apache trout (*Oncorhynchus apache*) has had its range reduced by habitat destruction and competition with introduced species. The species has also hybridized extensively with rainbow trout (*O. mykiss*), an introduced sport fish. Studies of the Pecos pupfish (*Cyprinodon pecosensis*), a rare endemic species of western Texas and New Mexico, show evidence of extensive hybridization with the introduced sheepshead minnow (*C. variegatus*), with hybrid individuals being more vigorous than genetically pure Pecos pupfish (Rosenfield et al. 2004).

> Where human development changes the environment, invasive species and undesirable native species may thrive. Hybridization between rare native species and invasive species may blur species boundaries.

Invasive species are considered to be the most serious threat facing the biota of the U.S. national park system. While the effects of habitat degradation, fragmentation, and pollution potentially can be corrected and reversed in a matter of years or decades as long as the original species are present, well-established exotic species may be impossible to remove from communities. They may have built up such large numbers and become so widely dispersed and so thoroughly integrated into the community that eliminating them may be extraordinarily difficult and expensive (King et al. 2009; Rinella et al. 2009). Also, the general public may resist efforts to control the numbers of introduced mammals that overgraze native plant communities. Animal rights groups, in particular, have objected to attempts to reduce large populations of deer, wild horses, mountain sheep, and wild boar. Yet sometimes these populations must be reduced if rare native species are to be saved from extinction. When invasive plant species and nonnative grazers are removed as part of a management plan, the native species may recover on their own. Recovery sometimes requires a comprehensive restoration program (see Chapters 13 and 19; **Figure 10.11**).

FIGURE 10.11 Removal of exotic species can lead to the recovery of native species: in this case, dune vegetation at Lanphere Dunes Unit of the Humboldt Bay National Wildlife Refuge, California, had become dominated by the exotic European beach grass (*Ammophila arenaria*) (A). Following the removal of the beach grass, native species recovered (B). (Photographs courtesy of Andrea Pickart.)

(A)

(B)

Control of Invasive Species

The threats posed by invasive species are so severe that reducing the rate of their introduction needs to become a greater priority for conservation efforts (**Figure 10.12**) (Chornesky et al. 2005; Keller et al. 2008). Governments must pass and enforce laws and customs restrictions prohibiting the transport and introduction of exotic species. In some cases this may require restrictions and inspections related to the movement of soil, wood, plants, animals, and other items across international borders and even through checkpoints within countries. Better ecological information is required prior to deliberate introductions of species thought to be beneficial or potentially desirable (Gordon and Gantz 2008). Currently, vast sums are spent controlling widespread outbreaks of exotics, but inexpensive, prompt control and eradication efforts at the time of first sighting can stop a species from getting established in the first place. Training citizens and protected-areas staff to monitor vulnerable habitats for the appearance of known invasive species, and promptly implementing intensive control efforts, can be an effective way to stop the establishment and early spread of a new exotic species. This may require a cooperative effort on the part of multiple levels of government and private landowners.

A thoroughly researched, ecologically grounded program of biological control, using species from the exotic's original range, may be necessary in the overall strategy in severe cases (Louda et al. 2005). Such programs require careful testing to determine the host specificity and likely ecological interactions of the biological control species. They also require careful monitoring after introduction of the control

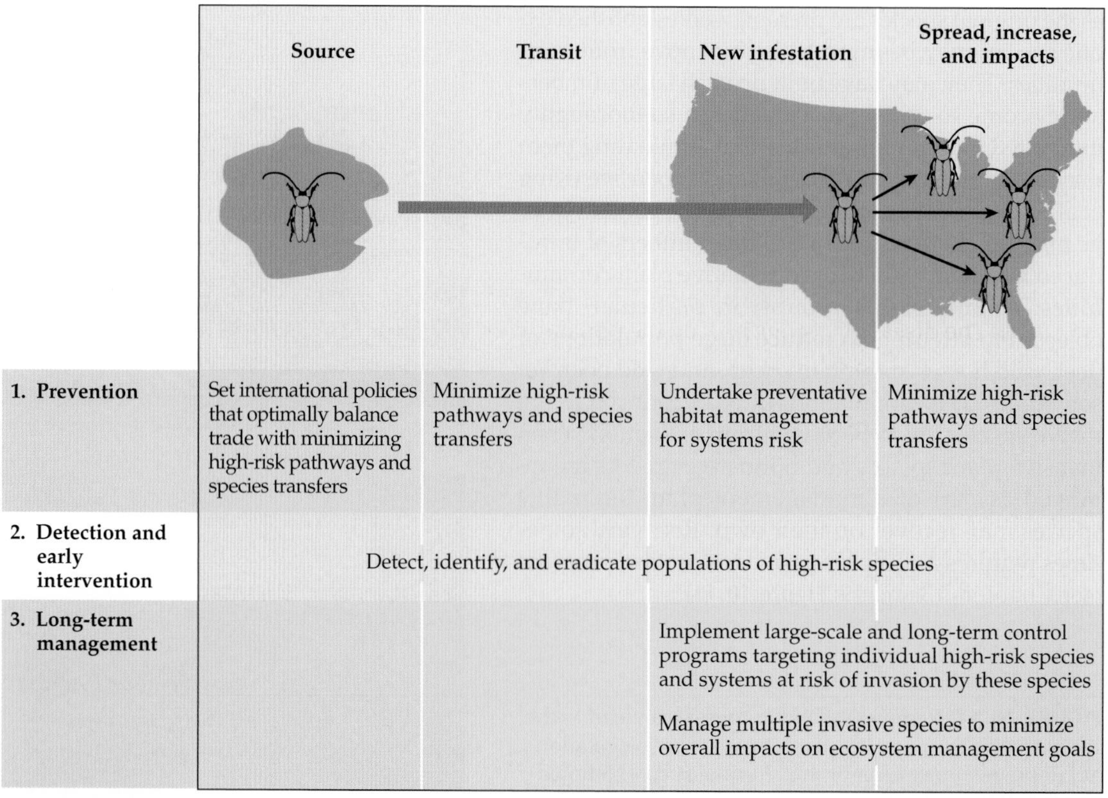

	Source	Transit	New infestation	Spread, increase, and impacts
1. Prevention	Set international policies that optimally balance trade with minimizing high-risk pathways and species transfers	Minimize high-risk pathways and species transfers	Undertake preventative habitat management for systems risk	Minimize high-risk pathways and species transfers
2. Detection and early intervention	Detect, identify, and eradicate populations of high-risk species			
3. Long-term management			Implement large-scale and long-term control programs targeting individual high-risk species and systems at risk of invasion by these species Manage multiple invasive species to minimize overall impacts on ecosystem management goals	

FIGURE 10.12 A strategy for reducing the impact of harmful invasive species involves a combination of prevention, detection, and early intervention as well as long-term management. This strategy is illustrated by the example of the Asian long-horned beetle (*Anoplophora glabripennis*). This species arrived in North America in wooden crates and other packing material from its native Asia. The beetle infects and kills a wide range of trees, especially maples. The only effective treatment is to cut down infected trees and destroy the wood. (After Chornesky et al. 2005.)

species, to determine its effectiveness in controlling the invasive species, as well as any nontarget effects on native species and communities. In some cases, land use practices will need to be changed in ways that favor the restoration of native species. In other cases, invasive species may be controlled through physical removal, trapping, and poisoning (Howald et al. 2007; King et al. 2009). When introduced rats were removed from the islands of New Zealand, populations of the tuatara (*Sphenodon punctatus*) showed a dramatic improvement (Towns et al. 2007). An extensive public education program is often necessary so that people are aware of why invasive species need to be removed or killed, especially when they are mammals such as goats, horses, and rabbits.

> Countries need to prevent the introduction of new invasive species, to monitor the arrival and spread of invasives, and to eradicate new populations of invasives.

Even though the impacts of invasive species are generally considered negative, they may provide some benefits as well. Invasive species can sometimes stabilize eroding lands, provide nectar for native insects such as bees, and supply nesting sites for birds and mammals. The trade-offs in such situations need to be evaluated to determine whether the potential benefits will outweigh the overall costs.

Disease

Another major threat to species and biological communities is the increased transmission of disease resulting from human activities and interaction with humans. Human-caused habitat destruction may increase disease-carrying vectors, and interaction with humans may cause populations of wild animals to acquire diseases from nearby domestic animals and people (Jones et al. 2008). Infections by disease organisms are common in both wild and captive populations and can reduce the size and density of vulnerable populations. Disease organisms can also have a major impact on the structure of an entire biological community if they eliminate keystone species or dominant species (Breed et al. 2009). Infections may come from tiny microparasites, such as viruses, bacteria, fungi, and protozoa; or from larger macroparasites, such as helminth worms and parasitic arthropods. While living inside or on the host, these parasites absorb nutrients and damage host tissue, weakening the host and lowering its chances of surviving and reproducing.

White nose syndrome is one such disease that is currently killing hundreds of thousands of bats across the eastern United States. In some caves, 90% of the bats have died. The disease is recognized by the powdery white fuzz or fungus on an infected bat's snout. Bats are apparently killed when the fungus causes skin irritation and the bat wakes up in midwinter instead of in spring, depleting its energy reserves and subsequently causing the bat to starve to death. Discovered in one cave in New York in 2006, this fungal disease has spread rapidly to populations and caves in other states when bats have migrated, and it is a threat to the endangered Indiana bat (*Myotis soldalis*). Scientists think that cave explorers or bat researchers may have accidentally introduced the fungus to the United States as a contaminant on their clothes, boots, or equipment following a visit to a European bat cave. At this point, the only effective way to protect bats is to close bat caves to all human visitors except for scientists who sterilize their clothes and equipment before entering.

The basic principles of epidemiology have three obvious practical implications for limiting disease in captive breeding and management of rare species (Scott 1988):

1. A high rate of contact between host and parasite encourages the spread of disease.

2. Indirect effects of habitat destruction increase susceptibility to disease.

3. Species in conservation programs may contract diseases from related species, and even from humans.

We'll examine each of these implications in turn, recognizing that increased levels of disease can be caused by the interactions of multiple factors. First, a high rate of contact between the host (such as a mountain sheep) and the parasite (such as an intestinal worm) is one factor that encourages the spread of disease. In general, as host population density increases, the parasite load also increases, as expressed by the percentage of hosts infected and the number of parasites per host. In addition, a high density of the infective stages of a parasite in the environment of the host population can lead to increased incidence of disease. In natural situations, the level of infection is typically reduced when animals migrate away from their droppings, saliva, old skin, dead animals, and other infection sources. However, in unnaturally confined situations, such as habitat fragments, zoos, or even parks, the animals remain in contact with the potential sources of infection, and disease transmission increases. At higher densities, animals have abnormally frequent contact, and once one animal becomes infected, the parasite can rapidly spread throughout the entire population.

Second, indirect effects of habitat destruction can increase an organism's susceptibility to disease. When a host population is crowded into a smaller area because of habitat destruction, there will often be a deterioration in habitat quality and food availability, leading to high contact rates, lowered nutritional status, weaker animals, and less resistance to infection. Young, very old, and pregnant individuals may be particularly susceptible to disease in such a situation. Plant populations can be similarly affected by fragmentation and degradation. Changes in plant microenvironments caused by habitat destruction or fragmentation, stress caused by air pollution, and direct injury occurring during logging or other human activities directly lead to increased levels of disease in plant populations. Aquatic species, including marine mammals, sea turtles, fish, coral animals, shellfish, and sea grasses, also have exhibited increased levels of disease due to water pollution, injury, and unusual environmental perturbations (Harvell et al. 2004). A recent insight is that biodiversity regulates disease—including diseases that can be transmitted to humans—by diluting the number of suitable host species or by constraining the size of host populations through predation and competition (Ostfeld 2009). For example, the increased incidence of Lyme disease and other tick-born pathogens has been linked to the local abundance of certain host rodent species and the overall loss of local species diversity (**Figure 10.13**).

Third, in many conservation areas and zoos, species come into contact with other species that they would rarely or never encounter in the wild, including humans,

> Increased incidence of infectious disease threatens wild and domestic species as well as humans. Transfer of disease between different species is the subject of special concern.

so infections can spread from one species to another. A species that is common and fairly resistant to a parasite can act as a reservoir for the disease, which can then infect a population of a highly susceptible species on contact. For example, apparently healthy African elephants can transmit a fatal herpes virus to related Asian elephants when they are kept together in zoos. Diseases can spread very rapidly between captive species kept in crowded conditions. An outbreak of a herpes virus spread across the captive colony at the International Crane Federation, killing cranes belonging to several rare species. The outbreak was apparently related to a high density of birds in the colony (Docherty and Romaine 1983).

Infectious disease also can spread from domestic animals into wild populations (**Figure 10.14**) (Tomley and Shirley 2009). A classic example from the late nineteenth century is that of rinderpest virus, which spread from domestic cattle to wild antelope, wildebeest, and other ungulates in eastern and southern Africa, killing off 75% of the animals. At Tanzania's Serengeti National Park, at least 25% of the lions were killed by canine distemper, a viral disease apparently contracted from one or more of the 30,000 domestic dogs living near the park (Kissui and Packer 2004). For endangered species, such outbreaks can be the final blow: The last population of

(A)

(B)

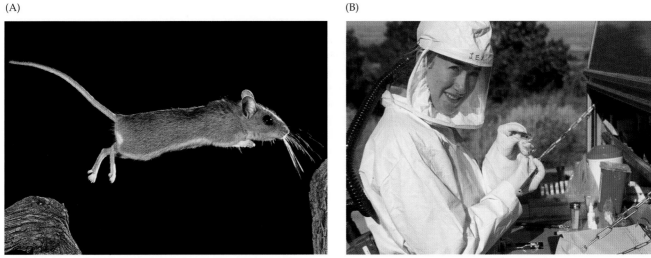

FIGURE 10.13 (A) A white-footed mouse, one of the main hosts for Lyme disease, increases in abundance in habitat fragments created by suburban development. (B) Field biologists are sampling mice for the presence of infectious diseases, such as plague. (C) A black-legged tick, which can transfer Lyme disease to human, after acquiring the disease from an infected animal. (A, photograph © Rolf Nussbaumer/Naturepl.com; B, photograph from Crowl et al. 2008; C, photograph courtesy of Michael L. Levin/CDC.)

(C)

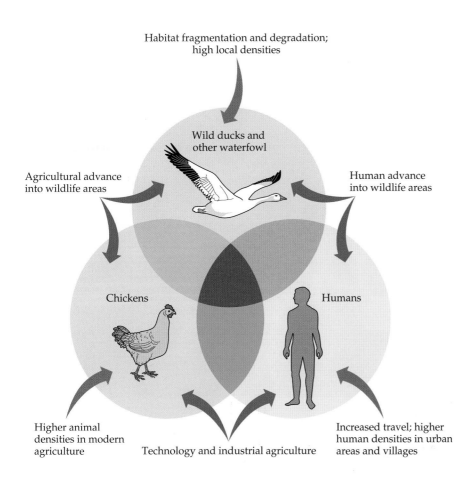

FIGURE 10.14 Infectious diseases—such as rabies, Lyme disease, influenza, bird flu, hantavirus, and canine distemper—spread among wildlife populations, domestic animals, and humans as a result of increasing population densities and the advance of agriculture and human settlements into wildlife areas. The figure illustrates the infection and transmission routes of bird flu—wild waterfowl, chickens, and humans are all susceptible to the virus. The shaded areas of overlap indicate that diseases can be shared among the three groups. Green arrows indicate factors contributing to higher rates of infection; blue arrows indicate factors contributing to the spread of disease among the three groups. (After Daszak et al. 2000.)

black-footed ferrets (*Mustela nigrepes*) known to occur in the wild was destroyed by the canine distemper virus in 1987. One of the main challenges of managing the captive breeding program for black-footed ferrets has been protecting the captives from canine distemper, human viruses, and other diseases; this is being done through rigorous quarantine measures and subdivision of the captive colony into geographically separate groups (see Figure 13.1). Infected humans have also been responsible for directly transmitting tuberculosis, measles, and influenza to captive orangutans, chimpanzees, colobus monkeys, ferrets, and other animals (Szentiks et al. 2009). Once infected with exotic diseases acquired from people or other species, such captive animals cannot be returned to the wild without threatening the entire wild population. Captive Arabian oryx infected with the bluetongue virus of domestic livestock and orangutans with human tuberculosis could not be reintroduced into the wild as planned, for fear of infecting free-ranging animals.

Diseases that spread to new regions of the world can decimate common species, as mentioned previously with white nose syndrome in bats. The North American chestnut tree (*Castanea dentata*), once a prominent component of the hardwood forests throughout the eastern United States, has been virtually obliterated by an ascomycete fungus carried by Chinese chestnut trees imported to New York City. Fungal diseases are also eliminating elm trees (*Ulmus americana*) and flowering dogwoods (*Cornus florida*) from these forests (**Figure 10.15**). Reports of widespread oak and pine tree deaths from fungal disease in the western United States are cause for serious concern because of their dominant role in many ecosystems (McKinney et al. 2007). Throughout Europe, native crayfish populations have been decimated by a funguslike pathogen, *Aphanomyces astaci*, introduced with intentionally stocked North American crayfish in the mid-nineteenth century (Edgerton et al. 2004). Introduced diseases have particularly powerful adverse effects on endemic island

FIGURE 10.15 Populations of flowering dogwood (*Cornus florida*) are declining in eastern North American forests because of anthracnose disease, which is caused by the introduced fungus *Discula destructiva*. (Photograph by Jonathan P. Evans.)

species (see Box 7.1) and frog species (see Box 8.1). An important factor in the decline and extinction of many endemic Hawaiian birds has been the introduction of the mosquito *Culex quinquefasciatus* and the malaria protozoan *Plasmodium relictum capistranoae*.

A number of actions can be taken to reduce the spread of disease:

1. Plants, animals, soils, and other biological materials need to be inspected, tested, and, if needed, quarantined and appropriately treated before they are allowed to cross borders. These procedures should include domestic and wild species and any equipment and clothing used by researchers.

2. Care must be taken to reduce the interaction of endangered species with humans, domesticated species, and closely related species. Such interactions can occur frequently in zoos, aquariums, and botanical gardens or in small protected areas. For example, people working with endangered mammals may need to wear face masks and sterile clothing (see Figures 10.13 and 13.1).

3. Endangered species need to be monitored to detect outbreaks of disease. If necessary, diseased individuals may have to be treated or removed from the population (Sandmeier et al. 2009).

4. Appropriate living conditions and population densities in both wild and captive situations will lower the susceptibility to disease vectors and reduce the rate of transmission.

Within populations, individuals vary in their susceptibility to particular diseases. Conservation biologists may face this dilemma in practice: Either protect all individuals of a rare species from a potential disease, in order to maintain population numbers and genetic variation, or let natural selection take its course and allow the individuals that are genetically most susceptible to the disease to die off. If the disease kills only a few individuals and the population is still large, the population may be more fit in the long term for having weathered the disease. However, if the disease kills large numbers of individuals, then the entire population might die out. It is often difficult to predict how virulent a disease will be in an isolated population of a rare species, especially if the environmental conditions and population have been altered by human activity.

> Steps must be taken to prevent the spread of disease in captive animals, and to ensure that new diseases are not accidentally introduced into wild populations.

Implications of Invasive Species and Diseases for Human Health

The presence of invasive species and disease-causing organisms also has serious, direct implications for humans. Invading killer bees (*Apis mellifera scutellata*) and fire ants (*Solenopsis invicta*) that are spreading in the New World not only displace native insect species from their ecological niches but also can cause serious injuries to humans. Also, as people move into wild areas through suburban and exurban development and associated habitat fragmentation, there is greater potential for disease movement among people, domestic animals, and wild species (Rwego et al. 2008; Tomley and Shirley 2009). The potential for the spread of serious pests and disease-causing organisms also increases dramatically with the increasing movement of people, pets, wildlife, and materials from one part of the world to another. The dramatic upsurge in Lyme disease and Rocky Mountain spotted fever, spread by infected ticks, and West Nile virus, spread by mosquitoes, has caused near panic in some regions of the United States. Hantavirus, Ebola virus, HIV/AIDS, bubonic plague, mad cow disease, and bird flu are additional diseases that can move between wild species and people. Bird flu, for example, moves from wild birds to domestic birds such as chickens, with the potential to spread to people on a large scale. Bird flu might also eliminate the remaining populations of susceptible endangered animals.

Such examples are likely to become more common as a result of human-induced changes to the environment. Recent warm years linked to global climate change have allowed many disease-carrying insects and associated diseases, such as malaria and dengue fever, to expand their ranges to higher elevations in tropical countries and farther from the equator. If world temperatures increase as predicted by global climate change models (see Chapter 9), the stage will be set for major range expansions of diseases now confined primarily to tropical climates (Lafferty 2009; Ostfeld 2009; Pongsiri et al. 2009). For example, bluetongue disease, a tropical virus that affects cattle, has been spreading through Europe over the past decade. Warmer and more polluted aquatic environments and unusually heavy rains are already allowing waterborne diseases, such as cholera, to ravage previously unaffected human and animal populations, and this range expansion will probably continue.

There is serious potential for the environment of the developed world to become a more dangerous place, as exotic stinging and disease-causing species arrive and thrive. In addition, if bird-watchers, hunters, swimmers, and hikers become frightened by and disenchanted with the outdoor experience, strong support for conservation efforts may be lost. Conservation biologists have an obligation to help prevent the spread of potentially invasive and dangerous species that threaten both people and biological diversity. Conservation biologists also need to keep the public engaged in conservation-related activities, in part to counter media reports that exaggerate the dangers of the outdoors.

Conclusion

As we've seen in Chapters 7–10, a combination of factors acting simultaneously or sequentially can overwhelm a species. Consider, for example, the large freshwater mussel *Margaritifera auricularia*. This species was formerly known from western Europe to the Mediterranean, but now it occurs only in isolated, remnant populations in a few rivers in France, Spain, and Morocco (Araujo and Ramos 2000). Its attractive shell and pearls were used as ornaments by humans as far back as the Neolithic age. Overcollecting, the main reason for the decline of the mussel, led to its disappearance from rivers in central Europe in the fifteenth and sixteenth centuries; pollution, destruction of freshwater habitats, and overcollecting continue to reduce its range and numbers in recent times. The mussel is also affected by the loss of other species, since its larval stage needs to attach to the gill filaments of salmonid fish to complete its life cycle. The lack of small individuals in some of the remaining populations indicates that the species is now unable to reproduce under present conditions. To save this species, a comprehensive conservation plan must be implemented, including preventing overcollection, controlling water quality, maintaining fish stocks, and protecting the habitat.

Comprehensive conservation efforts must recognize that biodiversity faces multiple threats.

Threats to biological diversity come from a number of different sources, but their underlying cause is the same: the magnitude of destructive human activity. It is often easy to blame a group of poor, rural people or a certain industry for the destruction of biological diversity, but the real challenge is to demonstrate that it is in people's best interest to establish and manage protected areas and to value biodiversity wherever it is found. In addition, we need to understand the economic conditions and national and international linkages that promote such destruction and to find viable alternatives. These alternatives must include stabilizing the size of the human population, finding a livelihood for rural people in developing countries that does not damage the environment, providing incentives and penalties that will convince people and industries to value and maintain the environment, restricting international trade in products that are obtained in ways that damage the environment, and persuading people in developed countries to reduce their consumption of the world's resources and to pay fair prices for products that are produced in a sustainable, nondestructive manner.

Summary

1. Overexploitation threatens about one-third of the endangered vertebrates in the world, as well as other groups of species. Poverty, more efficient methods of harvesting, and the globalization of the economy combine to encourage exploitation of species to the point of extinction; overharvesting of birds, mammals, and fish for food are of particular concern. Many traditional societies have customs to prevent overharvesting of resources, but these customs are breaking down. Methods are being developed to allow the sustainable harvesting of natural resources.

2. Humans have deliberately and accidentally moved many thousands of plant and animal species to new regions of the world. Some of these species have become invasive, increasing at the expense of native species. Invasive species can sometimes completely dominate ecosystems and exclude native species. Island species are particularly vulnerable to invasive exotic species. Preventing the establishment of invasive species and removing them if they do establish themselves are important priorities.

3. Human activities may increase the incidence of disease in wild species. The levels of disease and parasites often increase when animals are crowded together and under stress in a nature reserve or a habitat fragment rather than being able to disperse over a wide area. Animals held in captivity in zoos are prone to higher levels of disease, which sometimes spreads between related species of animals. Diseased captive animals cannot be returned to the wild, to prevent the spread of disease to the wild population.

4. Species may be threatened by a combination of factors, all of which must be addressed in a comprehensive conservation plan.

For Discussion

1. Learn about one endangered species in detail. What is the full range of immediate threats to this species? How do these immediate threats connect to larger social, economic, political, and legal issues?

2. Control of an invasive species may involve searching for specialized natural enemies, parasites, or predators of that species within its original range and releasing such organisms in an attempt to control the invasive species at the new location. For example, an attempt is currently underway to control exotic purple loosestrife in North America by releasing several European beetle species that eat the plant in its home area. As another example, biologists are talking about introducing an exotic fungus into Hawaii to eliminate the invasive Puerto Rican coqui frog. What if these biological control agents begin to attack native species rather than their intended hosts? How might such a consequence be predicted and avoided? Consider the biological, economic, and ethical issues involved in a decision to institute a biological control program.

3. Why is it so difficult to regulate the fishing industry in many places and maintain a sustainable level of harvesting? Consider fishing, hunting, logging, and other harvesting activities in your region. Are these well managed? Try to calculate what the sustainable harvest levels of these resources would be and consider how such harvesting levels could best be monitored and enforced.

4. Develop a verbal or computer model of how disease spreads in a population. The rate of spread could be determined by the density of the host, the percentage of host individuals infected, the rate of transmission of the disease, and the effects of the disease on the host's survival and rate of reproduction. How will an increase in the density of the host—caused by crowding in zoos or nature reserves or by an inability to migrate due to habitat fragmentation—affect the percentage of individuals that are infected and the overall population size?

Suggested Readings

Bennett, E. L. and 13 others. 2007. Hunting for consensus: Reconciling bushmeat harvest, conservation, and development policy in West and Central Africa. *Conservation Biology* 21: 884–887. Conservation agencies must develop a consistent approach to the development of bushmeat policy.

Christy, B. 2010. Asia's wildlife trade. *National Geographic* 217(1): 78–107. Wildlife trade, both legal and illegal, is a multibillion-dollar business that threatens biodiversity.

Cox, T. M., R. L. Lewiston, R. Zydelis, L. B. Crowder, C. Safina, and J. Reed. 2007. Comparing effectiveness of experimental and implemented bycatch reduction measures: The ideal and the real. *Conservation Biology* 21: 1155–1164. Cooperation and monitoring are needed to translate experimental results into actual bycatch reductions.

Davis, M. A. 2009. *Invasion Biology*. Oxford University Press, Oxford, UK. This book addresses the reality and theory of invasion biology.

Dichmont, C. M., S. Pascoe, T. Kompas, A. E. Punt, and R. Deng. 2010. On implementing maximum economic yield in commercial fisheries. *Proceedings of the National Academy of Sciences USA* 107: 16–21. Why is it so hard to manage fisheries?

Gordon, D. R. and C. A. Gantz. 2008. Screening new plant introductions for potential invasiveness. *Conservation Letters* 1: 227–235. Tools such as the Australian Weed Risk Assessment system are useful to predict invasiveness of species.

Keller, R. P. and D. M. Lodge. 2007. Species invasions from commerce in live aquatic organisms: Problems and possible solutions. *BioScience* 57: 428–436. Human activities result in species invasions on a large scale.

King, C. M., R. M. McDonald, R. D. Martin, and T. Dennis. 2009. Why is eradication of invasive mustelids so difficult? *Biological Conservation* 142: 806–816. Case study of the control of an invasive predator.

Link, J. S. 2007. Underappreciated species in ecology: "Ugly fish" in the northwest Atlantic Ocean. *Ecological Applications* 17: 2037–2060. Intensive harvesting changes species abundances and ecological relationships.

Lotze, H. K. and B. Worm. 2009. Historical baselines for large marine mammals. *Trends in Ecology and Evolution* 24: 254–262. Large marine mammals have declined by 89% because of exploitation; certain groups such as whales and seals have started to recover because of conservation measures.

Loucks, C. and 8 others. 2009. Wildlife decline in Cambodia, 1953–2005: Exploring the legacy of armed conflict. *Conservation Letters* 2: 82–92. Armed conflict and the availability of guns have harmed wildlife populations.

Mathiessen, P. 2000. *Tigers in the Snow*. North Point Press, New York. Account of the heroic struggle to protect Asian tigers from multiple threats.

Mora, C. and 9 others. 2009. Management effectiveness of the world's marine fisheries. *PLoS Biology* 7: e1000131. The key to sustainability is sometimes incorporating accurate scientific information into policy.

Pongsiri, M. J. and 8 others. 2009. Biodiversity loss affects global disease ecology. *BioScience* 59: 945–954. The loss of biodiversity is sometimes linked to disease outbreaks.

Snow, A. A. and 6 others. 2005. Genetically engineered organisms and the environment: Current status and recommendations. *Ecological Applications* 15: 377–404. Balanced treatment of the controversy regarding genetically modified organisms.

Strayer, D. L. 2009. Twenty years of zebra mussels: Lessons from the mollusk that made headlines. *Frontiers in Ecology and the Environment* 7: 135–141. This invader continues to spread and have impact.

Walther, G. R. and 28 others. 2009. Alien species in a warmer world: Risks and opportunities. *Trends in Ecology and Evolution* 24: 686–693. Climate change influences biological invasions.

CONSERVATION AT THE POPULATION AND SPECIES LEVELS

Chapter 11

Problems of Small Populations

No population lasts forever. Changing climate, succession, disease, and a range of rare events ultimately lead every population to the same fate: extinction. The real questions to consider are whether a population goes extinct sooner rather than later, what factors cause the extinction, and whether other populations of the same species will continue elsewhere. Will a population of African lions last for more than 1000 years and go extinct only after a change in climate, or will the population go extinct after 10 years because of hunting by humans and introduced disease? Will individual lions from the original population start new populations in currently unoccupied habitat, or has all potential lion habitat disappeared because of new human settlements?

As we discussed in Chapter 7, the extinction of species as a result of human activities is now occurring more than 100 times faster than the natural rate of extinction—far more rapidly than new species can evolve. Because an endangered species may consist of just a few populations, or even a single population, *protecting populations is the key to preserving species*; it is often the few remaining populations of a rare species that are targeted for conservation efforts. In order to successfully maintain species under the restricted conditions imposed by human activities, conservation biologists must determine the stability of populations under different circumstances. Will a population of an endangered species persist or even increase in a nature reserve? Is the species in rapid decline, and does it require special attention to prevent it from going extinct?

Many national parks and wildlife sanctuaries have been created to protect "charismatic" megafauna such as lions, tigers, rhinos, bison, and bears, which are important national symbols and attractions for the tourist industry. However, designating the habitats in which these species live as protected areas may not be enough to stop their decline and extinction, even when they are legally protected. Sanctuaries generally are created after most populations of the threatened species have been severely reduced by habitat loss, degradation, and fragmentation or by overharvesting. Under such circumstances, a species tends to dwindle rapidly toward extinction. Also, individuals outside park boundaries remain unprotected and at risk. What, then, is the best strategy for protecting the few remaining populations of an endangered species? Are there special concerns for protecting small populations?

Essential Concepts for Small Populations

An ideal conservation plan for an endangered species would protect as many individuals as possible within the greatest possible area of high-quality, protected habitat (Wilhere 2008). In practical terms, the planners, land managers, politicians, and wildlife biologists often must attempt to achieve realistic goals, guided by general principles. For example, they need to know how much longleaf pine habitat a red-cockaded woodpecker population requires to persist. Is it necessary to protect habitat containing 50, 500, 5000, 50,000, or more individuals to ensure the survival of the species? Furthermore, planners must reconcile conflicting demands on finite resources—somehow a compromise must be found that allows the economic development required by society while at the same time providing reasonable protection for biological diversity. This problem is vividly demonstrated by the current debate in the United States over the need to protect caribou and other wildlife in the vast Arctic National Wildlife Refuge and the equally compelling need to utilize the considerable oil resources of the area.

Minimum Viable Population (MVP)

In a groundbreaking paper, Shaffer (1981) defined the number of individuals necessary to ensure the long-term survival of a species as the **minimum viable population**, or **MVP**: "A minimum viable population for any given species in any given habitat is the smallest isolated population having a 99% chance of remaining extant for 1000 years despite the foreseeable effects of demographic, environmental, and genetic stochasticity, and natural catastrophes." In other words, the MVP is the smallest population size that can be predicted to have a very high chance of persisting for the foreseeable future. Shaffer emphasized the tentative nature of this definition, saying that the survival probabilities could be set at 95%, 99%, or any other percentage and that the time frame might similarly be adjusted, for example, to 100 or 500 years. The key point is that the MVP size allows a quantitative estimate to be made of how large a population must be to ensure long-term survival.

> Plans for protecting a species must determine the number of individuals—the minimum viable population—necessary to maintain the species in both average and harsh years. Protected habitats of adequate size to maintain the MVP can then be established.

Shaffer (1981) compares MVP protection efforts to flood control. It is not sufficient to use average annual rainfall as a guideline when planning flood control systems and developing regulations for building on wetlands; instead, we must plan for extreme situations of high rainfall and severe flooding, which may occur only once every 50 years. In protecting natural systems, we understand that certain catastrophic events, such as hurricanes, earthquakes, forest fires, epidemics, and die-offs of food items, may occur at even greater intervals. To plan for the long-term protection of endangered species, we must provide for their survival, not only in average years, but also in exceptionally harsh years. An accurate estimate of the MVP size for a species often requires a detailed demographic study of the population and an analysis of its environment. This can be expensive and require months, or even years, of research. Analyses of over 200 species for which adequate data were available indicated that most MVP values for long time periods fall in the range of 3000 to 5000 individuals, with a median of 4000 (Traill et al. 2007). For species with extremely variable population sizes, such as certain invertebrates and annual plants, protecting a population of about 10,000 individuals might be an effective strategy.

Unfortunately, many species, particularly endangered species, have population sizes smaller than these recommended minimums. For instance, a survey was done of two rare burrowing frog species in the genus *Geocrina*, which occur in swamps in southwestern Australia (Driscoll 1999). In one species, 4 of its 6 populations had fewer than 250 individuals, and in the other species, 48 of 51 populations had fewer than 50 individuals. As another example, most of the nesting sites for sea turtles in the Caribbean have fewer than 100 nesting females each year, and many have fewer than 10 individuals (McClenachan et al. 2006).

Field studies confirm that small populations are most likely to decline and go extinct (Grouios and Manne 2009). One of the best-documented studies of MVP size tracked the persistence of 120 bighorn sheep (*Ovis canadensis*) populations (some of which have been followed for 70 years) in the deserts of the southwestern United States (Berger 1990, 1999). The striking observation is that 100% of the unmanaged populations with fewer than 50 individuals went extinct within 50 years, while virtually all of the populations with more than 100 individuals persisted within the same time period (**Figure 11.1**). No single cause was evident for most of the populations that died out; rather, a wide variety of factors appears responsible for the extinctions. For bighorn sheep, the minimum population size is at least 100 individuals. Unmanaged populations below 50 could not maintain their numbers, even in the short term. Additional research on bighorn sheep populations suggests that

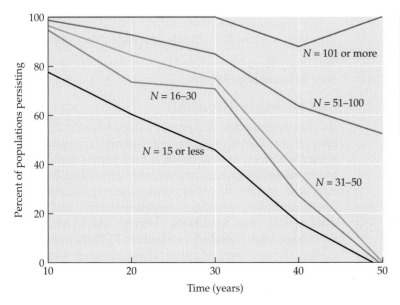

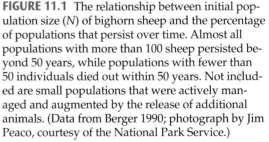

FIGURE 11.1 The relationship between initial population size (*N*) of bighorn sheep and the percentage of populations that persist over time. Almost all populations with more than 100 sheep persisted beyond 50 years, while populations with fewer than 50 individuals died out within 50 years. Not included are small populations that were actively managed and augmented by the release of additional animals. (Data from Berger 1990; photograph by Jim Peaco, courtesy of the National Park Service.)

populations have a greater chance of persisting when they occupy large habitats (which allow populations to increase in size) that are more than 23 km from domestic sheep, a source of disease (Singer et al. 2001). However, despite the factors hindering the survival of small populations, habitat management by government agencies and the release of additional animals have allowed some other small populations to persist that might otherwise have gone extinct.

> Small populations are more likely to go extinct than large populations.

Field evidence from long-term studies of birds on the Channel Islands off the California coast supports the fact that large populations are needed to ensure population persistence; only bird populations with more than 100 breeding pairs had a greater than 90% chance of surviving for 80 years (**Figure 11.2**). In spite of most evidence to the contrary, however, small populations sometimes prevail: many populations of birds apparently have survived for 80 years with 10 or fewer breeding pairs, and northern elephant seals have recovered to a population of about 150,000 individuals with breeding grounds on the Pacific coast of North America, after being reduced by hunting to only about 100 individuals in the late nineteenth century.

Once an MVP size has been established for a species, the **minimum dynamic area** (**MDA**)—the area of suitable habitat necessary for maintaining the minimum viable population—can be estimated by studying the home-range size of individuals and colonies of endangered species (Thiollay 1989). It has been estimated that reserves in Africa of 100 to 1000 km^2 are needed to maintain many small mammal populations (see Figure 16.2). To preserve populations of large carnivores, such as lions, reserves of 10,000 km^2 are needed.

Exceptions notwithstanding, large populations are needed to protect most species, and species with small populations are in real danger of going extinct. Small populations are subject to rapid decline in numbers and local extinction for three main reasons:

1. Loss of genetic variability and related problems of inbreeding depression and genetic drift

2. Demographic fluctuations due to random variations in birth and death rates

3. Environmental fluctuations due to variation in predation, competition, disease, and food supply and due to natural catastrophes that occur at irregular intervals, such as fires, floods, storms, or droughts

We'll now examine in detail each of these causes for decline in small populations.

Loss of Genetic Variability

As was described in Chapter 2, a population's ability to adapt to a changing environment depends on genetic variability, which occurs as a result of individuals' having different **alleles**—different forms of the same gene. Individuals with certain alleles or combinations of alleles may have just the characteristics needed to survive and reproduce under new conditions (Wayne and Morin 2004; Frankham 2005; Allendorf and Luikart 2007). Within a population, the frequency of a given allele can range from common to very rare. New alleles arise in a population either by random mutations or through the migration of individuals from other populations.

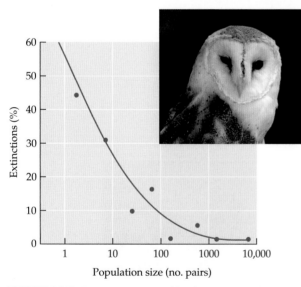

FIGURE 11.2 Extinction rates of bird species on the Channel Islands, with a barn owl (*Tyto alba*) as an example of one of the species. Each dot represents the extinction percentage of all the species in that population size class; extinction rate decreases as the size of the population increases. Populations with fewer than 10 breeding pairs had an overall 39% probability of extinction over 80 years, populations of between 10 and 100 pairs averaged about 10% probability of extinction, and populations of over 100 pairs had a very low probability of extinction. (After Jones and Diamond 1976; photograph courtesy of Thomas G. Barnes/U.S. Fish and Wildlife Service.)

In small populations, allele frequencies may change from one generation to the next simply because of chance—based on which individuals survive to sexual maturity, mate, and leave offspring. This random process of allele frequency change is known as **genetic drift**, and it is a separate process from changes in allele frequency caused by natural selection (Hedrick 2005). When an allele occurs at a low frequency in a small population, it has a significant probability of being lost in each generation. For example, if a rare allele occurs in 5% of all the genes present (the "gene pool") in a population of 1000 individuals, then 100 copies of the allele are present (1000 individuals × 2 copies per individual × 0.05 allele frequency), and the allele will probably remain in the population for many generations. However, in a population of 10 individuals, only 1 copy of the allele is present (10 individuals × 2 copies per individual × 0.05 allele frequency), and it is possible that the rare allele will be lost by chance from the population in the next generation.

Considering the general case of an isolated population in which there are two alleles of each gene in the gene pool, Wright (1931) proposed a formula to express the proportion of original heterozygosity remaining after each generation (H). The formula includes the **effective population size** (N_e)—the size of the population as estimated by the number of its breeding individuals:*

$$H = 1 - 1/[2 N_e]$$

According to this equation, a population of 50 breeding individuals would retain 99% of its original heterozygosity after one generation:

$$H = 1 - 1/100 = 1.00 - 0.01 = 0.99$$

The proportion of heterozygosity remaining after t generations (H_t) decreases over time:

$$H_t = H^t$$

For our population of 50 animals, then, the remaining heterozygosity would be 98% after two generations (0.99 × 0.99), 97% after three generations, and 90% after ten generations. A population of 10 individuals would retain 95% of its original heterozygosity after one generation, 90% after two generations, 86% after three generations, and 60% after ten generations (**Figure 11.3**).

This formula demonstrates that significant losses of genetic variability can occur in isolated small populations, particularly those on islands and fragmented landscapes. However, the amount of genetic variability within the population will increase over time through two means: regular mutation of genes and migration of even a few individuals from distant populations. Mutation rates found in nature are between 1 in 10,000 and 1 in 1 million per gene per generation; mutations therefore may make up for the random loss of alleles in large populations and, to a lesser extent, contribute to greater genetic diversity in small populations. However, mutations alone are not sufficient to counter genetic drift in populations of 100 individuals or less. Fortunately, even a low frequency of movement of individuals between populations minimizes the loss of genetic variability associated with small population size (**Figure 11.4**) (Corlatti et al. 2009; Bell et al. 2010). If even one or two immigrants arrive each generation in an isolated population of about 100 individuals, the impact of genetic drift will be greatly reduced. With four to ten migrants arriving per generation from nearby populations, the effects of genetic drift are

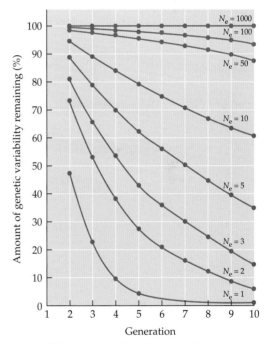

FIGURE 11.3 Genetic variability is lost randomly over time through genetic drift. This graph shows the average percentage of genetic variability remaining after ten generations in theoretical populations of various effective population sizes (N_e). After ten generations, there is a loss of genetic variability of approximately 40% with a population size of ten, 65% with a population size of five, and 95% with a population size of two. Blue lines indicate minimal loss of genetic variability in large populations; red lines indicate rapid loss of genetic variability in small populations. (After Meffe and Carroll 1997.)

---

*Factors affecting N_e, the effective population size, are discussed in detail beginning on page 257.

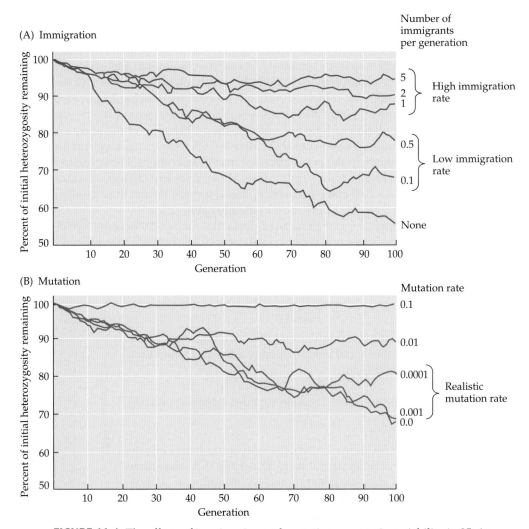

FIGURE 11.4 The effects of immigration and mutation on genetic variability in 25 simulated populations of size $N_e = 120$ individuals over 100 generations. (A) In an isolated population of 120 individuals, even low rates of immigration from a larger source population prevent the loss of heterozygosity from genetic drift. In the model, an immigration rate as low as 0.1 (1 immigrant per 10 generations) increases the level of heterozygosity, while genetic drift is negligible with an immigration rate of 1. (B) It is more difficult for mutation to counteract genetic drift. In the model, the mutation rate must be 1% (0.01) per gene per generation or greater to affect the level of heterozygosity. Because this mutation rate is far higher than what is observed in natural populations, mutation appears to play a minimal role in maintaining genetic variability in small populations. (After Lacy 1987.)

negligible. Gene flow from neighboring populations appears to be the major factor preventing the loss of genetic variability in small populations of Galápagos finches (Turner and Wilcove 2006; Grant and Grant 2008) and Scandinavian wolves (Ingvarsson 2001). Notably, genetic variation that increases fitness will tend to be retained longer in a population, even when there is genetic drift (McKay and Latta 2002).

Field data also show that lower effective population size leads to a more rapid loss of alleles from the population (Turner et al. 2006; Evans and Sheldon 2008). For example, a broad survey of 89 bird species showed levels of heterozygosity ranging from 30% to over 90%, with population sizes ranging from 40 breeding pairs to over 100

FIGURE 11.5 For 89 species of birds, the level of heterozygosity is lower with smaller population sizes. The Madagascar fish eagle (*Haliaeetus vociferoides*) represents one extreme with fewer than 40 breeding pairs and very low heterozygosity; at the other extreme, the willow grouse (*Lagopus lagopus*), the state bird of Alaska, has a population size of more than 10 million and high heterozygosity. (After Evans and Sheldon 2008; eagle photograph © Danita Delimont/Alamy; grouse photograph courtesy of Dave Menke/U.S. Fish and Wildlife Service.)

million individuals (**Figure 11.5**). Overall there was a strong tendency for abundant birds to have more heterozygosity than species with small populations. Almost all species with populations over 10 million have over 60% heterozygosity, in contrast to less than 60% heterozygosity in most species with less than 10,000 individuals.

Unfortunately, rare and endangered species often have small, isolated populations, leading to a rapid loss of genetic variation. In 170 paired comparisons, threatened taxa with narrow ranges had an average of 35% lower genetic diversity than taxonomically related non-threatened species of wide distribution (Spielman et al. 2004). In some cases, entire species lacked genetic variation. In the evolutionarily isolated Wollemi pine (*Wollemia nobilis*) in Australia, only 40 plants occur in two nearby populations. As might be predicted, an extensive investigation failed to find any genetic variation in this species (Peakall et al. 2003).

It seems safe to assume that to maintain genetic variability, conservation biologists should strive to preserve populations that are as large as possible. But how big should a given population be? How many individuals are needed to maintain genetic variability? Franklin (1980) suggested that 50 reproductive individuals might be the minimum number necessary to avoid short-term inbreeding depression, the lower fitness that results from matings between closely related individuals. This figure is based on the practical experience of animal breeders, and it indicates that animal stocks can be maintained with a loss of 2% to 3% of their heterozygosity per generation. However, because this figure is based on work with domestic animals, its applicability to the wide range of wild species is uncertain.

Using data on mutation rates in *Drosophila* fruit flies, Franklin further suggested that in populations of 500 reproductive individuals, the rate of new genetic variability arising through mutation might balance the variability being lost because of genetic drift in small population size. This range of values (at least 50 individuals to prevent inbreeding depression and at least 500 for mutation rates to balance genetic drift) has been referred to as the **50/500 rule**: isolated populations need to have at least 50 individuals, and preferably 500 individuals, to maintain genetic variability. This rule is now considered outdated, as empirical studies have found inbreeding depression in populations with effective sizes of even more than 50 individuals and the mutation rates of beneficial mutations are now considered to be much lower (Frankham et al. 2009) The best evidence now suggests that at least several thousand reproductive individuals must be protected to maintain the genetic variability and long-term survival of a population. While this work on genetic variation and MVPs gives us some practical guidelines, the ideal is still to protect as many individuals of rare and endangered species as possible, to maximize their chances of survival.

Consequences of Reduced Genetic Variability

> Once a small population loses genetic variation, it is likely to enter a downward spiral of reduced population size and even less genetic variation in each generation.

Small populations subjected to genetic drift have greater susceptibility to a number of deleterious genetic effects such as inbreeding depression, outbreeding depression, and loss of evolutionary flexibility. These factors may contribute to a decline in population size, leading to an even greater loss of genetic variability, a loss of fitness, and a greater probability of extinction (Frankham et al. 2009).

INBREEDING DEPRESSION   A variety of mechanisms prevents **inbreeding**, mating among close relatives, in most natural populations. In large populations of most animal species, individuals do not normally mate with close relatives; this tendency to mate with unrelated individuals of the same species is termed **outbreeding**. Individuals often disperse from their place of birth or are restrained from mating with relatives by behavioral inhibitions, unique individual odors, or other sensory cues. In many plants, numerous morphological and physiological mechanisms encourage cross-pollination and prevent self-pollination. In some cases, particularly when population size is small and no other mates are available, these mechanisms fail to prevent inbreeding. Mating among parents and their offspring, siblings, and cousins, and self-fertilization in hermaphroditic species, may result in **inbreeding depression**, a condition that occurs when an individual receives two identical copies of a defective allele from each of its parents. Inbreeding depression is characterized by higher mortality of offspring, fewer offspring, or offspring that are weak or sterile or have low mating success (Frankham et al. 2009; Jaquiéry et al. 2009). These factors result in even fewer individuals in the next generation, leading to more pronounced inbreeding depression.

Evidence for the existence of inbreeding depression comes from studies of human populations (in which there are records of marriages between close relatives for many generations), captive animal populations, and cultivated plants (Leberg and Firmin 2007; Frankham 2005). In a wide range of captive mammal populations, matings among close relatives, such as parent–offspring matings and sibling–sibling matings, resulted on average in offspring with a 33% higher mortality rate than in non-inbred animals (**Figure 11.6**). This lower fitness resulting from inbreeding is sometimes referred to as a "cost of inbreeding." Inbreeding depression can be a severe problem in small captive populations in zoos and domestic livestock breeding programs. Deleterious effects of inbreeding in the wild have also been demonstrated (Crnokrak and Roff 1999): Of over 150 valid data sets, 90% showed inbreeding to be detrimental. The scarlet gilia, *Ipomopsis aggregata*, provides an example. Plants that come from populations with fewer than 100 individuals produce smaller seeds with a lower rate of seed germination and exhibit greater susceptibility to environmental stress than do plants from larger populations (**Figure 11.7**) (Heschel and Paige

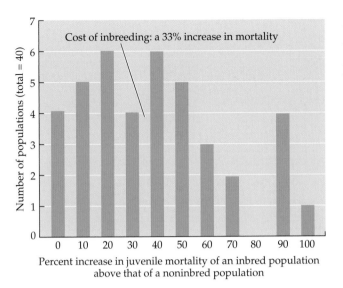

FIGURE 11.6 A high degree of inbreeding (such as matings between mother and son, father and daughter, brother and sister) results in a "cost of inbreeding." The data shown in the graph, based on a survey of 40 inbred mammal populations, express the cost as a percentage increase in juvenile mortality above the juvenile mortality rate of outbreeding animals of the same species. (After Ralls et al. 1988.)

1995). In a second study, Bouzat et al. (2008) examined isolated small populations of greater prairie chickens (*Tympanuchus cupido pinnatus*) in Illinois. These populations were showing the effects of declining genetic variation and inbreeding depression, including lowered fertility and lowered rates of egg hatching. However, when individuals from large, genetically diverse populations were released among the small populations, egg viability was restored and the populations began to increase in numbers. This result demonstrates the importance of maintaining genetic variation in existing populations and of restoring genetic variation in genetically impoverished populations as a conservation strategy.

OUTBREEDING DEPRESSION Individuals of different species rarely mate in the wild; there are strong ecological, behavioral, physiological, and morphological isolating mechanisms that ensure mating occurs only between individuals of the same species. However, when a species is rare or its habitat is damaged, outbreeding—mating between individuals of different populations or species—may occur

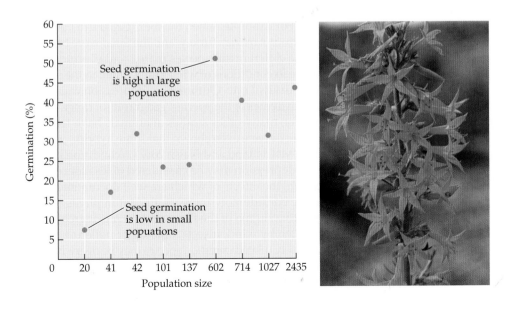

FIGURE 11.7 Seed germination in populations of the scarlet gilia (*Ipomopsis aggregata*) from montane Arizona is lower in small populations (fewer than 150 individuals) compared with larger populations. Seed germination is strongly reduced in the smallest populations. (After Heschel and Paige 1995; photograph © Bob Gibbons/Alamy.)

FIGURE 11.8 Mating between unrelated individuals of the same species often results in offspring with a high fitness (or heterosis) as measured by survival or high reproduction (number of offspring produced). Mating among close relatives (sibling–sibling or parent–offspring matings) or self-fertilization in hermaphroditic species leads to low fitness or inbreeding depression. Mating between individuals from widely different populations or even different species sometimes, but not always, results in lowered fitness or outbreeding depression. (After Groom et al. 2006.)

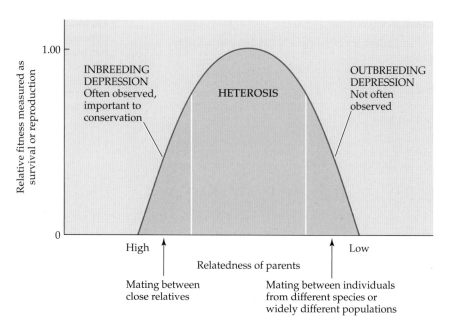

(**Figure 11.8**). Individuals unable to find mates within their own species may mate with individuals of related species. The resulting offspring sometimes exhibit **outbreeding depression**, a condition that results in weakness, sterility, or lack of adaptability to the environment. Outbreeding depression may be caused by incompatibility of the chromosomes and enzyme systems that are inherited from the different parents (Montalvo and Ellstrand 2001). To use an example from artificial selection, domestic horses and donkeys are commonly bred to produce mules. Although mules are not physically weak (on the contrary, they are quite strong, which is why humans find them useful), they are almost always sterile.

Outbreeding depression can also result from matings between different subspecies, or even matings between divergent genotypes or populations of the same species. Such matings might occur in a captive breeding program or when individuals from different populations are kept together in captivity. In such cases, the offspring of such different genotypes are unlikely to have the precise mixture of genes that allows individuals to survive and reproduce successfully in a particular set of local conditions (Frankham et al. 2009). For example, when the ibex (*Capra ibex*) population of Slovakia went extinct, ibex from Austria, Turkey, and the Sinai were brought in to start a new population. These different subspecies mated and produced hybrids that bore their young in the harsh conditions of winter rather than in the spring, and consequently they had a low survival rate. Outbreeding depression caused by the pairing of individuals from the extremes of the species' geographical range meant failure for the experiment. However, many other studies of animals have failed to demonstrate outbreeding depression or have even shown that some hybrids are *more* vigorous than their parent species (McClelland and Naish 2007), a condition known as **hybrid vigor**. Thus, outbreeding depression may be considered of less concern for animals than inbreeding depression, the effects of which are well documented.

Outbreeding depression may be considerably more significant in plants, where the arrival of pollen onto the receptive stigma of the flower is to some degree a matter of the chance movement of pollen by wind, insects, or another pollen vector. A rare plant species growing near a closely related common species may be overwhelmed by the pollen of the common species (Ellstrand 1992) and fail to produce seeds (Willi et al. 2007). Even when hybrids are produced by matings between a common and a rare species, the genetic identity of the rare species becomes lost as its small gene pool is mixed into the much larger gene pool of the common species. The seriousness of this threat is illustrated by the fact that more than 90% of California's threatened and endangered plants occur in close proximity to other species in the same genus, with which the rare plants could possibly hybridize. Such a loss of identity can also take place in gardens when individuals from different parts of a species' range are grown next to each other and are cross-pollinated, producing hybrid seed.

LOSS OF EVOLUTIONARY FLEXIBILITY It is important to understand that evolution is not directed; that is, individuals and populations cannot adapt to conditions they have not yet experienced. This fact makes the existence of genetic variation extremely important to a species' long-term survival. Rare alleles and unusual combinations of alleles that are harmless (or even slightly harmful) but confer no immediate advantage on the few individuals who carry them may turn out to be uniquely suited for a future set of environmental conditions. If such alleles and combinations do become advantageous, their incidence in the population will increase rapidly through natural selection, since the individuals who carry them will be those most likely to survive and reproduce successfully, passing on the formerly rare alleles to their offspring.

Loss of genetic variability in a small population may limit its ability to respond to new conditions and long-term changes in the environment, such as pollution, new diseases, and global climate change (Willi et al. 2007). According to the fundamental theorem of natural selection, the rate of evolutionary change in a population is directly related to the amount of genetic variation in the population. A small population is less likely than a large population to possess the genetic variation necessary for adaptation to long-term environmental changes and so will be more likely to go extinct. For example, in many plant populations, a few individuals have alleles that promote tolerance for high concentrations of toxic metals such as zinc and lead, even when these metals are not present. If toxic metals become abundant in the environment because of pollution, individuals with these alleles will be better able to adapt to them and to grow, survive, and reproduce better than typical individuals; consequently, frequency of these alleles in the population will increase dramatically. However, if the population has become small and the genotypes for metal tolerance have been lost, the population could go extinct.

Factors That Determine Effective Population Size

In this section we will discuss the factors that determine the effective population size, which is the size of the population as estimated by the number of its breeding individuals. The factors limiting the estimated number of breeding individuals in a population include unequal sex ratio, variation in reproductive output, and population fluctuations and bottlenecks.

The effective population size is lower than the total population size because many individuals do not reproduce, because of factors such as inability to find a mate, being too old or too young to mate, poor health, sterility, malnutrition, small body size, and social structures that restrict which individuals can mate. Many of the factors are initiated or aggravated by habitat degradation and fragmentation (Alò and Turner 2005). Furthermore, many plant, fungus, bacteria, and protist species have seeds, spores, or other structures in the soil that remain dormant unless stable conditions for germination appear. These individuals could be counted as members of the population, though they are obviously not part of the breeding population. Because of these factors, the effective population size (N_e) of breeding individuals is often sub-

> The effective population size N_e will be much smaller than the total population size N when there is great variation in reproductive output, an unequal sex ratio, or population fluctuations and bottlenecks.

stantially smaller than the actual population size (*N*). Because the rate of loss of genetic variability is based on the effective population size, the loss of genetic variability can be quite severe, even in a large population. For example, consider a population of 1000 alligators with 990 immature animals and only 10 mature breeding animals: 5 males and 5 females. In this case, the effective population size is 10, not 1000. For a rare oak species, there might be 20 mature trees, 500 saplings, and 2000 seedlings, resulting in a population size of 2520 but an effective population size of only 20.

A smaller-than-expected effective population size from a genetic perspective can also exist when there is an unequal sex ratio, large amount of variation in reproductive output, or population fluctuations and bottlenecks, as described below. The overall impact of these factors can be substantial. The effective population size can be smaller than might be expected from an initial count of reproductive individuals, under any of the following circumstances.

UNEQUAL SEX RATIO   A population may consist of unequal numbers of males and females due to chance, selective mortality, or the harvesting of only one sex by people. If, for example, a population of a goose species that is monogamous (with one male and one female forming a long-lasting pair bond) consists of 20 males and 6 females, then only 12 individuals—6 males and 6 females—will be mating. In this case, the effective population size is 12, not 26. In other animal species, social systems may prevent many individuals from mating even though they are physiologically capable of doing so. Among elephant seals, for example, a single dominant male usually mates with a large group of females and prevents other males from mating with them (**Figure 11.9**), whereas among African wild dogs, the dominant female in the pack often bears all of the pups.

FIGURE 11.9   A single male elephant seal (the larger animal with the extended snout, seen roaring in the left of the photograph) mates with large numbers of females; thus the effective population size is reduced because only one male is providing genetic input. (Photograph © Bert Gildart/Peter Arnold Images/Photolibrary.com.)

The effect of unequal numbers of breeding males and females on N_e can be described by this formula:

$$N_e = [4(N_f \times N_m)] / (N_f + N_m)$$

where N_m and N_f are the numbers of adult breeding males and breeding females, respectively, in the population. In general, as the sex ratio of breeding individuals becomes increasingly unequal, the ratio of the effective population size to the number of breeding individuals (N_e/N) also goes down (**Figure 11.10**). This occurs because only a few individuals of one sex are making a disproportionately large contribution to the genetic makeup of the next generation, rather than the equal contribution found in monogamous mating systems. In the case of Asian elephants, for example, males are hunted by poachers for their tusks at the Periyar Tiger Reserve in India (Ramakrishnan et al. 1998). In 1997, there were 1166 elephants, of which 709 were adults. Of these adults, 704 were female and 5 were male. If all of these elephants were breeding, this would result in an effective population size of only 20 from a genetic perspective, using the equation shown above.

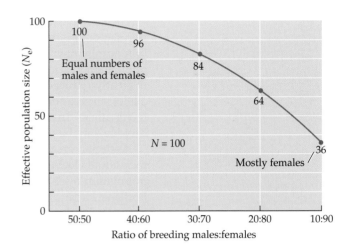

FIGURE 11.10 The effective population size (N_e) declines when the number of males and females in a breeding population (N) of 100 individuals is increasingly unequal. N_e is 100 when 50 males and 50 females breed, but it is only 36 when 10 males and 90 females breed.

VARIATION IN REPRODUCTIVE OUTPUT In many species the number of offspring varies substantially among individuals. This phenomenon is particularly true of highly fecund species, such as plants and fish (see Hedrick 2005), where many or even most individuals produce a few offspring while others produce huge numbers. Unequal production of offspring leads to a substantial reduction in N_e because a few individuals in the present generation will be disproportionately represented in the gene pool of the next generation. In general, the greater the variation in reproductive output, the more the effective population size is lowered. For a variety of species in the wild, Frankham (1995) estimated that variation in offspring number reduces effective population size by a factor of 54%. In many annual plant populations that consist of large numbers of tiny plants producing one or a few seeds and a few gigantic individuals producing thousands of seeds, N_e could be reduced even more.

POPULATION FLUCTUATIONS AND BOTTLENECKS In some species, population size varies dramatically from generation to generation. Particularly good examples of this are butterflies, annual plants, and amphibians. In extreme fluctuations, the effective population size is somewhere between the lowest and the highest numbers of individuals. This is often the most important factor reducing N_e below the census population size. The effective population size can be calculated over a period of t years using the number of individuals (N) breeding in any one year:

$$N_e = t / (1/N_1 + 1/N_2 + \ldots + 1/N_t)$$

Consider a butterfly population, monitored for 5 years, that has 10, 20, 100, 20, and 10 breeding individuals in the successive 5 years. In this case,

$$N_e = 5 / (1/10 + 1/20 + 1/100 + 1/20 + 1/10) = 5 / (31/100) = 5 (100/31) = 16.1$$

The effective population size over the course of 5 years is above the lowest population level (10) but well below the maximum number (100) and the arithmetically average population size (32).

The effective population size tends to be determined by the years in which the population has the smallest numbers. A single year of drastically reduced population numbers will substantially lower the value of N_e. This principle applies to a phenomenon known as a **population bottleneck**, which occurs when a population is greatly reduced in size and loses rare alleles if no individuals possessing those alleles survive and reproduce (Jamieson et al. 2006; Roman and Darling 2007). With fewer alleles present and a decline in heterozygosity, the overall fitness of the individuals in the population may decline.

A special category of bottleneck, known as the **founder effect**, occurs when a few individuals leave one population to establish another new population. The new population often has less genetic variability than the larger, original population. Bottlenecks can also occur when captive populations are established using relatively few individuals. For example, the captive population of the Speke's gazelle in the United States was established from one male and three females. If a population is fragmented by human activities, each of the resulting small subpopulations may lose genetic variation and go extinct. Such is the fate of many fish populations fragmented by dams (Wofford et al. 2005).

The lions (*Panthera leo*) of Ngorongoro Crater in Tanzania provide a well-studied example of a population bottleneck (Munson et al. 2008). The lion population in the crater consisted of 60 to 75 individuals until an outbreak of biting flies in 1962 reduced the population to 9 females and 1 male (**Figure 11.11**). Two years later, 7 additional males immigrated to the crater; there has been no further immigration since that time. The small number of founders, the isolation of the population, and the variation in reproductive success among individuals have apparently created a population bottleneck, leading to inbreeding depression. In comparison with the large Serengeti lion population nearby, the crater lions show reduced genetic variability, high levels of sperm abnormalities (**Figure 11.12**), reduced reproductive rates, increased cub mortality, and higher rates of infection (Munson et al. 2008). As a result, even though the population increased and contained 75 to 125 animals in 1983, the population has since declined. By 2003, the population dropped to 34 animals following an outbreak of canine distemper virus that had spread from domestic dogs kept by people living just outside the crater area.

Population bottlenecks do not always lead to greatly reduced heterozygosity. The effects of population bottlenecks will be most evident when the breeding pop-

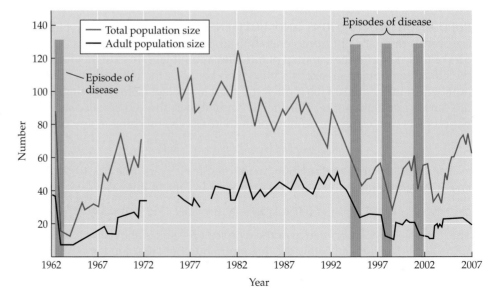

FIGURE 11.11 The Ngorongoro Crater lion population consisted of about 90 individuals in 1961 before crashing in 1962. Since that time, the population reached a peak of 125 individuals in 1983 before collapsing to fewer than 40 individuals (fewer than 20 of which were adults). Small population size, an isolated location, lack of immigration since 1962, and the impact of disease have apparently resulted in the loss of genetic variation caused by a population bottleneck. A lack of census data for certain years is the cause of gaps in the lines. The four green bars represent episodes of disease outbreak. (After Munson et al. 2008.)

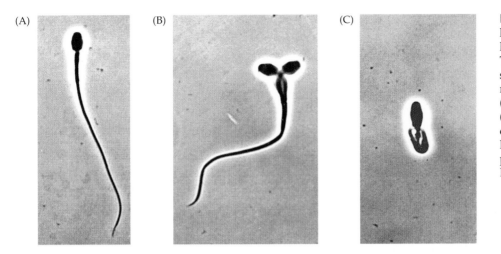

(A) (B) (C)

FIGURE 11.12 Males of the isolated and inbred population of lions at Ngorongoro Crater in Tanzania exhibit a high level of sperm abnormalities. (A) Normal lion sperm. (B) Bicephalic ("two-headed") sperm and (C) nonfunctional sperm with a coiled flagellum, both from lions of the Ngorongoro Crater population. (Photographs by D. Wildt.)

ulation is reduced below 10 individuals for several generations. If the population expands rapidly in size after a temporary bottleneck, average heterozygosity in the population may be restored even though the number of alleles present is severely reduced. An example of this phenomenon is the high level of heterozygosity found in the greater one-horned rhinoceros (*Rhinoceros unicornis*) in Nepal, even after the population passed through a bottleneck (**Box 11.1**). Population size declined from 800 individuals in Chitwan National Park to less than 100 individuals; fewer than 30 were breeding. With an effective population size of 30 individuals for one generation, the population would have lost only 1.7% of its heterozygosity after one generation. As a result of strict protection of the species by park guards, the population recovered to 400 individuals. The

> New populations established from only a few individuals may have reduced genetic variation. Genetic variation may be restored if the population expands rapidly in size.

Mauritius kestrel (*Falco punctatus*) represents an even more extreme case, with a long population decline that resulted in only one breeding pair remaining in 1974. An intensive conservation program has allowed the population to recover to about 1000 birds today. A study comparing the present birds with preserved museum specimens and kestrels living elsewhere has found that the Mauritius kestrel lost only about half of its genetic variation after passing through this bottleneck (Ewing et al. 2008).

These examples demonstrate that effective population size is often substantially less than the total number of individuals in a population. Particularly where there is a combination of factors such as fluctuating population size, numerous nonreproductive individuals, and an unequal sex ratio, the effective population size may be far lower than the number of individuals alive in a good year. A review of a wide range of wildlife studies revealed that the effective population size averaged only 11% of the total population size; that is, a population of 300 animals, seemingly large enough to maintain the population, might have an effective population size of only 33, which would indicate that it was in serious danger of extinction (Frankham 2005). If the goal of a conservation program is to protect 5000 reproductive individuals (see p. 249), then the effective population size might be about 550. For highly fecund species, such as fish, seaweed, and many invertebrates, the effective population size may be less than 1% (Frankham et al. 2009). Consequently, management aimed toward simply maintaining large populations may not prevent the loss of genetic variation unless the effective population size is also large. In the case of captive populations of rare and endangered species, genetic variation may be effectively maintained by con-

BOX 11.1   *Rhino Species in Asia and Africa: Genetic Diversity and Habitat Loss*

■ In recent decades, conservationists have focused extraordinary effort on protecting and restoring the numbers of rhinoceroses in parts of their original ranges (Amin et al. 2006). The task is monumental: Three of the five species of rhinoceros that inhabit Asia and Africa are critically endangered, and all five represent ancient and unusual adaptations for survival. Habitat destruction and poaching are serious threats to the three species of the Asian forests, while the illegal killing of rhinos for their horns (used for medicine and carving) is the main problem for the two African species.

Rhino losses are so severe that it is estimated that only 17,000 individuals of all five species survive today (Amin et al. 2006). These species exist in a tiny fraction of their former range. The most numerous of the five is the white rhinoceros, *Ceratotherium simum*; this species numbers approximately 11,300 wild animals, although there are only 4 individuals of the distinctive northern subspecies (www.rhinos-irf.org). The rarest species—the elusive Javan rhinoceros, *Rhinoceros sondaicus*—is thought to number about 50 animals on the very western end of the island of Java, with another 6 individuals in Vietnam. These two populations are genetically very distinct (IUCN 2008).

The overall decline of each species is alarming enough, but the problem is exacerbated by the fact that many of the remaining animals live in very small, isolated populations. The African black rhino, *Diceros bicornis*, for example, numbers about 4000, but these individuals are in approximately 75 small, widely separated subgroups. The existing populations of the Sumatran rhino (*Dicerorhinus sumatrensis*) each contain fewer than 100 individuals, with the total species count under 250. Some biologists fear that these small populations may not be viable over the long term, as a result of loss of genetic variability, inbreeding depression, and genetic diseases resulting from mating among closely related individuals.

The question of genetic viability in rhino populations is not as simple as it first appears. Genetic diversity varies greatly among rhino species. Studies of the greater one-horned, or Indian, rhinoceros (*Rhinoceros unicornis*) in Nepal indicate that despite its small total population—an estimated 2500 animals (see figure)—the genetic diversity in at least this population is relatively high, contradicting the common assumption that small populations automatically have low heterozygosity. The combination of long generation times and high individual mobility among genetically unique populations may have allowed the Indian rhino to maintain its genetic variability despite passing through a population bottleneck (Pluhácek et al. 2007). Current Indian rhino populations in parks, zoos, and sanctuaries have increased dramatically and are apparently genetically healthy; however, the species will probably always be limited to these small, heavily guarded remnant habitats, with no opportunity to return to its former range or numbers. Further, the rhinos' choice of mates will increasingly be determined by wildlife biologists concerned with maintaining genetic variation within the species.

> Understanding the genetic characteristics of a species is often needed for effective conservation planning.

As a contrast with the Indian rhino, the four recognized subspecies of the black rhino are genetically distinct, as shown by microsatellite DNA data; perhaps they represent adaptations to local environmental conditions throughout the species' range (Harley et al. 2005). If black rhinos from a number of different subspecies are placed together in a sanctuary to increase genetic diversity in the species, would the rhinos risk losing adaptive differences that might prove crucial to the survival of local subspecies? Maintaining genetic diversity is contingent on controlling outside threats to the breeding population, including illegal poaching for their horns. Optimal park conditions must also be maintained to ensure that all adult individuals reproduce. Captive breeding of endangered rhinos presents special challenges; white rhinos in particular often will not breed in zoo programs.

Genetic analysis has also been useful for making decisions on the conservation of the Sumatran rhinoceros, numbering fewer than 300 individuals and found in scattered populations. Analysis of mitochondrial DNA from blood and hair samples from eastern Sumatra, western Sumatra, peninsular Malaysia, and Borneo populations showed that the Borneo population represented a lineage distinct from the other three populations, which were genetically similar. The recommendation is that the Borneo rhinos should be treated as a separate population for breeding and conservation purposes, whereas the other three populations can be managed as one conservation unit (Morales et al. 1997). Because this species is under such great threat from logging and agriculture, breeding programs in the wild and in captivity will be needed.

As this research makes evident, there is no single, all-encompassing answer to rhino conservation; management must be tailored to the specific genetic and environmental circumstances of particular species and populations.

BOX 11.1 *(continued)*

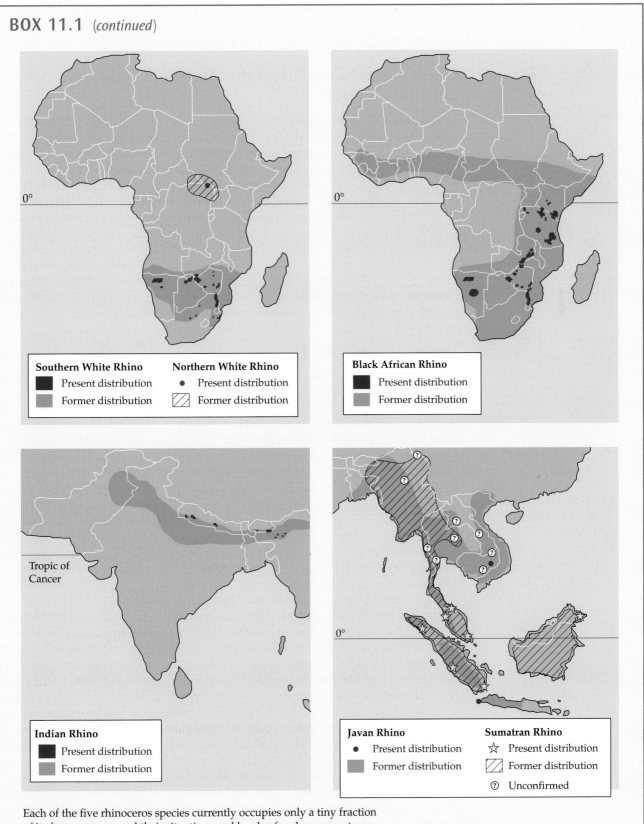

Each of the five rhinoceros species currently occupies only a tiny fraction of its former range, and their situations and levels of endangerment vary greatly. (After www.rhinos-irf.org.)

trolling breeding, perhaps by subdividing the population, periodically removing dominant males to allow subdominant males the opportunity to mate, and periodically transporting a few selected individuals among subpopulations.

Other Factors That Affect the Persistence of Small Populations

In this section we discuss some other factors that affect small populations. Random variation, or **stochasticity**, in the environment can cause variation in the population size of a species. For example, the population of an endangered butterfly species might be affected by fluctuations in the abundance of its food plants and the number of its predators. Variation in the physical environment might also strongly influence the butterfly population; in an average year, the weather may be warm enough for caterpillars to feed and grow, whereas a cold year might cause many caterpillars to become inactive and consequently starve. Such **environmental stochasticity** affects all individuals in the population and is linked to **demographic stochasticity** (or **demographic variation**), which is the variation in birth and death rates among individuals and across years within a given population.

> Random fluctuations in birth and death rates, disruption of social behavior following decreased population density, and environmental stochasticity all contribute to instability in the population size, often leading to local extinction.

Demographic Variation

In an ideal, stable environment, a population would increase until it reached the carrying capacity (K) of the environment, at which point the average birthrate (b) per individual would equal the average death rate (d) and there would be no net change in population size. In any real population, individuals do not usually produce the average number of offspring: they might leave no offspring, somewhat fewer than the average, or more than the average. For example, in an ideal, stable giant panda population, each female would produce an average of two surviving offspring in her lifetime, but field studies show that rates of reproduction among individual females vary widely around that number. However, as long as population size is large, the average birthrate provides an accurate description of the population. Similarly, the average death rate in a population can be determined only by examining large numbers of individuals, because some individuals die young and other individuals live a relatively long time. This variation in population size due to random variation in reproduction and mortality rates is known as demographic variation or demographic stochasticity.

Population size may fluctuate over time because of changes in the environment or other factors without ever approaching a stable value. In general, once population size drops below about 50 individuals, individual variation in birth and death rates begins to cause the population size to fluctuate randomly up or down (Schleuning and Matthies 2009). If population size fluctuates downward in any one year because of a higher than average number of deaths or a lower than average number of births, the resulting smaller population will be even more susceptible to demographic fluctuations in subsequent years. Random fluctuations upward in population size are eventually bounded by the carrying capacity of the environment, and the population may fluctuate downward again. Consequently, once a population decreases because of habitat destruction and fragmentation, demographic variation becomes important and the population has a higher probability of declining more and even going extinct due to chance alone (in a year with low reproduction and high mortality) (Melbourne and Hastings 2008). Species with highly variable birth and death rates, such as annual plants and short-lived insects, may be particularly susceptible to population extinction due to demographic stochasticity. The chance of extinction is also greater in species that have low birthrates, such as elephants, because these species take longer to recover from chance reductions in population size.

As a simple example, imagine a population of three hermaphroditic individuals; each lives for 1 year, needs to find a mate and reproduce, and then dies. Assume that each individual has a 33% probability of producing zero, one, or two offspring, resulting in an average birthrate of 1 per individual; in this instance, there is theoretically a stable population. However, when these individuals reproduce, there is a 1-in-27 chance ($0.33 \times 0.33 \times 0.33$) that no offspring will be produced in the next generation and the population will go extinct. Consider also that there is a 1-in-9 chance that only one offspring will be produced in the next generation ($0.33 \times 0.33 \times 0.33 \times 3$); because this individual will not be able to find a mate, the population will be doomed to extinction in the next generation. There is also a 22% chance that the population will decline to two individuals in the next generation. Thus, random variation in birthrates can lead to demographic stochasticity and extinction in small populations. Similarly, random fluctuations in the death rate can lead to fluctuations in population size. When populations are small, random high mortality in one year might eliminate the population altogether.

When populations drop below a critical number, deviations from an equal sex ratio may occur, leading to a declining birthrate and a further decrease in population size. For example, imagine a population of four birds that includes two mating pairs of males and females, in which each female produces an average of two surviving offspring in her lifetime. In the next generation, there is a 1-in-8 chance that only male or only female birds will be produced, in which case no eggs will be laid to produce the following generation. There is a 50% (8-in-16) chance that there will be either three males and one female or three females and one male in the next generation, in which case only one pair of birds will mate and the population will decline. This scenario is illustrated by the last five surviving individuals of the extinct dusky seaside sparrow (*Ammodramus maritimus nigrescens*); all individuals were males, so there was no opportunity to establish a captive breeding program. Such demograpic effects are also seen in the Spanish imperial eagle (*Aquila adalberti*); immature birds are more likely to breed when the population is small than when the population is large, when only mature birds breed. Such immature birds are in turn more likely to produce predominantly male offspring, contributing to further population decline and increasing the probability of local extinction (**Figure 11.13**) (Ferrer et al. 2009).

POPULATION DENSITY AND THE ALLEE EFFECT   Many small populations are demographically unstable because social interactions (especially those affecting mating) can be disrupted once population density falls below a certain level (Gascoigne et al. 2009). This interaction among population size, population density, and population growth rate is sometimes referred to as the **Allee effect**. Herds of grazing mammals and flocks of birds may be unable to find food and defend themselves against attack from predators when numbers fall below a certain level. Animals that hunt in packs, such as wild dogs and lions, may need a certain number of individuals to hunt effectively.

> The social systems and breeding systems of many animals can be disrupted when the population size or density falls below a certain level.

Perhaps the most significant aspect of the Allee effect for small populations involves reproductive behavior: many species that live in widely dispersed populations, such as bears, spiders, and tigers, have difficulty finding mates once the population density drops below a certain point. Even among plant species, as population size and density decrease, the distance between individual plants increases; polli-

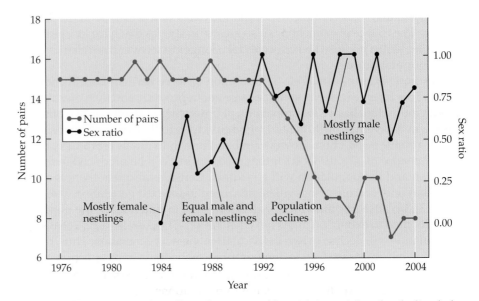

FIGURE 11.13 As the number of breeding pairs of Spanish imperial eagles declined, the sex ratio of nestlings changed from entirely female in 1984, to approximately equal, to almost exclusively male. This change was due to the tendency of immature male eagles to breed only when population size is small and for them to produce mainly male offspring. (After Ferrer et al. 2009.)

nating animals may not visit isolated, scattered plants, resulting in insufficient transfer of compatible pollen and a subsequent decline in seed production. In such cases, the birthrate will decline, population density will become lower yet, problems such as unequal sex ratio will worsen, and birthrates will drop even more. Once the birthrate falls to zero, extinction is guaranteed.

Environmental Variation and Catastrophes

Random variation in the biological and physical environment, known as **environmental stochasticity**, can also cause variation in the population size of a species. For example, the population of an endangered rabbit species might be affected by fluctuations in the population of a deer species that eats the same types of plants, fluctuations in the population of a fox species that feeds on the rabbits, and fluctuations in the populations of parasites and disease-causing organisms that affect the rabbits. Variation in the physical environment might also strongly influence the rabbit populations—rainfall during an average year might encourage plant growth and allow the population to increase, while dry years might limit plant growth and cause rabbits to starve. Environmental stochasticity affects all individuals in the population, unlike demographic stochasticity, which causes variation among individuals within the population.

Natural catastrophes that occur at unpredictable intervals, such as droughts, storms, earthquakes, and fires, along with cyclical die-offs of the surrounding biological community, can cause dramatic fluctuations in population levels. Natural catastrophes can kill part of a population or even eliminate an entire population from an area. Numerous examples exist of die-offs in populations of large mammals; in many cases 70% to 90% of the population dies (Young 1994). For a wide range of vertebrates, the frequency of catastrophes is about 15% per generation (Reed et al. 2003). Even

> Even though a population appears to be stable or increasing, an infrequent environmental event or catastrophe can severely reduce population size or even drive it to extinction. Such rare events need to be considered by conservation biologists.

though the probability of a natural catastrophe in any one year is low, over the course of decades and centuries, natural catastrophes have a high likelihood of occurring.

As an example of environmental variation, imagine a rabbit population of 100 individuals in which the average birthrate is 0.2 and an average of 20 rabbits are eaten each year by foxes. On average, the population will maintain its numbers at exactly 100 individuals, with 20 rabbits born each year and 20 rabbits eaten each year. However, if there are 3 successive years in which the foxes eat 40 rabbits per year, the population size will decline to 80 rabbits, 56 rabbits, and 27 rabbits in years 1, 2, and 3, respectively. If there are then 3 years of no fox predation, the rabbit population will increase to 32, 38, and 46 individuals in years 4, 5, and 6. Even though the same average rate of predation (20 rabbits per year) occurred over this 6-year period, variation in year-to-year predation rates caused the rabbit population size to decline by more than 50%. At a population size of 46 individuals, the rabbit population will probably go extinct within the next 5 to 10 years when subjected to the average rate of 20 rabbits eaten by foxes per year.

Modeling efforts by Menges (1992) and others have shown that random environmental variation is generally more important than random demographic variation in increasing the probability of extinction in populations of small to moderate size. Environmental variation can substantially increase the risk of extinction even in populations showing positive population growth under the assumption of a stable environment (Mangel and Tier 1994). In general, introducing environmental variation into population models, in effect making them more realistic, results in populations with lower growth rates, lower population sizes, and higher probabilities of extinction. For example, a model of a tropical palm using demographic variation predicted that the MVP size, the number of individuals needed to give the population a 95% probability of persisting for 100 years, was about 48 mature individuals (**Figure 11.14**). When moderate environmental variation was included, however, the MVP size increased to 380 individuals, meaning that a seven times larger population needs to be protected.

The interaction between population size and environmental variation was demonstrated using the biennial herb garlic mustard (*Alliaria petiolata*), an invasive plant in the United States, as an experimental subject (Drayton and Primack 1999). Populations of various sizes were assigned at random either to be left alone as controls or to be experimentally eradicated by removal of every flowering plant in each of the 4 years of the study; removal of all plants could be considered an extreme en-

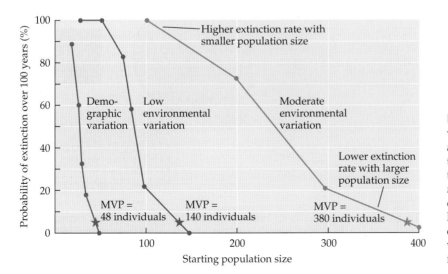

FIGURE 11.14 The effects of demographic variation, low environmental variation, and moderate environmental variation on the probability of extinction of a population of the Mexican palm, *Astrocaryum mexicanum*. In this study, the MVP size, indicated by a star, was defined as the population size at which there is a less than 5% chance of the population's going extinct within 100 years. (After Menges 1992; data from Piñero et al. 1984.)

vironmental event. Overall, the probability of an experimental population's going extinct over the 4-year period was 43% for small populations (<10 individuals initially), 9% for medium-sized populations (10 to 50), and 7% for large populations (>50 individuals). For control populations, the probability of going extinct for small, medium, and large populations was 11%, 0%, and 0%. Large numbers of dormant seeds in the soil apparently allowed most experimental populations to persist even when every flowering plant was removed in 4 successive years. However, small populations were far more susceptible to extinction than large populations.

Extinction Vortices

The smaller a population becomes, the more vulnerable it is to further demographic variation, environmental variation, and genetic factors that tend to lower reproduction, increase mortality rates, and so reduce population size even more, driving the population to extinction. This tendency of small populations to decline toward extinction has been likened to a vortex, a whirling mass of gas or liquid spiraling inward—the closer an object gets to the center, the faster it moves. At the center of an **extinction vortex** is oblivion: the local extinction of the species. Once caught in such a vortex, it is difficult for a species to resist the pull toward extinction (Fagan and Holmes 2006).

For example, a natural catastrophe, a new disease, or human disturbance could reduce a large population to a small size. This small population could then suffer from inbreeding depression with an associated lowered juvenile survival rate. This increased death rate could result in an even lower population size and more inbreeding. Similarly, demographic variation will often reduce population size, resulting in even greater demographic fluctuations and, once again, a greater probability of extinction.

These three forces—environmental variation, demographic variation, and loss of genetic variability—act together such that a decline in population size caused by one factor will increase the vulnerability of the population to the other two factors (**Figure 11.15**). For example, a decrease in orangutan population size caused by for-

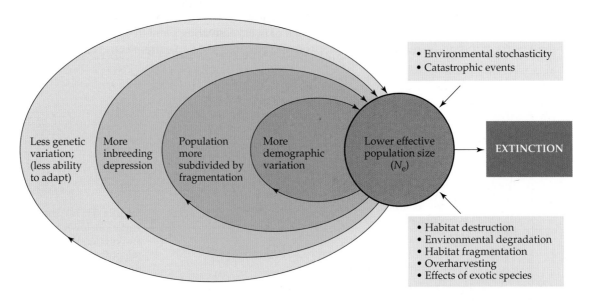

FIGURE 11.15 Once a population drops below a certain size, it enters an extinction vortex in which the factors that affect small populations tend to drive its size progressively lower. This downward spiral often leads to the local extinction of species. (After Gilpin and Soulé 1986 and Guerrant 1992.)

est fragmentation may cause inbreeding depression, decreasing population size; decreased population size may then disrupt the social structure and the ability to find mates, leading to an even lower population size; the smaller population is then more vulnerable to further population reduction and eventual extinction caused by unusual environmental events.

It is also important to remember that as a population becomes smaller, it also tends toward becoming ecologically extinct: once the orangutan population drops below a certain size, for example, the species would not be an effective seed disperser in the community.

An important implication of the extinction vortex is that addressing the original cause of population decline may not be sufficient to recover a threatened population. Such was the case with the greater prairie chicken population in Illinois described earlier. The original population of over 1 million prairie chickens declined to below 50 following the arrival of European settlers, with a decline in fertility and hatchability. Habitat restoration reversing one of the major original causes of decline failed to help the population recover. The Illinois prairie chicken population began to grow only after it was outcrossed to populations from other states to reverse inbreeding depression.

As the prairie chicken example illustrates, once a population has declined to a small size, it will probably go extinct unless unusual and highly favorable conditions allow the population size to increase (Schott et al. 2005). Such populations often require a careful program of population and habitat management, as described in later chapters, to increase population growth rate and allow the population to escape from the harmful effects of small population size.

> Often favorable conditions and active management are needed to help species recover from the problems of small populations.

Summary

1. In many cases, protecting populations is the key to protecting species from extinction. The minimum viable population (MVP) size is the smallest population size that can be predicted to have a high chance of persisting for the forseeable future. The MVP for many species is at least several thousand individuals.

2. Biologists have observed that small populations have a greater tendency to go extinct than large populations. Small populations are subject to a more rapid rate of extinction for three main reasons: loss of genetic variability and related problems of inbreeding depression and genetic drift, demographic fluctuations, and environmental variation or natural catastrophes.

3. To protect small populations, we need to determine the effective population size, which is a genetic estimate based on the number of individuals that are actually producing offspring. The calculated effective population size is often much lower than simply the number of living individuals because (1) many individuals are not reproducing, (2) there may be an unequal sex ratio, (3) there may be variation among individuals in number of offspring produced, and (4) populations may show large fluctuations in size over time.

4. Variations in reproductive and mortality rates can cause small populations to fluctuate randomly in size, leading to extinction. Environmental variation can also cause random fluctuations in population size, with infrequent natural catastrophes sometimes causing major reductions.

5. Once a population's size has been reduced by habitat destruction, fragmentation, and other human activities, it is even more vulnerable to random fluctuations in size

and eventual extinction. The combined effects of demographic variation, environmental variation, and loss of genetic variability on small populations create an extinction vortex that tends to accelerate the drive to extinction and may require population and habitat management, to be counteracted.

For Discussion

1. Imagine a species that has four populations, consisting of 4, 10, 40, and 100 individuals. Using Wright's formula, $H = 1 - 1/[2 N_e]$, calculate the loss in heterozygosity over 1, 2, 5, and 10 generations for each population. Calculate the effective population size, N_e, for each population, assuming that there are equal numbers of males and females; then calculate it assuming different proportions of males and females. Allow the population size of each group to fluctuate at random around its average value. Calculate how this affects the loss of heterozygosity and the effective population size.

2. Construct a simple population model of a rabbit that has a stable population size (see page 267); then add environmental variation (such as severe winter storms or predation) and demographic variation (number of offspring produced per rabbit per year), and determine whether the population would be able to persist over time. Use the methods shown in the text, computer simulations (see Shultz et al. 1999 and Donovan and Welden 2002 for ideas), or random-number generators (flipping coins is the easiest).

3. Find out about a species that is currently endangered in the wild. How is this species or how might it be affected by the problems of small populations? Address genetic, physiological, behavioral, and ecological aspects, as appropriate.

Suggested Readings

Bell, C. D., J. M. Blumenthal, A. C. Broderick, and B. J. Godley. 2010. Investigating potential for depensation in marine turtles: How low can you go? *Conservation Biology* 24: 226–235. High gene flow may explain why certain marine turtles can persist at low population densities.

Corlatti, L., K. Hacklander, and F. Frey-Roos. 2009. Ability of wildlife overpasses to provide connectivity and prevent genetic isolation. *Conservation Biology* 23: 548–556. Dispersal is needed to maintain genetic variation in fragmented populations.

Evans, S. R. and B. C. Sheldon. 2008. Interspecific patterns of genetic diversity in birds: Correlations with extinction risk. *Conservation Biology* 22: 1016–1025. Species with small populations have less genetic variation and have greater extinction risk.

Ewing, S. R., R. G. Nager, M. A. C. Nicoll, A. Aumjaud, C. G. Jones, and L. F. Keller. 2008. Inbreeding and loss of genetic variation in a reintroduced population of Mauritius kestrel. *Conservation Biology* 22: 395–404. The loss of genetic variation is a concern, despite the apparent success of this project.

Ferrer, M., I. Newton, and M. Pandolfi. 2009. Small populations and offspring sex-ratio deviations in eagles. *Conservation Biology* 23: 1017–1025. Small populations produce nestlings with a strong male bias.

Frankham, R. 2005. Genetics and extinction. *Biological Conservation* 126: 131–140. Small populations in the wild suffer from negative genetic effects.

Frankham, R., J. D. Ballou, and D. A. Briscoe. 2009. *Introduction to Conservation Genetics*, 2nd ed. Cambridge University Press, Cambridge, UK. Excellent introduction to the importance of genetics to conservation.

Hedrick, P. 2005. Large variance in reproductive success and the N_e/N ratio. *Evolution* 59: 1596–1599. A variety of factors can result in reduced effective population size.

Jamieson, I. G., G. P. Wallis, and J. V. Briskie. 2006. Inbreeding and endangered species management: Is New Zealand out of step with the rest of the world? *Conservation Biology* 20: 38–47. Population bottlenecks and inbreeding depression affect rare species recovery.

Melbourne, B. A. and A. Hastings. 2008. Extinction risk depends strongly on factors contributing to stochasticity. *Nature* 454: 100–103. Both environmental and demographic factors contribute to extinction risk.

Schleuning, M. and D. Matthies. 2009. Habitat change and plant demography: Assessing the extinction risk of a formerly common grassland perennial. *Conservation Biology* 23: 174–183. Habitat change and lack of proper management can increase the extinction risk of plants.

Schrott, G. R., K. A. With, and A. W. King. 2005. Demographic limitations on the ability of habitat restoration to rescue declining populations. *Conservation Biology* 19: 1181–1193. Intensive management is sometimes needed to rebuild small populations.

Wayne, R. K. and P. A. Morin. 2004. Conservation genetics in the new molecular age. *Frontiers in Ecology and the Environment* 2: 89–97. Modern molecular techniques can be used to assess population characteristics and suggest management strategies.

Wilhere, G. F. 2008. The how-much-is-enough myth. *Conservation Biology* 22: 514–517. The question of how much is enough is key to conservation science and cannot be answered only objectively.

Willi, Y., M. van Kleunen, S. Dietrich, and M. Fischer. 2007. Genetic rescue persists beyond first-generation outbreeding in small populations of a rare plant. *Proceedings of the Royal Society*, Series B 274: 2357–2364. Despite the risk of outbreeding depression, interpopulation outbreeding can be a beneficial conservation strategy.

Chapter 12

Applied Population Biology

H ow can conservation biologists determine whether a specific plan to manage an endangered or rare species has a good chance of succeeding? Even without human disturbance, a population of any species can be stable, increasing, decreasing, or fluctuating in number. In general, widespread human disturbance destabilizes populations of many native species, often sending them into sharp decline. But how can this disturbance be measured, and what actions should be taken to prevent or reverse it? This chapter discusses applied population biology, which seeks to answer these and other questions by examining the factors affecting the abundance and distribution of rare and endangered species.

In protecting and managing a rare or endangered species, it is vital to have a firm grasp of the ecology of the species, its distinctive characteristics (sometimes called its **natural history**), and the status of its populations, particularly the dynamic processes that affect population size and distribution (its **population biology**). With more information concerning a rare species' natural history and population biology, land managers are able to more effectively maintain the species and identify factors that place it at risk of extinction. As will be discussed later in the chapter, this information can be used to make mathematical predictions of the ability of species to persist in a protected area and the impact of alternative management options.

To help implement effective population-level conservation efforts, conservation biologists should try to answer as many questions as possible from the following categories. For most species, we're able to answer only a few of these questions without further investigation, yet management decisions may have to be made before this information is available or while it is being gathered:

- *Environment.* What are the habitat types where the species is found, and how much area is there of each? How variable is the environment in time and space? How frequently is the environment affected by catastrophic disturbance? How have human activities affected the environment?

- *Distribution.* Where is the species found in its habitat? Are individuals clustered together, distributed at random, or spaced out regularly? Do individuals of this species move and migrate among habitats or to different geographical areas over the course of a day or over a year? How efficient is the species at colonizing new habitats? How have human activities affected the distribution of the species?

- *Biotic interactions.* What types of food and other resources does the species need and how does it obtain them? What other species compete with it for these resources? What predators, parasites, or diseases affect its population size? What mutualists (pollinators, dispersers, etc.) does it interact with? Do juvenile stages disperse by themselves, or are they dispersed by other species? How have human activities altered the relationships among species in the community?

- *Morphology.* What does the species look like? What are the shape, size, color, surface texture, and function of its parts? How do the shapes of its body parts relate to their functions and help the species to survive in its environment? What are the characteristics that allow this species to be distingushed from species that are similar in appearance?

- *Physiology.* How much food, water, minerals, and other necessities does an individual need to survive, grow, and reproduce? How efficient is an individual at using its resources? How vulnerable is the species to extremes of climate, such as heat, cold, wind, and rain? When does the species reproduce, and what are its special requirements during reproduction?

> Knowledge of the natural history and population biology of a species is crucial to its protection, but urgent management decisions often must be made before all of this information is available, or while it is still being gathered.

- *Demography.* What is the current population size, and what was it in the past? Are the numbers of individuals stable, increasing, or decreasing? Does the population have a mixture of adults and juveniles, indicating that recruitment of new individuals is occurring? What is the age at first breeding?

- *Behavior.* How do the actions of an individual allow it to survive in its environment? How do individuals in a population mate and produce offspring? In what ways do individuals of a species interact, cooperatively or competitively? At what time of day or year is the species most visible for monitoring?

- *Genetics.* How much variation occurs in morphological, physiological, and behavioral characteristics? How is the variation spread across the species range? How much of this variation is genetically controlled? What percentage of the genes is variable? How many alleles does the population have for each variable gene? Are there genetic adaptations to local sites?

- *Interactions with humans.* How do human activities affect the species? What human activities are harmful or beneficial to the species? Do people harvest or use this species in any way? What do local people know about this species?

Methods for Studying Populations

Methods for the study of populations have developed largely from the study of land plants and animals. Small organisms such as protists, bacteria, and fungi have not been investigated in comparable detail. Species that inhabit soil, freshwater, and marine habitats are particularly poorly investigated for population characteristics. In this section we will examine how conservation biologists undertake their studies of populations, recognizing that methods need to be modified for each species.

Gathering Ecological Information

The basic information needed for an effort to conserve a species or determine its status can be obtained from three major sources: published literature, unpublished literature, and fieldwork.

PUBLISHED LITERATURE   Other people may have studied the same rare species (or a related species) or investigated a habitat type. Library indices such as BIO-SIS and Biological Abstracts are often accessible by computer and provide easy access to a variety of books, articles, and reports relating to a particular topic. This literature may contain records of previous population sizes and distributions that can be compared with the current status of the species. Some sections of the library will have related material shelved together, so finding one book often leads to others. The World Wide Web on the Internet provides ever-increasing access to databases, Web sites, electronic bulletin boards, journals, news articles, specialized discussion groups, and subscription databases such as the ISI Web of Science and Science Direct. Google Scholar may be the best place to start for searches on topics relating to conservation biology. Information on the Internet needs to be examined carefully to determine the accuracy and source of the data, because there is no control over what is posted. Asking biologists and naturalists for ideas on references is another way to locate published materials. Searching indexes of newspapers, magazines, and popular journals is also an effective strategy because results of important scientific research often appear first in the popular news media and are sometimes more clearly summarized there than in the professional journals.

Once one key reference is obtained, the bibliography often can be used to discover useful earlier references. The Science Citation Index, available in many libraries (and online via the ISI Web of Science, a subscription database), is a valuable tool for tracing the literature forward in time; for example, many recent scientific papers on the penguin conservation can be located by looking at the current Science Citation Index for the name P. D. Boersma, who wrote important papers on penguin ecology and conservation in the 1990s. Any recent paper citing Boersma's work will appear following a search of her name.

UNPUBLISHED LITERATURE   An enormous amount of information on conservation biology is contained in unpublished reports by individual scientists, enthusiastic citizens, government agencies, and conservation organizations such as national and regional forest and park departments, government fisheries and wildlife agencies, NatureServe, The Nature Conservancy, the IUCN, and the World Wildlife Fund. This so-called gray literature is sometimes cited in published literature or mentioned by leading authorities in conversations, lectures, or articles. For example, the unpublished series of the FAO's Tropical Forestry Action Plans contains some of the most comprehensive sources of information on conservation in tropical countries. Often a report known through word of mouth can be obtained through direct contact with the author or from the Internet. Governmental and conservation organizations sometimes are able to supply additional reports not found in the published literature. People working at these agencies and organizations are sometimes willing to share a considerable amount of knowledge about species, conservation, and management efforts that is not contained in reports. (A list of environmental organizations and other information sources is found in the Appendix.)

FIELDWORK   The natural history of a species usually must be learned through careful observations in the field (Feinsinger 2001). Fieldwork is necessary because only a tiny percentage of the world's species have been adequately studied, and the ecology of a species often changes from one place to another. Only in the field can the conservation status of a species be determined, as well as its relationships to the biological and physical environment. Fieldwork for species such as polar bears, humpback whales, or bog orchids can be time-consuming, expensive, and physically arduous, but it is crucial for developing conservation plans for endangered species, and it can be exhilarating and deeply satisfying as well. There is a long tradition, particularly in Britain, of dedicated amateurs conducting excellent studies of species in their immediate surroundings with minimal equipment or financial support. While much natural history information can be obtained through careful observation, many of the technical methods for investigating populations are very specialized and are best learned by studying under the supervision of an expert or by reading manuals. For example, ornithologists deploy mist nets to catch birds and then attach numbered bands to their legs. An important, and frequently neglected, part of fieldwork involves explaining the purpose of the study to people living in the area and listening to what they have to say about the project. In many cases, local people have surprising insights and observations that they are willing and eager to share with scientists (Smart et al. 2005).

> The natural history of a species must be learned in the field. Biologists census populations, conduct demographic studies, and complete population viability analyses as part of developing suitable plans to preserve species and communities.

The need for fieldwork is highlighted by recent work on Magellanic penguins in breeding colonies in Argentina that helped to define the foraging area the birds use when feeding their chicks (Boersma 2008; Boersma and Rebstock 2009). It had previously been thought that the birds forage within only 30 km of their nests, but using radiotelemetry and satellite tags attached to the penguins, field researchers discovered that the birds swim up to 600 km from their nesting sites (**Figure 12.1**). During the critical period when penguins are feeding their chicks, they forage primarily in a seasonal fishing exclusion zone where food is probably more abundant and they have reduced chances of getting caught in fishing nets. Based on this information, the Argentinian government agreed to extend the number of months of fishing exclusion. The survival and growth of young penguins subsequently improved.

Monitoring Populations

To learn the status of a species of special concern, scientists must survey its population in the field and monitor it over time (**Figure 12.2**). Survey methods range from making a complete count of every individual, often called a census, to estimating population size using sampling methods or indexes. By repeatedly taking a survey of a population on a regular basis, one can determine changes in population size and distribution (Marsh and Trenham 2008; Mattfeldt et al. 2009). Long-term sur-

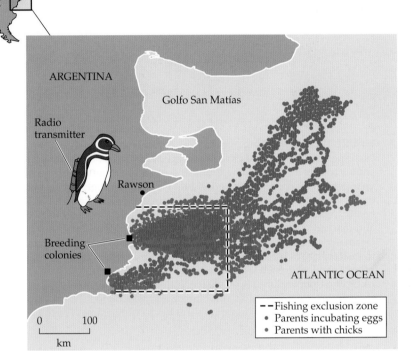

FIGURE 12.1 Satellite tracking of Magellanic penguins (*Spheniscus magellanicus*) off the coast of Argentina shows that penguins incubating eggs forage up to 600 km from their breeding colonies. When penguins are feeding chicks, foraging takes place mainly within a seasonal fishing exclusion zone that was established to protect spawning fish. Fieldwork provided this vital information about the penguins' foraging habits, which led to leaving the fishing zone closed until the chicks left their nests. (After Boersma et al. 2006.)

vey records can help to distinguish long-term population trends of increase or decrease (possibly caused by human disturbance) from short-term fluctuations caused by variations in weather or unpredictable natural events (Scholes et al. 2008). Survey records can also determine whether an endangered species is showing a positive response to conservation management or is responding negatively to present levels of harvest or the arrival of invasive species.

Observing a long-term decline in the species they study often motivates biologists to take vigorous action to conserve it (**Box 12.1**). Monitoring efforts can be targeted at particularly sensitive species, such as butterflies, using them as indicator species of the long-term stability of ecological communities (Wikström et al. 2008).

Monitoring has a long history in temperate countries, particularly in Britain, and it plays an important role in conservation biology. In North America, the Breeding Bird Survey has been recording bird abundance at approximately 1000 transects over the past 35 years. This information has been used to determine the stability of migrant songbird populations over time (Sauer et al. 2003). Some of the most elaborate projects involve establishing permanent research plots in tropical forests, such as the 50 ha site at Barro Colorado Island in Panama, to monitor changes in species and communities (Hardesty 2007). The Barro Colorado studies have shown that many tropical tree and bird species are more dynamic in numbers than had

(A)

(B)

(C)

FIGURE 12.2 Monitoring populations requires specialized techniques suited to each species. (A) Botanists monitor tagged lady's slipper orchid plants (*Cypripedium acaule*) for their changes in leaf size and number of flowers over a 10-year period. As shown here, individual leaves are monitored for their rates of carbon dioxide uptake, a measure of photosynthetic rate and an index of plant health. Note the numbered aluminum tag, anchored to the ground by a wire and marked with red flagging. (B) A radio transmitter is attached to a protected Hermann's tortoise (*Testudo hermanii*, subspecies *boettgeri*) in Romania to determine its range of movements in meadows. Researchers using portable radio receivers can locate each tagged animal. (The silver button is a data logger for recording temperature.) (C) Censusing the abundance and distribution of coral reef species using a quadrat and underwater writing tools. (A,B, photographs by Richard Primack; C, photograph © Tim Rock/Waterframe/Photolibrary.com.)

previously been suspected, suggesting that estimates of their minimum viable population sizes may need to be revised upward.

The number of monitoring studies has been increasing dramatically as government agencies and conservation agencies have become more concerned with protecting rare and endangered species. Some of these studies are mandated by law as part of management efforts. With some planning, monitoring can facilitate an estimate of the ability of a population to persist in the future, known as population viability analysis (PVA; discussed later in this chapter). The geographical range and intensity of monitoring has often been greatly extended through the use of volunteers (Danielson et al. 2009; Mueller et al. 2010). Training and educating citizens not only expands the data available to scientists but often transforms these citizens into advocates for conservation (Low et al. 2009). Examples of four programs that rely heavily on volunteers are the North American Amphibian Monitoring Program, Environment Canada, Project Nestwatch, and Frogwatch USA. Other programs target butterflies, birds, water quality, and endangered wildflowers. Journey North involves students in tracking the northward migration of birds and butterflies and other signs of spring (www.learner.org/jnorth).

Population monitoring often needs to be combined with monitoring of other parameters of the environment to understand the reasons behind population changes. The long-term monitoring of ecosystem processes (e.g., temperature, rainfall, humidity, soil acidity, water quality, discharge rates of streams, and soil erosion) and

BOX 12.1   *Three Primatologists Who Became Activists*

■ Human beings' closest living relatives are the great apes: chimpanzees, gorillas, and orangutans. Yet despite a fascination spanning centuries, most of what we know about them has been learned in the past 50 years. Much of the early foundation of our knowledge rests on the pioneering work of three primatologists: Jane Goodall, Dian Fossey, and Biruté Galdikas, sometimes called the "trimates." Their contributions are all the more valuable because they came at a time when prominent female scientists were a rare breed. These women pioneered the long-term study of their respective subjects, and all three eventually came to devote much of their time to conservation efforts rather than to the sole pursuit of scientific knowledge.

> Many researchers have started their careers by studying species and ecosystems in the field, and then have become involved in conservation activities.

The first of the trimates, Jane Goodall, began her study of chimpanzees in 1960 in Gombe National Park, Tanzania. Her fieldwork quickly paid off. Within three months, she had witnessed activities no researcher had ever seen, including chimpanzees eating meat that they had killed and extracting termites from nests, using plucked blades of grass. The latter finding caused a sensation: it was the first example of tool use in a primate other than humans (Morell 1993; Peterson 2006). Goodall's method of naming (rather than numbering) individual animals and focusing on each individual's unique characteristics in order to explain group dynamics was criticized by some primatologists, but in time it became the standard. By patiently following chimpanzee groups across generations, she gained new insights into their social structure. In her second decade of research, Goodall and her associates made more startling discoveries, including cannibalism within groups and elaborate, premeditated "warfare" between groups. Now completing its fifth decade, the work at Gombe is among the longest continuous field studies of animal behavior ever undertaken (Pusey et al. 2007).

The second trimate, Dian Fossey, studied mountain gorillas at Parc Nacional des Volcans in Rwanda, her research site and home from 1967 until her death 18 years later (Neinaber 2006). She was the first researcher to note females transferring between groups and to document males killing infant gorillas to bring females into estrus—two important keys to understanding gorilla social dynamics. Like Goodall at Gombe, Fossey developed her study site, Karisoke, into a major center for field research.

Biruté Galdikas, the youngest of the trimates, embarked on her pioneering work among orangutans in Borneo in 1971. Unlike chimps and gorillas, orangutans are largely solitary and arboreal, making them difficult to study. Nevertheless, over years of patient study, Galdikas uncovered basic information on the orangutan diet and documented the sometimes lengthy relationships between males and females, extended maternal care, and roving bands of juvenile males (Morell 1993).

The scientific success of the trimates rested in part on new study methods, which allowed these researchers to study the effects of individual differences on group social dynamics. These new methods included long-term, multi-year observations of the same individuals; the habituation of primate groups to the presence of humans; and an appreciation for the individuality of the animals being studied. Such methods, which led the researchers to develop empathy with the apes, ran counter to prevailing attitudes, which valued objectivity and emotional detachment as essential to "good science." For the work of the trimates, however, involvement with the study animals seemed less a barrier and more an aid to gaining scientific knowledge.

Empathy led the three researchers to fight for the conservation of the great ape species, all of which are endangered by poaching, habitat destruction, and human population growth. Jane Goodall was initially content to concentrate on research and leave direct conservation work to others. Eventually her attitude changed as a result of the direct threats to chimpanzees in and at her study site and elsewhere in Africa (Goodall 1999). Today Goodall devotes much of her time to conservation education, speaking out against habitat destruction, the illegal trade in chimpanzees, the hunting of chimpanzees for bushmeat, and the poor treatment of chimps in medical research.

Biruté Galdikas also became actively involved in conservation issues in Indonesian Borneo. The Orangutan Foundation International, which she directs, has established a rehabilitation center to take care of orangutans that have been displaced by forest clearing and to return them to the wild. (This approach has proved controversial, as it is uncertain whether these reintroduced animals are still surviving in the wild.) She was also instrumental in protecting her study site, now designated as the Tanjung Puting National Park (Galdikas 1995).

Dian Fossey did not have the luxury of gradually developing into a conservationist. Like many other field scien-

(*continued*)

BOX 12.1 (continued)

"Trimates" Dian Fossey (left), Jane Goodall (center), and Biruté Galdikas began by studying animal behavior but eventually devoted themselves to conservation activism. (Photograph courtesy of The Leakey Foundation.)

by local villagers to catch antelope, and farmers and their cattle were reducing and degrading the habitat both inside and outside the park. In the lack of official enforcement of park rules, Fossey began practicing "active conservation"—destroying poachers' snares, shooting cattle inside the park, and leading armed antipoaching patrols (Fossey 1990). Her murder in 1985 was probably motivated by revenge for these antipoaching activities, which included torturing and shooting poachers and kidnapping their children. Fossey's methods of personal and sometimes brutal law enforcement remain controversial, but some people see her efforts as essential, even heroic, steps in salvaging a gorilla population at the brink of extinction. Under such conditions, her supporters argued, detailed scientific study is beside the point. The well-known zoologist George Schaller believes Fossey had her priorities in order: "When you have any kind of rare species, the first priority is to work for its protection. Science is necessarily secondary" (Morell 1986).

The contributions of these three scientists are extensive. First, they have helped create an early body of knowledge on species that are our closest relatives. Second, they have made the international community aware of the desperate plight of these species, through magazine articles, television profiles, books, and movies. Third, they have taken prominent, active, and self-sacrificing stands on behalf of the apes. Fourth, their field sites have become tourist destinations and research centers that have brought needed income to poor areas and generated income for further research. Finally, they provide role models for young women, scientists, and students worldwide, inspiring them to enrich the scientific world with their own contributions.

tists, she saw her study subjects being slaughtered—in this case, trophy heads and hands of the extremely rare mountain gorillas were collected for sale to tourists, and adults were killed so that infants could be captured for European zoos. Gorillas were also killed accidentally by snares set

community characteristics (e.g., species present, percentage of vegetative cover, and amount of biomass present at each trophic level) allows scientists to determine the health of the ecosystem and the status of species of special concern. Monitoring these parameters allows managers to determine whether the goals of their projects are being achieved or whether adjustments must be made in the management plans (called adaptive management), as discussed in Chapter 17.

The most common types of monitoring conducted are censuses, surveys, and population demographic studies.

CENSUS A **census** is a count of the number of individuals present in a population. It is a comparitively inexpensive and straightforward method. By repeating a census over successive time intervals, biologists can determine whether a population is stable, increasing, or decreasing in number. In one example of a monitoring study, population censuses of the Hawaiian monk seal on the beaches of several islands in the Kure Atoll of the South Pacific documented a decline, from almost 100 adults in the 1950s to fewer than 14 in the late 1960s (**Figure 12.3**). The number of seal pups similarly declined during this period. On the basis of these trends, the Hawaiian monk

(A)

(B)

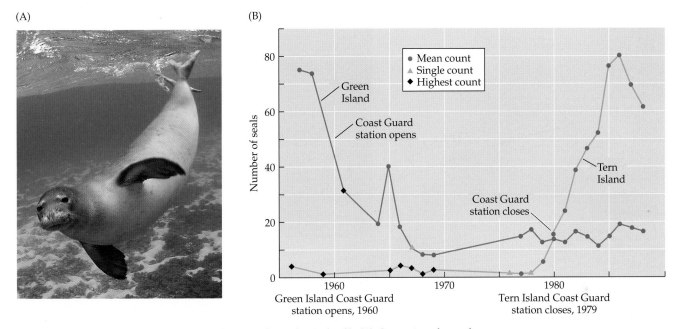

FIGURE 12.3 (A) A Hawaiian monk seal (*Monachus schauinslandi*). (B) Censusing the seal populations on Green Island, Kure Atoll (blue trace), and on Tern Island, French Frigate Shoals (green trace), revealed that this species was in danger of extinction. Population counts were plotted from a single count, the mean of several counts, or the maximum of several counts. Seal populations declined when a Coast Guard station was opened on Green Island in 1960 due to disturbance by people and dogs; populations increased on Tern Island after the closing of a Coast Guard station in 1979, and there was less disturbance to seals. (A, photograph by James D. Watt, courtesy of U.S. Department of the Interior; B, after Gerrodette and Gilmartin 1990.)

seal was declared endangered in 1976 under the U.S. Endangered Species Act (discussed in Chapter 20) (Baker and Thompson 2007). Conservation efforts were implemented that reversed the trend, but only for some populations. The Tern Island population showed a substantial recovery following the closing of a Coast Guard station in 1979, but it started to decline again in the 1990s because of high juvenile mortality (Baker and Johanos 2004).

Censuses of a community can be conducted to determine what species are currently present in a locality; a comparison of current occurrences with past censuses can highlight species that have been lost. Censuses conducted over a wide area can help to determine the range of a species and its areas of local abundance. Censuses taken over time can highlight changes in the ranges of species.

The most extensive censuses have been carried out in the British Isles by a large number of local amateur naturalists supervised by professional societies. The most detailed mapping efforts have involved recording the presence or absence of plants, lichens, and birds in a mosaic of 10 km squares covering the British Isles. The Biological Records Centre (BRC) at Monks Wood Experimental Station maintains and analyzes the 4.5 million distribution records, which contain information on 16,000 species. One part of these efforts involved the Botanical Society in the British Isles Monitoring Scheme, in which the British Isles were intensively surveyed from 1987 to 1988 by 1600 volunteers, who collected a million records of all plant species occurrences (Rich 2006). When the 1987–1988 data were compared with detailed censuses from 1930 to 1960, it was found that numerous species of grassland, heathland, aquatic, and swamp habitats had declined in frequency, while introduced weed species had increased (**Figure 12.4**).

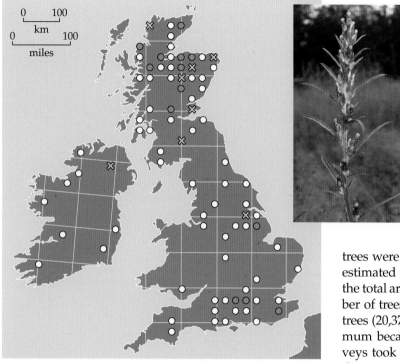

FIGURE 12.4 The British Isles Monitoring Scheme has documented the decline in the woodland cudweed (*Gnaphalium sylvaticum*), a perennial herb covered by silvery hairs. Large numbers of populations present from 1930 to 1960 were no longer present in the period from 1987 to 1988 (open circles), particularly in Ireland and England. Many populations in Scotland persisted during this interval (orange dots), and there were a few new populations (yellow crosses). (After Rich and Woodruff 1996; photograph © Bernd Haynold.)

SURVEYS A **survey** of a population involves using a repeatable sampling method to estimate the number of individuals or the density of a species in a part of a community. An area can be divided into sampling segments and the number of individuals in certain segments counted. These counts can then be used to estimate the actual population size. For example, the number of trees of the rare Florida torreya (*Torreya taxifolia*) was estimated in five separate ravine populations along the Apalachicola River of northern Florida and southern Georgia (Schwartz et al. 2000). A total of 365 trees were counted in the 1825 ha surveyed, leading to estimated tree density of 0.2 trees per hectare. Because the total area of ravines is 20,370 ha, the maximum number of trees in the whole region is estimated to be 4074 trees (20,370 ha × 0.2 trees/ha). This estimate is a maximum because the density of trees where the five surveys took place is probably higher than the density of the entire area. Similar methods can be used for different species in a variety of ecosystems; for instance, the number of crown-of-thorns starfish can be counted in a series of 10 m × 10 m quadrats (plots) to estimate the total starfish population on a coral reef. A survey might also count the number of bats caught in mist nets per hour or the density of a particular crustacean species per liter of seawater.

A variety of survey methods that includes observing animals, their footprints, and their scats; setting up automatic camera traps; and listening for animal calls is used to estimate population size and changes over time. A specialized type of survey, a mark–recapture survey, involves the capture, marking, release, and recapture of animals to estimate population size and individual movement (see Cowen et al. 2009 as an example). Surveys have expanded in recent years to include DNA analysis of scat and hair samples (Guschanski et al. 2009). In some cases, specially trained dogs are used to locate scat samples of rare animal species. Such DNA studies using dung have revealed that population size is often larger than previous estimates made using traditional survey methods, because some individuals have never been seen.

Survey methods are used when a population is very large or its range extensive. Although survey methods are time-consuming, they are a methodical and repeatable way to examine a population and determine whether it is changing in size. Such methods are particularly valuable when the species being studied has stages in its life cycle that are inconspicuous, tiny, or hidden, such as the seed and seedling stages of many plants or the larval stages of aquatic invertebrates. In the case of plants, the population may contain no adult individuals aboveground but still may be present because of viable seeds in the ground (Adams et al. 2005). Soil samples could be taken at fixed survey points and examined in the laboratory to determine the density of seeds, expressed as the number of seeds per cubic centimeter of soil. Disadvantages of survey methods are that they may be expensive (chartering a vessel to sample marine species), technically difficult (extracting seeds from the soil and identifying them), and inaccurate (missing or including infrequent aggregations of species). Conducting such surveys in the deep sea environment is particularly challenging.

DEMOGRAPHIC STUDIES **Demographic studies** follow known individuals of different ages and sizes in a population to determine their rates of growth, reproduction, and survival (Quintana-Ascencio et al. 2007). Either the whole population or a subsample can be followed. In a complete-population study, all individuals are counted, aged if possible, measured for size, sexed, and tagged or marked for future identification; their position on the site is mapped, and tissue samples sometimes are collected for genetic analysis. The techniques used to conduct a population study vary depending on the characteristics of the species and the purpose of the study. Each discipline has its own technique for following individuals over time; ornithologists band birds' legs, mammalogists often attach tags to animals' ears, and botanists nail aluminum tags to trees. Information from demographic studies can be used in standard mathematical formulae (life history formulae) to calculate the rate of population change and to identify critical stages in the life cycle (deRoos 2008).

An example of a specialized demographic study can be found in the work of researchers who use new techniques in bioacoustic recording to monitor populations of forest elephants, which are difficult to observe in their forest habitat. Bioacoustic recording allows researchers to track individual animals by tracking the characteristic sonograms of their display calls, which are outside the range of human hearing. This technique can be used to give a precise estimate of population size and to track animal movements, information critical for a conservation strategy (Joubert and Joubert 2008).

Demographic studies provide the most information of any monitoring method and, when analyzed thoroughly, suggest ways in which a site can be managed to ensure population persistence. The disadvantages of demographic studies are that they are often time-consuming, are expensive, require repeated visits, necessitate a knowledge of the species' life history, and can be quantitatively or statistically complex to analyze. Demographic data gathered over time can be used to predict whether the population will be present at different future dates and what the population size will be. If the population is predicted to go extinct, estimates can be made of the extent to which the survival and reproductive rates need to be increased through site management to maintain or enlarge the population.

Demographic studies can also provide information on the age structure of a population. A stable population typically has an age distribution with a characteristic ratio of juveniles, young adults, and older adults. The absence or low representation of any age class, particularly of juveniles, may indicate that the population is declining. Conversely, a large number of juveniles and young adults may indicate that the population is stable or even expanding. However, it is often difficult to determine the age of individuals for species such as plants, fungi, and colonial invertebrates. A small individual may be either young or slow-growing and old; a large individual may be either old or unusually fast-growing and young. For these species, the distribution of size classes is often taken as an approximate indicator of population stability, but this needs to be confirmed by following individuals over time to determine rates of growth and mortality. It is significant that for many long-lived species, such as trees, the establishment of new individuals in the population is an episodic event; there are many years of low reproduction and an occasional year with abundant reproduction. In such situations, careful analysis of long-term data is needed to determine population trends.

> Demographic studies provide data on the numbers, ages, sexes, conditions, and locations of individuals within a population. These data indicate whether a population is stable or declining and are the basis for statistical models used to predict a species' future.

Reproductive characteristics of populations—such as sex ratio, mating structure, percentage of breeding adults, number of offpsring, and monogamous or polygamous mating systems—will also affect the success of conservation strategies and should be thoroughly analyzed. For example, a strategy to increase genetic diversity in a highly inbred population such as the lions of Ngorongoro Crater (see Chapter 11) might include introducing individuals from outside this population to mate with the inbred animals. But if the "migrant" individuals do not fit into the social dynamics of the group, they may not breed and may even be driven out or killed by the native population.

Finally, demographic studies can supply clues to the maximum carrying capacity of the environment. These studies are important in determining how large a population the environment can support before it deteriorates and the population declines. Nature reserves may have abnormally large populations of certain species due to the recent loss of adjoining habitat or the inability of individuals to disperse from the nature reserve. Because of limited available space, many nature reserves are expected to support large populations over long periods of time. Data that help define the maximum carrying capacity of the reserves are crucial to preventing population and environmental stress, particularly in circumstances where natural population control mechanisms such as predators have been eliminated by humans.

MONITORING: SOME CASE STUDIES A few case studies provide an overview of how the various monitoring techniques have been used in the field.

- *Killer whales.* The killer whale (*Orcinus orca*) is an easily recognized top predator in marine systems. Observations of killer whales were compiled from a wide variety of sources to demonstrate that they only appeared in the Hudson Bay of northern Canada in the mid-1900s and have been increasing in abundance since that time. It is predicted that in coming years the killer whale will cause major shifts in the abundance of prey species such as seals and small whale species (**Figure 12.5**) (Higdon and Ferguson 2009).

- *Butterflies.* In Britain, butterfly censuses have been carried out on a grid of 2 km × 2 km squares covering Hertfordshire County (Thomas and Abery 1995). This amazingly detailed study documents a surprisingly high rate of

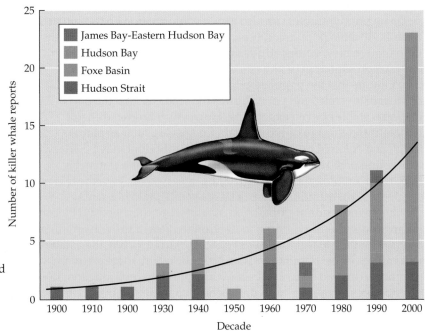

FIGURE 12.5 Number of killer whales sighted in the Hudson Bay region of eastern Canada has been increasing over the past 110 years, probably because of the reduction of winter sea ice. (From Higdon and Ferguson 2009).

local extinction—67% of the 2 km squares occupied by particular species before 1970 had no current population of that species.

- *Fish.* The distribution of fish in a marine protected area (MPA) in a South Africa lagoon was evaluated by attaching radio transmitters to 30 white stumpnose, a migratory fish. Tagged fish spent 50% of their time in the MPA even though it constituted only 4% of their total habitat (Kerwath et al. 2009).

Population Viability Analysis

Predictions of whether a species has the ability to persist in an environment can be made using **population viability analysis** (**PVA**), an extension of demographic analysis (Zabel et al. 2006). PVA can be thought of as risk assessment—using mathematical and statistical methods to predict the probability that a population or a species will go extinct at some point in the future. By looking at the range of a species' requirements and the resources available in its environment, one can identify the vulnerable stages in the natural history of the species. PVA can be useful in considering the effects of habitat loss, habitat fragmentation, and habitat deterioration on a rare species, such as the European bison (Beissinger et al. 2009; Naujokaitis-Lewis et al. 2009). An important part of PVA is estimating how management efforts such as reducing (or increasing) hunting or increasing (or decreasing) the area of protected habitat will affect the probability of extinction. PVA can model the effects of augmenting a population through the release of additional individuals caught in the wild elsewhere or raised in captivity (Kohlmann et al. 2005).

PVA begins by constructing a mathematical model of the population or species of concern, using data on average mortality rates, average recruitment rates, and the current age (or size) distribution of the population. The model can be readily constructed using a spreadsheet package, and it can be analyzed using the methods of matrix algebra. Because this initial model results in only one outcome—a population that is growing, declining, or stable—it is called a deterministic model. Environmental variability, as well as genetic and demographic variability, can then be added into the model by allowing model elements (such as the mortality rate) to vary at random within their observed ranges of annual values. Catastrophic events can be programmed to occur at random (**Figure 12.6**). Hundreds or thousands of simulations of individual populations can be run using this random vari-

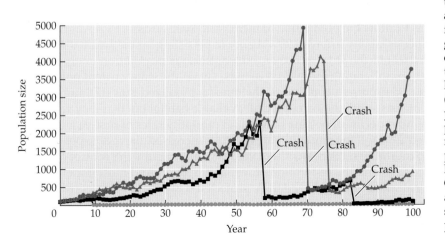

FIGURE 12.6 This PVA simulates the trajectory of four populations. Each population has an average growth rate of 5% per year, with fluctuations around this value due to demographic and environmental variation. In any one year, there is also a 2% chance of a catastrophe (or crash), in which 90% of the population dies. For example, one population (black squares) experienced catastrophes in years 55 and 82. After a catastrophe strikes, population size is often so small that environmental and demographic variations cause the population to go extinct. All four populations have experienced at least one catastrophe. One population (orange circles) went extinct after 10 years, and a second population (black squares) is on the verge of extinction after 100 years. (After Possingham et al. 2001.)

ation to determine the probability of population extinction within a certain period of time or the median time to extinction. Management regimes that affect population parameters can then be developed and analyzed (for example, a regime that increases adult survival by 10% and juvenile recruitment by 20%). Simulations of the impact of this management regime can be compared with the original population model to determine how it affects the probability that the population will persist in the future (Maschinski et al. 2006; Bakker and Doak 2009).

Existing computer simulation packages such as VORTEX and RAMAS can be used to run the models. Models can be tailored to include landscape information and a variety of independent environmental factors, such as addition of extra food, the frequency of storms, and removal of exotic competitors. The choice of models will depend on the goals of the analysis and the management options under consideration. A particularly useful feature of PVA—and of many models in general—is that the parameters of the model can be investigated using sensitivity analysis, a method that determines which parameter or combination of parameters most influences extinction probabilities. For example, sensitivity analysis might reveal that slight changes in adult mortality rates greatly affect the probability of extinction, whereas relatively large changes in juvenile mortality rates have minimal impact on the probability of extinction. Obviously, parameters that greatly influence the extinction rate should become the focus of conservation efforts, whereas parameters that have minimal effect on the extinction rate can be given less attention.

> PVA uses mathematical and statistical methods to predict the probability that a population or species will go extinct within a certain time period. PVA is also useful in modeling the effects of habitat degradation and management efforts.

Such statistical models must be used with caution and a large dose of common sense (Schultz and Hammond 2003). Generally, about 10 years of data are needed to obtain a PVA with good predictive power (McCarthy et al. 2003). The results of some models can often change dramatically with different model assumptions and slight changes in parameters. Another problem is that models are still not sophisticated enough to include all possible parameters and cannot incorporate unanticipated future events, such as unusual weather events or the arrival of an invasive species. PVA does have value in demonstrating the possible effectiveness of alternative management strategies (Pfab and Witkowski 2000; Traill et al. 2010). For this reason, attempts to utilize PVA as part of practical conservation efforts are increasingly common in mangement planning, as the following examples demonstrate. It will be valuable to revisit these studies in the future to determine whether their predictions were accurate.

- *The Hawaiian stilt.* The Hawaiian stilt (*Himantopus mexicanus knudseni*) is an endangered, endemic bird of the Hawaiian islands (see photo in Box 18.1). Hunting and coastal development 70 years ago reduced the number of birds to 200, but protection has allowed recovery to the present population size of about 1400 individuals (Reed et al. 2007). The goal of government protection efforts is to allow the population to increase to 2000 birds. A PVA was made of the species' ability to have a 95% chance of persisting for the next 100 years. Models treated the stilts as either one continuous population or six subpopulations inhabiting individual islands. Given the stilts' current positive growth under present conditions, the models predicted that stilt numbers would increase until they occupied all available habitat but that they would show a rapid decline if nesting failure and mortality rates of first-year birds exceeded 70% or if the mortality rate of adults increased above 30% per year. To keep mortality rates below these values would require the control of exotic predators and the restoration of wetland habitat. And most important, additional wetland would need to be protected if the goal of protecting 2000 stilts were to be achieved.

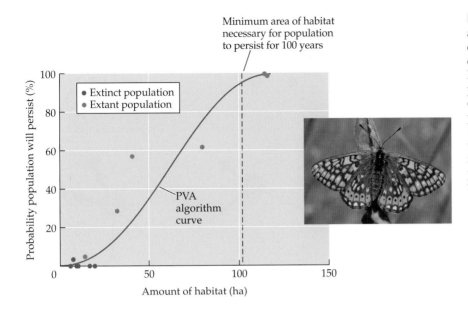

Minimum area of habitat
necessary for population
to persist for 100 years

- Extinct population
- Extant population

PVA
algorithm
curve

Probability population will persist (%)

Amount of habitat (ha)

FIGURE 12.7 Population viability analyses predict that it takes 100 ha to ensure (at 95% likelihood) the persistence of a marsh fritillary butterfly population for 100 years. All of the extinct populations occupied areas much smaller than 100 ha. Four of the six extant populations occupy areas smaller than 100 ha and are predicted to go extinct in the coming decade unless their habitat is increased. (After Bulman et al. 2007; photograph © Sergey Chushkin/ Shutterstock.)

- *Marsh fritillary butterfly.* The marsh fritillary butterfly (*Euphydryas aurinia*) is declining in abundance in the United Kingdom, where it occupies lightly grazed grasslands. The average area occupied by the six extant populations studied is larger than the average area formerly occupied by six extinct populations. A PVA showed that an area of at least 100 ha is necessary to ensure a 95% probability that a population will persist for 100 years (**Figure 12.7**). Only two of the extant populations encompass areas of this magnitude. The other four populations face a high probability of extinction unless the habitat is enlarged in area and managed to encourage the growth of food plants (Bulman et al. 2007).

- *Leadbeater's possum.* The most complete PVA ever undertaken is probably that of the Leadbeater's possum (*Gymnobelideus leadbeateri*), an endangered, arboreal marsupial inhabiting a rare type of eucalyptus forest in southeastern Australia (Lindenmayer 2000). Populations of this species are predicted to decline by more than 90% over the coming 20 to 30 years because of habitat destruction caused by logging. Population models have been developed for the spatial distribution of habitat patches and dispersal corridors, den requirements, and forest dynamics. These models are based on extensive field research, and they have been used to estimate the impact of different logging management plans on the persistence of populations and the extinction of the species. The analyses all point to the need to manage the species at a landscape scale and over the entire present range of the species.

These examples illustrate the application of PVA to management situations. To be convincing, PVA must begin with a clear understanding of the ecology of the species, the threats it faces, and its demographic characteristics. In addition, the limitations of the model should be well understood.

Metapopulations

Over time, populations of a species may become extinct on a local scale, while new populations may form nearby on other suitable sites. Often a species of ephemeral habitats, such as a streamside herb, is better characterized by a **metapopulation**

FIGURE 12.8 Possible metapopulation patterns, with the size of a population indicated by the size of the circle. The arrows indicate the direction and intensity of migration between populations. (After White 1996.)

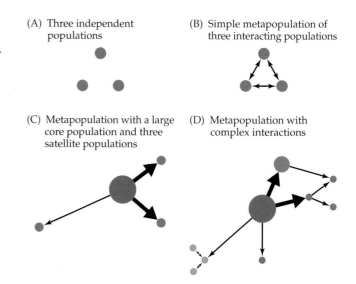

(A) Three independent populations

(B) Simple metapopulation of three interacting populations

(C) Metapopulation with a large core population and three satellite populations

(D) Metapopulation with complex interactions

(a "population of populations") that is made up of a shifting mosaic of populations linked by some degree of migration (Holt and Barfield 2010). In some species, every population in the metapopulation is short-lived, and the distribution of the species changes dramatically with each generation. In other species, the metapopulation may be characterized by one or more **source populations** (core populations) with fairly stable numbers and several **sink populations** (satellite populations) that fluctuate with arrivals of immigrants. Populations in the satellite areas may become extinct in unfavorable years, but the areas are recolonized, or rescued, by migrants from the more permanent core population when conditions become more favorable (**Figure 12.8**). Metapopulations might also involve relatively permanent populations that individuals occasionally move between. Metapopulation structures have a further complexity in migratory species in which there are separate summer breeding grounds and overwintering areas, which may or may not be shared among populations. Metapopulations also lend themselves to modeling efforts, and various programs have been developed for simulating them (Donovan and Welden 2002). In one approach, metapopulation dynamics can be simulated by using PVA combined with spatial information on multiple populations.

The target of a population study is typically one or several populations, but a metapopulation study may produce a more accurate portrayal of the species. Metapopulation studies recognize that local populations are dynamic; that is, the locations of populations change over time, and individuals can move between populations and colonize new sites. Sites within the range of the species may be occupied only because they are repeatedly colonized after local extinction occurs; a reduction in migration rates between sites, perhaps caused by intervening roads and farms, would gradually result in the permanent extinction of local populations across the range of the metapopulation. Such models are particularly effective at describing bird populations in fragmented landscapes. Metapopulation models recognize that infrequent colonization events in occupied sites and disperal of individuals between existing populations occur, which allows biologists to consider the impact of founder effects, genetic drift, and gene flow on the species. Even infrequent movement of individuals between populations can restore much of the lost genetic variation, in effect genetically "rescuing" a small population otherwise headed toward extinction. The following two examples demonstrate how evaluating species on the metapop-

> Populations of a species are often connected by dispersal, and can be considered as a metapopulation. In such a system, the loss of one population can negatively affect other populations.

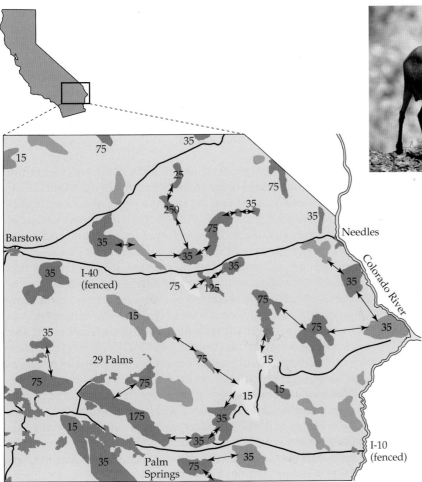

FIGURE 12.9 Mountain sheep (*Ovis canadensis*) in the southeastern California desert are an example of a metapopulation. The species has permanently occupied the mountain ranges shown in red, with populations of the sizes indicated. Mountain ranges shown in orange do not currently have permanent mountain sheep populations, though they may have been occupied in the past. The species has been reintroduced into the mountain ranges shown in purple; yellow indicates areas where natural recolonization has occurred in the past 15 years. Arrows indicate observed sheep migrations. Human settlements, major highways, and canals—all of which are barriers to the animals' movement—are shown in black or green. (After Epps et al. 2007; photograph courtesy of Ryan Hagerty/U.S. Fish and Wildlife Service.)

ulation level has proved to be more useful in understanding and managing many species than evaluating them on the single-population level.

- *California mountain sheep.* Mountain sheep (*Ovis canadensis*) in the desert of southeastern California offer a well-studied example of metapopulation dynamics, exhibiting the shifting mosaic of populations that defines a metapopulation. These sheep have been observed dispersing between mountain ranges and occupying previously unpopulated sites, while mountains that previously had sheep populations are now unoccupied (**Figure 12.9**). Migration and gene flow occurs primarily between populations less than 15 km apart and is greater when the intervening countryside is more hilly (Epps et al. 2005, 2007). Human-made barriers such as highways, irrigation canals, and urban areas almost completely eliminate movement between populations. Maintaining dispersal routes between existing population areas and potentially suitable sites is important in managing this species.

- *Furbish's lousewort.* The endemic Furbish's lousewort (*Pedicularis furbishiae*) occurs along the St. John's River in northern Maine and New Brunswick in a 200 km stretch that is subject to periodic flooding (**Figure 12.10**) (Schwartz 2003). Flooding often destroys some existing populations of this herb species but also creates exposed riverbank conditions suitable for establishing new

FIGURE 12.10 The rare Furbish's lousewort occurs as a series of temporary populations that are best protected as a metapopulation. (Courtesy of the U.S. Fish and Wildlife Service.)

populations. These populations eventually decline as the growth of shrubs and trees shade out the lousewort plants. Studies of any single population would give an incomplete picture of the species because the current populations are short-lived. Dispersal of seeds from existing populations to newly exposed soil suitable for colonization is a feature of the species. The metapopulation is really the appropriate unit of study for this species, and the watershed is the appropriate unit of management.

In a metapopulation, destruction of the habitat of one central, core population might result in the extinction of numerous smaller populations that depend on the core population for periodic colonization (Gutiérrez 2005). Also, human disturbances that inhibit migration, such as fences, power lines, roads, and dams, might reduce the rate of migration among habitat patches and so reduce the probability of recolonization after local extinction. Habitat fragmentation resulting from these and other human activities sometimes has the effect of changing a large, continuous population into a metapopulation in which small, temporary populations occupy habitat fragments. When population size within each fragment is small and the rate of migration among fragments is low, populations within each fragment will gradually go extinct and recolonization will not occur.

Metapopulation models highlight the dynamic nature of population processes and show how eliminating a few core populations or reducing the potential for migration could lead to the local extinction of a species over a much wider area. This actually occurred with the California checkerspot butterfly (*Euphydryas* sp.): A large core population went extinct after an unmanaged grassland habitat underwent succession, followed soon after by the extinction of the satellite populations. Maintaining the butterfly would have required managing the site using periodic controlled fires or cattle grazing to keep the area in grassland. Effective management of a species often requires an understanding of these metapopulation dynamics and a restoration of lost habitat and dispersal routes.

Long-Term Monitoring of Species and Ecosystems

Monitoring of populations needs to be combined with monitoring of other parameters of the environment. The long-term monitoring of ecosystem processes (e.g., temperature, rainfall, humidity, soil acidity, water quality, discharge rates of streams, and soil erosion) and community characteristics (species present, percentage of vegetative cover, amount of biomass present at each trophic level, etc.) allows scientists to determine the health of the ecosystem and the status of species of special concern (Sagarin and Pouchard 2009; Papworth et al. 2009). The Long-Term Ecological Research program in the United States focuses on such changes that occur on timescales ranging from months and years to decades and centuries (**Figure 12.11**) (Hobbie et al. 2003).

For example, many amphibian, insect, and annual plant populations are highly variable from year to year, so many years of data are required to determine whether a particular species is actually declining in abundance over time or merely experiencing a number of low population years that are in accord with its regular pattern

	Years	Research scales	Physical events	Biological phenomena
10^5	100 Millennia			Evolution of species
10^4	10 Millennia	Paleoecology and limnology	Continental glaciation	Bog succession Forest community migration
10^3	Millennium		Climate change	Species invasion Forest succession
10^2	Century		Forest fires CO_2-induced climate warming	Cultural eutrophication Population cycles
10^1	Decade		Sun spot cycle El Niño events Prairie fires Lake turnover Ocean upwelling	Prairie succession Annual plants Seasonal migration Plankton succession
10^0	Year			
10^{-1}	Month			
10^{-2}	Day	Most ecology	Storms Daily light cycle Tides	Algal blooms Daily movements
10^{-3}	Hour			

LTER { (bracketing rows 10^2 Century through 10^{-1} Month)

FIGURE 12.11 The Long-Term Ecological Research (LTER) program focuses on timescales ranging from years to centuries in order to understand changes in the structure, function, and processes of ecosystems that are not apparent from short-term observations. (From Magnuson 1990.)

of variation. In one instance, a salamander species' low population numbers (based on several years of low breeding numbers) initially made it appear to be very rare. But in a subsequent favorable year for breeding, its population numbers turned out to be surprisingly large (Pechmann 2003). In another instance, 40 years of observation of populations of two flamingo species (*Phoenicopterus ruber*, the greater flamingo, and *Phoeniconaias minor*, the lesser flamingo) in southern Africa revealed that large numbers of chicks fledged only in years with high rainfall (**Figure 12.12**). However, the number of chicks fledging in the current populations is much lower than in the past, indicating that the species may be heading toward local extinction.

The fact that environmental effects may lag for many years behind their initial causes creates a challenge to understanding change in ecosystems. For example, acid rain, nitrogen deposition, and other components of air pollution may gradually change the water chemistry, algal community, and oxygen content of forest streams, ultimately making the aquatic environment unsuitable for the larvae of certain rare insect species. In this case, the cause (air pollution) may have occurred decades before the effect (insect decline) is detectable. Even habitat fragmentation can have delayed effects on losses via gradual environmental degradation and metapopulation extinction.

> Long-term monitoring of populations and ecosystems is important as these may be changing slowly over time.

A major purpose of monitoring programs is to gather essential data on ecosystem functions and biological communities that can be used to monitor changes in natural communities. Monitoring in these studies allows managers to determine whether the goals of their projects are being achieved or whether adjustments must be made in the management plans. Increasingly, monitoring of biological diversity is being combined with the monitoring of social and economic characteristics of the same area—tracking, for example, people's annual income, adequacy of diet, education level, and amount and value of plant and animal materials people obtain from nearby ecosystems—in recognition of the linkages between people and conservation. People who live in the local area often join the monitoring program because they know the area well and have the greatest interest in ensuring that

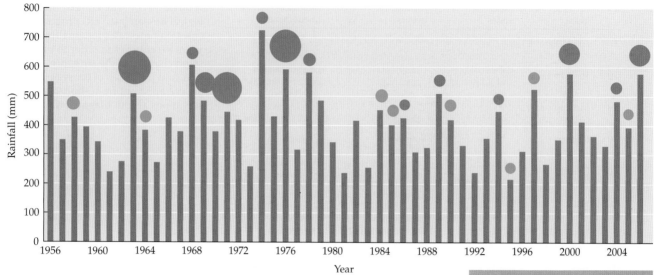

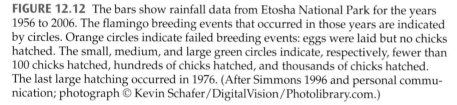

FIGURE 12.12 The bars show rainfall data from Etosha National Park for the years 1956 to 2006. The flamingo breeding events that occurred in those years are indicated by circles. Orange circles indicate failed breeding events: eggs were laid but no chicks hatched. The small, medium, and large green circles indicate, respectively, fewer than 100 chicks hatched, hundreds of chicks hatched, and thousands of chicks hatched. The last large hatching occurred in 1976. (After Simmons 1996 and personal communication; photograph © Kevin Schafer/DigitalVision/Photolibrary.com.)

the area is well managed (Low et al. 2009). Long-term monitoring provides an early-warning system for disruption or decline of ecosystem functions and the social systems of humans that depend on them. Magnuson (1990) expressed the need for long-term monitoring as follows:

> In the absence of the temporal context provided by long-term research, serious misjudgments can occur not only in our attempts to understand and predict change in the world around us, but also in our attempts to manage our environment. Although serious accidents in an instant of mismanagement can be envisioned that might cause the end of Spaceship Earth destruction is even more likely to occur at a ponderous pace in the secrecy of the invisible present.

Summary

1. Protecting and managing a rare or endangered species requires a firm grasp of its ecology and its distinctive characteristics, sometimes called its natural history. This essential knowledge covers the species' environment, distribution, biotic interactions, morphology, physiology, demography, behavior, genetics, and interactions

with people. This information can be obtained from the published and unpublished literature or from fieldwork. Long-term monitoring of a species in the field, using censuses, surveys, and demographic studies, can reveal temporal changes in population size and help to distinguish short-term fluctuations from long-term decline.

2. Population viability analysis (PVA) uses demographic, genetic, environmental, and natural-catastrophe data to estimate the probability of a population's persisting in an environment to some future date. PVA can also be used to predict the effects on population persistence of various management actions.

3. Many species that reside in ephemeral habitats are characterized by metapopulations made up of shifting mosaics of temporary populations that are linked by some degree of migration. In other species, a metapopulation may be characterized by one or more core populations with relatively stable numbers, linked by dispersal to satellite areas with unstable, temporary populations.

4. Long-term monitoring efforts provide an early warning system for threats to species, communities, ecosystem functions, and human communities.

For Discussion

1. Read the paper on the Arizona cliffrose by Maschinski et al. (2006), the paper on the South African plant by Pfab and Witkowski (2000), or another PVA study. What are the strengths and weaknesses of PVA?

2. Construct models of various metapopulations, using Figure 12.8 as a starting point. The simplest model would be an infinitely large core population that continuously sends out colonists to a satellite population, which is regularly destroyed by a catastrophic event such as a hurricane. Then include random variation in the frequency of hurricanes (destroying the population on average once every 4 years) and rate of colonization (sending out colonists on average once every 4 years). How realistic are your models? What do you assume?

3. (A) Construct your own PVA of an endangered toad species. This species formerly occupied many large islands but now occupies only one small, isolated island in the middle of the Atlantic Ocean. There are presently 10 toads on the island, and the island can support a maximum of 20 toads. In the spring, males and females form mating pairs, and each pair can produce zero, one, two, three, four, or five offspring, all of which survive and reach maturity the following year (for example, flip five coins for each mated pair; the number of heads is the number of offspring). Individuals not mated because of uneven sex ratios do not breed. After the breeding season, the adult toads die. The sex of the offspring is assigned at random (for example, flip a coin for each animal, with heads for males and tails for females, or use a random-number generator or simulation software such as VORTEX or RAMAS).

(B) Run ten population simulations of the island toad species for ten generations each, and chart population size over time. What percentage of populations go extinct? Try making the conditions more severe by lowering the island's carrying capacity to 15 (or even 10) or by imposing a 50% mortality on offspring every third year due to an introduced rat. Examine the impact of supplying extra food to the toads, which would allow more offspring to be produced per breeding pair. Make different variants of this basic model, corresponding to different ecological, genetic, and life history constraints. Use a computer program if possible.

Suggested Readings

Boersma, P. D. 2008. Penguins as marine sentinels. *BioScience* 58: 597–607. Penguins now have to swim farther because fish are being intensely harvested.

Bulman, C. R. and 6 others. 2007. Minimum viable metapopulation size, extinction debt, and the conservation of a declining species. *Ecological Applications* 17: 1460–1473. Metapopulation modeling can help identify areas most in need of conservation.

Feinsinger, P. 2001. *Designing Field Studies for Biodiversity Conservation.* Island Press, Washington, D.C. A guide to establishing a field research program.

Goodall, J. 1999. *Reason for Hope: A Spiritual Journey.* Warner Books, New York. This amazing woman explains her dedication to chimpanzees and people.

Guschanski, K., L. Vigilant, A. McNeilage, M. Gray, E. Kagoda, and M. M. Robbins. 2009. Counting elusive animals: Comparing field and genetic census of the entire mountain gorilla population of Bwindi Impenetrable National Park, Uganda. *Biological Conservation* 142: 290–300. Genetic techniques are providing new opportunities for censusing populations.

Higdon, J. W. and S. H. Ferguson. 2009. Loss of Arctic sea ice causing punctuated change in sightings of killer whales (*Orcinus orca*) over the past century. *Ecological Applications* 19: 1365–1375. Creative use of past observations to document the changing range of a species.

Holt, R. D. and M. Barfield. 2010. Metapopulation perspectives on the evolution of species' niches. In S. Cantrell, C. Cosner, and S. Ruan (eds.), *Spatial Ecology*, pp. 189–212. Chapman and Hall, Boca Raton, FL. Spatial features are essential for understanding species and their conservation.

Low, B., S. R. Sundaresan, I. R. Fischhoff, and D. I. Rubenstein. 2009. Partnering with local communities to identify conservation priorities for endangered Grevy's zebra. *Biological Conservation* 142: 1548–1555. Involving citizens in monitoring programs can both generate useful data and improve local attitudes about conservation.

Marsh, D. M. and P. C. Trenham. 2008. Current trends in plant and animal population monitoring. *Conservation Biology* 22: 647–655. Monitoring programs must have good agreement between their design and their objectives.

Maschinski, J., J. E. Baggs, P. F. Quintana-Ascencio, and E. S. Menges. 2006. Using population viability analysis to predict the effects of climate change on the extinction risk of an endangered limestone endemic shrub, Arizona cliffrose. *Conservation Biology* 20: 218–228. Models indicate that management efforts are required to prevent extinction of this species.

Mueller, J. G., I. H. B. Assanou, I. D. Guimbo, and A. M. Almedom. 2010. Evaluating rapid participatory rural appraisal as an assessment of ethnoecological knowledge and local biodiversity patterns. *Conservation Biology* 24: 140–150. Local people were able to contribute to monitoring efforts by providing accurate information on vegetation characteristics.

Papworth, S. K., J. Rist, L. Coad, and E. J. Milner-Gulland. 2009. Evidence for shifting baseline syndrome in conservation. *Conservation Letters* 2: 93–100. People often forget what biodiversity was like in the past.

Pfab, M. F. and E. T. F. Witkowski. 2000. A simple population viability analysis of the critically endangered *Euphorbia clivicola* R. A. Dyer under four management scenarios. *Biological Conservation* 96: 263–270. An example of PVA that is easy to understand.

Pusey, A. E., L. Pintea, M. L. Wilson, S. Kamenya, and J. Goodall. 2007. The contribution of long-term research at Gombe National Park to chimpanzee conservation. *Conservation Biology* 21: 623–634. Long-term research provides valuable conservation insights.

Scholes, R. J. and 8 others. 2008. Toward a global biodiversity observing system. *Science* 321: 1044–1045. The Group on Earth Observations Biodiversity Observation Network (GEO BON) proposes a new global tool for biodiversity monitoring.

Traill, L. W., B. W. Brook, R. R. Frankham, and C. J. A. Bradshaw. 2010. Pragmatic population viability targets in a rapidly changing world. *Biological Conservation* 143: 28–34. PVA studies often indicate that managers may need to protect thousands of individuals.

Zabel, R. W., M. D. Scheuerell, M. M. McClure, and J. G. Williams. 2006. The interplay between climate variability and density dependence in the population viability of Chinook salmon. *Conservation Biology* 20: 190–200. Many interacting factors determine the persistence of salmon in a changing world.

Establishing New Populations

In Chapters 11 and 12 we discussed the problems conservation biologists face in preserving naturally occurring populations of endangered species. This chapter discusses some exciting conservation methods to address those problems. These methods include establishing new wild and semiwild populations of rare and endangered species and increasing the size of existing populations. These approaches allow species that have persisted only in captivity or in small, isolated populations to regain their ecological and evolutionary roles within the biological community.

Many species benefit from the complementary approaches of establishing new populations in the wild and developing captive breeding programs. Widely dispersed populations in the wild may be less likely to be destroyed by catastrophes (such as earthquakes, hurricanes, disease, epidemics, or war) than captive populations confined to a single facility or isolated wild populations occupying only small areas. Furthermore, increasing the number and size of populations for a species will generally reduce its probability of extinction.

Establishment programs are unlikely to be effective, however, unless the factors leading to the decline of the original wild populations are clearly understood and eliminated, or at least controlled (Houston et al. 2007). For example, the peregrine falcon declined throughout its range due to the harmful effects of DDT. In order to establish new populations, DDT first had to be banned. Starting with birds raised in captivity, peregrine falcon populations are now recovering across North America, with notable increases in cities. For the endangered California condor, one of the main problems was the lead shot used by hunters. When condors ate dead animals shot by hunters, the condors suffered and even died from lead poisoning. In California, hunters now must use other types of ammunition when hunting, a key element in establishing new condor populations from captive-raised individuals.

Chapter 13

Three Approaches to Establishing New Populations

Three basic approaches have been used to establish new populations of animals and plants, many of which are coordinated by the IUCN Re-introduction Specialist Group (www.iucnsscrsg.org). All involve the relocation of existing individuals.

A **reintroduction program*** involves releasing captive-bred or wild-collected individuals into an ecologically suitable site within their historical range where the species no longer occurs. The principal objective of a reintroduction program is to create a new population in its original environment. For example, a program initiated in 1995 to reintroduce gray wolves into Yellowstone National Park aims to restore the equilibrium of predators and herbivores that existed prior to intervention in the region by American wildlife managers (**Box 13.1**). Frequently, individuals are released near the site where they or their ancestors were collected, to ensure genetic adaptation to their environment. Wild-collected individuals are also sometimes caught and later released elsewhere within the range of the species when a new protected area has been established, when an existing population is under a new threat and will no longer be able to survive in its present location, or when natural or artificial barriers to the normal dispersal tendencies of the species exist.

> Establishing new populations of endangered species can benefit the species itself, other species, and the ecosystem. Such programs must identify and attempt to eliminate the factors that led to the original population's decline.

A **restocking program** involves releasing individuals into an existing population to increase its size and gene pool. These released individuals may be raised in captivity or may be wild individuals collected elsewhere.

An **introduction program** involves moving captive-bred or wild-collected animals or plants to areas suitable for the species outside their historical range. This approach may be appropriate when the environment within the known range of a species has deteriorated to the point where the species can no longer survive there, or when reintroduction is impossible because the factor causing the original decline is still present. In the near future, introductions may be necessary for many species if those species can no longer survive within their current ranges because of a changing climate, especially warming temperatures as described in Chapter 9.

The introduction of a species to new sites needs to be carefully considered and evaluated in order to ensure that the species does not damage its new ecosystem or harm populations of any local endangered species (Ricciardi and Simberloff 2009). Care must be taken that released individuals have not acquired any diseases while in captivity that could spread to and decimate wild populations. For example, cap-

---

*Unfortunately, some confusion exists about the terms denoting the establishment of populations. Reintroduction programs sometimes are called "reestablishments" or "restorations." Another term, "translocation," usually refers to moving individuals from a location where they are about to be destroyed to another site that, hopefully, provides a greater degree of protection. Restocking programs are sometimes called "augmentations."

BOX 13.1 *Wolves Return to a Cold Welcome*

■ To the general public, *conservation* usually means saving endangered animal species on the verge of extinction—such as the California condor, with only about 130 wild individuals, or the giant panda, estimated at only 1600 in number. Although it is critical to try to prevent species extinctions, the ultimate goal of conservation is to restore damaged ecosystems to their previous balanced, functional state. Sometimes that involves reintroducing species into ecosystems—species that are abundant elsewhere and do not otherwise need reintroduction to protect them. An example of such a situation is the reintroduction of gray wolves into Yellowstone.

> The reintroduction of a keystone predator can have major impacts on lower trophic levels and can transform the structure of entire ecosystems.

Until 1995, Yellowstone National Park was an ecosystem out of balance, largely because of the systematic extermination of the gray wolf (*Canis lupus*) populations there 100 years ago. Wolves were believed to pose a threat to the herds of elk and other game animals inhabiting the park. The result of their extirpation was a burgeoning population of elk and other herbivores that damaged vegetation and starved during times of scarcity. From a biological perspective, reintroducing wolves was necessary to restore ecological balance in the Yellowstone area through their effects on populations of other wildlife.

When the U.S. Fish and Wildlife Service proposed in 1987 that the gray wolf be reintroduced into Yellowstone National Park and surrounding government lands known as the Greater Yellowstone Area (GYA), opposition erupted immediately. Ranchers in Montana, Wyoming, and Idaho argued that wolves would destroy livestock and possibly endanger humans as well (Smith et al. 2003). Hunters objected that wolves would reduce the supply of game animals, and logging and mining companies were concerned that the presence of a protected species would limit their ability to utilize resources on federal lands. Underpinning all these objections was the argument that the wolf, with an estimated population of 50,000 in Canada alone, is in no immediate danger of extinction. To accommodate these concerns, it was agreed that any wolf population at Yellowstone would be designated "experimental, nonessential," giving the wolves some degree of protection but allowing more flexible management to deal with wolves that left the park and attacked livestock.

In 1995 and 1996, elements of five wolf packs, as well as a few individuals, were transferred from Canada to the area (Berger 2007). The wolves were held in large pens for 10 weeks (to break their homing tendency) and then released. The wolves adapted well to the park, hunting prey and producing numerous pups. As of 2009, a total of 390 free-ranging wolves had formed 33 packs that resided within the GYA (Vonholdt et al. 2008), and over 1600 wolves inhabited the larger region (see figure).

The wolves' activities are reshaping the ecological structure of the park (Barber-Meyer et al. 2008; Hamlin et al. 2008). Elk are congregating in larger herds, and wolves are interacting with grizzly bears and coyotes. The availability of carrion from wolf kills is affecting the dynamics of scavengers, from grizzlies to carrion beetles. Some tree species are already recovering, forming dense stands of saplings, because of reduced grazing pressure. Now one of the major attractions of Yellowstone National Park, wolves are having a positive economic impact as the featured subject of books and souvenirs sold to park visitors. The ecology and impact of wolves on the ecosystem have proved to be worthy of intensive study, with the participation of numerous scientists and student volunteers.

Each year, wolves do kill some 400 cattle, sheep, and other domestic animals in this region of the northern Rockies. While not insignificant, these wolf kills constitute a small number compared with the 400,000 cattle alone living in the area. The number is also small in comparison with the millions of dollars invested in the project, its great ecological value to the Yellowstone area, and the tens of thousands of people who have visited the park or been exposed to the story of the Yellowstone wolves. In addition, an organization called Defenders of Wildlife has assumed responsibility for compensating ranchers for verified wolf kills, paying out over $1 million since 2000 (www.defenders.org), but ranchers' reactions remain mixed. Wolves that attacked livestock on private land had previously been released onto government lands far away, but now they are killed by park officials because there is no remaining land without wolves on which to release them (Baker et al. 2008; Harper et al. 2008). As the wolf population grows, so will the potential for depredations beyond park boundaries and for further conflict with ranchers; increasing numbers of wolves are killed by humans when they roam outside the park.

(continued)

BOX 13.1 *(continued)*

Already the Yellowstone wolf project has demonstrated that wolves can be reintroduced and the original ecosystem dynamics can be shifted back toward their original balance. In recognition of the success of this project, the wolf was removed from endangered species protection in Montana and Idaho, meaning that private citizens can kill wolves

that are chasing and attacking domestic animals (Bergstrom et al. 2009). In the end, the success or failure of this project may rest on finding a compromise that moves ranchers and other private landowners from opposing the project to supporting it.

(A)

(A) A gray wolf (*Canis lupus*) in Yellowstone Park wears a radio transmitter collar that allows researchers to follow its movements. (B) The number of wolves in Wyoming, Idaho, and Montana increased following the reintroduction of wolves to the Yellowstone area in 1995. There has also been an increase in the number of domestic animals, primarily sheep, killed by wolves and an increase in the number of problem wolves killed by government authorities. (A, photograph courtesy of William Campbell/U.S. Fish and Wildlife Service; B, after Musiani et al. 2003, with updates courtesy of M. Musiani and from Clark and Johnson 2009.)

(B)

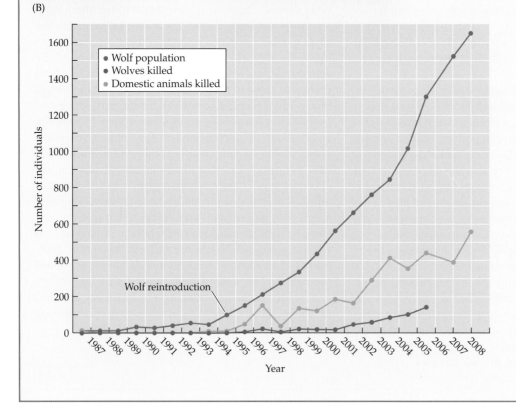

Legend:
- Wolf population
- Wolves killed
- Domestic animals killed

(x-axis: Year, 1987–2008; y-axis: Number of individuals; "Wolf reintroduction" labeled at 1994)

(A)

(B)

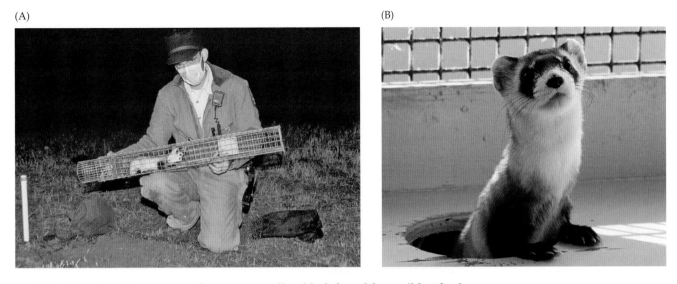

FIGURE 13.1 (A) Within a protected range, cages allow black-footed ferrets (*Mustela nigrepes*) to experience the environment into which they will eventually be released. The ferrets' caretaker is wearing a mask to reduce the chance of exposing the animals to human diseases. (B) A black-footed ferret raised at the captive colony in Colorado. (A, photograph by M. R. Matchett, courtesy of U.S. Fish and Wildlife Service; B, photograph by Ryan Hagerty/U.S. Fish and Wildlife Service.)

tive, endangered black-footed ferrets must be carefully handled and quarantined so they do not acquire diseases from people and dogs that they might transfer into wild populations upon their release in North American grasslands (**Figure 13.1**). Also, a species may adapt genetically to the new environment where it is being released such that the original gene pool is not actually being preserved.

New populations can be established using different approaches and experimental treatments that seek to help individuals make successful transitions to their new homes—for example, giving supplemental food and water to animals for a while as they learn about their new homes, or planting individual plants into habitats from which competing plants have been removed. By careful monitoring of a variety of approaches, existing management techniques can be evaluated and new techniques developed (Goossens et al. 2005). These management techniques can then be applied to better manage existing natural populations of the species.

One special method used in establishing new populations and restocking is "head-starting," an approach in which animals are raised in captivity during their vulnerable young stages and then are released into the wild. The release of sea turtle hatchlings produced from eggs collected from the wild and raised in nearby hatcheries is an example of this approach.

Successful Programs with Animals

Establishing new populations is often expensive and difficult because it requires a serious, long-term commitment. The programs to capture, raise, monitor, and release California condors, peregrine falcons, and black-footed ferrets, for example, have cost millions of dollars and have required years of work. When the animals involved are long-lived, the program may have to continue for many years before its outcome is known (Grenier et al. 2007).

Reintroduction programs can become highly emotional public issues, as demonstrated by the programs for the California condor, the black-footed ferret, the grizzly bear, and the gray wolf in the United States and comparable programs in Europe. Programs are often criticized on many different fronts. They may be attacked as a waste of money ("Millions of dollars for a few ugly birds!"), unnecessary ("Why do we need wolves here when there are so many elsewhere?"), intrusive ("We just want to go about our lives without the government telling us what to do!"), poorly run ("Look at all the ferrets that died of disease in captivity!"), or unethical ("Why can't the last animals just be allowed to live out their lives in peace without being captured and put into zoos?").

Because of the conflicts and high emotions, it is crucial that establishment programs include local people so that (ideally) the community has a stake in a program's success. (Indeed, this is true of any conservation project.) At a minimum, it is necessary to explain the need for the program and its goals, to convince local people to support it—or at least not to oppose it. In many cases, such programs have considerable educational value (Ausband and Foresman 2007). Programs are often more successful if they provide incentives to affected people rather than impose rigid restrictions and laws. For example, direct payments are made to Wyoming residents whose farms and domestic animals are injured by reintroduced wolves, and the few wolves that repeatedly attack livestock are either killed or moved in order to retain local support for the program (Haney et al. 2007; Nyhus et al. 2003).

Successful reintroduction programs often have considerable educational value. In Brazil, conservation and reintroduction efforts to protect golden lion tamarins have become a rallying point for the protection of the last remaining fragments of the Atlantic forest. In the Middle East and northern Africa, captive-bred Arabian oryx have been successfully reintroduced into many desert areas that they formerly occupied, providing signficant public attention, a source of national pride, and opportunities for employment.

There is an important genetic component in selecting plants or animals for reintroduction programs. Captive populations may have lost much of their genetic variability. Genetic adaptations to the benign captive environment may occur in populations that have been raised for several generations in captive conditions, such as has occurred in the Pacific salmon (Waples et al. 2004), and they may lower a species' ability to survive in the wild following release. Individuals have to be carefully selected to ensure against inbreeding depression and to produce the most genetically diverse release population (Vilas et al. 2006). Also, to increase the chances that the individuals can survive, they must be selected from an environment and climate that are as similar as possible to the release site (Olsson 2007).

> Reintroduction efforts have a greater chance of success if animals are able to become familiar with a site in the days and weeks before release and are given some care and assistance immediately after release.

For some species, animals may require special care and assistance immediately to increase survival prospects (Miskelly et al. 2009). This approach is known as **soft release** (see Figure 13.1). Animals may have to be fed and sheltered at the release point until they are able to subsist on their own, or they may need to be caged temporarily at the release point and introduced gradually, until they become familiar with the sights, sounds, smells, and layout of the area. Eighty-eight chicks of the Mauritius kestrel (*Falco punctatus*) raised in captivity by humans and then given a soft release into the wild, for example, had a survival rate that was not significantly different from that of 284 chicks born in the wild (**Figure 13.2**) (Nicoll et al. 2004). The population today, composed exclusively of wild-bred offpsring, is growing (Ewing et al. 2008).

Social groups abruptly released from captivity without assistance such as food supplementation (**hard release**) may disperse explosively from the protected area,

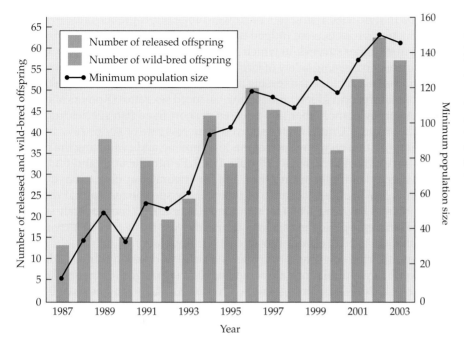

FIGURE 13.2 For the first four years of the Mauritius kestrel reintroduction program (1987–1990), all offspring were captive-reared. Kestrels living in the wild began to produce offspring in 1991, and by 1997 all new offspring were wild-bred. The number of new offspring and the minimum population size (the number of breeding adults plus the number of fledged offspring) has been gradually increasing. (After Ewing et al. 2008.)

resulting in a failed establishment effort. Intervention may be necessary if animals appear unable to survive, particularly during episodes of drought or low food abundance. Even when animals appear to have enough food to survive, supplemental feeding may help by increasing reproduction and allowing the population to increase and persist. Outbreaks of diseases and pests may have to be monitored and dealt with. The impact of human activities in the area, such as farming and hunting, needs to be observed and possibly controlled. In every case, a decision has to be made about whether it is better to give occasional temporary help to the species or to force the individuals to survive on their own.

Establishment programs for common game species have always been widespread and have contributed a great deal of knowledge for the development of new programs for threatened and endangered species. A number of generalizations can be made following analyses of about 200 establishment programs (Griffith et al. 1989; Fischer and Lindenmayer 2000):

1. Success was greater for releases in excellent-quality habitat (84%) than in poor-quality habitat (38%).

2. Success was greater in the core of the historical range (78%) than at the periphery of and outside the historical range (48%).

3. Success was greater with wild-caught (75%) than with captive-reared animals (38%).

4. Success was greater for herbivores (77%) than for carnivores (48%).

For these bird and mammal species studied, the probability of establishing a new population increased with the number of animals being released, up to about 100. Releasing more than 100 animals did not further enhance the probability of success. Certain of these results have been confirmed by later studies.

Another survey of reintroduction projects (Beck et al. 1994) analyzed a specific type of reintroduction: the release of captive-born animals within the historical range of the species. A program was judged a success if there was a self-maintaining population of 500 individuals. Using this narrower range of programs, only 16 out of 145 reintroduction projects were judged successful—a dramatically lower rate of success than in the other surveys, in which the majority of reintroductions were successful. An analysis consisting solely of larger grazers concluded that factors increasing the rate of success included: releasing at least 20 individuals, releasing a higher proportion of mature individuals, and having balanced sex ratios (Komers and Curman 2000). A survey of more than 400 releases of short-lived fish species into wild habitats of the western United States showed a success rate of about 26%, though incomplete information on many species made compiling and evaluating the results extremely difficult (Hendrickson and Brooks 1991). Reintroductions and translocations of endangered amphibians, reptiles, and invertebrates appear to have a success rate below 50%, perhaps because of their highly specialized habitat requirements (Griffiths and Pavajeau 2008; Germano and Bishop 2009). The moderate success rate for these different species emphasizes the need to use many sites to increase the probability that the species establishes at least one population.

Clearly, monitoring ongoing programs is crucial in determining whether efforts to establish new populations are achieving their stated goals (e.g., see Adamski and Witkowski 2007; Armstrong and Seddon 2008). Many studies have little or no documentation or subsequent monitoring, making evaluations difficult. Key elements of monitoring involve determining whether released individuals survive and establish a breeding population, then following that population over time to see whether it increases in numbers of individuals and geographical range. Monitoring of important ecosystem elements is also needed to determine the broader impact of a reintroduction; for example, when a predator is introduced, it will be crucial to determine its impact on prey species and competing species and its indirect impact on vegetation. In an otter reintroduction program, for instance, the returned otter populations appealed to the general public, but the otters reduced populations of fish and crustaceans, which angered commercial fishermen (Fanshawe et al. 2003). Monitoring may need to be carried out over many years, even decades, because many reintroductions that initially appear successful eventually fail. For example, a reintroduction of topminnows into a stream in the western United States resulted in a large, viable population; however, a flood eliminated the population 10 years later (Minckley 1995).

Research on establishing new populations has three urgent needs:

1. The costs of reintroduction must be tracked and published to determine whether this represents a cost-effective strategy. Reintroduction of wild dogs in South Africa, for instance, costs 20 times more than conserving existing packs in protected areas (Lindsey et al. 2005).

2. The great majority of research has been carried out on temperate, terrestrial species. More work is needed on tropical species and marine species.

3. As described in the next section, we need to develop ways of teaching learned behavior to increase the success rate in animal establishment programs. We also need to be able to compare the success rate for species that require such learned behavior with the rate for species that have primarily innate behaviors.

Learned Behavior of Released Animals

To be successful, both introduction and reintroduction programs must often address the behaviors of animals that are being released (Buchholz 2007). When social animals, including many mammals and some bird species, grow up in the wild, they learn from other members of their population, particularly their parents, about their environment and how to interact with other members of their species. They learn how to search their environment for food and how to gather, capture, and consume it. For carnivores such as lions and wild dogs, hunting techniques are complex and subtle and require considerable teamwork. To obtain the variety of food items necessary to stay alive and reproduce, frugivores such as hornbills and gibbons must learn seasonal migration patterns covering a wide area.

When mammals and birds are raised in captivity, their environment is limited to a cage or pen, so exploration is unnecessary. Searching for food and learning about new food sources is not needed, since the same food items come day after day, on schedule. Social behavior may become highly distorted when animals are raised alone or in unnatural social groupings (i.e., in small groups or single-age groups). In such cases, animals may lack the skills to survive in their natural environment and the social skills necessary to cooperatively find food, sense danger, find mating partners, and raise young (Brightsmith et al. 2005; Mathews et al. 2005).

To overcome these behavioral problems, captive-raised mammals and birds may require extensive training before and after release into the environment. They must learn how to find food and shelter, avoid predators, and interact in social groups. Training techniques have been developed for several mammals and a few birds. Captive chimps, for instance, have been taught how to use twigs to feed on termites and how to build nests in captivity. Red wolves are taught how to kill live prey. Captive animals are taught to fear potential predators by pairing a frightening stimulus with a dummy predator display.

> It is imperative that captive-bred mammals and birds learn predator avoidance and species-appropriate social behavior if they are to survive and reproduce after being released into the wild.

Social interaction is one of the most difficult behaviors to teach captive-bred mammals and birds, because for most species the subtleties of social behavior are poorly understood. Nevertheless, some successful attempts have been made to socialize captive-bred animals (Nicholson et al. 2007). In one technique, humans mimic the appearance and behavior of the wild species. This method is particularly important when dealing with very young animals. For example, captive-bred California condor hatchlings (*Gymnogyps californianus*) were originally unable to learn normal social bonds with other condors because they had imprinted on their human keepers. Newly hatched condors are now fed with condor puppets and kept from seeing human visitors so they learn to identify with their own species rather than a foster species or humans (**Figure 13.3**). However, even with such training, when captive-raised condors were released into the wild in protected areas, they often congregated around buildings, causing damage and frightening people. To break this association, condors are now being captive-reared in enclosed outdoor areas without any buildings.

When captive-bred animals are released into the wild as part of a restocking program, developing social relationships with wild animals may be crucial to their success. One approach employs wild individuals as "instructors" for captive individuals of the same species. For example, wild golden lion tamarins (*Leontopithecus rosalia*) are

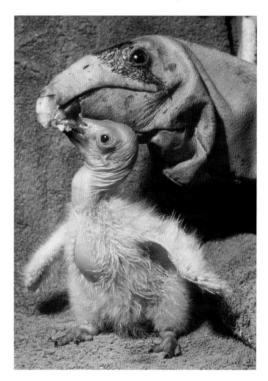

FIGURE 13.3 California condor chicks raised in captivity are fed by researchers using puppets that look like adult birds. Conservation biologists hope that minimizing human contact with the birds will improve their chances of survival when they are returned to the wild. (Photograph by Ron Garrison, courtesy of U.S. Fish and Wildlife Service.)

caught and held with captive-bred tamarins so that the captive-bred tamarins will learn appropriate behavior from the wild ones. After they form social groups, they are released together. These captive-reared animals then gain some knowledge of food items and potential danger by watching the wild animals in their group (Brightsmith et al. 2005).

ANIMAL REINTRODUCTION CASE STUDIES   The following five case studies illustrate the various approaches to animal species reintroductions:

- *Atlantic puffins.* Puffins (*Fratercula arctica*) were virtually eliminated from the Maine coast due to overharvesting for eggs and meat. In 1973, Project Puffin begin a program to reintroduce puffins to Eastern Egg Rock Island off the Maine coast. Over a 13-year period, researchers released over 900 chicks into artifical burrows and supplied them with a diet of fish and vitamins. Aggressive gulls had to be regularly chased from the island, and this continues every year. After a season of growing, fledged chicks left the island for the open ocean. To encourage them to return to the island and make the island appear to be occupied by an active puffin colony, researchers set up puffin decoys on the island (**Figure 13.4**). Puffins began to return to the island in 1977, and as of 2008, 101 pairs were breeding on the island.

- *Red wolves.* Red wolves (*Canis rufus*) have been reestablished in the Alligator River National Wildlife Refuge in northeastern North Carolina through the release of 42 captive-born animals starting in 1987. Over 100 animals currently occupy about 700,000 ha (1.7 million acres) of private and government land, including a military base. Animals in the program have produced pups and established packs and survive by hunting deer, raccoons, rabbits, and rodents (Kramer and Jenkins 2009). Even though the Red Wolf Recovery Program appears to be successful, many landowners remain unwilling to accept the presence of wolves on their land. Mating in the wild between red wolves and coyotes is probably the greatest threat to the species, because it obscures species differences.

FIGURE 13.4 Puffins have been reintroduced onto Eastern Egg Rock Island off the Maine coast. Management includes setting up these decoys to attract puffins to the island. (Photograph by Stephen W. Kress/ www.projectpuffin.org.)

- *Kemp's ridley sea turtles.* Attempts have been made to stop the rapid decline of Kemp's ridley sea turtles (*Lepidochelys kempii*) by collecting wild eggs, raising the hatchlings for 1 year in captivity in Texas, and tagging and releasing them into the Gulf of Mexico (Shaver and Wibbels 2007). Despite the release of nearly 24,000 head-started hatchlings between 1978 and 2000, as of 2004 only 23 of these turtles had nested in the wild. While this represents a minimum estimate because of insufficient monitoring and tag loss, large-scale releases of turtles have been discontinued because of the program's high cost and low rate of success. Modeling studies of sea turtle populations have subsequently shown that high mortality of turtles in commercial fishing operations is the cause of population decline and needs to be the primary target of conservation efforts (Lewison et al. 2003; Shaver and Wibbels 2007).

- *The kakapo.* The kakapo (*Strigops habroptilus*) is not only the largest parrot species in the world, it is also flightless, nocturnal, and solitary. The New Zealand kakapo was believed extinct because of introduced mammalian predators, but two small populations were discovered in the late 1970s. These populations were declining in numbers, requiring urgent action to save the species. Sixty-five kakapos were collected in the wild and released on three offshore islands that lacked most of their predators. Breeding success on the islands, while initially low, improved following supplemental feeding of adults with apples, sweet potatoes, and native seeds. Chick survival is gradually being improved by artificial incubation of eggs, raising of chicks in captivity, and release of young birds back into the wild. The current population size is 86 birds, which is expected to increase (Horrocks et al. 2008).

- *Big Bend gambusia.* The Big Bend gambusia (*Gambusia gaigei*), also called the Big Bend mosquitofish, is a small fish originally known from two small springs in Texas. One population was eliminated when one spring dried up in 1954; at the same time, the second population began to decline rapidly when its spring was diverted to create an artificial fishing pond, and by 1960 it too had disappeared. In the interim, however, two females and one male had been taken from the artificial pond to establish a captive breeding program. A combination of captive breeding and releases into new artificial ponds in Big Bend National Park helped this vulnerable species survive a series of droughts and invasions by exotic fish. The species is now reestablished in two spring pools with a population size of several thousand individuals, and the natural flow of the spring is mandated under the management plan for this protected species (Hubbs et al. 2002). A captive population is still maintained in a fish hatchery in New Mexico, however, in case the wild population declines again.

Establishing New Plant Populations

Methods used to establish new populations of rare and endangered plant species are fundamentally different from those used to establish terrestrial vertebrate animal species (Montalvo and Ellstrand 2001). Animals can disperse to new locations and actively seek out the most suitable microsite conditions. In the case of plants, seeds are dispersed to new sites by agents such as wind, animals, water, or the actions of conservation biologists (Bacles et al. 2006; Jordano et al. 2007). Once a seed lands on the ground or an adult is planted at a site, it is unable to move, even if a suitable microsite exists just a few meters away. The immediate microsite is crucial for plant survival—if the environmental conditions are in any way too sunny, too shady, too wet, or too dry, either the seed will not germinate or the resulting plant will not reproduce or will die. Botanists trying to establish a new plant population might simply scatter seeds of the target species on the ground of an appropriate unoccuppied site. Alternatively, either wild-collected or greenhouse-grown adults can be planted at the site to bypass the vulnerable seedling stage, a practice analagous to head-starting in animals.

Disturbance in the form of fire or tree falls may also be necessary for seedling establishment in many species; therefore, a site may be suitable for seedling establishment only once every several years. Careful site selection is thus critical in plant reintroductions. Plants and seeds need to be obtained from a site as similar as possible to the new site to ensure that they are genetically suited to the conditions of the new site (Vergeer et al. 2004). However, just as with animal reintroductions, identifying the factors that caused the original decline in the plant species is critical for success. In California, for example, many rare native plants are being outcompeted by introduced annual grasses. Developing management techniques to control or eliminate these grasses is an essential part of the reintroduction process.

Plant populations typically fail to establish from introduced seeds at most sites that appear to be suitable for them. In one study, large numbers of seeds of 6 species of annual plants were planted at 48 apparently suitable sites (Primack 1996). Of these 48 attempts, new populations persisted for 2 years at only 5 sites, and for 6 years at only 1 site. At this single, apparently successful site, the population had increased to more than 10,000 individuals and had spread 30 m around the margins of a marshy pond (**Figure 13.5**). Subsequent attempts to establish new populations of 35 species of perennial herbs by sowing seeds at 173 apparently suitable sites had an even lower rate of success: no seedlings at all were seen at 167 of the 173 sites, and no individuals at all were seen for 32 of the 35 species.

> New plant populations are established by sowing seeds or transplanting seedlings and adults. Site treatments such as burning off or physically removing competing plants are often necessary for success.

To increase their chances of success, botanists often germinate seeds in controlled environments and grow the young plants in protected conditions (**Figure 13.6**). Only after the plants are past the fragile seedling stage are they transplanted into the wild. Planting must be executed using the techniques appropriate to

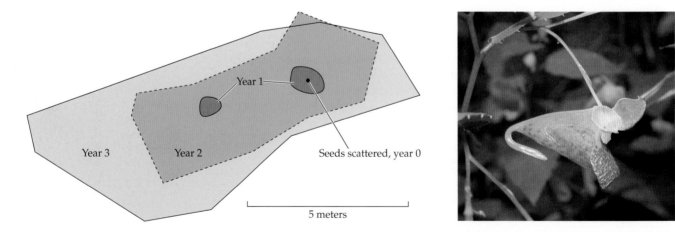

FIGURE 13.5 Sometimes a new plant population can be established by the introduction of seeds. In year 0, 100 seeds of *Impatiens capensis*, an annual species of jewelweed, were introduced into an unoccupied site in Hammond Woods, near Boston, Massachusetts. The seeds were scattered within 1 m of a stake (black dot). In year 1, two groups of plants separated by several meters had established themselves (darkest green areas). The populations continued to expand in year 2 (as shown by the limits in dashed lines) and year 3 (solid lines). By year 7, population size had grown to more than 10,000 individuals and had spread 30 m. (After Primack 1996, photograph by David McIntyre.)

FIGURE 13.6 Seedlings of rare plant species being grown on a greenhouse bench; they were subsequently planted in the wild. Plant reintroductions from seed usually fail; they are often more successful when plants are grown from seeds or cuttings in a separate location and then transplanted into their new home site as seedlings or mature plants. (Photograph by R. Primack.)

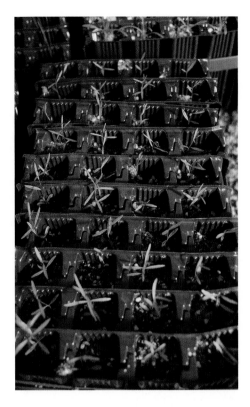

the species (planting depth, watering, time of day, time of year, site preparation, and so on) to ensure survival. Transplanted seedlings and adults often flower and fruit 1 or more years earlier than plants growing from seed sown directly into the wild, which increases the potential for seed dispersal and the formation of a second generation of plants (Guerrant et al. 2004). In other cases, plants are dug up from an existing wild population (usually either one that is threatened with destruction or one in which removing a small percentage of the plants is not expected to harm the population) and then transplanted into an unoccupied but apparently suitable site (Gunnarsson and Söderström 2007).

While transplanting seedlings and adults may generally have a better chance of ensuring that the species survives at a new location, it does not perfectly mimic a natural process, and the new population may fail to produce seed and form the next generation. Plant ecologists are currently trying to work out new techniques to overcome these difficulties, such as fencing to exclude animals, removal of some of the existing vegetation to reduce competition, controlled burning, planting other species to provide shade and leaf litter in arid regions, and adding mineral nutrients to the soil (Donath et al. 2007) (**Figure 13.7A**). Keys to suc-

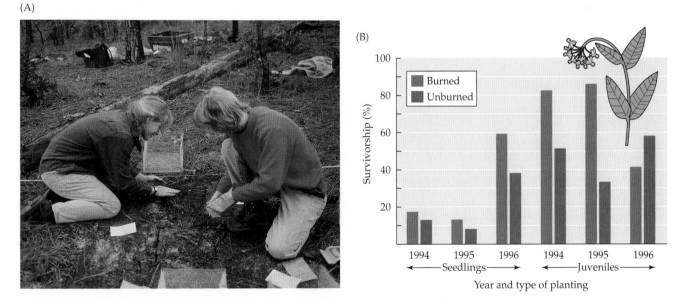

FIGURE 13.7 (A) Several methods are being used to create new populations of rare wildflower species on U.S. Forest Service land in South Carolina. Seeds are being planted in a pine forest from which the oak understory has been burned away. Wire cages will be placed over some plantings to determine whether excluding rabbits, deer, and other animals will help in plant establishment. (B) Seedlings and juvenile plants of Mead's milkweed (*Asclepias meadii*) are evaluated in a reintroduction experiment. Survivorship is greater for older juvenile plants than for seedlings and greater in burned habitat than in unburned habitat. Seedling survivorship was greatest in 1996, a year with high rainfall. (A, photograph by R. Primack; B, after Bowles et al. 1998.)

cess seem to be using multiple sites, using as many seeds or transplants as possible, and reintroducing species over several successive years at the same site. Reintroductions require careful monitoring of the numbers of seedlings and adults to determine whether the project is a success. A successful project (Guerrant et al. 2004) would have a self-maintaining—or even growing—population with subsequent generations of plants replacing the reintroduced individuals. In some cases, new populations that initially appeared to be well-established have died out in subsequent years. As research on this developing topic is published and synthesized, hopefully the chances for successful plant reintroductions will improve.

PLANT REINTRODUCTION CASE STUDIES The following two case studies illustrate experimental approaches to the reintroduction of plant species:

- *Mead's milkweed.* Mead's milkweed (*Asclepias meadii*) is a threatened perennial prairie plant in the Midwestern United States, characterized by low seed production. Populations were established using different techniques in an experimental approach (Bell et al. 2003). Survivorship was greater for older juvenile plants than for seedlings, and survival was higher in burned habitat than in unburned habitat (**Figure 13.7B**). Seedling survival was also higher in 1996, which had greater rainfall than average. As of 2009, plants in burned plots had shown much better growth and reproduction. Using this information, managers of this species now employ burning.

- *Knowlton's cactus.* Knowlton's cactus (*Pediocactus knowltonii*) is a tiny, perennial cactus known only from one narrow hilltop location in northwestern New Mexico (**Figure 13.8**). Despite the fact that the site is now owned by The Nature Conservancy, this threatened species remains vulnerable to human disturbance from oil and gas exploration, livestock grazing, and removal of plants by collectors. To reduce the possibility of extinction, two nearby, comparable sites were selected for introductions in 1985 (Sivinski and McDonald 2007). At one site, 150 individuals grown from cuttings were planted and watered. Eighteen years later, 40% of the plants were still alive, with about half of them flowering and fruiting, but only four second-generation individuals had developed.

FIGURE 13.8 Knowlton's cactus (*Pediocactus knowltonii*) growing in New Mexico. (Photograph courtesy of Robert Sivinski/U.S. Forest Service.)

The Status of New Populations

The establishment of new populations raises some novel issues at the intersection of scientific research, conservation efforts, government regulation, and ethics. These issues need to be addressed because reintroduction, introduction, and restocking programs will increase in the coming years, as the biological diversity crisis eliminates more species and populations from the wild and as many of the reintroduction programs for endangered species are mandated by official recovery plans set up by national governments. In addition, many species may need to be moved if their present ranges become too hot, too dry, or otherwise unsuitable because of global climate change (McLachlan et al. 2007).

Programs and research increasingly are being hampered by endangered species legislation that restricts the possession and use of endangered species (Reinartz 1995; Falk et al. 1996). If government officials rigidly apply these laws to scientific research programs, which was certainly not the original intent of the legislation, the programs will be blocked, and any possible creative insights and new approaches that could have come out of them will be lost. Projects to establish experimental populations sometimes have been delayed for more than 5 years while waiting for government approval. New scientific information is central to reintroduction programs and other conservation efforts. Government officials who block reasonable scientific projects need to consider whether their actions are really in the best interests of biodiversity protection and the citizens of their country. The potential harm to endangered species or local ecosystems caused by carefully planned scientific research is relatively insignificant when compared with the actual massive loss of biological diversity being caused by habitat destruction and fragmentation, pollution, and overexploitation.

Experimental populations of rare and endangered species—those that are successfully created by reintroduction and introduction programs—are given various degrees of legal protection. The U.S. Endangered Species Act (ESA) recognizes two categories of experimental populations: "Experimental, essential" populations are regarded as critical to the survival of endangered species and are as rigidly protected as naturally occurring populations. "Experimental, nonessential" populations are not considered essential to the survival of a species and are not protected under the ESA. Designating populations as nonessential, as was done for the gray wolves released in the greater Yellowstone area, means that local landowners are not limited by the provisions of the ESA and may be less inclined to oppose the creation of an experimental population. The disadvantage of this designation is that landowners can shoot or kill animals they perceive as a threat without any legal consequences.

Sometimes reintroduction programs are misused. In many cases, proposals are made by developers to create new habitat or new populations to compensate for the habitat damage or the eradication of populations of endangered species that occurred during development projects. This is generally referred to as **mitigation**. Mitigation is often directed at legally protected species and habitats and includes (1) reduction in the extent of damage, (2) establishment of new populations and habitat as compensation for what is being destroyed, and (3) enhancement of what remains after development.

Proposals to establish new populations of endangered species as part of the mitigation process merely for the convenience and profit of developers should be regarded with considerable skepticism. Claims that the loss of biodiversity can be mitigated are usually exaggerated. Given the poor success of most attempts to create new populations of rare species, protection of existing populations of rare species should be given the highest priority. While the replacement and restoration of damaged habitat may be beneficial, at least with respect to certain species and some ecosystem functions, artificially created habitat is generally neither as biologically rich nor as functionally useful as natural habitat. For example, artificially created wetlands generally do not have as much water storage capacity or ability to break down sewage and other human pollutants (Bellio et al. 2009). Legislators, environmental engineers, and scientists alike must understand that the establishment of new populations through reintroduction programs in no way reduces the need to protect the original populations of the endangered species. Original populations are more likely to have the most complete gene pool of the species and the most intact interactions with other members of the biological community. Reintroduction is not an alternative to the protection of existing populations and species; it is an additional tool to achieve a common end: increased survival probability in the wild. Finally, conservation biologists must be able to explain the benefits and limitations of reintroduction programs in a way that government officials and the general public can understand, and they must address the legitimate concerns of those groups (Musiani et al. 2003; Guerrant et al. 2004; Seddon et al. 2007). One way this can be facilitated is if biologists incorporate citizen groups, in particular school groups, into reintroduction efforts. When people have the experience of working on reintroduction projects, they become more knowledgeable about the issues and often become advocates for conservation.

> The establishment of new populations through reintroduction programs in no way reduces the need to protect the original populations of endangered species.

Summary

1. One approach to protect endangered species involves establishing new wild populations of those species. New populations of rare and endangered species can be established in the wild using captive-bred, captive-raised (caught as juveniles in the wild), or wild-caught animals. Reintroduction involves releasing individuals within the historical range of the species; introduction involves releasing individuals at a site outside of the historical range of the species; restocking involves releasing individuals into an existing population to increase population size and genetic variability.

2. Mammals and birds raised in captivity may lack the skills needed to survive in the wild. Some species require social and behavioral training before release and some degree of maintenance after release (soft release). Establishment of a new population of a rare animal species is often not successful, but the potential for success is enhanced when the release occurs in excellent habitat within the historical range of the species and when large numbers of wild-caught animals are used.

3. Reintroductions of plant species require a different approach because of their specialized environmental requirements and inability to move. Current research focuses on improving site selection, habitat management, and planting techniques.

4. Newly created populations of endangered species are sometimes given legal protection. Conservation biologists involved in establishing new populations of endangered species must be careful that their efforts do not weaken the legal protection currently given to natural populations of those species. Similarly, they must educate the public about the potential benefits and uncertainties of reintroduction efforts.

For Discussion

1. How do you judge whether a reintroduction project is successful? Develop simple and then increasingly detailed criteria to evaluate a project's success. Use demographic, environmental, and genetic factors in your evaluation.

2. Would it be a good idea to create new wild populations of African rhinos, elephants, and lions in Australia, South America, the southwestern United States, and other areas outside of their current range, as described by Donlan et al. (2006)? What would be some of the legal, economic, and ecological issues?

3. Does our increasing ability to create new populations of rare and endangered species mean that we do not have to be concerned with protecting the known sites where these species occur? What are the costs and benefits of reintroduction programs?

4. Many endangered plant species are currently being propagated by commercial growers and botanical gardens and then sold (as both plants and seeds) to government agencies, conservation organizations, garden clubs, and the general public, who then in effect create new populations of these legally protected species. There is little or no regulation of these sales or the subsequent plantings. What do you see as the advantages and disadvantages of this widespread activity? Should the propagation and planting of legally protected species be more closely regulated by the government?

5. What are the advantages and disadvantages of incorporating children into a local reintroduction project for wildflowers or butterflies? What concerns would their parents and teachers have?

Suggested Readings

Adamski, P. and Z. J. Witkowski. 2007. Effectiveness of population recovery projects based on captive breeding. *Biological Conservation* 140: 1–7. How to monitor and evaluate a recovery program.

Armstrong, D. P. and P. J. Seddon. 2008. Directions in reintroduction biology. *Trends in Ecology and Evolution* 23: 20–25. Poses the key questions to be asked when considering species reintroductions.

Bergstrom, B. J., S. Vignieri, S. R. Sheffield, W. Sechrest, and A. A. Carlson. 2009. The northern Rocky Mountain gray wolf is not yet recovered. *BioScience* 59: 991–999. The authors argue that legal protection of reintroduced wolves should not end until the ecosystem is also recovered.

Donlan, J. and 11 others. 2006. Re-wilding North America. *Nature* 436: 913–914. Some conservation biologists have suggested establishing large African game animals on the American plain.

Fischer, J. and D. B. Lindenmayer. 2000. An assessment of published results of animal relocations. *Biological Conservation* 96: 1–11. A review of 180 relocation studies highlights factors leading to success: using wild-caught animals, releasing numerous animals, and removing the original cause of population decline.

Grenier, M. B., D. B. McDonald, and S. W. Buskirk. 2007. Rapid population growth of a critically endangered carnivore. *Science* 317: 779. The black-footed ferret reintroduction program has faced many problems, but the efforts are now showing signs of success.

Griffiths, R. A. and L. Pavajeau. 2008. Captive breeding, reintroduction, and the conservation of amphibians. *Conservation Biology* 22: 852–861. Programs involving amphibians often have multiple goals and require a long-term commitment.

Lindsey, P. A., R. Alexander, J. T. DuToit, and M. G. L. Mills. 2005. The cost efficiency of wild dog conservation in South Africa. *Conservation Biology* 19: 1205–1214. Correctly done reintroduction is often very expensive.

Mathews, F., M. Orros, G. McLaren, M. Gelling, and R. Foster. 2005. Keeping fit on the ark: assessing the suitability of captive-bred animals for release. *Biological Conservation* 121: 569–577. Many animals raised in captivity have lost the behaviors needed to survive in the wild.

Minckley, W. L. 1995. Translocation as a tool for conserving imperiled fishes: Experiences in western United States. *Biological Conservation* 72: 297–309. Review of freshwater fish releases; also see other articles on fish conservation in this issue.

Miskelly, C. M., G. A. Taylor, H. Gummer, and R. Williams. 2009. Translocations of eight species of burrow-nesting seabirds (genera *Pterodroma*, *Pelecanoides*, *Pachyptila* and *Puffinus*: Family Procellariidae). *Biological Conservation* 142: 1965–1980. Evaluation of attempts to establish new colonies of seabirds using hand-fed chicks.

Ricciardi, A. and D. Simberloff. 2009. Assisted colonization is not a viable conservation strategy. *Trends in Ecology and Evolution* 24: 248–253. Some researchers argue for creating new populations in response to climate change; these scientists disagree.

Seddon, P. J., D. P. Armstrong, and R. F. Maloney. 2007. Developing the science of reintroduction biology. *Conservation Biology* 21: 303–312. Progress in the field will come from a greater use of an experimental approach and modeling.

Vilas, C., E. San Miguel, R. Amaro, and C. Garcia. 2006. Relative contribution of inbreeding depression and eroded adaptive diversity to extinction risk in small populations of shore campion. *Conservation Biology* 20: 229–238. Success in reintroduction is improved if seeds resulting from outbreeding are used.

Chapter 14

Ex Situ Conservation Strategies

The goal of conservation is to maintain biological diversity *in nature* for the continued health of ecosystems at all levels. For most species, the ideal strategy for the long-term protection of biological diversity would be the preservation of natural communities and populations in the wild, known as **in situ**, or on-site, **conservation**. Only in natural communities are such species able to continue their process of evolutionary adaptation to a changing environment. Ecosystem-level interactions among species, as discussed in Chapter 2, are often crucial to rare species' continued survival; these interactions can be quite complex and probably cannot be replicated under captive conditions. Furthermore, captive animal populations are generally not large enough to prevent the loss of genetic variability through genetic drift; the same can also be true of plant species established in cultivation when they have special requirements for pollination that might make it difficult to ensure adequate cross-pollination among individuals. For such species, in situ conservation involving careful habitat protection and management would be the best solution.

In the face of increasing human activities, however, relying solely on in situ conservation is not currently a viable option for most rare species, and species that are under conservation management in situ may still decline and go extinct in the wild for any of the reasons already discussed: habitat destruction, loss of genetic variation and inbreeding depression, demographic and environmental variability, deteriorating habitat quality, habitat fragmentation, climate change, competition from invasive species, disease, and excessive hunting and collecting. If a remnant population is too small to maintain the species, if it is still declining despite conservation efforts, or if the remaining individuals are found outside of protected areas, then in situ preservation may not be adequate. It is likely that the only way species in such circumstances can be prevented from going extinct is to maintain individuals in artificial conditions under human supervision (Russello and Amato 2007; Bowkett 2009).

> Integrated with efforts to protect existing populations and to establish new populations, ex situ conservation involving zoos, aquariums, and botanical gardens is an important conservation strategy to protect endangered species and educate the public.

Ex situ, or off-site, **conservation** used in place of or to complement in situ conservation can mean the difference between life and death for some species. Ex situ facilities for animal preservation include zoos, aquariums, sanctuaries, game farms, and private breeders, while plants are maintained in botanical gardens, arboretums, and seed banks. For certain species, ex situ conservation can actually be superior to in situ conservation in terms of both its lower overall cost and its ability to rapidly augment small populations with captive-grown individuals drawn from a larger gene pool. Although it is always preferable to have a population in situ (the point of conservation, after all, is to maintain biological diversity in nature, not under glass or behind fences), ex situ methods are best viewed not as "second best" strategies but as complementary components of a larger, more comprehensive, integrated conservation strategy (Conway et al. 2001; Zimmerman et al. 2008; Bowkett 2009). There are some species for which the original wild site or sites are so threatened or so badly degraded that attempting in situ conservation would be a death sentence for the species; ex situ methods are therefore more than simply a backup plan, as they can mean the difference between a viable conservation plan and one that is unworkable.

Already a number of species that went extinct in the wild have survived because of propagation in captive colonies. Examples include Père David's deer (*Elaphurus davidianus*) and Przewalski's horse, or takhi (*Equus caballus przewalski*) (**Figure 14.1**). The beautiful Franklin tree (*Franklinia alatamaha*) grows only in cultivation and is no longer found in the wild. In situations such as these, the long-term goal of many ex situ conservation programs is the eventual establishment of new populations in the wild, once sufficient numbers of individuals and a suitable habitat are available. In the case of Przewalski's horse, social groups based on 14 founder individuals were released in a national park in Mongolia starting in 1992. The population is showing steady growth, now numbering about 325 individuals (IUCN 2008; Adams et al. 2009).

An intermediate strategy that combines elements of both ex situ and in situ preservation is the monitoring and management of populations of rare and endangered species in small, protected areas; such populations are still somewhat wild, but human intervention may be necessary occasionally to prevent population decline.

As mentioned above, ex situ and in situ conservation are complementary strategies. Individuals from ex situ populations can be periodically released into the wild to establish new populations and to augment existing wild populations (**Figure 14.2**). Research on captive populations can provide insight into the basic biology, physiol-

FIGURE 14.1 The IUCN has declared Przewalski's horse (*Equus caballus przewalski*) to be extinct in the wild. Several zoos around the world have maintained populations and been successful in breeding these animals. Recent reintroductions of the wild horses into their natural range in Mongolia appear so far to have been successful. (Photograph © Erich Kuchling/Westend61/Alamy.)

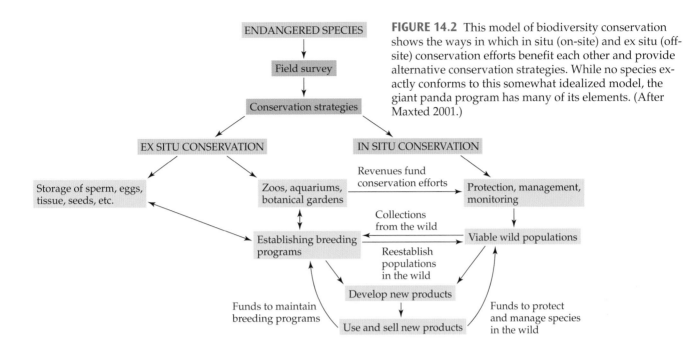

FIGURE 14.2 This model of biodiversity conservation shows the ways in which in situ (on-site) and ex situ (off-site) conservation efforts benefit each other and provide alternative conservation strategies. While no species exactly conforms to this somewhat idealized model, the giant panda program has many of its elements. (After Maxted 2001.)

ogy, and genetics of the species through research studies that would not be possible on wild animals. Results of these studies can suggest new conservation strategies for in situ populations. Similarly, the ease of access to individual animals in captivity allows scientists to develop and test relevant technologies (e.g., radio collars) that enhance the study and preservation of the species in the wild. Long-term, self-sustaining ex situ populations can also reduce the need to collect individuals from the wild for display and research. Captive-bred individuals on display can help to educate the public about the need to preserve the species and so protect other members of the species in the wild. The number of people visiting zoos is enormous; over 600 million people visit the world's zoos every year (**Figure 14.3**).

(A)

(B)

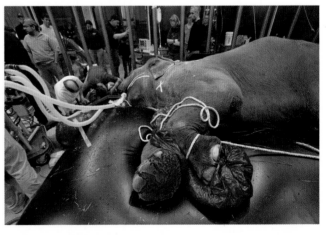

FIGURE 14.3 (A) Visitors to the Asahiyama Zoo on Japan's northern island of Hokkaido enjoy a parade of emperor penguins (*Aptenodytes forsteri*). Zoos can serve to educate the public about the need to protect wildlife as well as providing research facilities for in situ species preservation. (B) Veteri-narians carry out dental surgery on a captive Asian elephant. The knowledge gained can then potentially assist in helping the species in the wild. (A, photograph © JTB Photo Communications, Inc./Alamy; B © Richard Clement/Zuma Press.)

Zoos, aquariums, and botanical gardens, and the people who visit them, regularly contribute money to in situ conservation programs. In addition, ex situ programs can be used to develop new products that potentially can generate funds from profits or licensing fees to protect species in the wild. In situ preservation of species, in turn, is vital to the survival of species that are difficult to maintain in captivity, as well as to the continued ability of zoos, aquariums, and botanical gardens to display species that do not have self-sustaining ex situ populations.

Ex Situ Conservation Facilities

The most common types of ex situ conservation facilities currently in use are zoos, aquariums, botanical gardens, and seed banks. In this section, we'll examine each of these facilities to determine its role in conservation programs.

Zoos

A current goal of most major zoos is to establish viable, long-term captive breeding populations of rare and endangered animals. Zoos have traditionally focused on maintaining large vertebrates—especially mammals—since these species are of greatest interest to the general public. In the past, these animals were typically displayed as curiosities in cages, without any relationship to a natural environment. The world's 2000 zoos and aquariums are increasingly incorporating ecological themes and information about the threats to endangered species in their public displays and their research programs as part of the World Zoo Conservation Strategy, which seeks to link zoo programs with conservation efforts in the wild (Praded 2002). In North America, the National Zoo's Conservation & Research Center has joined with other zoos to form a program to develop scientifically focused approaches to endangered species conservation.

The variety of species displayed in zoos has increased in recent years, but the emphasis is still on "charismatic" megafauna such as pandas, giraffes, and elephants because it helps to attract the general public and influences them favorably toward conservation. In fact, over 90% of families enjoy seeing biodiversity at zoos and aquariums and believe they teach children about protecting species and habitat (www.aza.org). As such, ex situ individuals serve as "ambassadors" for the plight of their free-ranging counterparts. However, zoos must reach a better balance between displaying large animals to attract visitors and displaying smaller, lesser animals, such as insects, that comprise most of the world's animal species.

The potential educational and financial impact of zoos is enormous, considering that they receive approximately 600 million visitors per year. Educational programs at zoos, articles written about zoo programs, and zoo field projects all direct public attention to animals and habitats of conservation significance. A survey of visitors demonstrated that zoos and aquariums enhance public understanding of biodiversity and habitat conservation, which prompts people to reconsider their own role in solving conservation problems (Falk et al. 2007). If, for example, the general public becomes interested in protecting giant pandas after seeing them in zoos and reading about them, then money may be donated, pressure may be exerted on governments, and eventually appropriate habitat in China may be set aside as protected areas (Box 14.1). At the same time, thousands of other plant and animal species occupying these environments will be protected.

Zoos presently maintain over 2 million animals, including over 500,000 individual terrestrial vertebrates, representing over 7400 species and subspecies of mammals, birds, reptiles, and amphibians (Table 14.1; www.isis.org). While this number of captive animals may seem impressive, it is trivial in comparison to the tens of millions of domestic cats, dogs, and fish kept by people as pets. Zoos could establish breeding colonies of even more species if they directed more of their ef-

BOX 14.1 *Love Alone Cannot Save the Giant Panda*

■ The giant panda (*Ailuropoda melanoleuca*) is one of the most familiar endangered species in the world. It is so well known and so beloved by millions of people that its image is the symbol for the World Wide Fund for Nature (also known as the World Wildlife Fund), a prominent international conservation organization. Despite its popular appeal, the panda's future is in jeopardy. As with many endangered species, habitat destruction and fragmentation are the most significant threats to its survival (Shen et al. 2008). Moreover, human pressure appears to exacerbate some of the unusual traits of the panda's physical and behavioral makeup that make this species particularly vulnerable to extinction.

One of the most unusual features of pandas is their diet of bamboo. The problem for pandas is that while bamboo is not rare, bamboo species reproduce in long-term cycles of anywhere from 15 to over 100 years, and typically, nearly all individuals in a given species within a certain area will flower and die in a single season. In the past, on those rare years when bamboos died off, pandas would travel to find remaining bamboo stands, especially in lowland areas. Now, when agricultural areas, roads, and human settlements prevent them from migrating to lowland areas, pandas have nowhere to go during bamboo die-offs. In the 1970s, when several bamboo species flowered simultaneously over a large area of its range, at least 138 pandas starved, and the population declined by more than 23%.

Following this catastrophe, the Chinese government tried to establish a self-sustaining captive breeding population. However, the success was low, as giant pandas are extremely selective in choosing mates while in captivity, and pandas paired by zoos and other breeding facilities often proved uninterested in mating. Also, pandas typically only give birth to one cub per season. Thus the rate of population growth is very slow even under the best conditions. Despite these problems, however, giant panda breeding has recently proved more successful, due in part to a better understanding of nutrition, housing needs, and overall biology. Between 1963, when China first began to breed captive pandas, and 1989, only 90 cubs were born, of which only 37 survived for more than 6 months. After many methods were tried, artificial insemination emerged as the key to producing giant pandas in captivity. Currently, captive giant pandas at the Wolong Giant Panda Breeding Center in Sichuan Province, China, and other facilities are capable of producing over 2 dozen cubs per year. Breeding at Wolong was temporarily slowed by damage to the facilities caused by a massive earthquake in 2008. An eventual goal of the captive breeding program is to return some of the giant pandas to the wild. However,

Wolong National Reserve and other facilities in China have been successful at breeding giant pandas using artificial insemination and hand-rearing, but such captive-raised individuals may lack the needed behavioral skills to survive in the wild. (Photograph © LMR Group/Alamy.)

captive-bred pandas almost certainly lack the behavioral skills to ever be released back to wild populations in protected areas.

> Chinese scientists have successfully used modern veterinary medicine to breed captive giant pandas. The next challenge will be to develop methods for reintroducing these captive-borne animals back into the wild.

The captive breeding program is valuable in raising public interest and funds needed for in situ conservation. Currently, U.S. and European zoos with pairs of giant pandas on loan from China make large financial contributions for giant panda conservation programs in China. These contributions are required as part of the panda exchange program.

Fragmentation of habitat is another problem for the long-term survival of the species (Shen et al. 2008). There are about 1600 giant pandas occupying about 23,000 km² of habitat scattered among approximately 25 populations across six mountain ranges (see figure). As a result, the small populations, many with fewer than 20 individuals, may eventually suffer from inbreeding depression. Many of the panda reserves are becoming more isolated over time because of

(continued)

BOX 14.1 *(continued)*

habitat deterioration by government projects, including roads, dams, and tourist developments, and the activities of villagers at the borders of the reserves (Li et al. 2003). Poaching pandas for their skins was formerly a serious problem that is now less common because of stiff penalties imposed by the Chinese government, but pandas still die in snares set by hunters for antelope, deer, and other game.

The Chinese government has put significant financial resources into setting aside more habitat for the remaining wild pandas (Shen et al. 2008). There are now 40 reserves covering 45% of the pandas' current habitat. However, it will not be easy for the reserves to withstand the pressure of China's immense human population. The pandas need more forest to live in and bamboo to eat, as well as protection from hunters—difficult resources to provide as people keep encroaching into their mountain refuges. Time will tell whether they will get what they need.

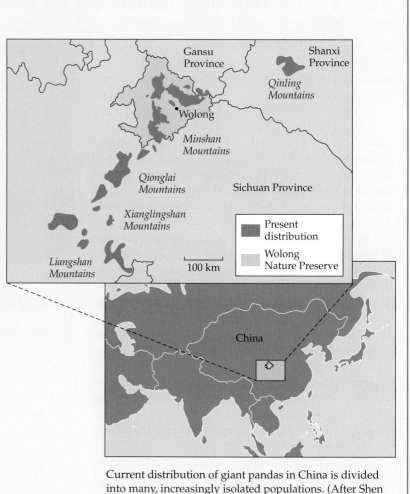

Current distribution of giant pandas in China is divided into many, increasingly isolated populations. (After Shen et al. 2008.)

forts to smaller-bodied species such as insects, amphibians, and reptiles, which are less expensive to maintain in large numbers than large-bodied mammals such as giant pandas, elephants, and rhinos (Balmford 1996). Many zoos are moving in this direction, with more displays of frogs and colorful butterflies that have popular appeal. For instance, seven North American zoos are joining with universities and the Defenders of Wildlife to form the Panama Amphibian Rescue and Conservation Project (www.aza.org), a major goal being to establish breeding populations of frogs and other amphibians being decimated in the wild by chytrid fungus (see Box 8.1).

Zoos working with affiliated universities, government wildlife departments, and conservation organizations are the logical choices to develop captive populations of rare and endangered species because they have the needed knowledge and experience in animal care, veterinary medicine, animal behavior, reproductive biology, and genetics. Zoos and affiliated conservation organizations have embarked on a major effort to build facilities and develop the technology necessary to establish breeding colonies of these animals, and to develop the new methods and programs needed to reintroduce species in the wild (Zimmermann et al. 2008). Some of these facilities are highly specialized, such as that run by the International Crane

TABLE 14.1 Number of Terrestrial Vertebrates Currently Maintained in Zoos, According to the International Species Information System (ISIS)

Location	Mammals	Birds	Reptiles	Amphibians	Total
Europe	93,482	109,903	26,778	13,661	243,824
North America	54,393	57,668	29,967	25,208	167,236
Central America	11,630	4175	1195	65	17,065
South America	2372	3927	1682	177	8158
Asia	8437	22,624	3637	529	35,137
Australasia	6266	8629	3188	1288	19,371
Africa	6235	15,018	1278	293	22,824
Totals					
All species	182,725	221,944	67,725	41,221	513,615
Number of taxa[a]	2238	3753	969	544	7486
Percent wild-born[c]	5%	9%	15%	5%	
Rare species[b]	59,030	37,748	22,474	3398	122,650
Number of taxa[a]	527	344	207	29	1107
Percent wild-born[c]	7%	9%	18%	7%	

Source: Data from ISIS as of February 2009, provided by Laurie Bingaman Lackey.

[a]The number of taxa is not exactly equivalent to species, because many species have more than one subspecies listed.

[b]Rare species are those covered by CITES (the Convention on International Trade in Endangered Species).

[c]The percentage of individuals born in the wild is approximate (particularly for reptiles and amphibians), since the origin of the animals is often not reported.

Foundation in Wisconsin, which is attempting to establish captive breeding colonies of all crane species. This effort has paid off. Currently, less than about 7% of the terrestrial mammals kept in zoos have been collected in the wild, and this number is declining as zoos gain more experience (see Table 14.1). For endangered mammals, again, about 10% of captive individuals were captured in the wild.

For common animals such as the raccoon and the white-tailed deer, there is no need to establish breeding colonies and conservation programs since individuals of these species can be readily obtained from the wild. The real need is for zoos to establish sustainable, captive populations of rare species that can no longer be readily captured in the wild, such as the orangutan, Chinese alligator, and snow leopard.

CAPTIVE BREEDING METHODS AND TARGETS The success of captive breeding programs has been enhanced by efforts to collect and disseminate knowledge about the maintenance of rare and endangered species. The Species Survival Commission's Conservation Breeding Specialist Group, a division of the IUCN, and affiliated organizations, such as the Association of Zoos and Aquariums, the European Association of Zoos and Aquaria, and the Australasian Regional Association of Zoological Parks and Aquaria, provide zoos with the necessary information for proper care and handling of these species, as well as updates on the status and behavior of animals in the wild (www.aza.org). This includes data on nutritional requirements, anesthetic techniques to immobilize animals and reduce stress during transport and medical procedures, optimal housing conditions, vaccinations and antibiotics to prevent the spread of disease, and breeding records. This effort is being aided by a central database called ARKS, the Animal Record Keeping System, maintained by the International Species Inventory System (ISIS), which keeps track of all relevant information on over 2 million animals belonging to 10,000 species at 825 member institutions in 76 countries (www.isis.org). Such a database is an important tool in monitoring health trends in zoo populations.

Most species provided with humane captive conditions reproduce with abandon; so much so that the use of contraceptives and other management programs to control populations are required. However, some rare animal species do not adapt or reproduce well in captivity. Zoos conduct extensive research and are constantly identifying managament conditions to overcome these problems and promote successful reproduction of genetically appropriate mates. In addition, new techniques are being developed to enhance the low reproductive rates of such species (Holt et al. 2003; Pukazhenthi et al. 2006; Wildt et al. 2009). Some of these come directly from human and veterinary medicine, while others are novel methods developed at special research facilities such as the Conservation & Research Center of the Smithsonian's National Zoological Park, San Diego Zoo's Center for Reproduction of Endangered Species, the Audubon Nature Institute's Species Survival Center in New Orleans, and the Durrell Wildlife Conservation Trust in Jersey, in the Channel Islands, UK. For example, foster parents from a common species can be used to raise the offspring of a rare species in an approach known as **cross-fostering**. Many bird species, such as the bald eagle, normally lay only one clutch of eggs per year, but if biologists remove this first clutch of eggs, the mother bird will lay and raise a second clutch. If the first clutch of eggs is given to another bird of a common related species, two clutches of eggs will be produced per year for each rare female. This technique, known informally as double-clutching, potentially doubles the number of offspring one female of a rare species can produce.

> Zoos often use the latest methods of veterinary medicine to establish healthy breeding colonies of endangered animals.

Another aid to reproduction, similar to cross-fostering, is **artificial incubation**. If a mother does not adequately care for her offspring, or if the offspring are readily attacked by predators, parasites, or disease, humans may care for them during their vulnerable early stages. This approach has been tried extensively with egg-laying species such as sea turtles, birds, fishes, and amphibians: Eggs are collected and placed in ideal hatching conditions; the hatchlings are protected and fed during their vulnerable early stages; and the young are then released into the wild or raised in captivity. This approach is sometimes called head-starting (see Chapter 13).

Individuals of some animal species lose interest in mating while in captivity, or a zoo may have only one or a few individuals of a rare species such as the giant panda. In these circumstances, **artificial insemination** can be used when an isolated female animal comes into breeding condition, either on her own or after being hormonally induced, similar to what occurs in a human fertility clinic. Biochemical tracking of hormonal levels in urine and feces can be used to determine the timing of sexual receptivity in females. Sperm are collected from suitable males, stored at low temperatures or frozen until needed, and then used for artificial insemination with a receptive female. While artificial insemination is performed routinely with many domesticated animal species, the exact techniques of sperm collection, sperm storage, recognition of female receptivity, and sperm delivery have to be worked out separately for each species in a conservation breeding program. Artificial insemination is used increasingly for maintaining genetic diversity, as females can be inseminated by distantly related males held at other facilities. The gene pool of cheetahs in North American zoos has even been augmented by inseminating females with semen collected from wild-born Namibian males (Comizzoli et al 2009). Transporting semen is preferable to removing endangered species from the wild and is much more cost-effective than transfering males between ex situ facilities. Recently, reproductive biologists have developed the ability to sort sperm cells based on sex for certain species (Behr et al. 2009). Using this new technology, ex situ facilities can maintain the ideal sex ratios needed to promote breeding and captive management.

Embryo transfer has been accomplished successfully in a few rare animals such as the bongo, gaur, tiger, ocelot, and Przewalski's horse. Superovulation, or production of multiple eggs, is induced using fertility drugs, and the extra eggs are surgically collected, fertilized with sperm, and laparoscopically implanted into surrogate mothers, sometimes of related common species. The surrogate mother carries the offspring to term and then gives birth (**Figure 14.4**). In the future, this technology may be used to increase the reproductive output of certain rare species.

Cutting-edge medical and veterinary technologies are being used to develop new approaches for some species that are difficult to breed in captivity (Holt and Lloyd 2009). These include cloning individuals from single cells (when only one or a few individuals remain), cross-species hybridization (when the remaining members of a species cannot breed among themselves), induced hibernation and induced dormancy as a way of maintaining dormant populations, and biochemical and surgical sexing of animals that have no external sex differences. One of the most unusual techniques, known as a **genome resource bank** (**GRB**), involves freezing purified DNA, eggs, sperm, embryos, and other tissues of species so they can be used to contribute to breeding programs, to maintain genetic diversity, and for scientific research. One such project is called the Frozen Ark (Clarke 2009). However, many of these techniques are expensive and species-specific. In any case, GRBs are no substitute for in situ and ex situ conservation programs that preserve ecological relationships and behaviors that are necessary for survival in the wild.

As we discussed in Chapter 11, genetic inbreeding is an important problem in small populations (such as those found in zoos). Traditionally, captive populations in zoos were usually extensively inbred (**Figure 14.5**), but zoo managers are more careful now to avoid potential genetic problems when assigning mates (Pelletier et al. 2009). Modern zoos now use global computerized databases provided by ISIS and special studbooks to carefully track the genetic lineages of endangered

FIGURE 14.4 A bongo calf (*Tragelaphus euryceros*, an endangered species) produced by embryo transfer using an eland (*Taurotragus oryx*) as a surrogate mother at the Cincinnati Zoo Center for the Reproduction of Endangered Wildlife. Bongos also breed successfully on their own in captive herds. (Photograph © Cincinnati Zoo and Botanical Garden.)

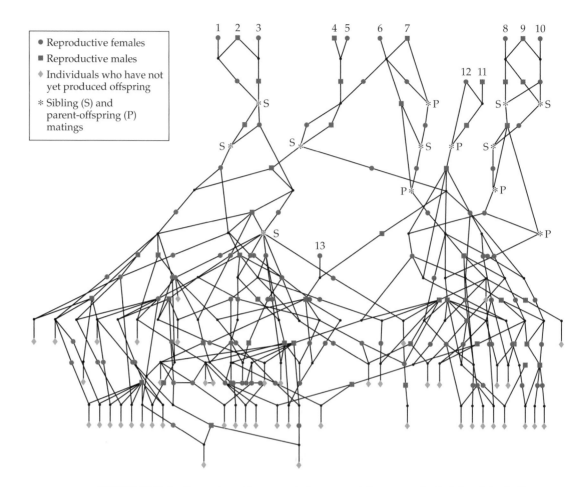

FIGURE 14.5 In the past, captive populations were often extensively inbred, including sibling–sibling matings and parent–offspring matings, as illustrated by this pedigree of a captive group of Przewalski's horses. The 13 "founder" individuals are indicated with numbers. (After Thomas 1995.)

captive animals as part of species survival plans, to prevent pairing of related animals and avoid inbreeding depression. Hundreds of studbooks currently exist, detailing the parentage of European, North American, Japanese, Australian, and other international captive animals. This system of pedigree construction can also be used to create a breeding program to prevent the gradual loss of genetic diversity over time in small populations (see Chapter 11).

Ex situ conservation efforts have been increasingly directed at saving endangered species of invertebrates as well. One of the most striking examples is the family of partulid snails of the Pacific island of Moorea (Miller et al. 2007; Lee et al. 2008). Most of the 33 species of this snail family became extinct in the wild after a predatory snail was introduced to control an agricultural pest. Currently 4 of the partulid species survive in a captive breeding program. Attempts to reintroduce the native species on Moorea have failed because of continued attacks from the predatory snail.

Other important targets for captive breeding programs are the breeds of domestic animals on which human societies depend for animal protein, dairy products, leather, wool, agricultural labor, transportation, and recreation. Even though enormous populations of domestic animals exist (over 1 billion cattle and 1 billion sheep, for example), diverse and distinctive breeds of domestic animals adapted to local

FIGURE 14.6 Soay sheep are a relict breed (a breed of an otherwise extinct group) of sheep living in the St. Kilda Islands, off the coast of Scotland. Soays retain characteristics of the first sheep brought to Britain more than 5000 years ago, and some of these characteristics may be valuable for low-maintenance animal husbandry in the future: small size (25–36 kg), robust health, and the ability to shed their fleece. (Photograph © Mark Boulton/Alamy.)

conditions are rapidly dying out as traditional agricultural practices are abandoned and intensive, high-yield agriculture is emphasized. For example, out of 3831 breeds of ass, water buffalo, cattle, goat, horse, pig, and sheep that existed during the last 100 years, 16% have already become extinct and an additional 23% are rare and in danger of extinction (Ruane 2000). Half of the breeds of domestic poultry are endangered. Preservation of the genetic variation from these local breeds for characteristics such as disease resistance, drought tolerance, general health, and meat production is crucial to animal breeding programs (**Figure 14.6**). Governments and conservation organizations are maintaining secure populations of some of these local breeds and developing frozen collections of sperm and embryos for later use. However, much more needs to be done to protect this global resource needed for healthy and productive domestic animals.

LIMITATIONS OF EX SITU CONSERVATION   Ex situ conservation should not be regarded as the ideal solution for preserving all or even most species on the verge of extinction. Short- and long-term costs, limited population size, adaptation to artificial environments, inability to learn survival skills, and potential genetic problems are all significant concerns with ex situ preservation (Miller et al. 2007; Zimmerman et al. 2008). We will now address some of the limitations of ex situ conservation in detail:

- *Cost*. Particularly with respect to large animals, ex situ conservation is not cheap. Zoos are considerably more expensive to operate than many other conservation programs, and protecting individual species in this setting simply isn't cost effective as a single strategy; for example, the cost of maintaining African elephants and black rhinos in zoos is 50 times greater than protecting the same number of individuals in East African national parks (Leader-Williams 1990), so it is obvious that protecting these animals in the wild is a more cost-effective option. In such cases, an entire community consisting of thousands or tens of thousands of species is preserved, along with a range of ecosystem services. But it is also true that zoos and aquariums are able to attract money from visitors and donors that allows them to maintain populations of captive animals and use high-profile species to raise money for the protection of their wild counterparts. For smaller animal species, or for plant or animal species for which habitat preservation and management is prohibitively expensive, ex situ conservation can be more effective than attempting to sustain a wild population. The cost of maintaining each new captive chick of the endangered Puerto Rican parrot is $22,000; while this sounds expensive, it compares favorably with the $1 million spent per year to protect the declining wild population of 30–35 birds (White et al. 2005; Morell 2008). To date, 62 birds have been raised in captivity and 46 have been released back to the wild.

- *Population size.* To prevent genetic drift, ex situ populations of at least several hundred and preferably several thousand individuals need to be maintained. Because of space limitations, no one zoo can maintain such large numbers of any of the larger animal species. Globally, only a few vertebrate species are maintained in captivity at such numbers, and these populations are distributed across tens and even hundreds of institutions. Zoos are working to maintain genetic variation by breeding distantly related individuals, in part through the transport of stored sperm and better record keeping. In botanical gardens, only one or a few individuals of most species typically are maintained, especially in the case of trees.

> Captive populations are expensive to maintain and present certain ethical issues. Also, animals raised in captivity may lose needed behaviors and be unable to survive if released back in the wild.

- *Adaptation.* Ex situ populations may undergo genetic adaptation to their artificial environment (Williams and Hoffman 2009). For example, animal species conditioned to rapidly flee a predator will often not thrive in a fenced-in enclosure. The more docile, less reactive individuals are more likely to reproduce, and so the zoo population will change genetically over time. If the animals from this captive population are later returned to the wild, they may no longer be able to evade their natural enemies.

- *Learning skills.* Individuals in ex situ populations may be ignorant of their natural environment and unable to survive in the wild. For example, captive-bred animals released back into the wild may no longer recognize wild foods as edible or their predators as dangerous, or be able to locate water sources. This problem is most likely to occur among social mammals and birds, whose juveniles learn survival skills and locations of critical resources from adult members of the population. Migratory animals may not know where or when to migrate. Providing appropriate training for captive animals may be needed before they can be released back in the wild, as described in Chapter 13.

- *Genetic variability.* Ex situ populations may represent only a limited portion of the gene pool of the species. If a captive population was started using individuals collected from a warm lowland site, for example, these animals may be unable to adapt physiologically to colder highland sites formerly occupied by the species. Also, small captive populations will lose genetic variation over time because of genetic drift, as discussed in Chapter 11.

- *Continuity.* Ex situ conservation efforts require a continuous supply of funds and a steady institutional policy. While this is also true to some extent for in situ conservation efforts, interruption of care in a zoo, aquarium, or greenhouse lasting only days or weeks can result in considerable losses of both individuals and species. Frozen and chilled collections of sperm, eggs, tissues, and seeds are particularly vulnerable to the loss of electric power. The 2010 earthquakes in Chile and Haiti and the recent decline of government services in many places illustrate how rapidly conditions can shift in a country. Zoos will not be able to maintain their collections under such circumstances.

- *Concentration.* Because ex situ conservation efforts are sometimes concentrated in one relatively small place, there is a danger that an entire population of an endangered species will be destroyed by a catastrophe such as a fire, hurricane, or epidemic. Hurricane Andrew, for example, flattened zoos all over South Florida, setting loose large numbers of captive animals.

- *Surplus animals.* Some species, such as small monkeys, breed too easily in captivity. What should be done with these surplus animals that no other zoo wants and that have no chance of surviving in the wild? This ethical issue must be addressed: the welfare of any animal taken into human custody is the responsibility of its captors. It is often unacceptable to kill or sell an individual animal, particularly when each animal in a highly threatened species might represent a key component of the species' future survival.

In spite of these limitations, ex situ conservation strategies may prove to be the best—perhaps the only—alternative when in situ preservation of a species is difficult or impossible. As Michael Soulé says, "There are no hopeless cases, only people without hope and expensive cases" (Soulé 1987).

ETHICAL ISSUES   Ex-situ techniques provide technological solutions to problems caused by human activities. Often the cheapest solution and the one most likely to succeed is protection of the species and its habitat in the wild so that it can recover naturally. Ex situ populations help support this solution through fundraising, research, and education programs and at the same time provide a safety net for those species that will become extinct without human intervention. When scientists consider ex situ methods for endangered species, they need to answer several ethical questions (Zimmermann et al. 2008):

1. How will establishing an ex situ population really benefit the wild population? Is it better to allow the last few individuals of a species to live out their days in the wild or to breed a captive population that may be unable to readapt to wild conditions?

2. Does a population of a rare species that has been raised in captivity and does not know how to survive in its natural environment really represent a victory for the species?

3. Are species held in captivity primarily for the benefit of these individuals or their entire species, the economic benefit of zoos, or the pleasure of zoo visitors?

4. Are the animals in captivity receiving appropriate care based on their biological needs? Does the benefit of the entire species outweigh any cost to the individual animals?

5. Are sufficient efforts being made to educate the public about conservation issues?

Even when the answers to these questions indicate a need for ex situ management, it is not always feasible to create ex situ populations of rare animal species. A species may have been so severely reduced in numbers that there is low breeding success and high infant mortality due to inbreeding depression. Certain animals, particularly marine mammals, are so large or require such specialized environments that there is no way to maintain population sizes large enough for long-term sustainability. Many invertebrates have complex life cycles in which their diets change as they grow and in which their environmental needs vary in subtle ways. Many of these species are impossible to raise through their life cycles given our present knowledge. Finally, certain species simply do not mate and produce offspring in captivity. As a result of these considerations, zoos are increasingly linking the animals in their exhibits to conservation projects in the wild.

Aquariums

Public aquariums have traditionally been oriented toward the display of unusual and attractive fish, sometimes supplemented with exhibits and performances of seals, dolphins, and other marine mammals (**Figure 14.7A**). However, as concern for the environment has increased, aquariums have made conservation a major educational theme in the displays, publications, and media outlets. Aquariums have

(A)

FIGURE 14.7 (A) Public aquariums participate in both in situ and ex situ conservation programs and provide a valuable function by educating people about marine conservation issues. (B,C) Aquariums are becoming more involved in breeding and raising marine animals other than fish, as illustrated by this hatchery, where baby sea turtles will be raised and later released into the ocean. (A, photograph © tororo reaction/Shutterstock; B,C, photographs by Richard Primack.)

(B)

(C)

also taken the lead in advising consumers about eating seafood that is managed sustainably. The need is great, since large numbers of marine and freshwater fish species are declining and threatened with extinction. In North America alone, 21 species are known to have gone extinct since the arrival of European settlers, and 154 species are now classified as endangered (Baillie et al. 2004). Large-scale extinctions of fishes are occurring worldwide in places such as the African Great Lakes, the Andean lakes, Madagascar, and the Philippines. Other groups or organisms, such as mollusks and coral species, are similarly threatened with extinction.

In response to this threat to aquatic species, ichthyologists, marine mammalogists, and coral reef experts who work for public aquariums are increasingly linking up with colleagues in marine research institutes, government fisheries departments, and conservation organizations to develop programs for the conservation of rich natural communities and species of special concern. Currently approximately 600,000 individual fish are maintained in aquariums, with most of these obtained from the wild. Major efforts are being made to develop breeding techniques so that rare species can be maintained in aquariums without further collection in the wild and in the hope that some can be released back into the wild. These breeding programs utilize indoor aquarium facilities, seminatural water bodies, and fish hatcheries and farms.

Many of the techniques for fish breeding were originally developed by fisheries biologists for large-scale stocking operations involving trout, bass, salmon, and other commercial species. Other techniques were discovered in the aquarium pet trade, when dealers attempted to propagate tropical fish for sale. These techniques are now being applied to endangered freshwater fauna. Programs for breeding endangered marine fishes and coral species are still in an early stage, but both public and private groups are making impressive efforts to unlock the secrets of propagating some of the more difficult species. Commercial production levels have been achieved for numerous species, and home aquarists can now expect fishes, corals, and other creatures to have been raised in captivity or be certified as having been sustainably collected from the wild.

Aquariums have an increasingly important role to play in the conservation of endangered cetaceans, manatees, sea turtles, and other large marine animals. Aquarium personnel often respond to public requests for assistance in handling animals stranded on beaches or disoriented in shallow waters. The lessons learned from working with common species may be used by the aquarium community to develop programs to aid endangered species. Extensive experience with captive populations of the bottle-nosed dolphin, the most popular aquarium species, is being applied to other species. Researchers are able to maintain colonies, breed them naturally or perform artificial insemination, hand-raise calves, and release captive-born animals into the natural environment. Some aquariums have established hatcheries where large numbers of baby sea turtles can be raised and later released back into the wild (**Figure 14.7B,C**). Such programs are of great interest to the public, and wind up attracting volunteers.

> Aquariums have made the conservation of marine species a significant priority, with a special focus on fish and marine mammals.

The ex situ preservation of aquatic biodiversity takes on additional significance due to the dramatic recent increase in aquaculture, which represents about 30% of fish and shellfish production worldwide. This aquaculture includes the extensive salmon, carp, and catfish farms of the temperate zones, the shrimp farms of the tropics, and the 12 million tons of aquatic products grown in China and Japan. As fish, frogs, mollusks, and crustaceans increasingly become domesticated and are raised to meet human needs, it becomes necessary to preserve the genetic stocks needed to continue improvements in these species—and to protect them against disease and unforeseeable threats. Ironically, fishes and invertebrates that have escaped from aquaculture present major threats to the diversity of indigenous species because these exotic species can become invasive, spread disease, and hybridize with local species (Frazer 2009). A challenge for the future will involve balancing the need to increase human food production from aquaculture with the need to protect aquatic biodiversity from increasing human threats.

Botanical Gardens and Arboretums

Gardening is enjoyed by millions of people worldwide and has a history that dates back thousands of years. Kitchen gardens have long provided a source of vegetables and herbs for households. In ancient times, doctors and healers kept gardens of medicinal plants to treat their patients. In more recent centuries, royal families established large private gardens for their personal enjoyment, and governments established botanical gardens for the urban public. In recognition of the vital role plants play in the economic activity of society, many European countries set up botanical gardens throughout their colonial empires. An **arboretum** is a specialized botanical garden focusing on trees and other woody plants. While the major purpose of many of these large gardens was the display of beautiful plants, they also illustrate the diversity of the living world and assist in the dissemination and propagation of plants that can be used in horticulture, agriculture, forestry, landscaping, and industry.

The world's 1775 botanical gardens now contain major collections of living plants and represent a crucial resource for plant conservation; they currently contain about 4 million living plants, representing 80,000 species—approximately 30% of the world's flora (Guerrant et al. 2004; www.bgci.org). When we add in the species grown in greenhouses, subsistence gardens, and hobby gardens, the numbers are increased. One of the world's largest botanical gardens, the Royal Botanic Gardens, Kew, in England, has over 30,000 species of plants under cultivation, about 10% of the world's total; 2700 of these are listed as threatened under the IUCN categories. One of the most exciting new botanical gardens is the Eden Project in southwest England, which focuses on displaying and explaining over 5000 species of rain forest, temperate, and Mediterranean plants in giant domes that comprise the world's largest greenhouse (**Figure 14.8**) (edenproject.com). The Eden Project currently receives about 1.4 million visitors per year.

FIGURE 14.8 The Eden Project in Cornwall, England, cultivates more than 5000 plant species of economic importance in a series of giant greenhouses. The project has an appealing public image, as seen by these visitors to the project's Mediterranean Biome. (Photograph © Jack Sullivan/Alamy.)

Botanical gardens increasingly focus their efforts on cultivating rare and endangered plant species, and many specialize in particular types of plants (Given 1995). The Arnold Arboretum of Harvard University grows thousands of different temperate tree species, and the New England Wild Flower Society has a collection of thousands of perennial temperate herbs at its Garden in the Woods location. South Africa's leading botanical garden has 25% of South Africa's plant species growing in cultivation. More than 250 botanical gardens maintain nature reserves that serve as important conservation areas in their own right. In addition, botanical gardens are able to educate an estimated 200 million visitors per year about conservation issues.

In many ways, plants are easier to maintain in controlled conditions than animals. Adequate population samples can often be established from seeds, shoot and root cuttings, and other plant parts and by using tissue culture techniques. Most plants have similar basic needs for light, water, and minerals, which can be readily supplied in greenhouses and gardens. Adjusting light, temperature, humidity levels, soil type, and soil moisture to suit species is the main concern, but this is often easily determined through knowledge of the plant's natural growing conditions. Since plants do not move, they often can be grown in high densities. If space is a limiting factor, plants can be pruned to a small size. Plants can often be maintained outdoors in gardens, where they need minimal care and weeding to survive. Some perennial plants, particularly shrubs and trees, are long-lived, so individuals can be kept alive for decades or centuries once they grow beyond the seedling stage. Species that are primarily inbreeders (self-fertilizing), such as wheat, need fewer individuals to maintain genetic variability than primarily outcrossing species such as maize, or corn. Many plant species readily produce seeds on their own, which can be collected and germinated to produce more plants. Wind, insects, and other animals cross-pollinate many plants in botanical gardens, while other species naturally self-pollinate. Simple hand pollination is used to produce seeds in some plant species. Botanical gardens and research institutes have developed collections of seeds, sometimes called **seed banks**, from both wild and cultivated plants, which provides a crucial backup to their living collections. Many plants, particularly those found in the temperate zone, in dry climates, and growing in disturbed conditions, have seeds that can lie dormant for years—even decades—in cool, dry conditions.

Botanical gardens are in a unique position to contribute to conservation efforts because living collections in botanical gardens and their associated herbaria of dried plant collections represent the best sources of information we have on plant distribution and habitat requirements. The staff members of botanical gardens are often recognized authorities on plant identification, distribution, and conservation status. Expeditions sent out by botanical gardens discover new species and determine the distribution and status of known species.

> Living collections of plants in botanical gardens provide ex situ protection and knowledge of plants that are either endangered or of economic importance.

The conservation of endangered species is becoming one of the major goals of botanical gardens as well as of zoos. In the United States, conservation efforts by a network of 34 botanical gardens are being coordinated by the Center for Plant Conservation based at the Missouri Botanical Garden (http://centerforplantconservation.org). These botanical gardens maintain joint collections of over 700 rare plant species. While most plant species occur in the tropics, the United States alone has 3000 species that are threatened in some way, and more than 450 of the threatened species are now being grown in cultivation in these botanical gardens. Their ultimate goal is to have adequate genetic material and expertise necessary to reintroduce a species back into the wild, should it become necessary to do so (Vitt et al. 2010). Ex situ materials can be thought of as "insurance policies," and like all insurance policies, it is best not to have to redeem them.

Botanical Gardens Conservation International (BGCI) represents and coordinates the conservation efforts of over 700 botanical gardens. Priorities of this program involve creating a worldwide database to coordinate collecting activity and identify important species that are underrepresented or absent from living collections. One project involves creating an online PlantSearch database that currently lists over 575,000 species and varieties growing in botanical gardens, of which about 3000 are rare or threatened. The data identify which botanical gardens grow the plant and provide links to the IUCN lists of threatened plants, along with image-search services for pictures of the plant (www.bgci.org).

Most botanical gardens are located in the temperate zone, even though most of the world's plant species are found in the tropics. A number of major gardens do exist in places such as Singapore, Sri Lanka, Java, and Colombia, but establishing new botanical gardens in the tropics should be a priority for the international community, along with training local plant taxonomists, geneticists, and horticulturalists to fill staff positions (Guerrant et al. 2004).

Seed Banks

Botanical gardens and research institutes have developed seed banks—collections of seeds from the wild and from cultivated plants (Johnson 2008). Seed banks have generally focused on the approximately 100 plant species that make up over 90% of human food consumption, but they are devoting more and more attention to a wider range of species that may be threatened with extinction or loss of genetic variability.

As mentioned earlier, seeds of most plant species can be stored in cold, dry conditions in seed banks for long periods of time and then later germinated to produce new plants (**Figure 14.9**). At low temperatures, a seed's metabolism slows down and the food reserves of the embryo are maintained. This property makes seeds extremely well suited to ex situ conservation efforts, since seeds of large numbers of rare species can be stored in a small space with minimal supervision and at a low cost. The U.S. Department of Agriculture Agricultural Research Service (USDA ARS) National Center for Genetic Resources Preservation (NCGRP), formerly called the National Seed Storage Laboratory, at Fort Collins, Colorado, stores some seeds in conditions as low as −196°C. The NCGRP stores over 500,000 seed samples from 7000 species (ars.usda.gov). The Institute of Crop Germplasm Resources in Beijing, China, has over 370,000 seed collections. More than 60 other major seed banks exist in the world, with their activities coordinated by the Consultative Group on International Agricultural Research (CGIAR). Along with 1300 smaller regional collections, these seed banks collectively maintain about 6 million seed samples (BGCI 2005). The focus of most of these facilities is on preserving the genetic variation needed for breeding purposes in crop species, such as wheat, rice, corn (maize), and soybeans.

> Seed banks represent an effective strategy for plant conservation because the seeds of many wild plant species and crop plants can be stored for years in cold dry conditions.

At present, somewhere around 30,000 wild plant species are represented in seed banks, just over 10% of the world's total species. To deal with the remaining species, many botanical gardens actively collect and store seeds, especially from species in danger of extinction. The seed banks maintained by botanical gardens allow a greater range of genetic variation to be preserved than exists in their living collections. The world's largest bank is the Millennium Seed Bank Project of the Royal Botanic Gardens, Kew, which has a goal of conserving the seeds of 25% of the world's estimated 250,000 species by the year 2020. The particular focus of the collection is species from dry climates of the world and the flora of the United Kingdom. A group of botanical gardens and the Bureau of Land Management in the United States have formed the Seeds of Success program, with a goal of collecting and preserving the seeds of all U.S. native species. Norway has recently established the newest seed bank, the Svalbard Global Seed Vault, in which millions of frozen seed samples will be stored below permafrost. Seed banks are also expanding their collections to include the pollen of seed plants and the spores of ferns, mosses, fungi, and microorganisms.

(A)

(B)

(C)

(D)

FIGURE 14.9 (A) The National Center for Genetic Resources Preservation (NCGRP) in Fort Collins, Colorado is an example of a modern seed bank facility. (B) At seed banks, seeds of many plant varieties are sorted, cataloged, and stored at freezing temperatures. (C) Seeds are also stored in liquid nitrogen at –196°C. (D) Seeds come in a wide variety of sizes and shapes. Each such seed represents a genetically unique, dormant individual. (Photographs courtesy of the U.S. Department of Agriculture.)

Organizations establishing seed banks have developed sampling strategies to ensure that they represent most of the genetic variability found within a species (Guerrant et al. 2004). To achieve this goal, seeds of each species should be collected from at least five populations, and 10–50 individuals should be sampled within each population. Also, collecting should not be so intensive that most of the seeds are removed from wild populations.

While seed banks have great potential for conserving species, they are limited by certain problems. If power supplies fail or equipment breaks down, an entire frozen collection may be damaged. Even seeds in storage gradually lose their ability to germinate after energy reserves are exhausted and harmful mutations are accumulated. Old seed supplies simply may not germinate. To overcome the gradual deterioration of quality, samples must be regenerated periodically by germinating seeds, growing new plants to maturity, controlling pollination, and storing new samples. The testing and rejuvenation of seed samples can be a formidable task for seed banks with large collections. Renewing seed vigor in species that have large individual plants and delayed maturity, such as trees, may be extremely expensive and time-consuming.

Approximately 10% of the world's plant species have recalcitrant seeds that either lack dormancy or do not tolerate low-temperature storage conditions and consequently cannot be stored in seed banks. Seeds of these species must germinate right away or die. Species with recalcitrant seeds are much more common in tropical forests than in the temperate zone, and the seeds of many economically important tropical fruit trees, timber trees, and plantation crops such as cocoa and rubber cannot be stored. Intensive investigations are underway to find ways of storing recalcitrant seeds; one possibility may be storing just the embryo from inside the seed, or the young seedling. One of the ways to preserve genetic variation in these species is to establish special botanical gardens known as **clonal repositories**, or clonal orchards, which require considerable area and expense. In the past, root crops such as cassava (manioc), yams, and sweet potatoes have not been well represented in seed banks because they often do not form seeds. Genetic variation in these species is being preserved by vegetative propagation in special gardens such as the International Potato Center in Peru and the International Center for Tropical Agriculture in Colombia. This undertaking is crucial, as these root crops are very important in the diets of people in developing tropical countries. An alternative method of conserving this genetic variability involves the in situ preservation of traditional agricultural practices (see Chapter 20). Vegetative propagation is also needed for plant species that have become so rare that in some cases only a single individual remains. For such species, parts of a single leaf can be grown in tissue culture and then used to propagate whole plants.

AGRICULTURAL SEED BANKS Seed banks have been embraced by agricultural research institutes and the agricultural industry as an effective resource for preserving and using the genetic variability that exists in agricultural crops and their wild relatives. Often resistance to particular diseases and pests is found in only one variety of a crop, known as a **landrace**, that is grown in only one small area of the world, or in a wild relative. Preserving the genetic variability represented by landraces is crucial to the agricultural industry's interest in maintaining and increasing the high productivity of modern crops and their ability to respond to changing environmental conditions such as acid rain, global climate change, and soil erosion. Agricultural researchers have been combing the world for landraces of major food crops that can be stored and later hybridized with modern varieties in crop improvement programs. Many of the major food crops such as wheat, maize (corn), oats, potatoes, and soybeans and other legumes are well represented in seed banks, and other important crops such as rice, millet, and sorghum are being intensively collected. Researchers are in a race against time to preserve genetic variability because traditional farmers throughout the world, who occupy only 10% to 15% of the world's cultivated land, are abandoning their diverse local crop varieties in favor of standard, high-yielding varieties (Altieri 2004) (**Box 14.2**). This worldwide phenomenon is illustrated by Sri Lankan farmers, who grew 2000 varieties of rice until the late 1950s, when they switched over to five high-yielding varieties.

To better understand the value of agricultural seed banks, consider the following classic example. Rice crops in Africa were being devastated by a virus called grassy stunt virus strain 1. To find a solution to this problem, agricultural researchers grew wild and cultivated rice plants from thousands of seed samples obtained from collections around the world (Lin and Yuan 1980). One seed sample of wild rice from India was found to contain a gene for resistance to this viral disease. These

> Some seed banks focus on the preservation of genetic variation found in major crop species, and play an important role in improving agriculture.

BOX 14.2 *Seed Savers and Crop Varieties*

■ Many common crop plants, including the fruits and vegetables that most people eat regularly, are potentially threatened by low genetic diversity. The reason for this is simple: Commercial farming tends to emphasize a few varieties that have high yield and appeal to consumer preferences for flavor, shape, size, and color. As such, many unique varieties of common crops have been ignored and are now relatively uncommon, even rare. Some varieties might have died out altogether, if not for the activities of ordinary gardeners and plant breeders, especially the efforts of a small Iowa-based organization, founded in 1975, called Seed Savers Exchange (SSE).

SSE concentrates on preserving many little-known "heirloom" varieties of crop plants that were brought to North America by settlers from other countries (www.seedsavers.org). Do you like cucumbers? What about mini-white cucumbers, Parisian pickling cucumbers, or Mexican sour gherkins? In the 35 years of its existence, SSE has organized a group of some 750 individual gardeners and plant breeders responsible for preserving over 12,000 different varieties of crop plants, which are offered in the SSE catalog, newsletters, and Web site to other interested gardeners, plant breeders, and historical preservation societies. Most of these varieties are offered by only one grower, who is specifically responsible for acting as curator for the variety, which shows just how unusual many of these varieties have become.

Many of these unique varieties of vegetables and fruits have long and fascinating histories, particularly the heirloom plants that can be traced back for centuries—even millennia—to the place of origin, perhaps a village or town in Europe. Other plants may be interesting to look at, have medicinal properties, or be unusually colorful or flavorful. These reasons alone are sufficient rationale for many gardeners to obtain these varieties. In addition, these varieties are of great potential value in breeding of new crop varieties to deal with future threats to agriculture.

SSE founders Kent and Diane Whealy run a farm in Iowa (appropriately called Heritage Farm) at which many of the different varieties are grown. To assure that no crop is left out because of habitat or climate limitations, growers are located in different parts of the United States and in different climatic zones. SSE makes a phenomenal number of interesting plants available to ordinary gardeners. One curator in Iowa offers almost 200 different types of squash and 53 varieties of watermelon. And for those growers seeking a particular variety—perhaps one they remember from childhood but for which they have no name—the "Plant Finder Service," appearing annually in the *Seed Savers Harvest Edition*, publishes growers' descriptions of the plants they want and appeals to the general membership for help finding them.

The SSE produces the *Garden Seed Inventory*, an inventory of hundreds of seed catalogs and thousands of vegetable varieties. The headquarters of SSE is the Heritage Farm in Iowa, where many unusual and hard-to-find vegetable varieties are grown. (Inset photograph © Judith Ann Griffith; farm photograph courtesy of John Torgrimson.)

wild plants were immediately incorporated into a major breeding program to transfer the gene for viral resistance into high-yielding varieties of rice. If the sample of wild rice had not been collected or had died out before being discovered, the future of rice cultivation in Africa would have been uncertain.

Despite their obvious successes in collecting and storing material, agricultural seed banks have several important limitations. Collections are often poorly documented regarding the locality of collection and growing conditions. Many of the seeds are of unknown quality and may not germinate. Crops of regional significance as well as medicinal plants, fiber plants, and other useful plants are not as well represented, even though these are economically significant to tropical countries.

Many agricultural seed banks are coordinated by the Consultative Group on International Agricultural Research (CGIAR) and the International Board for Plant Genetic Resources (www.cgiar.org; http://www.bioversityinternational.org/). One of the largest seed banks in the world, with about 80,000 separate collections of rice seeds, is maintained by the International Rice Research Institute, an organization with headquarters in the Philippines that was instrumental in the development of high-yielding, Green Revolution crop varieties. Other specialized seed collections are held by the International Maize and Wheat Improvement Center in Mexico, which holds 12,000 samples of maize and 100,000 samples of wheat, and by the Plant Genetic Resources Unit at the National Germplasm System repository in Geneva, New York. CGIAR is currently establishing a $260 million Global Crop Diversity Trust to help with the annual maintenance costs of these collections (www.croptrust.org).

A major controversy in the development of agricultural seed banks is who owns and controls the genetic resources of crops (Brush 2007). The genes of local landraces of crop plants and wild relatives of crop species represent the building blocks needed to develop elite, high-yielding varieties suitable for modern agriculture (Nabhan 2008). Approximately 96% of the raw genetic variation necessary for modern agriculture comes from developing countries such as India, Ethiopia, Peru, Mexico, Indonesia, and China, yet most corporate breeding programs for elite strains are located in the industrialized countries of North America and Europe (**Figure 14.10**). In the past, genetic material was perceived as free for the taking: The staffs of international seed banks freely collected seeds and plant tissue from developing countries and gave them to research stations and seed companies. Seed companies then developed new strains through sophisticated breeding programs and field trials. The resulting seeds were then sold at high prices to maximize profits that often totaled hundreds of millions of dollars a year, but the countries from which the original seeds were collected did not receive any profit from this activity.

> Countries, corporations, scientists and local people are working to determine who owns the genetic variation found in economically important crops and other plant species, and how the value can be fairly shared.

Developing countries now question why they should share their biological materials freely if they will have to pay for new seed varieties and cultivated plants based on those genetic resources. In fact, all countries of the world benefit from the free exchange of seeds and plant tissues. The modern varieties developed by international breeding centers, often using modern DNA technology, and now grown throughout the world have the best qualities of the landraces that were originally found in many different countries. Many countries contribute genetic resources to international breeding efforts, but they also receive benefits in terms of higher agricultural productivity. Indeed, two-thirds of the agriculture of developing countries uses crops that were first domesticated in other regions of the world.

In 1993, a group of countries drew up the Convention on Biological Diversity in an effort to provide a fair way of dealing with the situation (see Chapter 21). The convention, signed by 170 countries, sets forth a general framework for sharing the financial benefits of genetic resources more fairly and gives incentives for countries

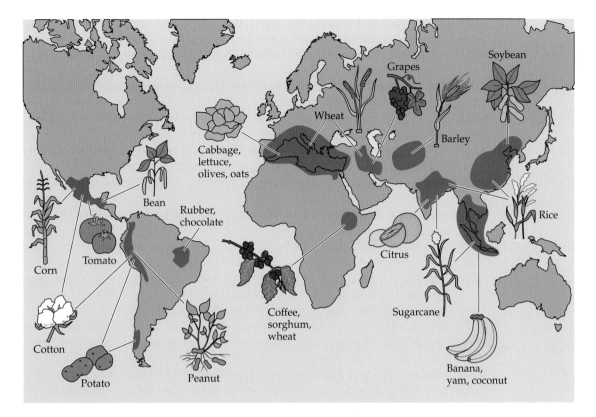

FIGURE 14.10 Crop species show high genetic diversity in certain areas of the world, often where the species was first domesticated or where the species is still grown in traditional agricultural settings. This genetic diversity is of international importance in maintaining the productivity of agricultural crops. (Map courtesy of Garrison Wilkes.)

that preserve biological diversity. Among the important policy recommendations of the Convention on Biological Diversity are the following:

- Countries have the right to control access to their biological diversity and should be paid for its use.

- Countries have a responsibility to inventory their biological diversity and protect it.

- Collectors must have permission to collect samples from the host country, the local community, and the landowners.

- As much as possible, research, breeding, processing, and production of new varieties should take place in the countries where the biological resources occur.

- The financial benefits, new products, and new varieties should be shared fairly with countries that contributed genetic resources used in the final product.

Many countries, international agencies, conservation organizations, and corporations are presently developing the financial and legal mechanisms to carry out the provisions of the Convention on Biological Diversity. Disagreements among these groups have been difficult to resolve, which has impeded implementation of the convention. However, contracts have now being negotiated, with countries such as Costa Rica and Brazil taking the lead (see Chapter 5), and these will be followed carefully to determine whether they are mutually beneficial and to see whether they can serve as models for future contracts and other countries.

CONSERVING THE GENETIC RESOURCES OF TREES   Forestry is a huge, global industry that depends on the genetic variation found in trees for its long-term success (Grattapaglia et al. 2009). Relying on wild-collected seeds for establishing plantations has its drawbacks because selective logging often removes the superior trees and leaves the inferior ones behind. The results of poor initial seed sample will only be seen years and decades later in slow-growing, misshapen, disease-ridden trees with poor wood quality. To conserve genetic variation in tree species, foresters have used cuttings and families of closely related seeds taken from the best trees to establish plantations of superior genetic varieties, called **clone banks**, for long-term maintenance and research of commercially important tree species. For loblolly pine (*Pinus taeda*) alone, 8000 clones are being grown in clone banks in the southeastern United States. Selected trees are used to establish seed orchards for producing commercial seed. Once produced, storage of seeds is difficult for many important genera of trees such as oaks (*Quercus*) and poplars (*Populus*). Even pine seeds cannot be stored indefinitely and must eventually be grown as trees.

Preserving areas where commercial tree species occur naturally is an important way to protect genetic variability. International cooperation is needed in forestry research and conservation because commercial species are often grown far from their countries of origin. For example, loblolly pine and Monterey pine (*Pinus radiata*) from North America are planted on about 6 million ha of land outside that continent. In New Zealand, 1.3 million ha are planted in Monterey pine, making it a key element in the national economy. In Hungary, 19% of the forested area is planted in North American shipmast locust (*Robinia pseudoacacia* var. *rectissima*), because the species produces durable wood and grows on degraded, low-nutrient sites. These forest plantations far from home still depend on natural populations of the species to supply the genetic variability required for continued improvements and survival in a hostile environment.

Conclusion

As more of the environment is dominated by human activities, ex situ populations are playing an ever-greater role in contributing to the conservation of species in the wild. Species maintained in captivity and in cultivation can serve as ambassadors for their wild counterparts through a variety of conservation, research, and education programs. In the cases of highly endangered species, captive individuals can be used to establish new populations in the wild, once the threats to the species have been identified and controlled. Although ex situ programs can be expensive, they can also generate income—through the display of species in zoos, aquariums, and botanical gardens, genetic improvements in domesticated species, and new products developed by the biotech and medical industries. Some of this income must be directed to support the protection of biodiversity in the wild by funding the creation and management of protected areas, which is the topic of Part 5.

Summary

1. Some species that are in danger of going extinct in the wild can be maintained off-site under human supervision; this is known as ex situ conservation. These captive colonies can sometimes be used later to reestablish species in the wild, and are important in educating the public concerning conservation issues.

2. Zoos are developing self-sustaining populations of many rare and endangered terrestrial vertebrates, often using modern techniques of veterinary medicine. Currently zoos maintain over 2 million individuals of over 7400 species and subspecies, most of which were born in captivity. Collections are also being maintained of endangered breeds of domestic animals.

3. Aquariums increasingly emphasize conservation themes in their displays and outside activities, with marine mammals being a particular focus.

4. The world's botanical gardens and arboretums now make it one of their main priorities to collect and grow rare and endangered species. The seeds of most species of plants can be stored for long periods of time under cold conditions in seed banks. Seed banks often specialize in the collection of major crop species, commercial timber species, and their close relatives in order to preserve material for genetic improvement programs.

For Discussion

1. What are the similarities and differences among the ex situ conservation methods used for plants, terrestrial animals, and aquatic species?

2. Would biological diversity be adequately protected if every species were raised in captivity? Is this possible? Practical? How would freezing biological samples of every individual help to protect biological diversity? Again, is this possible and is it practical?

3. Are the arguments for preserving the genetic variability in domesticated species of animals and plants (and their close relatives) the same arguments we would put forward for saving endangered wild species?

4. How much of an ex situ facility's resources should be devoted to conservation efforts in order for the institution to announce that it is a conservation organization? What sorts of conservation activities are appropriate for each institution? Visit a zoo, aquarium, or botanical garden and evaluate it for its conservation activities and efforts; use or modify some of the methods of Miller et al. 2004 to develop your ideas.

Suggested Readings

Altieri, M. A. 2004. Linking ecologists and traditional farmers in the search for sustainable agriculture. *Frontiers in Ecology and the Environment* 2: 35–42. Traditional farmers (and farmers and gardners in general) have a lot to teach ecologists.

Bowkett, A. E. 2009. Recent captive-breeding proposals and the return of the ark concept to global species conservation. *Conservation Biology* 23: 773–776. Zoos balance the need to protect endangered species using in situ and ex situ approaches.

Clarke, A. G. 2009. The Frozen Ark Project: The role of zoos and aquariums in preserving the genetic material of threatened animals. *International Zoo Yearbook* 43: 222–230. Major efforts are underway to freeze genetic material from endangered species; when should this be part of a conservation strategy?

Conway, W. G., M. Hutchins, M. Souza, Y. Kapentanakos, and E. Paul. 2001. *The AZA Field Conservation Resource Guide.* Zoo Atlanta, Atlanta, GA. Information on hundreds of projects supported or directed by zoo and aquarium personnel.

Frazer, L. N. 2009. Sea-cage aquaculture, sea lice, and declines of wild fish. *Conservation Biology* 23: 599–607. Aquaculture has the potential to reduce the harvesting of wild species, but it also has considerable environmental impact.

Guerrant, E. O., Jr., K. Havens, and M. Maunder. 2004. *Ex Situ Conservation: Supporting Species Survival in the Wild.* Island Press, Washington, D.C. Describes the linkages between botanical gardens and plant conservation.

Holt, W. V., A. R. Pickard, J. C. Rodger, and D. E. Wildt (eds.). 2003. *Reproductive Science and Integrated Conservation.* Conservation Biology Series, no. 8. Cambridge University Press, New York. Advances in reproductive technology are having a major impact on captive breeding programs.

Johnson, R. C. 2008. Gene banks pay big dividends to agriculture, the environment, and human welfare. *PLoS Biology* 6: e148. Genetic diversity of crop plants is crucial to human society, but who really owns it?

Miller, B. and 9 others. 2004. Evaluating the conservation mission of zoos, aquariums, botanical gardens, and natural history museums. *Conservation Biology* 18: 86–93. Eight tough questions are asked with hopes that these institutions can become more effective.

Morell, V. 2008. Into the wild: Reintroduced animals face daunting odds. *Science* 320: 742–743. When captive animals are released into the wild, they have a difficult time establishing new populations.

Pukazhenthi, B., P. Comizzoli, A. J. Travis, and D. E. Wildt. 2006. Applications of emerging technologies to the study and conservation of threatened and endangered species. *Reproduction Fertility and Development* 18: 77–90. High-tech medicine comes to the zoo.

Vitt, P., K. Havens, A. T. Kramer, D. Sollenberger, and E. Yates. 2010. Assisted migration of plants: Changes in latitudes, changes in attitudes. *Biological Conservation* 143: 18–27. Seed banks need to be established in anticipation of a changing climate.

Williams, S. E. and E. A. Hoffman. 2009. Minimizing genetic adaptation in captive breeding programs: A review. *Biological Conservation* 142: 2388–2400. Species begin to adapt genetically to captive conditions, but then they may not be adapted to the wild.

Zimmermann, A., M. Hatchwell, L. Dickie, and C. D. West (eds.) 2008. *Zoos in the 21st Century: Catalysts for Conservation.* Cambridge University Press, Cambridge. Many modern zoos see the advancement of in situ wildlife conservation as part of their mission.

Chapter 15

Establishing Protected Areas

Ecosystems vary from a very few that are virtually unaffected by human activities (such as communities found on the deep ocean floor or in the most remote parts of the Amazon rain forest) to the many that are heavily modified by human activity (urban areas, agricultural land, artificial ponds, and heavily polluted lakes and rivers). Even in the most remote areas of the world, human influence is apparent in the form of rising carbon dioxide levels, changing climate, air pollution, and the collection of valuable natural products; conversely, even the most modified of human environments often retain remnants of the original biota.

Habitats with intermediate levels of disturbance present some of the most interesting challenges and opportunities for conservation biology because they often cover large areas. Considerable biodiversity may remain in selectively logged forests, heavily fished oceans, and grasslands grazed by domestic livestock. Conservation often means finding a compromise between protecting biodiversity and ecosystem function on the one hand, and satisfying immediate and long-term human needs for resources on the other.

A **protected area** is an area of land or sea dedicated by law or tradition to, and managed for, the protection of biodiversity and associated natural and cultural resources (www.iucn.org).

FIGURE 15.1 The increasing numbers and area of worldwide protected areas over the past 135 years. The values increase in the final year with the addition of protected areas with no known year of establishment. Note that marine protected areas have only been established over the last 4 decades, and their area is much smaller than terrestrial protected areas. (After www.unep-wcmc.org/ protected_areas/pdf/stateOfThe-World'sProtectedAreas.pdf.)

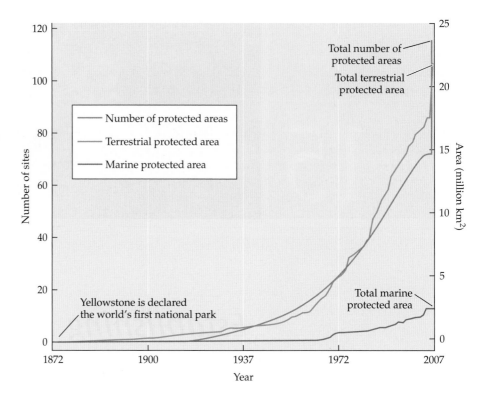

Protecting areas that contain healthy, intact ecosystems is the most effective way to preserve overall biodiversity. One could argue that it is ultimately the only way to preserve species, since we have the resources and knowledge to maintain only a small minority of the world's species in captivity. Preserving ecosystems involves establishing individual protected areas, creating networks of protected areas, managing those areas effectively, implementing conservation measures outside the protected areas, and restoring biological communities in degraded habitats (www.wri.org).

In this chapter we will discuss the critical first step in protecting biological communities—establishing legally designated protected areas governed by laws and regulations that allow widely varying degrees of commercial resource use, traditional use by local people, and recreational use. We'll begin our discussion by examining existing protected areas, and then we will explore the steps involved in creating new ones.

The momentum to establish protected areas has been increasing throughout the twentieth and early twenty-first centuries (**Figure 15.1**). Over 80% of the world's protected areas have been established since 1962, when the first World Parks Congress was held (Chape et al. 2003; www.wdpa.opg). Protected areas currently cover about 13% of the Earth's surface. This limited area of protected habitat emphasizes the biological significance of the 23% of the land that is managed for sustainable resource production, such as production forests, watersheds around reservoirs, and grazing lands, described in greater detail in Chapter 18.

Establishment and Classification of Protected Areas

Protected areas can be established in a variety of ways, but the most common mechanisms are these:

- Government action, usually at a national level, but often on regional or local levels as well

- Land purchases by private individuals and conservation organizations

- Actions of indigenous peoples and traditional societies

- Development of biological field stations (which combine biodiversity protection and research with conservation education) by universities and other research organizations

Although legislation and land purchases alone do not ensure habitat preservation, they can lay the groundwork for it. Partnerships among governments of developing countries, international conservation organizations, multinational banks, research and educational organizations, and governments of developed countries have developed many ways to bring together funding, training, and scientific and management expertise to establish new protected areas.

Each of these organizations has their own concerns and priorities that must be considered. At the time protected areas are being planned decisions must be made regarding what human activities and how much human disturbance will be allowed. In general, when greater amounts of human disturbance are permitted, a narrower scope of biodiversity is preserved. However, some aspects of biodiversity depend on a certain level of habitat disturbance, especially where humans have a long historical presence. For example, many plant and animal species require the ecosystem processes and structure created by traditional farming, as described in Chapter 18. When such farming is discontinued or intensified, sometimes these species can no longer survive.

The International Union for Conservation of Nature (IUCN) has developed a system of classifying protected areas that ranges from minimal (nature reserves, national parks, etc.) to intensive use of the habitat by humans, with six categories (**Table 15.1**). Of these categories, the first five can be defined as true protected areas, because their habitat is managed primarily for biological diversity. (However, a stricter definition would include only the first three categories.) Areas in the sixth category, managed-resource protected areas, are administered to conserve biological diversity, but the production of natural resources, such as timber and cattle, may take higher priority. Managed-resource protected areas can be particularly significant because they are often much larger in area than other categories of protected areas, because they still may contain many or even most of their original species, and because protected areas are often embedded in a matrix of areas managed for production.

> The IUCN has developed a classification system for protected areas ranging from strict nature reserves to managed-resource protected areas, depending on the level of human impact and the needs of society for resources.

Existing Protected Areas

At least 180 countries—and perhaps more—currently have protected areas (Chape et al. 2008; www.iucn.org). Among the countries without protected areas as of the year 2005 are Syria, Yemen, Equatorial Guinea, and Guinea-Bissau. While it could be argued that virtually all countries should have at least one national park, large countries with rich biotas and a variety of ecosystem types would obviously benefit from having many protected areas. As of 2009, more than 108,000 protected areas in IUCN categories I–VI had been designated worldwide, covering some 30 million km^2 on land and 2 million km^2 at sea (**Figure 15.2**).* This impressive total represents only about 13% of Earth's total land surface, which is about the same area as the land used to grow all of the world's crops. However, much of this protected land is not particularly valuable to people; the world's largest park is in

---

*Uncertainty about the number and size of protected areas stems from the different standards used throughout the world and degree of protection actually given to a designated area, and when the data was gathered.

TABLE 15.1 IUCN Protected Area Designations I–VI

Category	Description
Ia Strict nature reserves	Managed mainly for scientific research and monitoring; areas of land and/or sea possessing some outstanding or representative ecosystems, geological or physiological features, and/or species
Ib Wilderness areas	Managed mainly for wilderness protection; large areas of unmodified or slightly modified land and/or sea retaining their natural character and influence, without permanent or significant habitation, which are protected and managed so as to preserve their natural condition
II National parks	Managed mainly for ecosystem protection and recreation; natural areas of land and/or sea designated to (1) protect the ecological integrity of one or more ecosystems for present and future generations; (2) exclude exploitation or occupation inimical to the purposes of designation of the area; and (3) provide a foundation for spiritual, scientific, educational, recreational, and visitor opportunities, all of which must be environmentally and culturally compatible
III Natural monuments	Managed mainly for conservation of specific natural features; areas containing one or more-specific natural or natural/cultural features of outstanding or unique value because of inherent rarity, representative or aesthetic qualities, or cultural significance
IV Habitat/species management areas	Managed mainly for conservation through management intervention; areas of land and/or sea subject to active intervention for management purposes so as to ensure the maintenance of habitats and/or to meet the requirements of specific species
V Protected landscapes and seascapes	Managed mainly for landscape/seascape conservation and recreation; areas of land, with coast and sea as appropriate, where the interaction of people and nature over time has produced an area of distinct character with significant aesthetic, ecological, and/or cultural value, and often with high biological diversity
VI Managed-resource protected areas	Managed mainly for the sustainable use of natural ecosystems; areas containing predominantly unmodified natural systems, managed to ensure long-term protection and maintenance of biological diversity, while also providing a sustainable flow of natural products and services to meet community needs

Source: After www.iucn.org.

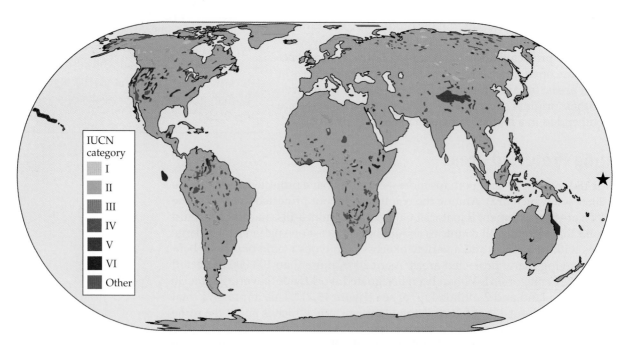

FIGURE 15.2 The world's terrestrial and marine protected areas. Although many small protected areas do not show up at this scale, all large areas in IUCN categories I–VI are indicated, as well as many areas that are protected in some manner (e.g., privately) but which do not have an official designation at the present time. Note the large protected areas in Greenland, the Hawaiian Islands, the Galápagos Islands, northern Alaska, northeastern Australia, and western China. The new Phoenix Island Protected Area is indicated by a star. (Based on World Database on Protected Areas 2005, www.wdpa.org.)

Greenland on inhospitable terrain and covers 970,000 km², accounting for about 3% of the global area protected. About 6% of the Earth's surface is in categories I–IV, *strictly protected* in scientific reserves and national parks.

The measurements of protected areas in individual countries and on continents are only approximate because sometimes the laws protecting national parks and wildlife sanctuaries are not strictly enforced; at the same time, there are sections of managed areas that, while not legally protected, are carefully protected in practice. Examples of this include the sections within U.S. national forests designated as wilderness areas. The coverage of strictly protected areas varies dramatically among countries: High proportions of land are protected in Germany (32%), Austria (36%), and the United Kingdom (15%), and surprisingly low proportions in Russia (8%), Greece (3%), and Turkey (3%). Even when a country has numerous protected areas, certain unique habitats of high economic value may remain unprotected (Dietz and Czech 2005; earthtrends.wri.org).

Marine Protected Areas

Marine conservation has lagged behind terrestrial conservation efforts; even establishing priorities has proved difficult (Salm et al. 2000; Game et al. 2009). Priorities also need to be established to protect freshwater ecosystems, such as streams, rivers, and lakes (Higgins et al. 2005). Only about 1% of the marine environment is included in protected areas, yet as much as 20% of it may need to be protected in order to manage declining commercial fishing stocks (**Figure 15.3**) (www.iucn.org; Spalding et al. 2008). Even more may be required to conserve the full range of coastal and marine biodiversity. Over 5000 marine and coastal protected areas have been estab-

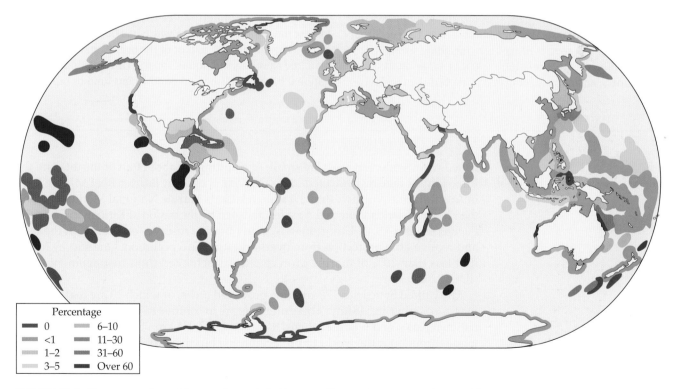

Percentage
- 0
- <1
- 1–2
- 3–5
- 6–10
- 11–30
- 31–60
- Over 60

FIGURE 15.3 The proportion of the continental shelf covered by marine protected areas. The colored areas extend out from the coast for ease of visualization. Note the high areas of coverage in the Hawaiian Islands, the west coast of North America, the Caribbean, the east coast of Australia, the Galápagos Islands, Greenland, and east Asia. (After Spalding et al. 2008.)

BOX 15.1 *The Phoenix Islands Protected Area: The World's Largest Marine Park*

■ The tiny Pacific islands nation of Kiribati (pronounced kirr-i-bas) has recently gained worldwide attention for its designation of the world's largest marine protected area (MPA). Located near the equator in the middle of the Pacific, the Republic of Kiribati first established the Phoenix Islands Protected Area (PIPA) in 2006 in conjunction with the New England Aquarium and Conservation International. Kiribati more than doubled the area of the reserve in 2008; now at 410,500 km² (about the size of the state of California or the country of Germany), the PIPA is the world's largest marine protected area and encompasses one of the last truly undisturbed oceanic coral archipelago ecosystems (Lilley 2008). The PIPA includes all eight Phoenix Island atolls and two submerged reef systems and is the first Pacific island MPA to contain significant deep sea habitat. It represents 16% of the global area of MPAs and has been nominated as a UNESCO World Heritage Site.

A veritable marine wilderness with very limited human exploitation (within the entire park, just 31 people reside on one atoll), the Phoenix Islands have survived unscathed from the water pollution and marine diseases that endanger less remote coral reefs, thus providing a glimpse into the prehuman past. The PIPA harbors over 120 species of coral and 514 species of reef fish, including strong representation of top predators, such as large sharks and groupers, an anomaly compared with overfished reefs else-

where in the world. The Islands also provide important habitat for migratory seabirds and turtles.

The remoteness of the Phoenix Islands makes them ideal for observing large-scale ecosystem functions: Since local anthropogenic impacts are so minimal, the effects of global phenomena such as a climate change and ocean acidification can be clearly seen, since these conditions affect the marine environment regardless of location. For instance, the corals of the archipelago suffered a massive bleaching event (when corals expel their symbiotic algae and then die) in 2002–2003 as a result of abnormally high sea surface temperatures (Alling et al. 2007). Based on the results of a recent research expedition, though, the ecosystem is recovering quickly.

> Marine protected areas are now being established throughout the world. Recently the Pacific island nation of Republic of Kirabati created the world's largest marine protected area in a region with minimal human impact.

Designating the protected area required the government to close the commercial fishery, which had been an economic mainstay for Kiribati; as part of the overall management plan, the New England Aquarium and Conservation International have established an endowment fund to replace

lished worldwide, but most are small. Accounting for about half of the total are the three largest marine protected areas (MPAs): the Great Barrier Reef Marine Park in Australia, the Northwestern Hawaiian Islands Marine National Monument, and the Phoenix Islands Protected Area (established by the nation of Kiribati in the South Pacific; see **Box 15.1**). Unfortunately, many marine reserves exist only on the map and receive little protection from overharvesting and pollution. One survey found that less than 10% of marine protected areas achieved their management goals (IUCN 2004).

The United States has 1700 marine protected areas, of which 13 are marine sanctuaries covering 46,548 km². These numbers are in contrast to the 906 national forests, national parks, and wildlife refuges that total 1,657,084 km². Urgent efforts are being made throughout the world to protect marine biodiversity by establishing marine parks that seek to protect the nursery grounds of commercial species and to maintain water quality and both physical and biological features of the ecosystem. In the process, high-quality protected areas can also maintain recreational activies such as swimming and diving and the economic benefits associated with tourism (**Figure 15.4**). However, many large marine areas remain completely unprotected at

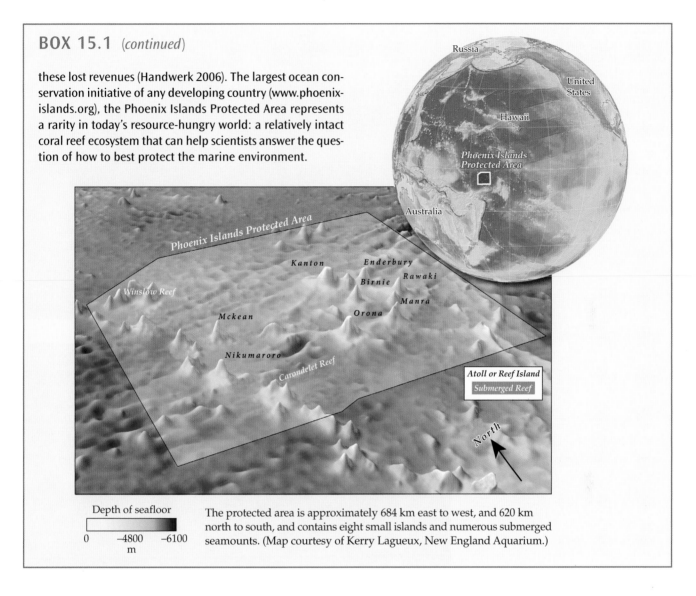

BOX 15.1 *(continued)*

these lost revenues (Handwerk 2006). The largest ocean conservation initiative of any developing country (www.phoenix-islands.org), the Phoenix Islands Protected Area represents a rarity in today's resource-hungry world: a relatively intact coral reef ecosystem that can help scientists answer the question of how to best protect the marine environment.

Depth of seafloor

0   −4800   −6100
m

The protected area is approximately 684 km east to west, and 620 km north to south, and contains eight small islands and numerous submerged seamounts. (Map courtesy of Kerry Lagueux, New England Aquarium.)

present (Guarderas et al. 2008). Conservation of freshwater environments shares many of the same challenges (Abell et al. 2008).

One approach to establishing marine protected areas involves protecting examples of each type of marine community. Determining biogeographical provinces for the marine environment is much more difficult than for the terrestrial environment, because boundaries between realms are less sharp, dispersal of larval and adult stages is more widespread, and the marine environment is less well known (Planes et al. 2009; Underwood et al. 2009). Marine biogeographical provinces are being identified using a combination of the distribution of related marine animals (coastal, shelf, ocean) and of the physical properties that affect species' ecology and distribution (currents, temperature).

The Effectiveness of Protected Areas

The value of protected areas in maintaining biological diversity is abundantly clear in many tropical countries; inside the park boundaries, forests and animal life abound, while outside the park, the land has been cleared and few animals are seen (Lee et al. 2007). Yet these protected areas still face threats from logging, hunting, and other

FIGURE 15.4 (A) The Monterey Bay National Marine Sanctuary (MBNMS) in California; (B) Feather worms and various coral species living on the ocean bottom at the Davidson Seamount, which is part of the MBNMS. (Photographs courtesy of NOAA.)

(A)

(B)

human activities. It is also true that some national parks have become even more degraded than neighboring areas, due to management problems and conflicts with local people (Wright et al. 2007). However, studies show that protected areas generally are effective in keeping land intact (Bruner et al. 2001; DeFries et al. 2005). In one study, land clearing in tropical forests in national parks was found to be far lower than in control areas surrounding those parks (**Figure 15.5**).

If national parks can be established where concentrations of species occur, an even higher percentage of species can be preserved. This explains why, in Mexico, 82% of mammal species are represented in protected areas that occupy only 4% of the coun-

> Although the number of species living within a protected area is an important indicator of its potential to protect biodiversity, protected areas need to maintain healthy ecosystems and viable populations of important species.

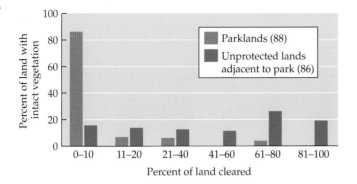

FIGURE 15.5 Land clearing of tropical forests in national parks is far lower than in control areas surrounding those parks. For example, the first two bars show that more than 80% of the parks have almost intact vegetation (<10% cleared), whereas less than 20% of nearby control areas have almost intact vegetation. (After Bruner et al. 2001.)

try (Ceballos 2007). Such locations are found along elevational gradients of mountains, at places where different geological formations are juxtaposed, in areas that are geologically old, and in places with an abundance of critical natural resources, such as streams and water holes. In addition, a system of protected areas can include a high percentage of a country's species if the system includes representatives of all habitats. In Britain, 88% of plant species occur in the protected area system, of which 26% are found exclusively within protected areas (Jackson et al. 2009).

Often a landscape contains large expanses of a fairly uniform habitat type and only a few small areas of rare habitat types. Protecting biological diversity in such a case probably depends not so much on preserving large areas of the common habitat type as on including representatives of all the habitats in a system of protected areas (Shafer 1999). Even though a protected area may be within the geographical range of an endangered species, that species may be absent if the habitat and land use patterns are not suited to the species (Rondinini et al. 2005).

It is also important to recognize that the long-term future of many species in protected areas, and even of the ecosystems themselves, remains in doubt. Populations of many species may be so reduced in size that they are likely to become extinct. Similarly, catastrophic events such as fires, outbreaks of disease, and episodes of poaching can rapidly eliminate particular species from isolated reserves. Consequently, although the number of species existing in a park is an important indicator of the park's potential in protecting biodiversity, the real value of the protected area lies in its ability to support viable long-term populations of species and maintain healthy ecosystems.

Creating New Protected Areas

As mentioned in the beginning of the chapter, protected areas can be established in a variety of ways, but the common mechanisms are (1) by government action (usually at a national level, but often at regional or local levels as well), (2) through purchases of land by private individuals and conservation organizations such as The Nature Conservancy (see Box 16.1), (3) via the established customs of indigenous people, and (4) through the development of biological field stations (which combine biodiversity protection and research with conservation education) by many universities and other research organizations (**Figure 15.6**).

National governments are the most important force in establishing and managing protected areas today. The international conservation community can help to establish guidelines and find opportunities to protect biological diversity, but in the end, national (and local) governments must determine their own priorities. Many countries are in the process of drafting, or have already prepared, national environmental action plans, national biodiversity action plans, or tropical forest action plans, which

FIGURE 15.6 Protected areas in Concord, a suburban town of 67 km² in eastern Massachusetts, have been established by different governmental agencies and private organizations. The area includes Walden Pond, where the naturalist Henry David Thoreau wrote his famous book, *Walden*. Note the wide variety in the sizes and shapes of protected areas. Many rare species (both native and nonnative) are found in these protected areas, but many are also found outside of these protected areas. (After Primack et al. 2009.)

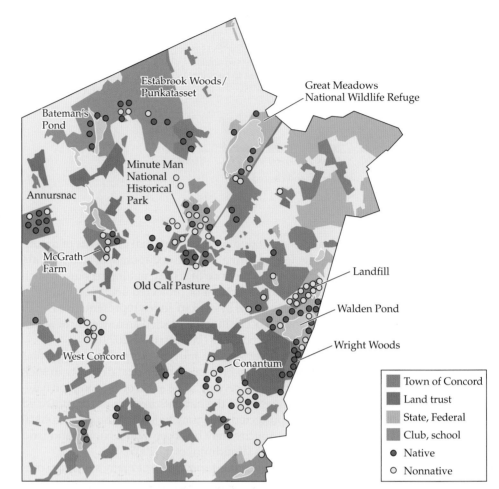

help identify priorities for protected areas. (National governments also determine the type of park management, a subject covered in detail in Chapters 17 and 18; park management is of central importance in ensuring that a protected area actually fulfills its goals and is not just a "paper park" that is soon destroyed and degraded.)

There are also important roles to be played by local and regional governments, conservation organizations, corporations, and even individuals. These organizations and individuals have often worked on their own, but they are increasingly forming partnerships to establish and manage new protected areas. Local people are often key partners in efforts to establish national parks. Traditional societies have established numerous protected areas to maintain their way of life or just to preserve their land. Many of these protected areas have been in existence for long periods and are linked to the religious beliefs of the people. Such "sacred sites" often have concentrations of rare plants and animals that have disappeared elsewhere and often include keystone resources such as springs and forested watersheds. National governments in many countries, including the United States, Canada, Colombia, Brazil, Australia, and Malaysia, have recognized the rights of traditional societies to own and manage the land on which they live, hunt, and farm, although in some cases recognition of land rights only results following conflict in the courts, in the press, and on the land. Many of these traditional societies are changing rapidly as they come into contact with modern society, and their attitudes toward the environment are changing as well.

Creating new protected areas requires the following steps, which we'll examine in detail in the following sections:

1. Identifying priorities for conservation

2. Determining those areas of each country that should be protected to meet conservation priorities

3. Linking new protected areas to existing conservation networks, using techniques such as gap analysis

Prioritization: What Should Be Protected?

In a crowded world with limited natural resources and limited government funding, it is crucial to establish priorities for conserving biological diversity. Although some conservationists would argue that no ecosystem or any portion of its species should ever be lost, the reality is that numerous species are in danger of going extinct and there are not enough resources available to save them all. The real challenge lies in finding ways to minimize the loss of biological diversity in an environment of limited financial and human resources (Bottrill et al. 2009). Conservation planners must address three interrelated questions: What needs to be protected? Where should it be protected? and How should it be protected? Three criteria can be used to answer the first two of these questions and set conservation priorities:

1. *Distinctiveness (or irreplaceability)*. An ecosystem composed primarily of rare endemic species or that has other unusual attributes (scenic value, geological features) is given higher priority for conservation than if it is composed primarily of common, widespread species. A species is often given more conservation value if it is taxonomically distinctive—that is, it is the only species in its genus or family—than if it is a member of a genus with many species (Faith 2008). Similarly, a population of a species having unusual genetic characteristics that distinguish it from other populations of the species might be a greater priority for conservation than a more typical population.

2. *Endangerment (or vulnerability)*. Species in danger of extinction are of greater concern than species that are not; thus, the whooping crane (*Grus americana*), with only about 382 individuals, requires more protection than the sandhill crane (*Grus canadensis*), with approximately 520,000 individuals. Ecosystems threatened with imminent destruction are also given priority, such as the rain forests of West Africa, the wetland ecosystems of the southeastern United States, and other ecosystems with numerous endemic and restricted-range species. Endangerment of an ecosystem can be estimated by the present size of its geographic range, the rate of decline in its range, and loss of its ecological functions (Nicholson et al. 2009).

3. *Utility*. Species that have present or potential value to people are given more conservation priority than species of no obvious use to people. For example, wild relatives of wheat, which are potentially useful in developing new, improved cultivated varieties, are given greater priority than species of grass that are not known to be related to any economically important plant. Species with major cultural significance, such as tigers in India and the bald eagle in the United States, are given high priority. Ecosystems of major economic value, such as coastal wetlands, are usually given greater priority for protection than less valuable communities such as dry scrubland.

FIGURE 15.7 The carnivorous Komodo dragon (*Varanus komodoensis*) of Indonesia is the largest living monitor lizard. Tourists flock to see these animals in the wild. Protecting this endangered species was an important reason for establishing the Komodo National Park. (Photograph © Stephen Frink Collection/Alamy.)

When these criteria are applied, the Komodo dragon of Indonesia (*Varanus komodoensis*) (**Figure 15.7**) surfaces as an example of a species that fits all three categories: it is the world's largest lizard (distinctive), it occurs on only a few small islands of a rapidly developing nation (endangered), and it has major potential as a tourist attraction in addition to being of great scientific interest (utility). Appropriately, these Indonesian islands are now protected within the Komodo National Park and are designated as one of the United Nations Educational, Scientific and Cultural Organization (UNESCO) World Heritage Sites (http://whc.unesco.org; see Chapter 21). These specially designated protected areas include diverse sites of overwhelming natural and/or cultural significance that are deemed to be "of outstanding value to humanity" and "irreplaceable sources of life and inspiration," transcending national boundaries.

The Western Ghats, a series of hills paralleling the southwestern coast of India, contain tropical forests that are similarly a high priority for conservation: These forests contain many endemic species, including the ancestors of several cultivated species, such as black pepper (distinctive); many of the products from these forests are necessary to the well-being of local villagers (utility); the forests perform vital watershed services that prevent flooding and provide hydroelectric power for the region (utility); and despite their importance, these forests are threatened by logging, by fires set by villagers to create forage for their animals, by the collection of fuelwood and other forest products, and by continuing fragmentation by human activities (endangered).

Determining Which Areas Should Be Protected

Using these three criteria, several prioritization systems have been developed at both national and international levels to target both species and ecosystems. These approaches are generally complementary; they differ more in their emphases than in fundamental principles. Such approaches are presently being reevaluated in relation to climate change.

THE SPECIES APPROACH One approach to establishing conservation priorities involves protecting particular species and, in doing so, protecting an entire biological community. Protected areas are often established to protect individual species of

FIGURE 15.8 The northern spotted owl (*Strix occidentalis caurina*) is an indicator species for old-growth forests in the Pacific Northwest, a habitat coveted for its rich timber sources. Protecting the owl protects many other species in the same habitat. (Photograph courtesy of John and Karen Hollingsworth/U.S. Fish and Wildlife Service.)

special concern, such as rare species, endangered species, keystone species, and culturally significant species; species that provide the impetus to protect an area and ecosystem are known as **focal species**. One type of focal species is an **indicator species**, a species that is associated with an endangered biological community or set of unique ecosystem processes, such as the endangered northern spotted owl in the U.S. Northwest (**Figure 15.8**) or the red-cockaded woodpecker in the U.S. Southeast. The goal of managing a site for indicator species is to protect the range of species and ecosystem processes with the same distribution (Halme et al. 2009); for example, when the red-cockaded woodpecker is protected, the last remaining stands of old-growth, longleaf pine forest in the Southeast will also be protected. Of course, research must be conducted to establish that the designated indicator species is consistently associated with the full range of species and ecosystem processes, and in many cases, it might be more effective to designate a group of indicator species to ensure the protection of a biological community (Lawton and Gaston 2001).

Another type of focal species is a **flagship species**, often a large, well-known species that is one of the "charismatic megafauna." Many national parks have been created to protect flagship species, which capture public attention, have symbolic value, and are crucial to ecotourism (Rabinowitz 2000). When flagship and indicator species are protected, whole ecosystems that may consist of thousands of other species and their associated ecosystem processes are also protected. Flagship and indicator species, whose protection automatically extends protection to other species and the community, are therefore known as **umbrella species** (Ozaki et al. 2006). For example, Project Tiger in India was begun in 1973 after a census revealed that the Indian tiger was in imminent danger of extinction. The establishment of 18 Project Tiger reserves, combined with strict protection measures, has slowed the rapid decline in the number of tigers (despite some recent setbacks) and in so doing has also protected many important and endangered ecosystems.

> Based on distinctiveness, endangerment, and utility, several approaches have been developed to prioritize the protection of species and ecosystems. Differing more in their emphases than their fundamental principles, these include the species approach, the ecosystem approach, and the hotspot approach.

The species approach follows from developing survival plans for individual species, which also identifies areas of high conservation priority. In the Americas, the Natural Heritage programs and the Conservation Data Centers, organized into the NatureServe network, are using information on rare and endangered species to target new localities for conservation—areas where there are concentrations of endangered species or where the last populations of a declining species exist (www.natureserve.org). Another important program is the IUCN Species Survival Commission's Action Plans. Approximately 7000 scientists are organized in over 100 specialist groups that provide evaluations, recommendations, and action plans for mammals, birds, invertebrates, reptiles, fishes, and plants and provide extensive information on their Web site: http://www.iucn.org. Using such action plans, conservation projects can be carried out within individual countries but coordinated across countries by international agencies and nongovernmental organizations.

THE ECOSYSTEM APPROACH A number of conservationists have argued that ecosystems and the biological communities that they contain, rather than species, should be targeted for conservation (Tallis and Polasky 2009). They claim that spending, say, $1 million on habitat protection and the management of a self-maintaining ecosystem might preserve more species and provide more value to people in the long run than spending the same amount of money on an intensive effort to save just one conspicuous species. It often is easy to demonstrate an ecosystem's economic value to policy makers and the public in terms of flood control, clean water, and recreation, whereas arguing for a particular species may be more difficult.

When using this ecosystem-based approach, officials should try to ensure that representative sites of as many types of ecosystems as possible are protected. A **representative site** includes the species and environmental conditions characteristic of the ecosystem. Although no site is perfectly representative, biologists working in the field can identify suitable sites for protection.

Determining which areas of the world urgently need additional protection is critical. Resources, research, and publicity must be directed to those areas. An analysis of 13 major terrestrial **biomes**—ecosystem types linked by the structure and characteristics of their vegetation, each of which supports unique biological communities—shows that the area of protected habitat and the percent of habitat converted to other uses can vary considerably (**Figure 15.9**). Based on the information in Figure 15.9, probably the greatest priority for conservation is increasing the area of protection for temperate grasslands, Mediterranean forests, and tropical dry forests because these communities are under significant threat and only a small percentage of their area is protected (Hoekstra et al. 2004; Jenkins and Joppa et al. 2009). The lowest priority for establishment of new protected areas would be tundra, boreal forests, and montane grasslands.

THE HOTSPOT APPROACH Certain organisms can be used as **biodiversity indicators** to guide protection efforts when specific data about whole ecosystems are unavailable. For example, a site with a high diversity of flowering plants often has a high diversity of mosses, snails, spiders, and fungi (Fleishman and Murphy 2009). Further, areas with high diversity often have a high percentage of **endemism**, that is, species occurring there and nowhere else. The hope is that by protecting centers of species diversity for one type of organism, the diversity of other species will also be preserved.

This approach is now being expanded in a systematic way. The IUCN Plant Conservation office in England is identifying and documenting about 250 global centers of plant diversity with large concentrations of species, with Important Plant Areas (IPAs) identified at a country level, starting in Europe (Hoffmann et al. 2008). BirdLife International is identifying Important Bird Areas (IBAs): localities with large concentrations of birds that have restricted ranges (Tushabe et al. 2006; www.birdlife.org). Over 200 localities containing more than 2400 restricted-range bird species have been identified. Many of these localities are islands and isolated mountain ranges that also have many endemic species of lizards, butterflies, and plants and thus represent priorities for conservation. Further analysis has highlighted IBAs that contain no protected areas and thus require urgent conservation measures to prevent imminent extinctions. The biodiversity indicator approach may not work for all species in all places; for instance, vascular plant richness in protected areas in Italy was found not to be an effective surrogate for predicting the species richness of fungi (Chiarucci et al. 2005).

Using a similar approach, the World Conservation Monitoring Centre, BirdLife International, Conservation International, World Wildlife Fund, and others have

> Many protected areas have been established to protect large, well-known species, and places where there are concentrations of species.

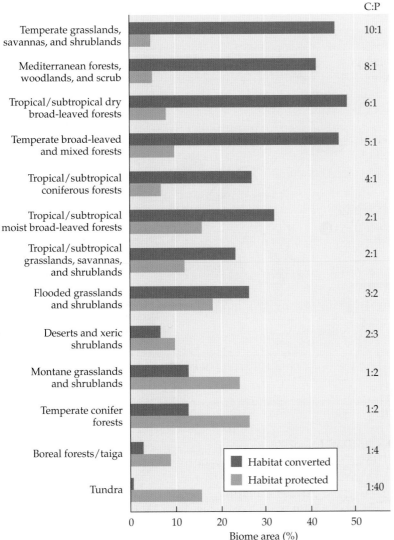

C:P

Biome	C:P
Temperate grasslands, savannas, and shrublands	10:1
Mediterranean forests, woodlands, and scrub	8:1
Tropical/subtropical dry broad-leaved forests	6:1
Temperate broad-leaved and mixed forests	5:1
Tropical/subtropical coniferous forests	4:1
Tropical/subtropical moist broad-leaved forests	2:1
Tropical/subtropical grasslands, savannas, and shrublands	2:1
Flooded grasslands and shrublands	3:2
Deserts and xeric shrublands	2:3
Montane grasslands and shrublands	1:2
Temperate conifer forests	1:2
Boreal forests/taiga	1:4
Tundra	1:40

■ Habitat converted
■ Habitat protected

Biome area (%)

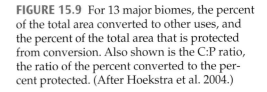

FIGURE 15.9 For 13 major biomes, the percent of the total area converted to other uses, and the percent of the total area that is protected from conversion. Also shown is the C:P ratio, the ratio of the percent converted to the percent protected. (After Hoekstra et al. 2004.)

attempted to identify key areas of the world that have great biological diversity and high levels of endemism and that are under immediate threat of species extinctions and habitat destruction: so-called hotspots for preservation (**Figure 15.10**) (Fonseca 2009; Laurance 2009; www.biodiversityhotspots.org). Using these criteria, 34 global hotspots have been identified that together encompass the entire ranges of 12,066 endemic species of terrestrial vertebrates (42% of the world's total) and at least part of the ranges of an additional 35% of the remaining terrestrial vertebrate species—all on only 2.3% of Earth's total land surface (**Table 15.2**).

Many of these hotspots are isolated tropical rain forest areas found in places such as the Atlantic coast of Brazil and West Africa. Hotspots also include island areas such as the Caribbean region, the Philippines, and New Zealand. Other hotspots are located in warm, seasonally dry areas in the temperate zone, such as the Mediterranean basin, the California region, and southwest Australia. Remaining areas are the dry forests and savannas of the Brazilian Cerrado, the eastern mountains of Kenya and Tanzania, and the mountains of south central China. Lastly, one of the Earth's major centers of biodiversity is the tropical Andes, in which at least 30,000 plant

(A)

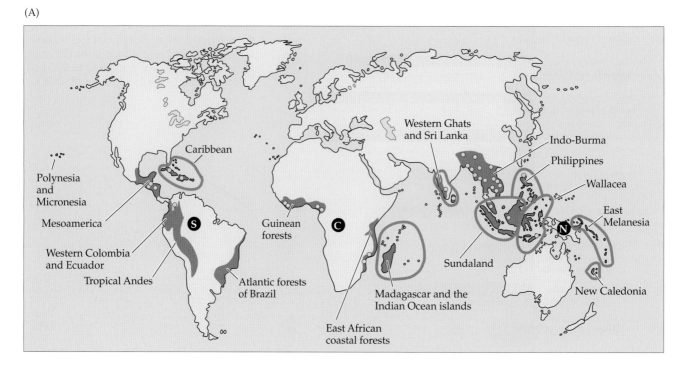

(B)

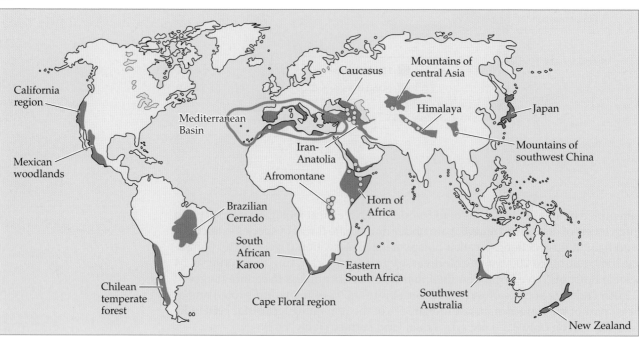

FIGURE 15.10 Hotspots are targets for protection because of their high biodiversity, endemism, and significant threat of imminent extinctions. (A) Sixteen tropical rain forest hotspots. Areas circled in green are island groups. The Polynesia/Micronesia region (not shown) covers a large number of Pacific Ocean islands, including the Hawaiian Islands, Fiji, Samoa, French Polynesia, and the Marianas. Black-circled letters indicate the only three remaining undisturbed rain forest areas of any extent, in South America (S), the Congo basin of Africa (C), and the island of New Guinea (N). (B) Eighteen hotspots representing other ecosystems. Yellow dots denote areas that have experienced armed conflicts between 1950 and 2000 with over 1000 casualties. (After Mittermeier et al. 2005; Hansen et al. 2009.)

TABLE 15.2 A Comparison of 34 Global Hotspots						
Location[a]	Original extent (×1000 km²)	Undisturbed vegetation remaining (%)	Included in protected areas (%)[b]	Number of species		
				Plants	Birds	Mammals
THE AMERICAS						
Central Chile	397	30	11	3892	226	65
Tropical Andes	1543	25	8	30,000	728	569
Western Colombia/Ecuador	275	24	7	11,000	892	283
Atlantic forest of Brazil	1234	8	2	20,000	936	263
Brazilian Cerrado	2032	22	1	10,000	605	195
Mexican pine–oak woodlands	461	20	2	5300	525	328
California region	294	25	10	3488	341	151
Mesoamerica	1130	20	6	17,000	1124	440
Caribbean islands	230	10	7	13,000	607	89
AFRICA						
Guinean forests of West Africa	620	15	3	9000	793	320
South African Karoo	103	29	2	6356	227	74
Cape region of South Africa	79	20	13	9000	324	90
Southeastern South Africa	274	24	7	8100	541	193
Madagascar and Indian Ocean islands	600	10	2	13,000	367	183
East African coastal forests	291	10	4	4000	639	198
East Afromontane	1018	10	6	7598	1325	490
Horn of Africa	1659	5	3	5000	704	219
EUROPE AND MIDEAST						
Mediterranean basin	2085	5	1	22,500	497	224
Caucasus Mountains region	863	20	1	6400	381	130
Iran–Anatolia	900	15	3	6000	364	141
CONTINENTAL ASIA						
Mountains of central Asia	863	20	7	5500	493	143
Himalaya	742	25	10	10,000	797	300
Western Ghats and Sri Lanka	190	23	11	5916	457	140
Indo–Burma	2373	5	6	13,500	1277	433
Mountains of southwest China	262	8	2	12,000	611	237
PACIFIC RIM						
Sundaland island region	1501	7	6	25,000	771	381
Wallacea island region	338	15	6	10,000	650	222
Philippines	297	7	6	9253	535	167
Southwest Australia	357	30	11	5571	285	57
East Melanesian islands	99	30	0	8000	365	86
New Caledonia	19	27	3	3270	105	9
New Zealand	270	22	22	2300	198	4
Japan	373	20	6	5600	368	91
Micronesia/Polynesia (includes Hawaii)	47	21	4	5330	300	15

Source: Based on data from Mittermeier et al. 2005 and www.biodiversityhotspots.org.

[a]Tropical rain forest hotspots are shown in blue; other hotspots encompass a variety of ecosystem types.

[b]Calculations are based on protected areas in IUCN categories I–IV.

species, 1728 bird species, 569 mammal species, 610 reptile species, and 1155 amphibian species persist in tropical forests and high-altitude grasslands on about 0.3% of the Earth's total land surface. The hotspot approach has generated a considerable amount of enthusiasm and funding during the last 10 years, and it will be worth watching to see how successful it is in advancing the goals of conservation in areas of intense human pressures with scarce and valuable biodiversity. Implementing conservation management in many of these areas is difficult because of armed conflicts and guerrilla insurgencies in remote, rugged landscapes (Hanson et al. 2009).

The hotspot approach can also be applied to individual countries (da Silva et al. 2005). In the United States, hotspots for rare and endangered species occur in the Hawaiian Islands, the southern Appalachians, the Florida Panhandle, the Death Valley region, the San Francisco Bay Area, and coastal and interior Southern California (**Figure 15.11**). The Nature Conservancy targets its land acquisiton funds to such centers of species richness (Fishburn et al. 2009). Despite the value of using the hotspot approach, it is also important to continue protecting endangered ecosystems and endemic species that lie outside these high-profile areas (Stohlgren et al. 2005). This can be done by protecting representative examples of all the world's biomes, which is estimated to cost $90 to $330 billion over the next 30 years (Pimm et al. 2001).

Another valuable approach has been to identify 17 "megadiversity" countries (out of a global total of almost 200) that together contain more than 70% of the world's biological diversity: Mexico, Colombia, Brazil, Peru, Ecuador, Venezuela, the United States, the Democratic Republic of the Congo, South Africa, Madagascar, Indonesia, Malaysia, the Philippines, India, China, Papua New Guinea, and Australia. Many of these countries are possible targets for increased conservation attention and international funding because of the weakness of their own economies, ineffectivenss of government conservation programs, and the urgency of threats to their biodiversity (Mittermeier et al. 1997; Shi et al. 2005; Liu 2009). A current priority is to establish comparable hotspot analyses for freshwater and marine ecosystems.

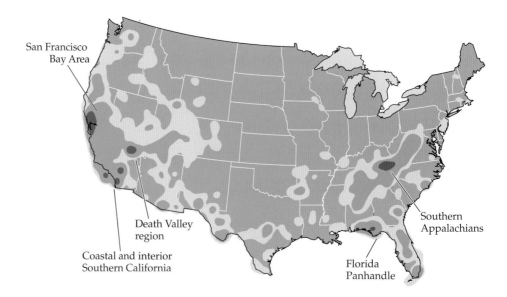

FIGURE 15.11 Peaks of species richness in the United States, calculated by employing an index that gives extra weighting to rare species. The Hawaiian Islands, not shown here, have the greatest concentration of rare species. Red shading indicates greater concentrations of rare species. (After Stein et al. 2000.)

WILDERNESS AREAS Wilderness areas are another high priority for establishing new protected areas. Large blocks of land that have been minimally affected by human activity, that have a low human population density, and that are not likely to be developed in the near future are perhaps the only places on Earth where large mammals can survive in the wild. These wilderness areas potentially could serve as "controls," showing what natural communities are like with minimal human influence. For example, large protected areas of wilderness in the Chang Tang Reserve of the Tibetan Plateau will be needed to preserve the remaining declining populations of the wild yak (*Bos grunniens*) from hunting, habitat encroachment, and hybridization with domesticated yaks. In the United States, proponents of the Wildlands Network, a private conservation policy group, are advocating the management of regional ecosystems to preserve viable populations of large carnivores such as grizzly bears, wolves, and large cats (www.wildlandsproject.org). In Europe, efforts are being made to protect the Bialowieza Forest, a 1500 km² tract of primeval forest on the border between Poland and Belarus (part of the former Soviet Union) (Daleszczyk and Bunevich 2009).

> Wilderness areas are valuable in demonstrating the nature of ecosystems processes in the absence of human influence.

Three large tropical wilderness areas occupying 6% of the Earth's land surface represent urgent conservation priorities (see Figure 15.10A) (Mittermeier et al. 2003). It is important to emphasize that even these so-called wilderness areas have had a long history of human occupation, and the structure of the forest and the densities of plants and animals have been affected by human activity. The following three large tropical forest wilderness areas are in danger of degradation:

- *South America.* One arc of wilderness containing rain forest, savanna, and mountains—but few people—runs through the southern Guianas, southern Venezuela, northern Brazil, Colombia, Ecuador, Peru, and Bolivia. The principal threat to this wilderness is the development of a modern road network, which will facilitate logging, migration, and agriculture (see Chapter 21). Experience has shown that this combination will in turn lead to widespread forest fires and other problems.

- *Congo basin in Africa.* A large area of equatorial Africa centered on the Congo River basin has a low population density and relatively undisturbed habitat, including large portions of Gabon, the Republic of the Congo, and the Democratic Republic of the Congo. Warfare and lack of government control prevent effective conservation activities in parts of the region but also reduce development pressures. However, construction of new roads and an increase in logging activity indicate that additional protection is required.

- *New Guinea.* The island of New Guinea has the largest tracts of relatively undisturbed forest in the Asian Pacific region despite the impacts of logging, mining, and transmigration programs (especially in the Indonesian province of West Papua, the western half of the island). The eastern half of the island is the independent nation of Papua New Guinea, with 6.7 million people on 460,000 km² of land, while West Papua has a population of 2.6 million people on 420,000 km². Large tracts of forest also occur on the island of Borneo, but logging, plantation agriculture, an expanding human population, and the development of a transportation network are rapidly reducing the area of undisturbed forest there.

A problem for conservation protection is that these wilderness areas act as a magnet for landless people living elsewhere. These areas currently have over 75 million people (1.1% of the world's total in 6% of the land area), but the population is rising at 3% per year, more than twice the global rate, in large part because of immigration (Cincotta et al. 2000).

ESTABLISHING PROTECTED AREAS WITH LIMITED DATA In general, new protected areas should encompass ecosystems that are rich in endemic species of restricted range, that contain ecosystems underrepresented in other protected areas, that support threatened species, and that contain resources of potential use to people, such as species of potential agricultural or medicinal use or ecosystem services that are easily understood by the public. The methods we have been describing for identifying areas of conservation assume knowledge of the areas in question. Sometimes taxonomists who collect plants, animals, and other species for museum specimens can provide data about species and the communities in which they live (van Gemerden et al. 2005). Unfortunately, such data typically do not exist or are incomplete. One approach to supplementing the lack of data is to convene groups of biologists to pool their collective knowledge, identifying localities that should be protected. Teams of biologists can also be dispatched to poorly known areas to make an inventory of species. Where decisions on park boundaries have to be made quickly, biologists are being trained to make **rapid biodiversity assessments** (**RBAs**) that involve mapping vegetation, making lists of species, checking for species of special concern, estimating the total number of species, and looking out for new species and features of special interest (Kerr et al. 2000).

Another way of circumventing the lack of data is to base decisions on general principles of ecology and conservation biology, as described more completely in Chapter 16. For example, a national park system could include elevational gradients that encompass diverse habitats, large parks to protect a large and charismatic species of significant public interest and tourist value, protection of representative habitats in different climatic zones, and individual biogeographical areas that have many endemic species.

CLIMATE CHANGE An important question being investigated is the extent to which present protected areas will allow species and ecosystems to persist in the face of climate change (Post et al. 2009). A target species may not be able to persist in a protected area if the climate becomes too different or the associated vegetation changes. New protected areas may need to be established in places where a species or ecosystem might be able to disperse and survive in coming decades. One of the best options is to preserve elevational and environmental gradients so that species and ecosystems can gradually spread in response to a changing climate.

Linking New Protected Areas to Reserve Networks

Once priorities are established, resources and personnel can be effectively directed to the protection of the most critical conservation areas. Prioritization should reduce the tendency of funding agencies, conservation organizations, and land trusts to cluster together in a few locations with high-profile projects. The decision of the MacArthur Foundation, one of the largest private sources of funds for conservation activities, to concentrate on different areas of the world for several years at a time—a "moving spotlight" approach—is a valuable counter to the tendency to concentrate resources on a few well-known places such as Costa Rica, Panama, and Kenya.

An additional step is to link new protected areas with existing protected areas to create a reserve network, because biological diversity is protected most efficiently by ensuring that all major ecosystem types are included in such a system. These ecosystem types should include those that are unaffected by human activity as well as those managed and dominated by human activity, such as plantation forests and pastures.

Gap Analysis

One way to determine the effectiveness of ecosystem and community conservation programs is to compare biodiversity priorities with existing and proposed protected areas (**Figure 15.12**) (Turner and Wilcove 2006; Langhammer et al. 2007). This comparison can identify gaps in biodiversity preservation that need to be filled in with new protected areas. In the past, this was done informally by establishing national parks in different regions with distinctive ecosystems and ecological features (Shafer 1999). At the present time, a more systematic conservation planning process, known as **gap analysis**, is sometimes used (Tognelli et al. 2009). Such complementary site selection increases the biodiversity of a network of protected areas. Gap analysis consists of the following steps:

1. Data are compiled on the species, ecosystems, and physical features of the region, which are sometimes referred to as **conservation units**. Information on human densities and economic factors can also be included.

2. Conservation goals are identified, such as the amount of area to be protected for each ecosystem or the number of individuals of rare species to be protected.

3. Existing conservation areas are reviewed to determine what is protected already and what is not (known as identifying gaps in coverage).

4. Additional areas are identified to help meet the conservation goals ("filling the gaps").

5. These additional areas are acquired for conservation, and a management plan is developed and implemented.

6. The new protected areas are monitored to determine whether they are meeting their stated goals. If not, the management plan can be changed, or possibly additional areas can be acquired to meet the goals.

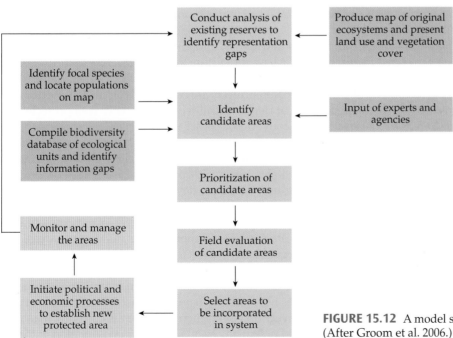

FIGURE 15.12 A model showing the process of gap analysis. (After Groom et al. 2006.)

Gap analysis has been applied to the detailed bird census records in Britain to identify potential sites for new nature reserves (Williams et al. 1996). Using 170,098 documented breeding records of 218 species located within 2827 census grid cells (each 10 km × 10 km) that cover all of Britain, three possible reserve systems were analyzed for their ability to protect breeding sites for British birds; each network included only 5% of the grid cells—approximately 5% of Britain's land area. These three systems were created to (1) protect hotspots of richness that contain the most species, (2) protect hotspots of rare species (narrowly distributed endemics), and (3) protect sets of **complementary areas**, areas in which each new cell added to the set includes one or more additional species. The results of the analysis show that while selecting species hotspots results in the greatest number of bird species per grid cell, it misses 11% of Britain's rare bird species. In contrast, selecting for complementary areas protects all of the bird species and is probably the most effective conservation strategy. In addition to using birds, this approach could be implemented using mammals, plants, unique ecosystems, or any other biodiversity component. The advantage of this approach is that each additional protected area adds to the total range of biological diversity protected (Cowling and Pressey 2003). Despite their sophistication, such theoretical approaches are often regarded as impractical by land managers, who are preoccupied with nuts-and-bolts issues such as fund-raising, public relations, political priorities, the development of management plans, and dealing with competing demands for land resources.

On an international scale, scientists are comparing the distribution of endangered species and protected areas (Maiorano et al. 2008). The Global Gap Analysis project is helping to determine how effectively protected areas include populations of the world's vertebrates (Maiorano et al. 2008). This project compared the distribution of 11,633 species of mammals, birds, amphibians, turtles, and tortoises with the distribution of protected areas throughout the world to identify 1424 **gap species**: species not protected in any part of their range. The distressing result is that hundreds of these gap species are threatened with extinction. Of all the groups, amphibians were the least well protected. A related study has mapped imminent extinctions of plant and animal species to highlight places urgently needing protection (**Figure 15.13**) (Ricketts et al. 2005).

Gap analysis can also be applied to major biome types (see Figure 15.9). On a global level, over 40% of major biomes such as temperate grasslands, Mediterranean-type forests and scrub, tropical dry forests, and temperate deciduous forests have been converted to other uses, such as agriculture and forestry; less than 10% of the area of these threatened habitats is currently protected (Hoekstra et al. 2005). Montane grasslands and temperate conifer forests are comparatively well protected and thus are less threatened. Tropical rain forests are comparatively well protected on those areas that have not been converted to other uses.

At the national level, it is possible to compare maps of vegetation types and biological communities with maps showing lands under government protection (Wright et al. 2001). In the western United States, where 62% of the land is publicly owned, the gap analysis programs of individual states have developed a comprehensive system of ecosystem mapping. In the 148 million ha covered by this mapping system, the 73 distinct vegetation types can be compared with maps of the 8% of government land legally maintained in a natural state (such as national parks, wilderness areas, and wildlife refuges). Twenty-five vegetation types (34% of the total number of vegetation types) had at least 10% of their total area in protected areas; many of these vegetation types were high-elevation types that are well represented in mountainous national parks. Of the 48 vegetation types not currently having at least 10% of their area protected, 43 of them occur extensively on government land that is currently managed for resource extraction and could potentially be managed for conservation in the future. For the remaining vegetation types, negotiations with private landowners would

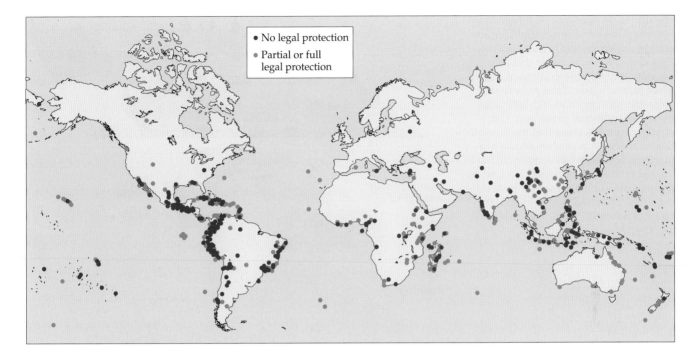

FIGURE 15.13 The imminent extinction of 794 animals and plant species is mapped at 595 sites around the world. Many of these species currently exist at sights with no legal protection, whereas others occur at sites with partial or full legal protection. Note the large number of imminent extinctions in Central America, the South American Andes, and the Atlantic coast of Brazil. (After Ricketts et al. 2005.)

be required to establish protection. It is important to note that no one federal agency has a complete representation of U.S. ecosystem types on its land; certain government agencies, such as the Department of Defense and the Bureau of Land Management, which have priorities other than conservation, may be important in efforts to preserve biological diversity. Cooperation among federal agencies, state and local governments, and private landowners is key to protecting biological communities.

Geographic information systems (**GIS**) represent the latest development in gap analysis technology, using computers to integrate the wealth of data on the natural environment with information on species distributions (Murray-Smith et al. 2009). GIS analyses make it possible to highlight critical areas that need to be included within national parks and areas that should be avoided by development projects. The basic GIS approach involves storing, displaying, and manipulating many types of mapped data such as vegetation types, climate, soils, topography, geology, hydrology, species distributions, human settlements, and resource use (**Figure 15.14**). This approach can point out correlations among the abiotic and biotic elements of the landscape, help plan parks that include a diversity of biological communities, and even suggest sites that are likely to support rare and protected species. Aerial photographs and satellite imagery are additional sources of data for GIS analysis, and they can highlight patterns of vegetation structure and distribution over local and regional scales. In particular, a series of images taken over time can reveal patterns of habitat fragmentation and destruction that need prompt attention. These images can dramatically illustrate when current government policies are not working and need to be changed.

> GIS is an effective tool for gap analysis, using a wide variety of information to pinpoint critical areas for protection within parks and other reserves, as well as areas outside of reserves that are priorities for protection.

FIGURE 15.14 Geographic information systems (GIS) provide a method for integrating a wide variety of data for analysis and display on maps. In this example, vegetation types, distributions of endangered animal species, and preserved areas are overlapped to highlight areas that need additional protection. The overlapped maps show that the distribution of Species A is predominantly in a preserve, Species B is only protected to a limited extent, and Species C is found entirely outside of the preserves. Establishing a new protected area to include the range of Species C would be the highest priority. (After Scott et al. 1991.)

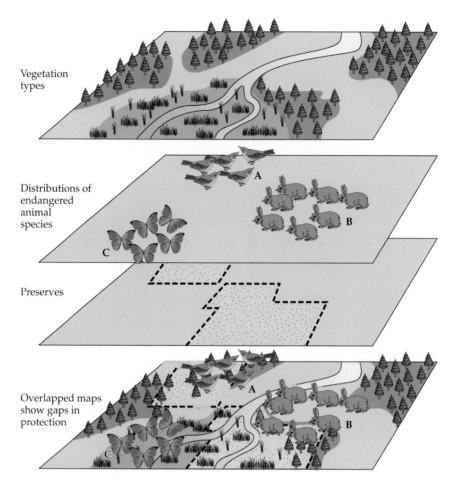

Vegetation
types

Distributions of
endangered
animal
species

Preserves

Overlapped maps
show gaps in
protection

It is also true that sometimes local people know where crucial resources and important species are located, and can be partners in establishing and managing protected areas. An approach that integrates science-based methods and community knowledge may sometimes be the best strategy (Ban et al. 2009). And, while this chapter has emphasized official protected areas, traditional peoples and private citizens protect sites that they value. Such sites are often not counted in official lists of protected areas. Yet these sites are important to the conservation of biodiversity and will be considered later in this book.

Summary

1. Protecting habitat is the most effective method for preserving biological diversity. Land can be protected by governments, private conservation organizations, groups of local people, or private individuals. Protected areas include nature reserves, national parks, wildlife sanctuaries, national monuments, protected landscapes and seascapes, and managed-resource protected areas.

2. About 13% of the Earth's surface is included in over 100,000 protected areas. Because of the real and perceived needs of human society for natural resources, strictly pro-

tected areas occupy only 6% of the Earth's surface. Therefore, the protection of biological diversity must be a priority on land and in water that is managed for resource production, including production forests, grazing lands, and fishing grounds. Many new marine protected areas are currently being established, though their effectiveness needs to be evaluated.

3. Government agencies and conservation organizations have set priorities for establishing new protected areas based on the relative distinctiveness, endangerment, and utility of the species and biological communities that occur in an area. Many protected areas are established to safeguard focal species of special concern, often preserving an entire community with its associated ecosystem processes. However, certain species may not be able to survive in these locations, because of climate change. New protected areas may need to be established in places where a species or ecosystem might be able to disperse and survive in coming decades.

4. International conservation organizations are identifying hotspots of large concentrations of animal and plant species. If these areas can be protected, then most of the world's biological diversity will be protected. Another conservation priority is protecting wilderness areas so that ecological processes and evolution can continue with minimal human impact.

5. Gap analysis is an approach that identifies additional protected areas that need to be added to an existing network of protected areas. New computer mapping technologies, known as geographical information systems, or GIS, can facilitate this process.

For Discussion

1. Obtain a map of a town, state, or nation that shows protected areas (such as nature reserves and parks) and multiple-use managed areas. Who is responsible for each parcel of land, and what is their purpose in managing it?

   (A) Consider aquatic habitats in this region (ponds, marshes, streams, rivers, lakes, estuaries, coastal zones, etc.). Who is responsible for managing these environments, and how do they balance the need for protecting biological diversity with the needs of society for natural resources?

   (B) If you could add protected areas to this region, where would you place them and why? Show their exact location, size, and shape, and justify your choices.

   (C) How will this system of protected areas be affected by climate change by the end of the century? What changes or additions in the protected areas would help protect species and ecosystems in coming decades?

2. Imagine that the only population of a rare and declining flamingo species lives along the shore of an isolated lake. This lake has numerous unique species of fish, crayfish, and insects. The lake and its shores are owned by a logging company that is planning to build a paper mill on the shore where the flamingos nest. This mill will seriously pollute the lake and destroy the food eaten by the flamingos. You have $1 million to spend on conservation in this area. The company is willing to sell the lake and its shores for $1 million. An effective flamingo management program involving captive breeding, release of new individuals into the population, habitat improvement, and natural history studies would cost $750,000. Is it better to buy the land and not devote resources to managing and researching the flamingo? Or would it be better to manage the flamingo and allow the lake to be destroyed? Can you suggest other alternatives or possibilities?

Suggested Readings

Abell, R., M. L. Thieme, C. Revenga, M. Bryer, M. Kottelat, N. Bogutskaya, et al. 2008. Freshwater ecoregions of the world: A new map of biogeographic units for freshwater biodiversity conservation. *BioScience* 58: 403–414. Freshwater conservation has received comparatively less attention; this new information should help.

Bottrill, M. C., L. N. Joseph, J. Carwardine, M. Bode, C. Cook, and E. T. Game. 2009. Finite conservation funds mean triage is unavoidable. *Trends in Ecology and Evolution* 24: 183–184. With limited funds, difficult choices need to be made concerning what to save.

Chape, S., M. D. Spalding, and M. D. Jenkins (eds.). 2008. *The World's Protected Areas: Status, Values, and Prospects in the Twenty-First Century.* University of California Press, Berkeley, CA. Massive source of information on protected areas.

DeFries, R., A. Hansen, A. C. Newton, and M. C. Hansen. 2005. Increasing isolation of protected areas in tropical forests of the past twenty years. *Ecological Applications* 15: 19–26. Protected areas are reasonably effective; however, the lands around them are often becoming degraded.

Faith, D. P. 2008. Threatened species and the potential loss of phylogenetic diversity: Conservation scenarios based on estimated extinction probabilities and phylogenetic risk analysis. *Conservation Biology* 22: 1461–1470. The evolutionary uniqueness of a species could be considered in deciding conservation priorities.

Fleishman, E. and D. D. Murphy. 2009. A realistic assessment of the indicator potential of butterflies and other charismatic taxonomic groups. *Conservation Biology* 23: 1109–1116. How effective is it to use indicator groups to determine patterns of biodiversity?

Game, E. T., H. S. Grantham, A. J. Hobday, R. L. Pressey, A. T. Lombard, L. E. Beckley, et al. 2009. Pelagic protected areas: The missing dimension in ocean conservation. *Trends in Ecology and Evolution* 24: 360–369. The largest unprotected ecosystem in the world is the open ocean, away from the continental shelves.

Hanson, T., T. M. Brooks, G. A. B. da Fonseca, M. Hoffmann, J. F. Lamoreux, G. Machlis, et al. 2009. Warfare in biodiversity hotspots. *Conservation Biology* 23: 578–587. Many of the world's biodiversity hotspots have also been the scene of fighting, creating difficulties for conservation.

Jackson, S. F., K. Walker, and K. J. Gaston. 2009. Relationship between distributions of threatened plants and protected areas in Britain. *Biological Conservation* 142: 1515–1522. Britain has an enormous number of small conservation areas, many of which are important for conservation.

Mittermeier, R. A., P. R. Gil, M. Hoffman, J. Pilgrim, T. Brooks, C. Goettsch, et al. 2005. *Hotspots Revisited: Earth's Biologically Richest and Most Endangered Terrestrial Ecoregions.* Conservation International, Washington, D.C. Check out the website for a comprehensive treatment by region: www.biodiversityhotspots.org/Pages/default.aspx.

Planes, S., G. P. Jones, and S. R. Thorrold. 2009. Larval dispersal connects fish populations in a network of marine protected areas. *Proceedings of the National Academy of Sciences USA* 106: 5693–5697. Further scientific study of dispersal patterns and species status undertaken to develop an effective system of protected areas.

Post, E., J. Brodie, M. Hebblewhite, A. D. Anders, J. A. K. Maier, and C. C. Wilmers. 2009. Global population dynamics and hot spots of response to climate change. *BioScience* 59: 489–497. Certain parts of a species' range are especially vulnerable to climate change.

Rabinowitz, A. 2000. *Jaguar: One Man's Struggle to Establish the World's First Jaguar Preserve.* Island Press, Washington, D.C. Sometimes one motivated individual makes a huge difference.

Spalding, M. D., L. Fish, and L. J. Wood. 2008. Towards representative protection of the world's coasts and oceans—progress, gaps, and opportunities. *Conservation Letters* 1: 217–226. Marine protected areas are now being established throughout the world, but efforts still lag far behind terrestrial conservation.

Turner, W. R. and D. S. Wilcove. 2006. Adaptive decision rules for the acquisition of nature reserves. *Conservation Biology* 20: 527–537. Site availability, site condition, and financial limitations are all important in establishing networks of protected areas.

Chapter 16

Designing Networks of Protected Areas

In this chapter we will examine some of the issues involved in designing effective protected areas. These issues are currently being investigated by conservation biologists, and they provide insight into the best methods for establishing new protected areas and reserve systems. Many protected areas are required to protect examples of all species and ecosystems. (These concepts were described briefly in Chapter 15.) A considerable body of ecological literature is now developing to address the most efficient way to design networks of conservation areas that more adequately protect the full range of biodiversity (Margules and Sarkar 2007; Nicholson and Possingham 2007). Existing and proposed networks also need to be evaluated for their ability to protect biodiversity in the future, as species and ecosystems change their abundance and distribution in response to climate change.

There is a need to be more organized in establishing new protected areas, as at present, protected areas are often created in a haphazard fashion. The size and placement of protected areas throughout the world are often determined by the distribution of people, potential land values, the political efforts of conservation-minded citizens, and historical factors (Armsworth et al. 2006).

In developed areas, the ability of private conservation groups and government departments to raise funds for land purchases is often the most important factor in determining what land is acquired (Lerner et al. 2007). In other cases, certain parcels of land may be purchased to protect a critical water supply or a charismatic species, but another parcel may be acquired simply because it adjoins the property of a wealthy donor.

Sometimes lands are set aside for conservation protection because they have no immediate commercial value—they are "the lands that nobody wants" (Scott et al. 2001). The largest parks usually occur in areas where few people live and where the land is considered unsuitable or too remote for agriculture, logging, urban development, or other human activities. Examples are the low heath forests on nutrient-poor soils at Bako National Park in Malaysia; the rugged, rocky mountain parks of Switzerland; the huge desert parks of the U.S. Southwest; and the 1 million km^2 of federal land in Alaska encompassing tundra and mountains. In other cases, small reserves are acquired in urban areas at great cost. Many of the conservation areas and parks in metropolitan areas of Europe and North America were formerly estates of wealthy citizens and royalty. In the U.S. Midwest, a number of the prairie nature reserves are former railroad rights-of-way and other oddly shaped pieces with unusual histories.

Issues of Reserve Design

Issues of reserve design have proved to be of great interest to governments, corporations, and private landowners, who are being urged—and mandated—to manage their properties for both the commercial production of natural resources and for the protection of biological diversity. However, consideration of such issues does not necessarily produce universal design guidelines: Conservation biologists need to be cautious about using simplistic, overly general guidelines for designing protected areas, because every conservation situation requires individual consideration (Cawardine et al. 2009). Everyone benefits from more communication between the academic scientists, who are developing theories of nature reserve design, and the managers, planners, and policy makers who are actually creating specific new reserves (Turner and Wilcove 2006).

Models are being developed and refined that describe the most effective ways to use available funds to optimize biodiversity protection. Conservation biologists often start by considering "the four *R*s":

- *Representation.* The protected areas should contain as many aspects of biodiversity (species, populations, habitats, etc.) as possible.

- *Resiliency.* Protected areas must be sufficiently large to maintain all aspects of biodiversity in a healthy condition for the foreseeable future, including the predicted impacts of climate change.

- *Redundancy.* Protected areas must include enough examples of each aspect of biodiversity to ensure the long-term existence of the unit in the face of future uncertainties.

- *Reality.* There must be sufficient funds and political will, not only to acquire and protect lands, but also to subsequently regulate and manage the protected areas.

The following more specific questions about reserve design are also useful for discussing how best to construct and network protected areas:

- How large must a nature reserve be to effectively protect biodiversity?

- Is it better to have a single large protected area or multiple smaller reserves?

- How many individuals of an endangered species must be included in a protected area to prevent the local extinction of a species?

- What is the best shape for a nature reserve?

- When a network of protected areas is created, should the areas be close together or far apart? Should they be isolated from one another or connected by corridors?

Some of these issues are being explored using the island biogeography model of MacArthur and Wilson (1967), described in Chapter 7. Many of them also have originated from the insights of wildlife and park managers (Shafer 2001; Tabarelli and Gascon 2005; Roux et al. 2008). The island biogeography approach makes the significant assumption, which is often invalid, that parks are habitat islands completely isolated by an unprotected matrix of inhospitable terrain. In fact, many species are capable of living in and dispersing through this habitat matrix. Researchers working with island biogeography models and data from protected areas have proposed some alterations to these models, but they are still being debated (**Figure 16.1**).

> Principles of design have been developed to guide land managers in establishing and maintaining networks of protected areas.

Also, all of these issues have been viewed mainly with land vertebrates, higher plants, and large invertebrates in mind. The applicability of these ideas to freshwater and marine nature reserves, where dispersal mechanisms are largely unknown, requires further investigation (Leathwick 2008; Planes et al. 2009). Recent evidence suggests that many widespread marine species actually only disperse their offspring a short distance. If this proves true for many species, additional protected areas will have to be established to protect the genetic variation found in specific localities. Protecting marine nature reserves requires particular attention to pollution control because of its subtle and widespread destructive effects. Various countries in the Caribbean and Pacific regions have made steps in the right direction: Many individual islands have half or even more of their coastlines designated as marine parks, and the entire island of Bonaire is a protected marine park, with ecotourism emerging as the leading industry.

Protected Area Size and Characteristics

An early debate in conservation biology occurred over whether species richness is maximized in one large nature reserve or in several smaller ones of an equal total area (Soulé and Simberloff 1986; McCarthy et al. 2006), known in the literature as the **SLOSS debate** (single *large* or *several small*). Is it better, for example, to set aside one reserve of 10,000 ha or four reserves of 2500 ha each? The proponents of large reserves argue that only large reserves have sufficient numbers of large, wide-ranging, low-density species (such as large carnivores) to maintain long-term populations (**Figure 16.2**). Large reserves also minimize the ratio of edge habitat to total habitat, encompass more species, and can have greater habitat diversity than small reserves.

The advantage of large parks is effectively demonstrated by an analysis of 299 mammal populations in 14 national parks in western North America (**Figure 16.3**) (Newmark 1995). Twenty-nine mammal species are now locally extinct, and seven species have recolonized or newly colonized the parks. Extinction rates have been very low or zero in parks with areas over 1000 km^2 and have been much higher in parks that are smaller than 1000 km^2. Extinction rates have been highest for species with low initial population numbers and small body size. It is also true that human population densities are lower on the edges of large reserves compared with human

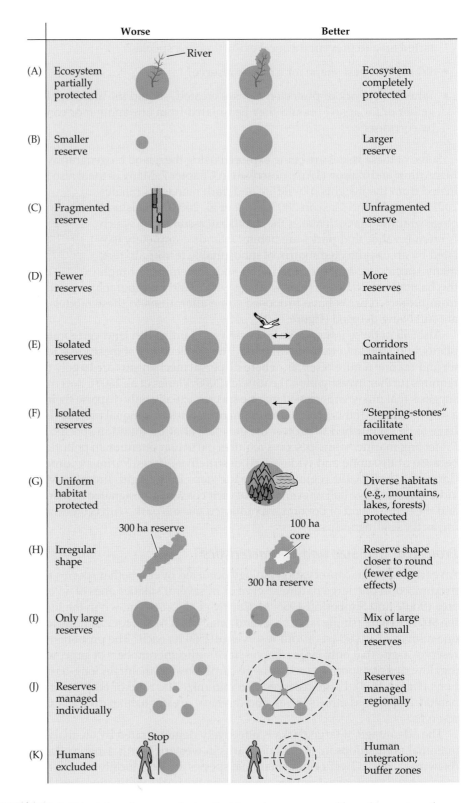

FIGURE 16.1 Principles of reserve design that have been proposed based in part on theories of island biogeography. Imagine that the reserves are "islands" of the original ecosystem surrounded by land that has been made uninhabitable by human activities such as farming, ranching, or industrial development. The practical application of these principles is still being studied and debated, but in general the designs shown on the right are considered to be preferable to those on the left. (After Shafer 1997.)

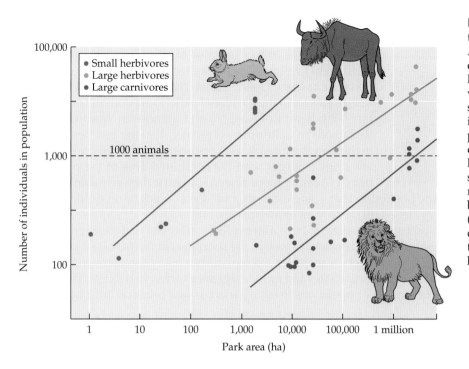

FIGURE 16.2 Population studies show that large parks and protected areas in Africa contain larger populations of each species than small parks; only the largest parks may contain long-term viable populations of many vertebrate species. Each symbol represents an animal population in a park. If the viable population size of a species is 1000 individuals (dashed line), parks of at least 100 ha will be needed to protect small herbivores (e.g., rabbits, squirrels), parks of more than 10,000 ha will be needed to protect large herbivores (e.g., zebras, wildebeests), and parks of at least 1 million ha will be needed to protect large carnivores (e.g., lions, hyenas). (From Schonewald-Cox 1983.)

densities on the edges of small reserves, and this could contribute to the higher extinction rates in small parks (Wiersma et al. 2004).

On the other hand, once a park reaches a certain size, the number of new species added with each increase in area starts to decline. At that point, creating a second large park, as well as a third or fourth park some distance away, may be an effective strategy for preserving additional species. The extreme proponents of large reserves argue that small reserves need not be maintained, because their inability to support long-term populations, ecosystem processes, and all successional stages gives them little value for conservation purposes. Other conservation biologists

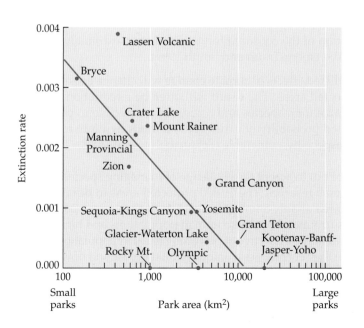

FIGURE 16.3 Each dot represents the extinction rate of animal populations for a particular U.S. national park, Canadian national park, or two or more adjacent parks. Mammals have higher extinction rates in smaller parks than in larger ones. The y-axis is the extinction rate per species per year. (After Newmark 1995.)

argue that well-placed small reserves are able to include a greater variety of habitat types and more populations of rare species than one large block of the same area

> It is generally accepted that large reserves are better able to maintain many species because such reserves support larger population sizes and greater variety of habitats. However, small reserves are important in protecting particular species and ecosystems.

(Maiorano et al. 2008). The value of several well-placed reserves in different habitats is demonstrated by a comparison of four national parks in the United States. The total number of large mammalian species in three national parks located in contrasting habitats—Big Bend in Texas, North Cascades in Washington, and Redwoods in California—is greater than the number of species in the largest U.S. park, Yellowstone, even though the area of Yellowstone is larger than the combined area of the other three parks. Creating more reserves, even if they are small ones, decreases the possibility that a single catastrophic force—such as an exotic animal, a disease, or fire—will destroy an entire species.

The consensus now seems to be that strategies for reserve size depend on the group of species under consideration, as well as the scientific circumstances. It generally is accepted that large reserves are better able to maintain many species because they can support larger population sizes and include a greater variety of habitats. The research on extinction rates of populations in large parks has four practical implications:

1. When a new park is being established, it should be made as large as possible—to preserve as many species as possible, contain large populations of each species, and provide a diversity of habitats and natural resources. Keystone resources should be included, in addition to habitat features that promote biodiversity, such as elevational gradients.

2. Whenever possible, land adjacent to protected areas should be acquired in order to reduce external threats to existing parks and to maintain critical buffer zones. For example, terrestrial habitats adjacent to wetlands are often necessary for semiaquatic species such as snakes and turtles. The best protection may be provided when natural ecological units, such as entire watersheds or mountains, are encompassed within reserve borders as a means of reducing external threats (Possingham et al. 2005).

3. Even though large parks have many advantages, well managed small nature reserves also have value, particularly for the protection of many species of plants, invertebrates, and small vertebrates (Pellens and Grandcolas 2007). For example, woodland remnants in an Australian agricultural landscape retained some native insect species when they were as small as 50 m², an amazing demonstration of the conservation value of even extremely small habitat fragments (Abensperg-Traun and Smith 1999).

4. The present and predicted effects of climate change will change ecosystems within existing protected areas. The result will often be a reduction in the area of habitat available for a species and a consequent decline in population size and increased probablity of extinction. Animals living in tropical mountain areas are especially vulnerable (Sekercioglou et al. 2008).

Often there is no choice but to accept the challenge of managing species and biological communities in small reserves. The 10,000 protected areas in Britain, for instance, have an average area of only 3 km² (**Figure 16.4**) (Jackson et al. 2009). Such small reserves often are surrounded by dense human populations and highly modified habitat. Small reserves may be effective at protecting isolated populations of rare species, particularly when they encompass a unique habitat type found nowhere else (Markovchick-Nicholls et al. 2008). Numerous countries have many more small protected areas (less than 100 ha) than medium and large ones, yet the combined area of these small reserves is only a tiny percentage of the total area under protection.

This is particularly true in places that have been intensively cultivated for centuries, such as Europe, China, and Java. Bukit Timah Nature Reserve in Singapore is an excellent example of a small reserve that provides long-term protection for numerous species. This 164 ha forest reserve represents 0.2% of the original forested area on Singapore and has been isolated from other forests since 1860, yet it still protects 74% of the original flora, 72% of the original bird species, and 56% of the fish (Corlett and Turner 1996). In addition, small reserves located near populated areas make excellent conservation education and nature study centers that further the long-range goals of conservation biology by developing public awareness of important issues. By 2030, over 60% of the world's population will live in urban areas; thus, there is a need to develop such reserves for public use and education.

Reserve Design and Species Preservation

Because population size is the best predictor of extinction probability, reserves should be sufficient in area to preserve large populations of important species (rare and endangered species, keystone species, economically important species, etc.). The best evidence to date suggests that populations of at least several hundred reproductive individuals are needed to ensure the long-term viability of most vertebrates, with several thousand individuals being a desirable goal (though it is also true that some small populations are able to persist for many decades; see Chapters 11 and 12). Having more than one population of a rare species within a protected area will increase the probability of survival for the species; if one population goes extinct, the species still remains in the reserve and can potentially recolonize its former range.

Several strategies exist to facilitate the survival of small populations of rare species in scattered, isolated nature reserves. The populations can be managed as one metapopulation, with efforts made to encourage natural migration between the nature reserves by maintaining connectivity among the reserves. Occasionally individuals can be collected from one nature reserve and added to the breeding population of another. Addressing the needs of wide-ranging species that cannot tolerate human disturbance is a more difficult aspect of ensuring viable populations in reserves. Ideally, a reserve should be large enough to include a viable population of the most wide-ranging species in it. Protection of the habitat of wide-ranging species, which are often large or conspicuous flagship or umbrella species, will often provide adequate protection for the other species in the community (see Chapter 15). Extensive areas of pine habitat surrounding the Savannah River nuclear processing plant in South Carolina are being protected to maintain the red-cockaded woodpecker (*Picoides borealis*), a species that needs large stands of mature longleaf pine trees (**Figure 16.5**). In the process, many endangered plant species are being protected as well.

The effective design of nature reserves requires a thorough knowledge of the natural history of important species and information on the distribution of biological communities. Knowledge about species' feeding requirements, nesting behavior, daily and seasonal movement patterns, potential predators and competitors, and susceptibility to disease and pests contributes to determining an effective conser-

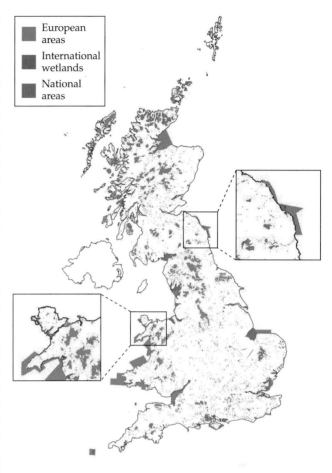

FIGURE 16.4 The geographic locations of protected areas in Britain managed for biodiversity conservation. Note their large number, varied sizes and shapes, and their scattered distribution. At the scale of this map, most of the small protected areas cannot be seen. Many of the protected areas are covered by two or more designations. There are other areas managed for other purposes, not shown on this map. (Courtesy of Sarah Little.)

(A)

(B)

FIGURE 16.5 Longleaf pine habitat in the southeastern United States, including areas of South Carolina, North Carolina, and Georgia, is being managed to protect the endangered red-cockaded woodpecker. Heavily logged areas lack older trees with the nesting holes that the woodpecker requires. (A) This USFWS worker is inserting a nesting box into a hole cut out of a pine tree. (B) An adult red-cockaded woodpecker landing at a nesting cavity. (A, photograph courtesy of John and Karen Hollingsworth/U.S. Fish and Wildlife Service; B, photograph © Derrick Hamrick/Photolibrary.com.)

vation strategy. A balance must be struck, between focusing on the needs of the indicator or flagship species to the exclusion of all other species, and managing only for maximum species diversity and ecosystem processes, which could result in the loss of the flagship species that interest the general public.

Minimizing Edge and Fragmentation Effects

It is generally agreed that protected areas should be designed to minimize harmful edge effects (see Chapter 9). Conservation areas that are rounded in shape minimize the edge-to-area ratio, and the center is farther from the edge than in other park shapes. Long, linear parks have the most edge, and all points in the park are close to the edge (Yamaura et al. 2008). Consequently, for parks with four straight sides, a square park is a better design than an elongated rectangle of the same area. Unfortunately, these ideas have rarely, if ever, been implemented. Most parks have irregular shapes because land acquisition is typically a matter of opportunity rather than a matter of design.

As discussed in Chapter 9, internal fragmentation of reserves by roads, fences, farming, logging, and other human activities should be avoided as much as possible because fragmentation often divides a large population into two or more smaller populations, each of which is more vulnerable to extinction than is the large population. Fragmentation alters the climate inside forest reserves, and it also provides entry points for invasive species that may harm native species, creates more undesirable edge effects, and creates barriers to dispersal that reduce the probability of colonization of new sites.

The forces promoting fragmentation are powerful because protected areas are often the only undeveloped land available for new projects such as agriculture, dams, and residential areas. This has been particularly true in densely settled areas such as western Europe, where undeveloped land is scarce and there is intense pressure for development. Undeveloped parkland near urban centers, for instance, may appear to be ideally positioned as a site for new industrial development, recreational facilities, schools, waste management sites, and government offices. In the eastern United States, many parks are crisscrossed by roads, railroad tracks, and power lines, which divide large areas of habitat like pieces of a roughly cut pie, in the process eliminating interior habitat needed by some species. Government planners often prefer to locate transportation networks and other infrastructure in protected areas because they assume there will be less political opposition to that than to locating the projects on privately owned, settled land. Indeed, park and forest supervisors are often rewarded for building infrastructure or increasing commodity production, regardless of whether it fragments their holdings and harms biodiversity. However, this situation is rapidly changing as conservation groups and some government officials become advocates for maintaining the integrity of protected areas.

> Fragmentation of protected areas can create many harmful side effects, and should be avoided if possible.

Networks of Protected Areas

Strategies do exist for aggregating small nature reserves into larger conservation networks (Wiersma 2007). Nature reserves are often embedded in a larger matrix of habitat managed for resource extraction (such as timber forest, grazing land, and farmland). If conservation biologists can make management for the protection of biological diversity a secondary priority of these areas, then larger habitat areas can be included in conservation plans and the effects of fragmentation can be reduced (Berry et al. 2005). Habitat managed for resource extraction can sometimes also be managed as an important secondary site for wildlife and as dispersal corridors between isolated nature reserves. Whenever possible, populations of rare species should be managed as a large metapopulation to facilitate gene flow and migration among populations. Cooperation among public and private landowners is particularly important in developed metropolitan areas, where there are often many small, isolated parks under the control of a variety of different government agencies and private organizations (**Box 16.1**).

An excellent example of cooperation to achieve conservation goals is the Chicago Wilderness project, which consists of more than 240 organizations collaborating to preserve more than 145,000 ha (360,000 acres) of tallgrass prairies, woodlands, rivers, streams, and other wetlands in metropolitan Chicago (**Figure 16.6**; www.chicago wildernessmag.org). These cooperating organizations include museums, zoos, forest preserve districts, national and local government agencies, and private conservation organizations. This network of natural areas is critical to the quality of life of residents, since it is the only undeveloped land available for recreation between the densely developed urban core of Chicago and the highly developed agricultural landscape outside of the metropolitan area. The Chicago Region Biodiversity Council coordinates conservation efforts, facilitates communication among members, develops policy and strategy related to land conservation, directs scientific research, and encourages volunteer participation. Among its many educational initiatives, Chicago Wilderness has produced the *Atlas of Biodiversity*, to publicize the diversity of habitats and species in the Chicago Wilderness network, and established the Mighty Acorns program to teach nature stewardship to schoolchildren.

Habitat Corridors

One intriguing suggestion for designing a system of nature reserves has been to link isolated protected areas into one large system through the use of **habitat corridors**: strips of land running between the reserves (Cushman et al. 2009). Such habi-

(A)

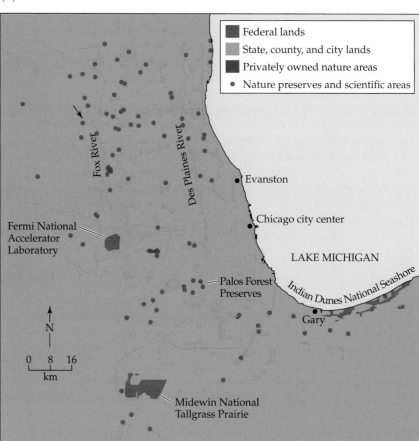

(B)

FIGURE 16.6 (A) The Chicago Wilderness project involves more than 240 organizations working to preserve biodiversity in a densely settled urban area surrounded by agriculture. Many of the linear areas are trails and the banks of rivers. (B) A family enjoys Lake-in-the-Hills Fen, a unique wilderness in the northwest corner of the project (arrow in A). (Courtesy of Chicago Regional Biodiversity Council and www.chicagowildernessmag.org; photograph by Stephen Packard.)

BOX 16.1   *Ecologists and Real Estate Experts Mingle at The Nature Conservancy*

■ Of the many nonprofit organizations that now strive to protect biological diversity, The Nature Conservancy (TNC) is set apart by a unique approach that applies the methods of private business to accomplish the conservation of native species and their habitats around the world (Birchard 2005; Fishburn et al. 2009). Simply put, TNC works collaboratively with individual landowners, indigenous peoples, governments, the business community, and others to find creative ways to conserve ecologically important wildlife habitat for people *and* nature. In many situations, TNC either buys threatened habitat outright or shows landowners how managing their land for conservation may be as profitable as developing it.

> Many conservation organizations are actively involved in establishing protected areas. The larger ones have even established their own networks of protected areas, and operate on an international scale.

Founded in 1951, TNC now has over 1 million members (www.nature.org). TNC is not as widely known as some conservation organizations, nor is it as vocal. TNC advocates a nonconfrontational, businesslike, and results-oriented approach that contrasts with the methods of some high-profile, activist environmental groups such as Greenpeace and Earth First! (McCormick 2004). Still, its methods have been quietly successful: In the United States alone, TNC has set aside more than 6 million ha. Some parcels of land that TNC owned were so ecologically valuable that they have been sold or donated to local, state, or federal units of government and designated as public land, including state wildlife areas, national wildlife refuges, national parks, and national forests. Outside the United States, the Conservancy has worked closely with local peoples, communities, nongovernmental organizations, and governments in over 30 countries to conserve biologically important areas totaling about 50 million ha.

To achieve its goals, TNC maintains a revolving fund of over $160 million, created predominantly from private donations, with which TNC can make direct land purchases and fund high-leverage strategies such as debt-for-nature swaps (see Chapter 21) when necessary. TNC invests a total of over $700 million per year in conservation (Goldman et al. 2008). Through these methods, the organization has created the largest system of private natural areas and wildlife sanctuaries in the world.

TNC, like other land trust organizations (see Chapter 20), uses creative approaches to accomplish its conservation mission. If TNC cannot purchase land outright for the protection of habitat, it seeks to offer alternatives to landowners that make conservation financially feasible. For example, 30 years ago, the U.S. Congress created tax incentives to encourage landowners to conserve ecologically important lands and waters by donating development rights to land trusts. These tax benefits provide landowners with valuable incentives to work with organizations such as TNC to conserve their lands. In recent years, the opportunity to earn tax benefits and other financial advantages has expanded to include a wide range of ecosystem services, such as carbon sequestration (Goldman et al. 2008).

Tina Buijs, a TNC park guard supervisor and operations manager, talks with Juan Antillanca, a farmer belonging to the Hurio indigenous community that borders The Nature Conservancy's Reserva Costera Valdiviana in Chile. The reserve is a 147,500-acre site comprising temperate rain forest and 36 km of Pacific coastline. Keeping in close contact with their neighbors helps TNC officials realize their conservation goals. (Photograph by Mark Godfrey/The Nature Conservancy.)

(continued)

BOX 16.1 (*continued*)

When it is compatible with their biodiversity conservation mission, TNC also may pursue conservation strategies that allow some of the preserves it owns to be financially self-supporting. For example, the cost of maintaining one South Dakota prairie preserve is partially defrayed by maintaining a resident bison herd. Carefully managed bison grazing enhances biological diversity in these grasslands, provided the herd does not become too large. When the herd grows to a size at which overgrazing becomes a possibility, the excess animals are sold for meat (www.buffalofield-campaign.org). The sale of bison brings roughly $25,000 annually to the preserve.

In addition, through its more than 700 staff scientists, TNC supports and encourages efforts to identify rare and at-risk species and habitats in the United States and in the more than 30 other countries in which the organization works (www.nature.org). In the United States, TNC played a key leadership role by working jointly with every state government to create Natural Heritage programs. Heritage staff inventory plant and animal populations in each state and add this information to a computerized database located in each state and at NatureServe, an independent organization spun off from TNC in 2001. With this database, biologists can monitor the status of species and populations throughout the nation. When Natural Heritage program biologists identify populations of species that are rare, unique, declining, or threatened, state agencies and conservation organizations such as TNC have the information to make wise decisions.

In recent years, The Nature Conservancy has designed portfolios of conservation areas within and across ecoregions. An ecoregion is a large unit of land and water typically defined by climate, geology, topography, and associations of plants and animals. Ecoregional portfolios represent the full distribution and diversity of native species, natural communities, and ecosystems.

TNC's businesslike approach to conservation is successful largely because the organization's science-based, collaborative approach is appealing to many, including those, such as developers and large corporations, who sometimes have no great love for environmentalists. In general, TNC avoids lawsuits, preferring to use market-based approaches, financial incentives, and other creative solutions to achieve on-the-ground conservation results. The fundamental principle of The Nature Conservancy is, in essence, "land and water conservation through private action"; so far, the idea has proved to be sound.

tat corridors, also known as **conservation corridors** or **movement corridors**, can allow plants and animals to disperse from one reserve to another, facilitating gene flow and colonization of suitable sites. Corridors can potentially transform a set of isolated protected areas by establishing a linked network, with populations of a species interacting as a metapopulation. Corridors are clearly needed to preserve animals that must migrate seasonally among different habitats to obtain food and water, such as the large grazing mammals of the African savanna; if these animals were confined to a single reserve, they could starve (Wilcove and Wikelski 2008). Observations on Brazilian arboreal mammals suggest that corridors of 30 to 40 m in width may be adequate for migration of most species, and a corridor width of 200 m of primary forest will be adequate for all species (Laurance and Laurance 1999). In agricultural landscapes, increasing the connectivity of fragments allows native species to persist at higher densities (Hilty and Merenlender 2004).

Some park managers have enthusiastically embraced the idea of corridors as a strategy for managing wide-ranging species. In Riverside, California, the preservation of dispersal corridors was a key component in a plan to establish a 17,400 ha reserve to protect the endangered Stephens' kangaroo rat (*Dipodomys stephensi*). In Florida, millions of dollars have been spent to establish corridors between tracts of land occupied by the endangered Florida panther (*Felis concolor coryi* or *Puma concolor coryi*). In many areas, culverts, tunnels, and overpasses create passages under and over roads and railways that allow for dispersal between habitats for lizards, amphibians, and mammals (Corlatti et al. 2009). An added benefit of these passageways is that collisions between animals and vehicles are reduced, which saves lives and money. In Canada's Banff National Park, road collisions involving deer,

(A)

FIGURE 16.7 (A) An overpass above a fenced-off divided highway allows animals to migrate safely between two forested areas. (B) Individuals of a species naturally disperse between two large protected areas (areas 1 and 2, left) by using smaller protected areas as stepping-stones. The right-hand panel shows that habitat destruction and a large edge effect zone caused by a new road have blocked a migration route. To offset the effects of the road, compensation sites have been added to the system of protected areas, and an overpass has been built over the highway to allow dispersal. (A, photograph © Joel Sartore; B after Cuperus et al. 1999.)

(B)

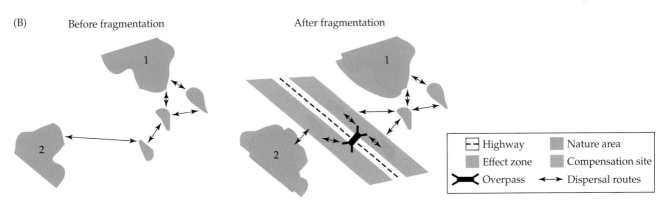

elk, and other large mammals declined by 96% after fences, overpasses, and underpasses were installed along a major highway (**Figure 16.7**). These corridor projects all involved a large expenditure of public funds. An important question to ask is whether these corridors provided a greater benefit to the target species than using the same amount of money to acquire new blocks of conservation land elsewhere.

Some conservation biologists have started to plan habitat corridors on a truly huge scale. Wildlands Network has a detailed plan called the Spine of the Continent Initiative that would link all large protected areas in the United States by habitat corridors, creating a system that would allow large and currently declining mammals to coexist with human society (Soulé and Terborgh 1999). In eastern North America, there are over 2000 national, state, and provincial protected areas, but only 14 of them are over 2700 km^2, which is the approximate area needed to maintain populations of large mammals (Gurd et al. 2001). Linking the largest protected areas by corridors and managing them as single conservation systems would be an effective strategy to maintain rare species.

> Establishing habitat corridors can potentially transform a set of isolated protected areas into a linked network within which populations can interact as a metapopulation.

Corridors that facilitate natural patterns of migration will probably be the most successful at protecting species (Caro et al. 2009). For example, large grazing animals often migrate in regular patterns across a rangeland in search of water and the best vegetation. In seasonally dry savanna habitats, animals often migrate along the riparian forests that grow along streams and rivers. In mountainous areas, many bird and mammal species regularly migrate to higher elevations during the warmer months of the year. To protect migrating birds, a corridor was established in Costa Rica to link two wildlife reserves, the Braulio Carrillo National Park and La Selva Biological Station. A 7700 ha corridor of forest several kilometers wide and 18 km long, known as the Zona Protectora Las Tablas, was set aside to provide an elevational link that allows at least 75 species of birds to migrate between the two large conservation areas (Bennett 1999).

As the global climate changes in the coming decades, many species will begin to migrate to higher elevations and to higher latitudes. Creating corridors to protect expected migration routes—such as north–south river valleys, ridges, and coastlines—would be a useful precaution. Extending existing protected areas in the direction of anticipated species movements would help to maintain long-term populations (Hannah 2010). Corridors that cross gradients of elevation, rainfall, and soils will also allow local migration of species to more favorable sites. Similarly, planning for marine protected areas should anticipate a change in climate, especially its effects on species distributions and sea level (McLeod et al. 2009).

Although the idea of corridors is intuitively appealing, there are some possible drawbacks (Simberloff et al. 1992; Orrock and Damschen 2005). Corridors may facilitate the movement of pest species and disease; a single infestation could quickly spread to all of the connected nature reserves and cause the extinction of all populations of a rare species. Also, animals dispersing along corridors may be exposed to greater risks of predation because human hunters as well as animal predators tend to concentrate on routes used by wildlife. Finally, buying land to use as corridors and building overpasses and underpasses across existing roads are expensive solutions: whenever a corridor project is being considered, the cost needs to be evaluated to determine whether this expenditure of money is the most effective way to reach the stated conservation objectives.

Some studies published to date support the conservation value of corridors, while other studies do not show any effect (Pardini et al. 2005). In general, maintaining existing corridors is probably worthwhile because many of them are along watercourses that may be biologically important habitats themselves. When new parks are being carved out of large blocks of undeveloped land, incorporating corridors by leaving small clumps of original habitat between large conservation areas may facilitate movement in a stepping-stone pattern. Similarly, forest species are more likely to disperse through a matrix of recovering secondary forest than through cleared farms and pastures (Castellón and Sieving 2006). Corridors are most obviously needed along known migration routes (Newmark 2008). Clearly, the abilities of different types of species to use corridors and intervening habitat areas to migrate between protected areas needs to be more thoroughly assessed.

Habitat Corridor Case Studies

Several case studies serve to illustrate the concept and practical applications of habitat corridors and some of the difficulties involved in establishing and maintaining such protected pathways.

BANFF NATIONAL PARK   In Banff National Park, the Canadian government has been building a variety of underpasses and overpasses across the four-lane Trans-Canada Highway to facilitate wildlife movement and at the same time to reduce the incidence of collision between vehicles and large mammals (Ford et al. 2009). Thirteen recent structures were evaluated for their use, which was measured as a function of animal tracks left in raked beds of soil. Certain mammals, such as grizzly bears, wolves, elks, and deer, used wide overpasses, whereas narrow underpasses were favored by black bears and cougars (see Figure 16.7). Cougars favored crossings with vegetation cover, but grizzly bears, elks, and deer preferred a more open landscape. The results demonstrate that a mixture of crossing types and associated vegetation covers are needed to allow connectivity across road barriers.

SELOUS–NIASSA WILDLIFE CORRIDOR, TANZANIA   The Selous–Niassa Wildlife Corridor (SNWC) connects the Selous Game Reserve in Tanzania with the Niassa Game Reserve in Mozambique. These two reserves are the largest protected areas in eastern Africa (Mpanduji et al. 2008). Studies of radio-collared elephants have demonstrated that these animals frequently use habitat areas within the corridor . While the corridor and its adjoining reserves represent important habitat areas for elephants and other migratory animals, the corridor is inconsistently protected, highlighting a significant barrier to effective conservation (Caro et al. 2009). The main threats to the corridor are agricultural expansion into the corridor, road building across the corridor, hunting for bushmeat, and lack of effective government action to protect the corridor. The SNWC is in better condition than many other wildlife corridors in Tanzania, but improvements are still needed to ensure its long-term integrity, especially in the face of an expanding human population near its borders (Mpanduji et al. 2008, Caro et al. 2009). One urgent need is to document wildlife migration routes and to provide this information to the relevant government officials.

COMMUNITY BABOON SANCTUARY   Corridors may be valuable on a small scale, linking isolated forest patches. Such an approach has been undertaken at the 47 km² Community Baboon Sanctuary (CBS) near the village of Bermudian Landing in Belize (**Figure 16.8**). Populations of black howler monkeys (*Alouatta pigra*) were declining because local landowners were clearing forest along the Belize River to

(A)

(B)

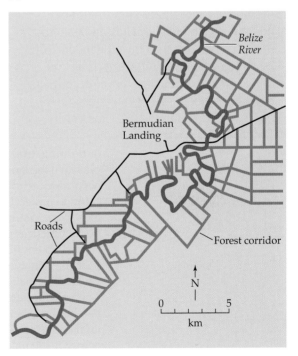

FIGURE 16.8 (A) Aerial bridges allow howler monkeys (baboons) to cross over roads and gaps in forests. These bridges have become popular viewing points for tourists. (B) The Community Baboon Sanctuary at Bermudian Landing, Belize, is attempting to preserve a network of forest corridors (dark green areas) along the Belize River and between fields. (A, photograph courtesy of R. P. Horwich and J. Lyon.)

create new agricultural land (Horwich and Lyon 2007), and the monkeys were unable to cross open fields between forest patches. As their food sources declined and their ability to move through the river forest became impaired, the monkey population underwent a serious decline. To reverse this trend, the 450 villagers living and owning land in the CBS made pledges in 1985 to maintain corridors of forest approximately 20 m wide along the watercourses and property boundaries. Forest corridors were also established across large fields and between forest patches. Other components of the plan include protecting trees that provide food for the monkeys and building aerial bridges over roads, so the monkeys can cross in safety. After 24 years, the results of the project are mixed. While the black howler monkey population has been steadily increasing as a result of greater habitat connectivity, the overall rate of deforestation in the CBS area continues at the same rate as nearby areas (Wyman and Stein 2009). Ecotourism associated with the project provides significant income to only a few of the many families in the village, as described in Chapter 20.

Landscape Ecology and Park Design

The interaction of actual land use patterns, conservation theory, and park design is evident in the discipline of **landscape ecology**, which investigates patterns of habitat types on a local and regional scale and their influence on species distribution and ecosystem processes (Koh et al. 2009; Wu and Hobbs 2009). A landscape is a repeating pattern of landforms or ecosystems, with each type of ecosystem in the landscape having its own distinctive vegetation structure and species composition (**Figure 16.9**). In many cases, conservation biologists need to consider protecting biodiversity within such a landscape context, not just a specific site where threatened species are found (Boyd et al. 2008; Ficetola et al. 2009).

Landscape ecology has been more intensively studied in the human-dominated environments of Europe, where long-term practices of traditional agricultural and forest management determine the landscape pattern, than it has been in North

> In some instances, long-term traditional human use has created landscape patterns that preserve and even increase biodiversity. Especially where agriculture, grazing and other traditional practices have recently been abandoned, management is sometimes effective in maintaining that biodiversity.

America, where research has emphasized single habitat types that are considered (often erroneously) to be minimally affected by people. In traditional farming, there are cultivated fields, pastures, woodlots, and hedges alternating to create a mosaic that affects the distribution of wild species (Fischer et al. 2008). In the traditional Japanese landscape, known as *satoyama*, flooded rice fields, hay fields, villages, and forests provide a rich diversity of habitat for wetland species such as dragonflies, amphibians, and waterfowl (**Figure 16.10**) (Kobori and Primack 2003; Kadoya et al. 2009). In many areas of Europe and Asia, traditional patterns of farming, grazing, and forestry are being abandoned. In some places, rural people leave the land completely and migrate to urban areas, or their farming practices become more intensive, involving more machinery and inputs of fertilizer. In such cases, to protect biological communities, conservation biologists have to adopt strategies to maintain the traditional landscapes, in some cases by subsidizing traditional practices or having volunteers manage the land.

In such environments, many species are not confined to a single habitat; rather, they move between habitats or live on borders where two habitats meet. For these species, the patterns of habitat types on a regional scale are of critical importance. The presence and density of many species may be affected by the size of habitat patches and their degree of linkage. For example, the population size of a rare animal species will be different in two 100 ha parks, one with an alternating checkerboard of 100 patches of field and forest, each 1 ha in area, the other with a checkerboard of four patches, each 25 ha in area (**Figure 16.11**). These alternative landscape

(A)

(B)

(C)

(D)

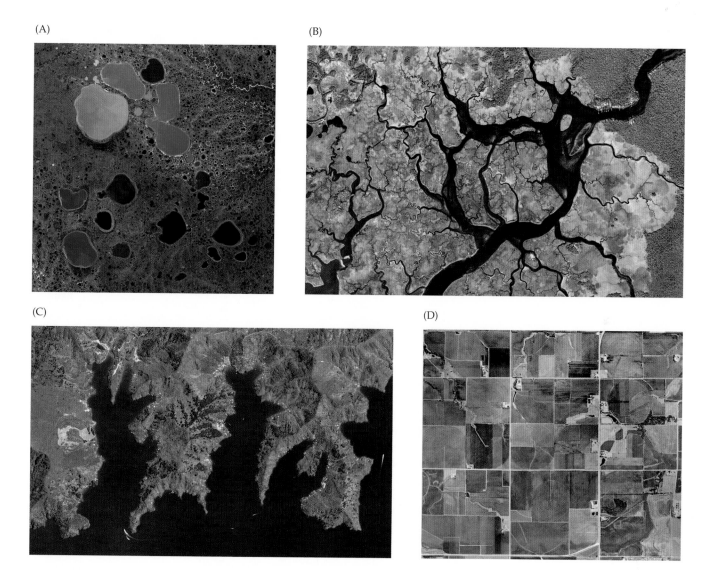

FIGURE 16.9 Four different landscape types in which interacting ecosystems or land uses form repetitive patterns. The discipline of landscape ecology focuses on such interactions rather than on a single habitat type. (A) These pothole lakes in Siberia illustrate scattered patch landscapes. (B) This aerial photograph of the wetlands off the Gulf Coast of Florida illustrates a network landscape. (C) This coastal image of the South Island of New Zealand illustrates an interdigitated landscape. (D) This Nebraska farmland forms a checkerboard landscape. (A, NASA image created by Jesse Allen, Earth Observatory; B, photograph courtesy of the U.S. Geological Survey; C, photograph © Digital Globe; D, photograph courtesy of the USDA Farm Service Agency.)

patterns may have very different effects on the microclimate (wind, temperature, humidity, and light), pest outbreaks, and animal movement patterns, as described in Chapter 9. Different land uses often result in dramatically contrasting landscape patterns. Forest areas cleared for shifting agriculture, permanent subsistence agriculture, plantation agriculture, or suburban development have differing distributions and sizes of remnant forest patches and different kinds of species. The patterns of the landscape can strongly influence species distributions. For example, certain species of frogs are more abundant when there is greater forest cover around ponds (Mazerolle et al. 2005).

FIGURE 16.10 Traditional rural landscape near Tokyo, Japan, with an alternating pattern of villages (black); secondary forest (dark green); padi, or wet rice fields (light green); and hay fields (beige). Such landscapes were common in the past but are now becoming rare because of the increasing mechanization of Japanese agriculture, the movement of the population away from farms, and the urbanization of the Tokyo area. The area covered is approximately 4 km × 4 km. (After Yamaoko et al. 1977.)

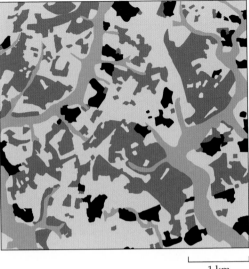

1 km

To increase the number and diversity of animals, wildlife managers sometimes create the greatest amount of landscape variation possible within the confines of their game management unit. Fields and meadows are created and maintained, small thickets are encouraged, groups of fruit trees and crops are planted, patches of forests are periodically cut, little ponds and dams are developed, and numerous trails and dirt roads meander across and along all of the patches. Such landscaping is often appealing to the public, who are the main visitors and financial contributors to the park. The result is a park transformed into a mass of edges where transition zones abound and animal life is abundant and easy to observe. However, the species in these landscapes are likely to be principally common species that depend on human disturbance—in some cases, invasive species. A reserve that contains the maximum amount of edge may lack many rare interior species that survive only in large blocks of undisturbed habitat (Horner-Devine et al. 2003; Crooks et al. 2004). The net result is that parks intensively managed for maximum wildlife

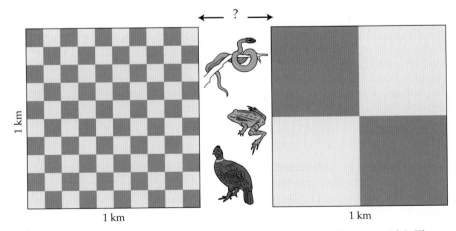

FIGURE 16.11 Two square nature reserves, each 100 ha in area (1 km on a side). They have equal areas of forest (shaded) and pasture (unshaded) but in patches that are of very different sizes. Which landscape pattern benefits which species? This is a question managers must endeavor to answer.

and habitat diversity could be inhospitable to certain species of true conservation significance.

To remedy this localized approach, biological diversity needs to be managed on a regional landscape level, in which the sizes of the landscape units more closely approximate the natural sizes and migration patterns of the species. An alternative to creating a miniature landscape of a variety of habitats on a small scale is to link all parks in an area in a regional plan, perhaps involving corridors, in which larger habitat units could be created (**Figure 16.12**).

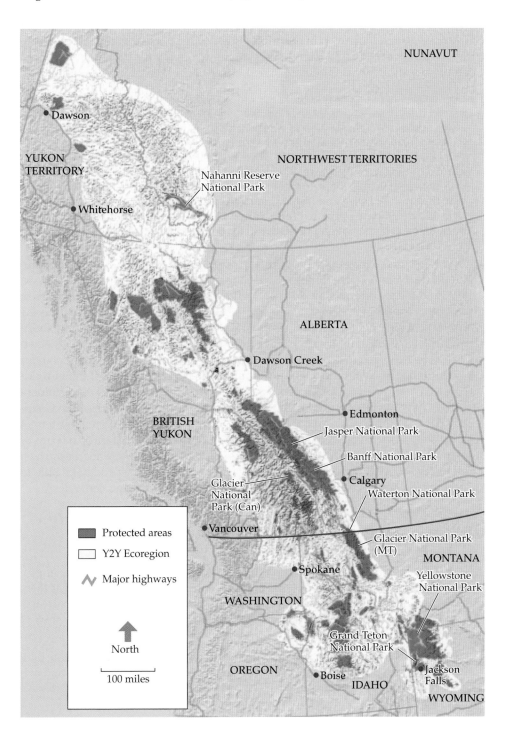

FIGURE 16.12 The Yellowstone to Yukon (Y2Y) Ecoregion plan proposes to link the national parks and other government lands along the Rocky Mountains of the United States and Canada. Managing at the regional scale might be the best way to control populations of large mammals. (After Yellowstone to Yukon Conservation Initiative.)

The Wildlands Network and the U.S. National Wildlife Refuge System are examples of a proposed and an actual linked park system. Some of these large habitat units would protect wide-ranging, rare species (such as grizzly bears, wolves, and large cats) that are unable to tolerate human disturbance and need large areas to exist.

Conclusion

Within the field of conservation biology, there is ongoing discussion of the optimal procedures for designing networks of protected areas. The publication of new research results and vigorous discussion are helping to provide greater insight into the various issues. However, in describing the desire of conservation biologists to provide land managers with simplified general guidelines for designing networks of nature reserves, David Ehrenfeld (1989), a leading conservation scientist, stated:

> I feel obliged to point out that there is a widespread obsession with a search for general rules of scientific conservation, the "genetic code of conservation" so to speak, and this finds expression in very general statements about extinction rates, viable population sizes, ideal reserve designs, and so forth. . . . Yet this kind of generality is easily abused, especially when would-be conservationists become bewitched by models of their own making. When this happens, the sight of otherwise intelligent people trying to extract non-obvious general rules about extinction from their own polished and highly simplified versions of reality becomes a spectacle that would have interested Lewis Carroll. . . . We should not be surprised when different conservation problems call for qualitatively different solutions.

At present, the managers of protected areas still must approach each land acquisition decision on its individual merits. Managers need to be aware of the best examples and the appropriate models, but in the end, the particular circumstances of a case, often involving such concerns as funding and politics, will determine the course of action (Knight and Cowling 2007; Zavaleta et al. 2008). The greatest short-term challenge in designing systems of protected areas is to anticipate how the network will be managed to achieve its goals. In many cases, the management plan for the protected areas will be more important than the size and shape of the individual protected areas. In addition, people living nearby may help meet management objectives or come into conflict with park managers (as will be discussed in Chapter 17). The greatest long-term challenge is to anticipate how the current system of reserves will protect biodiversity in an uncertain world that is changing in terms of human population growth, land use patterns, climate, invasive species, and a host of other factors. Will the network of protected areas established today be able to protect these same species and ecosystems in coming decades and centuries?

Summary

1. Conservation biologists are investigating the best way to design networks of protected areas. In some cases, investigations are based on the assumption that these areas have islandlike characteristics in a matrix of human-dominated landscape. The insight provided by these investigations can be combined with common sense and natural history data to develop a useful approach.

2. Conservation biologists have debated whether it is better to create a single large park or several small parks comprising equivalent area; convincing arguments and evidence have been presented on both sides. In general, though, a large park will have more species than a small park of equivalent habitat.

3. Parks need to be designed to minimize harmful edge effects, and if possible, a park should contain an entire ecosystem. The tendency to fragment parks with roads, fences, and other human developments should be avoided because they inhibit migration and facilitate the spread of exotic and other undesirable species and diseases. Whenever possible, government authorities and private landowners should coordinate their activities and manage adjoining parcels of land as one large unit.

4. Habitat corridors have been proposed to link isolated conservation areas. These corridors may allow the movement of animals between protected areas, which would facilitate gene flow as well as dispersal and colonization of new sites. Habitat corridors will be most effective when they protect existing routes of migratory animals. Networks of protected areas should be planned to account for changing climate in coming decades.

5. In the past, wildlife biologists advocated creating a mosaic of habitats with abundant edges. While this landscape design often increases the number of species and the overall abundance of animals, it may not favor some species of greatest conservation concern, which often occupy large blocks of undisturbed habitat.

For Discussion

1. The only known population of a rare beetle species has 50 individuals and exists in a 10 m × 10 m area in a 1 ha (100 m × 100 m) patch of metropolitan woodland. Should this woodland be established as a protected area, or is it too small to protect the species? How would you make this determination? What suggestions could you make for designing and managing a park that would increase the chances of survival for this beetle species?

2. Obtain a map of a national park or protected area. How does the shape and location of the protected area differ from the ideal designs discussed in this chapter? What would it take to improve the design of the park and/or coordinate its management with surrounding landholders so that it had a greater likelihood of preserving biodiversity?

3. Obtain a map of protected areas for a country or region. Consider how these protected areas could be linked by a system of habitat corridors. What would it accomplish? How much land would have to be acquired? How much would it cost? Would these corridors help species to disperse in response to a changing climate? Can you think of any other ways that the same funds could be spent more effectively to achieve the goals of conservation? To complete this exercise, you might have to make many assumptions.

Suggested Readings

Birchard, B. 2005. *Nature's Keepers: The Remarkable Story of How the Nature Conservancy Became the Largest Environmental Group in the World*. Jossey-Bass, San Francisco, CA. TNC is so large, wealthy, and influential that you have to know about it.

Cawardine, J., J. K. Carissa, K. A. Wilson, R. L. Pressey, and H. P. Possingham. 2009. Hitting the target and missing the point: Target-based conservation planning in context. *Conservation Letters* 2: 4–11. A more flexible planning approach is needed to accomplish conservation goals and avoid misunderstanding.

Corlatti, L., K. Hacklander, and F. Frey-Roos. 2009. Ability of wildlife overpasses to provide connectivity and prevent genetic isolation. *Conservation Biology* 23: 548–556. Wildlife overpasses are proving to be an effective conservation tool.

Goldman, R. L., H. Tallis, P. Kareiva, and G. C. Daily. 2008. Field evidence that ecosystem service projects support biodiversity and diversify options. *Proceedings of the National Academy of Sciences USA* 105: 9445–9448. The number of ecosystem service projects is rapidly increasing, and their impacts are positive.

Hannah, L. 2010. A global conservation system for climate-change adaptation. *Conservation Biology* 24: 70–77. The world's network of protected areas needs to be planned with climate change in mind.

Knight, A. and R. M. Cowling. 2007. Embracing opportunism in the selection of priority conservation areas. *Conservation Biology* 21: 1124–1126. Often establishing new protected areas depends on funding and political will, not an elaborate planning process.

Koh, L. P., P. Levang, and J. Ghazoul. 2009. Designer landscapes for sustainable biofuels. *Trends in Ecology and Evolution* 24: 431–438. The greatest biodiversity may be preserved in landscapes with heterogeneous vegetation and low-level cultivation.

Leathwick, J. 2008. Novel methods for the design and evaluation of marine protected areas in offshore waters. *Conservation Letters* 1: 91–102. Well-designed MPAs would be far more effective at achieving conservation goals.

Lerner, J., J. Mackey, and F. Casey. 2007. What's in Noah's wallet? Land conservation spending in the United States. *BioScience* 57: 419–423. The U.S. government spent $32 billion on land conservation from 1992 to 2001.

Margules, C. and S. Sarkar. 2007. *Systematic Conservation Planning*. Cambridge University Press, Cambridge, UK. Guide for the most efficient method for developing a comprehensive conservation network.

Markovchick-Nicholls, L. and 6 others. 2008. Relationships between human disturbance and wildlife land use in urban habitat fragments. *Conservation Biology* 22: 99–109. Many animal species can persist in urban areas if large habitat fragments exist there.

Nicholson, E. and H. P. Possingham. 2007. Making conservation decisions under uncertainty for the persistence of multiple species. *Ecological Applications* 17: 251–265. Principles of conservation design can guide the establishment of protected areas when complete information is not available.

Roux, D. J. and 10 others. 2008. Designing protected areas to conserve riverine biodiversity: Lessons from the hypothetical redesign of Kruger National Park. *Biological Conservation* 141: 100–117. With better management, Kruger National Park could be even more effective in protecting biodiversity.

Tabarelli, M. and C. Gascon. 2005. Lessons from fragmentation research: Improving management and policy guidelines for biodiversity conservation. *Conservation Biology* 19: 734–739. Fragmented landscapes need to be reconnected.

Wilcove, D. S. and M. Wikelski. 2008. Going, going, gone: Is animal migration disappearing? *PLoS Biology* 6: 1361–1364. In Africa and other places, human settlements and agriculture are blocking existing migration routes, with resulting harm to wildlife populations.

Wu, J. and R. J. Hobbs (eds.). 2009. *Key Topics in Landscape Ecology*. Cambridge University Press, Cambridge, UK. Current topics in the field presented by leading experts.

Chapter 17

Managing Protected Areas

Protected areas have different objectives depending on their legal status, establishment history, and individual characteristics. Some places are designated for biodiversity conservation and are managed to meet the needs of particular species, while others protect whole ecosystems. Other types of protected areas are designated for recreational and cultural value. A common misconception is that once protected areas are legally established, the work of conservation is largely complete, and nothing more needs to be done. Regardless of their objectives, most protected areas require active management, and it is important that the management be tailored to the goals of each individual protected area. This chapter examines some of the strategies employed in managing protected areas.

Although some people believe that "nature knows best" and that biodiversity is best served when humans do not intervene, the reality is often very different. In many cases, humans have already modified the environment so much that the remaining species and communities need human monitoring and intervention in order to survive.

Without human intervention, reserves exist in name only. The world is littered with "paper parks" created by government

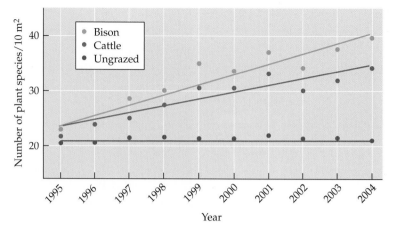

FIGURE 17.1 Large herbivores originally grazed the tallgrass prairies of the midwestern United States. The loss of these herbivores has altered the ecology of this ecosystem, with a resulting loss of plant species. Grazing by cattle and bison resulted in a gradual increase in plant species in prairie research plots over a 10-year period, compared with ungrazed control plots. (After Towne et al. 2005; photograph courtesy of Jim Peaco/U.S. National Park Service.)

decree but left to flounder without any management (Joppa et al. 2008). These protected areas have gradually—or sometimes rapidly—lost species as their habitat quality has been degraded. In some countries, people readily farm, log, mine, hunt, and fish in protected areas because they feel that government land is owned by "everyone," "anybody" can take whatever they want, and "nobody" is willing to intervene. The crucial point is that often parks must be actively managed to prevent deterioration.

In some countries, particularly Asian and European countries such as Japan and France, the habitats of interest, such as woodlands, meadows, and hedges, have been formed from hundreds and even thousands of years of human activity. These habitats support high species diversity as a result of traditional land management practices, which must be maintained if the species are to persist. If these areas are not managed, they will undergo succession and lose many of their characteristic species; effective management then becomes necessary to restore the lost species. For example, in prairie grasslands, moderate grazing by cattle and bison results in more species than in control areas that are ungrazed (**Figure 17.1**).

Many examples of successful park management come from the United Kingdom, where there is a history of scientists and volunteers successfully monitoring and managing small reserves such as the Monks Wood and Castle Hill nature reserves (Morris 2000; www.naturalengland.org.uk). At these sites, the effects of different grazing methods (sheep vs. cattle, light vs. heavy grazing) on populations of wildflowers, butterflies, and birds are closely followed. For example, in montane grasslands at Ben Lawers National Nature Reserve in Scotland, the response of a rare alpine gentian plant has been studied in relation to the intensity of sheep grazing (Miller et al. 1999). Gentian populations initially increase when sheep are excluded but decline after 3 years due to an inability to compete with taller plants and a lack of open sites for seedling establishment. Thus, the presence of moderate sheep grazing is critical to the maintenance of this rare wildflower. Livestock grazing may also be useful in reducing the abundance of certain invasive plant species and undesirable shrubs (Newton et al. 2009).

While such active management may be important in some places, in other places management practices are ineffective or even detrimental. Often, this comes from a lack of understanding of biological interactions or from unclear or conflicting management objectives. Here are some examples:

- Active management to promote the abundance of a game species such as deer to allow hunting and increase revenue for park management has frequently involved eliminating top predators such as wolves and cougars; without predators to control them, game populations (and, incidentally, rodents) sometimes increase far beyond expectations. The result is overgrazing, habitat degradation, and a collapse of the animal and plant communities.

- Overenthusiastic park managers who remove hollow trees, dead standing trees, rotting logs, and underbrush to "improve" a park's appearance may unwittingly remove critical resources needed by certain animal species for nesting and overwintering. Hollow trees, for instance, are used by birds, bats, and bears, and rotting logs are prime germination sites for the seeds of many orchids and an important source of ecosystem nutrients (Keeton et al. 2007). Rotting wood and sprouting fallen trees are also important in the overall ecology of aquatic environments (Gurnell et al. 2005). In these instances, a "clean" park equals a biologically sterile park.

- In many parks, fire is part of the natural ecology of the area. Attempts to suppress fire completely are expensive and waste scarce management resources. Suppressing the normal fire cycle may eventually lead to loss of fire-dependent species and to massive, uncontrollable fires of unnatural intensity, such as those that occurred in Yellowstone National Park in 1988.

Detrimental management practices aside, the crucial point is that parks often must be actively managed to prevent deterioration. The most effective parks are usually those whose managers have the benefit of information provided by research and monitoring programs and have funds available to implement management plans.

Small reserves, such as those found in long-settled areas and large cities, will generally require more active management than large reserves, because they often are surrounded by an altered environment, have less interior habitat, and are more easily affected by exotic species and human activities. Even in large reserves, active management may be required to control hunting and to regulate the frequency of fire and the number of visitors. Simply maintaining the park boundaries may not be sufficient except in the largest and most remote protected areas.

> Unmanaged "paper parks" often do not protect biodiversity. Management plans are needed that articulate conservation goals and practical methods for achieving them. Adequate funding and good leadership are also important.

In a symposium volume entitled *The Scientific Management of Animal and Plant Communities for Conservation* (Duffey and Watts 1971), Michael Morris of Monks Wood emphasized the importance of designing management objectives for each individual reserve:

> There is no inherently right or wrong way to manage a nature reserve . . . the aptness of any method of management must be related to the objects of management for any particular site. . . . Only when objects of management have been formulated can results of scientific management be applied.

The level and type of management needed must be based not only on the ecological objectives of the reserve but also on the social context of the area. Both can change over time. Protected areas in some countries may be extremely hard to manage, and management can break down with poor funding and inadequate leadership and even cease completely in times of war when the central government ceases to function (**Figure 17.2**). In such situations there is often severe and rapid

FIGURE 17.2 In the Rio Negro regions of northern Brazil, a sign on protected lands of the Waimiri Atroari native people asks motorists to drive carefully to avoid hitting wildlife. Bullet holes in the sign dramatically illustrate that illegal hunting is also a problem that needs to be addressed. (Photograph courtesy of Wiliam Laurance.)

degradation of natural resources when trees are cut down and animals are hunted. Examples of such breakdowns have occurred in Afghanistan, the Democratic Republic of the Congo, and Rwanda, though in some cases park officials remained and continued to do their work, without proper security and without being paid (Hart and Hart 2003; Zahler 2003).

Monitoring as a Management Tool

An important aspect of park management involves monitoring components that are crucial for biological diversity, such as the water level of ponds; the amount of soil being washed into streams; the number of individuals of rare and endangered species; the density of herbs, shrubs, and trees; and the dates migratory animals arrive at and leave the park. This monitoring may also include tracking the amount of natural materials being removed by local people. Basic monitoring methods include recording standard observations, performing surveys of key elements, taking photographs from fixed points, and conducting interviews with park users (see Chapter 12). Increasingly, monitoring an area's biodiversity is being combined with the monitoring of its social and economic characteristics, in recognition of the linkages between people and conservation. Factors such as residents' annual income, adequacy of diet, and education level and the amount and value of plant and animal materials people obtain from nearby ecosystems are all important features of this linkage.

The exact types of information gathered depend on the goals of park management. Not only does monitoring allow managers to determine the health of the park, it can also suggest which management practices are working and which are not (Bormann et al. 2007; Levin and Lubchenco 2008; de Bello et al. 2010). The effectiveness of park management practices can sometimes be investigated with carefully designed experiments involving comparisons with control areas or prior baseline data. Managers must continually refine the information they need on conditions inside, or sometimes outside, protected areas and be ready to adjust park management practices in an adaptive manner to achieve conservation objectives; this is sometimes referred to

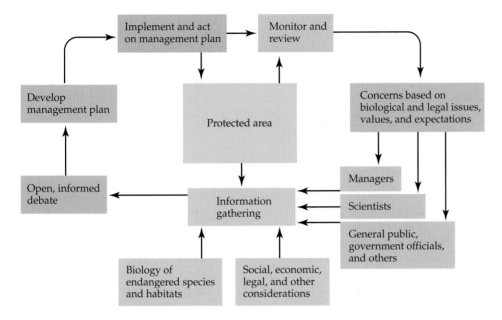

FIGURE 17.3 Model of an adaptive management process for protected areas, emphasizing the decision-making stages, during which input is solicited from many sources. (After Cork et al. 2000.)

as **adaptive management** (**Figure 17.3**). In some cases, this may mean that management plans need to demonstrate cost-effectiveness, that the money being spent is actually making a difference (Salafsky et al. 2002; Briggs 2009). In some protected areas, difficult choices may have to be made; for example, when protected sea lions are eating endangered yellow-eyed penguins in New Zealand, which species should be given priority in management practices (David et al. 2003; Lalas et al. 2007)?

The scale and methods of monitoring have to be appropriate for management needs. For large parks in remote areas, remote sensing using satellites and airplanes may be an effective method for monitoring logging, shifting cultivation, mining, and other activities, both authorized and unauthorized (Buchanan et al. 2009; Morgan et al. 2010). In some cases, local people can be trained to carry out the required monitoring at a local scale. Often these local people have extensive and useful knowledge of a protected area that they are willing to share as part of the monitoring process (Anadón et al. 2009).

> Parks must be monitored to determine if their goals are being met. Management plans may need to be adjusted based on new information from monitoring.

Managers may often gain insight into the appropriate actions needed by reading reports of comparable situations published in scientific journals. In many cases, scientists synthesize the results of a number of similar studies in the form of review articles. A new development is the systematic review, in which the evidence on a management topic is presented and analyzed according to an explicit procedure (www.environmentalevidence.org). Recent systematic reviews have included such practical topics as the effectiveness of herbicides and biological control agents at controlling invasive plants, such as ragwort (*Senecio*) species.

One species that has been intensively monitored for decades is the giant cactus, or saguaro (*Carnegiea gigantea*), an icon of the desert landscape. In 1933, the Saguaro National Park was established east of Tucson, Arizona, to protect this flagship species. Detailed observations, combined with precise photographic records, show that stands of large saguaros are declining within the park. Investigations over an 80-year period suggest that adult cacti are damaged or killed by periods of sub-freezing weather that occur about once a decade. Also, cattle grazing, which occurred from the 1880s until 1979, prevented regeneration, because cattle trampled seedlings and compacted the soil. After 30 years without cattle, large numbers of young saguaro plants have become established in permanent research plots within the park (Drezner 2007). These plots will be closely watched to see if new cactus forests appear later this century.

Identifying and Managing Threats

Management of protected areas must take into account factors that threaten the biological diversity and ecological health of the park. These include many of the threats detailed in Chapters 9 and 10, including exotic species; low population size among rare species; habitat destruction, fragmentation, and degradation; and human use. Even in a well-regulated park, air pollution, acid rain, water pollution, global climate change, and the changing composition of atmospheric gases influence natural communities and cause some species to increase and others to decrease or be eliminated (Hansen et al. 2010; Lawler et al. 2010). In the Atlantic Ocean east of Massachusetts endangered right whales in Stellwagen National Marine Sanctuary were frequently injured during collisions with commercial ships entering and leaving the port of Boston. When detailed maps monitoring whale sightings revealed that some of the highest densities of right whales and other baleen whales were directly in the path of shipping lanes, the shipping lanes were changed in 2007 to areas of lower whale density (**Figure 17.4**). The new shipping lanes have the potential to reduce contact with whales by 81%.

Managing Invasive Species

Invasion by exotic species is now recognized as a major threat to many protected areas, particularly wetlands, grasslands, and island ecosystems. In many places, exotic species may already be present inside a park, and new exotic species may be invading along its boundaries. If these species are allowed to increase unchecked, native species and even entire communities might be eliminated from the park. Where an invasive species threatens native species, it should be removed or at least reduced in frequency. An exotic species that has just arrived and has known invasive tendencies should be aggressively removed while it is still at low densities. Removing invasive species each year is often highly cost-effective compared with the expensive massive eradication programs that are required when the population of an exotic species explodes (Kingsford et al. 2009). European purple loosestrife (*Lythrum salicaria*), which invades North American wetlands, is an example of an invasive species that can outcompete many native plants, often forming pure stands along river and pond edges and in marshes. This species has a detrimental effect on wildlife, because it is not eaten by most waterfowl and it crowds out beneficial species that are.

Once such an exotic species becomes established in an area, it may be difficult (if not impossible) to eliminate it. The recovery of previously declining populations of native plants and animals has often been linked to the elimination of exotic animal species such as goats, rats, rabbits, and gulls from islands and other management areas. Common methods for controlling animals involve poisoning, shooting, capturing, and preventing reproduction. In such cases, a major effort in public relations is needed to explain the goal of the intervention and to respond to the concerns of the public. Invasive plants can sometimes be controlled by physical removal, herbicides, burning, adjusting levels of grazing, mowing, and releasing

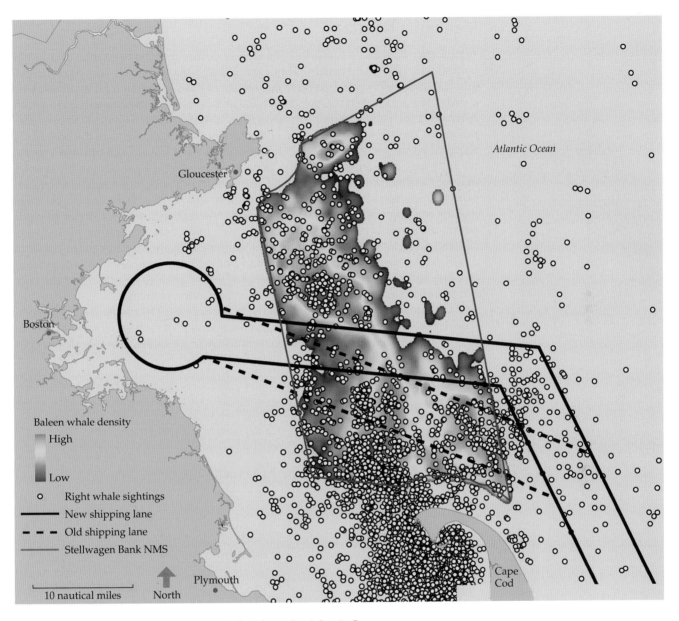

FIGURE 17.4 Ships coming into Boston harbor from the Atlantic Ocean pass through Stellwagen Bank National Marine Sanctuary, where there is a high density of endangered right whales and other baleen whales. To minimize whale strikes, the shipping lane (TSS) into the harbor was moved in 2007 to an area of lower whale density. (From Stellwagen Bank National Marine Sanctuary Web group.)

specialized insects and other biological controls agents. As an example of pest management, colonies of rare species of terns on an island off the Maine coast were displaced by expanding gull populations (Anderson and Devlin 1999). When the gulls were removed by poisoning and shooting, the terns returned to the island, and their numbers appear to be recovering. Constant vigilance is required, as the gulls would quickly return to the island if park managers did not shoot at them. Similarly, following removal of nonnative fish from ponds, native amphibian populations can sometimes recover within a few years (Pope 2008).

Managing Habitat

A park may have to be carefully managed to ensure that the full range of original habitat types are maintained (Rahmig et al. 2009). Many species occupy only specific habitats and specific successional stages of habitat. When land is set aside as a protected area, often the pattern of disturbance and human usage changes so markedly that many species previously found on the site fail to persist. Natural disturbances, including fires, grazing, and tree falls, are key elements in the ecosystem required for the presence of certain rare species (Lepczyk et al. 2008). In small parks, the full range of successional stages may not be present at a site, and many species may be missing for this reason. For example, in an isolated park dominated by old-growth trees, species characteristic of the early successional herb and shrub stage may be missing (**Figure 17.5**). If such a park is swept entirely by a fire or a windstorm, the species characteristic of old-growth forest may be eliminated. In many isolated protected areas in metropolitan locations, frequent human-caused fires and other human disturbances eliminate many of the late successional plant and animal species. However, early successional species may also be missing if they are not present in adjacent sites that serve as colonization sources.

Park managers sometimes must actively manage sites to ensure that all successional stages are present so that species characteristic of each stage have a place to persist and thrive (**Box 17.1**). One common way to do this is to set localized, con-

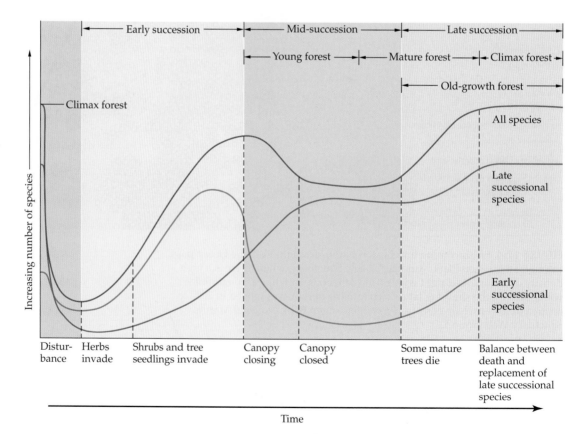

FIGURE 17.5 A general model of the change in species diversity during forest succession following a major disturbance such as a fire, hurricane, or clear-cut logging. Early successional species are generally fast-growing and intolerant of shade; late successional species grow more slowly and are shade tolerant. The full successional time span covers many decades or centuries. (After Norse 1986.)

BOX 17.1   *Habitat Management: The Key to Success in the Conservation of Endangered Butterflies*

■ In 1980 the heath fritillary butterfly (*Mellicta athalia*) had the dubious honor of being closer to extinction than any other butterfly species in England. The distribution of the species had declined steadily for 70 years as its preferred habitat became overgrown or was converted to farmland. The larvae of the heath fritillary feed on plants found in unimproved grasslands or where woodland has recently been cleared to create sunny glades. These habitats are ephemeral and patchy by nature; they require regular cutting of trees or grazing to maintain populations of the butterflies' food plants. The decline of traditional forestry practices and intensive farming have interrupted the processes that provide the necessary butterfly habitat (Dover and Settele 2009). The problem faced by the heath fritillary is similar to that of a number of butterfly species that must colonize specialized, ephemeral habitats—they survive as a network of temporary populations linked by dispersal, which is best described as a metapopulation. The silver-studded blue butterfly (*Plebejus argus*), found in the heathlands of East Anglia, and the silver-spotted skipper (*Hesperis comma*), of short-turf grasslands in southern England, are two additional species that require habitat management to survive.

In the case of the silver-studded blue, the species is only found in young stands of bell heather and heath, where adults feed on nectar and larvae feed on leaves. The specialization goes even further because the larvae must be tended by a certain type of black ant (*Lasius* sp.) to survive, and the distribution of these ants is variable. When the butterflies' habitats are fragmented by human activities, these natural patterns may be interrupted. Species may be unable to locate new suitable habitat because of limited dispersal abilities. The silver-studded blue in particular seems to be unable to disperse more than 1 km from existing populations (Harris 2008). Experimental attempts to establish new populations by carrying adults to unoccupied sites have had some degree of success.

> Active management is needed to maintain populations of many rare butterflies. Without such management, butterflies would decline and go extinct in many places.

Detailed ecological studies have provided the basis for species-specific management strategies. Areas with heath fritillary populations are now managed to encourage the habitat types that the species prefers, such as newly felled woodland and unimproved grasslands. Assessment of the fritillary's progress after nearly a decade of intervention to maintain early-succession food plants demonstrates that human intervention has been a significant factor in the success of the colonies. Where habitat management did not occur, the majority of colonies became extinct (Warren 1991; Hodgson et al. 2009). However, the practice of intensive management raises the disturbing issue of the extent to which endangered species depend on

Larvae of the heath fritillary butterfly (*Melicta athalia*) feed on early-succession plants and require the kind of patchy habitat that occurs when disturbances open up gaps in a forest. These types of sites are now being deliberately created by cutting trees in small patches. (Caterpillar photograph © FLPA/John Tinning/AGE Fotostock; butterfly photograph © Aleksander Bolbot/istockphoto.com; habitat photograph © Ian West/OSF/Photolibrary.com.)

(continued)

BOX 17.1 *(continued)*

human action. The heath fritillary now appears to be utterly dependent on human intervention for survival; the fate of many other species probably rests entirely in our hands as well.

The rare silver-spotted skipper has shown a 10-fold increase in the area it occupies due to the deliberate development of a grazing policy to favor the species and two serendipitous circumstances: an increasing rabbit population that keeps the turf short, and global warming, which also helps this species survive through the winter (Davies et al. 2006).

Roadsides dominated by exotic grasses are increasingly being replanted with native grasslands and wildflower species. The original purpose of such programs was to reduce roadside maintenance costs and make the roadsides more attractive. An indirect benefit has been a substan-

tial increase in the abundance and diversity of rare butterfly species, which benefit from the abundant nectar supply and whose catepillars feed on the diverse food plants (Collinge 2003; Dover 2008).

Butterflies are important to most human societies as symbols of beauty and freedom. If we want to have butterflies in our world, we need to include maintaining habitat for butterflies as an important management goal. In many cases this will mean continuing traditional land use practices, particularly in European countries where the landscape has been strongly influenced by human activities, or even deliberately restoring habitat favored by butterflies. However, hard decisions must sometimes be made, as there are many types of butterflies, and the management that helps one species may harm another (Pöyry et al. 2005).

(A)

(B)

trolled fires periodically in grassland, shrublands, and forests to reinitiate the successional process (Davies et al. 2009). In some wildlife sanctuaries, grasslands and fields are maintained by livestock grazing, burning, mowing, or shallow plowing in order to retain open habitat in the landscape. For example, many of the unique wildflowers of Nantucket Island off the coast of Massachusetts are found in the scenic heathland areas. These heathlands were previously maintained by grazing sheep; now they must be burned every few years to prevent scrub oak forest from taking over and shading out the wildflowers (**Figure 17.6A**). Obviously, such burning must be done in a legal and carefully controlled manner to prevent damage to nearby property. Also, prior to burning, land managers need to develop a program of public education to explain to local residents the role of fire in maintaining the balance of nature. In other situations, parts of protected areas

FIGURE 17.6 Conservation management: intervention versus leave-it-alone. (A) Heathland in protected areas of Nantucket Island, Massachusetts, is burned on a regular basis in order to maintain the open vegetation habitat and protect wildflowers and other rare species. (B) Sometimes management involves keeping human disturbance to an absolute minimum. Muir Woods National Monument is a forest of old-growth coast redwoods, protected in the midst of the heavily urbanized San Francisco Bay area. (A, photograph by Elise Smith, U.S. Fish and Wildlife Service; B, photograph courtesy of U.S. National Park Service.)

(A) (B)

FIGURE 17.7 (A) Overgrazing by cattle along the San Pedro River in Arizona had denuded the vegetation and exposed the river bed. (B) Following a management decision to remove the cattle, the vegetation has been restored and ecosystem processes have recovered. (Photographs by Dave Krueper, U.S. Fish and Wildlife Service.)

must be carefully managed *to minimize* human disturbance and fire, providing the conditions required by old-growth species (**Figure 17.6B**).

The type of controlled management that provides optimal results can be determined through field experiments. For example, chalk grasslands in Britain require specific management measures to maintain a biologically rich community. Experiments have shown that the number, relative abundance, and type of species present are determined by the management regime: whether the grassland is grazed, mowed, or burned; the time of year of the management; the amount of fertilizer applied; and whether the management is carried out continuously, annually, or rotationally (Bennie et al. 2006). Certain management regimes favor certain groups of species over others; for instance, biological communities can take on dramatically different appearances depending on how intensely they are grazed by domestic animals (Krueper et al. 2003; **Figure 17.7**).

> Active management involves specific activities, based on conditions within a given protected area. These activities can include controlled burns, maintaining traditional agriculture, and enforcing restrictions on human use.

Managing Water

Rivers, lakes, swamps, estuaries, and all other types of wetlands must receive a sufficient supply of clean water to maintain their ecosystem processes. In particular, maintaining healthy wetlands is necessary for populations of waterbirds, fish, amphibians, aquatic plants, and a host of other species (Greathouse et al. 2006; Deacon et al. 2007). Yet protected areas may end up directly competing for water resources with agricultural irrigation projects, demands for residential and industrial water supplies, flood control schemes, and hydroelectric dams. Wetlands are often interconnected, so a decision affecting water levels and quality in one place has ramifications for other areas. One strategy for maintaining wetlands is to include an entire watershed within the protected area.

Biological reserves most likely to be affected by human alterations of hydrology are those located in the lower part of a watershed, whereas biological reserves located in the upper parts of a watershed are somewhat less likely to be affected. Such upland protected areas may protect water for thousands or even millions of people living downstream; in these cases, it is often possible to manage large areas

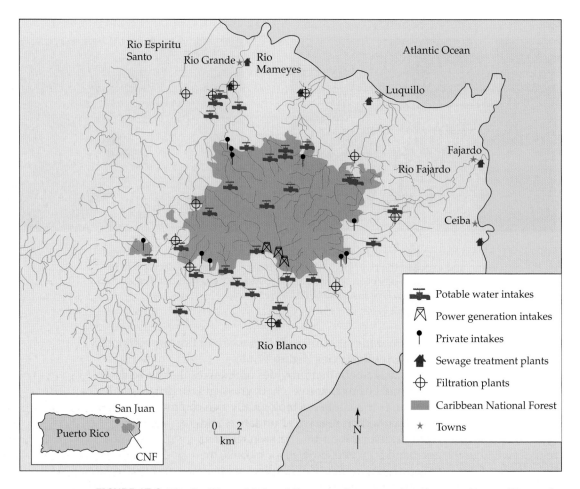

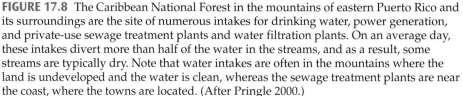

FIGURE 17.8 The Caribbean National Forest in the mountains of eastern Puerto Rico and its surroundings are the site of numerous intakes for drinking water, power generation, and private-use sewage treatment plants and water filtration plants. On an average day, these intakes divert more than half of the water in the streams, and as a result, some streams are typically dry. Note that water intakes are often in the mountains where the land is undeveloped and the water is clean, whereas the sewage treatment plants are near the coast, where the towns are located. (After Pringle 2000.)

for both biodiversity and watershed protection (Verhoeven et al. 2006). However, even remote sources of water may not be exempt from human demands. In the mountains of Puerto Rico, water intakes in the Caribbean National Forest divert stream water for use as drinking water and for power generation (**Figure 17.8**) (Pringle 2000). Six hundred thousand people are dependent on this diverted stream water. However, this means that more than 50% of the water is diverted on an average day. Many streams are dry for most of the year, dramatically impacting populations of fish and other aquatic animals and many other ecological processes.

The water in nature reserves can be contaminated from nearby agricultural, residential, and industrial areas. Such contamination can develop gradually over decades, as happened when the Everglades National Park in Florida was encircled by agricultural and urban development and its water source diverted and contaminated. An example of sudden contamination occurred in Spain in 1998 when a dam at a mine site collapsed, releasing approximately 150,000 m³ of acidic sludge with high concentrations of lead, zinc, and arsenic into the Doñana National Park wetlands. Huge numbers of fish and aquatic invertebrates died as a result. To deal with such situations, park managers may have to become politically sophisticated and effective at public relations to ensure that the wetlands under their supervision continue to receive the clean water they need to survive. Water quality monitoring can help to document alterations in quality and quantity of water in ecosystems and to provide the information needed to convince government officials and the public of the seriousness of the problem. Park managers must be effective advocates for maintaining the water needed for lands under their control (Roux et al. 2008).

Managing Keystone Resources

In many parks, it may be necessary to preserve, maintain, and supplement keystone resources on which many species depend. These resources include trees that supply fruit when little or no other food is available, pools of water during a dry season, exposed mineral licks, and so forth. For example, grain is supplied to rare Japanese cranes at feeding stations to replace a natural food source that was eliminated when wetlands were converted to cultivated fields (**Figure 17.9A**). Is it better to supply this additional food source and have the cranes survive the winter, or not feed the cranes and watch them starve to death?

Keystone resources and keystone species can be enhanced in managed conservation areas to increase the populations of species whose numbers have declined. By planting areas with food plants and building an artificial pond, it might be possible to maintain vertebrate species in a smaller conservation area and at higher densities than would be predicted based on studies of species distribution in undisturbed habitat. Artificial ponds not only provide needed habitat for attractive insects such as dragonflies, but they are also important centers of public education in urban areas (Kobori and Primack 2003). Another example is providing nesting boxes or drilling nesting holes in living and dead trees for birds and mammals as a substitute shelter resource when there are few dead trees with nesting cavities (see Figure 16.5) (Lindenmayer et al. 2009). Pond turtle populations may be increased by building artificial rafts for them to sun on and clearing away brushy vegetation at the pond edge to facilitate nests (**Figure 17.9B**). In these various ways, a viable population of a rare species might be established, whereas without such interventions the population size of the rare species might be too small to persist. In each case, a balance must be struck between estab-

(A)

(B)

FIGURE 17.9 (A) Food must be supplied to red-crowned cranes (*Grus japonicus*) in order for them to survive through the winter. (B) Specially designed rafts allow "sunning" behavior by rare pond turtles and facilitate population growth. (A, photograph © David Tipling/Alamy; B, photograph by Mark Primack.)

lishing nature reserves free from human influence and creating seminatural gardens in which the plants and animals are dependent on people.

Management and People

In both developed and developing countries, a central part of any park's management plan must be a policy on the use of the park resources by different groups of people (Redford and Sanderson 2000; Leischer 2008). Different interest groups often try to sway how park systems or even individual parks are managed. In most countries, some of the greatest threats to parks come from the policies of those same governments responsible for managing them. Large development projects (e.g., roads, dams), concessions for extractive activities (logging forests) or for exploration (oil, gas, minerals), or policies that conflict with management objectives can all threaten biodiversity within protected areas. Local residents may resent any loss of access to or use of resources: for example, ranchers used to grazing cattle and snowmobilers used to riding through roadless areas will not want to lose access. People living off the land who have traditionally used products from inside a protected area and are suddenly not allowed to enter the area will suffer from their loss of access to the basic resources that they need to stay alive. They will be understandably angry and frustrated, and people in such a position are unlikely to be strong supporters of conservation (Wilkie et al. 2006; Mascia and Claus 2009).

Thus, many parks flourish or are destroyed depending on the degree of support, neglect, or hostility they receive from the people who live in or near them. To encourage local people's support, the process of creating protected areas must involve many different stakeholders who should be given the opportunity to articulate what they want and why (see Figure 17.3). Such a process can combine top-down strategies, in which governments define conservation areas, with bottom-up programs, in which villages and other local groups formulate and identify their own conservation goals. If the purpose of a protected area is explained to local residents, and if most residents agree with the objectives and respect the rules of the park, then the area may better maintain its natural communities. This process will help clarify the purpose of the protected area, increasing the chances that the local residents will support different components of park creation and management, from boundary demarcation to ecological monitoring to restoration activities. It is also likely to help the park meet and maintain its objectives.

> The involvement of local people is often the crucial element missing from conservation strategies. Top-down strategies, in which governments and other organizations direct conservation projects, need to be integrated with bottom-up programs in which local people play a leadership role.

In the most positive scenario, local people become involved in park management and planning, are trained and employed by the park authority, and benefit from the protection of biodiversity and regulation of activity within the park. Local residents often support protected areas when they see that such areas can help protect their livelihoods and assist in maintaining their traditional culture and knowledge base. At the other extreme, if there is a history of bad relations and mistrust between local people and the government, or if the purpose of the park is not explained adequately, the local people may reject the park concept and ignore park regulations. In this case, the local people will come into conflict with park personnel, to the detriment of the park. Park personnel and even armed soldiers may have to patrol constantly to prevent illegal activity. In many protected areas local people have been arrested and jailed for activities that they regard as necessary for their livelihood. Escalating cycles of conflict can lead to outright violence by local people, and park personnel can be threatened, injured, and even killed.

The people coming into conflict with park personnel may not just be "locals." In many developing countries, recent migrants into areas who claim land and resources can pose a huge threat to both local residents and protected areas (**Box 17.2**). They

BOX 17.2   *Managing Leopards Together with People*

■ The challenges of protected area management are illustrated dramatically by Sanjay Gandhi National Park, surrounded by Mumbai, home to the Bollywood film industry and one of India's largest and most densely settled cities (Zerah 2007). The park is home to an important leopard population numbering about 33 individuals, many of which were released in the park after they were caught in settled areas by wildlife officials. Unfortunately, the 103 km^2 park is far too small for this number of leopards. Each leopard requires about 25 km^2 of habitat for its territory and feeding ground, so the current leopard population is about eight times too big for the area, forcing the leopards to leave the park to hunt for food. To make matters much worse, due to the lack of housing in Mumbai itself, 65,000 impoverished people are also living illegally in slums on park boundaries. These people hunt the same wildlife as the leopards do. When hungry leopards, with nothing else to eat, prey upon dogs, cats, and other domestic animals both inside and outside the park, people may also be attacked and killed: About 15 people are killed by leopards each year.

Park officers have the unenviable task of both protecting leopards, from angry people who have had relatives, friends, and neighbors attacked, killed, and eaten, and also protecting nearby people from hungry leopards. One short-

Wildlife officials in India are struggling to find the right compromise between protecting leopards and providing for the basic needs of people. (Photograph © Interfoto/Alamy.)

term solution involves releasing pigs and rabbits in the park for the leopards to eat. Two long-term solutions are to move the people outside of the park and enforce the park boundaries or to create a new park for the leopards far from the city. While no long-term decision will be universally popular, the illegal slums are scheduled to be demolished (Deshpande 2009), which will alleviate some of the human–wildlife conflicts.

---

may have little traditional knowledge of the area or its species, have no experience being part of a community or working together, and be motivated only by the prospect of immediate economic gain. One of the ironies of integrating local people into park planning is that a well-run program that provides economic benefits can act as a magnet for poor people from neighboring areas, overwhelming the structure of the project and putting even more pressure on the protected area. Such are the limitations to even an ideal program (Wittemyer et al. 2008).

Clear guidelines on who can use what resources within parks must be a central part of any management plan, in both developed and developing countries (Kothari et al. 1996; Terborgh et al. 2002). In some cases it is necessary to limit any extractive or consumptive uses of park resources by anyone, including local residents. This occurs most commonly when the integrity of the biological communities is being threatened; this strategy is sometimes referred to as "fences and fines." In Kenya, there has been an ongoing struggle between wildlife experts who advocate integrating local people into park management and others who favor excluding them from the parks. The result has been a shifting policy, which has left both wildlife officials and local people confused. Ideally, the benefits from tourism in a country like Kenya would be high enough to support park management, generate high levels of local employment, and provide revenue sharing with local communities. In countries with high levels of nature-based tourism, it should be possible to structure benefits to compensate people for any real opportunity costs to them, such as food not grown, cattle not grazed, and natural products not harvested. The reality is that only a small portion of the revenue from the tourism is typically used to benefit the people living around such protected areas. But this problem is beyond the scope of park management alone and demonstrates the need for government policies and political will to share the financial benefits of tourism.

Zoning to Separate Conflicting Demands

A possible way to deal with a variety of conflicting demands on a protected area is **zoning**, which considers the overall management objectives for a park and sets aside designated areas that permit or give priority to certain activities (Eigenbrod et al. 2009). Some areas of a forest may be designated for timber production, hunting, wildlife protection, nature trails, or watershed maintenance. A marine reserve might allow fishing in certain areas and strictly prohibit it in others; certain areas might be designated for surfing, water-skiing, and recreational diving, but these sports may be prohibited elsewhere (**Figure 17.10**).

Other commonly established zones are for the recovery of endangered species, restoration of degraded communities, and scientific research. For example, at the Cape Cod National Seashore in Massachusetts, protecting least tern and piping plover nesting habitat on beaches has been given priority over the desire of people to drive off-road vehicles and to fish on the beaches where birds are nesting (**Figure 17.11**). A hands-off policy by park managers that does not restrict beach access by fishermen and vehicles would result in the rapid destruction of the shorebird

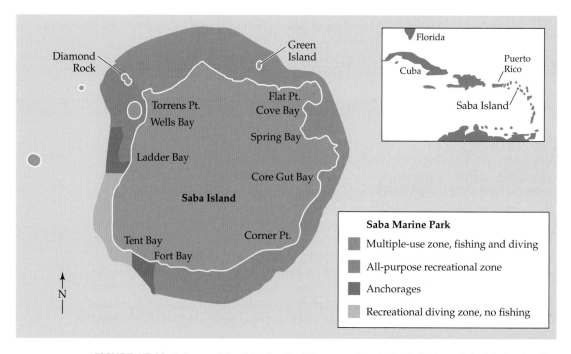

FIGURE 17.10 Saba, an island in the Caribbean under the jurisdiction of the Netherlands, has established a system of zoning to protect the marine environment and still allow fishing. The Saba Marine Park includes the entire coastal zone of the island. The designation of fishing exclusion zones is important to maintain the health of the coral reefs and fish populations that ecotourists come to see. (After Agardy 1997.)

(A)

(B)

FIGURE 17.11 (A) Within a coastal protected area, people may be excluded from certain areas due to the presence of nesting birds. (B) Other areas may be zoned for more intensive recreational uses such as driving off-road vehicles. (A, photograph © Martin Creasser/Alamy; B, photograph © imagebroker/Alamy.)

colonies. In this case, a compromise has been developed whereby prime nesting beaches are closed to human activities but other beaches remain open for recreational activities. Even quiet recreational use of protected areas, including people walking their dogs, may sometimes need to be regulated because of its distruptive impacts on wildlife (Reed and Merenlender 2008).

The challenge in zoning is to find a compromise that people are willing to accept that provides for the long-term, sustainable use of natural resources. Managers often need to spend considerable effort informing the public about what activities are acceptable in particular areas of a park, and then enforcing park regulations (Andersson et al. 2007).

Zoned marine reserves in the Philippines have proven an effective way to rebuild and maintain populations of fish and other marine organisms (**Figure 17.12**). These areas are also known as **marine protected areas** (**MPAs**), marine parks, and no-fishing zones (McClanahan et al. 2007; Leathwick et al. 2008). In comparison with nearby unprotected sites, marine parks often have greater total weight of commercially important fish, greater numbers of individual fish, and greater coral reef cover. Evidence shows that fish from marine reserves spill over into adjacent unprotected areas, where they can help rebuild populations and also be caught by fishermen. It has been demonstrated at various locations in the world that MPAs also foster healthy populations of large herbivorous fishes that reduce fleshy algal cover, a process that is key to the survival of reef-building corals. Before we completely embrace zoning for the fishing industry, though, further research is needed to determine whether concentrating fishing efforts into a few designated fishing zones will seriously damage those parts of the ecosystem. Enforcement of zoning is often a major challenge in marine reserves because fishermen will tend to move toward and into the fishing-exclusion zones, because those areas are where the fishing is best, and that leads to overfishing at the margins of the marine reserve. A combination of local involvement, publicity, education, clear posting of warning signs, and vis-

> Marine protected areas are often zoned with a no-fishing area where fish and other marine organisms can recover from harvesting. Zoning allows the separation of mutually incompatible activities.

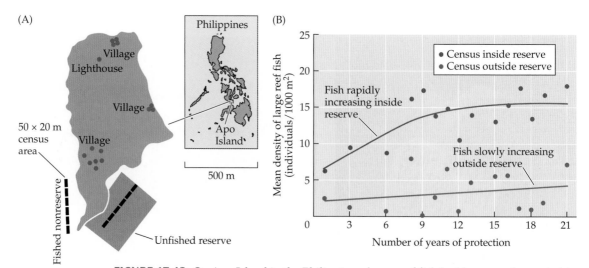

FIGURE 17.12 On Apo Island in the Philippines, large reef fish had been overharvested to the point where they were rarely seen. (A) In response to overharvesting, a reserve was set up (blue area) on the eastern side of the island, while fishing continued as before at a specified nonreserve area on the western side. A censusing study measured the number of large reef fish at each site (six underwater census areas are shown as black rectangles for each site). (B) Resulting data show that after the marine reserve was established, the number of fish observed in the unfished reserve increased substantially. The number of fish in the unprotected area did not increase initially, because the fish were still being intensively harvested; after about 8 years, however, an increase became detectable, originating from the spillover of fish from the reserve area. (After Abesamis and Russ 2005.)

ible enforcement significantly increases the success of any zoning plan, especially in the marine environment.

The Great Barrier Reef off the east coast of Australia provides an example of multiple use zoning to meet a variety of demands. The Great Barrier Reef Marine Park runs for 2300 km along the coast and is up to 400 km wide, protecting about 34 million ha, or 98.5%, of the Great Barrier Reef region. The current management plan recognizes 70 distinct bioregions; within each bioregion, at least 20% of the area is off-limits to commercial fishing, though in some cases traditional fishing is allowed. Separate zones are designated for commercial fishing, research, and traditional fishing. The example set by the Great Barrier Reef Marine Park Authority is now slowly being emulated in other parts of the world.

The United Nations Educational, Scientific and Cultural Organization (UNESCO) has pioneered approaches to balance human needs and conservation with its Man and the Biosphere Program (MAB). This program has designated hundreds of biosphere reserves worldwide in an attempt to integrate activities of local people, research, protection of the natural environment, and often tourism at the same location. The biosphere concept depends on a system of zoning that defines a core area, a surrounding buffer zone, and a transitional zone (**Figure 17.13**). In the core area, biological communities are strictly protected. In the surrounding buffer zone, nondestructive research is conducted and traditional human activities, such as the collection of thatch, medicinal plants, and small fuelwood, are carefully monitored for their impact on biodiversity. In the transitional zone, some forms of sustainable development (such as small-scale farming) are allowed, along with some extraction of natural resources (such as selective logging) and experimental research. In many areas, additional income is generated by providing food, lodging, and guiding services to visiting tourists.

While these zones are easy to draw on paper, in practice it has been difficult to inform residents who live in or near biosphere reserves about where the zones are and what uses are allowed in them and to reach agreement with them.

The general strategy of surrounding core conservation areas with buffer and transition zones is still being debated. The approach has benefits: local people may be more willing to support park activities if they are allowed zoned access to the park, and certain desirable features of the landscape created by human use may be maintained (such as farms, gardens, and early stages of succession). Also, buffer zones may facilitate animal dispersal between highly protected core conservation areas and human-dominated transitional areas. Yet zoning for multiple-use resource extraction including local residents may only work if the core area is large enough to protect viable populations of all key species and if people are willing to respect the zones and their designated uses. Respect for zones varies greatly in different parts of the world among different social situations. In places where park management, political will, and land tenure are weak, buffer zones often are seen as a commons or as unowned and unmanaged lands that are up for grabs. In many developing countries, one of the ironies of a well-managed park is that the economic benefits from the park act as a magnet for poor people from neighboring areas, overwhelming the structure of the project and putting even more pressure on the protected area. For this reason, greater attention is being given to protected areas as one unit in a mosaic of compatible land uses. Rather than trying to have parks conserve biodiversity *and* respond to development needs, broader planning is required that looks across large areas and considers the needs of both people and conservation.

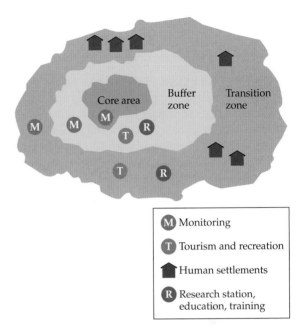

FIGURE 17.13 The general pattern of a MAB biosphere reserve: a core protected area is surrounded by a buffer zone, where human activities are monitored and managed and where research is carried out; this, in turn, is surrounded by a transition zone where sustainable development and experimental research take place.

Regulating Activities inside Protected Areas

Certain human activities are incompatible with maintaining biological diversity within a protected area. If these activities are allowed to continue, important elements of the biological communities eventually may be destroyed (**Box 17.3**) (Wells and McShane 2004). The following activities within protected areas must be regulated, or abolished altogether:

- *Commercial harvesting of game and fish.* Some regulated hunting and fishing may be acceptable for personal consumption and sport, as long as it is sustainable, but harvesting for commercial sale frequently leads to the elimination of species. Commercial hunting and fishing within a reserve, if it is allowed at all, must be carefully monitored by park officials to ensure that animal populations are not depleted. However, heavily armed local hunters operating in remote areas of parks at night are extremely difficult to monitor, and they frequently intimidate park officials. Regulating hunting is most effective when there are clear checkpoints that hunters must pass through, or when a village is so well organized and led that the community itself can regulate the hunting. The difficulties of regulating harvesting in parks are illustrated by the ongoing conflicts in the Galápagos Islands of Ecuador, one of the world's premier national parks (Hile 2004; www.galapagos.org).

BOX 17.3 *Is Arctic Wildlife Management Compatible with Oil Drilling?*

■ In the United States, there are over 500 national wildlife refuges protecting animals on 1 million km². In a national wildlife refuge, one might imagine the protection of biodiversity would have the highest management priority. However, in 60% of the refuges, potentially harmful activities are allowed, such as fishing, hunting, grazing, logging, mining, and drilling. In the United States, a highly emotional struggle is being waged over the future management of the Arctic National Wildlife Refuge (ANWR), a pristine wilderness so remote that few humans have visited there, much less left any marks on the landscape. This area is sometimes referred to as "America's Serengeti" because of its abundant wildlife, consisting of herds of caribou and musk oxen, nesting sites of tundra swans and seabirds, and bowhead whales just offshore (USFWS and Nodvin 2008). The ANWR sits on top of up to 7 billion barrels of oil, considered vital by many to the strategic energy needs of the United States. Environmentalists describe the potential for oil spills, the ugliness of drilling platforms, damage to the tundra, and the loss of a national treasure, while the business community and certain government officials emphasize the need to give the country additional options for energy independence. In the end, a compromise might allow oil extraction in a 15,000 km² area (out of a total refuge area of 192,000 km²), using methods that minimize the impact on the environment, such as slant drilling to reduce the number of drilling platforms, and trucking in supplies only in winter when the tundra is frozen and roads can be made of ice. It is unclear how this situation will be resolved; it continues to be debated after many years. However, whenever strong conservation concerns conflict with powerful business interests, any solution is bound to be imperfect.

Vast grasslands and herds of wildlife are a feature of the Arctic National Wildlife Refuge. Will the energy needs of the United States lead to oil explorations and extractions in this 60 million ha wilderness? (Photograph © Accent Alaska.com/Alamy.)

Fishermen have refused to accept quotas on catches of lobsters, sea cucumbers, sharks, and other marine species and have directed their anger at the park and scientists, threatening research workers and holding them hostage and destroying park offices, research labs, equipment, and data books. In less conflictive situations, establishment of marine protected areas with zones that regulate fishing has proved an effective way to rebuild and maintain populations of fish (see Figure 17.12).

- *Intensive harvesting of natural plant products.* As with hunting and fishing, collection of natural plant products such as fruits, fibers, resins, and mushrooms for personal use may be acceptable, but commercial harvesting can be detrimental. Even personal collecting can be unacceptable in national parks with tens of thousands of visitors per year and where the local human population is large in relation to the area of the park. Monitoring of plant populations is needed to ensure that overharvesting does not occur. A surprisingly large number of people are sometimes found in remote areas of parks illegally collecting forest products such as medicinal plants, ornamental plants, and mushrooms. Dealing with such a situation represents a great challenge for park managers, especially when there are links between illegal poaching or collection of high-value plants and organized criminal groups.

- *Logging and farming.* These activities sometimes degrade the habitat and eliminate species (Zarin et al. 2007). Where these activities are large in scale, commercial in nature, and controlled by outside interests, they must be stopped whenever possible. However, when local people need to clear forests for income or farms to supply basic human needs, it is very difficult for managers to ban these activities. Changing the park zones or park type or "swapping" transformed areas for intact places elsewhere have all been successful in some places. In certain contexts, some regulated harvesting and farming may even be useful to maintain successional stages and to preserve traditional agricultural systems. Such systems can often bring in needed revenue to protected areas and provide employment to local people.

- *Fire.* Widespread and highly destructive forest fires can result when fires are set to clear brush and open areas for farming. They are even more destructive when they follow selective logging. Occasional fires set accidentally or deliberately by local people can open up habitats, provide forage for livestock and wildlife, and reduce undesirable species, and they may help to create a variety of successional stages. Fires that are more frequent than would occur naturally can dry out a habitat, cause soil erosion, and eliminate many native species.

- *Recreational activities.* Popular recreational activities such as hiking off trails, camping outside designated areas, and riding motorcycles, off-road vehicles, and mountain bikes can eliminate sensitive plants and animals from protected lands and must be controlled and restricted to specified areas (**Figure 17.14**). Even such activities as bird-watching must sometimes be curtailed. In many heavily used parks, frequent traffic by hikers wearing heavy boots has degraded vegetation along trails and even killed trees. Redwood trees in California, for instance, are harmed when park visitors compress the soil too tightly by walking around the

FIGURE 17.14 Many parks, such as the one posting this sign in Romania, have signs and brochures that instruct visitors on behaviors that are encouraged or prohibited. (Photograph by Richard Primack.)

redwood trunks. In many parks, people are not allowed to bring dogs for walks, because the dogs frighten and chase animals. In tropical marine parks, swimmers and divers are often restricted to specific areas or trails to prevent widespread damage to delicate branching corals (DiFranco et al. 2009).

Challenges in Park Management

Human populations will continue to increase dramatically in the coming decades, while resources such as fuelwood, medicinal plants, and wild meat will become harder to find. Managers of protected areas in the developing world need to anticipate ever-greater demand for use of the remaining patches of natural habitat. Seventy percent of the buffer zones around protected areas have lost forest cover over the last four decades because of this ever-increasing demand for natural resources (Mayaux et al. 2005). Conflict is inevitable as more people live and farm closer to high concentrations of wildlife that, when food is scarce, have nowhere to go but out of the park and into nearby agricultural fields and villages. Elephants, primates, and flocks of birds can all be significant crop raiders, while carnivores such as tigers pose a different set of challenges to nearby residents.

For park management to be effective, there must be adequate funding for a sufficient number of well-equipped, properly trained, and motivated park personnel who are willing to carry out park policy (Aung 2007). Buildings, communications equipment, and other appropriate elements of infrastructure are necessary to manage a park. In many areas of the world, particularly in developing, but also in developed, countries, protected areas are understaffed, and they lack the equipment to patrol remote areas of the reserve. In most developing countries, conservation programs receive less than 10% of the funds they need to carry out their goals (Balmford et al. 2003). Without enough radios and vehicles, the park staff may be restricted to the vicinity of headquarters, unaware of what is happening in their own park.

> For park management to be effective, there must be adequate personnel, equipment, and funding to carry out the management goals. In many areas of the world, parks are underfunded and understaffed.

The importance of sufficient personnel and equipment should not be underestimated: In areas of Panama, for instance, a greater frequency of antipoaching patrols by park guards results in a greater abundance of large mammals and the seed dispersal services they provide (Wright et al. 2000; Brodie et al. 2009). In another study, of 86 tropical parks, the parks that were most effective at maintaining the vegetation of the park in good conditions had (1) the greatest number of guards per unit area, (2) clearly marked and maintained park borders, and (3) programs to compensate local people when park animals or other park activities damaged their crops (Bruner et al. 2001). (Interestingly, some parks were found to be effective at maintaining or even increasing the biological communities within their borders even with few park guards and poorly defined boundaries, because the legal designations of the national parks prevented private land development.) A third study, of African rain forest protected areas, shows that successful conservation is linked to a positive public attitude toward the park, effective enforcement of park regulations, large park size, low human populations, and the presence of conservation organizations at the park itself (Struhsaker et al. 2005). A fourth study, from Ghana, demonstrates that higher budgets, increased patrolling, and more supervision by senior officers reduce the level of poaching (Jachmann 2008).

The majority of the evidence shows that park personnel and equipment are integral to a park's success, but funding for these resources is often a problem (Bruner et al. 2004; Struhsaker et al. 2005; Steinmetz et al. 2010). For instance, compare the national parks and biological reserves of the United States and the Brazilian Ama-

TABLE 17.1 Comparison of Personnel and Resources Available for Protecting National Parks and Biological Reserves in the Brazilian Amazon and the United States

Feature	Brazilian Amazon	United States
Protected area (in km^2)	139,222	326,721
Number of park rangers	23	4002
Total number of park personnel[a]	65	19,000
Park ranger:km^2 ratio	1:6053	1:82
Park guard[b]	31	100
Administrative building[b]	45	100
Guard post[b]	52	100
Motor vehicle[b]	45	100

Source: After Peres and Terborgh 1995.
[a]Includes all office staff.
[b]Percentage of nature reserves with at least one.

zon (**Table 17.1**) (Peres and Terborgh 1995; Peres and Lake 2003). The United States employs about 4000 park rangers, while Brazil, because of inadequate funding, employs only 23! That is a ratio of approximately one ranger per every 82 km^2 of park in the United States compared with one ranger for every 6053 km^2 of park in Brazil. Half of Brazil's parks lack even basic transportation, such as motorized boats, trucks, or jeeps; it is clearly impossible for Brazil's tiny park staff to adequately patrol large, rugged parks on foot or by canoe, and so protected areas remain unmanaged. The situation is even more disconcerting in the Democratic Republic of the Congo, in which the already inadequate budget for protected area management is actually declining because of war and a deteriorating economy (Inogwabini et al. 2005). To remedy the situation, international conservation organizations are trying to make up for the shortfall, spending about 20 times more on conservation in the Democratic Republic of the Congo than the hard-pressed government does.

It is ironic that zoos and conservation organizations in the developed countries of the world spend vast sums on captive breeding and conservation programs while the biologically rich parks of so many developing countries languish for lack of resources. For instance, the Zoological Society of San Diego, largely occupied with keeping exotic animals on display for the public, has an annual budget of $80 million, which is about the same as the combined wildlife conservation budgets of all African countries south of the Sahara. In many cases, the annual management costs for endangered species and habitats are a bargain compared with the large costs of conservation efforts to save species on the verge of extinction or ecosystems on the verge of collapse. And at the end of the day, conservation biologists need to account for whether their management of protected areas achieved stated goals and whether money was spent effectively (Christensen 2003).

Throughout this chapter the principles and practices of management have been discussed. To implement management, people must be trained as conservation managers, learning both academic and practical skills. Positions for managers need to be created that provide a secure and adequate salary. These managers will then be in a position to carry out their responsibilities of protecting biological diversity.

Summary

1. Protected areas often must be managed to maintain biological diversity because the original conditions of the area have been and continue to be altered by human activities. Effective management begins with a clearly articulated statement of priorities. Monitoring can be used to determine whether management practices are working or need to be adjusted.

2. Parts of protected areas may have to be periodically burned, dug up, or otherwise disturbed by people to create the openings and successional stages that certain species need. Such management is crucial, for example, to some endangered butterfly species that need early successional food plants to complete their life cycle.

3. Keystone resources such as nesting sites and water holes often need to be preserved, restored, or even added to protected areas in order to maintain populations of some species.

4. An effective management tool is zoning, allowing and prohibiting certain kinds of uses in different parts of a park. In biosphere reserves, a core area of strict protection is surrounded by buffer and transition zones in which various human activities are allowed.

5. For park management to be effective, protected areas must have an adequate staff and resources. In many cases, personnel and resources are insufficient to accomplish management objectives.

For Discussion

1. Think about a national park or nature reserve you have visited. In what ways was it well run or poorly run? What were the goals of the park or reserve, and how could they be achieved through better management?

2. Imagine a public nature preserve in a metropolitan area that protects a number of endangered species. Would the nature preserve be more effectively run by a government agency, a group of scientists, the local residents living near the reserve, an environmental nongovernmental organization (NGO), or a council made up of all of them? What are the advantages and disadvantages of each of these possibilities?

3. Can you think of special challenges in the management of aquatic preserves such as coastal estuaries, islands, or freshwater lakes that would not be faced by managers of terrestrial protected areas?

4. Imagine you are a park ranger at Yellowstone National Park during the great fires of 1988. How would you explain the ecologically beneficial role of fire in mature lodgepole pine forests while reassuring park visitors that their park is not being destroyed?

Suggested Readings

Anadón, J. D., A. Gimenez, R. Ballestar, and I. Pérez. 2009. Evaluation of local ecological knowledge as a method for collecting extensive data on animal abundance. *Conservation Biology* 23: 617–625. Monitoring efforts can benefit from local people, who can often provide accurate information on the abundance and distribution of wildlife.

Davies, K. W., T. J. Svejcar, and J. D. Bates. 2009. Interaction of historical and nonhistorical disturbances maintains native plant communities. *Ecological Applications* 19: 1536–1545. Management of biodiversity sometimes needs combinations of old and new land use practices.

Jachmann, H. 2008. Monitoring law-enforcement performance in nine protected areas in Ghana. *Biological Conservation* 141: 89–99. Careful monitoring of staff performance and supervision by senior staff can reduce poaching levels.

Joppa, L. N., S. R. Loarie, and S. L. Pimm. 2008. On the protection of "protected areas." *Proceedings of the National Academy of Sciences USA* 105: 6673–6678. Management is needed to resist the large human impacts that are just outside the park boundaries.

Krueper, D., J. Bart, and T. D. Rich. 2003. Response of vegetation and breeding birds to the removal of cattle on the San Pedro River, Arizona (U.S.A.). *Conservation Biology* 17: 607–615. Amazing before-and-after pictures demonstrating how management affects biological communities.

Lawler, J. J. and 11 others. 2010. Resource management in a changing and uncertain climate. *Frontiers in Ecology and the Environment* 8: 35–43. Managers need to consider the coming impacts of climate change.

Levin, S. and J. Lubchenco. 2008. Resilience, robustness, and marine ecosystem-based management. *BioScience* 58: 27–32. The incentives for individuals to practice good stewardship need to be strengthened.

McClanahan, T. R., N. A. J. Graham, J. M. Calnan, and M. A. MacNeil. 2007. Toward pristine biomass: Reef fish recovery in coral marine protected areas in Kenya. *Ecological Applications* 17: 1055–1067. Biomass and species richness increase over periods of 10 years or more of protection.

Morgan, J. L., S. E. Gergel, and N. C. Coops. 2010. Aerial photography: A rapidly evolving tool for ecological management. *BioScience* 60: 47–59. Aerial photography allows researchers to monitor and manage ecosystems on a large scale.

Rahmig, C. J., W. E. Jensen, and K. A. With. 2009. Grassland bird responses to land management in the largest remaining tallgrass prairie. *Conservation Biology* 23: 420–432. Various management regimes should be used because of differing species responses to each of them.

Redford, K. H. and S. E. Sanderson. 2000. Extracting humans from nature. *Conservation Biology*: 1362–1364. The authors argue for the need to integrate local people in conservation strategies; other articles in the volume present the case for excluding local people or for giving local people greater rights.

Reed, S. E. and A. M. Merenlender. 2008. Quiet, non-consumptive recreation reduces protected area effectiveness. *Conservation Letters* 1: 146–154. Quiet, nonmotorized recreational use decreases wildlife in an area fivefold.

Salafsky, N., R. Margoluis, K. H. Redford, and J. G. Robinson. 2002. Improving the practice of conservation: A conceptual framework and research agenda for conservation science. *Conservation Biology* 16: 1469–1479. Conservation biologists must demonstrate that they have achieved their management goals and used their funds effectively.

Steinmetz, R., W. Chutipong, N. Seuaturien, E. Chirngsaard, and M. Khaengkhetkarn. 2010. Population recovery patterns of Southeast Asian ungulates after poaching. *Biological Conservation* 143: 42–51. Certain large mammals can recover once poaching is controlled.

Wilkie, D. S., G. A. Morelli, J. Demmer, M. Starkey, P. Telfer, and M. Steil. 2006. Parks and people: Assessing the human welfare effects of establishing protected areas for biodiversity conservation. *Conservation Biology* 20: 247–249. New national parks can have both positive and negative effects on local people.

Zarin, D. J., M. D. Schulze, E. Vidal, and M. Lentini. 2007. Beyond reaping the first harvest: Management objectives for timber production in the Brazilian Amazon. *Conservation Biology* 21: 916–925. Low-impact logging has the potential to protect biological diversity, but only if good management is maintained.

Conservation Outside Protected Areas

It is shortsighted to rely solely on protected areas to preserve biodiversity. Such reliance can create a paradoxical situation in which species and ecosystems inside the protected areas are preserved while the same species and ecosystems outside are allowed to be damaged, which in turn results in the decline of biodiversity *within* the protected areas (Boyd et al. 2008; Newmark 2008). This decline is due in part to the fact that many species must migrate across protected area boundaries to access resources that the protected area itself cannot provide. In India, for example, tigers sometimes leave their protected sanctuaries to hunt in the surrounding human-dominated landscape. A crucial component of conservation strategies must be the protection of biological diversity *outside* as well as inside protected areas. Such unprotected areas include government and private lands managed primarily for resource extraction, such as grazing lands and logged forests, privately owned farms and rangelands, and highly modified urban areas, and also oceans, lakes, rivers, and other aquatic systems where food is harvested.

Jeff McNeely (1989), an IUCN protected areas expert, suggests that the park boundary "is too often also a psychological boundary, suggesting that since nature is taken care of by the national park, we can abuse the surrounding lands, isolating the national park as an 'island' of habitat which is subject to the usual increased threats that go with insularity." Sharply demarcated borders between healthy and unhealthy ecosystems do little to preserve the overall welfare of either biological diversity or the human communities that, knowingly or not, rely on that biodiversity for food, materials, and ecosystem services. In many ways, conservation outside of protected areas should strive to blur the distinctions between protected and unprotected ecosystems as much as possible by maintaining unprotected areas in a state of reasonable ecological health (Radeloff et al. 2010). Such efforts will also help to keep the ecosystems within the parks healthier.

Some countries, such as Brazil and Indonesia, are establishing new, large national parks to protect their biodiversity, to maintain ecosystem services, and to provide a destination for ecotourism. However, if the areas outside parks are degraded, then the biological diversity within the protected areas will decline as well (Danby and Slocombe 2005). In general, the smaller a protected area is, the more dependent it is on neighboring unprotected lands for the long-term maintenance of biological diversity. Especially for large animals and migratory species, the number of individuals of any one species contained within park boundaries may be lower than the minimum viable population size. For such species, a management plan that includes neighboring lands outside the park is essential to the long-term maintenance of populations.

In the last chapter, we discussed principles of managing protected areas. In this chapter, we explore strategies to include biodiversity protection as a management objective for both unprotected areas immediately outside protected areas and all other areas that are not protected. Protected and unprotected areas provide complementary roles in conserving nature. They each contribute to a matrix in which species live and ecosystem services are maintained. In the worst case, a devastated landscape polluting the air and water will strangle the protected area it surrounds and will block the movement of dispersing animals and plants. In the best case, unprotected areas surrounding protected areas will provide additional space for ecosystem processes and new populations. Such unprotected areas can also provide corridors that allow individuals to disperse among protected areas.

> Many endangered species and unique ecosystems are found partly or entirely on unprotected lands. Consequently, the conservation of biodiversity in these places has to be considered.

Protecting these areas is essential because more than 80% of the world's land will remain outside of strictly protected areas, according to even the most optimistic predictions (Dinerstein et al. 2006). Human use of ecosystems varies greatly in these unprotected lands, but significant portions are not used intensively by humans and still harbor some of their original biota (**Figure 18.1**). Strategies for reconciling human needs and conservation interests in unprotected areas are critical to the success of conservation plans (Koh et al. 2009). In almost every country, numerous rare species and ecosystems exist primarily or exclusively on unprotected public lands or on lands that are privately owned. In the United States, 60% of species that are globally rare or listed under the U.S. Endangered Species Act occur on private forested lands (Robles et al. 2008). Even when endangered species occur on public land, it is often not land managed for biodiversity but rather land managed primarily for timber harvesting, grazing, mining, or other economic uses. For many other countries as well, a gap exists in the protected land system, with many rare and endangered ecosystems and species existing primarily or exclusively on private lands (Deguise and Kerr 2006).

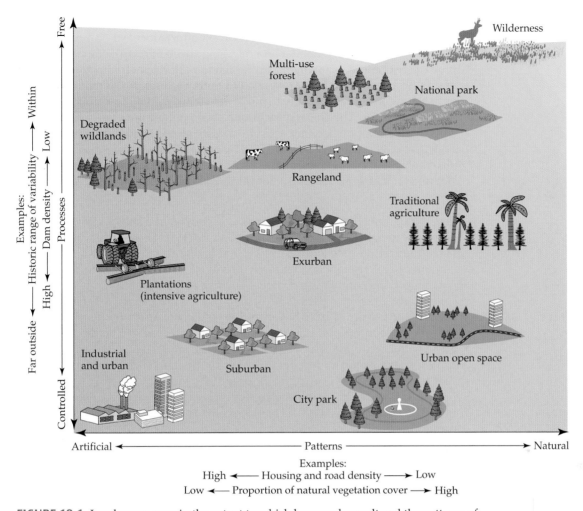

FIGURE 18.1 Landscapes vary in the extent to which humans have altered the patterns of species composition, natural vegetation cover, and ecosystem processes. Species composition and vegetation cover are changed by human activities such as agriculture, road construction, and housing. Ecosystem processes such as water flow and nutrient cycling are altered through human fire control, dam construction, and alteration of plant cover. Wilderness areas retain most of their original patterns and processes, and urban areas retain the least, with other landscapes retaining intermediate amounts to various extents. (After Theobald 2004.)

The Value of Unprotected Habitat

Strategies that encourage private landowners and government land managers to protect rare species and biological communities are obviously essential to the long-term survival of many species (Wilcove et al. 2004). In many countries, government programs inform road builders and developers of the locations of rare species or threatened communities and help them modify their plans to avoid damage to the sites. Public education programs and even financial subsidies may be needed to encourage conservation efforts. The following examples illustrate the importance of land outside protected areas.

- *Mountain sheep.* Mountain sheep (*Ovis canadensis*) often occur in isolated populations on steep, open terrain surrounded by large areas of unsuitable habitat (Epps et al. 2007). Since mountain sheep had been considered to be slow colonizers of new habitat, past conservation efforts focused on protecting known mountain sheep habitat and releasing sheep into areas that they had previously occupied. However, studies using radiotelemetry have revealed that mountain sheep often move well outside their normal territories and even show considerable ability to move across inhospitable terrain between mountain ranges. The isolated mountain sheep populations are really parts of a large metapopulation that occupies a much greater area (see Figure 12.9). Thus, not only must the land occupied by mountain sheep be protected, but also the habitat between populations must be protected because it acts as stepping-stones for dispersal, colonization, and gene flow.

- *The Florida panther.* With a population of fewer than 100 individuals, the Florida panther (*Felis* [*Puma*] *concolor coryi*) is an endangered subspecies of puma that lives in South Florida (Thatcher et al. 2009). This panther was designated the Florida state animal in 1982 and has since received a tremendous amount of government and research attention. Half of the land in the present range of the panther is privately owned, and animals tracked with radio collars have all spent at least some of their time on private lands (**Figure 18.2**). Private lands typically have better soils that support more prey species. Panthers that spend most of their time on private lands have a better diet and are in better condition than panthers on public land.

  While land acquisition programs have brought about 200,000 ha of panther habitat into public ownership since 1996, much more habitat must be protected in order to ensure the panther's continued survival. The acquisition of an additional 200,000 ha has been proposed (Kautz et al. 2006). In the meantime, though, even slowing down the pace of land development may be impractical. Two viable possibilities are educating private landowners on the value of conservation and paying willing landowners to practice management options that allow the continued existence of panthers—specifically, minimizing habitat fragmentation and maintaining preferred habitats of hardwood hammock forest, mixed hardwood swamp, and cypress swamp. In addition, special road underpasses have been built in the hopes of reducing panther deaths from collisions with motor vehicles.

Native species can often continue to live in unprotected areas, especially when those areas are set aside or managed for some other purpose that is not harmful to the ecosystem. Forests that are either selectively logged on a long cutting cycle or are cut down for farming using traditional shifting cultivation methods may still contain a considerable percentage of their original biota and maintain most of their ecosystem services (Clarke et al. 2005; Dias et al. 2010). In Malaysia, most forest bird species are still found in rain forests 30 years after selective logging has occurred where undisturbed forest is available nearby to act as a source of colonists (Peh et al. 2005). Primate species also appear to tolerate selective logging involving low levels of disturbance (Arnhem et al. 2008). However, more intensive logging can result in the loss of species such as woodpeckers that need large, older trees (Lammertink 2004).

The Forest Stewardship Council has been one of the leading organizations to promote the certification of timber produced from sustainably managed forests. Certification of forests is increasing rapidly, with demand, especially in Europe, exceeding supply. For certification to be granted by the Forest Stewardship Council and other comparable organizations, the forests need to be managed and monitored for their long-term environmental benefits, and the rights and well-being of local people and workers need to be recognized. At the same time, major industrial organizations rep-

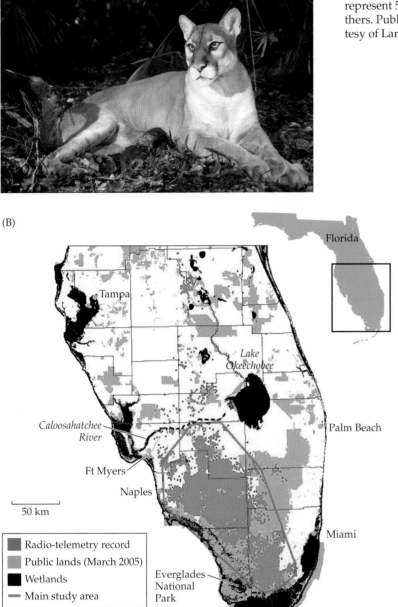

FIGURE 18.2 (A) The Florida panther is found on both public and private lands in South Florida. (B) The red dots represent 55,000 radio telemetry records of 79 collared panthers. Public lands are shaded brown. (A, photograph courtesy of Larry Richardson, USFWS; B from Kautz et al. 2006.)

resenting such industries as logging, mining, and agriculture also lobby for their own alternative certification programs, which generally have lower requirements for monitoring and weaker standards for judging practices to be sustainable.

The mown edges of roadsides often provide an open grassland community that is a critical resource for many species such as butterflies (Saarinen et al. 2005). A similar habitat is provided by the surprisingly large amount of mown fields occupied by power lines. In the United States, power line right-of-way corridors occupy over 2 million ha (5 million acres). Power line corridors managed with infrequent mowing and without herbicides maintain high densities of birds, insects, and other animals (King et al. 2009). If such management practices could be extended over a greater proportion of power line rights of way, these areas could become additional habitat for insects and a wide range of other species. Remnant prairies in the United States also represent an important habitat for many grassland species, especially where they can be managed with grazing or burning.

Many heavily altered ecosystems still have some value for conservation. Although dams, reservoirs, canals, dredging operations, port facilities, and coastal development destroy and damage aquatic communities, some bird, fish, and other aquatic species are capable of adapting to altered conditions, particularly if the water is not polluted. Similarly, in estuaries and seas managed for commercial fisheries, many noncommercial native species can survive, though often at reduced densities.

Excellent examples of natural habitat occur on large tracts of government-owned land managed for nonextractive purposes—for instance, on watersheds adjacent to metropolitan water supplies, such as the Quabbin Reservoir in Massachusetts. Se-

> Even ecosystems that are impacted by human use can retain considerable biodiversity, and have importance in conservation efforts.

curity zones surrounding government installations and military reservations are some of the most outstanding natural areas in the world. The U.S. Department of Defense manages more than 10 million ha, much of it undeveloped, containing over 200 threatened and endangered species of plants and animals (**Box 18.1**). For example, the White Sands Missile Range in New Mexico is almost 1 million ha in area, about the same size as Yellowstone National Park. While certain sections of military reservations may be damaged by military activities, much of the habitat remains as an undeveloped buffer zone with restricted access.

Other areas that are not protected by law may retain species because the human population density and degree of utilization are typically very low. Border areas such as the demilitarized zone between North and South Korea often have an abundance of wildlife because they remain undeveloped and depopulated. Mountain areas, often too steep and inaccessible for development, are frequently managed by governments as valuable watersheds that produce a steady supply of water and prevent flooding; they also harbor important natural communities. Likewise, desert and tundra species and ecosystems may be at less risk than other unprotected communities because such regions are marginal for human habitation and use (MEA 2005).

In many parts of the world, wealthy individuals have acquired large tracts of land for their personal estates and for private hunting. These private estates are frequently deliberately managed by the landowner to maintain large wildlife populations. Some estates in Europe, such as the Bialowieza Forest, have preserved unique old-growth forests that have been owned and protected for hundreds of years by royal families. In recent decades, many such estates have been taken over by government agencies and conservation organizations.

Conservation in Urban Areas

Many native species can persist even in urban areas, in small protected areas, streams, ponds, and other less altered habitats (Rubbo and Kiesecker 2005; Ellis and Ramankutty 2008; Vermonden et al. 2009). As suburban and urban communities expand at the margins of urban centers, this will become more common in the future. Protecting these remnants of biodiversity within a human-dominated matrix not only presents special challenges but provides unique opportunities to educate the public about biodiversity conservation. For example, discovery of a new species of salamander at a popular swimming site in Austin, Texas, has required a change in how the site is managed, to allow people and salamanders to coexist. In Europe, storks often nest in chimneys and towers. Villages have even erected special poles as stork nesting sites, now that the storks' natural nesting sites in forests are

BOX 18.1   *In Defense of Wildlife . . . Send in the Soldiers*

■ The thump of mortar fire and the thudding of tank treads hardly seem compatible with wildlife conservation, yet some of the largest expanses of undeveloped land in the United States are on military reservations located throughout the nation. The U.S. Department of Defense controls more than 10 million ha of land, nearly one-third the size of the 35 million ha of national park lands managed by the National Park Service. Whereas national parks host millions of visitors a year, access to military bases is limited to military personnel and authorized visitors; because of these restrictions, much of the land remains in its natural state. Moreover, the land used for military exercises often is not used intensively; for instance, the Air Force uses only 1,250 ha of its 44,000 ha base in Avon Park, Florida, and similarly small fractions are used at other sites. In other cases, the impact

> Military reservations sometimes have large areas of land with unique species and habitats. With encouragement and funding, military personnel can become participants in conservation activities.

of military training itself, including accidental fires, tank exercises, and artillery practice, provides the disturbance and open habitat required by certain species, such as the Karner blue butterfly and its host plants at Fort McCoy in Wisconsin. As a result, many military bases have become de facto refuges for about 300 species of endangered plants and animals, many of which have their largest populations on military bases (Stein et al. 2008). Rare and endangered desert tortoises, manatees, red-cockaded woodpeckers, bald eagles, Atlantic white cedars, and the least Bell's vireo all have found safe havens on military lands.

Obviously, military reservations differ from true wildlife refuges in one important aspect: They are sites for significant disturbances caused by military exercises. While much of the land may be left undisturbed as a security zone, large parts of the otherwise undeveloped land may be used periodically for acclimating troops to potential combat environments. Many bases contain toxic waste dumps and high levels of chemical pollutants, and human disturbance in the form of bomb explosions, artillery practice, or the use of heavy vehicles can have a significant negative effect on the resident wildlife.

The passage of the Legacy Resource Management Program in 1991 by Congress allowed the military to place greater emphasis on environmentally sound practices by giving them funding for research and conservation programs. Recent programs have ranged from helping individual species to restoring entire habitats (Efroymson et al. 2005). In some cases, conservation efforts simply mean protecting the stands of old-growth forest at the Jim Creek Radio Station in the Pacific Northwest, or the largest chunk of ungrazed tallgrass prairie in the West at Fort Sill, or the pine habitat that houses endangered red-cockaded woodpeckers at Fort Bragg. At the Naval Weapons Station at Charleston, South Carolina, Navy biologists have installed nest boxes and drilled holes in trees to provide future nest sites for the red-cockaded woodpecker. Abandoned underground bunkers are being modified to provide habitat for bats. Construction of a pipeline in San Pedro, California, was halted when workers found a population of the Palos Verdes blue butterfly, formerly thought to be extinct; Navy biologists are now monitoring the population and restoring its coastal scrub habitat. Habitat is also being restored at numerous bases around the

The endangered Hawaiian stilt (*Himantopus mexicanus knudseni*) lives on exposed mudflats in Nu'upia Wildlife Management Area of the Hawaiian Marine Corps base. The Marine Corps periodically uses amphibious assault vehicles to break up exotic woody plants that threaten to cover the mudflats and exclude the stilt. (Photographs courtesy of Mark J. Rauzon.)

(continued)

BOX 18.1 (*continued*)

country as trees are replanted and bulldozers reshape land that has been pitted with bomb craters and gouged with vehicle tracks. Personnel at the Barksdale Air Force Base in Shreveport, Louisiana, have reflooded drained wetlands along the Red River, restoring 830 ha of wetlands for thousands of wading birds. Contaminated sites are being cleaned up. The Army's Rocky Mountain Arsenal in Colorado has been transformed into the Rocky Mountain Arsenal National Wildlife Refuge, complete with its own bison herd. Fences are being installed at Fort Irwin in California to prevent the endangered desert tortoises from getting run down during tank training activities, and hundreds of tortoises inside the training area will be used to augment a declining population elsewhere.

Habitat preservation on military lands isn't a perfect conservation solution: Conflict still arises when military commanders resist involvement in nonmilitary activities, when Congress questions funding such conservation activities, or when military activities appear to be incompatible with species protection. For the time being, though, military reservations are encouraging preservation. At Camp Pendleton in California, a clear message is being sent: a sign warns people away from a tern nesting site "by order of the base commander."

no longer available (**Figure 18.3**). Endangered raptors such as the peregrine falcon and bald eagle make nests and raise young in the skyscrapers of downtown Boston and New York, where the presence of small mammals in the inner city park systems (along with the ubiquitous pigeons and rats common to urban centers) provide abundant food sources. Even ponds at golf courses in urban areas may be suitable habitats for certain newts, dragonflies, and other wetland species, as long as the water is not polluted (Colding et al. 2009).

As exciting as such examples of urban adaptations might be, we cannot assume that all species have the potential to live within human-dominated landscapes. We have a lot to learn about just what habitat and disturbance features are important for various species and how to integrate those into our urban and suburban landscapes. In general, increasing intensity of land use will decrease the number of native species found in a location. Also, the size and configuration of landscape features will determine the extent to which species and ecosystem processes are maintained. More work needs to be done in terms of how these general principles apply in specific locations.

Increasing the presence of wild animals in the urban landscape comes with fairly serious consequences for both animals and humans. Transmission of disease and other potentially harmful direct interactions among people, domestic animals, and wild animals is a major concern. For example, development of woodland areas and mountain canyons includes the creation of yards and gardens that attract deer. Deer may seem fairly innocuous to urbanites unused to wild animals, but they bring with them a host of problems: they can carry ticks that transmit illnesses to humans, such as Lyme disease and Rocky Mountain spotted fever; they are a significant potential road hazard; and males can become fairly aggressive toward humans during mating season. In some areas, deer that live with-

FIGURE 18.3 European storks (*Ciconia ciconia*) take advantage of village structures to make their nests, such as this chimney. (Photograph © Roland Vidmar/istockphoto.com.)

in developments also attract predators such as cougars, increasing the potential for human–wildlife conflicts for a scarce and ecologically important top carnivore.

Conservation in Agricultural Areas

Considerable biological diversity can also be maintained in traditional agricultural systems and forest plantations, characterized by their relatively small scale of operation and limited use of external inputs and machinery (see Chapter 20). Birds, insects, and other animal and plant species are often more abundant in traditional agricultural landscapes, with their mixture of small fields, hedges, and woodlands. Some species are only found in such highly modified habitat. In comparison with more intensive "modern" agricultural practices that emphasize high yields of crops for sale in the market, mechanization, and external inputs, these traditional landscapes experience less exposure to herbicides, fertilizers, and pesticides. Similarly, farmlands worked using organic methods have a greater abundance of birds than farmlands worked using nonorganic methods (Beecher et al. 2002).

In many areas of the world, however, the best agricultural lands are being more intensively used, while less optimal lands are abandoned as people leave for urban areas (West and Brockington 2006). Such agricultural intensification often leads to less wildlife (Ghilain and Bélisle 2008). In European countries, farmers are sometimes paid by the government to maintain traditional agricultural landscapes and farming practice under a program called Natura 2000 (Aviron et al. 2009). For example, farmers are paid to maintain the traditional wildflowers of farmland, such as cornflowers (*Centaurea cyanus*) and red poppies (*Papaver rhoeas*), which are eliminated by the applications of fertilizer and herbicides associated with intensive agriculture (**Figure 18.4**) (Buner et al. 2005). These wildflowers sometimes are maintained by establishing hedges in fields and creating wildflower strips. In the United States, the government has established set-aside programs in which

> Traditionally managed farmlands and organic farms often have more biodiversity than intensively managed farms. Government programs can compensate farmers for practices that maintain birds, wildflowers, and other elements of biodiversity.

FIGURE 18.4 The traditional wildflowers of European cultivated fields, such as cornflowers and red poppies, can be maintained when farmers are paid to reduce applications of herbicides and fertilizers and to reduce the intensity of cultivation. In this case, Swiss farmers maintain wildflower strips between their fields to support wildflower and animal populations. (Photograph © Agroscope Reckenholz-Tänikon ART.)

(A)

(B)

FIGURE 18.5 Two types of coffee management systems. (A) Shade coffee is grown under a diverse canopy of trees, providing a forest structure in which birds, insects, and other animals can live. (B) Sun coffee is grown as a monoculture, without shade trees. Animal life is greatly reduced. (A, photograph © John Warburton-Lee Photography/Alamy; B, photograph © Elder Vieira Salles/shutterStock.)

farmers are compensated for managing farmland to increase populations of grassland birds (Herkert 2009). In Japan, traditional rice fields subsidized by the government support much greater densities of winter bird populations than lands farmed by modern methods (Amano 2009).

Traditional tropical forest plantations, planted with crops such as coffee, cocoa, and many fruits, often retain considerable species diversity. In traditional plantations, coffee bushes are grown under a wide variety of shade trees, often as many as 40 tree species per farm (**Figure 18.5A**) (Philpott et al. 2007, 2008). In northern Latin America alone, shade coffee plantations cover 2.7 million ha. These plantations have structural complexity created by multiple vegetation layers and a diversity of birds and insects comparable to adjacent natural forest, and they represent a rich repository of biodiversity (Bakermans et al. 2009). However, a concern remains as to whether native tree species can regenerate in these altered environments. In many areas, the spread of a fungal disease called coffee leaf rust has encouraged conversion of shade plantations to high-yielding sun coffee plantations without shade trees, which incorporate coffee varieties that require more pesticides and fertilizers (**Figure 18.5B**). These sun coffee plantations have only a tiny fraction of the species diversity found in shade coffee areas and are far more prone to water runoff and soil erosion. Therefore, maintenance of species diversity in many tropical countries is being attempted by regulating and subsidizing shade coffee farmers to maintain practices that minimize forest clearing, monitoring the health of the forest species within shade-grown coffee plantations, and marketing the product at a premium price as "environmentally friendly" shade-grown coffee. A difficulty with this strategy is that the standards for shade coffee are not uniform, and some coffee marketed as "environmentally friendly, shade coffee" may actually be grown as sun coffee with a few small, interspersed trees.

Payments for ecosystem services (PES) programs in Florida are supported by private conservation organizations and government agencies; they compensate ranchers for maintaining unimproved pastures that are rich in wildlife, such as native wet prairie species. Such programs allow farmers an option other than changing to intensive agriculture, which would result in declines in biodiversity (Bohlen et al. 2009; Jordan and Weaver 2010).

Forests that are recovering from selective logging, clear-cutting, or the abandonment of agriculture may still contain a considerable percentage of their original biota and maintain most of their ecosystem services. This is particularly true when fires and erosion have not irreversibly damaged the soil and native species can migrate from nearby undisturbed lands, such as steep hillsides, swamps, and river forests, and colonize the sites. In tropical forests, primate species appear to tolerate selective logging that involves low levels of disturbance, though only when hunting levels can be controlled (Clark et al. 2009).

Multiple Use Habitat

In many countries, large parcels of government-owned land are designated for **multiple use**: they are managed to provide a variety of goods and services. The Bureau of Land Management in the United States oversees more than 110 million ha, including 83% of the state of Nevada and large amounts of Utah, Wyoming, Oregon, Idaho, and other western states (**Figure 18.6**). In the United States, national forests cover over 83 million ha, including the Rocky Mountains, the Cascade Range, the Sierra Nevada, the Appalachian Mountains, and the southern coast of Alaska. In the past, these lands have been managed for logging, mining, grazing, wildlife, and recreation. Increasingly, multiple use lands also are being valued and managed for their ability to protect species, biological communities, and ecosystem services (Gardner et al. 2007). The U.S. Endangered Species Act of 1973 and other similar laws, such as the 1976 National Forest Management Act, require landowners, including government agencies, to avoid activities that threaten listed species.

Laws and court systems are now being used by conservation biologists to halt government-approved activities on public lands that threaten the survival of endangered species. In the late 1980s in Wisconsin, for instance, conservation-oriented botanists questioned how the U.S. Forest Service was interpreting its multiple use mandate in the Chequamegon-Nicolet National Forest. This forest had been managed for a wide variety of uses by the U.S. Forest Service, but timber production and deer hunting tended to predominate. In this part of the country, few threatened and endangered species exist, but many migrant songbirds and forest wildflowers have been declining for decades (Rooney et al. 2004). Many of these declines appeared attributable to the loss of forest interior conditions and an overabundance of white-tailed deer, responding to plentiful food in specially created "wildlife openings." The Wisconsin botanists argued that an effective way to protect this biodiversity would be to forgo all logging, road construction, and wildlife openings in several large (200 to 400 km^2) blocks of land. The chief of the U.S. Forest Service rejected proposals to establish these "diversity maintenance areas." This prompted lawsuits involving not only the original scientists but also conservation groups such as the Sierra Club. The U.S. Forest Service eventually agreed to increase the emphasis it placed on conserving biodiversity. However, new regulations recently issued by the U.S. Forest Service appear to restrict the role of scientists and the general public in influencing decisions on how to manage federal lands and appear to place less emphasis on sustainable management (Noon et al. 2005). Thus, public forest management remains contentious in the United States.

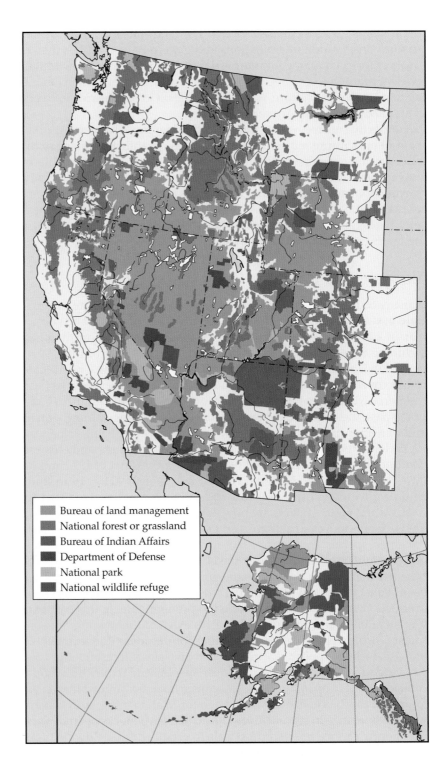

FIGURE 18.6 In Alaska and the western states, agencies of the U.S. government own the majority of the land, including some truly enormous blocks of land. The management of this multiple use land increasingly incorporates the protection of biodiversity as a major objective. (Data from National Geographic Society.)

Legend:
- Bureau of land management
- National forest or grassland
- Bureau of Indian Affairs
- Department of Defense
- National park
- National wildlife refuge

Ecosystem Management

In this chapter so far, the discussion has focused on conservation on a local scale or at a specific place. At the same time, resource managers around the world increasingly are being urged by their governments and conservation organizations to think on even larger geographic scales; these managers are being asked to expand their traditional emphasis on the maximum production of goods (such as volume of timber harvested) and services (such as the number of visitors to parks) and take a broader perspective that includes the conservation of biodiversity and the protection of ecosystem processes (Koontz and Bodine 2008; Levin et al. 2009). This viewpoint is encompassed in the concept of **ecosystem management**, a system of large-scale management involving multiple stakeholders, the primary goal of which is preserving ecosystem components and processes for the long term while still satisfying the current needs of society (**Figure 18.7**).

Rather than having each government agency, private conservation organization, business, or landowner acting in isolation and for its own interests, ecosystem management envisions them cooperating to achieve common objectives (Richmond et al. 2006; Armitage et al. 2009). For example, in a large forested watershed along a coast, ecosystem management would link all owners and users from the tops of the hills to the seashore, including foresters, farmers, business groups, townspeople, and the fishing industry. Some groups might also join this type of project in order to persuade the general public that their organizations are "green." Nonetheless, having public relations benefits on the side of ecosystem management for conservation would be a significant factor in promoting the next important step of putting the paradigm into practice.

> Ecosystem management links private and public landowners, businesses, and conservation organizations to plan and act on a larger scale.

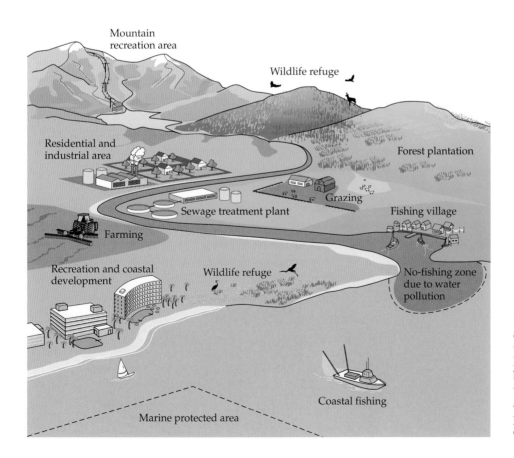

FIGURE 18.7 Ecosystem management involves linking all of the stakeholders that affect a large ecosystem and receive benefits from it. In this case, a watershed needs to be managed for a wide variety of purposes, many of which influence each other. (After Miller 1996.)

Important themes in ecosystem management include the following:

- Using the best science available to develop a coordinated plan for the area that is sustainable; that includes biological, economic, and social components; and that is shared by all levels of government, business interests, conservation organizations, and private citizens

- Ensuring viable populations of all species, representative examples of all biological communities and successional stages, and healthy ecosystem functions

- Seeking and understanding connections between all levels and scales in the ecosystem hierarchy—from the individual organism to the species, the community, the ecosystem, and even to regional and global scales

- Monitoring significant components of the ecosystem (numbers of individuals of significant species, vegetation cover, water quality, etc.), gathering the needed data, and then using the results to adjust management in an adaptive manner (sometimes referred to as adaptive management)

One example of ecosystem management is the work of the Malpai Borderlands Group, a nonprofit cooperative enterprise of ranchers and other local landowners who promote collaboration among conservation organizations such as The Nature Conservancy, private landowners, scientists, and government agencies (www.malpaiborderlandsgroup.org). The group is developing a network of cooperation across the Malpai planning area, nearly 400,000 ha of unique, rugged mountain and desert habitat along the Arizona and New Mexico border. This country of isolated mountains, or "sky islands," includes the San Bernardino Valley as well as the Animas and Peloncillo Mountains. This is one of the richest biological areas in the United States, supporting 265 species of birds, 90 species of mammals, and the most diverse lizard fauna in the United States (**Figure 18.8**). It includes six listed endangered species, including the Mexican jaguar, the Chiricahua leopard frog, the New Mexico ridge-nosed rattlesnake, the lesser long-nosed bat, and the Yaqui chub fish. It is also home to dozens of other rare and endemic species, such as the Gould's turkey. The Malpai Borderlands Group is using controlled burning as a range man-

FIGURE 18.8 The Malpai Borderlands Group encourages ecosystem management for 400,000 ha of desert and mountains in southern Arizona and New Mexico. Numerous rare and endangered species, including the Mexican jaguar (*Panthera onca*), are protected in the process. (Photograph by Warner Glenn, from *Eyes of Fire: Encounter with a Borderland Jaguar*.)

agement tool, reintroducing native grasses, applying innovative approaches to cattle grazing, incorporating scientific research into management plans, and taking action to avoid habitat fragmentation by using conservation easements (agreements not to develop land) to prevent residential development. Their goal is to create "a healthy, unfragmented landscape to support a diverse, flourishing community of human, plant and animal life in the Borderlands Region" (Allen 2006).

Most ecosystem management projects appear to be successful at improving cooperation among stakeholders and increasing public awareness of conservation issues (Keough and Blahna 2006). However, many attempts at ecosystem management have not succeeded, because of distrust among the participating groups. Certain groups, such as real estate developers and conservation activists, often have fundamentally different objectives. Forcing conservation-minded groups into alliances might weaken their ability to lobby the government for conservation measures and prevent them from taking cases to court (Peterson et al. 2005).

A logical extension of ecosystem management is **bioregional management**, which integrates protection with use and often focuses on a single large ecosystem, such as the Caribbean Sea or the Great Barrier Reef of Australia, or a series of linked ecosystems such as the protected areas of Central America (Schellnhuber et al. 2001). A bioregional approach is particularly appropriate where there is a single, continuous, large ecosystem that crosses international boundaries or when activity in one country or region will directly affect an ecosystem in another country. For the European Union and the 21 individual countries that participate in the Mediterranean Action Plan (MAP), for example, bioregional cooperation is absolutely necessary because the enclosed Mediterranean Sea has large human populations along the coasts, heavy oil tanker traffic, and weak tides that cannot quickly remove pollution resulting from cities, agriculture, and industry (**Figure 18.9**). This combina-

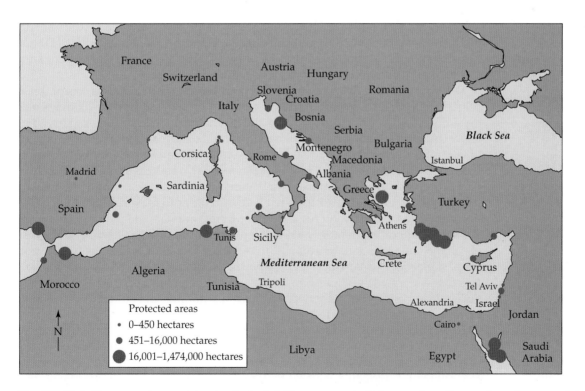

FIGURE 18.9 The countries participating in the Mediterranean Action Plan cooperate in monitoring and controlling pollution and coordinating their protected areas. Major protected areas along the coast are shown as dots. Note that there are no major protected areas on the coasts of France, Libya, and Egypt. (After Miller 1996.)

tion of problems threatens the health of the entire Mediterranean ecosystem, including the sea, its surrounding lands, and its associated tourist and fishing industries. Cross-boundary management is also necessary because pollution from one country can significantly damage the natural resources of neighboring countries. Participants in the plan agree to cooperate in carrying out research, monitoring and controlling pollution, and promoting sustainable development through integrated coastal zone planning (NOAA and Duffy 2008; Frantzi et al. 2009).

Case Studies

Throughout the world, the protection of biological diversity is being incorporated as an important objective of land management. We conclude the chapter by examining three case studies—old-growth forests in the Pacific Northwest of the United States, Kenya's large wildlife populations outside its parks, and a successful community-based program in Namibia—that demonstrate the problems of managing biological diversity outside protected areas.

Managed Coniferous Forests

The coniferous forests of the Pacific Northwest of the United States are managed for a variety of natural resources, but timber production traditionally has been considered the most important. In this ecosystem, the issue of timber production versus the conservation of unique species—the northern spotted owl (*Strix occidentalis caurina*), the marbled murrelet (*Brachyramphus marmoratus*), as well as the salmon—has been a highly emotional and political debate billed as "owls versus jobs." Some environmentalists want to stop all cutting in old-growth forests, while many local citizens want the logging industry to continue current practices without outside interference. A regional compromise has emerged in which most federal lands have been made into forest reserves to protect biodiversity and ecosystem services, with a reduced level of logging on the remaining lands (Carroll and Johnson 2008). Logging has continued on state and private lands under Habitat Conservation Plans, but in a way that reduces impacts on rare and endangered species and maintains water quality and fish populations.

Research on forest management techniques has contributed to this compromise solution: Many of the species characteristic of old-growth forests over 200 years old, including cavity-nesting birds such as the northern spotted owl, are also found at lower densities in young forests following natural disturbances (because even very young forests have at least a few old, large trees; some dead, standing trees; and fallen trees that remain after fires and storms). These resources are sufficient to support a complex community of plants and animals. However, clear-cutting techniques that remove living and dead trees of all ages in order to maximize wood production eliminate the places and resources that certain animals and plants need to live. Further, clear-cutting damages the adjacent streams and rivers, leading to the loss of salmon and other aquatic animals. In managed forests of the Pacific Northwest, the past practice of clear-cut, staggered patches of timber produced a landscape pattern that was a mosaic of forest fragments, with different tree ages across fragments and uniform ages within them. These tree plantations lacked the old trees that certain animal species needed to live in.

Research has been used to develop an approach in which conifer forests can be managed to both produce timber and maintain the most important elements of biodiversity. These lessons have been incorporated into "ecological forestry" or "green-tree retention," a logging method that has been developed for the Pacific Northwest (Halpern et al. 2005; Zarin et al. 2007). This method essentially involves removing most trees in the areas that are designated for logging but leaving a low density of medium to large live trees, standing dead trees, and some fallen trees to

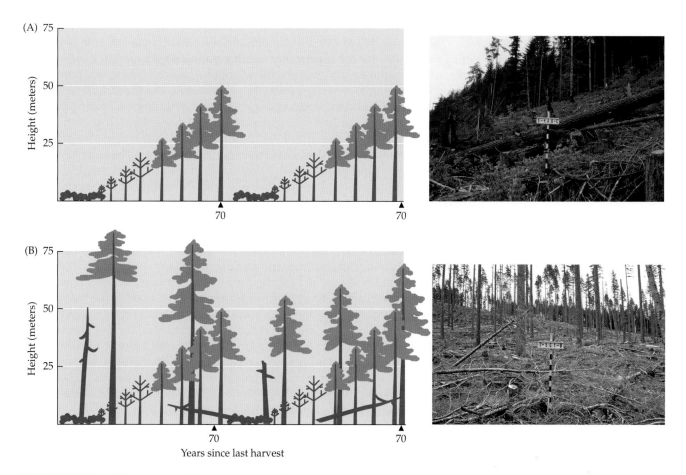

FIGURE 18.10 (A) Conventional clear-cutting involves removing all trees from an area on a 70-year cycle, thus reducing the structural diversity of the forest. The photo shows clear-cutting in the foreground, with some forest retained in the background. (B) New practices better maintain structural diversity by leaving behind some old trees, standing dead trees, and fallen trees. The photo shows logging with "green-tree" retention. (Graphs after Hansen et al. 1991; photographs courtesy of Charles Halpern and David Phillips.)

provide structural complexity (or what could be termed structural legacies) and to serve as habitat for animal species in the next forest cycle (**Figure 18.10**). Typically about 15% of the trees remain after this type of logging, but a greater percentage can remain, if necessary. By avoiding logging near streams, water quality and other ecosystem services can also be protected.

This change in logging has had major economic consequences. Large areas of national forest are now off-limits to logging, and ecological forestry is now practiced in most areas of federal forests still being logged and in some areas of state and private forests. Ecological forestry requires a reduced harvest of timber at the time of cutting and a somewhat longer cutting cycle, sometimes resulting in less short-term profit for the timber industry. Although strict environmentalists are still not satisfied, because some old-growth "big trees" continue to be cut down, United States citizens and their government have reached a hard-won compromise on the use of these forests and the development of the entire region. Many other such examples of selective logging, including methods known as low-impact logging and light-touch logging, are being developed in other forested areas throughout the world.

> Forestry practices are being modified to include biodiversity conservation as an important objective.

African Wildlife Outside Parks

Many East African and southern African countries such as Kenya, Tanzania, and South Africa are famous for the spectacular wildlife populations found in their national parks, which are the basis of the valuable ecotourist industry. Despite the fame of the parks, about two-thirds of Kenya's 650,000 large animals live outside the parks' boundaries in rangelands used by commercial ranches and as traditional grazing lands by local people (Young et al. 2005; Western et al. 2009). Among the well-known species found predominantly in the 70% of the country's rangelands outside the parks are giraffes, elephants, impalas, Grevy's zebras, oryx, and ostriches. The large herbivores found in the parks often graze seasonally outside them. However, the rangelands outside the parks are increasingly unavailable to wildlife because of fences, poaching, and agricultural development, leading to a gradual decline in numbers.

Even with these declines in wildlife populations, several factors contribute to the persistence of substantial populations of wildlife in unprotected areas of sub-Saharan Africa (Western 1989). Most important is that some species are protected outside parks by laws against hunting and trading, which are enforced by wildlife officials. Other species are valued for their meat, so their presence on rangeland is encouraged. In addition, certain traditional communities, such as the Masai, have prohibitions against hunting and eating wildlife, though killing large predators is allowed. In particular places, private ranching in which wildlife and livestock are managed together is more profitable than managing livestock alone. This is the case because cattle and many wild grazers eat different kinds of plants, and wild animals are often more drought tolerant. Many ranches have also developed facilities for foreign tourists who want to view wildlife, which creates an additional source of revenue and an additional incentive for protecting wildlife.

Community-Based Wildlife Management in Namibia

As an alternative to wildlife protection primarily as an activity for governments, it has been increasingly asserted, conservation works best when local people have a strong investment in its success. Many countries in East and southern Africa have tried to promote conservation by implementing Community-Based Natural Resource Management (CBNRM) programs in which local landowners and communal groups are given the authority to manage and profit from the wildlife on their own property. Prior to this policy, wildlife was often managed by government officials, often with no input from the local people, who gained little or no economic benefit from the wildlife on their own land. By changing the management system to CBNRM, African countries hope to counterbalance pressures threatening local wildlife while simultaneously contributing to rural economic development.

> In many African countries, wildlife on traditionally owned lands is being managed for ecotourism and trophy hunting. The hope is that people will protect the wildlife resource that provides them with revenue.

One of the most ambitious new programs for local communities managing wildlife is found in Namibia in southern Africa (Schumann et al. 2008). In this country of 1.8 million people, 14% of the land is in national parks and other protected areas, 45% is private land, and 41% is communal land. Beginning in 1996, the Namibian government granted traditional communal groups the right to use and manage the wildlife on their own lands. To obtain these rights, a group needs to form a management committee and determine the boundaries of its land. The government then designates the group as a "community conservancy." The benefits of forming a conservancy and participating in wildlife management are fourfold:

1. The conservancy can form joint ventures with tour operators, with about 5% to 10% of the gross earnings paid to the conservancy. A certain number of the employees in the tourist operation are hired from among the communal group. Revenues from the joint ventures are used to train and pay game

guards, again hired from the communal group, who monitor wildlife populations and prevent poaching.

2. Using funds from the joint ventures, the conservancy members can build and operate campsites for tourist groups, providing direct revenue, employment, and experience for the communal group.

3. The conservancy can apply to the government for a trophy-hunting quota. The quota will be granted if wildlife populations are large enough, as indicated by monitoring. This quota can then be sold or auctioned off to professional hunters, who bring in wealthy foreign tourists willing to pay a high price for an African hunting experience. One hundred percent of the trophy fees go directly to the conservancy, regardless of whether the animals are actually killed. Payments to the conservancy for high-value animals such as lions and elephants can be as large as $11,000 per animal. Meat from the hunted animals is distributed to the group members as an added benefit.

4. Once the conservancy has formed a wildlife management plan, four species of wildlife—gemsbok, springbok, kudu, and warthog—can be hunted for subsistence. In practice, the hunting is often done by game guards and professional hunters, with the meat distributed to everyone in the community.

Over the last 23 years, 50 conservancies in Namibia have been established, with 20–30 more in the process of forming (**Figure 18.11**). The total area covered is 119,000

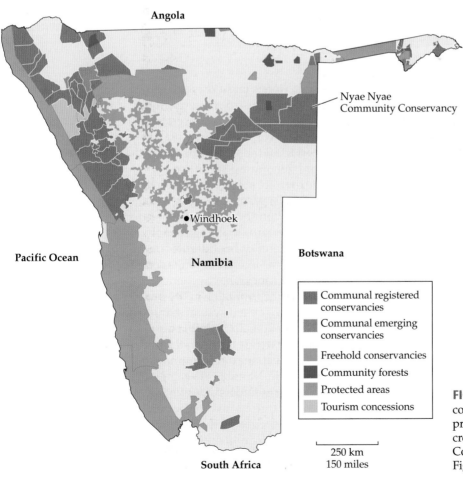

FIGURE 18.11 The distribution of community conservancies and state-protected lands in Namibia. The increase in wildlife at the Nyae Nyae Community Conservancy is shown in Figure 18.12. (After NASCO 2008.)

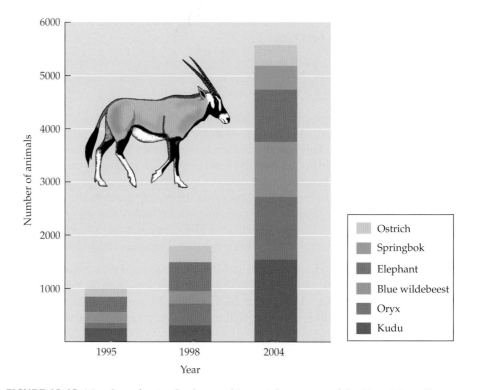

FIGURE 18.12 Number of animals observed in aerial censuses of the Nyae Nyae Community Conservancy in Namibia conducted in 1995, 1998, and 2004. See Figure 18.11 for the location of this site. (After Namibia Ministry of Environment and Tourism and WRI 2009.)

km², or 14% of Namibia's area (Jones and Weaver 2009). Help in the initial establishment of the conservancies has come from external funding agencies, such as the U.S. Agency for International Development. Conservancy members have received further training in tourism, financial and marketing skills, and training in effective advocacy to gain support from the government and the private sector.

Certain conservancies are generating significant revenue from their wildlife operations. With this income they are able to build more tourist facilities, erect communal structures such as schools, distribute money to their members, and even establish bank accounts. However, the conservancies depend on international tourism as their main income, a source that might not be secure in times of actual or perceived local and global instability. In addition, conservancies in more remote areas have had difficulty gaining the interest of tour operators and negotiating joint ventures. As a result, those conservancies have generated little income from tourists and trophy hunters and may not be profitable in the present system.

In general, the communal management system seems to be having positive conservation effects. Wildlife populations in Namibia are showing strong increasing trends (**Figure 18.12**). While these trends began in the mid-1980s following the end of a severe drought, wildlife populations have continued to increase during this period of communal management in Namibia. This may result in part from the increased likelihood of conservancy members' adopting livestock management techniques that reduce conflict with large carnivores (Schumann 2008).

Other African countries have programs that are like Namibia's, and they also often depend on continuing subsidies from outside donor governments to run their community wildlife programs. When these outside subsidies cease, the wildlife programs often end as well, suggesting that these programs, which are so dependent on foreign tourists and external subsidies, cannot really be profitable on their own. The ineffectiveness and corruption of some local government agencies is an additional factor causing such programs to fail. These community wildlife programs will be judged successful when they can demonstrate that they can both protect wildlife and provide a stable income source for the local people.

Summary

1. Considerable biological diversity exists outside of protected areas, particularly in habitat managed for multiple use resource extraction. Such unprotected habitats are vital for conservation because in almost all countries, protected areas account for only a small percentage of total area. Animal species living in protected areas often forage on or migrate to unprotected land, where they are vulnerable to hunting, habitat loss, and other threats from humans. Governments are increasingly encouraging the protection of biological diversity as a priority on multiple use land, including forests, grazing lands, agricultural areas, military reservations, and urban areas.

2. Government agencies, private conservation organizations, businesses, and private landowners are cooperating on large-scale ecosystem management projects to achieve conservation objectives and to use natural resources sustainably. Bioregional management involves cooperation between countries to manage large ecosystems that cross international borders.

3. In temperate forest ecosystems, biological diversity can be enhanced if logging operations avoid damage to streams and minimize fragmentation and if some late-successional components are left, including living trees, standing dead trees, and fallen trees.

4. In Africa, many of the characteristic large animals are found predominantly in rangeland outside the parks. Local people and landowners often maintain wildlife on their land for a variety of purposes. Local communities are now generating income by combining wildlife management and ecotourism, sometimes including trophy hunting.

For Discussion

1. Consider a national forest that has been used for decades for logging, hunting, and mining. If endangered plant species are discovered in this forest, should these activities be stopped? Can logging, hunting, and mining coexist with endangered species, and if so, how? If logging has to be stopped or scaled back, do logging companies or their employees deserve any compensation?

2. Imagine that you are informed by the government that the endangered Florida panther lives on a piece of land that you own and were planning to develop as a golf course. Are you happy, angry, confused, or proud? What are your options? What would be a fair compromise that would protect your rights, the rights of the public, and the rights of the panther?

3. Choose a large aquatic ecosystem that includes more than one country, such as the Black Sea, the Rhine River, the Caribbean, the St. Lawrence River, or the South China Sea. What agencies or organizations have responsibility for ensuring the long-term health of the ecosystem? In what ways do they, or could they, cooperate in managing the area?

Suggested Readings

Aviron, S., H. Nitsch, P. Jeanneret, S. Buholzer, H. Luka, L. Pfiffner, et al. 2009. Ecological cross compliance promotes farmland biodiversity in Switzerland. *Frontiers in Ecology and the Environment* 7: 247–252. Various government programs contribute to nature conservation.

Bohlen, P. J., S. Lynch, L. Shabman, M. Clark, S. Shukla, and H. Swain. 2009. Paying for environmental services from agricultural lands: An example from the northern Everglades. *Frontiers in Ecology and the Environment* 7: 46–55. Programs can support farmers using nonintensive practices and benefit the environment.

Boyd, C. and 9 others. 2008. Spatial scale and the conservation of threatened species. *Conservation Letters* 1: 37–43. Most threatened species need conservation at landscape levels; site protection by itself is insufficient.

Colding, J., J. Lundberg, S. Lundberg, and E. Andersson. 2009. Golf courses and wetland fauna. *Ecological Applications* 19: 1481–1491. Golf courses have features that can have a positive impact on wildlife.

Dias, M. S., W. E. Magnusson, and J. Zuanon. 2010. Effects of reduced-impact logging on fish assemblages in Central Amazonia. *Conservation Biology* 24: 278–286. Carefully done selective logging has far fewer impacts on biodiversity than ordinary logging, but how can such best practices become more common?

Dinerstein, E. and 14 others. 2006. The fate of wild tigers. *BioScience* 57: 508–514. An approach that includes both protected areas and unprotected lands will be needed to maintain tigers.

Jordan, N. and K. D. Warner. 2010. Enhancing the multifunctionality of U.S. agriculture. *BioScience* 60: 60–66. Agriculture can benefit society and improve its own economic viability by providing a range of ecosystem services.

Koontz, T. M. and J. Bodine. 2008. Implementing ecosystem management in public agencies: Lessons from the U.S. Bureau of Land Management and the Forest Service. *Conservation Biology* 22: 60–69. Often the barriers to effective management are political, cultural, and legal.

Levin, P. S., M. J. Fogarty, S. A. Murawski, and D. Fluharty. 2009. Integrated ecosystem assessments: Developing the scientific basis for ecosystem-based management of the ocean. *PLoS Biology* 7: 23–28. The authors show how the general concept of ecosystem management can be implemented in a practical way in marine systems.

Philpott, S. M., P. Bichier, R. Rice, and R. Greenberg. 2007. Field-testing ecological and economic benefits of coffee certification programs. *Conservation Biology* 21: 975–985. Programs in organic, fair trade, and shade certification are all needed to provide comprehensive benefits to farmers and biodiversity.

Radeloff, V. C. and 7 others. 2010. Housing growth in and near United States protected areas limits their conservation value. *Proceedings of the National Academy of Sciences USA* 107: 940–945. Areas next to national parks can contribute to conservation but can also threaten conservation if they are overdeveloped.

Richmond, R. H. and 9 others. 2006. Watersheds and coral reefs: Conservation science, policy, and implementation. *BioScience* 57: 598–607. Integrated watershed management is needed to prevent runoff and sedimentation.

Stein, B. A., C. Scott, and N. Benton. 2008. Federal lands and endangered species: The role of the military and other federal lands in sustaining biodiversity. *BioScience* 58: 339–347. Many endangered species occur on military lands, especially in Hawaii.

Wilcove, D. S., M. J. Bean, B. Long, W. J. Snape III, B. M. Beehler, and J. Eisenberg. 2004. The private side of conservation. *Frontiers in Ecology and the Environment* 2: 326–331. Private and public initiatives are both important in conservation.

Chapter 19

Restoration Ecology

Ecosystems can be damaged by natural phenomena such as hurricanes or fires triggered by lightning, but they typically recover to their original community structures and even similar species compositions through the process of ecological succession (see Chapter 2). However, some are too damaged or degraded to recover, and ecosystems destroyed by intensive human activities such as mining, ranching, and logging may have lost much of their natural ability to rebound. In other cases, natural recovery may require centuries or millennia. In these cases, it may be desirable to intervene to facilitate or speed the recovery of degraded ecosystems.

Damaged and degraded ecosystems provide important opportunities for conservation biologists to put research findings into practice by helping to restore historical species and communities (Clewell and Aronson 2008). Rebuilding damaged ecosystems has great potential for enlarging, enhancing, and connecting the current system of protected areas. **Ecological restoration** is the practice of restoring the species and ecosystems that occupied a site at some point in the past, but were degraded, damaged, or destroyed (www.ser.org). **Restoration ecology** is the science of restoration—the research and scientific study of restored populations, communities, and ecosystems (Falk et al. 2006). These are overlapping disciplines: ecological restoration provides useful scientific data in the process of its work, while restoration ecology interprets and evaluates restoration projects in a way that can lead to improved methods. In this chapter we examine these interconnected disciplines and the effects their practices are having on protecting biological diversity.

There are many different situations in which restoration ecology plays an important role (Clewell and Aronson 2008). For instance, in some cases, businesses are required by law to restore habitats they have degraded through activities such as strip-mining or waste disposal. Governments sometimes must restore ecosystems damaged by their own activities, including the dumping of sewage into rivers and estuaries by municipalities and chemical pollution on military bases. Restoration efforts are often part of **compensatory mitigation**, in which a new site, often incorporating wetland communities, is created or rehabilitated in compensation for a site that has been destroyed elsewhere by development (Clewell and Aronson 2006). At other times, ecological processes rather than ecosystems need to be restored; for example, annual floods disrupted by the construction of dams and levees and natural fires stopped by fire suppression efforts may need to be reintroduced if the absence of these processes proves harmful to local and regional ecosystems and communities. The 2005 destruction of New Orleans and other Gulf Coast cities by Hurricane Katrina, and to a lesser extent by Hurricane Rita that closely followed Katrina, was in part a result of the loss and overdevelopment of the region's wetlands. The ensuing natural disaster has become a classic example of the importance of such ecosystem services to biological and human communities alike. Ironically, the damage that followed these hurricanes had been predicted 7 years earlier in an assessment of coastal wetlands by the Louisiana Coastal Wetlands Conservation and Restoration Task Force (1998), which had stressed the urgent need for immediate action to restore lost wetlands (see Box 5.1).

Ecological restoration has its origins in older applied technologies that attempted to restore ecosystem functions or species of known economic value, such as wetland replication (to prevent flooding), mine site reclamation (to prevent soil erosion), range management of overgrazed lands (to increase production of grasses), and tree planting on cleared land (for timber, recreational, and ecosystem values) (**Figure 19.1**).

(A)   (B)

FIGURE 19.1 (A) Construction of a new railroad line through Glacier National Park in Canada created widespread habitat damage. (B) As part of the project, these areas were restored using native grasses and trees. (Photographs courtesy of David F. Polster.)

However, these technologies often produce only simplified biological communities or communities that cannot maintain themselves. As concern for biological diversity has grown, restoration plans have included as a major goal the reestablishment of original or historical species assemblages and processes. The input of conservation biologists is needed for these efforts to achieve their goals.

Damage and Restoration

In many cases, damaged ecosystems will not recover on their own without human intervention. For example, the original plant species will not be able to grow at a site if the soil has been washed away by erosion. Recovery is often unlikely when the damaging agent is still present in the ecosystem (Christian-Smith and Merenlender 2010). Restoration of degraded savanna woodlands in the western United States, for instance, is not possible as long as the land continues to be overgrazed by introduced cattle; reduction of the grazing pressure is obviously the key starting point in these restoration efforts.

Once the damaging agent is removed or controlled, the original communities may reestablish themselves by natural successional processes from remnant populations. However, recovery is unlikely when many of the original species have been eliminated over a large area so that there is no source of colonists. Prairie species, for instance, were eliminated from huge areas of the United States when the land was converted to agriculture. Even when an isolated patch of land is no longer cultivated, the original community is unlikely to reestablish itself, because there is no source of seeds and no potential colonizing animals of the original species. The site also may be dominated by invasive species, which often become established in disturbed areas; invasive species must be removed before native species can recover (Cuevas and Zalba 2010). Recovery also is unlikely when the physical environment has been so altered that the original species can no longer survive there; an example is mine sites, where the restoration of natural communities may be delayed by decades or even centuries because of soil erosion and the heavy-metal toxicity and low nutrient status of the remaining soil. In some cases, complete restoration may be biologically impossible or simply too expensive (Seastedt et al. 2008).

> Some ecosystems have been so degraded by human activity that their ability to recover on their own is severely limited. Ecological restoration may help return functioning ecosystems with some or all of the original species to such areas or encourage new valuable communities.

Restoration in such challenging habitats requires modification of the physical environment by adding soil, nutrients, and water; by removing invasive species; and by reintroducing native species to the point where the natural process of succession and recovery can begin (Zhang et al. 2008). Because restoration efforts need to be customized for individual sites, an approach in which different methods are tested experimentally is often advisable (Zedler 2005) (**Figure 19.2**). These restored sites then need to be monitored for years, even decades, to determine how well management goals are being achieved and whether further intervention is required, an approach that is called **adaptive restoration** (Wagner et al. 2008). In particular, native species may have to be introduced again if they have not survived, and invasive species may have to be removed again if they are still abundant.

In certain cases, entirely new environments have been created by human activity, such as reservoirs, canals, landfills, and industrial sites. If these sites are neglected, they often become dominated by invasive species, resulting in biological communities that are not useful to people, not typical of the surrounding areas, valueless or even damaging from a conservation perspective, and aesthetically unappealing (Suding et al. 2004). If these sites are properly prepared and native species are reintroduced, native communities possibly can be restored.

The goal of these and other restoration efforts often is to create new habitats that are comparable in ecosystem functions or species composition to existing **reference**

FIGURE 19.2 An experiment to test the effects of different treatments on the restoration at the Friendship Marsh in Tijuana Estuary, California. The marsh is divided into six experimental units, three with tidal creeks and three without creeks, to test the effects of drainage. Within each unit, restoration treatments in the small squares involve different species, different planting densities, and different soil additions. In the larger blocks, salt marsh grass was planted with or without kelp compost. The impact of these treatments on plants, fish and invertebrates, and algae are being evaluated. (After Zedler 2005.)

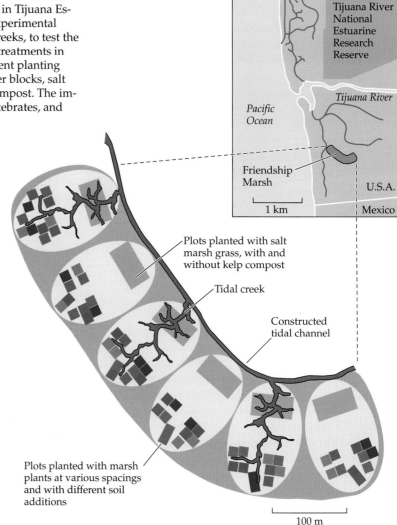

sites (Swetnam et al. 1999; Humphries and Winemiller 2009). Reference sites provide explicit goals for restoration and supply quantitative measures of the success of a project. Indeed, reference sites act as control sites and are central to the very concept of restoration. Another goal of restoration sometimes is to recreate a historic landscape or assemblage, such as a traditional agricultural landscape, using old photographs and journals to establish restoration objectives. The use of reference sites does not mean restoration goals are set in stone: since ecosystems change over time because of changing climate, plant succession, the varying abundance of common species, and other factors, the goals of restoration may have to change over time as well, to remain realistic.

To determine whether the goals of restoration projects are being achieved, clear goals are needed, and both the restoration and the reference sites need to be monitored over time (**Box 19.1**) (Burger 2008). If practical, the successfully restored ecosystem should be dominated by native species, contain representatives of all key functional groups of species, have a physical environment suitable for native species and ecosystem processes, and be secure from detrimental outside disturbances. In some cases, such as at arid and cold sites, ecosystem recovery might take decades or centuries. Monitoring is also needed to determine the efficacy of some methods versus

BOX 19.1   *Can Many Small Projects Clean Up the Chesapeake Bay?*

■ The Chesapeake Bay is one of the most important fishing grounds and recreational areas in the United States. However, pollution from residential, agricultural, and industrial lands enclosing the bay has been causing a dramatic decline in the quality of the marine environment, affecting all aspects of biodiversity. The immediate economic consequences of this pollution were also urgent when its effects first came to light: harvests of fish and shellfish were in decline, and the water was becoming unsafe for swimming. This type of general pollution from an entire landscape is referred to as nonpoint source pollution, and it requires a comprehensive restoration approach, since no single source of the pollution can be readily identified and contained. In 1987 the federal, state, and local government bodies responsible for the bay signed an agreement to reduce nutrient and sediment loads coming into the bay by 40%, to be achieved mainly through improving the health of streams and watersheds feeding water into the bay. Since that time, over 4700 individual restoration projects have been implemented, at a cost of over $400 million (Hassett et al. 2005; Craig et al. 2008; Stokstad 2009). The largest number of projects involve stream and river restorations that include regrading slopes and planting native vegetation. However, the most money has been spent on water treatment projects. A weakness of these projects is that only 5% of them have been monitored, mainly for vegetation structure, and even fewer have monitored water quality to determine whether they have been achieving the desired goals of reducing nutrient and sediment loads. The Chesapeake Bay project demonstrates that while society has accepted the need to restore large aquatic ecosystems, scientists need to do a better job of ensuring that the restoration jobs deliver the services as promised.

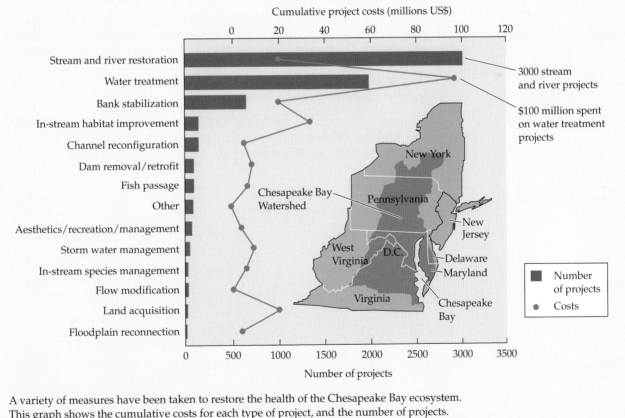

A variety of measures have been taken to restore the health of the Chesapeake Bay ecosystem. This graph shows the cumulative costs for each type of project, and the number of projects. Stream and river restoration is the most common type of project, and the most money has been spent on water treatment. The map shows the watersheds that drain into the bay. (After Hassett et al. 2005.)

their costs. For instance, roads are increasingly being removed in protected areas to restore ecosystem processes and reconnect fragmented landscapes; monitoring is needed to determine the effectiveness of this expensive activity (Switalski et al. 2004).

Ecological Restoration Techniques

Restoration ecology provides theory and techniques to restore various types of degraded ecosystems. Four main approaches are available in restoring biological communities and ecosystems (**Figure 19.3**) (Bradshaw 1990):

1. *No action.* Restoration is deemed too expensive, previous attempts have failed, or experience has shown that the ecosystem will recover on its own. Letting the ecosystem recover on its own, also known as passive restoration, is typical for old agricultural fields in eastern North America, which return to forest within a few decades after being abandoned.

2. *Rehabilitation.* Replacing a degraded ecosystem with another productive type, using just a few or many species. An example of this is replacing a degraded forest area with a productive pasture. Replacement at least establishes a biological community on a site and restores ecological functions such as flood control and soil retention. In the future, the new community might eventually come to incorporate a larger number of native species than its predecessor had.

3. *Partial restoration.* Restoring at least some of the ecosystem functions and some of the original, dominant species. An example is replacing a degraded forest with a tree plantation or replanting a degraded grassland with a few species that can survive. Partial restoration typically focuses on dominant species or particularly resilient species that are critical to ecosystem function, delaying action on the rare and less common species that are part of a complete restoration program.

4. *Complete restoration.* Restoring the area to its original species composition and structure by an active program of site modification and reintroduction of the original species. Restoration must first determine and reduce the source

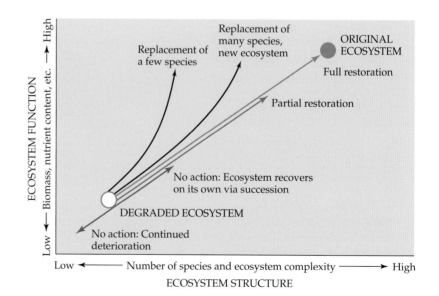

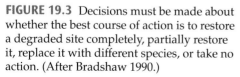

FIGURE 19.3 Decisions must be made about whether the best course of action is to restore a degraded site completely, partially restore it, replace it with different species, or take no action. (After Bradshaw 1990.)

of ecological degradation. For example, a source of pollution must be controlled before a lake ecosystem can be restored. Natural ecological processes must be reestablished and allowed to heal the system.

Practical Considerations

Restoration ecology projects often involve professionals from other fields who lend their expertise. These practitioners often have different goals than conservation biologists. For instance, civil engineers involved in major projects seek to find economical ways to permanently stabilize land surfaces, prevent soil erosion, make the site look better to neighbors and the general public, and if possible, restore the productive value of the land. Sewage treatment plants must be built as part of the restoration of lakes, rivers, and estuaries. To restore wetland communities needed for flood control and wildlife habitat, dams and channels may need to be altered to reestablish the original water flow patterns. Ecologists contribute to these restoration efforts by developing ways to restore the communities in terms of species diversity, species composition, vegetation structure, and ecosystem function (Dodds et al. 2008; Rodrigues et al. 2009). To be practical, ecological restoration must also consider the speed of restoration, the cost, the reliability of results, and the ability of the target community to persist with little or no further maintenance. Practitioners of ecological restoration must have a clear grasp of how natural systems work and what methods of restoration are feasible (Falk et al. 2006). Considerations of the cost and availability of seeds, when to water plants, how much fertilizer to add, how to remove invasive species, and how to prepare the surface soil may become paramount in determining a project's outcome. Permits will likely be needed, all regulations must be followed, and the public and nearby landowners must be convinced of the project's value. Dealing with such practical details generally has not been the focus of academic biologists in the past, but these details must be considered in ecological restoration.

> Restoration projects require evaluation to determine if goals are being met, including costs and speed of recovery. Such projects can also provide new insights into ecological processes.

Restoration ecology, the science of restoration, is valuable to the broader science of ecology because it provides a test of how well we understand a biological community, and the extent to which we can successfully reassemble a functioning ecosystem from its component parts demonstrates the depth of our knowledge and points out deficiencies. As Bradshaw (1990) has said, "Ecologists working in the field of ecosystem restoration are in the construction business, and like their engineering colleagues, can soon discover if their theory is correct by whether the airplane falls out of the sky, the bridge collapses, or the ecosystem fails to flourish." In this sense, restoration ecology can be viewed as an experimental methodology that complements existing basic research on intact systems. In addition to its role as a conservation strategy, restoration ecology provides opportunities to reassemble communities in different ways, to see how well they function, and to test ideas on a larger scale than would be possible otherwise (Wallace et al. 2005; Suding and Hobbs 2009). For example, it has been found that when more species are planted in restoration projects, there is subsequently more biomass accumulation, more plant cover, and a greater uptake of soil nutrients (Callaway et al. 2003).

Efforts to restore degraded terrestrial communities generally have emphasized the establishment of the original plant community. This emphasis is appropriate because the plant community typically contains the majority of the biomass and provides structure for the rest of the community. However, in the future, restoration ecology needs to devote more attention to the other major components of the community. Fungi and bacteria (see Box 5.3) play vital roles in soil decomposition and nutrient cycling; soil invertebrates are important in creating soil structure; herbivorous animals are important in reducing plant competition and maintaining species diversity; birds and insects are often essential pollinators; and many birds and mammals have vital functions as insect predators, soil diggers, and seed dispersers (Allen et al. 2003). Many of these nonplant species can be transferred to a restored site in sod samples. If an area is going to be destroyed and then restored later, as might occur during strip-mining, the top layer of soil, which contains the majority of buried seeds, soil invertebrates, and other soil organisms, can be carefully removed and stored for later use in restoration efforts. Such efforts to use local biological materials avoid the problems of introducing foreign genotypes that may not be adapted to the site (Hufford and Mazer 2003). While these methods are a step in the right direction, many species will still be lost during this process, and the community structure will be completely altered. Large animals and aboveground invertebrates may have to be reintroduced from existing populations or captive breeding populations if they are unable to disperse to the site on their own. These reintroductions need to be carefully planned and monitored to minimize the chance of species becoming invasive (see Chapter 13).

Restoration ecology will play an increasingly important role in the conservation of biological communities if degraded lands and aquatic communities can be restored to their original species compositions and added to the limited existing area under protection. While conservation of existing natural ecosystems is critical, it is often only through restoration that we can increase the area of ecosystems dominated by native species. Because degraded areas are unproductive and of little economic value, governments may be willing to restore them to increase their productive and conservation value.

Many restoration efforts are supported and even initiated by local conservation groups because they can see the direct connection between a healthy environment and their own personal and economic well-being. People can understand that planting trees produces firewood, timber, and food; prevents soil from washing away; and cools off the surrounding area in hot weather (**Figure 19.4**). An excellent ex-

FIGURE 19.4 Japanese students visiting Australia plant tree seedlings as part of an effort to restore rain forests. (Photograph by Hiromi Kobori.)

ample of a restoration effort with strong local support is the Green Belt Movement, a grassroots effort involving mainly rural women in Kenya that has planted over 30 million trees in degraded sites. The movement also organizes rural people, especially poor women, to have a voice in the political process, to maintain access to public forests, and to resist illegal logging.

Case Studies

The following case studies illustrate some of the problems and solutions of ecological restoration.

Wetlands Restoration in Japan

An informative example of wetlands restoration comes from Japan, where parents, teachers, and children have built over 500 small ponds next to schools and in public parks to provide habitat for dragonflies and other native aquatic species (Kobori 2009). Dragonflies are an important symbol in Japanese culture, and dragonfly ponds are useful as a starting point for teaching zoology, ecology, chemistry, and principles of conservation. These ponds provide a focus for an entire science and math curriculum. The ponds are planted with aquatic plants; many dragonflies colonize them on their own, and some species are carried in as nymphs from other ponds. The schoolchildren are responsible for the regular weeding and maintenance of these "living laboratories," which helps them to feel an ownership of the project and to develop environmental awareness.

The Grand Canyon–Colorado River Ecosystem

River damming has severe and extensive impacts on downstream ecosystems, and restoring river flow may allow these ecosystems to recover (Rood et al. 2005; Helfield et al. 2007). One high-profile case of restoration in the United States involves the Colorado River where it flows through the Grand Canyon. The river had been drastically altered in 1963 by the construction of the Glen Canyon Dam and the filling of Lake Powell. While those projects did provide water and electricity throughout the region, there was a major reduction in the spring floods that once surged through the canyon, creating new beaches and habitat for the unique Grand Canyon fish species. Without the flooding, beaches and banks either were worn away or became overgrown with woody vegetation, and introduced game fish began to replace native fish. To restore this crucial flooding event, the Bureau of Reclamation began experimenting with varying the rate of water release as a restoration technique, releasing an experimental flood of 900 million m^3 (1350 m^3/s) from the Glen Canyon Dam over the course of a week in March 1996 (Yanites 2006). The flood was effective in creating new beaches and habitat for native fish species, but by 2002 the river had mostly returned to its preflood condition, and a second controlled dam release of 1220 m^3/s was subsequently initiated in November 2004 (Yanites 2006). Research suggests that more such releases may be required to prevent debris buildup and maintain downstream habitats.

Restoration in Urban Areas

Highly visible restoration efforts are also taking place in many urban areas, to reduce the intense human impact on ecosystems and enhance the quality of life for city dwellers (Jordan 2003; Tzoulas et al. 2007). Local citizen groups often welcome the opportunity to work with government agencies and conservation groups to restore degraded urban areas. Unattractive drainage canals in concrete culverts can be replaced with winding streams bordered with large rocks and planted with native wetland species. Vacant lots and neglected lands can be replanted with native shrubs, trees, and wildflowers. Gravel pits can be packed with soil and restored as ponds. Establishing native plant species often leads to increases in populations of native birds and insects (Burghardt et al. 2009). These efforts have the additional benefits of fostering neighborhood pride, creating a sense of community, and enhancing property value. However, such restorations are often only partially successful because of their small size and the fact that they are embedded in the highly modified urban environment. Developing urban places in which people and biodiversity can coexist has been termed **reconciliation ecology**. It will increase in importance as urban areas expand (Chen and Wu 2009).

Restoring native communities on huge urban landfills presents one of the most unusual opportunities. In the United States, 150 million tons of trash are being buried in over 5000 active landfills each year. These eyesores can be the focus of conservation efforts. When they have reached their maximum capacity, these landfills are

(A)

(B)

FIGURE 19.5 (A) The Fresh Kills landfill on Staten Island while active dumping was still occurring. Note the large number of gulls. (B) The future planned restoration of the site, based on an artist's viewpoint. The restoration will include recreational sites, natural areas and re-built wetlands. (A, photograph from *Infrastructure: A Field Guide to the Industrial Landscape* © Brian Hayes; B, image courtesy of NYC Parks and Recreation.)

usually capped by sheets of plastic and layers of clay to prevent toxic chemicals and pollutants from seeping out. If these sites are left alone, they are often colonized by weedy, exotic species. However, planting native shrubs and trees attracts birds and mammals that will bring in and disperse the seeds of a wide range of native species.

Consider the ongoing restoration of the Fresh Kills landfill on Staten Island in New York City (Fresh Kills Park 2006; www.nycgovparks.org). The site occupies almost 1000 ha, has a volume 25 times that of the Great Pyramid of Giza, and has garbage mounds as tall as the Statue of Liberty. The landfill was closed in 2001 and is now undergoing restoration to create a huge public park with an intact ecosystem, a project that will be implemented in six phases over the next 30 years (Corner 2005). The project began by using bulldozers to contour the site, creating an appearance and drainage similar to natural coastal dunes. Next, 52,000 individuals of 18 species of trees and shrubs were planted to create distinctive native plant communities: an oak scrub forest, a pine–oak forest, and a low shrubland. Herbs were also planted within these communities. Right away, the trees provided perching places for fruit-eating birds that brought seeds of many new species to the site. After just a year, seedlings of 32 additional woody plant species had appeared on the site. Native birds of conservation interest, such as ospreys, hawks, and egrets, nest and feed there. Furthermore, Fresh Kills' location adjacent to an exisiting wildlife refuge and along the Atlantic migratory flyway means that it will provide a vital last link in the 3000-acre Staten Island Greenbelt (Sugarman 2009). The eventual goal is to create a large public parkland area (almost three times the size of Central Park) with abundant wildlife and many recreational, cultural, and educational amenities (**Figure 19.5**).

> Ecological restoration in highly degraded urban sites, such as landfills, can create new habitat for biodiversity near large human populations.

Restoration of Some Major Communities

Many efforts to restore ecological communities have focused on wetlands, lakes, prairies, and forests. These environments have suffered severe alteration from human activities and are good candidates for restoration work, as described below.

Wetlands

Some of the most extensive restoration work has been done on wetlands, including swamps and marshes (Halpern et al. 2007). Wetlands are often damaged, or even filled in, because their importance in flood control, maintenance of water quality, and preservation of biological communities is either not known or not appreciated. More than half of the original wetlands in the United States have already been lost, and in heavily populated states such as California, over 90% have been lost. While the loss of a single wetland seems unimportant in most years, the cumulative loss of many wetlands over periods of years and decades can result in massive flood damage to low-lying properties following heavy rains and hurricanes. Because of wetland protection under the Clean Water Act and the U.S. government policy of "no net loss of wetlands," large development projects that damage wetlands must repair them or create new wetlands to compensate for those damaged beyond repair (**Box 19.2**) (Robertson 2006). The focus of these efforts has been on recreating the natural hydrology of the area and then planting native species. Experience has shown that such efforts to restore wetlands often do not closely match the species composition or hydrologic characteristics of reference sites. The subtleties of species composition, water movement, and soils, as well as the site history, are too difficult to match. Often the restored wetlands are dominated by exotic, invasive species. However, the restored wetlands often do have some of the wetland plant species, or at least similar ones, and can provide some of the func-

BOX 19.2   *The Kissimmee River: Restoring a Channelized River to Its Natural State*

■ The Kissimmee River was formerly a long, meandering river that flowed from Lake Kissimmee to Lake Okeechobee in central Florida. Its loops and bends created a mosaic of wetlands and floodplains that supported a highly diverse community of waterfowl, wading birds, fish, and other wildlife. The hydrology of the Kissimmee River was unique. The large number of headwater lakes and streams that drain into the Kissimmee River, combined with flat floodplains, low riverbanks, and poor drainage, led to frequent, prolonged flooding, dense vegetation, and outstanding wildlife habitat.

But the annual floods that created such a unique ecosystem were not considered compatible with the rapid expansion of urban and agricultural development in Florida in the 1950s and 1960s. In response to the growing demand for flood protection, the Kissimmee River was channelized. The U.S. Army Corps of Engineers dug a 90-km-long drainage canal down the center of the floodplain, built levees and water control structures along the length of the canal, and regulated water flow from the feeder lakes. Two-thirds of the river's floodplain wetlands were drained, water flow was eliminated in the native river channel, and much of the drained land was converted to rangeland for cattle. As water flow was diverted through the canal, dissolved oxygen concentrations in the remaining sections of wetland declined, and an ecosystem that had been char-

acterized by highly variable water levels and patchy, diverse habitats became a stable, homogeneous environment.

The negative effects on biodiversity were almost immediate: The numbers of overwintering birds declined sharply, habitat for game fish was degraded, and a diverse natural community of wading birds and fish was replaced by a few dominant species such as cattle egrets, gar, and bowfin (Jones et al. 2010). As the impact of the channelization became apparent, pressure mounted from conservation groups to restore the Kissimmee River to its original state. Initial plans focused on restoring certain target species

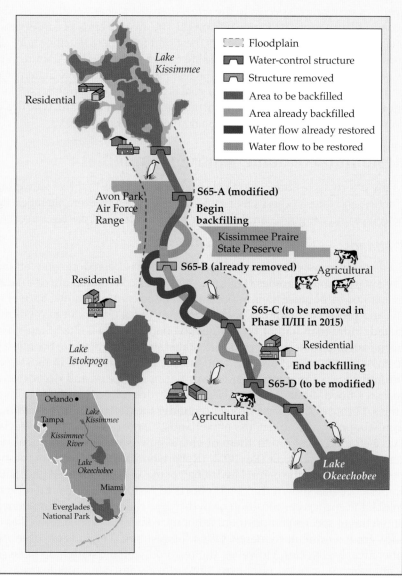

The Kissimmee River restoration project involves backfilling a total of 36 km of flood-control canal and removing two water-control structures (S-65B and S-65C). In the process, flow will be reestablished to 64 km of continuous river channel, and seasonal floodwaters will inundate the floodplain once again. In Phase I of the project, completed in 2001, control structure S-65B was removed, 13 km of canal was filled in, and 23 km of the river channel was reconnected. The map is not to scale. The distance from Lake Kissimmee to Lake Okeechobee is about 90 km. (From Jones et al. 2010).

BOX 19.2 *(continued)*

or functions of the river. Fishermen lobbied for restoration of the largemouth bass fishery. Residents clamored for improving water quality by restoring the filtering function of the wetlands. Hunters and bird-watchers focused on improving conditions for waterfowl. Ultimately it became clear that efforts needed to focus on restoring the ecological integrity of the ecosystem, rather than on individual characteristics such as species abundance. A demonstration project in 1984 that reflooded a section of floodplain provided evidence that such a restoration of the Kissimmee River was technically feasible.

> Restoration of large-scale wetlands can provide valuable ecosystem benefits, but can also be extremely expensive.

In 1992, the U.S. Congress authorized the restoration of approximately one-third of the Kissimmee River and floodplain through backfilling 36 km of the flood-control canal, removing two water-control structures, and recarving the old river channel (Jones et al. 2010). To accomplish this, more than 40,000 ha of land are being acquired by the state and federal governments. Important habitat will be provided for over 260 fish and wildlife species, including the threatened bald eagle, the endangered snail kite, and the endangered wood stork. The first phase of the reconstruction was completed between 1999 and 2001. It reestab-

lished flow in 23 km of winding river channel and allowed flooding over approximately 3800 ha of floodplain. Key aspects of the biotic and abiotic environment are being evaluated and monitored before, during, and after each phase of the project, to determine whether project goals are being achieved. Results for the first construction phase have been encouraging: dissolved oxygen levels have increased, game fish populations have almost doubled, densities of wading birds have increased more than threefold, and densities of ducks have increased by over 30 times.

Two additional phases of restoration construction were completed in 2009, with the final phase of construction scheduled to be completed by 2015, at which time a new schedule of water releases to the river from its headwaters lakes will be implemented. Ecological monitoring will continue for at least 5 years after completion of the project or until ecological responses stabilize. The total project cost is currently estimated at $987 million, shared equally between the federal government and the State of Florida. While this cost may seem enormous, the totality of ecosystem services provided by a healthy, restored Kissimmee River will be immensely valuable and will reestablish a significant part of Florida's natural heritage. The project will also serve as practice for the far larger Comprehensive Everglades Restoration Plan—begun in 2001 and slated to cost $8 billion—which is designed to rebuild this degraded, world famous wetland of South Florida (www.everglades-plan.org).

tions of the reference sites (Meyer et al. 2010). The restored wetlands also have some of the beneficial ecosystem characteristics such as flood control and pollution reduction, and they are often valuable for wildlife habitat. Additional research of restoration methods may result in further improvement.

An example from Iraq illustrates the potential for restoration. An enormous marsh formerly covered southeastern Iraq; this wetland was home to 75,000 people with a unique culture and was a regional center for bird, fish, and plant biodiversity. The previous Iraqi government drained over 80% of the marshland, converting it to agricultural land and expelling the local people. With the fall of President Saddam Hussein, local residents have opened the dikes, reflooding the area. Up to 20% of the marsh has been restored, returning former habitat and homes to wildlife and people (**Figure 19.6**)(Richardson et al. 2005; Mohamed et al. 2008). However, the recovery of the original plants and animals will take many decades.

Lakes

Limnologists (scientists who study the chemistry, biology, and physics of freshwater bodies) involved in multibillion-dollar efforts to restore lakes are already gaining valuable insights into community ecology and trophic structure that otherwise would not be possible (Sondergaard et al. 2007). One of the most common types of damage

(A) **1973** Before drainage   (B) **2000** After drainage   (C) **2005** After partial restoration

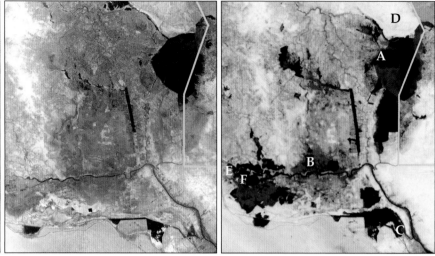

■ Permanent lake/reflooded marsh
■ Seasonal lake
■ Agriculture
■ Marsh vegetation

50 km

FIGURE 19.6 Marsh restoration in Iraq as shown by these Landsat images. The images have false color, with marsh land in red, agriculture in pink, and wetlands in black and blue. (A) In 1973, marshes covered extensive areas of southern Iraq and was home to about 400,000 Marsh Arabs. Three main marshes are labeled 1, 2, and 3. (B) As shown in the 2000 image, the marshes were drained by the government for political reasons. (C) Reflooding of lakes and wetlands in recent years has resulted in the restoration of some of the marsh vegetation, with major restored areas indicated as A, B and F. Other letters indicate sampling sites. The new canals are still visible. (From Richardson and Hussain 2006; courtesy of Curtis J. Richardson, Duke University Wetland Center.)

to lakes and ponds is **cultural eutrophication**, which occurs when there are excess mineral nutrients in the water resulting from human activity. Signs of eutrophication include increases in the algae population (particularly surface scums of blue-green algae), lowered water clarity, lowered oxygen content in the water, fish kills, and an eventual increase in the growth of floating plants and other water weeds.

In many lakes, the eutrophication process can be reversed by reducing amounts of mineral nutrients entering the water through better sewage treatment or by diverting polluted water. One of the most dramatic and expensive examples of lake restoration has been the effort to restore Lake Erie (LEPR 2008; Markham et al. 2008; Sponberg 2009). Lake Erie was the most polluted of the Great Lakes in the 1950s and 1960s, characterized by deteriorating water quality, extensive algal blooms, declining indigenous fish populations, the collapse of commercial fisheries, and oxygen depletion in deeper waters. To address this problem, the governments of the United States and Canada have invested billions of dollars since 1972 in wastewater treatment facilities, reducing the annual discharge of phosphorus into the lake from 15,260 tons in 1972 to 2449 tons in 1985. Once water quality began to improve, populations of native predatory fish began to increase on their own; additional individuals of these species were added to the lake by state agencies because the predatory fish eat the smaller fish that feed on **zooplankton** (single-celled, nonphotosynthetic organisms floating in the water). With fewer small fish, the zooplankton increased and consumed more algae, and the water quality improved substantially.

Ironically, increased water clarity in Lake Erie is probably also due in part to the devastating zebra mussel invasion (see Figure 10.10), because the millions of exotic

> Lake restorations are linked to both improving water quality and returning the original species composition and community structure.

mussels filter tons of algae out of the water. There is even some evidence of increased oxygen levels at the lower depths of the lake. Even though the lake may never return to its historical condition because of altered water chemistry and the large number of exotic species present, the investment of billions of dollars has resulted in a significant degree of restoration in this large, highly managed ecosystem.

Prairies

Many small parcels of former agricultural land in central North America have been restored to prairies. Because they are species rich, have many beautiful wildflowers, and can be established within a few years, prairies represent ideal subjects for restoration work (Foster et al. 2009).

Some of the earliest research on the restoration of prairies was carried out in Wisconsin, starting in the 1930s. A wide variety of techniques has been used in these prairie restoration attempts, but the basic method involves a site preparation of shallow plowing, burning, and raking, if prairie species are present, or eliminating all vegetation by plowing or applying herbicides, if only exotics are present. Native plant species are then established by transplanting them in prairie sods obtained elsewhere, planting individuals grown from seed, or scattering prairie seeds collected from the wild or from cultivated plants (**Figure 19.7**). The simplest method is gathering hay from a native prairie and spreading it on the prepared site. Such native species are more likely to become established in the absence of fertilizer, as its use tends to favor nonnative species. Of course, reestablishing the full range of plant species, soil structure, and invertebrates could take centuries or might never occur. In concluding his essay on five decades of Wisconsin experiments, Cottam (1990) said:

> Prairie restoration is an exciting and rewarding enterprise. It is full of surprises, fantastic successes, and abysmal failures. You learn a lot—usually more about what not to do than what to do. Success is seldom high, but prairie plants are resilient, and even a poor beginning will in time result in a beautiful prairie.

Prairie restoration projects are also useful for their educational value and for their ability to excite urban dwellers eager to volunteer in conservation efforts. Because the techniques used for prairie restoration are similar to common gardening and agriculture, such restorations are well suited to volunteer labor. People who have the experience of working on restoration projects often become strong advocates for conservation. The Chicago metropolitan area is particularly well known for such projects; some involve creating prairie grasslands with native prairie species, rather than lawns, in suburban neighborhoods, while others involve converting forests back to their historical condition as prairies. However, some of the proposed prairie restorations on public land in Chicago have encountered fierce opposition from neighborhood groups, who preferred their parks to remain as forests. Both government officials and biologists were

> Prairie restorations have proved popular in many urban areas, incorporating numerous volunteers. Large-scale prairie restorations involving large game animals have been proposed.

surprised by this reaction, which highlights the need to spend time talking with all stakeholders, especially local residents, before initiating restoration projects (Gobster and Hull 2009). In this particular case, many of the neighborhood groups prevailed, and certain forests proposed for prairie restoration have remained as forests.

One of the most ambitious proposed restorations involves re-creating a shortgrass prairie ecosystem, or "buffalo commons," on about 380,000 km^2 of the Great Plains states, from the Dakotas to Texas and from Wyoming to Nebraska (Adams 2006). Some of this land is currently used for environmentally damaging and often unprofitable agriculture and grazing supported by government subsidies. The human population of this region is declining as farmers and townspeople go out of business and young people move away. From the ecological, sociological, and even economic perspectives, the best long-term use of much of the region might be as a

FIGURE 19.7 (A) In the late 1930s, members of the Civilian Conservation Corps (one of the organizations created by President Franklin Roosevelt in order to boost employment during the Great Depression) participated in a University of Wisconsin project to restore the wild species of a midwestern prairie. (B) The prairie as it looks today. (A, photograph courtesy of the University of Wisconsin Arboretum and Archives; B, photograph courtesy of Molly Field Murray.)

(A)

(B)

restored prairie ecosystem. The human population of the region could stabilize around nondamaging core industries such as tourism, wildlife management, and low-level grazing by cattle and bison, leaving only the best lands in agriculture. The World Wildlife Fund has started to implement this concept with its American Prairie Restoration Project in Montana that will link government and private lands together in a regional conservation network.

A conundrum for restoration ecology, illustrated by work in the prairies, is to determine the target ecosystem state; in many ecosystems human impacts go back centuries or even millennia. For example, early humans hunted many North American mammals to extinction more than 12,000 years ago. An interesting thought experiment is to consider whether North American grasslands should be restored to a state resembling that before European colonization a few hundred years ago or before human colonization more than 12,000 yeas ago. Another dramatic proposal argues for releasing large game animals from Africa and Asia, such as elephants, cheetahs, camels, and even lions, into this area in an attempt to re-create the types of ecological interactions that occurred in North America before humans arrived on the continent (Hayward 2009). Both of these proposed projects are controversial because many of the farmers and ranchers in the region want to continue their present way of life without alteration, and they tend to be highly resentful of unwanted advice and/or interference from scientists or the government.

Tropical Dry Forest in Costa Rica

An exciting experiment in restoration ecology, begun in 1985, is ongoing in northwestern Costa Rica. The tropical dry forests of Central America have long suffered from large-scale conversion to cattle ranches and farms. Only a few fragments remain. Even in these fragments, logging, frequent fires, and hunting threaten remaining species. This destruction has gone largely unnoticed as international scientific and public attention has focused on the more glamorous rain forests elsewhere. The American ecologist Daniel Janzen has been working with Costa Rica's national park service and resident staff to restore 130,000 ha of land and 43,000 ha of overfished marine habitat in the Area de Conservación Guanacaste (ACG) **(Figure 19.8)** (Allen 2001; Ehrlich and Pringle 2008). The project also includes making inventories of key

(A)

(B)

(C)

FIGURE 19.8 The Area de Conservación Guanacaste is an experiment in restoration ecology—an attempt to restore the devastated and fragmented tropical dry forest of Costa Rica. (A) A barren grassland with scattered forest fragments was heavily grazed by cattle and frequently burned. (B) Native trees and other species became established once again in this young forest after 17 years without cattle and fire. (C) Daniel Janzen, an ecologist from the United States, is a driving force behind the restoration project in Guanacaste. Here he discusses a proposed ecotourist development with two Costa Rican businessmen. (Photographs courtesy of Daniel H. Janzen.)

insect groups, including flies, wasps, and moths and butterflies, using methods that combine traditional means of identification with the latest DNA bar coding techniques (Janzen et al. 2009).

Restoration of this area of marginal ranches, low-quality pastures, and forest fragments includes planting both native and exotic trees to shade out introduced invasive grasses, eliminating human-caused fires, and banning logging and hunting. Livestock grazing was initially used to lower the abundance of grasses and then was phased out as the forest invaded through natural animal- and wind-borne seed dispersal. In just 25 years, this process has converted tens of thousands of hectares of pastures to a species-rich, dense young forest, with abundant and growing populations of native animals. This process reestablishes the dry forest ecosystem and benefits the adjacent rain forest to which animals of the dry forest seasonally migrate, but it will require an estimated 200 to 500 years to regain the original forest structure.

An innovative aspect of this restoration is that all 95 members of the staff and administration of the ACG are Costa Ricans and reside in the area, with another 55 people working on research and other special projects. The ACG offers training and advancement for its staff, educational opportunities for their children, and the best economic use of these marginal lands, which were formerly ranch and farm lands. ACG selects its employees from the local community, rather than spending scarce resources on imported consultants. A key element in the restoration plan is what has been termed **biocultural restoration**, meaning that the ACG teaches basic biology and ecology in the field to community members. Each year, it teaches 2500 students in grades four through six from the neighboring schools and gives presentations to citizen groups. Janzen (quoted in Allen 1988) believes that, in rural areas such as Guanacaste, providing an opportunity for learning about nature can be one of the most valuable functions of national parks and restored areas:

> The public is starving for and responds immediately to presentations of complexity of all kinds—biology, music, literature, politics, education, et cetera. . . . The goal of biocultural restoration is to give back to people the understanding of the natural history around them that their grandparents had. These people are now just as culturally deprived as if they could no longer read, hear music, or see color.

This educational effort has created a community literate in conservation issues as well as a local viewpoint that the ACG offers something of value to everyone. Residents have begun to view the ACG as if it were a large ranch producing "wildland resources" for the community rather than an exclusionary "national park."

Funding for land purchases and park management for the ACG restoration project, totaling $56 million as of 2009, comes from the Costa Rican government and donations from over 8500 individuals, 40 institutions and foundations, and nine foreign governments. Ecotourism is playing a significant part in the $1.7 million annual budget because of the proximity of the park to the Pan-American Highway. Employment in the expanding research, ecotourist, and educational facilities is providing a significant source of income for the local community, particularly for those who are interested in nature and education. For continued success, the ACG must ensure that the plan for park development and management provides the proper integration of community needs and restoration needs in a way that satisfactorily fulfills both. Also, by having scientists involved in the design and implementation of the project, basic and applied information is being obtained that can be used to advance the science of restoration ecology.

This restoration effort has accomplished so many of its goals and has attracted so much media attention in large part because a highly articulate, well-known individual—Daniel Janzen—is committing all his time and resources to a cause in which he passionately believes (Laurance 2008a). His enthusiasm and vision have inspired many other people to join his cause, and he is a classic example of how potent a force for conservation one individual can be.

The Future of Restoration Ecology

Restoration ecology is one of the major growth areas in conservation biology. It has its own scientific society, the Society for Ecological Restoration, and journals, *Restoration Ecology* and *Ecological Restoration*. Ecosystems are being restored using methods developed by the discipline, books are being written about the subject, and more courses are being taught at more universities. Scientists are increasingly able to make use of the growing range of published studies and suggest improvements in how to carry out restoration projects. At its best, restored land can provide new opportunities for protecting biodiversity. However, conservation biologists in this field must take care to ensure that restoration efforts are legitimate, not just public relations covers by environmentally damaging corporations only interested in continuing business as usual (Ehrlich and Pringle 2008). A 5 ha "demonstration" project in a highly visible location does not compensate for thousands or tens of thousands of hectares damaged elsewhere and should not be accepted as adequate by conservation biologists. Attempts to mitigate the destruction of an intact biological community by the building of a similar species assemblage at a new location is almost certainly not going to provide a home for the same species and provide similar ecosystem functions; therefore, conservation biologists need to be wary of such projects. The best long-term strategy still is to protect and manage biological communities where they are found naturally; only in these places can we be sure that the requirements for the long-term survival of all species are available.

> Ecological restoration is an important and growing tool for conservation, but the protection of existing biodiversity is still the first priority.

Summary

1. Ecological restoration is the practice of reestablishing populations and whole ecosystems in degraded, damaged, or even destroyed habitat. Restoration ecology is the scientific study of such restorations. Partial restoration of certain species or ecosystem functions may be an appropriate goal if complete restoration is impossible or too expensive.

2. Establishment of new communities such as wetlands, forests, and prairies on degraded or abandoned sites provides an opportunity to enhance biological diversity in habitats that have little other value and can improve the quality of life for people living in the area. Restoration ecology can also provide insight into community ecology by testing our ability to reassemble a biological community from its native species.

3. Restoration projects begin by eliminating or neutralizing factors that prevent the system from recovering. Then some combination of site preparation, habitat management, and reintroduction of original species gradually allows the community to regain the species and ecosystem characteristics of designated reference sites. Attempts to restore habitat need to be monitored to determine whether they are reestablishing the historical species composition and ecosystem functions.

4. Creating new habitat in one place to replace lost habitat elsewhere, known as compensatory mitigation, has some value but is not an effective overall conservation strategy; the best strategy is still to protect populations and communities where they naturally occur.

For Discussion

1. Restoration ecologists are improving their ability to restore biological communities. Does this mean that biological communities can be moved around the landscape and positioned in convenient places that do not inhibit further expansion of human activities?

2. What methods and techniques could you use to monitor and evaluate the success of a restoration project? What timescale would you suggest using?

3. What do you think are some of the easiest ecosystems to restore? The most difficult? Why?

4. Conservation efforts are particularly difficult in areas of Africa where there is an increasing human population coupled with poverty, warfare, and environmental damage. Consider the plight of the mountain gorilla living in the Virunga Mountains of Africa. If it is not possible to protect this species in its native locality, why not use a range of African plants to restore a degraded site in a more stable place, such as the mountains of Costa Rica, Mexico, or Puerto Rico, and then release a population of gorillas onto the site? Is this feasible? What about extending the concept to create an entire African savanna ecosystem, complete with herds of grazing animals and predators, on degraded rangelands in Mexico? What are the advantages and disadvantages of such a restoration approach?

Suggested Readings

Adams, J. S. 2006. *The Future of the Wild: Radical Conservation for a Crowded World*. Beacon Press, Boston. The author proposes an approach to restore and manage large tracts of land for wildlife conservation.

Allen, W. 2001. *Green Phoenix: Restoring the Tropical Forests of Guanacaste, Costa Rica*. Oxford University Press, Oxford. Vivid description of Dan Janzen's mission to restore Costa Rica's dry forest.

Clewell, A. F. and J. Aronson. 2006. Motivations for the restoration of ecosystems. *Conservation Biology* 20: 420–428. A wide variety of people with different motivations contribute to the restoration of ecosystems.

Christian-Smith, J. and A. Merenlender. 2010. The disconnect between restoration goals and practices: A case study of watershed restoration in the Russian River basin. *Restoration Ecology* 18: 95–102. Hundreds of small restoration projects have not addressed the large drivers of degradation.

Craig, L. S., M. A. Palmer, D. C. Richardson, S. Filoso, E. S. Bernhardt, B. P. Bledsoe, et al. 2008. Stream restoration strategies for reducing river nitrogen loads. *Frontiers in Ecology and the Environment* 6: 529–538. Small streams with high nitrogen loads are the best targets for restorations aimed at reducing pollution.

Dodds, W. K. and 7 others. 2008. Comparing ecosystem goods and services provided by restored and native lands. *BioScience* 58: 837–845. Within 10 years of restoration, restored ecosystems provide 31%–93% of the benefits of native lands.

Falk, D. A., M. A. Palmer, and J. B. Zedler (eds.). 2006. *Foundations of Restoration Ecology: The Science and Practice of Ecological Restoration*. Island Press, Washington, D.C. A good source for more information about this rapidly developing field.

Gobster, P. H. and R. B. Hull. 2009. *Restoring Nature: Perspectives from the Social Sciences and Humanities*. Island Press, Washington, D.C. Includes an unusual discussion of who should be making decisions about urban restoration, and who should carry out the work.

Helfman, S. G. 2007. *Fish Conservation: A Guide to Understanding and Restoring Global Aquatic Biodiversity and Fishery Resources*. Island Press, Washington, D.C. A comprehensive overview of marine and freshwater fish diversity and fishery issues.

Humphries, P. and K. O. Winemiller. 2009. Historical impacts on river fauna, shifting baselines, and challenges for restoration. *BioScience* 59: 673–684. Like marine species, freshwater species have been overexploited and should be considered in restoration efforts.

Meyer, C. K., M. R. Whiles, and S. G. Baer. 2010. Plant community recovery following restoration in temporarily variable riparian wetlands. *Restoration Ecology* 18: 52–64. The diversity of habitats and weather create a highly variable response to restoration efforts.

Restoration Ecology and *Ecological Restoration*. Check out these journals to see what is really happening in the field. Available from many college and university libraries and from the Society for Ecological Restoration International, 285 W. 18th Street, Suite 1, Tucson AZ 85701 USA; or contact the society at www.ser.org.

Rodrigues, R. R., R. A. F. Lima, S. Gandolfi, and A. G. Nave. 2009. On the restoration of high diversity forests: 30 years of experience in the Brazilian Atlantic Forest. *Biological Conservation* 142: 1242–1251. Reducing costs, operating on a landscape level, and confronting social and political considerations are major challenges for practical restoration.

Suding, K. N. and R. J. Hobbs. 2009. Threshold models in restoration and conservation: A developing framework. *Trends in Ecology and Evolution* 24: 271–279. Ecosystems can change rapidly between various states, creating challenges for restoration.

Swetnam, T. W., C. D. Allen, and J. L. Betancourt. 1999. Applied historical ecology: Using the past to manage the future. *Ecological Applications* 9: 1189–1206. A knowledge of the history of a site is important in a restoration project.

Switalski, T. A., J. A. Bissonette, T. H. DeLuca, C. H. Luce, and M. A. Madej. 2004. Benefits and impacts of road removal. *Frontiers in Ecology and the Environment* 2: 21–28. Roads can be removed, but it is expensive and difficult.

CONSERVATION AND HUMAN SOCIETIES

Chapter 20

Conservation and Sustainable Development at the Local and National Levels

As we have seen, many problems in conservation biology require a multidisciplinary approach that addresses the need to protect biological diversity while simultaneously providing for the economic welfare of people (McShane and Wells 2004). The sea turtle conservation program described in Box 1.1 illustrates such an approach: Conservation biologists in Brazil are employing fisherfolk at the *local level* as conservation workers, developing tourist facilities and educational materials, providing medical care and aquaculture training for the local people, and supplying information the national government needs to establish new protected areas and conservation protection laws. Conservation biologists throughout the world are actively working at local and national levels to develop such innovative approaches. This chapter examines some of the strategies employed at local and national levels to promote conservation strategies that often involve action by combinations of government agencies, private conservation organizations, and local and indigenous peoples. The chapter also explores the efforts by traditional people to protect their lands, which is an important component of protecting biodiversity, since many traditional peoples live in the most biologically diverse areas of

FIGURE 20.1 Sustainable development seeks to address the conflict that exists between development to meet human needs and the preservation of the natural world. (Photographs © Lazar Mihai-Bogdan/shutterstock and George Burba/shutterstock.)

the world. Finally, the chapter concludes with a brief evaluation of some of these initiatives and suggests possible improvements.

As has been discussed, efforts to preserve biological diversity sometimes conflict with both real and perceived human needs (**Figure 20.1**). Increasingly, many conservation biologists, policy makers, and land managers are recognizing the need for **sustainable development**—economic development that satisfies both present and future needs for resources and employment while minimizing the impact on biological diversity (Holden and Linnerud 2007). Sustainable development can be contrasted with more typical development that is *unsustainable*. Unsustainable development cannot continue indefinitely, because it destroys or uses up the resources on which it depends (Pollan 2007).

> The goal of sustainable economic development is to provide for the current and future needs of human society while at the same time protecting species, ecosystems, and other aspects of biodiversity.

Sustainable development is needed because many current economic activities damage or deplete the environment in ways that cannot continue without causing irreparable harm to both natural and human communities. As defined by some environmental economists, **economic development** implies improvements in efficiency and organization *but not necessarily increases in resource consumption*. Economic development is clearly distinguished from **economic growth**, which is defined as material increases in the amount of resources used. Sustainable development is a useful and important concept in conservation biology because it emphasizes *improving current economic development and limiting unsustainable economic growth*.

By this definition, investing in national park infrastructure to improve protection of biological diversity and provide revenue opportunities for local communities would be an example of movement toward sustainable development, as would implementation of less destructive logging and fishing practices. Unfortunately, the term *sustainable development* has become overused and is often misappropriated. Few politicians or businesses are willing to proclaim themselves to be against sustainable development. Thus, many large corporations, and the policy organizations that they fund, misuse the notion of sustainable development to "greenwash" their industrial activities, with only limited change in practice.

For instance, a plan to establish a huge mining complex in the middle of a forest wilderness cannot justifiably be called sustainable development simply because a small percentage of the land area is set aside as a park. Similarly, building huge houses filled with "energy-efficient" appliances and oversize SUVs that boast the latest energy-saving technology cannot really be called sustainable development or "green technology" when the net result is increased energy use. Alternatively, some people champion the opposite extreme, claiming that sustainable development means that vast areas of the world must be kept off limits to all development and should remain as, or be allowed to return to, wilderness. As with all such disputes, informed scientists and citizens must study the issues carefully, identify which groups are advocating which positions and why, and then make careful decisions that best meet the seemingly contradictory demands—needs of human society and the protection of biological diversity. Such apparent contradiction necessitates compromise, and in most cases compromises form the basis of government policy and laws, with conflicts resolved by government agencies and in the courts (**Box 20.1**).

Conservation at the Local Level

One of the most powerful strategies in protecting biological diversity at the local level is the designation of intact biological communities as nature reserves or land for conservation. Governments often set aside public lands for various conservation purposes and to preserve future options. Government bodies buy land as local parks for recreation, conservation areas to maintain biological diversity, forests for timber production and other uses, and watersheds to protect water supplies. In some cases, land is purchased outright, but often it is donated to conservation organizations by public-spirited citizens. Many of these citizens receive significant tax benefits from the government to encourage these donations.

Land Trusts

In many countries, nonprofit, private conservation organizations are among the leaders in acquiring land for conservation (Gallo et al. 2009). In the Netherlands, about half of the protected areas are privately owned. In the United States alone, over 15 million ha of land are protected at the local level by about 1700 **land trusts**, which are private, nonprofit corporations established to protect land and natural resources (www.landtrustalliance.org). At a national level, major organizations such as The Nature Conservancy and the Audubon Society have protected an additional 10 million ha in the United States (see Box 16.1).

Land trusts are common in Europe. In Britain, the National Trust has more than 3.6 million members and 52,000 volunteers and owns about 250,000 ha of land, much of it farmland, including 57 National Nature Reserves, 466 Sites of Special Scientific Interest, 355 Areas of Outstanding Natural Beauty, and 40,000 archaeological sites (**Figure 20.2**). Among the many private land trusts in Britain, one of the most notable is the Royal Society for the Protection of Birds (RSPB), which has more than a million members and manages 200 reserves with an area of almost 130,000 ha (www.rspb.org). The RSPB has an annual income of about $45 million and is active in bird conservation issues around the world. A major emphasis of many of these reserves is nature education, often linked to school programs, whereas other land trusts focus on watershed protection, local farm preservation, or particular species. These private reserve networks are collectively referred to as CARTs—Conservation, Amenity, and Recreation Trusts.

FIGURE 20.2 Membership in the British National Trust has increased dramatically since the 1960s, with a corresponding increase in land ownership; membership is more than 3.6 million as of 2010. (After Dwyer and Hodge 1996.)

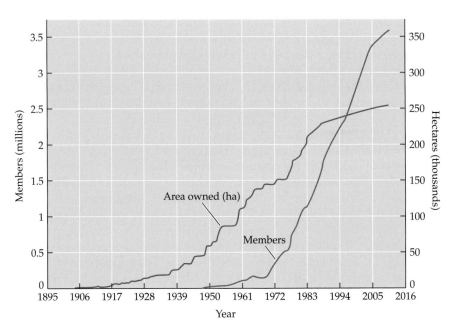

> Private conservation organizations protect millions of hectares as land trusts. Other arrangements with property owners, such as conservation easements and limited development agreements, further increase the area that can protect biodiversity.

In addition to purchasing land outright, both governments and conservation organizations protect land through **conservation easements**, in which landowners give up the right to develop, build on, or subdivide their property in exchange for a sum of money, lower real estate taxes, or some other tax benefit (Armsworth and Sanchirico 2008). Sometimes the government or conservation organization purchases the development rights to the land, compensating the landowner for not selling it to developers. For many landowners, accepting a conservation easement is an attractive option: They receive a financial advantage while still owning their land and are able to feel that they are assisting conservation objectives. Of course, the offer of lower taxes or money is not always necessary; many landowners will voluntarily accept conservation restrictions without compensation.

Another strategy that land trusts and governments use is **limited development**, also known as **conservation development** (Milder et al. 2008): A landowner, property developer, and conservation organization reach a compromise that allows part of the land to be commercially developed while the remainder is protected by a conservation easement. Limited development projects are often successful because the value of the developed lands is usually enhanced by being adjacent to conservation land. Limited development also allows the construction of necessary buildings and other infrastructures for an expanding human society.

Governments and conservation organizations can further encourage conservation on private lands through other mechanisms, including compensating private landowners for desisting from some damaging activity and implementing some positive activity (Matta et al. 2009). **Conservation leasing** involves providing payments to private landowners who actively manage their land for biodiversity protection. Tax deductions and payments can also be obtained for any costs of restoration or management, including weeding, controlled burning, establishing nest holes, and planting native species. In some cases, private landowners may still be allowed to develop their land later, even if endangered species come to live on the land. A related idea is **conservation banking**, in which a landowner deliberately preserves an endangered species or a protected habitat type such as wetlands, or even restores

BOX 20.1   *How Clean Is "Green" Energy?*

■ The enormous scale of global carbon emissions and the degree to which human infrastructure depends on the burning of carbon dioxide–emitting fossil fuels (coal, oil, and natural gas) mean that several interrelated strategies must be implemented to counter the damage caused by present and future climate change (McKibben 2007). Attention is now focused on myriad options for renewable energy sources, from wind to biofuels to solar power, but what is often lost in the debate is a discussion of the direct ecological impacts of "green" energy.

Wind energy has been promoted as a feasible global source of electricity (Lu et al. 2009), but wind turbines present an obvious danger to wildlife. Recent studies have reported that large numbers of migratory bats and birds, most notably eagles, are killed when they fly into or even near turbine blades, particularly when these are built on migration pathways (Kunz et al. 2007; Horn et al. 2008). The presence of wind turbines has also been shown to limit dispersal of sage grouse in the Great Plains and thus contribute to habitat fragmentation for these already rare animals (Pruett et al. 2009). The key to minimizing damage to wildlife is to build turbines with slower-moving blades that birds and bats can avoid and to build wind farms away from known migratory routes. Noise from spinning turbines may also be disturbing to people living in nearby residential areas, limiting where wind farms can be located.

Biofuels, such as ethanol from corn, are another perceived green energy panacea. Carbon in plants comes from the atmosphere rather than from fossil fuels, in theory making a completely biofuel-powered vehicle or power plant carbon neutral. Increasing corn production to meet a rising demand for ethanol, however, will magnify its negative environmental effects, including increasing soil erosion and releasing more herbicides and nitrogen fertilizers into the water supply. The increase in agricultural area to grow crops for biofuels will also come at the expense of native habitat and biodiversity (Danielson et al. 2009). Finally, calculations suggest the production of corn ethanol and other biofuels may actually require more fossil fuel than it displaces, further negating the purported environmental benefit (Bourne 2007). The greatest benefit to society may come when waste plant materials, produced as a by-product of agriculture and forestry, are used instead of crops to produce biofuels.

> Renewable energy sources, including wind, biofuels, and solar power, are needed to create a sustainable society, but they also need to be evaluated for their environmental impact.

Solar power, advocated as part of the solution to the energy crisis, is also not without environmental pitfalls. The construction and maintenance of solar mirrors on a large enough scale to contribute to national energy budgets will require huge amounts of land, water, and materials. Stirling Energy Systems, for instance, plans to erect about 60,000 of their SunCatchers at desert sites near Los Angeles and San Diego, with unknown and probably negative impacts on many desert ecosystems (Carroll 2009). The habitat of many rare and endangered species living in the area would certainly be impacted and fragmented. It would take about 30,000 km^2 of solar panels (about the size of the state of Vermont or the country of Belgium) to power the United States. While this sounds huge, such an area actually represents less than 25% of all roofs and paved areas in the country—locations where solar panels could potentially be installed instead of on open land (Parfit 2005).

The importance of reducing human consumption of fossil fuels and the resulting production of greenhouse gases cannot be overstated, but transitioning to renewable energy alone is hardly a silver bullet when it comes to protecting the environment. We must evaluate the ramifications of any energy source and carefully plan to achieve sustainability, rather than substitute one set of problems for another.

Sheep grazing below wind turbines that can supply energy to the town beyond. Such wind farms can have significant impacts on wildlife that need to be considered in their design and placement. (Photograph © Otmar Smit/Shutterstock.)

FIGURE 20.3 Different regulations and management styles can have different outcomes for conservation. (A) An agriculturally improved pasture in South Florida, with primarily nonnative plants and inputs of fertilizer. (B) Ranchers can maintain native Florida prairie pasture with many native plants and mimimal fertilizer if they are provided with conservation subsidies. (From Bohlen et al. 2009; photographs by Patrick Bohlen and Carlton Ward Jr.)

(A)

(B)

degraded habitat and creates new habitat (Dreschler and Watzold 2009). A developer can then pay the landowner or a conservation organization to protect this new habitat in compensation for a similar habitat that is being destroyed elsewhere by a construction project. The funds paid by the developer for such habitat mitigation can be used to pay for the management of the newly created, restored, or preserved habitat and endangered species living there (Robertson 2006). A related program is a **payments for ecosystem services** (**PES**) program, in which a landowner is paid for providing specific conservation services (**Figure 20.3**) (Bohlen et al. 2009). Utilities may also gain carbon credits by paying for habitat protection (e.g., paying a landowner for not cutting down a forest) and restoration (e.g., paying a landowner for planting trees and establishing a new forest); these carbon credits are then used to offset the carbon emissions produced through the burning of fossil fuels. At a larger scale, carbon offset payments by governments and international corporations can be used to compensate for greenhouse gas emissions (Kiesecker et al. 2009). **Conservation concessions** are an additional approach in which conservation organizations outbid logging companies or other extractive industries for the rights to use the land. The problem with all such conservation mechanisms is that they must be continuously monitored to make sure that the agreements are being carried out (Czech 2002; Wunder et al. 2008).

Public perception can also be a source of problems. Local efforts by land trusts to protect land are sometimes criticized as being elitist because they provide tax breaks only to those wealthy enough to take advantage of them while they lower the revenue collected from land and property taxes. Others argue that land used in other ways, such as for agriculture or commercial activity, is more productive. Although land in trust may initially yield lower tax revenues, the loss is often offset by the increased value and consequent increased property taxes of houses and land adjacent to the conservation area. In addition, the employment, recreational activities, tourist spending, and research projects associated with nature reserves and other protected areas generate revenue throughout the local economy, which benefits local residents. Finally, by preserving important features of the landscape and natural communities, local nature reserves also preserve and enhance the cultural heritage of the local society, a consideration that must be valued for sustainable development to be achieved.

The conservation measures described in this section and elsewhere in this book must be continuously monitored to make sure that regulations and laws are enforced and that agreements are being carried out, particularly in cases where destruction cannot be easily reversed. For example, a developer may agree to limit the amount of development and conserve an area of forest but then obtain construction permits, ignore the agreement, and clear all the trees. By the time action can be taken to stop the developer, the trees and the habitat they provided are gone and cannot be easily replaced. Even if sanctions such as fines or forfeiting of bonds are imposed, the developer may feel that the potential profits outweigh such considerations, and managers and officials usually take the "what's done is done" approach and allow the cleared land to be developed. Conservation workers need to raise awareness so that "breach of promise" against the environment is viewed by the public and the judicial system with the same seriousness as similar crimes against personal property.

> Conservation goals are not achieved simply by acquiring land. Like maintaining a home, growing vegetables, and paying your bills, conservation projects require ongoing management and continuous vigilance.

Local Legislation

Most efforts to find the right balance between the preservation of species and habitats and the needs of society rely on initiatives from concerned citizens, conservation organizations, and government officials. The result of these initiatives often end up codified into environmental regulations or laws. These efforts may take many forms, but they begin with individual and group decisions to prevent the destruction of habitats and species in order to preserve something of perceived economic, cultural, biological, scientific, or recreational value. One of the most significant developments of recent decades has been the rise of nongovernmental organizations (NGOs), many of which mobilize people to protect the environment and promote the welfare of citizens. Many NGOs have a local focus, but there are already over 40,000 international NGOs (**Figure 20.4**). These NGOs help to organize and educate citizens to achieve conservation objectives.

In modern societies, local (city and town) and regional (county, state, and provincial) governments pass laws to provide effective protection for species and habitats and at the same time provide development for the continued needs of society (Saterson 2001). Often, but not always, these local and regional laws are comparable to or stricter than national laws. Such laws are passed because citizens and political

FIGURE 20.4 There has been enormous growth in the number of international nongovernmental organizations since 1950; many of these organizations protect the environment, promote the welfare of people, and lobby the government to take actions relating to conservation. (After WRI 2003.)

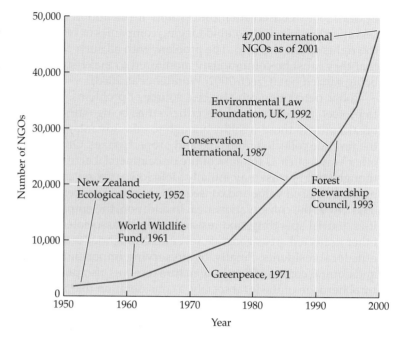

leaders feel that they represent the will of the majority and provide long-term benefits to society. Conservation laws regulate activities that directly affect species and ecosystems. The most prominent of these laws govern when and where hunting and fishing can occur; the size, number, and species of animals that can be taken; and the types of weapons, traps, and other equipment that can be used. Restrictions are enforced through licensing requirements and patrols by game wardens and police. In some settled and protected areas, hunting and fishing are banned entirely. Similar laws affect the harvesting of plants, seaweed, and shellfish. Related legislation includes prohibitions on trade in wild-collected animals and plants. Certification of origin of biological products may be required to ensure that wild populations are not depleted by illegal collection or harvest. These restrictions have long applied to certain animals such as trout and deer and to plants of horticultural interest such as orchids, azaleas, and cacti. New initiatives are being developed to certify the origin of additional products such as ornamental fish and timber.

Laws that control the ways in which land is used are another means of protecting biological diversity. These laws include restrictions on the extent of land use or access, type of land use, and generation of pollution. For example, vehicles and even people on foot may be restricted from habitats and resources that are sensitive to damage, such as bird nesting areas, bogs, sand dunes, wildflower patches, and sources of drinking water. Uncontrolled fires may severely damage habitats, so practices such as campfires that contribute to accidental fires are often rigidly controlled. Zoning laws sometimes prevent construction in sensitive areas such as barrier beaches and floodplains. Wetlands are often strongly protected because of their recognized value for flood protection, preserving water quality, and maintaining wildlife. Even where development is permitted, building permits are reviewed with increasing scrutiny to ensure that damage is not done to endangered species or ecosystems, particularly wetlands. For major regional and national projects, such as dams, canals, mining and smelting operations, oil extraction, and highway construction, environmental impact statements must be prepared that describe the damage that such projects could cause so that these projects may be conducted in a more environmentally sensitive manner. To prevent inadvertent damage to natural resources and human health, it is essential to consider all the potential environmental impacts before projects are initiated.

The passage and enforcement of conservation-related laws on a local level can become an emotional experience that divides a community and even leads to violence. To avoid such counterproductive outcomes, conservationists must be able to convince the public that using resources in a thoughtful and sustainable manner creates the greatest long-term benefit for the community. The general public must be made to look beyond the immediate benefits that come with rapid and destructive exploitation of resources. For example, towns often need to restrict development in watershed areas to protect water supplies; this may mean that houses and businesses are not built in these sensitive areas and landowners may have to be compensated for these lost opportunities. It is essential that conservation biologists clearly communicate the reasons for these restrictions. Those affected by the restrictions can become allies in the protection of resources if they understand the importance and long-term benefits of reduced access. These people must be kept informed and consulted throughout the decision-making process. The ability to negotiate, compromise, and explain positions, regulations, and restrictions—often using the best scientific evidence available—is an important skill for conservationists to develop. A fervent belief in one's cause is not enough.

Conservation at the National Level

Throughout much of the modern world, national governments play a leading role in conservation activities (Zimmerer 2006). Governments can use their revenues to buy new lands for conservation. Areas particularly targeted for conservation are the watersheds that protect drinking water, open lands near densely settled urban areas, areas occupied by endangered species, and lands adjacent to existing protected areas. In the United States, special funding mechanisms, such as the Lands Legacy Initiative and the Land and Water Conservation Fund, have been established to purchase land for conservation purposes. National governments can also strongly influence conservation practices on private land through the payment of cash subsidies and the granting of tax deductions to landowners who manage their lands for biological diversity.

The establishment of national parks is a particularly important conservation strategy. National parks are the single largest source of protected lands in many countries. For example, Costa Rica's national parks protect about 620,000 ha, or about 12% of the nation's land area (www.costarica-nationalparks.com). Outside the protected areas, deforestation is proceeding rapidly, and soon national parks may represent the only undisturbed habitat and source of natural products, such as timber, in the whole country. As of 2009, the U.S. National Park system protected about 8.4 million ha with 391 sites. The U.S. governement also protects biodiversity in its 550 National Wildlife Refuges covering 62 million ha, the Bureau of Land Management's National Landscape Conservation System with 886 sites covering 11 million ha, and many of the National Forests.

National Legislation

National legislatures and governing agencies are the principal bodies for developing policies that regulate environmental pollution. Laws are passed by legislatures and then implemented in the form of regulations by government agencies. Laws and regulations affecting air emissions, sewage treatment, waste dumping, and development of wetlands are often enacted to protect human health and property and resources such as drinking water, forests, and commercial and sport fisheries. The level of enforcement of these laws demonstrates a nation's determination to protect the health of its citizens and the integrity of its natural resources. At the same time, these laws protect biological communities that would otherwise be destroyed by pollution and other human activities. The air pollution that exacerbates human respiratory disease, for instance, also damages commercial forests and biological communities, and pollution that ruins drinking water also kills terrestrial and aquatic species such as turtles and fish.

National governments can also have a substantial effect on the protection of biological diversity through the control of their borders, ports, and commerce. To protect forests and regulate their use, governments can ban logging, as was done in Thailand following disastrous flooding; they can restrict the export of logs, as was done in Indonesia; and they can penalize timber companies that damage the environment. Certain kinds of environmentally destructive mining can be banned. Methods of shipping oil and toxic chemicals can be regulated. Conservation biologists can provide government officials key information for developing the needed policy framework and then use the resulting laws and regulations to protect biodiversity.

To prevent the exploitation of rare species, governments can restrict the possession of certain species and control all imports and exports of the species through laws and agreements such as the Convention on International Trade in Endangered Species (CITES) (Apensperg-Traun 2009). For example, the U.S. government restricts trade in endangered tropical parrots through the enforcement of CITES and the Wild Bird Conservation Act. Persons caught violating these laws can be fined or imprisoned. National governments can also regulate the importation of all exotic species into their countries as a way of preventing the accidental or intentional introduction of invasive species.

Finally, national governments can identify endangered species within their borders and take steps to conserve them, such as protecting and acquiring habitat for the species, controlling use of the species, developing research programs, and implementing in situ and ex situ recovery plans. In European countries, for example, endangered species conservation is accomplished through domestic enforcement of international agreements such as CITES and the Ramsar Convention on Wetlands. International Red Lists of endangered species, prepared by the International Union for Conservation of Nature (IUCN), and national Red Data Books also may be protected through legislation (Fontaine et al. 2007).

> National governments protect designated endangered species within their borders, establish national parks, and enforce legislation on environmental protection.

In addition, the Fauna Europaea database provides information on the distribution of 130,000 terrestrial and freshwater species. Countries in Europe protect species and habitats through directives adopted by the European Union; these directives implement the earlier Bern Convention. Some countries may have additional laws, such as the Wildlife and Countryside Act of 1981 in the United Kingdom, which protects habitat occupied by endangered species.

Many of the factors described so far come together to explain the recovery of green sea turtle (*Chelonia mydas*) populations at Tortuguero Beach, on the Caribbean coast of Costa Rica (**Figure 20.5**). Following decades of overcollection of sea turtle eggs and adult turtles, the Costa Rican government undertook a series of actions to protect this endangered species. First, the government banned the collecting of eggs and adults at Tortuguero Beach in 1963; then it stopped exports of turtle products in 1969. In 1970, the government established Tortuguero National Park to protect the whole area. Protection has gradually been extended by a ban on turtle fishing and the recognition of how valuable nesting turtles are to the tourist industry. Nicaragua and neighboring countries have signed the CITES treaty and are also implementing protection measures. As a result of these combined actions, nesting populations have more than tripled since 1970 (Troëng and Rankin 2005).

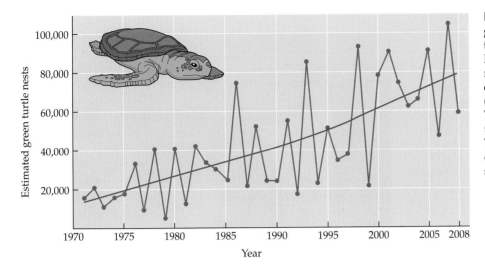

FIGURE 20.5 Greater numbers of green turtles have been nesting on the beach in Tortuguero in Costa Rica since a series of protective measures implemented by the government started in 1963. Nest counts (dots) are variable from year to year. The red curve tracks the general trend of increase in numbers. (After Troëng and Rankin 2005, with updates provided by Caribbean Conservation Corporation.)

It is interesting to note that national legal efforts to protect species are subject to cultural factors: Some species with cultural appeal receive extensive protection, while other species equally in danger may not get the protection they need. In the United Kingdom, for example, the beloved and relatively common hedgehog (*Erinaceous europaeus*) and the badger (*Meles meles*) receive far greater protection than many truly rare species of insects (Harrop 1999). Also, dilemmas may arise when conservation efforts for one endangered species would be detrimental to a second endangered species living in the same site. For example, one species may require protection from fires to survive, while another species may require frequent fires to maintain its populations. Despite the fact that many countries have enacted legislation to preserve biodiversity, it is also true that national governments are sometimes unresponsive to requests from conservation groups to protect the environment. In some cases national governments have acted to decentralize decision making, giving back control of natural resources and protected areas to local governments, village councils, and conservation organizations (WRI 2003). Because of the importance of laws and regulations in protecting biodiversity, conservation biologists need to have a thorough knowledge of this topic (Rohlf and Dobkin 2005).

The U.S. Endangered Species Act

Environmental laws are sometimes perceived as ineffective ("the law isn't going to help anyway"), unfair ("why should landowners be prevented from doing what they want?"), not feasible ("this law is too difficult to enforce"), or too costly ("protecting the environment is just too expensive"). However, in many cases, environmental laws have made a huge impact in protecting biodiversity. In the United States, the principal conservation law protecting species is the **Endangered Species Act (ESA)**, passed in 1973 and subsequently amended in 1978 and 1982. This legislation has been a model for other countries, though its implementation has often been controversial (Stem et al. 2005). The ESA was created by the U.S. Congress to "provide a means whereby the ecosystems upon which endangered species and threatened species depend may be conserved [and] to provide a program for the conservation of such species." Species are protected under the ESA if they are on the official list of endangered and threatened species. In addition, a recovery plan is generally required for each listed species.

As defined by law, "endangered species" are those likely to become extinct as a result of human activities and/or natural causes in all or a significant portion of

FIGURE 20.6 (A) Whooping cranes are protected by the U.S. Endangered Species Act and are intensively managed. Here captive-born juvenile whooping cranes are taught foraging and flying skills by a crane expert in a whooping crane costume. The birds will eventually join a flock in the wild without ever having seen an "unmasked" human. (B) Migrating cranes from a managed flock have been trained to follow an ultralight aircraft from their wintering ground in Florida to their summer breeding area in Wisconsin. (A, photograph courtesy of the International Crane Foundation; B, photograph courtesy of U.S. Fish and Wildlife Service.)

(A)

(B)

their range; "threatened species" are those likely to become endangered in the near future. The Secretary of the Interior Department, acting through the U.S. Fish and Wildlife Service (FWS), and the Secretary of the Commerce Department, acting through the National Marine Fisheries Service (NMFS), can add and remove species from the list based on information available to them. Since 1973, more than 1322 U.S. species have been added to the list, including many well-known species such as the whooping crane (*Grus americana*) and the manatee (*Trichechus manatus*), in addition to 576 endangered species from elsewhere in the world that face special restrictions when they are imported into the United States (**Figure 20.6**).

The ESA requires all U.S. government agencies to consult with the FWS and the NMFS to determine whether their activities will affect listed species, and it prohibits activities that will harm these species and their habitat—a critical feature, since many of the threats to species come from activities on federal lands, such as logging, cattle grazing, and mining. The ESA also prevents private individuals, businesses, and local governments from harming or "taking" listed animal species and damaging their habitat and prohibits all trade in listed species (Taylor et al. 2005). By protecting habitats, the ESA in effect uses listed species as indicator species to protect entire biological communities and the thousands of species that they contain. These restrictions on private land are important to species recovery because about 10% of endangered species are found exclusively on private land (Stein et al. 2000). Although the ESA provides legal recourse to protect species, obtaining the goodwill and cooperation of private landowners is important for recovery efforts (Langpap 2006).

An analysis of the listing process for the U.S. Endangered Species Act shows a number of revealing trends. The great majority of U.S. species listed under the ESA are plants (745 species) and vertebrates (over 300 species), despite the fact that most of the world's species are insects and other invertebrates. If the same proportion of insects were protected as vertebrates, an estimated 29,000 species would be protected under the ESA, an awesome number to contemplate (Dunn 2005). More than 40% of the 300 mussel species found in the United States are extinct or in danger of extinction, yet only 70 species are listed under the ESA. Clearly, greater efforts must be made to study the lesser known and underappreciated invertebrate groups and extend listing to those endangered species whenever necessary (Stankey and Shindler 2006). Another study of species covered by the ESA has shown that on average only about 1000 individuals remain at the time a given animal is listed, while plants have fewer than 120 individuals remaining when they are added to the list (Wilcove et al. 1993). Thirty-nine species were listed when they had 10 or fewer individuals remaining, and one freshwater mussel species was listed when it had only a single remaining population that was not reproducing. Species with dramatically reduced populations such as these may encounter genetic and demographic problems that can impede or prevent recovery. For the ESA to be most effective, endangered species must be given protection under the ESA before they decline to the point where recovery becomes virtually impossible. An early listing of a declining species might allow it to recover and thus become a candidate for removal from the list more quickly than if authorities were to wait for its status to worsen before adding it to the list.

> Species listed under the U.S. Endangered Species Act receive extensive protection. Earlier listing of species would facilitate their eventual recovery.

The ESA has become a source of contention between conservation and some business interests in the United States. One common viewpoint of many private and business landowners is that the government should not be telling anyone what they can and cannot do on private property. The protection afforded to species listed under the ESA is so strong and the economic costs can be so staggering that business interests and landowners often lobby strenuously against the listing of species in their area. At the extreme are landowners who destroy endangered species on their property to evade the provisions of the ESA, a practice informally known as "shoot, shovel, and shut up." Such was the fate of a quarter of the sites that contained habitat suitable for the threatened Preble's meadow jumping mouse (*Zapus hudsonius*) that lives in streamside habitats in Colorado and Wyoming (Brook et al. 2003). Clearly, landowners need to be compensated in some way and encouraged publicly to get them to support the provisions of the ESA.

THE ESA AND RECOVERY   At present over 249 species are candidates under consideration for listing; while awaiting official decision, numerous species have probably gone extinct. The reluctance of government agencies to put species on the list is caused primarily by the restrictions it places on economic activity, even though economic costs are not supposed to be a factor in listing. Another important obstacle to listing is the difficulty of species recovery—rehabilitating species or reducing the threats to species to the point where they can be removed from listing under the ESA, or "delisted." So far, only about 20 of more than 1300 listed U.S. species have been delisted, and another 20 species have shown enough recovery to be changed from endangered to threatened (Schwartz 2008). The most notable successes include the brown pelican, the American peregrine falcon, and the American alligator. In 2007, the bald eagle was removed from the federal list of threatened and endangered species because its numbers in the lower 48 states had increased from 400 breeding pairs in the 1960s to the current 7000 pairs. Seven species were delisted because they went extinct, and 11 species were delisted either because new populations were found or because biologists decided that they were not truly distinct species. Overall, just under half of the listed species are still declining in numbers, just under half are stable or increasing, and most surprisingly, the remaining approximately 100 species are of unknown status (Taylor et al. 2005). Due to their low numbers and consequent vulnerability, there is now recognition that even species that are candidates for delisting will still require some degree of conservation management to maintain their populations (**Figure 20.7**) (Scott et al. 2005).

The difficulty of implementing recovery plans for so many species is often not primarily biological but, rather, political, administrative, and ultimately financial (Hagen and Hodges 2006; Briggs 2009). For example, an endangered river clam species might need to be protected from pollution and the effects of an existing dam. Installing sewage treatment facilities and removing a dam are theoretically straightforward actions but expensive and difficult to carry out in practice. The U.S. Fish and Wildlife Service annually spends only about $350 million per year on activities related to the ESA. Increasing funding to $650 million per year would be needed to create a truly effective program, one that would implement effective recovery programs for all listed species (Miller et al. 2002; Taylor et al. 2005). The cost eventually might be higher if the U.S. government grants private landowners financial compensation for ESA-imposed restrictions on the use of their property, an option that is periodically discussed in the U.S. Congress.

While funding for the ESA has been growing steadily over the past 20 years, the number of species protected under the ESA has been growing even faster. As a

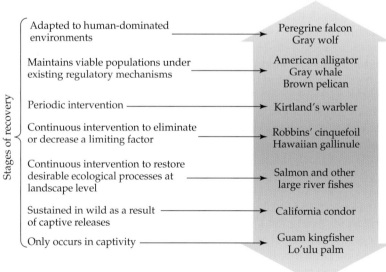

FIGURE 20.7 Endangered species will often require active management and intervention as part of the recovery process. There will be a continuum, with some species independent of humans and others dependent on human intervention. (After Scott et al. 2005.)

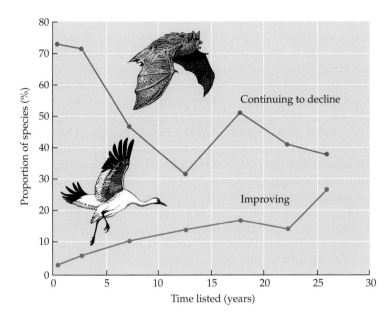

FIGURE 20.8 The longer species have been listed, protected, and managed under the Endangered Species Act, the greater their probability of improving in status (as shown by the whooping crane) and the lower their probability of continuing to decline in status (with the Indiana bat as an example). The numbers do not add up to 100% because some species are not changing in status and others are of unknown status. (After Taylor et al. 2005.)

result, there is less money available per species in need of recovery now than ever before, and new species will need to be included in coming decades due to the threats posed by a changing climate (Holtcamp 2010). The importance of adequate funding for species recovery is shown by a study demonstrating that species that receive a higher proportion of requested funding for their recovery plans have a higher probability of reaching a stable or improved status than species that receive a lower proportion of funding (Miller et al. 2002). The longer a species has been protected under the ESA, the higher the probability that it is improving (**Figure 20.8**) (Taylor et al. 2005). Also, species have a higher probability of improving if critical habitat and a recovery plan have been designated for them.

> Funding for the Endangered Species act has been inadequate. Increased funding would help species recover, and would lead to their removal from protection under the Endangered Species Act.

Even though funding is supposed to be allocated on a priority system according to the degree of threat a species faces, along with its potential for recovery and its taxonomic distinctiveness, certain species often receive disproportionately more funding because they are widely recognizable bird or mammal species with strong public support (such as the California condor and the West Indian manatee) or because they are umbrella species whose protection is linked to the protection of economically valuable ecosystems (such as the red-cockaded woodpecker in Southeastern pine forests). Other species are substantially underfunded because they are relatively unknown to the public, they have restricted distributions, they are not birds or mammals, or they are from geographical areas with weak or no political representation (Restani and Marzluff 2002).

CONFLICT AND THE ESA: COMPROMISE SOLUTIONS An attempt was made to find a compromise between economic interests and conservation priorities during a controversy over whether the protection of the snail darter, a small endangered fish species, should block a major dam project. As a result, the ESA was amended in 1978 to allow a cabinet-level committee, the so-called "God-Squad," to exclude certain endangered species from protection.

Despite the God-Squad amendment to the ESA, concerns about the implications of ESA protection have often forced business organizations, conservation groups, and governments to develop compromises that reconcile both conservation and business interests (Camacho 2007). To provide a legal mechanism to achieve this goal, Congress amended the ESA in 1982 to allow the design of **Habitat Conservation Plans** (**HCPs**). HCPs are regional plans that allow development in designated areas but also protect remnants of biological communities or ecosystems that contain groups of actual and/or potentially endangered species. These plans are drawn up by the concerned parties—developers, conservation groups, citizen groups, and local governments—and given final approval by the U.S. Fish and Wildlife Service. An important feature of these plans is a "no surprises" clause, whereby developers have only limited financial responsibility if the conservation plan does not succeed in protecting the designated endangered species. Also, if any changes to the plan are subsequently needed, the government agrees to pay for them. About 650 HCPs covering about 16 million ha and over 500 species have been approved. In one case, an innovative program in Riverside County, California, allows developers to build within the historic range of the endangered Stephens' kangaroo rat (*Dipodomys stephensi*) if they contribute to a fund that will be used to buy wildlife sanctuaries. Already, more than $42 million has been used to secure 41,000 ha, with a long-term goal of raising $100 million. As a result of the HCP and the resulting new reserves, this species is being considered for removal from the endangered species list; however, the effectiveness of these measures remains to be seen (Brock and Kelt 2004). In this case and others, the result is a compromise in which developers may proceed after paying additional fees into the fund to support conservation activities. Such plans need to be carefully monitored to determine whether they are meeting their stated objectives.

> The U.S. Endangered Species Act mandates such strong protection for species that conservation and business groups often agree to compromises that allow some species protection along with limited development.

In 1991 the State of California passed the Natural Community Conservation Planning Act, a law similar to the federal law establishing Habitat Conservation Plans. One such plan addresses development in the coastal sage scrub habitat of southern California, which includes almost 100 rare, sensitive, threatened, or endangered plants and animals, most notably the coastal California gnatcatcher, a flagship species protected under the ESA (**Figure 20.9**) (Winchell and Doherty 2008). As a result of

(A)

(B)

FIGURE 20.9 (A) A California gnatcatcher (*Polioptila californica*). (B) In southern California, a habitat conservation plan has been established to protect portions of the gnatcatchers' coastal sage scrub community (center of photo) from the uncontrolled development and fragmentation seen in this photo. (A, photograph by B. Morse Peterson; B, photograph by Claire Dobert; A,B courtesy of U.S. Fish and Wildlife Service.)

agricultural development and more recent urban development, less than 20% of the original coastal sage scrub habitat still exists, divided into small habitat fragments. Negotiating the plan has proved to be a challenge, since three-fourths of the habitat is privately owned and the planning area includes 50 cities and five counties. The plan that has been developed for the area involves protecting permanent reserves in high-quality habitat and allowing regions within the plan to develop up to 5% of their lower-quality habitat.

While HCPs are not perfect, they are at least attempts to create the next generation of conservation planning: approaches that seek to protect many species, entire ecosystems, or whole communities and that extend over a wide geographical region that includes many projects, landowners, and jurisdictions. The difficulty with such an approach is that attempting to create a consensus among groups with clearly different goals prevents conservation biologists from pursuing their goals with single-minded intensity. Indeed, in some cases, conservation biologists have been incorporated into ineffective bureaucratic structures without having had a significant impact on protecting endangered species.

Traditional Societies, Conservation, and Sustainable Use

In this section of the chapter, we examine the attitudes held by traditional societies toward conservation, discuss how some traditional societies regulate their own resource use, and review some conservation projects that involve traditional societies (Shackeroff and Campbell 2007). Human activities are sometimes compatible with the conservation of biological diversity. There are many highly diverse biological communities existing in places where people have practiced a traditional way of life for many generations, using the resources of their environment in a sustainable manner. But it is also true that many traditional societies have degraded their environment and driven species to extinction, just as modern societies have, both in the past and even more so in the present, once they have acquired modern tools such as guns and chain saws.

Societies that practice a traditional way of life in rural areas, with relatively little outside influence in terms of modern technology, are variously referred to as "tribal people," "indigenous people," "native people," or more generally "traditional people" (Timmer and Juma 2005; www.iwgia.org). These people regard themselves as original inhabitants or long-standing residents of the region and are often organized at the community or village level. Even remote regions of tropical rain forests, rugged mountains, and deserts designated as "wilderness" by governments and conservation groups often have sparse human populations. It is necessary to distinguish these established traditional peoples from more-recent settlers, who may not be as concerned with the health of surrounding biological communities or as knowledgeable about the species present and ecological limits of the land. In many countries, such as India and Mexico, there is a striking correspondence between areas occupied by traditional people and the areas of high conservation value and intact forest (Toledo 2001). Such local people often have established systems of rights to natural resources, which sometimes are recognized by their governments, and they are potentially important partners in conservation efforts (Nepstad et al. 2006; West and Brockington 2006). Worldwide, there are approximately 370 million traditional people living in more than 70 countries, occupying 12% to 19% of the Earth's land surface (Redford and Mansour 1996; indigenouspeople.net). About 2 million km^2 of tropical forest are protected in some way by traditional people, with half of this total in the Brazilian Amazon (Nepstad et al. 2006). However, people who practice their traditional culture are on the decline. In most areas of the world, local people are increasingly becoming integrated into the modern world, resulting in changing belief systems (particularly among the younger members of society) and greater use of outside manufactured goods. Sometimes this shift can lead

FIGURE 20.10 Lacandon Maya from Southern Mexico practice traditional shifting cultivation of maize (corn), vegetables, and other useful crops. This type of small-scale agriculture, combined with selective planting and weeding of trees and other species, creates a heterogeneous forest with many useful plants. (Photograph courtesy of James D. Nations.)

to a weakening of ties to the land and conservation ethics. However, as described later in this section, there are also cases where indigenous peoples are reworking traditional values and organizations into forms influenced by modern ideas about conservation.

Rather than being a threat to the "pristine" environment in which they live, in some cases traditional peoples have been an integral part of these environments for thousands of years (Borghesio 2009). The present mixture and relative densities of plants and animals in many biological communities may reflect the historic activities—such as fishing, selective hunting of game animals, and planting or encouraging of useful plant species in fallow agricultural plots—of people in the area, as shown by the traditional agroecosystems and forests of the Lacandon Maya of Chiapas, Mexico (**Figure 20.10**) (Diemont and Martin 2009). In addition to their permanent agricultural fields and swidden agriculture, the Lacandon maintain managed forests on slopes, along watercourses, and in other areas that are either fragile or unsuitable for intensive agriculture. These forests contain hundreds of species of plants from which the people obtain food, wood, and other products. Species composition in the forest is altered in favor of useful species by planting and periodic selective weeding. Forest resources provide Lacandon families with the means to survive the failure of their cultivated crops should they encounter a season of bad weather or an insect outbreak. Comparable examples of such intensively managed village forests exist in traditional societies throughout the world (Heckenberger 2009).

> In many parts of the world, areas with high biodiversity are inhabited by indigenous people with long-standing systems for resource protection and use. These people are important, and possibly essential, to conservation efforts in those areas.

Conservation Beliefs

The conservation ethics of traditional societies have been viewed from a variety of perspectives by Western civilization. At one extreme, local people are viewed as destroyers of biological diversity who cut down forests and overharvest game. This destruction is accelerated when these people acquire guns, chain saws, and outboard motors. At the other extreme, traditional peoples are viewed as "noble savages" living in harmony with nature and minimally disturbing the natural environment. A middle view is that traditional societies are highly varied and that there is no one simple description of their relationship to their environment that fits all groups (Berkes 2004; Hames 2007). In addition to the variation among traditional societies, these societies vary from within; they are changing rapidly as they encounter outside influences, and there are often sharp differences between older and younger generations.

Many traditional societies do have strong conservation ethics. These ethics are subtler and less clearly stated than Western conservation beliefs, but they tend to affect people's actions in their day-to-day lives, perhaps more than Western beliefs (Schwartzman and Zimmerman 2005; Abensperg-Traun 2009). In such societies, people use their traditional ecological knowledge to create management practices that are linked to belief systems and enforced by village consent and the authority of leaders. These practices might include restricting harvesting seasons and methods of farming, restricting certain locations from harvesting, or restricting the age, size, and sex of animals harvested. If they are approached with respect for their traditional rules, such people have the potential to become strong allies of conservation biologists. One well-documented example of such a conservation perspective is that of the Tukano Indians, who live in a reserve for indigenous people in northwest Brazil (Andrew-Essien and Bisong 2009), subsisting on a diet of root crops and river fish. They have strong religious and cultural prohibitions against cutting the forest along the Upper Río Negro, which they recognize as important to the maintenance of fish populations: The Tukano believe that these forests belong to the fish and cannot be cut by people. They have also designated extensive refuges for fish and permit fishing along less than 40% of the river margin. Anthropologist Janet M. Chernela (Chernela 1999) observes, "As fishermen dependent upon river systems, the Tukano are aware of the relationship between their environment and the life cycles of the fish, particularly the role played by the adjacent forest in providing nutrient sources that maintain vital fisheries."

(A)

In Papua New Guinea, the establishment and linking of multiple protected areas in the TransFly Ecoregion of wetlands, grasslands, and tropical rain forest has resulted in over 2 million ha of protected wild lands. Over 60 different groups of indigenous people live in or have cultural ties to this region, and most have joined the World Wildlife Fund in supporting and celebrating the protection of biodiversity (www.panda.org). The TransFly is a biodiversity hotspot (see Chapter 15), being home to many endemic species, including the beautiful and intriguing birds of paradise (**Figure 20.11A**). New Guinea tribesmen have long hunted birds of paradise and other native species for the males' fabulous feathers, which are used in headdresses and other regalia (**Figure 20.11B**). Now that many species of these birds are threatened, the people are eager to learn about and support efforts to maintain their populations, including limiting harvesting of feathers and eggs.

(B)

FIGURE 20.11 (A) Many bird of paradise species, such as Goldie's bird of paradise (*Paradisaea decora*) shown here, are endemic to New Guinea. (B) Payakona and other New Guinea tribesmen use bird of paradise feathers in ceremonial costumes. Local people are cooperating with international conservation organizations to create a huge international reserve that will protect these birds and other wildlife. (Photographs © Tim Laman.)

Local people who support conservation as an integral part of their livelihoods and traditional values are often inspired to take the lead in protecting biological diversity. In many parts of the world, people have designated areas as sacred forests whose protection is linked to their religious beliefs (Dudley et al. 2009). The destruction of sacred and communally owned forests by government-sanctioned logging operations has been a frequent target of protests by traditional people throughout the world. Algonquins in Canada have banned logging in a huge area of Quebec under their traditional jurisdiction (Matchewan 2009). In India, followers of the Chipko movement hug trees to prevent logging. In Borneo, the Penans, a small tribe of hunter-gatherers, have attracted worldwide attention by blockading logging roads that enter their traditional forests. In Thailand, Buddhist priests are working with villagers to protect communal forests and sacred groves from commercial logging operations. As stated by a Tambon leader in Thailand (quoted in Alcorn 1991):

> This is our community forest that was just put inside the new national park. No one consulted us. We protected this forest before the roads were put in. We set up a roadblock on the new road to stop the illegal logging. We caught the district police chief and arrested him for logging. We warned him not to come again.

Empowering such local people and helping them to obtain **legal title**—the right to ownership that is recognized by the government—to their traditionally owned lands is often an important component of efforts to establish locally managed protected areas in developing countries (Bhagwat and Rutte 2006).

Conservation Efforts That Involve Traditional Societies

In the developing world and even in many developed countries such as Australia and Canada, it is often not possible to create a rigid separation between lands used by local people to obtain natural resources and those designated by governments as protected areas. Local people often live in and/or traditionally use the resources found in protected areas. Also, considerable biological diversity often occurs on traditionally managed land owned by local people. For example, indigenous communities own 97% of the land in Papua New Guinea. Amerindian reserves in the Amazon basin of Brazil occupy over 100 million ha (22%) of its incredibly diverse habitats—a greater area than in the national parks. The Inuit people (formerly known as the Eskimos) govern one-fifth of Canada. In Australia, tribal people control 90 million ha, including many of the most important areas for conservation. The challenge, then, is to develop strategies for incorporating these local peoples in conservation programs and policy development (Blaustein 2007). The partnership of traditional people, government agencies, and conservation organizations working in protected areas has been termed **co-management** (Borrini-Feyerabend et al. 2004). Co-management involves sharing of decisions and the consequences of management decisions (**Table 20.1**). Such new approaches have been developed in an effort to avoid **ecocolonialism**, the common practice by some governments and conservation organizations of disregarding the traditional rights and practices of local people in order to establish new conservation areas. This practiced is called ecocolonialism because of its similarity to the historical abuses of native rights by colonial powers of past eras (Cox and Elmqvist 1997).

There are many examples of reserves involving resident traditional peoples who were there before the reserves were established and of reserves in which people are allowed to enter periodically to obtain natural products or are compensated for preserving and managing biological diversity. In Biosphere Reserves, an international land use designation, local people are allowed to use resources from designated buffer zones. For instance, arrangements have been negotiated between local peo-

TABLE 20.1	Good Governance Principles for Protected Areas and Their Relationship with Local People

Consideration of rights The rights of local people should be considered and respected in decisions affecting a protected area.

Legitimacy and voice Local people should be able to influence decisions and have the rights to freedom of speech and association.

Access to authority Government agents at the protected area should have the authority to make decisions, especially on matters that affect local people; the lines of authority of both government officials and local leaders need to be clear.

Fairness The benefits and costs of the protected area should be shared fairly, with an agreed upon method to resolve disputes.

Direction Long-term goals for the protected area need to be developed and agreed upon.

Accountability Financial transactions and the decision-making process need to be transparent.

Information sharing Information and reports about the protected area should be readily available to everyone.

Source: Modified from Borrini-Feyerabend et al. 2004.

ple and governments allowing cattle to graze inside certain African national parks in exchange for agreement from the local people not to harm wild animals outside the parks.

In some projects, the economic needs of local people are included in conservation management plans, to the benefit of both the people and the reserves. Such projects, known as **integrated conservation development projects (ICDPs)**, are now regarded as worthy of serious consideration, though in practice they are often problematic to implement, as described later in the chapter (Baral et al. 2007; Linkie et al. 2008). In particular, to be successful, actions often have to occur at the local, national, and international levels; if any of these actions does not work, the project may fail.

Integrated conservation and development projects (ICDPs) involve local people in sustainable activities that combine biodiversity conservation and economic development.

There are many possible strategies that could be classified as ICDPs, ranging from wildlife management projects to ecotourism. These projects normally attempt to combine the protection of biological diversity and the customs of traditional societies with aspects of economic development, including poverty reduction, job creation, health improvement, and food security. A large number of such programs have been initiated over the last 15 years, and they have provided opportunities for evaluation and improvement. A critical component of these projects must be the ongoing monitoring of biological, social, and economic factors to determine how effective these programs are in meeting their goals. Involving local people in these monitoring efforts may increase information and also help to determine how the people themselves perceive the benefits and problems of the project (Braschler 2009). The hope of such projects is that the local people will decide that sustainable use of their local resources is more valuable than destructive use of those resources and that these people will become involved in biodiversity conservation. The following are some examples of the types of ICDPs currently in practice:

BIOSPHERE RESERVES UNESCO's Man and the Biosphere (MAB) Program, described in Chapter 17, includes among its goals the maintenance of "samples of varied and harmonious landscapes resulting from long-established land use pat-

FIGURE 20.12 Locations of recognized Biosphere Reserves (dots). Yellow regions indicate tropical rain forest habitats in the Amazon basin and New Guinea that remain underrepresented in terms of these reserves. The Kuna Yala Indigenous Reserve of Panama (discussed in the text) is marked with a red dot. (Data from www.unesco.org.)

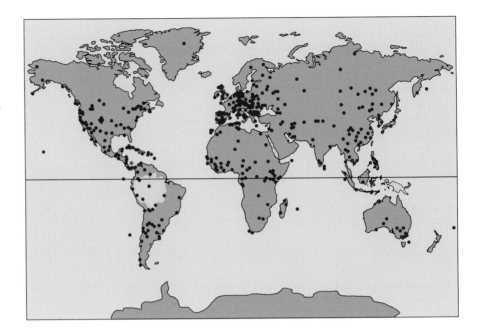

terns" (Batisse 1997). This program is a successful example of the ICDP approach, at least in terms of its adoption of land use zoning as a model of conservation; there are 553 Biosphere Reserves in 107 countries, covering over 260 million ha (**Figure 20.12**). The MAB Program recognizes the role of people in shaping the natural landscape, as well as the need to find ways in which people can sustainably use natural resources without degrading the environment. The research framework, applied in its worldwide network of designated Biosphere Reserves, integrates natural science and social science research. It includes investigations of how biological communities respond to different human activities, how humans respond to changes in their natural environment, and how degraded ecosystems can be restored to their former condition. A desirable feature of Biosphere Reserves is a system of land use zoning in which there are varying levels of use, from complete protection to areas where farming and logging are permitted (see Figure 17.13).

One instructive example of a Biosphere Reserve is the Kuna Yala Indigenous Reserve on the northeast coast of Panama. In this protected area comprising 60,000 ha of tropical forest and coral islands, 50,000 Kuna people in 60 villages practice traditional medicine, fishing, agriculture, and forestry (**Figure 20.13**). Scientists from outside institutions carry out management research, in the process training and hiring local people as guides and research assistants. The Kuna local government attempts to control the type and rate of economic development in the reserve. However, a change appears to be occurring in the Kuna: Traditional conservation beliefs are eroding in the face of outside influences, often associated with the growing tourism industry, and younger Kuna are beginning to question the need to rigidly protect the reserve (Posey and Balick 2006). Also, the Kuna people have had difficulties establishing a stable organization that can administer the reserve and work with external conservation and donor groups, and scientists working on marine studies have been ejected by the Kuna from the Biosphere Reserve. Furthermore, rising sea levels and declining marine resources are forcing village leaders to consider other options for their future (Guzmán et al. 2003; Posey and Balick 2006). This

FIGURE 20.13 Kuna people still practice traditional methods of catching fish in the Kuna Yala Indigenous Reserve. (Photograph © Andoni Canela/AGE Fotostock.)

example illustrates that empowering traditional people is no guarantee that biodiversity will be preserved. This is particularly true when traditions change or disappear, economic pressures for exploitation increase, and programs are mismanaged. The challenge will be to determine a way to integrate conservation into the cultural evolution of Kuna society, which cannot—and from an ethical standpoint, should not—be prevented.

IN SITU AGRICULTURAL CONSERVATION   The long-term health of modern agriculture depends on the preservation of the genetic variability maintained in local varieties of crops cultivated by traditional farmers (Bisht et al. 2007; see Chapter 14). One innovative suggestion has been for an international agricultural body, such as the Consultative Group on International Agricultural Research, to subsidize villages as in situ (in place) landrace custodians (Brush 2004). The cost of subsidizing villages to maintain the genetic variation of major crops such as wheat, maize, and potatoes would be a relatively modest investment in the long-term health of world agriculture. In China, the genetic variability of rice is maintained by a government program that involves interplanting high-quality traditional and high-yielding hybrid rice varieties (Zhu et al. 2003). Villages that participate in such programs have an opportunity to maintain their culture in the face of a rapidly changing world (**Figure 20.14**).

A different approach linking traditional agriculture and genetic conservation is being used in arid regions of the American Southwest, with a focus on dryland crops with drought tolerance (www.nativeseeds.org). A private organization, Native Seeds/SEARCH, collects the seeds of 1800 traditional crop cultivars for long-term preservation. The organization also encourages a network of 4600 farmers and other members to grow traditional crops, provides them with the seeds of traditional cultivars, and buys their unsold production.

Countries have also established special reserves to conserve areas containing wild relatives and ancient landraces of commercial crops (Barazani et al. 2008). One

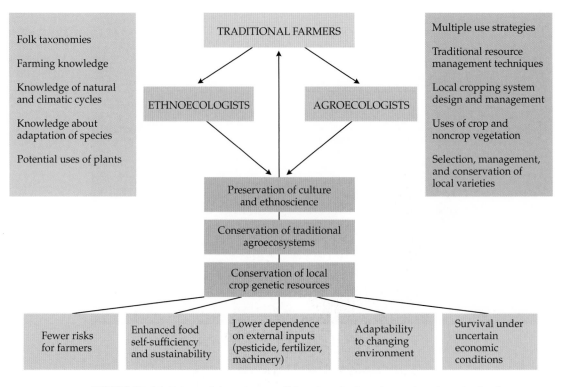

FIGURE 20.14 It is useful to view traditional agricultural practices from both a human cultural and an agricultural perspective. A synthesis of these viewpoints can lead to theoretical and methodological approaches that seek to conserve the environment, the culture, and the genetic variation found in these traditional agroecosystems. (After Altieri and Anderson 1992; Altieri 2004.)

such place is Nokrek Biosphere Reserve in northeastern India, which was created to protect wild trees of oranges, lemons, pomelo, and other citrus relatives. Villages in the mountains of Peru are cooperating with the International Potato Center and various international conservation organizations to create a Potato Park in which about 1200 potato varieties are being grown and traditional cultivation and cultural practices are being maintained.

EXTRACTIVE RESERVES In many areas of the world, traditional people have extracted products from natural communities for decades and even centuries. The sale and barter of these natural products are a major part of people's livelihoods. Understandably, local people are very concerned about retaining their rights to continue collecting natural products from the surrounding countryside (**Box 20.2**). In areas where such collection represents an integral part of traditional society, the establishment of a national park that excludes the traditional collection of products will meet with as much resistance from the local community as will a land-grab that involves exploitation of the natural resources and their conversion to other uses. A type of protected area known as an **extractive reserve** may present a sustainable solution to this problem. However, these programs need to be evaluated to determine whether they are able to maintain a sustainable level of harvesting without damaging the underlying resource base.

The Brazilian government is trying to address the legitimate demands of local citizens through extractive reserves from which settled people collect natural ma-

BOX 20.2 *People-Friendly Conservation in the Hills of Southwest India: Successes and Failures*

■ For local people living in the developing world, leaves, fruits, roots, and other nontimber forest products (NTFPs) collected from the wild are often essential food and medicine and a crucial subset of cash income. As forests shrink in size and become degraded, it is uncertain whether NTFP collection is sustainable in particular areas; if not, alternative sources of income and supplies must be found to support rural families. An important research study of NTFPs initiated by the Ashoka Trust for Research in Ecology and the Environment (ATREE), based in Bangalore, India, began by monitoring the amount of forest products collected by the Soligas, a group of 4500 tribal people, from the Biligiri Rangaswamy Temple (BRT) Wildlife Sanctuary in southwestern India (Setty et al. 2008). But then these researchers took a huge step beyond the norm by training the local people to monitor the health of the forest and to process and sell the forest products themselves. Over time, the Soligas themselves became the principal focus of this conservation project, which came to include economic and sociological elements (Shankar et al. 2005).

A little background information is needed first. The inhabitants of these hilly forests, the Soliga people, are from a tribe that has survived in this remote, species-rich area since ancient times. Thousands of Soligas lived here as shifting cultivators and gathering NTFPs, but they were forced by the Indian Forest Department to become sedentary agriculturists in and around the reserve when the 540 km^2 BRT sanctuary was established in 1974.

The current conservation project began in 1993 when researchers used surveys to determine that NTFPs from the forest constituted about 50% of an average Soliga household's cash income (Hegde et al. 1996). The study also found poor regeneration of many edible and medicinal plants due to overharvesting. Unregulated harvesting of wild honey resulted in the death of bee larvae, with negative consequences for the hives. Another problem was that the Soligas sold the raw NTFPs through government-controlled cooperatives, missing the larger income that could be obtained from processing and selling the products themselves.

> Researchers are working with local people to integrate conservation and development, as described in this example from India. Good communications among participants and long-term commitment are key elements in such programs.

In response to these concerns, researchers developed a project with a simple concept: If the Soligas processed the raw materials themselves and sold the products directly in nearby towns, they could substantially increase their income. They would also be able to harvest less from the forest to make ends meet. Several such enterprises were undertaken that generated employment for numerous

Frequent village meetings are held to exchange ideas with researchers and to develop a consensus on current activites and future directions. As part of a project, Soligas are producing furniture from local plant materials that can be sold in nearby towns. Such activities provide employment for villagers and funds for village projects. (Photographs courtesy of Siddappa Setty.)

(continued)

BOX 20.2 *(continued)*

individuals and profits for the community. Honey collected from wild bees, jams and pickles made from wild fruit, and herbal medicines made from wild plants were sold directly to consumers using the Soligas' own brand name *Prakruti*, which means "nature." The Soligas and the researchers also began to monitor the health of forest resources and the status of project finances (Setty et al. 2008). Over time, Soligas were assuming positions of responsibility for these enterprises. Many local residents could see that conserving forest resources was in their best long-term interest. However, in 2005, the Indian Forest Department banned the commercial collection of nontimber forest products in the BRT sanctuary, curtailing the initial successes of the project.

Since the ban took effect, researchers have focused on helping the Soligas assert their rights for use and management of NTFPs under a newly enacted Forest Rights Act. Planning and training for this effort occurs at the new community conservation center, a facility established specifically to facilitate the two-way transfer of information between researchers and villagers. Researchers are also working with the Soligas to establish new commercial products of food, medicine, and furniture based on agricultural and wild plants growing on their lands and invasive species growing in forests adjoining the sanctuary. This example illustrates the potential and problems of developing community-based management of natural resources within a government-controlled protected area.

---

terials such as medicinal plants, edible seeds, rubber, resins, and Brazil nuts in ways that minimize damage to the forest ecosystem (Posey and Balick 2006; Wadt et al. 2008). Such extractive areas in Brazil, which comprise about 3 million ha, guarantee the ability of local people to continue their way of life and guard against the possible conversion of the land to cattle ranching and farming. At the same time, the government protection afforded to the local population serves to protect the biological diversity of the area, because the ecosystem remains basically intact.

Extractive reserves appear to be appropriate for the Amazon rain forest, where about 68,000 rubber tapper families live. The rubber tappers, or *seringueiros*, live at a density of only about one family per 300 to 500 ha, of which they clear only a few hectares for growing food and a few cattle (**Figure 20.15**). The efforts of Chico

> The challenge of extractive reserves is to find the right balance that allows local people to harvest enough natural resources to get an adequate income without damaging the local ecosystem.

Mendes and his subsequent assassination in 1988 drew worldwide attention to the plight of the rubber tappers (see Box 22.2). In response to both local and international concern, in 1999 the Brazilian government established extractive reserves in rubber-tapping areas and began subsidizing rubber and Brazil nut production, in some cases with support from international conservation organizations (Rosendo 2007). To many people, establishing the reserves made sense because the rubber collection system was already in place and had been operating for over 100 years. The hope was that the rubber tappers themselves would have a strong vested interest against habitat destruction because it also would destroy their livelihood. This has generally been true, with low rates of deforestation in some of the extractive reserves that have been studied (Ruiz-Pérez et al. 2005).

Extractive reserve policies are based on the idea that the extraction of nontimber resources is a sustainable land use, an assumption that may not always be correct. For example, populations of large animals in extractive reserves are often substantially reduced or eliminated altogether by subsistence and commercial hunting (Posey and Balick 2006). Also, the density of Brazil nut seedlings is often reduced because of the intense collection of Brazil nuts (Peres et al. 2003). Further, during hard times, when resource prices are low, rubber tappers may need to cut down their forests and sell the timber just to survive. Despite these concerns, extractive

FIGURE 20.15 Extractive reserves established in Brazil provide a reason to maintain forests. The trunks of wild rubber trees are cut for their latex which flows down the grooves into the cup. Later the latex will be processed and used to make natural rubber products. (Photograph © Edward Parker/Alamy.)

reserves in Brazil appear to be a realistic alternative to large-scale logging and agriculture. Further, extraction of forest resources is also practiced within some Indian reserves, making this an important land use.

These types of efforts are not limited to Latin America. Many countries in East and southern Africa are aggressively applying community development and sustainable harvesting strategies in their efforts to preserve wildlife populations, as described in Chapter 18 for Namibia. These governments are attempting to develop programs to generate income from safari hunting and wildlife tourism that can be used to run conservation programs and provide clear benefits to local people (Lindsey et al. 2007). Much of the funding to support, develop, and administer these programs comes from agencies of developed countries, such as the United States, Germany, Japan, and the United Kingdom; large conservation organizations, such as the World Wildlife Fund; and international funding institutions, such as the World Bank and the Global Environment Facility.

It is unknown how long such programs would persist if the substantial subsidies provided by foreign governments were reduced or withdrawn. Some of these programs are also expected to depend on tourism for much of their revenue, a prospect that is uncertain given political and economic instabilities within the countries themselves and internationally. Finally, it is unclear whether wildlife populations could be maintained in the face of constant levels of harvesting. Future generations of conservation biologists will need to evaluate these programs to determine whether they are meeting their stated short- and long-term goals of both conservation and economic development.

COMMUNITY-BASED INITIATIVES In many cases, local people already protect natural areas and resources such as forests, wildlife, rivers, and coastal waters in the vicinity of their homes. Protection of such areas, sometimes called **community con-**

served areas, is often enforced by village elders because of their clear benefit to the local people, in terms of maintaining natural resources such as food supplies and drinking water. Protection is also sometimes justified on the basis of religious and traditional beliefs (Borrini-Feyerabend et al. 2004). Governments and conservation organizations can assist local conservation initiatives by providing legal title to traditional lands, access to scientific expertise, and financial assistance to develop needed infrastructure. One example of a local initiative is the Community Baboon Sanctuary in eastern Belize, created by a collective agreement among a group of villages to maintain the forest habitat required by the local population of black howler monkeys (known locally as baboons) (see Figure 16.7) (Waters and Ulloa 2007). Ecotourists visiting the sanctuary pay a fee to the village organization, and additional payments are made if they stay overnight and eat meals with a local family. Conservation biologists working at the site have provided training for local nature guides, a body of scientific information on the local wildlife, funds for a local natural history museum, and business training for the village leaders.

In the Pacific islands of Samoa, much of the rain forest land and marine area is under "customary ownership"—it is owned by communities of indigenous people (Boydell and Holzknecht 2003). Villagers are under increasing pressure to sell logs from their forests to pay for schools and other necessities. Despite this situation, the local people have a strong desire to preserve the land because of the forest's religious and cultural significance, as well as its value for medicinal plants and other products. A variety of solutions are being developed to meet these conflicting needs: In American (or Eastern) Samoa, where about 90% of the land is under customary ownership (www.fao.org), the U.S. government in 1988 leased forest and coastal land from the villages to establish a new national park. In this case, the villages retained ownership of the land and traditional hunting and collecting rights (www.nps.gov). Village elders were also assigned places on the park advisory board so they would have a voice in issues of governance and management. In Western Samoa, where over 70% of the land is under customary ownership (www.fao.org), international conservation organizations and various donors agreed to build schools, medical clinics, and other public works projects that the villages needed in exchange for stopping all commercial logging. Thus, each dollar donated did double service, both protecting the forest and providing humanitarian aid to the villages.

PAYMENTS FOR ECOSYSTEM SERVICES A new creative strategy being developed involves direct payments to individual landowners and local communities that protect critical ecosystems, in effect paying the community to be good land stewards (Chen et al. 2009; Tallis et al. 2009; Zabel and Roe 2009). Such an approach has the advantage of greater simplicity than programs that attempt to link conservation with economic development. These types of programs are sometimes referred to as payments for ecosystem services (PES) and are increasing in abundance (**Figure 20.16**). Governments, nongovernmental conservation organizations, and businesses develop markets in which local landowners can participate through protecting and restoring ecosystems. One such example is the Cauca Valley in Colombia, where landowners in upland areas of the valley were cutting down trees and overgrazing the slopes with cattle, leading to flooding and erratic stream flows in the valley below (WWF and McGinley 2007). The downstream landowners had invested in establishing sugar plantations but recognized that they needed to protect their water supply. With the help of a local NGO, almost 4000 landowners organized a water users association, which established a series of initiatives targeted toward upland landowners, including a social program to provide education and training, a production

> New markets are being developed in which local people are paid for providing ecosystem services such as protecting forests to maintain water supplies and planting trees to absorb carbon dioxide. Programs that address climate change issues are predicted to become more common in coming years.

program involving reforestation and sustainable agriculture, and an infrastructure program to improve water quality and reduce erosion. Since the 1980s, almost $5 million has been raised by the water users association and spent on the upland areas (Porras and Neves 2006).

Rural people can also be drawn into newly developing international markets for ecosystem services (www.ecosystem-marketplace.com). In the Scolel Té project in Chiapas, Mexico, begun in 1996, farmers agree to maintain their existing forest land and restore degraded land in order to increase natural carbon sequestration. Farmers participating in the plan receive payments from a European car racing association, the World Bank, and religious groups seeking carbon credits to offset their own carbon dioxide emissions. Farmers gain additional income by planting high-value shade-grown coffee under the trees. This program is a good example of combining conservation and carbon dioxide mitigation with sustainable development; so far, 700 farmers have agreed to participate, and annual income is about US$120,000. Programs addressing carbon sequestration and climate change are likely to expand greatly in coming years, and may provide substantial funds for land protection. However, at present such programs are sometimes unable to pay enough money to prevent landowners from converting their land to other uses (Butler et al. 2009).

Evaluating Conservation Initiatives That Involve Traditional Societies

A key element in the success of many of the projects discussed in the preceding sections is the opportunity for conservation biologists to build on and work with stable, flexible, local communities with effective leaders and competent government agencies. Certain projects appear to be successful at combining biodiversity protection with sustainable development and poverty reduction. The Equator Initiative of the United Nations is cosponsored by many leading conservation organizations, businesses, and governments and is helping to fund and publicize such efforts. In 2008, the initiative recognized 25 of the most outstanding projects in the world, and they received its Equator Prize (www.equatorinitiative.org).

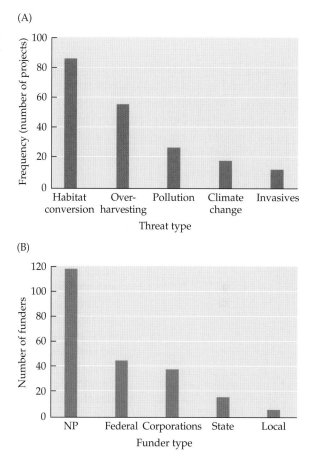

FIGURE 20.16 Patterns of ecosystem services projects. (A) Number of projects addressing different types of threat. Most projects address issues of habitat conversion (from forests to agricultural land, for example) and overharvesting (trees, for example). (B) Funding sources for the projects are primarily nonprofit (NP) conservation organizations, and also include government agencies at national, state, and local levels, as well as corporations. (After Tallis et al. 2009.)

However, many such conservation projects have failed because of the need to carry out projects at multiple levels and scales. In many other cases a local community may have internal conflicts and poor leadership, making it incapable of administering a successful conservation program (Linkie et al. 2008). Also, conservation initiatives involving recent immigrants or impoverished, disorganized local people may be difficult to carry out. Additionally, government agencies working on the project may be ineffective or even corrupt. In such cases, conservation biologists, government officials, and local people may have difficulty establishing common objectives during the projects, leading to misunderstanding, mistrust, and miscommunication (Castillo et al. 2005). These factors will tend to prevent conservation programs from succeeding. An additional negative factor is the increasing population pressure that is generated not only by high local birth rates but by the tendency of successful programs to attract immigrants to the program areas (Stem et al. 2005; Struhsaker et al. 2005). This increasing population leads to further environmental degradation and a breakdown of social structures. For example, newly established panda reserves in China have attracted additional people to those areas because of the rapidly growing ecotourist activity, with deforestation resulting from the increased demand for timber to build and heat new tourist lodges. Consequently, while working with local people may be a desirable goal, in some cases this simply is not possible. Sometimes the only way to preserve biological diversity is to exclude people from protected areas and rigorously patrol their boundaries, although this may be politically difficult and impractical in many countries (Schmidt-Soltau 2009).

> Conservation projects involving local people have often failed due to problems with funding, management, and changing circumstances. Developing a better approach to working with local people is an important challenge for conservation biologists and organizations.

In many cases, projects that initially appeared very promising were terminated when external funding and management ended, because the projected income stream never developed. Even for projects that appear successful, there is often no monitoring of ecological and social parameters to determine whether project goals are being achieved. It is essential that any conservation program design include mechanisms for evaluating the progress and success of measures taken (Kapos et al. 2008). Projects can also be undermined by external forces, such as political instability and economic downturns.

The catchphrase "think globally, act locally" is a true measure of how conservation must work. In the preceding examples, one factor is consistently true: Whether they are supporting conservation activities or opposing them, ordinary people with no strong feelings about conservation are more likely to respond to issues that affect their day-to-day lives. If people learn that a species or habitat to which they are accustomed to having access might be taken away from them because of pressures to develop the land (or to conserve a species), they may feel compelled to take direct action. This reaction can be a double-edged sword; when harm to the environment is viewed by local inhabitants as a threat to their well-being, it can be used to the advantage of conservation, but it is often the case that conservation activities are initially perceived as threatening the local way of life or obstructing the community from beneficial economic development. The challenge for conservation biologists is to energize local people in support of long-term conservation goals while recognizing and addressing the objections of those who oppose them. In many cases, improving the economic conditions of people's lives and helping them obtain secure rights to their land are essential to preserving biological diversity in developing countries.

Summary

1. Legal efforts to protect biodiversity occur at local, regional, and national levels and regulate activities affecting both privately and publicly owned lands. Governments and private land trusts may buy land for conservation purposes or acquire conservation easements and development rights for future protection. Associated laws limit pollution, curtail or ban certain types of development, and set rules for hunting and other recreational activities—all with the aim of preserving biodiversity and protecting human health.

2. National governments protect biodiversity by establishing national parks and refuges, controlling imports and exports at their borders, and creating regulations for air and water pollution. The most effective law in the United States for protecting species is the Endangered Species Act. The protection afforded under the ESA is so strong that probusiness and development groups are often forced to work with conservation organizations and government agencies to create compromises that protect species and allow some development.

3. In many countries, traditional people own large areas of undeveloped land and have beliefs which are compatible with biodiversity conservation.

4. Conservation biologists and local people are collaborating on many projects to achieve the combined objectives of protecting biological diversity, preserving cultural diversity, and providing new economic opportunities. Initiatives that allow people to use park resources in a sustainable manner without harming biological diversity are sometimes called integrated conservation development projects. New initiatives called payments for ecosystem services programs are now being explored for their feasibility.

For Discussion

1. Apply the concepts of development and growth to aspects of the economy that you know about. Are there industries practicing or at least approaching sustainable development? Are there industries or aspects of the economy that are clearly not sustainable? Are development and unsustainable growth always linked, or can there be growth that is sustainable, or development without growth at all? Consider industries such as logging, mining, education, road construction, home construction, and nature tourism.

2. What are the roles of government agencies, private conservation organizations, businesses, community groups, and individuals in the conservation of biological diversity? Can they work together, or are their interests necessarily opposed to each other?

3. Imagine that a new tribe of hunting-and-gathering people is discovered in a remote area of the Amazon that has previously been designated for a logging and mining project. The area is also found to contain numerous species new to science. Should the project go forward as planned and the people be given whatever employment they are suited for? Should the area be closed to all outsiders and the people and new species allowed to live undisturbed? Should the tribe be contacted by social workers, educated in special schools, and eventually incorporated into modern society? Can you think of a possible compromise that would integrate conservation and development? In such a case, who should decide what actions should be taken?

4. Programs in Namibia, Zambia, and Zimbabwe have tried to generate rural income through safari hunting and wildlife tourism. Elephants and lions are hunted in these programs, despite the fact that they are protected species under the Convention on International Trade in Endangered Species. What ethical, economic, political, ecological, and social issues are raised by these programs?

Suggested Readings

Abensperg-Traun, M. 2009. CITES, sustainable use of wild species and incentive-driven conservation in developing countries, with an emphasis on southern Africa. *Biological Conservation* 142: 948–963. Local communities may sometimes be better able to manage wildlife and other resources than government agencies are.

Armsworth, P. R. and J. N. Sanchirico. 2008. The effectiveness of buying easements as a conservation strategy. *Conservation Letters* 1: 182–189. Easements are most effective when developers have other lands to buy.

Bohlen, P. J., S. Lynch, L. Shabman, M. Clark, S. Shukla, and H. Swain. 2009. Paying for environmental services from agricultural lands: An example from the northern Everglades. *Frontiers in Ecology and the Environment* 7: 46–55. Farmers will manage their lands in an environmentally responsible way if supported financially.

Braschler, B. 2009. Successfully implementing a citizen-scientist approach to insect monitoring in a resource-poor country. *BioScience* 59: 103–104. Volunteer involvement in conservation is an important outreach approach.

Briggs, S. V. 2009. Priorities and paradigms: Directions in threatened species recovery. *Conservation Letters* 2: 101–108. Species recovery must be cost-effective.

Danielson, F. and 10 others. 2009. Biofuel plantations on forested lands: Double jeopardy for biodiversity and climate. *Conservation Biology* 23: 348–358. The production of biofuels can have significant environmental impacts.

Diemont, S. A. W. and J. F. Martin. 2009. Lacandon Maya ecosystem management: Sustainable design for subsistence and environmental restoration. *Ecological Applications* 19: 254–266. Traditional people have important lessons to teach conservation biologists.

Dudley, N., L. Higgins-Zogin, and S. Mansourian. 2009. The links between protected areas, faith, and sacred natural sites. *Conservation Biology* 23: 568–577. Traditional people are already carrying out conservation efforts that should be encouraged.

Holtcamp, W. 2010. Silence of the pikas. *BioScience* 60: 8–12. The pika is threatened by a warming climate and may require protection under the U.S. Endangered Species Act.

Kiesecker, J. M. and 7 others. 2009. A framework for implementing biodiversity offsets: Selecting sites and determining scale. *BioScience* 59: 77–84. Sites must be selected carefully to make sure there is a positive outcome.

Kunz, T. H. and 8 others. 2007. Ecological impacts of wind energy development on bats: Questions, research needs, and hypotheses. *Frontiers in Ecology and the Environment* 5: 315–324. Biologists grapple with compromises between development and conservation.

Schwartz, M. W. 2008. The performance of the Endangered Species Act. *Annual Review of Ecology, Evolution, and Systematics* 39: 279–299. Many listed species are recovering, but certain goals have not been achieved.

Stem, C., R. Margoluis, N. Salafsky, and M. Brown. 2005. Monitoring and evaluation in conservation: A review of trends and approaches. *Conservation Biology* 19: 295–309. Conservation projects involving local people need to be monitored and evaluated to determine whether they are meeting their goals.

Struhsaker, T. T., P. J. Struhsaker, and K. S. Siex. 2005. Conserving Africa's rain forests: Problems in protected areas and possible solutions. *Biological Conservation* 123: 45–54. Excellent study of why certain projects succeed.

Tallis, H., R. Goldman, M. Uhl, and B. Brosi. 2009. Integrating conservation and development in the field: Implementing ecosystem service projects. *Frontiers in Ecology and the Environment* 7: 12–20. New types of projects are being developed; which ones will be successful?

Chapter 21

An International Approach to Conservation and Sustainable Development

Biological diversity is concentrated in developing countries, which tend to have weak governments and relatively high poverty, economic and social inequality, population growth, and habitat destruction. Despite these problems, developing countries may be willing to preserve biological diversity: many have established protected areas and have ratified the Convention on Biological Diversity (discussed in detail later in this chapter). Ultimately it is the responsibility of each country to protect its own natural environment, which is the source of products, ecosystem services, recreation, and culture—since many species and biological communities are a source of national pride and figure prominently in stories, songs, and art. Until their economies are stronger, developing countries may be unable to pay for the habitat preservation, research, and management required for the task. Even though developing countries receive many benefits from biodiversity conservation, many of the benefits of conservation also accrue globally, supplying natural products for agriculture, medicine, and industry and genetic materials for breeding and research. Consequently, it is fair for the developed countries of the world (including the United States, Canada, Japan, Australia, and many European nations) to pay for protecting biodiversity. Tropical regions are also important in the global ecosystem through their influence on carbon dioxide levels and weather patterns. And it is also true that many of the benefits of biological diversity have flowed back to developing countries. In this chapter, we examine the question of how countries can work together to preserve biological diversity.

> International cooperation and agreements are often needed to protect biodiversity and to address issues of pollution and climate change. Countries can collectively manage shared areas, such as coastal zones, and shared resources, such as migratory animals and fishing grounds.

The protection of biological diversity must be addressed at multiple levels of government. Although the major control mechanisms that presently exist in the world are based within individual countries, international agreements among countries are increasingly used to protect species and habitats. International cooperation is an absolute requirement for several reasons:

1. *Species migrate across international borders.* Conservation efforts must protect species at all points in their ranges; efforts in one country will be ineffective if critical habitats are destroyed in a second country to which an animal migrates (Bradshaw et al. 2008). For example, efforts to protect migratory bird species in northern Europe will not work if the birds' overwintering habitat in Africa is destroyed. Efforts to protect whales in U.S. coastal waters will not be effective if these species are killed or harmed in international waters. Species are particularly vulnerable when they are migrating, as they may be more conspicuous, more tired, or more desperately in need of food and water. Globally, international parks, often called "peace parks," have been created to protect species living and moving through border areas, such as the Waterton–Glacier International Peace Park on the border of the United States and Canada, that protects grizzly bears and lynx.

2. *International trade in biological products is commonplace.* A strong demand for a product in one country can result in the overexploitation of the species by another country to supply this demand. When people are willing to pay high prices for exotic pets or plants or for wildlife products such as tiger bones and rhino horn, poachers looking for easy profits, or poor, desperate people looking for any source of income, will take or kill even the very last animal to obtain this income. To prevent overexploitation, consumers who buy wildlife products, and the people who collect and trade biological products, need to be educated about the consequences of overuse of wild species. When poverty is the root of overexploitation, it is sometimes possible to provide people with economic alternatives while strictly controlling resource use. Helping people to sustainably manage collection and use is sometimes possible depending on the characteristics of the species (e.g., how quickly it reproduces) and the ability of people to organize and control trade. Where it is simply a question of greedy people seeking to make a profit by flouting the law, enforcement efforts and border checks should be strengthened (World Bank 2005).

3. *The benefits of biological diversity are of international importance.* The community of nations is helped by the species and varieties used in agriculture, medicine, and industry; by the ecosystems that help regulate climate; and by the national parks and other protected areas of international scientific and tourist value. Biological diversity is also widely recognized to have intrinsic value, existence value, and option value. The developed countries of the world that use and rely on the value from biological diversity and ecosystem services in poor tropical countries provide limited, inadequate funding to help the less wealthy countries of the world manage and protect these globally significant resources (Balmford and Whitten 2003). Funding levels need to be increased and used more effectively.

4. *Many problems of environmental pollution that threaten ecosystems are international in scope and require international cooperation.* Such threats include atmospheric pollution and acid rain; the pollution of lakes, rivers, and oceans; greenhouse gas production exchange and global climate change; and ozone depletion (Srinivasan et al. 2008). Additionally, the costs of many of these problems do not fall on countries in proportion to their role in causing them. Consider the River Danube, which flows through Germany, Austria, Slovakia, Hungary, Croatia, Serbia, Montenegro, Bulgaria, Romania, and Ukraine and carries the pollution of a vast agricultural and industrial region before emptying into the Black Sea—another international body of water, this one bordered by four additional countries. Only countries working together can solve problems such as these.

International Agreements to Protect Species

We begin by discussing the key international agreements that exist to protect species. To address the protection of biological diversity, countries of the world have signed international agreements, as described earlier in this book. International agreements have provided a framework for countries to cooperate in protecting species, habitats, ecosystem processes, and genetic variation. Treaties are negotiated at international conferences and come into force when they are ratified by a certain number of countries (**Figure 21.1**), often under the authority of international bodies, such as the United Nations Environment Programme (UNEP), the Food and Agriculture Organization of the United Nations, and the International Union for Conservation of Nature (IUCN). One of the most important treaties protecting species at an in-

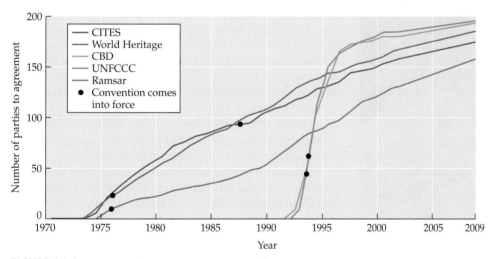

FIGURE 21.1 Major multinational environmental agreements (MEA) are negotiated and then ratified by the governments of individual countries, which become "parties," or participants, in the provisions of the agreements or treaties. A treaty comes into force (i.e., countries begin to follow the provisions of the treaty) when it has been signed by a certain number of countries (indicated by a dot). The plot lines show the numbers of countries that have ratified various treaties that provide for biodiversity protection by protecting habitat (the Ramsar Convention on Wetlands of International Importance, the World Heritage Convention concerning the Protection of the World Cultural and Natural Heritage), species (Convention on International Trade in Endangered Species/CITES, the Convention on Biological Diversity/CBD), and the environment (United Nations Framework Convention on Climate Change/UNFCCC). (After WRI 2003.)

ternational level is the **Convention on International Trade in Endangered Species** (**CITES**), established in 1973 in association with UNEP (Doukakis et al. 2009; www.cites.org). The treaty has currently been ratified by 175 countries. CITES, headquartered in Switzerland, establishes lists (known as Appendices) of species for which international trade is to be controlled or monitored. Member countries agree to restrict trade in and destructive exploitation of these species. Appendix I includes over 800 animals and plants for which commercial trade is prohibited. Appendix II includes about 4400 animals and 28,000 plants whose international trade is regulated and monitored. For plants, Appendices I and II cover important horticultural species such as orchids, cycads, cacti, carnivorous plants, and tree ferns; timber species and wild-collected seeds are increasingly being considered for regulation as well. For animals, closely regulated groups include parrots, large cats, whales, sea turtles, birds of prey, rhinos, bears, and primates. Species collected for the pet, zoo, and aquarium trades and species harvested for their fur, skin, or other commercial products also are closely monitored. Appendix III covers 170 additional species that are protected in one country; the countries that protect them are seeking conservation help from additional countries.

International treaties such as CITES are implemented when a country signing the treaty passes laws to enforce it. Countries may also establish Red Data Books of endangered species, which are national versions of the international Red Lists prepared by the IUCN. Laws may protect species listed by both CITES and the national Red Data books. Once species protection laws are passed within a country, the police, customs inspectors, wildlife officers, and other government agents can arrest and prosecute individuals possessing or trading in protected species and can seize the products or organisms involved (**Figure 21.2**). In one recent case in California, the owner of a reptile business was arrested at the Los Angeles airport with 15 protected Australian lizards strapped to his chest; he will face criminal charges and a fine. The CITES Secretariat periodically sends out bulletins aimed at publicizing specific illegal activities. In recent years, the CITES Secretariat has recommended to its member nations that they halt wildlife trade with the country of Vietnam because of its unwillingness to restrict the illegal export of wildlife from its territory.

Member countries are required to establish their own management and scientific authorities to implement their CITES obligations. Technical advice is provided by nongovernment organizations such as the IUCN (also known as the World Conservation Union) Wildlife Trade Program, the TRAFFIC network run by the World Wildlife Fund (WWF), and UNEP's World Conservation Monitoring Centre (WCMC). CITES is particularly active in encouraging cooperation among countries, in addition to fostering conservation efforts by development agencies. The treaty has been instrumental in restricting the trade in certain endangered wildlife species. Its most notable success was a global ban on the ivory trade when poaching was causing severe declines in African elephant populations (**Box 21.1**) (Wasser et al. 2007). Recently, countries in southern Africa

FIGURE 21.2 A customs official shows wildlife products seized at the U.S. border. For some products, such as the sea turtle, the type of animal involved can be easy to determine, but for other products, such as bags and shoes, the type of animal used to make them may be hard to determine. (Photograph by John and Karen Hollingsworth, courtesy of U.S. Fish and Wildlife Service.)

BOX 21.1   *The War for the Elephant: Is the Armistice Over?*

■ The trade in elephant ivory has existed for hundreds of years and is thought to have contributed to local extinctions of African elephants as early as the fourth century AD (Lee and Graham 2006). Fueled by the rising buying power of East Asian consumers, the demand for ivory carvings grew rapidly during the 1970s and early 1980s to over 800 tons annually. Ivory sales generated large tax revenues for struggling countries and provided considerable local income for poor rural people. However, it has also been estimated that more than 80% of the ivory being exported from Africa in the late 1980s came from elephants killed by poachers and and that it contributed to overall lawless and even armed conflicts. The intense illegal hunting during this period, known as the "ivory crisis" (Lee and Graham 2006), reduced the total elephant population on the African continent from an estimated high of 1.6 million to less than 600,000 (van Kooten 2008).

To deal with this threat, wildlife services instituted new policies that allowed well-armed game wardens to aggressively confront poachers. Combined with incentives such as higher pay, this was intended to increase the wardens' commitment to their job. The East African countries and conservation organizations also joined together to ask the member nations of CITES to halt ivory imports. When the ban was finally instituted in 1989, the price of ivory dropped dramatically, and so did the rate of poaching.

Yet the elephant was not entirely safe. Antipoaching aid from Western nations quickly dried up, and by 2006 poaching had arguably become worse than before the ban, spurred by rising demand that drove the price of ivory to $6,500/kg by 2009 (Wasser et al. 2009). Poaching continues to be sustained by the ongoing war and political instability in central Africa, including the involvement of major crime syndicates in the increasingly lucrative ivory trade. The ivory is shipped to Japan, China, and other East Asian countries, where it is passed off as legal ivory from sanctioned one-time auctions. It is estimated that 8% of the African elephant population is wiped out annually, a figure that surpasses its modest 6% annual reproductive rate under optimal conditions.

In the face of this continued threat, a high-tech measure is now part of the antipoaching arsenal: the use of DNA to trace illegal shipments of ivory and to distiguish it from legal ivory. Teams of scientists have genetically mapped ele-

Illegal hunting of elephants for their tusks has contributed to elephant decline in many countries. Restricting the sale of ivory may help to reduce poaching. (Photograph © Photoshot Holdings Ltd/Alamy.)

phant populations all over Africa using the unique DNA signatures in their dung, ivory, and tissue samples. DNA from seized undocumented ivory anywhere in the world can then be matched to this map, thereby tracing illegal ivory shipments to their source. Law enforcement and conservation measures can then be concentrated where they are needed most (Wasser et al. 2009).

While the major cause of elephant decline has traditionally been poaching, habitat fragmentation and loss caused by agricultural expansion may be a more important long-term threat (Blanc 2008). As a result of new farms, fences, and roads, traditional migration routes are gradually being blocked. Elephant populations are increasing inside nation-

> Protection under the CITES treaty, identifying the source country of illegal ivory shipments using DNA analysis, and increased patrolling on the ground have combined to reduce illegal elephant poaching. Agricultural expansion and habitat fragmentation may be a greater long-term threat to elephants.

(continued)

BOX 21.1 *(continued)*

al parks, but they are unable to leave the protected areas without coming into conflict with farmers and settlements, often leading to overgrazing inside the parks.

The damage done to the East African elephant herds by decades of poaching and habitat fragmentation is more than a matter of mere numbers. Elephants are social animals with complex behaviors that elders teach to younger elephants (Poole 1996). Because the poachers selectively killed older elephants (which have the largest tusks), the transmission of knowledge from mature animals to the next generation has been disrupted. Elephants also have a profound impact on the development of microhabitats on which many other animals depend: As they feed, elephants strip leaves, knock down trees, and trample brush. These foraging patterns open up forest areas of East African bush for grazing animals and encourage the growth of vegetation favored by gorillas and other forest animals. With fewer elephants available to perform this service, less open habitat is created, and other species suffer as a consequence.

Will the combination of low-tech patrolling and high-tech DNA sleuthing successfully prevent further poaching? Will enough habitat be preserved to sustain recovering elephant populations? Only time will tell for certain, but the eyes of many people concerned with the fate of these majestic animals will be watching closely.

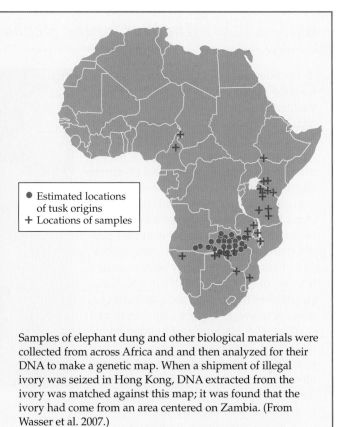

● Estimated locations of tusk origins
+ Locations of samples

Samples of elephant dung and other biological materials were collected from across Africa and and then analyzed for their DNA to make a genetic map. When a shipment of illegal ivory was seized in Hong Kong, DNA extracted from the ivory was matched against this map; it was found that the ivory had come from an area centered on Zambia. (From Wasser et al. 2007.)

with increasing elephant populations have been allowed to resume limited ivory sales, resulting in an increase in illegal harvesting.

> The Convention on Trade in Endangered Species (CITES) establishes lists of species for which trade is prohibited, controlled or monitored. Countries agree to enforce the provisions of the treaties within their borders.

While trade in wildlife may not sound important, it is a huge illegal business, estimated between US$10 to US$20 billion per year, excluding aquatic species. It remains a major problem and is sometimes linked to illegal trade in timber, drugs smuggling, and arms. Unsurprisingly, compiling accurate data is a challenge (Blundell and Mascia 2005). A difficulty with enforcing CITES is that shipments of both living plants and animals and preserved parts of plants and animals are often mislabeled, either because of an ignorance of species names or in a deliberate attempt to avoid the restrictions of the treaty. Also, sometimes countries fail to enforce the restrictions of the treaty because of a lack of trained staff, or corruption. Finally, many restrictions are difficult to enforce because of remote borders, for example, those between Laos and Vietnam (Nooren and Claridge 2001). The result is that the illegal wildlife trade continues to represent one of the most serious threats to biological diversity, particularly in Asia.

Another key treaty is the Convention on the Conservation of Migratory Species of Wild Animals, often referred to as the Bonn Convention, signed by 42 countries, with a primary focus on bird species. This convention complements CITES by encouraging international efforts to conserve bird species that migrate across international borders and by emphasizing regional approaches to research, management, and hunting regulations. The convention now includes protection of bats and their habitats and cetaceans in the Baltic and North seas. Other important international agreements that protect species include

- Convention on the Conservation of Antarctic Marine Living Resources (www.ccamlr.org)

- International Convention for the Regulation of Whaling, which established the International Whaling Commission (see Box 10.1) (www.iwcoffice.org)

- International Convention for the Protection of Birds and the Benelux (Belgium/Netherlands/Luxembourg) Convention Concerning Hunting and the Protection of Birds

- Convention for the Conservation and Management of Highly Migratory Fish Stocks in the Western and Central Pacific Ocean (www.wcpfc.int)

- Additional agreements protecting specific groups of animals, such as prawns, lobsters, crabs, fur seals, Antarctic seals, salmon, and vicuña

A number of international agreements with broader focuses are also increasingly seeking direct protection of endangered species. The Convention on Biological Diversity, described later in this chapter, for example, now includes recommendations for the protection of IUCN Red Listed species (www.iucnredlist.org).

A weakness of all these international treaties is that they operate through consensus, so necessary strong measures often are not adopted if one or more countries are opposed to the measures. Also, any nation's participation is voluntary, and countries can ignore these conventions to pursue their own interests when they find the conditions of compliance too difficult (Carraro et al. 2006). This flaw was highlighted when several countries decided not to comply with the International Whaling Commission's 1986 ban on whale hunting, and the Japanese government announced its fleet would continue hunting whales under the dubious claim that further data were needed to evaluate the status of whale populations. Persuasion and public pressure are the principal means used to induce countries to enforce treaty provisions and prosecute violators, though funding through treaty organizations can also help. A further problem is that many conventions are underfunded and consequently ineffective in achieving their goals. There is frequently no monitoring mechanism in place to determine whether countries are even enforcing the treaties.

International Agreements to Protect Habitat

Habitat conventions at the international level complement species conventions by emphasizing unique biological communities and ecosystem features that need to be protected (and within these habitats, a multitude of individual species can be protected). Three of the most important are the **Ramsar Convention on Wetlands**, the **Convention concerning the Protection of the World Cultural and Natural Heritage** (or the **World Heritage Convention**), and the awkwardly titled **UNESCO Man and the Biosphere Program** (also known as the **Biosphere Reserves Program**). Countries designating protected areas under these conventions voluntarily agree to administer them under the terms detailed in the conventions; countries do not give up sovereignty over these areas to an international body but retain full control over them. Such conventions have been found to be effective at protecting lands and meeting conservation goals (www.panda.org).

> Countries can gain international recognition for protected areas through the Ramsar Convention, the World Heritage Convention, and the Biosphere Reserves Program. Transfrontier parks in border areas provide opportunities for both conservation and international cooperation.

FIGURE 21.3 Los Lípez is a Ramsar-listed site in Bolivia covering 1.5 million ha and noted for its populations of two flamingo species. (Photograph © J. Marshall-Tribaleye Images/Alamy.)

The Ramsar Convention on Wetlands was established in 1971 to halt the continued destruction of wetlands, particularly those that support migratory waterfowl, and to recognize the ecological, scientific, economic, cultural, and recreational values of wetlands. The Ramsar Convention covers freshwater, estuarine, and coastal marine habitats and includes 1867 sites with a total area of more than 180 million ha (**Figure 21.3**). The 159 countries that have signed the Ramsar Convention agree to conserve and protect their wetland resources and designate for conservation purposes at least one wetland site of international significance (www.ramsar.org). Twenty-eight Ramsar countries have joined together to form the Mediterranean Wetlands Initiative for regional cooperation. A comparable program, the Western Hemisphere Shorebird Reserve Network, focuses on protecting the declining wetland habitat of the Americas.

The World Heritage Convention is associated with UNESCO, IUCN, and the International Council on Monuments and Sites (whc.unesco.org). This convention has received unusually wide support, with 186 countries participating. The goal of the convention is to protect cultural areas and natural areas of international significance through its World Heritage Site program. The convention is unique because it emphasizes the cultural as well as the biological significance of natural areas and recognizes that the world community has an obligation to support the sites financially. Limited funding for World Heritage Sites comes from the United Nations Foundation, which also supplies technical assistance. As with the Ramsar Convention, this convention seeks to give international recognition and support to protected areas that are established initially by national legislation. The 890 World Heritage Sites protecting natural areas cover about 142 million ha and include some of the world's premier conservation areas (**Figure 21.4**): Serengeti National Park in Tanzania, Sinharaja Forest Reserve in Sri Lanka, Iguaçu Falls in Brazil, Manu National Park in Peru, the Queensland Rain Forest of Australia, Komodo National Park in Indonesia, and Great Smoky Mountains National Park in the United States, to name a few.

UNESCO's Man and the Biosphere Program (MAB) began in 1971. Biosphere Reserves are designed to be models that demonstrate the compatibility of conservation efforts and sustainable development for the benefit of local people, as described in Chapter 20. A total of 553 Biosphere Reserves have been created in 107 countries, covering more than 263 million ha and including 47 reserves in the United States, 37 in Russia, 17 in Bulgaria, 26 in China, 14 in Germany, and 34 in Mexico (see Figure 20.12). The largest biosphere reserve, located in Greenland, is over 97 million ha in area.

These three conventions, along with provisions of the Convention on Biological Diversity, establish an overarching consensus regarding appropriate conservation of protected areas and certain habitat types. More limited international agreements protect unique ecosystems and habitats in particular regions, including the Western Hemisphere, the Antarctic, the South Pacific, Africa, the Caribbean, and the European Union (WRI 2003). Other international agreements have been ratified to prevent or limit pollution that poses regional and international threats to the environment. The Convention on Long-Range Transboundary Air Pollution in the European region recognizes the role that long-range transport of air pollution plays

(A)   (B)

FIGURE 21.4 World Heritage Sites include some of the most revered and well-known conservation areas in the world. (A) Iguaçu Falls, Iguaçu National Park, Brazil. (B) Cacti and a blue-footed booby in the Galápagos National Park in Ecuador. (A, photograph © Joris Van Ostaeyen/istock; B, photograph courtesy of Andrew Sinauer.)

in acid rain, lake acidification, and forest dieback. The Convention for the Protection of the Ozone Layer was signed in 1985 to regulate and phase out the use of chlorofluorocarbons. The Convention on the Law of the Sea promotes the peaceful use and conservation of the world's oceans.

Conservation measures can also potentially contribute to promoting cooperation between governments. Such is often the case when countries need to manage areas collectively. In many areas of the world largely uninhabited mountain ranges mark the boundaries between countries. Such rugged border areas have often become highly militarized and have even led to armed conflicts. As an alternative, countries can establish transfrontier parks on both sides of boundaries to cooperatively manage whole ecosystems and promote conservation on a larger scale (Rosen and Bath 2009). An early example of this collaboration was the decision to manage Glacier National Park in the United States and Waterton Lakes National Park in Canada as the Waterton–Glacier International Peace Park. Today, intensive efforts are being made to link national parks and protected areas in Zimbabwe, Mozambique, and South Africa into larger management units (**Figure 21.5**). This joint management would have the added advantage of protecting the seasonal migratory routes of large animals. The establishment of the Red Sea Marine Peace Park between Israel and Jordan is important, not only for conservation, but also for its potential for building trust in a war-ravaged region.

Marine pollution is another issue of vital concern because of the extensive areas of international waters not under national control and because of the ease with which pollutants released in one area can spread to another area. Agreements covering marine pollution include the Convention on the Prevention of Marine Pollution by Dumping of Wastes and Other Matter, the Convention on the Law of the Sea, and the Regional Seas Program of UNEP. Regional agreements cover the north-

FIGURE 21.5 The Greater Limpopo Transfrontier Park has the potential to unite wildlife management activities in national parks and conservation areas of South Africa, Mozambique, and Zimbabwe. A larger conservation area will include national parks, private game reserves, and private farms and ranches. (After www.sanpark.org.)

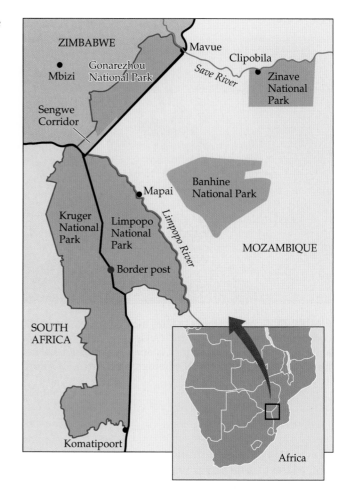

eastern Atlantic, the Baltic, and other specific locations, particularly in the North Atlantic region. The pelagic zone of the open ocean is still largely unexplored and unregulated at this point and is in urgent need of protection.

International Earth Summits

Progress can sometimes be made on conservation issues by bringing together leaders at international meetings. A significant step made in adopting a global approach to sound environmental management was the international conference held for 12 days in June 1992 in Rio de Janeiro, Brazil. Known officially as the United Nations Conference on Environment and Development (UNCED), and unofficially as the **Earth Summit** or the **Rio Summit**, the conference brought together representatives from 178 countries, including heads of state, leaders of the United Nations, major conservation organizations, and other groups representing religions and indigenous peoples. Their purpose was to discuss ways of combining increased protection of the environment with more effective economic development in less wealthy countries (United Nations 1993a,b). The conference successfully heightened awareness of the seriousness of the environmental crisis by placing the issue at the center of world attention. Also, the conference established a clear linkage between the protection of the environment and the need to alleviate poverty in the developing world through increased levels of financial assistance from developed countries

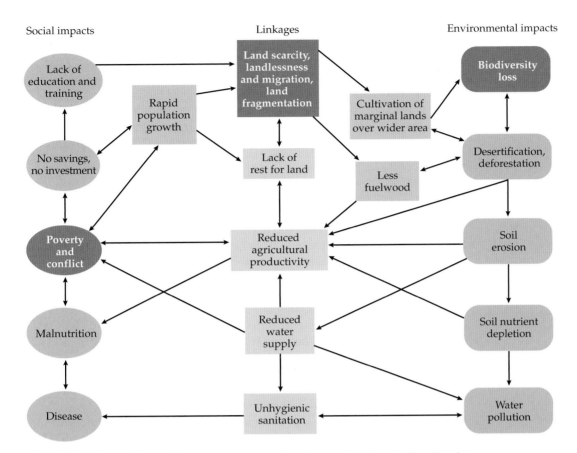

Social impacts   Linkages   Environmental impacts

FIGURE 21.6 Some linkages between poverty and environmental degradation. Breaking the linkages is a focus of national and international funding efforts by the World Bank and other donor organizations. (After Goodland 1994.)

(**Figure 21.6**). While the developed countries of the world potentially have the resources to provide for their citizens and protect the environment, many poor countries believe that economic progress can only come from rapidly exploiting natural resources to spur development and reduce poverty. While this strategy provides a short-term gain, it is often costly over the long term. At the Earth Summit, the developed countries collectively agreed that they would assist the developing countries of the world in the long-term goal of protecting the global environment and biodiversity.

In addition to initiating many new projects, conference participants discussed, and most countries eventually signed, four major documents:

1. *The Rio Declaration.* This nonbinding declaration provides general principles to guide the actions of both wealthy and poor nations on issues of the environment and development. The right of nations to utilize their own resources for economic and social development is recognized, as long as the environments of other nations are not harmed in the process. The declaration affirms the "polluter pays" principle, in which companies and governments take financial responsibility for the environmental damage that they cause. The declaration declares, "States shall cooperate in a spirit of global partnership to conserve, protect, and restore the health and integrity of the Earth's ecosystem."

2. *The United Nations Framework Convention on Climate Change (UNFCCC).* Almost universally ratified (194 signatories), this agreement requires industrialized countries to reduce their emissions of carbon dioxide and other greenhouse gases and to make regular reports on their progress. While specific emission limits were not decided upon, the convention states that greenhouse gases should be stabilized at levels that will not interfere with the Earth's climate. The most recent conference, the Copenhagen Climate Change Summit, was convened in December 2009 to discuss and update the agreement.

3. *Convention on Biological Diversity.* The Convention on Biological Diversity has three objectives: protecting the various components of biological diversity, using them sustainably, and sharing the benefits of new products made with genetic resources of wild and domestic species (www.cbd.int). The first two objectives recognize that countries have an obligation to protect their biological diversity and to use it responsibly. While individual countries have the primary responsibility of protecting their own biological diversity, substantial international funding has been provided to assist developing countries in these efforts. The convention also recognizes that indigenous people should share in the benefits derived from biological diversity, particularly when they have contributed their own local knowledge about the species. Developing international intellectual property rights laws that fairly share the financial benefits of biological diversity among countries, biotechnology companies, and local people is proving to be a major challenge to the convention. Because of concerns about how biological materials will be used or misused, certain developing countries have established highly restrictive procedures for granting permits to scientists who want to collect biological samples for their research (Kothamasi and Kiers 2009). The effect has sometimes been to halt legitimate research on ecology, taxonomy, and biodiversity. In other cases, new research facilities have been built in developing countries and local people trained in scientific procedures so biological samples do not have to be exported.

> International meetings have allowed countries to create agreements to protect biodiversity. Under the Convention on Biological Diversity, each country has an obligation to protect the biodiversity within its borders and the right to obtain benefits from the use of that biodiversity.

4. *Agenda 21.* This 800-page document is an innovative attempt to comprehensively describe the policies needed by governments for environmentally sound development. Agenda 21 links the environment with other development issues that are often considered separately, such as child welfare, poverty, gender issues, technology transfer, and the unequal division of wealth. Plans of action address problems of the atmosphere, land degradation and desertification, mountain development, agriculture and rural development, deforestation, aquatic environments, and pollution. Financial, institutional, technological, legal, and educational mechanisms that governments can use to implement these action plans are also described.

Following the Earth Summit, two important agreements—the Convention on Biological Diversity and the United Nations Framework Convention on Climate Change—were ratified by many countries and have formed the basis for many specific actions on the parts of governments and conservation organizations. Follow-up meetings indicated a willingness on the part of governments to continue the discussion (**Figure 21.7**). For example, the Convention on Biological Diversity includes significant provisions for establishing, managing, and financing protected areas, although targets are far from being met. The most significant success is the inter-

FIGURE 21.7 In December 2009, many international leaders attended the United Nations Climate Change Conference in Copenhagen, Denmark, along with observers from intergovernmental and nongovernmental organizations. Development of the next comprehensive agreement to reduce greenhouse gas emissions—a successor to the Kyoto Protocol—dominated the conference discussions. (Photograph by Pete Souza.)

national agreement, reached at Kyoto in December of 1997, to reduce global greenhouse gas emissions to below 1990 levels. The Kyoto Protocol was finally ratified in 2004 under the UNFCCC (see above), and many countries have put in place policies that have reduced their emissions of greenhouse gases, primarily carbon dioxide. However, the United States has not ratified the Kyoto treaty, and many developing countries such as China and India are rapidly increasing their rates of greenhouse gas emission. Because of this, countries have been focusing beyond Kyoto and have held talks in Bali in December 2007 and in Copenhagen in December 2009. The 2009 Copenhagen conference did produce an agreement on climate change, but environmentalists, countries, and industries hoping for serious action were disappointed by its weak provisions. Further international meetings will be needed to produce an environmental agreement that deals with this issue.

There have been related efforts to put the ideas of the Earth Summit into force. One example is the Aarhus Convention of 1998, signed by 40 countries, recognizing the right of all people to a healthy environment. The convention requires governments to make environmental data available, and it gives citizens, organizations, and countries the right to investigate causes of pollution and to take action to reduce environmental damage. Another initiative is the organization Green Cross International established by former Soviet leader Mikhail Gorbachev, which is active in negotiating environmental agreements in regions of conflict. In August 2002, another major environment summit was held: The World Summit on Sustainable Development in Johannesburg, South Africa, with representatives of 191 countries and 20,000 participants (WRI 2003). Although the conference emphasized the need to reduce the rate of biodiversity loss, the main focus was on achieving the social and economic goals of sustainability. This shift in focus from the Rio Summit highlights a significant, ongoing debate over whether the emphasis in conservation should be to promote sustainable use of natural resources for the benefit of poor people or should be to protect areas and biodiversity (Lapham and Livermore 2003; Naughton-Treves et al. 2005).

Another set of international agreements are the Millennium Development Goals (MDGs), aimed at reducing extreme poverty by half by 2015. MDG 7, "ensuring environmental sustainability," has the reduction of biodiversity loss by 2010 as a key target, and protected areas are important indicators of monitoring progress toward this goal. Although there is no formal treaty between countries, another positive development is international certification of products, such as timber and coffee, documenting that they have been produced sustainably, without damaging the environment or harming local people.

Funding for Conservation

One of the most contentious issues resulting from these international conferences and treaties has been deciding how to fund the proposals, particularly the Convention on Biological Diversity and other programs related to sustainable development and conservation. At the time of the Earth Summit, the cost of these programs was estimated to be about $600 billion per year, of which $125 billion was to come from developed countries as part of their overseas development assistance (ODA). Because the level of ODA from all countries in the early 1990s totaled approximately $60 billion per year, implementing these conventions would have required a severalfold increase of the aid commitment at that time. The developed countries did not agree to this increase in funding. As an alternative, they offered that each country would increase its level of foreign assistance to 0.7% of its gross national product (GNP) by the year 2000, which would have roughly doubled the ODA from developed nations. While the major developed countries agreed in principle to this figure, no schedule was set to meet the target date. As of the year 2008, of 22 donor countries, only a few wealthy northern European countries has met the 0.7% of GNP target percentage: Sweden (0.98%), Luxembourg (0.92%), Norway (0.88%), Denmark (0.82%), and the Netherlands (0.80%). Many of the larger developed countries have actually lowered the percentage of GNP that they give as foreign assistance over the past 10 years, such as the United States, at 0.18% of GNP (Shah 2008; www.oecd.org).

Following the Earth Summit, international funding for conservation has increased, though not as much as originally promised. Much of this increase in funding has been channeled through the Global Environment Facility, administered by the World Bank and UNEP, as will be discussed later in the chapter. Funding priorities have also shifted significantly during this period (Quintero 2007). What is the process that identifies projects for funding? Often it begins when a conservation biologist, conservation organization, or government identifies a conservation need, such as protecting a species, establishing a nature reserve, or training park personnel. This often initiates a lengthy process of analysis, discussion, planning, project design, proposal writing, fund-raising, and implementation that involves different types of conservation organizations (Martín-López et al. 2009). Private foundations (e.g., the MacArthur Foundation), international organizations (e.g., the World Bank), and government agencies (e.g., the U.S. Agency for International Development) often provide money for conservation programs through direct grants to the institutions that implement the projects (e.g., **nongovernmental organizations [NGOs]**, universities, museums, and national parks departments).

Conservation work is often carried out when foundations, development banks such as the World Bank, and government agencies give money to fund the activities of local, national, and international conservation organizations. Major international conservation NGOs (e.g., the World Wildlife Fund, Conservation International, BirdLife International, The Nature Conservancy, and the Wildlife Conservation Society) implement conservation activities directly, often through a carefully articulated set of priorities and programs. These NGOs have also emerged as leading sources of conservation funding, raising funds from membership dues, donations from wealthy individuals, sponsorship from corporations, and grants from foundations and international development banks (**Figure 21.8**). The big international conservation organizations (sometimes called BINGOs), such as The Nature Conservancy and BirdLife International, raise money from private sources, governments, and corporations, and then use these funds for scientific research and training. The international NGOs are often active in establishing, strengthening, and funding both local NGOs and government agencies in the developing world that run conservation programs; see the Appendix for a list of major conservation NGOs (Zavaleta et al. 2008; Martín-López et al. 2009). Yet the international NGOs and the local NGOs sometimes have different conservation priorities, goals, and policies (Halpern et al. 2006).

From the perspective of a BINGO such as the World Wildlife Fund, working with local organizations in developing countries is an effective strategy because it relies on local knowledge, and it trains and supports groups of citizens within the country who can then be advocates for conservation for years to come. NGOs are often perceived to be more effective at carrying out conservation projects than government departments, but programs initiated by NGOs may end after a few years when funding runs out, and often they do not achieve a lasting effect. Also, the income of NGOs can be quite variable, depending on the state of the economy. In the recent recession, many conservation organizations have had to dramatically cut back on their activities and staffing because of lower revenues.

Government and foundation funding for conservation projects has increased in recent decades. Nongovernmental conservation organizations (NGOs) have emerged as important players in international conservation projects.

Governments of developed countries and international banks have provided 90% of the conservation funding to Latin America, demonstrating the great importance of those institutions to funding (**Figure 21.9**) (Castro et al. 2000). Although foundations and conservation organizations provided only 10% of the funding for

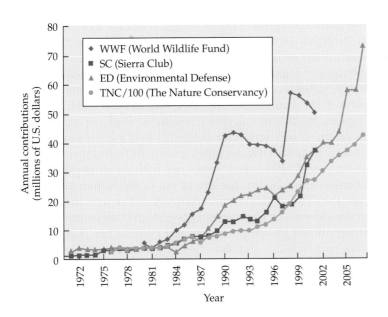

FIGURE 21.8 Over the past four decades, there has been a dramatic increase in the annual contributions of many conservation organizations, as illustrated by four large NGOs from the U.S.A.: The Nature Conservancy, World Wildlife Fund, Environmental Defense, and Sierra Club. Note that the values for The Nature Conservancy should be multiplied by 100; for 2007, its contributions are approximately $4 billion. (After Zaradic et al. 2009)

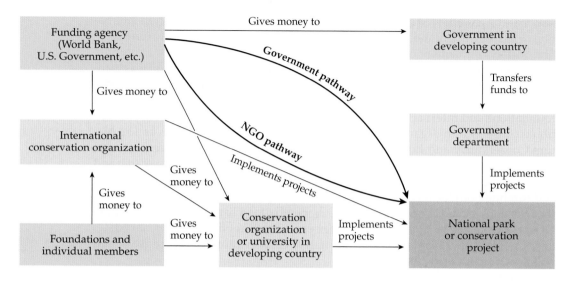

FIGURE 21.9 Conservation projects are funded by development banks, governments, foundations, and members of conservation organizations and implemented by international and local nongovernmental conservation organizations and government departments in developing countries.

Latin America, they can sometimes be more flexible and can fund innovative small projects and provide more intensive management. The growing importance of private funding throughout the world is illustrated by a $260 million donation given by the Moore Foundation to the NGO Conservation International to support its activities.

An unfortunate reality of the present method of funding projects is that conservation organizations compete intensely for a limited amount of funds (Wilson et al. 2009). As a result, there is sometimes a duplication of conservation efforts and a lack of coordination between similar organizations and projects. In the drive for greater funding, conservation organizations have often emphasized the successful aspects of their projects and ignored their failures, missing the opportunity to learn from mistakes. Conservation organizations have begun to emphasize the need to cooperate to achieve shared, long-term goals, which is clearly a positive sign (Stem et al. 2005; Open Standards for the Practice of Conservation, version 2.0, 2007).

An active local conservation program in a developing country often receives money from one or more conservation foundations and foreign governments, maintains scientific links to international conservation NGOs, and has affiliations with local and overseas research institutions (Rodrigues 2004). In such a manner, the world conservation community is knit together through networks of money, expertise, and mutual interests. The Program for Belize (PFB) is a good example of this international networking capacity (www.pfbelize.org). At first glance the PFB is a Belizean organization, staffed by Belizean personnel, with the main purpose of managing a Belizean conservation facility, the Rio Bravo Conservation and Management Area. However, the PFB has an extensive network of research, institutional, and financial connections to various government agencies in other countries (e.g., the U.S. Agency for International Development), major foundations (MacArthur Foundation), universities both in Belize and elsewhere (e.g., Boston University), international conservation NGOs (e.g., The Nature Conservancy) and even major industrial corporations (e.g., Coca-Cola Enterprises). In such situations, there is a genuine concern that wealthy international organizations might be involved in an asymmetric power relationship with a local conservation organization struggling to survive; the fear is that the local NGO might wind up giving priority to international goals rather than local ones.

The Role of International Development Banks

The rates of deforestation, habitat destruction, and loss of aquatic ecosystems have often been greatly accelerated by poorly conceived large-scale projects that are internationally financed. Such projects include dams, hydroelectric power, and the resettlements of large rural populations, roads and transportation, mines, manufacturing, logging, agriculture and irrigation projects, and the oil, coal, and gas industries. These projects may be financed by the international development agencies of major industrial nations, as well as by the major **multilateral development banks** (**MDBs**), which are governed mainly by major developed countries. Among the largest MDBs are the World Bank, which lends to developing countries in all regions of the globe, the Inter-American Development Bank, the Asian Development Bank, and the African Development Bank.

These multilateral development banks have committed more than $100 billion in loans to 151 countries to finance development projects in 2009 and 2010 (www.export.gov). The impact of the MDBs is actually even greater than that yearly total suggests, however, because their funding is often linked to financing from donor countries, private banks, and other government agencies: the $100 billion in funding from the MDBs attracts about another $50 billion in loans, which makes the MDBs major players in the developing world. Related to the MDBs are international financial institutions, such as the International Monetary Fund and the International Finance Corporation, as well as government-supported export credit agencies, such as the U.S. Export-Import Bank, Japan's Export-Import Bank, Germany's Hermes Guarantee, Britain's Export Credits Guarantee Department, France's Coface, and Italy's SACE. These international institutions collectively support $400 billion of foreign investments and exports each year, although it is important to remember this is an amount equivalent to just 2% of total world trade (World Trade Report 2009). These export credit agencies exist primarily to support the corporations of developed countries in selling manufactured goods and services to developing countries.

Even though the official goals of the MDBs include sustainable economic development and poverty alleviation, which are important and admirable goals, many of the projects they fund lead to overexploitation and loss of natural resources to create export goods for international consumer and industrial markets (Cernea 2006; Norlen and Gordon 2007). During the 1970s and 1980s, many of the MDB-funded projects resulted in the destruction of ecosystems over a wide area, involving soil erosion, flooding, water pollution, health problems, loss of income for local people, and loss of biological diversity (Norlen and Gordon 2007). Forestry, agriculture, mining, dam construction, power generation, and other components of economic development are certainly needed to supply human needs. It is also true that conservation organizations need to be involved to ensure that such activities are carried out in ways that minimize the harm to the environment and the local people living in the area.

The Brazilian Amazon has lost huge areas of natural habitat from development on a large scale (Adeney et al. 2008). Over the past 40 years, road construction across previously inaccessible areas of the Amazon basin, financed in part by international banks, has been followed by large-scale clearing of rain forests, massive forest fires, and dislocation of indigenous people (**Figure 21.10**; see also Figure 9.7). A new round of construction of 6245 km of roads funded by international development

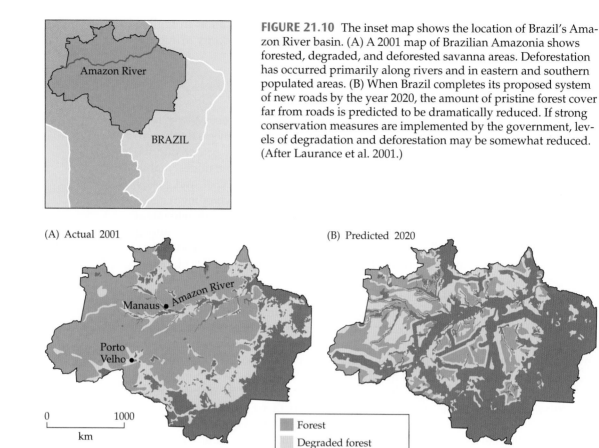

FIGURE 21.10 The inset map shows the location of Brazil's Amazon River basin. (A) A 2001 map of Brazilian Amazonia shows forested, degraded, and deforested savanna areas. Deforestation has occurred primarily along rivers and in eastern and southern populated areas. (B) When Brazil completes its proposed system of new roads by the year 2020, the amount of pristine forest cover far from roads is predicted to be dramatically reduced. If strong conservation measures are implemented by the government, levels of degradation and deforestation may be somewhat reduced. (After Laurance et al. 2001.)

(A) Actual 2001

(B) Predicted 2020

Forest

Degraded forest

Highly degraded forest and savanna

banks is just beginning and will double the amount of forest area accessible by road, greatly expanding the amount of new farmland for growing crops such as soybeans, but also increasing forest fragmentation, forest clearing, loss of biodiversity, and fires leading to the release of carbon dioxide (Soares-Filho et al. 2006; Malhi et al. 2008). The value of ecosystem services that the Amazon provides, both to Brazil and globally, needs to be compared with the value and jobs provided by soybean fields, low-level agriculture, or ranching. Current conservation efforts in the region emphasize protection of huge blocks of contiguous forest in a vast, but underfunded, network of protected areas and indigenous reserves and support of sustainable development outside of these areas. Additional approaches to promote poverty alleviation and development include addressing issues regarding land tenure that leads to migration into the Amazon, improving agriculture in existing cultivated lands, and promoting reforestation.

Another major class of projects financed by the international development banks is the construction of dams and irrigation systems. Dams can provide important benefits, including water for agricultural activities, flood control, and hydroelectric power. Generating hydroelectricity from dams means there is less need to build fossil fuel power plants that create air pollution and greenhouse gases. However, dams can also damage large aquatic ecosystems by changing water depth, temperature, flood regimes, and watershed patterns, thereby increasing sedimentation, eliminat-

FIGURE 21.11 The World Bank has funded the Nam Theun 2 Dam in Laos despite objections from many environmental groups, including the Worldwatch Institute, the Environmental Defense Fund, and International Rivers, regarding the negative impacts to biodiversity and people living along the river. (Photograph © Associated Press.)

ing habitat for many species, and creating barriers to animal dispersal (**Box 21.2**). In addition, the reservoirs behind the dams displace people who live in the areas that are flooded. Such people can become impoverished and/or forced to move to cities unless appropriate planning and long-term attention are provided. The World Bank's Involuntary Resettlement policy addresses this issue.

Large dam projects remain controversial. For example, the Nam Theun 2 Dam in Laos on a tributary of the Mekong River, funded by the World Bank, the Asian Development Bank, and various governments and other banks, will generate significant electrical power and income for Laos (**Figure 21.11**). However, the dam will flood 410 km^2 of river habitat, displace 6200 local people, and have unknown impacts downriver on ecosystems and approximately 100,000 people. The World Bank and the Laotian government have announced plans for new protected areas adjacent to the reservoir and programs for displaced people. However, international environmental groups, such as the Worldwatch Institute and the Environmental Defense Fund, point out the failures of past agreements made for similar dam projects, past broken promises made to local people, and the uncertainty of downstream impacts.

Reforming Development Lending

In order to act more responsibly, for the last 15 years the World Bank and other MDBs have added environmental and social requirements to the projects that they are financing (Mohamed and Al-Thukair 2009). The World Bank now requires new projects to be more environmentally responsible; they have hired ecological and environmental staff to review new and ongoing projects, conducted more thorough environmental analyses, and adopted a management policy that recognizes the linkages between economic development and environmental sustainability (World Bank 2006; Norlen and Gordon 2007). The World Bank incorporates biodiversity protection activities into its large projects, a practice they describe as "mainstreaming"

BOX 21.2   *How Much Will the Three Gorges Dam Really Cost?*

■ On paper, it sounds like a great idea: build a dam to control flooding, improve navigation, and provide clean hydroelectric power to millions of people (Cleveland and Black 2008; Stone 2008). The Yangtze River is one of the largest rivers in the world, running from the Tibetan plateau through China and emptying into the East China Sea. Flooding is a serious problem for the people living near the Yangtze: a series of floods in 1954 killed more than 30,000 people, and flooding in 1991 claimed at least another 3000 victims. The area is economically depressed, and per capita income is low. In 1992, the Chinese government gave final approval to build a dam downriver of the Three Gorges area of the Yangtze River in central China, with the aims of improving navigation, protecting approximately 10 million people from floods, and generating electricity for industrial development. The dam began generating electricity in 2003 and was mostly complete by 2009. It is estimated that the electricity generated by the dam will reduce coal consumption (the primary source of electricity in China) by 30–50 million tons each year, which will significantly reduce air pollution. This will also potentially reduce carbon dioxide emissions by 100 million tons annually. Slower currents and a more stable water flow will also potentially improve navigability for shipping.

But the costs of building the dam are high—by the time of its completion, the construction will have cost about US$30 billion. In addition to funding by Chinese banks, substantial support is coming from government-sponsored finance agencies such as Germany's Hermes Guarantee and

> International banks provided some funding for the Three Gorges Dam, a project that flooded 600 km of the Yangtze River valley, displaced 2 million people, and altered the ecology of a vast ecosystem. The project will provide needed electricity, flood control and improved navigation, but the environmental costs remain to be determined.

Japan's Export-Import Bank, with private banks such as Citigroup, Chase Manhattan Bank, Credit Suisse, First Boston, Merrill Lynch, Deutsche Bank, and Barclays Capital assisting with placing Chinese government bonds for the project. The long, narrow reservoir behind the dam will stretch across more than 600 km of the Yangtze Valley, from Yichang westward to Chongqing, one of China's largest cities. As the reservoir fills, it is flooding low-lying areas, necessitating the resettlement of entire villages, towns, and cities—eventually almost 2 million people in all (Cleveland 2008). About a million of these people are being moved uphill from their former locations. However, those uphill sites that

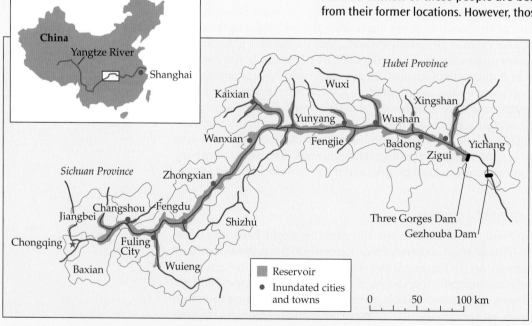

The Three Gorges Dam is flooding a 600 km stretch of the Yangtze River Valley in central China. Because the terrain comprises gorges, ravines, and mountain slopes, the resulting reservoir will be narrow and deep. (After Chau 1995.)

BOX 21.2 *(continued)*

are not already in use are typically steep, are thinly covered with infertile soil, and lack sufficient water for agriculture. It is estimated that five times the present farmland will be needed to yield the same amount of food. As steep hillsides are deforested, erosion will accelerate, increasing the buildup of silt behind the dam and the likelihood of dangerous landslides. Temples, pagodas, and other important cultural sites are being submerged by up to 175 m of water. The Yangtze River basin also contains a freshwater fishery that provides two-thirds of the country's catch and agricultural lands that yield 40% of the country's crops—much of which will be affected, probably negatively, by the dam (Xie et al. 2007).

The waters of the Yangtze River have already submerged many of the fields in this area and will continue up these steep slopes, almost reaching the houses. The village shown in this photograph is a new village, built to replace an old one across the river that is now almost underwater. (Photograph © Tina Manley/Alamy.)

The dam's effect on natural communities and the environment is likely to be profound and detrimental. Dams block the movement of nutrients downriver, slow water flow, decrease variations in the water level, and allow sediments to build up (Yang et al. 2007). Slower currents decrease oxygen levels and decrease the ability of the river to flush out pollutants. As the hydrology changes, so will the composition of the plant and animal communities (Xie et al. 2007; Cleveland and Black 2008). With the construction of the Three Gorges Dam, the rare Chinese sturgeon (*Acipenser sinensis*) probably will be unable to swim up the Yangtze River to spawn.

Some of these concerns have been addressed by the dam's planners (Stone 2008). Little is known, however, about how suitable marginal lands are for farming, how fast silt will build up behind the dam, or how endangered species

in the drainage basin will adapt to the altered hydrology. Perhaps the best emblem of the Three Gorges Dam is the endangered Siberian crane (*Grus leucogeranus*), symbolic of well-being among the Chinese, that feeds in shallow waters along the Yangtze River basin. Changing water levels may affect its survival—and the prosperity of the Chinese people as well. In coming years, we will be better able to determine whether the clear benefits of the dam, in terms of electric power, flood control, and navigation, are balanced by the cost of construction, its environmental impacts, and the social disruption it will cause.

(Quintero 2007). As a result, many environmental NGOs now want the MDBs involved in lending so that environmental and social assessments are required. Otherwise, countries and the private sector have few requirements for environmental standards and there is little or no project monitoring. Additionally, the MDBs recognize the need for open public discussions from all interested parties before projects are implemented (Rosenberg and Korsmo 2001). They have moved in this direction by allowing public examination, independent evaluations, and discussion of environmental impact reports by local organizations that will be affected by projects being considered for funding (WRI 2003). However, many conservation organizations and independent observers remain skeptical that the World Bank will apply this policy of open review to the bulk of its investments.

Careful scrutiny of actions of the World Bank and related MDBs in the future is required, particularly the lending done by the affiliated International Finance Corporation and especially the import-export banks, which lend to the private sector. Conservation organizations, the media, and the public must continue to monitor the funding decisions of the MDBs—made by representatives of the ministries of finance of the donor and recipient countries—and particpate in discussions if necessary before the decisions are made. The World Bank and other banks have Web-based public information centers in which information on pending projects can be found. Conservation groups should also seek to engage with MDB teams in the field. It should also be noted that the MDBs have no enforcement authority: Once a country receives funds for a project, it can violate the environmental provisions in the legal agreements, despite local and international protests. In such instances, one of the MDBs' few effective options is to cancel further stages of funding for these projects and delay new projects.

> The World Bank and related development banks fund large projects in developing countries, many of which have created environmental damage. New projects are now reviewed and monitored for social and environmental impacts.

One important project to watch is the mammoth Hidrovia Project in South America, in which the Paraguay–Parana river system is being dredged and channeled so that large ships can carry cargo from Buenos Aires on the Argentine coast 3400 km north into Bolivia, Paraguay, and Brazil and then return carrying soybeans and other agricultural products from southern Brazil to world markets (Desbiez et al. 2009; Zeilhofera and de Mourab 2009). This river system drains the Pantanal in South America, the world's largest wetland, covering 140,000 km^2 in southwestern Brazil, eastern Bolivia, and northeastern Paraguay—an area larger than England, Wales, and the Netherlands combined (**Figure 21.12**). The wetland consists of vast, unspoiled everglades fabulously rich in endangered wildlife such as jaguars, tapirs, maned wolves, and giant otters. Environmentalists believe the Hidrovia Project will

FIGURE 21.12 The Pantanal in South America is the world's largest wetland, with an exceptional diversity and abundance of plant and aquatic life. This area is now being transformed by an enormous project involving improved river transportation, industrial development, and the expansion of soybean agriculture. (Photograph © Malcolm Schuyl/ Alamy.)

completely alter the hydrology of the area—submerging some areas, drying out others—and lead to an enormous loss of biological diversity (Baigún et al. 2008; Desbiez et al. 2009). In Argentina, unprecedented flooding downriver could result, though maintenance of wetlands could minimize some of the adverse impacts. The final cost of the project is estimated to be $1 billion, with $3 billion in added maintenance costs over the next 25 years. As part of the total project, a natural gas pipeline from Bolivia to the coast of Brazil is currently being constructed, along with associated steel and petrochemical plants, with unknown environmental consequences to the region. Funding, publicity, and opposition to the project all go through cycles—the project moves forward, is stalled for a time, then starts again in a somewhat different form. On the positive side, the World Bank and conservation NGOs have been establishing Biosphere Reserves and new national parks in the area to protect some of the region's rich biodiversity (WWF and McGinley 2007b).

The MDBs have shown some commitment to reducing environmental degradation. For example, in Papua New Guinea, the World Bank refused to provide development loans until the government carried out a number of measures that would ensure more prudent forest management practices, which led to a full review of forestry practices and a subsequent moratorium on opening additional areas for logging. Unfortunately, another trend is for the World Bank and the MDBs to finance "clean" projects that can be publicly justified on environmental and social grounds, while the far larger import-export banks quietly support the huge projects that damage the environment and benefit large corporations. Given that the MDBs have funded some dubious projects, a vital role for conservation biologists is to track and report the actual environmental impacts. This will help ensure that the countries' implementing agencies and their financial backers pursue an environmentally responsible path both within the project concerned and within their broader strategies in the future.

Funding Sources and Programs

Over the last 20 years, the World Bank has emerged as a leading source of conservation funding. About 8% of the World Bank's recent investments are for environmental projects, with a major focus on pollution abatement and control, but its investments also include funding for biodiversity conservation, forest management, and the conservation of natural resources. From 1988 to 2008, the World Bank provided grants and loans totaling about $6 billion to support almost 500 biodiversity projects (**Figure 21.13**) (www.worldbank.org). The World Bank is currently sup-

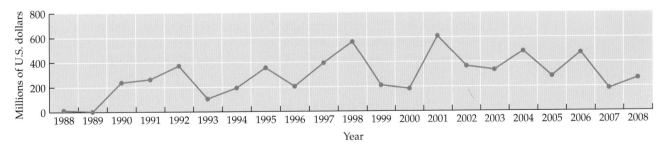

FIGURE 21.13 World Bank funding for biodiversity projects on an annual basis for the period 1988 to 2008. Annual fluctuations in funding are caused by the tendency to bunch large projects together. The total funding is $6 billion, of which 32% is loans, 23% is grants, and 45% is cofinancing from other sources. (After www.worldbank.org.)

porting conservation projects in 105 countries, as well as 39 multi-country regional programs. In the process, the World Bank has emerged as one of the largest sources of funding for international conservation efforts.

Much of the World Bank's investment involves joint financing with other sources, often national governments. Activities funded by the World Bank include establishing protected areas, protecting endangered species, restoring degraded habitats, training conservation staff, developing conservation infrastructure, addressing global climate change, managing and protecting forests, and managing freshwater and marine resources. In addition, the World Bank provides independent funding to many conservation organizations that carry out such projects. A recent trend is toward funding a larger number of smaller projects, which often have more specific goals and are managed on a local level.

The scale of World Bank activities is illustrated by its joint Forest Alliance program with the World Wildlife Fund, which has already established 47 million ha of newly protected forest. Upcoming goals include establishing 25 million more ha of protected forest and instituting effective management for an additional 70 million ha of forest that is currently protected (www.worldwildlife.org/alliance). The management of a further 300 million ha of forest will be improved through a combination of forest certification of good practices, forest restoration, and community forestry. The World Bank is also one of the leaders in efforts to reduce carbon dioxide emissions caused by deforestation in tropical countries such as Indonesia. Through its Forest Carbon Partnership Facility, companies and developed countries are able to offset their present production of greenhouse gases by purchasing carbon credits for maintaining these tropical forests. The World Bank has also partnered with the World Wildlife Fund and other large NGOs in implementing such programs.

Another major source of funds for the protection of biodiversity is the **Global Environment Facility** (**GEF**). The GEF was created in 1991 to fund the goals of the Convention on Biological Diversity and is based in Washington, D.C. (www.thegef.org/gef). It does not carry out projects itself but rather has a number of implementing agencies that manage its projects, such as the World Bank, United Nations Development Programme (UNDP), UNEP, and regional development banks. The GEF has provided funding of over \$8.6 billion for more than 2400 projects in 165 countries, making it, along with the World Bank, one of the largest sources of conservation funding. Many of these projects involve the conservation of biodiversity and the development of renewable energy sources as a way to reduce greenhouse gas emissions. Using funds from the GEF, the World Bank, MacArthur Foundation, and the Japanese government, the NGO Conservation International manages the Critical Ecosystem Partnership Fund to undertake conservation projects in biodiversity hotspots (www.cepf.net). Both the World Bank and the GEF have extensive Web sites that list and describe the individual projects that they fund and provide overviews of their programs. The GEF also provides reports that evaluate their past projects. One GEF report concluded that their funding was probably a contributing factor in recent additions to the global system of protected areas, but their level of funding was not sufficient to influence global carbon emissions.

National Environmental Funds

In addition to direct grants and loans for projects, another important mechanism used to provide secure, long-term support for conservation activities in developing countries is the **national environmental fund** (**NEF**). NEFs are typically set up as conservation trust funds or foundations in which a board of trustees—composed of representatives of the host government, conservation organizations, and donor agencies—allocates the annual income from an endowment to support inadequately funded government departments and nongovernment conservation organizations and activities. NEFs have been established in over 50 developing countries with funds contributed by developed countries and by major organizations such as the World Bank, the Global Environment Facility, and the World Wildlife Fund.

One important early example of an NEF, the Bhutan Trust Fund for Environmental Conservation (BTF), was established in 1991 by the government of Bhutan in cooperation with the World Bank and the World Wildlife Fund. The BTF has already received about $26 million (exceeding its goal of $20 million). The fund provides $1 million per year for surveying the rich biological resources of this eastern Himalayan country; training foresters, ecologists, and other environmental professionals; promoting environmental education; establishing and managing protected areas; and designing and implementing integrated conservation development projects.

NEFs have proliferated in recent years, with the Latin American and Caribbean Network of Environmental Funds (RedLAC) alone comprising 13 countries and over 3000 projects supported by an annual budget of over $70 million (www.redlac.org).

Debt-for-Nature Swaps

Many countries in the developing world have accumulated huge international debts that they are unable to repay. As a result, some developing countries have rescheduled their loan payments, unilaterally reduced them, or stopped making them altogether. Because of the low expectation of repayment, the commercial banks that hold these debts are selling the debts at a steep discount on the international secondary debt market. For example, Costa Rican debt has traded for only 14% to 18% of its face value.

In a creative approach, debt from the developing world is used as a vehicle for financing projects to protect biological diversity, so-called **debt-for-nature swaps** (Greiner and Lankester 2007). In one common type of debt-for-nature swap, an NGO in the developed world (such as Conservation International) buys up the debts of a developing country; the NGO agrees to forgive the debt in exchange for the country's carrying out a conservation activity. This activity could involve land acquisition for conservation purposes, park management, development of park facilities, conservation education, or sustainable development projects.

> The World Bank and the Global Environment Facility currently fund and manage hundreds of environmental and sustainable development programs. National environmental funds and debt-for-nature swaps provide additional mechanisms for funding conservation activities.

Costa Rica has taken the lead in debt swaps. In the 1980s and early 1990s, outside conservation organizations spent $12 million to purchase over $79 million of Costa Rican debt, which was then exchanged for nearly $43 million in bonds for use in conservation activities at La Amistad Biosphere Reserve, Braulio Carillo National Park, Corcovado National Park, Guanacaste National Park, Tortuguero National Park, and Monteverde Cloud Forest, a private reserve (Sheikh 2004). The interest on the bonds was used to establish a fund administered by the Costa Rican government and several local NGOs, including the Costa Rican National Parks Foundation.

In another type of swap, a government of a developed country that is owed money directly by a developing country may decide to cancel a certain percentage of the debt if the developing country will agree to contribute to a national environmental fund or to some other conservation activity. Such programs have converted debt valued at $1.5 billion into conservation and sustainable development activities in Colombia, Poland, the Philippines, Madagascar, and a dozen other countries. Debt swaps are being incorporated into major U.S. foreign assistance programs such as the Enterprise for the Americas and the Tropical Forest Conservation Act. As one example, the U.S. government agreed to forgive $26 million in Costa Rican debt in exchange for the Costa Rican government's undertaking forest conservation programs (www.nature.org).

While debt-for-nature swaps have great potential advantages, they present a number of potential limitations to both the donor and the recipient (Ferraro and Simpson 2006). Debt swaps will not change the underlying problems associated with poverty and mismanagement if these are the causes of environmental degradation. Also, spending money on conservation programs might divert money from other necessary domestic programs such as medical care, schools, and agricultural development.

Marine Environments

Innovative funding programs such as NEFs and debt-for-nature swaps are particularly needed for marine protected areas, which have lagged behind terrestrial protected areas in conservation efforts. The ease with which the marine environment can be polluted, the high value of seashore real estate, and the open access to marine resources mean that such protected areas will require special attention. Establishing low-impact ecotourism facilities and setting up restricted fishing zones are among the types of activities being funded. Funding for marine conservation from the World Bank, conservation foundations, and government sources has greatly increased during the past decade and remains a high priority. For example, The Nature Conservancy is currently increasing its leasing and ownership of submerged ocean and coastal areas and resources and has already acquired over 25,000 acres in 22 countries.

How Effective Is Conservation Funding?

Conservation organizations have developed a number of tools to evaluate the effectiveness of funded projects (Kapos et al. 2008; Leverington et al. 2008). Evaluations of the GEF provide one such example: the World Bank has judged the GEF projects funded so far to be a mixture of positives and negatives (see various reports at www.thegef.org/gef). On the positive side, the GEF provided increased funding for conservation and biodiversity projects, reviewed biodiversity-related legislation, transferred conservation information, planned national biodiversity strategies, identified and protected important ecosystems and habitats, and enhanced the capacity to carry out biodiversity projects. However, the lack of participation by community groups, local scientists, and government leaders; an overreliance on foreign consultants; an elaborate and time-consuming application procedure; and a lack of understanding of GEF objectives by people in the recipient countries were identified as major problems. An additional problem was the mismatch of funding over short periods with the long-term needs of poor countries.

Many of these problems apply to international conservation funding more broadly: a major shortcoming is that only a small fraction of available support ends up paying for what is arguably the foundation for conservation efforts worldwide—actual management of protected areas. Grant money is diverted for salaries, infrastructure, and overhead at administrative headquarters. Indeed, in countries from Peru to Ghana, even during periods of significant donor support, protected areas may still find themselves without funding to buy gas for vehicles, pay staff salaries, and meet other basic needs.

It must be recognized that many environmental projects supported by international aid do not provide lasting solutions to the problems, because of failure to deal with the "4 Cs"—concern, contracts, capacity, and causes. Environmental aid will be effective only when applied to situations in which both donors and recipients have a genuine *concern* to solve the problems (Do key people really want the project to be successful, or do they just want the money?); when mutually satisfactory and enforceable *contracts* for the project can be agreed on (Will the work actually be done once the money is given out? Will money be siphoned off into private hands?);

where there is the *capacity* to undertake the project in terms of institutions, personnel, and infrastructure (Do people have the skills to do the work, and do they have the necessary resources, such as vehicles, research equipment, buildings, and access to information, to carry out the work?); and when the *causes* of the problem are addressed (Will the project treat the underlying causes of the problem or just provide temporary relief of the symptoms?). Despite these problems, international funding of conservation projects continues. Past experiences are informing new projects, which are more effective, but with the result that the application and accounting processes can be extremely cumbersome and time-consuming.

Increased Funding Is Necessary for the Future

The need for increased funding for biodiversity remains great at the local, national, and international levels. At present, about $6 billion is spent each year on budgets for terrestrial protected areas, yet it would take $13 billion to expand and effectively manage systems protecting terrestrial biological diversity in the tropics alone (Brooks et al. 2009). Simply managing the existing protected areas in developing countries would cost perhaps $2.1 billion, approximately three times the current expenditure (Bruner et al. 2004). While $13 billion is an enormous amount of money, it is comparable to the $16 billion spent annually just on agricultural subsidies in the United States, and it is dwarfed by the whopping $1 trillion spent on U.S. military defense in 2010 (**Figure 21.14**). Similarly, while the conservation funds provided by the World Bank seem large, they are small compared with the other activities supported by the World Bank and related organizations. Certainly the world's priorities could be modestly adjusted to give more resources to the protection of biological diversity (Bottrill et al. 2009). Instead of countries rushing forward in a race to supply themselves with the next generation of fighter aircraft, missiles, and other weapons systems, what about spending what it takes to protect biological diversity? Instead of the world's affluent consumers buying the latest round of consumer luxuries and electronic gadgets to re-

> While the recent increased funding for the protection of biodiversity is welcome, further funding is needed to accomplish the task.

(A) Huge amounts of money are spent on military defense

(B) Far less money is spent on biodiversity conservation

FIGURE 21.14 (A) Countries spend huge amounts of money on military defense and agricultural subsidies. (B) Far less money is spent on biodiversity conservation and environmental protection. (A, photograph courtesy of Micah P. Blechner/U.S. Navy; B, photograph © Steve Bloom Images/Alamy.)

place things that still work, what about contributing more money to conservation organizations and causes?

There is also a role to be played by conservation organizations and businesses working together to market "green products." Already the Forest Stewardship Council and similar organizations are certifying wood products from sustainably managed forests, and coffee companies are marketing shade-grown coffee. If consumers are educated to buy these products at a somewhat higher price, this could be a strong force in international conservation efforts.

Finally, a potentially huge new funding source to protect tropical forests is being adopted as part of the 2009 Copenhagen accords. Because about 20% of global greenhouse gas emission results from tropical forest destruction, a funding mechanism called **REDD—Reducing Emissions from Deforestation and Forest Degradation—** could pay to protect tropical forests (Gullison et al. 2007). REDD would reward poorer nations for preserving forests by paying them for the carbon that is stored in their forests. There are huge concerns about whether this money will be well spent in protecting forests and reducing poverty in developing countries, or whether it will be diverted to other purposes or cause worse deforestation in other places. Organizations at all scales will be involved in designing, implementing, and monitoring what happens as REDD becomes a reality.

Summary

1. International agreements and conventions that protect biological diversity are needed for the following reasons: species migrate across borders, there is an international trade in biological products, the benefits of biological diversity are of international importance, and the threats to diversity are often international in scope and require international cooperation. The Convention on International Trade in Endangered Species (CITES) regulates and monitors trade in individuals and products from endangered species of plants and animals; in some cases, all trade is prohibited. Other international agreements protect habitat, such as the Ramsar Convention on Wetlands, the World Heritage Convention, and the UNESCO Biosphere Reserves Program.

2. Major environmental agreements include the Convention on Biological Diversity, which gives countries the rights to profit from biological diversity within their borders but the responsibility to protect it, and the UN Framework Convention on Climate Change, which establishes targets for stabilizing and reducing emissions of CO_2 and other greenhouse gases. Climate change, park management, and the rights of local people have been the subject of further international agreements and meetings.

3. Major new development projects approved by multilateral development banks, such as the World Bank and the closely associated Global Environment Facility, now include reviews and funding to address environmental and social issues. Because of the huge impact of World Bank funding, and because of past problems with some of their projects, environmental groups are closely monitoring their activities.

4. The World Bank, the Global Environmental Facility, and governments in developed countries are providing substantial funding to protect biological diversity in developing countries. While the increased levels of international funding are welcome, the amount of money is still not sufficient to deal with the loss of biological diversity that is taking place. Many international conservation projects are being carried out by nongovernmental conservation organizations.

5. Innovative approaches are being developed to finance the preservation of biodiversity. One approach involves setting up national environmental funds (NEFs) in which

the annual income from endowments is used to finance conservation activities. A second approach involves debt-for-nature swaps, in which the foreign debt obligations of a government are canceled in exchange for the government's providing increased conservation funding.

For Discussion

1. Imagine that Brazil, Indonesia, China, or India builds an expensive dam to provide electricity and water for irrigation. It will take decades to pay back the costs of construction and lost ecosystem services—or those costs may never be paid back. Who are the winners with such a project, and who are the losers? Consider the local people who had to move, newly arrived settlers, construction companies, timber companies, local banks, international banks, the urban poor, government leaders, environmental organizations, and anyone else that you think will be affected. Consider also the animals and plants that lived in the watershed before the dam was built. Can they survive in the same region? Can they migrate to another place?

2. Which is a more important cause of biodiversity loss, consumption in developed countries or poverty in developing countries? Are poverty and the conservation of biological diversity linked, and if so, how? Should these problems be attacked together or separately?

3. How do national governments decide on an acceptable amount of money to spend on protecting biological diversity? How much money should a particular country spend on protecting biological diversity? Can you calculate an amount? What are the most cost-effective measures governments can take to protect biological diversity?

4. Suppose a species was discovered in Peru that could potentially cure a major disease affecting millions of people if it were grown on a large scale in cultivation and then widely marketed. If the government of Peru did not show interest in protecting this wonderful species, what could the international community do to protect the species and to fairly compensate the country for doing so? Come up with a variety of offers, suggestions, or alternatives that could be used to convince the government and people of Peru to protect the species and to become involved in its commercial development.

5. Do you think that the purchase of "green" (environmentally responsible) products is an effective way to promote the conservation of biodiversity? Would people be willing to spend more money for wood, coffee, and other products that have been produced in a sustainable manner, and if so, how much more? How could you determine whether the purchase of such products was really making a difference?

Suggested Readings

Botrill, M. C. and 13 others. 2009. Finite conservation funds mean triage is unavoidable. *Trends in Ecology and Evolution* 24: 183–184. Because conservation funding is currently inadequate, managers must establish clear priorities for conservation.

Bruner, A. G., R. E. Gullison, and A. Balmford. 2004. Financial costs and shortfalls of managing and expanding protected-area systems in developing countries. *BioScience* 54: 1119–1126. Budgets for managing protected areas in developing countries are inadequate and need to be increased.

Gullison, R. E. and 10 others. 2007. Tropical forests and climate policy. *Science* 316: 985–986. Protecting tropical forests is needed to stabilize carbon dioxide levels and reduce global warming.

Kapos, V., A. Balmford, R. Aveling, P. Bubb, P. Carey, A. Entwistle, et al. 2008. Calibrating conservation: New tools for measuring success. *Conservation Letters* 1: 155–164. A methodology for evaluating whether conservation projects have achieved their goals.

Kothamasi, D. and E. T. Kiers. 2009. Emerging conflicts between biodiversity conservation laws and scientific research: The case of the Czech entomologists in India. *Conservation Biology* 23: 1328–1330. The conflict between scientific research and government regulations is illustrated by two Czech entomologists arrested for collecting butterflies.

Martín-López, B., C. Montes, L. Ramirez, and J. Benayas. 2009. What drives policy decision-making related to species conservation? *Biological Conservation* 142: 1370–1380. Policy is closely linked to scientific research, funding, and public perception.

Naughton-Treves, L., M. B. Holland, and K. Brandon. 2005. The role of protected areas in conserving biodiversity and sustaining local livelihoods. *Annual Review of Environmental Resources* 30: 219–252. Discussion of a major controversy: Should protected areas exist for biodiversity or for the benefit of people?

Rosen, T. and A. Bath. 2009. Transboundary management of large carnivores in Europe: From incident to opportunity. *Conservation Letters* 2: 109–114. The social context of reintroductions and management of large carnivores must be considered.

Soares-Filho, B. S. and 9 others. 2006. Modelling conservation in the Amazon basin. *Nature* 440: 520–523. The rapid expansion of highways and agriculture will eliminate 40% of the Amazon basin's forests by the year 2050.

Stem, C., R. Margoluis, N. Salafsky, and M. Brown. 2005. Monitoring and evaluation in conservation: A review of trends and approaches. *Conservation Biology* 19: 295–309. Conservation organizations would benefit from cooperating in project evaluations to see what works best.

Stone, R. 2008. China's environmental challenges: Three Gorges Dam: Into the unknown. *Science* 321: 628–632. The dam is engineering on an enormous scale, but its environmental impacts are still uncertain.

Wasser, S. K., B. Clark, and C. Laurie. 2009. The ivory trail. *Scientific American* 301: 68–76. DNA technology is being used to track the country of origin of illegal ivory.

World Bank. 2006. *Mountains to Coral Reefs: The World Bank and Biodiversity 1988–2005.* World Bank, Washington, D.C. An official statement of the World Bank's efforts on behalf of the environment; see earlier reports and related documents.

Zavaleta, E., D. C. Miller, N. Salafsky, E. Fleishman, M. Webster, B. Gold, et al. 2008. Enhancing the engagement of the U.S. private foundations with conservation science. *Conservation Biology* 22: 1477–1484. Private foundations have emerged as an important alternate source of conservation funding.

Chapter 22

An Agenda for the Future

As we have seen throughout this book, the causes of the rapid, worldwide decline in biological diversity are no mystery. Biological communities are destroyed and species are driven to extinction because of human resource use, which is propelled by the need of poor people to survive, by the excessive consumption of resources by affluent people and countries, and by the desire to make money (Sachs 2008). The destruction may be caused by local people in the region, people recently arrived from outside the region, local business interests, large businesses in urban centers, suburban sprawl into rural areas, multinational corporations in other countries, military conflicts, or governments. People may also be unaware of or apathetic toward the impact of human activities on the natural world.

In order for conservation policies to work, people at all levels of society must see that it is in their own interest to work for conservation (Charnley 2006). If conservationists can demonstrate that the protection of biological diversity has more value than its destruction, people and their governments will be more willing to preserve biological diversity. This assessment should include not only immediate monetary value but also less tangible aspects, including existence value, option value, and intrinsic value.

Ongoing Problems and Possible Solutions

There is a consensus among conservation biologists that there are several major problems involved in preserving biological diversity and that certain changes in policies and practices are needed (Sutherland et al. 2009, 2010). We list these problems, and suggested solutions, below. Note that, for the purposes of this text, the responses are simplified; they leave out many of the intricacies that would need to be addressed to provide comprehensive, real-world answers to these problems.

Problem: Protecting biological diversity is difficult when most of the world's species remain undescribed by scientists and are not known by the general public. Furthermore, most biological communities are not being monitored to determine how they are changing over time.

Solution: More scientists and enthusiastic nonscientists need to be trained to identify, classify, and monitor species and biological communities, and funding should be increased in this area (Cohn 2008). There is a particular need for training more scientists and establishing research institutes in developing countries. Enthusiastic nonscientists often can play an important role in protecting and monitoring biodiversity once they are given some training and guidance by scientists (Low et al. 2009; Sullivan et al. 2009). People interested in conservation biology should be taught basic skills, such as species identification and environmental monitoring techniques, and such people will often join and support local, national, and international conservation organizations (**Box 22.1**). Conservation education targeting particular audiences, such as schoolchildren or senior citizens, with specific information can help promote conservation-oriented behaviors (Jacobson et al. 2006). Information on biological diversity must be made more accessible; this may be accomplished in part through the new Encyclopedia of Life (www.eol.org) and Tree of Life Web Project (tolweb.org), which serve as central clearinghouses for data.

Problem: Many conservation issues are global in scope and involve many countries.

Solution: Countries are increasingly willing to discuss international conservation issues, as shown by the 2009 climate change conference in Copenhagen. Nations are also more willing to sign and implement treaties such as the Convention on Biological Diversity, the United Nations Framework Convention on Climate Change, and the Convention on International Trade in Endangered Species. International conservation efforts are expanding, and further participation in these activities by conservation biologists and the general public should be encouraged. One positive development is the trend toward establishing transfrontier parks that straddle borders; these parks are good for wildlife and encourage cooperation between countries. Citizens and governments of developed countries must also become aware that they bear a direct responsibility for the destruction of biological diversity through their overconsumption of the world's resources and the specific products that they purchase (**Figure 22.1**). Conservation professionals need to demonstrate how changes in the actions and lifestyles of individuals on the local level can have a positive influence far beyond their immediate community.

Problem: Developing countries often want to protect their biological diversity but are under pressure to develop their natural resources.

Solution: Conservation organizations, zoos, aquariums, botanical gardens, and governments in developed countries and international organizations such as the United Nations and the World Bank should continue to provide technical and financial support to developing countries for conservation activities, in particular establishing and maintaining national parks and other protected areas. It is also important that they support the training of conservation biologists in developing countries

BOX 22.1   *Conservation Education: Shaping the Next Generation into Conservationists*

■ Television, newspapers, and the Internet are filled with high-profile information regarding the importance of protecting the Earth on a daily basis, yet most people know relatively little about conservation. One of the best ways to educate people about conservation is to involve them in local conservation projects. Such efforts involving direct outreach to ordinary citizens require creativity and attention to popular concerns, yet sometimes they can be very successful (Jacobson 2006). A common feature of many of these projects is the involvement of scientists with groups of citizens in fieldwork. Another rapidly expanding feature is the use of Websites that allow citizens to enter their data online and to track the results of the project.

Many of these citizen science conservation projects involve birds. Project Feeder-Watch (www.birds.cornell.edu/pfw) is a Cornell Lab of Ornithology and Bird Studies Canada initiative that recruits people for annual winter surveys of bird populations at their feeders. Another venture de-

---

Conservation biologists can spread the conservation message and do better science by educating the public and including them in projects. These citizens then often become advocates for protecting biodiversity.

---

veloped by Cornell and the National Audubon Society is eBird (www.ebird.org), a database on bird presence and abundance as observed by bird-watchers throughout North America (Sullivan et al. 2009). Finally, Journey North (www.learner.org/jnorth) is a global study of migration and seasonal change that is geared toward student observations of migration patterns, plant flowering times, and other natural events that signal the change of seasons. For example, using this site, students can enter data online about when they see the first ruby-throated hummingbird and monarch butterfly in the spring, and then they can see maps of dates of first appearance across North America.

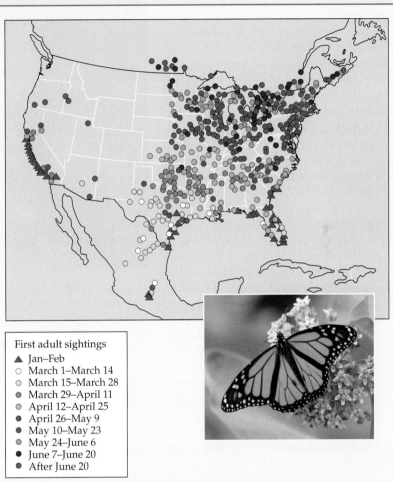

First adult sightings
- ▲ Jan–Feb
- ○ March 1–March 14
- ○ March 15–March 28
- ◔ March 29–April 11
- ◑ April 12–April 25
- ◕ April 26–May 9
- ● May 10–May 23
- ◕ May 24–June 6
- ● June 7–June 20
- ● After June 20

Each spring, thousands of citizen observers, especially students, contribute their observations to the Journey North website. This map presents the observations of the first appearance of monarch butterflies across North America in the spring of 2009. The butterflies primarily overwinter in central Mexico and start migrating into southern United States in March, arriving in northern United States and southern Canada in late May and June. There are secondary overwintering sites in California, Florida, and Texas. (After www.learner.org/jnorth; butterfly photograph by David McIntyre.)

Certain case studies provide examples of how community-based programs can dramatically improve awareness and influence conservation efforts. For example, community residents in the Gulf of Saint Lawrence have traditionally lived by fishing and collecting seabird eggs for food. Unfortunately for the endangered birds in the area, community residents continued to feast on bird eggs even though it was no longer a necessary food source. As a result of human predation, seabird populations were in steep decline (Blanchard 2005). Between 1955 and 1978, populations of the Atlantic puffin

(continued)

BOX 22.1 *(continued)*

decreased from about 62,000 individuals to about 15,000.

The Quebec–Labrador Foundation, working with the Canadian Wildlife Service in their quest to save endangered seabirds, decided that the best way to save the seabirds was to convince the public to stop consuming birds and their eggs. Their plan included education programs for children, who participated in clubs and theater productions that addressed the plight of the seabirds. Children aged 8 to 17 spent 5 days at Cape Saint Mary Ecological Reserve learning to appreciate seabirds through interactive activities. These children were crucial in convincing their parents to protect birds, reaching out to adults by performing a play about the importance of conservation. The foundation also turned to the media in its education program, producing television specials and making posters and calendars. The Canadian Wildlife Service contributed by hiring local townspeople to work in the seabird conservation program. Within a few years, this program was successful in changing attitudes about seabird conservation. While 54% of locals supported hunting the Atlantic puffin in 1981, this number dropped to 27% as early as 1988. Partly because of reduced hunting and egg collecting, the population of Atlantic puffins in the Gulf of Saint Lawrence more than doubled from 1977 to 1988 and has since returned to its original size (Savenkoff et al. 2004).

Another waterbird, the West Indian whistling-duck, is an example of how a species can become a flagship for wetlands conservation. These ducks have become rare in their native Caribbean island habitats because of combined effects of wetland habitat loss, overhunting, and predation by introduced rats and mongooses (Sorenson et al. 2004). Because wetlands have long been regarded as marginal land to be filled in and developed, conservationists with the Society for the Conservation and Study of Caribbean Birds (www.scscb.org) recognized that the first step to saving this species was changing perceptions of the duck's habitat. With support from local and international NGOs and the U.S. Fish and Wildlife Service, a regionwide public education and awareness program was developed to train local teachers and educators to raise awareness of and appreciation for the value of local wetlands. The project developed and distributed a teacher's manual called *The Wondrous West Indian Wetlands: Teachers' Resource Book* that contains com-

Bahamian schoolteachers try out a plant sampling technique during the wetlands field trip portion of a wetlands education training workshop. (Photograph courtesy of Lisa Sorenson, West Indies Whistling-Duck and Wetlands Conservation Project.)

prehensive information and educational activities relating to the ecology and conservation of Caribbean wetlands. Companion materials include a slide show, puppet show, poster, coloring book, conservation buttons, postcard, wetland field trip notebook, mangrove identification booklet, and wetland and seabird identification cards. These materials provide teachers with the essential tools needed to incorporate conservation themes into their classrooms and reach an enormous number of schoolchildren and their parents. One teacher's comment conveys the reaction of many: "Prior to the workshop I viewed wetlands as murky, stagnant, mosquito-infested areas to be avoided. Now I am fully aware of their importance to the environment." The educational materials and associated workshops have helped to raise the profile of the whistling-duck, which now has increased species and habitat protection in many Caribbean islands. The duck has responded well; populations on most islands are now stable or increasing. The whistling-duck has even extended its breeding range to the island of Guadeloupe, which is exciting news from a conservation standpoint.

To implement conservation education within schools, a variety of approaches are available, such as environment-based education, service learning, and action projects (Jacobson 2006). The Global Rivers Environmental Education Network (GREEN) exemplifies an effective action project that

BOX 22.1 *(continued)*

demonstrates the importance of a practical, hands-on approach. This program has allowed children in over 60 countries to learn about evaluating water quality and to help protect local water reserves. GREEN began when students at Huron High School in Michigan contracted hepatitis A after participating in water sports in the Huron River. To investigate the source of the disease, students tested the river water and found large amounts of fecal coliform bacteria that indicate the presence of untreated sewage. The city identified defective storm drains as the cause of the problem, and these were subsequently repaired.

Many other schools enthusiastically adopted this program, eventually expanding GREEN into a global environmental network in which parents and teachers are connected through the Internet (Earth Force 2010). Through the

GREEN Website (www.earthforce.org/section/programs/green), teachers can access resources for water quality research, and schools can post data they have collected from local watersheds. The program urges students to think critically about the possible causes of water pollution and to take action by urging the community and the government to stop pollution (Hamann and Drossman 2006; Earth Force 2010). GREEN not only teaches children about science but also shapes a new generation of children into activists.

Public education programs such as those described here have proven to be effective in teaching children and adults about science and encouraging people to protect environmental resources. All such programs would greatly benefit from increased participation from conservation biologists.

so that they can become advocates for biodiversity within their own countries (Wrangham and Ross 2008). This support should continue until countries are able to protect biodiversity with their own resources and personnel. This is fair and reasonable since developed countries have the funds to support these parks and because they will make use of the protected biological resources in their agriculture, industry, research programs, zoos, aquariums, botanical gardens, and educational systems. Economic and social problems in developing countries must be addressed at the same time, particularly those relating to reducing poverty and ending armed conflicts. A variety of financial mechanisms exist to achieve these goals, including direct grants, payments for ecosystem services, debt-for-nature swaps, and trust funds. Individ-

FIGURE 22.1 The lifestyle of people in developed countries affects the natural world. For example, driving automobiles contributes to global warming through the production of carbon dioxide. The resources used to make and operate automobiles impact the environment as well. (Photograph © Tim Graham / Alamy.)

ual citizens in developed countries can donate money and participate in organizations and programs that further advance these conservation goals.

Problem: Economic analyses often paint a falsely encouraging picture of development projects that are environmentally damaging. Ecosystem services are often not assigned value in economic decision making.

Solution: Development projects must be evaluated using comprehensive cost-benefit analyses that compare potential project benefits with environmental and human costs such as soil erosion, pollution, deterioration of water quality, loss of natural products and other ecosystem services, and loss of places for people to live.

> Conservation biologists need to develop approaches that provide benefits for people and protect biological diversity. A new approach is to compensate landowners and local people for the ecosystem services that their land provides.

Local communities and the general public should be presented with all available information and asked to provide input into the decision process. The "polluter pays" principle, in which industries, governments, and individual citizens pay for cleaning up the environmental damage their activities have caused, must be adopted (Pope and Owen 2009; Szlávik and Füle 2009). Financial subsidies to industries that damage the environment—such as the pesticide, transportation, petrochemical, logging, fishing, and tobacco industries—should end, particularly to the industries that damage human health as well. Those funds should be redirected to activities that enhance the environment and human well-being, especially to people whose lands are providing ecosystem services to the public.

Problem: Poor people who are simply trying to survive are frequently blamed for the destruction of the world's biological diversity.

Solution: Changing the government policies that act as the root causes of biodiversity loss can improve conservation and the lives of local people. In many cases, this involves better zoning of land uses and enforcement of environmental laws. In places where local actions are leading to losses, conservationists can help bring in the development and humanitarian organizations with the skills to assist local people in organizing and developing sustainable economic activities that do not damage biological diversity. Conservation biologists and conservation organizations are increasing their participation in programs for poor rural areas that promote smaller families, a more reliable food supply, and more training in economically useful skills (Sachs 2005; Setty et al. 2008). These programs should be closely linked to efforts aimed at recognizing basic human rights, especially ownership of the land where the local people live.

Conservation organizations and businesses should also play a role by working together to market "green" products produced by rural communities, with some of the profits shared with those communities. Already the Forest Stewardship Council and similar organizations are certifying wood products that derive from sustainably managed forests, and coffee companies are marketing shade-grown coffee (McMurtry 2009). Aquariums and ocean conservation organizations are developing lists of seafood that are harvested sustainably and should be selected by consumers (Kaiser and Edwards-Jones 2006). Products that meet environmental, labor, and developmental standards can be Fair Trade Certified; as of 2010, over 700 organizations in 58 developing countries were certified to sell products as such (www.fairtrade.net) (**Figure 22.2**). If consumers choose to buy these certified products instead of noncertified products, even if they are slightly more expensive, their purchases could be a strong force in local and international conservation efforts and provide tangible benefits to poor people in rural areas.

Problem: Decisions about the establishment and management of protected areas are often made by central governments with little input from people and local or-

(A)

(B)

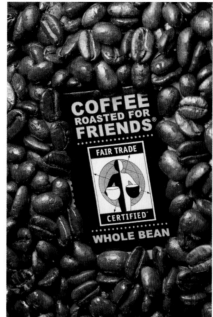

FIGURE 22.2 (A) A farmer growing and processing sustainably produced coffee berries hopes to receive a higher price for the crop. (B) Sustainably produced and certified coffee is available for purchase in an increasing number of stores and has a recognizable logo on the package. (A, photograph © Randy Plett/istockphoto. com; B, photograph by David McIntyre.)

ganizations in the region being affected. Consequently, local people sometimes feel alienated from conservation projects and do not support them.

Solution: In order for a conservation project to be successful, it is imperative that local people believe that they will benefit from it and that their involvement is important. To achieve this goal, environmental impact statements and other project information should be made publicly available, to encourage open discussion at all steps of a project. Local people should be provided with whatever assistance they may need in order to understand and evaluate the implications of the project being presented to them. Local people often want to protect biodiversity and associated ecosystem services because they know that their own survival depends on the protection of the natural environment (MEA 2005). Mechanisms should be established to ensure that the rights, responsibilities, and if possible, the decisions for management are shared between government agencies, conservation organizations, and local communities and businesses (Salafsky et al. 2001). Conservation biologists working in national parks should periodically explain the purpose and results of their work to nearby communities and school groups and listen to what the local people have to say. In some cases, a regional strategy such as a habitat conservation plan or a natural community conservation plan may have to be developed to reconcile the need for some development (and resulting loss of habitat) with the need to protect species and ecosystems.

Problem: Revenues, business activities, and scientific research associated with national parks and other protected areas do not directly benefit the surrounding communities.

Solution: Local communities often bear the costs but do not receive the benefits of living near protected areas, and mechanisms to benefit local communities need to be developed. For example, local people should be trained and employed in parks as a way of utilizing local knowledge and providing income. Local people can be assisted to develop businesses related to tourism and other park activities. A portion of park revenues should be used to fund local community projects such as schools, clinics, roads, cultural activities, sports programs and facilities, and community businesses—infrastructure that benefits a whole village, town, or region; this establishes a link between conservation programs and the improvement of local lives.

Problem: National parks and conservation areas often have inadequate budgets to pay for conservation activities.

Solution: It is often possible to increase funds for park management by raising rates for admission, lodging, or meals so that rates reflect the actual cost of maintaining the area. Concessions selling goods and services may be required to contribute a percentage of their income to the park's operation. Also, zoos and conservation organizations in the developed world should continue to make direct financial contributions to conservation efforts in developing countries. For example, members of the American Zoo and Aquarium Association and their partners participate in over 3700 in situ conservation projects in 100 countries worldwide.

Problem: Many endangered species and biological communities are on private land and on government land that is managed for timber production, grazing, mining, and other activities. Timber companies that lease forests and ranchers who rent rangeland from the government often damage biological diversity and reduce the productive capacity of the land in pursuit of short-term profits. Private landowners often regard endangered species on their land as restrictions on the use of it.

Solution: Change the laws so that people can obtain leases to harvest trees and use rangelands only as long as the health of the biological community is maintained (Stocks 2005). Eliminate tax subsidies that encourage the overexploitation of natural resources, and establish payments for land management, especially on private land, that enhances conservation efforts (Environmental Defense 2000). Alternatively, educate landowners to protect endangered species, and praise them publicly for their efforts. Develop connections among farmers, ranchers, conservation biologists, and perhaps even hunting groups because biodiversity, wildlife, and the rural way of life are all threatened by the process of economic growth.

Problem: In many countries, governments are inefficient and are bound by excessive regulation. Consequently, governments are often slow and ineffective at protecting biological communities.

Solution: Local NGOs (nongovernmental organizations) and citizen groups are often the most effective agents for promoting conservation (Posa et al. 2008). Accordingly, these groups should be encouraged and supported politically, scientifically, and financially. Conservation biologists need to educate citizens about local environmental issues and encourage them to take action when necessary. Building the capacity of universities, the national media, and NGOs to evaluate, propose, and implement policies is also an effective way to encourage national-level action. New foundations should be started by individuals, organizations, and businesses to financially support conservation efforts. One of the most important trends in conservation funding and policy is the increased strength of international NGOs, such as the World Wide Fund for Nature (with about 5 million members) and the Royal Society for the Protection of Birds. The number of NGOs has risen dramatically in past decades, and the ability of NGOs to influence local conservation programs and environmental policy at the national and international levels is often substantial (WRI 2003).

Problem: Many businesses, banks, and governments are uninterested in and unresponsive to conservation issues.

Solution: Leaders may become more willing to support conservation efforts once they receive additional information about the benefits of more sustainable practices or perceive strong public support for conservation initiatives. In countries with fairly open societies, lobbying and similar efforts may be effective in changing the policies of unresponsive institutions, because most will want to avoid bad publicity. Petitions, rallies, letter-writing campaigns, and economic boycotts all have their place when requests for change are ignored (**Box 22.2**). In many situations, radical environmental groups such as Greenpeace and Earth First! dominate media attention with dramatic, publicity-grabbing actions, while mainstream conservation organizations follow behind to negotiate a compromise. In closed societies, identifying and educating key leaders is usually a better strategy. A better understanding of the diverse values that different cultures attribute to biodiversity also can help in promoting sustainable practices.

The Role of Conservation Biologists

The problems and solutions we just discussed underscore the importance of conservation biologists—they will be among the primary participants in solving these problems. Conservation biology differs from many other scientific disciplines in that it plays an active role in the preservation of biological diversity in all its forms: species, genetic variability, biological communities, and ecosystem functions. Members of the diverse disciplines that contribute to conservation biology share the common goal of protecting biological diversity in practice, rather than simply investigating it and talking about it (Scott et al. 2007). However, they must work together to provide practical solutions that can be used to deal with real-world situations (Fazey et al. 2005).

Challenges for Conservation Biologists

The ideas and theories of conservation biology are increasingly being incorporated into decisions about park management and species protection. At the same time, botanical gardens, museums, nature centers, zoos, national parks, and aquariums are reorienting their programs to meet the challenges of protecting biological diversity. The need for large parks and the need to protect large populations of endangered species are two particular topics that have received widespread attention in both academic and popular literature. The vulnerability of small populations to local extinction, even when they are carefully protected and managed, and the alarming rates of species extinction and destruction of unique biological communities worldwide have also been highly publicized. The sense of urgency has been heightened with a recognition that many endangered species of cold climates, such as polar bears and penguins, are faced with immediate threats due to a warming climate and the melting of sea ice. As a result of this publicity, the need to protect biological diversity is entering political debate and has been targeted as a priority for government conservation programs. What is ultimately required, however, is to include the principles of conservation biology in the broader domestic policy arena and in the economic planning process (Czech 2004). Incorporating conservation biology into economic policy or reprioritizing domestic policy goals will take substantial public education and political effort.

One of the most serious challenges facing conservation biology is reconciling the needs of local people with the need to preserve biological diversity. How can poor people—particularly in the developing world but also in rural areas of developed countries—be convinced to forgo the exploitation of nature reserves and biological diversity when they are desperate to obtain the food, wood, and other natural products that they need for their daily survival? Park managers in particular need to

BOX 22.2   *Environmental Activism Confronts the Opposition*

■ The past two decades have witnessed a tremendous increase in popular awareness of environmental issues (Humes 2009). Many conservation organizations such as the Sierra Club, the World Wildlife Fund, and The Nature Conservancy, to name only a few, have gained millions of new members while attempting to achieve conservation goals within the current political and social systems. Other organizations have tried to take a more direct approach: Greenpeace International, with 2.8 million members and an annual budget of about $30 million, actively prevents environmental destruction. The surge in environmental activism, however, has triggered a disturbing backlash from those industries, business interests, labor organizations, and even some governments that resent and fear any restrictions on the use of natural resources (Rohrman 2004). Conservation of natural resources may be linked, in some peoples' minds, to a loss in profits and job opportunities. When people fear losing their jobs or businesses because of conservation measures, they sometimes direct their anger at environmental activists. This tends to be more prevalent during economic recessions, such as the one much of the world has confronted starting in 2008. Incidents of intimidation, threats, and physical harassment of environmental activists, sometimes frighteningly violent, have been reported worldwide.

Perhaps the best known violent incident occurred in 1988, when Chico Mendes, a Brazilian activist organizing rubber tappers to resist the encroachment of cattle ranching and logging in the Amazon rain forest, was assassinated by ranchers. Mendes's martyrdom created a worldwide uproar and focused global attention on the destruction of the rain forest. Many other environmental and social activists in Brazil have been beaten or killed, both before and since Mendes's death.

In many countries, people who protest destructive activities have been branded as subversives, traitors, or foreign agents by their own governments for fighting government policies that promote unrestricted development at the expense of the environment. In 1995, nine environmental ac-

> Activists have taken strong stands on protecting the environment, sometimes at serious cost to their personal safety. Their activities have brought needed attention to certain unresolved problems, such as whaling, cutting of old growth forests, and poorly regulated oil drilling.

tivists were hanged in Nigeria after a secret trial; they were members of the Ogoni tribe, whose land is being destroyed by a massive oil production operation sanctioned by the Nigerian government.

Environmental activists fighting industrial pollution and the destruction of important biological communities in North America, Europe, and other developed countries have sometimes resorted to radical action to publicize their cause. In 1997, national media attention was drawn to a young, articulate woman, Julia "Butterfly" Hill, who decided to protest the logging of old-growth forest in northern California by sitting and living in a tall, 1000-year-old redwood tree she named Luna. After 2 years in the tree and ever-increasing levels of publicity and tension, Hill finally descended from her tree perch when the logging company agreed to stop logging in some of the old-growth forests (Hill 2001). Building on this publicity, Hill established an environmental group, the Circle of Life, which promotes an outlook on life that could be described as a variation of deep ecology. Their activities include environmental festivals, tours, campaigns, and social justice. The goal of the group is to "transform the way humans interact with the Earth and all living beings" (www.circleoflifefoundation.org).

Indigenous people and other environmental activists in Panama join forces to protest the construction of a new hydroelectric dam, and the damage it might cause to their way of life. (Photograph © EFE/ZUMA Press.)

BOX 22.2 *(continued)*

Some radical environmental groups advocate acts of civil disobedience to stop harm to biodiversity and the environment. This is sometimes referred to as "passionate activism" by its proponents and as "ecoterrorism" by its opponents. In a few extreme cases, protestors have engaged in ecosabotage, destroying vehicles and buildings (Rohrman 2004). Some radical conservation measures have even become popularized in mainstream media. The activities of the Sea Shepherd Conservation Society, for instance, are chronicled in part by the television series *Whale Wars* on Animal Planet. Founded in 1977 by Paul Watson, a Greenpeace cofounder, Sea Shepherd bills itself as "defending ocean wildlife and habitats worldwide" (www.seashepherd.org). The series follows as Sea Shepherd crews expose and confront illegal activities on the high seas, which can include challenging, damaging, and blocking ships involved in whaling, sealing, and shark-finning operations. While these activities are highly controversial, the drama makes the series popular with average citizens and demonstrates how to use environmental activism as a conservation tool.

Greenpeace activists in small inflatable boats try to interfere with the hunting activities of a Japanese whaling ship. Crew members on the whaling ship use water cannons to keep the activists away. (Photograph © Kate Davison/eyevine/ZUMA Press.)

find compromises, such as those exemplified by biosphere reserves and integrated conservation development projects, that allow people to obtain the natural resources that they need to support their families yet not damage the park's natural communities. In each instance, a balance must be achieved between excluding people to protect vulnerable species and encouraging people to freely use park resources. At national and international levels, the world's resources must be distributed more fairly to end the inequalities that exist today. Effective programs must be established to stabilize the world's human population. At the same time, the destruction of natural resources by industries must be halted so that the short-term quest for profits does not lead to a long-term ecological catastrophe (Cowling et al. 2008). Management strategies to preserve biological diversity also need to be developed for the 87% of the terrestrial environment that remains outside of protected areas, as well as for the vast and largely unprotected marine environment.

Achieving the Agenda

If these challenges are to be met successfully, conservation biologists must take on several active roles. They must become more effective *educators* and *leaders* in the public forum as well as in the classroom (**Figure 22.3**). Conservation biologists need to educate as broad a range of people as possible about the problems that stem from

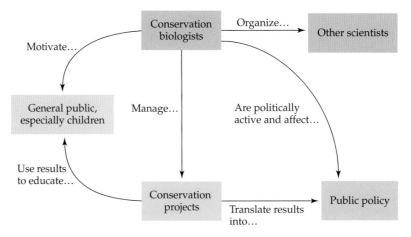

FIGURE 22.3 Conservation biologists need to be active in various ways to achieve the goals of conservation biology and the protection of biological diversity. Not every conservation biologist can be active in each role, but all of the roles are important.

loss of biological diversity (Van Heezik and Seddon 2005; de Groot and Steg 2009). The Society for Conservation Biology has even made the dissemination of knowledge the first item in its new code of ethics. Conservation biologists need to convey a positive message about what has been accomplished and what can be accomplished to protect biological diversity by delivering a sense of realistic optimism to counter the pessimism and passivity so frequently encountered in modern society. Other groups, such as fishers, hunters, bird-watchers, and hikers, may be motivated to help conservation efforts once they become aware of the issues or recognize that their self-interest or emotional well-being is dependent upon conservation (Granek et al. 2008).

Conservation biologists often teach college students and write technical papers addressing these issues, but they reach only a limited audience in this way: Remember that only a few hundred or a few thousand people read most scientific papers. In contrast, millions of adults watch nature programs on television, especially ones produced by the National Geographic Society, the Public Broadcasting Service, and the British Broadcasting Corporation, and tens of millions of children watch the television channel Animal Planet and movies such as *Finding Nemo* and *Avatar*, which often have powerful conservation themes. Conservation biologists need to reach a wider range of people through speaking in villages, towns, cities, elementary and secondary schools, parks, neighborhood gatherings, and religious organizations (Swanson et al. 2008). Also, the themes of conservation need to be even more widely incorporated into public discussions. Conservation biologists must spend more of their time writing articles and editorials for newspapers, magazines, and blogs, as well as effectively speaking on radio, television, and other mass media, in ways the public can understand (Jacobson 2009). Conservation biologists need to make a special effort to talk to children's groups and to write versions of their work that children can read. Hundreds of millions of people visit zoos, aquariums, and botanical gardens, making these another prime venue for communicating conservation messages to the public. Conservation biologists must continue to seek out creative ways to reach wider audiences and avoid repeatedly "preaching to the converted."

The efforts of Merlin Tuttle and Bat Conservation International (BCI) illustrate how public attitudes toward even unpopular species can be changed. BCI has campaigned throughout the United States and the world to educate people on the importance of bats in ecosystem health, emphasizing their roles as insect eaters, pollinators, and seed dispersers. A valuable part of this effort has involved producing bat photographs and films of exceptional beauty. In Austin, Texas, Tuttle intervened when citizens petitioned the city government to exterminate the hundreds of thousands of Mexican free-tailed bats (*Tadarida brasiliensis*) that lived under a downtown bridge. He and his colleagues were able to convince people that the bats are both fun to watch and critical in controlling noxious insect populations over a wide area. The situation has changed so drastically that now the government protects the bats as a matter of civic pride and practical pest control, and citizens and tourists gather every night to watch the bats emerge from under the bridge on their nightly expeditions (**Figure 22.4**).

Conservation biologists must also become *politically active leaders* in order to influence public policy (Beier 2008; Manolis et al. 2009). Involvement in the political process allows conservation biologists to influence the passage of new laws to support the preservation of biological diversity or to argue against legislation that would prove harmful to species or ecosystems. An important first step in this process is joining conservation organizations or mainstream political parties to gain strength by working in a group and to learn more about the issues. It is important to note that there is also room for people who prefer to work by themselves. Difficulties in getting the U.S. Congress to reauthorize the Endangered Species Act and to ratify the Convention on Biological Diversity and the United Nations Framework Convention on Climate Change dramatically illustrate the need for greater political activism on the part of scientists who understand the implications of not taking action now. Though much of the political process is time-consuming and tedious, it is often the only way to accomplish major conservation goals such as acquiring new land for reserves or preventing overexploitation of old-growth forests. Conservation biologists need to master the language and methods of the legal process and form ef-

FIGURE 22.4 Citizens and tourists gather in the evening to watch Mexican free-tailed bats emerge from their roosts beneath the Congress Avenue bridge in Austin, Texas. (Photograph © Merlin D. Tuttle, Bat Conservation International, www.batcon.org.)

fective alliances with environmental lawyers, citizen groups, and politicians. They also must be clear about when they are presenting objective scientific evidence and when they are expressing personal opinions.

A key role is for conservation biologists to become *translational scientists*, that is, scientists who can take the data and results of conservation science and translate them into legislation and other public policy (Barbour and Poff 2008). To be effective, conservation biologists have to demonstrate the relevance of their research and show that their findings are unbiased and respectful of the values and concerns of all stakeholders. Conservation scientists have to be aware of the full range of issues that may affect their programs and be able to speak to a general audience in terms that they can understand. Conservation biologists must take the lead, as their expertise is needed.

> The goal of conservation biology is not just to reveal new knowledge, but to use that knowledge to protect biodiversity. Conservation biologists must learn to show the practical application of their work.

Conservation biologists need to become *organizers* within the scientific community. Many professional biologists, and biologists in training, in universities, colleges, museums, high schools, and government agencies concentrate their energies on the specialized needs of their professional niche. They may feel that their institutions want them to concentrate on "pure science" and "not get involved in politics." These biologists may not realize that the world's biological diversity is under imminent threat of destruction and that their contributions are urgently needed to save it (Scott et al. 2008). Or they may feel that they are too busy with career goals or too unimportant to get involved in the struggle. By stimulating interest among their colleagues, conservation biologists can increase the ranks of trained professional advocates fighting the destruction of natural resources. These professional biologists may also find their involvement to be personally and professionally beneficial, as their new interests may result in heightened scientific creativity and more inspired teaching.

Conservation biologists should become *motivators,* convincing a range of people to support conservation efforts. At a local level, conservation programs have to be created and presented in ways that provide incentives for local people to support them. Local people need to be shown that protecting the environment not only saves species and biological communities but also improves the long-term health of their families, their own economic well-being, and their quality of life (Liu 2007). Public discussions, education, and publicity need to be a major part of any such program. The scientists may present their knowledge as expert witnesses at public panels and in testimony. Careful attention must be devoted in particular to convincing business leaders and politicians to support conservation efforts. Many of these people will support conservation efforts when they are presented in the right way. Sometimes conservation is perceived to have good publicity value, or supporting it is perceived to be better than a confrontation that may otherwise result. National leaders may be among the most difficult people to convince, since they must respond to a diversity of interests. However, whether it is due to reason, sentiment, or professional self-interest, once converted to the conservation cause, these leaders may be in a position to make major contributions.

Finally, and most important, conservation biologists need to become effective *managers* and *practitioners* of conservation projects (Shanley and López 2009). They must be willing to walk on the land and go out on the water to find out what is really happening, to get dirty, to talk with local people, to knock on doors, and to take risks. Conservation biologists must learn everything they can about the species and ecosystems that they are trying to protect and then make that knowledge available to others in a form that can be readily understood and can affect decision making.

If conservation biologists are willing to put their ideas into practice, and to work with park managers, land use planners, politicians, and local people, then progress will follow. Getting the right mix of models, new theories, innovative approaches, and practical examples is necessary for the success of the discipline. Once this balance is found, conservation biologists, working with energized citizens and government officials, will be in a position to protect the world's biological diversity during this unprecedented era of change.

Summary

1. There are major problems involved in protecting biological diversity; to address these problems, many changes must be made in policies and practices. These changes must occur at local, national, and international levels and require action on the part of individuals, conservation organizations, and governments.

2. Conservation biologists must demonstrate the practical value of the theories and approaches of their new discipline and actively work with all components of society to protect biological diversity and restore the degraded elements of the environment.

3. To achieve the long-term goals of conservation biology, practitioners need to become involved in conservation education and the political process.

For Discussion

1. Sutherland and colleagues (2009) posed 100 questions for conservation biology. Provide answers for the questions you consider to be the most urgent and important.

2. As a result of studying conservation biology, have you decided to change your lifestyle or your level of political activity? Do you think you can make a difference in the world, and if so, in what way?

3. Go to the library or search online to find articles that interest you in journals such as *Conservation Biology, Biological Conservation, BioScience, Conservation Letters, Ecological Applications,* and *National Geographic.* What is appealing about the articles you selected?

4. How can conservation biologists provide links between basic science and a public environmental movement? What suggestions can you make for ways in which conservation biologists and environmental activists can energize and enrich each other in working toward an economically and environmentally stable world?

5. Wind farms are gaining importance as sources of renewable energy, yet the wind turbines kill large numbers of birds and bats (see Kunz et al. 2007). How can the need for sustainable energy be balanced by the need to protect endangered wildlife?

Suggested Readings

Beier, C. M. 2008. Influence of political opposition and compromise on conservation outcomes in the Tongass National Forest, Alaska. *Conservation Biology* 22: 1485–1496. Prolonged and complex negotiations were the key to protecting wilderness in this valuable example.

Cohn, J. P. 2008. Citizen science: Can volunteers do real research? *BioScience* 58: 192–197. Volunteers assisting with research projects can both enhance data collection and increase their awareness of wildlife in their communities.

Granek, E. F., E. M. P. Madin, M. A. Brown, W. Figueira, D. S. Cameron, and Z. Hogan. 2008. Engaging recreational fishers in management and conservation: Global case studies. *Con-*

servation Biology 22: 1125–1134. Recreational fishers can become strong advocates for conservation.

Hill, J. 2001. *The Legacy of Luna: The Story of a Tree, a Woman, and the Struggle to Save the Redwoods*. Harper, San Francisco, CA. From a specific political action, this remarkable woman established her own environmental group.

Jacobson, S. K., M. McDuff, and M. Monroe. 2006. *Conservation Education and Outreach Techniques*. Oxford University Press, Oxford, UK. Practical ways for enlarging public support for conservation.

Manolis, J. C., K. M. Chan, M. E. Finkelstein, S. Stephens, C. R. Nelson, J. B. Grant, et al. 2009. Leadership: A new frontier in conservation science. *Conservation Biology* 23: 879–886. Conservation biologists need to integrate their science into policy, management, and the broader society.

Scott, J. M., J. L. Rachlow, R. T. Lackey, A. B. Pidgorna, J. L. Aycrigg, G. R. Feldman, et al. 2007. Policy advocacy in science: Prevalence, perspectives, and implications for conservation biologists. *Conservation Biology* 21: 29–35. The authors argue for carrying out research that is relevant to conservation policy, and widely conveying the results.

Sullivan, B., C. L. Wood, M. J. Iliff, R. E. Bonney, D. Fink, and S. Kelling. 2009. eBird: A citizen-based bird observation network in the biological sciences. *Biological Conservation* 142: 2282–2292. eBird is engaging tens of thousands of bird-watchers due to its user-friendly approach.

Sutherland, W. J. and 43 others. 2009. One hundred questions of importance to the conservation of global biological diversity. *Conservation Biology* 23: 557–567. Presents 100 scientific questions whose answers would have the greatest impact on conservation practice and policy.

Sutherland, W. J. and 22 others. 2010. A horizon scan of global conservation issues for 2010. *Trends in Ecology and Evolution* 25: 1–6. A review of key emerging topics in conservation biology, such as assisted colonization, Reduced Emissions from Deforestation and Degradation (REDD) in non-forest ecosystems, and trans-Arctic dispersal.

Van Heezik, Y. and P. J. Seddon. 2005. Conservation education structure and content of graduate wildlife management and conservation biology programs: An international perspective. *Conservation Biology* 19: 7–14. Conservation education programs are increasing and are highly diverse.

Appendix

Selected Environmental Organizations and Sources of Information

The best single reference on conservation activities is the *Conservation Directory 2005–2006*, (www.nwf.org/conservationdirectory). Available online or through Island Press, this directory lists over 4000 local, national, and international conservation organizations; conservation publications; and more than 18,000 leaders and officials in the field of conservation. Another publication of interest is *The ECO Guide to Careers that Make a Difference: Environmental Work for a Sustainable World* (2004), also published by Island Press. Online searches, especially using Google, provide a powerful way to search for information concerning people, organizations, places, and topics.

The following are a few searchable databases on species and countries:

Encyclopedia of Life
www.eol.org
Developing resource for species biology.

Global Biodiversity Information Facility
www.gbif.org
Free and open access to biodiversity data.

Below is a list of some major organizations and resources:

Association of Zoos and Aquariums (AZA)
8403 Colesville Road, Suite 710
Silver Spring, MD 20910 USA
www.aza.org
Preservation and propagation of captive wildlife.

BirdLife International
Wellbrook Court, Girton Road
Cambridge, CB3 0NA, UK
www.birdlife.org
Determines status, priorities, and conservation plans for birds throughout the world.

Center for Plant Conservation/Missouri Botanical Garden
4344 Shaw Boulevard
St. Louis, MO 63110 USA
www.centerforplantconservation.org,
www.mobot.org
Major center for worldwide plant conservation activities.

Convention on Biological Diversity Secretariat
413 Rue Saint-Jacques, Suite 800
Montreal, Quebec, H2Y 1N9, Canada
www.cbd.int
Promotes the goals of the CBD: sustainable development, biodiversity conservation, and equitable sharing of genetic resources.

CITES Secretariat of Wild Fauna and Flora
International Environment House
15 Chemin des Anémones
CH-1219 Châtelaine, Geneva, Switzerland
www.cites.org
Regulates trade in endangered species.

Conservation International (CI)
2011 Crystal Drive, Suite 500
Arlington, VA 22202 USA
www.conservation.org
Active in international conservation efforts and developing conservation strategies; home of the Center for Applied Biodiversity Science.

Earthwatch Institute
3 Clock Tower Place, Suite 100, Box 75
Maynard, MA 01754 USA
www.earthwatch.org
Clearinghouse for international conservation projects in which volunteers can work with scientists.

Environmental Defense Fund (EDF)
257 Park Avenue South
New York, NY 10010 USA
www.edf.org
Involved in scientific, legal, and economic issues.

Employment Opportunities
Various organizations have websites with environmental and conservation opportunities and internships throughout the world: www.webdirectory.com/employment, www.eco-jobs.com, etc. A publication of interest is *Careers in the Environment* by Mike Fasulo and Paul Walker, published by McGraw-Hill.

European Center for Nature Conservation (ECNC)
P.O. Box 90154
5000 LG Tilburg, the Netherlands
www.ecnc.nl
Provides the scientific expertise that is required for formulating conservation policy.

Fauna & Flora International
Jupiter House, 4th Floor
Station Road
Cambridge, CB1 2JD, UK
www.fauna-flora.org
Long-established international conservation body acting to protect species and ecosystems.

Food and Agriculture Organization of the United Nations (FAO)
Viale delle Terme di Caracalla
00513 Rome, Italy
www.fao.org
A UN agency supporting sustainable agriculture, rural development, and resource management.

Friends of the Earth
1717 Massachusetts Avenue, Suite 600
Washington, DC 20036 USA
www.foe.org
Attention-grabbing organization working to improve and expand environmental policy.

Global Environment Facility (GEF) Secretariat
1818 H Street NW, MSN G6-602
Washington, DC 20433 USA
www.thegef.org/gef
Funds international biodiversity and environmental projects.

Greenpeace International
Ottho Heldringstraat 5
1006 AZ Amsterdam, the Netherlands
www.greenpeace.org/international
Activist organization known for grassroots efforts and dramatic protests against environmental damage.

National Audubon Society
225 Varick Street, 7th floor
New York, NY 10014 USA
www.audubon.org
Involved in wildlife conservation, public education, research, and political lobbying, with emphasis on birds.

National Council for Science and the Environment (NCSE)
1101 17th Street NW, Suite 250
Washington, DC 20036 USA
www.ncseonline.org
Works to improve the scientific basis for environmental decision making; their website provides extensive environmental information.

National Wildlife Federation (NWF)
11100 Wildlife Center Drive
Reston, VA 20190 USA
www.nwf.org
Advocates for wildlife conservation. Publishes the *Conservation Directory 2005–2006*, as well as children's publications *Ranger Rick* and *Your Big Backyard*.

Natural Resources Defense Council (NRDC)
40 West 20th Street
New York, NY 10011 USA
www.nrdc.org
Uses legal and scientific methods to monitor and
influence government actions and legislation.

The Nature Conservancy (TNC)
4245 North Fairfax Drive, Suite 100
Arlington, VA 22203 USA
www.nature.org
Emphasizes land preservation.

NatureServe
1101 Wilson Boulevard, 15th floor
Arlington, VA 22209 USA
www.natureserve.org
Maintains databases of endangered species for North
America.

**The New York Botanical Garden (NYBG) Institute of
Economic Botany (IEB)**
International Plant Science Center, the New York
Botanical Garden
200th Street and Kazimiroff Boulevard
Bronx, NY 10458 USA
www.nybg.org
Conducts research and conservation programs
involving plants that are useful to people.

Rainforest Action Network
221 Pine Street, 5th floor
San Francisco, CA 94104 USA
www.ran.org
Works for rain forest conservation and human rights.

Ocean Conservancy
1300 19th Street NW, 8th floor
Washington, DC 20036 USA
www.oceanconservancy.org
Focuses on marine wildlife and ocean and coastal
habitats.

Royal Botanic Gardens, Kew
Richmond, Surrey, TW9 3AB, UK
www.kew.org
The famous Kew Gardens are home to a leading botanical research institute and an enormous plant collection.

Sierra Club
85 Second Street, 2nd floor
San Francisco, CA 94105 USA
www.sierraclub.org
Leading advocate for the preservation of wilderness
and open space.

Smithsonian National Zoological Park
3001 Connecticut Avenue NW
Washington, DC 20008 USA
www.nationalzoo.si.edu
The National Zoo and the nearby U.S. National
Museum of Natural History represent a vast
resource of literature, biological materials, and
skilled professionals.

Society for Conservation Biology (SCB)
1017 O Street NW
Washington, DC 20001 USA
www.conbio.org
Leading scientific society for the field. Develops and
publicizes new ideas and scientific results through
the journal *Conservation Biology* and annual
meetings.

Student Conservation Association (SCA)
689 River Road
P.O. Box 550
Charlestown, NH 03603 USA
www.thesca.org
Places volunteers and interns with conservation organizations and public agencies.

United Nations Development Programme (UNDP)
1 United Nations Plaza
New York, NY 10017 USA
www.undp.org
Funds and coordinates international economic development activities.

United Nations Environment Programme (UNEP)
United Nations Avenue, Gigiri
P.O. Box 30552, 00100
Nairobi, Kenya
www.unep.org
International program of environmental research and
management.

United Nations Environment Programme World Conservation Monitoring Centre (UNEP-WCMC)
219 Huntingdon Road
Cambridge, CB3 0DL, UK
www.unep-wcmc.org
Monitors global wildlife trade, the status of endangered species, natural resource use, and protected areas.

United States Fish and Wildlife Service (USFWS)
Department of the Interior
1849 C Street NW
Washington, DC 20240 USA
www.fws.gov
The leading U.S. government agency concerned with conservation research and management; with connections to state governments and other government units, including the National Marine Fisheries Service, the U.S. Forest Service, and the Agency for International Development, which is active in developing nations. The *Conservation Directory 2005–2006*, mentioned above, shows how these units are organized.

Wetlands International
Horapark 9, 6717 LZ Ede, the Netherlands
www.wetlands.org
Focus on the conservation and management of wetlands.

The Wilderness Society
1615 M Street NW
Washington, DC 20036 USA
www.wilderness.org
Devoted to preserving wilderness and wildlife.

Wildlife Conservation Society (WCS)
2300 Southern Boulevard
Bronx, NY 10460 USA
www.wcs.org
Leaders in wildlife conservation and research.

The World Bank
1818 H Street NW
Washington, DC 20433 USA
www.worldbank.org
Multinational bank involved in economic development; increasingly concerned with environmental issues.

World Conservation Union (IUCN)
Rue Mauverney 28
Gland, 1196, Switzerland
www.iucn.org
Coordinating body for international conservation efforts. Produces directories of specialists and the Red List of endangered species.

World Resources Institute (WRI)
10 G Street NE, Suite 800
Washington, DC 20002 USA
www.wri.org
Produces environmental, conservation, and development reports.

World Wildlife Fund (WWF)
1250 24th Street NW
P.O. Box 97180
Washington, DC 20077 USA
www.worldwildlife.org, www.wwf.org
Major conservation organization, with branches throughout the world. Active in national park management.

The Xerces Society
4828 Southeast Hawthorne Boulevard
Portland, OR 97215 USA
www.xerces.org
Focuses on the conservation of insects and other invertebrates.

Zoological Society of London (ZSL)
Regent's Park
London, England NW1 4RY
www.zsl.org
Center for worldwide activities to preserve nature.

Chapter Opener Photograph Credits

CHAPTER 1
A field biologist reburies sea turtle eggs confiscated from a poacher. (Photograph © The Palm Beach Post/ZUMA Press.)

CHAPTER 2
The variations in patterns on the shells of the marine snail *Neritina communis* are indicative of the genetic diversity within this species. (Photograph by David McIntyre.)

CHAPTER 3
Many of Earth's undescribed species live in relatively inaccessible tropical tree canopies. (Photograph by Andrew D. Sinauer.)

CHAPTER 4
While most sea creatures are gathered for food, these fish are used as ornaments in a seafood restaurant. (Photograph by Richard Primack.)

CHAPTER 5
Wetlands, such as this salt marsh on Cape Cod, provide ecosystem services valued in the trillions of dollars per year. (Photograph by David McIntyre.)

CHAPTER 6
The beauty of nature enhances people's lives, as illustrated by the cherry blossom festival in Tokyo. (Photograph by Richard Primack.)

CHAPTER 7
The extinct Carolina parakeet (*Conuropsis carolinensis*) was the only parrot species native to the eastern United States. The last one died in captivity in 1918. (Hand-colored engraving by John James Audubon.)

CHAPTER 8
The blue poison dart frog (*Dendrobates azureus*) is listed as Vulnerable on the IUCN Red List. (Photograph © John Arnold/Shutterstock.)

CHAPTER 9
Polar bears (*Ursus maritimus*) face multiple threats, including climate change. (Photograph courtesy of Susanne Miller/U.S. Fish and Wildlife Service.)

CHAPTER 10
The common water hyacinth (*Eichhornia* spp.), though beautiful, is invasive outside its native range in South America. (Photograph © JTB Photo Communications, Inc./Alamy.)

CHAPTER 11
Cheetahs (*Acinonyx jubatus*) and other large cats are particularly vulnerable to genetic problems associated with small populations. (Photograph © Hilton Kotze/istockphoto.com.)

CHAPTER 12
Endangered European tortoises are individually numbered as part of a demographic study. (Photograph by Richard Primack.)

CHAPTER 13
A sea otter (*Enhydra lutris*) floating on his back at Monterey Bay National Marine Sanctuary, California. (Photograph © David Gomez/istockphoto.com.)

CHAPTER 14
This young orangutan (*Pongo pygmaeus*) is being raised in a rescue facility in Indonesia. (Photograph © Berndt Fischer/OSF/Photolibrary.com.)

CHAPTER 15
The blue sea star (*Linckia laevigata*) and other coral reef species live in the Apo Island Marine Reserve, Philippines. (Photograph © ArteSub/Alamy.)

CHAPTER 16
The Hawley Bog, a nature reserve in Massachusetts, is owned and managed by The Nature Conservancy. (Photograph by David McIntyre.)

CHAPTER 17

A firefighter uses a driptorch to ignite a controlled fire as a management tool at the Pea Island National Wildlife Refuge in North Carolina. (Photograph courtesy of the U.S. Fish and Wildlife Service.)

CHAPTER 18

This World Heritage Site along the Rhine River in Austria includes villages, vineyards, fields, forests, and wetlands. (Photograph by Richard Primack.)

CHAPTER 19

Volunteers plant trees on former farmland in the Missouri River floodplains in order to re-establish original natural habitat. (Photograph courtesy of Steve Hillebrand/U.S. Fish and Wildlife Service.)

CHAPTER 20

The American alligator (*Alligator mississippiensis*) increased so dramatically in numbers following its listing on the U.S. Endangered Species Act that it has been removed from protection. (Photograph by Andrew D. Sinauer.)

CHAPTER 21

After being confiscated by the Kenyan government, this illegally harvested ivory will soon be burned, sending a message that Kenya is not a place to harvest ivory. (Photograph © Photoshot Holdings Ltd/Alamy.)

CHAPTER 22

Education is an important part of conservation biology. Here, children are working to create a new wetland at the Harpers Ferry National Historical Park in the U.S. (Photograph courtesy of Todd Harless/U.S. Fish and Wildlife Service.)

Glossary

A

adaptive management Implementing a management plan, monitoring how well it works, and then using the results to adjust the management plan.

adaptive radiation An evolutionary process whereby different populations of a species adapt to local conditions, followed by speciation.

adaptive restoration Using monitoring data to adjust management plans in order to achieve restoration goals.

affluenza The unsatisfying and unending pursuit of increasing material wealth.

Allee effect Inability of a species' social structure to function once a population of that species falls below a certain number or density of individuals.

alleles Different forms of the same gene (e.g., different alleles of the genes for certain blood proteins produce the different blood types found among humans).

alpha diversity The number of different species in a community or specific location.

amenity value Recreational value of biodiversity, including ecotourism.

arboretum Specialized botanical garden focusing on trees and other woody plants.

artificial incubation Conservation strategy that involves humans taking care of eggs or newborn animals.

artificial insemination Introduction of sperm into a receptive female animal by humans; used to increase the reproductive output of endangered species.

artificial selection Selective breeding by humans to produce desired and useful characteristics in domesticated plants and animals.

augmentation See **restocking**.

autotroph See **primary producer**.

B

bequest value The amount people are willing to pay to protect something of value for their own descendants or for future generations in general. Also known as beneficiary value.

beta diversity Rate of change of species composition along a gradient or transect.

binomial The unique two-part Latin name taxonomists bestow on a species, such as *Canis lupus* (gray wolf) or *Homo sapiens* (humans).

binomial nomenclature System of scientific names in which each species has a two-part name consisting of a genus name and a species name.

biocultural restoration Restoring lost ecological knowledge to people to give them an appreciation of the natural world.

biodiversity The complete range of species, biological communities and their ecosystem interactions, and genetic variation within species. Also known as biological diversity.

biodiversity indicators Species or groups of species that provide an estimate of the biodiversity in an area or that can be used to guide protection efforts when data on the whole community is unavailable. Also known as **surrogate species**.

biological community A group of species that occupies a particular locality.

biological definition of a species Among biologists, the most generally used of several definitions of "species." A group of individuals that can potentially breed among themselves in the wild and that do not breed with individuals of other groups. Compare with **morphological definition of a species**.

biomagnification Process whereby toxins become more concentrated in animals at higher levels in the food chain.

biomass Total weight of living material in a place; often expressed as weight per unit area.

biome Ecosystem characterized by the structure and characteristics of its vegetation, which supports unique biological communities.

biophilia The postulated predisposition in humans to feel an affinity for the diversity of the living world.

biopiracy Collecting and using biological materials for commercial, scientific, or personal use without obtaining the necessary permits.

bioprospecting Collecting biological materials as part of a search for new products.

bioregional management Management system that focuses on a single large ecosystem or a series of linked ecosystems, particularly where they cross political boundaries.

Biosphere Reserves Program Global network of biosphere reserves established by the United Nations to demonstrate the compatibility of biodiversity conservation and sustainable development to benefit local people.

biota A region's plants and animals.

bushmeat crisis The sharp decline in wild animal populations caused by humans hunting them for food.

bycatch Animals, including fish, marine mammals, sea turtles, and seabirds, caught and/or killed unintentionally during fishing operations.

C

carnivore An animal species that consumes other animals to survive. Also known as **secondary consumer** or **predator**. Compare with **herbivore**.

carrying capacity The number of individuals or biomass of a species that an ecosystem can support.

CARTs (Conservation, Amenity, and Recreation Trusts) Land trusts established for one of various purposes.

census A count of the number of individuals in a population.

CITES See **Convention on International Trade in Endangered Species**.

class Unit of classification; related orders of species are contained in a class.

clonal repository Special botanical garden or facility that preserves genetic variation for plants with seeds that cannot be stored or for plants that are long-lived. Also known as a clonal orchard.

clone banks Cuttings and families of closely related seeds taken from the best plants to establish plantations of superior genetic varieties; used by foresters to conserve genetic variation in tree species.

co-management Local people working as partners with government agencies and conservation organizations in protected areas.

commodity value See **direct use value**.

common property Natural resources that are not controlled by individuals but collectively owned by society. Also known as **open-access resources or common-pool resources**.

community conserved areas Protected areas managed and sometimes established by local people.

compensatory mitigation Creating, restoring, or enhancing a site in compensation for a site damaged or destroyed elsewhere.

competition A contest between individuals or groups of animals for resources. Occurs when individuals or a species uses a limiting resource in a way that prevents others from using it.

complementary areas Conservation strategy in which each newly established protected area adds additional species or other aspects of biodiversity to an existing system of protected areas.

conservation banking A system in which developers pay landowners for the preservation of an endangered species or protected habitat type (or even restoration of a degraded habitat) to compensate for a species or habitat that is destroyed elsewhere.

conservation biology Scientific discipline that draws on diverse fields in order to research, identify threats to, and preserve biodiversity.

conservation concession Method of protecting land whereby a conservation organization pays a government or other landowner to preserve habitat rather than allow an extractive industry to damage the habitat.

conservation corridor or **movement corridor** See **corridors**.

conservation development See **limited development**.

conservation easement Method of protecting land in which landowners give up the right to develop or build on their property, often in exchange for financial or tax benefit.

conservation leasing Providing payments to private landowners who actively manage their land for biodiversity protection.

conservation units Species, ecosystems, and physical features of a region; data about them are gathered and stored by conservation organizations.

consumptive use value Value assigned to goods that are collected and consumed locally.

Convention on Biological Diversity (CBD) A treaty that obligates countries to protect the biodiversity within their borders and gives them the right to benefit economically from the use of that biodiversity.

Convention on International Trade in Endangered Species (CITES) International treaty that establishes lists (known as Appendices) of species for which international trade is to be prohibited, regulated, or monitored.

corridor Connections between protected areas that allow for dispersal and migration. Also known as **conservation corridors, habitat corridors, or movement corridors**.

cost-benefit analysis Comprehensive analysis that compares values gained against the costs of a project or resource use.

cross-fostering Conservation strategy in which individuals from a common species raise the offspring of a rare, related species.

cryptic biodiversity The existence of one or more genetically distinct species that look similar to, and consequently have been mistaken for, a described species.

cultural eutrophication Algal blooms and associated impacts caused by excess mineral nutrients released into the water from human activity.

D

debt-for-nature swap Agreement in which a developing country agrees to fund conservation activities in exchange for some of its discounted debt being cancelled by a conservation organization or developed country.

decomposer A species that feeds or grows on dead plant and animal material. Also known as **detritivore**.

deep ecology Philosophy emphasizing biodiversity protection through personal lifestyle changes and political change.

demographic stochasticity Random variation in birth, death, and reproductive rates in small populations, sometimes causing further decline in population size. Also known as **demographic variation**.

demographic study Study in which individuals and populations are monitored over time to determine rates of growth, reproduction, and survival.

demographic variation See **demographic stochasticity**.

desertification Process by which dry ecosystems are degraded by human activities into deserts.

detritivore See **decomposer**.

direct use value Value assigned to products, such as timber and animals, that are harvested. Also known as **commodity value** or **private goods**.

discount rate Method for reducing the current value of a resource that is going to be used at some point in the future.

E

Earth Summit An international conference held in 1992 in Rio de Janeiro that resulted in new environmental agreements. Also known as the **Rio Summit**.

ecocolonialism Practice of governments and conservation organizations disregarding the land rights and traditions of local people in order to establish new conservation areas.

ecological economics Discipline that includes valuations of biodiversity in economic analyses.

ecological footprint The influence that people's patterns of consumption and lifestyle have on the surrounding ecosystem and across the globe.

ecological restoration Altering a site to reestablish the original ecosystem.

ecologically extinct A species that has been so reduced in numbers that it no longer has a significant ecological impact on the ecosystem.

ecologically functional A species that is sufficiently abundant to have a significant impact on other species in an ecosystem.

ecology The scientific study of interactions between organisms and their environment.

economic development Economic activity focused on improvements in efficiency and organization but not necessarily on increases in resource consumption.

economic growth Economic activity characterized by increases in the amount of resources used and in the amount of goods and services produced.

ecosystem A biological community together with its associated physical and chemical environment.

ecosystem diversity The variety of ecosystems present in a place or geographic area.

ecosystem health The condition of an ecosystem in which all processes are functioning normally.

ecosystem integrity The state of an ecosystem when it is complete and functional and has not been damaged by human activity.

ecosystem management Large-scale management that often involves multiple stakeholders, the primary goal of which is the preservation of ecosystem components and processes.

ecosystem services Range of benefits provided to people from ecosystems, including flood control, clean water, and reduction of pollution.

ecotourism Tourism, especially in developing countries, focused on viewing unusual and/or especially charismatic ecosystems and species that are unique to a country or region.

edge effects Altered environmental and biological conditions at the edges of a fragmented habitat.

effective population size The number of breeding individuals in a population.

embryo transfer The surgical implantation of embryos into a surrogate mother; used to increase the number of individuals of a rare species. Often, a common species is used as the surrogate mother.

endangered species A species that has a high risk of extinction in the wild in the near future; a category in the IUCN system and under the U.S. Endangered Species Act.

Endangered Species Act (ESA) An important U.S. law passed to protect endangered species and the ecosystems in which they live.

endemic Occurring in a place naturally, without the influence of people (e.g., gray wolves are endemic to Canada).

endemic species Species found in one place and nowhere else (e.g., the many lemur species found only on the island of Madagascar).

environmental and economic impact assessment Evaluation of a project that considers its possible present and future impacts on the environment and the economy.

environmental ethics Discipline of philosophy that articulates the intrinsic value of the natural world and people's responsibility to protect the environment.

environmental justice Movement that seeks to empower and assist poor and politically weak people in protecting their own environments; their well-being and the protection of biological diversity are enhanced in the process.

environmental stochasticity Random variation in the biological and physical environment. Can increase the risk of extinction in small populations.

environmentalism A widespread movement, characterized by political activism, with the goal of protecting the natural environment.

eutrophication Process of degradation in aquatic environments caused by nitrogen and phosphorus pollution and characterized by algal blooms and oxygen depletion.

ex situ conservation Preservation of species under artificial conditions, such as in zoos, aquariums, and botanical gardens.

existence value Amount of money that people are willing to pay to protect biodiversity for the sole purpose of its continued existence.

exotic species A species that occurs outside of its natural range due to human activity. Compare with **endemic**.

extant Presently alive; not extinct.

externalities Hidden costs or benefits that result from an economic activity to individuals or a society not directly involved in that activity.

extinct A species with no members currently living.

extinct in the wild A species no longer found in the wild. Individuals may remain alive in zoos, botanical gardens, or other artificial environments.

extinction cascade A series of linked extinctions whereby the extinction of one species leads to the extinction of one or more additional species.

extinction debt The inevitable extinction of many species in coming years as the result of current human activities.

extinction vortex Tendency of small populations to decline toward extinction.

extirpation Local extinction of a population, even though the species may still exist elsewhere.

extractive reserve Protected area in which sustainable extraction of certain natural products is allowed.

F

50/500 rule Proposed rule that at least 50 and up to 500 reproductive individuals are needed to prevent the loss of genetic variability in a population; larger numbers are now considered necessary for wild populations.

family A unit of classification; related genera are contained in a family.

fitness An individual's ability to grow, survive, and reproduce.

flagship species A species that captures public attention and aids in conservation efforts, such as establishing a protected area.

focal species Species that provides a reason for establishing a protected area.

food chains Specific feeding relationships between species at different trophic levels.

food web A network of feeding relationships among species.

founder effect Reduced genetic variability that occurs when a new population is established ("founded") by a small number of individuals.

G

gamma diversity The number of species in a large geographic area.

gap analysis Comparing the distribution of endangered species and ecosystems with existing and proposed protected areas to determine gaps in protection.

gap species A species that is not protected in any part of its range.

gene A unit (DNA sequence) on a chromosome that codes for a specific protein.

gene flow The transfer of new alleles and genetic combinations between populations that results from the movement of individuals.

gene frequency Percentage of different allele forms within a population.

gene pool The total array of genes and alleles in a population.

genetic diversity The range of genetic variation found within a species.

genetic drift Loss of genetic variation and change in allele frequencies that occur by chance in small populations.

genetic variation Genetic differences among individuals in a population or species.

genetically modified organism (GMO) An organism whose genetic code has been altered by scientists using recombinant DNA technology.

genome resource bank (GRB) Frozen collection of DNA, eggs, sperm, embryos, and other tissues of species that can be used in breeding programs and scientific research.

genotype Particular combination of alleles that an individual possesses.

genus Unit of classification that includes one or more species.

geographic information systems (GIS) Computer analyses that integrate and display spatial data; for example, showing the distribution of ecosystems, species, protected areas, and human activities.

global climate change Climate characteristics that are changing now and will continue to change in the future, resulting in part from human activity.

Global Environment Facility (GEF) A large international program, associated with the World Bank, involved in funding conservation activities in developing countries.

global warming The current and future increases in average surface temperatures caused by higher atmospheric concentrations of carbon dioxide and other greenhouse gases produced by human activities.

globalization The increasing interconnectedness of the world's economy.

globally extinct No individuals of the species are presently alive anywhere.

greenhouse effect Warming of the Earth caused by carbon dioxide and other greenhouse gases in the atmosphere that allow the sun's radiation to penetrate and warm the Earth but that slow the re-radiation of this heat. Heat is thus trapped near the surface, raising the planet's temperature.

greenhouse gases Gases in the atmosphere, primarily carbon dioxide, that are transparent to sunlight but that trap heat near the Earth's surface.

guild A group of species at the same trophic level that uses approximately the same environmental resources.

H

Habitat Conservation Plans (HCPs) Regional plans that allow development in designated areas while protecting biodiversity in other areas.

habitat corridors See **corridors**.

habitat fragmentation Process whereby a continuous area of habitat is both reduced in area and divided into two or more fragments.

hard release In the establishment of a new population, when individuals from an outside source are released in a new location without assistance.

healthy ecosystem Ecosystem in which processes are functioning normally, whether or not there are human influences.

herbivore A species that eats green plants or other photosynthetic organisms. Also known as **primary consumer**.

heterosis Increased fitness of individuals resulting from outbreeding. Also known as **hybrid vigor**.

heterozygous Condition of an individual having two different allele forms of the same gene.

homozygous Condition of an individual having two identical allele forms of the same gene.

hybrid Intermediate offspring resulting from the mating of individuals of two different species.

hybrid vigor See **heterosis**.

I

in situ conservation Preservation of endangered species and other aspects of biodiversity in the wild.

inbreeding Self-fertilization or mating among close relatives.

inbreeding depression Lowered reproduction or production of weak offspring following self-fertilization or mating among close relatives.

indicator species Species used in a conservation plan to identify and often protect a biological community or set of ecosystem processes.

indigenous people See **traditional people**.

indirect use values Values provided by biodiversity that do not involve harvesting or destroying the resource (such as water quality, soil protection, recreation, and education). Also known as **public goods**.

integrated conservation and development project (ICDP) Conservation project that also provides for the economic needs and welfare of local people.

Intergovernmental Panel on Climate Change (IPCC) A group of leading scientists organized by the United Nations to study the impacts and implications of human activity on climate and ecosystems.

intrinsic value Value of a species and other aspects of biodiversity for their own sake, unrelated to human needs.

introduction Release of a species outside of its natural range either accidentally or deliberately.

introduction program Moving individuals to areas outside their historical range in order to create a new population of an endangered species.

invasive species Introduced species that increases in abundance at the expense of native species.

inventory A count of the number of individuals in a population.

island biogeography model Formula for the relationship between island size and the number of species living on the island; the model can be used to predict the impact of habitat destruction on species extinctions, viewing remaining habitat as an "island" in the "sea" of a degraded ecosystem.

IUCN The World Conservation Union, a major international conservation organization; previously known as the International Union for the Conservation of Nature.

K

keystone resource A resource in an ecosystem that is crucial to the survival of many species; for example, a water hole.

keystone species A species that has a disproportionate impact (relative to its numbers or biomass) on the organization of an ecosystem. Loss of a keystone species has far-reaching consequences for the ecosystem.

kingdom A large unit of classification; for example, the Animal kingdom includes all animals.

L

land ethic Aldo Leopold's philosophy advocating human use of natural resources that is compatible with or even enhances ecosystem health.

land trust Conservation organization that protects and manages land.

landrace A variety of crop that has unique genetic characteristics.

landscape ecology Discipline that investigates patterns of habitat types and their influence on species distribution and ecosystem processes.

legal title The right of ownership, recognized by a government and/or judicial system; traditional people often struggle to achieve this kind of recognition for their land.

limited development Compromise involving a landowner, a property developer, and a conservation organization that combines some development with protection of the remaining land.

limiting resource Any requirement whose presence or absence limits a population's size. In the desert, for example, water is a limiting resource.

limnology The study of the chemistry, biology, and physics of freshwater.

locally extinct A species that no longer exists in a place where it used to occur but still exists elsewhere.

locus Location on a chromosome where a gene is found.

M

marine protected area (MPA) Protected area of ocean and/or coastline established to maintain and restore marine biodiversity.

market failure Misallocation of resources in which certain individuals or businesses benefit from using a common property resource, such as water, the atmosphere, or a forest, but other individuals, businesses, or the society at large bear the cost.

maximum sustainable yield (MSY) The greatest amount of a resource that can be harvested each year and naturally replaced through population growth without detriment to the population.

metapopulation Mosaic of populations of the same species linked by some degree of migration; a "population of populations."

minimum dynamic area (MDA) Area needed for a population to have a high probability of surviving into the future.

minimum viable population (MVP) Number of individuals necessary to ensure a high probability that a population will survive for a certain number of years into the future.

mitigation Process by which a new population or habitat is created to compensate for a habitat damaged or destroyed elsewhere.

morpho-species Individuals that are probably a distinct species based on their appearance but that do not currently have a scientific name.

morphological definition of a species A group of individuals, recognized as a species, that is morphologically, physiologically, or biochemically distinct from other groups. Compare with **biological definition of a species**.

multilateral development banks The World Bank and other regional banks established by developed countries to promote economic development in developing countries.

multiple-use habitat An area managed to provide a variety of goods and services.

mutalistic relationship A biological interaction between two organisms that is beneficial to both.

mutations Changes that occur in genes and chromosomes resulting in new allele forms and genetic variation.

N

national environmental fund (NEF) A trust fund or foundation that uses its annual income to support conservation activities.

natural history The ecology and distinctive characteristics of a species.

natural resources Commodities and qualities found in nature that are used and valued by people.

natural selection Genetic changes that occur in a population as it adapts over time to its environment; a key mechanism of evolution.

neoendemic Species that occupies a small area because it has only recently evolved from a closely related species.

non-use value Value of something that is not presently used; for example, **existence value**.

nonconsumptive use value Value assigned to benefits provided by some aspect of biodiversity that does not involve harvesting or destroying the resource (such as water quality, soil protection, recreation, and education).

nongovernmental organization (NGO) A private organization that acts to benefit society in some way; many conservation organizations are NGOs.

normative A perspective that embraces ethical commitment rather than ethical neutrality.

O

omnivore A species that consumes both plants and animals.

open-access resources See **common property**.

option value Value of biodiversity in providing possible future benefits for human society (such as new medicines).

order Unit of classification; an order includes one or more related families.

outbreeding Mating and production of offspring by individuals that are not closely related, such as individuals from different populations of the same species. In general, outbreeding leads to **heterosis**, a level of genetic variation that improves individual evolutionary fitness.

outbreeding depression Lowered evolutionary fitness that occasionally occurs when individuals of different species or widely different populations mate and produce offspring.

overexploitation Intense harvest of a resource or species that results in its decline or loss.

P

paleoendemic Ancient species with a narrow geographical range and no closely related extant species.

parasite A predator that grows and feeds on or in a host individual without immediately killing it.

payment for ecosystem services (PES) Direct payment to individual landowners and local communities that protect critical ecosystem characteristics.

perverse subsidies Government payments or other financial incentives to industries that result in environmentally destructive activities.

phenotype The morphological, physiological, anatomical, and biochemical characteristics of an individual that result from the expression of its genotype in a particular environment.

photochemical smog Visible air pollution resulting from chemicals released from human activities being transformed in sunlight.

photosynthetic species See **primary producer**.

phyletic evolution Gradual transformation of one species into another over time.

phylum Large unit of classification; a phylum contains related classes of species.

polymorphic gene Within a population, a gene that has more than one form or allele.

polyploidy Individual with an extra set of chromosomes; important in the evolution of new plant species.

population A geographically defined group of individuals of the same species that mate and otherwise interact with one another. Compare with **metapopulation**.

population biology Study of the ecology and genetics of populations, often with a focus on population numbers.

population bottleneck A radical reduction in population size (e.g., following an outbreak of infectious disease) for one or more generations, sometimes leading to the loss of genetic variation.

population viability analysis (PVA) Demographic analysis that predicts the probability of a population persisting in an environment for a certain period of time; sometimes linked to various management scenarios.

precautionary principle Principle stating that it may be better to avoid taking a particular action due to the possibility of causing unexpected harm.

predation Act of killing and consuming another organism for food.

predator See **carnivore**; **parasite**.

preservationist ethic A belief in the need to preserve wilderness areas for their intrinsic value.

primary consumer See **herbivore**.

primary producer An organism such as green plants, alga, or seaweed that obtains its energy directly from the sun via photosynthesis. Also known as an **autotroph** or **photosynthetic species**.

private goods See **direct use value**.

productive use value Values assigned to products that are sold in markets.

protected areas Habitats managed primarily, or in large part, for biodiversity.

public goods See **indirect use value**.

R

rain forest See **tropical rain forest**.

Ramsar Convention on Wetlands A treaty that promotes the protection of wetlands of international importance.

rapid biodiversity assessments Species inventories and vegetation maps made by teams of biologists when urgent decisions must be made on where to establish new protected areas. Also known as rapid assessment plans (RAPs).

recombination Mixing of the genes on the two copies of a chromosome that occurs during meiosis (i.e., in the formation of egg and sperm, which contain only one copy of each chromosome). Recombination is an important source of genetic variation.

reconciliation ecology The science of developing urban places in which people and biodiversity can coexist.

Red Data Books Compilations of lists ("Red Lists") of endangered species prepared by the IUCN, other conservation organizations, and countries.

Red List criteria Quantitative measures of threats to species based on the probability of extinction.

Reducing Emissions from Deforestation and Degradation (REDD) Program using financial incentives to reduce the emissions of greenhouse gases from deforestation.

reference site Control site that provides goals for restoration in terms of species composition, community structure, and ecosystem processes.

regionally extinct A species is no longer found in part of its former range but still lives elsewhere.

reintroduction program The release of captive-bred or wild-collected individuals at a site within their historical range where the species does not presently occur.

representative site Protected area that includes species and ecosystem properties characteristic of a larger area.

resilience The ability of an ecosystem to return to its original state following disturbance.

resistance The ability of an ecosystem to remain in the same state even with ongoing disturbance.

resource conservation ethic Natural resources should be used for the greatest good of the largest number of people for the longest time.

restocking program The release of additional individuals into an existing population to increase population size and introduce genetic variation. Also known as **augmentation**.

restoration ecology The scientific study of restored populations, communities, and ecosystems.

Rio Summit See **Earth Summit**.

S

secondary consumer See **carnivore**.

seed bank Collection of stored seeds collected from wild and cultivated plants; used in conservation and agricultural programs.

shifting cultivation Farming method in which farmers cut down trees, burn them, plant crops for a few years, and then abandon the site when soil fertility declines. Also called "slash-and-burn" agriculture.

sink population A population that receives an influx of new individuals from a source population.

SLOSS debate Controversy concerning the relative advantages of a *single large or several small* conservation areas.

soft release In the establishment of a new population, when individuals from an outside source are given assistance when released in a new location. Compare with **hard release**.

source population An established population from which individuals disperse to new locations.

speciation Process whereby one species is transformed into one or more new species.

species From the Latin word *specie*, meaning "kind." The base unit of taxonomic classification, a species is a group of genetically and physically similar individuals. Most commonly in biology, a species encompasses all (and only) those individuals that could potentially interbreed among themselves in the wild (see **biological definition of species**). Gene sequencing techniques now allow scientists to identify distinct species with a high degree of precision.

species–area relationship The number of species found in an area increases with the size of the area; i.e., more species are found on large islands than on small islands.

species diversity The entire range of different species found in a particular place.

species richness The number of species found in a community.

stable ecosystem An ecosystem that is able to remain in roughly the same compositional state despite human intervention or stochastic events such as unseasonable weather.

stochasticity Random variation; variation happening by chance.

substitute cost approach Valuing a resource by estimating how much people would have to pay for an equivalent product in the marketplace if their local supply were no longer available.

succession The gradual process of change in species composition, vegetation structure, and ecosystem characteristics following natural or anthropogenic disturbance.

surrogate species See **biodiversity indicators**.

survey Repeatable sampling method to estimate population size, density, or some other aspect of biodiversity.

sustainable development Economic development that meets present and future human needs without damaging the environment and biodiversity.

symbiotic relationship A close, long-term biological relationship in which two species are always found living together (e.g., a lichen is a symbiotic association between an alga and a fungus).

T

taxonomist Scientist involved in the identification and classification of species.

taxonomy Science of identifying and classifying living things.

threatened In the IUCN system refers to species in the endangered, vulnerable, or extinction categories. Under the U.S. Endangered Species Act, refers to species at risk of extinction, but at a lower risk than endangered species.

total economic value The combined direct, indirect, and existence values of some aspect of biodiversity.

traditional people People who regard themselves as the original inhabitants of a region; often organized by social groups and villages. Also known as **indigenous people**, local people, native people, or tribal people.

tragedy of the commons The unregulated use of a common property resource that results in its degradation.

trophic cascade Major changes in vegetation and biodiversity resulting from the loss of a keystone species.

trophic levels Levels of biological communities representing ways in which energy is captured and moved through the ecosystem by the various types of species. See **primary producer; herbivore; carnivore; detritivore**.

tropical rain forest Tropical forest whose trees have leaves throughout the year and where there is substantial rainfall in most months. Characterized by immense species richness, these are areas of great importance for biodiversity.

U

umbrella species Protecting an umbrella species results in the protection of other species.

use value The direct and indirect values provided by some aspect of biodiversity.

V

vulnerable species In the IUCN system, species that has a high risk of extinction in the medium-term future and may become endangered.

W

wilderness area A large area that experiences a bare minimum of human impact.

World Bank International bank established to support economic development in developing countries.

World Conservation Union See **IUCN**.

World Heritage Convention A treaty that protects cultural and natural areas of international significance.

Z

zoning A method of managing protected areas that allows or prohibits certain activities in designated places.

zooplankton Single-celled, heterotrophic (nonphotosynthetic) organisms that drift in bodies of both fresh and salt water.

Bibliography

The numbers in parentheses at the end of each reference indicate the chapter where the main citation can be found.

Abell, R., M. L. Thieme, C. Revenga, M. Bryer, M. Kottelat, N. Bogutskaya, et al. 2008. Freshwater ecoregions of the world: a new map of biogeographic units for freshwater biodiversity conservation. *BioScience* 58: 403–414. (15)

Abensperg-Traun, M. 2009. CITES, sustainable use of wild species and incentive-driven conservation in developing countries, with an emphasis on southern Africa. *Biological Conservation* 142: 948–963. (20)

Abensperg-Traun, M. and G. T. Smith. 1999. How small is too small for small animals? Four terrestrial arthropod species in different-sized remnant woodlands in agricultural Western Australia. *Biodiversity and Conservation* 8: 709–726. (16)

Abesamis, R. A. and G. R. Russ. 2005. Density-dependent spillover from a marine reserve: long-term evidence. *Ecological Applications* 15: 1798–1812. (17)

Adams, G. P., M. H. Ratto, C. W. Collins, and D. R. Bergfelt. 2009. Artificial insemination in South American camelids and wild equids. *Theriogenology* 71: 166–175. (14)

Adams, J. S. 2006. *The Future of the Wild: Radical Conservation for a Crowded World*. Beacon Press, Boston. (19)

Adamski, P. and Z. J. Witkowski. 2007. Effectiveness of population recovery projects based on captive breeding. *Biological Conservation* 140: 1–7. (13)

Adeney, J. M., N. L. Christensen, Jr., and S. L. Pimm. 2009. Reserves protect against deforestation fires in the Amazon. *PLoS One* 4: e5014. (21)

Agar, N. 2001. *Life's Intrinsic Value: Science, Ethics, and Nature*. Columbia University Press, New York. (6)

Agardy, T. S. 1997. *Marine Protected Areas and Ocean Conservation*. R.G. Landes Company, Austin, TX. (17)

Alcock, J. 1993. *Animal Behavior: An Evolutionary Approach*. Sinauer Associates, Sunderland, MA. (2)

Alcorn, J. B. 1991. Ethics, economies and conservation. *In* M. L. Oldfield and J. B. Alcorn (eds.), *Biodiversity: Culture, Conservation and Ecodevelopment*, pp. 317–349. Westview Press, Boulder, CO. (20)

Alexander, S. (ed.). 2009. *Voluntary Simplicity: The Poetic Alternative to Consumer Culture*. Stead and Daughters, Whanganui, New Zealand. (6)

Allen, C., R. S. Lutz, and S. Demarais. 1995. Red imported fire ant impacts on northern bobwhite populations. *Ecological Applications* 5: 632–638. (10)

Allen, E., M. F. Allen, L. Egerton-Warburton, L. Corkidi, and A. Gómez-Pompa. 2003. Impacts of early- and late-seral mycorrhizae during restoration in seasonal tropical forest, Mexico. *Ecological Applications* 13: 1701–1717. (19)

Allen, L. S. 2006. Collaboration in the borderlands: the Malpai Borderlands Group. *Society for Range Management* 17–21. (18)

Allen, W. H. 1988. Biocultural restoration of a tropical forest: architects of Costa Rica's emerging Guanacaste National Park plan to make it an integral part of local culture. *BioScience* 38: 156–161. (19)

Allen, W. H. 2001. *Green Phoenix: Restoring the Tropical Forests of Guanacaste, Costa Rica*. Oxford University Press, Oxford. (19)

Allendorf, F. W. and G. Luikart. 2007. *Conservation and the Genetics of Populations*. Blackwell Publishing, Oxford, UK. (11)

Alling, A., O. Doherty, H. Logan, L. Feldman, and P. Dustan. 2007. Catastrophic coral mortality in the remote Central Pacific Ocean: Kirabati Phoenix Islands. *Atoll Research Bulletin* 545–555. (15)

Allnutt, T. F., S. Ferrier, G. Manion, G.V.N. Powell, T. H. Ricketts, B. L. Fisher, et al. 2008. A method for quantifying biodiversity loss and its application to a 50–year record of deforestation across Madagascar. *Conservation Letters* 1: 173–181. (7)

Almeida, A. P. and S. L. Mendes. 2007. An analysis of the role of local fishermen in the conservation of the loggerhead turtle (*Caretta caretta*) in Pontal do Ipiranga, Linhares, ES, Brazil. *Biological Conservation* 134: 106–112. (1)

Alò, D. and T. F. Turner. 2005. Effects of habitat fragmentation on effective population size in the endangered Rio Grande silvery minnow. *Conservation Biology* 19: 1138–1148. (11)

Alter, S. E., E. Rynes, and S. R. Palumbi. 2007. DNA evidence for historic population size and past ecosystem impacts of gray whales. *Proceedings of the National Academy of Sciences USA* 104: 15162–15167. (10)

Altieri, M. A. 2004. Linking ecologists and traditional farmers in the search for sustainable agriculture. *Frontiers in Ecology and the Environment* 2: 35–42. (14, 20)

Altieri, M. A. and M. K. Anderson. 1992. Peasant farming systems, agricultural modernization and the conservation of crop genetic resources in Latin America. *In* P. L. Fiedler and S. K. Jain (eds.), *Conservation Biology: The Theory and Practice of Nature Conservation, Preservation and Management*, pp. 49–64. Chapman and Hall, New York. (20)

Alvarez-Filip, L., N. K. Dulvy, J. A. Gill, I. M. Côté, and A. R. Watkinson. 2009. Flattening of Caribbean coral reefs: region-wide declines in architectural complexity. *Proceedings of the Royal Society B* 276: 3019–3025. (2)

Amano, T. 2009. Conserving bird species in Japanese farmland: past achievements and future challenges. *Biological Conservation* 142: 1913–1921. (18)

American Cetacean Society. 2010. *http://www.acsonline.org* (10)

Amin, R., K. Thomas, R. H. Emslie, T. J. Foose, and N. van Strien. 2006. An overview of the conservation status of and threats to rhinoceros species in the wild. *International Zoo Yearbook* 40: 96–117. (11)

Anadón, J. D., A. Gimenez, R. Ballestar, and I. Pérez. 2009. Evaluation of local ecological knowledge as a method for collecting extensive data on animal abundance. *Conservation Biology* 23: 617–625. (17)

Anderson, D. M. 2009. Approaches to monitoring, control and management of harmful algal blooms (HABs). *Ocean and Coastal Management* 52: 342–347. (5)

Anderson, J.G.T. and C. M. Devlin. 1999. Restoration of a multi-species seabird colony. *Biological Conservation* 90: 175–181. (17)

Andrew-Essien, E. and F. Bisong. 2009. Conflicts, conservation and natural resource use in protected area systems: an analysis of recurrent issues. *European Journal of Scientific Research* 25: 118–129. (20)

Araujo, R. and M. A. Ramos. 2000. Status and conservation of the giant European freshwater pearl mussel (*Margaritifera auricularia*) (Spengler, 1793) (Bivalvia: Unionoidea). *Biological Conservation* 96: 233–239. (10)

Armitage, D. R., R. Plummer, F. Berkes, R. I. Arthur, A. T. Charles, I. J. Davidson-Hunt, et al. 2009. Adaptive co-management for social-ecological complexity. *Frontiers in Ecology and the Environment* 7: 95–102. (18)

Armstrong, D. P. and P. J. Seddon. 2008. Directions in reintroduction biology. *Trends in Ecology and Evolution* 23: 20–25. (13)

Armsworth, P. R., G. C. Daily, P. Kareiva, and J. N. Sanchirico. 2006. Land market feedbacks can undermine biodiversity conservation. *Proceedings of the National Academy of Sciences USA* 103: 5403–5408. (16)

Armsworth, P. R. and J. N. Sanchirico. 2008. The effectiveness of buying easements as a conservation strategy. *Conservation Letters* 1: 182–189. (20)

Arnhem, E., J. Dupain, R. V. Drubbel, C. Devos, and M. Vercauteren. 2008. Selective logging, habitat quality and home range use by sympatric gorillas and chimpanzees: a case study from an active logging concession in Southeast Cameroon. *Folia Primatologica* 79: 1–14. (18)

Arnold, A. E. and F. Lutzoni. 2007. Diversity and host range of foliar fungal endophytes: are tropical leaves biodiversity hotspots? *Ecology* 88: 541–549. (3)

Association of Zoos & Aquariums. 2009. *http://www.aza.org* (14)

Atkinson, G. and S. Mourato. 2008. Environmental cost-benefit analysis. *Annual Review of Environment and Resources* 33: 317–344. (4)

Aung, U. M. 2007. Policy and practice in Myanmar's protected area system. *Journal of Environmental Management* 84: 188–203. (17)

Ausband, D. E. and K. R. Foresman. 2007. Swift fox reintroductions on the Blackfeet Indian Reservation, Montana, USA. *Biological Conservation* 136: 423–430. (13)

Aviron, S., H. Nitsch, P. Jeanneret, S. Buholzer, H. Luka, L. Pfiffner, et al. 2009. Ecological cross compliance promotes farmland bio-diversity in Switzerland. *Frontiers in Ecology and the Environment* 7: 247–252. (18)

Azam, F. and A. Z. Worden. 2004. Oceanography: microbes, molecules, and marine ecosystems. *Science* 303: 1622–1624. (3)

Bacles, C.F.E., A. F. Lowe, and R. A. Ennos. 2006. Effective seed dispersal across a fragmented landscape. *Science* 311: 628–628. (13)

Bagstad, K. J., K. Stapleton, and J. R. D'Agostino. 2007. Taxes, subsidies, and insurance as drivers of United States coastal development. *Ecological Economics* 63: 285–298. (4)

Baigún, C.R.M., A. Puig, P. G. Minotti, P. Kandus, R. Quintana, and R. Vicari. 2008. Resource use in the Parana River Delta (Argentina): moving away from an ecohydrological approach? *Ecohydrology and Hydrobiology* 8: 245–262. (21)

Baillie, J.E.M., B. Collen, R. Amin, H. R. Akçakaya, S.H.M. Butchart, N. Brummitt, et al. 2008. Toward monitoring global biodiversity. *Conservation Letters* 1: 18–26. (8)

Baillie, J.E.M., C. Hilton-Taylor, and S. N. Stuart (eds.). 2004. *2004 IUCN Red List of threatened species: a global species assessment.* IUCN/SSC Red List Programme, Cambridge, UK. (7, 14)

Baker, J. D. and T. C. Johanos. 2004. Abundance of the Hawaiian monk seal in the main Hawaiian Islands. *Biological Conservation* 116: 103–110. (12)

Baker, J. D. and P. M. Thompson. 2007. Temporal and spatial variation in age-specific survival rates of a long-lived mammal, the Hawaiian monk seal. *Proceedings of the Royal Society B* 274: 407–415. (12)

Bakermans, M. H., A. C. Vitz, A. D. Rodewald, and C. G. Rengifo. 2009. Migratory songbird use of shade coffee in the Venezuelan Andes with implications for conservation of cerulean warbler. *Biological Conservation* 142: 2476–2483. (18)

Bakker, V. J. and D. F. Doak. 2009. Population viability management: ecological standards to guide adaptive management for rare species. *Frontiers in Ecology and the Environment* 7: 158–165. (12)

Balick, M. J. and P. A. Cox. 1996. *Plants, People and Culture: The Science of Ethnobotany.* Scientific American Library, New York. (4)

Balmford, A. 1996. Extinction filters and current resilience: the significance of past selection pressures for conservation biology. *Trends in Ecology and Evolution* 11: 193–196. (8, 14)

Balmford, A., J. Beresford, J. Green, R. Naidoo, M. Walpole, and A. Manica. 2009. A global perspective on trends in nature-based tourism. *PLoS Biology* 7: e1000144. (5)

Balmford, A., A. Bruner, P. Cooper, R. Costanza, S. Farber, R. E. Green, et al. 2002. Economic reasons for conserving wild nature. *Science* 297: 950–953. (4, 5)

Balmford, A., R. E. Green, and M. Jenkins. 2003. Measuring the changing state of nature. *Trends in Ecology and Evolution* 18: 326–330. (7, 17)

Balmford, A. and T. Whitten. 2003. Who should pay for tropical conservation, and how could the costs be met? *Oryx* 37: 238–250. (21)

Ban, N. C., C. R. Picard, and A.C.J. Vincent. 2009. Comparing and integrating community-based and science-based approaches to prioritizing marine areas for protection. *Conservation Biology* 23: 899–910. (15)

Bani, L., D. Massimino, L. Bottonni, and R. Massa. 2006. A multi-scale method for selecting indicator species and priority conservation areas: a case study for broadleaved forests in Lombardy, Italy. *Conservation Biology* 20: 512–526. (15)

Baral, N., M. J. Stern, and J. T. Heinen. 2007. Integrated conservation and development project life cycles in the Annapurna Conservation Area, Nepal: is development overpowering conservation? *Biodiversity and Conservation* 16: 2903–2917. (20)

Barazani, O., A. Perevolotsky, and R. Hadas. 2008. A problem of the rich: prioritizing local plant genetic resources for ex situ conservation in Israel. *Biological Conservation* 141: 596–600. (20)

Barbier, E. B., J. C. Burgess, and C. Folke. 1994. *Paradise Lost? The Ecological Economics of Biodiversity.* Earthscan Publications, London. (4)

Barbier, E. B., E. W. Koch, B. R. Silliman, S. D. Hacker, E. Wolanski, J. Primavera, et al. 2008. Coastal ecosystem-based management with nonlinear ecological functions and values. *Science* 319: 321–323. (5)

Barbour, M. T. and N. L. Poff. 2008. Perspective: communicating our science to influence public policy. *Journal of the North American Benthological Society* 27: 562–569. (22)

Barbour, R. C., J. M. O'Reilly-Wapstra, D. W. De Little, G. J. Jordan, D. A. Steane, J. R. Humphreys, et al. 2009. A geographic mosaic of genetic variation within a foundation tree species and its community-level consequences. *Ecology* 90: 1762–1772. (2)

Barlow, J. and C. A. Peres. 2004. Ecological responses to El Nino-induced surface fires in central Brazilian Amazonia: management implications for flammable tropical forests. *Philosophical Transactions of the Royal Society B* 359: 367–380. (9)

Barnhill, D. L., S. Sarkar, and L. Kalof. 2006. Deep ecology. *In* C. J. Cleveland (ed.), *Encyclopedia of Earth*. Environmental Information Coalition, National Council for Science and the Environment, Washington, D.C. *http://www.eoearth.org/article/Deep_ecology* (6)

Baskin, Y. 1997. *The Work of Nature: How the Diversity of Life Sustains Us.* Island Press, Washington, D.C. (4)

Bass, M. S., M. Finer, C. N. Jenkins, H. Kreft, D. F. Cisneros-Heredia, S. F. McCracken, et al. 2010. Global conservation significance of Ecuador's Yasuní National Park. *PLoS One* 5: e8767. (3)

Bassett, L. (ed.). 2000. *Faith and Earth: A Book of Reflection for Action.* United Nations Environment Programme, New York. (6)

Batisse, M. 1997. A challenge for biodiversity conservation and regional development. *Environment* 39: 7–33. (20)

Bearzi, G. 2009. When swordfish conservation biologists eat swordfish. *Conservation Biology* 23: 1–2. (6)

Beck, B. B., L. G. Rapport, M.R.S. Price, and A. C. Wilson. 1994. Reintroduction of captive-born animals. *In* P. J. Olney, G. M. Mace, and A.T.C. Feistner (eds.), *Creative Conservation: Interactive Management of Wild and Captive Animals*, pp. 265–286. Chapman and Hall, London. (13)

Becker, C .G., C. R. Fonseca, C.F.B. Haddad, and P. I. Prado. 2010. Habitat split as a cause of local population declines of amphibians with aquatic larvae. *Conservation Biology* 24: 287–294. (9)

Beecher, N. A., R. J. Johnson, J. R. Brandle, R. M. Case, and L. J. Young. 2002. Agroecology of birds in organic and nonorganic farmland. *Conservation Biology* 16: 1620–1631. (18)

Behr, B., D. Rath, P. Mueller, T. B. Hildebrandt, F. Goeritz, B. C. Braun, et al. 2009. Feasibility of sex-sorting sperm from the white and the black rhinoceros (*Ceratotherium simum, Diceros bicornis*). *Theriogenology* 72: 353–364. (14)

Beier, C. M. 2008. Influence of political opposition and compromise on conservation outcomes in the Tongass National Forest, Alaska. *Conservation Biology* 22: 1485–1496. (22)

Beier, P., M. van Drielen, and B. O. Kankam. 2002. Avifaunal collapse in West African forest fragments. *Conservation Biology* 16: 1097–1111. (9)

Beissinger, S. R., E. Nicholson, and H. P. Possingham. 2009. Application of population viability analysis to landscape conservation planning. *In* J. J. Millspaugh and F. R. Thompson, III (eds.), *Models for Planning Wildlife Conservation in Large Landscapes*, pp. 33–50. Academic Press, San Diego, CA. (12)

Bell, C. D., J. M. Blumenthal, A. C. Broderick, and B. J. Godley. 2010. Investigating potential for depensation in marine turtles: how low can you go? *Conservation Biology* 24: 226–235. (11)

Bell, T. J., M. L. Bowles, and K. A. McEachern. 2003. Projecting the success of plant population restoration with viability analysis. *In* C. A. Brigham and M. M. Schwartz (eds.), *Population Viability in Plants*, pp. 313–348. Springer-Verlag, Heidelberg. (13)

Bellio, M. G., R. T. Kingsford, and S. W. Kotagama. 2009. Natural versus artificial wetlands and their waterbirds in Sri Lanka. *Biological Conservation* 142: 3076–3085. (13)

Benayas, J.M.R., J. M. Bullock, and A. C. Newton. 2008. Creating woodland islets to reconcile ecological restoration, conservation, and agricultural land use. *Frontiers in Ecology and the Environment* 6: 329–336. (17)

Benítez, P. C., L. McCallum, M. Obersteiner, and Y. Yamagata. 2007. Global potential for carbon sequestration: geographical distribution, country risk and policy implications. *Ecological Economics* 60: 572–583. (4)

Bennett, A. F. 1999. *Linkages in the Landscape: The Role of Corridors and Connectivity in Wildlife Conservation*. IUCN, Gland, Switzerland. (16)

Bennett, E. L., E. Blencowe, K. Brandon, D. Brown, R. W. Burn, G. Cowlishaw, et al. 2007. Hunting for consensus: reconciling bushmeat harvest, conservation, and development policy in West and Central Africa. *Conservation Biology* 21: 884–887. (10)

Bennie, J., M. O. Hill, R. Baxter, and B. Huntley. 2006. Influence of slope and aspect on long-term vegetation change in British chalk grasslands. *Journal of Ecology* 94: 355–368. (17)

Berger, J. 1990. Persistence of different-sized populations: an empirical assessment of rapid extinctions in bighorn sheep. *Conservation Biology* 4: 91–98. (11)

Berger, J. 1999. Intervention and persistence in small populations of bighorn sheep. *Conservation Biology* 13: 432–435. (11)

Berger, J. 2007. Carnivore repatriation and holarctic prey: narrowing the deficit in ecological effectiveness. *Conservation Biology* 21: 1105–1116. (13)

Bergstrom, B. J., S. Vignieri, S. R. Sheffield, W. Sechrest, and A. A. Carlson. 2009. The northern Rocky Mountain gray wolf is not yet recovered. *BioScience* 59: 991–999. (13)

Berkes, F. 2001. Religious traditions and biodiversity. *In* S. A. Levin (ed.), *Encyclopedia of Biodiversity*, vol. 5, pp. 109–120. Academic Press, San Diego, CA. (4)

Berkes, F. 2004. Rethinking community-based conservation. *Conservation Biology* 18: 621–630. (20)

Berkessy, S. A. and B. A. Wintle. 2008. Using carbon investment to grow the biodiversity bank. *Conservation Biology* 22: 510–513. (5)

Berry, O., M. D. Tocher, D. M. Gleeson, and S. D. Sarre. 2005. Effect of vegetation matrix on animal dispersal: genetic evidence from a study of endangered skinks. *Conservation Biology* 19: 855–864. (16)

Bertness, M. D., C. Holdredge, and A. H. Altieri. 2009. Substrate mediates consumer control of salt marsh cordgrass on Cape Cod, New England. *Ecology* 90: 2108–2117. (2)

Beschta, R. L. and W. J. Ripple 2009. Large predators and trophic cascades in terrestrial ecosystems of the western United States. *Biological Conservation* 142: 2401–2414. (2)

Beyer, H. L., E. H. Merrill, N. Varley, and M. S. Boyce. 2007. Willow on Yellowstone's northern range: evidence for a trophic cascade? *Ecological Applications* 17: 1563–1571. (2)

Bhagwat, S. A. and C. Rutte. 2006. Sacred groves: potential for biodiversity management. *Frontiers in Ecology and the Environment* 4: 519–524. (20)

Bhatti, S., S. Carrizosa, P. McGuire, and T. Young (eds.). 2009. *Contracting for ABS: The Legal and Scientific Implications of Bioprospecting Contracts*. IUCN, Gland, Switzerland. (5)

Bickford, D., D. J. Lohman, N. S. Sodhi, P.K.L. Ng, R. Meier, K. Winker, et al. 2007. Cryptic species as a window on diversity and conservation. *Trends in Ecology and Evolution* 22: 148–55. (2)

Big Marine Fish. 2008. *http://www.bigmarinefish.com* (10)

Billington, H. L. 1991. Effect of population size on genetic variation in a dioecious conifer. *Conservation Biology* 5: 115–119. (11)

Bilney, R. J., R. Cooke, and J. G. White. 2010. Underestimated and severe: small mammal decline from the forests of south-eastern Australia since European settlement, as revealed by a top-order predator. *Biological Conservation* 143: 52–59. (7)

Biodiversity International. *http://www.biodiversityinternational.org* (14)

Birchard, B. 2005. *Nature's Keepers: The Remarkable Story of How the Nature Conservancy Became the Largest Environmental Group in the World*. Jossey-Bass, San Francisco, CA. (16)

BirdLife International. 2010. *http://www.birdlife.org* (15)

Bisht, I. S., P. S. Mehta, and D. C. Bhandari. 2007. Traditional crop diversity and its conservation on-farm for sustainable agricultural production in Kumaon Himalaya of Uttaranchal state: a case study. *Genetic Resources and Crop Evolution* 54: 345–357. (20)

Blanc, J. 2008. *Loxodonta africana. In* IUCN Red List of Threatened Species, Version 2009.2. *http://www.iucnredlist.org* (21)

Blanchard, K. A. 2005. Seabird populations of the North Shore of the Gulf of St. Lawrence: culture and conservation. *In* B. Child and M. W. Lyman (eds.), *Natural Resources As Community Assets: Lessons From Two Continents*, pp. 211–236. The Sand County Foundation, Madison, WI and The Aspen Institute, Washington, D.C. (22)

Blaustein, R. J. 2007. Protected areas and equity concerns. *BioScience* 57: 216–221. (20)

Blue Lists. 2009. *http://www.bluelists.ethz.ch* (8)

Blundell, A. G. and M. B. Mascia. 2005. Discrepancies in reported levels of international wildlife trade. *Conservation Biology* 19: 2020–2025. (21)

Boersma, M., A. M. Malzahn, W. Greve, and J. Javidpour. 2007. The first occurrence of the ctenophore *Mnemiopsis leidyi* in the North Sea. *Helgoland Marine Research* 61: 153–155. (10)

Boersma, P. D. 2006. Landscape-level conservation for the sea. *In* M. J. Groom, G. K. Meffe, and C. R. Carroll (eds.), *Principles of Conservation Biology*, 3rd ed, pp. 447–448. Sinauer Associates, Sunderland, MA. (12)

Boersma, P. D. 2008. Penguins as marine sentinels. *BioScience* 58: 597–607. (12)

Boersma, P. D. and G. A. Rebstock. 2009. Foraging distance affects reproductive success in Magellanic penguins. *Marine Ecology Progress Series* 375: 263–275. (12)

Bohlen, P. J., S. Lynch, L. Shabman, M. Clark, S. Shukla, and H. Swain. 2009. Paying for environmental services from agricultural lands: an example from the northern Everglades. *Frontiers in Ecology and the Environment* 7: 46–55. (18, 20)

Borghesio, L. 2009. Effects of fire on the vegetation of a lowland heathland in North-western Italy. *Plant Ecology* 201: 723–731. (20)

Bormann, B. T., R. W. Haynes, and J. R. Martin. 2007. Adaptive management of forest ecosystems: did some rubber hit the road? *BioScience* 57: 186–191. (17)

Borrini-Feyerabend, G., M. Pimbert, T. Farvar, A. Kothari, and Y. Renard. 2004. *Sharing Power: Learning by Doing in Co-Management of Natural Resources throughout the World*. IIED and IUCN/CEESP/CMWG, Cenesta, Tehran. (20)

Botanic Gardens Conservation International (BGCI). 2005. *http://www.bgci.org* (14)

Bottrill, M. C., L. N. Joseph, J. Carwardine, M. Bode, C. Cook, and E. T. Game. 2009. Finite conservation funds mean triage is unavoidable. *Trends in Ecology and Evolution* 24: 183–184. (15, 21)

Boucher, G. and P.J.D. Lambshead. 1995. Ecological biodiversity of marine nematodes in samples from temperate, tropical and deep-sea regions. *Conservation Biology* 9: 1594–1605. (3)

Bouchet, P., G. Falkner, and M. B. Seddon. 1999. Lists of protected land and freshwater molluscs in the Bern Convention and European Habitats Directive: are they relevant to conservation? *Biological Conservation* 90: 21–31. (7)

Bourne, J. K., Jr. 2004. Gone with the water (Louisiana's wetlands). *National Geographic Magazine* 206(October): 88–105. (5)

Bourne, J. K. 2007. Green dreams. *National Geographic Magazine* 212(October): 38–59. (20)

Bouzat, J. L., J. A. Johnson, J. E. Toepfer, S. A. Simpson, T. L. Ekser, and R. L. Westemeier. 2008. Beyond the beneficial effects of translocations as an effective tool for the genetic restoration of isolated populations. *Conservation Genetics* 10: 191–201. (11, 12)

Bowkett, A. E. 2009. Recent captive-breeding proposals and the return of the ark concept to global species conservation. *Conservation Biology* 23: 773–776. (14)

Bowles, M. L., J. L. McBride, and R. F. Betz. 1998. Management and restoration ecology of Mead's milkweed. *Annals of the Missouri Botanical Garden* 85: 110–125. (13)

Boyd, C., T. M. Brooks, S.H.M. Butchart, G. J. Edgar, G.A.B. da Fonseca, F. Hawkins, et al. 2008. Spatial scale and the conservation of threatened species. *Conservation Letters* 1: 37–43. (16, 18)

Boydell, S. and H. Holzknecht. 2003. Land-caught in the conflict between custom and commercialism. *Land Use Policy* 20: 203–207. (20)

Bradshaw, A. D. 1990. The reclamation of derelict land and the ecology of ecosystems. *In* W. R. Jordan III, M. E. Gilpin, and J. D. Aber (eds.), *Restoration Ecology: A Synthetic Approach to Ecological Research*, pp. 53–74. Cambridge University Press, Cambridge. (19)

Bradshaw, C.J.A., B M Fitzpatrick, C. C Steinberg, B. W. Brook, and M. G. Meekan. 2008. Decline in whale shark size and abundance at Ningaloo Reef over the past decade: the world's largest fish is getting smaller. *Biological Conservation* 141: 1894–190. (21)

Bradshaw, C.J.A., N. S. Sodhi, and B. W. Brook. 2009. Tropical turmoil: a biodiversity tragedy in progress. *Frontiers in Ecology and the Environment* 7: 79–87. (7, 9)

Braithwaite, R. W. 2001. Tourism, role of. *In* S. A. Levin (ed.), *Encyclopedia of Biodiversity*, vol. 5, pp. 667–679. Academic Press, San Diego, CA. (5)

Brandt, A. A., A. J. Gooday, S. N. Brandão, S. Brix, W. Brökeland, T. Cedhagen, et al. 2007. First insights in the biodiversity and biogeography of the Southern Ocean deep sea. *Nature* 447: 307–311. (3)

Braschler, B. 2009. Successfully implementing a citizen-scientist approach to insect monitoring in a resource-poor country. *BioScience* 59:103–104. (20)

Brashares, J. S., P. Arcese, M. K. Sam, P. B. Coppolillo, A.R.E. Sinclair, and A. Balmford. 2004. Bushmeat hunting, wildlife declines, and fish supply in West Africa. *Science* 306: 1180–1183. (10)

Breed, A. C., R. K. Plowright, D.T.S. Hayman, D. L. Knobel, F. M. Molenaar, D. Gardner-Roberts, et al. 2009. Disease management in endangered mammals. *In* R. J. Delahay, G. C. Smith, M. R. Hutchings, S. Rossi, G. Marion, et al. (eds.), *Management of Disease in Wild Mammals*, pp. 215–239. Springer, Japan. (10)

Brennan, A. and Y. S. Lo. 2008. Environmental ethics. *Stanford Encyclopedia of Philosophy*. *http://plato.stanford.edu/entries/ethics-environmental* (6)

Brennan, A. J. 2008. Theoretical foundations of sustainable economic welfare indicators – ISEW and political economy of the disembedded system. *Ecological Economics* 67: 1–19. (4)

Breshears D. D., O. B. Myers, C. W. Meyer, F. J. Barnes, C. B. Zhou, C. D. Allen, et al. 2009. Tree die-off in response to global change-type drought: mortality insights from a decade of plant water potential measurements. *Frontiers in Ecology and the Environment* 7: 185–189. (9)

Briggs. S. V. 2009. Priorities and paradigms: directions in threatened species recovery. *Conservation Letters* 2: 101–108. (17, 20)

Brightsmith, D., J. Hilburn, A. del Campo, J. Boyd, M. Frisius, R. Frisius, et al. 2005. The use of hand-raised psittacines for reintroduction: a case study of scarlet macaws (*Ara macao*) in Peru and Costa Rica. *Biological Conservation* 121: 465–472. (13)

Brock, R. E. and D. A. Kelt. 2004. Influence of roads on the endangered Stephens' kangaroo rat (*Dipodomys stephensi*): are dirt and gravel roads different? *Biological Conservation* 118: 633–640. (20)

Brodie, J. F., O. E. Helmy, W. Y. Brockelman, and J. L. Maron. 2009. Bushmeat poaching reduces the seed dispersal and population growth rate of a mammal-dispersed tree. *Ecological Applications* 19: 854–863. (17)

Brook, A., M. Zint, and R. DeYoung. 2003. Landowner's response to an Endangered Species Act listing and implications for encouraging conservation. *Conservation Biology* 17: 1638–1649. (20)

Brooke, A. D., S.H.M. Butchart, S. T. Garnett, G. M. Crowley, N. B. Mantilla-Beniers, and A. Stattersfield. 2008. Rates of movement of threatened bird species between IUCN Red List categories and toward extinction. *Conservation Biology* 22: 417–427. (8)

Brooks, T. M., R. A. Mittermeier, C. G. Mittermeier, G.A.B. da Fonseca, A. B. Rylands, W. R. Konstant, et al. 2002. Habitat loss and extinction in the hotspots of biodiversity. *Conservation Biology* 16: 909–923. (7)

Brooks, T. M., S. L. Pimm, and J. O. Oyugi. 1999. Time lag between deforestation and bird extinction in tropical forest fragments. *Conservation Biology* 13: 1140–1150. (7)

Brooks, T. M., S. J. Wright, and D. Sheil. 2009. Evaluating the success of conservation actions in safeguarding tropical forest biodiversity. *Conservation Biology* 23: 1448–1457. (21)

Bruner, A. G., R. E. Gullison, and A. Balmford. 2004. Financial costs and shortfalls of managing and expanding protected-area systems in developing countries. *BioScience* 54: 1119–1126. (17, 21)

Bruner, A. G., R. E. Gullison, R. E. Rice, and G.A.B. da Fonseca. 2001. Effectiveness of parks in promoting tropical diversity. *Science* 291: 125–128. (15, 17)

Bruno, J. F. and J. B. Cardinale. 2008. Cascading effects of predator richness. *Frontiers in Ecology and the Environment* 6: 539–546. (2)

Brush, S. B. 2004. Growing biodiversity. *Nature* 430: 967–968. (20)

Brush, S. B. 2007. Farmers' rights and protection of traditional agricultural knowledge. *World Development* 35: 1499–1514. (14)

Bryant, D., L. Burke, J. McManus, and M. Spalding. 1998. *Reefs at Risk: A Map-Based Indicator of Threats to the World's Coral Reefs.* World Resources Institute, Washington, D.C. (9)

Brys, R., H. Jacquemyn, P. Endels, G. De Blust, and M. Hermy. 2005. Effect of habitat deterioration on population dynamics and extinction risks in a previously common perennial. *Conservation Biology* 19: 1633–1643. (9)

Buchanan, G. M., P. F. Donald, L.D.C. Fishpool, J. A. Arinaitwe, M. Balman, and P. Mayaux. 2009. An assessment of land cover and threats in Important Bird Areas in Africa. *Bird Conservation International* 19: 49–61. (17)

Buchholz, R. 2007. Behavioral biology: an effective and relevant conservation tool. *Trends in Ecology and Evolution* 22: 401407. (13)

Buckley, M. C. and E. E. Crone. 2008. Negative off-site impacts of ecological restoration: understanding and addressing the conflict. *Conservation Biology* 22: 1118–1124. (4)

Buckley, R. 2009. Parks and tourism. *PLoS Biology* 7: e1000143. (5)

Buffalo Field Campaign. 2010. *http://www.buffalofieldcampaign.org* (16)

Bull, A. T. 2004. *Microbial Diversity and Bioprospecting.* ASM Press, Washington, D.C. (5)

Bulman, C. R., R. J. Wilson, A. R. Holt, A. L. Galvez-Bravo, R. I. Early, M. S. Warren et al. 2007. Minimum viable population size, extinction debt, and the conservation of declining species. *Ecological Applications* 17: 1460–1473. (8, 12)

Buner, F., M. Jenny, N. Zbinden, and B. Naef-Daenzer. 2005. Ecologically enhanced areas—a key habitat structure for re-introduced grey partridges *Perdix perdix*. *Biological Conservation* 124: 373–381. (18)

Burger, J. 2008. Environmental management: integrating ecological evaluation, remediation, restoration, natural resource damage assessment and long-term stewardship on contaminated lands. *Science of the Total Environment* 400: 16–19. (19)

Burghardt, K. T., D. W. Tallamy, and W. G. Shriver. 2009. Impact of native plants on bird and butterfly biodiversity in suburban landscapes. *Conservation Biology* 23: 219–224. (19)

Burgman, M. A., D. Keith, S. D. Hopper, D. Widyatmoko, and C. Drill. 2007. Threat syndromes and conservation of the Australian flora. *Biological Conservation* 134: 73–82. (9)

Burton, A. 2005. Microbes muster pollution power. *Frontiers in Ecology and the Environment* 3: 182. (5)

Bushmeat Crisis Task Force. 2009. *http://www.bushmeat.org* (10)

Butchart, S. H. and J. P. Bird. 2010. Data Deficient birds on the IUCN Red List: what don't we know and why does it matter? *Biological Conservation* 143: 239–247. (8)

Butler, R. A., L. P. Koh, and J. Ghazoul. 2009. REDD in the red: palm oil could undermine carbon payment schemes. *Conservation Letters* 2: 67–73. (5, 20)

Butler, R. A. and W. F. Laurance. 2008. New strategies for conserving tropical forests. *Trends in Ecology and Evolution* 23: 469–472. (9, 10)

Bytnerowicz, A., K. Omasa, and E. Paoletti. 2007. Integrated effects of air pollution and climate change on forests: a northern hemisphere perspective. *Environmental Pollution* 147: 438–445. (9)

Cafaro, P. 2010. Economic growth or the flourishing of life: the ethical choice global climate change puts to humanity in the 21st century. *Essays in Philosophy* 11: 6. (6)

Cafaro, P. and W. Staples. 2009. The environmental argument for reducing immigration into the United States. *Environmental Ethics* 31: 5–30. (6)

Cain, M. L., W. D. Bowman, and S. D. Hacker. 2008. *Ecology.* Sinauer Associates, Sunderland, MA. (2)

Callaway, J. C., G. Sullivan, and J. B. Zedler. 2003. Species-rich plantings increase biomass and nitrogen accumulation in a wetland restoration experiment. *Ecological Applications* 13: 1626–1639. (19)

Callaway, R. M., G. C. Thelen, A. Rodriguez, and W. E. Holben. 2004. Soil biota and exotic plant invasion. *Nature* 427: 731–733. (10)

Callicott, J. B. 1990. Whither conservation ethics? *Conservation Biology* 4: 15–20. (1)

Calver, M., S. Thomas, S. Bradley, and H. McCutcheon. 2007. Reducing the rate of predation on wildlife by pet cats: the efficacy and practicability of collar-mounted pounce protectors. *Biological Conservation* 137: 341–348. (9)

Camacho, A. E. 2007. Can regulation evolve? Lessons from a study in maladaptive management. *UCLA Law Review* 55: 293–358. (20)

Campbell, L., P. Verburg, D. G. Dixon, and R. E. Hecky. 2008. Mercury biomagnification in the food web of Lake Tanganyika (Tanzania, East Africa). *Science of the Total Environment* 402: 184–191. (9)

Cardillo, M., G. M. Mace, J. L. Gittleman, K. E. Jones, J. Bielby, and A. Purvis. 2008. The predictability of extinction: biological and external correlates of decline in mammals. *Proceedings of the Royal Society B* 275: 1441–1448. (8)

Carlton, J. T. 2001a. Endangered marine invertebrates. *In* S.A. Levin (ed.), *Encyclopedia of Biodiversity*, vol. 2, pp. 455–464. Academic Press, San Diego, CA. (10)

Carlton, J. T. 2001b. Introduced species in U.S. coastal waters: environmental impacts and management priorities. Pew Oceans Commission, Arlington, VA. (10)

Caro, T., T. Jones, and T.R.B. Davenport. 2009. Realities of documenting wildlife corridors in tropical countries. *Biological Conservation* 142: 2807–2811. (16)

Caron, D. A. 2009. New accomplishments and approaches for assessing protistan diversity and ecology in natural ecosystems. *BioScience* 59: 287–299. (3)

Carpenter, K. E., M. Abrar, G. Aeby, R. B. Aronson, S. Banks, A. Bruckner, et al. 2008. One-third of reef-building coral face elevated extinction risk from climate change and local impacts. *Science* 321: 560–563. (7, 9)

Carraro, C., J. Eyckmans, and M. Finus. 2006. Optimal transfers and participation decisions in international environmental agreements. *The Review of International Organizations* 1: 379–396. (21)

Carroll, C. 2009. Can solar save us? *National Geographic Magazine* 216(September): 52. (20)

Carroll, C. and D. S. Johnson. 2008. The importance of being spatial (and reserved): assessing northern spotted owl habitat relationships with hierarchical Bayesian methods. *Conservation Biology* 22: 1026–1036. (18)

Carruthers, E. H., D. C. Schneider, and J. D. Neilson. 2009. Estimating the odds of survival and identifying mitigation opportunities for common bycatch in pelagic longline fisheries. *Biological Conservation* 142: 2620–2630. (10)

Carson, R. 1962. *Silent Spring.* Houghton Mifflin, Boston. (1)

Carson, R. L. 1965. *The Sense of Wonder*. Harper & Row, New York. (6)

Castelletta, M., J. M. Thiollay, and N. S. Sodhi. 2005. The effects of extreme forest fragmentation on the bird community of Singapore Island. *Biological Conservation* 121: 135–155. (7)

Castellón, T. D. and K. E. Sieving. 2006. An experimental test of matrix permeability and corridor use by an endemic understory bird. *Conservation Biology* 20: 135–145. (16)

Castillo, A., A. Torres, A. Velázquez, and G. Bocco. 2005. The use of ecological science by rural producers: a case study in Mexico. *Ecological Applications* 15: 745–756. (20)

Castro, G., I. Locker, V. Russell, L. Cornwell, and E. Fajer. 2000. *Mapping Conservation Investments: An Assessment of Biodiversity Funding in Latin America and the Caribbean*. World Wildlife Fund, Washington, D.C. (21)

Cawardine, J., J. K. Carissa, K. A. Wilson, R. L. Pressey, and H. P. Possingham. 2009. Hitting the target and missing the point: target-based conservation planning in context. *Conservation Letters* 2: 4–11. (16)

Ceballos, G. 2007. Conservation priorities for mammals in megadiverse Mexico: the efficiency of reserve networks. *Ecological Applications* 17: 569–578. (15)

Center for Plant Conservation: Recovering America's Vanishing Flora. *http://centerforplantconservation.org* (14)

Cernea, M. 2006. Re-examining "displacement": a redefinition of concepts in development and conservation policies. *Social Change* 36: 8–35. (21)

Chan, K.M.A. 2008. Value and advocacy in conservation biology: crisis discipline or discipline in crisis? *Conservation Biology* 22: 1–3. (1)

Chape, S., S. Blyth, L. Fish, P. Fox, and M. Spaulding. 2003. *2003 United Nations List of Protected Areas*. IUCN and UNEP-WCMC, Gland, Switzerland. (15)

Chape, S., M. D. Spalding, and M. D. Jenkins (eds.). 2008. *The World's Protected Areas: Status, Values, and Prospects in the Twenty-First Century*. University of California Press, CA. (15)

Chapman, J. W., T. W. Miller, and E. V. Coan. 2003. Live seafood species as recipes for invasion. *Conservation Biology* 17: 1386–1395. (10)

Charnley, S. 2006. The Northwest Forest Plan as a model for broad-scale ecosystem management: a social perspective. *Conservation Biology* 20: 330–340. (22)

Chau. K. C. 1995. The Three Gorges Project of China: resettlement prospects and problems. *Ambio* 24: 98–102. (21)

Chen, X. and J. Wu. 2009. Sustainable landscape architecture: implications of the Chinese philosophy of "unity of man with nature" and beyond. *Landscape Ecology* 24: 1015–1026. (19)

Chen, X. D., F. Lupi, G. M. He, and J. G. Liu. 2009. Linking social norms to efficient conservation investment in payments for ecosystem services. *Proceedings of the National Academy of Sciences USA* 106: 11812–11817. (20)

Chen, Y. H. 2009. Combining the species-area habitat relationship and environmental cluster analysis to set conservation priorities: a study in the Zhoushan Archipelago, China. *Conservation Biology* 23: 537–545. (7)

Chernela, J. 1999. Indigenous knowledge and Amazonian blackwaters of hunger. *In* D. Posey (ed.), *Cultural and Spiritual Values of Biodiversity*, pp. 423–426. United Nations Environment Programme (UNEP), London. (20)

Chiarucci, A., F. D'auria, V. De Dominicis, A. Laganà, C. Perini, and E. Salerni. 2005. Using vascular plants as a surrogate taxon to maximize fungal species richness in reserve design. *Conservation Biology* 19: 1644–1652. (15)

Chicago Regional Biodiversity Council. 2001. *Chicago Wilderness, An Atlas of Biodiversity*. Chicago Regional Biodiversity Council, Chicago, IL. (16)

Chicago Wilderness Habitat Project. 2009. *http://www.habitatproject.org* (16)

Chicago Wilderness Magazine. 2004. *http://chicagowildernessmag.org* (16)

Chittaro, P. M., I. C. Kaplan, A. Keller, and P. S. Levin. 2010. Trade-offs between species conservation and the size of marine protected areas. *Conservation Biology* 24: 197–206. (7)

Chivian, E. and A. Bernstein (eds.). 2008. *Sustaining Life: How Human Health Depends on Biodiversity*. Oxford University Press, New York. (2, 3, 4, 5)

Chornesky, E. A., A. M. Bartuska, G. H. Aplet, K. O. Britton, J. Cummings-Carlson, F. W. Davis, et al. 2005. Science priorities for reducing the threat of invasive species to sustainable forestry. *BioScience* 55: 335–348. (10)

Chown, S. L. and K. J. Gaston. 2000. Areas, cradles and museums: the latitudinal gradient in species richness. *Trends in Ecology and Evolution* 15: 311–315. (3)

Christensen, J. 2003. Auditing conservation in an age of accountability. *Conservation in Practice* 4: 12–19. (17)

Christian-Smith, J. and A. Merenlender. 2010. The disconnect between restoration goals and practices: a case study of watershed restoration in the Russian River basin. *Restoration Ecology* 18: 95–102. (19)

Christy, B. 2010. Asia's wildlife trade. *National Geographic Magazine* 217(January): 78–107. (10)

Cincotta, R. P., J. Wisnewski, and R. Engelman. 2000. Human population in biodiversity hotspots. *Nature* 404: 990–992. (15)

Cinner, J. E. and S. Aswani. 2007. Integrating customary management into marine conservation. *Biological Conservation* 140: 201–216. (10)

Cinner, J. E., M. J. Marnane, T. R. McClanahan, T. H. Clark, and J. Ben. 2005. Trade, tenure, and tradition: influence of sociocultural factors on resource use in Melanesia. *Conservation Biology* 19: 1469–1477. (10)

Circle of Life. 2007. *http://www.circleoflife.org* (22)

Clapham, P. and K. van Waerebeek. 2007. Bushmeat and bycatch: the sum of the parts. *Molecular Ecology* 16: 2607–2609. (10)

Clark, C. J., J. R. Poulsen, R. Malonga, and P. W. Elkan, Jr. 2009. Logging concessions can extend the conservation estate for central African tropical forests. *Conservation Biology* 23: 1281–1293. (18)

Clarke, A. G. 2009. The Frozen Ark Project: the role of zoos and aquariums in preserving the genetic material of threatened animals. *International Zoo Yearbook* 43: 222–230. (14)

Clarke, F. M., D. V. Pio, and P. A. Racey. 2005. A comparison of logging systems and bat diversity in the Neotropics. *Conservation Biology* 19: 1194–1204. (18)

Clarke, S. 2008. Use of shark fin trade data to estimate historic total shark removals in the Atlantic Ocean. *Aquatic Living Resources* 21: 73–381. (6)

Clausen, R. and R. York. 2008. Economic growth and marine diversity: influence of human social structure on decline of marine trophic levels. *Conservation Biology* 22: 458–466. (9)

Clausnitzer, V., V. J. Kalkman, M. Ram, B. Collen, J.E.M. Baillie, M. Bedjanic, et al. 2009. Odonata enter the biodiversity crisis debate: the first global assessment of an insect group. *Biological Conservation* 142: 1864–1869. (8)

Clavero, M., L. Brotons, P. Pons, and D. Sol. 2009. Prominent role of invasive species in avian biodiversity loss. *Biological Conservation* 142: 2043–2049. (7, 10)

Clavero, M. and E. García-Berthou. 2005. Invasive species are a leading cause of animal extinctions. *Trends in Ecology and Evolution* 20: 110–110. (10)

Cleland, E. E., I. Chuine, A. Menzel, H. A. Mooney, and M. D. Schwartz. 2007. Shifting plant phenology in response to global change. *Trends in Ecology and Evolution* 22: 357–365. (9)

Cleveland, C. J. and B. Black. 2008. Three Gorges Dam, China. *In* C. J. Cleveland (ed.), *Encyclopedia of Earth*. Environmental Information Coalition, National Council for Science and the Environment, Washington, D.C. *http://www.eoearth.org/article/Three_Gorges_Dam%2C_China* (21)

Cleveland, C. J., M. Betke, P. Federico, J. D. Frank, T. G. Hallam, J. Horn, et al. 2006. Economic value of the pest control service provided by Brazilian free-tailed bats in south-central Texas. *Frontiers in Ecology and the Environment* 4: 238–243. (5)

Clewell, A. F. and J. Aronson. 2006. Motivations for the restoration of ecosystems. *Conservation Biology* 20: 420–428. (19)

Clewell, A. F. and J. Aronson. 2008. *Ecological Restoration: Principles, Values, and Structure of an Emerging Profession.* Island Press, Washington, D.C. (19)

Cohn, J. P. 2008. Citizen science: can volunteers do real research? *BioScience* 58: 192–197. (22)

Colding, J., J. Lundberg, S. Lundberg, and E. Andersson. 2009. Golf courses and wetland fauna. *Ecological Applications* 19: 1481–1491. (18)

Coleman, D. C. 2008. From peds to paradoxes: linkages between soil biota and their influences on ecological processes. *Soil Biology and Biochemistry* 40: 271–289. (5)

Coleman, J. M., O. K. Huh, and D. Braud. 2008. Wetland loss in world deltas. *Journal of Coastal Research* 24 (1A): 1–14. (9)

Collaboration for Environmental Evidence. 2009. *http://www.environ mentalevidence.org* (17)

Collen, B., J. Loh, S. Whitmee, L. McRae, R. Amin, and J.E.M. Baillie. 2009. Monitoring change in vertebrate abundance: the Living Planet Index. *Conservation Biology* 23: 317–327. (8)

Collinge, S. K., K. L. Prudic, and J. C. Oliver. 2003. Effects of local habitat characteristics and landscape context on grassland butterfly diversity. *Conservation Biology* 17: 178–187. (17)

Colwell R. K., G. Brehm, C. L. Cardelús, A. C. Gilman, and J. T. Longino. 2008. Global warming, elevational range shifts, and lowland biotic attrition in the wet tropics. *Science* 322: 258–261. (9)

Comizzoli, P., A. E. Crosier, N. Songsasen, M. S. Gunther, J. G. Howard, and D. E. Wildt. 2009. Advances in reproductive science for wild carnivore conservation. *Reproduction in Domestic Animals* 44: 47–52. (14)

Commission for the Conservation of Antarctic Marine Living Resources (CCAMLR). *http://www.ccamlr.org* (21)

Common, M. and S. Stagl. 2005. *Ecological Economics: An Introduction.* Cambridge University Press, New York. (4)

Comprehensive Everglades Restoration Plan (CERP): The Journey to Restore America's Everglades. *http://www.evergladesplan.org* (19)

Congressional Research Service and P. Saundry. 2009. Wilderness areas in the United States. *In* C. J. Cleveland (ed.), *Encyclopedia of Earth.* Environmental Information Coalition, National Council for Science and the Environment, Washington, D.C. *http://www.eoearth.org/article/Wilderness_areas_in_the_United_States* (1)

Connor, E. F. and E. D. McCoy. 2001. Species-area relationships. *In* S. A. Levin (ed.), *Encyclopedia of Biodiversity* 5: 397–412. Academic Press, San Diego, CA. (7)

Conservation International Biodiversity Hotspots. 2007. *http://www.biodiversityhotspots.org* (15)

Conservation International and K. J. Caley. 2008. Biological diversity in the Mediterranean Basin. *In* C. J. Cleveland (ed.), *Encyclopedia of Earth.* Environmental Information Coalition, National Council for Science and the Environment, Washington, D.C. *http://www.eoearth.org/article/Biological_diversity_in_the_Mediter ranean_Basin* (3)

Conservation Measures Partnership (CMP). 2007. Open Standards for the Practice of Conservation, Version 2.0. *http://www.conserva tionmeasures.org* (21)

Consultative Group on International Agricultural Research. 2009. *http://www.cgiar.org* (14)

Convention on Biological Diversity. 2010. *http://www.cbd.int* (21)

Convention on International Trade in Endangered Species of Wild Flora and Fauna (CITES). *http://www.cites.org* (10, 21)

Conway, W. G., M. Hutchins, M. Souza, Y. Kapentanakos, and E. Paul. 2001. *The AZA Field Conservation Resource Guide.* Zoo Atlanta, Atlanta, GA. (14)

Cooper, N. S. 2000. How natural is a nature reserve?: an ideological study of British nature conservation landscapes. *Biological Conservation* 9: 1131–1152. (1)

Cork, S. J., T. W. Clark, and N. Mazur. 2000. Introduction: an interdisciplinary effort for koala conservation. *Conservation Biology* 14: 606–609. (17)

Corlatti, L., K. Hacklander, and F. Frey-Roos. 2009. Ability of wildlife overpasses to provide connectivity and prevent genetic isolation. *Conservation Biology* 23: 548–556. (11, 16)

Corlett, R. T. 2009. Seed dispersal distances and plant migration potential in tropical East Asia. *Biotropica* 41: 592–598. (9)

Corlett, R. T. and R. B. Primack. 2010. *Tropical Rain Forests: An Ecological and Biogeographical Comparison,* 2nd ed. Blackwell Publishing, Malden, MA. (3, 4, 9)

Corlett, R. T. and I. M. Turner. 1996. The conservation value of small, isolated fragments of lowland tropical rain forest. *Trends in Ecology and Evolution* 11: 330–333. (16)

Corral-Verdugo, V., M. Bonnes, C. Tapia-Fonllem, B. Fraijo-Sing, M. Frias-Armenta, and G. Carrus. 2009. Correlates of pro-sustainability orientation: the affinity towards diversity. *Journal of Environmental Psychology* 29: 34–43. (1)

Costa Rica National Parks, National System of Conservation Areas. 2005. *http://www.costarica-nationalparks.com* (20)

Costanza, R., R. d'Arge, R. de Groot, S. Farber, M. Grasso, B. Hannon, et al. 1997. The value of the world's ecosystem services and natural capital. *Nature* 387: 253–260. (5)

Costello, C., J. M. Drake, and D. M. Lodge. 2007. Evaluating an invasive species policy: ballast water exchange in the Great Lakes. *Ecological Applications* 17: 655–662. (10)

Cottam, G. 1990. Community dynamics on an artificial prairie. *In* W. R. Jordan III, M. E. Gilpin, and J. D. Aber (eds.), *Restoration Ecology: A Synthetic Approach to Ecological Research,* pp. 257–270. Cambridge University Press, Cambridge MA. (19)

Cowen, L., S. J. Walsh, C. J. Schwarz, N. Cadigan, and J. Morgan. 2009. Estimating exploitation rates of migrating yellowtail flounder (*Limanda ferruginea*) using multistate mark-recapture methods incorporating tag loss and variable reporting rates. *Canadian Journal of Fisheries and Aquatic Sciences* 66: 1245–1255. (12)

Cowling, R. M., B. Egoh, A. T. Knight, P. J. O'Farrell, B. Reyers, M. Rouget, et al. 2008. An operational model for mainstreaming ecosystem services for implementation. *Proceedings of the National Academy of Sciences USA* 105: 9483–9488. (22)

Cowling, R. M. and R. L. Pressey. 2003. Introduction to systematic conservation planning in the Cape Floristic Region. *Biological Conservation* 112: 1–13. (15)

Cox, G. W. 1993. *Conservation Ecology.* W.C. Brown, Dubuque, IA. (9)

Cox, P. A. 2001. Pharmacology, biodiversity and. *In* S. A. Levin (ed.), *Encyclopedia of Biodiversity,* vol. 4, pp. 523–536. Academic Press, San Diego, CA. (4)

Cox, P. A. and T. Elmqvist. 1997. Ecocolonialism and indigenous-controlled rainforest preserves in Samoa. *Ambio* 26: 84–89. (20)

Cox, T. M., R. L. Lewison, R. Zydelis, L. B. Crowder, C. Safina, and A. J. Read. 2007. Comparing effectiveness of experimental and implemented bycatch reduction measures: the ideal and the real. *Conservation Biology* 21: 1155–1164. (10)

Craft, C., J. Clough, J. Ehman, S. Joye, R. Park, S. Pennings, et al. 2009. Forecasting the effects of accelerated sea-level rise on tidal marsh ecosystem services. *Frontiers in Ecology and the Environment* 7: 73–78. (5)

Craig, G. R., G. C. White, and J. H. Enderson. 2004. Survival, recruitment, and rate of population change of the peregrine falcon population in Colorado. *The Journal of Wildlife Management* 68: 1032–1038. (9)

Craig, L. S., M. A. Palmer, D. C. Richardson, S. Filoso, E. S. Bernhardt, B. P. Bledsoe, et al. 2008. Stream restoration strategies for reducing river nitrogen loads. *Frontiers in Ecology and the Environment* 6: 529–538. (19)

Critical Ecosystem Partnership Fund (CEPF). 2009. *http://www.cepf.net* (21)

Crnokrak, P. and D. A. Roff. 1999. Inbreeding depression in the wild. *Heredity* 83: 260–270. (11)

Crooks, K. R., A. V. Suarez, and D. T. Bolger. 2001. Extinction and colonization of birds on habitat islands. *Conservation Biology* 15: 159–172. (9)

Crooks, K. R., A. V. Suarez, and D. T. Bolger. 2004. Avian assemblages along a gradient of urbanization in a highly fragmented landscape. *Biological Conservation* 115: 451–462. (16)

Crowl, T. A., T. O. Crist, R. R. Parmenter, G. Belovsky, and A. E. Lugo. 2008. The spread of invasive species and infectious disease as drivers of ecosystem change. *Frontiers in Ecology and the Environment* 6: 238–246. (10)

Cuevas, Y. A. and S. M. Zalba. 2010. Recovery of native grasslands after removing invasive pines. *Restoration Ecology* In press (19)

Cuperus, R., K. J. Canters, H.A.V. de Hars, and D. S. Friedman. 1999. Guidelines for ecological compensation associated with highways. *Biological Conservation* 90: 41–51. (16)

Cushman, S. A., K. S. McKelvey, and M. K. Schwartz. 2009. Use of empirically derived source-destination models to map regional conservation corridors. *Conservation Biology* 23: 368–376. (16)

Czech, B. 2002. A transdisciplinary approach to conservation land acquisition. *Conservation Biology* 16: 1488–1497. (20)

Czech, B. 2004. Policies for managing urban growth and landscape change: a key to conservation in the 21st century. USDA Forest Service General Technical Report North Central 265: 8–13. (22)

Czech, B. 2008. Prospects for reconciling the conflict between economic growth and biodiversity conservation with technological progress. *Conservation Biology* 22: 1389–1398. (1)

da Silva, J.M.C., A. B. Rylands, and G.A.B. da Fonseca. 2005. The fate of the Amazonian areas of endemism. *Conservation Biology* 19: 689–694. (15)

Dahles, H. 2005. A trip too far: ecotourism, politics, and exploitation. *Development Change* 36: 969–971. (5)

Daleszczyk, K. and A. N. Bunevich. 2009. Population viability analysis of European bison populations in Polish and Belarusian parts of Bialowieza Forest with and without gene exchange. *Biological Conservation* 142: 3068–3075. (15)

Daly, G. L., Y. D. Lei, C. Teixeira, D.C.G. Muir, L. E. Castillo, and F. Wania. 2007. Accumulation of current-use pesticides in neotropical montane forests. *Environmental Science and Technology* 41: 1118–1123. (9)

Danby, R. K. and D. S. Slocombe. 2005. Regional ecology, ecosystem geography, and transboundary protected areas in the St. Elias Mountains. *Ecological Applications* 15: 405–422. (18)

Danielson, F., H. Beukema, N. D. Burgess, F. Parish, C. A. Brühl, P. F. Donald, et al. 2009. Biofuel plantations on forested lands: double jeopardy for biodiversity and climate. *Conservation Biology* 23: 348–358. (20)

Darwin, C. R. 1859. *On the Origin of Species*. John Murray, London. (2, 8)

Daszak, P., A. A. Cunningham, and A. D. Hyatt. 2000. Emerging infectious diseases of wildlife—threats to biodiversity and human health. *Science* 287: 443–449. (10)

David, J.H.M., P. Cury, R.J.M. Crawford, R. M. Randall, L. G. Underhill, and M. A. Meÿer. 2003. Assessing conservation priorities in the Benguela ecosystem, South Africa: analysing predation by seals on threatened seabirds. *Biological Conservation* 114: 289–292. (17)

Davidar, P., M. Arjunan, and J. Puyravaud. 2008. Why do local households harvest forest products? A case study from the southern Western Ghats, India. *Biological Conservation* 141: 1876–1884. (4)

Davies, A. R. 2008. Does sustainability count? Environmental policy, sustainable development and the governance of grassroots sustainability enterprise in Ireland. *Sustainable Development* 17: 174–182. (1)

Davies, K. W., T. J. Svejcar, and J. D. Bates. 2009. Interaction of historical and nonhistorical disturbances maintains native plant communities. *Ecological Applications* 19: 1536–1545. (17)

Davies, Z. G., R. J. Wilson, S. Coles, and C. D. Thomas. 2006. Changing habitat associations of a thermally constrained species, the silver-spotted skipper butterfly, in response to climate warming. *Journal of Animal Ecology* 75: 247–256. (17)

Davis, M. A. 2009. *Invasion Biology*. Oxford University Press, Oxford, UK. (10)

Dawson, M. R., L. Marivaux, C. K. Li, K. C. Beard, and G. Métais. 2006. *Laonastes* and the "Lazarus effect" in recent mammals. *Science* 311: 1456–1458. (3)

de Bello, F., S. Lavorel, P. Gerhold, Ü. Reier, and M. Pärtel. 2010. A biodiversity monitoring framework for practical conservation of grasslands and shrublands. *Biological Conservation* 143: 9–17. (17)

De Grammont, P. C. and A. D. Cuarón. 2006. An evaluation of threatened species categorization systems used on the American continent. *Conservation Biology* 20: 14–27. (8)

de Groot, J.I.M. and L. Steg. 2009. Morality and prosocial behavior: the role of awareness, responsibility, and norms in the norm activation model. *Journal of Social Psychology* 149: 425–49. (22)

Deguise, I. E. and J. T. Kerr. 2006. Protected areas and prospects for endangered species conservation in Canada. *Conservation Biology* 20: 48–55. (18)

De Merode, E. and G. Cowlishaw. 2006. Species protection, the changing informal economy, and the politics of access to the bushmeat trade in the Democratic Republic of Congo. *Conservation Biology* 20: 1262–1271. (10)

De Roos, A. M. 2008. Demographic analysis of continuous-time life-history models. *Ecology Letters* 11: 1–15. (12)

De'ath, G., J. M. Lough, and K. E. Fabricius. 2009. Declining coral calcification on the Great Barrier Reef. *Science* 323: 116–119. (9)

Deacon, J. E., A. E. Williams, C. D. Williams, and J. E. Williams. 2007. Fueling population growth in Las Vegas: how large-scale groundwater withdrawal could burn regional biodiversity. *BioScience* 57: 688–698. (17)

Dearborn, D. C. and S. Kark. 2010. Motivations for conserving urban biodiversity. *Conservation Biology* 24: 432–440. (9)

Decker, D. J., M. E. Krasny, G. R. Goff, C. R. Smith, and D. W. Gross (eds.). 1991. *Challenges in the Conservation of Biological Resources: A Practitioner's Guide*. Westview Press, Boulder, CO. (9)

DeFries, R. S., A. Hansen, A. C. Newton, and M. C. Hansen. 2005. Increasing isolation of protected areas in tropical forests of the past twenty years. *Ecological Applications* 15: 19–26. (15)

Desbiez, A.L.J., R. E. Bodmer, and S. A. Santos. 2009. Wildlife habitat selection and sustainable resources management in a Neotropical wetland. *International Journal of Biodiversity and Conservation* 1: 11–20. (21)

Deshpande, S. 2009. Bombay HC free to decide on national park encroachment: SC. *The Times of India*. http://timesofindia.indiatimes.com/Mumbai/Bombay-HC-free-to-decide-on-national-park-encroachment-SC/articleshow/4230913.cms (17)

Devall, B. and G. Sessions. 1985. *Deep Ecology*. Gibbs Smith Publishers, Salt Lake City, UT. (6)

Di Franco, A., M. Milazzo, P. Baiata, A. Tomasello, and R. Chemello. 2009. Scuba diver behaviour and its effects on the biota of a Mediterranean marine protected area. *Environmental Conservation* 36: 32–40. (17)

Diamond, J. 1999. *Guns, Germs and Steel: The Fates of Human Societies*. W.W. Norton & Company, New York. (1)

Diamond, J. 2005. *Collapse: How Societies Choose to Fail or Succeed*. Penguin Books, New York. (1, 6)

Diana, J. S. 2009. Aquaculture production and biodiversity conservation. *BioScience* 59: 27–38. (10)

Dias, M. S., W. E. Magnusson, and J. Zuanon. 2010. Effects of reduced-impact logging on fish assemblages in Central Amazonia. *Conservation Biology* 24: 278–286. (18)

Dichmont, C. M., S. Pascoe, T. Kompas, A. E. Punt, and R. Deng. 2010. On implementing maximum economic yield in commercial fisheries. *Proceedings of the National Academy of Sciences USA* 107: 16–21. (10)

Dicken, M. L., A. J. Booth, and M. J. Smale. 2008. Estimates of juvenile and adult raggedtooth shark (*Carcharias taurus*) abundance along the east coast of South Africa. *Canadian Journal of Fisheries and Aquatic Sciences* 65: 621–632. (6)

Diemont, S.A.W. and J. F. Martin. 2009. Lacandon Maya ecosystem management: sustainable design for subsistence and environmental restoration. *Ecological Applications* 19: 254–266. (20)

Dietz, R. W. and B. Czech. 2005. Conservation deficits for the continental United States: an ecosystem gap analysis. *Conservation Biology* 19: 1478–1487. (15)

Dietz, T., E. A. Rosa, and R. York. 2007. Driving the human ecological footprint. *Frontiers in Ecology and the Environment* 5: 13–18. (9)

Dinerstein, E., C. Loucks, E. Wikramanayake, J. Ginsberg, E. Sanderson, J. Seidensticker, et al. 2006. The fate of wild tigers. *BioScience* 57: 508–514. (18)

Dobson, A. 1995. Biodiversity and human health. *Trends in Ecology and Evolution* 10: 390–392. (4)

Docherty, D.E. and R. I. Romaine. 1983. Inclusion body disease of cranes: a serological follow-up to the 1978 die-off. *Avian Diseases* 27: 830–835. (10)

Dodds, W. K., K. C. Wilson, R. L. Rehmeier, G. L. Knight, S. Wiggam, J. A. Falke, et al. 2008. Comparing ecosystem goods and services provided by restored and native lands. *BioScience* 59: 837–845. (19)

Donath, T. W., S. Bissels, N. Hölzel, and A. Otte. 2007. Large scale application of diaspore transfer with plant material in restoration practice: impact of seed and microsite limitation. *Biological Conservation* 138: 224–234. (13)

Donlan, C. J., K. Campbell, W. Cabrera, C. Lavoie, V. Carrion, and F. Cruz. 2007. Recovery of the Galápagos rail (*Laterallus spilonotus*) following the removal of invasive mammals. *Biological Conservation* 138: 520–524. (7)

Donlan, J., H. W. Greene, J. Berger, C. E. Bock, J. H. Bock, D. A. Burney, et al. 2006. Re-wilding North America. *Nature* 436: 913–914. (13)

Donoghue, M. J. and W. S. Alverson. 2000. A new age of discovery. *Annals of the Missouri Botanical Garden* 87: 110–126. (3)

Donovan, T. M. and C. W. Welden. 2002. *Spreadsheet Exercises in Conservation Biology and Landscape Ecology*. Sinauer Associates, Sunderland, MA. (11, 12)

Doukakis, P., E.C.M. Parsons, W.C.G. Burns, A. K. Salomon, E. Hines, and J. A. Cigliano. 2009. Gaining traction: retreading the wheels of marine conservation. *Conservation Biology* 23: 841–846. (21)

Dover, J. and J. Settele. 2009. The influences of landscape structure on butterfly distribution and movement: a review. *Journal of Insect Conservation* 13: 3–27. (17)

Drayton, B. and R. B. Primack. 1999. Experimental extinction of garlic mustard (*Alliaria petiolata*) populations: implications for weed science and conservation biology. *Biological Invasions* 1: 159–167. (11)

Dreschler, M. and F. Wätzold. 2009. Applying tradable permits to biodiversity conservation: effects of space-dependent conservation benefits and cost heterogeneity on habitat allocation. *Ecological Economics* 68: 1083–1092. (20)

Drezner, T. D. 2007. Variation in age and height of onset of reproduction in the saguaro cactus (*Carnegiea gigantea*) in the Sonoran Desert. *Plant Ecology* 194: 223–229. (17)

Driscoll, C. T., Y. J. Han, C. Y. Chen, D. C. Evers, K. F. Lambert, T. M. Holsen, et al. 2007. Mercury contamination in forest and freshwater ecosystems in the northeastern United States. *BioScience* 57: 17–28. (9)

Driscoll, D. A. 1999. Genetic neighbourhood and effective population size for two endangered frogs. *Biological Conservation* 88: 221–229. (11)

Dudley, N., L. Higgins-Zogib, and S. Mansourian. 2009. The links between protected areas, faiths, and sacred natural sites. *Conservation Biology* 23: 568–577. (1, 20)

Dudley, R. K. and S. P. Platania. 2007. Flow regulation and fragmentation imperil pelagic-spawning riverine fishes. *Ecological Applications* 17: 2074–2086. (9)

Duffey, E. and A. S. Watts (eds.). 1971. *The Scientific Management of Animal and Plant Communities for Conservation*. Blackwell Scientific Publications, Oxford, UK. (17)

Duffus, D. A. and P. Dearden. 1990. Non-consumptive wildlife-oriented recreation: a conceptual framework. *Biological Conservation* 53: 213–231. (5)

Dulvy, N. K., J. K. Baum, S. Clarke, L.J.V. Compagno, E. Cortés, A. Domingo, et al. 2008. You can swim but you can't hide: the global status and conservation of oceanic pelagic sharks and rays. *Aquatic Conservation: Marine and Freshwater Ecosystems* 18: 459–482. (6)

Duncan, J. R. and J. L. Lockwood. 2001. Extinction in a field of bullets: a search for causes in the decline of the world's freshwater fishes. *Biological Conservation* 102: 97–105. (8)

Dunn, R. R. 2005. Modern insect extinctions, the neglected majority. *Conservation Biology* 19: 1030–1036. (20)

Dunn, R. R., N. C. Harris, R. K. Colwell, L. P. Koh, and N. S. Sodhi. 2009. The sixth mass coextinction: are most endangered species parasites and mutualists? *Proceedings of the Royal Society B* 276: 3037–3045. (8)

Dwyer, J. C. and I. D. Hodge. 1996. *Countryside in Trust: Land Management by Conservation, Recreation and Amenity Organizations*. John Wiley and Sons, Chichester, UK. (20)

Earth Charter Initiative. *http://www.earthcharterinaction.org* (6)

Earth Force. 2010. *http://www.earthforce.org* (22)

Ebbin, S. A. 2009. Institutional and ethical dimensions of resilience in fishing systems: perspectives from co-managed fisheries in the Pacific Northwest. *Marine Policy* 33: 264–270. (1)

eBird. *http://ebird.org* (22)

Ecosystem Marketplace. 2010. The Katoomba Group. *http://ecosystemmarketplace.com* (20)

Eden Project. *http://www.edenproject.com* (14)

Edgar, G. J., C. R. Samson, and N. S. Barrett. 2005. Species extinction in the marine environment: Tasmania as a regional example of overlooked losses in biodiversity. *Conservation Biology* 19: 1294–1300. (7)

Edgerton, B. F., P. Henttonen, J. Jussila, A. Mannonen, P. Paasonen, T. Taugbøl, et al. 2004. Understanding the causes of disease in freshwater crayfish. *Conservation Biology* 18: 1466–1474. (10)

Efroymson, R. A., V. H. Dale, L. M. Baskaran, M. Chang, M. Aldridge, and M. W. Berry. 2005. Planning transboundary ecological risk assessments at military installations. *Human and Ecological Risk Assessment* 11: 1193–1215. (18)

Egoh, B., B. Reyers, M. Rouget, M. Bode, and D. M. Richardson. 2009. Spatial congruence between biodiversity and ecosystem services in South Africa. *Biological Conservation* 142: 553–562. (5)

Ehrenfeld, D. W. 1970. *Biological Conservation*. Holt, Rinehart and Winston, New York. (8)

Ehrenfeld, D. W. 1989. Hard times for diversity. *In* D. Western and M. Pearl (eds.), *Conservation for the Twenty-first Century*, pp. 247–250. Oxford University Press, New York. (16)

Ehrlich, P. R. and A. H. Ehrlich. 1981. *Extinction: The Causes and Consequences of the Disappearance of Species*. Random House, New York. (6)

Ehrlich, P. R. and L. H. Goulder. 2007. Is current consumption excessive? A general framework and some indications for the United States. *Conservation Biology* 21: 1145–1154. (9)

Ehrlich, P. R. and R. M. Pringle. 2008. Where does biodiversity go from here? A grim business-as-usual forecast and a hopeful portfolio of partial solutions. *Proceedings of the National Academy of Sciences USA* 105: 11579–11586. (19)

Eigenbrod, F., B. J. Anderson, P. R. Armsworth, A. Heinemeyer, S. F. Jackson, M. Parnell, et al. 2009. Ecosystem service benefits of contrasting conservation strategies in a human-dominated region. *Proceedings of the Royal Society B* 276: 2903–2911. (17)

Elfring, C. 1989. Preserving land through local land trusts. *BioScience* 39: 71–74. (20)

Elkinton, J. S., D. Parry, and G. H. Boettner. 2006. Implicating an introduced generalist parasitoid in the invasive browntail moth's enigmatic demise. *Ecology* 87: 2664–2672. (10)

Elliot, R. 1992. Intrinsic value, environmental obligation and naturalness. *The Monist* 75: 138–160. (6)

Elliott, J. E., M. J. Miller, and L. K. Wilson. 2005. Assessing breeding potential of peregrine falcons based on chlorinated hydrocarbon concentrations in prey. *Environmental Pollution* 134: 353–361. (9)

Ellis, E. C. and N. Ramankutty. 2008. Putting people in the map: anthropogenic biomes of the world. *Frontiers in Ecology and the Environment* 6: 439–447. (18)

Ellstrand, N. C. 1992. Gene flow by pollen: implications for plant conservation genetics. *Oikos* 63: 77–86. (11)

Emerson, R. W. 1836. *Nature*. James Monroe and Co., Boston. (1)

Emerton, L. 1999. Balancing the opportunity costs of wildlife conservation for communities around Lake Mburo National Park, Uganda. Evaluating Eden Series Discussion Paper No. 5, International Institute for Environment and Development, London. (4)

Encyclopedia of Life. 2010. *http://eol.org* (22)

Encyclopedia of the Nations. 2009. India. *http://www.nationsencyclopedia.com/economies/Asia-and-the-Pacific/India.html* (1)

Environmental Defense. 2000. *Progress on the Back Forty: An analysis of three incentive-based approaches to endangered species conservation on private land.* Environmental Defense, Washington, D.C. (22)

Epps, C. W., P. J. Palsboll, J. D. Wehausen, G. K. Goderick, R. R. Ramey, and D. R. McCullough. 2005. Highways block gene flow and cause a rapid decline in genetic diversity of desert bighorn sheep. *Ecology Letters* 8: 1029–1038. (12)

Epps, C. W., J. D. Wehausen, V. C. Bleich, S. G. Torres, and J. S. Brashares. 2007. Optimizing dispersal and corridor models using landscape genetics. *Journal of Applied Ecology* 44: 714–724. (12, 18)

Equator Initiative. *http://www.equatorinitiative.org* (20)

Estes, J. A., D. F. Doak, A. M. Springer, and T. M. Williams. 2009. Causes and consequences of marine mammal population declines in southwest Alaska: a food-web perspective. *Philosophical Transactions of the Royal Society B* 364: 1647–1658. (2)

Esty, D. C., M. Levy, T. Srebotnjak, and A. de Sherbinin. 2005. *Environmental Sustainability Index: Benchmarking National Environmental Stewardship.* Yale Center for Environmental Law & Policy, New Haven, CT. (4)

Evans, S. R. and B. C. Sheldon. 2008. Interspecific patterns of genetic diversity in birds: correlations with extinction risk. *Conservation Biology* 22: 1016–1025. (11)

Ewel, K. C. 2010. Appreciating tropical coastal wetlands from a landscape perspective. *Frontiers in Ecology and the Environment* 8: 20–26. (5)

Ewing, S. R., R. G. Nager, M.A.C. Nicoll, A. Aumjaud, C. G. Jones, and L. F. Keller. 2008. Inbreeding and loss of genetic variation in a reintroduced population of Mauritius Kestrel. *Conservation Biology* 22: 395–404. (11, 13)

Export.gov: Helping U.S. Companies Export. *http://www.export.gov* (21)

Fa, J. E., C. A. Peres, and J. Meeuwig. 2002. Bushmeat exploitation in tropical forests: an intercontinental comparison. *Conservation Biology* 16: 232–237. (4)

Faeth, S. H., P. S. Warren, E. Shochat, and W. A. Marussich. 2005. Trophic dynamics in urban communities. *BioScience* 55: 399–407. (2)

Fagan, W. F. and E. E. Holmes. 2006. Quantifying the extinction vortex. *Ecology Letters* 9: 51–60. (11)

Fairtrade Labelling Organizations International (FLO): Tackling Poverty and Empowering Producers through Trade. 2009. *http://www.fairtrade.net* (22)

Faith, D. P. 2008. Threatened species and the potential loss of phylogenetic diversity: conservation scenarios based on estimated extinction probabilities and phylogenetic risk analysis. *Conservation Biology* 22: 1461–1470. (15)

Falk, D.A., C.I. Millar, and M. Olwell (eds.). 1996. *Restoring Diversity: Strategies for Reintroduction of Endangered Plants.* Island Press, Washington, D.C. (13)

Falk, D. A., M. A. Palmer, and J. B. Zedler (eds.). 2006. *Foundations of Restoration Ecology: The Science and Practice of Ecological Restoration.* Island Press, Washington, D.C. (19)

Falk, J. H., E. M. Reinhard, C. L. Vernon, K. Bronnenkant, J. E. Heimlich, and N. L. Deans. 2007. *Why Zoos & Aquariums Matter: Assessing the Impact of a Visit to a Zoo or Aquarium.* Association of Zoos & Aquariums, Silver Spring, MD. (14)

Fanshawe, S., G. R. Vanblaricom, and A. A. Shelly. 2003. Restored top carnivores as detriments to the performance of marine protected areas intended for fishery sustainability: a case study with red abalones and sea otters. *Conservation Biology* 17: 273–283. (2, 13)

FAO Forestry Country Profiles—American Samoa. 2010. *http://www.fao.org* (20)

FAOSTAT. 2009. Food and Agriculture Organization (FAO) of the United Nations. *http://faostat.fao.org* (9)

Fazey, I., J. Fischer, and D. B. Lindenmayer. 2005. What do conservation biologists publish? *Conservation Biology* 124: 63–73. (22)

Feagin, R. A., D. J. Sherman, and W. E. Grant. 2005. Coastal erosion, global sea-level rise, and the loss of sand dune plant habitats. *Frontiers in Ecology and the Environment* 3: 359–364. (9)

Feinsinger, P. 2001. *Designing Field Studies for Biodiversity Conservation.* Island Press, Washington, D.C. (12)

Feldhamer, G. A. and A. T. Morzillo. 2008. Relative abundance and conservation: is the golden mouse a rare species? *In* G. W. Barrett and G. A. Feldhamer (eds.), *The Golden Mouse*, pp. 117–133. Springer, New York. (8)

Fenberg, P. B. and K. Roy. 2008. Ecological and evolutionary consequences of size-selective harvesting: how much do we know? *Molecular Ecology* 17: 209–220. (2)

Fennell, D. A. 2007. *Ecotourism*, 3rd ed. Routledge, New York. (5)

Ferraro, P. J. and R. D. Simpson. 2006. Cost-effective conservation: a review of what works to preserve biodiversity. *In* W. E. Oates (ed.), *The RFF Reader in Environmental and Resource Policy*, pp. 163–170. Resources for the Future, Washington, D.C. (21)

Ferraz, G., G. J. Russell, P. C. Stouffer, R. O. Bierregaard, S. L. Pimm, and T. E. Lovejoy. 2003. Rates of species loss from Amazonian forest fragments. *Proceedings of the National Academy of Sciences USA* 100: 14069–14073. (7)

Ferrer. M., I. Newton, and M. Pandolfi. 2009. Small populations and offspring sex-ratio deviations in eagles. *Conservation Biology* 23: 1017–1025. (11)

Ferry, L. 1995. *The New Ecological Order*. University of Chicago Press, Chicago. (6)

Ficetola, G. F., E. Padoa-Schioppa, and F. De Bernardi. 2009. Influence of landscape elements in riparian buffers on the conservation of semiaquatic amphibians. *Conservation Biology* 23: 114–123. (16)

Fischer, A. and R. van der Wal. 2007. Invasive plant suppresses charismatic seabird: the construction of attitudes towards biodiversity management options. *Biological Conservation* 135: 256–267. (6)

Fischer, J. and D. B. Lindenmayer. 2000. An assessment of published results of animal relocations. *Biological Conservation* 96: 1–11. (13)

Fischer, M., K. Rudmann-Maurer, A. Weyand, and J. Stöcklin. 2008. Agricultural land use and biodiversity in the Alps: how cultural tradition and socioeconomically motivated changes are shaping grassland biodiversity in the Swiss Alps. *Mountain Research and Development* 28: 148–155. (16)

Fishburn, I. S., P. Kareiva, K. J. Gaston, K. L. Evans, and P. R. Armsworth. 2009. State-level variation in conservation investment by a major nongovernmental organization. *Conservation Letters* 2: 74–81. (15, 16)

Fitzpatrick, B. M. and H. B. Shaffer. 2007. Hybrid vigor between native and introduced salamanders raises new challenges for conservation. *Proceedings of the National Academy of Sciences USA* 104: 15793–15798. (2)

Fleishman, E. and D. D. Murphy. 2009. A realistic assessment of the indicator potential of butterflies and other charismatic taxonomic groups. *Conservation Biology* 23: 1109–1116. (15)

Flombaum, P. and O. E. Sala. 2008. Higher effect of plant species diversity on productivity in natural than artificial systems. *Pro-

ceedings of the National Academy of Sciences USA 105: 6087–6090. (5)

Flory, S. L. and K. Clay. 2009. Effects of roads and forest succession-al age on experimental plant invasions. *Biological Conservation* 142: 2531–2537. (9)

Foley, J. A., G. P. Asner, M. H. Costa, M. T. Coe, R. DeFries, H. K. Gibbs, et al. 2007. Amazonia revealed: forest degradation and loss of ecosystem goods and services in the Amazon Basin. *Frontiers in Ecology and the Environment* 5: 25–32. (5)

Foley, J. A., R. DeFries, G. P. Asner, C. Barford, G. Bonan, S. R. Carpenter, et al. 2005. Global consequences of land use. *Science* 309: 570–574. (5)

Foltz, R., F. M. Denny, and A. Baharuddin (eds), 2003. *Islam and Ecology: A Bestowed Trust.* Harvard Divinity School, Cambridge, MA. (6)

Fonseca, C. R. 2009. The silent mass extinction of insect herbivores in biodiversity hotspots. *Conservation Biology* 23: 1507–1515. (15)

Fontaine, B., P. Bouchet, K. Van Achterberg, M. A. Alonso-Zarazaga, R. Araujo, M. Asche, et al. 2007. The European Union's 2010 target: putting rare species in focus. *Biological Conservation* 139: 167–185. (20)

Ford, A. T., A. P. Clevenger, and A. Bennett. 2009. Comparison of methods of monitoring wildlife crossing structures on highways. *Journal of Wildlife Management* 73: 1213–1222. (16)

Fossey, D. 1990. *Gorillas in the Mist.* Houghton Mifflin, Boston. (12)

Foster, B. L., K. Kindscher, G. R. Houseman, and C. A. Murphy. 2009. Effects of hay management and native species sowing on grassland community structure, biomass, and restoration. *Ecological Applications* 19: 1884–1896. (19)

Foster, S. J. and A.C.J. Vincent. 2005. Enhancing sustainability of the international trade in seahorses with a single minimum size limit. *Conservation Biology* 19: 1044–1050. (10)

Fox, C. W., K. L. Scheilbly, and D. H. Reed. 2008. Experimental evolution of the genetic load and its implications for the genetic basis of inbreeding depression. *Evolution* 62: 2236–2249. (10)

Frankham, R. 1995. Effective population size/adult population size ratios in wildlife: a review. *Genetical Research* 66: 95–107. (11)

Frankham, R. 2005. Genetics and extinction. *Biological Conservation* 126: 131–140. (11)

Frankham, R., J. D. Ballou, and D. A. Briscoe. 2009. *Introduction to Conservation Genetics,* 2nd ed. Cambridge University Press, Cambridge, UK. (11)

Franklin, I. R. 1980. Evolutionary change in small populations. *In* M. E. Soulé and B. A. Wilcox (eds.), *Conservation Biology: An Evolutionary-Ecological Perspective,* pp. 135–149. Sinauer Associates, Sunderland, MA. (11)

Frantzi, S., N. T. Carter, and J. C. Lovett. 2009. Exploring discourses on international environmental regime effectiveness with Q methodology: a case study of the Mediterranean Action Plan. *Journal of Environmental Management* 90: 177–186. (18)

Frazer, L. N. 2009. Sea-cage aquaculture, sea lice, and declines of wild fish. *Conservation Biology* 23: 599–607. (14)

Frenot, Y., S. L. Chown, J. Whinam, P. M. Selkirk, P. Convey, M. Skotnicki, et al. 2005. Biological invasions in the Antarctic: extent, impacts and implications. *Biological Reviews* 80: 45–72. (10)

Fresh Kills Park: Lifescape. 2006. Staten Island, New York. Draft Master Plan, March 2006. Field Operations, New York. (19)

Fricke, H. and K. Hissmann. 1990. Natural habitat of the coelacanths. *Nature* 346: 323–324. (3)

Frisvold, G. B., J. Sullivan, and A. Raneses. 2003. Genetic improvements in major US crops: the size and distribution of benefits. *Agricultural Economics* 28: 109–119. (5)

Frohlich, J. and K. D. Hyde. 1999. Biodiversity of palm fungi in the tropics: are global fungal diversity estimates realistic? *Biodiversity and Conservation* 8: 977–1004. (3)

Funch, P. and R. Kristensen. 1995. Cycliophora is a new phylum with affinities to Entoprocta and Ectoprocta (*Symbion pandora*). *Nature* 378: 711–714. (3)

Futuyma, D. J. 2009. *Evolution,* 2nd ed. Sinauer Associates, Sunderland, MA. (2)

Futuyma, D. J. 2009. What everyone needs to know about evolution. *Trends in Ecology and Evolution* 24: 356–357. (2)

Gadgil, M. and R. Guha. 1992. *This Fissured Land: An Ecological History of India.* Oxford University Press, Oxford, UK. (1)

Galapagos Conservancy. 2008. *http://www.galapagos.org/2008* (17)

Galbraith, C. A., P. V. Grice, G. P. Mudge, S. Parr, and M. W. Pienkowski. 1998. The role of statutory bodies in ornithological conservation. *Ibis* 137: S224–S231. (1)

Galdikas, B. 1995. *Reflections of Eden: My Years with the Orangutans of Borneo.* Little, Brown and Company, Boston. (12)

Gales, N. J., P. J. Clapman, and C. S. Baker. 2007. A case for killing humpback whales? *Nature Precedings http://hdl.handle.net/10101/npre.2007.1313.1* (10)

Gallant, A. L., R. W. Klaver, G. S. Casper, and M. J. Lannoo. 2007. Global rates of habitat loss and implications for amphibian conservation. *Copeia* 2007: 967–979. (9)

Gallo, J. A., L. Pasquini, B. Reyers, and R. M. Cowling. 2009. The role of private conservation areas in biodiversity representation and target achievement within the Little Karoo region, South Africa. *Biological Conservation* 142: 446–454. (20)

Game, E. T., H. S. Grantham, A. J. Hobday, R. L. Pressey, A. T. Lombard, L. E. Beckley, et al. 2009. Pelagic protected areas: the missing dimension in ocean conservation. *Trends in Ecology and Evolution* 24: 360–369. (15)

Gardiner, M. M., D. A. Landis, C. Gratton, C. D. DiFonzo, M. O'Neal, J. M. Chacon, et al. 2009. Landscape diversity enhances biological control of an introduced crop pest in the north-central USA. *Ecological Applications* 19: 143–154. (5)

Gardiner, S., S. Caney, D. Jamieson, and H. Shue. 2010. *Climate Ethics: Essential Readings.* Oxford University Press, New York. (6)

Gardiner, S. M. 2004. Ethics and global climate change. *Ethics* 114: 555–600. (6)

Gardner, T. A., T. Caro, E. B. Fitzherbert, T. Banda, and P. Lalbha. 2007. Conservation value of multiple-use areas in East Africa. *Conservation Biology* 21: 1516–1525. (18)

Gascoigne, J., L. Berec, S. Gregory, and F. Courchamp. 2009. Dangerously few liaisons: a review of mate-finding Allee effects. *Population Ecology* 51: 355–372. (11)

Gaston, K. J. 2005. Biodiversity and extinction: species and people. *Progress in Physical Geography* 29: 239–247. (9)

Gaston, K. J. and J. I. Spicer. 2004. *Biodiversity: An Introduction,* 2nd ed. Blackwell Publishing, Oxford, UK. (3)

Gates, D. M. 1993. *Climate Change and Its Biological Consequences.* Sinauer Associates, Sunderland, MA. (9)

Gault, A., Y. Meinard, and F. Courchamp. 2008. Consumers' taste for rarity drives sturgeons to extinction. *Conservation Letters* 1: 199–207. (10)

Gentry, A. H. 1986. Endemism in tropical versus temperate plant communities. *In* M. E. Soulé (ed.), *Conservation Biology: The Science of Scarcity and Diversity,* pp. 153–181. Sinauer Associates, Sunderland, MA. (7, 8)

Gering, J. C., K. A. DeRennaux, and T. O. Crist. 2007. Scale dependence of effective specialization: its analysis and implications for estimates of global insect species richness. *Diversity and Distributions* 13: 115–125. (3)

German, C. R., D. R. Yoerger, M. Jakuba, T. M. Shank, C. H. Langmuir, and K. Nakamura. 2008. Hydrothermal exploration with the Autonomous Benthic Explorer. *Deep-Sea Research Part I: Oceanographic Research Papers* 55: 203–219. (3)

Germano, J. M. and P. J. Bishop. 2009. Suitability of amphibians and reptiles for translocation. *Conservation Biology* 23: 7–15. (13)

Gerrodette, T. and W. G. Gilmartin. 1990. Demographic consequences of changing pupping and hauling sites of the Hawaiian monk seal. *Conservation Biology* 4: 423–430. (12)

Ghilain, A. and M. Bélisle. 2008. Breeding success of tree swallows along a gradient of agricultural intensification. *Ecological Applications* 18: 1140–1154. (18)

Ghimire, S. K., D. McKey, and Y. Aumeeruddy-Thomas. 2005. Conservation of Himalayan medicinal plants: harvesting patterns and ecology of two threatened species, *Nardostachys grandiflora* DC. and *Neopicrorhiza scrophulariiflora* (Pennell) Hong. *Biological Conservation* 124: 463–475. (10)

Giese, M. 1996. Effects of human activity on Adelie penguin *Pygoscelis adeliae* breeding success. *Biological Conservation* 75: 157–164. (5)

Gigon, A., R. Langenauer, C. Meier, and B. Nievergelt. 2000. Blue Lists of threatened species with stabilized or increasing abundance: a new instrument for conservation. *Conservation Biology* 14: 402–413. (8)

Gillett, N. P., F. W. Zwiers, A. J. Weaver, and P. A. Stott. 2003. Detection of human influence on sea-level pressure. *Nature* 422: 292–294. (9)

Gilpin, M. E. and M. E. Soulé. 1986. Minimum viable populations: processes of species extinction. *In* M. E. Soulé (ed.), *Conservation Biology: The Science of Scarcity and Diversity*, pp. 19–34. Sinauer Associates, Sunderland, MA. (11)

Given, D. R. 1995. *Principles and Practice of Plant Conservation*. Timber Press, Portland, OR. (14)

Glenn, W. 1996. *Eyes of Fire: Encounter with a Borderland Jaguar*. Treasure Chest Books, Tucson, AZ. (18)

Global Crop Diversity Trust: A Foundation for Food Security. 2006. *http://www.croptrust.org* (14)

Global Environment Facility (GEF): Investing in Our Planet. 2009. *http://www.thegef.org/gef* (1, 21)

Global Footprint Network: Advancing the Science of Sustainability. 2009. *http://www.footprint.org* (9)

Global Forest Resources Assessment 2005: Progress towards sustainable forest management. FAO Forestry Paper 147. Food and Agriculture Organization (FAO) of the United Nations, Rome. (9)

Gobster, P. H. and R. B. Hull. 2009. *Restoring Nature: Perspectives from the Social Sciences and Humanities*. Island Press, Washington D.C. (19)

Goetz, S. J., M. C. Mack, K. R. Gurney, J. T. Randerson, and R. A. Houghton. 2007. Ecosystem responses to recent climate change and fire disturbance at northern high latitudes: observations and model results contrasting northern Eurasia and North America. *Environmental Research Letters* 2: 045031. (9)

Goldman, R. L., H. Tallis, P. Kareiva, and G. C. Daily. 2008. Field evidence that ecosystem service projects support biodiversity and diversify options. *Proceedings of the National Academy of Sciences USA* 105: 9445–9448. (16)

Goodall, J. 1999. *Reason for Hope: A Spiritual Journey*. Warner Books, New York. (12)

Gooden, B., K. French, P. J. Turner, and P. O. Downey. 2009. Impact threshold for an alien plant invader, *Lantana camara* L., on native plant communities. *Biological Conservation* 142: 2631–2641. (10)

Goodland, R. 1994. Ethical priorities in environmentally sustainable energy systems: the case of tropical hydropower. *International Conferences on Energy Needs in the Year 2000 and Beyond: Ethical and Environmental Perspectives*, 13–14 May 1993, Montreal, Canada. (21)

Goodman, S. M. and J. P. Benstead. 2005. Updated estimates of biotic diversity and endemism for Madagascar. *Oryx* 39: 73–77. (8)

Goossens, B., J. M. Setchell, E. Tchidongo, E. Dilambaka, C. Vidal, M. Ancrenaz, et al. 2005. Survival, interactions with conspecifics and reproduction in 37 chimpanzees released into the wild. *Biological Conservation* 123: 461–475. (13)

Gordon, D. R. and C. A. Gantz. 2008. Screening new plant introductions for potential invasiveness. *Conservation Letters* 1: 227–235 (10)

Gore, A. 2006. *An Inconvenient Truth: The Planetary Emergency of Global Warming and What We Can Do About It*. Rodale Books, New York. (1, 9)

Gössling, S. 1999. Ecotourism: a means to safeguard biodiversity and ecosystem functions? *Ecological Economics* 29: 303–320. (5)

GradSchools.com: the most comprehensive online resource of graduate school information. 2010. *http://www.gradschools.com* (1)

Granek, E. F., E.M.P. Madin, M. A. Brown, W. Figueira, D. S. Cameron, and Z. Hogan. 2008. Engaging recreational fishers in management and conservation: global case studies. *Conservation Biology* 22: 1125–1134. (22)

Granek, E. F., S. Polasky, C. V. Kappel, D. J. Reeds, D. M. Stoms, E. W. Koch, et al. 2010. Ecosystem services as a common language for coastal ecosystem-based management. *Conservation Biology* 24: 207–216. (5)

Grant, B. R. and P. R. Grant. 2008. Fission and fusion of Darwin's finches populations. *Philosophical Transactions of the Royal Society B* 363: 2821–2829. (11)

Grant, P. R., B. R. Grant, and L. F. Keller. 2005. Extinction behind our backs: the possible fate of one of the Darwin's finch species on Isla Floreana, Galápagos. *Biological Conservation* 122: 499–503. (7)

Grassle, J. F. 2001. Marine ecosystems. *In* S. A. Levin (ed.), *Encyclopedia of Biodiversity*, vol. 4, pp. 13–26. Academic Press, San Diego, CA. (3)

Grattapaglia, D., C. Plomion, M. Kirst, and R. R. Sederoff. 2009. Genomics of growth traits in forest trees. *Current Opinion in Plant Biology* 12: 148–156. (14)

Greathouse, E. A., C. M. Pringle, W. H. McDowell, and J. G. Holmquist. 2006. Indirect upstream effects of dams: consequences of migratory consumer extirpation in Puerto Rico. *Ecological Applications* 16: 339–352. (17)

Greene, R. M., J. C. Lehrter, and J. D. Hagy. 2009. Multiple regression models for hindcasting and forecasting midsummer hypoxia in the Gulf of Mexico. *Ecological Applications* 19: 1161–1175. (9)

Gregg, W. P., Jr. 1991. MAB Biosphere reserves and conservation of traditional land use systems. *In* M. L. Oldfield and J. B. Alcorn (eds.), *Biodiversity: Culture, Conservation and Ecodevelopment*, pp. 274–294. Westview Press, Boulder, CO. (1)

Greiner, R., and A. Lankester. 2007. Supporting on-farm biodiversity conservation through debt-for-conservation swaps: concept and critique. *Land Use Policy* 24: 458–471. (21)

Grenier, M. B., D. B. McDonald, and S. W. Buskirk. 2007. Rapid population growth of a critically endangered carnivore. *Science* 317: 779. (13)

Greuter, W. 1995. Extinction in Mediterranean areas. *In* J.H. Lawton and R.M. May (eds.), *Extinction Rates*, pp. 88–97. Oxford University Press, Oxford, UK. (8)

Griffith, B., J. M. Scott, J. W. Carpenter, and C. Reed. 1989. Translocation as a species conservation tool: status and strategy. *Science* 245: 477–480. (13)

Griffiths, R. A. and L. Pavajeau. 2008. Captive breeding, reintroduction, and the conservation of amphibians. *Conservation Biology* 22: 852–861. (13)

Grilo, C., J. A. Bissonette, and M. Santos-Reis. 2009. Spatial-temporal patterns in Mediterranean carnivore road casualties: consequences for mitigation. *Biological Conservation* 142: 301–313. (9)

Grimm, N. B., D. Foster, P. Groffman, J. M. Grove, C. S. Hopkinson, K. J. Nadelhoffer, et al. 2008. The changing landscape: ecosystem responses to urbanization and pollution across climatic and societal gradients. *Frontiers in Ecology and the Environment* 6: 264–272. (9)

Groom, M. J., G. K. Meffe, and C. R. Carroll (eds.). 2006. *Principles of Conservation Biology*, 3rd ed. Sinauer Associates, Sunderland, MA. (1, 2, 4, 5, 9, 11, 15)

Gross, L. 2008a. Can farmed and wild salmon coexist? *PLoS Biology* 6: e46. (4)

Gross, L. 2008b. Rethinking dams: Pacific salmon recovery may rest on other factors. *PLoS Biology* 6: e279. (9)

Grouios, C. P. and L. L. Manne. 2009. Utility of measuring abundance versus consistent occupancy in predicting biodiversity persistence. *Conservation Biology* 23: 1260–1269. (8, 11)

Grumbine, R. E. 2007. China's emergences and the prospects for global sustainability. *BioScience* 57: 249–255. (9)

Guarderas, A. P., S. D. Hacker, and J. Lubchenco. 2008. Current status of marine protected areas in Latin America and the Caribbean. *Conservation Biology* 22: 1630–1640. (15)

Gude, P. H., A. J. Hansen, R. Rasker, and B. Maxwell. 2006. Rates and drivers of rural residential development in the Greater Yellowstone. *Landscape and Urban Planning* 77: 131–151. (4)

Guerrant, E. O. 1992. Genetic and demographic considerations in the sampling and reintroduction of rare plants. *In* P. L. Fiedler and S. K. Jain (eds.), *Conservation Biology: The Theory and Practice of Nature Conservation, Preservation and Management*, pp. 321–344. Chapman and Hall, New York. (11)

Guerrant, E. O. Jr., K. Havens, and M. Maunder. 2004. *Ex Situ Conservation: Supporting Species Survival in the Wild*. Island Press, Washington, D.C. (13, 14)

Gullison, R. E., P. C. Frumhoff, J. G. Canadell, C. B. Field, D. C. Nepstad, K. Hayhoe, et al. 2007. Tropical forests and climate policy. *Science* 316: 985–986. (21)

Gunnarsson, U. and L. Söderström. 2007. Can artificial introductions of diaspore fragments work as a conservation tool for maintaining populations of the rare peatmoss *Sphagnum angermanicum*? *Biological Conservation* 135: 450–458. (13)

Gurd, D. B., T. D. Nudds, and D. H. Rivard. 2001. Conservation of mammals in eastern North American wildlife reserves: how small is too small? *Conservation Biology* 15: 1355–1363. (16)

Gurnell, A., K. Tockner, P. Edwards, and G. Petts. 2005. Effects of deposited wood on biocomplexity of river corridors. *Frontiers in Ecology and the Environment* 3: 377–382. (2, 17)

Guschanski, K., L. Vigilant, A. McNeilage, M. Gray, E. Kagoda, and M. M. Robbins. 2009. Counting elusive animals: comparing field and genetic census of the entire mountain gorilla population of Bwindi Impenetrable National Park, Uganda. *Biological Conservation* 142: 290–300. (12)

Gutiérrez, D. 2005. Effectiveness of existing reserves in the long-term protection of a regionally rare butterfly. *Conservation Biology* 19: 1586–1597. (12)

Guzmán, H.M., C. Guevara, and A. Castillo. 2003. Natural disturbances and mining of Panamanian coral reefs by indigenous people. *Conservation Biology* 17: 1396–1401. (20)

Haberl, H., K. H. Erb, F. Krausmann, V. Gaube, A. Bondeau, C. Plutzar, et al. 2007. Quantifying and mapping the human appropriation of net primary production in earth's terrestrial ecosystems. *Proceedings of the National Academy of Sciences USA* 104: 12942–12945. (7)

Hagen, A. N. and K. E. Hodges. 2006. Resolving critical habitat designation failures: reconciling law, policy, and biology. *Conservation Biology* 20: 399–407. (20)

Haig, S. M., E. A. Beever, S. M. Chambers, H. M. Draheim, B. D. Dugger, S. Dunham, et al. 2006. Taxonomic considerations in listing subspecies under the U.S. Endangered Species Act. *Conservation Biology* 20: 1584–1594. (2)

Halfar J. and R. M. Fujita. 2007. Danger of deep-sea mining. *Science* 316: 987. (9)

Hall, J. A. and E. Fleishman. 2010. Demonstration as a means to translate conservation science into practice. *Conservation Biology* 24: 120–127. (1)

Halme, P., M. Monkkonen, J. S. Kotiaho, A. L. Ylisirnio, and A. Markkanen. 2009. Quantifying the indicator power of an indicator species. *Conservation Biology* 23: 1008–1016. (15)

Halpern, B. S., C. R. Pyke, H. E. Fox, J. C. Haney, M. A. Schlaepfer, and P. Zaradic. 2006. Gaps and mismatches between global conservation priorities and spending. *Conservation Biology* 20: 56–64. (21)

Halpern, B. S., K. A. Selkoe, F. Micheli, and C. V. Kappel. 2007. Evaluating and ranking the vulnerability of global marine ecosystems to anthropogenic threats. *Conservation Biology* 21: 1301–1315. (9, 19)

Halpern, C. B., D. McKenzie, S. A. Evans, and D. A. Maguire. 2005. Initial responses of forest understories to varying levels and patterns of green-tree retention. *Ecological Applications* 15: 175–195. (18)

Hamann, H. B. and H. Drossman. 2006. Integrating watershed management with learning: the role of information transfer in linking educators and students with community watershed partners. *Comparative Technology Transfer and Society* 4: 305–339. (22)

Hames, R. 2007. The ecologically noble savage debate. *Annual Review of Anthropology* 36: 177–190. (20)

Hammond, P. M. 1992. Species inventory. *In* B. Groombridge (ed.), *Global Diversity: Status of the Earth's Living Resources*, pp. 17–39. Chapman and Hall, London. (3)

Handwerk, B. 2006. Giant marine reserve created in South Pacific. *National Geographic News*. *http://news.nationalgeographic.com/news/2006/03/0329_060329_reef_reserve.htm* (15)

Haney, J. C., T. Kroeger, F. Casey, A. Quarforth, G. Schrader, and S. A. Stone. 2007. Wilderness discounts on livestock compensation costs for imperiled gray wolf *Canis lupus*. *USDA Forest Service Proceedings* RMRS-P-49. (13)

Hannah, L. 2010. A global conservation system for climate-change adaptation. *Conservation Biology* 24: 70–77. (16)

Hansen, A. J., T. A. Spies, F. J. Swanson, and J. L. Ohmann. 1991. Conserving biodiversity in managed forests. *BioScience* 41: 382–392. (18)

Hansen, L., J. Hoffman, C. Drews, and E. Mielbrecht. 2010. Designing climate-smart conservation: guidance and case studies. *Conservation Biology* 24: 63–69. (17)

Hansen, M. C., S. V. Stehman, P. V. Potapov, B. Arunarwati, F. Stolle, and K. Pittman. 2009. Quantifying changes in the rates of forest clearing in Indonesia from 1990 to 2005 using remotely sensed data sets. *Environmental Research Letters* 4: 034001. (9)

Hansen, M. C., S. V. Stehman, P. V. Potapov, T. R. Loveland, J.R.G. Townshend, R. S. DeFries, et al. 2008b. Humid tropical forest clearing from 2000 to 2005 quantified by using multitemporal and multiresolution remotely sensed data. *Proceedings of the National Academy of Sciences USA* 105: 9439–9444. (9)

Hanson, T., T. M. Brooks, G.A.B. da Fonseca, M. Hoffmann, J. F. Lamoreux, G. Machlis, et al. 2009. Warfare in biodiversity hotspots. *Conservation Biology* 23: 578–587. (15)

Hardesty, B. D. 2007. How far do offspring recruit from parent plants? A molecular approach to understanding effective dispersal. *In* A. J. Dennis, E. W. Schrupp, R. A. Green, and D. A. Westcott (eds.), *Seed Dispersal: Theory and Its Application in a Changing World*, pp. 277–299. CAB International, Oxfordshire, UK. (12)

Hardin, G. 1985. *Filters against Folly: How to Survive Despite Economists, Ecologists and the Merely Eloquent*. Viking Press, New York. (4)

Harley, E. H., I. Baumgarten, J. Cunningham, and C. O'Ryan. 2005. Genetic variation and population structure in remnant populations of black rhinoceros, *Diceros bicornis*, in Africa. *Molecular Ecology* 14: 2981–2990. (11)

Harris, J. E. 2008. Translocation of the silver-studded blue *Plebejus argus* to Cawston Heath, Norfolk, England. *Conservation Evidence* 5: 1–5. (17)

Harrison, S., H. D. Safford, J. B. Grace, J. H. Viers, and K. F. Davies. 2006. Regional and local species richness in an insular environment: serpentine plants in California. *Ecological Monographs* 76: 41–56. (3)

Harrison, S., J. H. Viers, J. H. Thorne, and J. B. Grace. 2008. Favorable environments and the persistence of naturally rare species. *Conservation Letters* 1: 65–74. (8)

Harrop, S. R. 1999. Conservation regulation: a backward step for biodiversity? *Biodiversity and Conservation* 8: 679–707. (20)

Hart, J. and T. Hart. 2003. Rules of engagement for conservation. *Conservation in Practice* 4: 14–22. (17)

Hart, M. M. and J. T. Trevors. 2005. Microbe management: application of mycorrhizal fungi in sustainable agriculture. *Frontiers in Ecology and the Environment* 10: 533–539. (5)

Harvell, D., R. Aronson, N. Baron, J. Connell, A. Dobson, S. Ellner, et al. 2004. The rising tide of ocean diseases: unsolved problems and research priorities. *Frontiers in Ecology and the Environment* 2: 375–382. (10)

Hassett, B, M. Palmer, E. Bernhardt, S. Smith, J. Carr, and D. Hart. 2005. Restoring watersheds project by project: trends in Chesapeake Bay tributary restoration. *Frontiers in Ecology and Environment* 3: 259–267. (19)

Hay, J. M., C. H. Daughtery, A. Cree, and L. R. Maxson. 2003. Low genetic divergence obscures phylogeny among populations of *Sphenodon*, remnant of an ancient reptile lineage. *Molecular Phylogenetics and Evolution* 29: 1–19. (2)

Hayward, M. W. 2009. Conservation management for the past, present, and future. *Biodiversity and Conservation* 18: 765–775. (19)

Heckenberger, M. J. 2009. Lost cities of the Amazon. *Scientific American* 301(4): 64–71. (20)

Hedges, S., M. J. Tyson, A. F. Sitompul, M. F. Kinnaird, D. Gunaryadi, and Aslan. 2005. Distribution, status, and conservation needs of Asian elephants (*Elephas maximus*) in Lampung Province, Sumatra, Indonesia. *Biological Conservation* 124: 35–48. (7)

Hedrick, P. 2005. Large variance in reproductive success and the N_e/N ratio. *Evolution* 59: 1596–1599. (11)

Hedrick, P. W. 2005. *Genetics of Populations*, 3rd ed. Jones and Bartlett Publishers, Sudbury, MA. (11)

Hegde, R., S. Suryaprakash, L. Achoth, and K. S. Bawa. 1996. Extraction of non-timber forest products in the forests of Biligiri Rangan Hills, India. *Economic Botany* 50: 243–251. (20)

Heleno, R. H., R. S. Ceia, J. A. Ramos, and J. Memmott. 2009. Effects of alien plants on insect abundance and biomass: a food-web approach. *Conservation Biology* 23: 410–419. (10)

Helfield, J. M., S. J. Capon, C. Nilsson, R. Jansson, and D. Palm. 2007. Restoration of rivers used for timber floating: effects on riparian plant diversity. *Ecological Applications* 17: 840–851. (19)

Helfman, S. G. 2007. *Fish Conservation: A Guide to Understanding and Restoring Global Aquatic Biodiversity and Fishery Resources*. Island Press, Washington, D.C. (19)

Heller, N. E. and E. S. Zavaleta. 2009. Biodiversity management in the face of climate change: a review of 22 years of recommendations. *Biological Conservation* 142: 14–32. (9)

Hellmann, J. J., J. E. Byers, B. G. Bierwagen, and J. S. Dukes. 2008. Five potential consequences of climate change for invasive species. *Conservation Biology* 22: 534–543. (10)

Hendrickson, D. A. and J. E. Brooks. 1991. Transplanting short-lived fishes in North American deserts: review, assessment and recommendations. *In* W.L. Minckley and J.E. Deacon (eds.), *Battle against Extinction: Native Fish Management in the American West*, pp. 283–302. University of Arizona Press, Tucson, AZ. (13)

Herkert, J. R. 2009. Response of bird populations to farmland set-aside programs. *Conservation Biology* 23: 1036–1040. (18)

Heschel, M. S. and K. N. Paige. 1995. Inbreeding depression, environmental stress and population size variation in scarlet gilia (*Ipomopsis aggregata*). *Conservation Biology* 9: 126–133. (11)

Higdon, J. W. and S. H. Ferguson. 2009. Loss of Arctic sea ice causing punctuated change in sightings of killer whales (*Orcinus orca*) over the past century. *Ecological Applications* 19: 1365–1375. (12)

Higgins, J. V., M. T. Bryer, M. L. Khoury, and T. W. Fitzhugh. 2005. A freshwater classification approach for biodiversity conservation planning. *Conservation Biology* 19: 432–445. (15)

Higuchi, H. and R. B. Primack 2009. Conservation and management of biodiversity in Japan: an introduction. *Biological Conservation* 142: 1881–1883. (1)

Hile, J. 2004. Illegal fishing threatens Galapagos Islands waters. *National Geographic On Assignment.*

http://news.nationalgeographic.com/news/2004/03/0312_040312_TV galapagos.html (17)

Hill, J. 2001. *The Legacy of Luna: The Story of a Tree, a Woman, and the Struggle to Save the Redwoods*. Harper, San Francisco, CA. (22)

Hilty, J. A. and A. M. Merenlender. 2004. Use of riparian corridors and vineyards by mammalian predators in northern California. *Conservation Biology* 18: 126–135. (16)

Hinz, H., V. Prieto, and M. J. Kaiser. 2009. Trawl disturbance on benthic communities: chronic effects and experimental predictions. *Ecological Applications* 19: 761–773. (9)

Hobbie, J. E., S. R. Carpenter, N. B. Grimm, J. R. Gosz, and T. R. Seastedt. 2003. The US long term ecological research program. *BioScience* 53: 21–32. (12)

Hockey, P.A.R. and O. E. Curtis. 2009. Use of basic biological information for rapid prediction of the response of species to habitat loss. *Conservation Biology* 23: 64–71. (8)

Hodgson, G. and J. A. Dixon 1988. Logging versus fisheries and tourism in Palawan. East-West Environmental Policy Institute Occasional Paper No. 7, East-West Center, Honolulu, HI. (4)

Hodgson, J. A., A. Moilanen, N.A.D. Bourn, C. R. Bulman, and C. D. Thomas. 2009. Managing successional species: modelling the dependence of heath fritillary populations on the spatial distribution of woodland management. *Biological Conservation* 142: 2743–2751. (17)

Hoeinghaus, D. J., A. A. Agostinho, L. C. Gomes, F. M. Pelicice, E. K. Okada, J. D. Latini, et al. 2009. Effects of river impoundment on ecosystem services of large tropical rivers: embodied energy and market value of artisanal fisheries. *Conservation Biology* 23: 1222–1231. (4)

Hoekstra, J. M., T. M. Boucher, T. H. Ricketts, and C. Roberts. 2004. Are we losing ground? *Conservation in Practice* 5: 28–29. (15)

Hoekstra, J. M., T. M. Boucher, T. H. Ricketts, and C. Roberts. 2005. Confronting a biome crisis: global disparities of habitat loss and protection. *Ecology Letters* 8: 23–29. (15)

Hoffman, S. W. and J. P. Smith. 2003. Population trends of migratory raptors in western North America, 1977–2001. *Condor* 105: 397–419. (9)

Hoffmann, M., T. M. Brooks, G.A.B. da Fonseca, C. Gascon, A.F.A. Hawkins, R. E. James, et al. 2008. Conservation planning and the IUCN Red List. *Endangered Species Research* 6: 113–125. (15)

Hogan, C. M., World Wildlife Fund, S. Sarkar, and M. McGinley. 2008. Madagascar dry deciduous forests. *In* C. J. Cleveland (ed.), *Encyclopedia of Earth*. Environmental Information Coalition, National Council for Science and the Environment, Washington, D.C.
http://www.eoearth.org/article/Madagascar_dry_deciduous_forests (9)

Holden, E. and K. G. Hoyer. 2005. The ecological footprints of fuels. *Transportation Research Part D: Transport and Environment* 10: 395–403. (9)

Holden, E. and K. Linnerud. 2007. The sustainable development area: satisfying basic needs and safeguarding ecological sustainability. *Sustainable Development* 15: 174–187. (20)

Holland, T. G., G. D. Peterson, and A. Gonzalez. 2009. A cross-national analysis of how economic inequality predicts biodiversity loss. *Conservation Biology* 23: 1304–1313. (9)

Holt, R. D. and M. Barfield. 2010. Metapopulation perspectives on the evolution of species' niches. *In* S. Cantrell, C. Cosner, and S. Ruan (eds.), *Spatial Ecology*, pp. 189–212. Chapman and Hall, Boca Raton, FL. (12)

Holt, W. V. and R. E. Lloyd. 2009. Artificial insemination for the propagation of CANDES: the reality! *Theriogenology* 71: 228–235. (14)

Holt, W. V., A. R. Pickard, J. C. Rodger, and D. E. Wildt. (eds.). 2003. *Reproductive Science and Integrated Conservation*. Conservation Biology Series, No. 8. Cambridge

Holtcamp, W. 2010. Silence of the pikas. *BioScience* 60: 8–12. (20)

Horn, J. W., E. B. Arnett, and T. H. Kunz. 2008. Behavioral responses of bats to operating wind turbines. *Journal of Wildlife Management* 72: 123–132. (20)

Horner-Devine, M. C., G. C. Daily, P. R. Ehrlich, and C. L. Boggs. 2003. Countryside biogeography of tropical butterflies. *Conservation Biology* 17: 168–177. (16)

Horrocks, M., J. Salter, J. Braggins, S. Nichol, R. Moorhouse, and G. Elliott. 2008. Plant microfossil analysis of coprolites of the critically endangered kakapo (*Strigops habroptilus*) parrot from New Zealand. *Review of Paleobotany and Palynology* 149: 229–245. (13)

Horwich, R. H. and J. Lyon. 2007. Community conservation: practitioners' answer to critics. *Oryx* 41: 376–385. (16)

Houston, D., K. Mcinnes, G. Elliott, D. Eason, R. Moorhouse, and J. Cockrem. 2007. The use of a nutritional supplement to improve egg production in the endangered kakapo. *Biological Conservation* 138: 248–255. (13)

Howald, G., C. J. Donlan, J. P. Galván, J. C. Russell, J. Parkes, A. Samaniego, et al. 2007. Invasive rodent eradication on islands. *Conservation Biology* 21: 1258–1268. (10)

Howarth, F. G. 1990. Hawaiian terrestrial arthropods: an overview. *Bishop Museum Occasional Papers* 30: 4–26. (7)

Hubbs, C., R. J. Edwards, and G. P. Garrett. 2002. Threatened fishes of the world: *Gambusia heterochir* Hubbs, 1957 (Poeciliidae). *Environmental Biology of Fishes* 65: 422. (13)

Hufford, K. M. and S. J. Mazer. 2003. Plant ecotypes: genetic differentiation in the age of ecological restoration. *Trends in Ecology and Evolution* 18: 147–155. (19)

Hughes, A. R., S. L. Williams, C. M. Duarte, K. L. Heck, Jr., and M. Waycott. 2009. Associations of concern: declining seagrasses and threatened dependent species. *Frontiers in Ecology and the Environment* 7: 242–246. (2)

Hughes, J. B. and J. Roughgarden. 2000. Species diversity and biomass stability. *American Naturalist* 155: 618–627. (7)

Hulse, D. and R. Ribe. 2000. Land conversion and the production of wealth. *Ecological Applications* 10: 679–682. (4)

Humes, E. 2009. *Eco Barons: The Dreamers, Schemers, and Millionaires Who Are Saving Our Planet.* Ecco, New York. (22)

Humphries, P. and K. O. Winemiller. 2009. Historical impacts on river fauna, shifting baselines, and challenges for restoration. *BioScience* 59: 673–684. (19)

Ibáñez, I., J. A. Silander Jr., A. M. Wilson, N. LaFleur, N. Tanaka, and I. Tsuyama. 2009. Multivariate forecasts of potential distributions of invasive plant species. *Ecological Applications* 19: 359–375. (10)

Indigenous Peoples Literature. 2009. *http://indigenouspeople.net* (20)

Ingvarsson, P. K. 2001. Restoration of genetic variation lost: the genetic rescue hypothesis. *Trends in Ecology and Evolution* 16: 62–63. (11)

Inogwabini, B. I., O. Ilambu, and M. A. Gbanzi. 2005. Protected areas of the Democratic Republic of Congo. *Conservation Biology* 19: 15–22. (17)

Inoue, J. G., M. Miya, B. Venkatesh, and M. Nishida. 2005. The mitochondrial genome of Indonesian coelacanth *Latimeria menadoensis* (Sarcopterygii: Coelacanthiformes) and divergence time estimation between the two coelacanths. *Gene* 11: 227–235. (3)

International Ecotourism Society (TIES). 2010. *http://www.ecotourism.org* (5)

International Monetary Fund (IMF). 2010. *http://www.imf.org* (9)

International Rhino Foundation (IRF). *http://www.rhinos-irf.org* (11)

International Species Information System (ISIS). 2008. *http://www.isis.org* (14)

International Tropical Timber Organization (ITTO): Sustaining Tropical Forests. 2010. *http://www.itto.int* (9)

International Union for Conservation of Nature (IUCN). 2008. *http://www.iucnredlist.org* (14)

International Union for Conservation of Nature (IUCN). 2010. *http://iucn.org* (15)

International Whaling Commission (IWC). 2009. *http://www.iwcoffice.org* (21)

International Work Group for Indigenous Affairs (IWGIA). *http://www.iwgia.org* (20)

IPCC. 2007. *Climate Change 2007: The physical science basis. Contribution of Working Group I to the Fourth Assessment Report of the Intergovernmental Panel on Climate Change.* S. Solomon, D. Qin, M. Manning, Z. Chen, M. Marquis, K. B. Averyt, M. Tignor, and H. L. Miller (eds.). Cambridge University Press, Cambridge, UK. (5, 9)

IUCN. 2001. IUCN Red List Categories and Criteria: Version 3.1. IUCN Species Survival Commission. IUCN, Gland, Switzerland. *http://www.iucnredlist.org/technical-documents/categories-and-criteria/2001–categories-criteria* (8)

IUCN. 2004. 2004 IUCN Red List of Threatened Species. *http://www.iucnredlist.org* (9, 15)

IUCN. 2009. IUCN Red List of Threatened Species. Version 2009.2. *http://www.iucnredlist.org* (3, 7, 8, 10, 21)

IUCN Red List. 2008. *http://www.iucnredlist.org* (11)

IUCN/SSC Re-introduction Specialist Group. 2007. *http://iucnsscrsg.org* (13)

IUCN Species Survival Commission (SSC). 2010. *http://www.iucn.org* (15)

Jachmann, H. 2008. Monitoring law-enforcement performance in nine protected areas in Ghana. *Biological Conservation* 141: 89–99. (17)

Jackson, J.B.C. 2008. Ecological extinction and evolution in the brave new ocean. *Proceedings of the National Academy of Sciences USA* 105: 11458–11465. (7)

Jackson, S. T., J. L. Betancourt, R. K. Booth, and S. T. Gray. 2009. Ecology and the ratchet of events: climate variability, niche dimensions, and species distributions. *Proceedings of the National Academy of Sciences USA* 106: 19685–19692. (9)

Jackson, S. F., K. Walker, and K. J. Gaston. 2009. Relationship between distributions of threatened plants and protected areas in Britain. *Biological Conservation* 142: 1515–1522. (15, 16)

Jacob, J., E. Jovic, and M. B. Brinkerhoff. 2009. Personal and planetary well-being: mindfulness meditation, pro-environmental behavior and personal quality of life in a survey from the social justice and ecological sustainability movement. *Social Indicators Research* 93: 275–294. (6)

Jacobson, S. K. 2006. The importance of public education for biological conservation. *In* M. J. Groom, G. K. Meffe, and C. R. Carroll (eds.), *Principles of Conservation Biology,* 3rd ed, pp. 681–683. Sinauer Associates, Sunderland, MA. (22)

Jacobson, S. K. 2009. *Communication Skills for Conservation Professionals,* 2nd ed. Island Press, Washington, D.C. (22)

Jacobson, S. K., M. D. McDuff, and M. C. Monroe. 2006. *Conservation Education and Outreach Techniques.* Oxford University Press, Oxford. (22)

Jaeger, I., H. Hop, and G. W. Gabrielsen. 2009. Biomagnification of mercury in selected species from an Arctic marine food web in Svalbard. *Science of the Total Environment* 407: 4744–4751. (9)

Jaffe, M. 1994. *And No Birds Sing: A True Ecological Thriller Set in a Tropical Paradise.* Simon and Schuster, New York. (10)

Jamieson, I. G., G. P. Wallis, and J .V. Briskie. 2006. Inbreeding and endangered species management: is New Zealand out of step with the rest of the world? *Conservation Biology* 20: 38–47. (11)

Janzen, D. H. 2001. Latent extinctions—the living dead. *In* S.A. Levin (ed.), *Encyclopedia of Biodiversity* 3: 689–700. Academic Press, San Diego, CA. (7)

Janzen, D.H., W. Hallwachs, P. Blandin, J.M. Burns, J.M. Cadiou, I. Chacon, et al. 2009. Integration of DNA barcoding into an ongoing inventory of complex tropical biodiversity. *Molecular Ecology Resources* 9(s1): 1–26. (2, 19)

Jaquiéry, J., F. Guillaume, and N. Perrin. 2009. Predicting the deleterious effects of mutation load in fragmented populations. *Conservation Biology* 23: 207–218. (11)

Jenkins, C. N. and L. Joppa. 2009. Expansion of the global terrestrial protected area system. *Biological Conservation* 142: 2166–2174. (15)

Jenkins, M., R. E. Green, and J. Madden. 2003. The challenge of measuring global change in wild nature: are things getting better or worse? *Conservation Biology* 17: 20–23. (9)

Jenkins, M., S. J. Scherr, and M. Inbar. 2004. Markets for biodiversity services: potential roles and challenges. *Environment* 46: 32–42. (4)

Jentsch, A., J. Kreyling, and C. Beierkuhnlein. 2007. A new generation of climate-change experiments: events, not trends. *Frontiers in Ecology and the Environment* 5: 365–374. (9)

Johnson, C. 2009. Megafaunal decline and fall. *Science* 326: 1072–1073. (7)

Johnson, C. N. 2009. Ecological consequences of late Quaternary extinctions of megafauna. *Proceedings of the Royal Society B* 276: 2509–2519. (8)

Johnson, J. A. and P. O. Dunn. 2006. Low genetic variation in the heath hen prior to extinction and implications for the conservation of prairie-chicken populations. *Conservation Genetics* 7: 37–48. (12)

Johnson, P.T.J., J. D. Olden, and M.J.V. Zanden. 2008. Dam invaders: impoundments facilitate biological invasions into freshwaters. *Frontiers in Ecology and the Environment* 6: 357–363. (10)

Johnson, R. C. 2008. Gene banks pay big dividends to agriculture, the environment, and human welfare. *PLoS Biology* 6: e148. (14)

Jones, B. and L. C. Weaver. 2009. CBNRM in Namibia: growth, trends, lessons, and constraints. *In* H. Suich, B. Child, and A. Spenceley (eds.), *Evolution and Innovation in Wildlife Conservation: Parks and Game Ranches to Transfrontier Conservation Areas*, pp. 223–242. IUCN Earthscan, London. (18)

Jones, B. L., B. Anderson, D. H. Anderson, S. G. Bousquin, C. Carlson, M. D. Cheek, et al. 2010. Kissimmee River Basin. *In* M. W. Sole and C. A. Wehle (eds.), *2010 South Florida Environmental Report*, pp. 1–75. South Florida Water Management District, West Palm Beach, FL. (19)

Jones, H. L. and J. M. Diamond. 1976. Short-time-base studies of turnover in breeding birds of the California Channel Islands. *Condor* 76: 526–549. (11)

Jones, K. E., N. G. Patel, M. A. Levy, A. Storeygard, D. Balk, J. L. Gittleman, et al. 2008. Global trends in emerging infectious diseases. *Nature* 451: 990–994. (10)

Joppa, L.N., S. R. Loarie, and S. L. Pimm. 2008. On the protection of "protected areas." *Proceedings of the National Academy of Sciences USA* 105: 6673–6678. (17)

Jordan, N. and K. D. Warner. 2010. Enhancing the multifunctionality of U.S agriculture. *BioScience* 60: 60–66. (18)

Jordan, W. R., III. 2003. *The Sunflower Forest: Ecological Restoration and the New Communion with Nature*. University of California Press, Berkeley, CA. (19)

Jordano, P., C. Garcia, J. A. Godoy, and J. L. Garcia-Castano. 2007. Differential contribution of frugivores to complex seed dispersal patterns. *Proceedings of the National Academy of Sciences USA* 104: 3278–3282. (13)

Joubert, B. and D. Joubert. 2008. *Face to Face with Elephants*. National Geographic Books, Washington, D.C. (12)

Journey North: A Global Study of Wildlife Migration and Seasonal Change. 2010. *http://www.learner.org/jnorth* (12, 22)

Jovan, S. and B. McCune. 2005. Air-quality bioindication in the greater central valley of California, with epiphytic macrolichen communities. *Ecological Applications* 15: 1712–1726. (5)

Justus, J., M. Coyvan, H. Regan, and L. Maguire. 2009. Buying into conservation: intrinsic versus instrumental value. *Trends in Ecology and Evolution* 24: 187–191. (6)

Kadoya, T., S. Suda, and I. Washitani. 2009. Dragonfly crisis in Japan: a likely consequence of recent agricultural habitat degradation. *Biological Conservation* 142: 1899–1905. (16)

Kahn, P. H., Jr. and S. R. Kellert (eds.). 2002. *Children and Nature: Psychological, Sociocultural, and Evolutionary Investigations*. MIT Press, Cambridge, MA. (6)

Kaiser, M. J. and G. Edwards-Jones. 2006. The role of ecolabeling in fisheries management and conservation. *Conservation Biology* 20: 392–398. (22)

Kampa, M. and E. Castanas. 2008. Human health effects of air pollution. *Environmental Pollution* 151: 362–367. (9)

Kannan, R. and D. A. James. 2009. Effects of climate change on global biodiversity: a review of key literature. *Tropical Ecology* 50: 31–39. (9)

Kapos, V., A. Balmford, R. Aveling, P. Bubb, P. Carey, A. Entwistle, et al. 2008. Calibrating conservation: new tools for measuring success. *Conservation Letters* 1: 155–164. (20, 21)

Kareiva, P. and M. Marvier. 2003. Conserving biodiversity coldspots: recent calls to direct conservation funding to the world's biodiversity hotspots may be bad investment advice. *American Scientist* 91: 344–351. (15)

Kareiva, P. and S. A. Levin (eds.). 2003. *The Importance of Species: Perspectives on Expendability and Triage*. Princeton University Press, Princeton, NJ. (4)

Karesh, W. B., R. A. Cook, E. L. Bennett, and J. Newcomb. 2005. Wildlife trade and global disease emergence. *CDC Emerging Infectious Diseases* 11: 1000–1002. (10)

Karl, T. R. 2006. Written statement for an oversight hearing: Introduction to Climate Change before the Committee on Government Reform, U.S. House of Representatives, Washington, D.C. (9)

Karl, T. R. and K. E. Trenberth. 2003. Modern global climate change. *Science* 302: 1719–1723. (9)

Karnosky, D. F., J. M. Skelly, K. E. Percy, and A. H. Chappelka. 2007. Perspectives regarding 50 years of research on effects of tropospheric ozone air pollution on U.S. forests. *Environmental Pollution* 147: 489–506. (9)

Kautz, R., R. Kawula, T. Hoctor, J. Comiskey, D. Jansen, D. Jennings, et al. 2006. How much is enough? Landscape-scale conservation for the Florida panther. *Biological Conservation* 130: 118–133. (18)

Keeton, W. S., C. E. Kraft, and D. R. Warren. 2007. Mature and old-growth riparian forests: structure, dynamics, and effects on Adirondack stream habitats. *Ecological Applications* 17: 852–868. (17)

Keller, R. P., K. Frang, and D. M. Lodge. 2008. Preventing the spread of invasive species: economic benefits of intervention guided by ecological predictions. *Conservation Biology* 22: 80–88. (10)

Keller, R. P. and D. M. Lodge. 2007. Species invasions from commerce in live aquatic organisms: problems and possible solutions. *BioScience* 57: 428–436. (10)

Kellert, S. R. 1997. *Kinship to Mastery: Biophilia in Human Evolution and Development*. Island Press, Washington, D.C. (1)

Kelly, B. C., M. G. Ikonomou, J. D. Blair, A. E. Morin, and F.A.P.C. Gobas. 2007. Food-web specific biomagnification of persistent organic pollutants. *Science* 317: 236–239. (9)

Kelm, D. H., K. R. Wiesner, and O. von Helversen. 2008. Effects of artificial roosts for frugivorous bats on seed dispersal in a Neotropical forest pasture mosaic. *Conservation Biology* 22: 733–741. (2)

Keough, H. L. and D. J. Blahna. 2006. Achieving integrative, collaborative ecosystem management. *Conservation Biology* 20: 1373–1382. (18)

Kerr, J. T., A. Sugar, and L. Packer. 2000. Indicator taxa, rapid biodiversity assessment, and nestedness in an endangered ecosystem. *Conservation Biology* 14: 1726–1734. (15)

Kerwath, S. E., E. B. Thorstad, T. F. Næsje, P. D. Cowley, F. Økland, C. Wilke, et al. 2009. Crossing invisible boundaries: the effectiveness of the Langebaan Lagoon Marine Protected Area as a harvest refuge for a migratory fish species in South Africa. *Conservation Biology* 23: 653–661. (12)

Kiesecker, J. M., H. Copeland, A. Pocewicz, N. Nibbelink, B. McKenney, J. Dahlke, et al. 2009. A framework for implementing biodiversity offsets: selecting sites and determining scale. *BioScience* 59: 77–84. (20)

Killilea, M. E., A. Swei, R. S. Lane, C. J. Briggs, and R. S. Ostfeld. 2008. Spatial dynamics of Lyme disease: a review. *EcoHealth* 5: 167–195. (9)

Kindvall, O. and U. Gärdenfors. 2003. Temporal extrapolation of PVA results in relation to the IUCN Red List criterion E. *Conservation Biology* 17: 316–321. (8)

King, C. M., R. M. McDonald, R. D. Martin, and T. Dennis. 2009. Why is eradication of invasive mustelids so difficult? *Biological Conservation* 142: 806–816. (10)

King, D. I., R. B. Chandler, J. M. Collins, W. R. Petersen, and T. E. Lautzenheiser. 2009. Effects of width, edge and habitat on the abundance and nesting success of scrub-shrub birds in power-line corridors. *Biological Conservation* 142: 2672–2680. (18)

Kingsford, R. T., J.E.M. Watson, C. J. Lundquist, O. Venter, L. Hughes, E. L. Johnston, et al. 2009. Major conservation policy issues for biodiversity in Oceania. *Conservation Biology* 23: 834–840. (17)

Kissui, B. M. and C. Packer. 2004. Top-down population regulation of a top predator: lions in the Ngorongoro Crater. *Proceedings of the Royal Society B* 271: 1867–1874. (10)

Klass, K. D., O. Zompro, N. P. Kristensen, and J. Adis. 2002. Mantophasmatodea: a new insect order with extant members in the Afrotropics. *Science* 296: 1456–1459. (3)

Knapp, R. A., C. P. Hawkins, J. Ladau, and J. G. McClory. 2005. Fauna of Yosemite National Park lakes has low resistance but high resilience to fish introductions. *Ecological Applications* 15: 835–847. (2)

Knight, A. and R. M. Cowling. 2007. Embracing opportunism in the selection of priority conservation areas. *Conservation Biology* 21: 1124–1126. (16)

Knight, R. L., E. A. Odell, and J. D. Maetas. 2006. Subdividing the West. *In* M. J. Groom, G. K. Meffe, and C. R. Carroll (eds.), *Principles of Conservation Biology*, 3rd ed, pp. 241–243. Sinauer Associates, Sunderland, MA. (9)

Knowlton, N. and J.B.C. Jackson. 2008. Shifting baselines, local impacts, and global change on coral reefs. *PLoS Biology* 6: e54. (3)

Knutsen, H., P. E. Jorde, H. Sannæs, A. R. Hoelzel, O. A. Bergstad, S. Stefanni, et al. 2009. Bathymetric barriers promoting genetic structure in the deepwater demersal fish tusk (*Brosme brosme*). *Molecular Ecology* 18: 3151–3162. (3)

Kobori, H. 2009. Current trends in conservation education in Japan. *Biological Conservation* 142: 1950–1957. (19)

Kobori, H. and R. Primack. 2003. Participatory conservation approaches for Satoyama: the traditional forest and agricultural landscape of Japan. *Ambio* 32: 307–311. (16, 17)

Koh, L. P., P. Levang, and J. Ghazoul. 2009. Designer landscapes for sustainable biofuels. *Trends in Ecology and Evolution* 24: 431–438. (16, 18)

Koh, L. P. and D. S. Wilcove. 2007. Cashing in palm oil for conservation. *Nature* 448: 993–994. (9)

Kohlmann, S. G., G. A. Schmidt, and D. K. Garcelon. 2005. A population viability analysis for the island fox on Santa Catalina Island, California. *Ecological Modeling* 183: 77–94. (12)

Kolb, A. and M. Diekmann. 2005. Effects of life-history traits on responses of plant species to forest fragmentation. *Conservation Biology* 19: 929–938. (8)

Komers, P. E. and G. P. Curman. 2000. The effect of demographic characteristics on the success of ungulate re-introductions. *Biological Conservation* 93: 187–193. (13)

Koontz, T. M. and J. Bodine. 2008. Implementing ecosystem management in public agencies: lessons from the U.S. Bureau of Land Management and the Forest Service. *Conservation Biology* 22: 60–69. (18)

Kothamasi, D. and E. T. Kiers. 2009. Emerging conflicts between biodiversity conservation laws and scientific research: the case of the Czech entomologists in India. *Conservation Biology* 23: 1328–1330. (21)

Kothari, A., N. Singh, and S. Suri (eds.). 1996. *People and Protected Areas: Toward Participatory Conservation in India*. Sage Publications, New Delhi, India. (17)

Kramer, R. and A. Jenkins. 2009. Ecosystem services, markets, and red wolf habitats: results from a farm operator survey. *Ecosystem Services Series*, Nicholas Institute for Environmental Policy Solutions, Duke University, Durham, NC. (13)

Kremen, C. and R. S. Ostfeld. 2005. A call to ecologists: measuring, analyzing and managing ecosystem services. *Frontiers in Ecology and the Environment* 10: 539–548. (5)

Kristensen, R. M., I. Heiner, and R. P. Higgins. 2007. Morphology and life cycle of a new loriciferan from the Atlantic coast of Florida with an emended diagnosis and life cycle of Nanaloricidae (Loricifera). *Invertebrate Biology* 126: 120–137. (3)

Krueper, D., J. Bart, and T. D. Rich. 2003. Response of vegetation and breeding birds to the removal of cattle on the San Pedro River, Arizona (U.S.A.). *Conservation Biology* 17: 607–615. (17)

Kulkarni, M. V., P. M. Groffman, and J. B. Yavitt. 2008. Solving the global nitrogen problem: it's a gas! *Frontiers in Ecology and the Environment* 6: 199–206. (9)

Kunz, T. H., E. B. Arnett, W. P. Erickson, A. R. Hoar, G. D. Johnson, R. P. Larkin, et al. 2007. Ecological impacts of wind energy development on bats: questions, research needs, and hypotheses. *Frontiers in Ecology and the Environment* 5: 315–324. (20, 22)

Kuparinen, A., F. Schurr, O. Tackenberg, and R. B. O'Hara. 2007. Air-mediated pollen flow from genetically modified to conventional crops. *Ecological Applications* 17: 431–440. (10)

Kuussaari, M., R. Bommarco, R. K. Heikkinen, A. Helm, J. Krauss, R. Lindborg, et al. 2009. Extinction debt: a challenge for biodiversity conservation. *Trends in Ecology and Evolution* 24: 564–571. (7)

Lacy, R. C. 1987. Loss of genetic diversity from managed populations: interacting effects of drift, mutation, immigration, selection and population subdivision. *Conservation Biology* 1: 143–158. (11)

Laetz, C. A., D. H. Baldwin, T.K. Collier, V. Hebert, J. D. Stark, and N. L. Scholz. 2009. The synergistic toxicity of pesticide mixtures: implications for risk assessment and the conservation of endangered Pacific salmon. *Environmental Health Perspectives* 117: 348–353. (9)

Lafferty, K. D. 2009. The ecology of climate change and infectious diseases. *Ecology* 90: 888–900. (10)

Laikre, L., F. W. Allendorf, L. C. Aroner, C. S. Baker, D. P. Gregovich, M. M. Hansen, et al. 2010. Neglect of genetic diversity in implementation of the Convention on Biological Diversity. *Conservation Biology* 24: 86–88. (2)

Lake Erie Protection and Restoration Plan (LEPR) 2008. Ohio Lake Erie Commission, Toledo, OH. (19)

Lalas, C., H. Ratz, K. McEwan, and S. D. McConkey. 2007. Predation by New Zealand sea lions (*Phocarctos hookeri*) as a threat to the viability of yellow-eyed penguins (*Megadyptes antipodes*) at Otago Peninsula, New Zealand. *Biological Conservation* 135: 235–246. (17)

Lammertink, M. 2004. A multiple-site comparison of woodpecker communities in Bornean lowland and hill forests. *Conservation Biology* 18: 746–757. (18)

Lamoreux, J. F., J. C. Morrison, T. H. Ricketts, D. M. Olson, E. Dinerstein, M. W. McKnight, and H. H. Shugart. 2006. Global tests of biodiversity concordance and the importance of endemism. *Nature* 440: 212–214. (3)

Lampila, P., M. Monkkonen, and A. Desrochers. 2005. Demographic responses by birds to forest fragmentation. *Conservation Biology* 19: 1537–1546. (9)

Land Trust Alliance. 2009. *http://www.landtrustalliance.org* (20)

Langhammer, P. F., M. I. Bakarr, L. A. Bennun, T. M. Brooks, R. P. Clay, W. Darwall, et al. 2007. *Identification and Gap Analysis of Key Biodiversity Areas: Targets for Comprehensive Protected Area Systems*. Best Practice Protected Area Guidelines Series No. 15, IUCN, Gland, Switzerland. (15)

Langpap, C. 2006. Conservation of endangered species: can incentives work for private landowners? *Ecological Economics* 57: 558–572. (20)

Lant, C. L., J. B. Ruhl, and S. E. Kraft. 2008. The tragedy of ecosystem services. *BioScience* 58: 969–974. (4)

Lanza, R. P., B. L. Dresser, and P. Damiani. 2000. Cloning Noah's Ark. *Scientific American* 283(5): 84–89. (14)

Lapham, N. P. and R. J. Livermore. 2003. *Striking a Balance: Ensuring Conservation's Place on the International Biodiversity Agenda*. Conservation International, Washington, D.C. (21)

Larssen, T., E. Lydersen, D. Tang, Y. He, J. Gao, H. Liu, et al. 2006. Acid rain in China. *Environmental Science and Technology* 40: 418–425. (9)

Latin American and Caribbean Network of Environmental Funds (RedLAC). 2008. *http://www.redlac.org* (21)

Laurance, S. G. and W. F. Laurance. 1999. Tropical wildlife corridors: use of linear rainforest remnants by arboreal mammals. *Biological Conservation* 91: 231–239. (16)

Laurance, W. F. 1991. Ecological correlates of extinction proneness in Australian tropical rain forest mammals. *Conservation Biology* 5: 79–89. (8)

Laurance, W. F. 2007a. Forest destruction in tropical Asia. *Current Science* 93: 1544–1550. (9)

Laurance, W. F. 2007b. Have we overstated the tropical biodiversity crisis? *Trends in Ecology and Evolution* 22: 65–70. (7)

Laurance, W. F. 2008a. Adopt a forest. *Biotropica* 40: 3–6. (19)

Laurance, W. F. 2008b. Theory meets reality: how habitat fragmentation research has transcended island biogeographic theory. *Biological Conservation* 141: 1731–1744. (8, 9)

Laurance, W. F. 2009. Conserving the hottest of the hotspots. *Biological Conservation* 142: 1137. (15)

Laurance, W. F., M. A. Cochrane, S. Bergen, P. M. Fearnside, P. Delamônica, C. Barber, et al. 2001. The future of the Brazilian Amazon. *Science* 291: 438–439. (21)

Laurance, W. F., M. Goosem, and S.G.W. Laurance. 2009. Impacts of roads and linear clearings on tropical forests. *Trends in Ecology and Evolution* 24: 659–679. (9)

Laurance, W. F., S. G. Laurance, and D. W. Hilbert. 2008. Long-term dynamics of a fragmented rainforest mammal assemblage. *Conservation Biology* 22: 1154–1164. (7, 9)

Laurance, W. F., T. E. Lovejoy, H. L. Vasconcelos, E. M. Bruna, R. K. Didham, P. C. Stouffer, et al. 2002. Ecosystem decay of Amazonian forest fragments: a 22–year investigation. *Conservation Biology* 16: 605–618. (9)

Laurance, W. F. and R. C. Luizão. 2007. Driving a wedge into the Amazon. *Nature* 448: 409–10. (7, 9)

Lawler, J. J., S. L. Shafer, B. A. Bancroft, and A. R. Blaustein. 2010. Projected climate impacts for the amphibians of the Western Hemisphere. *Conservation Biology* 24: 38–50. (8)

Lawler, J. J., T. H. Tear, C. Pyke, M. R. Shaw, P. Gonzalez, P. Kareiva, et al. 2010. Resource management in a changing and uncertain climate. *Frontiers in Ecology and the Environment* 8: 35–43. (17)

Lawrence, A. J., R. Afif, M. Ahmed, S. Khalifa, and T. Paget. 2010. Bioactivity as an options value of sea cucumbers in the Egyptian Red Sea. *Conservation Biology* 24: 217–225. (5)

Lawton, J. H. and K. Gaston. 2001. Indicator species. *In* S. A. Levin (ed.), *Encyclopedia of Biodiversity* 3: 437–450. Academic Press, San Diego, CA. (15)

Le Page, Y., J.M.C. Pereira, R. Trigo, C. da Camara, D. Oom, and B. Mota. 2007. Global fire activity patterns (1996–2006) and climatic influence: an analysis using the World Fire Atlas. *Atmospheric Chemistry and Physics Discussions* 7: 17299–17338. (9)

Leader-Williams, N. 1990. Black rhinos and African elephants: lessons for conservation funding. *Oryx* 24: 23–29. (14)

Leathwick, J. 2008. Novel methods for the design and evaluation of marine protected areas in offshore waters. *Conservation Letters* 1: 91–102. (16)

Leathwick, J. R., J. Elith, W. L. Chadderton, D. Rowe, and T. Hastie. 2008. Dispersal, disturbance and the contrasting biogeographies of New Zealand's diadromous and non-diadromous fish species. *Journal of Biogeography* 35: 1481–1497. (17)

Leberg, P. L. and B. D. Firmin. 2008. Role of inbreeding depression and purging in captive breeding and restoration programs. *Molecular Ecology* 17: 334–343. (11)

Lee, J. E. and S. L. Chown. 2009. Breaching the dispersal barrier to invasion: quantification and management. *Ecological Applications* 19: 1944–1959. (10)

Lee, P. C. and M. D. Graham. 2006. African elephants *Loxodonta africana* and human-elephant interactions: implications for conservation. *International Zoo Yearbook* 40: 9–19. (14)

Lee, T., J. Y. Meyer, J. B. Burch, P. Pearce-Kelly, and D. Ó Foighil. 2008. Not completely lost: two partulid tree snail species persist on the highest peak of Raiatea, French Polynesia. *Oryx* 42: 615–619. (14)

Lee, T. M., N. S. Sodhi, and D. M. Prawiradilaga. 2007. The importance of protected areas for the forest and endemic avifauna of Sulawesi (Indonesia). *Ecological Applications* 17: 1727–1741. (15)

Legendre P., D. Borcard, and P. R. Peres-Neto. 2005. Analyzing beta diversity: partitioning the spatial variation of community composition data. *Ecological Monographs* 75: 435–450. (2)

Lehtiniemi, M., T. Hakala, S. Saesmaa, and M. Viitasalo. 2007. Prey selection by the larvae of three species of littoral fishes on natural zooplankton assemblages. *Aquatic Ecology* 41:85–94. (10)

Leisher, C. 2008. What Rachel Carson knew about marine protected areas. *BioScience* 58: 478–479. (1, 17)

Leopold, A. 1939a. A biotic view of land. *Journal of Forestry* 37: 113–116. (1)

Leopold, A. 1939b. The farmer as a conservationist. *American Forests* 45: 294–299, 316, 323. (1)

Leopold, A. 1949. *A Sand County Almanac and Sketches Here and There*. Oxford University Press, New York. (1, 6)

Leopold, A. C. 2004. Living with the land ethic. *BioScience* 54: 149–154. (1)

Lepczyk, C.A., C.H. Flather, V.C. Radeloff, A.M. Pidgeon, R.B. Hammer, and J.G. Liu. 2008. Human impacts on regional avian diversity and abundance. *Conservation Biology* 22: 405–416. (17)

Lepczyk, C. A., A. G. Mertig, and J. Liu. 2003. Landowners and cat predation across rural-to-urban landscapes. *Biological Conservation* 115: 191–201. (9)

Leprieur, F., O. Beauchard, S. Blanchet, T. Oberdorff, and S. Brosse. 2008. Fish invasions in the world's river systems: when natural processes are blurred by human activities. *PLoS Biology* 6: e28. (10)

Lerner, J., J. Mackey and F. Casey. 2007. What's in Noah's wallet? Land conservation spending in the United States. *BioScience* 57: 419–423. (16)

Letnic, M., F. Koch, C. Gordon, M. S. Crowther, and C. R. Dickman. 2009. Keystone effects of an alien top-predator stem extinctions of native mammals. *Proceedings of the Royal Society B* 276: 3249–3256. (2)

Leu, M., S. E. Hanser, and S. T. Knick. 2008. The human footprint in the west: a large-scale analysis of anthropogenic impacts. *Ecological Applications* 18: 1119–1139. (9)

Leverington, F., M. Hockings, and K. L. Costa. 2008. Management effectiveness evaluation in protected areas: a global study. Report for "Global study into management effectiveness evaluation of protected areas." IUCN, WCPA, TNC, and WWF, the University of Queensland, Gatton, Australia. (21)

Levin, P. S., M. J. Fogarty, S. A. Murawski, and D. Fluharty. 2009. Integrated ecosystem assessments: developing the scientific basis for ecosystem-based management of the ocean. *PloS Biology* 7: 23–28. (18)

Levin, S. and J. Lubchenco. 2008. Resilience, robustness, and marine ecosystem-based management. *BioScience* 58: 27–32. (17)

Levin, S. A. (ed.). 2001. *Encyclopedia of Biodiversity*. Academic Press, San Diego, CA. (2)

Levy, S. 2007. Cannery Row revisited: impacts of overfishing on the Pacific. *BioScience* 57: 8–13. (2)

Lewis, D. M. 2004. Snares vs. Hoes: Why Food Security is Fundamental to Wildlife Conservation. Presentation to the Africa Biodiversity Collaborative Group, Food Security and Wildlife Conservation in Africa Meeting, 29 October 2004, Washington, D.C. (10)

Lewis, O. T. 2009. Biodiversity change and ecosystem function in tropical forests. *Basic and Applied Ecology* 10: 97–102. (2)

Lewison, R. L., L. B. Crowder, and D. J. Shaver. 2003. The impact of turtle excluder devices and fisheries closures on loggerhead and Kemp's ridley strandings in the western Gulf of Mexico. *Conservation Biology* 17: 1089–1097. (13)

Li, L., C. Kato, and K. Horikoshi. 1999. Bacterial diversity in deep-sea sediments from different depths. *Biodiversity and Conservation* 8: 659–677. (3)

Li, Y. and D. S. Wilcove. 2005. Threats to vertebrate species in China and the United States. *BioScience* 55: 147–153. (10)

Li, Y. M., Z. W. Guo, Q. S. Yang, Y. S. Wang, and J. Niemela. 2003. The implications of poaching for giant panda conservation. *Biological Conservation* 111: 125–136. (14)

Lilley, R. 2008. World's largest marine reserve declared. *National Geographic News.* *http://news.nationalgeographic.com/news/2008/02/080215–AP Marine-Res.html* (15)

Lin, S. C. and L. P. Yuan. 1980. Hybrid rice breeding in China. *In Innovative Approaches to Rice Breeding: Selected Papers from the 1979 International Rice Research Conference*, pp. 35–52. International Rice Research Institute, Manila, Philippines. (14)

Lindenmayer, D. B. 2000. Factors at multiple scales affecting distribution patterns and their implications for animal conservation—Leadbeater's Possum as a case study. *Biodiversity and Conservation* 9: 15–35. (12)

Lindenmayer, D. B., A. Welsh, C. Donnelly, M. Crane, D. Michael, C. Macgregor, et al. 2009. Are nest boxes a viable alternative source of cavities for hollow-dependant animals? Long-term monitoring of nest box occupancy, pest use and attrition. *Biological Conservation* 142: 33–42. (17)

Lindholm, J. and B. Barr. 2001. Comparison of marine and terrestrial protected areas under federal jurisdiction in the United States. *Conservation Biology* 15: 1441–1444. (15)

Lindsey, P. A., R. Alexander, J. T. duToit, and M.G.L. Mills. 2005. The cost efficiency of wild dog conservation in South Africa. *Conservation Biology* 19: 1205–1214. (13)

Lindsey, P. A., P. A. Roulet, and S. S. Romañach. 2007. Economic and conservation significance of the trophy hunting industry in sub-Saharan Africa. *Biological Conservation* 134: 455–469. (4, 20)

Link, J. S. 2007. Underappreciated species in ecology: "ugly fish" in the northwest Atlantic Ocean. *Ecological Applications* 17: 2037–2060. (10)

Linkie, M., R. Smith, Y. Zhu, D. J. Martyr, B. Suedmeyer, J. Pramono, et al. 2008. Evaluating biodiversity conservation around a large Sumatran protected area. *Conservation Biology* 22: 683–690. (20)

Little, C.T.S. 2010. Life at the bottom: the prolific afterlife of whales. *Scientific American* 302(2): 78–84. (3)

Liu, D. 2009. BioDiversifying the curriculum. *CBE Life Sciences Education* 8: 100–107. (15)

Liu, J. G. 2007. Coupled human and natural systems. *Ambio* 36: 639–649. (22)

Lloyd, P., T. E. Martin, R. L. Redmond, U. Langer, and M. M. Hart. 2005. Linking demographic effects of habitat fragmentation across landscapes to continental source-sink dynamics. *Ecological Applications* 15: 1504–1514. (9)

Lobell, D. B., M. B. Burke, C. Tebaldi, M. D. Mastrandrea, W. P. Falcon, and R. L. Naylor. 2008. Prioritizing climate change adaptation needs for food security in 2030. *Science* 319: 607–610. (9)

Lotze, H. K. and B. Worm. 2009. Historical baselines for large marine mammals. *Trends in Ecology and Evolution* 24: 254–262. (10)

Loucks, C., M. B. Mascia, A. Maxwell, K. Huy, K. Duong, N. Chea, et al. 2009. Wildlife decline in Cambodia, 1953–2005: exploring the legacy of armed conflict. *Conservation Letters* 2: 82–92. (10)

Loucks, C. L. and R. F. Gorman. 2004. Regional ecosystem services and the rating of investment opportunities. *Frontiers in Ecology and the Environment* 2: 207–216. (4)

Louda, S. M., A. E. Arnett, T. A. Rand, and F. L. Russell. 2003. Invasiveness of some biological control insects and adequacy of their ecological risk assessment and regulation. *Conservation Biology* 17: 73–82. (10)

Louda, S. M., T. A. Rand, A. E. Arnett, A. S. McClay, K. Shea, and A. K. McEachern. 2005. Evaluation of ecological risk to populations of a threatened plant from an invasive biocontrol insect. *Ecological Applications* 15: 234–249. (10)

Louisiana Coastal Wetlands Conservation and Restoration Task Force and the Wetlands Conservation and Restoration Authority. 1998. *Coast 2050: Toward a Sustainable Coastal Louisiana.* Louisiana Department of Natural Resources, Baton Rouge, LA. (19)

Lourie, S. A. and A.C.J. Vincent. 2004. Using biogeography to help set priorities in marine conservation. *Conservation Biology* 18: 1004–1020. (15)

Low, B., S. R. Sundaresan, I. R. Fischhoff, and D. I. Rubenstein. 2009. Partnering with local communities to identify conservation priorities for endangered Grevy's zebra. *Biological Conservation* 142: 1548–1555. (12, 22)

Lowman, M. D., E. Burgess, and J. Burgess. 2006. *It's a Jungle Up There: More Tales from the Treetops.* Yale University Press, New Haven, CT. (3)

Lu, X., M. B. McElroy, and J. Kiviluoma. 2009. Global potential for wind-generated electricity. *Proceedings of the National Academy of Sciences USA* 106: 10933–10938. (20)

Luck, G. W., R. Harrington, P. A. Harrison, C. Kremen, P. M. Berry, R. Bugter, et al. 2009. Quantifying the contribution of organisms to the provision of ecosystem services. *BioScience* 59: 223–235. (5)

Luther, D. A. and R. Greenberg. 2009. Mangroves: a global perspective on the evolution and conservation of their terrestrial vertebrates. *BioScience* 59: 602–612. (9)

Lynch, J. A., V. C. Bowersox, and J. W. Grimm. 2000. Acid rain reduced in eastern United States. *Environmental Science and Technology* 6: 940–949. (9)

MacArthur, R. H. and E. O. Wilson. 1967. *The Theory of Island Biogeography.* Princeton University Press, Princeton, NJ. (7, 16)

Mace, G. M. 1995. Classification of threatened species and its role in conservation planning. *In* J. H. Lawton and R. M. May (eds.), *Extinction Rates*, pp. 131–146. Oxford University Press, Oxford, UK. (7)

Mace, G. M. 2005. Biodiversity—an index of intactness. *Nature* 434: 32–33. (7)

Mace, G. M., N. J. Collar, K. J. Gaston, C. Hilton-Taylor, H. R. Akçakaya, N. Leader-Williams, et al. 2008. Quantification of extinction risk: IUCN's system for classifying threatened species. *Conservation Biology* 22: 1424–1442. (8)

Mace, G. M., H. Masundire, J. Baillie, T. Ricketts, T. Brooks, M. Hoffmann, et al. 2005. Biodiversity. *In Millennium Ecosystem Assessment (MEA), Ecosystems and Human Well-Being: Current State and Trends* 1: 77–122. Island Press, Washington D.C. (7)

Magnuson, J. J. 1990. Long-term ecological research and the invisible present. *BioScience* 40: 495–501. (12)

Magnussen, J. E., E. K. Pikitch, S. C. Clarke, C. Nicholson, A. R. Hoelzel, and M. S. Shivji. 2007. Genetic tracking of basking shark products in international trade. *Animal Conservation* 10: 199–207. (6)

Maiorano, L., A. Falcucci, and L. Boitani. 2008. Size-dependent resistance of protected areas to land-use change. *Proceedings of the Royal Society B* 275: 1297–1304. (15, 16)

Malhi, Y., J. T. Roberts, R. A. Betts, T. J. Killeen, W. Li, and C. A. Nobre. 2008. Climate change, deforestation, and the fate of the Amazon. *Science* 319: 169–172. (9, 21)

Malpai Borderlands Group. 2010. *http://www.malpaiborderlandsgroup.org* (18)

Mangel, M. and C. Tier. 1994. Four facts every conservation biologist should know about persistence. *Ecology* 75: 607–614. (11)

Manolis, J. C., K. M. Chan, M. E. Finkelstein, S. Stephens, C. R. Nelson, J. B. Grant, et al. 2009. Leadership: a new frontier in conservation science. *Conservation Biology* 23: 879–886. (22)

Marcovaldi, M. A. and M. Chaloupka. 2007. Conservation status of the loggerhead sea turtle in Brazil: an encouraging outlook. *Endangered Species Research* 3: 133–143. (1)

Marcovaldi, M. Â. and G. G. Marcovaldi. 1999. Marine turtles of Brazil: the history and structure of Projeto TAMAR-IBAMA. *Biological Conservation* 91: 35–41. (1)

Margules, C. and S. Sarkar. 2007. *Systematic Conservation Planning.* Cambridge University Press, Cambridge, UK. (16)

Markham, J. L., A. Cook, T. MacDougall, L. Witzel, K. Kayle, C. Murray, et al. 2008. A strategic plan for the rehabilitation of lake trout in Lake Erie, 2008–2020. Great Lakes Fishery Commission Miscellaneous Publication 2008–02, Great Lakes Fishery Commission, Ann Arbor, MI. (19)

Markovchick-Nicholls, L., H. M. Regan, D. H. Deutschman, A. Widyanata, B. Martin, L. Noreke, et al. 2008. Relationships between human disturbance and wildlife land use in urban habitat fragments. *Conservation Biology* 22: 99–109. (16)

Marquard, E. A. Weigelt, V. M. Temperton, C. Roscher, J. Schumacher, N. Buchmann, et al. 2009. Plant species richness and functional composition drive overyielding in a six-year grassland experiment. *Ecology* 90: 3290–3302. (2, 5)

Marris, E. 2007. What to let go. *Nature* 450: 152–155. (1)

Marsh, D. M. and P. C. Trenham. 2008. Current trends in plant and animal population monitoring. *Conservation Biology* 22: 647–655. (12)

Marsh, G. P. 1865. *Man and Nature: Or, Physical Geography as Modified by Human Action.* Scribner, New York. (1)

Marshall, J. D., J. M. Blair, D.P.C. Peters, G. Okin, A. Rango, and M. Williams. 2008. Predicting and understanding ecosystem responses to climate change at continental scales. *Frontiers in Ecology and the Environment* 6: 273–280. (5)

Martín-López, B., C. Montes, and J. Benayas. 2007. The non-economic motives behind the willingness to pay for biodiversity conservation. *Biological Conservation* 139: 67–82. (5)

Martin-López, B., C. Montes, L. Ramirez, and J. Benayas. 2009. What drives policy decision-making related to species conservation? *Biological Conservation* 142: 1370–1380. (21)

Martinuzzi, S., W. A. Gould, A. E. Lugo, and E. Medina. 2009. Conversion and recovery of Puerto Rican mangroves: 200 years of change. *Forest Ecology and Management* 257: 75–84. (9)

Maschinski, J., J. E. Baggs, P. F. Quintana-Ascencio, and E. S. Menges. 2006. Using population viability analysis to predict the effects of climate change on the extinction risk of an endangered limestone endemic shrub, Arizona cliffrose. *Conservation Biology* 20: 218–228. (12)

Mascia, M. B. and C. A. Claus. 2009. A property rights approach to understanding human displacement from protected areas: the case of Marine Protected Areas. *Conservation Biology* 23: 16–23. (17)

Master, L. L., S. R. Flack, and B. A. Stein. 1998. *Rivers of Life: Critical Watersheds for Protecting Freshwater Biodiversity.* The Nature Conservancy, Arlington, VA. (7)

Matchewan, N. 2009. Algonquin ban logging in vast traditional territory until Quebec and Canada respect agreements. *Indigenous Peoples Issues and Resources.* http://www.indigenousportal.com (20)

Mathews, F., M. Orros, G. McLaren, M. Gelling, and R. Foster. 2005. Keeping fit on the ark: assessing the suitability of captive-bred animals for release. *Biological Conservation* 121: 569–577. (13)

Matta, J. R., J.R.R. Alavalapati, and D. E. Mercer. 2009. Incentives for biodiversity conservation beyond the best management practices: are forestland owners interested? *Land Economics* 85: 132–143. (20)

Mattfeldt, S. D., L. L. Bailey, and E.H.C. Grant. 2009. Monitoring multiple species: estimating state variables and exploring the efficacy of a monitoring program. *Biological Conservation* 142: 720–737. (12)

Mawdsley, J. R., R. O'Malley, and D. S. Ojima. 2009. A review of climate change adaptation strategies for wildlife management and biodiversity conservation. *Conservation Biology* 23: 1080–1089. (9)

Maxted, N. 2001. *Ex situ, in situ* conservation. *In* S. A. Levin (ed.), *Encyclopedia of Biodiversity* 2: 683–696. Academic Press, San Diego, CA. (14)

Mayaux, P., P. Holmgren, F. Achard, H. Eva, H. J. Stibig, and A. Branthomme. 2005. Tropical forest cover change in the 1990s and options for future monitoring. *Philosophical Transactions of the Royal Society B* 360: 373–384. (17)

Mazerolle, M. J., A. Desrochers, and L. Rochefort. 2005. Landscape characteristics influence pond occupancy by frogs after accounting for detectability. *Ecological Applications* 15: 824–834. (16)

McCarthy, M. A., S. J. Andelman, and H. P. Possingham. 2003. Reliability of relative predictions in population viability analysis. *Conservation Biology* 17: 982–989. (12)

McCarthy, M. A., C. J. Thompson, and N.S.G. Williams. 2006. Logic for designing nature reserves for multiple species. *American Naturalist* 167: 717–727. (16)

McClanahan, T. and G. M. Branch (eds.). 2008. *Food Webs and the Dynamics of Marine Reefs.* Oxford University Press, Oxford, UK. (2)

McClanahan, T. R., J. E. Cinner, N.A.J. Graham, T. M. Daw, J. Maina, S. M. Stead, et al. 2009. Identifying reefs of hope and hopeful actions: contextualizing environmental, ecological, and social parameters to respond effectively to climate change. *Conservation Biology* 23: 662–671. (9)

McClanahan, T. R., J. E. Cinner, J. Maina, N.A.J. Graham, T. M. Daw, S. M. Stead, et al. 2008. Conservation action in a changing climate. *Conservation Letters* 1: 53–59. (9)

McClanahan, T. R., N.A.J. Graham, J. M. Calnan, and M. A. MacNeil. 2007. Toward pristine biomass: reef fish recovery in coral marine protected areas in Kenya. *Ecological Applications* 17: 1055–1067. (17)

McClanahan, T. R., C. C. Hicks, and E. S. Darling. 2008. Malthusian overfishing and efforts to overcome it on Kenyan coral reefs. *Ecological Applications* 18: 1516–1529. (10)

McClelland, E. K. and K. A. Naish. 2007. What is the fitness outcome of crossing unrelated fish populations? A meta-analysis and an evaluation of future research directions. *Conservation Genetics* 8: 397–416. (11)

McClenachan, L. 2009. Documenting loss of large trophy fish from the Florida Keys using historical photographs. *Conservation Biology* 23: 636–643. (10)

McClenachan, L., J.B.C. Jackson, and M.J.H. Newman. 2006. Conservation implications of historic sea turtle nesting beach loss. *Frontiers in Ecology and the Environment* 4: 290–296. (11)

McConkey, K. R. and D. R. Drake. 2006. Flying foxes cease to function as seed dispersers long before they become rare. *Ecology* 87: 271–276. (7)

McCormick, S. 2004. *Conservation by Design: A Framework for Mission Success.* The Nature Conservancy, Washington, D.C. (16)

McKay, J. K. and R. G. Latta. 2002. Adaptive population divergence: markers, TL and traits. *Trends in Ecology and Evolution* 17: 285–291. (11)

McKibben, B. 2007. *Deep Economy: The Wealth of Communities and the Durable Future.* Henry Holt, New York. (6)

McKibben, B. 2007. Carbon's new math. *National Geographic Magazine* 212(October): 32–37. (20)

McKinney, M. A., S. De Guise, D. Martineau, P. Beland, M. Lebeuf, and R. J. Letcher. 2006. Organohalogen contaminants and metabolites in beluga whale (*Delphinapterus leucas*) liver from two Canadian populations. *Environmental Toxicology and Chemistry* 25: 1246–1257. (10)

McKinney, S. T. and D. F. Tomback. 2007. The influence of white pine blister rust on seed dispersal in whitebark pine. *Canadian Journal of Forest Research* 37: 1044–1057. (10)

McLachlan, J. S., J. J. Hellmann, and M. W. Schwartz. 2007. A framework for debate of assisted migration in an era of climate change. *Conservation Biology* 21: 297–302. (13)

McLeod, E., R. Salm, A. Green, and J. Almany. 2009. Designing marine protected area networks to address the impacts of climate change. *Frontiers in Ecology and the Environment* 7: 362–370. (16)

McMurtry, J. J. 2009. Ethical value-added: fair trade and the case of Café Femenino. *Journal of Business Ethics* 86: 27–49. (22)

McNeely, J. A. 1989. Protected areas and human ecology: how national parks can contribute to sustaining societies of the twenty-first century. *In* D. Western and M. Pearl (eds.), *Conservation for the Twenty-first Century*, pp. 150–165. Oxford University Press, New York. (18)

McNeely, J. A., K. R. Miller, W. Reid, R. Mittermeier, and T. B. Werner. 1990. *Conserving the World's Biological Diversity*. IUCN, World Resources Institute, CI, WWF-US, and the World Bank. Gland, Switzerland and Washington, D.C. (4, 5)

McShane, T. O. and M. P. Wells. 2004. *Getting Biodiversity Projects to Work: Towards More Effective Conservation and Development*. Columbia University Press, New York. (20)

Meffe, G. C., C. R. Carroll, and contributers. 1997. *Principles of Conservation Biology*, 2nd ed. Sinauer Associates, Sunderland, MA. (11)

Meijaard, E. and S. Wich. 2007. Putting orangutan population trends into perspective. *Current Biology* 17: R540. (9)

Meine, C. 2001. Conservation movement, historical. *In* S. A. Levin (ed.), *Encyclopedia of Biodiversity*, vol. 1, pp. 883–896. Academic Press, San Diego, CA. (1)

Meine, C., M. Soulé, and R. F. Noss. 2006. A mission-driven discipline: the growth of conservation biology. *Conservation Biology* 20: 631–651. (1)

Melbourne, B. A. and A. Hastings. 2008. Extinction risk depends strongly on factors contributing to stochasticity. *Nature* 454: 100–103. (11)

Menges, E. S. 1992. Stochastic modeling of extinction in plant populations. *In* P. L. Fiedler and S. K. Jain (eds.), *Conservation Biology: The Theory and Practice of Nature Conservation, Preservation and Management*, pp. 253–275. Chapman and Hall, New York. (11)

Menz, F. C. and H. M. Seip. 2004. Acid rain in Europe and the United States: an update. *Environmental Science and Policy* 7: 253–265. (9)

Messina, J. P. and M. A. Cochrane. 2007. The forests are bleeding: how land use change is creating a new fire regime in the Ecuadorian Amazon. *Journal of Latin American Geography* 6.1: 85–100. (9)

Meyer, C. K., M. R. Whiles, and S. G. Baer. 2010. Plant community recovery following restoration in temporarily variable riparian wetlands. *Restoration Ecology* 18: 52–64. (19)

Milder, J. C., J. P. Lassoie, and B. L. Bedford. 2008. Conserving biodiversity and ecosystem function through limited development: an empirical evaluation. *Conservation Biology* 22: 70–79. (20)

Millennium Ecosystem Assessment (MEA). 2005. *Ecosystems and Human Well-being*. 4 volumes. Island Press, Covelo, CA. (1, 2, 3, 4, 5, 7, 9, 10, 18, 22)

Miller, B., W. Conway, R. P. Reading, C. Wemmer, D. Wildt, D. Kleiman, et al. 2004. Evaluating the conservation mission of zoos, aquariums, botanical gardens, and natural history museums. *Conservation Biology* 18: 86–93. (14)

Miller, G. R., C. Geddes, and D. K. Mardon. 1999. Response of the alpine gentian *Gentiana nivalis* L. to protection from grazing by sheep. *Biological Conservation* 87: 311–318. (17)

Miller, J. K., J. M. Scott, C. R. Miller, and L. P Waits. 2002. The Endangered Species Act: dollars and sense? *BioScience* 52: 163–168. (20)

Miller, K. R. 1996. *Balancing the Scales: Guidelines for Increasing Biodiversity's Chances through Bioregional Management*. World Resources Institute, Washington, D.C. (18)

Miller-Rushing, A. J. and R. B. Primack. 2008. Global warming and flowering times in Thoreau's Concord: a community perspective. *Ecology* 89: 332–341. (7)

Mills, S. 2003. *Epicurean Simplicity*. Island Press, Washington, D.C. (6)

Minckley, W. L. 1995. Translocation as a tool for conserving imperiled fishes: experiences in western United States. *Biological Conservation* 72: 297–309. (13)

Minteer, B. A. and J. P. Collins. 2008. From environmental to ecological ethics: toward a practical ethics for ecologists and conservationists. *Science and Engineering Ethics* 14: 483–501. (6)

Miskelly, C. M., G. A. Taylor, H. Gummer, and R. Williams. 2009. Translocations of eight species of burrow-nesting seabirds (genera *Pterodroma, Pelecanoides, Pachyptila* and *Puffinus*: Family Procellariidae). *Biological Conservation* 142: 1965–1980. (13)

Mittermeier, R. A., P. R. Gil, M. Hoffman, J. Pilgrim, T. Brooks, C. Goettsch, et al. 2005. *Hotspots Revisited: Earth's Biologically Richest and Most Endangered Terrestrial Ecoregions*. Conservation International, Washington, D.C. (15)

Mittermeier, R. A., P. R. Gil, and C. G. Mittermeier. 1997. *Megadiversity: Earth's Biologically Wealthiest Nations*. Conservation International, Washington, D.C. (15)

Mittermeier, R. A., C. G. Mittermeier, P. R. Gil, and J. Pilgrim. 2003. *Wilderness: Earth's Last Wild Places*. Conservation International, Washington, D.C. (15)

Mohamed, A. R. M., N. A. Hussain, S. S. Al-Noor, F. M. Mutlak, I. M. Al-Sudani, A. M. Mojer, et al. 2008. Fish assemblage of restored Al-Hawizeh marsh, southern Iraq. *Ecohydrology and Hydrobiology* 8: 375–384. (19)

Mohamed, L. and A. A. Al-Thukair. 2009. Environmental assessments in the oil and gas industry. *Water, Air, and Soil Pollution Focus* 9: 99–105. (21)

Molnar, J. L., R. L Gamboa, C. Revenga, and M. D. Spalding. 2008. Assessing the global threat of invasive species to marine biodiversity. *Frontiers in Ecology and the Environment* 9: 485–492. (10)

Montalvo, A. M. and N. C. Ellstrand. 2001. Nonlocal transplantation and outbreeding depression in the subshrub *Lotus scoparius* (Fabaceae). *American Journal of Botany* 88: 258–269. (11, 13)

Mora, C. 2009. Degradation of Caribbean coral reefs: focusing on proximal rather than ultimate drivers. Reply to Rogers. *Proceedings of the Royal Society B* 276: 199–200. (9)

Mora, C., R. A. Myers, M. Coll, S. Libralato, T. J. Pitcher, R. U. Sumaila, et al. 2009. Management effectiveness of the world's marine fisheries. *PloS Biology* 7: e1000131. (10)

Morales, J. C., P. M. Andau, J. Supriatna, Z. Z. Zainuddin, and D.J. Melnick. 1997. Mitochondrial DNA variability and conservation genetics of the Sumatran rhinoceros. *Conservation Biology* 11: 539–543. (11)

Morell, V. 1986. Dian Fossey: field science and death in Africa. *Science* 86: 17–21. (12)

Morell, V. 1993. Called "trimates," three bold women shaped their field. *Science* 260: 420–425. (12)

Morell, V. 1999. The variety of life. *National Geographic Magazine* 195(February): 6–32. (1, 2)

Morell, V. 2007. Marine biology—killing whales for science? *Science* 316:532–534. (10)

Morell, V. 2008. Into the wild: reintroduced animals face daunting odds. *Science* 320: 742–743. (14)

Morgan, J. L., S. E. Gergel, and N. C. Coops. 2010. Aerial photography: a rapidly evolving tool for ecological management. *BioScience* 60: 47–59. (17)

Morris, M.G. 2000. The effects of structure and its dynamics on the ecology and conservation of arthropods in British grasslands. *Biological Conservation* 95: 129–142. (17)

Moseley, L. (ed.). 2009. *Holy Ground: A Gathering of Voices on Caring for Creation*. Sierra Club Books, San Francisco, CA. (6)

Moyle, P. B. and J. J. Cech, Jr. 2004. *Fishes: An Introduction to Ichthyology*, 5th ed. Prentice-Hall, NJ. (7)

Mpanduji, D. G., M. East, and H. Hofer. 2008. Analysis of habitat use by and preference of elephants in the Selous-Niassa wildlife corridor, southern Tanzania. *African Journal of Ecology* 47: 257–260. (16)

Mueller, J. G., I.H.B. Assanou, I. D. Guimbo, and A. M. Almedom. 2010. Evalutating rapid participatory rural appraisal as an assessment of ethnoecological knowledge and local biodiversity patterns. *Conservation Biology* 24: 140–150. (12)

Muir, J. 1901. *Our National Parks.* Houghton Mifflin, Boston. (1)

Muir, J. 1916. *A Thousand-Mile Walk to the Gulf.* Houghton Mifflin, Boston. (1)

Munilla, I., C. Diez, and A. Velando. 2007. Are edge bird populations doomed to extinction? A retrospective analysis of the common guillemot collapse in Iberia. *Biological Conservation* 137: 359–371. (8)

Munson, L., K. A. Terio, R. Kock, T. Mlengeya, M. E. Roelke, E. Dubovi, et al. 2008. Climate extremes promote fatal co-infections during canine distemper epidemics in African lions. *PLoS One* 3: e2545. (11)

Murray, K. A., L. F. Skerratt, R. Speare, and H. McCallum. 2009. Impact and dynamics of disease in species threatened by the amphibian chytrid fungus, *Batrachochytrium dendrobatidis.* *Conservation Biology* 23: 1242–1252. (8)

Murray-Smith, C., N. A. Brummitt, A. T. Oliveira-Filho, S. Bachman, J. Moat, E.M.N. Lughadha, et al. 2009. Plant diversity hotspots in the Atlantic coastal forests of Brazil. *Conservation Biology* 23: 151–163. (15)

Musiani, M., C. Mamo, L. Boitani, C. Callaghan, C. C. Gates, L. Mattei, et al. 2003. Wolf depredation trends and the use of fladry barriers to protect livestock in western North America. *Conservation Biology* 17: 1538–1547. (13)

Muths, E. and M. P. Scott. 2000. American burying beetle (*Nicrophorus americanus*). *In* R. P. Reading and B. Miller (eds.), *Endangered Animals*, pp. 10–15. Greenwood Press, Westport, CT. (7)

Myers, N. and J. Kent. 2001. *Perverse Subsidies: How Tax Dollars Can Undercut the Environment and the Economy.* Island Press, Washington, D.C. (4)

Myers, N. and J. Kent. 2004. *New Consumers: The Influence of Affluence on the Environment.* Island Press, Washington, D.C. (9)

Myers, N. and A. Knoll. 2001. The biotic crisis and the future of evolution. *Proceedings of the National Academy of Sciences USA* 98: 5389–5392. (2)

Myers, N., N. Golubiewski, and C. J. Cleveland. 2007. Perverse subsidies. *In* C. J. Cleveland (ed.), *Encyclopedia of Earth.* Environmental Information Coalition, National Council for Science and the Environment, Washington, D.C. *http://www.eoearth.org/article/ Perverse_subsidies* (4)

Myers, R. A., J. K. Baum, T. D. Shepherd, S. P. Powers, and C. H. Peterson. 2007. Cascading effects of the loss of apex predatory sharks from a coastal ocean. *Science* 315: 1846–1850. (10)

Nabhan, G. P. 2008. *Where Our Food Comes From: Retracing Nicolay Vavilov's Quest to End Famine.* Island Press, Washington, D.C. (5, 14)

Naeem, S., D. E. Bunker, A. Hector, M. Loreau, and C. Perrings (eds.). 2009. *Biodiversity, Ecosystem Functioning, & Human Wellbeing: An Ecological and Economic Perspective.* Oxford University Press, Oxford, UK. (5)

Naess, A. 1986. Intrinsic value: will the defenders of nature please rise? *In* M. E. Soulé (ed.), *Conservation Biology: The Science of Scarcity and Diversity*, pp. 153–181. Sinauer Associates, Sunderland, MA. (6)

Naess, A. 1989. *Ecology, Community and Lifestyle.* Cambridge University Press, Cambridge, MA. (6)

Naess, A. 2008. *The Ecology of Wisdom: Writings by Arne Naess.* A. Drengson and B. Devall (eds.). Counterpoint, Berkeley, CA. (6)

Naidoo, R. and W. L. Adamowicz. 2006. Modeling opportunity costs of conservation in transitional landscapes. *Conservation Biology* 20: 490–500. (4)

Namibia Association of CBNRM Support Organisations (NACSO). 2008. *Namibia's Communal Conservancies: a review of progress in 2008.* NACSO, Windhoek, Namibia. (18)

Namibia Ministry of Environment and Tourism (MET). 2009. *http://www.met.gov.na/* (18)

NASA. *http://www.nasa.gov* (9)

Nash, S. 2009. Ecotourism and other invasions. *BioScience* 59: 106–110. (5)

National Environmental Education Foundation. 2008. *http://www.neetf.org* (5)

National Oceanic and Atmospheric Administration (NOAA) and J. E. Duffy. 2008. Mediterranean Sea large marine ecosystem. *In* C. J. Cleveland (ed.), *Encyclopedia of Earth.* Environmental Information Coalition, National Council for Science and the Environment, Washington, D.C. *http://www.eoearth.org/article/ Mediterranean_Sea_large_marine_ecosystem* (18)

Native Seeds SEARCH: Southwestern Endangered Aridland Resource Clearing House. 2009. *http://www.nativeseeds.org* (20)

Natural England. *http://www.naturalengland.org.uk* (17)

Nature Conservancy, The. 2010. *http://www.nature.org* (16)

NatureServe Explorer. 2009. *http://www.natureserve.org/explorer* (8)

NatureServe: A Network Connecting Science with Conservation. 2009. *http://www.natureserve.org* (8, 15)

NatureServe. 2009. 2009 IUCN Red List highlights continued extinction threat. *http://www.natureserve.org/projects/iucn.jsp* (8)

Naughton-Treves, L., M. B. Holland, and K. Brandon. 2005. The role of protected areas in conserving biodiversity and sustaining local livelihoods. *Annual Review of Environmental Resources* 30: 219–252. (21)

Naujokaitis-Lewis, I. R., J.M.R. Curtis, P. Arcese, and J. Rosenfeld. 2009. Sensitivity analyses of spatial population viability analysis models for species at risk and habitat conservation planning. *Conservation Biology* 23: 225–229. (12)

Nee, S. 2003. Unveiling prokaryotic diversity. *Trends in Ecology and Evolution* 18: 62–63. (3)

Neff, J. C., R. L. Reynolds, J. Belnap, and P. Lamothe. 2005. Multidecadal impacts of grazing on soil physical and biogeochemical properties in southeast Utah. *Ecological Applications* 15: 87–95. (9)

Nellemann, C., I. Vistnes, P. Jordhoy, and O. Strand. 2001. Winter distribution of wild reindeer in relation to power lines, roads, and resorts. *Biological Conservation* 101: 351–360. (9)

Nelson, M. P. and J. A. Vucetich. 2009. On advocacy by environmental scientists: what, whether, why, and how. *Conservation Biology* 23: 1090–1101. (1)

Nepstad, D., S. Schwartzman, B. Bamberger, M. Santilli, D. Ray, P. Schlesinger, et al. 2006. Inhibition of Amazon deforestation and fire by parks and indigenous lands. *Conservation Biology* 20: 65–73. (9, 20)

New York City Department of Parks and Recreation. *http://www.nyc-govparks.org* (19)

Newbold, S. C. and J. Siikamäki. 2009. Prioritizing conservation activities using reserve site selection methods and population viability analysis. *Ecological Applications* 19: 1774–1790. (4)

Newmark, W. D. 1995. Extinction of mammal populations in western North American national parks. *Conservation Biology* 9: 512–527. (16)

Newmark, W. D. 2008. Isolation of African protected areas. *Frontiers in Ecology and the Environment* 6: 321–328. (16, 18)

Newton, A. C., G. B. Stewart, G. Myers, A. Diaz, S. Lake, J. M. Bullock, et al. 2009. Impacts of grazing on lowland heathland in north-west Europe. *Biological Conservation* 142: 935–947. (17)

Ng, Y. K. 2008. Environmentally responsible Happy Nation Index: towards an internationally acceptable national success indicator. *Social Indicators Research* 85: 425–446. (6)

Nicholson, E., D. A. Keith, and D. S. Wilcove. 2009. Assessing the threat status of ecological communities. *Conservation Biology* 23: 259–274. (15)

Nicholson, T. E., K. A. Mayer, M. M. Staedler, and A. B. Johnson. 2007. Effects of rearing methods on survival of released free-ranging juvenile southern sea otters. *Biological Conservation* 138: 313–320. (13)

Nicholson, E. and H. P. Possingham. 2007. Making conservation decisions under uncertainty for the persistence of multiple species. *Ecological Applications* 17: 251–265. (16)

Nicoll, M.A.C., C. G. Jones, and K. Norris. 2004. Comparison of survival rates of captive-reared and wild-bred Mauritius kestrels (*Falco punctatus*) in a re-introduced population. *Biological Conservation* 118: 539–548. (13)

Nienaber, G. 2006. *Gorilla Dreams: The Legacy of Dian Fossey*. Universe Inc., Bloomington, IN. (12)

Niles, L. J. 2009. Effects of horseshoe crab harvest in Delaware Bay on red knots: are harvest restrictions working? *BioScience* 59: 153–164. (4)

Noon, B. R., P. Parenteau, and S. C. Trombulak. 2005. Conservation science, biodiversity, and the 2005 U.S. forest service regulations. *Conservation Biology* 19: 1359–1361. (18)

Nooren, H. and G. Claridge. 2001. *Wildlife Trade in Laos: the End of the Game*. Netherlands Committee for IUCN, Amsterdam. (21)

Norden, N., J. Chave, P. Belbenoit, A. Caubère, P. Châtelet, P. M. Forget, et al. 2009. Interspecific variation in seedling responses to seed limitation and habitat conditions for 14 Neotropical woody species. *Journal of Ecology* 97: 186–197. (2)

Norlen, D. and D. Gordon. 2007. *Eschrichtius* (whale) and *hucho* (salmon): multilateral development banks' EIA process and the costs to biodiversity. *Natural Resources and Environment* 22: 30–35. (21)

Norris, S. 2007. Ghosts in our midst: coming to terms with amphibian extinctions. *BioScience* 57: 311–316. (9)

Norse, E. A. 1986. *Conserving Biological Diversity in Our National Forests*. The Wilderness Society, Washington, D.C. (17)

Norton, B. G. 2003. *Searching For Sustainability: Interdisciplinary Essays in the Philosophy of Conservation Biology*. Cambridge University Press, New York. (6)

Noss, R. F. 1992. Essay: Issues of scale in conservation biology. *In* P. L. Fiedler and S. K. Jain (eds.), *Conservation Biology: The Theory and Practice of Nature Conservation, Preservation and Management*, 239–250. Chapman and Hall, New York. (6)

Noss, R. F., E. T. La Roe III, and J. M. Scott. 1995. *Endangered Ecosystems of the United States: A Preliminary Assessment of Loss and Degradation. Biological Report 28*. U.S. Department of the Interior, National Biological Service, Washington, D.C. (9)

Novacek, M. J. 2008. Engaging the public in biodiversity issues. *Proceedings of the National Academy of Sciences USA* 105: 11571–11578. (6)

Novotny, V., Y. Basset, S. E. Miller, G. D. Weiblen, B. Bremer, L. Cizek, et al. 2002. Low host specificity of herbivorous insects in a tropical forest. *Nature* 416: 841–844. (3)

Nunes, P., J. Van Den Bergh, and P. Nijkamp. 2003. *The Ecological Economics of Biodiversity*. Edward Elgar, UK. (4)

Nunez-Iturri, G., O. Olsson, and H. F. Howe. 2008. Hunting reduces recruitment of primate-dispersed trees in Amazonian Peru. *Biological Conservation* 141: 1536–1546. (2)

Nuzzo, V. A., J. C. Maerz, and B. Blossey. 2009. Earthworm invasion as the driving force behind plant invasion and community change in northeastern North American forests. *Conservation Biology* 23: 966–974. (10)

NYC Environmental Protection. 2010. *http://www.nyc.gov/watershed* (5)

Nyhagen, D. F., S. D. Turnbull, J. M. Olesen, and C. G. Jones. 2005. An investigation into the role of the Mauritian flying fox, *Pteropus niger*, in forest regeneration. *Biological Conservation* 122: 491–497. (2)

Nyhus, P., H. Fischer, F. Madden, and S. Osofsky. 2003. Taking the bite out of wildlife damage: the challenges of wildlife compensation schemes. *Conservation in Practice* 4: 37–40. (13)

O'Grady, J. J., D. H. Reed, B. W. Brook, and R. Frankham. 2004. What are the best correlates of predicted extinction risk? *Biological Conservation* 118: 513–520. (8)

O'Meilla, C. 2004. Current and reported historical range of the American burying beetle. U.S. Fish and Wildlife Services, Oklahoma Ecological Services Field Office, OK. (7)

Oates, J. F., M. Abedi-Lartey, W. S. McGraw, T. T. Struhsaker, and G. H. Whitesides. 2000. Extinction of a West African red colobus monkey. *Conservation Biology* 14: 1526–1532. (7)

Ødegaard, F. 2000. How many species of arthropods? Erwin's estimate revised. *Biological Journal of the Linnean Society* 71: 583–597. (3)

Odell, J., M. E. Mather, and R. M. Muth. 2005. A biosocial approach for analyzing environmental conflicts: a case study of horseshoe crab allocation. *BioScience* 55: 735–748. (4)

Oehlmann J., U. Schulte-Oehlmann, W. Kloas, O. Jagnytsch, I. Lutz, K. O. Kusk, et al. 2009. A critical analysis of the biological impacts of plasticizers on wildlife. *Philosophical Transactions of the Royal Society B* 364: 2047–2062. (9)

Okin, G. S., A. Parsons, J. Wainwright, J. E. Herrick, B. T. Bestelmeyer, D. Peters, et al. 2009. Do changes in connectivity explain desertification? *BioScience* 59: 237–244. (9)

Olsson, O. 2007. Genetic origin and success of reintroduced white storks. *Conservation Biology* 21: 1196–1206. (13)

Ong, P. S. 2002. Current status and prospects of protected areas in the light of the Philippine biodiversity conservation priorities. Proceedings of IUCN/WCPA-EA-4 Taipei Conference, March 18–23, 2002, Taipei, Taiwan. (4)

Organisation for Economic Co-operation and Development (OECD). *http://www.oecd.org* (21)

Orr, D. W. 2007. Optimism and hope in a hotter time. *Conservation Biology* 21: 1392–1395. (1)

Orrock, J. L. and E. I. Damschen. 2005. Corridors cause differential seed predation. *Ecological Applications* 15: 793–798. (16)

Osborn, F. 1948. *Our Plundered Planet*. Little, Brown and Company, Boston. (1)

Osterlind, K. 2005. Concept formation in environmental education: 14–year olds' work on the intensified greenhouse. *International Journal of Science Education* 27: 891–908. (5)

Ostfeld, R. S. 2009. Climate change and the distribution and intensity of infectious diseases. *Ecology* 4: 903–905. (10)

Ozaki, K., M. Isono, T. Kawahara, S. Iida, T. Kudo, and K. Fukuyama. 2006. A mechanistic approach to evaluation of umbrella species as conservation surrogates. *Conservation Biology* 20: 1507–1515. (15)

Pacific Whale Foundation. 2003. Exploring Hawaii's Coral Reefs. *http://www.pacificwhale.org/printouts/coral_reef_guide.pdf* (3)

Paddack, M. J. and J. A. Estes. 2000. Kelp forest fish populations in marine reserves and adjacent exploited areas of central California. *Ecological Applications* 10: 855–870. (2)

Paine, R. T. 1966. Food web complexity and species diversity. *American Naturalist* 100: 65–75. (2)

Palumbi, S. R., P. A Sandifer, J. D. Allan, M. W. Beck, D. G. Fautin, M. J. Fogarty, et al. 2009. Managing for ocean biodiversity to sustain marine ecosystem services. *Frontiers in Ecology and the Environment* 7: 204–211. (2, 5)

Papworth, S. K., J. Rist, L. Coad, and E. J. Milner-Gulland. 2009. Evidence for shifting baseline syndrome in conservation. *Conservation Letters* 2: 93–100. (1, 12)

Pardini, R., S. M. de Souza, R. Braga-Neto, and J. P. Metzger. 2005. The role of forest structure, fragment size and corridors in maintaining small mammal abundance and diversity in an Atlantic forest landscape. *Biological Conservation* 12: 253–266. (16)

Parfit, M. 2005. Future power: where will the world get its next energy fix? *National Geographic Magazine* 208(August): 2–31. (20)

Parmesan, C. and G. Yohe. 2003. A globally coherent fingerprint of climate change impacts across natural systems. *Nature* 421: 37–42. (9)

Parry, L., J. Barlow, and C. A. Peres. 2009. Allocation of hunting effort by Amazonian smallholders: implications for conserving wildlife in mixed-use landscapes. *Biological Conservation* 142: 1777–1786. (10)

Parsons, E.C.M., S. J. Dolman, A. J. Wright, N. A Rose, and W.C.G. Burns. 2008. Navy sonar and cetaceans: just how much does the gun need to smoke before we act? *Marine Pollution Bulletin* 56: 1248–1257. (10)

Pärtel, M., R. Kalamees, Ü. Reier, E. Tuvi, E. Roosaluste, A. Vellak, et al. 2005. Grouping and prioritization of vascular plant species for conservation: combining natural rarity and management need. *Biological Conservation* 123: 271–278. (8)

Peakall, R., D. Ebert, L. J. Scott, P. F. Meagher, and C. A. Offord. 2003. Comparative genetic study confirms exceptionally low genetic variation in the ancient and endangered relictual conifer, *Wollemia nobilis* (Araucariaceae). *Molecular Ecology* 12: 2331–2343. (11)

Pearce, J. B. 2000. The New York Bight. *Marine Pollution Bulletin* 41: 44–45. (5)

Pearman, P. B., M. R. Penskar, E. H. Schools, and H. D. Enander. 2006. Identifying potential indicators of conservation value using Natural Heritage occurrence data. *Ecological Applications* 16: 186–201. (8)

Pechmann, J.H.K. 2003. Natural population fluctuations and human influences: null models and interactions. *In* R. D. Semlitsch (ed.), *Amphibian Conservation*, pp. 85–93. Smithsonian Institution Press, Washington, D.C. (12)

Peery, M. Z., S. R. Beissinger, S. H. Newman, E. B. Burkett, and T. D. Williams. 2004. Applying the declining population paradigm: diagnosing causes of poor reproduction in the marbled murrelet. *Conservation Biology* 18: 1088–1098. (8)

Peh, K.S.H., J. de Jong, N. S. Sodhi, S.L.H. Lim, and C.A.M. Lap. 2005. Lowland rainforest avifauna and human disturbance: persistence of primary forest birds in selectively logged forests and mixed-rural habitats of southern Peninsular Malaysia. *Biological Conservation* 123: 489–505. (18)

Pellens, R. and P. Grandcolas. 2007. The conservation-refugium value of small and disturbed Brazilian Atlantic forest fragments for the endemic ovoviviparous cockroach *Monastria biguttata* (Insecta: Dictyoptera, Blaberidae, Blaberinae). *Zoological Science* 24: 11–19. (16)

Pelletier F., D. Reale, J. Watters, E. H. Boakes, and D. Garant. 2009. Value of captive populations for quantitative genetics research. *Trends in Ecology and Evolution* 24: 263–270. (14)

Pellow, D. 2005. Endangering development: politics, projects, and environment in Burkina Faso. *Economic Development and Cultural Change* 53: 757–759. (6)

Peres, C. A. 2005. Why we need megareserves in Amazonia. *Conservation Biology* 19: 728–733. (15)

Peres, C. A., C. Baider, P. A. Zuidema, L.H.O. Wadt, K. A. Kainer, D.A.P. Gomes-Silva, et al. 2003. Demographic threats to the sustainability of Brazil nut exploitation. *Science* 302: 2112–2114. (20)

Peres, C. A. and I. R. Lake. 2003. Extent of nontimber resource extraction in tropical forests: accessibility to game vertebrates by hunters in the Amazon Basin. *Conservation Biology* 17: 521–535. (17)

Peres, C. A. and J. W. Terborgh. 1995. Amazonian nature reserves: an analysis of the defensibility status of existing conservation units and design criteria for the future. *Conservation Biology* 9: 34–46. (17)

Pergams, O. R., B. Czech, J. C. Haney, and D. Nyberg. 2004. Linkage of conservation activity to trends in the U.S. economy. *Conservation Biology* 18: 1617–1623. (21)

Perry, G. and D. Vice. 2009. Forecasting the risk of brown tree snake dispersal from Guam: a mixed transport-establishment model. *Conservation Biology* 23: 992–1000. (10)

Perry, M. 2009. Sharks, not humans, most at risk in ocean. Reuters. *http://www.reuters.com/article/idUSTRE50F0NH20090116* (6)

Peterson, D. 2006. *Jane Goodall: The Woman Who Redefined Man*. Houghton Mifflin, New York. (12)

Peterson, M. J., D. M. Hall, A. M. Feldpausch-Parker, and T. R. Peterson. 2010. Obscuring ecosystem function with the application of the ecosystem services concept. *Conservation Biology* 24: 113–119. (5)

Peterson, M. N., M. J. Peterson, and T. R. Peterson. 2005. Conservation and the myth of consensus. *Conservation Biology* 19: 762–767. (18)

Pfab, M. F. and E.T.F. Witkowski. 2000. A simple PVA of the Critically Endangered *Euphorbia clivicola* R.A. Dyer under four management scenarios. *Biological Conservation* 96: 263–270. (12)

Philpott, S. M., P. Bichier, R. Rice, and R. Greenberg. 2007. Field-testing ecological and economic benefits of coffee certification programs. *Conservation Biology* 21: 975–985. (18)

Philpott, S. M., P. Bichier, R. A. Rice, and R. Greenberg. 2008. Biodiversity conservation, yield, and alternative products in coffee agroecosystems in Sumatra, Indonesia. *Biodiversity and Conservation* 17: 1805–1820. (18)

Philpott, S.M., O. Soong, J. H. Lowenstein, A. L. Pulido, D. T. Lopez, D.F.B. Flynn, et al. 2009. Functional richness and ecosystem services: bird predation on arthropods in tropical agroecosystems. *Ecological Applications* 19: 1858–1867. (5)

Phoenix Islands Protected Area (PIPA). 2007. *http://phoenixislands.org* (15)

Phua, M. H., S. Tsuyuki, N. Furuya, and J. S. Lee. 2008. Detecting deforestation with a spectral change detection approach using multitemporal Landsat data: a case study of Kinabalu Park, Sabah, Malaysia. *Journal of Environmental Management* 88: 784–795. (9)

Picco, A. M. and J. P. Collins. 2008. Amphibian commerce as a likely source of pathogen pollution. *Conservation Biology* 22: 1582–1589. (8)

Piessens, K., O. Honnay, and M. Hermy. 2005. The role of fragment area and isolation in the conservation of heathland species. *Biological Conservation* 122: 61–69. (9)

Pimentel, D., C. Harvey, P. Resosudarmo, K. Sinclair, D. Kurtz, M. McNair, et al. 1995. Environmental and economic costs of soil erosion and conservation benefits. *Science* 267: 1117–1121. (5)

Pimentel, D., C. Wilson, C. McCullum, R. Huang, P. Dwen, J. Flack, et al. 1997. Economic and environmental benefits of diversity. *BioScience* 47: 747–757. (5)

Pimentel, D., R. Zuniga, and D. Morrison. 2005. Update on the environmental and economic costs associated with alien-invasive species in the United States. *Ecological Economics* 52: 273–288. (10)

Pimm, S. L., M. Ayres, A. Balmford, G. Branch, K. Brandon, T. Brooks, et al. 2001. Can we defy nature's end? *Science* 293: 2207–2208. (15)

Pimm, S. L. and J. H. Brown. 2004. Domains of diversity. *Science* 304: 831–833. (3)

Pimm, S. L. and C. Jenkins. 2005. Sustaining the variety of life. *Scientific American* 293(33): 66–73. (3, 7)

Pimm, S. L., M. P. Moulton, and L. J. Justice. 1995. Bird extinction in the Central Pacific. *In* J. H. Lawton and R. M. May (eds.), *Extinction Rates*, pp. 75–87. Oxford University Press, Oxford, UK. (7)

Pinchot, G. 1947. *Breaking New Ground*. Harcourt Brace, New York. (1)

Piñero, D., M. Martinez-Ramos, and J. Sarukhan. 1984. A population model of *Astrocaryum mexicanum* and a sensitivity analysis of its finite rate of increase. *Journal of Ecology* 72: 977–991. (11)

Planes, S., G. P. Jones, and S. R. Thorrold. 2009. Larval dispersal connects fish populations in a network of marine protected areas. *Proceedings of the National Academy of Sciences USA* 106: 5693–5697. (15, 16)

Pluhácek, J., S. P. Sinha, L. Bartos, and P. Sipek. 2007. Parity as a major factor affecting infant mortality of highly endangered Indian rhinoceros: evidence from zoos and Dudhwa National Park, India. *Biological Conservation* 139: 457–461. (11)

Pongsiri, M. J., J. Roman, V. O. Ezenwa, T. L. Goldberg, H. S. Koren, S. C. Newbold, et al. 2009. Biodiversity loss affects global disease ecology. *BioScience* 59: 945–954. (10)

Poole, A. 1996. *Coming of Age with Elephants: A Memoir.* Hyperion, New York. (21)

Pope, J. and A. D. Owen. 2009. Emission trading schemes: potential revenue effects, compliance costs and overall tax policy issues. *Energy Policy* 37: 4595–4603. (22)

Pope, K. L. 2008. Assessing changes in amphibian population dynamics following experimental manipulations of introduced fish. *Conservation Biology* 22: 1572–1581. (17)

Porras, I. and N. Neves 2006. Valle del Cauca—land acquisition and land management contracts. Markets for Watershed Services—Country Profile. *http://www.watershedmarkets.org/documents/Colombia_Valle_del_Cauca_E.pdf* (20)

Posa, M.R.C., A. C. Diesmos, N. Sodhi, and T. M. Brooks. 2008. Hope for threatened tropical biodiversity: lessons from the Philippines. *BioScience* 58: 231–240. (22)

Posey, D. A. and M. J. Balick (eds.). 2006. *Human Impacts on Amazonia: The Role of Traditional Ecological Knowledge in Conservation and Development.* Columbia University Press, New York. (20)

Possingham, H., D. B. Lindenmayer, and M. A. McCarthy. 2001. Population viability analysis. *In* S. A. Levin (ed.), *Encyclopedia of Biodiversity* 4: 831–844. Academic Press, San Diego, CA. (12)

Possingham, H. P., J. Franklin, K. Wilson, and T. J. Regan. 2005. The roles of spatial heterogeneity and ecological processes in conservation planning. *In* G. M. Lovett, C. G. Jones, M. G. Turner, and K. C. Weathers, (eds.), *Ecosystem Function in Heterogeneous Landscapes.* Springer-Verlag, New York. (16)

Post, E., J. Brodie, M. Hebblewhite, A. D. Anders, J.A.K. Maier, and C. C. Wilmers. 2009. Global population dynamics and hot spots of response to climate change. *BioScience* 59: 489–497. (9, 17)

Potapov, P., M. C. Hansen, S. V. Stehman, T. R. Loveland, and K. Pittman. 2008. Combining MODIS and Landsat imagery to estimate and map boreal forest cover loss. *Remote Sensing of Environment* 112: 3708–3719. (9)

Power, M. E., D. Tilman, J. A. Estes, B. A. Menge, W. J. Bond, L. S. Mills, et al. 1996. Challenges in the quest for keystones. *BioScience* 46: 609–620. (2)

Power, T. M. 1991. Ecosystem preservation and the economy in the Greater Yellowstone area. *Conservation Biology* 5: 395–404. (4)

Power, T. M. and R. N. Barret. 2001. *Post-Cowboy Economics: Pay and Prosperity in the New American West.* Island Press, Washington, D.C. (4)

Pöyry, J., S. Lindgren, J. Salminen, and M. Kuussaari. 2005. Responses of butterfly and moth species to restored cattle grazing in semi-natural grasslands. *Biological Conservation* 122: 465–478. (17)

Praded, J. 2002. Reinventing the zoo. *E: The Environmental Magazine* 13: 24–31. (14)

Prescott-Allen, C. and R. Prescott-Allen. 1986. *The First Resource: Wild Species in the North American Economy.* Yale University Press, New Haven, CT. (4)

Priess, J. A., M. Mimler, A. M. Klein, S. Schwarze, T. Tscharntke, and I. Steffan-Dewenter. 2007. Linking deforestation scenarios to pollination services and economic returns in coffee agroforestry systems. *Ecological Applications* 17: 407–417. (5)

Primack, R. B. 1996. Lessons from ecological theory: dispersal, establishment and population structure. *In* D. A. Falk, C. I. Millar, and M. Olwell (eds.), *Restoring Diversity: Strategies for Reintroduction of Endangered Plants*, pp. 209–234. Island Press, Washington, D.C. (13)

Primack, R. B., A. J. Miller-Rushing, and K. Dharaneeswaran. 2009. Changes in the flora of Thoreau's Concord. *Biological Conservation* 142: 500–508. (7, 15)

Pringle, C. M. 2000. Threats to U.S. public lands from cumulative hydrologic alterations outside of their boundaries. *Ecological Applications* 10: 971–989. (17)

Programme for Belize. 2008. *http://www.pfbelize.org* (21)

Project FeederWatch. 2009. *http://www.birds.cornell.edu/pfw* (22)

Pruett, C. L., M. A. Patten, and D. H. Wolfe. 2009. Avoidance behavior by prairie grouse: implications for development of wind energy. *Conservation Biology* 23: 1253–1259. (20)

Pukazhenthi, B., P. Comizzoli, A. J. Travis, and D. E. Wildt. 2006. Applications of emerging technologies to the study and conservation of threatened and endangered species. *Reproduction, Fertility, and Development* 18: 77–90. (14)

Pusey, A. E., L. Pintea, M. L. Wilson, S. Kamenya, and J. Goodall. 2007. The contribution of long-term research at Gombe National Park to chimpanzee conservation. *Conservation Biology* 21: 623–634. (12)

Quammen, D. 1996. *The Song of the Dodo: Island Biogeography in an Age of Extinctions.* Scribner, New York. (7)

Quayle, J. F., L. R. Ramsay, and D. F. Fraser. 2007. Trend in the status of breeding bird fauna in British Columbia, Canada, based on the IUCN Red List Index method. *Conservation Biology* 21: 1241–1247. (8)

Quinn, R. M., J. H. Lawton, B. C. Eversham, and S. N. Wood. 1994. The biogeography of scarce vascular plants in Britain with respect to habitat preference, dispersal ability and reproductive biology. *Biological Conservation* 70: 149–157. (8)

Quintana-Ascencio, P. F., C. W. Weekley, and E. S. Menges. 2007. Comparative demography of a rare species in Florida scrub and road habitats. *Biological Conservation* 137: 263–270. (12)

Quintero, J. 2007. *Mainstreaming Conservation in Infrastructure Projects: Case Studies for Latin America.* World Bank, Washington, D.C. (21)

Quist, M. C., P. A. Fay, C. S. Guy, A. K. Knapp, and B. N. Rubenstein. 2003. Military training effects on terrestrial and aquatic communities on a grassland military installation. *Ecological Applications* 13: 432–442. (5)

Rabinowitz, A. 2000. *Jaguar: One Man's Struggle to Establish the World's First Jaguar Preserve.* Island Press, Covelo, CA. (15)

Radeloff, V. C., S. I. Stewart, T. J. Hawbaker, U. Gimmi, A. M. Pidgeon, C. H. Flather, et al. 2010. Housing growth in and near United States protected areas limits their conservation value. *Proceedings of the National Academy of Sciences USA* 107: 940–945. (18)

Ragavan, S. 2008. New paradigms for protection of biodiversity. *Journal of Intellectual Property Rights* 13: 514–522. (5)

Rahmig, C. J., W. E. Jensen, and K. A. With. 2009. Grassland bird responses to land management in the largest remaining tallgrass prairie. *Conservation Biology* 23: 420–432. (17)

Ralls, K., J. D. Ballou, and A. Templeton. 1988. Estimates of lethal equivalents and the cost of inbreeding in mammals. *Conservation Biology* 2: 185–193. (11)

Raloff, J. 2005. Empty nests: fisheries may be crippling themselves by targeting the big ones. *Science News* 167: 360–362. (6)

Ramakrishnan, U., J. A. Santosh, U. Ramakrishnan, and R. Sukumar. 1998. The population and conservation status of Asian elephants in the Periyar Tiger Reserve, southern India. *Current Science India* 74: 110–113. (11)

Ramsar Convention on Wetlands. *http://www.ramsar.org* (21)

Randolph, J. and G. M. Masters. 2008. *Energy for Sustainability: Technology, Planning, Policy.* Island Press, Washington, D.C. (9)

Rao, M. and P. McGowan. 2002. Wild-meat use, food security, livelihoods, and conservation. *Conservation Biology* 16: 580–583. (4)

Raup, D. M. 1979. Size of the Permo-Triassic bottleneck and its evolutionary implications. *Science* 206: 217–218. (7)

Red Wolf Coalition. 2009. *http://www.redwolves.com* (2)

Redford, K. H. 1992. The empty forest. *BioScience* 42: 412–422. (2)

Redford, K. H. and W. M. Adams. 2009. Payment for ecosystem services and the challenge of saving nature. *Conservation Biology* 23: 785–787. (4, 6)

Redford, K. H. and J. A. Mansour (eds.). 1996. *Traditional Peoples and Biodiversity Conservation in Large Tropical Landscapes.* The Nature Conservancy, Arlington, VA. (20)

Redford, K. H. and S. E. Sanderson. 2000. Extracting humans from nature. *Conservation Biology* 2000: 1362–1364. (17)

Redford, K. H. and M. A. Sanjayan. 2003. Retiring Cassandra. *Conservation Biology* 17: 1473–1474. (1)

Reed, D. H., E. H. Lowe, D. A. Briscoe, and R. Frankham. 2003. Fitness and adaptability in a novel environment: effect of inbreeding, prior environment, and lineage. *Evolution* 57: 1822–1828. (11)

Reed, J. M. 1999. The role of behavior in recent avian extinctions and endangerments. *Conservation Biology* 13: 232–241. (8)

Reed, J. M., C. S. Elphick, and L. W. Oring. 1998. Life-history and viability analysis of the endangered Hawaiian stilt. *Biological Conservation* 84: 35–45. (12)

Reed, J. M., C. S. Elphick, A. F. Zuur, E. N. Ieno, and G. M. Smith. 2007. Time series analysis of Hawaiian waterbirds. *In* A. F. Zuur, E. N. Ieno, and G. M. Smith (eds.), *Analysis of Ecological Data.* Springer-Verlag, the Netherlands. (12)

Reed, S. E. and A. M. Merenlender. 2008. Quiet, nonconsumptive recreation reduces protected area effectiveness. *Conservation Letters* 1: 146–154. (17)

Regan, H. M., R. Lupia, A. N. Drinan, and M. A. Burgman. 2001. The currency and tempo of extinction. *American Naturalist* 157: 1–10. (7)

Regan, T. 2004. *The Case for Animal Rights*, 2nd ed. University of California Press, Berkeley, CA. (6)

Régnier, C., B. Fontaine, and P. Bouchet. 2009. Not knowing, not recording, not listing: numerous unnoticed mollusk extinctions. *Conservation Biology* 23: 1214–1221. (7, 8)

Reinartz, J. A. 1995. Planting state-listed endangered and threatened plants. *Conservation Biology* 9: 771–781. (13)

Relyea, R. A. 2005. The impact of insecticides and herbicides on the biodiversity and productivity of aquatic communities. *Ecological Applications* 15: 618–627. (9)

Restani, M. and M. Marzluff. 2002. Funding extinction? Biological needs and political realities in the allocation of resources to endangered species recovery. *BioScience* 52: 169–177. (20)

Reynisdottir, M., H. Song, and J. Agrusa. 2008. Willingness to pay entrance fees to natural attractions: an Icelandic case study. *Tourism Management* 29: 1076–1083. (5)

Ricciardi, A. 2003. Predicting the impacts of an introduced species from its invasion history: an empirical approach applied to zebra mussel invasions. *Freshwater Biology* 48: 972–981. (10)

Ricciardi, A. 2007. Are modern biological invasions an unprecedented form of global change? *Conservation Biology* 21: 329–336. (10)

Ricciardi, A. and D. Simberloff. 2009. Assisted colonization is not a viable conservation strategy. *Trends in Ecology and Evolution* 24: 248–253. (13)

Rich, T.C.G. 2006. Floristic changes in vascular plants in the British Isles: geographical and temporal variation in botanical activity 1836–1988. *Botanical Journal of the Linnean Society* 152: 303–330. (12)

Rich, T.C.G. and E. R. Woodruff. 1996. Changes in the vascular plant floras of England and Scotland between 1930–1960 and 1987–1988: the BSBI monitoring scheme. *Biological Conservation* 75: 217–229. (12)

Richardson, C. J., P. Reiss, N. A. Hussain, A. J. Alwash, and D. J. Pool 2005. The restoration potential of the Mesopotamian marshes of Iraq. *Science* 307: 1307–1311. (19)

Richardson, C. J. and N. J. Hussain. 2006. Restoring the Garden of Eden: an ecological assessment of the marshes of Iraq. *BioScience* 56: 477–489. (19)

Richmond, R. H., T. Rongo, Y. Golbuu, S., Victor, N. Idechong, G. Davis, et al. 2006. Watersheds and coral reefs: conservation science, policy, and implementation. *BioScience* 57: 598–607. (18)

Ricketts, T. H., E. Dinerstein, T. Boucher, T. M. Brooks, S.H.M. Butchart, M. Hoffmann, et al. 2005. Pinpointing and preventing imminent extinctions. *Proceedings of the National Academy of Sciences USA* 102: 18497–18501. (15)

Ricketts, T. H., E. Dinerstein, D. M. Olson, C. J. Loucks, W. Eichbaum, D. DellaSala, et al. 1999. *Terrestrial Ecoregions of North America: A Conservation Assessment.* Island Press, Washington, D.C. (3)

Rinella, M. F., B. D. Maxwell, P. K. Fay, T. Weaver, and R. L. Sheley. 2009. Control effort exacerbates invasive-species problem. *Ecological Applications* 19: 155–162. (10)

Roark, E. B., T. P. Guilderson, R. B. Dunbar, and B. L. Ingram. 2006. Radiocarbon-based ages and growth rates of Hawaiian deep-sea corals. *Marine Ecology Progress Series* 327: 1–14. (3)

Robbins, J. 2009. Between the devil and the deep blue sea. *Conservation* 10: 12–19. (9)

Roberge, J. M. and P. Angelstam. 2004. Usefulness of the umbrella species concept as a conservation tool. *Conservation Biology* 18: 76–85. (15)

Robertson, G. P. and S. M. Swinton. 2005. Reconciling agricultural productivity and environmental integrity: a grand challenge for agriculture. *Frontiers in Ecology and the Environment* 3: 38–46. (4)

Robertson, M. M. 2006. Emerging ecosystem service markets: trends in a decade of entrepreneurial wetland banking. *Frontiers in Ecology and the Environment* 4: 297–302. (5, 19, 20)

Robinson, R. A., H.P.Q. Crick, J. A. Learmonth, I.M.D. Maclean, C. D. Thomas, F. Bairlein, et al. 2008. Travelling through a warming world: climate change and migratory species. *Endangered Species Research* 7: 87–99. (9)

Robles, M. D., C. H. Flather, S. M Stein, M. D. Nelson, and A. Cutko. 2008. The geography of private forests that support at-risk species in the conterminous United States. *Frontiers in Ecology and the Environment* 6: 301–307. (18)

Rockström, J., W. Steffen, K. Noone, Å. Persson, F. S. Chapin III, E. F. Lambin, et al. 2009. A safe operating space for humanity. *Nature* 461: 472–475. (9)

Rodrigues, A.S.L., H. R. Akçakaya, S. J. Andelman, M. I. Bakarr, L. Boitani, T. M. Brooks, et al. 2004. Global gap analysis: priority regions for expanding the global protected-area network. *BioScience* 54: 1092–1100. (15)

Rodrigues, A.S.L., R. M. Ewers, L. Parry, C. Souza, Jr., A. Veríssimo, and A. Balmford. 2009. Boom-and-bust development patterns across the Amazon deforestation frontier. *Science* 324: 1435–1437. (9)

Rodrigues, M.G.M. 2004. Advocating for the environment: local dimensions of transnational networks. *Environment* 46: 15–25. (21)

Rodrigues, R. R., R.A.F. Lima, S. Gandolfi, and A. G. Nave. 2009. On the restoration of high diversity forests: 30 years of experience in the Brazilian Atlantic Forest. *Biological Conservation* 142: 1242–1251. (19)

Rohlf, D. J. and D. S. Dobkin. 2005. Legal ecology: ecosystem function and the law. *Conservation Biology* 19: 1344–1348. (20)

Rohrman, D. F. 2004. Environmental terrorism. *Frontiers in Ecology and the Environment* 2: 332. (22)

Roldán, G. 1988. *Guía para el Estudio de los Macroinvertebrados Acuáticos del Departamento de Antioquia.* Fondo-FEN Colombia, Editorial Presencia, Santa Fe de Bogotá. (2)

Rolston, H., III. 1988. *Environmental Ethics: Values In and Duties To the Natural World.* Temple University Press, Philadelphia, PA. (6)

Rolston, H., III. 1989. *Philosophy Gone Wild: Essays on Environmental Ethics.* Prometheus Books, Buffalo, NY. (6)

Rolston, H., III. 1994. *Conserving Natural Value.* Columbia University Press, New York. (6)

Rolston, H., III. 1995. Duties to endangered species. *In* W.A. Nierenberg (ed.), *Encyclopedia of Environmental Biology* 1: 517–528. Harcourt/Academic Press, San Diego, CA. (6)

Rolston, H., III. 2000. The land ethic at the turn of the millennium. *Biodiversity and Conservation* 9: 1045–1058. (6)

Roman, J. and J. A. Darling. 2007. Paradox lost: genetic diversity and the success of aquatic invasions. *Trends in Ecology and Evolution* 22: 454–464. (11)

Roman, J. and S. R. Palumbi. 2003. Whales before whaling in the North Atlantic. *Science* 301: 508–510. (10)

Rombouts, I., G. Beaugrand, F. Ibanez, S. Gasparini, S. Chiba, and L. Legendre. 2009. Global latitudinal variations in marine copepod diversity and environmental factors. *Proceedings of the Royal Society B* 276: 3053–3062. (3)

Rompré, G., W. D. Robinson, A. Desrochers, and G. Angehr. 2009. Predicting declines in avian species richness under nonrandom patterns of habitat loss in a Neotropical landscape. *Ecological Applications* 19: 1614–1627. (7)

Rondinini, C., S. Stuart, and L. Boitani. 2005. Habitat sustainability models and the shortfall in conservation planning for African vertebrates. *Conservation Biology* 19: 1488–1497. (15)

Rood, S. B., G. M. Samuelson, J. H. Braatne, C. R. Gourley, F.M.R. Hughes, and J. M. Mahoney. 2005. Managing river flows to restore floodplain forests. *Frontiers in Ecology and the Environment* 3: 193–201. (19)

Rooney, T. P., S. M. Wiegmann, D. A. Rogers, and D. M. Waller. 2004. Biotic impoverishment and homogenization in unfragmented forest understory communities. *Conservation Biology* 18: 787–798. (7, 18)

Rosen, T. and A. Bath. 2009. Transboundary management of large carnivores in Europe: from incident to opportunity. *Conservation Letters* 2: 109–114. (21)

Rosenberg, J. and F. L. Korsmo. 2001. Local participation, international politics, and the environment: the World Bank and the Grenada Dove. *Journal of Environmental Management* 62: 283–300. (21)

Rosenberg, M. 2009. Current world population. *http://geography.about.com/od/obtainpopulationdata/a/worldpopulation.htm* (1)

Rosendo, S. 2007. Partnerships across scales: lessons from extractive reserves in Brazilian Amazonia. *In* M.A.F. Ros-tonen (ed.), *Partnerships in Sustainable Forest Resource Management: Learning from Latin America*, pp. 229–253. Koninklijke Brill NV, Leiden, the Netherlands. (20)

Rosenfield, J. A., S. Nolasco, S. Lindauer, C. Sandoval, and A. Kodric-Brown. 2004. The role of hybrid vigor in the replacement of Pecos pupfish by its hybrids with sheepshead minnow. *Conservation Biology* 18: 1589–1598. (10)

Rosenzweig, C., D. Karoly, M. Vicarelli, P. Neofotis, Q. Wu, G. Casassa, et al. 2008. Attributing physical and biological impacts to anthropogenic climate change. *Nature* 453: 353–358. (9)

Roux, D. J., J. L. Nel, P. J. Ashton, A. R. Deacon, F. C. de Moor, D. Hardwick, et al. 2008. Designing protected areas to conserve riverine biodiversity: lessons from the hypothetical redesign of Kruger National Park. *Biological Conservation* 141: 100–117. (16, 17)

Royal Society for the Protection of Birds (RSPB). 2010. *http://www.rspb.org* (20)

Ruane, J. 2000. A framework for prioritizing domestic animal breeds for conservation purposes at the national level: a Norwegian case study. *Conservation Biology* 14: 1385–1393. (14)

Rubbo, M. J. and J. M. Kiesecker. 2005. Amphibian breeding distribution in an urbanized landscape. *Conservation Biology* 19: 504–511. (18)

Ruiz-Perez, M., M. Almeida, S. Dewi, E.M.L. Costa, M. C. Pantoja, A. Puntodewo, et al. 2005. Conservation and development in Amazonian extractive reserves: the case of Alto Juruá. *Ambio* 34: 218–223. (20)

Russello, M. A. and G. Amato. 2007. On the horns of a dilemma: molecular approaches refine ex situ conservation in crisis. *Molecular Ecology* 16: 2405–2406. (14)

Rwego, I. B, G. Isabirye-Basuta, T. R. Gillespie, and T. L. Goldberg. 2008. Gastrointestinal bacterial transmission among humans, mountain gorillas, and livestock in Bwindi Impenetrable National Park, Uganda. *Conservation Biology* 22: 1600–1607. (10)

Saarinen, K., A. Valtonen, J. Jantunen, and S. Saarino. 2005. Butterflies and diurnal moths along road verges: does road type affect diversity and abundance? *Biological Conservation* 123: 403–412. (18)

Sachs, J. 2005. *The End of Poverty: Economic Possibilities for Our Time.* Penguin Group, East Rutherford, N.J. (22)

Sachs, J. D. 2008. *Common Wealth: Economics for a Crowded Planet.* Penguin Press, New York. (1, 4, 22)

Safina, C. and D. H. Klinger. 2008. Collapse of bluefin tuna in the Western Atlantic. *Conservation Biology* 22: 243–246. (10)

Sagarin, R. and A. Pauchard. 2009. Observational approaches in ecology open new ground in a changing world. *Frontiers in Ecology and the Environment* (online in advance of print) (12)

Sagoff, M. 2008. On the compatibility of a conservation ethic with biological science. *Conservation Biology* 21: 337–345. (6)

Sairam, R., S. Chennareddy, and M. Parani. 2005. OBPC Symposium: Maize 2004 & Beyond—plant regeneration, gene discovery, and genetic engineering of plants for crop improvement. *In Vitro Cellular and Developmental Biology—Plant* 41: 411. (5)

Salafsky, N., R. Margolius, and K. H. Redford. 2001. *Adaptive Management: A Tool for Conservation Practitioners.* Biodiversity Support Program, Washington, D.C. (22)

Salafsky, N., R. Margolius, K. H. Redford, and J. G. Robinson. 2002. Improving the practice of conservation: a conceptual framework and research agenda for conservation science. *Conservation Biology* 16: 1469–1479. (17)

Salm, R. V., J. R. Clark, and E. Siirila. 2000. *Marine and Coastal Protected Areas: A Guide for Planners and Managers*, 3rd ed. IUCN Marine Programme, Gland, Switzerland. (15)

Sánchez-Azofeifa, G. A., A. Pfaff, J. A. Robalino, and J. P. Boomhower. 2007. Costa Rica's payment for environmental services program: intention, implementation, and impact. *Conservation Biology* 21: 1165–1173. (5)

Sanderson, E., M. Jaiteh, M. A. Levy, K. H. Redford, A. V. Wannebo, and G. Woolmer. 2002. The human footprint and the last of the wild. *BioScience* 52: 891–904. (9)

Sanderson, E. W., K. H. Redford, B. Weber, K. Aune, D. Baldes, J. Berger, et al. 2008. The ecological future of the North American bison: conceiving long-term, large-scale conservation of wildlife. *Conservation Biology* 22: 252–266. (9)

Sandler, R. L. 2007. *Character and Environment: A Virtue-Oriented Approach to Environmental Ethics.* Columbia University Press, New York. (6)

Sandmeier, F. C., R. Tracey, S. duPré, and K. Hunter. 2009. Upper respiratory tract disease (URTD) as a threat to desert tortoise populations: a reevaluation. *Biological Conservation* 142: 1255–1268. (10)

Saterson, K. 2001. Government legislation and regulation. *In* S.A. Levin (ed.), *Encyclopedia of Biodiversity* 3: 233–246. Academic Press, San Diego, CA. (20)

Sauer, J. R., J. E. Fallon, and R. Johnson. 2003. Use of North American Breeding Bird Survey data to estimate population change for bird conservation regions. *Journal of Wildlife Management* 67: 372–389. (12)

Savenkoff, C., H. Bourdages, M. Castonguay, L. Morissette, D. Chabot, and M. O. Hammill. 2004. Input data and parameter estimates for ecosystem models of the northern Gulf of St. Lawrence (mid-1990s). *Canadian Technical Report of Fisheries and Aquatic Sciences* 2531: 5–93. (22)

Schaal, G., P. Rieraa, and C. Lerou. 2009. Trophic significance of the kelp Laminaria digitata (Lamour.) for the associated food web: a between-sites comparison. *Estuarine, Coastal and Shelf Science* 85: 565–572. (2)

Scheckenbach, F., K. Hausmann, C. Wylezich, M. Weitere, and H. Arndt. 2010. Large-scale patterns in biodiversity of microbial eukaryotes from the abyssal sea floor. *Proceedings of the National Academy of Sciences USA* 107: 115–120. (3)

Schellnhuber, H. J., J. Kokott, F. O. Beese, K. Fraedrich, P. Klemmer, L. Kruse-Graumann, et al. 2001. *World in Transition: Conservation and Sustainable Use of the Biosphere.* IUCN Earthscan, London. (18)

Schlaepfer, M. A., C. Hoover, and C. K. Dodd, Jr. 2005. Challenges in evaluating the impact of the trade in amphibians and reptiles on wild populations. *BioScience* 55: 256–262. (10)

Schlenker, W., and M. J. Roberts. 2009. Nonlinear temperature effects indicate severe damages to US crop yields under climate change. *Proceedings of the National Academy of Sciences USA* 106: 15594–15598. (9)

Schleuning, M. and D. Matthies. 2009. Habitat change and plant demography: assessing the extinction risk of a formerly common grassland perennial. *Conservation Biology* 23: 174–183. (11)

Schmidt-Soltau, K. 2009. Is the displacement of people from parks only "purported", or is it real? *Conservation and Society* 7: 46–55. (20)

Schmidtz, D. 2005. Using, respecting, and appreciating nature? *Conservation Biology* 19: 1672–1678. (6)

Schmit, J. P., G. M. Mueller, P. R. Leacock, J. L. Mata, Q. Wu, and Y. Huang. 2005. Assessment of tree species richness as a surrogate for macrofungal species richness. *Biological Conservation* 121: 99–110. (3)

Scholes, R. J., G. M. Mace, W. Turner, G. N. Geller, N. Jürgens, A. Larigauderie, et al. 2008. Toward a global biodiversity observing system. *Science* 321: 1044–1045. (12)

Schonewald-Cox, C. M. 1983. Conclusions: Guidelines to management: A beginning attempt. *In* C. M. Schonewald-Cox, S. M. Chambers, B. MacBryde and L. Thomas (eds.), *Genetics and Conservation: A Reference for Managing Wild Animal and Plant Populations*, pp. 414–445. Benjamin/Cummings, Menlo Park, CA. (16)

Schrott, G. R., K. A. With, and A. W. King. 2005. Demographic limitations on the ability of habitat restoration to rescue declining populations. *Conservation Biology* 19: 1181–1193. (11)

Schultz, C. B. and P. C. Hammond. 2003. Using population viability analysis to develop recovery criteria for endangered insects: case study of the Fender's blue butterfly. *Conservation Biology* 17: 1372–1385. (12)

Schulz, H. N., T. Brinkhoff, T. G. Ferdelman, M. H. Marine, A. Teske, and B. B. Jorgensen. 1999. Dense populations of a giant sulfur bacterium in Namibian shelf sediments. *Science* 284: 493–495. (11)

Schumann, M., L. H. Watson, and B. D. Schumann. 2008. Attitudes of Namibian commercial farmers toward large carnivores: the influence of conservancy membership. *South African Journal of Wildlife Research* 38: 123–132. (18)

Schwartz, M. W. 2003. Assessing population viability in long-lived plants. *In* I. T. Baldwin, M. M. Caldwell, G. Heldmaier, O. L. Lange, H. A. Mooney, E. D. Schulze, and U. Sommer (eds.), *Population Viability in Plants: Conservation, Management, and Modeling of Rare Plants*, pp. 239–266. Springer, Germany. (12)

Schwartz, M. W. 2008. The performance of the Endangered Species Act. *Annual Review of Ecology, Evolution, and Systematics* 39: 279–299. (20)

Schwartz, M. W., S. M. Hermann, and P. J. van Mantgem. 2000. Estimating the magnitude of decline of the Florida torreya (*Torreya taxifolia* Arn.). *Biological Conservation* 95: 77–84. (12)

Schwartzman, S. and B. Zimmerman. 2005. Conservation alliances with indigenous peoples of the Amazon. *Conservation Biology* 19: 721–727. (20)

Science and Spirit. 2001. *http://www.science-spirit.org* (6)

Scott, J. M., B. Csuti, and F. Davis. 1991. Gap analysis: an application of Geographic Information Systems for wildlife species. *In* D. J. Decker, M. E. Krasny, G. R. Goff, C. R. Smith, and D. W. Gross (eds.), *Challenges in the Conservation of Biological Resources: A Practitioner's Guide*, pp. 167–179. Westview Press, Boulder, CO. (15)

Scott, J. M., F. W. Davis, R. G. McGhie, R. G. Wright, C. Groves, and J. Estes. 2001. Nature reserves: do they capture the full range of America's biological diversity? *Ambio* 11: 999–1007. (16)

Scott, J. M., D. D. Goble, J. A. Wiens, D. S. Wilcove, M. Bean, and T. Male. 2005. Recovery of imperiled species under the Endangered Species Act: the need for a new approach. *Frontiers in Ecology and the Environment* 3: 383–389. (20)

Scott, J. M., R. T. Lackey, and J. L. Rachlow. 2008. The science-policy interface: what is an appropriate role for professional societies? *BioScience* 58: 865–869. (22)

Scott, J. M., J. L. Rachlow, R. T. Lackey, A. B. Pidgorna, J. L. Aycrigg, G. R. Feldman, et al. 2007. Policy advocacy in science: prevalence, perspectives, and implications for conservation biologists. *Conservation Biology* 21: 29–35. (22)

Scott, M. E. 1988. The impact of infection and disease on animal populations: implications for conservation biology. *Conservation Biology* 2: 40–56. (10)

Sea Shepherd Conservation Society. 2010. *http://www.seashepherd.org* (22)

Seastedt, T. R., R. J. Hobbs, and K. N. Suding. 2008. Management of novel ecosystems: are novel approaches required? *Frontiers in Ecology and the Environment* 6: 547–553. (19)

SEDAC: Socioeconomic Data and Applications Center. 2010. Environmental sustainability index. Columbia University, New York. *http://sedac.ciesin.columbia.edu/es/ESI* (4)

Seddon, P. J., D. P. Armstrong, and R. F. Maloney. 2007. Developing the science of reintroduction biology. *Conservation Biology* 21: 303–312. (13)

Seed Savers Exchange. 2009. *http://www.seedsavers.org* (14)

Seidel, R. A., B. K. Lang, and D. J. Berg. 2009. Phylogeographic analysis reveals multiple cryptic species of amphipods (Crustacea: Amphipoda) in Chihuahuan Desert springs. *Biological Conservation* 142: 2303–2313. (2)

Sekercioglu, C. H., S. H. Schneider, J. P. Fay, and S. R. Loarie. 2008. Climate change, elevational range shifts, and bird extinctions. *Conservation Biology* 22: 140–150. (8, 9, 16)

Sethi, P. and H. F. Howe. 2009. Recruitment of hornbill-dispersed trees in hunted and logged forests of the eastern Indian Himalaya. *Conservation Biology* 23: 710–718. (5)

Setty, R. S., K. Bawa, T. Ticktin, and C. M. Gowda. 2008. Evaluation of a participatory resource monitoring system for nontimber forest products: the case of amla (*Phyllanthus* spp.) fruit harvest by Soligas in South India. *Ecology and Society* 13: 19. (20, 22)

Shackeroff, J. M. and L. M. Campbell. 2007. Traditional ecological knowledge in conservation research: problems and prospects for their constructive engagement. *Conservation and Society* 5: 343–360. (20)

Shafer, C. L. 1997. Terrestrial nature reserve design at the urban/rural interface. *In* M. W. Schwartz (ed.), *Conservation in Highly Fragmented Landscapes*, pp. 345–378. Chapman and Hall, New York. (16)

Shafer, C. L. 1999. History of selection and system planning for U.S. natural area national parks and monuments: beauty and biology. *Biodiversity and Conservation* 8: 189–204. (15)

Shafer, C. L. 2001. Conservation biology trailblazers: George Wright, Ben Thompson, and Joseph Dixon. *Conservation Biology* 15: 332–344. (1, 16)

Shaffer, M. L. 1981. Minimum population sizes for species conservation. *BioScience* 31: 131–134. (11)

Shah, A. 2008. US and foreign aid assistance. *Global Issues*. *http://www.globalissues.org/article/35/us-and-foreign-aid assistance#RichNationsAgreedatUNto07ofGNPToAid* (21)

Shankar, K., A. Hiremath, and K. Bawa. 2005. Linking biodiversity conservation and livelihoods in India. *PLoS Biology* 3: 1879–1880. (20)

Shanks, N. 2004. *God, the Devil, and Darwin: A Critique of Intelligent Design Theory*. Oxford University Press, New York. (2)

Shanley, P. and C. López. 2009. Out of the loop: why research rarely reaches policy makers and the public and what can be done? *Biotropica* 41: 535–544. (22)

Shanley, P. and L. Luz. 2003. The impacts of forest degradation on medicinal plant use and implications for health care in eastern Amazonia. *BioScience* 53: 573–584. (4)

Shaver, D. J. and T. Wibbels. 2007. Head-starting Kemp's ridleys. *In* P. T. Plotkin (ed.), *Biology and Conservation of Ridley Sea Turtles*, pp. 297–319. Johns Hopkins University Press, Baltimore, MD. (13)

Sheikh, P. A. 2004. Debt-for-nature initiatives and the Tropical Forest Conservation Act: status and implementation. Congressional Research Service (CRS) Report for Congress, Washington, D.C. (21)

Shen, G., C. Feng, Z. Xie, Z. Ouyang, J. Li, and M. Pascal. 2008. Proposed conservation landscape for giant pandas in the Minshan Mountains, China. *Conservation Biology* 22: 1144–1153. (14)

Shi, H., A. Singh, S. Kant, Z. Zhu, and E. Waller. 2005. Integrating habitat status, human population pressure, and protection status into biodiversity conservation priority setting. *Conservation Biology* 19: 1273–1285. (15)

Shogren, J. F., J. Tschirhart, T. Anderson, A. W. Ando, S. R. Beissinger, D. Brookshire, et al. 1999. Why economics matters for endangered species protection. *Conservation Biology* 13: 1257–1261. (4)

Siche, J. R., F. Agostinho, E. Ortega, and A. Romeiro. 2008. Sustainability of nations by indices: comparative study between environmental sustainability index, ecological footprint and the energy performance indices. *Ecological Economics* 66: 628–637. (4)

Simberloff, D. S., J. A. Farr, J. Cox, and D. W. Mehlman. 1992. Movement corridors: conservation bargains or poor investments? *Conservation Biology* 6: 493–505. (16)

Simmons, R. E. 1996. Population declines, variable breeding areas and management options for flamingos in Southern Africa. *Conservation Biology* 10: 504–515. (12)

Sin, H. and A. Radford. 2007. Coquí frog research and management efforts in Hawaii. USDA National Wildlife Research Center Symposia: Managing Vertebrate Invasive Species. University of Nebraska, Lincoln, NE. (10)

Singer, F. J., L. C. Zeigenfuss, and L. Spicer. 2001. Role of patch size, disease, and movement in rapid extinction of bighorn sheep. *Conservation Biology* 15: 1347–1354. (11)

Singer, P. 1979. Not for humans only. *In* K. E. Goodpaster and K. M. Sayre (eds.), *Ethics and Problems of the Twenty-first Century*, pp. 191–206. University of Notre Dame, Notre Dame, IN. (6)

Sivinski, R. C. and C. McDonald. 2007. Knowlton's cactus (*Pediocactus knowltonii*): eighteen years of monitoring and recovery actions. New Mexico Forestry Division and USDA Forest Service, 98–107. (13)

Smart, S. M., R.G.H. Bunce, R. Marrs, M. LeDuc, L. G. Firbank, L. C. Maskell, et al. 2005. Large-scale changes in the abundance of common higher plant species across Britain between 1978, 1990, and 1998 as a consequence of human activity: tests of hypothesised changes in trait representation. *Biological Conservation* 124: 355–371. (12)

Smith, A. 1909. *An Inquiry into the Nature and Causes of the Wealth of Nations.* J. L. Bullock (ed.), P.F. Collier & Sons, New York. (4)

Smith, D. W., R. O. Peterson, and D. B. Houston. 2003. Yellowstone after wolves. *BioScience* 53: 330–340. (13)

Smith, V. H. and D. W. Schindler. 2009. Eutrophication science: where do we go from here? *Trends in Ecology and Evolution* 24: 201–207. (9)

Snelgrove, P.V.R. 2001. Marine sediments. *In* S. A. Levin (ed.). *Encyclopedia of Biodiversity.* Academic Press, San Diego, CA. (9)

Snow, A. A., D. A. Andow, P. Gepts, E. M. Hallerman, A. Power, J. M. Tiedje, et al. 2005. Genetically engineered organisms and the environment: current status and recommendations. *Ecological Applications* 15: 377–404. (10)

Soares-Filho, B. S, D. C. Nepstad, L. M. Curran, G. C. Cerqueira, R. A. Garcia, C. A. Ramos, et al. 2006. Modelling conservation in the Amazon basin. *Nature* 440: 520–523. (21)

Society for Conservation Biology. 2010. *http://www.conbio.org* (1)

Society for Ecological Restoration International. *http://www.ser.org* (19)

Society for the Conservation and Study of Caribbean Birds. *http://www.scscb.org* (22)

Sondergaard, M., E. Jeppesen, T. L. Lauridsen, C. Skov, E. H. van Nes, R. Roijackers, et al. 2007. Lake restoration: successes, failures and long-term effects. *Journal of Applied Ecology* 44: 1095–1105. (19)

Sorenson, L. G., P. E. Bradley, and A. H. Sutton. 2004. The West Indian whistling-duck and wetlands conservation project: a model for species and wetlands conservation and education. *The Journal of Caribbean Ornithology Special Issue* 72–80. (22)

Soulé, M. E. 1980. Thresholds for survival: maintaining fitness and evolutionary potential. *In* M. E. Soulé and B. A. Wilcox (eds.), *Conservation Biology: An Evolutionary-Ecological Perspective*, pp. 151–170. Sinauer Associates, Sunderland, MA. (2)

Soulé, M. E. 1985. What is conservation biology? *BioScience* 35: 727–734. (1)

Soulé, M. E. (ed.). 1987. *Viable Populations for Conservation.* Cambridge University Press, Cambridge. (14)

Soulé, M. E. and D. Simberloff. 1986. What do genetics and ecology tell us about the design of nature reserves? *Biological Conservation* 35: 19–40. (16)

Soulé, M. E. and J. Terborgh. 1999. *Continental Conservation: Scientific Foundations of Regional Reserve Networks.* Island Press, Washington, D.C. (16)

SourceWatch: Your Guide to the Names Behind the News. 2010. Monsanto and the roundup ready controversy. *http://www.sourcewatch.org* (10)

South African National Parks. 2010. *http://www.sanparks.org* (21)

Spalding, M. D., L. Fish, and L. J. Wood. 2008. Towards representative protection of the world's coasts and oceans—progress, gaps, and opportunities. *Conservation Letters* 1: 217–226. (15)

Spencer, C. N., B. R. McClelland, and J. A. Stanford. 1991. Shrimp stocking, salmon collapse and eagle displacement. *BioScience* 41: 14–21. (10)

Spielman, D., B. W. Brook, and R. Frankham. 2004. Most species are not driven to extinction before genetic factors impact them. *Proceedings of the National Academy of Sciences USA* 101: 15261–15264. (11)

Sponberg, A. F. 2009. Great Lakes: sailing to the forefront of national water policy? *BioScience* 59: 372. (19)

Srinivasan, J. T. and V. R. Reddy. 2009. Impact of irrigation water quality on human health: a case study in India. *Ecological Economics* 68: 2800–2807. (9)

Srinivasan, U. T., S. P. Carey, E. Hallstein, P.A.T. Higgins, A. C. Kerr, L. E. Koteen, et al. 2008. The debt of nations and the distribution of ecological impacts from human activities. *Proceedings of the National Academy of Sciences USA* 105: 1768–1773. (5, 21)

Stankey, G. H. and B. Shindler. 2006. Formation of social acceptability judgments and their implications for management of rare and little-known species. *Conservation Biology* 20: 28–37. (20)

Steadman, D. W., G. K. Pregill, and D. V. Burley. 2002. Rapid prehistoric extinction of iguanas and birds in Polynesia. *Proceedings of the National Academy of Sciences USA* 99: 3673–3677. (10)

Stein, B. A., L. S. Kutner, and J. S. Adams (eds.). 2000. *Precious Heritage: The Status of Biodiversity in the United States.* Oxford University Press, New York. (8, 9, 15, 20)

Stein, B. A., C. Scott, and N. Benton. 2008. Federal lands and endangered species: the role of the military and other federal lands in sustaining biodiversity. *BioScience* 58: 339–347. (18)

Stein, E. D., F. Tabatabai, and R. F. Ambrose. 2000. Wetland mitigation banking: a framework for crediting and debiting. *Environmental Management* 26: 233–250. (8)

Steinmetz, R., W. Chutipong, N. Seuaturien, E. Chirngsaard, and M. Khaengkhetkarn. 2010. Population recovery patterns of Southeast Asian ungulates after poaching. *Biological Conservation* 143: 42–51. (17)

Stem, C., R. Margoluis, N. Salafsky, and M. Brown. 2005. Monitoring and evaluation in conservation: a review of trends and approaches. *Conservation Biology* 19: 295–309. (20, 21)

Stocks, A. 2005. Too much for too few: problems of indigenous land rights in Latin America. *Annual Review of Anthropology* 34: 85–104. (22)

Stohlgren, T. J., D. A. Guenther, P. H. Evangelista, and N. Alley. 2005. Patterns of plant species richness, rarity, endemism, and uniqueness in an arid landscape. *Ecological Applications* 15: 715–725. (15)

Stokes, D. and P. Morrison. 2003. GIS-based conservation planning. *Conservation in Practice* 4: 38–41. (15)

Stokstad, E. 2007. Gambling on a ghost bird. *Science* 317: 888–892. (7)

Stokstad, E. 2009. Obama moves to revitalize Chesapeake Bay restoration. *Science* 324: 1138–1139. (19)

Stone, R. 2008. China's environmental challenges: Three Gorges Dam: into the unknown. *Science* 321: 628–632. (9, 21)

Strayer, D. L. 2009. Twenty years of zebra mussels: lessons from the mollusk that made headlines. *Frontiers in Ecology and the Environment* 7: 135–141. (10)

Struhsaker, T. T., P. J. Struhsaker, and K. S. Siex. 2005. Conserving Africa's rain forests: problems in protected areas and possible solutions. *Biological Conservation* 123: 45–54. (17, 20)

Stuart, S. N., J. S. Chanson, N. A. Cox, B. E. Young, A.S.L. Rodrigues, D. L. Fischman, et al. 2004. Status and trends of amphibian declines and extinctions worldwide. *Science* 306: 1783–1787. (8)

Suárez, E., M. Morales, R. Cueva, V. U. Bucheli, G. Zapata-Ríos, E. Toral, et al. 2009. Oil industry, wild meat trade and roads: indirect effects of oil extraction activities in a protected area in northeastern Ecuador. *Animal Conservation* 12: 364–373. (10)

Subashchandran, M. D. and T. V. Ramachandra. 2008. Social and ethical dimensions of environmental conservation. From *Environmental challenges of the 21st century—the role of academic institutions*. 17–18 October 2008, Government Arts and Sciences Colleges, Karwar, India. (1)

Suding, K. N., K. L. Gross, and G. R. Houseman. 2004. Alternative states and positive feedbacks in restoration ecology. *Trends in Ecology and Evolution* 19: 46–53. (19)

Suding, K. N. and R. J. Hobbs. 2009. Threshold models in restoration and conservation: a developing framework. *Trends in Ecology and Evolution* 24: 271–279. (19)

Sugarman, J. 2009. Environmental and community health: a reciprocal relationship. *Restorative Commons* 138–153. (19)

Sullivan, B., C. L. Wood, M. J. Iliff, R. E. Bonney, D. Fink, and S. Kelling. 2009. eBird: a citizen-based bird observation network in the biological sciences. *Biological Conservation* 142: 2282–2292. (22)

Sutherland, W.J., W.M. Adams, R.B. Aronson, R. Aveling, T.M. Blackburn, S. Broad, et al. 2009. One hundred questions of importance to the conservation of global biological diversity. *Conservation Biology* 23: 557–567. (22)

Sutherland, W. J., M. Clout, I. M. Côté, P. Daszak, M. H. Depledge, L. Fellman, et al. 2010. A horizon scan of global conservation issues for 2010. *Trends in Ecology and Evolution* 25: 1–6. (22)

Swanson, F. J., C. Goodrich, and K. D. Moore. 2008. Bridging boundaries: scientists, creative writers, and the long view of the forest. *Frontiers in Ecology and the Environment* 6: 499–504. (6, 22)

Swetnam, T. W., C. D. Allen, and J. L. Betancourt. 1999. Applied historical ecology: using the past to manage the future. *Ecological Applications* 9: 1189–1206. (19)

Switalski, T. A., J. A. Bissonette, T. H. DeLuca, C. H. Luce, and M. A. Madej. 2004. Benefits and impacts of road removal. *Frontiers in Ecology and the Environment* 2: 21–28. (19)

Szentiks, C. A., S. Kondgen, S. Silinski, S. Speck, and F. H. Leendertz. 2009. Lethal pneumonia in a captive juvenile chimpanzee (*Pan troglodytes*) due to human-transmitted human respiratory syncytial virus (HRSV) and infection with *Streptococcus pneumoniae*. *Journal of Medical Primatology* 38: 236–240. (10)

Szlávik, J. and M. Füle. 2009. Economic consequences of climate change. American Institute of Physics Conference Proceedings, Sustainability 2009: The Next Horizon 1157: 73–82. (22)

Tabarelli, M. and C. Gascon. 2005. Lessons from fragmentation research: improving management and policy guidelines for biodiversity conservation. *Conservation Biology* 19: 734–739. (16)

Tait, C. J., C. B. Daniels, and R. S. Hill. 2005. Changes in species assemblages within the Adelaide metropolitan area, Australia, 1836–2002. *Ecological Applications* 15: 346–359. (7)

Talberth, J., C. Cobb, and N. Slattery. 2007. *The Genuine Progress Indicator 2006: a tool for sustainable development*. Redefining Progress: The Nature of Economics, Oakland, CA. (4)

Tallis, H., R. Goldman, M. Uhl, and B. Brosi. 2009. Integrating conservation and development in the field: implementing ecosystem service projects. *Frontiers in Ecology and the Environment* 7: 12–20. (20)

Tallis, H. and S. Polasky. 2009. Mapping and valuing ecosystem services as an approach for conservation and natural-resource management. *Annals of the New York Academy of Sciences* 1162: 265–283. (15)

Taylor, M.F.J., K. F. Suckling, and J. J. Rachlinski. 2005. The effectiveness of the Endangered Species Act: a quantitative analysis. *BioScience* 55: 360–366. (20)

Teel, T. L. and M. J. Manfredo. 2010. Understanding the diversity of public interests in wildlife conservation. *Conservation Biology* 24: 128–139. (6)

Temple, S. A. 1991. Conservation biology: new goals and new partners for managers of biological resources. *In* D. J. Decker, M. Krasny, G. R. Goff, C. R. Smith, and D. W. Gross (eds.), *Challenges in the Conservation of Biological Resources: A Practitioner's Guide*, pp. 45–54. Westview Press, Boulder, CO. (1)

Terborgh, J., L. C. Davenport, and C. Van Schaik (eds.). 2002. *Making Parks Work: Identifying Key Factors to Implementing Parks in the Tropics*. Island Press, Covelo, CA. (17)

Thatcher, C. A., F. T. van Manen, and J. D. Clark. 2009. A habitat assessment for Florida panther population expansion into central Florida. *Journal of Mammalogy* 90: 918–925. (18)

Theobald, D. M. 2004. Placing exurban land-use change in a human modification framework. *Frontiers in Ecology and the Environment* 2: 139–144. (18)

Thiere, G., S. Milenkovski, P. E. Lindgren, G. Sahlén, O. Berglund, and S.E.B. Weisner. 2009. Wetland creation in agricultural landscapes: biodiversity benefits on local and regional scales. *Biological Conservation* 142: 964–973. (2)

Thiollay, J. M. 1989. Area requirements for the conservation of rainforest raptors and game birds in French Guiana. *Conservation Biology* 3: 128–137. (11)

Thomas, A. 1995. Genotypic inference with the Gibbs sampler. *In* J. Ballou, M. Gilpin, and T. J. Foose (eds.), *Population Management for Survival and Recovery*, pp. 261–272. Columbia University Press, New York. (14)

Thomas, C. D. and J.C.G. Abery. 1995. Estimating rates of butterfly decline from distribution maps: the effect of scale. *Biological Conservation* 73: 59–65. (12)

Thomas, J. A., M. G. Telfer, D. B. Roy, C. D. Preston, J.J.D. Greenwood, J. Asher, et al. 2004. Comparative losses of British butterflies, birds, and plants and the global extinction crisis. *Science* 303: 1879–1881. (7, 9)

Thomas, K. S. 1991. *Living Fossil: The Story of the Coelacanth*. Norton, New York. (3)

Thompson, D. M. and R. van Woesik. 2009. Corals escape bleaching in regions that recently and historically experienced frequent thermal stress. *Proceedings of the Royal Society B* 276: 2893–2901. (9)

Thompson, J. D., M. Gaudeul, and M. Debussche. 2010. Conservation value of site of hybridization in peripheral populations of rare plant species. *Conservation Biology* 24: 236–245. (2)

Thoreau, H. D. 1854. *Walden; or, Life in the Woods*. Ticknor and Fields, Boston. (6)

Thoreau, H. D. 1863. *Excursions*. Ticknor and Fields, Boston. (1)

Thoreau, H. D. 1971 (reprint). *Walden*. Princeton University Press, Princeton, NJ. (1)

Thoreau, H. D. 2009. *The Journal of Henry David Thoreau 1837–1861.* D. Searls (ed.). New York Review of Books Classics, New York. (6)

Thorp, J. H., J. E. Flotemersch, M. D. Delong, A. F. Casper, M. C. Thoms, F. Ballantyne, et al. 2010. Linking ecosystem services, rehabilitation, and river hydrogeomorphology. *BioScience* 60: 67–74. (5)

Tierney, G. L., D. Faber-Langendoen, B. R. Mitchell, W. G. Shriver, and J. P. Gibbs. 2009. Monitoring and evaluating the ecological integrity of forest ecosystems. *Frontiers in Ecology and the Environment* 7: 308–316. (2)

Tilman, D. 1999. The ecological consequences of change in biodiversity: a search for general principles. *Ecology* 80: 1455–1474. (5)

Timmer, V. and C. Juma. 2005. Biodiversity conservation and poverty reduction come together in the tropics: lessons learned from the Equator Initiative. *Environment* 47: 25–44. (20)

Tognelli, M. F., M. Fernández, and P. A. Marquet. 2009. Assessing the performance of the existing and proposed network of marine protected areas to conserve marine biodiversity in Chile. *Biological Conservation* 142: 3147–3153. (15)

Toledo, V. M. 2001. Indigenous peoples, biodiversity and. *In* S. A. Levin (ed.), *Encyclopedia of Biodiversity* 3: 451–464. Academic Press, San Diego, CA. (20)

Tomley, F. M. and M. W. Shirley. 2009. Livestock infection diseases and zoonoses. *Philosophical Transactions of the Royal Society B* 364: 2637–2642. (10)

Towne, E. G., D .C. Hartnett, and R. C. Cochran. 2005. Vegetation trends in tallgrass prairie from bison and cattle grazing. *Ecological Applications* 15: 1550–1559. (17)

Towns, D. R., R. Parrish, C. L. Tyrrell, G. T. Ussher, A. Cree, D. G. Newman, et al. 2007. Responses of tuatara (*Sphenodon punctatus*) to removal of introduced Pacific rats from islands. *Conservation Biology* 21: 1021–1031. (10)

Traffic: The Wildlife Trade Monitoring Network. 2008. *http://www.traffic.org* (10)

Traill, L.W., C.J.A. Bradshaw, and B. W. Brook. 2007. Minimum viable population size: a meta-analysis of 30 years of published estimates. *Biological Conservation* 139: 159–166. (11)

Traill, L. W., B. W. Brook, R. R. Frankham, and C.J.A. Bradshaw. 2010. Pragmatic population viability targets in a rapidly changing world. *Biological Conservation* 143: 28–34. (12)

Tree of Life Web Project. 2007. *http://www.tolweb.org* (2, 22)

Triantis, K., D. Nogues-Bravo, J. Hortal, A. V. Borges, H. Adsersen, J. Maria Fernandez-Palacios, et al. 2008. Measurements of area and the (island) species-area relationship: new directions for an old pattern. *Oikos* 117: 1555–1559. (7)

Troëng, S. and E. Rankin. 2005. Long-term conservation efforts contribute to positive green turtle *Chelonia mydas* nesting trend at Tortuguero, Costa Rica. *Biological Conservation* 121: 111–116. (20)

Turner, W. R. and D. S. Wilcove. 2006. Adaptive decision rules for the acquisition of nature reserves. *Conservation Biology* 20: 527–537. (11, 15, 16)

Tushabe, H., J. Kalema, A. Byaruhanga, J. Asasira, P. Ssegawa, A. Balmford, et al. 2006. A nationwide assessment of the biodiversity value of Uganda's Important Bird Areas network. *Conservation Biology* 20: 85–99. (15)

Tzoulas, K., K. Korpela, S. Venn, V. Yli-Pelkonen, A. Kaêmierczak, J. Niemela, et al. 2007. Promoting ecosystem and human health in urban areas using Green Infrastructure: a literature review. *Landscape and Urban Planning* 81: 167–178. (19)

U.S. Census Bureau. *http://www.census.gov* (1)

U.S. EPA Environmental Education (EE). 2010. *http://www.epa.gov/enviroed* (5)

U.S. Fish and Wildlife Service (USFWS) and S. C. Nodvin. 2008. Arctic National Wildlife Refuge, United States. *In* C. J. Cleveland (ed.), *Encyclopedia of Earth*. Environmental Information Coalition, National Council for Science and the Environment, Washington, D.C.

http://www.eoearth.org/article/Arctic_National_Wildlife_Refuge%2C_ United_States (17)

U.S. National Park Service. 2009. National Park of American Samoa. *http://www.nps.gov/npsa/index.htm* (20)

Underwood, J. N., L. D. Smith, M.J.H. van Oppen, and J. P. Gilmour. 2009. Ecologically relevant dispersal of corals on isolated reefs: implications for managing resilience. *Ecological Applications* 19: 18–29. (15)

UNESCO. 2010. *http://www.unesco.org* (20)

UNESCO World Heritage Centre. 2010. *http://whc.unesco.org* (15, 21)

Union of Concerned Scientists: Citizens and Scientists for Environmental Solutions. 2009. *http://www.ucsusa.org* (9)

United Nations. 1993a. *Agenda 21: Rio Declaration and Forest Principles*. Post-Rio Edition. United Nations Publications, New York. (21)

United Nations. 1993b. *The Global Partnership for Environment and Development*. United Nations Publications, New York. (21)

United Nations Department of Economic and Social Affairs, Population Division. *http://www.un.org/esa/population* (9)

United Nations Development Programme. 2006. *http://www.undp.org* (9)

Uthicke, S., B. Schaffelke, and M. Byrne. 2009. A boom-bust phylum? Ecological and evolutionary consequences of density variations in echinoderms. *Ecological Monographs* 79: 3–24. (10)

Valdés, L., W. Peterson, J. Church, K. Brander, and M. Marcos. 2009. Our changing oceans: conclusions of the first international symposium on the effects of climate change on the world's oceans. *ICES Journal of Marine Science* 66: 1435–1438. (9)

Valeila, I., and P. Martinetto. 2007. Changes in bird abundance in eastern North America: urban sprawl and global footprint? *BioScience* 57: 360–370. (9)

Valentini, A., F. Pompanon, and P. Taberlet. 2009. DNA barcoding for ecologists. *Trends in Ecology and Evolution* 24: 110–117. (2)

van de Kerk, G., A. R. Manuel, and G. Douglas. 2009. Sustainable Society Index. *In* C. J. Cleveland (ed.), *Encyclopedia of Earth*. Environmental Information Coalition, National Council for Science and the Environment, Washington, D.C. *http://www.eoearth.org/article/Sustainable_Society_Index* (4)

van Gemerden, B. S., R. S. Etienne, H. Olff, P.W.F.M. Hommel, and F. van Langevelde. 2005. Reconciling methodologically different biodiversity assessments. *Ecological Applications* 15: 1747–1760. (15)

Van Heezik, Y. and P. J. Seddon. 2005. Structure and content of graduate wildlife management and conservation biology programs: an international perspective. *Conservation Biology* 19: 7–14. (1, 22)

van Kooten, G. C. 2008. Protecting the African elephant: a dynamic bioeconomic model of ivory trade. *Biological Conservation* 141: 2012–2022. (21)

van Kooten, G. C. and B. Sohngen. 2007. Economics of forest ecosystem carbon sinks: a review. Working Paper 2007–02, Resource Economics and Policy Analysis (REPA) Research Group, Department of Economics, University of Victoria, British Columbia. (4, 5)

Van Turnhout, C.A.M., R.P.B. Foppen, R.S.E.W. Leuven, A. Van Strien, and H. Siepel. 2010. Life-history and ecological correlates of population change in Dutch breeding birds. *Biological Conservation* 143: 173–181. (8)

Vaughn, C. C. 2010. Biodiversity losses and ecosystem function in freshwaters: emerging conclusions and research directions. *BioScience* 60: 25–35. (2)

Venter, O., J.E.M. Watson, E. Meijaard, W. F. Laurance, and H. P. Possingham. 2010. Avoiding unintended outcomes from REDD. *Conservation Biology* 24: 5–6. (5)

Vergeer, P., E. Sonderen, and N. J. Ouborg. 2004. Introduction strategies put to the test: local adaptation versus heterosis. *Conservation Biology* 18: 812–821. (13)

Verhoeven, J.T.A., B. Arheimer, C. Yin, and M. M. Hefting. 2006. Regional and global concerns over wetlands and water quality. *Trends in Ecology and Evolution* 21: 96–103. (17)

Vermonden, K., R.S.E.W. Leuven, G. van der Velde, M. M van Katwijk, J.G.M. Roelofs, and A. J. Hendriks. 2009. Urban drainage systems: an undervalued habitat for aquatic macroin-vertebrates. *Biological Conservation* 142: 1105–1115. (18)

Verstraete, M. M., R. J. Scholes, and M. S. Smith. 2009. Climate and desertification: looking at an old problem through new lenses. *Frontiers in Ecology and the Environment* 7: 421–428. (9)

Veteto, J. R. 2008. The history and survival of traditional heirloom vegetable varieties in the southern Appalachian Mountains of western North Carolina. *Agriculture and Human Values* 25: 121–134. (7)

Vilas, C., E. San Miguel, R. Amaro, and C. Garcia. 2006. Relative contribution of inbreeding depression and eroded adaptive diversity to extinction risk in small populations of shore campion. *Conservation Biology* 20: 229–238. (13)

Vistnes, I. I., C. Nellemann, P. Jordhøy, and O. Støen. 2008. Summer distribution of wild reindeer in relation to human activity and insect stress. *Polar Biology* 31: 1307–1317. (9)

Vitt, P., K. Havens, A. T. Kramer, D. Sollenberger, and E. Yates. 2010. Assisted migration of plants: changes in latitudes, changes in attitudes. *Biological Conservation* 143: 18–27. (14)

Vonholdt, B. M., D. R. Stahler, D. W. Smith, D. A. Earl, J. P. Pollinger, and R. K. Wayne. 2008. The geneaology and genetic viability of reintroduced Yellowstone grey wolves. *Molecular Ecology* 17: 252–274. (13)

Vredenburg, V. T. 2004. Reversing introduced species effects: experimental removal of introduced fish leads to rapid recovery of a declining frog. *Proceedings of the National Academy of Sciences USA* 101: 7646–7650. (10)

Wadt, L.H.O., K. A. Kainer, C. L. Staudhammer, and R.O.P. Serrano. 2008. Sustainable forest use in Brazilian extractive reserves: natural regeneration of Brazil nut in exploited populations. *Biological Conservation* 141: 332–346. (20)

Wagner, K. I., S. K. Gallagher, M. Hayes, B. A. Lawrence, and J. B. Zedler. 2008. Wetland restoration in the new millennium: do research efforts match opportunities? *Restoration Ecology* 16: 367–372. (19)

Wake, D. B. and V. T. Vredenburg. 2008. Are we in the midst of the sixth mass extinction? A view from the world of amphibians. *Proceedings of the National Academy of Sciences USA* 105: 11466–11473. (7)

Walker, B. G., P. D. Boersma, and J. C. Wingfield. 2005. Physiological and behavioral differences in Magellanic penguin chicks in undisturbed and tourist-visited locations of a colony. *Conservation Biology* 19: 1571–1577. (5)

Wallace, K., J. Callaway, and J. Zedler. 2005. Evolution of tidal creek networks in a high sedimentation environment: a 5–year experiment at Tijuana Estuary, California. *Estuaries* 28: 795–811. (19)

Wallach, A. D., B. Murray, and A. J. O'Neill. 2009. Can threatened species survive where the top predator is absent? *Biological Conservation* 142: 43–52. (2)

Walther, G. R., A. Roques, P. E. Hulme, M. T. Sykes, P. Pysek, I. Kühn, et al. 2009. Alien species in a warmer world: risks and opportunities. *Trends in Ecology and Evolution* 24: 686–693. (10)

Waples, R. S., D. J. Teel, J. Myers, and A. Marshall. 2004. Life history divergence in Chinook salmon: historic contingency and parallel evolution. *Evolution* 58: 386–403. (13)

Ward, P. 2004. The father of all mass extinctions. *Conservation* 5: 12–17. (7)

Warkentin, I. G., D. Bickford, N. S. Sodhi, and C.J.A. Bradshaw. 2009. Eating frogs to extinction. *Conservation Biology* 23:1056–1059. (10)

Warren, M. S. 1991. The successful conservation of an endangered species, the heath fritillary butterfly *Mellicta athalia*, in Britain. *Biological Conservation* 55: 37–56. (17)

Wasser, S. K., W. J. Clark, O. Drori, E. S. Kisamo, C. Mailand, B. Mutayoba, et al. 2008. Combating the illegal trade in African elephant ivory with DNA forensics. *Conservation Biology* 22: 1065–1071. (2)

Wasser, S. K., B. Clark, and C. Laurie. 2009. The ivory trail. *Scientific American* 301(1): 68–76. (21)

Wasser, S. K., C. Mailand, R. Booth, B. Mutayoba, E. Kisamo, B. Clark, et al. 2007. Using DNA to track the origin of the largest ivory seizure since the 1989 trade ban. *Proceedings of the National Academy of Sciences USA* 104: 4228–4333. (21)

Waters, S. S. and O. Ulloa. 2007. Preliminary survey on the current distribution of primates in Belize. *Neotropical Primates* 14: 80–82. (20)

Wayne, R. K. and P. A. Morin. 2004. Conservation genetics in the new molecular age. *Frontiers in Ecology and the Environment* 2: 89–97. (11)

Weis, J. S. and C.J. Cleveland. 2008. DDT. *In* C. J. Cleveland (ed.), *Encyclopedia of Earth*. Environmental Information Coalition, National Council for Science and the Environment, Washington, D.C. *http://www.eoearth.org/article/DDT* (9)

Wells, M. P. and T. O. McShane. 2004. Integrating protected area management with local needs and aspirations. *Ambio* 33: 513–519. (17)

West, P. and D. Brockington. 2006. An anthropological perspective on some unexpected consequences of protected areas. *Conservation Biology* 20: 609–616. (18, 20)

Western, D. 1989. Conservation without parks: wildlife in the rural landscape. *In* D. Western and M. Pearl (eds.), *Conservation for the Twenty-first Century*, pp. 158–165. Oxford University Press, New York. (18)

Western, D., R. Groom, and J. Worden. 2009. The impact of subdivision and sedentarization of pastoral lands on wildlife in an African savanna ecosystem. *Biological Conservation* 142: 2538–2546. (18)

Western and Central Pacific Fisheries Commission (WCPFC). 2009. *http://www.wcpfc.int* (21)

White, P. S. 1996. Spatial and biological scales in reintroduction. *In* D. A. Falk, C. I. Millar, and M. Olwell (eds.), *Restoring Diversity: Strategies for Reintroduction of Endangered Plants*, pp. 49–86. Island Press, Washington, D.C. (12)

White, R. P., S. Murray, and M. Rohweder. 2000. *Pilot Assessment of Global Ecosystems: Grassland Ecosystems*. World Resources Institute, Washington, D.C. (9)

White, T., J. A. Collazo, and F. J. Vilella. 2005. Survival of captive-reared Puerto Rican parrots released in the Caribbean National Forest. *The Condor* 107: 424–432. (14)

Whittier, T. R., P. L. Ringold, A. T. Herlihy, and S. M. Pierson. 2008. A calcium-based invasion risk assessment for zebra and quagga mussels (*Driessena* spp). *Frontiers in Ecology and the Environment* 6: 180–184. (10)

Wiersma, Y. F. 2007. The effect of target extent on the location of optimal protected areas networks in Canada. *Landscape Ecology* 22: 1477–1487. (16)

Wiersma, Y. F., T. D. Nudds, and D. H. Rivard. 2004. Models to distinguish effects of landscape patterns and human population pressures associated with species loss in Canadian national parks. *Landscape Ecology* 19: 773–786. (16)

Wikström, L., P. Milberg, and K. Bergman. 2008. Monitoring of butterflies in semi-natural grasslands: diurnal variation and weather effects. *Journal of Insect Conservation* 13: 203–211. (12)

Wilcove, D. S., M. J. Bean, B. Long, W. J. Snape, III, B. M. Beehler, and J. Eisenberg. 2004. The private side of conservation. *Frontiers and Ecology and the Environment* 2: 326–331. (18)

Wilcove, D. S. and L. L. Master. 2005. How many endangered species are there in the United States? *Frontiers in Ecology and the Environment* 3: 414–420. (9)

Wilcove, D. S., M. McMillan, and K. C. Winston. 1993. What exactly is an endangered species? An analysis of the U.S. Endangered Species List: 1985–1991. *Conservation Biology* 7: 87–93. (20)

Wilcove, D. S. and M. Wikelski. 2008. Going, going, gone: is animal migration disappearing? *PLoS Biology* 6: 1361–1364. (8, 16)

Wild, R. and C. McLeod (eds.). 2008. *Sacred natural sites: guidelines for protected area managers.* IUCN Task Force on the Cultural and Spiritual Values of Protected Areas. Thanet Press Ltd., Margate, UK. (9)

Wildlands Network: Reconnecting Nature in North America. *http://www.wildlandsproject.org* (15)

Wildt, D. E., P. Comizzoli, B. Pukazhenthi, and N. Songsasen. 2009. Lessons from biodiversity—the value of nontraditional species to advance reproductive science, conservation, and human health. *Molecular Reproduction and Development* 77: 397–409. (14)

Wilhere, G. F. 2008. The how-much-is-enough myth. *Conservation Biology* 22: 514–517. (11)

Wilkie, D. S., G. A., Morelli, J. Demmer, M. Starkey, P. Telfer, and M. Steil. 2006. Parks and people: assessing the human welfare effects of establishing protected areas for biodiversity conservation. *Conservation Biology* 20: 247–249. (17)

Willi, Y., M. van Kleunen, S. Dietrich, and M. Fischer. 2007. Genetic rescue persists beyond first-generation outbreeding in small populations of a rare plant. *Proceedings of the Royal Society B* 274: 2357–2364. (11)

Williams, P., D. Gibbons, C. Margules, A. Rebelo, C. Humphries, and R. Pressey. 1996. A comparison of richness hotspots, rarity hotspots and complementary areas for conserving the diversity of British birds. *Conservation Biology* 10: 155–174. (15)

Williams, S. E. and E. A. Hoffman. 2009. Minimizing genetic adaptation in captive breeding programs: a review. *Biological Conservation* 142: 2388–2400. (14)

Willis, C. G., B. Ruhfel, R. B. Primack, A. J. Miller-Rushing, and C. C. Davis. 2008. Phylogenetic patterns of species loss in Thoreau's woods are driven by climate change. *Proceedings of the National Academy of Sciences USA* 105: 17029–17033. (7, 9)

Wilson, E. O. 1989. Threats to biodiversity. *Scientific American* 261(3): 108–116. (7)

Wilson, E. O. 1992. *The Diversity of Life.* The Belknap Press of Harvard University Press, Cambridge, MA. (3)

Wilson, E. O. 2003. The encyclopedia of life. *Trends in Ecology and Evolution* 18: 77–80. (2)

Wilson, J.R.U., E. E. Dormontt, P. J. Prentis, A. J. Lowe, and D. M. Richardson. 2009. Something in the way you move: dispersal pathways affect invasion success. *Trends in Ecology and Evolution* 24: 136–144. (10)

Wilson, K. A., J. Cawardine, and H. P. Possingham. 2009. Setting conservation priorities. *Annals of the New York Academy of Sciences* 1162: 237–264. (21)

Winchell, C. S. and P. F. Doherty, Jr. 2008. Using California gnatcatcher to test underlying models in habitat conservation plans. *Journal of Wildlife Management* 72: 1322–1327. (20)

Winker, K. 2009. Reuniting phenotype and genotype in biodiversity research. *BioScience* 59: 657–665. (2)

Wirzba, N. 2003. *The Paradise of God: Renewing Religion in an Ecological Age.* Oxford University Press, Oxford, UK. (6)

Wittemyer, G., P. Elsen, W. T. Bean, A. Coleman, O. Burton and J. S. Brashares. 2008. Accelerated human population growth at protected area edges. *Science* 321: 123–126. (17)

Wofford, J.E.B., R. E. Gresswell, and M. A. Banks. 2005. Influence of barriers to movement on within-watershed genetic variation of coastal cutthroat trout. *Ecological Applications* 15: 628–637. (2, 11)

Woodhams, D. C. 2009. Converting the religious: putting amphibian conservation in context. *BioScience* 59: 463–464. (6)

Wooldridge, S. A. and T. J. Done. 2009. Improved water quality can ameliorate effects of climate change on corals. *Ecological Applications* 19: 1492–1499. (9)

World Bank. 2005. *Going, Going, Gone: The Illegal Trade in Wildlife in East and Southeast Asia.* Environment and Social Development Department East Asia and Pacific Region Discussion Paper. The World Bank, Washington, D.C. (21)

World Bank. 2006. *Mountains to Coral Reefs – The World Bank and Biodiversity 1988–2005.* World Bank, Washington, D.C. (21)

World Bank. 2010. *http://www.worldbank.org* (21)

World Commission on Environment and Development (WCED). 1987. *Our Common Future.* Oxford University Press, Oxford, UK. (1)

World Database on Protected Areas. *http://www.wdpa.org* (15)

World Resources Institute (WRI) Earth Trends: Environmental Information. 2007. *http://earthtrends.wri.org* (15)

World Resources Institute (WRI): Working at the Intersection of Environment and Human Needs. *http://www.wri.org* (15)

World Resources Institute (WRI). 1998. *World Resources 1998–1999.* Oxford University Press, New York. (7)

World Resources Institute (WRI). 2000. *World Resources 2000–2001.* World Resources Institute, Washington, D.C. (8, 9)

World Resources Institute (WRI). 2003. *World Resources 2002–2004: Decisions for the Earth: balance, voice, and power.* World Resources Institute, Washington, D.C. (4, 20, 21, 22)

World Resources Institute (WRI). 2005. *World Resources 2005: The Wealth of the Poor—Managing Ecosystems to Fight Poverty.* World Resources Institute, Washington, D.C. (4, 10, 18)

World Trade Organization. 2009. *World Trade Report 2009: Trade Policy Commitments and Contingency Measures.* Switzerland. (21)

World Wildlife Fund (WWF). 1999. *Religion and Conservation.* Full Circle Press, New Delhi, India. (6)

World Wildlife Fund (WWF) International. *http://www.panda.org* (20, 21)

World Wildlife Fund (WWF) and M. McGinley. 2007a. Cauca Valley dry forests. *In* C. J. Cleveland (ed.), *Encyclopedia of Earth.* Environmental Information Coalition, National Council for Science and the Environment, Washington, D.C. *http://www.eoearth.org/article/Cauca_Valley_dry_forests* (20)

World Wildlife Fund (WWF) and M. McGinley. 2007b. Pantanal. *In* C. J. Cleveland (ed.), *Encyclopedia of Earth.* Environmental Information Coalition, National Council for Science and the Environment, Washington, D.C. *http://www.eoearth.org/article/Pantanal* (21)

World Wildlife Fund (WWF) and M. McGinley. 2009. Central American dry forests. *In* C. J. Cleveland (ed.), *Encyclopedia of Earth.* Environmental Information Coalition, National Council for Science and the Environment, Washington, D.C. *http://www.eoearth.org/article/Central_American_dry_forests* (9)

Worldwatch Institute. 2008. Making better energy choices. *http://www.worldwatch.org* (1)

Wrangham, R. and E. Ross (eds.). 2008. *Science and Conservation in African Forests: The Benefits of Long-Term Research.* Cambridge University Press, Cambridge, MA. (22)

Wright, R., J. M. Scott, S. Mann, and M. Murray. 2001. Identifying unprotected and potentially at risk plant communities in the western USA. *Biological Conservation* 98: 97–106. (15)

Wright, S. 1931. Evolution in Mendelian populations. *Genetics* 16: 97–159. (11)

Wright, S. J., G. A. Sanchez-Azofeifa, C. Portillo-Quintero, and D. Davies. 2007. Poverty and corruption compromise tropical forest reserves. *Ecological Applications* 17: 1259–1266. (15)

Wright, S. J., H. Zeballos, I. Domínguez, M. M. Gallardo, M. C. Moreno, and R. Ibáñez. 2000. Poachers alter mammal abundance, seed dispersal, and seed predation in a Neotropical forest. *Conservation Biology* 14: 227–239. (17)

Wu, J. and R. J. Hobbs (eds.). 2009. *Key Topics in Landscape Ecology.* Cambridge University Press, Cambridge, UK. (16)

Wunder, S., B. Campbell, P.G.H. Frost, J. A. Sayer, R. Iwan, and L. Wollenberg. 2008. When donors get cold feet: the community conservation concession in Setulang (Kalimantan, Indonesia) that never happened. *Ecology and Society* 13: 12. (20)

WWF/World Bank Alliance. 2010. *http://www.worldwildlife.org/what/globalmarkets/forests/world-bankalliance.html* (21)

Wyman, M. S. and T. V. Stein. 2009. Modeling social and land-use/land-cover change data to assess drivers of smallholder deforestation in Belize. *Applied Geography* In press. (16)

Xie, S. G., Z. J. Li, J. S. Liu, S. Q. Xie, H. Z. Wang, and B. R. Murphy. 2007. Fisheries of the Yangtze River show immediate impacts of the Three Gorges Dam. *Fisheries* 32: 343–344. (21)

Xu, H., J. Wu, Y. Liu, H. Ding, M. Zhang, Y. Wu, et al. 2008. Biodiversity congruence and conservation strategies: a national test. *BioScience* 58: 632–639. (3)

Yamaoko, K., H. Moriyama, and T. Shigematsu. 1977. Ecological role of secondary forests in the traditional farming area in Japan. *Bulletin of Tokyo University* 20: 373–384. (16)

Yamaura, Y., T. Kawahara, S. Iida, and K. Ozaki. 2008. Relative importance of the area and shape of patches to the diversity of multiple taxa. *Conservation Biology* 22: 1513–1522. (16)

Yang, S. L., J. Zhang, and X. J. Xu. 2007. Influence of the Three Gorges Dam on downstream delivery of sediment and its environmental implications, Yangtze River. *Geophysical Research Letters* 34: L10401. (21)

Yanites. B., R. H. Webb, P. G. Griffiths, and C. S. Magirl. 2006. Debris flow deposition and reworking by the Colorado River in Grand Canyon, Arizona. *Water Resources Research* 42: W11411. (19)

Yodzis, P. 2001. Trophic levels. *In* S. A. Levin (ed.), *Encyclopedia of Biodiversity*, vol. 5, pp. 695–700. Academic Press, San Diego, CA. (2)

Young, T. P. 1994. Natural die-offs of large mammals: implications for conservation. *Conservation Biology* 8: 410–418. (11)

Young T. P., T. M. Palmer, and M. E. Gadd. 2005. Competition and compensation among cattle, zebras, and elephants in a semi-arid savanna in Laikipia, Kenya. *Biological Conservation* 112: 251–259. (18)

Zabel, A. and B. Roe. 2009. Optimal design of pro-conservation incentives. *Ecological Economics* 69: 126–134. (20)

Zabel, R. W., M. D. Scheuerell, M. M. McClure, and J. G. Williams. 2006. The interplay between climate variability and density dependence in the population viability of Chinook salmon. *Conservation Biology* 20: 190–200. (12)

Zahler, P. 2003. Top-down meets bottom-up: conservation in a post-conflict world. *Conservation in Practice* 4: 23–29. (17)

Zaradic, P. A., O.R.W. Pergams, and P. Kareiva. 2009. The impact of nature experience on willingness to support conservation. *PLoS One* 4: e7367. (21)

Zarin, D. J., M. D. Schulze, E. Vidal, and M. Lentini. 2007. Beyond reaping the first harvest: management objectives for timber production in the Brazilian Amazon. *Conservation Biology* 21: 916–925. (17, 18)

Zavaleta, E., D. C. Miller, N. Salafsky, E Fleishman, M. Webster, B. Gold, et al. 2008. Enhancing the engagement of U.S. private foundations with conservation science. *Conservation Biology* 22: 1477–1484. (16, 21)

Zedler, J. B. 2005. Restoring wetland plant diversity: a comparison of existing and adaptive approaches. *Wetlands Ecology and Management* 13: 5–14. (19)

Zeilhofera, P. and R. M. de Mourab. 2009. Hydrological changes in the northern Pantanal caused by the Manso dam: impact analysis and suggestions for mitigation. *Ecological Engineering* 35: 105–117. (21)

Zerah, M. H. 2007. Conflict between green space preservation and housing needs: the case of the Sanjay Gandhi National Park in Mumbai. *Cities* 24: 122–132. (17)

Zhang, Y., S. Tachibana, and S. Nagata. 2006. Impact of socio-economic factors on the changes in forest areas in China. *Forest Policy and Economics* 9: 63–76. (9)

Zhao, S., L. Da, Z. Tang, H. Fang, K. Song, and J. Fang. 2006. Ecological consequences of rapid urban expansion: Shanghai, China. *Frontiers in Ecology and the Environment* 4: 341–346. (9)

Zhu, Y. Y., Y. Y. Wang, H. R. Che, and B. R. Lu. 2003. Conserving traditional rice varieties through management for crop diversity. *BioScience* 53: 158–162. (20)

Zimmerer, K. S. 2006. Cultural ecology: at the interface with political ecology – the new geographies of environmental conservation and globalization. *Progress in Human Geography* 30: 63–78. (20)

Zimmermann, A., M. Hatchwell, L. Dickie, and C. D. West (eds.) 2008. *Zoos in the 21st Century: Catalysts for Conservation.* Cambridge University Press, Cambridge. (14)

Zonneveld, I. S. and R. T. Forman (eds.). 1990. *Changing Landscapes: An Ecological Perspective.* Springer-Verlag, New York. (16)

Zoological Society of London (ZSL). *http://www.zsl.org* (10)

Zydelis, R., B. P. Wallace, E. L. Gilman, and T. B. Werner. 2009. Conservation of marine megafauna through minimization of fisheries bycatch. *Conservation Biology* 23: 608–616. (10)

Index

The letter f after a page number indicates that the entry is included in a figure;
t after a page number indicates that the entry is included in a table.

About the Author

Richard B. Primack is a Professor in the Biology Department at Boston University. He received his B.A. at Harvard University in 1972 and his Ph.D. at Duke University in 1976, and then was a postdoctoral fellow at the University of Canterbury and Harvard University. He has served as a visiting professor at the University of Hong Kong and Tokyo University, and has been awarded Bullard and Putnam Fellowships from Harvard University and a Guggenheim Fellowship. Dr. Primack was President of the Association for Tropical Biology and Conservation, and is currently Editor-in-Chief of the journal *Biological Conservation*. Twenty-five foreign-language editions of his textbooks have been produced, with various coauthors adding in local examples. He is an author of rain forest books, most recently *Tropical Rain Forests: An Ecological and Biogeographical Comparison* (with Richard Corlett). Dr. Primack's research interests include: the biological impacts of climate change; the loss of species in protected areas; tropical forest ecology and conservation; and conservation education. He is currently writing a popular book about changes in Concord since the time of Henry David Thoreau and Walden.

About the Book

Editor: Andrew D. Sinauer

Project Editors: Sydney Carroll and Kathaleen Emerson

Production Manager: Christopher Small

Book Design and Composition: Joan Gemme

Cover Design: Jefferson Johnson

Photo Research: David McIntyre

Book and Cover Manufacture: World Print LTD